MW01042073

UNIVERSITY CASEBOOK SERIES®

CIVIL RIGHTS ACTIONS:

ENFORCING THE CONSTITUTION

THIRD EDITION

by

JOHN C. JEFFRIES, JR.
David and Mary Harrison Distinguished Professor of Law
University of Virginia

PAMELA S. KARLAN
Kenneth and Harle Montgomery Professor of Public Interest Law
Stanford University

PETER W. LOW
Hardy Cross Dillard Professor of Law
University of Virginia

GEORGE A. RUTHERGLEN
John Barbee Minor Distinguished Professor of Law
Earle K. Shawe Professor of Employment Law
University of Virginia

FOUNDATION PRESS

610 Opperman Drive
St. Paul, MN 55123
1-800-313-9378

Printed in the United States of America

ISBN: 978–1–60930–275–7

Mat # 41381343

PREFACE

The Third Edition incorporates developments that have occurred since publication of its predecessor edition in 2007. Many of these developments have been noted in the annual supplements, which keep the casebook up to date. The integration of these changes with existing materials—as distinct from simply adding materials on each new development—required substantial revision, which justified a new edition.

Prominent among the changes that the user might notice is the provision of alternative treatments of the relation of state sovereign immunity under the Eleventh Amendment to officer suits under § 1983. That topic is handled fairly summarily in Chapter 1, Section 3. The main case there is *Hafer v. Melo* (1991) on the importance of officer suits. For those who desire a more extensive foray into state sovereign immunity and the Eleventh Amendment, suitable materials are provided in Chapter 3, Section 1, which features *Edelman v. Jordan* (1974) as a main case, plus extensive notes. Explicit directions are given in Chapter 3 on how to combine this extended treatment of the Eleventh Amendment with *Hafer* and the accompanying Chapter 1 materials.

Other notable changes from the Second Edition include materials on *Ashcroft v. Iqbal* (2009) and new requirements for pleading civil rights cases; *Pearson v. Callahan* (2009) and the abrogation of mandatory merits-first adjudication in qualified immunity cases; expanded materials on exhaustion of remedies in civil rights actions, including discussion of the PLRA and habeas corpus; *Wal-Mart Stores v. Dukes* (2011) in the materials on Title VII; and *Brown v. Plata* (2011), which upheld a lower-court order requiring California to release prisoners, if need be, to relieve prison overcrowding. All of these cases are excerpted fairly fully and are analyzed in accompanying notes.

Additionally, many more recent developments are covered in notes, which also feature updated citations to the secondary literature.

PERMISSION TO DUPLICATE

Although the two books have grown in different directions, there remain intersections between **Civil Rights Actions: Enforcing the Constitution** (3rd ed. 2013) and Low, Jeffries, and Bradley, **Federal Courts and the Law of Federal-State Relations** (7th ed. 2012). Occasionally, a teacher using one book may wish to use material from the other or from its annual supplement. To facilitate such borrowings, we authorize teachers who have adopted either book to duplicate limited portions of the other or its annual supplement for distribution to their students. We are grateful to Foundation Press for making this option available.

JCJjr
PSK
PWL
GAR

March 2013

SUMMARY OF CONTENTS

TABLE OF CONTENTS

TABLE OF CASES

The principal cases are in bold type.

Cases

TABLE OF SECONDARY AUTHORITIES

Other Authorities

UNIVERSITY CASEBOOK SERIES ®

CIVIL RIGHTS ACTIONS:

ENFORCING THE CONSTITUTION

THIRD EDITION

CHAPTER 1

42 U.S.C. § 1983

1. "UNDER COLOR OF" LAW

Monroe v. Pape

Supreme Court of the United States, 1961.
365 U.S. 167.

■ MR. JUSTICE DOUGLAS delivered the opinion of the Court.

This case presents important questions concerning the construction of R.S. § 1979, 42 U.S.C. § 1983,[a] which reads as follows:

> Every person who, under color of any statute, ordinance, regulation, custom, or usage, of any State or Territory, subjects, or causes to be subjected, any citizen of the United States or other person within the jurisdiction thereof to the deprivation of any rights, privileges, or immunities secured by the Constitution and laws, shall be liable to the party injured in an action at law, suit in equity, or other proper proceeding for redress.

The complaint alleges that 13 Chicago police officers broke into petitioners' home in the early morning, routed them from bed, made them stand naked in the living room, and ransacked every room, emptying drawers and ripping mattress covers. It further alleges that Mr. Monroe was then taken to the police station and detained on "open" charges for 10 hours, while he was interrogated about a two-day-old murder, that he was not taken before a magistrate, though one was accessible, that he was not permitted to call his family or attorney, that he was subsequently released without criminal charges being preferred against him. It is alleged that the officers had no search warrant and no arrest warrant and that they acted "under color of the statutes, ordinances, regulations, customs and usages" of Illinois and of the city of Chicago. Federal jurisdiction was asserted under 42 U.S.C. § 1983, which we have set out above, and 28 U.S.C. § 1343[1] and 28 U.S.C. § 1331.

[D]efendants moved to dismiss, alleging that the complaint alleged no cause of action under those acts or the federal Constitution. The District Court dismissed the complaint. The Court of Appeals affirmed. . . .

---

[a] Subsequent citations in the Court's opinion to § 1979 of the Revised Statutes have been replaced with the now more conventional reference to title 42 of the United States Code, § 1983.—[Footnote by eds.]

[1] This section provides in material part:

The district courts shall have original jurisdiction of any civil action authorized by law to be commenced by any person . . .

(3) To redress the deprivation, under color of any state law, statute, ordinance, regulation, custom or usage, of any right, privilege or immunity secured by the Constitution of the United States or by any act of Congress providing for equal rights of citizens or of all persons within the jurisdiction of the United States.

I

Petitioners claim that the invasion of their home and the subsequent search without a warrant and the arrest and detention of Mr. Monroe without a warrant and without arraignment constituted a deprivation of their "rights, privileges, or immunities secured by the Constitution" within the meaning of § 1983. . . .

Section 1983 came onto the books as § 1 of the Ku Klux Act of April 20, 1871. . . . Its purpose is plain from the title of the legislation, "An Act to enforce the Provisions of the Fourteenth Amendment to the Constitution of the United States, and for other Purposes." Allegation of facts constituting a deprivation under color of state authority of a right guaranteed by the Fourteenth Amendment satisfies to that extent the requirement of § 1983. See Douglas v. City of Jeannette, 319 U.S. 157 (1943). So far petitioners are on solid ground. For the guarantee against unreasonable searches and seizures contained in the fourth amendment has been made applicable to the states by reason of the Due Process Clause of the Fourteenth Amendment. Wolf v. Colorado, 338 U.S. 25 (1949).

II

There can be no doubt at least since Ex parte Virginia, 100 U.S. 339 (1879), that Congress has the power to enforce provisions of the Fourteenth Amendment against those who carry a badge of authority of a state and represent it in some capacity, whether they act in accordance with their authority or misuse it. See Home Tel. & Tel. Co. v. Los Angeles, 227 U.S. 278, 287–96 (1913). The question with which we now deal is the narrower one of whether Congress, in enacting § 1983, meant to give a remedy to parties deprived of constitutional rights, privileges and immunities by an official's abuse of his position. We conclude that it did so intend.

It is argued that "under color of" enumerated state authority excludes acts of an official or policeman who can show no authority under state law, state custom, or state usage to do what he did. In this case it is said that these policemen, in breaking into petitioners' apartment, violated the Constitution and laws of Illinois. It is pointed out that under Illinois law a simple remedy is offered for that violation and that, so far as it appears, the courts of Illinois are available to give petitioners that full redress which the common law affords for violence done to a person; and it is earnestly argued that no "statute, ordinance, regulation, custom or usage" of Illinois bars that redress. . . .

The legislation—in particular the section with which we are now concerned—had several purposes. There are threads of many thoughts running through the debates. One who reads them in their entirety sees that the present section had three main aims.

First, it might, of course, override certain kinds of state laws. Mr. Sloss of Alabama, in opposition, spoke of that object and emphasized that it was irrelevant because there were no such laws:

> The first section of this bill prohibits any invidious legislation by states against the rights or privileges of citizens of the United States. The object of this section is not very clear, as it is not pretended by its advocates on this floor that any state has passed any laws endangering the rights or privileges of colored people.

Second, it provided a remedy where state law was inadequate. That aspect of the legislation was summed up by Senator Sherman of Ohio:

> [I]t is said the reason is that any offense may be committed upon a negro by a white man, and a negro cannot testify in any case against a white man, so that the only way by which any conviction can be had in Kentucky in those cases is in the United States courts, because the United States courts enforce the United States laws by which negroes may testify.

But the purposes were much broader. The third aim was to provide a federal remedy where the state remedy, though adequate in theory, was not available in practice. . . .

This Act of April 20, 1871, sometimes called "the third 'force bill,' " was passed by a Congress that had the Klan "particularly in mind." The debates are replete with references to the lawless conditions existing in the South in 1871. There was available to the Congress during these debates a report, nearly 600 pages in length, dealing with the activities of the Klan and the inability of the state governments to cope with it. This report was drawn on by many of the speakers. It was not the unavailability of state remedies but the failure of certain states to enforce the laws with an equal hand that furnished the powerful momentum behind this "force bill." Mr. Lowe of Kansas said:

> While murder is stalking abroad in disguise, while whippings and lynchings and banishment have been visited upon unoffending American citizens, the local administrations have been found inadequate or unwilling to apply the proper corrective. Combinations, darker than the night that hides them, conspiracies, wicked as the worst of felons could devise, have gone unwhipped of justice. Immunity is given to crime, and the records of the public tribunals are searched in vain for any evidence of effective redress. . . .

While one main scourge of the evil—perhaps the leading one—was the Ku Klux Klan, the remedy created was not a remedy against it or its members but against those who representing a state in some capacity were *unable* or *unwilling* to enforce a state law. . . . There was, it was said, no quarrel with the state laws on the books. It was their lack of enforcement that was the nub of the difficulty. . . .

Senator Pratt of Indiana spoke of the discrimination against Union sympathizers and Negroes in the actual enforcement of the laws:

> Plausibly and sophistically it is said [that] the laws of North Carolina do not discriminate against them; that the provisions in favor of rights and liberties are general; that the courts are open to all; that juries, grand and petit, are commanded to hear and redress without distinction as to color, race, or political sentiment.
>
> But it is a fact, asserted in the report, that of the hundreds of outrages committed upon loyal people through the agency of this Ku Klux organization not one has been punished. This defect in the administration of the laws does not extend to other cases. Vigorously enough are the laws enforced against Union people. They only fail in efficiency when a man of known Union sentiments, white or black, invokes their aid. Then Justice closes the door of her temple.

It was precisely that breadth of the remedy which the opposition emphasized. . . . Senator Thurman of Ohio [said] about the section we are now considering:

> It authorizes any person who is deprived of any right, privilege, or immunity secured to him by the Constitution of the United States, to bring an action against the wrongdoer in the federal courts, and that without any limit whatsoever as to the amount in controversy. The deprivation may be of the slightest conceivable character, the damages in the estimation of any sensible man may not be five dollars or even five cents; they may be what lawyers call merely nominal damages; and yet by this section jurisdiction of that civil action is given to the federal courts instead of its being prosecuted as now in the courts of the states.

The debates were long and extensive. It is abundantly clear that one reason the legislation was passed was to afford a federal right in federal courts because, by reason of prejudice, passion, neglect, intolerance or otherwise, state laws might not be enforced and the claims of citizens to the enjoyment of rights, privileges, and immunities guaranteed by the Fourteenth Amendment might be denied by the state agencies. . . .

Although the legislation was enacted because of the conditions that existed in the South at that time, it is cast in general language and is as applicable to Illinois as it is to the states whose names were mentioned over and again in the debates. It is no answer that the state has a law which if enforced would give relief. The federal remedy is supplementary to the state remedy, and the latter need not be first sought and refused before the federal one is invoked. Hence the fact that Illinois by its Constitution and laws outlaws unreasonable searches and seizures is no barrier to the present suit in the federal court.

We had before us in United States v. Classic, 313 U.S. 299 (1941), 18 U.S.C. § 242, which provides a criminal punishment for anyone who "under color of any law, statute, ordinance, regulation, or custom" subjects any inhabitant of a state to the deprivation of "any rights, privileges, or immunities secured by the Constitution or laws of the United States." Section 242 first came into the law as § 2 of the Civil Rights Act, Act of April 9, 1866. After passage of the Fourteenth Amendment, this provision was re-enacted and amended by §§ 17, 18, Act of May 31, 1870. The right involved in the *Classic* case was the right of voters in a primary to have their votes counted. The laws of Louisiana required the defendants "to count the ballots, to record the result of the count, and to certify the result of the election." But according to the indictment they did not perform their duty. In an opinion written by Mr. Justice (later Chief Justice) Stone, in which Mr. Justice Roberts, Mr. Justice Reed, and Mr. Justice Frankfurter joined, the Court ruled, "Misuse of power, possessed by virtue of state law and made possible only because the wrongdoer is clothed with the authority of state law, is action taken 'under color of' state law." There was a dissenting opinion; but the ruling as to the meaning of "under color of" state law was not questioned.

That view of the meaning of the words "under color of" state law, 18 U.S.C. § 242, was reaffirmed in Screws v. United States, 325 U.S. 91 (1945)[b]. . . .

---

[b] Screws was a Georgia sheriff who, with two other law enforcement officers, brutally beat an African–American man in the course of an apparently bogus arrest, then threw him in jail without medical care. The man died within the hour. When prosecuted under 18 U.S.C. § 242, the defendants claimed that their actions were not "under color of" law because they had not been commanded or authorized by state law. The Supreme Court rejected that argument in favor of the construction of § 242 adopted in *Classic*.—[Footnote by eds.]

We conclude that the meaning given "under color of" law in the *Classic* case and in the *Screws* . . . was the correct one; and we adhere to it.

In the *Screws* case we dealt with a statute that imposed criminal penalties for acts "wilfully" done. We construed that word in its setting to mean the doing of an act with "a specific intent to deprive a person of a federal right." We do not think that gloss should be placed on § 1983 which we have here. The word "wilfully" does not appear in § 1983. Moreover, § 1983 provides a civil remedy while in the *Screws* case we dealt with a criminal law challenged on the ground of vagueness. Section 1983 should be read against the background of tort liability that makes a man responsible for the natural consequences of his actions.

So far, then, the complaint states a cause of action. . . . [S]ince the complaint should not have been dismissed against the officials[c] the judgment must be and is

Reversed.

■ MR. JUSTICE HARLAN, whom MR. JUSTICE STEWART joins, concurring.

Were this case here as one of first impression, I would find the "under color of any statute" issue very close indeed. However, in *Classic* and *Screws* this Court considered a substantially identical statutory phrase to have a meaning which, unless we now retreat from it, requires that issue to go for the petitioners here. . . .

Those aspects of Congress' purpose which are quite clear in the earlier congressional debates, as quoted by my Brothers Douglas and Frankfurter in turn, seem to me to be inherently ambiguous when applied to the case of an isolated abuse of state authority by an official. One can agree with the Court's opinion that

> [i]t is abundantly clear that one reason the legislation was passed was to afford a federal right in federal courts because, by reason of prejudice, passion, neglect, intolerance or otherwise, state laws might not be enforced and the claims of citizens to the enjoyment of rights, privileges, and immunities guaranteed by the Fourteenth Amendment might be denied by the state agencies

without being certain that Congress meant to deal with anything other than abuses so recurrent as to amount to "custom, or usage." One can agree with my Brother Frankfurter in dissent, that Congress had no intention of taking over the whole field of ordinary state torts and crimes, without being certain that the enacting Congress would not have regarded actions by an official, made possible by his position, as far more serious than an ordinary state tort, and therefore as a matter for federal concern. If attention is directed at the rare specific references to isolated abuses of state authority, one finds them neither so clear nor so disproportionately divided between favoring the positions of the majority or the dissent as to make either position seem plainly correct. . . .

The dissent considers that the "under color of" provision of § 1983 distinguishes between unconstitutional actions taken without state authority, which only the state should remedy, and unconstitutional actions authorized by the state, which the federal act was to reach. If so, then the controlling difference for the enacting legislature must have been either that the

[c] The Court's treatment of the plaintiff's claim against the City of Chicago, as distinct from his claims against its officers, is postponed until Section 5 of this Chapter, where the issue of municipal liability under § 1983 is considered in detail.—[Footnote by eds.]

state remedy was more adequate for unauthorized actions than for authorized ones or that there was, in some sense, greater harm from unconstitutional actions authorized by the full panoply of state power and approval than from unconstitutional actions not so authorized or acquiesced in by the state. I find less than compelling the evidence that either distinction was important to that Congress.

I

If the state remedy was considered adequate when the official's unconstitutional act was unauthorized, why should it not be thought equally adequate when the unconstitutional act was authorized? . . .

Since the suggested narrow construction of § 1983 presupposes that state measures were adequate to remedy unauthorized deprivations of constitutional rights and since the identical state relief could be obtained for state-authorized acts with the aid of Supreme Court review, this narrow construction would reduce the statute to having merely a jurisdictional function, shifting the load of federal supervision from the Supreme Court to the lower courts and providing a federal tribunal for fact findings in cases involving authorized action. Such a function could be justified on various grounds. It could, for example, be argued that the state courts would be less willing to find a constitutional violation in cases involving "authorized action" and that therefore the victim of such action would bear a greater burden in that he would more likely have to carry his case to this Court, and once here, might be bound by unfavorable state court findings. But the legislative debates do not disclose congressional concern about the burdens of litigation placed upon the victims of "authorized" constitutional violations contrasted to the victims of unauthorized violations. Neither did Congress indicate an interest in relieving the burden placed on this Court in reviewing such cases.

The statute becomes more than a jurisdictional provision only if one attributes to the enacting legislature the view that a deprivation of a constitutional right is significantly different from and more serious than a violation of a state right and therefore deserves a different remedy even though the same act may constitute both a state tort and the deprivation of a constitutional right. This view, by no means unrealistic as a commonsense matter,[5] is, I believe, more consistent with the flavor of the legislative history than is a view that the primary purpose of the state was to grant a lower court forum for fact findings. . . .

II

I think this limited interpretation of § 1983 fares no better when viewed from the other possible premise for it, namely that state-approved constitutional deprivations were considered more offensive than those not so approved. For one thing, the enacting Congress was not unaware of the

---

[5] There will be many cases in which the relief provided by the state to the victim of a use of state power which the state either did not or could not constitutionally authorize will be far less than what Congress may have thought would be a fair reimbursement for deprivation of a constitutional right. I will venture only a few examples. There may be no damage remedy for the loss of voting rights or for the harm from psychological coercion leading to a confession. And what is the dollar value of the right to go to unsegregated schools? Even the remedy for such an unauthorized search and seizure as Monroe was allegedly subjected to may be only the nominal amount of damages to physical property allowable in an action for trespass to land. It would indeed be the purest coincidence if the state remedies for violation of common-law rights by private citizens were fully appropriate to redress those injuries which only a state official can cause and against which the Constitution provides protection.

fact that there was a substantial overlap between the protections granted by state constitutional provisions and those granted by the Fourteenth Amendment. Indeed one opponent of the bill, Senator Trumbull, went so far as to state in a debate with Senators Carpenter and Edmunds that his research indicated a complete overlap in every state, at least as to the protections of the due process clause. Thus, in one very significant sense, there was no ultimate state approval of a large portion of otherwise authorized actions depriving a person of due-process rights. . . .

These difficulties in explaining the basis of a distinction between authorized and unauthorized deprivations of constitutional rights fortify my view that the legislative history does not bear the burden which stare decisis casts upon it. For this reason and for those stated in the opinion of the Court, I agree that we should not now depart from the holdings of the *Classic* and *Screws* cases.

■ MR. JUSTICE FRANKFURTER, dissenting. . . .

This case squarely presents the question whether the intrusion of a city policeman for which that policeman can show no such authority at state law as could be successfully interposed in defense to a state-law action against him, is nonetheless to be regarded as "under color" of state authority within the meaning of § 1983. Respondents, in breaking into the Monroe apartment, violated the laws of the state of Illinois. Illinois law appears to offer a civil remedy for unlawful searches; petitioners do not claim that none is available. Rather they assert that they have been deprived of due process of law and of equal protection of the laws under color of state law, although from all that appears the courts of Illinois are available to give them the fullest redress which the common law affords for the violence done them, nor does any "statute, ordinance, regulation, custom, or usage" of the state of Illinois bar that redress. Did the enactment by Congress of § 1 of the Ku Klux Act of 1871 encompass such a situation?

That section, it has been noted, was patterned on the similar criminal provision of § 2, Act of April 9, 1866 [now 18 U.S.C. § 242]. The earlier act had as its primary object the effective nullification of the Black Codes, those statutes of the Southern legislatures which had so burdened and disqualified the Negro as to make his emancipation appear illusory. The act had been vetoed by President Johnson, whose veto message describes contemporary understanding of its second section; the section, he wrote

> seems to be designed to apply to some existing or future law of a state or territory which may conflict with the provisions of the bill. . . . It provides for counteracting such forbidden legislation by imposing fine and imprisonment upon the legislators who may pass such conflicting laws, or upon the officers or agents who shall put, or attempt to put, them into execution. It means an official offense, not a common crime committed against law upon the persons or property of the black race. Such an act may deprive the black man of his property, but not of the right to hold property. It means a deprivation of the right itself, either by the state judiciary or the state legislature.

And Senator Trumbull, then Chairman of the Senate Judiciary Committee, in his remarks urging its passage over the veto, expressed the intendment of the second section as those who voted for it read it:

> If an offense is committed against a colored person simply because he is colored, in a state where the law affords him the same protection as if he were white, this act neither has nor was intended to have any-

> thing to do with his case, because he has adequate remedies in the state courts; but if he is discriminated against under color of state laws because he is colored, then it becomes necessary to interfere for his protection. . . .

The original text of the present § 1983 contained words, left out in the Revised Statutes, which clarified the objective to which the provision was addressed:

> That any person who, under color of any law, statute, ordinance, regulation, custom, or usage of any state, shall subject or cause to be subjected, any person within the jurisdiction of the United States to the deprivation of any rights, privileges, or immunities secured by the Constitution of the United States, shall, *any such law, statute, ordinance, regulation, custom, or usage of the state to the contrary notwithstanding*, be liable to the party injured. . . .

The Court now says, however, that "It was not the unavailability of state remedies but the failure of certain states to enforce the laws with an equal hand that furnished the powerful momentum behind this 'force bill.' " Of course, if the notion of "unavailability" of remedy is limited to mean an absence of statutory, paper right, this is in large part true. Insofar as the Court undertakes to demonstrate—as the bulk of its opinion seems to do—that § 1983 was meant to reach some instances of action not specifically authorized by the avowed, apparent, written law inscribed in the statute books of the states, the argument knocks at an open door. No one would or could deny this, for by its express terms the statute comprehends deprivations of federal rights under color of any "statute, ordinance, regulation, *custom, or usage*" of a state. (Emphasis added.) The question is, *what* class of cases other than those involving state statute law were meant to be reached. And, with respect to this question, the Court's conclusion is undermined by the very portions of the legislative debates which it cites. For surely the misconduct of individual municipal police officers, subject to the effective oversight of appropriate state administrative and judicial authorities, presents a situation which differs toto coelo from one in which "Immunity is given to crime, and the records of the public tribunals are searched in vain for any evidence of effective redress," or in which murder rages while a state makes "no successful effort to bring the guilty to punishment or afford protection or redress". . . . These statements indicate that Congress—made keenly aware by the post-bellum conditions in the South that states through their authorities could sanction offenses against the individual by settled practice which established state law as truly as written codes—designed § 1983 to reach, as well, official conduct which, because engaged in "permanently and as a rule," or "systematically," came through acceptance by law-administering officers to constitute "custom, or usage" having the cast of law. They do not indicate an attempt to reach, nor does the statute by its terms include, instances of acts in defiance of state law and which no settled state practice, no systematic pattern of official action or inaction, no "custom, or usage, of any state," insulates from effective and adequate reparation by the state authorities.

Rather, all the evidence converges to the conclusion that Congress by § 1983 created a civil liability enforceable in the federal courts only in instances of injury for which redress was barred in the state courts because some "statute, ordinance, regulation, custom, or usage" sanctioned the grievance complained of. . . .

The present case comes here from a judgment sustaining a motion to dismiss petitioners' complaint. That complaint, insofar as it describes the police intrusion, makes no allegation that that intrusion was authorized by state law other than the conclusory and unspecific claim that "[d]uring all times herein mentioned the individual defendants and each of them were acting under color of the statutes, ordinances, regulations, customs, and usages of the state of Illinois, of the county of Cook and of the defendant city of Chicago." In the face of Illinois decisions holding such intrusions unlawful and in the absence of more precise factual averments to support its conclusion, such a complaint fails to state a claim under § 1983.

However, the complaint does allege, as to the 10–hour detention of Mr. Monroe, that "it was, and it is now, the custom or usage of the Police Department of the city of Chicago to arrest and confine individuals in the police stations and jail cells of the said department for long periods of time on 'open' charges." . . . Such averments do present facts which, admitted as true for purposes of a motion to dismiss, seem to sustain petitioners' claim that Mr. Monroe's detention—as contrasted with the night-time intrusion into the Monroe apartment—was "under color" of state authority. . . . [b]

NOTES ON 42 U.S.C. § 1983

1. BACKGROUND

Before *Monroe v. Pape*, § 1983 was remarkable for its insignificance. Indeed, one commentator found only 21 suits brought under this provision in the years between 1871 and 1920.[a] During the 1920s and 30s, the statute was invoked in a handful of cases involving racial discrimination and the franchise.[b] The prospect of broader application was signaled in Hague v. Committee for Industrial Organization, 307 U.S. 496 (1939), where the Court affirmed an injunction against a local ordinance used to harass labor organizers. In all of these cases, however, the acts complained of were affirmatively authorized by statute or local ordinance and thus fit even the narrowest reading of "under color of" law. None raised the issue of unauthorized misconduct by state officials. *Monroe v. Pape* was the first Supreme Court vindication of the use of § 1983 as an independent federal remedy against acts that violated both state law and the federal Constitution.

(i) The Mind–Set of the Civil Rights Cases

Monroe did not overrule precedent, but it did overturn a longstanding assumption that § 1983 reached only misconduct either officially authorized or so widely tolerated as to amount to "custom or usage." The origins of this assumption apparently lay in restrictive constitutional interpretations of the nineteenth century. In a number of cases, the Supreme Court insisted that federal legislative power to enforce the guarantees of the Fourteenth Amendment could

---

[b] In a portion of his opinion omitted here, Justice Frankfurter said that although he thought *Classic* and *Screws* had been wrongly decided, stare decisis did not require that he perpetuate the error.—[Footnote by eds.]

[a] Comment, The Civil Rights Act: Emergence of an Adequate Federal Civil Remedy?, 26 Ind.L.J. 361, 363 (1951).

[b] See, e.g., Nixon v. Herndon, 273 U.S. 536 (1927) (awarding damages against Texas officials for enforcing a statute barring African–Americans from the Democratic primary); Lane v. Wilson, 307 U.S. 268 (1939) (vindicating rights of African–Americans against enforcement of racially discriminatory laws governing the franchise).

be exercised only against "state action" and struck down Reconstruction-era efforts to reach purely private misconduct.[c] In the famous Civil Rights Cases, 109 U.S. 3 (1883), the Court struck down the attempt in the Civil Rights Act of 1875 to prohibit racial discrimination by private parties in the provision of public accommodations:

> [U]ntil some state law has been passed or some state action through its officers and agents has been taken, adverse to the rights of citizens sought to be protected by the Fourteenth Amendment, no legislation of the United States under said amendment, nor any proceeding under such legislation, can be called into activity; for the prohibitions of the amendment are against state laws and acts done under state authority. . . . In this connection it is proper to state that civil rights, such as are guarantied by the Constitution against state aggression, cannot be impaired by the wrongful acts of individuals, unsupported by state authority in the shape of laws, customs or judicial or executive proceedings.

Nowhere did the Court explicitly say that the acts of a state officer in violation of state law could not constitute the required state action, but this decision, and others, seemed to imply as much.[d] In fact, several lower courts explicitly so concluded.[e] In light of this background, a nineteenth-century observer might reasonably have thought that § 1983 would be unconstitutional unless it were limited to acts explicitly or impliedly authorized by state law.[f]

(ii) Home Telephone & Telegraph

By 1961 the notion of a *constitutional* incapacity to reach unauthorized misconduct of state officials had long since died. The demise of this idea dates from Home Telephone & Telegraph Co. v. Los Angeles, 227 U.S. 278 (1913) (cited in *Monroe*). In that case, the telephone company went to federal court to enjoin enforcement of a city ordinance setting telephone rates. The company charged that the rates were so unreasonably low as to be confiscatory and hence violative of the Fourteenth Amendment guarantee of due process of law. The city answered that, if that were true, the rates would also violate a parallel provision of the state constitution. In that event, said the city, the rates would be forbidden by state law and therefore their adoption would not constitute "state action." Since the Fourteenth Amendment guarantees due process only against state action, the city argued, the federal court would have no power to consider the matter "until, by final action of an appropriate state court, it was

---

[c] This was the fate of that part of § 2 of the Act of 1871 (of which § 1983 was originally § 1) that imposed criminal penalties for private conspiracy to deprive any person of "the equal protection of the laws, or of equal privileges or immunities under the law." United States v. Harris, 106 U.S. 629 (1882).

[d] Cf. Virginia v. Rives, 100 U.S. 313 (1879), in which the Supreme Court considered a provision of the Civil Rights Act of 1866 authorizing removal to federal court of a state criminal prosecution "[a]gainst any person who is denied or cannot enforce in the courts of such state a right under any law providing for the equal civil rights of citizens of the United States, or of all persons within the jurisdiction thereof." The Court held that the right to removal applied only where the denial of equal rights was accomplished by legislation rather than by the unauthorized acts of a state official. See also Barney v. New York, 193 U.S. 430 (1904).

[e] See the cases cited in Developments in the Law—Section 1983 and Federalism, 90 Harv.L.Rev. 1133, 1160–61 n.138 (1977), which summarizes the grounds for thinking that acts violative of state law could not be state action.

[f] For an effort to solve the "mystery" of *Monroe*—that is, why § 1983 had been so unimportant before that decision—see Louise Weinberg, The *Monroe* Mystery Solved: Beyond the "Unhappy History" Theory of Civil Rights Litigation, 1991 B.Y.U.L.Rev. 737 (1991).

decided that such acts were authorized by the state. . . . " The Supreme Court rejected this view and embraced a much broader conception of "state action."

"To speak broadly," said the Court, "the difference between the proposition insisted upon and the true meaning of the amendment is this, that the one assumes that the amendment virtually contemplates alone wrongs authorized by a state, and gives only power accordingly, while in truth the amendment contemplates the possibility of state officers abusing the powers lawfully conferred upon them by doing wrongs prohibited by the amendment." The Court therefore concluded that the Fourteenth Amendment reached not only unconstitutional acts authorized by state law but also those committed when "state powers [were] abused by those who possessed them."

Home Telephone & Telegraph established that conduct violative of state law could constitute state action within the meaning of the Fourteenth Amendment. This decision undermined the notion of a *constitutional* bar to a broad reading of § 1983, but it gave no indication whether the statute should in fact be so read. That possibility was first raised in *United States v. Classic* and *Screws v. United States*, both of which broadly interpreted the parallel "under color of" law language in 18 U.S.C. § 242 (quoted in *Monroe*). As the *Monroe* opinion recounts, 18 U.S.C. § 242 is a criminal provision, originally enacted as § 2 of the Civil Rights Act of 1866. The statute that ultimately became § 1983 was modeled on this earlier law, and provided civil remedies for conduct that had been prohibited by the penal statute. Given the close historical and textual association of the two provisions, it is not surprising that the interpretation placed on one would also be applied to the other, as *Monroe* held.

(iii) Implications of the Civil Rights Act of 1866

The connection between § 1983 and the 1866 Act introduces still further complexities in the interpretation of both statutes, explored in detail in Chapter 4. The 1866 Act has had a history of neglect and revival very much like § 1983, resulting eventually in the application of the Act to entirely private forms of racial discrimination. In its current form, in 42 U.S.C. § 1981(c), it protects "against impairment by nongovernmental discrimination and impairment under color of State law." This provision for coverage goes far beyond the actions of the police officers in *Monroe v. Pape*, and reaches purely private forms of discrimination. A recent study summarizes the intricate developments under the 1866 Act in these terms:

> Those developments can be traced back to the act's origins in the Thirteenth Amendment. This amendment is unique among constitutional provisions in directly regulating private activity. It prohibits all forms of slavery and involuntary servitude, whether public or private. Private contracts selling an individual into slavery are as illegal as formal slave codes. Few other clauses in the Constitution apply directly to private individuals. . . . Since the amendment directly regulates private activity, enforcement legislation can do so as well. Moreover, since Congress can legislate against the "badges and incidents of slavery," it can reach far beyond the abolition of slavery itself, to prohibit a wide range of discriminatory practices.

George Rutherglen, Civil Rights in the Shadow of Slavery: The Constitution, Common Law, and the Civil Rights Act of 1866 13–14 (2013).

Between the extremes of the *Civil Rights Cases* and the modern version of the 1866 Act, the degree of innovation involved in *Monroe* becomes still harder to pin down. The majority's reading of the statute may well have been consistent with the intent of its drafters, though that issue has been debated.[g] The decision was foreshadowed by *Classic* and *Screws* and therefore should have been predictable. On the other hand, during much of the life of the statute, the interpretation placed on it in *Monroe v. Pape* would have been thought at least surprising and probably unconstitutional. And it seems plain that the practicing bar was not aware of the potential uses of § 1983 until *Monroe* pointed the way. Thus, in an important sense, and regardless of whether it restored or perverted the original intention, *Monroe v. Pape* began a new chapter in federal court supervision of state officials.

2. "SECURED BY THE CONSTITUTION"

One reason why § 1983 was used infrequently before *Monroe* was the Supreme Court's constricted view of rights "secured by the Constitution." Michael G. Collins, "Economic Rights," Implied Constitutional Actions, and the Scope of Section 1983, 77 Geo. L.J. 1493 (1989), suggests that the turn-of-the-century Court distinguished between rights that were "granted and created" by the Constitution and those that were merely "recognized and declared"—such as the right to contract. Under this approach, § 1983 would not reach state violations of common-law property rights or liberty interests. In addition, the early roster of constitutional rights protected by the courts was much smaller than it is today. For one thing, the provisions of the Bill of Rights that have given rise to the greatest number of § 1983 actions, such as the First and Fourth Amendments, were not applied to the states until well into the twentieth century. For another, many of the rights protected by those amendments were either unrecognized or nascent in the decades prior to *Monroe*. Indeed, it is probably not coincidence that the *Monroe* remedy was first recognized by the Supreme Court in the early 1960s, a period during which constitutional rights were being greatly enlarged.

In this connection, it may be useful to consider what would have happened if the *Monroe* plaintiffs had brought the lawsuit they would have been entitled to bring under Illinois law. At common law, state officials were presumptively responsible for injuries they caused in performing their duties, but they could raise a defense of statutory authorization or official authority. If they were acting pursuant to a state statute, they could avoid personal liability. Thus, one question that a state court would have addressed in the Monroes' case was whether Illinois law authorized the officers' behavior. If the answer to that question was "no," the officers could be held liable in tort, in essentially the same way that private individuals who broke into and ransacked the Monroes' house, assaulted, and then kidnaped them would be. If Illinois law purported to authorize the officers' behavior, the plaintiffs would have argued that the stat-

---

[g] Compare Eric H. Zagrans, "Under Color of" *What* Law: A Reconstructed Model of § 1983 Liability, 71 Va.L.Rev. 499 (1985) (concluding that, "[a]s a matter of statutory construction, *Monroe* is flatly wrong"), with Steven L. Winter, The Meaning of "Under Color of" Law, 91 Mich. L. Rev. 323 (1992) (concluding that the "Frankfurter–Zagrans misinterpretation of section 1983 is not only wrong, but wildly ahistorical"), and David Achtenberg, A "Milder Measure of Villainy": The Unknown History of 42 U.S.C. § 1983 and the Meaning of "Under Color of" Law, 1999 Utah L. Rev. 1 (seeking to "dispel the remarkably persistent myth that the Forty-second Congress never intended the provision to cover constitutional wrongs unless those wrongs were actually authorized by state law").

ute or policy pursuant to which the officers acted was unconstitutional. In that case, the state law would be overridden, and the defense of official authority would fail. As Professor Collins explains, "In such a case, the officer was not liable because he had violated the Constitution; he was liable because he had committed a common law harm."[h]

3. QUESTIONS AND COMMENTS ON *MONROE V. PAPE*

Justice Douglas identified three main aims for § 1983: (1) to "override certain kinds of state laws," (2) to provide "a remedy where state law was inadequate," and (3) most importantly, "to provide a federal remedy where the state remedy, though adequate in theory, was not available in practice." Which of these purposes applies to the facts of *Monroe* ? More generally, why did the Court declare that "the federal remedy is supplementary to the state remedy, and the latter need not be first sought and refused before the federal one is invoked?" What is the rationale for a "supplementary" federal remedy that does not depend on the inadequacy of state law? Does the *Monroe* opinion answer provide an answer? Under Justice Frankfurter's view, the federal courts would have to distinguish between an isolated abuse of authority by a state official and an abuse so widely practiced or tolerated as to amount to "custom or usage." Do the difficulties in making this inquiry justify across-the-board federal relief?

A different rationale for an independent federal remedy was suggested by Justice Harlan. He "attribute[d] to the enacting legislature the view that a deprivation of a constitutional right is significantly different from and more serious than a violation of a state right and therefore deserves a different remedy even though the same act may constitute both a state tort and the deprivation of a constitutional right." Is this persuasive? Is deprivation of a constitutional right always more serious than the kinds of injuries against which state law protects? And why is a separate remedy needed when the same act accomplishes both wrongs?

4. JURISDICTION OVER CIVIL RIGHTS ACTIONS

The jurisdictional counterpart of § 1983 is 28 U.S.C. § 1343(3), which was also derived from Section 1 of the 1871 Civil Rights Act and which is quoted in footnote 1 of the *Monroe* opinion. A related provision is 28 U.S.C. § 1343(4), which provides jurisdiction over suits brought under "any act of Congress providing for the protection of civil rights." Of course, these cases are also covered by the general "federal question" statute, 28 U.S.C. § 1331, but until 1980 that provision required a minimum amount in controversy. The elimination of the amount-in-controversy requirement of § 1331 has made the special jurisdictional provisions for civil rights actions redundant and unnecessary.

Under whatever statute, the plaintiff's option to sue in federal court is significant. Comparison between state and federal judiciaries is inevitably subjective, but differences can arise. Federal judges may be more qualified, more expert in the adjudication of federal claims, more independent of popular sentiment, more sympathetic to federal rights, and less reluctant to award damages against state officials. Or they may be none of these things. It seems clear,

---

[h] For extensive inquiry into the common-law antecedents of the damages remedy authorized by *Monroe*, see Sina Kian, The Path of the Constitution: The Original System of Remedies, How It Changed, and How the Court Responded, 87 N.Y.U. L. Rev. 132 (2012).

however, that for whatever reason civil rights plaintiffs typically prefer federal court and that at certain times and in certain places the advantage of federal court may be real and substantial. See Burt Neuborne, The Myth of Parity, 90 Harv.L.Rev. 1105 (1977).

Whatever the perceived advantages of the choice to litigate in federal court, § 1983 actions may also be brought in state court.[i] Indeed, in recent years, resort to state court has become increasingly common.[j]

5. IMPACT OF *MONROE V. PAPE*

Some crude measure of the impact of *Monroe v. Pape* can be derived from the annual statistics on the business of the federal courts. In the year of the *Monroe* decision, fewer than 300 suits were brought in federal court under all civil rights acts. Ten years later, that figure had risen to 8,267, including 3,129 civil rights actions filed by prisoners. In the year ending on September 30, 2010, nearly 35,000 suits were brought under civil rights acts (chiefly § 1983). In addition, prisoners filed more than 25,000 civil rights cases (including conditions of confinement claims).[k]

Qualitative assessment is more difficult. Since Ex parte Young, 209 U.S. 123 (1908) (discussed in detail in the Introduction), injunctive relief against unconstitutional state action had been available simply by the expedient of naming the appropriate state officer as defendant. With respect to prospective relief, therefore, *Monroe* recharacterized rather than created a federal remedy. What was really new was the prospect of damage actions for violation of constitutional rights. Of course, § 1983 applies only to persons acting under color of statute, etc., "of any State or Territory or the District of Columbia."[l] It creates no right of action against federal officers, unless they act in concert with state officials and under the authority of state law.[m] Thus, although the damage

---

[i] Absent congressional direction to the contrary, state courts are *permitted* to hear federal claims. Accordingly, the Supreme Court has recognized the authority of state courts to hear § 1983 cases. A different question is whether state courts are *required* to hear § 1983 claims even when they would prefer not to do so. This question was resolved in Howlett v. Rose, 496 U.S. 356 (1990), where the Court held that state courts *must* hear § 1983 claims brought in a court otherwise competent to hear that type of claim. The state courts may refuse to hear a § 1983 case only if, under local law, they have a "valid excuse." A "valid excuse" must be a neutral procedural policy (the standard example is forum non conveniens) applicable to all cases (not just federal ones) heard in the court in question and not otherwise inconsistent with any governing federal policy.

[j] For analysis of possible tactical advantages in the choice of a state court and specific issues that may arise there, see Steven H. Steinglass, Section 1983 Litigation in State Courts (1989), and Susan Herman, Beyond Parity: Section 1983 and the State Courts, 54 Brooklyn L.Rev. 1057 (1989).

[k] These figures are found in the Annual Reports on the Judicial Business of the United States Courts published each year by the Administrative Office of the U.S. Courts. For one of the few empirical studies of § 1983 litigation, see Theodore Eisenberg and Stewart Schwab, The Reality of Constitutional Tort Litigation, 72 Corn.L.Rev. 641 (1987).

[l] In 1979, the statute was amended to treat the District of Columbia as a state for suit under § 1983. The amendment also declares that "any act of Congress applicable exclusively to the District of Columbia shall be considered to be a statute of the District of Columbia" for this purpose. Before that, the District of Columbia was outside the scope of § 1983, see District of Columbia v. Carter, 409 U.S. 418 (1973), even though the statute had been interpreted to cover acts under the laws of Puerto Rico. See Marin v. University of Puerto Rico, 377 F.Supp. 613 (D.P.R.1973).

[m] Parallel damages actions against federal officers are known as "*Bivens* actions," a label derived from the Supreme Court's decision in Bivens v. Six Unknown Named Agents, 403 U.S.

remedy is constrained in important ways, the availability of money damages for the unconstitutional acts of state and local government officers is the heart of § 1983.

Finally, mention should be made that § 1983 is not limited to constitutional violations. It applies in terms to deprivation of rights, privileges, or immunities "secured by the Constitution *and laws*" of the United States. On its face, it seems to create a private right of action for every violation of federal statute or regulation by a person acting under color of state authority. The extent to which this is true is examined in *Maine v. Thiboutot*, and the notes following, in Section 6 of this Chapter.

NOTES ON "UNDER COLOR OF" LAW AND STATE ACTION

1. INTRODUCTION

As a statutory matter, § 1983 requires that the defendant act "under color of" state law. Most constitutional rights have a similar limitation, which is usually described as the requirement of "state action." In United States v. Price, 383 U.S. 787, 794, n.7 (1966), the Supreme Court described the two concepts as essentially synonymous: "In cases under § 1983, 'under color' of law has consistently been treated as the same thing as the 'state action' required under the Fourteenth Amendment."[a]

For the vast majority of § 1983 claims, the question of state action is straightforward. There are, however, borderline cases. Questions can arise over whether a private individual or entity should be considered to have been acting under color of state law with regard to a particular practice or conduct. And when the defendant is a public officer, the question may arise whether he or she was acting in a purely private capacity when the wrong was committed. These questions are examined in turn below.

2. PRIVATE ACTORS AS PUBLIC ACTORS

It has long been settled that private parties engaged in concerted action with government officials are subject to liability under § 1983. See, e.g., Adickes v. S.H. Kress & Co., 398 U.S. 144 (1970) (department store potentially liable under § 1983 for collaboration in enforcing racial segregation laws against the plaintiff). A more modern example of this question concerns the availability of § 1983 to sue media defendants who participate in the kind of ride-alongs

388 (1971). The availability of *Bivens* actions against federal officers is discussed in Section 2 of this Chapter.

[a] The "under color of" clause refers to more than state law. It also refers to action under the "custom" or "usage" of any state. These terms have been interpreted to mean custom or usage of state officials. Adickes v. S.H. Kress Co., 398 U.S. 144, 166–68 (1970). Custom and usage, however, have a long history as sources of law independent of official action. For examination of this history and how it bears on the interpretation of § 1983 and the Fourteenth Amendment, see George Rutherglen, Custom and Usage as Action Under Color of State Law: An Essay on the Forgotten Terms of Section 1983, 89 Va. L. Rev. 925 (2003) (arguing that § 1983 was directed against "custom" and "usage" in the sense of pervasive practices, both public and private, that sought to perpetuate the inferior status of blacks in the South).

found unconstitutional in Wilson v. Layne, 526 U.S. 603 (1999) (discussed in Chapter I, Section 4 on qualified immunity).[b]

Additionally, a private actor or entity will be treated as governmental insofar as its conduct fulfills a "public function." A good example is Brentwood Academy v. Tennessee Secondary School Athletic Ass'n, 531 U.S. 288 (1001), where an association governing high school athletics was treated as state actor under § 1983, because a large portion of the association's membership consisted of public schools. In general, however, the public function concept has been construed narrowly. See, e.g., Rendell–Baker v. Kohn, 457 U.S. 830 (1982) (a private school furnishing instruction to students with special needs was not treated as a state actor despite the fact that public school districts referred students to the school and paid their tuition).

The most important contemporary context where private actors will be treated as state actors is in the industry of private prisons.[c] Private prisons are undoubtedly state actors, as their sole authority to confine inmates is the delegation of power from the state. But although this conferral of authority is sufficient to make them amenable to suit under § 1983, the Supreme Court has not treated private and public prison guards identically in all respects. See, e.g., Richardson v. McKnight, 521 U.S. 399 (1997) (refusing to extend the protections of qualified immunity that public officers enjoy to the employees of a private prison).

3. PUBLIC ACTORS AS PRIVATE ACTORS

Not everything done by a public official occurs "under color of" law. Public officials have private lives, and the line between state action and private behavior can sometimes be fuzzy. An area of particular controversy involves off-duty police officers. Consider, for example, the decision in Parilla–Burgos v. Hernandez–Rivera, 108 F.3d 445 (1st Cir. 1997). The defendant was an off-duty police officer (indeed, he was on medical leave) who killed another bar patron with his service revolver, which department policy required him to carry at all times. The plaintiff's estate brought suit under § 1983. The court of appeals held that the officer was not acting under color of law, because his actions were unrelated to his official duties.

Parilla–Burgos may well state the result that other courts would reach on similar facts, but different facts produce different results. For example, in United States v. Tarpley, 945 F.2d 806 (5th Cir. 1991), the court held that a deputy sheriff acted under color of law when he assaulted his wife's former lover, because the officer claimed special authority from his official status, summoned another police officer for assistance, and used a police car to chase the victim.

One of the most unusual cases of public officers found not to be acting "under color of" law involves public defenders—criminal defense lawyers provided by the state to defendants who cannot afford representation. In Polk

---

[b] See Sheila M. Lombardi, Note, Media In The Spotlight: Private Parties Liable For Violating the Fourth Amendment, 6 Roger Williams U. L. Rev. 393 (2000) (collecting conflicting cases on this question).

[c] See generally Ahmed A. White, Rule of Law and the Limits of Sovereignty: The Private Prison in Jurisprudential Perspective, 38 Am. Crim. L. Rev. 111 (2001); Paul Howard Morris, Note, The Impact of Constitutional Liability on the Privatization Movement After *Richardson v. McKnight*, 52 Vand. L. Rev. 489 (1999).

County v. Dodson, 454 U.S. 312 (1981), the Supreme Court held that a criminal defendant could not sue his public defender under § 1983. *Polk County* is the only case in which the Court has held that a public employee, while performing the function for which he or she was paid, is not a state actor. In West v. Atkins, 487 U.S. 42 (1988), the Court refused to extend *Polk County* to private physicians providing services to prison inmates pursuant to a contract with the state. Unlike public defenders, whose exercise of independent judgment would often lead them to positions that conflicted with the state's interest—thus making it inappropriate to hold the state responsible for their acts—prison physicians, even though they exercised independent medical judgment, were viewed as engaged in a fundamentally cooperative relationship with the state.

Does *Polk County* make sense? Particularly in light of the fact that the government is "responsible" for public defenders' serious shortcomings under established Sixth Amendment doctrine requiring effective assistance of counsel? What problems would arise if public defenders were liable to suit under § 1983?

4. QUASI–PUBLIC FUNCTIONS AND QUASI–PUBLIC OFFICIALS: THE CASE OF POLICING

In addition to cases where an officer is clearly off-duty, questions arise concerning officers who, although technically off-duty, are nonetheless acting in a quasi-police capacity. Consider the prevalent use of off-duty officers, sometimes in uniform and carrying service revolvers, as private security guards. See David A. Sklansky, The Private Police, 46 U.C.L.A. L. Rev. 1165 (1999). Sklansky notes that "an estimated 150,000 police officers moonlight as private security guards, often in police uniform. This practice, too, appears to have escalated sharply; more than half of the officers in many metropolitan police departments now supplement their income with private security work. In a growing number of cases police departments themselves contract to supply their personnel to groups of merchants or residents, and then pay the officers out of the proceeds." Id. at 1176.

Are these moonlighting officers acting with "apparent authority" for purposes of § 1983? If so, what about those who are not sworn officers but are employed full-time in the private security industry? Sklansky points out that there are more private security guards in the United States than sworn law enforcement officers and that, in some areas, they perform much of the traditional police job of patrolling neighborhoods. For the most part, courts have refused to find that private "police" are state actors. As Sklansky suggests, this result may flow from a concern far removed from the question of liability under § 1983. If private police are engaged in state action, then the exclusionary rules of the Fourth, Fifth, and Sixth Amendments would apply to the searches or questioning they conducted. In declining to find state action, courts seem primarily concerned with the general applicability of these constitutional protections. The finding of no state action also means, however, that private police also are not liable for damages under § 1983. Sklansky concludes, id. at 1183, that

> the main legal limitations on the private police today are [state law-based] tort and criminal doctrines of assault, trespass, and false imprisonment—variants of the same doctrines that once defined the principal boundaries

of permissible public policing. Unless the owner has given consent, a security guard's search of private property will generally constitute a trespass. And arrests or detentions not authorized by state law generally will expose a security guard to civil and criminal liability for false imprisonment and, if force is involved, for assault.

5. WHY IT MATTERS

Why might § 1983 be advantageous in such cases? Usually, state action is essential to establishing a constitutional violation that would trigger damages liability. In Brentwood Academy v. Tennessee Secondary School Athletic Ass'n, 531 U.S. 288 (2001), for example, the plaintiff's claim that the Association's rules violated the First Amendment required showing state action because the First Amendment does not bind private parties. By contrast, a person assaulted by an off-duty police officer would have a state-law tort claim against the officer, whether or not a claim would also lie § 1983. Even when damages may be available through a different route, § 1983 offers several potential advantages. Most obviously, § 1983 claims can be litigated in federal court, regardless of the citizenship of the parties or the amount in controversy. Docket congestion, different jury pools, non-elected judges, and various procedural differences may make federal courts more plaintiff-friendly than some state courts. More importantly, prevailing plaintiffs under § 1983 are entitled to their damages plus reasonable attorney's fees under 42 U.S.C. § 1988, while state tort plaintiffs are usually subject to the "American rule," under which the attorney for a successful plaintiff typically takes a share of the recovery.

2. SUITS AGAINST FEDERAL OFFICERS

Bivens v. Six Unknown Named Agents of Federal Bureau of Narcotics[a]

Supreme Court of the United States, 1971.
403 U.S. 388.

■ MR. JUSTICE BRENNAN delivered the opinion of the Court.

The Fourth Amendment provides that:

> The right of the people to be secure in their persons, houses, papers, and effects, against unreasonable searches and seizures, shall not be violated. . . .

In Bell v. Hood, 327 U.S. 678 (1946), we reserved the question whether violation of that command by a federal agent acting under color of his authority gives rise to a cause of action for damages consequent upon his unconstitutional conduct. Today we hold that it does.

This case has its origin in an arrest and search carried out on the morning of November 26, 1965. Petitioner's complaint alleged that on that day respondents, agents of the Federal Bureau of Narcotics acting under claim of federal authority, entered his apartment and arrested him for alleged narcotics violations. The agents manacled petitioner in front of his wife and children, and threatened to arrest the entire family. They

[a] The defendants' brief in the Supreme Court explained that after the plaintiff had filed his complaint, the United States Attorney supplied the agents' names to the clerk of the court.—[Footnote by eds.]

searched the apartment from stem to stern. Thereafter, petitioner was taken to the federal courthouse in Brooklyn, where he was interrogated, booked, and subjected to a visual strip search.

On July 7, 1967, petitioner brought suit in Federal District Court. In addition to the allegations above, his complaint asserted that the arrest and search were effected without a warrant, and that unreasonable force was employed in making the arrest; fairly read, it alleges as well that the arrest was made without probable cause. Petitioner claimed to have suffered great humiliation, embarrassment, and mental suffering as a result of the agents' unlawful conduct, and sought $15,000 damages from each of them. . . .

I

Respondents do not argue that petitioner should be entirely without remedy for an unconstitutional invasion of his rights by federal agents. In respondents' view, however, the rights that petitioner asserts—primarily rights of privacy—are creations of state and not of federal law. Accordingly, they argue, petitioner may obtain money damages to redress invasion of these rights only by an action in tort, under state law, in the state courts. In this scheme the Fourth Amendment would serve merely to limit the extent to which the agents could defend the state law tort suit by asserting that their actions were a valid exercise of federal power: if the agents were shown to have violated the Fourth Amendment, such a defense would be lost to them and they would stand before the state law merely as private individuals. Candidly admitting that it is the policy of the Department of Justice to remove all such suits from the state to the federal courts for decision,[b] respondents nevertheless urge that we uphold dismissal of petitioner's complaint in federal court, and remit him to filing an action in the state courts in order that the case may properly be removed to the federal court for decision on the basis of state law.

We think that respondents' thesis rests upon an unduly restrictive view of the Fourth Amendment's protection against unreasonable searches and seizures by federal agents, a view that has consistently been rejected by this Court. Respondents seek to treat the relationship between a citizen and a federal agent unconstitutionally exercising his authority as no different from the relationship between two private citizens. In so doing, they ignore the fact that power, once granted, does not disappear like a magic gift when it is wrongfully used. An agent acting—albeit unconstitutionally—in the name of the United States possesses a far greater capacity for harm than an individual trespasser exercising no authority other than his own. . . .

[R]espondents' argument that the Fourth Amendment serves only as a limitation on federal defenses to a state law claim, and not as an independent limitation upon the exercise of federal power, must be rejected.

. . . That damages may be obtained for injuries consequent upon a violation of the Fourth Amendment by federal officials should hardly seem a surprising proposition. Historically, damages have been regarded as the ordinary remedy for an invasion of personal interests in liberty. Of course, the Fourth Amendment does not in so many words provide for its enforcement by an award of money damages for the consequences of its violation. But "it is . . . well settled that where legal rights have been invaded, and

[b] Removal to federal court of state criminal prosecutions of federal officers is authorized by 28 U.S.C. § 1442.—[Footnote by eds.]

a federal statute provides for a general right to sue for such invasion, federal courts may use any available remedy to make good the wrong done." Bell v. Hood, 327 U.S., at 684 (footnote omitted). The present case involves no special factors counselling hesitation in the absence of affirmative action by Congress. . . . [W]e cannot accept respondents' formulation of the question as whether the availability of money damages is necessary to enforce the Fourth Amendment. For we have here no explicit congressional declaration that persons injured by a federal officer's violation of the Fourth Amendment may not recover money damages from the agents, but must instead be remitted to another remedy, equally effective in the view of Congress. The question is merely whether petitioner, if he can demonstrate an injury consequent upon the violation by federal agents of his Fourth Amendment rights, is entitled to redress his injury through a particular remedial mechanism normally available in the federal courts. "The very essence of civil liberty certainly consists in the right of every individual to claim the protection of the laws, whenever he receives an injury." Marbury v. Madison, 5 U.S. (1 Cranch) 137, 163 (1803). Having concluded that petitioner's complaint states a cause of action under the Fourth Amendment, we hold that petitioner is entitled to recover money damages for any injuries he has suffered as a result of the agents' violation of the Amendment.

. . .

■ MR. JUSTICE HARLAN, concurring in the judgment. . . .

For the reasons set forth below, I am of the opinion that federal courts do have the power to award damages for violation of "constitutionally protected interests" and I agree with the Court that a traditional judicial remedy such as damages is appropriate to the vindication of the personal interests protected by the Fourth Amendment.

I

[T]he interest which Bivens claims—to be free from official conduct in contravention of the Fourth Amendment—is a federally protected interest. Therefore, the question of judicial power to grant Bivens damages is not a problem of the "source" of the "right"; instead, the question is whether the power to authorize damages as a judicial remedy for the vindication of a federal constitutional right is placed by the Constitution itself exclusively in Congress' hands.

II

The contention that the federal courts are powerless to accord a litigant damages for a claimed invasion of his federal constitutional rights until Congress explicitly authorizes the remedy cannot rest on the notion that the decision to grant compensatory relief involves a resolution of policy considerations not susceptible of judicial discernment. Thus, in suits for damages based on violations of federal statutes lacking any express authorization of a damage remedy, this Court has authorized such relief where, in its view, damages are necessary to effectuate the congressional policy underpinning the substantive provisions of the statute. J. I. Case Co. v. Borak, 377 U.S. 426 (1964).

. . . I do not think that the fact that the interest is protected by the Constitution rather than statute or common law justifies the assertion that federal courts are powerless to grant damages in the absence of explicit congressional action authorizing the remedy. Initially, I note that it would be at least anomalous to conclude that the federal judiciary—while competent to choose among the range of traditional judicial remedies to implement statutory and common-law policies, and even to generate substantive rules governing primary behavior in furtherance of broadly formulated policies articulated by statute or Constitution—is powerless to accord a damages remedy to vindicate social policies which, by virtue of their inclusion in the Constitution, are aimed predominantly at restraining the Government as an instrument of the popular will. More importantly, the presumed availability of federal equitable relief against threatened invasions of constitutional interests appears entirely to negate the contention that the status of an interest as constitutionally protected divests federal courts of the power to grant damages absent express congressional authorization. . . .

III

The major thrust of the Government's position is that, where Congress has not expressly authorized a particular remedy, a federal court should exercise its power to accord a traditional form of judicial relief at the behest of a litigant, who claims a constitutionally protected interest has been invaded, only where the remedy is "essential," or "indispensable for vindicating constitutional rights." . . .

The question . . . is, as I see it, whether compensatory relief is "necessary" or "appropriate" to the vindication of the interest asserted. In resolving that question, it seems to me that the range of policy considerations we may take into account is at least as broad as the range of those a legislature would consider with respect to an express statutory authorization of a traditional remedy. In this regard I agree with the Court that the appropriateness of according Bivens compensatory relief does not turn simply on the deterrent effect liability will have on federal official conduct. Damages as a traditional form of compensation for invasion of a legally protected interest may be entirely appropriate even if no substantial deterrent effects on future official lawlessness might be thought to result. Bivens, after all, has invoked judicial processes claiming entitlement to compensation for injuries resulting from allegedly lawless official behavior. . . . I do not think a court of law—vested with the power to accord a remedy—should deny him his relief simply because he cannot show that future lawless conduct will thereby be deterred. . . .

Putting aside the desirability of leaving the problem of federal official liability to the vagaries of common-law actions, it is apparent that some form of damages is the only possible remedy for someone in Bivens' alleged position. It will be a rare case indeed in which an individual in Bivens' position will be able to obviate the harm by securing injunctive relief from any court. However desirable a direct remedy against the Government might be as a substitute for individual official liability, the sovereign still remains immune to suit. Finally, assuming Bivens' innocence of the crime charged, the "exclusionary rule" is simply irrelevant. For people in Bivens' shoes, it is damages or nothing.

The only substantial policy consideration advanced against recognition of a federal cause of action for violation of Fourth Amendment rights by federal officials is the incremental expenditure of judicial resources that will be necessitated by this class of litigation. There is, however, something ultimately self-defeating about this argument. For if, as the Government contends, damages will rarely be realized by plaintiffs in these cases because of jury hostility, the limited resources of the official concerned, etc., then I am not ready to assume that there will be a significant increase in the expenditure of judicial resources on these claims. Few responsible lawyers and plaintiffs are likely to choose the course of litigation if the statistical chances of success are truly de minimis. And I simply cannot agree with my Brother Black that the possibility of "frivolous" claims—if defined simply as claims with no legal merit—warrants closing the courthouse doors to people in Bivens' situation. There are other ways, short of that, of coping with frivolous lawsuits. . . .

■ MR. CHIEF JUSTICE BURGER, dissenting.

I dissent from today's holding which judicially creates a damage remedy not provided for by the Constitution and not enacted by Congress. We would more surely preserve the important values of the doctrine of separation of powers—and perhaps get a better result—by recommending a solution to the Congress as the branch of government in which the Constitution has vested the legislative power. [Chief Justice Burger continued by examining the *Bivens* issue in the larger context of remedies in general for violations of the Fourth Amendment. He launched an attack on the exclusionary rule, and concluded:]

Congress should develop an administrative or quasi-judicial remedy against the government itself to afford compensation and restitution for persons whose Fourth Amendment rights have been violated. The venerable doctrine of respondeat superior in our tort law provides an entirely appropriate conceptual basis for this remedy. If, for example, a security guard privately employed by a department store commits an assault or other tort on a customer such as an improper search, the victim has a simple and obvious remedy—an action for money damages against the guard's employer, the department store. . . .

A simple structure would suffice. For example, Congress could enact a statute along the following lines:

(a) a waiver of sovereign immunity as to the illegal acts of law enforcement officials committed in the performance of assigned duties;

(b) the creation of a cause of action for damages sustained by any person aggrieved by conduct of governmental agents in violation of the Fourth Amendment or statutes regulating official conduct;

(c) the creation of a tribunal, quasi-judicial in nature or perhaps patterned after the United States Court of Claims, to adjudicate all claims under the statute;

(d) a provision that this statutory remedy is in lieu of the exclusion of evidence secured for use in criminal cases in violation of the Fourth Amendment; and

(e) a provision directing that no evidence, otherwise admissible, shall be excluded from any criminal proceeding because of violation of the Fourth Amendment. . . .

■ MR. JUSTICE BLACK, dissenting.

[T]here can be no doubt that Congress could create a federal cause of action for damages for an unreasonable search in violation of the Fourth Amendment. Although Congress has created such a federal cause of action against state officials acting under color of state law [in 42 U.S.C. § 1983], it has never created such a cause of action against federal officials. . . . For us to do so is, in my judgment, an exercise of power that the Constitution does not give us.

Even if we had the legislative power to create a remedy, there are many reasons why we should decline to create a cause of action where none has existed since the formation of our Government. The courts of the United States as well as those of the States are choked with lawsuits. The number of cases on the docket of this Court have reached an unprecedented volume in recent years. A majority of these cases are brought by citizens with substantial complaints. . . . Unfortunately, there have also been a growing number of frivolous lawsuits, particularly actions for damages against law enforcement officers whose conduct has been judicially sanctioned by state trial and appellate courts and in many instances even by this Court. My fellow Justices on this Court and our brethren throughout the federal judiciary know only too well the time-consuming task of conscientiously poring over hundreds of thousands of pages of factual allegations of misconduct by police, judicial, and corrections officials. Of course, there are instances of legitimate grievances, but legislators might well desire to devote judicial resources to other problems of a more serious nature. . . .

The task of evaluating the pros and cons of creating judicial remedies for particular wrongs is a matter for Congress and the legislatures of the States. Congress has not provided that any federal court can entertain a suit against a federal officer for violations of Fourth Amendment rights occurring in the performance of his duties. A strong inference can be drawn from creation of such actions against state officials that Congress does not desire to permit such suits against federal officials. Should the time come when Congress desires such lawsuits, it has before it a model of valid legislation, 42 U.S.C. § 1983, to create a damage remedy against federal officers. Cases could be cited to support the legal proposition which I assert, but it seems to me to be a matter of common understanding that the business of the judiciary is to interpret the laws and not to make them.

■ MR. JUSTICE BLACKMUN, dissenting.

[T]he judicial legislation, which the Court by its opinion today concededly is effectuating, opens the door for another avalanche of new federal cases. Whenever a suspect imagines, or chooses to assert, that a Fourth Amendment right has been violated, he will now immediately sue the federal officer in federal court. This will tend to stultify proper law enforcement and to make the day's labor for the honest and conscientious officer even more onerous and more critical. Why the Court moves in this direction at this time of our history, I do not know. The Fourth Amendment was adopted in 1791, and in all the intervening years neither the Congress nor the Court has seen fit to take this step. I had thought that for the truly aggrieved person other quite adequate remedies have always been available. If not, it is the Congress and not this Court that should act.

NOTES ON SUITS AGAINST FEDERAL OFFICERS

1. INTRODUCTION

Prior to *Bivens*, individuals injured by unconstitutional conduct by federal officials were not entirely without remedy, at least not in cases where the unconstitutional conduct also violated state law. Injured individuals could sue the federal officers under state law, often bringing suit in state court (from which the federal officers would typically remove the case).[a] Moreover, in a variety of

[a] See, e.g., Wheeldin v. Wheeler, 373 U.S. 647, 652 (1963) (noting that "when it comes to suits for damages for abuse of power, federal officials are usually governed by local law"). One scholar, however, has pointed to the Court's "amnesia" in *Bivens* in "supposing that, in the absence of an express congressional remedy, a damages remedy for constitutional violations is

circumstances, the federal government had waived sovereign immunity, permitting direct lawsuits against it rather than against federal officers. For example, the Tucker Act, enacted in 1887, conferred jurisdiction on the federal Court of Claims to hear "any claim against the United States founded either upon the Constitution, or any Act of Congress or any regulation of an executive department, or upon any express or implied contract with the United States, or for liquidated or unliquidated damages in cases not sounding in tort." 28 U.S.C. § 1491(a). The Tucker Act did not reach the facts of *Bivens*, because it expressly excluded claims "sounding in tort."

That gap was partially filled by the Federal Tort Claims Act, enacted in 1946, which made the United States liable for any injury "caused by the negligent or wrongful act or omission of any employee of the Government while acting within the scope of his office or employment, under circumstances where the United States, if a private person, would be liable to the claimant in accordance with the law of the place where the act or omission occurred." 28 U.S.C. § 1346(b). But this provision has been construed not to extend to constitutional (as opposed to common-law) violations, since a private party would not be liable under for constitutional violations absent conduct under the color of law. See FDIC v. Meyer, 510 U.S. 471, 477–78 (1994) ("[T]he United States simply has not rendered itself liable under § 1346(b) for constitutional tort claims."). Thus, on the facts of *Bivens*, it was damages or nothing, so far as federal damage remedies were concerned.

Bivens was not the first time the Court addressed the availability of a damages action against federal officers. As Justice Brennan noted, the Supreme Court had reserved this question in Bell v. Hood, 327 U.S. 678 (1946), a case with roughly similar facts involving an allegedly unconstitutional search by federal officers. In *Bell*, the Court held that federal district courts had subject-matter jurisdiction over claims that federal officers had violated the Constitution, but remanded the case to determine whether the petitioners had stated a cause of action for money damages. On remand, the district court held that they had not. Bell v. Hood, 71 F. Supp. 813 (S.D. Cal. 1947). The district court's analysis is instructive. It noted that the constitutional constraints of the Fourth and Fifth Amendments apply only to government actors. As the officers were sued as individuals, the court reasoned, the Constitution provided no cause of action against them:

> The defendants are sought to be held as individuals, not as federal officers. But inasmuch as the prohibitions of the Fourth and Fifth Amendments do not apply to individual conduct, the Amendments themselves, when violated, cannot be the basis of any cause of action against individuals.
>
> There being "no federal general common law," Erie R. v. Tompkins, 304 U.S. 64 (1938), before a federal court can afford a remedy in an action at law where no diversity of citizenship exists, the right or cause of action must be one given by the Constitution or a federal statute.

---

only a by-product of the Court's invention of implied constitutional rights of action against federal officers." See Michael G. Collins, "Economic Rights," Implied Constitutional Acts, and the Scope of Section 1983, 77 Geo. L.J. 1493, 1496 (1989) (discussing earlier cases in which litigants recovered damages in federal court from federal officers on the basis of federal question jurisdiction statute). For inquiry into the common-law antecedents of the remedy authorized in *Bivens*, see Sina Kian, The Path of the Constitution: The Original System of Remedies, How It Changed, and How the Court Responded, 87 N.Y.U. L. Rev. 132 (2012).

> Plaintiffs are unable to point to any constitutional provision or federal statute giving one who has suffered an unreasonable search and seizure or false imprisonment by federal officers any federal right or cause of action to recover damages from those officers as individuals.

Bivens obviously held to the contrary.

2. *BIVENS* AND JUDICIAL POWER

Whatever the wisdom of *Bivens*, the Court's assertion of the power to grant a damages remedy should not have been terribly surprising. A damages action against state officers had already been provided under § 1983. Additionally, Ex parte Young, 209 U.S. 123 (1908), had established that injunctive relief could be granted against a state officer, notwithstanding the absence of express statutory authority. Finally, at the time it was also established—though this has subsequently been controverted—that the Court could infer a private cause of action for money damages under a federal statute that did not specifically authorize damages relief. J.I. Case Co. v. Borak, 377 U.S. 426 (1964) (permitting private damages actions for misleading proxy statements filed in violation of § 14 of the Securities and Exchange Act of 1934, despite the absence of explicit statutory authority). And of course, the Court had created an exclusionary remedy for violations of Fourth Amendment rights, first for federal courts in Weeks v. United States, 232 U.S. 383 (1914), and then for state courts in Mapp v. Ohio, 367 U.S. 643 (1961).

Does it follow from these decisions that the Court had the constitutional authority to do what it did in *Bivens*? Note that *J.I. Case* was unanimous. What reason would Justice Black have for voting in *J.I. Case* to create a damages remedy to enforce a federal statute, yet saying that *Bivens* involved the "exercise of a power that the Constitution does not give us"?

In the years since *J.I. Case*, several Justices—including notably Justice Powell in dissent in Cannon v. University of Chicago, 441 U.S. 677 (1979)—have argued that the Court should not—and perhaps constitutionally cannot—infer a private cause of action from a federal statute absent a clear indication of congressional intent. If this position is correct, does it follow that *Bivens* is incorrect? Or is the Court perhaps more justified in supplying a remedy for a constitutional violations than for violations of federal statutes?

3. THE ROLE PLAYED BY § 1983 IN *BIVENS* SUITS

Bivens was decided a decade after *Monroe v. Pape*. While one explanation for the emergence of *Monroe* nearly a century after the original enactment of § 1983 may be the incorporation of the Bill of Rights' protections against the states during the mid-twentieth century, that does not explain the late emergence of damages actions against federal officers, since the Bill of Rights had always constrained federal actors. More consequential seems to have been a shift in the understanding of the nature of constitutional rights and the corresponding importance of remedies for their violation. So long as federal constitutional rights were thought of as analogues to common-law concepts, the common-law damages remedies available under state law seemed adequate. As the Court began to think of federal rights and remedies as more than common-law concepts, independent federal damage actions seemed appropriate, whether against state officers under § 1983 or against federal officers under *Bivens*.[b] In this respect, *Monroe* and the revivification of § 1983 provided a model for the subsequent innovation in *Bivens*.

4. DECISIONS EXTENDING *BIVENS* ACTIONS: *DAVIS V. PASSMAN* AND *CARLSON V. GREEN*

The narrow holding of *Bivens* was that violations of the Fourth Amendment by federal officials give rise to a damages cause of action. In subsequent cases, the Supreme Court decided whether other constitutional provisions also support *Bivens* actions.

In Davis v. Passman, 442 U.S. 228 (1979), the Court permitted the petitioner, an administrative assistant to a congressman, to bring a *Bivens* action based on allegations that she had been discharged because of her sex. Doctrinally, this claim arose under the equal protection component of the Fifth Amendment Due Process Clause. The Court had previously determined that a cause of action for injunctive relief existed under that provision, see Bolling v. Sharpe, 347 U.S. 497 (1954), and concluded in *Davis* that a damages remedy was also appropriate. The case presented a "focused remedial issue without difficult questions of valuation or causation." Moreover, because the Congressman had lost his bid for reelection, equitable relief in the form of reinstatement was unavailable. "For Davis, as for Bivens, 'it is damages or nothing.' "

In Carlson v. Green, 446 U.S. 14 (1980), the Supreme Court again upheld a *Bivens* action, permitting the plaintiff to sue on behalf of the estate of her deceased son for damages under the Eighth Amendment. She alleged that federal prison officials had caused the son's death by failing to provide adequate medical attention. Although *Carlson* vindicated the right to sue for damages, the Court noted that *Bivens* actions might be foreclosed in either of two situations—where there were "special factors counselling hesitation in the absence of affirmative action by Congress" or where Congress had created an alternative remedial structure.

5. DECISIONS REJECTING *BIVENS* ACTIONS

Subsequent decisions have turned against extending *Bivens*. The grounds for doing so seem to have advanced from the exceptional circumstances identified in *Carlson v. Green* to broader hostility to *Bivens* itself.

(i) Bush v. Lucas

An alternative remedial structure foreclosed a *Bivens* claim in Bush v. Lucas, 462 U.S. 367 (1983). Bush was a NASA aerospace engineer who made a number of statements critical of NASA's policies. As a result, Lucas, the director of the facility at which Bush worked, approved a demotion that decreased his salary. Bush appealed this determination through the federal administrative process and was eventually restored to his position, receiving substantial back pay as well. In the meantime, Bush filed a *Bivens* action against Lucas seeking to recover damages for defamation and violation of his constitutional rights. Ultimately, the Supreme Court, in an opinion by Justice Stevens, held that the damages action was foreclosed.

---

[b] See Susan Bandes, Reinventing *Bivens*: The Self–Executing Constitution, 68 S. Cal. L. Rev. 289 (1995).

> Federal civil servants are now protected by an elaborate, comprehensive scheme that encompasses substantive provisions forbidding arbitrary action by supervisors and procedures—administrative and judicial—by which improper action may be redressed. They apply to a multitude of personnel decisions that are made daily by federal agencies. Constitutional challenges to agency action, such as the First Amendment claims raised by petitioner, are fully cognizable within this system. . . .
>
> Given the history of the development of civil service remedies and the comprehensive nature of the remedies currently available, it is clear that the question we confront today is quite different from the typical remedial issue confronted by a common-law court. The question is not what remedy the court should provide for a wrong that would otherwise go unredressed. It is whether an elaborate remedial system that has been constructed step by step, with careful attention to conflicting policy considerations, should be augmented by the creation of a new judicial remedy for the constitutional violation at issue. That question obviously cannot be answered simply by noting that existing remedies do not provide complete relief for the plaintiff. The policy judgment should be informed by a thorough understanding of the existing regulatory structure and the respective costs and benefits that would result from the addition of another remedy for violations of employees' First Amendment rights.
>
> The costs associated with the review of disciplinary decisions are already significant—not only in monetary terms, but also in the time and energy of managerial personnel who must defend their decisions. Respondent argues that supervisory personnel are already more hesitant than they should be in administering discipline, because the review that ensues sues inevitably makes the performance of their regular duties more difficult. Whether or not this assessment is accurate, it is quite probable that if management personnel face the added risk of personal liability for decisions that they believe to be a correct response to improper criticism of the agency, they would be deterred from imposing discipline in future cases. In all events, Congress is in a far better position than a court to evaluate the impact of a new species of litigation between federal employees on the efficiency of the civil service. Not only has Congress developed considerable familiarity with balancing governmental efficiency and the rights of employees, but it also may inform itself through factfinding procedures such as hearings that are not available to the courts.

Justice Marshall, joined by Justice Blackmun, concurred. He rejected Bush's claim that a *Bivens* action should be permitted because civil service remedies were substantially less effective than an individual damages remedy:

> To begin with, the procedure provided by the civil service scheme is in many respects preferable to the judicial procedure under a *Bivens* action. For example, the burden of proof in an action before the Civil Service Commission (now the Merit Systems Protection Board) must be borne by the agency, rather than by the discharged employee. Moreover, the employee is not required to overcome the qualified immunity of executive officials as he might be required to in a suit for money damages. Finally, an administrative action is likely to prove speedier and less costly than a lawsuit. These advantages are not clearly outweighed by the obvious and significant disadvantages of the civil service procedure—that it denies the

claimant the option of a jury trial, and that it affords only limited judicial review rather than a full trial in federal court. . . . [c]

(ii) *Correctional Services Corp. v. Malesko*

In Correctional Services Corp. v. Malesko, 534 U.S. 61 (2001), the Court offered a more sweeping limitation of *Bivens*. The CSC operated a variety of facilities under contract with the federal Bureau of Prisons (BOP). Malesko was serving part of his sentence in one of CSC's halfway houses and was assigned to living quarters on the fifth floor. CSC instituted a policy requiring inmates residing below the sixth floor to use the staircase rather than the elevator. Malesko, who had a heart condition, was exempted from the policy, but one day, a CSC employee forbade him from using the elevator. Malesko had a heart attack as he climbed the stairs and filed a *Bivens* action, claiming an Eighth Amendment violation by CSC.

In a previous case, FDIC v. Meyer, 510 U.S. 471 (1994), the Court had refused to extend *Bivens* to actions against federal agencies, even where Congress had waived sovereign immunity. The opinion emphasized that "the purpose of *Bivens* was to deter *the officer*," not the agency. Id. at 485 (emphasis in original). Ordinarily, plaintiffs would prefer to sue agencies rather than officers, since the latter would be able to assert qualified immunity. Extending *Bivens* actions to agencies, therefore, would mean that potential plaintiffs had less reason to sue individuals, and "the deterrent effects of the *Bivens* remedy would be lost."

In *Malesko*, the Court applied and extended the reasoning of *Meyer*:

> In 30 years of *Bivens* jurisprudence we have extended its holding only twice, to provide an otherwise nonexistent cause of action against *individual officers* alleged to have acted unconstitutionally, or to provide a cause of action for a plaintiff who lacked *any alternative remedy* for harms caused by an individual officer's unconstitutional conduct. Where such circumstances are not present, we have consistently rejected invitations to extend *Bivens*, often for reasons that foreclose its extension here.
>
> The purpose of *Bivens* is to deter individual federal officers from committing constitutional violations. *Meyer* made clear that the threat of litigation and liability will adequately deter federal officers for *Bivens* purposes no matter that they may enjoy qualified immunity, are indemnified by the employing agency or entity, or are acting pursuant to an entity's policy. *Meyer* also made clear that the threat of suit against an individual's employer was not the kind of deterrence contemplated by *Bivens*. This case is, in every meaningful sense, the same. For if a corporate defendant is available for suit, claimants will focus their collection efforts on it, and not the individual directly responsible for the alleged injury. . . .
>
> Inmates in respondent's position also have full access to remedial mechanisms established by the BOP, including suits in federal court for injunctive relief and grievances filed through the BOP's Administrative Remedy Program. This program provides yet another means through which allegedly unconstitutional actions and policies can be brought to the

[c] For another decision rejecting a *Bivens* action on grounds of the elaborate, if incomplete, remedial scheme adopted by Congress, see Schweiker v. Chilicky, 487 U.S. 412 (1988).—[Footnote by eds.]

attention of the BOP and prevented from recurring. And unlike the *Bivens* remedy, which we have never considered a proper vehicle for altering an entity's policy, injunctive relief has long been recognized as the proper means for preventing entities from acting unconstitutionally.

In sum, respondent is not a plaintiff in search of a remedy as in *Bivens* and *Davis*. Nor does he seek a cause of action against an individual officer, otherwise lacking, as in *Carlson*. Respondent instead seeks a marked extension of *Bivens*, to contexts that would not advance *Bivens*' core purpose of deterring individual officers from engaging in unconstitutional wrongdoing. The caution toward extending *Bivens* remedies into any new context, a caution consistently and repeatedly recognized for three decades, forecloses such an extension here.

Justice Scalia, joined by Justice Thomas, concurred:

Bivens is a relic of the heady days in which this Court assumed common-law powers to create causes of action—decreeing them to be "implied" by the mere existence of a statutory or constitutional prohibition. [W]e have abandoned that power to invent "implications" in the statutory field, see Alexander v. Sandoval, 532 U.S. 275 (2001). There is even greater reason to abandon it in the constitutional field, since an "implication" imagined in the Constitution can presumably not even be repudiated by Congress. I would limit *Bivens* and its two follow-on cases (*Davis v. Passman* and *Carlson v. Green)* to the precise circumstances that they involved.

Justice Stevens, joined by Justices Souter, Ginsburg, and Breyer, dissented. He challenged the Court's claim that imposing liability on CSC would not serve *Bivens*' deterrence rationale:

It cannot be seriously maintained . . . that tort remedies against corporate employers have less deterrent value than actions against their employees. As the Court has previously noted, the "organizational structure" of private prisons "is one subject to the ordinary competitive pressures that normally help private firms adjust their behavior in response to the incentives that tort suits provide—pressures not necessarily present in government departments." Richardson v. McKnight, 521 U.S. 399, 412 (1997). Thus, the private corporate entity at issue here is readily distinguishable from the federal agency in *Meyer*. Indeed, a tragic consequence of today's decision is the clear incentive it gives to corporate managers of privately operated custodial institutions to adopt cost-saving policies that jeopardize the constitutional rights of the tens of thousands of inmates in their custody. . . .

It is apparent . . . that the driving force behind the Court's decision is a disagreement with the holding in *Bivens* itself. There are at least two reasons why it is improper for the Court to allow its decision in this case to be influenced by that predisposition. First, . . . Congress has effectively ratified the *Bivens* remedy; surely Congress has never sought to abolish it. Second, a rule that has been such a well-recognized part of our law for over 30 years should be accorded full respect by the Members of this Court, whether or not they would have endorsed that rule when it was first announced. For our primary duty is to apply and enforce settled law, not to revise that law to accord with our own notions of sound policy.

Malesko treats *Bivens* as a primarily concerned with deterrence rather than compensation. To what extent does that differentiate *Bivens* from § 1983?

Consider also the persuasiveness of the Court's separation-of-powers rationale. Note that the presence of a variety of forms of injunctive or equitable relief seems to play a significant role in the Court's conclusion that a damages remedy is unnecessary. In some circumstances, might not the widespread availability of injunctive relief actually intrude more significantly on the executive branch than an after-the-fact damages remedy? See Pamela S. Karlan, The Irony of Immunity: The Eleventh Amendment, Irreparable Injury, and Section 1983, 53 Stan. L. Rev. 1311 (2001); see also Gene R. Nichol, *Bivens*, *Chilicky*, and Constitutional Damages Claims, 75 Va. L. Rev. 1117, 1135 (1989) (arguing that the relationship between equitable and monetary relief in *Bivens* cases "gets the traditional interplay between law and equity exactly backwards").[d]

6. EXPERIENCE WITH *BIVENS*

The success of the *Bivens* remedy in vindicating violations of constitutional rights by federal officers is a matter of dispute. It is often said that of roughly 12,000 *Bivens* actions filed between 1971 and 1985, only four plaintiffs obtained judgments that were not reversed on appeal.[e] In more recent years, the rate of success—either through litigated judgments or monetary settlements—has been estimated at below two percent. See Cornelia T.L. Pillard, Taking Fiction Seriously: The Strange Results of Public Officials' Individual Liability Under *Bivens*, 88 Geo. L.J. 65 (1999). Given these findings, it is not surprising that the *Bivens* remedy is often derided as ineffective.

An important recent study reaches a different conclusion. See Alexander A. Reinert, Measuring the Success of *Bivens* Litigation and Its Consequences for the Individual Liability Model, 62 Stan. L. Rev. 809 (2010). Reinert describes his article as "the first attempt to systematically study the success of *Bivens* litigation," as distinct from civil rights actions more generally, and reports that "*Bivens* cases are much more successful than has been assumed by the legal community." In the districts he studied, he found success rates (including settlements) ranging from 16 to more than 40 percent. These findings and the disciplined empirical research that supports them will likely revolutionize the way *Bivens* actions are understood.

Even under Reinert's figures, however, *Bivens* actions enjoy modestly lower rates of success than § 1983 actions against state and local officers. One possible reason may be that potential claimants with meritorious claims are diverted into other remedial venues. Federal employees with federal constitutional claims for damages will nearly always have a remedy under the Civil Service Reform Act. The availability of that remedy precludes resort to *Bivens*. See Bush v. Lucas, 462 U.S. 367 (1983). State and local employees often also

---

[d] In Minneci v. Pollard, 132 S.Ct. 617, the Court followed *Malesco* in refusing to create a *Bivens* remedy against employees of a privately operated federal prison. Speaking through Justice Breyer, the Court reasoned that state-law damages remedies provided adequate compensation and deterrence and therefore obviated the to recognize a federal cause of action. Only Justice Ginsburg dissented.

[e] This statistic seems to have originated in a statement made by the Director of the Civil Division of the Department of Justice, which was quoted in Cornelia T.L. Pillard, Taking Fiction Seriously: The Strange Results of Public Officials' Individual Liability Under *Bivens*, 88 Geo. L.J. 65, 6 n.5 (1999), and from there migrated to court opinions and law review articles.

have administrative remedies, but they are not required to pursue or exhaust such remedies before suing under § 1983. Another category of potential claimants against federal officers will choose to litigate against the government directly under the Federal Tort Claims Act. Finally, a large percentage of *Bivens* actions involve prisoner suits, and these suits, whether brought by state or federal inmates, have notably low success rates.

3. THE ELEVENTH AMENDMENT AND § 1983

INTRODUCTORY NOTES ON THE ELEVENTH AMENDMENT

1. FEDERAL LEGISLATIVE POWER AND STATE SOVEREIGN IMMUNITY

As mentioned in connection with *Bivens*, the United States government can be sued directly only if and to the extent that it waives sovereign immunity. States also enjoy sovereign immunity, at least insofar as the claims are based on state law. Whether states retain some form of sovereign immunity against claims based on federal law and if so, what the scope and dimensions of that immunity should be, are durably controversial questions. If read broadly, state sovereign immunity might even preclude officer liability for constitutional violations. The integration of constitutional tort liability with sovereign immunity is therefore a critically important issue.

Doctrinally, this issue is bound up with interpretation of the Eleventh Amendment, which is a complex and arcane corner of constitutional law. These notes provide the necessary introduction to that topic. For those who wish to cover this subject in greater depth, Chapter III, Section 1, provides that option. The materials in Chapter III, Section 1 may be assigned in lieu of these Introductory Notes. Coverage of this section would then resume with the next main case, *Hafer v. Melo*, and the associated notes.

2. ORIGINS

The Eleventh Amendment was adopted in response to Chisholm v. Georgia, 2 U.S. (2 Dall.) 419 (1793). In *Chisholm*, the executor of a South Carolina merchant sued the state of Georgia to recover for supplies furnished under a contract. The Supreme Court had original jurisdiction of diversity actions between a state and a citizen of another state. It heard the case and held that the suit could go forward despite Georgia's claim of sovereign immunity.

The reaction was swift and hostile. The concern, according to Charles Warren, was not merely the affront to state sovereignty but a practical fear of exhausting state treasuries: "In the crucial condition of the finances of most of the states at that time, only disaster was to be expected if suits could be successfully maintained by holders of state issues of paper and other credits, or by Loyalist refugees to recover property confiscated or sequestered by the states; and that this was no theoretical danger was shown by the immediate institution of such suits against the states in South Carolina, Georgia, Virginia and Massachusetts." 1 Charles Warren, The Supreme Court in United States History 99 (1922). The Commonwealth of Massachusetts adopted a resolution calling for the overturn of *Chisholm*, and the Georgia House of Representatives passed a bill to the effect that any persons attempting to execute process in the *Chisholm* case should be hanged. Id. at 100–01.

Constitutional amendments were proposed in the House of Representatives on the second and third days after *Chisholm* was announced. The proposal adopted by Congress in the next session and ultimately ratified as the Eleventh Amendment to the Constitution reads as follows:

> The Judicial power of the United States shall not be construed to extend to any suit in law or equity, commenced or prosecuted against one of the United States by Citizens of another State, or by Citizens or Subjects of any Foreign State.

3. *HANS V. LOUISIANA*

For three-quarters of a century, the Eleventh Amendment was of little consequence, but it again became important after Reconstruction. The Civil War had left the southern states economically destitute, yet saddled with debt. As the northern armies withdrew, one of the first goals of the restored local leadership was to repudiate public bonds. The bondholders sought to hold the states to their obligations by suit in federal court. Influenced by the similar history of *Chisholm,* Supreme Court refurbished and extended the Eleventh Amendment to defeat recovery.

One case from this period became the cornerstone of Eleventh Amendment law. In Hans v. Louisiana, 134 U.S. 1 (1890), a citizen of Louisiana sued to recover unpaid interest on state bonds. Hans claimed that a state constitutional amendment disavowing the obligation to pay interest was a "Law impairing the Obligation of Contracts" in violation of Art. I, § 10, of the federal Constitution. His case was not a diversity action, as *Chisholm* had been, but a claim arising under the Constitution or laws of the United States. Moreover, it was brought by a citizen of the defendant state and so was not covered by the literal terms of the Eleventh Amendment. The Court nevertheless found that that provision barred recovery. Speaking through Justice Bradley, the Court said:

> Can we suppose that, when the Eleventh Amendment was adopted, it was understood to be left open for citizens of a State to sue their own state in the federal courts, whilst the idea of suits by citizens of other states, or of foreign states, was indignantly repelled? Suppose that Congress, when proposing the Eleventh Amendment, had appended to it a proviso that nothing therein contained should prevent a State from being sued by its own citizens in cases arising under the Constitution or laws of the United States: can we imagine that it would have been adopted by the States? The supposition that it would is almost an absurdity on its face.

Hans thus embraced a constitutional notion of state sovereign immunity, an immunity which *Chisholm* had erroneously disregarded and which the Eleventh Amendment was meant to restore.[a]

4. LOCAL GOVERNMENTS

On the same day it decided *Hans v. Louisiana,* the Supreme Court held in Lincoln County v. Luning, 133 U.S. 529 (1890), that the Eleventh Amendment did not protect a county from suit in federal court. Subsequent cases have

---

[a] In addition to *Hans,* the Court decided several other cases rejecting various stratagems for evading the Eleventh Amendment. These included mandamus actions against state officials, Louisiana ex rel. Elliott v. Jumel, 107 U.S. 711 (1883); suits by other states, New Hampshire v. Louisiana and New York v. Louisiana, 108 U.S. 76 (1883); and attachment of state property, Christian v. Atlantic & North Carolina R., 133 U.S. 233 (1890).

extended this holding to other units of local government.[b] Though the disparity between states and their political subdivisions may seem anomalous, it appears to have a foundation in history. At the time the Eleventh Amendment was adopted, municipal corporations were analogized to private corporations and were deemed to lack the attributes of sovereignty possessed by states. By the time the municipal corporation came to be seen as a distinct legal form exercising governmental powers delegated by the state, the amenability of local governments to damage actions had long been established.

5. *EX PARTE YOUNG*

Hans prohibited private damage actions against states in federal court, absent consent. It might be thought that state immunity would also bar suits for declaratory and injunctive relief. The well-settled rule to the contrary dates at least from Ex parte Young, 209 U.S. 123 (1908).

Young was a suit brought by railroad shareholders who claimed that Minnesota legislation setting railroad rates was unconstitutional. They sued Edward T. Young, the Attorney General of Minnesota, seeking to enjoin enforcement of the state statute. The federal court granted that relief. In the Supreme Court, the chief question was whether enjoining enforcement of a state statute contravened the Eleventh Amendment. In dissent, Justice Harlan argued that the suit was really against the state and therefore barred by the Eleventh Amendment:

> Let it be observed that the suit instituted . . . in the Circuit Court of the United States was, as to the defendant Young, one against him *as, and only because he was,* Attorney General of Minnesota. No relief was sought against him individually but only in his capacity *as* Attorney General. And the manifest, indeed the avowed and admitted, object of seeking such relief was *to tie the hands* of the *State*. . . . It would therefore seem clear that within the true meaning of the Eleventh Amendment the suit brought in the Federal court was one, in legal effect, against the State—as much so as if the State had been formally named on the record as a party—and therefore it was a suit to which, under the Amendment, so far as the State or its Attorney General was concerned, the judicial power of the United States did not and could not extend. . . .

The majority disagreed. Speaking through Justice Peckham, the Court explained why the Eleventh Amendment was no bar to an injunction against the Attorney General:

> It is contended that the complainants do not complain and they care nothing about any action which Mr. Young might take or bring as an ordinary individual, but that he was complained of as an officer, to whose discretion is confided the use of the name of the State of Minnesota so far as litigation is concerned, and that when or how he shall use it is a matter resting in his discretion and cannot be controlled by any court.
>
> The answer to all this is the same as made in every case where an official claims to be acting under the authority of the State. The act to be enforced is alleged to be unconstitutional, and if it be so, the use of the name of the State to enforce an unconstitutional act to the injury of complain-

[b] See, e.g., Workman v. New York, 179 U.S. 552 (1900) (cities); Mount Healthy City School District v. Doyle, 429 U.S. 274 (1977) (school boards).

ants is a proceeding without the authority of and one which does not affect the State in its sovereign or governmental capacity. It is simply an illegal act upon the part of a state official in attempting by the use of the name of the State to enforce a legislative enactment which is void because unconstitutional. *If the act which the state Attorney General seeks to enforce be a violation of the Federal Constitution, the officer in proceeding under such enactment comes into conflict with the superior authority of the Constitution, and he is in that case stripped of his official or representative character and is subjected in his person to the consequences of his individual conduct.* The State has no power to impart to him any immunity from responsibility to the supreme authority of the United States. . . . [Emphasis added.]

The italicized sentence states what is often described as the "fiction" of *Ex parte Young*. The approval of injunctions against state officers created (or at least confirmed) a substantial exception to state sovereign immunity. For most purposes, a state can be sued in federal court for prospective relief by the simple expedient of naming the appropriate state officer as the defendant.[c]

6. *EDELMAN V. JORDAN*

In Edelman v. Jordan, 415 U.S. 651 (1974), plaintiffs sought to extend *Ex parte Young* to an order requiring refund of illegally withheld welfare benefits. The case arose under the Aid to the Aged, Blind or Disabled Act (AABD), a federal welfare statute offering states matching federal funds for administration of the program in accord with federal law. Illinois accepted federal funds and thereby became obligated to follow federal law. The trial court found, however, that the state had failed to process AABD applications within prescribed time limits and had failed to make the benefits retroactive to the date of initial eligibility, as required by federal regulations. The court therefore ordered relevant state officials to abide by the regulations in the future *and* to refund the benefits that had wrongfully been withheld.

Everyone agreed that prospective relief was valid under *Ex parte Young*, but the Supreme Court ruled that retrospective relief was barred by the Eleventh Amendment. The Court's opinion, authored by Justice Rehnquist, endorsed Judge Carl McGowan's comments when faced with a similar situation in Rothstein v. Wyman, 467 F.2d 226 (2d Cir. 1972):

> It is not pretended that these payments are to come from the personal resources of these appellants. Appellees expressly contemplate that they will, rather, involve substantial expenditures from the public funds of the state. . . .
>
> It is one thing to tell the Commissioner of Social Services that he must comply with the federal standards for the future if the state is to have the benefit of federal funds in the programs he administers. It is quite another thing to order the Commissioner to use state funds to make reparation for the past. The latter would appear to us to fall afoul of the

---

[c] Note also that the complainants in *Ex parte Young* sued to prevent violation of their constitutional rights without the aid of any statute specifically authorizing such an action. Where did the cause of action come from? Though the answer to this question is not entirely clear, *Ex parte Young* has come to be cited for the proposition that a cause of action for equitable relief to prevent violation of constitutional rights exists independent of explicit congressional authorization.

Eleventh Amendment if that basic constitutional provision is to be conceived of as having any present force.

The Court also found that Illinois had not waived its immunity or consented to suit in federal court. Plaintiffs had argued that waiver or constructive consent to suit could be implied from the state's acceptance of federal funds, governed as they were by federal law. The Court, however, found that waiver of a constitutional protection would be found only where stated "by the most express language" and that constructive consent was "not a doctrine commonly associated with the surrender of constitutional rights."[d]

Together *Ex parte Young* and *Edelman v. Jordan* draw a sharp line between prospective and retrospective relief. The former is permitted, but the latter is not.

7. FEDERAL LEGISLATIVE POWER AND § 1983

It may be surprising to learn that although states have a constitutionally based sovereign immunity, Congress can override it. Under Fitzpatrick v. Bitzer, 427 U.S. 445 (1976), Congress can abrogate state immunity if it is exercising its enforcement powers under the Thirteenth, Fourteenth, or Fifteenth Amendments. These Amendments were adopted after the Eleventh Amendment and were construed to operate as limitations on its reach. Article I powers, however, were held not to have the same effect and therefore cannot be used to override state sovereign immunity. Seminole Tribe v. Florida, 517 U.S. 44 (1996).

Generally speaking, § 1983 is used to enforce individual rights derived from the Fourteenth Amendment (or incorporated by that Amendment and applied to the states). One could argue, therefore, that § 1983 triggers the rule of *Fitzpatrick v. Bitzer*. That is, § 1983 could be seen to fall within Congress's Fourteenth Amendment power to abrogate the immunity of states and make them pay money damages.

Whether § 1983 should be so construed was raised in *Edelman*, where the Court held that § 1983 was not intended to override state immunity. A few years later, this conclusion was reconfirmed in Quern v. Jordan, 440 U.S. 332 (1979), where the Court said that § 1983 "does not explicitly and by clear language indicate on its face an intent to sweep away the immunity of the States. . . . " Together *Edelman* and *Quern* settled that § 1983 does not authorize damage actions against states as such, even though it clearly would have been within Congress's power to do so.[e]

Even after these decisions, the idea nevertheless persisted that perhaps § 1983 might authorize damage actions against states in *state* court, where the Eleventh Amendment in terms does not apply. This would have created the bizarre situation of a federal statute enforceable *only* in state court. That oddity was avoided in Will v. Michigan Department of State Police, 491 U.S. 58 (1989), where the Court held that, "neither a State or its officials acting in

---

[d] Justices Marshall and Blackmun dissented on the waiver issue. Justices Douglas and Brennan also dissented, arguing that the Eleventh Amendment did not bar damages actions to enforce federal law.

[e] See United States v. Georgia, 546 U.S. 151 (2006) (stating that "no one doubts" that § 5 of the Fourteenth Amendment grants Congress the power to abrogate state sovereign immunity and impose damages liability for Fourteenth Amendment violations).

their official capacities are 'persons' under § 1983." Speaking for the Court, Justice White argued that the intent to make states directly liable had not been shown with the clarity required to alter the "usual constitutional balance" between the states and the national government. As to state officials, he said:

> Obviously, state officials literally are persons. But a suit against a state official in his or her official capacity is not a suit against the official but rather is a suit against the official's office. As such, it is no different from a suit against the State itself.

INTRODUCTORY NOTE ON THE IMPORTANCE OF OFFICER SUITS

The holding in Will v. Michigan Department of State Police, 491 U.S. 58 (1989), that states cannot be sued as "persons" under § 1983 created an obvious tension with *Ex parte Young.* That case allowed suits for injunctions against state officers and automatic substitution of the officer's successor if the officer dies or leaves office. Justice White addressed the inconsistency in a footnote in *Will*:

> Of course a state official in his or her official capacity, when sued for injunctive relief, would be a person under § 1983 because "official-capacity actions for prospective relief are not treated as actions against the State." Kentucky v. Graham, 473 U.S. 159, 167 n. 14 (1985); Ex parte Young, 209 U.S. 123 (1908). This distinction is "commonplace in sovereign immunity doctrine," L. Tribe, American Constitutional Law § 3–27, p. 190 n. 3 (2d ed. 1988), and would not have been foreign to the 19th-century Congress that enacted § 1983.

When the plaintiff seeks only prospective relief, therefore, there is no sovereign immunity problem. Whether such suits are thought of as against the officer in his or her "official" capacity or against the officer in his or her "personal" (aka "individual") capacity does not matter. Under *Ex parte Young* and *Will*, suits for prospective relief can go forward regardless of such characterizations.

The distinction between "personal" capacity suits and "official" capacity suits is, however, crucially important in actions for money damages. Damage actions may be brought against state officers personally (i.e., as individuals), but actions against state officers in their official capacity are suits against the state itself and are barred by the Eleventh Amendment. Although this rule is well settled as a matter of precedent, its meaning is not at all obvious. Given that personal-capacity suits are allowed and official-capacity suits are not, the question arises: How does one tell the difference?

Hafer v. Melo

Supreme Court of the United States, 1991.
502 U.S. 21.

■ JUSTICE O'CONNOR delivered the opinion of the Court.

In Will v. Michigan Dept. of State Police, 491 U.S. 58 (1989), we held that state officials "acting in their official capacities" are outside the class of "persons" subject to liability under 42 U.S.C. § 1983. Petitioner takes this language to mean that § 1983 does not authorize suits against state officers for damages arising from official acts. We reject this reading of *Will*, and hold that state officials sued in their individual capacities are "persons" for purposes of § 1983.

I

In 1988, petitioner Barbara Hafer sought election to the post of Auditor General of Pennsylvania. Respondents allege that, during the campaign, United States Attorney James West gave Hafer a list of 21 employees in the Auditor General's Office who secured their jobs through payments to a former employee of the office. They further allege that Hafer publicly promised to fire all employees on the list if elected.

Hafer won the election. Shortly after becoming Auditor General, she dismissed 18 employees, including named respondent James Melo, Jr., on the basis that they "bought" their jobs. Melo and seven other terminated employees sued Hafer and West in Federal District Court. They asserted state and federal claims, including a claim under § 1983, and sought monetary damages. . . .

[T]he District Court dismissed all claims. In relevant part, the court held that the § 1983 claims against Hafer were barred because, under *Will*, she could not be held liable for employment decisions made in her official capacity as Auditor General.

The Court of Appeals for the Third Circuit reversed. . . . We granted certiorari to address the question whether state officers may be held personally liable for damages under § 1983 based upon actions taken in their official capacities.

II

In Kentucky v. Graham, 473 U.S. 159 (1985), the Court sought to eliminate lingering confusion about the distinction between personal- and official-capacity suits. We emphasized that official-capacity suits " 'generally represent only another way of pleading an action against an entity of which an officer is an agent.' " A suit against a state official in her official capacity should be treated as a suit against the State. Indeed, when an official sued in this capacity in federal court dies or leaves office, her successor automatically assumes her role in the litigation. See Fed. Rule Civ. Proc. 25(d)(1). . . . Personal-capacity suits, on the other hand, seek to impose individual liability upon a government officer for actions taken under color of state law. . . .

A

Will itself made clear that the distinction between official-capacity suits and personal-capacity suits is more than "a mere pleading device." State officers sued for damages in their official capacity are not "persons" for purposes of the suit, because they assume the identity of the government that employs them. By contrast, officers sued in their personal capacity come to court as individuals. A government official in the role of personal-capacity defendant thus fits comfortably within the statutory term "person."

Hafer seeks to overcome the distinction between official- and personal-capacity suits by arguing that § 1983 liability turns not on the capacity in which state officials are sued, but on the capacity in which they acted when injuring the plaintiff. Under *Will*, she asserts, state officials may not be held liable in their personal capacity for actions they take in their official capacity. . . .

Through § 1983, Congress sought "to give a remedy to parties deprived of constitutional rights, privileges, and immunities by an official's abuse of his position." Monroe v. Pape, 365 U.S. 167, 172 (1961). Accordingly, it authorized suits to redress deprivations of civil rights by persons acting "under color of any [state] statute, ordinance, regulation, custom, or usage." 42 U.S.C. § 1983. The requirement of action under color of state law means that Hafer may be liable for discharging respondents precisely because of her authority as Auditor General. We cannot accept the novel proposition that this same official authority insulates Hafer from suit.

In an effort to limit the scope of her argument, Hafer distinguishes between two categories of acts taken under color of state law: those outside the official's authority or not essential to the operation of state government, and those both within the official's authority and necessary to the performance of governmental functions. Only the former group, she asserts, can subject state officials to personal liability under § 1983; the latter group (including the employment decisions at issue in this case) should be considered acts of the State that cannot give rise to a personal-capacity action.

The distinction Hafer urges finds no support in the broad language of § 1983. To the contrary, it ignores our holding that Congress enacted § 1983 "to enforce provisions of the Fourteenth Amendment against those who carry a badge of authority of a State and represent it in some capacity, whether they act in accordance with their authority or misuse it." Scheuer v. Rhodes, 416 U.S. 232, 243 (1974) (quoting *Monroe v. Pape*, supra, at 171–72). Because of that intent, we have held that, in § 1983 actions, the statutory requirement of action "under color of" state law is just as broad as the Fourteenth Amendment's "state action" requirement. Lugar v. Edmondson Oil Co., 457 U.S. 922, 929 (1982). . . .

B

Hafer further asks us to read *Will*'s language concerning suits against state officials as establishing the limits of liability under the Eleventh Amendment. She asserts that imposing personal liability on officeholders may infringe on state sovereignty by rendering government less effective; thus, she argues, the Eleventh Amendment forbids personal-capacity suits against state officials in federal court.

Most certainly, *Will*'s holding does not rest directly on the Eleventh Amendment. Whereas the Eleventh Amendment bars suits in federal court . . . , *Will* arose from a suit in *state* court. We considered the Eleventh Amendment in *Will* only because the fact that Congress did not intend to override state immunity when it enacted § 1983 was relevant to statutory construction: "Given that a principal purpose behind the enactment of § 1983 was to provide a federal forum for civil rights claims," Congress' failure to authorize suits against States in federal courts suggested that it also did not intend to authorize such claims in state courts.

To the extent that Hafer argues from the Eleventh Amendment itself, she makes a claim that failed in *Scheuer v. Rhodes*, supra. In *Scheuer*, personal representatives of the estates of three students who died at Kent State University in May, 1970, sought damages from the Governor of Ohio and other state officials. The District Court dismissed their complaints on the theory that the suits, although brought against state officials in their personal capacities, were in substance actions against the State of Ohio, and therefore barred by the Eleventh Amendment.

We rejected that view. "[S]ince Ex parte Young, 209 U.S. 123 (1908)," we said, "it has been settled that the Eleventh Amendment provides no shield for a state official confronted by a claim that he had deprived another of a federal right under color of state law." While the doctrine of *Ex parte Young* does not apply where a plaintiff seeks damages from the public treasury, damages awards against individual defendants in federal courts "are a permissible remedy in some circumstances notwithstanding the fact that they hold public office." 416 U.S., at 238. That is, the Eleventh Amendment does not erect a barrier against suits to impose "individual and personal liability" on state officials under § 1983. . . . Insofar as respondents seek damages against Hafer personally, the Eleventh Amendment does not restrict their ability to sue in federal court.

We hold that state officials, sued in their individual capacities, are "persons" within the meaning of § 1983. The Eleventh Amendment does not bar such suits. . . .

The judgment of the Court of Appeals is affirmed.

■ JUSTICE THOMAS took no part in the consideration or decision of this case.

NOTES ON PERSONAL VS. OFFICIAL CAPACITY

1. QUESTIONS AND COMMENTS ON *HAFER V. MELO*

The *Hafer* Court was quite clear on the *consequences* of suing an officer in his or her personal rather than official capacity, but completely silent on the premises of that characterization. How does one tell the difference? The most obvious answer is how the plaintiff words the complaint. Although Justice O'Connor insisted that "the distinction between official-capacity suits and personal-capacity suits is more than 'a mere pleading device,' " her reasoning suggests exactly the opposite. It is not the capacity in which the action was taken that matters, but rather the capacity in which the defendant is sued. And that is controlled, at least in the first instance, by the plaintiff's pleading.

2. EXPERIENCE IN THE LOWER COURTS

Academic research supports this conclusion. See John C. Jeffries, Jr., In Praise of the Eleventh Amendment and Section 1983, 84 Va. L. Rev. 47 (1998). The article surveyed lower court decisions looking for suits properly pleaded against a state officer in his or her personal capacity but nevertheless treated as "really" or "in essence" an official-capacity suit and therefore barred by the Eleventh Amendment. At least for constitutional violations, the plaintiff's characterization of the suit as being against the officer in his or her personal capacity was almost always allowed to stand: "Almost never did the courts refuse to accept a properly pleaded complaint by coercively recharacterizing the complaint as being 'really' against the state and therefore barred by the Eleventh Amendment." Id. at 65.

Yet it is clear that in some exceptional cases, the plaintiff's attempt to sue an officer in his or her personal capacity will be disallowed. Edelman v. Jordan, 415 U.S. 651 (1974), illustrates the point. The plaintiffs challenging Illinois' administration of the Aid to the Aged, Blind or Disabled Act did not sue the state in name but sued an appropriate state officer. Nevertheless, the suit was found to be in substance against the state itself and therefore barred by the Eleventh Amendment. The "rule has evolved," the Court said, "that a suit by private parties seeking to impose a liability which must be paid from public funds in the state treasury is barred by the Eleventh Amendment."

Unfortunately, the exceptional circumstances that triggered this result are nowhere clearly stated. Perhaps the most important factor is an analogy to the distinction between tort and contract. Traditional agency law declares that a servant is liable for torts committed in the master's business, but a servant is not responsible for performance of the master's contracts. Courts that follow this rule routinely allow suits against a state official in "constitutional tort" cases and refuse to allow such suits where the underlying claim sounds more in contract than in tort. In practice this means that claims to redress almost all constitutional violations (excepting the occasional Contract Clause claim) are allowed to go forward as personal-capacity officer suits, because such actions resemble tort. Claims based on failure to adhere to an obligation created by statute, however, are more likely to seem analogous to contract actions and therefore are more often found to be against the officer in his or her official capacity, with the resulting potential of being barred by the Eleventh Amendment. The law has been summarized as follows:

> As an approximation, one might say that [an attempt to bring a personal-capacity officer suit is more likely to be disallowed] in statutory rather than constitutional cases, in cases where the underlying claim is more like contract than tort, and in cases where the fiction that any resulting judgment will be paid by the officer personally is impossible to maintain. In most recent cases disallowing officer suits, all three factors are present. Outside that (not very crisply defined) context, the alternative of suing a state officer under § 1983 is freely available. [Jeffries, 84 Va. L. Rev. at 67.]

3. DEFENSE AND INDEMNIFICATION

What actually happens when a government officer is sued under § 1983? Formally, the defendant is an individual who has to defend the action and pay any adverse judgment from his or her personal assets. But what really occurs? Do the deputy sheriffs, school principals, and welfare workers sued under § 1983 go out and hire their own lawyers? Do they find themselves bankrupted if they lose?

The answers to these questions are not immediately apparent. In most jurisdictions, policies of defense and indemnification are informal and hard to verify, and there is a notable dearth of scholarly attention to the subject.[a] One attempt to investigate the question concluded as follows:

> Very generally, a suit against a state officer is functionally a suit against the state, for the state defends the action and pays any adverse

[a] An important, but dated, exception is Lant B. Davis, John H. Small & David J. Wohlberg, Project, Suing the Police in Federal Court, 88 Yale L.J. 781, 810–11 (1979) (reporting that Connecticut police officers sued under § 1983 were provided counsel and indemnified against loss). See also Cornelia T.L. Pillard, Taking Fiction Seriously: The Strange Results of Public Officials' Individual Liability Under *Bivens*, 88 Geo. L.J. 65 (1999) (examining the analogous question of *Bivens* actions against federal officers and reporting that "virtually without exception, the government represents or pays for representation of federal officials accused of constitutional violations and pays the costs of judgments or settlements"). For an argument that juries should be told of the prospect of indemnification, see Martin A. Schwartz, Should Juries Be Informed that Municipality Will Indemnify Officer's § 1983 Liability for Constitutional Wrongdoing?, 86 Iowa L. Rev. 1209 (2001).

judgment. So far as can be assessed, this is true not occasionally and haphazardly but pervasively and dependably. . . .

Some years ago, Peter Schuck concluded, in the best summary of this subject, that indemnification of state and local officials sued under § 1983 was "neither certain nor universal" [citing Peter H. Schuck, Suing Government: Citizen Remedies for Official Wrongs 85 (1983)]. He is surely still right about the uncertainty—if only because indemnification so often depends on local practice or decision rather than on contract or statute. He may also be right about the incompleteness of indemnification—at least if one takes account of the occasional cases of flamboyantly bad actors. State officers who become targets of criminal prosecution are unlikely to receive financial subvention for civil liability. Such cases aside, the state or local government officer who is acting within the scope of his or her employment in something other than extreme bad faith can count on government defense and indemnification. [Jeffries, 84 Va. L. Rev. at 49–50 (footnotes omitted).]

4. DOES IT MATTER?

If state officers sued personally under § 1983 are routinely defended and indemnified by their employers, what is left of the Eleventh Amendment? Does it simply not matter?

The answer is that the Eleventh Amendment does matter, but in ways more indirect and attenuated than at first appear. Functionally, the Eleventh Amendment does not completely bar redress for constitutional violations by state governments. Rather, it forces constitutional tort plaintiffs to sue state officers under § 1983. When damages judgments entered against officers personally are in fact paid by their employers, officer-suits are an indirect way of holding states liable for constitutional violations.

That is not to say that the defendant's identity is completely irrelevant. Juries may well react differently to a life-and-blood defendant than they would to the (presumably deep-pocketed) government. Additionally, there may be circumstances where individual officers doubt the competence or loyalty of government lawyers and feel compelled to hire their own. Most importantly, a personal-capacity suit against the officer as an individual may trigger an absolute or a qualified immunity from liability under common law principles that the Court has read into § 1983. The law of absolute and qualified immunity, the topic covered in the next Section, spells out limitations on damages actions against government officers that are often quite restrictive. Generally speaking, as will be discussed, the same immunities apply to state and local officers sued under § 1983 and to federal officers sued under *Bivens*. The content of those immunities is the subject of the next Section.

4. OFFICIAL IMMUNITY

SUBSECTION A: ABSOLUTE IMMUNITY

Bogan v. Scott–Harris

Supreme Court of the United States, 1998.
523 U.S. 44.

■ JUSTICE THOMAS delivered the opinion of the Court.

It is well established that federal, state, and regional legislators are entitled to absolute immunity from civil liability for their legislative activities. In this case, petitioners argue that they, as local officials performing legislative functions, are entitled to the same protection. They further argue that their acts of introducing, voting for, and signing an ordinance eliminating the government office held by respondent constituted legislative activities. We agree on both counts and therefore reverse the judgment below.

I

Respondent Janet Scott–Harris was administrator of the Department of Health and Human Services (DHHS) for the city of Fall River, Massachusetts, from 1987 to 1991. In 1990, respondent received a complaint that Dorothy Biltcliffe, an employee serving temporarily under her supervision, had made repeated racial and ethnic slurs about her colleagues. After respondent prepared termination charges against Biltcliffe, Biltcliffe used her political connections to press her case with several state and local officials, including petitioner Marilyn Roderick, the vice president of the Fall River City Council. The city council held a hearing on the charges against Biltcliffe and ultimately accepted a settlement proposal under which Biltcliffe would be suspended without pay for 60 days. Petitioner Daniel Bogan, the mayor of Fall River, thereafter substantially reduced the punishment.

While the charges against Biltcliffe were pending, Mayor Bogan prepared his budget proposal for the 1992 fiscal year. Anticipating a 5 to 10 percent reduction in state aid, Bogan proposed freezing the salaries of all municipal employees and eliminating 135 city positions. As part of this package, Bogan called for the elimination of DHHS, of which respondent was the sole employee. The City Council Ordinance Committee, which was chaired by Roderick, approved an ordinance eliminating DHHS. The city council thereafter adopted the ordinance by a vote of 6 to 2, with petitioner Roderick among those voting in favor. Bogan signed the ordinance into law.

Respondent then filed suit under 42 U.S.C. § 1983, against . . . Bogan [and] Roderick. . . . She alleged that the elimination of her position was motivated by racial animus and a desire to retaliate against her for exercising her First Amendment rights in filing the complaint against Biltcliffe. The District Court denied Bogan's and Roderick's motions to dismiss on the ground of legislative immunity, and the case proceeded to trial.

The jury returned a verdict in favor of all defendants on the racial discrimination charge, but found . . . Bogan and Roderick liable on respondent's First Amendment claim, concluding that respondent's constitutionally protected speech was a substantial or motivating factor in the elimination of her position. On a motion for judgment notwithstanding the verdict, the

District Court again denied Bogan's and Roderick's claims of absolute legislative immunity, reasoning that "the ordinance amendment passed by the city council was an individually-targeted administrative act, rather than a neutral, legislative elimination of a position which incidentally resulted in the termination of plaintiff."

The United States Court of Appeals for the First Circuit . . . affirmed the judgments against Roderick and Bogan. Although the court concluded that petitioners have "absolute immunity from civil liability for damages arising out of their performance of legitimate legislative activities," it held that their challenged conduct was not "legislative." Relying on the jury's finding that "constitutionally sheltered speech was a substantial or motivating factor" underlying petitioners' conduct, the court reasoned that the conduct was administrative, rather than legislative, because Roderick and Bogan "relied on facts relating to a particular individual [respondent] in the decision-making calculus." We granted certiorari.

II

The principle that legislators are absolutely immune from liability for their legislative activities has long been recognized in Anglo–American law. This privilege "has taproots in the Parliamentary struggles of the Sixteenth and Seventeenth Centuries" and was "taken as a matter of course by those who severed the Colonies from the Crown and founded our Nation." Tenney v. Brandhove, 341 U.S. 367, 372 (1951). The Federal Constitution, the constitutions of many of the newly independent States, and the common law thus protected legislators from liability for their legislative activities. See U.S. Const., Art. I, § 6; *Tenney v. Brandhove*, supra, at 372–75.

Recognizing this venerable tradition, we have held that state and regional legislators are entitled to absolute immunity from liability under § 1983 for their legislative activities. See *Tenney v. Brandhove*, supra (state legislators); see also Kilbourn v. Thompson, 103 U.S. 168, 202–04 (1881) (interpreting the federal Speech and Debate Clause, U.S. Const., Art. I, § 6, to provide similar immunity to Members of Congress). We explained that legislators were entitled to absolute immunity from suit at common law and that Congress did not intend the general language of § 1983 to "impinge on a tradition so well grounded in history and reason." *Tenney v. Brandhove*, supra, at 376. Because the common law accorded local legislators the same absolute immunity it accorded legislators at other levels of government, and because the rationales for such immunity are fully applicable to local legislators, we now hold that local legislators are likewise absolutely immune from suit under § 1983 for their legislative activities.

The common law at the time § 1983 was enacted deemed local legislators to be absolutely immune from suit for their legislative activities. New York's highest court, for example, held that municipal aldermen were immune from suit for their discretionary decisions. Wilson v. New York, 1 Denio 595 (N.Y. 1845). The court explained that when a local legislator exercises discretionary powers, he "is exempt from all responsibility by action for the motives which influence him, and the manner in which such duties are performed. If corrupt, he may be impeached or indicted, but the law will not tolerate an action to redress the individual wrong which may have been done."[2] These principles, according to the court, were "too familiar and well settled to require illustration or authority."

---

[2] The court distinguished "discretionary" duties, which were protected absolutely, and "ministerial" duties, which were not. Although the Court described the former as "judicial" in

Shortly after § 1983 was enacted, the Mississippi Supreme Court reached a similar conclusion, holding that town aldermen could not be held liable under state law for their role in the adoption of an allegedly unlawful ordinance. Jones v. Loving, 55 Miss. 109 (1877). The court explained that "it certainly cannot be argued that the motives of the individual members of a legislative assembly, in voting for a particular law, can be inquired into, and its supporters be made personally liable, upon an allegation that they acted maliciously towards the person aggrieved by the passage of the law." The court thus concluded that "whenever the officers of a municipal corporation are vested with legislative powers, they hold and exercise them for the public good, and are clothed with all the immunities of government, and are exempt from all liability for their mistaken use."

Treatises of that era confirm that this was the pervasive view. A leading treatise on municipal corporations explained that "where the officers of a municipal corporation are invested with legislative powers, they are exempt from individual liability for the passage of any ordinance within their authority, and their motives in reference thereto will not be inquired into." 1 J. Dillon, Law of Municipal Corporations § 313, pp. 326–27 (3d ed. 1881). Thomas Cooley likewise noted in his influential treatise on the law of torts that the "rightful exemption" of legislators from liability was "very plain" and applied to members of "inferior legislative bodies, such as boards of supervisors, county commissioners, city councils, and the like." Thomas Cooley, Law of Torts 376 (1880).

Even the authorities cited by respondent are consistent with the view that local legislators were absolutely immune for their legislative, as distinct from ministerial, duties. In the few cases in which liability did attach, the courts emphasized that the defendant officials lacked discretion, and the duties were thus ministerial. Respondent's heavy reliance on our decision in Amy v. Supervisors, 78 U.S. 136 (1871), is misguided for this very reason. In that case, we held that local legislators could be held liable for violating a court order to levy a tax sufficient to pay a judgment, but only because the court order had created a ministerial duty. ("The rule is well settled that where the law requires absolutely a ministerial act to be done by a public officer, and he neglects or refuses to do such act, he may be compelled to respond in damages to the extent of the injury arising from his conduct"). The treatises cited by respondent confirm that this distinction between legislative and ministerial duties was dispositive of the right to absolute immunity.

Absolute immunity for local legislators under § 1983 finds support not only in history, but also in reason. The rationales for according absolute immunity to federal, state, and regional legislators apply with equal force to local legislators. Regardless of the level of government, the exercise of legislative discretion should not be inhibited by judicial interference or distorted by the fear of personal liability. See Spallone v. United States, 493 U.S. 265, 279 (1990) (noting, in the context of addressing local legislative action, that "any restriction on a legislator's freedom undermines the 'public good' by interfering with the rights of the people to representation in the

---

nature, it was merely using the term broadly to encompass the "discretionary" acts of officials. See *Wilson v. New York*, supra, at 599 ("If his powers are discretionary, to be exerted or withheld, according to his own view of what is necessary and proper, they are in their nature judicial"). The legislators' actions in *Wilson* were unquestionably legislative in both form and substance. Thus, *Wilson* was widely, and correctly, cited as a leading case regarding *legislative* immunity.

democratic process"). Furthermore, the time and energy required to defend against a lawsuit are of particular concern at the local level, where the part-time citizen-legislator remains commonplace. See *Tenney v. Brandhove*, supra, at 377 (citing "the cost and inconvenience and distractions of a trial"). And the threat of liability may significantly deter service in local government, where prestige and pecuniary rewards may pale in comparison to the threat of civil liability. See Harlow v. Fitzgerald, 457 U.S. 800, 816 (1982).

Moreover, certain deterrents to legislative abuse may be greater at the local level than at other levels of government. Municipalities themselves can be held liable for constitutional violations, whereas States and the Federal Government are often protected by sovereign immunity. And, of course, the ultimate check on legislative abuse—the electoral process—applies with equal force at the local level, where legislators are often more closely responsible to the electorate. Cf. *Tenney*, supra, at 378 (stating that "self-discipline and the voters must be the ultimate reliance for discouraging or correcting such abuses").

Any argument that the rationale for absolute immunity does not extend to local legislators is implicitly foreclosed by our opinion in Lake Country Estates v. Tahoe Regional Planning Agency, 440 U.S. 391 (1979). There, we held that members of an interstate regional planning agency were entitled to absolute legislative immunity. Bereft of any historical antecedent to the regional agency, we relied almost exclusively on *Tenney*'s description of the purposes of legislative immunity and the importance of such immunity in advancing the "public good." Although we expressly noted that local legislators were not at issue in that case, we considered the regional legislators at issue to be the functional equivalents of local legislators, noting that the regional agency was "comparable to a county or municipality" and that the function of the regional agency, regulation of land use, was "traditionally a function performed by local governments." Thus, we now make explicit what was implicit in our precedents: Local legislators are entitled to absolute immunity from § 1983 liability for their legislative activities.

III

Absolute legislative immunity attaches to all actions taken "in the sphere of legitimate legislative activity." *Tenney*, supra, at 376. The Court of Appeals held that petitioners' conduct in this case was not legislative because their actions were specifically targeted at respondent. Relying on the jury's finding that respondent's constitutionally protected speech was a substantial or motivating factor behind petitioners' conduct, the court concluded that petitioners necessarily "relied on facts relating to a particular individual" and "devised an ordinance that targeted [respondent] and treated her differently from other managers employed by the City." Although the Court of Appeals did not suggest that intent or motive can overcome an immunity defense for activities that are, in fact, legislative, the court erroneously relied on petitioners' subjective intent in resolving the logically prior question of whether their acts were legislative.

Whether an act is legislative turns on the nature of the act, rather than on the motive or intent of the official performing it. The privilege of absolute immunity "would be of little value if [legislators] could be subjected to the cost and inconvenience and distractions of a trial upon a conclusion of the pleader, or to the hazard of a judgment against them based upon a jury's speculation as to motives." *Tenney*, 341 U.S. at 377. Furthermore, it simply is "not consonant with our scheme of government for a court to inquire into the motives of legislators." We therefore held that the defendant in *Tenney* had acted in a legislative capacity even though he allegedly singled out the plaintiff for investigation in order "to intimidate and silence plaintiff and deter and prevent him from effectively exercising his constitutional rights."

This leaves us with the question whether, stripped of all considerations of intent and motive, petitioners' actions were legislative. We have little trouble concluding that they were. Most evidently, petitioner Roderick's acts of voting for an ordinance were, in form, quintessentially legislative. Petitioner Bogan's introduction of a budget and signing into law an ordinance also were formally legislative, even though he was an executive official. We have recognized that officials outside the legislative branch are entitled to legislative immunity when they perform legislative functions, see Supreme Court of Va. v. Consumers Union of United States, Inc., 446 U.S. 719, 731–34 (1980); Bogan's actions were legislative because they were integral steps in the legislative process. Cf. Edwards v. United States, 286 U.S. 482, 490 (1932) (noting "the legislative character of the President's function in approving or disapproving bills"); Smiley v. Holm, 285 U.S. 355, 372–73 (1932) (recognizing that a governor's signing or vetoing of a bill constitutes part of the legislative process).

Respondent, however, asks us to look beyond petitioners' formal actions to consider whether the ordinance was legislative in substance. We need not determine whether the formally legislative character of petitioners' actions is alone sufficient to entitle petitioners to legislative immunity, because here the ordinance, in substance, bore all the hallmarks of traditional legislation. The ordinance reflected a discretionary, policymaking decision implicating the budgetary priorities of the city and the services the city provides to its constituents. Moreover, it involved the termination of a position, which, unlike the hiring or firing of a particular employee, may have prospective implications that reach well beyond the particular occupant of the office. And the city council, in eliminating DHHS, certainly governed "in a field where legislators traditionally have power to act." *Tenney*, supra, at 379. Thus, petitioners' activities were undoubtedly legislative.

* * *

For the foregoing reasons, the judgment of the Court of Appeals is reversed.

NOTES ON ABSOLUTE LEGISLATIVE IMMUNITY

1. BACKGROUND

Liability of public officials under § 1983 involves two different levels of immunity from the award of damages. First, as *Bogan v. Scott–Harris* illustrates, certain officials are absolutely immune, at least when performing certain functions. Second, the default rule for officials who are not entitled to absolute immunity is qualified immunity.

Where applicable, absolute immunity offers the public official complete protection from damage actions, no matter how wrongful the act or how malicious the motivation. The effect of absolute immunity is therefore to vindicate fully the public's interest in unintimidated decisionmaking by its officials, but only at a correspondingly complete sacrifice of the interests of those who may be injured by abuse. By contrast, qualified immunity offers a more limited protection to decisionmaking by public officials. In effect, it establishes a standard of culpability, exonerating the public official from damages liability in the case of non-culpable behavior. The precise content of qualified immunity is addressed in considerable detail in the next section. For now, the issues are whether absolute immunity is ever appropriate, and if so when.

2. *TENNEY V. BRANDHOVE*

Absolute legislative immunity under § 1983 stems from Tenney v. Brandhove, 341 U.S. 367 (1951). In that case, members of an Un–American Activities Committee of the California Senate were sued under § 1983 for alleged harassment and intimidation in violation of the plaintiff's rights of free speech, due process, and equal protection. Justice Frankfurter's opinion found that § 1983 did not impose liability on the facts before the Court "once they are related to the presuppositions of our political history." He began by tracing the English and early American history of the Speech or Debate Clause (Art. I, § 6) and its counterparts in state constitutions. He said that the "reason for the privilege is clear":

> It was well summarized by James Wilson, an influential member of the Committee of Detail which was responsible for the provision in the federal Constitution. "In order to enable and encourage a representative of the public to discharge his public trust with firmness and success, it is indispensably necessary, that he should enjoy the fullest liberty of speech, and that he should be protected from the resentment of every one, however powerful, to whom the exercise of that liberty may occasion offence." 2 Works of James Wilson 38 (Andrews ed. 1896).

With respect to § 1983, Justice Frankfurter concluded:

> Did Congress by the general language of its 1871 statute mean to overturn the tradition of legislative freedom achieved in England by Civil War and carefully preserved in the formation of state and national governments here? Did it mean to subject legislators to civil liability for acts done within the sphere of legislative activity? Let us assume, merely for the moment, that Congress has constitutional power to limit the freedom of state legislators acting within their traditional sphere. That would be a big assumption. But we would have to make an even rasher assumption to find that Congress thought it had exercised the power. These are difficulties we cannot hurdle. The limits of [§ 1983] were not spelled out in debate. We cannot believe that Congress—itself a staunch advocate of legislative freedom—would impinge on a tradition so well grounded in history and reason by covert inclusion in the general language before us.

3. LEVEL VS. SCOPE

"Absolute" immunity refers to the level of immunity, not to its scope. No officer enjoys absolute immunity for all acts. Rather, the act complained of must be within the sphere of activity for which the immunity has been recognized. The determinative factor is the function performed, not the office held. Absolute legislative immunity protects legislators when they are engaged in such activities as voting on bills, holding hearings, participating in committee debates, and so on. And, as *Bogan v. Scott–Harris* indicates, absolute immunity also protects non-legislators when they are engaged in legislative functions. But when a legislator is not acting in a legislative capacity, he or she would have only qualified immunity. In Davis v. Passman, 442 U.S. 228 (1979), for example, the Supreme Court rejected a congressman's claim of absolute legislative immunity in a *Bivens* action brought by a staff member whom he had fired. Representative Passman's termination letter informed the plaintiff that, although she was "able, energetic and a very hard worker," he had concluded "that it was essential that the understudy to my Administrative Assistant be a man." The Court held that she had stated a cause of action under the equal protection component of the Fifth Amendment's Due Process Clause, which prohibits gender discrimination.

4. WHEN DOES IT MATTER?

Practically speaking, absolute legislative immunity often does not matter. In most cases, legislative actions must be implemented or enforced by executive officers, and the executive officers generally are amenable to suit under § 1983. If, for example, a city council were to pass a law barring pregnant teachers from the classroom, a dismissed teacher could sue the school superintendent who implemented that rule. The fact that she could not obtain damages from, or an injunction against, members of the city council would be more or less irrelevant, provided that her claim could be brought against another defendant. In most cases, therefore, the consequence of absolute legislative immunity is not to bar claims altogether, but rather to redirect them toward other defendants.

Bogan v. Scott–Harris, however, is an unusual case where there seems to be no executive officer who could be sued. In such circumstances, the effect of absolute immunity is not just to redirect litigation to another defendant but to bar absolutely the plaintiff's opportunity to recover damages for the constitutional violation. Note that the Supreme Court did not consider this issue. Should it have? Does the absence of an alternative defendant suggest that absolute immunity should have been construed more narrowly? Does it suggest that some other remedy should be available?[a]

In any event, *Bogan v. Scott–Harris* illustrates a potentially important characteristic of local government. At the state or federal level, legislation is unlikely to target a single individual, and there is usually a clear separation of powers between legislative and executive action. By contrast, local governments often vest legislative and executive power in the same body, see, e.g., Holder v. Hall, 512 U.S. 874, 876 (1994) (discussing the Georgia "single commissioner" form of county government in which one individual "performs all of the executive and legislative functions of the county government"). For that reason and for reasons of (usually) smaller scale, it is more likely that local governments will enact legislative policies that affect only one individual.

[a] If the ordinance was unconstitutional and if the retaliatory motive that rendered it so could be attributed to the municipality, as distinct from some individuals, recovery might be had from the city itself. The subject of direct governmental liability under § 1983 is covered in detail in Section 5 of this Chapter.

Stump v. Sparkman

Supreme Court of the United States, 1978.
435 U.S. 349.

■ MR. JUSTICE WHITE delivered the opinion of the Court.

This case requires us to consider the scope of a judge's immunity from damages liability when sued under 42 U.S.C. § 1983.

I

The relevant facts underlying respondents' suit are not in dispute. On July 9, 1971, Ora Spitler McFarlin, the mother of respondent Linda Kay Spitler Sparkman, presented to Judge Harold D. Stump of the Circuit Court of DeKalb County, Ind., a document captioned "Petition To Have Tubal Ligation Performed On Minor and Indemnity Agreement." The document had been drafted by her attorney, a petitioner here. In this petition Mrs. McFarlin stated under oath that her daughter was 15 years of age and was "somewhat retarded," although she attended public school and had been promoted each year with her class. The petition further stated that Linda had been associating with "older youth or young men" and had stayed out overnight with them on several occasions. As a result of this behavior and Linda's mental capabilities, it was stated that it would be in the daughter's best interest if she underwent a tubal ligation in order "to prevent unfortunate circumstances. . . . " In the same document Mrs. McFarlin also undertook to indemnify and hold harmless Dr. John Hines, who was to perform the operation, and the DeKalb Memorial Hospital, where the operation was to take place, against all causes of action that might arise as a result of the performance of the tubal ligation.

The petition was approved by Judge Stump on the same day. . . .

On July 15, 1971, Linda Spitler entered the DeKalb Memorial Hospital, having been told that she was to have her appendix removed. The following day a tubal ligation was performed upon her. She was released several days later, unaware of the true nature of her surgery.

Approximately two years after the operation, Linda Spitler was married to respondent Leo Sparkman. Her inability to become pregnant led her to discover that she had been sterilized during the 1971 operation. As a result of this revelation, the Sparkmans filed suit in the United States District Court for the Northern District of Indiana against Mrs. McFarlin, her attorney, Judge Stump, the doctors who had performed and assisted in the tubal ligation, and the DeKalb Memorial Hospital. Respondents sought damages for the alleged violation of Linda Sparkman's constitutional rights[2]; also asserted were pendent state claims for assault and battery, medical malpractice, and loss of potential fatherhood.

---

[2] The District Court gave the following summary of the constitutional claims asserted by the Sparkmans: ". . . (1) that the actions were arbitrary and thus in violation of the due process clause of the Fourteenth Amendment; (2) that Linda was denied procedural safeguards required by the Fourteenth Amendment; (3) that the sterilization was permitted without the promulgation of standards; (4) that the sterilization was an invasion of privacy; (5) that the sterilization violated Linda's right to procreate; (6) that the sterilization was cruel and unusual punishment; (7) that the use of sterilization as punishment for her alleged retardation or lack of self-discipline violated various constitutional guarantees; (8) that the defendants failed to follow certain Indiana statutes, thus depriving Linda of due process of law; and (9) that defendants violated the equal protection clause, because of the differential treatment accorded Linda on account of her sex, marital status, and allegedly low mental capacity."

Ruling upon the defendants' various motions to dismiss the complaint, the District Court concluded that each of the constitutional claims asserted by respondents required a showing of state action and that the only state action alleged in the complaint was the approval by Judge Stump, acting as Circuit Court Judge, of the petition presented to him by Mrs. McFarlin. The Sparkmans sought to hold the private defendants liable on a theory that they had conspired with Judge Stump to bring about the allegedly unconstitutional acts. The District Court, however, held that no federal action would lie against any of the defendants because Judge Stump, the only state agent, was absolutely immune from suit under the doctrine of judicial immunity. The court stated that "whether or not Judge Stump's 'approval' of the petition may in retrospect appear to have been premised on an erroneous view of the law, Judge Stump surely had jurisdiction to consider the petition and to act thereon." Accordingly, under Bradley v. Fisher, 80 U.S. (13 Wall.) 335, 351 (1872), Judge Stump was entitled to judicial immunity.[3]

On appeal, the Court of Appeals for the Seventh Circuit reversed the judgment of the District Court, holding that the "crucial issue" was "whether Judge Stump acted within his jurisdiction" and concluding that he had not. He was accordingly not immune from damages liability under the controlling authorities. The Court of Appeals also held that the judge had forfeited his immunity "because of his failure to comply with elementary principles of procedural due process."

We granted certiorari to consider the correctness of this ruling. We reverse.

II

The governing principle of law is well established and is not questioned by the parties. As early as 1872, the Court recognized that it was "a general principle of the highest importance to the proper administration of justice that a judicial officer, in exercising the authority vested in him, [should] be free to act upon his own convictions, without apprehension of personal consequences to himself." *Bradley v. Fisher*, supra, at 347. For that reason the Court held that "judges of courts of superior or general jurisdiction are not liable to civil actions for their judicial acts, even when such acts are in excess of their jurisdiction, and are alleged to have been done maliciously or corruptly."[6] Later we held that this doctrine of judicial immunity was applicable in suits under . . . 42 U.S.C. § 1983, for the legislative record gave no indication that Congress intended to abolish this long-established principle. Pierson v. Ray, 386 U.S. 547 (1967).

The Court of Appeals correctly recognized that the necessary inquiry in determining whether a defendant judge is immune from suit is whether at the time he took the challenged action he had jurisdiction over the sub-

---

[3] The District Court granted the defendants' motion to dismiss the federal claims for that reason and dismissed the remaining pendent state claims for lack of subject-matter jurisdiction.

[6] In holding that a judge was immune for his judicial acts, even when such acts were performed in excess of his jurisdiction, the Court in *Bradley* stated: "A distinction must be here observed between excess of jurisdiction and the clear absence of all jurisdiction over the subject-matter. Where there is clearly no jurisdiction over the subject-matter any authority exercised is a usurped authority, and for the exercise of such authority, when the want of jurisdiction is known to the judge, no excuse is permissible. But where jurisdiction over the subject-matter is invested by law in the judge, or in the court which he holds, the manner and extent in which the jurisdiction shall be exercised are generally as much questions for his determination as any other questions involved in the case, although upon the correctness of his determination in these particulars the validity of his judgments may depend."

ject matter before him. Because "some of the most difficult and embarrassing questions which a judicial officer is called upon to consider and determine relate to his jurisdiction . . . ," *Bradley*, supra, at 352, the scope of the judge's jurisdiction must be construed broadly where the issue is the immunity of the judge. A judge will not be deprived of immunity because the action he took was in error, was done maliciously, or was in excess of his authority; rather, he will be subject to liability only when he has acted in the "clear absence of all jurisdiction." [7] Id., at 351.

We cannot agree that there was a "clear absence of all jurisdiction" in the DeKalb County Circuit Court to consider the petition presented by Mrs. McFarlin. As an Indiana Circuit Court Judge, Judge Stump had "original exclusive jurisdiction in all cases at law and in equity whatsoever . . . ," jurisdiction over the settlement of estates and over guardianships, appellate jurisdiction as conferred by law, and jurisdiction over "all other causes, matters and proceedings where exclusive jurisdiction thereof is not conferred by law upon some other court, board or officer." Ind. Code § 33–4–4–3 (1975). This is indeed a broad jurisdictional grant; yet the Court of Appeals concluded that Judge Stump did not have jurisdiction over the petition authorizing Linda Sparkman's sterilization.

In so doing, the Court of Appeals noted that the Indiana statutes provided for the sterilization of institutionalized persons under certain circumstances, see Ind. Code §§ 16–13–13–1 through 16–13–13–4 (1973), but otherwise contained no express authority for judicial approval of tubal ligations. It is true that the statutory grant of general jurisdiction to the Indiana circuit courts does not itemize types of cases those courts may hear and hence does not expressly mention sterilization petitions presented by the parents of a minor. But in our view, it is more significant that there was no Indiana statute and no case law in 1971 prohibiting a circuit court, a court of general jurisdiction, from considering a petition of the type presented to Judge Stump. The statutory authority for the sterilization of institutionalized persons in the custody of the state does not warrant the inference that a court of general jurisdiction has no power to act on a petition for sterilization of a minor in the custody of her parents, particularly where the parents have authority under the Indiana statutes to "consent to and contract for medical or hospital care or treatment of [the minor] including surgery." Ind. Code § 16–8–4–2 (1973). The District Court concluded that Judge Stump had jurisdiction under § 33–4–4–3 to entertain and act upon Mrs. McFarlin's petition. We agree with the District Court, it appearing that neither by statute nor by case law has the broad jurisdiction granted to the circuit courts of Indiana been circumscribed to foreclose consideration of a petition for authorization of a minor's sterilization.

The Court of Appeals also concluded that support for Judge Stump's actions could not be found in the common law of Indiana, relying in particular on the Indiana Court of Appeals' intervening decision in A.L. v. G.R.H., 163 Ind.App. 636, 325 N.E.2d 501 (1975). In that case the Indiana court held that a parent does not have a common-law right to have a minor child sterilized, even though the parent might "sincerely believe the child's

[7] In *Bradley*, the Court illustrated the distinction between lack of jurisdiction and excess of jurisdiction with the following examples: if a probate judge, with jurisdiction over only wills and estates, should try a criminal case, he would be acting in the clear absence of jurisdiction and would not be immune from liability for his action; on the other hand, if a judge of a criminal court should convict a defendant of a nonexistent crime, he would merely be acting in excess of his jurisdiction and would be immune.

adulthood would benefit therefrom." The opinion, however, speaks only of the rights of the parents to consent to the sterilization of their child and does not question the jurisdiction of a circuit judge who is presented with such a petition from a parent. Although under that case a circuit judge would err as a matter of law if he were to approve a parent's petition seeking the sterilization of a child, the opinion in *A.L. v. G.R.H.* does not indicate that a circuit judge is without jurisdiction to entertain the petition. Indeed, the clear implication of the opinion is that, when presented with such a petition, the circuit judge should deny it on its merits rather than dismiss it for lack of jurisdiction.

Perhaps realizing the broad scope of Judge Stump's jurisdiction, the Court of Appeals stated that, even if the action taken by him was not foreclosed under the Indiana statutory scheme, it would still be "an illegitimate exercise of his common law power because of his failure to comply with elementary principles of procedural due process." This misconceives the doctrine of judicial immunity. A judge is absolutely immune from liability for his judicial acts even if his exercise of authority is flawed by the commission of grave procedural errors. The Court made this point clear in *Bradley*, where it stated: "[T]his erroneous manner in which [the court's] jurisdiction was exercised, however it may have affected the validity of the act, did not make the act any less a judicial act; nor did it render the defendant liable to answer in damages for it at the suit of the plaintiff, as though the court had proceeded without having any jurisdiction whatever. . . . "

We conclude that the Court of Appeals, employing an unduly restrictive view of the scope of Judge Stump's jurisdiction, erred in holding that he was not entitled to judicial immunity. Because the court over which Judge Stump presides is one of general jurisdiction, neither the procedural errors he may have committed nor the lack of a specific statute authorizing his approval of the petition in question rendered him liable in damages for the consequences of his actions.

The respondents argue that even if Judge Stump had jurisdiction to consider the petition presented to him by Mrs. McFarlin, he is still not entitled to judicial immunity because his approval of the petition did not constitute a "judicial" act. It is only for acts performed in his "judicial" capacity that a judge is absolutely immune, they say. We do not disagree with this statement of the law, but we cannot characterize the approval of the petition as a nonjudicial act.

Respondents themselves stated in their pleadings before the District Court that Judge Stump was "clothed with the authority of the state" at the time that he approved the petition and that "he was acting as a county circuit court judge." They nevertheless now argue that Judge Stump's approval of the petition was not a judicial act because the petition was not given a docket number, was not placed on file with the clerk's office, and was approved in an ex parte proceeding without notice to the minor, without a hearing, and without the appointment of a guardian ad litem. . . .

The relevant cases demonstrate that the factors determining whether an act by a judge is a "judicial" one relate to the nature of the act itself, i. e., whether it is a function normally performed by a judge, and to the expectations of the parties, i.e., whether they dealt with the judge in his judicial capacity. Here, both factors indicate that Judge Stump's approval of the sterilization petition was a judicial act.[11] State judges with general jurisdiction not infrequently are called upon in their official capacity to approve petitions relating to the affairs of minors, as for example, a petition to settle a minor's claim. Furthermore, as even respondents have admitted, at the time he approved the petition presented to him by Mrs. McFarlin, Judge Stump was "acting as a county circuit court judge." We may infer from the record that it was only because Judge Stump served in that position that Mrs. McFarlin, on the advice of counsel, submitted the petition to him for his approval. Because Judge Stump performed the type of act normally performed only by judges and because he did so in his capacity as a Circuit Court Judge, we find no merit to respondents' argument that the informality with which he proceeded rendered his action nonjudicial and deprived him of his absolute immunity.[12]

Both the Court of Appeals and the respondents seem to suggest that, because of the tragic consequences of Judge Stump's actions, he should not be immune. For example, the Court of Appeals noted that "[t]here are actions of purported judicial character that a judge, even when exercising general jurisdiction, is not empowered to take," and respondents argue that Judge Stump's action was "so unfair" and "so totally devoid of judicial concern for the interests and well-being of the young girl involved" as to disqualify it as a judicial act. Disagreement with the action taken by the judge, however, does not justify depriving that judge of his immunity. Despite the unfairness to litigants that sometimes results, the doctrine of judicial immunity is thought to be in the best interests of "the proper administration of justice [, for it allows] a judicial officer, in exercising the authority vested in him [to] be free to act upon his own convictions, without apprehension of personal consequences to himself." *Bradley v. Fisher*, supra, at 347. The fact that the issue before the judge is a controversial one is all the more reason that he should be able to act without fear of suit. . . .

---

[11] Mr. Justice Stewart, in dissent, complains that this statement is inaccurate because it nowhere appears that judges are normally asked to approve parents' decisions either with respect to surgical treatment in general or with respect to sterilizations in particular. Of course, the opinion makes neither assertion. Rather, it is said that Judge Stump was performing a "function" normally performed by judges and that he was taking "the type of action" judges normally perform. The dissent makes no effort to demonstrate that Judge Stump was without jurisdiction to entertain and act upon the specific petition presented to him. Nor does it dispute that judges normally entertain petitions with respect to the affairs of minors. Even if it is assumed that in a lifetime of judging, a judge has acted on only one petition of a particular kind, this would not indicate that his function in entertaining and acting on it is not the kind of function that a judge normally performs. If this is the case, it is also untenable to claim that in entertaining the petition and exercising the jurisdiction with which the statutes invested him, Judge Stump was nevertheless not performing a judicial act or was engaging in the kind of conduct not expected of a judge under the Indiana statutes governing the jurisdiction of its courts.

[12] Mr. Justice Stewart's dissent suggests that Judge Stump's approval of Mrs. McFarlin's petition was not a judicial act because of the absence of what it considers the "normal attributes of a judicial proceeding." These attributes are said to include a "case," with litigants and the opportunity to appeal, in which there is "principled decisionmaking." But under Indiana law, Judge Stump had jurisdiction to act as he did; the proceeding instituted by the petition placed before him was sufficiently a "case" under Indiana law to warrant the exercise of his jurisdiction, whether or not he then proceeded to act erroneously. That there were not two contending litigants did not make Judge Stump's act any less judicial. Courts and judges often act ex parte. They issue search warrants in this manner, for example, often without any "case" having been instituted, without any "case" ever being instituted, and without the issuance of the warrant being subject to appeal. Yet it would not destroy a judge's immunity if it is alleged and offer of proof is made that in issuing a warrant he acted erroneously and without principle.

The Indiana law vested in Judge Stump the power to entertain and act upon the petition for sterilization. He is, therefore, under the controlling cases, immune from damages liability even if his approval of the petition was in error. Accordingly, the judgment of the Court of Appeals is reversed, and the case is remanded for further proceedings consistent with this opinion.[13]

It is so ordered.

■ MR. JUSTICE BRENNAN took no part in the consideration or decision of this case.

■ MR. JUSTICE STEWART, with whom MR. JUSTICE MARSHALL and MR. JUSTICE POWELL join, dissenting.

It is established federal law that judges of general jurisdiction are absolutely immune from monetary liability "for their judicial acts, even when such acts are in excess of their jurisdiction, and are alleged to have been done maliciously or corruptly." Bradley v. Fisher, 80 U.S. (13 Wall.) 335, 351 (1872). It is also established that this immunity is in no way diminished in a proceeding under 42 U.S.C. § 1983. Pierson v. Ray, 386 U.S. 547 (1967). But the scope of judicial immunity is limited to liability for "judicial acts," and I think that what Judge Stump did on July 9, 1971, was beyond the pale of anything that could sensibly be called a judicial act.

Neither in *Bradley v. Fisher* nor in *Pierson v. Ray* was there any claim that the conduct in question was not a judicial act, and the Court thus had no occasion in either case to discuss the meaning of that term. Yet the proposition that judicial immunity extends only to liability for "judicial acts" was emphasized no less than seven times in Mr. Justice Field's opinion for the Court in the *Bradley* case. And if the limitations inherent in that concept have any realistic meaning at all, then I cannot believe that the action of Judge Stump in approving Mrs. McFarlin's petition is protected by judicial immunity.

The Court finds two reasons for holding that Judge Stump's approval of the sterilization petition was a judicial act. First, the Court says, it was "a function normally performed by a judge." Second, the Court says, the act was performed in Judge Stump's "judicial capacity." With all respect, I think that the first of these grounds is factually untrue and that the second is legally unsound.

When the Court says that what Judge Stump did was an act "normally performed by a judge," it is not clear to me whether the Court means that a judge "normally" is asked to approve a mother's decision to have her child given surgical treatment generally, or that a judge "normally" is asked to approve a mother's wish to have her daughter sterilized. But whichever way the Court's statement is to be taken, it is factually inaccurate. In Indiana, as elsewhere in our country, a parent is authorized to arrange for and consent to medical and surgical treatment of his minor child. Ind. Code Ann. § 16–8–4–2 (1973). And when a parent decides to call a physician to care for his sick child or arranges to have a surgeon remove his child's tonsils, he does not, "normally" or otherwise, need to seek the approval of a judge.[3] On the other hand, Indiana did in 1971 have statutory procedures

[13] The issue is not presented and we do not decide whether the District Court correctly concluded that the federal claims against the other defendants were required to be dismissed if Judge Stump, the only state agent, was found to be absolutely immune.

[3] This general authority of a parent was held by an Indiana Court of Appeals in 1975 not to include the power to authorize the sterilization of his minor child. A.L. v. G.R.H., 163

for the sterilization of certain people who were *institutionalized*. But these statutes provided for *administrative proceedings* before a board established by the superintendent of each public hospital. Only if after notice and an evidentiary hearing, an order of sterilization was entered in these proceedings could there be review in a circuit court. See Ind. Code Ann. §§ 16–13–13–1 through 16–13–13–4 (1973).[4]

In sum, what Judge Stump did on July 9, 1971, was in no way an act "normally performed by a judge." Indeed, there is no reason to believe that such an act has ever been performed by any other Indiana judge, either before or since.

When the Court says that Judge Stump was acting in "his judicial capacity" in approving Mrs. McFarlin's petition, it is not clear to me whether the Court means that Mrs. McFarlin submitted the petition to him only because he was a judge, or that, in approving it, he said that he was acting as a judge. But however the Court's test is to be understood, it is, I think, demonstrably unsound.

It can safely be assumed that the Court is correct in concluding that Mrs. McFarlin came to Judge Stump with her petition because he was a County Circuit Court Judge. But false illusions as to a judge's power can hardly convert a judge's response to those illusions into a judicial act. In short, a judge's approval of a mother's petition to lock her daughter in the attic would hardly be a judicial act simply because the mother had submitted her petition to the judge in his official capacity.

If, on the other hand, the Court's test depends upon the fact that Judge Stump said he was acting in his judicial capacity, it is equally invalid. It is true that Judge Stump affixed his signature to the approval of the petition as "Judge, DeKalb Circuit Court." But the conduct of a judge surely does not become a judicial act merely on his own say-so. A judge is not free, like a loose cannon, to inflict indiscriminate damage whenever he announces that he is acting in his judicial capacity.[5]

If the standard adopted by the Court is invalid, then what is the proper measure of a judicial act? Contrary to implications in the Court's opinion, my conclusion that what Judge Stump did was not a judicial act is not based upon the fact that he acted with informality, or that he may not have

---

Ind.App. 636, 325 N.E.2d 501 (1975). Contrary to the Court's conclusion, that case does not in the least demonstrate that an Indiana judge is or ever was empowered to act on the merits of a petition like Mrs. McFarlin's. The parent in that case did not petition for judicial approval of her decision, but rather "filed a complaint for declaratory judgment seeking declaration of her right under the common-law attributes of the parent-child relationship to have her son . . . sterilized." 163 Ind.App., at 636–37, 325 N.E.2d, at 501. The Indiana Court of Appeals' decision simply established a limitation on the parent's common-law rights. It neither sanctioned nor contemplated any procedure for judicial "approval" of the parent's decision. Indeed, the procedure followed in that case offers an instructive contrast to the judicial conduct at issue here: "At the outset, we thank counsel for their excellent efforts in representing a seriously concerned parent and in providing the guardian ad litem defense of the child's interest." Id., at 638, 325 N.E.2d, at 502.

[4] These statutes were repealed in 1974.

[5] Believing that the conduct of Judge Stump on July 9, 1971, was not a judicial act, I do not need to inquire whether he was acting in "the clear absence of all jurisdiction over the subject matter." *Bradley v. Fisher*, supra, at 351. "Jurisdiction" is a coat of many colors. I note only that the Court's finding that Judge Stump had jurisdiction to entertain Mrs. McFarlin's petition seems to me to be based upon dangerously broad criteria. Those criteria are simply that an Indiana statute conferred "jurisdiction of all . . . causes, matters and proceedings," and that there was not in 1971 any Indiana law specifically prohibiting what Judge Stump did.

been "in his judge's robes," or "in the courtroom itself." And I do not reach this conclusion simply "because the petition was not given a docket number, was not placed on file with the clerk's office, and was approved in an ex parte proceeding without notice to the minor, without a hearing, and without the appointment of a guardian ad litem."

It seems to me, rather, that the concept of what is a judicial act must take its content from a consideration of the factors that support immunity from liability for the performance of such an act. Those factors were accurately summarized by the Court in *Pierson v. Ray*, supra, at 554:

> [I]t "is . . . for the benefit of the public, whose interest it is that the judges should be at liberty to exercise their functions with independence and without fear of consequences". . . . It is a judge's duty to decide all cases within his jurisdiction that are brought before him, including controversial cases that arouse the most intense feelings in the litigants. His errors may be corrected on appeal, but he should not have to fear that unsatisfied litigants may hound him with litigation charging malice or corruption. Imposing such a burden on judges would contribute not to principled and fearless decisionmaking but to intimidation.

Not one of the considerations thus summarized in the *Pierson* opinion was present here. There was no "case," controversial or otherwise. There were no litigants. There was and could be no appeal. And there was not even the pretext of principled decision-making. The total absence of any of these normal attributes of a judicial proceeding convinces me that the conduct complained of in this case was not a judicial act.

The petitioners' brief speaks of "an aura of deism which surrounds the bench . . . essential to the maintenance of respect for the judicial institution." Though the rhetoric may be overblown, I do not quarrel with it. But if aura there be, it is hardly protected by exonerating from liability such lawless conduct as took place here. And if intimidation would serve to deter its recurrence, that would surely be in the public interest.

■ MR. JUSTICE POWELL, dissenting.

While I join the opinion of Mr. Justice Stewart, I wish to emphasize what I take to be the central feature of this case—Judge Stump's preclusion of any possibility for the vindication of respondents' rights elsewhere in the judicial system.

Bradley v. Fisher, 80 U.S. (13 Wall.) 335 (1872), which established the absolute judicial immunity at issue in this case, recognized that the immunity was designed to further the public interest in an independent judiciary, sometimes at the expense of legitimate individual grievances. The *Bradley* Court accepted those costs to aggrieved individuals because the judicial system itself provided other means for protecting individual rights:

> Against the consequences of [judges'] erroneous or irregular action, from whatever motives proceeding, the law has provided for private parties numerous remedies, and to those remedies they must, in such cases, resort.

Underlying the *Bradley* immunity, then, is the notion that private rights can be sacrificed in some degree to the achievement of the greater public good deriving from a completely independent judiciary, because there exist alternative forums and methods for vindicating those rights.

But where a judicial officer acts in a manner that precludes all resort to appellate or other judicial remedies that otherwise would be available, the underlying assumption of the *Bradley* doctrine is inoperative.[2] In this case, as Mr. Justice Stewart points out, Judge Stump's unjudicial conduct insured that "[t]here was and could be no appeal." The complete absence of normal judicial process foreclosed resort to any of the "numerous remedies" that "the law has provided for private parties." *Bradley*, supra, at 354.

In sum, I agree with Mr. Justice Stewart that petitioner judge's actions were not "judicial," and that he is entitled to no judicial immunity from suit under 42 U.S.C. § 1983.

NOTES ON ABSOLUTE JUDICIAL IMMUNITY

1. *PIERSON V. RAY*

The question of judicial immunity under § 1983 first came before the Supreme Court in Pierson v. Ray, 386 U.S. 547 (1967). The plaintiffs, some of whom were black, were ministers who sought to use segregated facilities at an interstate bus terminal in Jackson, Mississippi. They were arrested, charged with congregating in a public place in a manner that threatened a breach of the peace and failing to move on when ordered to do so by a police officer, and convicted in a proceeding held before a municipal police justice. On a trial de novo in the County Court, a motion for a directed verdict was granted in favor of one of the ministers after the city's evidence was heard. The charges against the others were dismissed.

The ministers then filed a § 1983 action in federal court against the arresting officers and the municipal police justice. A jury found for the defendants. On appeal, the Circuit Court held that the judge was immune from a § 1983 suit, but that the police officers were liable if the statute that served as the basis for the arrest was unconstitutional as applied, even if they had acted in good faith.[a]

With only Justice Douglas dissenting, Chief Justice Warren concluded for the Court that the municipal police justice was absolutely immune from § 1983 damages liability:

> We find no difficulty in agreeing with the Court of Appeals that Judge Spencer is immune from liability for damages for his role in these convictions. The record is barren of any proof or specific allegation that Judge Spencer played any role in these arrests and convictions other than to adjudge petitioners guilty when their cases came before his court. Few doctrines were more solidly established at common law than the immunity of judges from liability for damages for acts committed within their judicial jurisdiction, as this Court recognized when it adopted the doctrine, in Bradley v. Fisher, 80 U.S. (13 Wall.) 335 (1872). This immunity applies even when the judge is accused of acting maliciously and corruptly, and it "is not for the protection or benefit of a malicious or corrupt judge, but for the benefit of the public, whose interest it is that the judges should be at liberty to exercise their functions with independence and without fear of

[2] In both *Bradley* and Pierson v. Ray, 386 U.S. 547 (1967), any errors committed by the judges involved were open to correction on appeal.

[a] Four years after the arrests in *Pierson*, the statute was held unconstitutional as applied to similar facts. Thomas v. Mississippi, 380 U.S. 524 (1965).

consequences." (Scott v. Stansfield, L.R. 3 Ex. 220, 223 (1868), quoted in *Bradley v. Fisher*, supra, at 349–50 note ‡.) It is a judge's duty to decide all cases within his jurisdiction that are brought before him, including controversial cases that arouse the most intense feelings in the litigants. His errors may be corrected on appeal, but he should not have to fear that unsatisfied litigants may hound him with litigation charging malice or corruption. Imposing such a burden on judges would contribute not to principled and fearless decisionmaking but to intimidation.

We do not believe that this settled principle of law was abolished by § 1983, which makes liable "every person" who under color of law deprives another person of his civil rights. The legislative record gives no clear indication that Congress meant to abolish wholesale all common-law immunities. Accordingly, this Court held in Tenney v. Brandhove, 341 U.S. 367 (1951), that the immunity of legislators for acts within the legislative role was not abolished. The immunity of judges for acts within the judicial role is equally well established, and we presume that Congress would have specifically so provided had it wished to abolish the doctrine.[b]

2. Level vs. Scope

As with legislative immunity, "absolute" judicial immunity refers to the level of immunity, not to its scope. Both the majority and the dissent in *Stump* agree that if judges act outside the judicial functions of their office, they lose their absolute immunity. To use the example from footnote 7 of Justice White's opinion, "if a probate judge, with jurisdiction over only wills and estates, should try a criminal case, he would be acting in the clear absence of jurisdiction and would not be immune from liability for his action." The emphasis on function performed, rather than office held, was reconfirmed in Forrester v. White, 484 U.S. 219 (1988), where the Court unanimously held that a state judge was not entitled to absolute immunity for the allegedly unconstitutional discharge of a court employee. That act was administrative in nature and thus outside the scope of absolute judicial immunity. See also Zarcone v. Perry, 572 F.2d 52 (2d Cir. 1978) (judge who ordered a sandwich vendor to be handcuffed and brought before him for selling "putrid" coffee held liable for compensatory and punitive damages).

In this connection, consider Archie v. Lanier, 95 F.3d 438 (6th Cir. 1996). Several women who had been sexually assaulted in chambers by David Lanier, a state-court judge, brought suit under § 1983, alleging that Lanier had deprived them of their right to personal security and bodily integrity without due process of law and that they were deprived of the equal protection of the laws and of their right of access to the courts. Lanier moved to dismiss on grounds of absolute judicial immunity. On appeal, the Sixth Circuit denied the defense. Relying on Mireles v. Waco, 502 U.S. 9, 11 (1991), which had held that judicial immunity does not extend to "liability for nonjudicial actions, i.e., actions not taken in the judge's judicial capacity," the Court of Appeals held that "stalking and sexually assaulting a person, no matter the circumstances, do not constitute 'judicial acts.' The fact that, regrettably, Lanier happened to be a judge when he committed these reprehensible acts is not relevant to the

---

[b] As to the police officers, the result was different. The Court determined that the police officers, in common with other executive officers, were entitled only to qualified immunity from damages liability, the immunity resting on proof of good faith and probable cause. Qualified immunity is covered in detail in the next Subsection.—[Footnote by eds.]

question of whether he is entitled to immunity. Clearly he is not." *Archie*, supra, at 441. Note that Lanier was nonetheless clearly acting under color of state law and was therefore amenable to suit under § 1983. One of the assaults, for example, occurred while Archie was being interviewed in the judge's chambers for a secretarial position.

3. IMMUNITY FROM PROSPECTIVE RELIEF

Most immunity decisions involve claims for damages. Prospective relief is different. The traditional view, dating at least from Ex parte Young, 209 U.S. 123 (1908), is that unconstitutional acts by state officials may be enjoined. The Eleventh Amendment difficulty is avoided by the rule that the official who acts unconstitutionally "is in that case stripped of his official or representative character and is subjected in his person to the consequences of his individual conduct." Moreover, the rationales behind the common-law immunities recognized for damage actions under § 1983 do not apply to actions for prospective relief. Whatever may be said with respect to liability for money damages, there is certainly no injustice in ordering an official not to engage in unconstitutional conduct in the future. Nor is there the worry that the threat of declaratory or injunctive relief would deter an official from the disinterested discharge of assigned responsibilities. Generally speaking, therefore, it has been assumed that immunity from award of damages does not mean there is immunity from prospective relief.

In Supreme Court of Virginia v. Consumers Union, 446 U.S. 719 (1980), the Court confronted the question whether the Supreme Court of Virginia and its Chief Justice were absolutely immune from a § 1983 action challenging the court's disciplinary rules governing the conduct of attorneys. One such rule barred attorney advertising. Consumers Union sued the state Supreme Court and the Chief Justice for declaratory and injunctive relief, claiming that the advertising ban violated the First and Fourteenth Amendments. When that claim was successful, the plaintiffs applied for award of attorney's fees under the Civil Rights Attorney's Fees Awards Act of 1976, now codified at 42 U.S.C. § 1988(b). As is discussed more fully in the next chapter, that statute makes attorney's fees more or less automatically available to a prevailing plaintiff in a § 1983 action. If the Virginia Supreme Court and its Chief Justice were absolutely immune from suits for prospective relief under § 1983, the action against them could not support an award of attorney's fees. The question of absolute immunity under § 1983 therefore determined the availability of attorney's fees under § 1988.

In resolving this question, the United States Supreme Court distinguished among several kinds of authority exercised by the Virginia court. First, the Virginia court issued a Code of Professional Responsibility to govern the conduct of lawyers licensed in that state. In performing that function, said the Supreme Court, the Virginia judges were acting in a legislative capacity and were absolutely protected not only against the award of damages, but also against declaratory or injunctive relief.

The second function concerned the delegation of enforcement authority to the Virginia State Bar. When the State Bar brought disciplinary actions against Virginia attorneys, adverse determinations could be reviewed in court and appealed to the Supreme Court of Virginia. In reviewing those appeals, the state Supreme Court Justices were acting in a judicial capacity. The Court found it unnecessary to address absolute judicial immunity from prospective relief in light of its conclusion on the third point, summarized below.

Third, notwithstanding the delegation of enforcement authority to the state bar, the courts of Virginia also retained independent authority to initiate disciplinary proceedings against attorneys. In exercising this authority, the Virginia judges were acting in an enforcement capacity that was neither legislative nor judicial. Under the rule of *Ex parte Young*, enforcement officers have no immunity against declaratory or prospective relief. The judges of the Virginia Supreme Court would likewise have no immunity when acting in that capacity and were therefore amenable to an order of prospective relief that would trigger attorney's fees.

Of these several rulings, perhaps the most interesting is the recognition of absolute legislative immunity for § 1983 actions seeking prospective relief. Of course, federal legislators had already been granted immunity from prospective relief under the Speech or Debate Clause. Given the generally parallel character of immunities for state and federal officials, it was perhaps predictable that the Court would extend this approach to state legislators sued under § 1983. Is this position sound? Are suits for declaratory or injunctive relief against legislators barred because they are troublesome, or because they are unnecessary? Under what circumstances would the absence of a legislative defendant preclude a litigant from securing prospective relief?

Perhaps less obvious was the decision to include within the scope of legislative immunity at least some of those who exercise delegated legislative power. The reach of this inclusion is uncertain, but potentially quite significant. Does it mean, for example, that officials of administrative agencies are absolutely immune from both damages and prospective relief for the exercise of rulemaking authority? Or might *Supreme Court of Virginia* be read to say less than that? For examples of Court of Appeals decisions finding administrative rulemakers absolutely immune because they acted in a legislative capacity, see, e.g., Redwood Village Partnership v. Graham, 26 F.3d 839 (8th Cir. 1994) (state agency officials who set reimbursement rates for health care facilities were immune from § 1983 liability); Jayvee Brand v. United States, 721 F.2d 385 (D.C. Cir. 1983) (members of the Consumer Product Safety Commission were absolutely immune from *Bivens* actions predicated on their promulgation of regulations in the Code of Federal Regulations).

4. JUDICIAL IMMUNITY FROM PROSPECTIVE RELIEF

Although *Supreme Court of Virginia* dodged the issue of absolute judicial immunity from prospective relief, the question arose against in Pulliam v. Allen, 466 U.S. 522 (1984). There the Court held that absolute judicial immunity from the award of damages did not extend to declaratory or injunctive relief. The holding in *Pulliam* was modified by the Federal Courts Improvement Act of 1996, which amended § 1983 to provide that "in any action brought against a judicial officer for an act or omission taken in such officer's judicial capacity, injunctive relief shall not be granted unless a declaratory decree was violated or declaratory relief was unavailable." The Federal Courts Improvement Act also amended § 1988(b) to limit the award of attorney's fees against judges by adding an exceptions clause: "[I]n any action brought against a judicial officer for an act or omission taken in such officer's judicial capacity, such officer shall not be held liable for any costs, including attorney's fees, unless such action was clearly in excess of such officer's jurisdiction." Thus, even if declaratory relief is available against a judge—because, for example, the judge seeks to implement an unconstitutional policy—attorney's fees will not be available as long as the policy is within the scope of the judge's judicial function. In *Pulliam*, for example, the defendant was a magistrate who incarcerated defendants who could not afford bail even when they were charged with non-jailable offenses. The District Court found that practice unconstitutional. But the practice was arguably not outside Magistrate Pulliam's jurisdiction, since setting bail was one of the tasks state court magistrates in her position conventionally perform.

INTRODUCTORY NOTES ON PROSECUTORIAL IMMUNITY

1. *IMBLER V. PACHTMAN*

Prosecutorial immunity came before the Court in Imbler v. Pachtman, 424 U.S. 409 (1976). Imbler was convicted of a felony-murder committed in 1961. Nine years later he secured his release on federal habeas corpus on the ground, among others, that Pachtman, the prosecutor, had culpably (i.e., knowingly or negligently) used misleading or false testimony at the trial.[a] The state chose not to retry him, and he filed a § 1983 damages action against Pachtman in April of 1972.

Writing for the Court, Justice Powell said that although he was dealing with a statute that "on its face admits of no immunities," previous cases had recognized absolute immunity "predicated upon a considered inquiry into the immunity historically accorded the relevant official at common law and the interests behind it." At common law absolute prosecutorial immunity in suits for malicious prosecution was "well settled." Powell then asked "whether the same considerations of public policy that underlie the common-law rule likewise countenance absolute immunity under § 1983":

> If a prosecutor had only a qualified immunity, the threat of § 1983 suits would undermine performance of his duties no less than would the threat of common-law suits for malicious prosecution. A prosecutor is duty bound to exercise his best judgment both in deciding which suits to bring and in conducting them in court. The public trust of the prosecutor's office would suffer if he were constrained in making every decision by the consequences in terms of his own potential liability in a suit for damages. Such suits could be expected with some frequency, for a defendant often will transform his resentment at being prosecuted into the ascription of improper and malicious actions to the state's advocate. Further, if the prosecutor could be made to answer in court each time such a person charged him with wrongdoing, his energy and attention would be diverted from the pressing duty of enforcing the criminal law.
>
> Moreover, suits that survived the pleadings would pose substantial danger of liability even to the honest prosecutor. The prosecutor's possible knowledge of a witness' falsehoods, the materiality of evidence not revealed to the defense, the propriety of a closing argument, and ultimately in every case the likelihood that

[a] Ironically, the initial habeas litigation on these issues was prompted by a letter to the governor in which Pachtman—in discharge of his duty, as he described it, to be "fair"—disclosed exculpatory evidence that he and an investigator had discovered after the trial.

prosecutorial misconduct so infected a trial as to deny due process, are typical of issues with which judges struggle in actions for post-trial relief, sometimes to differing conclusions. The presentation of such issues in a § 1983 action often would require a virtual retrial of the criminal offense in a new forum, and the resolution of some technical issues by the lay jury. It is fair to say, we think, that the honest prosecutor would face greater difficulty in meeting the standards of qualified immunity than other executive or administrative officials. Frequently acting under serious constraints of time and even information, a prosecutor inevitably makes many decisions that could engender colorable claims of constitutional deprivation. Defending these decisions, often years after they were made, could impose unique and intolerable burdens upon a prosecutor responsible annually for hundreds of indictments and trials.

The affording of only a qualified immunity to the prosecutor also could have an adverse effect upon the functioning of the criminal justice system. Attaining the system's goal of accurately determining guilt or innocence requires that both the prosecution and the defense have wide discretion in the conduct of the trial and the presentation of evidence. The veracity of witnesses in criminal cases frequently is subject to doubt before and after they testify, as is illustrated by the history of this case. If prosecutors were hampered in exercising their judgment as to the use of such witnesses by concern about resulting personal liability, the triers of fact in criminal cases often would be denied relevant evidence.[24]

The ultimate fairness of the operation of the system itself could be weakened by subjecting prosecutors to § 1983 liability. Various post-trial procedures are available to determine whether an accused has received a fair trial. These procedures include the remedial powers of the trial judge, appellate review, and state and federal post-conviction collateral remedies. In all of these the attention of the reviewing judge or tribunal is focused primarily on whether there was a fair trial under law. This focus should not be blurred by even the subconscious knowledge that a post-trial decision in favor of the accused might result in the prosecutor's being called upon to respond in damages for his error or mistaken judgment.[25]

We conclude that the considerations outlined above dictate the same absolute immunity under § 1983 that the prosecutor enjoys at common law. . . .

---

[24] A prosecutor often must decide, especially in cases of wide public interest, whether to proceed to trial where there is a sharp conflict in the evidence. The appropriate course of action in such a case may well be to permit a jury to resolve the conflict. Yet, a prosecutor understandably would be reluctant to go forward with a close case where an acquittal likely would trigger a suit against him for damages.

[25] The possibility of personal liability also could dampen the prosecutor's exercise of his duty to bring to the attention of the court or of proper officials all significant evidence suggestive of innocence or mitigation. At trial this duty is enforced by the requirements of due process, but after a conviction the prosecutor also is bound by the ethics of his office to inform the appropriate authority of after-acquired or other information that casts doubt upon the correctness of the conviction. Indeed, the record in this case suggests that respondent's recognition of this duty led to the post-conviction hearing which in turn resulted ultimately in the District Court's granting of the writ of habeas corpus.

> We emphasize that the immunity of prosecutors from liability in suits under § 1983 does not leave the public powerless to deter misconduct or to punish that which occurs. This Court has never suggested that the policy considerations which compel civil immunity for certain governmental officials also place them beyond the reach of the criminal law. Even judges, cloaked with absolute civil immunity for centuries, could be punished criminally for willful deprivations of constitutional rights on the strength of 18 U.S.C. § 242, the criminal analog of § 1983. The prosecutor would fare no better for his willful acts. Moreover, a prosecutor stands perhaps unique, among officials whose acts could deprive persons of constitutional rights, in his amenability to professional discipline by an association of his peers. These checks undermine the argument that the imposition of civil liability is the only way to insure that prosecutors are mindful of the constitutional rights of persons accused of crime.

Justice Powell turned finally to the "boundaries of our holding." He noted the Court of Appeals' focus on "the functional nature of the activities rather than respondent's status" so as to "distinguish and leave standing those [Circuit Court] cases . . . which hold that a prosecutor engaged in certain investigative activities enjoys, not the absolute immunity associated with the judicial process, but only a good-faith defense comparable to the policeman's." He concluded:

> We agree with the Court of Appeals that respondent's activities were intimately associated with the judicial phase of the criminal process, and thus were functions to which the reasons for absolute immunity apply with full force. We have no occasion to consider whether like or similar reasons require immunity for those aspects of the prosecutor's responsibility that cast him in the role of an administrator or investigative officer rather than that of advocate. We hold only that in initiating a prosecution and in presenting the state's case, the prosecutor is immune from a civil suit for damages under § 1983.

Justice Stevens did not participate in the decision. Justice White, joined by Justices Brennan and Marshall, concurred in the judgment. He agreed that absolute prosecutorial immunity was appropriate for claims arising from the presentation of evidence in court. He wrote separately to disassociate himself from "any implication that *absolute* immunity for prosecutors extends to suits based on claims of unconstitutional suppression of evidence. . . . " Justice Powell's opinion expressly rejected this distinction in a footnote.

2. SUBSEQUENT DECISIONS

The boundaries of the holding in *Imbler* have been litigated in three subsequent cases.[b]

Burns v. Reed, 500 U.S. 478 (1991), held that a prosecutor was absolutely immune from damages liability based upon positions taken in a probable cause hearing for a search warrant. The same prosecutor was held not entitled

---

[b] For an argument that absolute prosecutorial immunity should be limited if not abandoned, see Margaret Z. Johns, Reconsidering Absolute Prosecutorial Immunity, 2005 B.Y.U. L. Rev. 535. For a more general attack on official immunities from civil damages, see Donald L. Doernberg, Taking Supremacy Seriously: The Contrariety of Official Immunities, 80 Fordham L. Rev. 443 (2011).

to absolute immunity for giving legal advice to the police about the legality of an investigative practice. Joined by Justices Blackmun and Marshall, Justice Scalia wrote separately to resolve an issue the Court thought not before it. He would have held the prosecutor not entitled to absolute immunity for claims arising out of the decision to initiate a search warrant proceeding.

In Buckley v. Fitzsimmons, 509 U.S. 259 (1993), the Court was unanimous that a prosecutor was not entitled to absolute immunity for making statements at a press conference. But the Court held five-four that a prosecutor charged with conspiring with the police to manufacture false evidence was, in the particular context, also not entitled to absolute immunity.

Finally, Kalina v. Fletcher, 522 U.S. 118 (1997), concerned whether absolute prosecutorial immunity covered false sworn statements made in support of a motion for an arrest warrant. Because the false statements were made to a judge, they might have been thought "intimately associated with the judicial phase of the criminal process" under *Imbler v. Pachtman*. The trouble was that in Malley v. Briggs, 475 U.S. 335 (1986), the Court had ruled that police officers had only qualified immunity for sworn statements made to secure arrest warrants. If absolute prosecutorial immunity had been extended to such conduct, prosecutors and police would have enjoyed different levels of protection for *precisely the same conduct*. In *Kalina*, the Court avoided this embarrassment by saying that the prosecutor's sworn statements in support of a motion for an arrest warrant were not part of the prosecutorial function but were analogous to the role of a complaining witness and therefore triggered only qualified immunity.

Van de Kamp v. Goldstein

Supreme Court of the United States, 2009.
555 U.S. 335.

■ JUSTICE BREYER delivered the opinion of the Court.

We here consider the scope of a prosecutor's absolute immunity from claims asserted under 42 U. S. C. § 1983. See Imbler v. Pachtman, 424 U. S. 409 (1976). We ask whether that immunity extends to claims that the prosecution failed to disclose impeachment material, see Giglio v. United States, 405 U. S. 150 (1972), due to: (1) a failure properly to train prosecutors, (2) a failure properly to supervise prosecutors, or (3) a failure to establish an information system containing potential impeachment material about informants. We conclude that a prosecutor's absolute immunity extends to all these claims.

I

In 1998, respondent Thomas Goldstein (then a prisoner) filed a habeas corpus action in the Federal District Court for the Central District of California. He claimed that in 1980 he was convicted of murder; that his conviction depended in critical part upon the testimony of Edward Floyd Fink, a jailhouse informant; that Fink's testimony was unreliable, indeed false; that Fink had previously received reduced sentences for providing prosecutors with favorable testimony in other cases; that at least some prosecutors in the Los Angeles County District Attorney's Office knew about the favorable treatment; that the office had not provided Goldstein's attorney with that information; and that, among other things, the prosecution's failure to provide Goldstein's attorney with this potential impeachment information had led to his erroneous conviction.

After an evidentiary hearing the District Court agreed with Goldstein that Fink had not been truthful and that if the prosecution had told Goldstein's lawyer that Fink had received prior rewards in return for favorable testimony it might have made a difference. The court ordered the State either to grant Goldstein a new trial or to release him. The Court of Appeals affirmed the District Court's determination. And the State decided that, rather than retry Goldstein (who had already served 24 years of his sentence), it would release him.

Upon his release Goldstein filed this § 1983 action against petitioners, the former Los Angeles County district attorney and chief deputy district attorney. Goldstein's complaint (which for present purposes we take as accurate) asserts in relevant part that the prosecution's failure to communicate to his attorney the facts about Fink's earlier testimony-related rewards violated the prosecution's constitutional duty to "insure communication of all relevant information on each case [including agreements made with informants] to every lawyer who deals with it." *Giglio*, at 154. Moreover, it alleges that this failure resulted from the failure of petitioners (the office's chief supervisory attorneys) adequately to train and to supervise the prosecutors who worked for them as well as their failure to establish an information system about informants. And it asks for damages based upon these training, supervision, and information-system related failings.

Petitioners, claiming absolute immunity from such a § 1983 action, asked the District Court to dismiss the complaint. The District Court denied the motion to dismiss on the ground that the conduct asserted amounted to "administrative," not "prosecutorial," conduct; hence it fell outside the scope of the prosecutor's absolute immunity to § 1983 claims. The Ninth Circuit, considering petitioners' claim on an interlocutory appeal, affirmed the District Court's "no immunity" determination. We now review the Ninth Circuit's decision, and we reverse its determination.

II

A half-century ago Chief Judge Learned Hand explained that a prosecutor's absolute immunity reflects "a balance" of "evils." Gregoire v. Biddle, 177 F. 2d 579, 581 (2d Cir. 1949). "[I]t has been thought in the end better," he said, "to leave unredressed the wrongs done by dishonest officers than to subject those who try to do their duty to the constant dread of retaliation." In *Imbler*, supra, this Court considered prosecutorial actions that are "intimately associated with the judicial phase of the criminal process." And, referring to Chief Judge Hand's views, it held that prosecutors are absolutely immune from liability in § 1983 lawsuits brought under such circumstances.

The § 1983 action at issue was that of a prisoner freed on a writ of habeas corpus who subsequently sought damages from his former prosecutor. His action, like the action now before us, tracked the claims that a federal court had found valid when granting his habeas corpus petition. In particular, the prisoner claimed that the trial prosecutor had permitted a fingerprint expert to give false testimony, that the prosecutor was responsible for the expert's having suppressed important evidence, and that the prosecutor had introduced a misleading artist's sketch into evidence.

In concluding that the prosecutor was absolutely immune, the Court pointed out that legislators have long "enjoyed absolute immunity for their official action," that the common law granted immunity to "judges and . . . jurors acting within the scope of their duties," and that the law had also granted prosecutors absolute immunity from common-law tort actions, say, those underlying a "decision to initiate a prosecution." The Court then held that the "same considerations of public policy that underlie" a prosecutor's common-law immunity "countenance absolute immunity under § 1983." Those considerations, the Court said, arise out of the general common-law "concern that harassment by unfounded litigation" could both "cause a deflection of the prosecutor's energies from his public duties" and also lead the prosecutor to "shade his decisions instead of exercising the independence of judgment required by his public trust."

Where § 1983 actions are at issue, the Court said, both sets of concerns are present and serious. The "public trust of the prosecutor's office would suffer" were the prosecutor to have in mind his "own potential" damages "liability" when making prosecutorial decisions—as he might well were he subject to § 1983 liability. This is no small concern, given the frequency with which criminal defendants bring such suits, and the "substantial danger of liability even to the honest prosecutor" that such suits pose when they survive pretrial dismissal. A "prosecutor," the Court noted, "inevitably makes many decisions that could engender colorable claims of constitutional deprivation. Defending these decisions, often years after they were made, could impose unique and intolerable burdens upon a prosecutor responsible annually for hundreds of indictments and trials." The Court thus rejected the idea of applying the less-than-absolute "qualified immunity" that the law accords to other "executive or administrative officials," noting that the "honest prosecutor would face greater difficulty" than would those officials "in meeting the standards of qualified immunity." Accordingly, the immunity that the law grants prosecutors is "absolute."

The Court made clear that absolute immunity may not apply when a prosecutor is not acting as "an officer of the court," but is instead engaged in other tasks, say, investigative or administrative tasks. To decide whether absolute immunity attaches to a particular kind of prosecutorial activity, one must take account of the "functional" considerations discussed above. See Burns v. Reed, 500 U. S. 478, 486 (1991) (collecting cases applying "functional approach" to immunity); Kalina v. Fletcher, 522 U. S. 118, 127, 130 (1997). In *Imbler*, the Court concluded that the "reasons for absolute immunity appl[ied] with full force" to the conduct at issue because it was "intimately associated with the judicial phase of the criminal process." The fact that one constitutional duty at issue was a positive duty (the duty to supply "information relevant to the defense") rather than a negative duty (the duty not to "use . . . perjured testimony") made no difference. After all, a plaintiff can often transform a positive into a negative duty simply by reframing the pleadings; in either case, a constitutional violation is at issue.

Finally, the Court specifically reserved the question whether or when "similar reasons require immunity for those aspects of the prosecutor's responsibility that cast him in the role of an administrator . . . rather than that of advocate." It said that "[d]rawing a proper line between these functions may present difficult questions, but this case does not require us to anticipate them."

In the years since *Imbler*, we have held that absolute immunity applies when a prosecutor prepares to initiate a judicial proceeding, *Burns*, supra, at 492,or appears in court to present evidence in support of a search warrant application, *Kalina*, at 126. We have held that absolute immunity does not apply when a prosecutor gives advice to police during a criminal investigation, see *Burns*, at 496, when the prosecutor makes statements to the press, Buckley v. Fitzsimmons, 509 U. S. 259, 277 (1993), or when a prosecutor acts as a complaining witness in support of a warrant application, *Kalina*, at132 (Scalia, J., concurring). This case, unlike these earlier cases, requires us to consider how immunity applies where a prosecutor is engaged in certain administrative activities.

III

Goldstein claims that the district attorney and his chief assistant violated their constitutional obligation to provide his attorney with impeachment-related information, see *Giglio*,because, as the Court of Appeals wrote, they failed "to adequately train and supervise deputy district attorneys on that subject," 481 F. 3d, at 1176, and because, as Goldstein's complaint adds, they "failed to create any system for the Deputy District Attorneys handling criminal cases to access information pertaining to the benefits provided to jailhouse informants and other impeachment information." We agree with Goldstein that, in making these claims, he attacks the office's administrative procedures. We are also willing to assume with Goldstein, but purely for argument's sake, that *Giglio* imposes certain obligations as to training, supervision, or information-system management.

Even so, we conclude that prosecutors involved in such supervision or training or information-system management enjoy absolute immunity from the kind of legal claims at issue here. Those claims focus upon a certain kind of administrative obligation—a kind that itself is directly connected with the conduct of a trial. Here, unlike with other claims related to administrative decisions, an individual prosecutor's error in the plaintiff's specific criminal trial constitutes an essential element of the plaintiff's claim. The administrative obligations at issue here are thus unlike administrative duties concerning, for example, workplace hiring, payroll administration, the maintenance of physical facilities, and the like. Moreover, the types of activities on which Goldstein's claims focus necessarily require legal knowledge and the exercise of related discretion, e.g., in determining what information should be included in the training or the supervision or the information-system management. And in that sense also Goldstein's claims are unlike claims of, say, unlawful discrimination in hiring employees. Given these features of the case before us, we believe absolute immunity must follow.

A

We reach this conclusion by initially considering a hypothetical case that involves supervisory or other office prosecutors but does not involve administration. Suppose that Goldstein had brought such a case, seeking damages not only from the trial prosecutor but also from a supervisory prosecutor or from the trial prosecutor's colleagues—all on the ground that they should have found and turned over the impeachment material about Fink. *Imbler* makes clear that all these prosecutors would enjoy absolute immunity from such a suit. The prosecutors' behavior, taken individually or separately, would involve "[p]reparation . . . for . . . trial," and would be "intimately associated with the judicial phase of the criminal process" because it concerned the evidence presented at trial. And all of the considerations that this Court found to militate in favor of absolute immunity in *Imbler* would militate in favor of immunity in such a case.

The only difference we can find between *Imbler* and our hypothetical case lies in the fact that, in our hypothetical case, a prosecutorial supervisor or colleague might himself be liable for damages instead of the trial prosecutor. But we cannot find that difference (in the pattern of liability among prosecutors within a single office) to be critical. Decisions about indictment or trial prosecution will often involve more than one prosecutor within an office. We do not see how such differences in the pattern of liability among a group of prosecutors in a single office could alleviate *Imbler*'s basic fear, namely, that the threat of damages liability would affect the way in which prosecutors carried out their basic court-related tasks. Moreover, this Court has pointed out that "it is the interest in protecting the proper functioning of the office, rather than the interest in protecting its occupant, that is of primary importance." *Kalina*, 522 U. S., at 125. Thus, we must assume that the prosecutors in our hypothetical suit would enjoy absolute immunity.

B

Once we determine that supervisory prosecutors are immune in a suit directly attacking their actions related to an individual trial, we must find they are similarly immune in the case before us. We agree with the Court of Appeals that the office's general methods of supervision and training are at issue here, but we do not agree that that difference is critical for present purposes. That difference does not preclude an intimate connection between prosecutorial activity and the trial process. The management tasks at issue, insofar as they are relevant, concern how and when to make impeachment information available at a trial. They are thereby directly connected with the prosecutor's basic trial advocacy duties. And, in terms of *Imbler*'s functional concerns, a suit charging that a supervisor made a mistake directly related to a particular trial, on the one hand, and a suit charging that a supervisor trained and supervised inadequately, on the other, would seem very much alike.

That is true, in part, for the practical reason that it will often prove difficult to draw a line between general office supervision or office training (say, related to *Giglio*) and specific supervision or training related to a particular case. To permit claims based upon the former is almost inevitably to permit the bringing of claims that include the latter. It is also true because one cannot easily distinguish, for immunity purposes, between claims based upon training or supervisory failures related to Giglio and similar claims related to other constitutional matters (obligations under Brady v. Maryland, 373 U. S. 83 (1963), for example). And that being so, every consideration that *Imbler* mentions militates in favor of immunity.

As we have said, the type of "faulty training" claim at issue here rests in necessary part upon a consequent error by an individual prosecutor in the midst of trial, namely, the plaintiff's trial. If, as *Imbler* says, the threat of damages liability for such an error could lead a trial prosecutor to take account of that risk when making trial-related decisions, so, too, could the threat of more widespread liability throughout the office (ultimately traceable to that trial error) lead both that prosecutor and other office prosecutors as well to take account of such a risk. Indeed, members of a large prosecutorial office, when making prosecutorial decisions, could have in mind the "consequences in terms of" damages liability whether they are making general decisions about supervising or training or whether they are making individual trial-related decisions.

Moreover, because better training or supervision might prevent most, if not all, prosecutorial errors at trial, permission to bring such a suit here would grant permission to criminal defendants to bring claims in other similar instances, in effect claiming damages for (trial-related) training or supervisory failings. Further, given the complexity of the constitutional issues, inadequate training and supervision suits could, as in *Imbler*, "pose substantial danger of liability even to the honest prosecutor." Finally, as *Imbler* pointed out, defending prosecutorial decisions, often years after they were made, could impose "unique and intolerable burdens upon a prosecutor responsible annually for hundreds of indictments and trials."

At the same time, to permit this suit to go forward would create practical anomalies. A trial prosecutor would remain immune, even for intentionally failing to turn over, say *Giglio* material; but her supervisor might be liable for negligent training or supervision. Small prosecution offices where supervisors can personally participate in all of the cases would likewise remain immune from prosecution; but large offices, making use of more general office-wide supervision and training, would not. Most important, the ease with which a plaintiff could restyle a complaint charging a trial failure so that it becomes a complaint charging a failure of training or supervision would eviscerate *Imbler*.

We conclude that the very reasons that led this Court in *Imbler* to find absolute immunity require a similar finding in this case. We recognize, as Chief Judge Hand pointed out, that sometimes such immunity deprives a plaintiff of compensation that he undoubtedly merits; but the impediments to the fair, efficient functioning of a prosecutorial office that liability could create lead us to find that *Imbler* must apply here.

C

We treat separately Goldstein's claim that the Los Angeles County District Attorney's Office should have established a system that would have permitted prosecutors "handling criminal cases to access information pertaining to the benefits provided to jailhouse informants and other impeachment information." We do so because Goldstein argues that the creation of an information management system is a more purely administrative task, less closely related to the "judicial phase of the criminal process," than are supervisory or training tasks. He adds that technically qualified individuals other than prosecutors could create such a system and that they could do so prior to the initiation of criminal proceedings.

In our view, however, these differences do not require a different outcome. The critical element of any information system is the information it contains. Deciding what to include and what not to include in an information system is little different from making similar decisions in respect to training. Again, determining the criteria for inclusion or exclusion requires knowledge of the law.

Moreover, the absence of an information system is relevant here if, and only if, a proper system would have included information about the informant Fink. Thus, were this claim allowed, a court would have to review the office's legal judgments, not simply about whether to have an information system but also about what kind of system is appropriate, and whether an appropriate system would have included *Giglio*-related information about one particular kind of trial informant. Such decisions—whether made prior to or during a particular trial—are "intimately associated with the judicial phase of the criminal process." And, for the reasons set out above, all *Im-*

bler's functional considerations (and the anomalies we mentioned earlier) apply here as well.

We recognize that sometimes it would be easy for a court to determine that an office's decision about an information system was inadequate. Suppose, for example, the office had no system at all. But the same could be said of a prosecutor's trial error. Immunity does not exist to help prosecutors in the easy case; it exists because the easy cases bring difficult cases in their wake. And, as *Imbler* pointed out, the likely presence of too many difficult cases threatens, not prosecutors, but the public, for the reason that it threatens to undermine the necessary independence and integrity of the prosecutorial decision-making process. Such is true of the kinds of claims before us, to all of which *Imbler*'s functional considerations apply. Consequently, where a § 1983 plaintiff claims that a prosecutor's management of a trial-related information system is responsible for a constitutional error at his or her particular trial, the prosecutor responsible for the system enjoys absolute immunity just as would the prosecutor who handled the particular trial itself.

* * *

For these reasons we conclude that petitioners are entitled to absolute immunity in respect to Goldstein's claims that their supervision, training, or information-system management was constitutionally inadequate. Accordingly, the judgment of the Court of Appeals is reversed, and the case is remanded for further proceedings consistent with this opinion.

It is so ordered.

ADDITIONAL NOTES ON ABSOLUTE IMMUNITY

1. WITNESS IMMUNITY: *BRISCO V. LAHUE*

It was alleged in Brisco v. LaHue, 460 U.S. 325 (1983), that police officers had given false testimony leading to the conviction of a criminal defendant. The Court held that they were entitled to absolute immunity.

Justice Stevens' opinion for the Court began by asking whether § 1983 damages would be available against a private-party witness. He answered "no" for two reasons. First, the private party would not (absent collusion with the prosecutor or the police) be acting "under color of law." Second, there was a well-established common law privilege protecting the testimony of witnesses from damages liability "even if the witness knew the statements were false and made them with malice." This rule was based on the fear that a "witness's apprehension of subsequent damages liability might induce . . . self-censorship":

> [W]itnesses might be reluctant to come forward to testify. And once a witness is on the stand, his testimony might be distorted by the fear of subsequent liability. Even within the constraints of the witness's oath there may be various ways to give an account or to state an opinion. These alternatives may be more or less detailed and may differ in emphasis and certainty. A witness who knows that he might be forced to defend a subsequent lawsuit, and perhaps to pay damages, might be inclined to shade his testimony in favor of the potential plaintiff, to magnify uncertainties, and

> thus to deprive the finder of fact of candid, objective, and undistorted evidence.

Justice Stevens reviewed the Court's prior holdings that prosecutors and judges were absolutely immune for their participation in judicial proceedings, and observed:

> In short, the common law provided absolute immunity from subsequent damages liability for all persons—governmental or otherwise—who were integral parts of the judicial process. It is equally clear that § 1983 does not authorize a damages claim against private witnesses on the one hand, or against judges or prosecutors in the performance of their respective duties on the other. When a police officer appears as a witness, he may reasonably be viewed as acting like any other witness sworn to tell the truth—in which event he can make a strong claim to witness immunity. . . .

Justice Stevens then turned to the plaintiffs' argument that a special rule should apply to police officers:

> Petitioners, finally, urge that we should carve out an exception to the general rule of immunity in cases of alleged perjury by police officer witnesses. They assert that the reasons supporting common law immunity—the need to avoid intimidation and self-censorship—apply with diminished force to police officers. Policemen often have a duty to testify about the products of their investigations, and they have a professional interest in obtaining convictions which would assertedly counterbalance any tendency to shade testimony in favor of potentially vindictive defendants. In addition, they are subject to § 1983 lawsuits for the performance of their other duties, as to which they have only qualified immunity, and their defense is generally undertaken by their governmental employers. Further, petitioners urge that perjured testimony by police officers is likely to be more damaging to constitutional rights than such testimony by ordinary citizens, because the policeman in uniform carries special credibility in the eyes of jurors. And, in the case of police officers, who cooperate regularly with prosecutors in the enforcement of criminal law, prosecution for perjury is alleged to be so unlikely that it is not an effective substitute for civil damages.
>
> These contentions have some force. But our cases clearly indicate that immunity analysis rests on functional categories, not on the status of the defendant. A police officer on the witness stand performs the same functions as any other witness; he is subject to compulsory process, takes an oath, responds to questions on direct examination and cross-examination, and may be prosecuted subsequently for perjury. . . .
>
> Section 1983 lawsuits against police officer witnesses, like lawsuits against prosecutors, "could be expected with some frequency." Imbler v. Pachtman, 424 U.S. 409, 425 (1976). Police officers testify in scores of cases every year, and defendants often will transform resentment at being convicted into allegations of perjury by the state's official witnesses. . . .[29]

[29] Moreover, lawsuits alleging perjury on the stand in violation of the defendant's due process rights often raise material questions of fact, inappropriate for disposition at the summary judgment stage. The plaintiff's complaint puts in issue the falsity and materiality of the

> It is not sufficient to assert that the burdens on defendants and the courts could be alleviated by limiting the cause of action to those former criminal defendants who have already vindicated themselves in another forum, either on appeal or by collateral attack. We rejected a similar contention in *Imbler*. Petitioner contended that "his suit should be allowed, even if others would not be, because the District Court's issuance of the writ of habeas corpus shows that his suit has substance." Id., at 428 n.27. We declined to carve out such an exception to prosecutorial immunity, noting that petitioner's success in a collateral proceeding did not necessarily establish the merits of his civil rights action. Moreover, we noted that "using the habeas proceeding as a 'door-opener' for a subsequent civil rights action would create the risk of injecting extraneous concerns into that proceeding." We emphasized that, in determining whether to grant post-conviction relief, the tribunal should focus solely on whether there was a fair trial under law. "This focus should not be blurred by even the subconscious knowledge that a post-trial decision in favor of the accused might result in the prosecutor's being called upon to respond in damages for his error or mistaken judgment." Id., at 427. The same danger exists in the case of potential liability for police officer witnesses.
>
> Justices Brennan, Marshall, and Blackmun dissented.

2. GRAND JURY WITNESSES: *REHBERG V. PAULK*

Absolute witness immunity was extended to grand jury proceedings in Rehberg v. Paulk, 132 S.Ct. 1497. That witness immunity ordinarily would apply to both trial and grand jury proceedings seems obvious. Questions arose because the witness, a district attorney's investigator, was the sole "complaining witness" in three successive grand jury proceedings. Absolute immunity for a "complaining witness" seemed to conflict with decisions holding that police and prosecutors have only qualified immunity for sworn statements made as a "complaining witness" in seeking an arrest warrant. See Malley v. Briggs, 475 U.S. 335 (1986) (police); Kalina v. Fletcher, 522 U.S. 118 (1997) (prosecutors).

James Paulk launched a criminal investigation of Charles Rehberg, who had been making anonymous allegations about the management of a local hospital. Three times Paulk appeared before a grand jury, resulting in indictments of Rehberg for burglary, assault of a hospital physician, and making harassing telephone calls. All the indictments were dismissed. Rehberg then sued Paulk, claiming that his status as a law enforcement officer and a "complaining witness" warranted lesser immunity than that afforded ordinary grand jury witnesses. The Supreme Court unanimously disagreed. Speaking through Justice Alito, the Court first equated grand jury and trial witnesses: "In both contexts, a witness' fear of retaliatory litigation may deprive the tribunal of critical evi-

---

allegedly perjured statements, and the defendant witness's knowledge and state of mind at the time he testified. Sometimes collateral estoppel principles will permit dismissal at the pretrial stage. But if the truth of the allegedly perjured statement was not necessarily decided in the previous criminal verdict, if there is newly-discovered evidence of falsity, or if the defendant concedes that the testimony was inaccurate, the central issue will be the defendant's state of mind. Summary judgment is usually not feasible under these circumstances. If summary judgment is denied, the case must proceed to trial and must traverse much of the same ground as the original criminal trial.

dence. And in neither context is the deterrent of civil liability needed to prevent perjurious testimony."

The idea that a "complaining witness" should receive lesser protection was treated as little more than a play on words. Police and prosecutors who file affidavits to initiate criminal prosecutions (and who receive only qualified immunity for doing so) might not be witnesses at all. Historically, the term "complaining witness" referred to someone who "procured an arrest and initiated a criminal prosecution." A law enforcement officer who testifies before a grand jury is "not at all comparable" to a complaining witness in that sense:

> By testifying before a grand jury, a law enforcement officer does not perform the function of applying for an arrest warrant; nor does such an officer make the critical decision to initiate a prosecution. It is of course true that a detective or case agent who has performed or supervised most of the investigative work in a case may serve as an important witness in the grand jury proceeding and may very much want the grand jury to return an indictment. But such a witness, unlike a complaining witness at common law, does not make the decision to press criminal charges.
>
> Instead, it is almost always a prosecutor who is responsible for the decision to present a case to a grand jury, and in many jurisdictions, even if an indictment is handed up, a prosecution cannot proceed unless the prosecutor signs the indictment. It would thus be anomalous to permit a police officer who testifies before a grand jury to be sued for maliciously procuring an unjust prosecution when it is the prosecutor, who is shielded by absolute immunity, who is actually responsible for the decision to prosecute."

With this decision, the Supreme Court preserved the uniform treatment of police and prosecutors performing similar functions. Under *Malley v. Briggs* and *Kalina v. Fletcher*, both police and prosecutors enjoy only qualified immunity for sworn statements made to secure arrest warrants. Under *Brisco v. LaHue* and *Rehberg v. Paulk*, both police and prosecutors enjoy absolute immunity for testimony before grand and petit juries. This parallelism between police and prosecutors, however, requires rather fine distinctions among the functions performed by both. Thus, a police officer has qualified immunity for sworn statements made in support of an arrest warrant but absolute immunity for sworn statements made to a grand jury. And a prosecutor likewise has only qualified immunity for sworn statements made to secure an arrest but absolute immunity for bringing a case to a grand jury to secure an indictment. Is there any obvious rationale for these distinctions? Do they make sense?

3. IMMUNITIES FOR FEDERAL OFFICIALS

Section 1983 applies in terms only to persons acting under color of "state" law; federal officials are not covered. In Butz v. Economou, 438 U.S. 478, 504 (1978), however, the Court concluded that it would be "untenable to draw a distinction for purposes of immunity law between suits brought against state officials under § 1983 and [*Bivens*] suits brought directly under the Constitution against federal officers." For most purposes, therefore, the immunities accorded state and federal officers are the same. Indeed, the two lines of cases are often cited interchangeably.

There are, however, a few respects in which federal officers are treated specially. Members of Congress are protected by Art. I, § 6, which provides in part that senators and representatives "shall in all Cases, except Treason, Felony and Breach of the Peace, be privileged from Arrest during their Attendance at the Sessions of their respective Houses, and in going to and returning from the same; and for any Speech or Debate in either House, they shall not be questioned in any other Place." The privilege from arrest has been read narrowly to permit the operation against senators and congressmen of ordinary criminal laws, see Gravel v. United States, 408 U.S. 606 (1972), but the Speech or Debate Clause had been construed quite broadly. As a general matter, the Speech or Debate Clause protects federal legislators and their aides from being prosecuted or punished in relation to any official acts. See generally Robert J. Reinstein and Harvey A. Silverglate, Legislative Privilege and the Separation of Powers, 86 Harv.L.Rev. 1113 (1973).

Another special feature of the law governing federal officers is the President's absolute immunity from award of damages for official misconduct. See Nixon v. Fitzgerald, 457 U.S. 731 (1982). No comparable immunity extends to state executives. In the *Nixon* case, the Court, speaking through Justice Powell, found that the "President occupies a unique position in the constitutional scheme" and is "entrusted with supervisory and policy responsibilities of utmost discretion and sensitivity" on a wide range of matters. In the Court's view, the President's "unique status under the Constitution" and the "singular importance" of the duties of the office called for a broader immunity than that enjoyed by state governors and other executive officials:

> [D]iversion of [the president's] energies by concern with private lawsuits would raise unique risks to the effective functioning of government. . . . This concern is compelling where the officeholder must make the most sensitive and far-reaching decisions entrusted to any official under our constitutional system. Nor can the sheer prominence of the President's office be ignored. In view of the visibility of his office and the effect of his actions on countless people, the president would be an easily identifiable target for suits for civil damages. Cognizance of this personal vulnerability frequently could distract a president from his public duties, to the detriment not only of the President and his office but also the nation that the presidency was designed to serve.

The Court concluded, therefore, that the President should have an absolute immunity against award of damages and that this immunity should apply to all acts within the "outer perimeter" of presidential responsibility.[a]

---

[a] Justice White dissented in an opinion joined by Justices Brennan, Marshall, and Blackmun. The dissenters argued that the scope of presidential immunity should be determined by function, not office. Thus, while absolute immunity might be appropriate for certain acts (e.g., presidential participation in prosecutorial decisions), qualified immunity should be applied to others. In the view of the dissenters, absolute immunity effectively placed the President above the law.

The implications of *Nixon v. Fitzgerald* for President Clinton subsequently excited much comment. Paula Jones sued the President under § 1983 and state law for various alleged wrongs that occurred while he was Governor of Arkansas. In response the President claimed executive immunity for pre-presidential conduct. For an endorsement of that claim, see Akhil Reed Amar and Neal Kumar Katyal, Executive Privileges and Immunities: The *Nixon* and *Clinton* Cases, 108 Harv. L. Rev. 701 (1995). The trial court ruled that the President was immune from trial during his term but allowed pre-trial discovery to go forward at once. Both sides objected and appealed this ruling to the Eighth Circuit, which held that both trial and discovery could go forward. The Supreme Court unanimously endorsed this conclusion in

Aside from the somewhat broader immunity accorded federal legislators and the absolute immunity of the president, most federal officials are treated the same as are their state and local counterparts under § 1983. Thus, federal judges and law enforcement officers and executive personnel generally are entitled to the same absolute or qualified immunity, as the case may be, as exists under § 1983. The meaning of those levels of immunity is generally the same in both contexts.

4. QUESTIONS AND COMMENTS ON ABSOLUTE IMMUNITY

Should the Court have recognized absolute immunity for legislators, judges, prosecutors, and witnesses in the absence of any basis in the language of § 1983 or its legislative history? Is it appropriate for the Court to assume that this is what Congress would have done had it thought about the problem? If so, should the Court determine the nature and scope of the immunity purely by historical considerations, or should it also examine the competing policies?

If some public officials are to be entitled to absolute immunity for functions performed in connection with their office, has the Court has identified the right ones? Should state governors, for example, be entitled to the same immunity as the president and as legislators and judges? How about federal and state cabinet officials?

Finally, there are questions about the concrete application of the Court's immunity principles. Even if judges are entitled to absolute immunity for at least some acts, one might question whether the Court reached the right conclusion in *Stump v. Sparkman*.

For representative criticism of the law of absolute immunity, see John C. Jeffries, Jr., The Liability Rule for Constitutional Torts, 99 Va. L. Rev. 207 (2013) (criticizing the current scope of legislative, judicial, and prosecutorial immunity); Margaret Z. Johns, A Black Robe Is Not a Big Tent: The Improper Expansion of Absolute Judicial Immunity to Non-Judges in Civil Rights Cases, 59 S.M.U.L. Rev. 265 (2006); Margaret Johns, Reconsidering Absolute Prosecutorial Immunity, 2005 B.Y.U.L. Rev. 53; Bennett L. Gershman, Bad Faith Exception to Prosecutorial Immunity for *Brady* Violations, Amicus: Harv. C.R.-C.L. L. Rev's Online Companion 1 (Aug. 10, 2010).

SUBSECTION B: QUALIFIED IMMUNITY

Scheuer v. Rhodes

Supreme Court of the United States, 1974.
416 U.S. 232.

■ MR. CHIEF JUSTICE BURGER delivered the opinion of the Court.

We granted certiorari in these cases to resolve whether the District Court correctly dismissed civil damage actions, brought under 42 U.S.C.

Clinton v. Jones, 520 U.S. 681 (1997). Rather than recognize any immunity for unofficial acts, the Court relied on the sound discretion of district judges to protect sitting Presidents from harassment and frivolous litigation.

Most observers assume that *Clinton* would come out differently if the allegedly unconstitutional sexual harassment had occurred during the President's term of office. In that circumstance, might a plaintiff be able to avoid absolute immunity by foregoing claims based on the Constitution and instead alleging only state-law tort claims?

§ 1983, on the ground that these actions were, as a matter of law, against the state of Ohio, and hence barred by the Eleventh Amendment to the Constitution and, alternatively, that the actions were against state officials who were immune from liability for the acts alleged in the complaints. These cases arise out of the . . . period of alleged civil disorder on the campus of Kent State University in Ohio during May 1970. . . .

In these cases the personal representatives of the estates of three students who died in that episode seek damages against the governor, the adjutant general, and his assistant, various named and unnamed officers and enlisted members of the Ohio National Guard, and the president of Kent State University. The complaints in both cases allege a cause of action under the Civil Rights Act of 1871, 42 U.S.C. § 1983. . . .

The District Court dismissed the complaints for lack of jurisdiction over the subject matter on the theory that these actions, although in form against the named individuals, were, in substance and effect, against the state of Ohio and thus barred by the Eleventh Amendment. The Court of Appeals affirmed the action of the District Court, agreeing that the suit was in legal effect one against the State of Ohio and, alternatively, that the common-law doctrine of executive immunity barred action against the state officials who are respondents here. We are confronted with the narrow threshold question whether the District Court properly dismissed the complaints. We hold that dismissal was inappropriate at this stage of the litigation and accordingly reverse the judgments and remand for further proceedings. We intimate no view on the merits of the allegations since there is no evidence before us at this stage.

I

The complaints in these cases are not identical but their thrust is essentially the same. In essence, the defendants are alleged to have "intentionally, recklessly, wilfully and wantonly" caused an unnecessary deployment of the Ohio National Guard on the Kent State campus and, in the same manner, ordered the Guard members to perform allegedly illegal actions which resulted in the death of plaintiffs' decedents. Both complaints allege that the action was taken "under color of state law" and that it deprived the decedents of their lives and rights without due process of law. Fairly read, the complaints allege that each of the named defendants, in undertaking such actions, acted either outside the scope of his respective office, or, if within the scope, acted in an arbitrary manner, grossly abusing the lawful powers of office. . . .

II

The Eleventh Amendment to the Constitution of the United States provides: "The Judicial power of the United States shall not be construed to extend to any suit in law or equity, commenced or prosecuted against one of the United States by Citizens of another State. . . . " It is well established that the amendment bars suits not only against the state when it is the named party but also when it is the party in fact. . . .

However, since Ex parte Young, 209 U.S. 123 (1908), it has been settled that the Eleventh Amendment provides no shield for a state official confronted by a claim that he had deprived another of a federal right under the color of state law. . . .

Ex parte Young involved a question of the federal courts' injunctive power, not, as here, a claim for monetary damages. While it is clear that the doctrine of *Ex parte Young* is of no aid to a plaintiff seeking damages from the public treasury, Edelman v. Jordan, 415 U.S. 651 (1974), damages against individual defendants are a permissible remedy in some circumstances notwithstanding the fact that they hold public office. In some situations a damage remedy can be as effective a redress for the infringement of a constitutional right as injunctive relief might be in another.

Analyzing the complaints in light of these precedents, we see that petitioners allege facts that demonstrate they are seeking to impose individual and personal liability on the *named defendants* for what they claim—but have not yet established by proof—was a deprivation of federal rights by these defendants under color of state law. Whatever the plaintiffs may or may not be able to establish as to the merits of their allegations, their claims, as stated in the complaints, given the favorable reading required by the Federal Rules of Civil Procedure, are not barred by the Eleventh Amendment. . . .

III

The Court of Appeals relied upon the existence of an absolute "executive immunity" as an alternative ground for sustaining the dismissal of the complaints by the District Court. If the immunity of a member of the executive branch is absolute and comprehensive as to all acts allegedly performed within the scope of official duty, the Court of Appeals was correct; if, on the other hand, the immunity is not absolute but rather one that is qualified or limited, an executive officer may or may not be subject to liability depending on all the circumstances that may be revealed by the evidence. The concept of the immunity of government officers from personal liability springs from the same root considerations that generated the doctrine of sovereign immunity. While the latter doctrine—that the "king can do no wrong"—did not protect all government officers from personal liability, the common law soon recognized the necessity of permitting officials to perform their official functions free from the threat of suits for personal liability. This official immunity apparently rested, in its genesis, on two mutually dependent rationales: (1) the injustice, particularly in the absence of bad faith, of subjecting to liability an officer who is required, by the legal obligations of his position, to exercise discretion; (2) the danger that the threat of such liability would deter his willingness to execute his office with the decisiveness and the judgment required by the public good. . . .

Although the development of the general concept of immunity, and the mutations which the underlying rationale has undergone in its application to various positions are not matters of immediate concern here, it is important to note, even at the outset, that one policy consideration seems to pervade the analysis: the public interest requires decisions and action to enforce laws for the protection of the public. Mr. Justice Jackson expressed this general proposition succinctly, stating "it is not a tort for government to govern." Public officials, whether governors, mayors or police, legislators or judges, who fail to make decisions when they are needed or who do not act to implement decisions when they are made do not fully and faithfully perform the duties of their offices. Implicit in the idea that officials have some immunity—absolute or qualified—for their acts, is a recognition that they may err. The concept of immunity assumes this and goes on to assume that it is better to risk some error and possible injury from such error than not to decide or act at all. In Barr v. Matteo, 360 U.S. 564, 572–73 (1959), the Court observed, in the somewhat parallel context of the privilege of public officers from defamation actions, "The privilege is not a badge or emolument of exalted office, but an expression of a policy designed to aid in the effective functioning of government."

For present purposes we need determine only whether there is an absolute immunity, as the Court of Appeals determined, governing the specific allegations of the complaint against the chief executive officer of a state, the senior and subordinate officers and enlisted personnel of that state's National Guard, and the president of a state-controlled university. If the immunity is qualified, not absolute, the scope of that immunity will necessarily be related to facts as yet not established either by affidavits, admissions or a trial record. Final resolution of this question must take into account the functions and responsibilities of these particular defendants in their capacities as officers of the state government, as well as the purposes of 42 U.S.C. § 1983. . . .

Soon after Monroe v. Pape, 365 U.S. 167 (1961), Mr. Chief Justice Warren noted in Pierson v. Ray, 386 U.S. 547 (1967), that the "legislative record [of § 1983] gives no clear indication that Congress meant to abolish wholesale all common-law immunities." The Court had previously recognized that the Civil Rights Act of 1871 does not create civil liability for legislative acts by legislators "in a field where legislators traditionally have power to act." Tenney v. Brandhove, 341 U.S. 367 (1951). . . .

In similar fashion, *Pierson v. Ray*, supra, examined the scope of judicial immunity under this statute. Noting that the record contained no "proof or specific allegation" that the trial judge had "played any role in these arrests and convictions other than to adjudge petitioners guilty when their cases came before his court," the Court concluded that, had the Congress intended to abolish the common-law "immunity of judges for acts within the judicial role," it would have done so specifically. . . .

The *Pierson* Court was also confronted with whether immunity was available to that segment of the executive branch of a state government that is most frequently and intimately involved in day-to-day contacts with the citizenry and, hence, most frequently exposed to situations which can give rise to claims under § 1983—the local police officer. . . . The Court noted that the "common law has never granted police officers an absolute and unqualified immunity," but that "the prevailing view in this country [is that] a peace officer who arrests someone with probable cause is not liable for false arrest simply because the innocence of the suspect is later proved"; the Court went on to observe that a "policeman's lot is not so unhappy that he must choose between being charged with dereliction of duty if he does not arrest when he has probable cause, and being mulcted in damages if he does." The Court then held:

> that the defense of good faith and probable cause, which the Court of Appeals found available to the officers in the common-law action for false arrest and imprisonment, is also available to them in the action under 1983.

When a court evaluates police conduct relating to an arrest its guideline is "good faith and probable cause." In the case of higher officers of the executive branch, however, the inquiry is far more complex since the range of decisions and choices—whether the formulation of policy, of legislation, of budgets, or of day-to-day decisions—is virtually infinite. In common with police officers, however, officials with a broad range of duties and authority must often act swiftly and firmly at the risk that action deferred will be futile or constitute virtual abdication of office. Like legislators and judges, these officers are entitled to rely on traditional sources for the factual information on which they decide and act. When a condition of civil disorder in fact exists, there is obvious need for prompt action, and decisions must be made in reliance on factual information supplied by others. While both federal and state laws plainly contemplate the use of force when the necessity arises, the decision to invoke military power has traditionally been viewed with suspicion and skepticism since it often involves the temporary suspension of some of our most cherished rights—government by elected civilian leaders, freedom of expression, of assembly, and of association. Decisions in such situations are more likely than not to arise in an atmosphere of confusion, ambiguity, and swiftly moving events and when, by the very existence of some degree of civil disorder, there is often no consensus as to the appropriate remedy. In short, since the options which a chief executive and his principal subordinates must consider are far broader and far more subtle than those made by officials with less responsibility, the range of discretion must be comparably broad. . . .

These considerations suggest that, in varying scope, a qualified immunity is available to officers of the executive branch of government, the variation being dependent upon the scope of discretion and responsibilities of the office and all the circumstances as they reasonably appeared at the time of the action on which liability is sought to be based. It is the existence of reasonable grounds for the belief formed at the time and in light of all the circumstances, coupled with good-faith belief, that affords a basis for qualified immunity of executive officers for acts performed in the course of official conduct. . . .

IV

These cases, in their present posture, present no occasion for a definitive exploration of the scope of immunity available to state executive officials nor, because of the absence of a factual record, do they permit a determination as to the applicability of the foregoing principles to the respondents here. The District Court acted before answers were filed and without any evidence other than the copies of the proclamations issued by respondent [Governor] Rhodes and brief affidavits of the adjutant general and his assistant. In dismissing the complaints, the District Court and the Court of Appeals erroneously accepted as a fact the good faith of the governor, and took judicial notice that "mob rule existed at Kent State University." There was no opportunity afforded petitioners to contest the facts assumed in that conclusion. There was no evidence before the courts from which such a finding of good faith could be properly made and, in the circumstances of these cases, such a dispositive conclusion could not be judicially noticed. We can readily grant that a declaration of emergency by the chief executive of a state is entitled to great weight but it is not conclusive.

The documents properly before the District Court at this early pleading stage specifically placed in issue whether the governor and his subordinate officers were acting within the scope of their duties under the Constitution and laws of Ohio; whether they acted within the range of discretion permitted the holders of such office under Ohio law and whether they acted in good faith both in proclaiming an emergency and as to the actions taken to cope with the emergency so declared. Similarly, the complaints place directly in issue whether the lesser officers and enlisted personnel of the Guard acted in good-faith obedience to the orders of their superiors. Further proceedings, either by way of summary judgment or by trial on the merits, are required. . . .

The judgments of the Court of Appeals are reversed and the cases are remanded for further proceedings consistent with this opinion.

■ MR. JUSTICE DOUGLAS took no part in the decision of these cases.[a]

NOTES ON THE RATIONALES FOR QUALIFIED IMMUNITY

1. THE EMERGENCE OF QUALIFIED IMMUNITY UNDER § 1983

Soon after the Supreme Court revived § 1983 as a source for damages actions against government officers, it confronted the question whether § 1983 incorporated certain common law-based defenses. Pierson v. Ray, 386 U.S. 547 (1967), which is discussed in *Scheuer*, involved the question whether police officers could be sued for damages under § 1983 for arresting the plaintiffs pursuant to an unconstitutional statute. The Court held that they could, but went on to state that "the defense of good faith and probable cause," which would have been "available to the officers in the common-law action for false arrest and imprisonment, is also available to them in the action under § 1983."

The availability and contours of the good-faith-and-probable-cause defense were thus taken from the common-law analogue to the plaintiffs' constitutional claim and were not articulated as a freestanding requirement of § 1983. Nonetheless, as *Scheuer* shows, the Supreme Court quickly transformed the claim-specific defense in *Pierson* into a general defense applicable to *all* § 1983 claims that the defendant officer had "reasonable grounds . . . coupled with good-faith belief" for believing his actions to be constitutional.

2. RATIONALES FOR QUALIFIED IMMUNITY

As the Court has developed the law of qualified immunity, it has identified several distinct, and sometimes cross-cutting, considerations that underlie that defense.

(i) Compensation

The Supreme Court has identified compensation of the victims of official misconduct as "the basic purpose of a § 1983 damages award." Carey v. Piphus, 435 U.S. 247, 254 (1978). Yet many factors, including the Court's own decisions, undercut the effectiveness of § 1983 as a compensatory remedy.

One restrictive factor is the Eleventh Amendment protection of states and state agencies from the award of damages. See Edelman v. Jordan, 415 U.S. 651 (1974). It is true that Congress can override this immunity in enforcing Fourteenth Amendment rights, but the Court has not found any such intent behind § 1983. See Quern v. Jordan, 440 U.S. 332 (1979). It is also true, after Monell v. New York City Department of Social Services, 436 U.S. 658 (1978) (a main case in the next Section), that local governments may sometimes be held directly liable under § 1983, but only in very restricted circumstances. In most cases compensation for official misconduct must be sought from the individual public official, rather than from the government itself.

---

[a] Following the Supreme Court's remand in *Scheuer*, the cases were tried on the merits. After a trial of nearly four months' duration, the jury returned a verdict in favor of all defendants. This verdict was set aside on appeal because of threats made against a juror by some unknown person. Krause v. Rhodes, 570 F.2d 563 (6th Cir. 1977). The cases were then remanded for a second trial, but were eventually settled out of court. See Krause v. Rhodes, 535 F.Supp. 338 (N.D.Ohio 1979).—[Footnote by eds.]

While these defendants are routinely reimbursed by the government that employs them,[a] the fact that an individual will be the named defendant has important implications.

In some cases, plaintiffs may have trouble identifying the persons who should be sued. Where injury results from systemic failure rather than individual misconduct, the necessity of proceeding against named individuals may prove especially burdensome. Defendants who seem to face personal liability for government acts may well arouse the sympathy of juries. Perhaps most important of all, the fact that § 1983 actions ordinarily must be brought against public officials as individuals introduces the perceived unfairness of imposing personal liability for good faith error as a limitation on the plaintiff's claim to compensation. Thus, the *Scheuer* Court identified as the first rationale for official immunity "the injustice, particularly in the absence of bad faith, of subjecting to liability an officer who is required, by the legal obligations of his position, to exercise discretion." The resulting grant of qualified immunity to individual officials sharply curtails the availability of money damages for injured plaintiffs.[b]

(ii) Deterrence

Another, arguably more important, objective of money damages is to deter future misconduct. An award of damages against one official conveys to others a threat of similar treatment if they too misbehave. Any limitation on the award of damages, such as the defense of qualified immunity, reduces the deterrent effect of liability under § 1983. Under current doctrine, qualified immunity shields government officers and the governments that employ them from damages liability for a substantial range of unconstitutional conduct. Why has the Supreme Court embraced qualified immunity, despite the obvious reduction in the incentives to avoid unconstitutional behavior?

Part of the answer lies in a fear of overdeterrence. To the extent that the standards of liability are uncertain or the mechanisms of enforcement unpredictable, the prospect of liability will be difficult for officers to assess. Officials will have an incentive to avoid all acts that might lead to civil liability or to the necessity of litigation. This unintended inhibitory effect is what the *Scheuer*

---

[a] For obvious reasons, governments generally choose to protect their employees against damage liability, either by themselves providing defense counsel and indemnifying the employees against loss or, less commonly, by purchasing insurance. As no such arrangements are required by federal law, the availability of counsel, indemnification, and insurance depend on the statutes, ordinances, and practices in each jurisdiction. See, e.g., Project, Suing the Police in Federal Court, 88 Yale L.J. 781, 811 (1979) (reporting that a survey of § 1983 actions against police showed that the officers were provided with counsel and indemnified, either by the municipality or by its insurance carrier, against the cost of a settlement or adverse judgment). Quite commonly, the act giving rise to liability must have been within the scope of employment and often must have been performed in good faith. Moreover, the availability of free legal counsel is often not guaranteed, but may depend on a decision by the state attorney general or some analogous local officer. See generally Rolando del Carmen and Carol M. Veneziano, Legal Liabilities, Representation, and Indemnification of Probation and Parole Officers, 17 U.S.F.L. 227, 243–45 (1983).

[b] Whether this limitation on recovery is consistent with the goal of compensation, properly understood, is a conceptual issue of some subtlety. It is presented most clearly in Owen v. City of Independence, 445 U.S. 622 (1980), where the Supreme Court held that, in the limited circumstances when municipalities are directly liable under § 1983, they are strictly liable and have no defense of qualified immunity. *Owen* is a main case in the next Section of this Chapter, and the role of fault in a regime aimed at compensation is considered more closely at that point.

Court had in mind when it identified as the second rationale for official immunity "the danger that the threat of such liability would deter [the official's] willingness to execute his office with the decisiveness and the judgment required by the public good."

Of course, the problem of unintended deterrence is not unique to this context. In much the same way, ordinary tort liability will inhibit some non-tortious conduct that the actor finds difficult to segregate from potentially tortious activity. In most situations, society relies on private decisionmakers to evaluate the expected costs and benefits of their actions, including the possibility of civil liability, and to make decisions roughly congruent with the social interest. In the context of damage actions against government officials, however, some observers think that the prospect of personal liability will induce government officials to engage in excessive defensive activity and thus to sacrifice the public good in favor of individual protection. These factors are detailed in an analysis of the working environment of the street-level official by Peter H. Schuck in Suing Government: Citizen Remedies for Official Wrongs 60–77 (1983).

The person most likely to be sued under § 1983 is, in Schuck's parlance, the "street-level official." Examples include police officers, prison authorities, public school officials, and welfare administrators. Because these officials personally and directly deliver basic government services, they constantly interact with individual citizens on matters of intense concern. Many of these interactions are non-consensual and thus likely to be characterized by conflict and mutual suspicion. The goals that these officials are directed to pursue—maintaining order, educating students, and the like—are often complex and ambiguous, and the choice of means to attain them is irreducibly judgmental.

Moreover, the official often has a duty to act. While the private citizen is usually free to do nothing, if that seems the best course, the public official may be commanded by law to intervene on behalf of the public interest. Since government action is likely to be coercive, it is especially productive of conflict and harm. Indeed, virtually any choice of action or inaction risks harm to someone. The decision to discipline a student risks unfairness to that student; the decision not to discipline may impair the educational opportunities of others. The decision to arrest may violate the rights of the arrestee; the decision not to arrest may sacrifice the protection of the public.

Not only are such decisions potentially harmful to others; they are also likely to be attended by significant risk of error. Many officials must act more or less instantly, in situations that border on emergency, and on the basis of inadequate information. Under such circumstances, it is difficult to capture appropriate decisionmaking in clear rules. Not that the effort is lacking. As Schuck points out, the street-level official is typically required to administer and to abide by a host of rules, but rules "so voluminous, ambiguous, contradictory, and in flux that officials can only comply with or enforce them selectively." In short, says Schuck, the officials "are actually awash in discretion."

Most important of all, public officials are typically unable to appropriate to themselves the benefits that flow from their decisions. The costs of malfeasance or mistake can be visited upon the official by a suit for damages, but the benefits of good performance tend to run to the public at large. The resulting incentive structure may conduce to defensive, cost-minimizing behavior, even if it entails a net loss in social benefits. Schuck explains the point as follows:*

> Most private actors would decide to incur any cost if the expected value of the correlative benefit were great enough, but officials tend to reject any course of action that would drive their personal costs above some minimum level, what I call a "duty threshold." The duty threshold, of course, varies from official to official, for it is defined by one's idiosyncratic attitudes toward (and trade-offs among) certain values and interests, some altruistic, some more narrowly self-interested . . .—feelings of professionalism; moral duty; programmatic mission; fear of criticism, discipline, or reprisals for self-protective behavior; concern for professional reputation; habituation to routine; personal convenience; and the like. Officials tend to orient their decisions about whether, when, and how to act less toward maximizing . . . net benefits, which they cannot appropriate, than toward minimizing (subject to their duty threshold) those costs that they would incur personally. [Id. at 68–69.]

Among these costs is the risk of being sued. The magnitude of this risk depends not only on the expected cost of adverse judgments, but also on the expected cost of having to defend such actions and on the demoralization or other nonpecuniary cost of being sued. Schuck concludes that officials have strong incentives to minimize costs, including the risk of being sued, even if a strategy of cost-minimization means foregoing social benefits.

Finally, it is worth noting that the expected costs and benefits to officials of their own decisions are typically not symmetrical. Action is likely to be more costly than inaction. This imbalance is due in part to what Jerry Mashaw has termed a "cause of action" problem. See Jerry L. Mashaw, Civil Liability of Government Officers: Property Rights and Official Accountability, 42 Law & Contemp. Probs. 8 (1978). The individual who is injured by affirmative misconduct is likely to be able to state a cause of action against the responsible official. The harm to the citizen and its connection to the official's conduct are likely to be clear. By contrast, persons injured by an official's failure to act may find it more difficult to state a claim for relief. The connection between harm to the citizen and official inaction may be indirect and obscure, and causation therefore difficult to establish. Furthermore, enforcement authority is typically discretionary in nature. As a result, the official may be protected from liability for an omission by the absence of any duty to act. For these reasons, the likelihood of being sued for erroneous action exceeds the risk for erroneous inaction, and the incentives of government officials, given a realistic threat of civil liability, may therefore be skewed toward defensive behavior.

For these reasons, the prospect of unintended deterrence of legitimate government activity has loomed very large in the debates over official immunities. It is chiefly on this ground that the Supreme Court has established, both under § 1983 and under analogous *Bivens*-type actions against federal officers, that virtually every government official is entitled to at least a qualified defense of good faith and reasonable belief against actions for money damages.[c]

---

* Reprinted by permission of the author from Peter H. Schuck, Suing Government: Citizen Remedies for Official Wrongs (1983).

[c] The applicability to governments of general deterrence theory is challenged in Daryl Levinson, Making Government Pay: Markets, Politics, and the Allocation of Constitutional Costs, 67 U. Chi. L. Rev. 345 (2000). Levinson argues that government officers do not neces-

(iii) The Effects of Indemnification

One problem with this argument is that it slights the importance of employer indemnification in affecting officer incentives. While it is true that government officers ordinarily cannot appropriate to themselves the full benefits of good performance, it is also true that they do not personally bear the full costs of mistakes. The incentives of individual officers may be *reduced*, but it does not necessarily follow that they would be *skewed*. As compared to actors in the private sector, government officers may simply have less to gain *or* lose.

This argument is considered in John C. Jeffries, Jr., In Praise of the Eleventh Amendment and Section 1983, 84 Va. L. Rev. 47 (1998), which focuses on indemnification and treats § 1983 damages actions against officers as an indirect way of imposing liability on the governments that employ them. Despite indemnification, Jeffries concludes, "the incentives of government officers are skewed, as compared to actors in the private sector, toward inaction, passivity, and defensive behavior":

> At least three factors play a role. First is government employment law. The tradition of the civil service, powerfully reinforced by doctrines of procedural due process, makes government workers hard to fire. Generally, the absence of good performance is not a sufficient reason. Much more than their colleagues in private industry, government employees are protected against discharge for relative inefficiency or lack of productivity. For government workers, the risk of job loss is overwhelmingly linked to bad performance, to the provable act of misconduct or neglect that will justify a civil service termination. Government workers might, therefore, rationally be more concerned with avoiding mistakes than with maximizing social benefits.
>
> Second, to the extent that this characteristic of the civil service is recognized by prospective employees, there may be psychological self-selection. Persons willing to take risks in pursuit of gains may gravitate toward private industry, where successful risk-taking is more likely to be rewarded. Those who place a premium on job security may be drawn to government work. If, as a result, government workers are relatively risk-averse, the skewed incentives toward defensiveness and inaction may be reinforced by psychological predisposition.

---

sarily respond to liability rules in the same way as private actors. "Because government actors respond to political, not market, incentives, we should not assume that government will internalize social costs just because it is forced to make a budgetary outlay." Moreover, even if government officers do respond to the prospect of money damages, deterrence will still fail if constitutional violations create benefits for a majority of citizens that outweigh the costs imposed on a few. Levinson's arguments suggest a profound skepticism about the utility of money damages in enforcing constitutional rights.

These ideas are examined in a symposium in the Georgia Law Review. Included is a Foreword by Thomas A Eaton, 35 Ga. L. Rev. 837 (2001), and an Afterword by Marshall Shapo, id., at 931. Articles in the symposium include: Myriam E. Gilles, In Defense of Making Government Pay: The Deterrent Effect of Constitutional Tort Remedies, 35 Ga. L. Rev. 845 (2001); Brian J. Serr, Turning Section 1983's Protection of Civil Rights Into an Attractive Nuisance: Extra–Textual Barriers in Municipal Liability Under *Monell*, 35 Ga. L. Rev. 881 (2001); Bernard P. Dauenhauer & Michael L. Wells, Corrective Justice and Constitutional Torts, 35 Ga. L. Rev. 903 (2001). For another response to Levinson, see Mark R. Brown, Deterring Bully Government: A Sovereign Dilemma, 76 Tul. L. Rev. 149 (2001) (using game theory to argue that government can be deterred by the prospect of damages liability).

> Third, and to my mind most important, is the political tendency to give greater weight to costs that must be accounted for in the budget and to discount costs that fall elsewhere. On-budget costs mean higher taxes, and the political penalties for raising taxes can be severe. Acts that give rise to § 1983 claims trigger on-budget costs and are therefore subject to the political disincentives of higher taxes. Government inaction may be just as costly, but the burdens fall elsewhere. The failure to arrest a suspected criminal or to discipline an unruly student may have error costs just as great as would result from taking those actions, but those costs are born by subsequent crime victims and by other students. If, as seems likely, the political culture punishes on-budget costs more than those that are borne elsewhere, government managers may reinforce their workers's incentives toward caution and constraint.

Jeffries notes that the risk of overdeterrence would be "manageable, or at any rate less acute, if constitutional law were precise and rule-like":

> It is the combination of skewed incentives and constitutional indeterminacy that makes the risk of unintended deterrence so severe. An unconstitutional search and seizure may differ only slightly from good police work. Conduct on the right side of the line is not only legally permissible, but socially desirable, even essential to maintaining adequate order and security. The obvious response to strict liability based on uncertain standards is to draw well back from the danger zone. However tolerable that reaction may be in some contexts, in others it is very costly. By limiting damages liability to acts that clearly cross the line, qualified immunity moderates unintended deterrence.[d]

NOTES ON THE EVOLUTION OF QUALIFIED IMMUNITY

1. INTRODUCTION

The current state of the law of qualified is illustrated by *Brosseau v. Haugen*, the next main case. The notes below explore the evolution of the doctrine in prior decisions. The result of this history is that qualified immunity has come to be defined in terms quite different from its common-law antecedents.

2. *WOOD V. STRICKLAND*

Wood v. Strickland, 420 U.S. 308 (1975), involved two high school students who sued the school board members who had expelled them for "spiking" punch served at a school event. The District Court ruled that the school board members could be held liable only if they acted with "malice," which it had defined to mean "ill will against a person—a wrongful act done intentionally without just cause or excuse."

Speaking through Justice White, the Supreme Court disagreed:

> [W]e hold that a school board member is not immune from liability for damages under § 1983 if he knew or reasonably should have known that the action he took within his sphere of official responsibility would violate the constitutional rights of the student affected, or if he took the action with the malicious intention to cause a deprivation of constitutional

[d] For criticism of this argument, see Mark R. Brown, The Failure of Fault Under § 1983: Municipal Liability for State Law Enforcement, 84 Cornell L. Rev. 1503 (1999).

> rights or other injury to the student. That is not to say that school board members are "charged with predicting the future course of constitutional law." Pierson v. Ray, 386 U.S. 547, 557 (1967). A compensatory award will be appropriate only if the school board member has acted with such an impermissible motivation or with such disregard of the student's clearly established constitutional rights that his action cannot reasonably be characterized as being in good faith.

Justice Powell, joined by Chief Justice Burger and Justices Blackmun and Rehnquist, dissented. They objected to the majority's insistence that liability could be based on a school official's lack of knowledge of constitutional rights, as distinct from the official's subjective bad faith.

3. *HARLOW V. FITZGERALD*

Although the *Wood v. Strickland* dissenters anticipated difficulty with the objective branch of qualified immunity, the subjective inquiry proved, if anything, the more troublesome. The problem was the substantial pre-trial proceedings sometimes required to determine whether an allegation of subjective bad faith had adequate foundation to proceed to trial. The Court addressed this problem in Harlow v. Fitzgerald, 457 U.S. 800 (1982).

Fitzgerald was a notorious "whistle-blower" in the Department of Defense. Following the abolition of his job in an Air Force reorganization, Fitzgerald brought a *Bivens* action against a number of people, including Bryce Harlow, a presidential aide primarily responsible for congressional relations. Fitzgerald claimed that Harlow and others had participated in a conspiracy to discharge Fitzgerald in retaliation for testifying to Congress concerning cost overruns in the Air Force. The alleged conspiracy took place in the years preceding Fitzgerald's dismissal in 1970. Fitzgerald filed suit in 1973, and Harlow was added as a defendant in 1978. Harlow denied any involvement in the decision to fire Fitzgerald, and at the conclusion of extensive discovery, the evidence of Harlow's involvement "remained inferential." The trial court denied a motion for summary judgment, and an appeal was taken before trial to resolve the disputed issue of Harlow's immunity.

The Supreme Court concluded that qualified immunity should be recrafted to "permit the defeat of insubstantial claims without resort to trial." Speaking for the Court, Justice Powell said:

> The resolution of immunity questions inherently requires a balance between the evils inevitable in any available alternative. In situations of abuse of office, an action for damage may offer the only realistic avenue for vindication of constitutional guarantees. It is this recognition that has required the denial of absolute immunity to most public officers. At the same time, however, it cannot be disputed seriously that claims frequently run against the innocent as well as the guilty—at a cost not only to the defendant officials, but to society as a whole. These social costs include the expenses of litigation, the diversion of official energy from pressing public issues, and the deterrence of able citizens from acceptance of public office. Finally, there is the danger that fear of being sued will "dampen the ardor of all but the most resolute, or the most irresponsible [public officials] in the unflinching discharge of their duties." Gregoire v. Biddle, 177 F.2d 579, 581 (2d Cir. 1949).

In identifying qualified immunity as the best attainable accommodation of competing values, in Butz v. Economou, 438 U.S. 478 (1978), and Scheuer v. Rhodes, 416 U.S. 232 (1974), we relied on the assumption that this standard would permit "[i]nsubstantial lawsuits [to] be quickly terminated." Yet petitioners advance persuasive arguments that the dismissal of insubstantial lawsuits without trial—a factor presupposed in the balance of competing interests struck by our prior cases—requires an adjustment of the "good faith" standard established by our decisions. . . .

In the context of *Butz's* attempted balancing of competing values, it now is clear that substantial costs attend the litigation of the subjective good faith of government officials. Not only are there the general costs of subjecting officials to the risks of trial—distraction of officials from their governmental duties, inhibition of discretionary action, and deterrence of able people from public service. There are special costs to "subjective" inquiries of this kind. Immunity generally is available only to officials performing discretionary functions. In contrast with the thought processes accompanying "ministerial" tasks, the judgments surrounding discretionary action almost inevitably are influenced by the decisionmaker's experiences, values, and emotions. These variables explain in part why questions of subjective intent so rarely can be decided by summary judgment. Yet they also frame a background in which there often is no clear end to the relevant evidence. Judicial inquiry into subjective motivation therefore may entail broad-ranging discovery and the deposing of numerous persons, including an official's professional colleagues. Inquiries of this kind can be peculiarly disruptive of effective government.

Consistently with the balance at which we aimed in *Butz*, we conclude today that bare allegations of malice should not suffice to subject government officials either to the costs of trial or to the burdens of broad-reaching discovery. We therefore hold that government officials performing discretionary functions generally are shielded from liability for civil damages insofar as their conduct does not violate clearly established statutory or constitutional rights of which a reasonable person would have known.

Reliance on the objective reasonableness of an official's conduct, as measured by reference to clearly established law, should avoid excessive disruption of government and permit the resolution of many insubstantial claims on summary judgment. On summary judgment, the judge appropriately may determine, not only the currently applicable law, but whether that law was clearly established at the time an action occurred. If the law at that time was not clearly established, an official could not reasonably be expected to anticipate subsequent legal developments, nor could he fairly be said to "know" that the law forbade conduct not previously identified as unlawful. Until this threshold immunity question is resolved, discovery should not be allowed. If the law was clearly established, the immunity defense ordinarily should fail, since a reasonably competent public official should know the law governing his conduct. Nevertheless, if the official pleading the defense claims extraordinary circumstances and can prove that he neither knew nor should have known of the relevant legal standard, the defense should be sustained. But again, the defense would turn primarily on objective factors.

The case was remanded to the District Court for reconsideration of the summary judgment issue in light of these standards.

Justice Brennan, with whom Justices Marshall and Blackmun joined, wrote a separate concurrence, agreeing with the majority's effort to facilitate summary judgment but adding that "it seems inescapable to me that some measure of discovery may sometimes be required to determine exactly what a public-official defendant did 'know' at the time of his actions."

Harlow left an ambiguity. Did the Court mean only that something more than "bare allegations" of malice should be required before permitting discovery? Or did the Court mean, as it seemed to say, that summary judgment should always be granted when the law was unclear at the time of the action, regardless of credible and detailed allegations of bad faith? The definitive answer came in Crawford–El v. Britton, 523 U.S. 574 (1998), which is reprinted below as a main case. There the Court read *Harlow* to say that "a defense of qualified immunity may not be rebutted by evidence that the defendant's conduct was malicious or otherwise improperly motivated. Evidence concerning the defendant's subjective intent is simply irrelevant to that defense."

4. *ANDERSON V. CREIGHTON*

Given elimination of the subjective branch of qualified immunity, the crucial question became just how clearly established a constitutional right had to be before the defendant could be held liable for violating it and, more importantly, at what level of specificity that inquiry should be made. Those questions were addressed in Anderson v. Creighton, 483 U.S. 635 (1987).

Anderson was an F.B.I. agent who participated in a warrantless search of the Creightons' home in search of a suspected bank robber. The Creightons sued Anderson and others, claiming damages for violation of their Fourth Amendment rights and alleging high-handed and abusive behavior during the search. The Court of Appeals ruled that Anderson was not entitled to summary judgment because the right against warrantless searches of the home without exigent circumstances was clearly established at the time of the search, but the Supreme Court disagreed. Speaking through Justice Scalia, a divided Court read *Harlow* to say that "whether an official protected by qualified immunity may be held personally liable for an allegedly unlawful official action generally turns on the 'objective legal reasonableness' of the action, assessed in light of the legal rules that were 'clearly established' at the time it was taken":

> The operation of this standard, however, depends substantially upon the level of generality at which the relevant "legal rule" is to be identified. For example, the right to due process of law is quite clearly established by the Due Process Clause, and thus there is a sense in which any action that violates that clause (no matter how unclear it may be that the particular action is a violation) violates a clearly established right. Much the same could be said of any other constitutional or statutory violation. But if the test of "clearly established law" were to be applied at this level of generality, it would bear no relationship to the "objective legal reasonableness" that is the touchstone of *Harlow*. Plaintiffs would be able to convert the rule of qualified immunity that our cases plainly establish into a rule of virtually unqualified liability simply by alleging violation of extremely abstract rights. . . . It should not be surprising, therefore, that our cases establish that the right the official is alleged to have violated must have

been "clearly established" in a more particularized, and hence more relevant, sense: The contours of the right must be sufficiently clear that a reasonable official would understand that what he is doing violates that right. This is not to say that an official action is protected by qualified immunity unless the very action in question has previously been held unlawful, but it is to say that in the light of pre-existing law the unlawfulness must be apparent.

Justices Steven, Brennan, and Marshall dissented.

5. *HUNTER V. BRYANT*

The *Anderson* approach to *Harlow* immunity was reconfirmed in Hunter v. Bryant, 502 U.S. 224 (1991). Secret Service Agents Hunter and Jordan arrested Bryant because they believed he had threatened the life of President Reagan. Bryant was arraigned before a magistrate and held without bond. After the criminal complaint was dismissed on the government's motion, Bryant brought a *Bivens* action against the agents for making the arrest without probable cause. The District Court denied summary judgment on the agents' claim of qualified immunity and the Court of Appeals affirmed, reasoning that "[w]hether a reasonable officer could have believed he had probable cause is a question for the trier of fact. . . . " The Supreme Court summarily reversed:

> The decision of the Ninth Circuit . . . is wrong for two reasons. First, it routinely places the question of immunity in the hands of the jury. Immunity ordinarily should be decided by the court long before trial. Second, the court should ask whether the agents acted reasonably under settled law in the circumstances, not whether another reasonable, or more reasonable, interpretation of the events can be constructed five years after the fact.
>
> Under settled law, Secret Service agents Hunter and Jordan are entitled to immunity if a reasonable officer could have believed that probable cause existed to arrest Bryant.

The Court then examined the facts known to the officers at the time of the arrest and concluded that they were entitled to qualified immunity.[a]

6. APPEALABILITY OF IMMUNITY DENIALS: *MITCHELL V. FORSYTH*

An important aspect of the administration of immunity defenses was settled in Mitchell v. Forsyth, 472 U.S. 511 (1985). Former Attorney General John Mitchell was sued by a person whose telephone conversations had been intercepted in a "national security" wiretap. Mitchell claimed qualified immunity based on the uncertain legality of such wiretaps at the time of the authorization, but the District Court held that Mitchell should have anticipated the Supreme Court's rejection of such wiretaps in United States v. United States District Court (the *Keith* case), 407 U.S. 297 (1972). The District Court then granted summary judgment against Mitchell on liability and scheduled a trial on damages.

This raised the question whether rejection of the immunity defense was immediately appealable or whether Mitchell had to wait until a final judgment

[a] Justices Stevens and Kennedy dissented on the ground that the case should be scheduled for full briefing and argument.

to challenge the court's ruling. The Supreme Court found interlocutory appeal justified under the "collateral order" doctrine of Cohen v. Beneficial Industrial Loan Corp., 337 U.S. 541 (1949):[b]

> [T]he *Harlow* Court refashioned the qualified immunity doctrine in such a way as to "permit the resolution of many insubstantial claims on summary judgment" and to avoid "subject[ing] government officials either to the costs of trial or to the burdens of broad-reaching discovery" in cases where the legal norms the officials are alleged to have violated were not clearly established at the time. . . . *Harlow* thus recognized an entitlement not to stand trial or face the other burdens of litigation, conditioned on the resolution of the essentially legal question whether the conduct of which the plaintiff complains violated clearly established law. The entitlement is an *immunity from suit* rather than a mere defense to liability; and like an absolute immunity, it is effectively lost if a case is erroneously permitted to go to trial. Accordingly, the reasoning that underlies the immediate appealability of an order denying absolute immunity indicates to us that the denial of qualified immunity should be similarly appealable: in each case, the district court's decision is effectively unreviewable on appeal from a final judgment.

On the merits, the Court overturned the District Court's ruling and held that Mitchell was entitled to summary judgment on his claim of qualified immunity.

Justice Brennan, joined by Justice Marshall, argued that the denial of the defense of qualified immunity was not immediately appealable and hence that the interpretation of that immunity was not properly before the Court.

7. THE LIMITS OF *MITCHELL*: *JOHNSON V. JONES*

In an opinion by Justice Breyer, the Court unanimously limited the immediate appealability of immunity denials in Johnson v. Jones, 515 U.S. 304 (1995). Jones, a diabetic, suffered an insulin seizure on a public street. He was arrested by several police officers who thought him drunk and later found himself in a hospital with several broken ribs. Jones brought suit against five policemen whom he accused of using excessive force during the arrest and beating him at the police station.

Three of the officer-defendants moved for summary judgment on the ground that Jones had no evidence that they either beat him or were present while others did. Jones contested these factual assertions, and the District Court denied the summary judgment motion on the ground that the record revealed genuine issues of disputed fact. The three officers immediately appealed, but the Circuit Court distinguished *Mitchell* and refused to accept jurisdiction. The Supreme Court affirmed. It held that courts were required to separate a "reviewable determination (that a given set of facts violates clearly established law) from [an] unreviewable determination (that an issue of fact is 'genuine')." A "simple 'we didn't do it' case," in the Court's view, presented an easy illustra-

---

[b] *Cohen* held that a decision is "final" for purposes of appeal if it falls within "that small class which finally determines claims of right separable from, and collateral to, rights asserted in the action, too important to be denied review, and too independent of the cause itself to require that appellate consideration be deferred until the whole case is adjudicated."

tion of an inappropriate interlocutory appeal. Nor, the Court added, will a distinction along these lines prove unworkable in practice.[c]

8. CONCLUSION

Even though the administration of *Harlow* qualified immunity now seems to be reasonably well settled as a matter of precedent, it remains controversial.[d] It may be surprising, therefore, to note the near unanimity of the Court in the next main case.

Brosseau v. Haugen

Supreme Court of the United States, 2004.
543 U.S. 194.

■ PER CURIAM.

Officer Rochelle Brosseau, a member of the Puyallup, Washington, Police Department, shot Kenneth Haugen in the back as he attempted to flee from law enforcement authorities in his vehicle. Haugen subsequently filed this action in the United States District Court for the Western District of Washington pursuant to 42 U.S.C. § 1983. He alleged that the shot fired by Brosseau constituted excessive force and violated his federal constitutional rights. The District Court granted summary judgment to Brosseau after finding she was entitled to qualified immunity. The Court of Appeals for the Ninth Circuit reversed. [The Ninth Circuit] found, first, that Brosseau had violated Haugen's Fourth Amendment right to be free from excessive force and, second, that the right violated was clearly established and thus Brosseau was not entitled to qualified immunity. Brosseau then petitioned for writ of certiorari, requesting that we review both of the Court of Appeals' determinations. We grant the petition on the second, qualified immunity question and [summarily] reverse.

The material facts, construed in a light most favorable to Haugen, are as follows. On the day before the fracas, Glen Tamburello went to the police station and reported to Brosseau that Haugen, a former crime partner of his, had stolen tools from his shop. Brosseau later learned that there was a felony no-bail warrant out for Haugen's arrest on drug and other offenses. The next morning, Haugen was spray-painting his Jeep Cherokee in his mother's driveway. Tamburello learned of Haugen's whereabouts, and he

---

[c] In a subsequent case, the Court held that state courts do not have to provide the opportunity for interlocutory appeal made available in federal courts by *Mitchell*. In Johnson v. Fankell, 520 U.S. 911 (1997), Justice Stevens wrote for a unanimous Court: "The right to have the trial court rule on the merits of the qualified immunity defense presumably has its source in § 1983, but the right to immediate appellate review of that ruling in a federal case has its source in § 1291. The former right is fully protected by Idaho. The latter right, however, is a federal procedural right that simply does not apply in a nonfederal forum." Of course, if summary judgment is denied and interlocutory appeal is not taken, or because of material facts in dispute, cannot be taken, appellate review after final judgment is based on the full record developed at trial, not just the material available at the time of the pre-trial motion. This is the general rule for civil litigation and is fully applicable to summary judgment motions based on qualified immunity. See Ortiz v. Jordan, 131 S.Ct. 884.

[d] See, e.g., Laura Oren, Immunity and Accountability in Civil Rights Litigation: Who Should Pay?, 50 U.Pitt.L.Rev. 935 (1989); David Rudovsky, The Qualified Immunity Doctrine in the Supreme Court: Judicial Activism and the Restriction of Constitutional Rights, 138 U.Pa.L.Rev. 23 (1989). For early efforts to assess the implementation of *Harlow,* see Kit Kinports, Qualified Immunity in Section 1983 Cases: The Unanswered Questions, 23 Ga.L.Rev. 597 (1989); Karen M. Blum, Qualified Immunity: A User's Manual, 26 Ind.L.Rev. 187 (1993).

and cohort Matt Atwood drove a pickup truck to Haugen's mother's house to pay Haugen a visit. A fight ensued, which was witnessed by a neighbor who called 911.

Brosseau heard a report that the men were fighting in Haugen's mother's yard and responded. When she arrived, Tamburello and Atwood were attempting to get Haugen into Tamburello's pickup. Brosseau's arrival created a distraction, which provided Haugen the opportunity to get away. Haugen ran through his mother's yard and hid in the neighborhood. Brosseau requested assistance, and, shortly thereafter, two officers arrived with a K–9 to help track Haugen down. . . .

An officer radioed from down the street that a neighbor had seen a man in her backyard. Brosseau ran in that direction, and Haugen appeared. He ran past the front of his mother's house and then turned and ran into the driveway. With Brosseau still in pursuit, he jumped into the driver's side of the Jeep and closed and locked the door. Brosseau believed that he was running to the Jeep to retrieve a weapon.

Brosseau arrived at the Jeep, pointed her gun at Haugen, and ordered him to get out of the vehicle. Haugen ignored her command and continued to look for the keys so that he could get the Jeep started. Brosseau repeated her commands and hit the driver's side window several times with her handgun, which failed to deter Haugen. On the third or fourth try, the window shattered. Brosseau unsuccessfully attempted to grab the keys and struck Haugen on the head with the barrel and butt of her gun. Haugen, still undeterred, succeeded in starting the Jeep. As the Jeep started or shortly after it began to move, Brosseau jumped back and to the left. She fired one shot through the rear driver's side window at a forward angle, hitting Haugen in the back. She later explained that she shot Haugen because she was " 'fearful for the other officers on foot who [she] believed were in the immediate area, [and] for the occupied vehicles in [Haugen's] path and for any other citizens who might be in the area.' "

Despite being hit, Haugen, in his words, " 'st[ood] on the gas' " . . . ; swerved across the neighbor's lawn; and continued down the street. After about a half block, Haugen realized that he had been shot and brought the Jeep to a halt. He suffered a collapsed lung and was airlifted to a hospital. He survived the shooting and subsequently pleaded guilty to the felony of "eluding." Wash. Rev. Code § 46.61.024 (1994). By so pleading, he admitted that he drove his Jeep in a manner indicating "a wanton or wilful disregard for the lives . . . of others." He subsequently brought this § 1983 action against Brosseau.

* * *

. . . As the Court of Appeals recognized, the constitutional question in this case is governed by the principles enunciated in Tennessee v. Garner, 471 U.S. 1 (1985), and Graham v. Connor, 490 U.S. 386 (1989). These cases establish that claims of excessive force are to be judged under the Fourth Amendment's "objective reasonableness" standard. Specifically, with regard to deadly force, we explained in *Garner* that it is unreasonable for an officer to "seize an unarmed, nondangerous suspect by shooting him dead." But "[w]here the officer has probable cause to believe that the suspect poses a threat of serious physical harm, either to the officer or to others, it is not constitutionally unreasonable to prevent escape by using deadly force."

We express no view as to the correctness of the Court of Appeals' decision on the constitutional question itself. We believe that, however that question is decided, the Court of Appeals was wrong on the issue of qualified immunity.

Qualified immunity shields an officer from suit when she makes a decision that, even if constitutionally deficient, reasonably misapprehends the law governing the circumstances she confronted. . . . It is important to emphasize that this inquiry "must be undertaken in light of the specific context of the case, not as a broad proposition." Saucier v. Katz, 533 U.S. 194, 206 (2001). As we previously said in this very context:

> [T]here is no doubt that *Graham v. Connor*, supra, clearly establishes the general proposition that use of force is contrary to the Fourth Amendment if it is excessive under objective standards of reasonableness. Yet that is not enough. Rather, we emphasized in Anderson v. Creighton, 483 U.S. 635, 640 (1997), "that the right the official is alleged to have violated must have been 'clearly established' in a more particularized, and hence more relevant, sense: The contours of the right must be sufficiently clear that a reasonable official would understand that what he is doing violates that right.' ". . . .

The Court of Appeals acknowledged this statement of law, but then proceeded to find fair warning in the general tests set out in *Graham* and *Garner*. In so doing, it was mistaken. . . .

We therefore turn to ask whether, at the time of Brosseau's actions, it was "clearly established" in this more "particularized" sense that she was violating Haugen's Fourth Amendment right. The parties point us to only a handful of cases relevant to the "situation [Brosseau] confronted": whether to shoot a disturbed felon, set on avoiding capture through vehicular flight, when persons in the immediate area are at risk from that flight.[5] Specifically, Brosseau points us to Cole v. Bone, 993 F.2d 1328 (8th Cir. 1993), and Smith v. Freland, 954 F.2d 343 (6th Cir. 1992).

In these cases, the courts found no Fourth Amendment violation when an officer shot a fleeing suspect who presented a risk to others. *Smith* is closer to this case. There, the officer and suspect engaged in a car chase, which appeared to be at an end when the officer cornered the suspect at the back of a dead-end residential street. The suspect, however, freed his car and began speeding down the street. At this point, the officer fired a shot, which killed the suspect. The court held the officer's decision was reasonable and thus did not violate the Fourth Amendment. It noted that the suspect, like Haugen here, "had proven he would do almost anything to avoid capture" and that he posed a major threat to, among others, the officers at the end of the street.

Haugen points us to Estate of Starks v. Enyard, 5 F.3d 230 (7th Cir. 1993), where the court found summary judgment inappropriate on a Fourth Amendment claim involving a fleeing suspect. There, the court concluded that the threat created by the fleeing suspect's failure to brake when an officer suddenly stepped in front of his just-started car was not a sufficiently grave threat to justify the use of deadly force.

These . . . cases taken together undoubtedly show that this area is one in which the result depends very much on the facts of each case. None

[5] The parties point us to a number of other cases in this vein that postdate the conduct in question. These decisions, of course, could not have given fair notice to Brosseau and are of no use in the clearly established inquiry.

of them squarely governs the case here; they do suggest that Brosseau's actions fell in the " 'hazy border between excessive and acceptable force.' " *Saucier v. Katz*, 533 U.S., at 206. The cases by no means "clearly establish" that Brosseau's conduct violated the Fourth Amendment.

The judgment of the United States Court of Appeals for the Ninth Circuit is therefore reversed, and the case is remanded for further proceedings consistent with this opinion.

■ [The concurring opinion of JUSTICE BREYER, with whom JUSTICES SCALIA and GINSBURG joined, is omitted.]

■ JUSTICE STEVENS dissenting.

In my judgment, the answer to the constitutional question presented by this case is clear: Under the Fourth Amendment, it was objectively unreasonable for Officer Brosseau to use deadly force against Kenneth Haugen in an attempt to prevent his escape. What is not clear is whether Brosseau is nonetheless entitled to qualified immunity because it might not have been apparent to a reasonably well trained officer in Brosseau's shoes that killing Haugen to prevent his escape was unconstitutional. In my opinion that question should be answered by a jury. . . .

An officer is entitled to qualified immunity, despite having engaged in constitutionally deficient conduct, if, in doing so, she did not violate "clearly established statutory or constitutional rights of which a reasonable person would have known." Harlow v. Fitzgerald, 457 U.S. 800, 818 (1982). The requirement that the law be clearly established is designed to ensure that officers have fair notice of what conduct is proscribed. See Hope v. Pelzer, 536 U.S. 730, 739 (2002). Accordingly, we have recognized that "general statements of the law are not inherently incapable of giving fair and clear warning," United States v. Lanier, 520 U.S. 259, 271 (1997), and have firmly rejected the notion that "an official action is protected by qualified immunity unless the very action in question has previously been held unlawful." Anderson v. Creighton, 483 U.S. 635, 640 (1987).

Thus, the Court's search for relevant case law applying the Tennessee v. Garner, 471 U.S. 1 (1985), standard to materially similar facts is both unnecessary and ill-advised. See *Hope*, 536 U.S., at 741 ("Although earlier cases involving 'fundamentally similar' facts can provide especially strong support for a conclusion that the law is clearly established, they are not necessary to such a finding").

Rather than uncertainty about the law, it is uncertainty about the likely consequences of Haugen's flight—or, more precisely, uncertainly about how a reasonable officer making the split-second decision to use deadly force would have assessed the foreseeability of a serious accident—that prevents me from answering the question of qualified immunity that this case presents. This is a quintessentially "fact-specific" question, not a question that judges should try to answer "as a matter of law." Although it is preferable to resolve the qualified immunity question at the earliest possible stage of litigation, this preference does not give judges license to take inherently factual questions away from the jury. . . .

In sum, the constitutional limits on an officer's use of deadly force have been well settled in this Court's jurisprudence for nearly two decades, and, in this case, Officer Brosseau acted outside of those clearly delineated bounds. Nonetheless, in my judgment, there is a genuine factual question as to whether a reasonably well-trained officer standing in Brosseau's shoes could have concluded otherwise, and the question plainly falls within the purview of the jury.

For these reasons, I respectfully dissent.

NOTES ON "CLEARLY ESTABLISHED LAW"

1. REQUIRED SIMILARITY OF PRIOR PRECEDENT: *HOPE V. PELZER*

Hope v. Pelzer, 536 U.S. 730 (2002), concerned the Alabama Department of Corrections' (ADOC) use of a "hitching post" to punish state prison inmates who refused to work or disrupted work squads. (Alabama was apparently the only state to use this practice.) According to his complaint, Hope was handcuffed to a hitching post on two occasions. The first time, he was attached to the post for two hours. Due to his height, his arms were pinioned above his shoulders and "[w]henever he tried moving his arms to improve his circulation, the handcuffs cut into his wrists, causing pain and discomfort." The second time, Hope was required to remove his shirt and remained handcuffed to the post for seven hours. He was given little water, denied bathroom breaks, and taunted by guards, and he suffered sunburn.

Hope filed a § 1983 suit against three guards involved in these incidents. Both the District Court and the Court of Appeals held that the guards were entitled to qualified immunity. The Court of Appeals agreed with Hope that the alleged conduct would violate the Eighth Amendment. Nonetheless, because the facts in the cases on which Hope relied, "though analogous," were not "*materially similar*," they did not create clearly established law.

The Supreme Court reversed. Justice Stevens's opinion for the Court agreed that Alabama's practices violated the Eighth Amendment. Given the facts as alleged by Hope, the guards' actions involved the "unnecessary and wanton infliction of pain" that Whitley v. Albers, 475 U.S. 312 (1986), had held violative of the Cruel and Unusual Punishment Clause. With respect to qualified immunity, the Court rejected the Eleventh Circuit's requirement that § 1983 plaintiffs point to a decision involving "materially similar" facts as a "rigid gloss on the qualified immunity standard . . . not consistent with our cases." Such a requirement, the Court stated, was not necessary "to ensure that before they are subjected to suit, officers are on notice their conduct is unlawful."

The Court drew a parallel to United States v. Lanier, 520 U.S. 259 (1997), which involved criminal prosecution under 18 U.S.C. § 242 of a state-court judge who sexually assaulted a number of women. Section 242 makes it a crime for a state official to "willfully" deprive a person of rights protected by the Constitution. Lanier argued that he had not received "fair warning" that his conduct violated the statute because no prior case had held that sexual assaults committed under color of state law violated the Fourteenth Amendment, but the Supreme Court disagreed. The lesson drawn from *Lanier* in *Hope* was "that officials can still be on notice that their conduct violates established law even in novel factual circumstances":

> Indeed, in *Lanier*, we expressly rejected a requirement that previous cases be "fundamentally similar." Although earlier cases involving "fundamentally similar" facts can provide especially strong support for a conclusion that the law is clearly established, they are not necessary to such a find-

ing. The same is true of cases with "materially similar" facts. Accordingly, pursuant to *Lanier* the salient question that the Court of Appeals ought to have asked is whether the state of the law in 1995 gave respondents fair warning that their alleged treatment of Hope was unconstitutional.

The Court held that it did. It pointed to a 1974 court of appeals decision, binding on the Eleventh Circuit, that had held unconstitutional several forms of corporal punishment inflicted within the Mississippi prison system, including "handcuffing inmates to the fence and to cells for long periods of time, . . . and forcing inmates to stand, sit or lie on crates, stumps, or otherwise maintain awkward positions for prolonged periods":

> [For] the purpose of providing fair notice to reasonable officers administering punishment for past misconduct, [there is no] reason to draw a constitutional distinction between a practice of handcuffing an inmate to a fence for prolonged periods and handcuffing him to a hitching post for seven hours. The Court of Appeals' conclusion to the contrary exposes the danger of a rigid, overreliance on factual similarity. As the Government submits in its brief amicus curiae: "No reasonable officer could have concluded that the constitutional holding of [Gates v. Collier, 501 F.2d 1291 (5th Cir. 1974)] turned on the fact that inmates were handcuffed to fences or the bars of cells, rather than a specially designed metal bar designated for shackling. If anything, the use of a designated hitching post highlights the constitutional problem." Brief for United States as Amicus Curiae 22. In light of *Gates*, the unlawfulness of the alleged conduct should have been apparent to the respondents.
>
> Our conclusion that "a reasonable person would have known," Harlow v. Fitzgerald, 457 U.S. 800, 818 (1982), of the violation is buttressed by the fact that the [United States Department of Justice (DOJ)] specifically advised the ADOC of the unconstitutionality of its practices before the incidents in this case took place. . . . The ADOC replied that it thought the post could permissibly be used "to preserve prison security and discipline." In response, the DOJ informed the ADOC that, "although an emergency situation may warrant drastic action by corrections staff, our experts found that the 'rail' is being used systematically as an improper punishment for relatively trivial offenses. Therefore, we have concluded that the use of the 'rail' is without penological justification." Although there is nothing in the record indicating that the DOJ's views were communicated to respondents, this exchange lends support to the view that reasonable officials in the ADOC should have realized that the use of the hitching post under the circumstances alleged by Hope violated the Eighth Amendment prohibition against cruel and unusual punishment.
>
> The obvious cruelty inherent in this practice should have provided respondents with some notice that their alleged conduct violated Hope's constitutional protection against cruel and unusual punishment. Hope was treated in a way antithetical to human dignity—he was hitched to a post for an extended period of time in a position that was painful, and under circumstances that were both degrading and dangerous.

Justice Thomas, joined by Chief Justice Rehnquist and Justice Scalia, dissented:

The right not to suffer from "cruel and unusual punishments" is an extremely abstract and general right. In the vast majority of cases, the text of the Eighth Amendment does not, in and of itself, give a government official sufficient notice of the clearly established Eighth Amendment law applicable to a particular situation. Rather, one must look to case law. . . .

Previous litigation over Alabama's use of the restraining bar, however, did nothing to warn reasonable Alabama prison guards that attaching a prisoner to a restraining bar was unlawful, let alone that the illegality of such conduct was clearly established. . . . In the face of these decisions, and the absence of contrary authority, I find it impossible to conclude that respondents either were "plainly incompetent" or "knowingly violating the law" when they affixed petitioner to the restraining bar. Malley v. Briggs, 475 U.S. 335, 341 (1986). . . .

Moreover, if the application of this Court's general Eighth Amendment jurisprudence to the use of a restraining bar was as "obvious" as the Court claims, one wonders how Federal District Courts in Alabama could have repeatedly arrived at the opposite conclusion, and how respondents, in turn, were to realize that these courts had failed to grasp the "obvious.". . . .

The Department of Justice report referenced by the Court does nothing to demonstrate that it should have been clear to respondents that attaching petitioner to a restraining bar violated his Eighth Amendment rights. To begin with, the Court concedes that there is no indication the Justice Department's recommendation that the ADOC stop using the restraining bar was ever communicated to respondents, prison guards in the small town of Capshaw, Alabama. In any event, an extraordinarily well-informed prison guard in 1995, who had read both the Justice Department's report and Federal District Court decisions addressing the use of the restraining bar, could have concluded only that there was a dispute as to whether handcuffing a prisoner to a restraining bar constituted an Eighth Amendment violation, not that such a practice was clearly unconstitutional.

Note that *Brosseau v. Haugen* was decided after *Hope v. Pelzer*. Are they consistent?

2. THE SOURCES OF CLEARLY ESTABLISHED LAW

A decision by the Supreme Court of the United States that particular conduct violates the Constitution "clearly establishes" the law regarding that conduct. And within a particular circuit, a decision by the court of appeals creates clearly established law for purposes of qualified immunity. There is a split among the courts of appeals, however, on whether persuasive authority from other circuits is relevant to the question of qualified immunity. The Eleventh Circuit categorically refuses to look to out-of-circuit authority on questions of qualified immunity.[a] The Second Circuit has recently adopted the same approach, though there is also prior circuit authority taking the opposite view.[b] Seven other circuits agree that persuasive out-of-circuit authority, at least un-

[a] See Thomas ex rel. Thomas v. Roberts, 323 F.3d 950, 955 (11th Cir. 2003).

[b] See Moore v. Vega, 371 F.3d 110, 114 (2d Cir. 2004); African Trade & Info. Ctr., Inc. v. Abromaitis, 294 F.3d 355, 361 (2d Cir.2002).

der some circumstances, can clearly establish a constitutional right.[c] In thinking about how to resolve this conflict, consider the views of Chief Judge Posner in Burgess v. Lowery, 201 F.3d 942, 945 (7th Cir. 2000), that "[t]o rule that until the Supreme Court has spoken, no right of litigants in this circuit can be deemed established before we have decided the issue would discourage anyone from being the first to bring a damages suit in this court; he would be *certain* to be unable to obtain any damages."[d]

3. *ASHCROFT V. AL-KIDD*

Questions about the authority for clearly established law can arise even when there is precedent precisely on point. Suppose that a federal district or circuit court explicitly holds a particular police practice unconstitutional, and suppose further that the decision was made a month before identical behavior subsequently challenged in a § 1983 damages action. Should qualified immunity be denied? Might it be reasonable for an officer not to know about very recent legal developments? Would that depend on the court involved?

Similar questions arose in Ashcroft v. al-Kidd, 131 S.Ct. 2074. Al–Kidd, a United States citizen, was detained under a material witness warrant when he attempted to board a flight to Saudi Arabia.[e] He subsequently brought a *Bivens* action against Attorney General John Ashcroft and others, claiming that they used the material witness statute pretextually—that is, without the intention of calling him as a witness. The real purpose, al-Kidd alleged, was simply to detain him on suspicion of terrorism in the absence of sufficient evidence to bring a criminal charge.

---

[c] See Owens v. Lott, 372 F.3d 267, 279–80 (4th Cir. 2004) ("[W]e look ordinarily to 'the decisions of the Supreme Court, this court of appeals, and the highest court of the state in which the case arose," but "[w]hen there are no such decisions from courts of controlling authority, we may look to 'a consensus of cases of persuasive authority' from other jurisdictions, if such exists."); McClendon v. City of Columbia, 305 F.3d 314, 331 (5th Cir. 2002) (looking to "cases from our sister circuits" to determine whether the relevant law was clearly established); Walton v. City of Southfield, 995 F.2d 1331, 1336 (6th Cir. 1993) ("In an extraordinary case, it may be possible for the decisions of other courts to clearly establish a principle of law."); Cleveland–Purdue v. Brutsche, 881 F.2d 427, 431 (7th Cir. 1989) (stating that "[i]n the absence of a controlling precedent" the court would "look to all relevant caselaw" in determining whether the law was clearly established); Buckley v. Rogerson, 133 F.3d 1125, 1129 (8th Cir. 1998) ("In the absence of binding precedent, a court should look to all available decisional law, including decisions of state courts, other circuits and district courts."); Boyd v. Benton County, 374 F.3d 773, 781 (9th Cir. 2004) ("[I]n the absence of binding precedent, we look to whatever decisional law is available to ascertain whether the law is clearly established for qualified immunity purposes. . . . "); Peterson v. Jensen, 371 F.3d 1199, 1202 (10th Cir. 2004) ("A right is clearly established . . . if the clearly established weight of authority from other circuits found a constitutional violation from similar actions.").

[d] The question of what sources can create "clearly established" law for qualified immunity is in some respects analogous to a question in the law of habeas corpus. The Antiterrorism and Effective Death Penalty Act of 1996 provided that "[a]n application for a writ of habeas corpus . . . shall not be granted with respect to any claim that was adjudicated on the merits in State court proceedings unless the adjudication of the claim . . . resulted in a decision that was contrary to, or involved an unreasonable application of, clearly established Federal law, as determined by the Supreme Court of the United States." 28 U.S.C. § 2254(d)(1). See generally Kit Kinports, Habeas Corpus, Qualified Immunity, and Crystal Balls: Predicting the Course of Constitutional Law, 33 Ariz. L. Rev. 115 (1991) (discussing parallels between the clearly established law inquiries in § 1983 and habeas cases).

[e] The federal material-witness statute authorizes judges to order the arrest of someone whose testimony "is material in a criminal proceeding . . . if it is shown that it may become impracticable to secure the presence of the person by subpoena." 18 U.S.C. § 3144.

The Ninth Circuit ruled for al-Kidd, finding both that pretextual use of the material witness statute violated the Fourth Amendment and that the Attorney General was not entitled to immunity, 580 F.3d 949 (2009), and, with eight judges dissenting, denied rehearing en banc. 598 F.3d 1129 (2010). The Supreme Court unanimously reversed. All eight Justices (Justice Kagan not participating) agreed that Ashcroft was entitled to qualified immunity because he had not violated a "clearly established" constitutional right. Five Justices went further and found the Fourth Amendment claim lacking on the merits. On that issue, Justices Ginsburg, Breyer, and Sotomayor reserved judgment.

The Ninth Circuit found the right against pretextual use of a material witness warrant "clearly established," based largely on a footnote from the Southern District of New York, even though al-Kidd's arrest did not occur there. Speaking through Justice Scalia, the majority responded with barely concealed contempt:

> At the time of al-Kidd's arrest, not a single judicial opinion had held that pretext could render an objectively reasonable arrest pursuant to a material-witness warrant unconstitutional. A district-court opinion had suggested, in a footnoted dictum devoid of supporting citation, that using such a warrant for preventive detention of suspects "is an illegitimate use of the statute". . . . United States v. Awaddallah, 202 F. Supp.2d 55, 77 n.28 (S.D.N.Y. 2002). The Court of Appeals thought nothing could "have given John Ashcroft fair[er] warning" that his conduct violated the Fourth Amendment, because the footnoted dictum "*call[ed] out Ashcroft by name*"! 580 F.3d, at 972–73 (emphasis added). We will indulge the assumption (though it does not seem to us realistic) that Justice Department lawyers bring to the Attorney General's personal attention all district judges' footnoted speculations that boldly "call him out by name." On that assumption, would it prove that for him (and for him only?) it became clearly established that pretextual use of the material-witness statute rendered the arrest unconstitutional? An extraordinary proposition. Even a district judge's ipse dixit of a holding is not "controlling authority" in any jurisdiction, much less in the entire United States; and his ipse dixit of a footnoted dictum falls far short of what is necessary absent controlling authority: a robust "consensus of cases of persuasive authority." Wilson v. Layne, 526 U.S. 617 (1999). . . .
>
> The Court of Appeals also found clearly established law lurking in the broad "history and purposes of the Fourth Amendment." 580 F.3d, at 971. We have repeatedly told courts—and the Ninth Circuit in particular—not to define clearly established law at a high level of generality. . . .
>
> Qualified immunity gives government officials breathing room to make reasonable but mistaken judgments about open legal questions. When properly applied, it protects "all but the plainly incompetent or those who knowingly violate the law." Malley v. Briggs, 475 U.S. 335, 341 (1986). Ashcroft deserves neither label, not least because eight Court of Appeals judges agreed with his judgment in a case of first impression.

Justice Kennedy wrote a concurrence in which (on this point speaking only for himself) he elaborated on the significance of the office held by the defendant in determining whether a right is "clearly established":

> [T]he Attorney General occupies a national office and so sets policies implemented in many jurisdictions throughout the country. The official with responsibilities in many jurisdictions may face ambiguous and sometimes inconsistent sources of decisional law. . . .
>
> When faced with inconsistent legal rules in different jurisdictions, national officeholders should be given some deference for qualified immunity purposes, at least if they implement policies consistent with the governing law of the jurisdiction where the action is taken. . . .
>
> The proceedings in this case illustrate these concerns. The Court of Appeals for the Ninth Circuit appears to have reasoned that a Federal District Court sitting in New York had authority to establish a legal rule binding on the Attorney General and, therefore, on federal law-enforcement operations conducted nationwide. Indeed, this case involves a material witness warrant issued in Boise, Idaho, and an arrest near Washington, D.C. Of course, district court decisions are not precedential to this extent. But nationwide security operations should not have to grind to a halt even when an appellate court finds those operations unconstitutional. The doctrine of qualified immunity does not so constrain national officeholders entrusted with urgent responsibilities.

Justices Ginsburg, Breyer, and Sotomayor agreed that qualified immunity applied in this case, but concurred in the judgment to record their unease with the majority's view of the underlying Fourth Amendment claim.

NOTES ON QUALIFIED IMMUNITY IN RIGHTS OF "REASONABLENESS"

1. THE PROBLEM

As the Supreme Court said in Baker v. McCollan, 443 U.S. 137, 144 n.3 (1979), § 1983 "is not itself a source of substantive rights, but a method for vindicating federal rights elsewhere conferred." Thus, a § 1983 action raises the question whether the defendant violated the Constitution as well as the question whether the defendant is entitled to qualified immunity. As a conceptual matter, those questions are entirely independent, but "reasonableness" may arise in both. Qualified immunity depends on whether a *reasonable* officer would have known that his or her conduct was unconstitutional, and in some circumstances whether the conduct was unconstitutional also depends on whether it was *reasonable*. The Fourth Amendment, for example, protects against "unreasonable searches and seizures." If a court has determined, in the context of adjudicating a Fourth Amendment issue, that the defendant behaved unreasonably, is there anything left to consider with respect to qualified immunity?

2. *ANDERSON V. CREIGHTON*

Anderson v. Creighton, 483 U.S. 635 (1987), was a *Bivens* action involving a Fourth Amendment claim. Anderson and other federal agents conducted a warrantless search of the Creightons' home. The Creightons sued, alleging abusive and high-handed behavior during the search. The Court, in an opinion by Justice Scalia, held that the defendants would be entitled to qualified immunity unless the unconstitutionality of their conduct was clearly established at the time of the search.

Justice Stevens, joined by Justices Brennan and Marshall, dissented. They argued that the majority had adopted a "double standard of reasonableness" in applying qualified immunity to Fourth Amendment claims. "By double standard," Stevens explained, "I mean a standard that affords a law enforcement official two layers of insulation from liability or other adverse consequence, such as suppression of evidence." Stevens argued that allowance for reasonable error was already made in Fourth Amendment doctrine and quoted Judge Posner's comments in Llaguno v. Mingey, 763 F.2d 1520, 1569 (7th Cir. 1985) (en banc):

> The question whether they had probable cause depends on what they reasonably believed with reference to the facts that confronted them. . . . To go on and instruct the jury further that even if they police acted without probable cause they should be exonerated if they reasonably (though erroneously) believed that they were acting reasonably is to confuse the jury and give the defendants two bites at the apple.

The majority answered that Stevens' objection to finding that an officer who had violated the Fourth Amendment had been "reasonably unreasonable" was little more than a play on words:

> Its surface appeal is attributable to the circumstance that the Fourth Amendment's guarantees have been expressed in terms of "unreasonable" searches and seizures. Had an equally serviceable term, such as "undue" searches and seizures been employed, what might be termed the "reasonably unreasonable" argument against application of *Harlow* to the Fourth Amendment would not be available—just as it would be available against application of *Harlow* to the Fifth Amendment if the term "reasonable process of law" had been employed there. The fact is that, regardless of the terminology used, the precise content of most of the Constitution's civil-liberties guarantees rests upon an assessment of what accommodation between governmental need and individual freedom is reasonable. . . . We have frequently observed, and our many cases on the point amply demonstrate, the difficulty of determining whether particular searches or seizures comport with the Fourth Amendment. Law enforcement officers whose judgments in making these difficult determinations are objectively legally reasonable should no more be held personally liable in damages than should officials making analogous determinations in other areas of law.

3. *SAUCIER V. KATZ*

The Court revisited this question with respect to a question of excessive force in Saucier v. Katz, 533 U.S. 194 (2001). Katz protested at a speech given by Vice President Gore at a military base. He alleged that Saucier, a military policeman, had used excessive force in removing him to a police van.

The district court held that a dispute of material fact existed concerning whether petitioner had used excessive force. It denied petitioner's claim of qualified immunity, holding that in this context qualified immunity merely duplicated the merits inquiry into whether the use of force was unreasonable and therefore violative of the Fourth Amendment. See Graham v. Connor, 490

U.S. 386, (1989) (holding that objective reasonableness is the appropriate test for a claim of excessive force). The Ninth Circuit affirmed, but the Supreme Court, in an opinion by Justice Kennedy, reversed:

> The Court of Appeals concluded that qualified immunity is merely duplicative in an excessive force case, eliminating the need for the second step where a constitutional violation could be found based on the allegations. . . . Graham v. Connor, 490 U.S. 386, (1989), in respondent's view, sets forth an excessive force analysis indistinguishable from qualified immunity, rendering the separate immunity inquiry superfluous and inappropriate. Respondent asserts that, like the qualified immunity analysis applicable in other contexts, the excessive force test already affords officers latitude for mistaken beliefs as to the amount of force necessary. . . .
>
> [In *Graham*, we] set out a test that cautioned against the "20/20 vision of hindsight" in favor of deference to the judgment of reasonable officers on the scene. *Graham* sets forth a list of factors relevant to the merits of the constitutional excessive force claim, "requiring careful attention to the facts and circumstances of each particular case, including the severity of the crime at issue, whether the suspect poses an immediate threat to the safety of the officers or others, and whether he is actively resisting arrest or attempting to evade arrest by flight." If an officer reasonably, but mistakenly, believed that a suspect was likely to fight back, for instance, the officer would be justified in using more force than in fact was needed.
>
> The qualified immunity inquiry, on the other hand, has a further dimension. The concern of the immunity inquiry is to acknowledge that reasonable mistakes can be made as to the legal constraints on particular police conduct. It is sometimes difficult for an officer to determine how the relevant legal doctrine, here excessive force, will apply to the factual situation the officer confronts. An officer might correctly perceive all of the relevant facts but have a mistaken understanding as to whether a particular amount of force is legal in those circumstances. If the officer's mistake as to what the law requires is reasonable, however, the officer is entitled to the immunity defense. . . .
>
> The deference owed officers facing suits for alleged excessive force is not different in some qualitative respect from the probable cause inquiry in *Anderson*. Officers can have reasonable, but mistaken, beliefs as to the facts establishing the existence of probable cause or exigent circumstances, for example, and in those situations courts will not hold that they have violated the Constitution. Yet, even if a court were to hold that the officer violated the Fourth Amendment by conducting an unreasonable, warrantless search, *Anderson* still operates to grant officers immunity for reasonable mistakes as to the legality of their actions. The same analysis is applicable in excessive force cases, where in addition to the deference officers receive on the underlying constitutional claim, qualified immunity can apply in the event the mistaken belief was reasonable. . . .

Ultimately, the Supreme Court decided that the petitioner had "substantial grounds" to conclude that he had legitimate justification under the existing law for using the force he did:

> A reasonable officer in petitioner's position could have believed that hurrying respondent away from the scene, where the Vice President was speaking and respondent had just approached the fence designed to separate the public from the speakers, was within the bounds of appropriate police responses. . . .
>
> As for the shove respondent received when he was placed into the van, those same circumstances show some degree of urgency. . . . In the circumstances presented to this officer, which included the duty to protect the safety and security of the Vice President of the United States from persons unknown in number, neither respondent nor the Court of Appeals has identified any case demonstrating a clearly established rule prohibiting the officer from acting as he did, nor are we aware of any such rule. Our conclusion is confirmed by the uncontested fact that the force was not so excessive that respondent suffered hurt or injury. On these premises, petitioner was entitled to qualified immunity, and the suit should have been dismissed at an early stage in the proceedings.

Justice Ginsburg, joined by Justices Stevens and Breyer, concurred in the judgment. She felt that application of the objective reasonableness standard laid out in *Graham* as a matter of substantive Fourth Amendment law was "both necessary, under currently governing precedent, and, in my view, sufficient to resolve cases of this genre." She disapproved of the Court's decision to "tac[k] on to a *Graham* inquiry a second, overlapping objective reasonableness inquiry purportedly demanded by qualified immunity doctrine." She noted that the lower federal courts had recognized that "the same 'objectively reasonable' standard [governs] . . . both the constitutional test of liability and the . . . standard for qualified immunity":

> Double counting "objective reasonableness," the Court appears to suggest, is demanded by *Anderson*, which twice restated that qualified immunity shields the conduct of officialdom "across the board." 483 U.S. at 642, 645 (quoting Harlow v. Fitzgerald, 457 U.S. 800, 821 (1982) (Brennan, J., concurring)). As I see it, however, excessive force cases are not meet for *Anderson*'s two-part test. . . .
>
> The Court fears that dispensing with the duplicative qualified immunity inquiry will mean "leaving the whole matter to the jury." Again, experience teaches otherwise. Lower courts, armed with *Graham*'s directions, have not shied away from granting summary judgment to defendant officials in Fourth Amendment excessive force cases where the challenged conduct is objectively reasonable based on relevant, undisputed facts. See, e.g., Wilson v. Spain, 209 F.3d 713, 716 (8th Cir. 2000) ("addressing in one fell swoop both [defendant's] qualified immunity and the merits of [plaintiff's] Fourth Amendment [excessive force] claim" and concluding officer's conduct was objectively reasonable in the circumstances, so summary judgment for officer was proper). Indeed, this very case, as I earlier explained, fits the summary judgment bill. Of course, if an excessive force claim turns on which of two conflicting stories best captures what happened on the street, *Graham* will not permit summary judgment in favor of the defendant official. And that is as it should be. When a plaintiff proffers evidence that the official subdued her with a chokehold even though she complied at all times with his orders, while the official proffers evi-

dence that he used only stern words, a trial must be had. In such a case, the Court's two-step procedure is altogether inutile. . . .

A major practical effect of *Saucier* to reinforce the idea that judges, near the outset of the litigation, rather than juries towards the end, have the power to decide reasonableness. Is that a by-product of the law-based definition of qualified immunity, or is that the point?

Crawford–El v. Britton

Supreme Court of the United States, 1998.
523 U.S. 574.

■ JUSTICE STEVENS delivered the opinion of the Court.

Petitioner, a long-time prison inmate, seeks damages from a corrections officer based on a constitutional claim that requires proof of improper motive. The broad question presented is whether the courts of appeals may craft special procedural rules for such cases to protect public servants from the burdens of trial and discovery that may impair the performance of their official duties. The more specific question is whether, at least in cases brought by prisoners, the plaintiff must adduce clear and convincing evidence of improper motive in order to defeat a motion for summary judgment.

I

Petitioner is serving a life sentence in the District of Columbia's correctional system. During his confinement he has filed several lawsuits and has assisted other prisoners with their cases. He has also provided interviews to reporters who have written news stories about prison conditions. He is a litigious and outspoken prisoner.

The events that gave rise to this case occurred in 1988 and 1989. Because of overcrowding in the District of Columbia prison in Lorton, Virginia, petitioner and other inmates were transferred to the county jail in Spokane, Washington. Thereafter, he was moved, first to a Washington State prison, later to a facility in Cameron, Missouri, next back to Lorton, then to Petersburg, Virginia, and ultimately to the federal prison in Marianna, Florida. Three boxes containing his personal belongings, including legal materials, were transferred separately. When the District of Columbia Department of Corrections received the boxes from the Washington State facility, respondent, a District correctional officer, asked petitioner's brother-in-law to pick them up rather than sending them directly to petitioner's next destination. The boxes were ultimately shipped to Marianna by petitioner's mother, at petitioner's expense, but he was initially denied permission to receive them because they had been sent outside official prison channels. He finally recovered the property several months after his arrival in Florida.

Petitioner contends that respondent deliberately misdirected the boxes to punish him for exercising his First Amendment rights and to deter similar conduct in the future. Beyond generalized allegations of respondent's hostility, he alleges specific incidents in which his protected speech had provoked her.[1] His claimed injury caused by the delay in receiving his boxes

[1] In 1986, petitioner had invited a Washington Post reporter to visit the Lorton prison and obtained a visitor application for the reporter, which resulted in a front-page article on the prison's overcrowding "crisis." Respondent had approved the visitor application, which did not

includes the costs of having the boxes shipped and purchasing new clothes and other items in the interim, as well as mental and emotional distress. Respondent denies any retaliatory motive and asserts that she entrusted the property to petitioner's brother-in-law, who was also a District of Columbia corrections employee, in order to ensure its prompt and safe delivery.

Although the factual dispute is relatively simple, it engendered litigation that has been both protracted and complex. [The plaintiff filed an action for damages under § 1983, alleging as his main claim that the defendant had diverted his boxes of legal materials in order to interfere with his constitutional right of access to the courts. Prior to discovery, the defendant moved for dismissal of the complaint or, in the alternative, for summary judgment, based partly on the defense of qualified immunity. When motion was denied, the defendant appealed and the court of appeals found the complaint inadequate under a heightened standard for pleading civil rights claims. The court, however, remanded the case to allow the plaintiff to replead. After he did so, the district court again dismissed his complaint, and upon another appeal, the court of appeals took the case en banc. A majority of judges, writing in five separate opinions, ordered the case to be remanded to the district court for still further proceedings. On this appeal, the en banc court held that the plaintiff did not have to satisfy any heightened pleading standard, but that in order to prevail at trial, he had to establish an unconstitutional motive by clear and convincing evidence. The court of appeals also held that Harlow v. Fitzgerald, 457 U.S. 800 (1982), required special procedures to be implemented in unconstitutional-motive cases in order to protect the defendant from the costs of litigation. The Supreme Court granted certiorari to settle the "correct understanding of the relationship between our holding in *Harlow v. Fitzgerald*, and the plaintiff's burden when his or her entitlement to relief depends on proof of an improper motive."]

II

The Court of Appeals' requirement of clear and convincing evidence of improper motive is that court's latest effort to address a potentially serious problem: because an official's state of mind is "easy to allege and hard to disprove," insubstantial claims that turn on improper intent may be less amenable to summary disposition than other types of claims against government officials. This category of claims therefore implicates obvious concerns with the social costs of subjecting public officials to discovery and trial, as well as liability for damages. . . .

Harlow's Specific Holding

[The scope of the qualified immunity defense] had been the subject of debate within the Court in Wood v. Strickland, 420 U.S. 308 (1975), a case involving a constitutional claim against the members of a school board. A bare majority in that case concluded that the plaintiff could overcome the defense of qualified immunity in two different ways, either if (1) the defendant "knew or reasonably should have known that the action he took within his sphere of official responsibility would violate the constitutional rights of the student affected," or (2) "he took the action with the malicious intention to cause a deprivation of constitutional rights or other injury to the student." . . .

disclose the visitor's affiliation with the newspaper; she allegedly accused petitioner of tricking her and threatened to make life "as hard for him as possible." . . .

In *Harlow*, the Court reached a consensus on the proper formulation of the standard for judging the defense of qualified immunity. Speaking for the Court, Justice Powell announced a single objective standard:

> [W]e conclude today that bare allegations of malice should not suffice to subject government officials either to the costs of trial or to the burdens of broad-reaching discovery. We therefore hold that government officials performing discretionary functions generally are shielded from liability for civil damages insofar as their conduct does not violate clearly established statutory or constitutional rights of which a reasonable person would have known.

Under that standard, a defense of qualified immunity may not be rebutted by evidence that the defendant's conduct was malicious or otherwise improperly motivated. Evidence concerning the defendant's subjective intent is simply irrelevant to that defense.

Our holding that "bare allegations of malice" cannot overcome the qualified immunity defense did not implicate the elements of the plaintiff's initial burden of proving a constitutional violation. It is obvious, of course, that bare allegations of malice would not suffice to establish a constitutional claim. It is equally clear that an essential element of some constitutional claims is a charge that the defendant's conduct was improperly motivated. Thus, although evidence of improper motive is irrelevant on the issue of qualified immunity, it may be an essential component of the plaintiff's affirmative case. Our holding in *Harlow*, which related only to the scope of an affirmative defense, provides no support for making any change in the nature of the plaintiff's burden of proving a constitutional violation. . . .

The Reasoning in *Harlow*

Two reasons that are explicit in our opinion in *Harlow*, together with a third that is implicit in the holding, amply justified *Harlow*'s reformulation of the qualified immunity defense. First, there is a strong public interest in protecting public officials from the costs associated with the defense of damages actions. That interest is best served by a defense that permits insubstantial lawsuits to be quickly terminated. Second, allegations of subjective motivation might have been used to shield baseless lawsuits from summary judgment. The objective standard, in contrast, raises questions concerning the state of the law at the time of the challenged conduct—questions that normally can be resolved on summary judgment. Third, focusing on "the objective legal reasonableness of an official's acts" avoids the unfairness of imposing liability on a defendant who "could not reasonably be expected to anticipate subsequent legal developments, nor . . . fairly be said to 'know' that the law forbade conduct not previously identified as unlawful," 457 U.S., at 818. That unfairness may be present even when the official conduct is motivated, in part, by hostility to the plaintiff.

This last rationale of fairness does not provide any justification for the imposition of special burdens on plaintiffs who allege misconduct that was plainly unlawful when it occurred. While there is obvious unfairness in imposing liability—indeed, even in compelling the defendant to bear the burdens of discovery and trial—for engaging in conduct that was objectively reasonable when it occurred, no such unfairness can be attributed to holding one accountable for actions that she knew, or should have known, violated the constitutional rights of the plaintiff. *Harlow* itself said as much: "If the law was clearly established, the immunity defense ordinarily should fail, since a reasonably competent public official should know the law governing his conduct."

The first two reasons underlying our holding in *Harlow*, however, would provide support for a procedural rule that makes it harder for any plaintiff, especially one whose constitutional claim requires proof of an improper motive, to survive a motion for summary judgment. But there are countervailing concerns that must be considered before concluding that the balance struck in the context of defining an affirmative defense is also appropriate when evaluating the elements of the plaintiff's cause of action. . . .

There are several reasons why we believe that here, unlike *Harlow*, the proper balance does not justify a judicial revision of the law to bar claims that depend on proof of an official's motive. Initially, there is an important distinction between the "bare allegations of malice" that would have provided the basis for rebutting a qualified immunity defense under *Wood v. Strickland* and the allegations of intent that are essential elements of certain constitutional claims. Under *Wood*, the mere allegation of intent to cause any "other injury," not just a deprivation of constitutional rights, would have permitted an open-ended inquiry into subjective motivation. When intent is an element of a constitutional violation, however, the primary focus is not on any possible animus directed at the plaintiff; rather, it is more specific, such as an intent to disadvantage all members of a class that includes the plaintiff, see, e.g., Washington v. Davis, 426 U.S. 229, 239–48 (1976), or to deter public comment on a specific issue of public importance. [For example, in] this case proof that respondent diverted the plaintiff's boxes because she hated him would not necessarily demonstrate that she was responding to his public comments about prison conditions, although under *Wood* such evidence might have rebutted the qualified immunity defense.

Moreover, existing law already prevents this more narrow element of unconstitutional motive from automatically carrying a plaintiff to trial. The immunity standard in *Harlow* itself eliminates all motive-based claims in which the official's conduct did not violate clearly established law. Even when the general rule has long been clearly established (for instance, the First Amendment bars retaliation for protected speech), the substantive legal doctrine on which the plaintiff relies may facilitate summary judgment in two different ways. First, there may be doubt as to the illegality of the defendant's particular conduct (for instance, whether a plaintiff's speech was on a matter of public concern). Second, at least with certain types of claims, proof of an improper motive is not sufficient to establish a constitutional violation—there must also be evidence of causation. Accordingly, when a public employee shows that protected speech was a "motivating factor" in an adverse employment decision, the employer still prevails by showing that it would have reached the same decision in the absence of the protected conduct. Mt. Healthy City Bd. of Ed. v. Doyle, 429 U.S. 274, 287 (1977). Furthermore, various procedural mechanisms already enable trial judges to weed out baseless claims that feature a subjective element, as we explain in more detail in Part IV, infra.[6]

---

[6] These various protections may not entirely foreclose discovery on the issue of motive, and the Court of Appeals adopted its heightened proof standard in large part to facilitate the resolution of summary judgment motions before any discovery at all. Discovery involving public officials is indeed one of the evils that *Harlow* aimed to address, but neither that opinion nor subsequent decisions create an immunity from *all* discovery. *Harlow* sought to protect

Thus, unlike the subjective component of the immunity defense eliminated by *Harlow*, the improper intent element of various causes of action should not ordinarily preclude summary disposition of insubstantial claims. The reasoning in *Harlow*, like its specific holding, does not justify a rule that places a thumb on the defendant's side of the scales when the merits of a claim that the defendant knowingly violated the law are being resolved. . . .

III

In fashioning a special rule for constitutional claims that require proof of improper intent, the judges of the Court of Appeals relied almost entirely on our opinion in *Harlow*, and on the specific policy concerns that we identified in that opinion. As we have explained, neither that case nor those concerns warrant the wholesale change in the law that they have espoused. Without such precedential grounding, for the courts of appeals or this Court to change the burden of proof for an entire category of claims would stray far from the traditional limits on judicial authority. . . .

IV

In *Harlow* we noted that a " 'firm application of the Federal Rules of Civil Procedure' is fully warranted" and may lead to the prompt disposition of insubstantial claims. 457 U.S., at 819–20 n.35 (quoting *Butz v. Economou*, supra, at 508). Though we have rejected the Court of Appeals' solution, we are aware of the potential problem that troubled the court. It is therefore appropriate to add a few words on some of the existing procedures available to federal trial judges in handling claims that involve examination of an official's state of mind.

When a plaintiff files a complaint against a public official alleging a claim that requires proof of wrongful motive, the trial court must exercise its discretion in a way that protects the substance of the qualified immunity defense. It must exercise its discretion so that officials are not subjected to unnecessary and burdensome discovery or trial proceedings. The district judge has two primary options prior to permitting any discovery at all. First, the court may order a reply to the defendant's or a third party's answer under Federal Rule of Civil Procedure 7(a), or grant the defendant's motion for a more definite statement under Rule 12(e). Thus, the court may insist that the plaintiff "put forward specific, nonconclusory factual allegations" that establish improper motive causing cognizable injury in order to survive a prediscovery motion for dismissal or summary judgment. Siegert v. Gilley, 500 U.S. 226, 236 (1991) (Kennedy, J., concurring in judgment). This option exists even if the official chooses not to plead the affirmative defense of qualified immunity. Second, if the defendant does plead the immunity defense, the district court should resolve that threshold question before permitting discovery. *Harlow*, 457 U.S., at 818. To do so, the court must determine whether, assuming the truth of the plaintiff's allegations, the official's conduct violated clearly established law. Because the former option of demanding more specific allegations of intent places no burden on the defendant-official, the district judge may choose that alternative before resolving the immunity question, which sometimes requires complicated analysis of legal issues.

---

officials from the costs of "broad-reaching" discovery, 457 U.S., at 818, and we have since recognized that limited discovery may sometimes be necessary before the district court can resolve a motion for summary judgment based on qualified immunity. Anderson v. Creighton, 483 U.S. 635, 646, n. 6 (1987).

If the plaintiff's action survives these initial hurdles and is otherwise viable, the plaintiff ordinarily will be entitled to some discovery. Rule 26 vests the trial judge with broad discretion to tailor discovery narrowly and to dictate the sequence of discovery. On its own motion, the trial court

> may alter the limits in [the Federal Rules] on the number of depositions and interrogatories and may also limit the length of depositions under Rule 30 and the number of requests under Rule 36. The frequency or extent of use of the discovery methods otherwise permitted under these rules . . . shall be limited by the court if it determines that . . . (iii) the burden or expense of the proposed discovery outweighs its likely benefit, taking into account the needs of the case, the amount in controversy, the parties' resources, the importance of the issues at stake in the litigation, and the importance of the proposed discovery in resolving the issues.

Rule 26(b)(2). Additionally, upon motion the court may limit the time, place, and manner of discovery, or even bar discovery altogether on certain subjects, as required "to protect a party or person from annoyance, embarrassment, oppression, or undue burden or expense." Rule 26(c). And the court may also set the timing and sequence of discovery. Rule 26(d).

These provisions create many options for the district judge. For instance, the court may at first permit the plaintiff to take only a focused deposition of the defendant before allowing any additional discovery. Alternatively, the court may postpone all inquiry regarding the official's subjective motive until discovery has been had on objective factual questions such as whether the plaintiff suffered any injury or whether the plaintiff actually engaged in protected conduct that could be the object of unlawful retaliation. The trial judge can therefore manage the discovery process to facilitate prompt and efficient resolution of the lawsuit; as the evidence is gathered, the defendant-official may move for partial summary judgment on objective issues that are potentially dispositive and are more amenable to summary disposition than disputes about the official's intent, which frequently turn on credibility assessments. Of course, the judge should give priority to discovery concerning issues that bear upon the qualified immunity defense, such as the actions that the official actually took, since that defense should be resolved as early as possible.

Beyond these procedures and others that we have not mentioned, summary judgment serves as the ultimate screen to weed out truly insubstantial lawsuits prior to trial. At that stage, if the defendant-official has made a properly supported motion, the plaintiff may not respond simply with general attacks upon the defendant's credibility, but rather must identify affirmative evidence from which a jury could find that the plaintiff has carried his or her burden of proving the pertinent motive. Finally, federal trial judges are undoubtedly familiar with two additional tools that are available in extreme cases to protect public officials from undue harassment: Rule 11, which authorizes sanctions for the filing of papers that are frivolous, lacking in factual support, or "presented for any improper purpose, such as to harass"; and 28 U.S.C.A. § 1915(e)(2) (Supp.1997), which authorizes dismissal "at any time" of in forma pauperis suits that are "frivolous or malicious."

It is the district judges rather than appellate judges like ourselves who have had the most experience in managing cases in which an official's intent is an element. Given the wide variety of civil rights and "constitutional tort" claims that trial judges confront, broad discretion in the management of the factfinding process may be more useful and equitable to all the parties than the categorical rule imposed by the Court of Appeals.

The judgment of the Court of Appeals is vacated, and the case is remanded for further proceedings consistent with this opinion.

■ JUSTICE KENNEDY, concurring.

Prisoner suits under 42 U.S.C. § 1983 can illustrate our legal order at its best and its worst. The best is that even as to prisoners the government must obey always the Constitution. The worst is that many of these suits invoke our basic charter in support of claims which fall somewhere between the frivolous and the farcical and so foster disrespect for our laws. . . . The analysis by the Chief Justice addresses these serious concerns. I am in full agreement with the Court, however, that the authority to propose those far-reaching solutions lies with the legislative branch, not with us.

■ CHIEF JUSTICE REHNQUIST, with whom JUSTICE O'CONNOR joins, dissenting.

The petition on which we granted certiorari in this case presents two questions. The first asks:

> In a case against a government official claiming she retaliated against the plaintiff for his exercise of First Amendment rights, does the qualified immunity doctrine require the plaintiff to prove the official's unconstitutional intent by "clear and convincing" evidence?

The Court's opinion gives this question an extensive treatment, concluding that our cases applying the affirmative defense of qualified immunity provide no basis for placing "a thumb on the defendant's side of the scales when the merits of a claim that the defendant knowingly violated the law are being resolved."

The second question presented asks:

> In a First Amendment retaliation case against a government official, is the official entitled to qualified immunity if she asserts a legitimate justification for her allegedly retaliatory act and that justification would have been a reasonable basis for the act, even if evidence—no matter how strong—shows the official's actual reason for the act was unconstitutional?

The Court does not explicitly discuss this question at all. Its failure to do so is both puzzling and unfortunate. Puzzling, because immunity is a "threshold" question that must be addressed prior to consideration of the merits of a plaintiff's claim. Harlow v. Fitzgerald, 457 U.S. 800, 818 (1982). Unfortunate, because in assuming that the answer to the question is "no," the Court establishes a precedent that is in considerable tension with, and significantly undermines, *Harlow*.

I would address the question directly, and conclude . . . that a government official who is a defendant in a motive-based tort suit is entitled to immunity from suit so long as he can offer a legitimate reason for the action that is being challenged, and the plaintiff is unable to establish, by reliance on objective evidence, that the offered reason is actually a pretext. This is the only result that is consistent with *Harlow* and the purposes of the qualified immunity doctrine. . . .

[In *Harlow*], we "purged" qualified immunity doctrine of its subjective component and remolded it so that it turned entirely on "objective legal reasonableness," measured by the state of the law at the time of the challenged act. Mitchell v. Forsyth, 472 U.S. 511, 517 (1985); *Harlow*, supra, at 819. This new rule eliminated the need for the disruptive inquiry into subjective intent, ensured that insubstantial suits would still be subject to dismissal prior to trial, and had the additional benefit of allowing officials to predict when and under what circumstances they would be required to stand trial for actions undertaken in the course of their work. Since then we have held that qualified immunity was to apply "across the board" without regard to the "precise nature of various officials' duties or the precise character of the particular rights alleged to have been violated." Anderson v. Creighton, 483 U.S. 635, 642–43 (1987).

Applying these principles to the type of motive-based tort suit at issue here, it is obvious that some form of qualified immunity is necessary, and that whether it applies in a given case must turn entirely on objective factors. It is not enough to say that because (1) the law in this area is "clearly established," and (2) this type of claim always turns on a defendant official's subjective intent, that (3) qualified immunity is therefore never available. Such logic apparently approves the "protracted and complex" course of litigation in this case, runs afoul of *Harlow*'s concern that insubstantial claims be prevented from going to trial, and ensures that officials will be subject to the "peculiarly disruptive" inquiry into their subjective intent that the *Harlow* rule was designed to prevent. Such a rule would also allow plaintiffs to strip defendants of *Harlow*'s protections by a simple act of pleading—any minimally competent attorney (or pro se litigant) can convert any adverse decision into a motive-based tort, and thereby subject government officials to some measure of intrusion into their subjective worlds.

Such a result is quite inconsistent with the logic and underlying principles of *Harlow*. In order to preserve the protections that *Harlow* conferred, it is necessary to construct a qualified immunity test in this context that is also based exclusively on objective factors, and prevents plaintiffs from engaging in "peculiarly disruptive" subjective investigations until after the immunity inquiry has been resolved in their favor. The test I propose accomplishes this goal. Under this test, when a plaintiff alleges that an official's action was taken with an unconstitutional or otherwise unlawful motive, the defendant will be entitled to immunity and immediate dismissal of the suit if he can offer a lawful reason for his action and the plaintiff cannot establish, through objective evidence, that the offered reason is actually a pretext.

The Court's interpretation of *Harlow* does not differ from mine. ("Under [the *Harlow*] standard, a defense of qualified immunity may not be rebutted by evidence that the defendant's conduct was malicious or otherwise improperly motivated. Evidence concerning the defendant's subjective intent is simply irrelevant to that defense.") The Court does not, however, carry the *Harlow* principles to their logical extension. Its failure to discuss the issue explicitly makes it difficult to understand exactly why it rejects my position, but there appear to be two possibilities.

First, the Court appears concerned that an extension of *Harlow* qualified immunity to motive-based torts will mean that some meritorious claims will go unredressed. This is perhaps true, but it is not a sufficient reason to refuse to apply the doctrine. Every time a privilege is created or an immunity extended, it is understood that some meritorious claims will be dismissed that otherwise would have been heard. Courts and legislatures craft these immunities because it is thought that the societal benefit they confer outweighs whatever cost they create in terms of unremedied meritorious claims. In crafting our qualified immunity doctrine, we have always considered the public policy implications of our decisions.

In considering those implications here, it is desirable to reflect on the subspecies of First Amendment claims which we address in this case. Respondent Britton is a D.C. corrections officer; petitioner Crawford–El is a D.C. prisoner who was transferred from Spokane, Washington, to Marianna, Florida, with intermediate stops along the way. The action of Britton's that gave rise to this lawsuit was asking Crawford–El's brother-in-law to pick up boxes of the former's belongings for delivery to him, rather than shipping them directly to him in Florida. This act, considered by itself, would seem to be about as far from a violation of the First Amendment as can be conceived. But Crawford–El has alleged that Britton's decision to deliver his belongings to a relative was motivated by a desire to punish him for previous interviews with reporters that he had given, and lawsuits that he had filed. This claim of illicit motive, Crawford–El asserts, transforms a routine act in the course of prison administration into a constitutional tort.

The Court cites Pickering v. Board of Ed., 391 U.S. 563 (1968), as an example of this sort of tort. But *Pickering* is but a distant cousin to the present case; there the school board plainly stated that its reason for discharging the plaintiff teacher was his writing of a letter to a newspaper criticizing the board. It was not motivation that was disputed, but whether the First Amendment protected the writing of the letter. Closer in point is Branti v. Finkel, 445 U.S. 507 (1980), also cited by the Court, but there the act complained of was the dismissal of Republican assistants by the newly appointed Democratic public defender. Objective evidence—the discharging of members of one party by the newly appointed supervisor of another party, and their replacement by members of the supervisor's party—would likely have served to defeat a claim of qualified immunity had the defendant official attempted to offer a legitimate reason for firing the Republican assistants. Thus, the defendants in neither *Pickering* nor *Branti* would have been entitled to qualified immunity under the approach that I propose.

[Chief Justice Rehnquist distinguished the present case from the large category of "primary First Amendment cases, where the constitutional claim does not depend on motive at all."] The great body of our cases involving freedom of speech would, therefore, be unaffected by this approach to qualified immunity. It would apply prototypically to a case such as the present one: A public official is charged with doing a routine act in the normal course of her duties—an act which by itself has absolutely no connection with freedom of speech—but she is charged with having performed that act out of a desire to retaliate against the plaintiff because of his previous exercise of his right to speak freely. In this case, there was surely a legitimate reason for respondent's action, and there is no evidence in the record before ut that shows it to be pretextual. Under the Court's view, only a factfinder's ultimate determination of the motive with which she acted will resolve this case. I think the modest extension of *Harlow* which I propose should result in a judgment of qualified immunity for the respondent. . . .

The costs of the extension of *Harlow* that I propose would therefore be minor. The benefits would be significant, and we have recognized them before. As noted above, inquiries into the subjective state of mind of government officials are "peculiarly disruptive of effective government" and the threat of such inquiries will in some instances cause conscientious officials to shrink from making difficult choices. . . . This result is simply not faithful to *Harlow*'s underlying concerns.

■ JUSTICE SCALIA, with whom JUSTICE THOMAS joins, dissenting.

As I have observed earlier, our treatment of qualified immunity under § 1983 has not purported to be faithful to the common-law immunities that existed when § 1983 was enacted, and that the statute presumably intended to subsume. See Burns v. Reed, 500 U.S. 478, 498 n.1 (1991) (Scalia, J., concurring in judgment in part and dissenting in part). That is perhaps just as well. The § 1983 that the Court created in 1961 bears scant resemblance to what Congress enacted almost a century earlier. I refer, of course, to the holding of Monroe v. Pape, 365 U.S. 167 (1961), which converted an 1871 statute covering constitutional violations committed "*under color of* any statute, ordinance, regulation, custom, or usage of any State," 42 U.S.C. § 1983 (emphasis added), into a statute covering constitutional violations committed *without* the authority of any statute, ordinance, regulation, custom, or usage of any state, and indeed even constitutional violations committed in stark violation of state civil or criminal law. Applying normal common-law rules to the statute that *Monroe* created would carry us further and further from what any sane Congress could have enacted.

We find ourselves engaged, therefore, in the essentially legislative activity of crafting a sensible scheme of qualified immunities for the statute we have invented—rather than applying the common law embodied in the statute that Congress wrote. My preference is, in undiluted form, the approach suggested by Judge Silberman's concurring opinion in the Court of Appeals: extending the "objective reasonableness" test of Harlow v. Fitzgerald, 457 U.S. 800 (1982), to qualified immunity insofar as it relates to intent-based constitutional torts.

The Chief Justice's opinion . . . differs in a significant respect: it would allow the introduction of "objective evidence" that the constitutionally valid reason offered for the complained-of action "is actually a pretext." This would consist, presumably, of objective evidence regarding the state official's subjective intent—for example, remarks showing that he had a partisan-political animus against the plaintiff. The admission of such evidence produces a less subjective-free immunity than the one established by *Harlow*. Under that case, once the trial court finds that the constitutional right was not well established, it will not admit any "objective evidence" that the defendant *knew* he was violating the Constitution. The test I favor would apply a similar rule here: once the trial court finds that the asserted grounds for the official action were objectively valid (e.g., the person fired for alleged incompetence was indeed incompetent), it would not admit any proof that something other than those reasonable grounds was the genuine motive (e.g., the incompetent person fired was a Republican). This is of course a more severe restriction upon "intent-based" constitutional torts; I am less put off by that consequence than some may be, since I believe that *no* "intent-based" constitutional tort would have been actionable under the § 1983 that Congress enacted.

NOTES ON CLAIMS OF UNCONSTITUTIONAL MOTIVE AND ASHCROFT V. IQBAL

1. QUESTIONS AND COMMENTS ON *CRAWFORD–EL*

The progression of cases from *Harlow* through *Crawford–El* is arguably schizophrenic. It applies different standards to arguably analogous questions.

Recall that *Harlow* originally was susceptible to two readings. The Court said that "bare allegations of malice should not suffice to subject government officials either to the costs of trial or to the burdens of far-reaching discovery" and that officers "generally are shielded from liability for civil damages insofar as their conduct does not violate clearly established statutory or constitutional rights of which a reasonable person would have been aware." At the time of *Harlow*, no one could know for sure whether the Court meant to eliminate the subjective branch of qualified immunity entirely or only to require something more than "bare allegations of malice" before allowing claims to proceed to discovery.

Crawford–El adopted the more radical interpretation, concluding that evidence of the defendant's subjective intent is "simply irrelevant" to the defense of qualified immunity. But *Crawford–El* also said that the reasons for eliminating improper motive from qualified immunity did not apply to improper motive in the definition of constitutional violations. Proof that is "simply irrelevant" to the defense of qualified immunity (apparently because it is so difficult to manage) is nevertheless critical to establishing a motive-based constitutional violation.

Might it have been more sensible for the Court to follow the same approach to both issues? The question might be asked in two directions. On the one hand, if it is necessary to eliminate altogether the subjective branch of qualified immunity rather than deal with proof of improper motive, why is it not equally necessary to disallow such proof when it seeks to establish an unconstitutional motive for an otherwise legitimate act? On the other hand, if the palliatives described in *Crawford–El* are sufficient to enable trial courts to monitor the problems of proving improper motive when motive relates to the underlying right, why are those same techniques not also sufficient for the defense of qualified immunity? It seems odd to think that the drastic solution of making subjective bad faith irrelevant is required in the one context but not in the other.

2. HEIGHTENED PROOF VS. HEIGHTENED PLEADING

Crawford–El clearly rejected a heightened burden of proof for claims of unconstitutional motivation but was perhaps less clear in resolving the question of heightened pleading. On the one hand, the Court insisted that "questions regarding pleading, discovery, and summary judgment are most frequently and most effectively resolved either by the rulemaking process or the legislative process." On the other hand, the Court cited Justice Kennedy's concurrence in the judgment in Siegert v. Gilley, 500 U.S. 226, 236 (1991), for the ability of trial courts to "insist that the plaintiff 'put forward specific, nonconclusory factual allegations' that establish improper motive causing cognizable injury in order to survive a prediscovery motion for dismissal or summary judgment."

In *Siegert*, Kennedy approved a heightened pleading standard for malice alleged to overcome the defense of qualified immunity. (The *Siegert* majority did not reach this question.) In *Crawford–El*, the Court said that *no* allegation of malice, however specific and nonconclusory, can overcome qualified immunity once the defendant's actions have been shown to be objectively reasonable, but the Court refused to extend that approach to substantive claims that require proof of unconstitutional motivation. The Court nevertheless cited Kennedy's endorsement of heightened pleading as something on which a trial judge may insist. Does that mean that the Court approves a heightened pleading (but not proof) standard for claims involving unconstitutional motivation? Or only that the Court thinks that some requirement along these lines lies within the discretion of a trial judge? These questions arose in Ashcroft v. Iqbal, 556 U.S. 662 (2009), which is considered below.

3. *ASHCROFT V. IQBAL*

In Ashcroft v. Iqbal, 556 U.S. 662 (2009), the Court approached these questions from a third direction, interpreting the existing rules of procedure to impose a more demanding pleading standard in all cases, not just civil rights cases. *Iqbal* itself was a civil rights case in which the plaintiff, an alien detained following the terrorist attacks on September 11, 2001, brought a *Bivens* action against various federal officials. These included Attorney General John Ashcroft and FBI Director Robert Mueller, who allegedly violated Iqbal's constitutional rights by acting in their supervisory capacity to allow discrimination against him because he was an Arab and Muslim. Iqbal alleged that he was brutally treated after being designated a "person of interest" and confined to a detention facility that went under the acronym of ADMAX SHU, denoting the maximum security conditions of confinement in the federal prison system.

The defendants moved to dismiss the complaint for failure to state a claim. The District Court denied this motion and, on interlocutory appeal, was affirmed by the Court of Appeals. Although several lower-level officials at ADMAX SHU were also named as defendants, only the claims against Ashcroft and Mueller reached the Supreme Court. The Court ordered dismissal of these claims, subject only to the possibility that the plaintiff might be granted leave to amend his complaint.

Writing for the Court, Justice Kennedy first analyzed the elements of a claim of supervisory liability:

> The factors necessary to establish a *Bivens* violation will vary with the constitutional provision at issue. Where the claim is invidious discrimination in contravention of the First and Fifth Amendments, our decisions make clear that the plaintiff must plead and prove that the defendant acted with discriminatory purpose. Under extant precedent purposeful discrimination requires more than "intent as volition or intent as awareness of consequences." Personnel Administrator of Mass. v. Feeney, 442 U. S. 256, 279 (1979). It instead involves a decisionmaker's undertaking a course of action " 'because of,' not merely 'in spite of,' [the action's] adverse effects upon an identifiable group." Ibid. It follows that, to state a claim based on a violation of a clearly established right, respondent must plead sufficient factual matter to show that petitioners adopted and implemented the detention policies at issue not for a neutral, investigative reason

> but for the purpose of discriminating on account of race, religion, or national origin.
>
> Respondent disagrees. He argues that, under a theory of "supervisory liability," petitioners can be liable for "knowledge and acquiescence in their subordinates' use of discriminatory criteria to make classification decisions among detainees." That is to say, respondent believes a supervisor's mere knowledge of his subordinate's discriminatory purpose amounts to the supervisor's violating the Constitution. We reject this argument. Respondent's conception of "supervisory liability" is inconsistent with his accurate stipulation that petitioners may not be held accountable for the misdeeds of their agents. In a § 1983 suit or a *Bivens* action—where masters do not answer for the torts of their servants—the term "supervisory liability" is a misnomer. Absent vicarious liability, each Government official, his or her title notwithstanding, is only liable for his or her own misconduct. In the context of determining whether there is a violation of clearly established right to overcome qualified immunity, purpose rather than knowledge is required to impose *Bivens* liability on the subordinate for unconstitutional discrimination; the same holds true for an official charged with violations arising from his or her superintendent responsibilities.

The dissent by Justice Souter, joined by three other justices, framed the issue differently. They relied upon the concession by Ashcroft and Mueller in their brief "that they would be subject to supervisory liability if they 'had actual knowledge of the assertedly discriminatory nature of the classification of suspects as being "of high interest" and they were deliberately indifferent to that discrimination.' " Because of this concession, there had been "no briefing or argument on the proper scope of supervisory liability, much less the full-dress argument we normally require." Justice Souter accordingly would have assessed the sufficiency of the complaint based on a broader theory of supervisory liability than the majority allowed.

Having set a high bar for substantive liability, the Court easily found the allegations of the complaint inadequate. Because the plaintiff claimed discrimination only in the conditions of detention—as persons of "high interest" placed in a maximum security facility—the complaint had to "contain facts *plausibly showing* that petitioners purposefully adopted a policy of classifying post-September–11 detainees as 'of high interest' because of their race, religion, or national origin [emphasis added]." The requirement of plausibility came from an earlier decision dismissing a complaint for failure to contain plausible allegations of a conspiracy in restraint of trade in violation of the antitrust laws. Bell Atlantic Corp. v. Twombly, 550 U.S. 544 (2007). The *Iqbal* Court interpreted *Twombly* as requiring that conclusory allegations be disregarded:

> We begin our analysis by identifying the allegations in the complaint that are not entitled to the assumption of truth. Respondent pleads that petitioners "knew of, condoned, and willfully and maliciously agreed to subject [him]" to harsh conditions of confinement "as a matter of policy, solely on account of [his] religion, race, and/or national origin and for no legitimate penological interest." The complaint alleges that Ashcroft was the "principal architect" of this invidious policy, and that Mueller was "instrumental" in adopting and executing it. These bare assertions, much like the pleading of conspiracy in *Twombly*, amount to nothing more than a

"formulaic recitation of the elements" of a constitutional discrimination claim, 550 U.S., at 555, namely, that petitioners adopted a policy " 'because of,' not merely 'in spite of,' its adverse effects upon an identifiable group." *Feeney*, 442 U.S., at 279. As such, the allegations are conclusory and not entitled to be assumed true. *Twombly*, 550 U.S., at 554–55. To be clear, we do not reject these bald allegations on the ground that they are unrealistic or nonsensical. . . . It is the conclusory nature of respondent's allegations, rather than their extravagantly fanciful nature, that disentitles them to the presumption of truth.

We next consider the factual allegations in respondent's complaint to determine if they plausibly suggest an entitlement to relief. The complaint alleges that "the [FBI], under the direction of Defendant Mueller arrested and detained thousands of Arab Muslim men . . . as part of its investigation of the events of September 11." It further claims that "[t]he policy of holding post-September–11th detainees in highly restrictive conditions of confinement until they were 'cleared' by the FBI was approved by Defendants Ashcroft and Mueller in discussions in the weeks after September 11, 2001." Taken as true, these allegations are consistent with petitioners' purposefully designating detainees "of high interest" because of their race, religion, or national origin. But given more likely explanations, they do not plausibly establish this purpose.

The September 11 attacks were perpetrated by 19 Arab Muslim hijackers who counted themselves members in good standing of al Qaeda, an Islamic fundamentalist group. Al Qaeda was headed by another Arab Muslim—Osama bin Laden—and composed in large part of his Arab Muslim disciples. It should come as no surprise that a legitimate policy directing law enforcement to arrest and detain individuals because of their suspected link to the attacks would produce a disparate, incidental impact on Arab Muslims, even though the purpose of the policy was to target neither Arabs nor Muslims. On the facts respondent alleges the arrests Mueller oversaw were likely lawful and justified by his non-discriminatory intent to detain aliens who were illegally present in the United States and who had potential connections to those who committed terrorist acts. As between that "obvious alternative explanation" for the arrests, *Twombly*, 550 U.S., at 567, and the purposeful, invidious discrimination respondent asks us to infer, discrimination is not a plausible conclusion.

But even if the complaint's well-pleaded facts give rise to a plausible inference that respondent's arrest was the result of unconstitutional discrimination, that inference alone would not entitle respondent to relief. It is important to recall that respondent's complaint challenges neither the constitutionality of his arrest nor his initial detention in the MDC. Respondent's constitutional claims against petitioners rest solely on their ostensible "policy of holding post-September–11th detainees" in the ADMAX SHU once they were categorized as "of high interest." To prevail on that theory, the complaint must contain facts plausibly showing that petitioners purposefully adopted a policy of classifying post-September–11 detainees as "of high interest" because of their race, religion, or national origin.

This the complaint fails to do. Though respondent alleges that various other defendants, who are not before us, may have labeled him a person "of high interest" for impermissible reasons, his only factual allegation against petitioners accuses them of adopting a policy approving "restrictive conditions of confinement" for post-September–11 detainees until they were " 'cleared' by the FBI." Accepting the truth of that allegation, the complaint does not show, or even intimate, that petitioners purposefully housed detainees in the ADMAX SHU due to their race, religion, or national origin. All it plausibly suggests is that the Nation's top law enforcement officers, in the aftermath of a devastating terrorist attack, sought to keep suspected terrorists in the most secure conditions available until the suspects could be cleared of terrorist activity. Respondent does not argue, nor can he, that such a motive would violate petitioners' constitutional obligations. He would need to allege more by way of factual content to "nudg[e]" his claim of purposeful discrimination "across the line from conceivable to plausible." *Twombly*, 550 U.S., at 570. . . .

It is important to note, however, that we express no opinion concerning the sufficiency of respondent's complaint against the defendants who are not before us. Respondent's account of his prison ordeal alleges serious official misconduct that we need not address here. Our decision is limited to the determination that respondent's complaint does not entitle him to relief from petitioners.

4. QUESTIONS AND COMMENTS ON *IQBAL*

Iqbal lies at the intersection of pleading, supervisory liability, and qualified immunity. Different threads in the decision lead to different interpretations of its significance. As a pleading case, it contradicts the decisions disavowing any requirement of special pleading for civil rights claims.[a] In effect, it requires specificity in the plaintiff's allegations in order to achieve the greater "plausibility" now required to survive a motion to dismiss. As a case on supervisory liability, *Iqbal* goes to the circumstances in which high officials will be held liable for the actions of their subordinates, imposing the same requirements for proof of claims against them as for claims against lower-level officials. As a case on qualified immunity, *Iqbal* is narrowly focused on the burdens of litigation on high officials, singling them out for special protection because of the inevitable burdens that discovery would impose upon them. Claims against lower-level officials were not before the Court.

Purely as a pleading case, *Iqbal* is contextually far removed from the *Twombly* precedent on which it is based. *Twombly* was an antitrust case involving claims of a conspiracy in restraint of trade, which typically require detailed allegations of business practices and which, if not dismissed, often lead to massive discovery. A civil rights claim of discrimination, by contrast, normally focuses on the issue of discriminatory intent, which plaintiffs are allowed to plead generally under Federal Rule of Civil Procedure 9(b). Without discovery, the

---

[a] In several previous decisions, the Court insisted that the ordinary rules of pleading apply to civil rights cases. See Leatherman v. Tarrant County Narcotics Intelligence & Coordination Unit, 507 U.S. 163 (1993) (no requirement of special pleading for civil rights cases); Gomez v. Toledo, 446 U.S. 635 (1980) (defendant has burden of raising qualified immunity as an affirmative defense). These decisions suggested that any exceptional treatment for civil rights cases had to be made by the standard process of amending the rules, which requires approval by the Supreme Court on recommendation by a series of committees composed of judges, lawyers, and law professors. Any such change is then transmitted to Congress and takes effect only if Congress does not reject it within six months. See 28 U.S.C. §§ 2073–74. No such proposal for exceptional treatment of civil rights cases has emerged from the rulemaking process, nor has Congress enacted legislation on that subject.

plaintiff may have little way of substantiating more detailed allegations of discriminatory intent, particularly on the part of high-level officials such as Ashcroft and Mueller. All of these points were made by Justice Souter in dissent.

Together, *Iqbal* and *Twombly* mark a sharp departure from the previously accepted standards for pleading under the Federal Rules. Those standards went under the label of "notice pleading" and came from a case, like *Iqbal*, involving a civil rights claim. In Conley v. Gibson, 355 U.S. 41 (1957), the Court took an expansive approach to pleading in an era when it was also taking an expansive approach to civil rights. In *Conley*, the Court observed "that a complaint should not be dismissed for failure to state a claim unless it appears beyond doubt that the plaintiff can prove no set of facts in support of the claim which would entitle him to relief." Although this statement was widely quoted in subsequent decisions, it was not always accepted at face value, which would effectively have required that no complaints be dismissed. Even so, *Conley* greatly constrained the power of district judges to dismiss at the pleading stage, leaving most cases to proceed to discovery and summary judgment. *Iqbal* and *Twombly* lifted those constraints and restored to district judges the power to curtail litigation when they deem the plaintiff's allegations implausible.

Civil rights claims alleging supervisory liability, as in *Iqbal*, are particularly susceptible to dismissal for this reason. This form of liability raises many of the same issues as municipal liability, discussed later in this chapter. Officials such as Ashcroft and Mueller act almost exclusively through their subordinates. Those subordinates remain available as targets for civil rights actions. Adding supervisory officials as defendants certainly increases the visibility of the litigation and may perhaps increase the size of award in the event that liability is established. Claims against the Attorney General and the Director of the FBI can more readily be litigated as claims against the Department of Justice, even if they remain formally only claims against these officers in their individual capacities. Claims against high officials also raise questions about vicarious liability under the common law theory of respondeat superior for the actions of lower-level officials within the scope of their employment, or liability for various omissions, such as deliberate indifference to the known wrongful acts of lower-level officials. The Court rejected both of these theories of supervisory liability in *Iqbal*, as it has rejected similar theories of municipal liability under § 1983. The Court instead insisted that liability for supervisors conform to the same theories as liability for their subordinates.

As a pleading problem, *Iqbal* emerged as a solution to the problem posed in *Crawford–El*: how to reconcile a constitutional violation that requires proof of subjective motivation with a defense of qualified immunity that raises only the objective issue whether violation of a clearly established constitutional right which would have been known to a reasonable person. After *Iqbal*, the baseline requirements for pleading a constitutional violation based on improper motive require allegations of intent that are neither conclusory nor implausible. Without quite saying so, the Supreme Court has read into the requirements of a sufficient complaint some version of heightened pleading. Bald allegations of intent are likely to be ignored. The complaint now has to contain much more than a conclusory allegation of "discriminatory intent." Moreover, the allegations must go beyond recounting practices of government that can plausibly be construed as the legitimate response of public officials to the problems that they confront.

Detailed allegations of unconstitutional motive, if plausible, are likely to meet the objective requirements for defeating qualified immunity. Iqbal himself alleged that the defendants' policies had a disparate impact on Arabs and Muslims, allegations which the Court found insufficient to plead intentional discrimination on the basis of race, national origin, and religion. But what if he had alleged that all, or nearly all, detainees sent to ADMAX SHU were Arabs or Muslims? Would that have been sufficient to allow the case to go forward to discovery and trial? If proved, would these allegations have overcome a defense of qualified immunity? Recall that the claims against lower-level officials were not addressed in *Iqbal*. Are the allegations of discrimination against these officials, based on the details recounted in the complaint of the particularly harsh treatment the plaintiff received, more plausible than those against the Attorney General and the Director of the FBI?

In the absence of a curative amendment, dismissal of a complaint for failure to state a claim precludes further litigation, thus avoiding all the attendant costs that litigation imposes on high officials. Moreover, the defendant can make the motion to dismiss early in the litigation, before raising the defense of qualified immunity, or alternatively, by raising it along with the defense of immunity in the answer. The defendants in *Iqbal* chose the former alternative, and their motion was denied. The Supreme Court allowed an interlocutory appeal for much the same reasons that it allows an appeal from denial of qualified immunity. In a preliminary holding on this issue, the Court emphasized the role of qualified immunity in protecting government officials from the burdens of litigation, especially those in high office with broad responsibilities. The Court returned to this theme at the end of its opinion. Responding to the plaintiff's argument that discovery against such officials could be limited, the Court reasoned that discovery would inevitably be burdensome: "Even if petitioners are not yet themselves subject to discovery orders, then, they would not be free from the burdens of discovery." On the contrary, the Court felt "impelled to give real content to the concept of qualified immunity for high-level officials who must be neither deterred nor distracted from the vigorous performance of their duties."

Like the Court's holding on supervisory liability, its discussion of qualified immunity raises the question of just how broad its holding really is. If this were only a pleading case, then the requirement of nonconclusory, plausible pleading would apply across the board, to any kind of claim, whether or not it involved civil rights, supervisory liability, or qualified immunity. Yet the Court's focus on the particular kind of claim before it and the particular officials involved suggests that the holding might be narrower. If *Iqbal* is regarded as the solution to the problem posed by *Crawford–El*, should it be limited to that context? Or does the Court's reliance on general standards of pleading, derived from the antitrust litigation in *Twombly*, necessarily make the decision applicable to civil litigation generally? These questions are likely to be authoritatively answered only in future cases.

5. BIBLIOGRAPHY ON *IQBAL*

Iqbal has generated a cottage industry of commentary among civil rights and procedure scholars. Several symposia have examined aspects of the decision. See Reflections on *Iqbal*: Discerning Its Rule, Grappling with Its Implications, 114 Penn St. L. Rev. 1143 (2010) (with articles, in addition to those cited above, by Justin Houser, Nancy A. Welsh, Nancy A. Welsh, Ray

Worthy Campbell, Jeffrey J. Rachlinski, James R. Maxeiner, Victor C. Romero, Ramzi Kassem, Shoba Sivaprasad Wadhia, Lee H. Rosenthal); Pondering *Iqbal*, 14 Lewis & Clark L. Rev. 1 (2010) (with articles, in addition to those cited above, by Edward Brunet, Suja A. Thomas, Scott Dodson, Suzette M. Malveaux, Hillel Y. Levin, A. Benjamin Spencer, Michael C. Dorf, Juliet P. Stumpf, and Stephen I. Vladeck).

An important study from the Federal Judicial Center has examined pleading decisions after *Iqbal* and found no increase in the rate at which complaints have been dismissed. The study did find an increase in the rate of filing motions to dismiss, but not the rate at which such motions were granted without leave to amend. This finding specifically included both civil rights and employment discrimination cases (although it excluded prisoner and pro se cases). Joe S. Cecil et al., Motions to Dismiss for Failure to State A Claim after *Iqbal*: Report to the Judicial Conference Advisory Committee on Civil Rules, available at http://ssrn.com/abstract=1878646. If this study is correct, does it imply that the concern about *Iqbal* is much ado about nothing? Or might the decision have discouraged precisely the complaints that would not survive a motion to dismiss?

For articles concerned with the implications of *Iqbal* for civil rights cases, see, e.g., John M. Greabe, *Iqbal*, *Al–Kidd* and Pleading Past Qualified Immunity: What the Cases Mean and How They Demonstrate a Need to Eliminate the Immunity Doctrines from Constitutional Tort Law, 20 Wm. & Mary Bill of Rts. J. 1 (2011); Kit Kinports, *Iqbal* and Supervisory Immunity, 114 Penn St. L. Rev. 1291 (2010) (criticizing *Iqbal* for abandoning supervisory liability and analyzing how qualified immunity should apply in such cases); Sheldon Nahmod, Constitutional Torts, Over–Deterrence, and Supervisory Liability After *Iqbal*, 14 Lewis & Clark L. Rev. 279 (2010) (approving the conclusion, although not the reasoning, of the opinion in requiring proof of supervisors' intent when it is an element of the underlying constitutional violation); James E. Pfander, *Iqbal*, *Bivens*, and the Role of Judge–Made Law in Constitutional Litigation, 114 Penn St. L. Rev. 1387 (2010) (contrasting the judicial creativity evident in *Iqbal* and in qualified immunity cases with the disclaimer of judicial authority to allow recovery against federal officers under *Bivens*); Howard W. Wasserman, *Iqbal*, Procedural Mismatches, and Civil Rights Litigation, 14 Lewis & Clark L. Rev. 157 (2010) (arguing that *Iqbal* will lead to a substantial decrease in the enforcement of civil rights because of the specificity it requires for a plausible claim).[b]

6. GENERAL BIBLIOGRAPHY

The general subject of qualified immunity has generated an enormous literature, most of it critical of current law. Even limiting the search to recent publications produces a long list, including: Michael Avery, Paying for Silence:

---

[b] For additional articles on *Iqbal* as a case on general rules of pleading, see Kevin M. Clermont, Three Myths About *Twombly–Iqbal,* 45 Wake Forest L. Rev. 1337 (2010); Scott Dodson, New Pleading, New Discovery, 109 Mich. L. Rev. 53 (2010); Robin J. Effron, The Plaintiff Neutrality Principle: Pleading Complex Litigation in the Era of *Twombly* and *Iqbal*, 51 Wm. & Mary L. Rev. 1997 (2010); Richard A. Epstein, Of Pleading and Discovery: Reflections on *Twombly* and *Iqbal* with Special Reference to Antitrust, 2011 U. Ill. L. Rev. 187 (2011); Peter Julian, Comment, Charles E. Clark and Simple Pleading: Against a "Formalism of Generality," 104 Nw. U. L. Rev. 1179 (2010); Arthur R. Miller, From *Conley* to *Twombly* to *Iqbal*: A Double Play on the Federal Rules of Civil Procedure, 60 Duke L.J. 1 (2010); Adam N. Steinman, The Pleading Problem, 62 Stan. L. Rev. 1293 (2010).

The Liability of Police Officers under Section 1983 for Suppressing Exculpatory Evidence, 13 Temple Pol. & C.R. L. Rev. 1 (2003); Barbara E. Armacost, Qualified Immunity: Ignorance Excused, 51 Vand. L. Rev. 583 (1998) (focusing on the function of clearly established law in providing notice of illegality to government officers); Alan K. Chen, Rosy Pictures and Renegade Officials: The Slow Death of *Monroe v. Pape*, 78 U.M.K.C. L. Rev. 889 (2010) (examining alternative remedies in evaluating the law of § 1983); Alan K. Chen, The Facts About Qualified Immunity, 55 Emory L.J. 229 (2006) (describing the unresolvable tension between the desire to resolve unmeritorious claims pre-trial and the inevitably fact-specific nature of many qualified immunity issues); Alan K. Chen, The Ultimate Standard: Qualified Immunity in the Age of Constitutional Balancing Tests, 81 Iowa L. Rev. 261 (1995) (examining qualified immunity in terms of the familiar distinction between rules and standards and concluding that it should be more rule-like); John M. Greabe, A Better Path for Constitutional Tort Law, 25 Const. Commentary 189 (2008) (arguing that the *defense* of qualified immunity should be eliminated and replaced by a reconceptualized *cause of action* that would deploy § 1983 to remedy a range of entitlements narrower than the underlying constitutional rights); John C. Jeffries, Jr., The Liability Rule for Constitutional Torts, 99 Va. L. Rev. 207 (2013) (criticizing application of qualified immunity to certain rights); John C. Jeffries, Jr., What's Wrong With Qualified Immunity?, 62 Fla. L. Rev. 1 (2010) (criticizing qualified immunity as administered by the lower courts as "complicated, unstable, and overprotective of government officers"); John C. Jeffries, Jr., Disaggregating Constitutional Torts, 110 Yale L.J. 259 (2000) (arguing that qualified immunity should take account of the presence or absence of alternative remedies); Sheldon Nahmod, The Restructuring of Narrative and Empathy in Section 1983 Cases, 72 Chi.–Kent L. Rev. 819 (1997) (interpreting the law of § 1983 as instructing the "judge, and *not* the jury, to empathize with the defendant . . . , thus forcing § 1983 plaintiffs to bear their own losses even when their constitutional rights are violated"); Cornelia T.L. Pillard, Taking Fiction Seriously: The Strange Results of Public Officials' Individual Liability Under *Bivens*, 88 Geo. L.J. 65 (1999) (criticizing qualified immunity and the entire scheme of officer liability); Teressa E. Ravenell, Cause and Conviction: The Role of Causation in § 1983 Wrongful Conviction Claims, 81 Temp. L. Rev. 689 (2008) (examining proximate cause in wrongful conviction cases and concluding that the limitations of proximate cause are unnecessary and redundant for defendants enjoying qualified immunity).

NOTES ON QUALIFIED IMMUNITY AND PRIVATE ACTORS

1. INTRODUCTION

Section 1983 imposes liability only when a person acts "under color" of state law. Thus, § 1983 defendants are usually public officials or entities. Nonetheless, private individuals *can* be held liable under § 1983 when they act in concert with state actors or when they exercise power delegated by the state.[a] The question then arises whether private actors potentially liable under § 1983 are entitled to the same qualified immunity that officers of the state would enjoy. The Supreme Court has addressed this question twice.

[a] The question of state action is addressed below in Section 7 of this Chapter.

2. *WYATT V. COLE*

Wyatt v. Cole, 504 U.S. 158 (1992), involved private parties who invoked state attachment statutes and were sued under § 1983 when those statutes were later declared unconstitutional. The Court held that they were not entitled to qualified immunity.

Writing for the Court, Justice O'Connor said that "the qualified immunity recognized in Harlow v. Fitzgerald, 457 U.S. 800 (1982), acts to safeguard government, and thereby to protect the public at large, not to benefit its agents." She continued:

> These rationales are not transferable to private parties. Although principles of equality and fairness may suggest . . . that private citizens who rely unsuspectingly on state laws they did not create and may have no reason to believe are invalid should have some protection from liability, as do their government counterparts, such interests are not sufficiently similar to the traditional purposes of qualified immunity to justify such an expansion. [P]rivate parties hold no office requiring them to exercise discretion; nor are they principally concerned with enhancing the public good. Accordingly, extending *Harlow* qualified immunity to private parties would have no bearing on whether public officials are able to act forcefully and decisively in their jobs or on whether qualified applicants enter public service. Moreover, unlike with government officials performing discretionary functions, the public interest will not be unduly impaired if private individuals are required to proceed to trial to resolve their legal disputes. In short, the nexus between private parties and the historic purposes of qualified immunity is simply too attenuated to justify such an extension of our doctrine of immunity.

The Court's decision, however, was narrow:

> The precise issue [we decide] is whether qualified immunity, as enunciated in *Harlow*, is available for private defendants faced with § 1983 liability for invoking a state replevin, garnishment, or attachment statute. That answer is no. In so holding, however, we do not foreclose the possibility that private defendants faced with § 1983 liability . . . could be entitled to an affirmative defense based on good faith and/or probable cause or that § 1983 suits against private, rather than governmental parties, could require plaintiffs to carry additional burdens. Because those issues are not before us, . . . we leave them to another day.

Justice Kennedy, joined by Justice Scalia, concurred in a separate opinion. Kennedy said that "the essence of the wrong itself" alleged to have occurred on the facts of *Wyatt* required the plaintiffs to prove that the defendants acted "with malice and without probable cause." He agreed that the Court's qualified immunity decisions that had removed the "malice" component from the equation should not be extended to private defendants. The Chief Justice, joined by Justices Souter and Thomas, dissented.

3. *RICHARDSON V. MCKNIGHT*

In Richardson v. McKnight, 521 U.S. 399 (1997), the Court considered whether guards at a privately run correctional facility were entitled to the same qualified immunity that prison guards at a state-run facility enjoy under

Procunier v. Navarette, 434 U.S. 555 (1978). In a five-to-four decision, the Court held that they were not.

Justice Breyer's opinion for the Court found no " 'firmly rooted' tradition of immunity applicable to privately employed prison guards." As for the policy question, the Court held that qualified immunity for private prison guards was not necessary to serve the central goal of qualified immunity, namely "protecting the public from unwarranted timidity on the part of public officials." Butz v. Economou, 438 U.S. 478, 506 (1978). Breyer identified market forces as the key distinction between public and private guards:

> First, the most important special government immunity-producing concern—unwarranted timidity—is less likely present, or at least is not special, when a private company subject to competitive market pressures operates a prison. Competitive pressures mean not only that a firm whose guards are too aggressive will face damages that raise costs, thereby threatening its replacement, but also that a firm whose guards are too timid will face threats of replacement by other firms with records that demonstrate their ability to do both a safer and a more effective job.
>
> These ordinary marketplace pressures are present here. The private prison guards before us work for a large, multistate private prison management firm. . . . It must buy insurance sufficient to compensate victims of civil rights torts. And, since the firm's first contract expires after three years, its performance is disciplined, not only by state review, but also by pressure from potentially competing firms who can try to take its place.
>
> In other words, marketplace pressures provide the private firm with strong incentives to avoid overly timid, insufficiently vigorous, unduly fearful, or "non-arduous" employee job performance. And the contract's provisions—including those that might permit employee indemnification and avoid many civil-service restrictions—grant this private firm freedom to respond to those market pressures through rewards and penalties that operate directly upon its employees. To this extent, the employees before us resemble those of other private firms and differ from government employees. . . .
>
> Second, "privatization" helps to meet the immunity-related need "to ensure that talented candidates" are "not deterred by the threat of damages suits from entering public service." Wyatt v. Cole, 504 U.S. 158, 167 (1992). It does so in part because of the comprehensive insurance-coverage requirements just mentioned. The insurance increases the likelihood of employee indemnification and to that extent reduces the employment-discouraging fear of unwarranted liability potential applicants face. Because privatization law also frees the private prison-management firm from many civil service law restraints, it permits the private firm, unlike a government department, to offset any increased employee liability risk with higher pay or extra benefits. In respect to this second government-immunity-related purpose then, it is difficult to find a *special* need for immunity, for the guards' employer can operate like other private firms; it need not operate like a typical government department.

The Court closed its opinion with several caveats, the most important of which left open the question whether private defendants might assert "a special 'good faith' defense" in the terms anticipated in *Wyatt*.

Justice Scalia's dissent took issue with both the majority's account of the history of immunity for private prison guards and with its policy analysis:

> First of all, it is fanciful to speak of the consequences of "market" pressures in a regime where public officials are the only purchaser, and other people's money the medium of payment. . . . Secondly and more importantly, however, if one assumes a political regime that *is* bent on emulating the market in its purchase of prison services, it is almost certainly the case that, short of mismanagement so severe as to provoke a prison riot, *price* (not discipline) will be the predominating factor in such a regime's selection of a contractor. A contractor's price must depend upon its costs; lawsuits increase costs; and "fearless" maintenance of discipline increases lawsuits. The incentive to down-play discipline will exist, moreover, even in those states where the politicians' zeal for market-emulation and budget-cutting has waned, and where prison-management contract renewal is virtually automatic: the more cautious the prison guards, the fewer the lawsuits, the higher the profits. In sum, it seems that "market-competitive"private prison managers have even greater need than civil-service prison managers for immunity as an incentive to discipline.
>
> [O]ne more possible rationale for denying immunity to private prison guards [is] worth discussing, albeit briefly. It is a theory so implausible that the Court avoids mentioning it, even though it was the primary reason given in the Court of Appeals decision that the Court affirms. It is that officers of private prisons are more likely than officers of state prisons to violate prisoners' constitutional rights because they work for a profit motive, and hence an added degree of deterrence is needed to keep these officers in line. The Court of Appeals offered no evidence to support its bald assertion that private prison guards operate with different incentives than state prison guards, and gave no hint as to how prison guards might possibly increase their employers' profits by violating constitutional rights. One would think that private prison managers, whose § 1983 damages come out of their own pockets, as compared with public prison managers, whose § 1983 damages come out of the public purse, would, if anything, be more careful in training their employees to avoid constitutional infractions. And in fact, States having experimented with prison privatization commonly report that the overall caliber of the services provided to prisoners has actually improved in scope and quality. Matters Relating To The Federal Bureau Of Prisons: Hearing before the Subcommittee on Crime of the House Committee on the Judiciary, 104th Cong., 1st Sess., 110 (1995).

4. QUESTIONS AND COMMENTS

How ought the issue of a qualified immunity for private defendants to be analyzed? In his dissent in *Wyatt*, Chief Justice Rehnquist questioned whether "some practical difference will result from recognizing a defense but not an immunity." If suits involving private defendants are to involve issues of "good faith and/or probable cause," as forecast in *Wyatt*, are there practical differences between viewing the issues as: (a) part of the description of the wrong; (b) an affirmative defense; or (c) a qualified immunity? If choice among these options does make a practical difference, which more accurately reflects the policies that ought to control the liability of private defendants sued under § 1983? Is it sound to make a different choice for public officials?

SUBSECTION C: THE SEQUENCE OF DECISION IN QUALIFIED IMMUNITY CASES

Wilson v. Layne

Supreme Court of the United States, 1999.
526 U.S. 603.

■ CHIEF JUSTICE REHNQUIST delivered the opinion of the Court.

While executing an arrest warrant in a private home, police officers invited representatives of the media to accompany them. We hold that such a "media ride along" does violate the Fourth Amendment, but that because the state of the law was not clearly established at the time the search in this case took place, the officers are entitled to the defense of qualified immunity.

I

In early 1992, the Attorney General of the United States approved "Operation Gunsmoke," a special national fugitive apprehension program in which United States Marshals worked with state and local police to apprehend dangerous criminals. . . . One of the dangerous fugitives identified as a target of "Operation Gunsmoke" was Dominic Wilson, the son of petitioners Charles and Geraldine Wilson. Dominic Wilson had violated his probation on previous felony charges of robbery, theft, and assault with intent to rob, and the police computer listed "caution indicators" that he was likely to be armed, to resist arrest, and to "assault police." The computer also listed his address as 909 North StoneStreet Avenue in Rockville, Maryland. Unknown to the police, this was actually the home of petitioners, Dominic Wilson's parents. Thus, in April 1992, the Circuit Court for Montgomery County issued three arrest warrants for Dominic Wilson, one for each of his probation violations. The warrants were each addressed to "any duly authorized peace officer," and commanded such officers to arrest him and bring him "immediately" before the Circuit Court to answer an indictment as to his probation violation. The warrants made no mention of media presence or assistance.

In the early morning hours of April 16, 1992, a Gunsmoke team of Deputy United States Marshals and Montgomery County police officers assembled to execute the Dominic Wilson warrants. The team was accompanied by a reporter and a photographer from the *Washington Post*, who had been invited by the marshals to accompany them on their mission as part of a Marshal's Service ride-along policy.

At around 6:45 a.m., the officers, with media representatives in tow, entered the dwelling at 909 North StoneStreet Avenue in the Lincoln Park neighborhood of Rockville. Petitioners Charles and Geraldine Wilson were still in bed when they heard the officers enter the home. Petitioner Charles Wilson, dressed only in a pair of briefs, ran into the living room to investigate. Discovering at least five men in street clothes with guns in his living room, he angrily demanded that they state their business, and repeatedly cursed the officers. Believing him to be an angry Dominic Wilson, the officers quickly subdued him on the floor. Geraldine Wilson next entered the living room to investigate, wearing only a nightgown. She observed her husband being restrained by the armed officers.

When their protective sweep was completed, the officers learned that Dominic Wilson was not in the house, and they departed. During the time that the officers were in the home, the *Washington Post* photographer took numerous pictures. The print reporter was also apparently in the living room observing the confrontation between the police and Charles Wilson. At no time, however, were the reporters involved in the execution of the arrest warrant. The *Washington Post* never published its photographs of the incident.

Petitioners sued the law enforcement officials in their personal capacities for money damages under Bivens v. Six Unknown Fed. Narcotics Agents, 403 U.S. 388 (1971) (the U.S. Marshals Service respondents) and 42 U.S.C. § 1983 (the Montgomery County Sheriff's Department respondents). They contended that the officers' actions in bringing members of the media to observe and record the attempted execution of the arrest warrant violated their Fourth Amendment rights. The District Court denied respondents' motion for summary judgment on the basis of qualified immunity.

On interlocutory appeal to the Court of Appeals, a divided panel reversed and held that respondents were entitled to qualified immunity. The case was twice reheard en banc, where a divided Court of Appeals again upheld the defense of qualified immunity. The Court of Appeals declined to decide whether the actions of the police violated the Fourth Amendment. It concluded instead that because no court had held (at the time of the search) that media presence during a police entry into a residence violated the Fourth Amendment, the right allegedly violated by petitioners was not "clearly established" and thus qualified immunity was proper. Five judges dissented, arguing that the officers' actions did violate the Fourth Amendment, and that the clearly established protections of the Fourth Amendment were violated in this case.

Recognizing a split among the Circuits on this issue, we granted certiorari . . . and now affirm the Court of Appeals, although by different reasoning.

II

The petitioners sued the federal officials under *Bivens* and the state officials under § 1983. Both *Bivens* and § 1983 allow a plaintiff to seek money damages from government officials who have violated his Fourth Amendment rights. But government officials performing discretionary functions generally are granted a qualified immunity and are "shielded from liability for civil damages insofar as their conduct does not violate clearly established statutory or constitutional rights of which a reasonable person would have known." Harlow v. Fitzgerald, 457 U.S. 800, 818 (1982).

Although this case involves suits under both § 1983 and *Bivens*, the qualified immunity analysis is identical under either cause of action. A court evaluating a claim of qualified immunity "must first determine whether the plaintiff has alleged the deprivation of an actual constitutional right at all, and if so, proceed to determine whether that right was clearly established at the time of the alleged violation." Conn v. Gabbert, 526 U.S. 286, 290 (1999). This order of procedure is designed to "spare a defendant not only unwarranted liability, but unwarranted demands customarily imposed upon those defending a long drawn-out lawsuit." Siegert v. Gilley, 500 U.S. 226, 232 (1991). Deciding the constitutional question before addressing the qualified immunity question also promotes clarity in the legal standards for official conduct, to the benefit of both the officers and the general public. See County of Sacramento v. Lewis, 523 U.S. 833, 840–42, n.5 (1998). We now turn to the Fourth Amendment question.

In 1604, an English court made the now-famous observation that "the house of every one is to him as his castle and fortress, as well for his defence against injury and violence, as for his repose." Semayne's Case, 77 Eng. Rep. 194, 5 Co. Rep. 91a, 91b, 195 (K.B.). . . . The Fourth Amendment embodies this centuries-old principle of respect for the privacy of the home. . . . Our decisions have applied these basic principles of the Fourth Amendment to situations, like those in this case, in which police enter a home under the authority of an arrest warrant in order to take into custody the suspect named in the warrant. In Payton v. New York, 445 U.S. 573, 602 (1980), we . . . decided that "an arrest warrant founded on probable cause implicitly carries with it the limited authority to enter a dwelling in which the suspect lives when there is reason to believe the suspect is within."

Here, of course, the officers had such a warrant, and they were undoubtedly entitled to enter the Wilson home in order to execute the arrest warrant for Dominic Wilson. But it does not necessarily follow that they were entitled to bring a newspaper reporter and a photographer with them. In Horton v. California, 496 U.S. 128, 140 (1990), we held "if the scope of the search exceeds that permitted by the terms of a validly issued warrant or the character of the relevant exception from the warrant requirement, the subsequent seizure is unconstitutional without more." While this does not mean that every police action while inside a home must be explicitly authorized by the text of the warrant, the Fourth Amendment does require that police actions in execution of a warrant be related to the objectives of the authorized intrusion.

Certainly the presence of reporters inside the home was not related to the objectives of the authorized intrusion. Respondents concede that the reporters did not engage in the execution of the warrant, and did not assist the police in their task. The reporters therefore were not present for any reason related to the justification for police entry into the home—the apprehension of Dominic Wilson.

This is not a case in which the presence of the third parties directly aided in the execution of the warrant. . . . Respondents argue that the presence of the *Washington Post* reporters in the Wilsons' home nonetheless served a number of legitimate law enforcement purposes. . . . It may well be that media ride-alongs further the law enforcement objectives of the police in a general sense, but that is not the same as furthering the purposes of the search. Were such generalized "law enforcement objectives" themselves sufficient to trump the Fourth Amendment, the protections guaranteed by that Amendment's text would be significantly watered down. . . . We hold that it is a violation of the Fourth Amendment for police to bring members of the media or other third parties into a home during the execution of a warrant when the presence of the third parties in the home was not in aid of the execution of the warrant.

III

Since the police action in this case violated the petitioners' Fourth Amendment right, we now must decide whether this right was clearly established at the time of the search. As noted above, government officials performing discretionary functions generally are granted a qualified immunity and are "shielded from liability for civil damages insofar as their conduct does not violate clearly established statutory or constitutional rights of which a reasonable person would have known." *Harlow v. Fitzgerald*, 457 U.S. at 818. What this means in practice is that "whether an official protected by qualified immunity may be held personally liable for an allegedly unlawful official action generally turns on the 'objective legal reasonableness' of the action, assessed in light of the legal rules that were 'clearly established' at the time it was taken." Anderson v. Creighton, 483 U.S. 635, 639 (1987) (citing *Harlow*, supra, at 819).

In *Anderson*, we explained that what "clearly established" means in this context depends largely "upon the level of generality at which the relevant 'legal rule' is to be established." "Clearly established" for purposes of qualified immunity means that "the contours of the right must be sufficiently clear that a reasonable official would understand that what he is doing violates that right. This is not to say that an official action is protected by qualified immunity unless the very action in question has previously been held unlawful, but it is to say that in the light of pre-existing law the unlawfulness must be apparent."

It could plausibly be asserted that any violation of the Fourth Amendment is "clearly established," since it is clearly established that the protections of the Fourth Amendment apply to the actions of police. Some variation of this theory of qualified immunity is urged upon us by the petitioners and seems to have been at the core of the dissenting opinion in the Court of Appeals. However, as we explained in *Anderson*, the right allegedly violated must be defined at the appropriate level of specificity before a court can determine if it was clearly established. In this case, the appropriate question is the objective inquiry of whether a reasonable officer could have believed that bringing members of the media into a home during the execution of an arrest warrant was lawful, in light of clearly established law and the information the officers possessed.

We hold that it was not unreasonable for a police officer in April 1992 to have believed that bringing media observers along during the execution of an arrest warrant (even in a home) was lawful. First, the constitutional question presented by this case is by no means open and shut. The Fourth Amendment protects the rights of homeowners from entry without a warrant, but there was a warrant here. The question is whether the invitation to the media exceeded the scope of the search authorized by the warrant. Accurate media coverage of police activities serves an important public purpose, and it is not obvious from the general principles of the Fourth Amendment that the conduct of the officers in this case violated the Amendment.

Second, although media ride-alongs of one sort or another had apparently become a common police practice, in 1992 there were no judicial opinions holding that this practice became unlawful when it entered a home. The only published decision directly on point was a state intermediate court decision which, though it did not engage in an extensive Fourth Amendment analysis, nonetheless held that such conduct was not unreasonable. Prahl v. Brosamle, 98 Wis. 2d 130, 154–55, 295 N.W.2d 768, 782

(App. 1980). From the federal courts, the parties have only identified two unpublished District Court decisions dealing with media entry into homes, each of which upheld the search on unorthodox non-Fourth Amendment right to privacy theories. Moncrief v. Hanton, 10 Media L. Rep. 1620 (N.D. Ohio 1984); Higbee v. Times–Advocate, 5 Media L. Rep. 2372 (S.D. Cal. 1980). These cases, of course, can not "clearly establish" that media entry into homes during a police ride-along violates the Fourth Amendment.

At a slightly higher level of generality, petitioners point to Bills v. Aseltine, 958 F.2d 697 (6th Cir. 1992), in which the Court of Appeals for the Sixth Circuit held that there were material issues of fact precluding summary judgment on the question of whether police exceeded the scope of a search warrant by allowing a private security guard to participate in the search to identify stolen property other than that described in the warrant. *Bills*, which was decided a mere five weeks before the events of this case, did anticipate today's holding that police may not bring along third parties during an entry into a private home pursuant to a warrant for purposes unrelated to those justifying the warrant. However, we cannot say that even in light of *Bills*, the law on third-party entry into homes was clearly established in April 1992. Petitioners have not brought to our attention any cases of controlling authority in their jurisdiction at the time of the incident which clearly established the rule on which they seek to rely, nor have they identified a consensus of cases of persuasive authority such that a reasonable officer could not have believed that his actions were lawful.

Finally, important to our conclusion was the reliance by the United States marshals in this case on a Marshal's Service ride-along policy which explicitly contemplated that media who engaged in ride-alongs might enter private homes with their cameras as part of fugitive apprehension arrests. The Montgomery County Sheriff's Department also at this time had a ride-along program that did not expressly prohibit media entry into private homes. Such a policy, of course, could not make reasonable a belief that was contrary to a decided body of case law. But here the state of the law as to third parties accompanying police on home entries was at best undeveloped, and it was not unreasonable for law enforcement officers to look and rely on their formal ride-along policies.

Given such an undeveloped state of the law, the officers in this case cannot have been "expected to predict the future course of constitutional law." Procunier v. Navarette, 434 U.S. 555, 556 (1978). Between the time of the events of this case and today's decision, a split among the federal circuits in fact developed on the question whether media ride-alongs that enter homes subject the police to money damages [citing cases]. If judges thus disagree on a constitutional question, it is unfair to subject police to money damages for picking the losing side of the controversy.

For the foregoing reasons, the judgment of the Court of Appeals is affirmed.

■ JUSTICE STEVENS, concurring in part and dissenting in part.

Like every other federal appellate judge who has addressed the question, I share the Court's opinion that it violates the Fourth Amendment for police to bring members of the media or other third parties into a private dwelling during the execution of a warrant unless the homeowner has consented or the presence of the third parties is in aid of the execution of the warrant. I therefore join Parts I and II of the Court's opinion.

In my view, however, the homeowner's right to protection against this type of trespass was clearly established long before April 16, 1992. My sincere respect for the competence of the typical member of the law enforcement profession precludes my assent to the suggestion that "a reasonable officer could have believed that bringing members of the media into a home during the execution of an arrest warrant was lawful." I therefore disagree with the Court's resolution of the conflict in the circuits on the qualified immunity issue.[1] . . .

I

In its decision today the Court has not announced a new rule of constitutional law. Rather, it has refused to recognize an entirely unprecedented request for an exception to a well-established principle. Police action in the execution of a warrant must be strictly limited to the objectives of the authorized intrusion. That principle, like the broader protection provided by the Fourth Amendment itself, represents the confluence of two important sources: our English forefathers' traditional respect for the sanctity of the private home and the American colonists' hatred of the general warrant. . . .

During my service on the Court, I have heard lawyers argue scores of cases raising Fourth Amendment issues. Generally speaking, the members of the Court have been sensitive to the needs of the law enforcement community. In virtually all of them at least one Justice thought that the police conduct was reasonable. In fact, in only a handful did the Court unanimously find a Fourth Amendment violation. That the Court today speaks with a single voice on the merits of the constitutional question is unusual and certainly lends support to the notion that the question is indeed "open and shut."

But the more important basis for my opinion is that it should have been perfectly obvious to the officers that their "invitation to the media exceeded the scope of the search authorized by the warrant." Despite reaffirming that clear rule, the Court nonetheless finds that the mere presence of a warrant rendered the officers' conduct reasonable. The Court fails to cite a single case that even arguably supports the proposition that using official power to enable news photographers and reporters to enter a private home for purposes unrelated to the execution of a warrant could be regarded as a "reasonable" invasion of either property or privacy.

II

The absence of judicial opinions expressly holding that police violate the Fourth Amendment if they bring media representatives into private homes provides scant support for the conclusion that in 1992 a competent officer could reasonably believe that it would be lawful to do so. Prior to our decision in United States v. Lanier, 520 U.S. 259 (1997), no judicial opinion specifically held that it was unconstitutional for a state judge to use his official power to extort sexual favors from a potential litigant. Yet, we unanimously concluded that the defendant had fair warning that he was violating his victim's constitutional rights. Id., at 271 ("The easiest cases don't even arise").

Nor am I persuaded that the absence of rulings on the precise Fourth Amendment issue presented in this case can plausibly be explained by the

---

[1] It is important to emphasize that there is no split in circuit authority on the merits of the constitutional issue. . . . Any conflict was limited to the qualified immunity issue. . . .

assumption that the police practice was common. I assume that the practice of allowing media personnel to "ride along" with police officers was common, but that does not mean that the officers routinely allowed the media to enter homes without the consent of the owners. . . .

In addition to this case, the Court points to three lower court opinions—none of which addresses the Fourth Amendment—as the ostensible basis for a reasonable officer's belief that the rule in *Semayne's Case* was ripe for reevaluation. Two of the cases were decided in 1980 and the third in 1984. In view of the clear restatement of the rule in the later opinions of this Court, those three earlier decisions could not possibly provide a basis for a claim by the police that they reasonably relied on judicial recognition of an exception to the basic rule that the purposes of the police intrusion strictly limit its scope.

That the two federal decisions were not officially reported makes such theoretical reliance especially anomalous. Moreover, as the Court acknowledges, the claim rejected in each of those cases was predicated on the media's alleged violation of the plaintiffs' "unorthodox non-Fourth Amendment right to privacy theories," rather than a claim that the officers violated the Fourth Amendment by allowing the press to observe the execution of the warrant. Moncrief v. Hanton, 10 Media L. Rep. 1620 (N.D. Ohio 1984); Higbee v. Times–Advocate, 5 Media L. Rep. 2372 (S.D. Cal. 1980). As for the other case, Prahl v. Brosamle, 98 Wis. 2d 130, 295 N.W.2d 768 (App. 1980)—cited by the Court for the proposition that the officer's conduct was "not unreasonable"—it actually held that the defendants' motion to dismiss should have been denied because the allegations supported the conclusion that the officer committed a trespass when he allowed a third party to enter the plaintiff's property. Since that conclusion was fully consistent with a number of common-law cases holding that similar conduct constituted a trespass, it surely does not provide any support for an officer's assumption that a similar trespass would be lawful.

The Court is correct that the Wisconsin Court of Appeals upheld dismissal of the plaintiff's 42 U.S.C. § 1983 claim against the newscaster because he was not acting under color of state law. As the basis for rejecting the § 1983 action "for invasion of privacy based on disclosure of the incident," the court further held that "we are unwilling to accept the proposition that the filming and television broadcast of a reasonable search and seizure, without more, result in unreasonableness." Important to its conclusion was its observation that . . . "neither the search of Dr. Prahl and his premises nor the film or its broadcast has been shown to include intimate, offensive or vulgar aspects." The reporter in question was stationed in the entryway of the building and was able to film into the plaintiff's office during the police interview.

Far better evidence of an officer's reasonable understanding of the relevant law is provided by the testimony of the Sheriff of Montgomery County, the commanding officer of three of the respondents: " 'We would never let a civilian into a home. . . . That's just not allowed.' "

III

The most disturbing aspect of the Court's ruling on the qualified immunity issue is its reliance on a document discussing "ride-alongs" apparently prepared by an employee in the public relations office of the United States Marshals Service. The text of the document . . . makes it quite clear that its author was not a lawyer, but rather a person concerned with developing the proper public image of the service, with a special interest in creating a favorable impression with the Congress. Although the document . . . suggests handing out free Marshals Service T–Shirts and caps to "grease the skids," it contains no discussion of the conditions which must be satisfied before a newsperson may be authorized to enter private property during the execution of a warrant. . . .

* * *

The defense of qualified immunity exists to protect reasonable officers from personal liability for official actions later found to be in violation of constitutional rights that were not clearly established. The conduct in this case, as the Court itself reminds us, contravened the Fourth Amendment's core protection of the home. In shielding this conduct as if it implicated only the unsettled margins of our jurisprudence, the Court today authorizes one free violation of the well-established rule it reaffirms.

I respectfully dissent.

NOTE ON THE REQUIREMENT OF MERITS–FIRST ADJUDICATION

In *Wilson v. Layne* and again in Saucier v. Katz, 533 U.S. 194 (2001), a *Bivens* action alleging excessive use of force, the Court emphasized the sequence in which various issues should be addressed. As Justice Kennedy explained for the Court in *Saucier*:

> In a suit against an officer for an alleged violation of a constitutional right, the requisites of a qualified immunity defense must be considered in proper sequence. . . .
>
> A court required to rule upon the qualified immunity issue must consider, then, this threshold question: Taken in the light most favorable to the party asserting the injury, do the facts alleged show the officer's conduct violated a constitutional right? This must be the initial inquiry. In the course of determining whether a constitutional right was violated on the premises alleged, a court might find it necessary to set forth principles which will become the basis for a holding that a right is clearly established. This is the process for the law's elaboration from case to case, and it is one reason for our insisting upon turning to the existence or nonexistence of a constitutional right as the first inquiry. The law might be deprived of this explanation were a court simply to skip ahead to the question whether the law clearly established that the officer's conduct was unlawful in the circumstances of the case.
>
> If no constitutional right would have been violated were the allegations established, there is no necessity for further inquiries concerning qualified immunity. On the other hand, if a violation could be made out on a favorable view of the parties' submissions, the next, sequential step is to ask whether the right was clearly established. . . .

The requirement of merits-first adjudication quickly drew criticism. The reasons for that criticism are revealed in the next main case.

Pearson v. Callahan

Supreme Court of the United States, 2009.
555 U.S. 223.

■ JUSTICE ALITO delivered the opinion of the Court.

This is an action brought by respondent under 42 U.S.C. § 1983, against state law enforcement officers who conducted a warrantless search of his house incident to his arrest for the sale of methamphetamine to an undercover informant whom he had voluntarily admitted to the premises. The Court of Appeals held that petitioners were not entitled to summary judgment on qualified immunity grounds. Following the procedure we mandated in Saucier v. Katz, 533 U.S. 194 (2001), the Court of Appeals held, first, that respondent adduced facts sufficient to make out a violation of the Fourth Amendment and, second, that the unconstitutionality of the officers' conduct was clearly established. In granting review, we required the parties to address the additional question whether the mandatory procedure set out in *Saucier* should be retained.

We now hold that the *Saucier* procedure should not be regarded as an inflexible requirement and that petitioners are entitled to qualified immunity on the ground that it was not clearly established at the time of the search that their conduct was unconstitutional. We therefore reverse.

I

A

The Central Utah Narcotics Task Force is charged with investigating illegal drug use and sales. In 2002, Brian Bartholomew, who became an informant for the task force after having been charged with the unlawful possession of methamphetamine, informed Officer Jeffrey Whatcott that respondent Afton Callahan had arranged to sell Bartholomew methamphetamine later that day.

That evening, Bartholomew arrived at respondent's residence at about 8 p.m. Once there, Bartholomew went inside and confirmed that respondent had methamphetamine available for sale. Bartholomew then told respondent that he needed to obtain money to make his purchase and left.

Bartholomew met with members of the task force at about 9 p.m. and told them that he would be able to buy a gram of methamphetamine for $100. After concluding that Bartholomew was capable of completing the planned purchase, the officers searched him, determined that he had no controlled substances on his person, gave him a marked $100 bill and a concealed electronic transmitter to monitor his conversations, and agreed on a signal that he would give after completing the purchase.

The officers drove Bartholomew to respondent's trailer home, and respondent's daughter let him inside. Respondent then retrieved a large bag containing methamphetamine from his freezer and sold Bartholomew a gram of methamphetamine, which he put into a small plastic bag. Bartholomew gave the arrest signal to the officers who were monitoring the conversation, and they entered the trailer through a porch door. In the enclosed porch, the officers encountered Bartholomew, respondent, and two other persons, and they saw respondent drop a plastic bag, which they later determined contained methamphetamine. The officers then conducted a protective sweep of the premises. In addition to the large bag of methamphetamine, the officers recovered the marked bill from respondent and a small bag containing meth-amphetamine from Bartholomew, and they found drug syringes in the residence. As a result, respondent was charged with the unlawful possession and distribution of methamphetamine.

B

The trial court held that the warrantless arrest and search were supported by exigent circumstances. On respondent's appeal from his conviction, the Utah attorney general conceded the absence of exigent circumstances, but urged that the inevitable discovery doctrine justified introduction of the fruits of the warrantless search. The Utah Court of Appeals disagreed and vacated respondent's conviction. See State v. Callahan, 93 P. 3d 103 (2004). Respondent then brought this damages action under 42 U.S.C. § 1983 in the United States District Court for the District of Utah, alleging that the officers had violated the Fourth Amendment by entering his home without a warrant.

In granting the officers' motion for summary judgment, the District Court noted that other courts had adopted the "consent-once-removed" doctrine, which permits a warrantless entry by police officers into a home when consent to enter has already been granted to an undercover officer or informant who has observed contraband in plain view. Believing that this doctrine was in tension with our intervening decision in Georgia v. Randolph, 547 U.S. 103 (2006), the District Court concluded that "the simplest approach is to assume that the Supreme Court will ultimately reject the [consent-once-removed] doctrine and find that searches such as the one in this case are not reasonable under the Fourth Amendment." The Court then held that the officers were entitled to qualified immunity because they could reasonably have believed that the consent-once-removed doctrine authorized their conduct.

On appeal, a divided panel of the Tenth Circuit held that petitioners' conduct violated respondent's Fourth Amendment rights. The panel majority stated that "[t]he 'consent-once-removed' doctrine applies when an undercover officer enters a house at the express invitation of someone with authority to consent, establishes probable cause to arrest or search, and then immediately summons other officers for assistance." The majority took no issue with application of the doctrine when the initial consent was granted to an undercover law enforcement officer, but the majority disagreed with decisions that "broade[n] this doctrine to grant informants the same capabilities as undercover officers."

The Tenth Circuit panel further held that the Fourth Amendment right that it recognized was clearly established at the time of respondent's arrest. "In this case," the majority stated, "the relevant right is the right to be free in one's home from unreasonable searches and arrests." The Court determined that, under the clearly established precedents of this Court and the Tenth Circuit, "warrantless entries into a home are per se unreasonable unless they satisfy the established exceptions." In the panel's words, "the Supreme Court and the Tenth Circuit have clearly established that to allow police entry into a home, the only two exceptions to the warrant requirement are consent and exigent circumstances." Against that backdrop, the panel concluded, petitioners could not reasonably have believed that their conduct was lawful because petitioners "knew (1) they had no warrant; (2) [respondent] had not consented to their entry; and (3) [respondent's] consent to the entry of an informant could not reasonably be interpreted to extend to them."

In dissent, Judge Kelly argued that "no constitutional violation occurred in this case" because, by inviting Bartholomew into his house and participating in a narcotics transaction there, respondent had compromised the privacy of the residence and had assumed the risk that Bartholomew would reveal their dealings to the police. Judge Kelly further concluded that, even if petitioners' conduct had been unlawful, they were nevertheless entitled to qualified immunity because the constitutional right at issue—"the right to be free from the warrantless entry of police officers into one's home to effectuate an arrest after one has granted voluntary, consensual entry to a confidential informant and undertaken criminal activity giving rise to probable cause"—was not "clearly established" at the time of the events in question.

As noted, the Court of Appeals followed the *Saucier* procedure. The *Saucier* procedure has been criticized by Members of this Court and by lower court judges, who have been required to apply the procedure in a great variety of cases and thus have much firsthand experience bearing on its advantages and disadvantages. Accordingly, in granting certiorari, we directed the parties to address the question whether *Saucier* should be overruled.

II

A

The doctrine of qualified immunity protects government officials "from liability for civil damages insofar as their conduct does not violate clearly established statutory or constitutional rights of which a reasonable person would have known." Harlow v. Fitzgerald, 457 U.S. 800, 818 (1982). Qualified immunity balances two important interests—the need to hold public officials accountable when they exercise power irresponsibly and the need to shield officials from harassment, distraction, and liability when they perform their duties reasonably. . . .

In *Saucier*, this Court mandated a two-step sequence for resolving government officials' qualified immunity claims. First, a court must decide whether the facts that a plaintiff has alleged (see Fed. Rules Civ. Proc. 12(b)(6), (c)) or shown (see Rules 50, 56) make out a violation of a constitutional right. Second, if the plaintiff has satisfied this first step, the court must decide whether the right at issue was "clearly established" at the time of defendant's alleged misconduct. Qualified immunity is applicable unless the official's conduct violated a clearly established constitutional right.

Our decisions prior to *Saucier* had held that "the better approach to resolving cases in which the defense of qualified immunity is raised is to determine first whether the plaintiff has alleged a deprivation of a constitutional right at all." County of Sacramento v. Lewis, 523 U.S. 833, n.5 (1998). *Saucier* made that suggestion a mandate. For the first time, we held that whether "the facts alleged show the officer's conduct violated a constitutional right . . . *must* be the initial inquiry" in every qualified immunity case. (Emphasis added). Only after completing this first step, we said, may a court turn to "the next, sequential step," namely, "whether the right was clearly established." Ibid.

This two-step procedure, the Saucier Court reasoned, is necessary to support the Constitution's "elaboration from case to case" and to prevent constitutional stagnation. "The law might be deprived of this explanation were a court simply to skip ahead to the question whether the law clearly established that the officer's conduct was unlawful in the circumstances of the case."

B

In considering whether the *Saucier* procedure should be modified or abandoned, we must begin with the doctrine of stare decisis. . . . Although "[w]e approach the reconsideration of [our] decisions . . . with the utmost caution," "[s]tare decisis is not an inexorable command." State Oil Co. v. Khan, 522 U.S. 3, 20 (1997). Revisiting precedent is particularly appropriate where, as here, a departure would not upset expectations, the precedent consists of a judge-made rule that was recently adopted to improve the operation of the courts, and experience has pointed up the precedent's shortcomings. . . .

Lower court judges, who have had the task of applying the *Saucier* rule on a regular basis for the past eight years, have not been reticent in their criticism of *Saucier*'s "rigid order of battle." See, e.g., Purtell v. Mason, 527 F.3d 615, 622 (7th Cir. 2008) ("This 'rigid order of battle' has been criticized on practical, procedural, and substantive grounds"); Leval, Judging Under the Constitution: Dicta About Dicta, 81 N.Y.U.L. Rev. 1249, 1275, 1277 (2006) (referring to *Saucier*'s mandatory two-step framework as "a new and mischievous rule" that amounts to "a puzzling misadventure in constitutional dictum"). . . .

Members of this Court have also voiced criticism of the *Saucier* rule. See Morse v. Frederick, 551 U.S. 393, 431 (2007) (Breyer, J., concurring in judgment in part and dissenting in part) ("I would end the failed *Saucier* experiment now"); Bunting v. Mellen, 541 U.S. 1019 (2004) (Stevens, J., joined by Ginsburg and Breyer, JJ., respecting denial of certiorari) (criticizing the "unwise judge-made rule under which courts must decide whether the plaintiff has alleged a constitutional violation before addressing the question whether the defendant state actor is entitled to qualified immunity"); Id., at 1025 (Scalia, J., joined by Rehnquist, C. J., dissenting from denial of certiorari) ("We should either make clear that constitutional determinations are *not* insulated from our review . . . or else drop any pretense at requiring the ordering in every case" (emphasis in original)); Brosseau v. Haugen, 543 U.S. 194, 201–02 (2004) (Breyer, J., joined by Scalia and Ginsburg, JJ., concurring) (urging Court to reconsider *Saucier*'s "rigid 'order of battle,' " which "requires courts unnecessarily to decide difficult constitutional questions when there is available an easier basis for the decision (e.g., qualified immunity) that will satisfactorily resolve the case before the court") . . .

Where a decision has "been questioned by Members of the Court in later decisions and [has] defied consistent application by the lower courts," these factors weigh in favor of reconsideration. Payne v. Tennessee, 501 U.S. 808, 829–30. Collectively, the factors we have noted make our present reevaluation of the *Saucier* two-step protocol appropriate.

III

On reconsidering the procedure required in *Saucier*, we conclude that, while the sequence set forth there is often appropriate, it should no longer be regarded as mandatory. The judges of the district courts and the courts of appeals should be permitted to exercise their sound discretion in deciding which of the two prongs of the qualified immunity analysis should be addressed first in light of the circumstances in the particular case at hand.

A

Although we now hold that the *Saucier* protocol should not be regarded as mandatory in all cases, we continue to recognize that it is often beneficial. For one thing, there are cases in which there would be little if any conservation of judicial resources to be had by beginning and ending with a discussion of the "clearly established" prong. "[I]t often may be difficult to decide whether a right is clearly established without deciding precisely what the constitutional right happens to be." Lyons v. Xenia, 417 F. 3d 565, 581 (6th Cir. 2005) (Sutton, J., concurring). In some cases, a discussion of why the relevant facts do not violate clearly established law may make it apparent that in fact the relevant facts do not make out a constitutional violation at all. In addition, the *Saucier* Court was certainly correct in noting that the two-step procedure promotes the development of constitutional precedent and is especially valuable with respect to questions that do not frequently arise in cases in which a qualified immunity defense is unavailable.

B

At the same time, however, the rigid *Saucier* procedure comes with a price. The procedure sometimes results in a substantial expenditure of scarce judicial resources on difficult questions that have no effect on the outcome of the case. There are cases in which it is plain that a constitutional right is not clearly established but far from obvious whether in fact there is such a right. District courts and courts of appeals with heavy caseloads are often understandably unenthusiastic about what may seem to be an essentially academic exercise.

Unnecessary litigation of constitutional issues also wastes the parties' resources. Qualified immunity is "an immunity from suit rather than a mere defense to liability." Mitchell v. Forsyth, 472 U.S. 511, 526 (emphasis deleted). *Saucier*'s two-step protocol "disserve[s] the purpose of qualified immunity" when it "forces the parties to endure additional burdens of suit—such as the costs of litigating constitutional questions and delays attributable to resolving them—when the suit otherwise could be disposed of more readily." Brief for Nat. Assn. of Criminal Defense Lawyers as Amicus Curiae 30.

Although the first prong of the *Saucier* procedure is intended to further the development of constitutional precedent, opinions following that procedure often fail to make a meaningful contribution to such development. For one thing, there are cases in which the constitutional question is so fact-bound that the decision provides little guidance for future cases.

A decision on the underlying constitutional question in a § 1983 damages action or a Bivens v. Six Unknown Fed. Narcotics Agents, 403 U.S. 388 (1971), action may have scant value when it appears that the question will soon be decided by a higher court. When presented with a constitutional question on which this Court had just granted certiorari, the Ninth Circuit elected to "bypass *Saucier*'s first step and decide only whether [the alleged right] was clearly established." Motley v. Parks, 432 F.3d 1072, 1078, and n.5 (2005) (en banc). Similar considerations may come into play when a court of appeals panel confronts a constitutional question that is pending before the court en banc or when a district court encounters a constitutional question that is before the court of appeals.

A constitutional decision resting on an uncertain interpretation of state law is also of doubtful precedential importance. As a result, several courts have identified an "exception" to the *Saucier* rule for cases in which resolution of the constitutional question requires clarification of an ambiguous state statute. Egolf v. Witmer, 526 F. 3d 104, 109–11 (3rd Cir. 2008) [and others]. Justifying the decision to grant qualified immunity to the defendant without first resolving, under *Saucier*'s first prong, whether the defendant's conduct violated the Constitution, these courts have observed that *Saucier*'s "underlying principle" of encouraging federal courts to decide unclear legal questions in order to clarify the law for the future "is not meaningfully advanced . . . when the definition of constitutional rights depends on a federal court's uncertain assumptions about state law." 526 F.3d at 110.

When qualified immunity is asserted at the pleading stage, the precise factual basis for the plaintiff's claim or claims may be hard to identify. Accordingly, several courts have recognized that the two-step inquiry "is an uncomfortable exercise where . . . the answer [to] whether there was a violation may depend on a kaleidoscope of facts not yet fully developed" and have suggested that "[i]t may be that *Saucier* was not strictly intended to cover" this situation. Dirranne v. Brookline Police Dept., 315 F. 3d 65, 69–70 (1st Cir. 2002).

There are circumstances in which the first step of the *Saucier* procedure may create a risk of bad decisionmaking. The lower courts sometimes encounter cases in which the briefing of constitutional questions is woefully inadequate. See Lyons, 417 F. 3d, at 582 (Sutton, J., concurring) (noting the "risk that constitutional questions may be prematurely and incorrectly decided in cases where they are not well presented").

Although the *Saucier* rule prescribes the sequence in which the issues must be discussed by a court in its opinion, the rule does not—and obviously cannot—specify the sequence in which judges reach their conclusions in their own internal thought processes. Thus, there will be cases in which a court will rather quickly and easily decide that there was no violation of clearly established law before turning to the more difficult question whether the relevant facts make out a constitutional question at all. In such situations, there is a risk that a court may not devote as much care as it would in other circumstances to the decision of the constitutional issue.

Rigid adherence to the *Saucier* rule may make it hard for affected parties to obtain appellate review of constitutional decisions that may have a serious prospective effect on their operations. Where a court holds that a defendant committed a constitutional violation but that the violation was not clearly established, the defendant may face a difficult situation. As the winning party, the defendant's right to appeal the adverse holding on the constitutional question may be contested. See Bunting v. Mellen, 541 U.S. 1019, 1025 (Scalia, J., dissenting from denial of certiorari) ("The perception of unreviewability undermines adherence to the sequencing rule we . . . created" in *Saucier*).[2] In cases like *Bunting*, the "prevailing" defendant fac-

---

[2] In *Bunting*, the Court of Appeals followed the *Saucier* two-step protocol and first held that the Virginia Military Institute's use of the word "God" in a "supper roll call" ceremony violated the Establishment Clause, but then granted the defendants qualified immunity because the law was not clearly established at the relevant time. Although they had a judgment in their favor below, the defendants asked this Court to review the adverse constitutional ruling. Dissenting from the denial of certiorari, Justice Scalia, joined by Chief Justice Rehnquist, criticized "a perceived procedural tangle of the Court's own making." The "tangle" arose from the Court's " 'settled refusal' to entertain an appeal by a party on an issue as to which he prevailed" below, a practice that insulates from review adverse merits decisions that are "locked inside" favorable qualified immunity rulings.

es an unenviable choice: "compl[y] with the lower court's advisory dictum without opportunity to seek appellate [or certiorari] review," or "def[y] the views of the lower court, adher[e] to practices that have been declared illegal, and thus invit[e] new suits" and potential "punitive damages." Horne v. Coughlin, 191 F. 3d, 244, 247–48 (2nd Cir. 1999).

Adherence to *Saucier*'s two-step protocol departs from the general rule of constitutional avoidance and runs counter to the "older, wiser judicial counsel 'not to pass on questions of constitutionality . . . unless such adjudication is unavoidable.' " Scott, 550 U.S., at 388 (Breyer, J., concurring) (quoting Spector Motor Service, Inc. v. McLaughlin, 323 U.S. 101, 105 (1944)); see Ashwander v. TVA, 297 U.S. 288, 347 (1936) (Brandeis, J., concurring) ("The Court will not pass upon a constitutional question although properly presented by the record, if there is also present some other ground upon which the case may be disposed of").

In other analogous contexts, we have appropriately declined to mandate the order of decision that the lower courts must follow. For example, in Strickland v. Washington, 466 U.S. 668 (1984), we recognized a two-part test for determining whether a criminal defendant was denied the effective assistance of counsel: The defendant must demonstrate (1) that his counsel's performance fell below what could be expected of a reasonably competent practitioner; and (2) that he was prejudiced by that substandard performance. After setting forth and applying the analytical framework that courts must use in evaluating claims of ineffective assistance of counsel, we left it to the sound discretion of lower courts to determine the order of decision. ("Although we have discussed the performance component of an ineffectiveness claim prior to the prejudice component, there is no reason for a court deciding an ineffective assistance claim to approach the inquiry in the same order or even to address both components of the inquiry if the defendant makes an insufficient showing on one.")

In United States v. Leon, 468 U.S. 897 (1984), we created an exception to the exclusionary rule when officers reasonably rely on a facially valid search warrant. In that context, we recognized that a defendant challenging a search will lose if either: (1) the warrant issued was supported by probable cause; or (2) it was not, but the officers executing it reasonably believed that it was. Again, after setting forth and applying the analytical framework that courts must use in evaluating the good-faith exception to the Fourth Amendment warrant requirement, we left it to the sound discretion of the lower courts to determine the order of decision. ("There is no need for courts to adopt the inflexible practice of always deciding whether the officers' conduct manifested objective good faith before turning to the question whether the Fourth Amendment has been violated.")

This flexibility properly reflects our respect for the lower federal courts that bear the brunt of adjudicating these cases. Because the two-step *Saucier* procedure is often, but not always, advantageous, the judges of the district courts and the courts of appeals are in the best position to determine the order of decisionmaking will best facilitate the fair and efficient disposition of each case.

C

Any misgivings concerning our decision to withdraw from the mandate set forth in *Saucier* are unwarranted. Our decision does not prevent the lower courts from following the *Saucier* procedure; it simply recognizes that those courts should have the discretion to decide whether that procedure is worthwhile in particular cases. Moreover, the development of constitutional law is by no means entirely dependent on cases in which the defendant may seek qualified immunity. Most of the constitutional issues that are presented in § 1983 damages actions and *Bivens* cases also arise in cases in which that defense is not available, such as criminal cases and § 1983 cases against a municipality, as well as § 1983 cases against individuals where injunctive relief is sought instead of or in addition to damages. . . .

IV

Turning to the conduct of the officers here, we hold that petitioners are entitled to qualified immunity because the entry did not violate clearly established law. An officer conducting a search is entitled to qualified immunity where clearly established law does not show that the search violated the Fourth Amendment. This inquiry turns on the "objective legal reasonableness of the action, assessed in light of the legal rules that were clearly established at the time it was taken." Wilson v. Layne, 526 U.S. 603, 614 (1999) (internal quotation marks omitted).

When the entry at issue here occurred in 2002, the "consent-once-removed" doctrine had gained acceptance in the lower courts. This doctrine had been considered by three Federal Courts of Appeals and two State Supreme Courts starting in the early 1980's. See, e.g., United States v. Diaz, 814 F.2d 454, 459 (7th Cir. 1987); United States v. Bramble, 103 F.3d 1475 (9th Cir. 1996); United States v. Pollard, 215 F.3d 643, 648–49 (6th Cir. 2000); State v. Henry, 133 N. J. 104, 627 A.2d 125 (1993); State v. Johnston, 184 Wis. 2d 794, 518 N.W.2d 759 (1994). It had been accepted by every one of those courts. Moreover, the Seventh Circuit had approved the doctrine's application to cases involving consensual entries by private citizens acting as confidential informants. See United States v. Paul, 808 F. 2d, 645, 648 (1986). The Sixth Circuit reached the same conclusion after the events that gave rise to respondent's suit, see United States v. Yoon, 398 F. 3d 802, 806–08 (2005), and prior to the Tenth Circuit's decision in the present case, no court of appeals had issued a contrary decision.

The officers here were entitled to rely on these cases, even though their own Federal Circuit had not yet ruled on "consent-once-removed" entries. The principles of qualified immunity shield an officer from personal liability when an officer reasonably believes that his or her conduct complies with the law. Police officers are entitled to rely on existing lower court cases without facing personal liability for their actions. In *Wilson*, we explained that a Circuit split on the relevant issue had developed after the events that gave rise to suit and concluded that "[i]f judges thus disagree on a constitutional question, it is unfair to subject police to money damages for picking the losing side of the controversy." Likewise, here, where the divergence of views on the consent-once-removed doctrine was created by the decision of the Court of Appeals in this case, it is improper to subject petitioners to money damages for their conduct.

Because the unlawfulness of the officers' conduct in this case was not clearly established, petitioners are entitled to qualified immunity. We therefore reverse the judgment of the Court of Appeals.

It is so ordered.

NOTES ON SEQUENCING IN QUALIFIED IMMUNITY CASES

1. THE RATIONALE FOR "UNNECESSARY" MERITS DECISIONS

The opinion in *Pearson* explores the many difficulties that were or might have been encountered under *Saucier* but pays relatively little attention to the rationale for that decision. Perhaps that was because the merits-first "order of battle" was disapproved only to the extent that it was mandatory. The *Pearson* Court apparently still contemplates that it is permissible for courts to address the merits first and that in many cases they should do so.

Why? Why should adjudication of the merits of a constitutional claim ever come before the determination of qualified immunity? When qualified immunity bars recovery, what justification exists for reaching a merits conclusion that does not affect the outcome?

A pre-*Pearson* answer to these questions was attempted in John C. Jeffries, Jr., The Right–Remedy Gap in Constitutional Law, 109 Yale L.J. 87 (1999). Jeffries pointed out that the limitation on money damages imposed by the law of qualified immunity is a two-edged sword. On the one hand, qualified immunity reduces the incentives for government officers to comply with existing constitutional requirements. That follows from the fact that some existing requirements will be found not to have been "clearly established" on the facts of the case and therefore not sufficient to support damages liability. On the other hand, qualified immunity reduces the cost of expanding or clarifying constitutional rights. Since damages liability is triggered only by conduct violating "clearly established" rights, a constitutional rule can be refined or clarified without risk of imposing potentially large damages liability for conduct previously thought lawful. The result, Jeffries argued, is to facilitate the development of the law by allowing courts to impose new or refined constitutional requirements, without triggering potentially debilitating and arguably unfair liability for past conduct.

This argument was necessarily abstract. In a subsequent article, Jeffries applied it quite specifically to the facts of *Pearson*:

> The intended operation of *Saucier* can be illustrated on the facts of *Pearson*. If the Supreme Court had followed *Saucier*'s order of battle, a split in the circuits would have been resolved. "Consent-once-removed" would have been accepted or rejected, and the Tenth Circuit's distinction between officers and informants would have been adopted or reversed. The specific defendants sued in *Pearson* would have been protected by qualified immunity, but that defense would have become irrelevant to future cases. The asserted right against warrantless search, despite the undercover invitee's report of contraband in plain view, would have become either clearly established or clearly non-existent. If the former, money damages would have become routinely available; if the latter, there would have been no claim. One way or the other, qualified immunity would have been eliminated for consent-once-removed searches.
>
> The role of the merits-first order of battle in development of the law is thus easily seen. What may not be quite so obvious, but is in fact far more important, is the degradation of constitutional rights that may result when *Saucier* is not followed and constitutional tort claims are resolved solely on grounds of qualified immunity. For rights that depend on vindi-

> cation through money damages, the repeated invocation of qualified immunity will reduce the meaning of the Constitution to the lowest plausible conception of its content. Functionally, the Constitution will be defined not by what judges, in their wisdom, think it does or should mean, but by the most grudging conception that an executive officer could reasonably entertain. This effect will be ameliorated for rights that also arise in settings that do not trigger qualified immunity, but for rights that depend on vindication through money damages, abandoning merits adjudication will reduce constitutional protections to the least-common-denominator understanding of their meaning.

John C. Jeffries, Jr., Reversing the Order of Battle in Constitutional Torts, 2009 Sup. Ct. Rev. 115, 120–21.

In this analysis, much depends on whether damages actions are important vehicles for defining and enforcing particular constitutional rights. For rights defined and enforced chiefly in other contexts—such as motions to suppress illegally seized evidence—the elimination of merits-first adjudication in constitutional tort cases may have relatively low costs. But for rights—such as the protection against excessive force—that depend for their vindication on actions for money damages, the merits-avoidance authorized by *Pearson* will have potentially high costs:

> These costs are not measured solely, or even chiefly, in the persistence of uncertainty in the law. The greater problem is the underenforcement of constitutional rights while such uncertainty continues. The perpetuation of qualified immunity dilutes the meaning of constitutional protections from whatever the legitimate authorities believe the Constitution requires to some lesser standard of reasonable misperception. For that, *Pearson* has no good answer. [Id. at 131.]

2. *REICHLE V. HOWARDS*

The merits-avoidance approach of *Pearson v. Callahan* was repeated in Reichle v. Howards, 132 S.Ct. 2088. At a meet-and-greet in a Colorado shopping mall, Dan Howards told Vice President Cheney that his Iraq war policies were "disgusting" and touched (in what manner was disputed) the Vice President on the shoulder. A Secret Service agent subsequently interviewed Howards, who falsely denied having touched Cheney. Howards was arrested and charged under state law, but the charge was dropped. Howards then sued the Secret Service agents (under *Bivens*) and the local officers (under § 1983), claiming that his First Amendment rights had been violated by a retaliatory arrest. The courts found that there had been probable cause to arrest Howards for making a materially false statement to a federal officer in violation of 18 U.S.C. § 1001. The question then became whether Howards could pursue a First Amendment claim for retaliatory arrest, despite the existence of probable cause.

Tenth Circuit precedent said that he could. Arguably, however, that precedent had been called into question by the Supreme Court's decision in Hartman v. Moore, 547 U.S. 250 (2006), which held that a First Amendment claim for retaliatory *prosecution* could not proceed if the charges were supported by probable cause. The Tenth Circuit held that *Hartman* applied only to retaliatory prosecution, as distinct from arrest, and that Howards' claim of a retaliatory motive for his arrest raised a material factual dispute that could go to trial. The

Supreme Court unanimously disagreed. Speaking through Justice Thomas, the Court concluded that *Hartman* had unsettled the law on retaliatory arrest and that the defendants were therefore entitled to qualified immunity. Justices Ginsburg and Breyer concurred in the judgment on narrow grounds, and Justice Kagan did not participate.

Reichle and *Pearson* have at least two similarities. In both cases, the Tenth Circuit took an aggressively expansive view of "clearly established" law and a correspondingly narrow view of qualified immunity, and in both cases the Supreme Court unanimously reversed without reaching the merits of the constitutional claims. In both cases, the Court therefore left circuit splits intact, thereby foregoing the opportunity to create "clearly established" law for future cases.

3. APPEAL BY PREVAILING PARTIES: *CAMRETA V. GREENE*

Of all the objections to *Saucier*, none attracted more attention than the question of appealability. Could a defendant who prevailed on qualified immunity nevertheless seek appellate review of an adverse ruling on the merits?

The question arose in Bunting v. Mellen, 541 U.S. 1019 (2004). Cadets at the Virginia Military Institute challenged the practice of conducting a prayer before the evening meal. They sued Bunting, then Superintendent of VMI, for declaratory and injunctive relief, as well as nominal damages. The District Court enjoined Bunting from continuing to sponsor the prayer, but said he was entitled to qualified immunity on damages. Both sides appealed. Meanwhile, Bunting retired, and the cadets graduated. The Court of Appeals therefore vacated the injunction as moot but affirmed the finding of qualified immunity. That left VMI officials in the unusual situation of having prevailed on the only claim adjudicated by the Court of Appeals but still being saddled with an adverse ruling on the unconstitutionality of the supper prayer. Under traditional practices, the Supreme Court would not grant certiorari to a prevailing party, and in fact the Court did deny the petition, but several Justices commented on the "procedural tangle" of reviewing merits rulings at the behest of a prevailing party. See *Pearson*, n.2.

The appealability issue reached the Supreme Court again in Camreta v. Greene, 131 S.Ct. 2020. The case arose in the aftermath of suspected child abuse. Camreta, a state child protective services worker, accompanied by a deputy sheriff, interviewed a girl at her elementary school about allegations that she had been sexually abused by her father. The father was tried for that crime, but the jury could not reach a verdict and the charges were dismissed. The girl's mother then sued the officials for damages, claiming a violation of her daughter's constitutional rights. The Ninth Circuit agreed, ruling that the officials had violated the Fourth Amendment by failing to obtain a warrant (or parental permission) to conduct the interview. The Ninth Circuit also ruled, however, that the defendants were protected by qualified immunity. As in *Bunting*, the prevailing defendants then sought Supreme Court review of the adverse ruling on the merits.

Speaking through Justice Kagan, the Court found that "this Court generally may review a lower court's constitutional ruling at the behest of a government official granted immunity." The Court noted first that 28 U.S.C. § 1254(1) authorized certiorari "upon the petition of *any* party" (emphasis by the Court). Article III presented no obstacle, so long as the case presented a genuine case or controversy. That would often be true "when immunized officials seek to challenge a ruling that their conduct violated the Constitution," because such a ruling would have prospective effect on their future conduct:

> The court in such a case says: "Although this official is immune from damages today, what he did violates the Constitution and he or anyone else who does that thing again will be personally liable." If the official regularly engages in that conduct as part of his job (as Camreta does), he suffers injury caused by the adverse constitutional ruling. So long as it continues in effect, he must either change the way he performs his duties or risk a meritorious damages action. Only by overturning the ruling on appeal can the official gain clearance to engage in the conduct in the future. He thus can demonstrate, as we demand, injury, causation, and redressability.

Moreover, Justice Kagan added, judicial policy "places qualified immunity cases in a special category when it comes to this Court's review of appeals brought by winners":

> The constitutional determinations that prevailing parties ask us to consider in these cases are not mere dicta or "statements in opinions." They are rulings that have a significant future effect on the conduct of public officials—both the prevailing parties and their co-workers—and the policies of the government units to which they belong. And more: they are rulings self-consciously designed to produce this effect, by establishing controlling law and preventing invocations of immunity in later cases. And still more: they are rulings designed this way with this Court's permission, to promote clarity—and observance—of constitutional rules. . . . [T]aken together, [these considerations] support bending our usual rule to permit consideration of immunized officials' petitions.

Despite this general conclusion, the Court found that this particular case had become moot and therefore declined to proceed to merits review. The Court also noted, without further explanation, that it "need not decide if an appellate court can also entertain an appeal from a party who has prevailed on immunity grounds." Apparently, the question of a prevailing party's appeal from the District Court to a Court of Appeals remains for another day.

Justice Sotomayor, joined by Justice Breyer, concurred in the judgment on the ground that since the case was moot, the Court should go no further in specifying whether a prevailing party could seek review.

Justice Kennedy, joined by Justice Thomas, dissented:

> As today's decision illustrates, our recent qualified immunity cases tend to produce decisions that are in tension with conventional principles of case-or-controversy adjudication. This Court has given the Courts of Appeals "permission" to find constitutional violations when ordering dismissal or summary judgment based on qualified immunity. This invitation, as the Court is correct to note, was intended to produce binding constitutional holdings on the merits. The goal was to make dictum precedent, in order to hasten the gradual process of constitutional interpretation and alter the behavior of government defendants. The present case brings the difficulties of that objective into perspective. In express reliance on the permission granted in *Pearson*, the Court of Appeals went out of its way to announce what may be an erroneous interpretation of the Constitu-

tion; and, under our case law, the Ninth Circuit must give that dictum legal effect as precedent in future cases. . . .

The Court's analysis appears to rest on the premise that the reasoning of the decision below in itself causes Camreta injury. Until today, however, precedential reasoning of general applicability divorced from a particular adverse judgment was not thought to yield "standing to appeal." Parr v. United States, 351 U. S. 513, 516, 517 (1956) (opinion for the Court by Harlan, J.). . . .

The conclusion that precedent of general applicability cannot in itself create standing to sue or appeal flows from basic principles. Camreta's asserted injury is caused not by the Court of Appeals or by respondent but rather by "the independent action of some third party not before the court"—that is, by the still-unidentified private plaintiffs whose lawsuits Camreta hopes to avoid. This circumstance distinguishes the present case from requests for declaratory or injunctive relief filed against officeholders who threaten legal enforcement. An inert rule of law does not cause particular, concrete injury; only the specific threat of its enforcement can do so. That is why the proper defendant in a suit for prospective relief is the party prepared to enforce the relevant legal rule against the plaintiff. Without an adverse judgment from which to appeal, Camreta has in effect filed a new declaratory judgment action in this Court against the Court of Appeals. This is no more consistent with Article III than filing a declaratory judgment action against this Court for its issuance of an adverse precedent or against Congress in response to its enactment of an unconstitutional law.

If today's decision proves to be more than an isolated anomaly, the Court might find it necessary to reconsider its special permission that the Courts of Appeals may issue unnecessary merits determinations in qualified immunity cases with binding precedential effect. . . .

There will be instances where courts discuss the merits in qualified immunity cases. It is sometimes a better analytic approach and a preferred allocation of judicial time and resources to dismiss a claim on the merits rather than to dismiss based on qualified immunity. And "[i]t often may be difficult to decide whether a right is clearly established without deciding precisely what the existing constitutional right happens to be." *Pearson*, supra, at 236 (internal quotation marks omitted). This Court should not superintend the judicial decisionmaking process in qualified immunity cases under special rules, lest it make the judicial process more complex for civil rights suits than for other litigation. It follows, however, that the Court should provide no special permission to reach the merits. If qualified immunity cases were treated like other cases raising constitutional questions, settled principles of constitutional avoidance would apply. So would conventional rules regarding dictum and holding. Judicial observations made in the course of explaining a case might give important instruction and be relevant when assessing a later claim of qualified immunity. But as dicta those remarks would not establish law and would not qualify as binding precedent.

. . . I would dismiss this case and note that our jurisdictional rule against hearing appeals by prevailing parties precludes petitioners' attempt to obtain review of judicial reasoning disconnected from a judgment.

4. BIBLIOGRAPHY

The merits-first "order of battle" requirement by *Wilson* and *Saucier* produced considerable commentary, both before and after *Pearson v. Callahan*. For judicial criticism of the requirement of merits adjudication, see Judge Pierre Leval, Judging Under the Constitution: Dicta About Dicta, 81 N.Y.U.L. Rev. 1249, 1275–81 (2006), and an influential opinion by Judge Jeffrey Sutton in Lyons v. City of Xenia, 417 F.3d 565, 580 (6th Cir. 2005) (Sutton, J., concurring). For academic criticism, see Thomas Healy, The Rise of Unnecessary Constitutional Rulings, 83 N.C.L. Rev. 847 (2005) (arguing that "unnecessary" merits adjudication is improper as well as unwise); and Nancy Leong, The *Saucier* Qualified Immunity Experiment: An Empirical Analysis, 36 Pepperdine L. Rev. 667 (2009) (concluding on the basis of empirical investigation that merits-first adjudication is unlikely to result in the clarification or development of constitutional rights). Cf. Paul W. Hughes, Not a Failed Experiment: *Wilson–Saucier* Sequencing and the Articulation of Constitutional Rights, 80 U. Colo. L. Rev. 401 (2009) (reaching the opposite conclusion, also on the basis of empirical investigation).

For pre-*Pearson* articles supporting merits-first adjudication, see John M.M. Greabe, *Mirabule Dictum*!: The Case for "Unnecessary" Constitutional Ruling in Civil Rights Damages Actions, 74 Notre Dame L. Rev. 403 (1999) (arguing against "merits by-pass" and in favor of "not-strictly-necessary" constitutional adjudication); Michael L. Wells, The "Order-of-Battle" in Constitutional Litigation, 60 S.M.U. L. Rev. 1539 (2005) (arguing that "deciding immunity issues first stunts the growth of substantive law to the detriment of the vindication and deterrent goals of constitutional tort law"); and Sam Kamin, An Article III Defense of Merits–First Decisionmaking in Civil Rights Litigation: The Continued Viability of *Saucier v. Katz*, 16 Geo. Mason L. Rev. 53 (2008) (anticipating and criticizing *Pearson v. Callahan*).

For post-*Pearson* commentary, see Jack M. Beermann, Qualified Immunity and Constitutional Avoidance, 2009 Sup. Ct. Rev. 139 (exploring the problems of unguided judicial discretion in deciding whether to address the merits in constitutional tort cases and calling for legal standards to provide guidance and prevent strategic behavior); Karen M. Blum, Section 1983 Litigation: Post–*Pearson* and Post–*Iqbal*, 26 Touro L. Rev. 433 (2010), and Karen M. Blum, Qualified Immunity: Further Developments in the Post–*Pearson* Era, 27 Touro L. Rev. 243 (2011) (providing early assessments of the post-*Pearson* experience in the lower courts); Michael T. Kirkpatrick & Joshua Matz, Avoiding Permanent Limbo: Qualified Immunity and the Elaboration of Constitutional Rights from *Saucier* to *Camreta* (and Beyond), 80 Fordham L. Rev. 643 (2011) (providing a generally favorable assessment of the Supreme Court's decisions on the order of battle in constitutional torts); Nancy Leong, Rethinking the Order of Battle in Constitutional Torts: A Reply to John Jeffries, 105 Nw. U. L. Rev. 969 (2011) (extending and defending the argument that cognitive dissonance impairs the ability of judges to resolve the merits of constitutional claims correctly in cases where the outcome is dictated by qualified immunity); James E. Pfander, Resolving the Qualified Immunity Dilemma: Constitutional Tort Claims for Nominal Damages, 111 Colum. L. Rev. 1601 (2011) (suggesting that the barrier to merits adjudication raised by qualified immunity be circumvented by suits for nominal damages).

5. GOVERNMENTAL LIABILITY

INTRODUCTORY NOTE ON MONROE V. PAPE

In Monroe v. Pape, 365 U.S. 1 (1965) (excerpted in Chapter I), the plaintiffs sued not only Chicago police officers but also the city itself. *Monroe* held that § 1983 provided a federal cause of action against the officers even if their conduct was unauthorized by, or even in violation of, state law. *Monroe* also held, however, that city of Chicago could not be sued. The basis for this conclusion, explained Justice Douglas, was the 1871 Congress's rejection of the Sherman Amendment:

> When the bill that became the Act of April 20, 1871, was being debated in the Senate, Senator Sherman of Ohio proposed an amendment which would have made "the inhabitants of the county, city, or parish" in which certain acts of violence occurred liable "to pay full compensation" to the person damaged or his widow or legal representative. The amendment was adopted by the Senate. The House, however, rejected it. The Conference Committee reported another version. The House rejected the Conference report. In a second conference the Sherman amendment was dropped. . . . Mr. Poland, speaking for the House Conferees about the Sherman proposal to make municipalities liable, said:
>
> > We informed the conferees on the part of the Senate that the House had taken a stand on that subject and would not recede from it; that that section imposing liability upon towns and counties must go out or we should fail to agree.
>
> The objection to the Sherman amendment stated by Mr. Poland was that "the House had solemnly decided that in their judgment Congress had no constitutional power to impose any obligation upon county and town organizations, the mere instrumentality for the administration of state law."

The *Monroe* Court expressly declined to consider policy arguments for or against municipal liability and also declined to reach the question whether Congress has the constitutional power to make municipalities liable for the acts of their officers. Instead, the Court rested squarely on its understanding of legislative intent:

> The response of the Congress to the proposal to make municipalities liable for certain actions being brought within federal purview by the Act of April 20, 1871, was so antagonistic that we cannot believe that the word "person" was used in this particular act to include them. Accordingly we hold that the motion to dismiss the complaint against the city of Chicago was properly granted.

On this point, *Monroe* was unanimous. Nevertheless, the issue was reconsidered in the next main case.

Monell v. New York City Department of Social Services

Supreme Court of the United States, 1978.
436 U.S. 658.

■ MR. JUSTICE BRENNAN delivered the opinion of the Court.

Petitioners, a class of female employees of the Department of Social Services and of the Board of Education of the city of New York, commenced this action under 42 U.S.C. § 1983 in July, 1971. The gravamen of the complaint was that the board and the Department had as a matter of official policy compelled pregnant employees to take unpaid leaves of absence before such leaves were required for medical reasons. Cf. Cleveland Board of Education v. LaFleur, 414 U.S. 632 (1974). The suit sought injunctive relief and backpay for periods of unlawful forced leave. Named as defendants in the action were the Department and the commissioner, the board and its chancellor, and the city of New York and its Mayor. In each case, the individual defendants were sued solely in their official capacities.

On cross-motions for summary judgment, the District Court for the Southern District of New York held moot petitioners' claims for injunctive and declaratory relief since the City of New York and the board, after the filing of the complaint, had changed their policies relating to maternity leaves so that no pregnant employee would have to take leave unless she was medically unable to perform her job. No one now challenges this conclusion. The court did conclude, however, that the acts complained of were unconstitutional under *LaFleur*. Nonetheless plaintiffs' prayers for backpay were denied because any such damages would come ultimately from the city of New York and, therefore, to hold otherwise would be to "circumven[t]" the immunity conferred on municipalities by Monroe v. Pape, 365 U.S. 167 (1961). . . .

I

In *Monroe v. Pape*, we held that "Congress did not undertake to bring municipal corporations within the ambit of [§ 1983]." The sole basis for this conclusion was an inference drawn from Congress' rejection of the "Sherman amendment" to the bill which became the Civil Rights Act of 1871—the precursor of § 1983—which would have held a municipal corporation liable for damage done to the person or property of its inhabitants by *private* persons "riotously and tumultuously assembled."[8]

Although the Sherman amendment did not seek to amend § 1 of the Act, which is now § 1983, and although the nature of the obligation created by that amendment was vastly different from that created by § 1, the Court nonetheless concluded in *Monroe* that Congress must have meant to exclude municipal corporations from the coverage of § 1 because " 'the House [in voting against the Sherman amendment] had solemnly decided that in their judgment Congress had no constitutional power to impose any *obligation* upon county and town organizations, the mere instrumentality for the administration of state law,' " (emphasis added), quoting Rep. Poland. This statement, we thought, showed that Congress doubted its "constitutional power . . . to impose *civil liability* on municipalities" (emphasis added), and that such doubt would have extended to any type of civil liability.

[8] We expressly declined to consider "policy considerations" for or against municipal liability.

A fresh analysis of debate on the Civil Rights Act of 1871, and particularly of the case law which each side mustered in its support, shows, however, that *Monroe* incorrectly equated the "obligation" of which Representative Poland spoke with "civil liability." . . .

House opponents of the Sherman amendment—whose views are particularly important since only the House voted down the amendment—. . . argued that the local units of government upon which the amendment fastened liability were not obligated to keep the peace at state law and further that the federal government could not constitutionally require local governments to create police forces, whether this requirement was levied directly, or indirectly by imposing damages for breach of the peace on municipalities. The most complete statement of this position is that of Representative Blair:

> The proposition known as the Sherman amendment . . . is entirely new. It is altogether without a precedent in this country. . . . That amendment claims the power in the general government to go into the states of this union and lay such obligations as it may please upon the municipalities, which are the creatures of the states alone. . . .
>
> Here it is proposed not to carry into effect an obligation which rests upon the municipalities, but to create that obligation, and that is the provision I am unable to assent to. . . .
>
> Now, only the other day, the Supreme Court . . . decided [in Collector v. Day, 78 U.S. (11 Wall.) 113 (1871)] that there is no power in the government of the United States, under its authority to tax, to tax the salary of a state officer. Why? Simply because the power to tax involves the power to destroy, and it was not the intent to give the government of the United States power to destroy the government of the states in any respect. It was also held in the case of Prigg v. Pennsylvania, 41 U.S. (16 Pet.) 539 (1842), that it is not within the power of the Congress of the United States to lay duties upon a state officer; that we cannot command a state officer to do any duty whatever, as such; and I ask . . . the difference between that and commanding a municipality, which is equally a creature of the state, to perform a duty.

Any attempt to impute a unitary constitutional theory to opponents of the Sherman amendment is, of course, fraught with difficulties, not the least of which is that most members of Congress did not speak to the issue of the constitutionality of the amendment. Nonetheless, two considerations lead us to conclude that opponents of the Sherman amendment found it unconstitutional substantially because of the reasons stated by Representative Blair: First, Blair's analysis is precisely that of Poland, whose views were quoted as authoritative in *Monroe*, and that analysis was shared in large part by all House opponents who addressed the constitutionality of the Sherman amendment. Second, Blair's exegesis of the reigning constitutional theory of his day, as we shall explain, was clearly supported by precedent—albeit precedent that has not survived. . . .

Collector v. Day, cited by Blair, was the clearest and, at the time of the debates, the most recent pronouncement of a doctrine of coordinate sovereignty that, as Blair stated, placed limits on even the enumerated powers of the national government in favor of protecting state prerogatives. There, the Court held that the United States could not tax the income of Day, a

Massachusetts state judge, because the independence of the states within their legitimate spheres would be imperiled if the instrumentalities through which states executed their powers were "subject to the control of another and distinct government." [And in] Kentucky v. Dennison, 65 U.S. (24 How.) 66 (1861), . . . the Court was asked to require Dennison, the Governor of Ohio, to hand over Lago, a fugitive from justice wanted in Kentucky, as required by § 1 of the Act of Feb. 12, 1793, which implemented Art. IV, § 2, Cl. 2 of the Constitution. Mr. Chief Justice Taney, writing for a unanimous Court, refused to enforce that section of the act:

> [W]e think it clear, that the federal government, under the Constitution, has no power to impose on a state officer, as such, any duty whatever, and compel him to perform it; for if it possessed this power, it might overload the officer with duties which would fill up all his time, and disable him from performing his obligations to the state, and might impose on him duties of a character incompatible with the rank and dignity to which he was elevated by the state.

The rationale of *Dennison*—that the nation could not impose duties on state officers since that might impede states in their legitimate activities—is obviously identical to that which animated the decision in *Collector v. Day*. And, as Blair indicated, municipalities as instrumentalities through which states executed their policies could be equally disabled from carrying out state policies if they were also obligated to carry out federally imposed duties. Although no one cited *Dennison* by name, the principle for which it stands was well known to Members of Congress, many of whom discussed *Day*, as well as a series of state supreme court cases in the mid–1860s which had invalidated a federal tax on the process of state courts on the ground that the tax threatened the independence of a vital state function. Thus, there was ample support for Blair's view that the Sherman amendment, by putting municipalities to the Hobson's choice of keeping the peace or paying civil damages, attempted to impose obligations on municipalities by indirection that could not be imposed directly, thereby threatening to "destroy the government of the states."

If municipal liability under § 1 of the Civil Rights Act of 1871 created a similar Hobson's choice, we might conclude, as *Monroe* did, that Congress could not have intended municipalities to be among the "persons" to which that section applied. But that is not the case.

First, opponents expressly distinguished between imposing an obligation to keep the peace and merely imposing civil liability for damages on a municipality that was obligated by state law to keep the peace, but which had not in violation of the Fourteenth Amendment. Representative Poland, for example, reasoning from Contract Clause precedents, indicated that Congress could constitutionally confer jurisdiction on the federal courts to entertain suits seeking to hold municipalities liable for using their authorized powers in violation of the Constitution—which is as far as § 1 of the Civil Rights Act went:

> I presume . . . that where a state had imposed a duty [to keep the peace] upon [a] municipality . . . an action would be allowed to be maintained against them in the courts of the United States under the ordinary restrictions as to jurisdiction. But enforcing a liability, existing by their own contract, or by a state law, in the courts, is a very widely different thing from devolving a new duty or liability upon them by the national government, which has no power either to create or destroy them, and no power or control over them whatever. . . .

Second, the doctrine of dual sovereignty apparently put no limit on the power of the federal courts to enforce the Constitution against municipalities that violated it. . . . The limits of the principles defined in *Dennison* and *Day* are not so well defined in logic, but are clear as a matter of history. It must be remembered that the same Court which rendered *Day* also vigorously enforced the Contract Clause against municipalities—an enforcement effort which included various forms of "positive" relief, such as ordering that taxes be levied and collected to discharge federal-court judgments, once a constitutional infraction was found. Thus, federal judicial enforcement of the Constitution's express limits on state power, since it was done so frequently, must, notwithstanding anything said in *Dennison* or *Day*, have been permissible. . . . Since § 1 of the Civil Rights Act simply conferred jurisdiction on the federal courts to enforce § 1 of the Fourteenth Amendment—a situation precisely analogous to the grant of diversity jurisdiction under which the Contract Clause was enforced against municipalities—there is no reason to suppose that opponents of the Sherman amendment would have found any constitutional barrier to § 1 suits against municipalities. . . .

From the foregoing discussion it is readily apparent that nothing said in the debates on the Sherman amendment would have prevented holding a municipality liable under § 1 of the Civil Rights Act for its own violations of the Fourteenth Amendment. The question remains, however, whether the general language describing those to be liable under § 1—"any person"—covers more than natural persons. An examination of the debate on § 1 and application of appropriate rules of construction show unequivocally that § 1 was intended to cover legal as well as natural persons. . . .

In both Houses, statements of the supporters of § 1 corroborated that Congress, in enacting § 1, intended to give a broad remedy for violations of federally protected civil rights. Moreover, since municipalities through their official acts could, equally with natural persons, create the harms intended to be remedied by § 1, and, further, since Congress intended § 1 to be broadly construed, there is no reason to suppose that municipal corporations would have been excluded from the sweep of § 1. One need not rely on this inference alone, however, for the debates show that members of Congress understood "persons" to include municipal corporations.

Representative Bingham, for example, in discussing § 1 of the bill, explained that he had drafted § 1 of the Fourteenth Amendment with the case of Barron v. Mayor of Baltimore, 32 U.S. (7 Pet.) 243 (1833), especially in mind. "In [that] case the *city* had taken private property for public use, without compensation . . . , and there was no redress for the wrong. . . . " (Emphasis added.) Bingham's further remarks clearly indicate his view that such takings by cities, as had occurred in *Barron*, would be redressable under § 1 of the bill. More generally, and as Bingham's remarks confirm, § 1 of the bill would logically be the vehicle by which Congress provided redress for takings, since that section provided the only civil remedy for Fourteenth Amendment violations and that amendment unequivocally prohibited uncompensated takings. Given this purpose, it beggars reason to suppose that Congress would have exempted municipalities from suit, insisting instead that compensation for a taking come from an officer in his individual capacity rather than from the government unit that had the benefit of the property taken.

In addition, by 1871, it was well understood that corporations should be treated as natural persons for virtually all purposes of constitutional and statutory analysis. . . .

That the "usual" meaning of the word "person" would extend to municipal corporations is also evidenced by an act of Congress which had been passed only months before the Civil Rights Act was passed. The act provided that

> in all acts hereafter passed . . . the word "person" may extend and be applied to bodies politic and corporate . . . unless the context shows that such words were intended to be used in a more limited sense.

Municipal corporations in 1871 were included within the phrase "bodies politic and corporate" and, accordingly, the "plain meaning" of § 1 is that local government bodies were to be included within the ambit of the persons who could be sued under § 1 of the Civil Rights Act. . . .

II

Our analysis of the legislative history of the Civil Rights Act of 1871 compels the conclusion that Congress *did* intend municipalities and other local government units to be included among those persons to whom § 1983 applies.[54] Local governing bodies, therefore, can be sued directly under § 1983 for monetary, declaratory, or injunctive relief where, as here, the action that is alleged to be unconstitutional implements or executes a policy statement, ordinance, regulation, or decision officially adopted and promulgated by that body's officers. Moreover, although the touchstone of the § 1983 action against a government body is an allegation that official policy is responsible for a deprivation of rights protected by the Constitution, local governments, like every other § 1983 "person," by the very terms of the statute, may be sued for constitutional deprivations visited pursuant to governmental "custom" even though such a custom has not received formal approval through the body's official decisionmaking channels. . . .

On the other hand, the language of § 1983, read against the background of the same legislative history, compels the conclusion that Congress did not intend municipalities to be held liable unless action pursuant to official municipal policy of some nature caused a constitutional tort. In particular, we conclude that a municipality cannot be held liable *solely* because it employs a tortfeasor—or, in other words, a municipality cannot be held liable under § 1983 on a respondeat superior theory.

We begin with the language of § 1983 as passed:

> [*A*]*ny person who*, under color of any law, statute, ordinance, regulation, custom, or usage of any state, *shall subject, or cause to be subjected*, any person . . . to the deprivation of any rights, privileges, or immunities secured by the Constitution of the United States, shall, any such law, statute, ordinance, regulation, custom, or usage of the state to the contrary notwithstanding, be liable to the party injured in

54 There is certainly no constitutional impediment to municipal liability. "The Tenth Amendment's reservation of nondelegated powers to the states is not implicated by a federal-court judgment enforcing the express prohibitions of unlawful state conduct enacted by the Fourteenth Amendment." For this reason, National League of Cities v. Usery, 426 U.S. 833 (1976), is irrelevant to our consideration of this case. Nor is there any basis for concluding that the Eleventh Amendment is a bar to municipal liability. See, e.g., Fitzpatrick v. Bitzer, 427 U.S. 445 (1976). Our holding today is, of course, limited to local government units which are not considered part of the state for Eleventh Amendment purposes.

> any action at law, suit in equity, or other proper proceeding for redress. . . . [Emphasis added.]

The italicized language plainly imposes liability on a government that, under color of some official policy "causes" an employee to violate another's constitutional rights. At the same time, the language cannot be easily read to impose liability vicariously on governing bodies solely on the basis of the existence of an employer-employee relationship with a tortfeasor. Indeed, the fact that Congress did specifically provide that A's tort became B's liability if B "caused" A to subject another to a tort suggests that Congress did not intend § 1983 liability to attach where such causation was absent.

Equally important, creation of a federal law of respondeat superior would have raised all the constitutional problems associated with the obligation to keep the peace, an obligation Congress chose not to impose because it thought imposition of such an obligation unconstitutional. To this day, there is disagreement about the basis for imposing liability on an employer for the torts of an employee when the sole nexus between the employer and the tort is the fact of the employer-employee relationship. Nonetheless, two justifications tend to stand out. First is the commonsense notion that no matter how blameless an employer appears to be in an individual case, accidents might nonetheless be reduced if employers had to bear the cost of accidents. Second is the argument that the cost of accidents should be spread to the community as a whole on an insurance theory.

The first justification is of the same sort that was offered for statutes like the Sherman amendment: "The obligation to make compensation for injury resulting from riot is, by arbitrary enactment of statutes, affirmatory law, and the reason of passing the statute is to secure a more perfect police protection." (Sen. Frelinghuysen) This justification was obviously insufficient to sustain the amendment against perceived constitutional difficulties and there is no reason to suppose that a more general liability imposed for a similar reason would have been thought less constitutionally objectionable. The second justification was similarly put forward as a justification for the Sherman amendment: "we do not look upon [the Sherman amendment] as a punishment. . . . It is a mutual insurance." (Rep. Butler) Again, this justification was insufficient to sustain the amendment.

We conclude, therefore, that a local government may not be sued under § 1983 for an injury inflicted solely by its employees or agents. Instead, it is when execution of a government's policy or custom, whether made by its lawmakers or by those whose edicts or acts may fairly be said to represent official policy, inflicts the injury that the government as an entity is responsible under § 1983. Since this case unquestionably involves official policy as a moving force of the constitutional violation found by the District Court, we must reverse the judgment below. . . .

III

Although we have stated before that stare decisis has more force in statutory analysis than in constitutional adjudication because, in the former situation, Congress can correct our mistakes through legislation, we have never applied stare decisis mechanically to prohibit overruling our earlier decisions determining the meaning of statutes. . . .

[Justice Brennan gave four reasons why stare decisis should not be applied in this situation.

[First, *Monroe* "was a departure from prior practice." Brennan cited a number of cases in which injunctive relief had been sought against municipalities. "Moreover," he continued, "the constitutional defect that led to the rejection of the Sherman amendment would not have distinguished between municipalities and school boards, each of which is an instrumentality of state administration." For this reason, prior cases decided both before and after *Monroe* holding school boards liable in § 1983 actions were inconsistent with *Monroe*.

[Second, "recent expressions of Congressional intent" indicated that a broad implementation of the principle of *Monroe* was unsound. Here he cited the rejection of efforts to strip the federal courts of jurisdiction over school boards, the enactment of legislation to assist school boards in complying with federal court decrees, and a provision in attorney-fee legislation indicating that Congress expected attorney fees in § 1983 suits to be collectable from state or local governments.

[Third, unlike in a commercial situation, "municipalities can assert no reliance claim." Surely, he said, *Monroe* cannot be read as allowing local governments to rely on their ability to adopt unconstitutional policies.

[And finally, he argued that even under the most stringent test for when a statutory interpretation should be overruled, *Monroe* qualified. It is "beyond doubt," he said, that *Monroe* is wrong and "there is no justification" given the legislative history "for excluding municipalities from the 'persons' covered by § 1983."]

IV

Since the question whether local government bodies should be afforded some form of official immunity was not presented [or] briefed . . . we express no views on the scope of any municipal immunity beyond holding that municipal bodies sued under § 1983 cannot be entitled to an absolute immunity, lest our decision that such bodies are subject to suit under § 1983 "be drained of meaning."

V

For the reasons stated above, the judgment of the Court of Appeals is

Reversed.

■ MR. JUSTICE POWELL, concurring. . . .

Few cases in the history of the Court have been cited more frequently than Monroe v. Pape, 365 U.S. 167 (1961), decided less than two decades ago. Focusing new light on 42 U.S.C. § 1983, that decision widened access to the federal courts and permitted expansive interpretations of the reach of the 1871 measure. But *Monroe* exempted local governments from liability at the same time it opened wide the courthouse door to suits against officers and employees of those entities—even where they act pursuant to express authorization. The oddness of that result and the weakness of the historical evidence relied on by the *Monroe* Court in support of it, are well demonstrated by the Court's opinion today. . . .

The Court correctly rejects a view of the legislative history that would produce the anomalous result of immunizing local government units from monetary liability for action directly causing a constitutional deprivation, even though such actions may be fully consistent with, and thus not remediable under, state law. No conduct of government comes more clearly within the "under color of" state law language of § 1983. It is most unlikely that Congress intended public officials acting under the command or the specific authorization of the government employer to be *exclusively* liable for resulting constitutional injury. . . .

[This is not] the usual case in which the Court is asked to overrule a precedent. Here considerations of stare decisis cut in both directions. On the one hand, we have a series of rulings that municipalities and counties are not "persons" for purposes of § 1983. On the other hand, many decisions of this Court have been premised on the amenability of school boards and similar entities to § 1983 suits. . . .

If now, after full consideration of the question, we continued to adhere to *Monroe*, grave doubt would be cast upon the Court's exercise of § 1983 jurisdiction over school boards. . . . Although there was an independent basis of jurisdiction in many of the school board cases because of the inclusion of individual public officials as nominal parties, the opinions of this Court make explicit reference to the school board party, particularly in discussions of the relief to be awarded. [T]he exercise of § 1983 jurisdiction over school boards . . . has been longstanding. Indeed, it predated *Monroe*. . . .

The Court of Appeals in this case suggested that we import, by analogy, the Eleventh Amendment fiction of *Ex parte Young* into § 1983. That approach . . . would require "a bifurcated application" of "the generic word 'person' in § 1983" to public officials "depending on the nature of the relief sought against them." A public official sued in his official capacity for carrying out official policy would be a "person" for purposes of injunctive relief, but a non-"person" in an action for damages. The Court's holding avoids this difficulty.

Finally, if we continued to adhere to a rule of absolute municipal immunity under § 1983, we could not long avoid the question whether "we should, by analogy to our decision in *Bivens*, imply a cause of action directly from the Fourteenth Amendment. . . . " In light of the Court's persuasive re-examination in today's decision of the 1871 debates, I would have difficulty inferring from § 1983 "an explicit congressional declaration" against municipal liability for the implementation of official policies in violation of the Constitution. Rather than constitutionalize a cause of action against local government that Congress intended to create in 1871, the better course is to confess error and set the record straight, as the Court does today. . . .

■ MR. JUSTICE STEVENS, concurring in part.

[Justice Stevens declined to join those portions of the majority opinion dealing with respondeat superior on the ground that discussion of that issue was "merely advisory" and "not necessary to explain the Court's decision."]

■ MR. JUSTICE REHNQUIST, with whom THE CHIEF JUSTICE joins, dissenting.

Seventeen years ago in Monroe v. Pape, 365 U.S. 167 (1961), this Court held that the 42d Congress did not intend to subject a municipal corporation to liability as a "person" within the meaning of 42 U.S.C. § 1983. Since then, the Congress has remained silent, but this Court has reaffirmed that holding on at least three separate occasions. Today, the Court abandons this long and consistent line of precedents, offering in justification only an elaborate canvass of the same legislative history which was before the Court in 1961. . . .

I

[O]ur only task is to discern the intent of the 42d Congress. That intent was first expounded in *Monroe*, and it has been followed consistently ever since. This is not some esoteric branch of the law in which congressional silence might reasonably be equated with congressional indifference. Indeed, this very year, the Senate has been holding hearings on a bill which would remove the municipal immunity recognized by *Monroe*. In these circumstances, it cannot be disputed that established principles of stare decisis require this Court to pay the highest deference to its prior holdings. *Monroe* may not be overruled unless it has been demonstrated "beyond doubt from the legislative history of the 1871 statute that [*Monroe*] misapprehended the meaning of the controlling provision," [quoting Justice Harlan's remark in his *Monroe* concurrence about overruling the interpretation of "under color of" law adopted in *Screws* and *Classic*]. The Court must show not only that Congress, in rejecting the Sherman amendment, concluded that municipal liability was not unconstitutional, but also that in enacting § 1, it intended to impose that liability. I am satisfied that no such showing has been made.

II

Any analysis of the meaning of the word "person" in § 1983, which was originally enacted as § 1 of the Ku Klux Klan Act of April 20, 1871, must begin, not with the Sherman amendment, but with the Dictionary Act. The latter act, which supplied rules of construction for all legislation, provided:

> That in all acts hereafter passed . . . the word "person" may extend and be applied to bodies politic and corporate . . . unless the context shows that such words were intended to be used in a more limited sense. . . .

There are . . . factors . . . which suggest that the Congress which enacted § 1983 may well have intended the word "person" "to be used in a more limited sense," as *Monroe* concluded. It is true that this Court had held that both commercial corporations and municipal corporations were "citizens" of a state within the meaning of the jurisdictional provisions of Art. III. Congress, however, also knew that this label did not apply in all contexts, since this Court had held commercial corporations not to be "citizens" within the meaning of the Privileges and Immunities Clause, U.S. Const., Art. IV, § 2. Thus, the Congress surely knew that, for constitutional purposes, corporations generally enjoyed a different status in different contexts. Indeed, it may be presumed that Congress intended that a corporation should enjoy the same status under the Ku Klux Klan Act as it did under the Fourteenth Amendment, since it had been assured that § 1 "was so very simple and really reenacting the Constitution." At the time § 1983 was enacted the only federal case to consider the status of corporations under the Fourteenth Amendment had concluded, with impeccable logic, that a corporation was neither a "citizen" nor a "person."

Furthermore, the state courts did not speak with a single voice with regard to the tort liability of municipal corporations. Although many members of Congress represented states which had retained absolute municipal tort immunity, other states had adopted the currently predominant distinction imposing liability for proprietary acts. Nevertheless, no state court had ever held that municipal corporations were always liable in tort in precisely the same manner as other persons.

The general remarks from the floor on the liberal purposes of § 1 offer no explicit guidance as to the parties against whom the remedy could be enforced. As the Court concedes, only Representative Bingham raised a concern which could be satisfied only by relief against governmental bodies. Yet he never directly related this concern to § 1 of the act. Indeed, Bingham stated at the outset, "I do not propose now to discuss the provisions of the bill in detail," and, true to his word, he launched into an extended discourse on the beneficent purposes of the Fourteenth Amendment. While Bingham clearly stated that Congress could "provide that no citizen in any state shall be deprived of his property by state law or the judgment of a state court without just compensation therefore," he never suggested that such a power was exercised in § 1.[4] . . .

Thus, it ought not lightly to be presumed, as the Court does today, that § 1983 "should prima facie be construed to include 'bodies politic' among the entities that could be sued." Neither the Dictionary Act, the ambivalent state of judicial decisions, nor the floor debate on § 1 of the act gives any indication that any Member of Congress had any inkling that § 1 could be used to impose liability on municipalities. . . .

The Court is probably correct that the rejection of the Sherman amendment does not lead ineluctably to the conclusion that Congress intended municipalities to be immune from liability under all circumstances. Nevertheless, it cannot be denied that the debate on that amendment, the only explicit consideration of municipal tort liability, sheds considerable light on the Congress' understanding of the status of municipal corporations in that context. . . . Whatever the merits of the constitutional arguments against it, the fact remains that Congress rejected the concept of municipal tort liability on the only occasion in which the question was explicitly presented. Admittedly this fact is not conclusive as to whether Congress intended § 1 to embrace a municipal corporation within the meaning of "person," and thus the reasoning of *Monroe* on this point is subject to challenge. The meaning of § 1 of the Act of 1871 has been subjected in this case to a more searching and careful analysis than it was in *Monroe*, and it may well be that on the basis of this closer analysis of the legislative debates a conclusion contrary to the *Monroe* holding could have been reached when that case was decided 17 years ago. But the rejection of the Sherman amendment remains instructive in that here alone did the legislative debates squarely focus on the liability of municipal corporations, and that liability was rejected. . . .

The decision in *Monroe v. Pape* was the fountainhead of the torrent of civil rights litigation of the last 17 years. Using § 1983 as a vehicle, the courts have articulated new and previously unforeseeable interpretations of the Fourteenth Amendment. At the same time, the doctrine of municipal immunity enunciated in *Monroe* has protected municipalities and their limited treasuries from the consequences of their officials' failure to predict the course of this Court's constitutional jurisprudence. None of the members of this Court can foresee the practical consequences of today's removal of that protection. Only the Congress, which has the benefit of the advice of every

[4] It has not been generally thought, before today, that § 1983 provided an avenue of relief from unconstitutional takings. Those federal courts which have granted compensation against state and local governments have resorted to an implied right of action under the Fifth and Fourteenth Amendments. Since the Court today abandons the holding of *Monroe* chiefly on the strength of Bingham's arguments, it is indeed anomalous that § 1983 will provide relief only when a local government, not the state itself, seizes private property. See note 54, supra.

segment of this diverse nation, is equipped to consider the results of such a drastic change in the law. It seems all but inevitable that it will find it necessary to do so after today's decision. . . .

NOTES ON GOVERNMENTAL LIABILITY UNDER § 1983

1. QUESTIONS AND COMMENTS ON *MONELL*

Before *Monell*, damages could be obtained from a police officer who violated constitutional rights but not from the city that ordered the officer to do so. Justice Powell commented on the "oddness" of that result. There is something odd, is there not, in holding an agent exclusively liable for acts specifically authorized by, and perhaps even commanded by, the principal? And yet, exactly this situation prevails with respect to state officials. They can be sued for damages under § 1983, but the state itself is immune from suit. Does this make sense? Is there any justification for treating states and municipalities differently?[a]

As a practical matter, the issue of state or municipal liability for the *authorized* acts of its employees matters chiefly when the official cannot be held personally liable. Where liability can be imposed on the official as an individual, the government will have a strong incentive to indemnify its employees against loss incurred in implementing official policy. Not only may the government feel a moral obligation to hold its employee harmless for following orders; but it will also find that indemnification is necessary to recruit and retain qualified employees. Few would be so bold as to accept government office without protection against personal liability for government error. Perhaps for that reason, states almost always follow the policy of defending state officers in actions under § 1983 and reimbursing them for any damages assessed, despite the formal immunity of the Eleventh Amendment.

Monell held that municipalities could be sued under § 1983, but only for actions taken pursuant to an official policy or custom. The Court specifically rejected the theory of respondeat superior. In essence, the *Monell* Court adopted for municipalities the test proposed for all § 1983 defendants by Justice Frankfurter's dissent in *Monroe*. Why? Is that result compelled by the language of the statute? Is it indicated by the rejection of the Sherman amendment? Is it consistent with the purposes of § 1983, as interpreted in *Monroe*.[b]

2. STATE AS "PERSON" UNDER § 1983: *WILL V. MICHIGAN DEPARTMENT OF STATE POLICE*

Before *Monell*, the Court assumed that *Monroe*'s conclusion that municipalities were not "persons" under § 1983 also applied to states. When *Monell*

---

[a] See William D. Murphy, Reinterpreting "Person" in Section 1983: The Hidden Influence of *Brown v. Board of Education*, 9 Black L.J. 97 (1985). Murray contends that *Monell* was necessary to remove the "very serious danger" of derailing desegregation suits against school boards. By contrast, Murphy suggests, the exclusion of states from the concept of "person" in § 1983 has no large impact on desegregation litigation.

[b] On the historical basis for rejecting respondeat superior, see Ronald M. Levin, The Section 1983 Municipal Immunity Doctrine, 65 Geo.L.J. 1483 (1977). For speculation that *Monroe* reflected Justice Powell's untimely agreement with the Frankfurter position in *Monroe v. Pape*, see David Jacks Achtenberg, Frankfurter's Champion: Justice Powell, *Monell*, and the Meaning of "Color of Law," 80 Ford. L. Rev. 681 (2011).

reversed that rule for localities, the question arose whether states might also be held directly liable under § 1983.

The question is entangled with the Eleventh Amendment, which has been read to deprive federal courts of jurisdiction over damage actions against states, except when Congress makes a very clear statement of the intent to impose such liability pursuant to its powers under the Reconstruction-era amendments. In Quern v. Jordan, 440 U.S. 332 (1979), the Court ruled that § 1983 was not such a legislative override of Eleventh Amendment immunity. That settled the matter for federal courts, but since the Eleventh Amendment does not apply in state court, the question remained open whether states might be sued there under § 1983.

The Supreme Court answered that question in Will v. Michigan Department of State Police, 491 U.S. 58 (1989). *Will* held that "person" in § 1983 does not include states or state officials acting in their official capacities.[c] Writing for the Court, Justice White argued that the legislative intent to make states directly liable had not been shown with the clarity required to alter the "usual constitutional balance" between the states and the national government. Nothing in the history or purpose of § 1983 clearly showed such intent.[d]

3. COMMENT ON JUDICIAL METHODOLOGY UNDER § 1983

In holding that a municipality is a "person" within the meaning of § 1983, *Monell* overruled part of *Monroe v. Pape*. Although the two decisions reach opposite conclusions on this point, they are alike in methodology. In both cases, the Supreme Court treated the issue as a straightforward exercise in statutory construction. Both decisions locate the question in the textual ambiguity of the word "person" as used in § 1983, and both purport to resolve the issue by resort to legislative history. The decisions read that history differently, but both seem to regard it as dispositive. Neither opinion discusses the policies involved. In fact, the *Monroe* Court specifically disavowed analysis of the "policy considerations" for or against municipal liability.

Perhaps this is just as it should be. Section 1983 is an act of Congress, and a traditional (though increasingly contested) means of resolving statutory ambiguity is to refer to the intent of the enacting legislature. Indeed, the Court might have opened itself to criticism if it had taken any other approach. Conventional wisdom would say that the Court's job in interpreting acts of Congress (at least in the absence of constitutional infirmity) is to give effect to the legislative meaning, not to consult its own perceptions of sound public policy.

And yet there is something a bit unsettling about the relentless historicity of § 1983 opinions. For one thing, the legislative history is often less clear than it is made out to be. In *Monroe* and *Monell*, for example, despite a seemingly thorough search, neither side was able to produce the "smoking gun" that clear-

---

[c] For an article lamenting the result in that case, see William Burnham & Michael C. Fayz, The State as a "Non–Person" Under Section 1983: Some Comments on *Will* and Suggestions for the Future, 70 Ore.L.Rev. 1 (1991). For an analysis of *Will* as legal pragmatism, see Gene R. Shreve, Symmetries of Access in Civil Rights Litigation: Politics, Pragmatism, and *Will*, 66 Ind.L.J. 1 (1990).

[d] Subsequently, the Court relied on *Will* to conclude that an Indian tribe cannot sue under § 1983 to contest the seizure of tribal records by state law enforcement officers. The Court found that tribes, like states, are not "persons" who can sue or be sued under § 1983. Inyo County v. Paiute–Shoshone Indians of the Bishop Community of the Bishop Colony, 538 U.S. 701 (2003).

ly demonstrated legislative intent one way or the other—not for the meaning of "under color of" law and not for the scope of the word "person." If, for example, the 42d Congress had considered and rejected a proposal to exclude municipalities from the coverage of the word "person," the debates might have been dispositive. But in fact the legislative history does not include this kind of focused and collective consideration of the issue. Instead, inferences must be drawn from scattered statements of individual legislators, whose views may or may not have been representative and who may or may not have had this issue precisely in mind when they spoke. To treat such evidence as controlling may be placing more reliance on history than it can fairly bear.[e]

Moreover, the uncertainty of historical reconstruction increases with remoteness in time. The legislators who spoke and voted in 1871 did so against a background of political experience and constitutional interpretation vastly different from what we know today. Projecting their views forward in time inevitably distorts them. Ultimately, what the Court is asking is not merely what the 42d Congress thought with respect to the kinds of problems then before it, but also what it would have thought if confronted with the issues now at hand. The more radical the change between that day and this, the less likely that the question is susceptible to meaningful answer.

Finally, these problems are compounded by the accumulation of precedent. The original meaning of a statute may be obscured by layers of interpretation. Each decision builds on the others. At some point, the statutory scheme, although grounded in a legislative act, is more nearly the product of judicial construction. Reversion to expressions of original intent to resolve some remaining ambiguity may have the effect of projecting the utterances of original enactment onto a pattern of legal regulation that has been substantially altered by subsequent interpretation.

Whether these concerns warrant deemphasis of the traditional model of statutory interpretation is a matter of controversy, both on and off the Supreme Court. Some think that § 1983 should be treated as a specie of federal common law, with the Supreme Court setting the terms of federal court supervision of state officials as it thinks best, but leaving the matter open for congressional correction. Others may think that the model of federal common law invites inappropriate innovation and that the wiser course is for the Court to stick close to the traditional tasks of statutory construction.

Whatever the merits of this debate, this much is clear: From *Monroe* to *Monell*, the Supreme Court has anchored its interpretations of § 1983 in the traditional mode. Many decisions are explained chiefly, if not exclusively, in terms of statutory language, legislative history, and original intent. Often the policy justifications for deciding an issue one way or the other are slighted or ignored or refracted through the historical prism of what the framers "must have thought." As a result, students of § 1983 are often left to uncover the underlying policies for themselves and to reach their own conclusions on the wisdom of the Court's judgments substantially unaided by judicial explication.

---

[e] See Richard A. Matasar, Personal Immunities Under § 1983: The Limits of the Court's Historical Analysis, 40 Ark.L.Rev. 741 (1987).

Owen v. City of Independence

Supreme Court of the United States, 1980.
445 U.S. 622.

■ MR. JUSTICE BRENNAN delivered the opinion of the Court.

Monell v. New York City Dept. of Social Services, 436 U.S. 658 (1978), overruled Monroe v. Pape, 365 U.S. 167 (1961), insofar as *Monroe* held that local governments were not among the "persons" to whom 42 U.S.C. § 1983 applies and were therefore wholly immune from suit under the statute. *Monell* reserved decision, however, on the question whether local governments, although not entitled to absolute immunity, should be afforded some form of official immunity in § 1983 suits. In this action brought by petitioner in the District Court for the Western District of Missouri, the Court of Appeals for the Eighth Circuit held that respondent City of Independence, Mo., "is entitled to qualified immunity from liability" based on the good faith of its officials. . . . We reverse.

I

The events giving rise to this suit are detailed in the District Court's findings of fact. On February 20, 1967, Robert L. Broucek, then City Manager of respondent City of Independence, Mo., appointed George D. Owen to an indefinite term as Chief of Police.[2] In 1972, Owen and a new City Manager, Lyle W. Alberg, engaged in a dispute over petitioner's administration of the Police Department's property room. In March of that year, a handgun, which the records of the Department's property room stated had been destroyed, turned up in Kansas City in the possession of a felon. This discovery prompted Alberg to initiate an investigation of the management of the property room. Although the probe was initially directed by petitioner, Alberg soon transferred responsibility for the investigation to the city's Department of Law, instructing the City Counselor to supervise its conduct and to inform him directly of its findings.

Sometime in early April 1972, Alberg received a written report on the investigation's progress, along with copies of confidential witness statements. Although the City Auditor found that the Police Department's records were insufficient to permit an adequate accounting of the goods contained in the property room, the City Counselor concluded that there was no evidence of any criminal acts or of any violation of state or municipal law in the administration of the property room. Alberg discussed the results of the investigation at an informal meeting with several City Council members and advised them that he would take action at an appropriate time to correct any problems in the administration of the Police Department.

On April 10, Alberg asked petitioner to resign as Chief of Police and to accept another position within the Department, citing dissatisfaction with the manner in which petitioner had managed the Department, particularly his inadequate supervision of the property room. Alberg warned that if petitioner refused to take another position in the Department his employment would be terminated, to which petitioner responded that he did not intend to resign.

---

[2] Under § 3.3(1) of the city's charter, the City Manager has sole authority to "[a]ppoint, and when deemed necessary for the good of the service, lay off, suspend, demote, or remove all directors, or heads, of administrative departments and all other administrative officers and employees of the city. . . . "

On April 13, Alberg issued a public statement addressed to the Mayor and the City Council concerning the results of the investigation. After referring to "discrepancies" found in the administration, handling, and security of public property, the release concluded that "[t]here appears to be no evidence to substantiate any allegations of a criminal nature" and offered assurances that "[s]teps have been initiated on an administrative level to correct these discrepancies." Although Alberg apparently had decided by this time to replace petitioner as police chief, he took no formal action to that end and left for a brief vacation without informing the City Council of his decision.

While Alberg was away on the weekend of April 15 and 16, two developments occurred. Petitioner, having consulted with counsel, sent Alberg a letter demanding written notice of the charges against him and a public hearing with a reasonable opportunity to respond to those charges. At approximately the same time, City Councilman Paul L. Roberts asked for a copy of the investigative report on the Police Department property room. Although petitioner's appeal received no immediate response, the Acting City Manager complied with Roberts' request and supplied him with the audit report and the witness statements.

On the evening of April 17, 1972, the City Council held its regularly scheduled meeting. After completion of the planned agenda, Councilman Roberts read a statement he had prepared on the investigation.[5] Roberts charged that petitioner had misappropriated Police Department property for his own use, that narcotics and money had "mysteriously disappeared" from his office, that traffic tickets had been manipulated, that high ranking police officials had made "inappropriate" requests affecting the police court, and that "things have occurred causing the unusual release of felons." At the close of his statement, Roberts moved that the investigative reports be released to the news media and turned over to the prosecutor for presentation to the grand jury, and that the City Manager "take all direct and appropriate action" against those persons "involved in illegal, wrongful, or gross inefficient activities brought out in the investigative reports." After some discussion, the City Council passed Roberts' motion with no dissents and one abstention.

City Manager Alberg discharged the petitioner the very next day. Petitioner was not given any reason for his dismissal; he received only a written notice stating that his employment as Chief of Police was "[t]erminated

---

[5] Roberts' statement . . . in part recited:

On April 2, 1972, the City Council was notified of the existence of an investigative report concerning the activities of the Chief of Police of the city of Independence, certain police officers and activities of one or more other city officials. On Saturday, April 15th for the first time I was able to see these 27 voluminous reports. The contents of these reports are astoundingly shocking and virtually unbelievable. They deal with the disappearance of two or more television sets from the Police Department and [a] signed statement that they were taken by the Chief of Police for his own personal use.

The reports show that numerous firearms properly in the Police Department custody found their way into the hands of others including undesirables and were later found by other law enforcement agencies.

Reports whow [sic] that narcotics held by the Independence Missouri Chief of Police have mysteriously disappeared. Reports also indicate money has mysteriously disappeared. Reports show that traffic tickets have been manipulated. The reports show inappropriate requests affecting the police court have come from high ranking police officials. Reports indicate that things have occurred causing the unusual release of felons. The reports show gross inefficiencies on the part of a few of the high ranking officers of the Police Department. . . .

under the provisions of section 3.3(1) of the city charter." Petitioner's earlier demand for a specification of charges and a public hearing was ignored, and a subsequent request by his attorney for an appeal of the discharge decision was denied by the city on the grounds that "there is no appellate procedure or forum provided by the charter or ordinances of the city of Independence, Missouri, relating to the dismissal of Mr. Owen."

The local press gave prominent coverage both to the City Council's action and petitioner's dismissal, linking the discharge to the investigation. As instructed by the City Council, Alberg referred the investigative reports and witness statements to the prosecuting attorney of Jackson County, Mo., for consideration by a grand jury. The results of the audit and investigation were never released to the public, however. The grand jury subsequently returned a "no true bill," and no further action was taken by either the City Council or City Manager Alberg.

II

Petitioner named the city of Independence, City Manager Alberg, and the present members of the City Council in their official capacities as defendants in this suit.[9] Alleging that he was discharged without notice of reasons and without a hearing in violation of his constitutional rights to procedural and substantive due process, petitioner sought declaratory and injunctive relief, including a hearing on his discharge, backpay from the date of discharge, and attorney's fees. The District Court, after a bench trial, entered judgment for respondents.[10]

The Court of Appeals initially reversed the District Court. Although it agreed with the District Court that under Missouri law petitioner possessed no property interest in continued employment as Police Chief, the Court of Appeals concluded that the city's allegedly false public accusations

---

9 Petitioner did not join former Councilman Roberts in the instant litigation. A separate action seeking defamation damages was brought in state court against Roberts and Alberg in their individual capacities. Petitioner dismissed the state suit against Alberg and reached a financial settlement with Roberts.

10 The District Court, relying on Monroe v. Pape, 365 U.S. 167 (1961), . . . held that § 1983 did not create a cause of action against the city, but that petitioner could base his claim for relief directly on the Fourteenth Amendment. On the merits, however, the court determined that petitioner's discharge did not deprive him of any constitutionally protected property interest because, as an untenured employee, he possessed neither a contractual nor a de facto right to continued employment as Chief of Police. Similarly, the court found that the circumstances of petitioner's dismissal did not impose a stigma of illegal or immoral conduct on his professional reputation, and hence did not deprive him of any liberty interest.

The District Court offered three reasons to support its conclusion: First, because the actual discharge notice stated only that petitioner was "[t]erminated under the provisions of Section 3.3(1) of the city charter," nothing in his official record imputed any stigmatizing conduct to him. Second, the court found that the City Council's actions had no causal connection to petitioner's discharge, for City Manager Alberg had apparently made his decision to hire a new police chief before the Council's April 17th meeting. Lastly, the District Court determined that petitioner was "completely exonerated" from any charges of illegal or immoral conduct by the City Counselor's investigative report, Alberg's public statements, and the grand jury's return of a "no true bill."

As an alternative ground for denying relief, the District Court ruled that the city was entitled to assert, and had in fact established, a qualified immunity against liability based on the good faith of the individual defendants who acted as its agents: "[D]efendants have clearly shown by a preponderance of the evidence that neither they, nor their predecessors, were aware in April 1972, that, under the circumstances the Fourteenth Amendment accorded plaintiff the procedural rights of notice and a hearing at the time of his discharge. Defendants have further proven that they cannot reasonably be charged with constructive notice of such rights since plaintiff was discharged prior to the publication of the Supreme Court decisions in Board of Regents v. Roth, 408 U.S. 564 (1972) and Perry v. Sindermann, 408 U.S. 593 (1972)."

had blackened petitioner's name and reputation, thus depriving him of liberty without due process of law. That the stigmatizing charges did not come from the City Manager and were not included in the official discharge notice was, in the court's view, immaterial. What was important, the court explained, was that "the official actions of the city council released charges against [petitioner] contemporaneous and, in the eyes of the public, connected with that discharge."[12]

Respondents petitioned for review of the Court of Appeals' decision. Certiorari was granted, and the case was remanded for further consideration in light of our supervening decision in Monell v. New York City Dept. of Social Services, 436 U.S. 658 (1978). The Court of Appeals on the remand reaffirmed its original determination that the city had violated petitioner's rights under the Fourteenth Amendment, but held that all respondents, including the city, were entitled to qualified immunity from liability [stating]:

> The Supreme Court's decisions in Board of Regents v. Roth, 408 U.S. 564 (1972), and Perry v. Sindermann, 408 U.S. 593 (1972), crystallized the rule establishing the right to a name-clearing hearing for a government employee allegedly stigmatized in the course of his discharge. The Court decided those two cases two months after the discharge in the instant case. Thus, officials of the city of Independence could not have been aware of [petitioner's] right to a name-clearing hearing in connection with the discharge. The city of Independence should not be charged with predicting the future course of constitutional law. . . . We extend the limited immunity the district court applied to the individual defendants to the city as well, because its officials acted in good faith and without malice. We hold the city not liable for actions it could not reasonably have known violated [petitioner's] constitutional rights.

We turn now to the reasons for our disagreement with this holding.

III

Because the question of the scope of a municipality's immunity from liability under § 1983 is essentially one of statutory construction, the starting point in our analysis must be the language of the statute itself. By its terms, § 1983 "creates a species of tort liability that on its face admits of no immunities." Imbler v. Pachtman, 424 U.S. 409, 417 (1976). Its language is absolute and unqualified; no mention is made of any privileges, immunities, or defenses that may be asserted. Rather, the act imposes liability upon "*every* person" who, under color of state law or custom, "subjects, or causes to be subjected, any citizen of the United States . . . to the deprivation of any rights, privileges, or immunities secured by the Constitution and laws." And *Monell* held that these words were intended to encompass municipal corporations as well as natural "persons."

---

[12] As compensation for the denial of his constitutional rights, the Court of Appeals awarded petitioner damages in lieu of backpay. The court explained that petitioner's termination without a hearing must be considered a nullity, and that ordinarily he ought to remain on the payroll and receive wages until a hearing is held and a proper determination on his retention is made. But because petitioner had reached the mandatory retirement age during the course of the litigation, he could not be reinstated to his former position. Thus the compensatory award was to be measured by the amount of money petitioner would likely have earned to retirement had he not been deprived of his good name by the city's actions, subject to mitigation by the amounts actually earned, as well as by the recovery from Councilman Roberts in the state defamation suit. . . .

Moreover, the congressional debates surrounding the passage of § 1 of the Civil Rights Act of 1871—the forerunner of § 1983—confirm the expansive sweep of the statutory language. . . .

However, notwithstanding § 1983's expansive language and the absence of any express incorporation of common-law immunities, we have, on several occasions, found that a tradition of immunity was so firmly rooted in the common law and was supported by such strong policy reasons that "Congress would have specifically so provided had it wished to abolish the doctrine." Pierson v. Ray, 386 U.S. 547, 555 (1967). . . . Subsequent cases have required that we consider the personal liability of various other types of government officials. . . .

In each of these cases, our finding of § 1983 immunity "was predicated upon a considered inquiry into the immunity historically accorded the relevant official at common law and the interests behind it." Where the immunity claimed by the defendant was well established at common law at the time § 1983 was enacted, and where its rationale was compatible with the purposes of the Civil Rights Act, we have construed the statute to incorporate that immunity. But there is no tradition of immunity for municipal corporations, and neither history nor policy [supports] a construction of § 1983 that would justify the qualified immunity accorded the city of Independence by the Court of Appeals. We hold, therefore, that the municipality may not assert the good faith of its officers or agents as a defense to liability under § 1983.

A

Since colonial times, a distinct feature of our nation's system of governance has been the conferral of political power upon public and municipal corporations for the management of matters of local concern. As *Monell* recounted, by 1871, municipalities—like private corporations—were treated as natural persons for virtually all purposes of constitutional and statutory analysis. In particular, they were routinely sued in both federal and state courts. Local governmental units were regularly held to answer in damages for a wide range of statutory and constitutional violations, as well as for common-law actions for breach of contract. And although, as we discuss below, a municipality was not subject to suit for all manner of tortious conduct, it is clear that at the time § 1983 was enacted, local governmental bodies did not enjoy the sort of "good-faith" qualified immunity extended to them by the Court of Appeals.

As a general rule, it was understood that a municipality's tort liability in damages was identical to that of private corporations and individuals:

> There is nothing in the character of a municipal corporation which entitles it to an immunity from liability for such malfeasances as private corporations or individuals would be liable for in a civil action. A municipal corporation is liable to the same extent as an individual for any act done by the express authority of the corporation, or of a branch of its government, empowered to act for it upon the subject to which the particular act relates, and for any act which, after it has been done, has been lawfully ratified by the corporation.

Thomas G. Shearman & Amasa A. Redfield, A Treatise on the Law of Negligence § 120, p. 139 (1869).

. . . Under this general theory of liability, a municipality was deemed responsible for any private losses generated through a wide variety of its operations and functions, from personal injuries due to its defective sewers, thoroughfares, and public utilities, to property damage caused by its trespasses and uncompensated takings.

Yet in the hundreds of cases from that era awarding damages against municipal governments for wrongs committed by them, one searches in vain for much mention of a qualified immunity based on the good faith of municipal officers. Indeed, where the issue was discussed at all, the courts had rejected the proposition that a municipality should be privileged where it reasonably believed its actions to be lawful. . . .

That municipal corporations were commonly held liable for damages in tort was also recognized by the 42d Congress. See *Monell*, 436 U.S., at 688. For example, Senator Stevenson, in opposing the Sherman amendment's creation of a municipal liability for the riotous acts of its inhabitants, stated the prevailing law: "Numberless cases are to be found where a statutory liability has been created against municipal corporations for injuries resulting from a neglect of corporate duty." Nowhere in the debates, however, is there a suggestion that the common law excused a city from liability on account of the good faith of its authorized agents, much less an indication of a congressional intent to incorporate such an immunity into the Civil Rights Act. . . .

To be sure, there were two doctrines that afforded municipal corporations some measure of protection from tort liability. The first sought to distinguish between a municipality's "governmental" and "proprietary" functions; as to the former, the city was held immune, whereas in its exercise of the latter, the city was held to the same standards of liability as any private corporation. The second doctrine immunized a municipality for its "discretionary" or "legislative" activities, but not for those which were "ministerial" in nature. A brief examination of the application and rationale underlying each of these doctrines demonstrates that Congress could not have intended them to limit a municipality's immunity under § 1983.

The governmental-proprietary distinction owed its existence to the dual nature of the municipal corporation. On the one hand, the municipality was a corporate body, capable of performing the same "proprietary" functions as any private corporation, and liable for its torts in the same manner and to the same extent, as well. On the other hand, the municipality was an arm of the state, and when acting in that "governmental" or "public" capacity, it shared the immunity traditionally accorded the sovereign. But the principle of sovereign immunity—itself a somewhat arid fountainhead for municipal immunity—is necessarily nullified when the state expressly or impliedly allows itself, or its creation, to be sued. Municipalities were therefore liable not only for their "proprietary" acts, but also for those "governmental" functions as to which the state had withdrawn their immunity. And, by the end of the 19th century, courts regularly held that in imposing a specific duty on the municipality either in the charter or by statute, the state had impliedly withdrawn the city's immunity from liability for the nonperformance or misperformance of its obligation. Thus, despite the nominal existence of an immunity for "governmental" functions, municipalities were found liable in damages in a multitude of cases involving such activities.

That the municipality's common-law immunity for "governmental" functions derives from the principle of sovereign immunity also explains why that doctrine could not have served as the basis for the qualified privilege respondent city claims under § 1983. First, because sovereign immunity insulates the municipality from unconsented suits altogether, the presence or absence of good faith is simply irrelevant. The critical issue is whether injury occurred while the city was exercising governmental, as opposed to proprietary, powers or obligations—not whether its agents reasonably believed they were acting lawfully in so conducting themselves. More fundamentally, however, the municipality's "governmental" immunity is obviously abrogated by the sovereign's enactment of a statute making it amenable to suit. Section 1983 was just such a statute. By including municipalities within the class of "persons" subject to liability for violations of the Federal Constitution and laws, Congress—the supreme sovereign on matters of federal law—abolished whatever vestige of the state's sovereign immunity the municipality possessed.

The second common-law distinction between municipal functions—that protecting the city from suits challenging "discretionary" decisions—was grounded not on the principle of sovereign immunity, but on a concern for separation of powers. A large part of the municipality's responsibilities involved broad discretionary decisions on issues of public policy—decisions that affected large numbers of persons and called for a delicate balancing of competing considerations. For a court or jury, in the guise of a tort suit, to review the reasonableness of the city's judgment on these matters would be an infringement upon the powers properly vested in a coordinate and coequal branch of government. In order to ensure against any invasion into the legitimate sphere of the municipality's policymaking processes, courts therefore refused to entertain suits against the city "either for the nonexercise of, or for the manner in which in good faith it exercises, *discretionary powers* of a public or legislative character."

Although many, if not all, of a municipality's activities would seem to involve at least some measure of discretion, the influence of this doctrine on the city's liability was not as significant as might be expected. For just as the courts implied an exception to the municipality's immunity for its "governmental" functions, here, too, a distinction was made that had the effect of subjecting the city to liability for much of its tortious conduct. While the city retained its immunity for decisions as to whether the public interest required acting in one manner or another, once any particular decision was made, the city was fully liable for injuries incurred in the execution of its judgment. Thus, the municipalities remained liable in damages for a broad range of conduct implementing their discretionary decisions.

Once again, an understanding of the rationale underlying the common-law immunity for "discretionary" functions explains why that doctrine cannot serve as the foundation for a good-faith immunity under § 1983. That common-law doctrine merely prevented courts from substituting their own judgment on matters within the lawful discretion of the municipality. But a municipality has no "discretion" to violate the Federal Constitution; its dictates are absolute and imperative. And when a court passes judgment on the municipality's conduct in a § 1983 action, it does not seek to second-guess the "reasonableness" of the city's decision nor to interfere with the local government's resolution of competing policy considerations. Rather, it looks only to whether the municipality has conformed to the requirements of the Federal Constitution and statutes. . . .

In sum, we can discern no "tradition so well grounded in history and reason" that would warrant the conclusion that in enacting § 1 of the Civil Rights Act, the 42d Congress sub silentio extended to municipalities a qualified immunity based on the good faith of their officers. Absent any clearer indication that Congress intended so to limit the reach of a statute expressly designed to provide a "broad remedy for violations of federally protected civil rights," *Monell*, we are unwilling to suppose that injuries occasioned by a municipality's unconstitutional conduct were not also meant to be fully redressable through its sweep.

B

Our rejection of a construction of § 1983 that would accord municipalities a qualified immunity for their good-faith constitutional violations is compelled both by the legislative purpose in enacting the statute and by considerations of public policy. The central aim of the Civil Rights Act was to provide protection to those persons wronged by the " '[m]isuse of power, possessed by virtue of state law and made possible only because the wrongdoer is clothed with the authority of state law.' " *Monroe v. Pape*, 365 U.S. at 184. By creating an express federal remedy, Congress sought to "enforce provisions of the Fourteenth Amendment against those who carry a badge of authority of a state and represent it in some capacity, whether they act in accordance with their authority or misuse it." Id. at 172.

How "uniquely amiss" it would be, therefore, if the government itself—"the social organ to which all in our society look for the promotion of liberty, justice, fair and equal treatment, and the setting of worthy norms and goals for social conduct"—were permitted to disavow liability for the injury it has begotten. A damages remedy against the offending party is a vital component of any scheme for vindicating cherished constitutional guarantees, and the importance of assuring its efficacy is only accentuated when the wrongdoer is the institution that has been established to protect the very rights it has transgressed. Yet owing to the qualified immunity enjoyed by most government officials, see Scheuer v. Rhodes, 416 U.S. 232 (1974), many victims of municipal malfeasance would be left remediless if the city were also allowed to assert a good-faith defense. Unless countervailing considerations counsel otherwise, the injustice of such a result should not be tolerated.[33]

Moreover, § 1983 was intended not only to provide compensation to the victims of past abuses, but to serve as a deterrent against future constitutional deprivations, as well. The knowledge that a municipality will be liable for all of its injurious conduct, whether committed in good faith or not, should create an incentive for officials who harbor doubts about the lawfulness of their intended actions to err on the side of protecting citizens' constitutional rights. Furthermore, the threat that damages might be levied against the city may encourage those in a policymaking position to institute internal rules and programs designed to minimize the likelihood of unintentional infringements on constitutional rights. Such procedures are particularly beneficial in preventing those "systemic" injuries that result not so much from the conduct of any single individual, but from the interactive behavior of several government officials, each of whom may be acting in good faith.[36]

---

[33] The absence of any damages remedy for violations of all but the most "clearly established" constitutional rights could also have the deleterious effect of freezing constitutional law in its current state of development, for without a meaningful remedy, aggrieved individuals will have little incentive to seek vindication of those constitutional deprivations that have not previously been clearly defined.

[36] In addition, the threat of liability against the city ought to increase the attentiveness with which officials at the higher levels of government supervise the conduct of their subordinates. The need to institute system-wide measures in order to increase the vigilance with which otherwise indifferent municipal officials protect citizens' constitutional rights is, of

Our previous decisions conferring qualified immunities on various government officials are not to be read as derogating the significance of the societal interest in compensating the innocent victims of governmental misconduct. Rather, in each case we concluded that overriding considerations of public policy nonetheless demanded that the official be given a measure of protection from personal liability. The concerns that justified those decisions, however, are less compelling, if not wholly inapplicable, when the liability of the municipal entity is at issue.

In *Scheuer v. Rhodes*, supra, the Chief Justice identified the two "mutually dependent rationales" on which the doctrine of official immunity rested:

> (1) the injustice, particularly in the absence of bad faith, of subjecting to liability an officer who is required, by the legal obligations of his position, to exercise discretion; (2) the danger that the threat of such liability would deter his willingness to execute his office with the decisiveness and the judgment required by the public good.

The first consideration is simply not implicated when the damages award comes not from the official's pocket, but from the public treasury. It hardly seems unjust to require a municipal defendant which has violated a citizen's constitutional rights to compensate him for the injury suffered thereby. Indeed, Congress enacted § 1983 precisely to provide a remedy for such abuses of official authority. Elemental notions of fairness dictate that one who causes a loss should bear the loss.

It has been argued, however, that revenue raised by taxation for public use should not be diverted to the benefit of a single or discrete group of taxpayers, particularly where the municipality has at all times acted in good faith. On the contrary, the accepted view is that stated in Thayer v. Boston, 36 Mass. 511, 515 (1837)—"that the city, in its corporate capacity, should be liable to make good the damage sustained by an [unlucky] individual, in consequence of the acts thus done." After all, it is the public at large which enjoys the benefits of the government's activities, and it is the public at large which is ultimately responsible for its administration. Thus, even where some constitutional development could not have been foreseen by municipal officials, it is fairer to allocate any resulting financial loss to the inevitable costs of government borne by all the taxpayers, than to allow its impact to be felt solely by those whose rights, albeit newly recognized, have been violated.[39]

The second rationale mentioned in *Scheuer* also loses its force when it is the municipality, in contrast to the official, whose liability is at issue. At the heart of this justification for a qualified immunity for the individual official is the concern that the threat of *personal* monetary liability will in-

---

course, particularly acute where the front-line officers are judgment-proof in their individual capacities.

[39] *Monell v. New York Dept of Social Services* indicated that the principle of loss-spreading was an insufficient justification for holding the municipality liable under § 1983 on a respondeat superior theory. Here, of course, quite a different situation is presented. Petitioner does not seek to hold the city responsible for the unconstitutional actions of an individual official "*solely* because it employs a tortfeasor." Rather, liability is predicated on a determination that "the action that is alleged to be unconstitutional implements or executes a policy statement, ordinance, regulation, or decision officially adopted and promulgated by the body's officers." In this circumstance—when it is the local government itself that is responsible for the constitutional deprivation—it is perfectly reasonable to distribute the loss to the public as a cost of the administration of government, rather than to let the entire burden fall on the injured individual.

troduce an unwarranted and unconscionable consideration into the decisionmaking process, thus paralyzing the governing official's decisiveness and distorting his judgment on matters of public policy. The inhibiting effect is significantly reduced, if not eliminated, however, when the threat of personal liability is removed. First, as an empirical matter, it is questionable whether the hazard of municipal loss will deter a public officer from the conscientious exercise of his duties; city officials routinely make decisions that either require a large expenditure of municipal funds or involve a substantial risk of depleting the public fisc. More important, though, is the realization that consideration of the *municipality's* liability for constitutional violations is quite properly the concern of its elected or appointed officials. Indeed, a decisionmaker would be derelict in his duties if, at some point, he did not consider whether his decision comports with constitutional mandates and did not weigh the risk that a violation might result in an award of damages from the public treasury. As one commentator aptly put it: "Whatever other concerns should shape a particular official's actions, certainly one of them should be the constitutional rights of individuals who will be affected by his actions. To criticize § 1983 liability because it leads decisionmakers to avoid the infringement of constitutional rights is to criticize one of the statute's raisons d'etre."[41]

IV

In sum, our decision holding that municipalities have no immunity from damages liability flowing from their constitutional violations harmonizes well with developments in the common law and our own pronouncements on official immunities under § 1983. Doctrines of tort law have changed significantly over the past century, and our notions of governmental responsibility should properly reflect that evolution. No longer is individual "blameworthiness" the acid test of liability; the principle of equitable loss-spreading has joined fault as a factor in distributing the costs of official misconduct.

We believe that today's decision, together with prior precedents in this area, properly allocates these costs among the three principals in the scenario of the § 1983 cause of action: the victim of the constitutional deprivation; the officer whose conduct caused the injury; and the public, as represented by the municipal entity. The innocent individual who is harmed by an abuse of governmental authority is assured that he will be compensated for his injury. The offending official, so long as he conducts himself in good faith, may go about his business secure in the knowledge that a qualified immunity will protect him from personal liability for damages that are more appropriately chargeable to the populace as a whole. And the public will be forced to bear only the costs of injury inflicted by the "execution of a government's policy or custom, whether made by its lawmakers or by those whose edicts or acts may fairly be said to represent official policy." *Monell v. New York City Dept. of Social Services*, supra.

Reversed.

■ MR. JUSTICE POWELL, with whom the CHIEF JUSTICE, MR. JUSTICE STEWART, and MR. JUSTICE REHNQUIST joined, dissenting.

The Court today holds that the city of Independence may be liable in damages for violating a constitutional right that was unknown when the events in this case occurred. It finds a denial of due process in the city's

[41] Note, Developments in the Law—Section 1983 and Federalism, 90 Harv.L.Rev. 1133, 1244 (1977).

failure to grant petitioner a hearing to clear his name after he was discharged. But his dismissal involved only the proper exercise of discretionary powers according to prevailing constitutional doctrine. The city imposed no stigma on petitioner that would require a "name clearing" hearing under the Due Process Clause.

On the basis of this alleged deprivation of rights, the Court interprets 42 U.S.C. § 1983 to impose strict liability on municipalities for constitutional violations. This strict liability approach inexplicably departs from this Court's prior decisions under § 1983 and runs counter to the concerns of the 42d Congress when it enacted the statute. The Court's ruling also ignores the vast weight of common-law precedent as well as the current state law of municipal immunity. For these reasons, and because this decision will hamper local governments unnecessarily, I dissent.

I

The Court does not question the District Court's statement of the facts surrounding Owen's dismissal. It nevertheless rejects the District Court's conclusion that no due process hearing was necessary because "the circumstances of [Owen's] discharge did not impose a stigma of illegal or immoral conduct on his professional reputation." Careful analysis of the record supports the District Court's view that Owen suffered no constitutional deprivation. . . . [3]

Due process requires a hearing on the discharge of a government employee "if the employer creates and disseminates a false and defamatory impression about the employee in connection with his termination. . . . " Codd v. Velger, 429 U.S. 624, 628 (1977) (per curiam). This principle was first announced in Board of Regents v. Roth, 408 U.S. 564 (1972), which was decided in June 1972, 10 weeks *after* Owen was discharged. The pivotal question after *Roth* is whether the circumstances of the discharge so blackened the employee's name as to impair his liberty interest in his professional reputation.

The events surrounding Owen's dismissal "were prominently reported in local newspapers." Doubtless, the public received a negative impression of Owen's abilities and performance. But a "name clearing" hearing is not necessary unless the employer makes a public statement that "might seriously damage [the employee's] standing and associations in his community." *Roth*, 408 U.S. at 564. No hearing is required after the "discharge of a public employee whose position is terminable at the will of the employer when there is no public disclosure of the reasons for the discharge." Bishop v. Wood, 426 U.S. 341 (1976).

The City Manager gave no specific reason for dismissing Owen. Instead, he relied on his discretionary authority to discharge top administrators "for the good of the service." Alberg did not suggest that Owen "had been guilty of dishonesty, or immorality." *Roth*, 408 U.S. at 573. Indeed, in his "property room" statement of April 13, Alberg said that there was "no evidence to substantiate any allegations of a criminal nature." This exoneration was reinforced by the grand jury's refusal to initiate a prosecution in the matter. Thus, nothing in the actual firing cast such a stigma on Owen's professional reputation that his liberty was infringed.

[3] Owen initially claimed that his property interests in the job also were violated. The Court of Appeals affirmed the District Court's rejection of that contention, and petitioner has not challenged that ruling in this Court.

The Court does not address directly the question whether any stigma was imposed by the discharge. Rather, it relies on the Court of Appeals' finding that stigma derived from the events "connected with" the firing. That court attached great significance to the resolution adopted by the City Council at its April 17 meeting. But the resolution merely recommended that Alberg take "appropriate action," and the District Court found no "causal connection" between events in the City Council and the firing of Owen. Two days before the Council met, Alberg already had decided to dismiss Owen. Indeed, Councilman Roberts stated at the meeting that the City Manager had asked for Owen's resignation.

Even if the Council resolution is viewed as part of the discharge process, Owen has demonstrated no denial of his liberty. Neither the City Manager nor the Council cast any aspersions on Owen's character. Alberg absolved all connected with the property room of any illegal activity, while the Council resolution alleged no wrongdoing. That events focused public attention upon Owen's dismissal is undeniable; such attention is a condition of employment—and of discharge—for high government officials. Nevertheless, nothing in the actions of the City Manager or the City Council triggered a constitutional right to a name-clearing hearing.

The statements by Councilman Roberts were neither measured nor benign, but they provide no basis for this action against the city of Independence. Under Monell v. New York City Dept. of Social Services, 436 U.S. 658, 691 (1978), the city cannot be held liable for Roberts' statements on a theory of respondeat superior. That case held that § 1983 makes municipalities liable for constitutional deprivations only if the challenged action was taken "pursuant to official municipal policy of some nature. . . . " As the Court noted, "a municipality cannot be held liable *solely* because it employs a tortfeasor. . . . " The statements of a single Councilman scarcely rise to the level of municipal policy.

As the District Court concluded, "[a]t most, the circumstances . . . suggested that, as Chief of Police, [Owen] had been an inefficient administrator." This Court now finds unconstitutional stigma in the interaction of unobjectionable official acts with the unauthorized statements of a lone Councilman who had no direct role in the discharge process. The notoriety that attended Owen's firing resulted not from any city policy, but solely from public misapprehension of the reasons for a purely discretionary dismissal. There was no constitutional injury.

II

Having constructed a constitutional deprivation from a valid exercise of governmental authority, the Court holds that municipalities are strictly liable for their constitutional torts. Until two years ago, municipal corporations enjoyed absolute immunity from § 1983 claims. Monroe v. Pape, 365 U.S. 167 (1961). But *Monell v New York City Dept. of Social Services*, supra, held that local governments are "persons" within the meaning of the statute, and thus are liable in damages for constitutional violations inflicted by municipal policies. *Monell* did not address the question whether municipalities might enjoy a qualified immunity or good-faith defense against § 1983 actions.

After today's decision, municipalities will have gone in two short years from absolute immunity under § 1983 to strict liability. As a policy matter, I believe that strict municipal liability unreasonably subjects local governments to damages judgments for actions that were reasonable when performed. It converts municipal governance into a hazardous slalom through constitutional obstacles that are unknown and unknowable.

The Court's decision also impinges seriously on the prerogatives of municipal entities created and regulated primarily by the states. At the very least, this Court should not initiate a federal intrusion of this magnitude in the absence of explicit congressional action. Yet today's decision is supported by nothing in the text of § 1983. Indeed, it conflicts with the apparent intent of the drafters of the statute, with the common law of municipal tort liability, and with the current state law of municipal immunities.

A

1

Section 1983 provides a private right of action against "[e]very person" acting under color of state law who imposes or causes to be imposed a deprivation of constitutional rights. Although the statute does not refer to immunities, this Court has held that the law "is to be read in harmony with general principles of tort immunities and defenses rather than in derogation of them." Imbler v. Pachtman, 424 U.S. 409, 418 (1976). . . .

The Court today abandons any attempt to harmonize § 1983 with traditional tort law. It points out that municipal immunity may be abrogated by legislation. Thus, according to the Court, Congress "abolished" municipal immunity when it included municipalities "within the class of "persons' subject to liability" under § 1983.

This reasoning flies in the face of our prior decisions under this statute. We have held repeatedly that "immunities 'well grounded in history and reason' [were not] abrogated 'by covert inclusion in the general language' of 1983." Imbler v. Pachtman, 424 U.S. 409, 418 (1976), quoting Tenney v. Brandhove, 341 U.S. 367, 376 (1951). The peculiar nature of the Court's position emerges when the status of executive officers under § 1983 is compared with that of local governments. State and local executives are personally liable for bad-faith or unreasonable constitutional torts. Although Congress had the power to make those individuals liable for all such torts, this Court has refused to find an abrogation of traditional immunity in a statute that does not mention immunities. Yet the Court now views the enactment of § 1983 as a direct abolition of traditional municipal immunities. Unless the Court is overruling its previous immunity decisions, the silence in § 1983 must mean that the 42d Congress mutely accepted the immunity of executive officers, but silently rejected common-law municipal immunity. I find this interpretation of the statute singularly implausible.

2

Important public policies support the extension of qualified immunity to local governments. First, as recognized by the doctrine of separation of powers, some governmental decisions should be at least presumptively insulated from judicial review. . . . The allocation of public resources and the operational policies of the government itself are activities that lie peculiarly within the competence of executive and legislative bodies. When charting those policies, a local official should not have to gauge his employer's possible liability under § 1983 if he incorrectly—though reasonably and in good faith—forecasts the course of constitutional law. Excessive judicial intrusion into such decisions can only distort municipal decisionmaking and discredit the courts. Qualified immunity would provide presumptive protection for discretionary acts, while still leaving the municipality liable for bad faith or unreasonable constitutional deprivations. . . .

The Court now argues that local officials might modify their actions unduly if they face personal liability under § 1983, but that they are unlikely to do so when the locality itself will be held liable. This contention denigrates the sense of responsibility of municipal officers, and misunderstands the political process. Responsible local officials will be concerned about potential judgments against their municipalities for alleged constitutional torts. Moreover, they will be accountable within the political system for subjecting the municipality to adverse judgments. If officials must look over their shoulders at strict municipal liability for unknowable constitutional deprivations, the resulting degree of governmental paralysis will be little different from that caused by fear of personal liability.[9]

In addition, basic fairness requires a qualified immunity for municipalities. The good-faith defense recognized under § 1983 authorizes liability only when officials acted with malicious intent or when they "knew or should have known that their conduct violated the constitutional norm." The standard incorporates the idea that liability should not attach unless there was notice that a constitutional right was at issue. This idea applies to governmental entities and individual officials alike. Constitutional law is what the courts say it is, and—as demonstrated by today's decision and its precursor, *Monell*—even the most prescient lawyer would hesitate to give a firm opinion on matters not plainly settled. Municipalities, often acting in the utmost good faith, may not know or anticipate when their action or inaction will be deemed a constitutional violation.

The Court nevertheless suggests that, as a matter of social justice, municipal corporations should be strictly liable even if they could not have known that a particular action would violate the Constitution. After all, the Court urges, local governments can "spread" the costs of any judgment across the local population. The Court neglects, however, the fact that many local governments lack the resources to withstand substantial unanticipated liability under § 1983. Even enthusiastic proponents of municipal liability have conceded that ruinous judgments under the statute could imperil local governments. By simplistically applying the theorems of welfare economics and ignoring the reality of municipal finance, the Court imposes strict liability on the level of government least able to bear it. For some municipalities, the result could be a severe limitation on their ability to serve the public.

B

The Court searches at length—and in vain—for legal authority to buttress its policy judgment. Despite its general statements to the contrary, the Court can find no support for its position in the debates on the civil rights legislation that included § 1983. Indeed, the legislative record suggests that the members of the 42d Congress would have been dismayed by this ruling. Nor, despite its frequent citation of authorities that are only marginally relevant, can the Court rely on the traditional or current law of municipal tort liability. Both in the 19th century and now, courts and legislatures have recognized the importance of limiting the liability of local gov-

---

[9] The Court's argument is not only unpersuasive, but also is internally inconsistent. The Court contends that strict liability is necessary to "create an incentive for officials . . . to err on the side of protecting citizens' constitutional rights." Yet the Court later assures us that such liability will not distort municipal decisionmaking because "[t]he inhibiting effect is significantly reduced, if not eliminated . . . when the threat of personal liability is removed." Thus, the Court apparently believes that strict municipal liability is needed to modify public policies, but will not have any impact on those policies anyway.

ernments for official torts. Each of these conventional sources of law points to the need for qualified immunity for local governments.

1

The modern dispute over municipal liability under § 1983 has focused on the defeat of the Sherman amendment during the deliberations on the Civil Rights Act of 1871. Senator Sherman proposed that local governments be held vicariously liable for constitutional deprivations caused by riots within their boundaries. As originally drafted, the measure imposed liability even if municipal officials had no actual knowledge of the impending disturbance. The amendment, which did not affect the part of the Civil Rights Act that we now know as § 1983, was approved by the Senate but rejected by the House of Representatives. After two revisions by conference committees, both houses passed what is now codified as 42 U.S.C. § 1986. The final version applied not just to local governments but to all "persons," and it imposed no liability unless the defendant knew that a wrong was "about to be committed."

Because Senator Sherman initially proposed strict municipal liability for constitutional torts, the discussion of his amendment offers an invaluable insight into the attitudes of his colleagues on the question now before the Court. Much of the resistance to the measure flowed from doubts as to Congress' power to impose vicarious liability on local governments. But opponents of the amendment made additional arguments that strongly support recognition of qualified municipal immunity under § 1983.

First, several legislators expressed trepidation that the proposal's strict liability approach could bankrupt local governments. . . .

Most significant, the opponents objected to liability imposed without any showing that a municipality knew of an impending constitutional deprivation. Senator Sherman defended this feature of the amendment as a characteristic of riot acts long in force in England and this country. But Senator Stevenson argued against creating "a corporate liability for personal injury which no prudence or foresight could have prevented." In the most thorough critique of the amendment, Senator Thurman carefully reviewed the riot acts of Maryland and New York. He emphasized that those laws imposed liability only when a plaintiff proved that the local government had both notice of the impending injury and the power to prevent it.

> Is not that right? Why make the county, or town, or parish liable when it had no reason whatsoever to anticipate that any such crime was about to be committed, and when it had no knowledge of the commission of the crime until after it was committed? What justice is there in that?

These concerns were echoed in the House of Representatives. . . .

Partly in response to these objections, the amendment as finally enacted conditioned liability on a demonstration that the defendant knew that constitutional rights were about to be denied. . . .

These objections to the Sherman amendment apply with equal force to strict municipal liability under § 1983. Just as the 42d Congress refused to hold municipalities vicariously liable for deprivations that could not be known beforehand, this Court should not hold those entities strictly liable for deprivations caused by actions that reasonably and in good faith were thought to be legal. The Court's approach today, like the Sherman amendment, could spawn onerous judgments against local governments and distort the decisions of officers who fear municipal liability for their actions. Congress' refusal to impose those burdens in 1871 surely undercuts any historical argument that federal judges should do so now.

The Court declares that its rejection of qualified immunity is "compelled" by the "legislative purpose" in enacting § 1983. One would expect powerful documentation to back up such a strong statement. Yet the Court notes only three features of the legislative history of the Civil Rights Act. Far from "compelling" the Court's strict liability approach, those features of the congressional record provide scant support for its position.

First, the Court [relies on] statements by Congressmen attesting to the broad remedial scope of the law. In view of our many decisions recognizing the immunity of officers under § 1983, those statements plainly shed no light on the congressional intent with respect to immunity under the statute. Second, the Court cites Senator Stevenson's remark that frequently "a statutory liability has been created against municipal corporations for injuries resulting from a neglect of corporate duty." The Senator merely stated the unobjectionable proposition that municipal immunity could be qualified or abolished by statute. This fragmentary observation provides no basis for the Court's version of the legislative history.

Finally, the Court emphasizes the lack of comment on municipal immunity when opponents of the bill did discuss the immunities of government officers. "Had there been a similar common-law immunity for municipalities, the bill's opponents would have raised the spectre of its destruction as well." This is but another example of the Court's continuing willingness to find meaning in silence. This example is particularly noteworthy because the very next sentence in the Court's opinion concedes: "To be sure, there were two doctrines that afforded municipal corporations some measure of protection from tort liability." Since the opponents of the Sherman amendment repeatedly expressed their conviction that strict municipal liability was unprecedented and unwise, the failure to recite the theories of municipal immunity is of no relevance here. In any event, that silence cannot contradict the many contemporary judicial decisions applying that immunity.

2

The Court's decision also runs counter to the common law in the 19th century, which recognized substantial tort immunity for municipal actions. Nineteenth-century courts generally held that municipal corporations were not liable for acts undertaken in their "governmental," as opposed to their "proprietary," capacity. Most states now use other criteria for determining when a local government should be liable for damages. Still, the governmental/proprietary distinction retains significance because it was so widely accepted when § 1983 was enacted. It is inconceivable that a Congress thoroughly versed in current legal doctrines, see *Monell*, 436 U.S. at 669, would have intended through silence to create the strict liability regime now imagined by this Court.

More directly relevant to this case is the common-law distinction between the "discretionary" and "ministerial" duties of local governments. This Court wrote in Harris v. District of Columbia, 256 U.S. 650, 652 (1921): "[W]hen acting in good faith municipal corporations are not liable for the manner in which they exercise their discretionary powers." The rationale for this immunity derives from the theory of separation of powers. . . .

That reasoning, frequently applied in the 19th century, parallels the theory behind qualified immunity under § 1983. This Court has recognized the importance of preserving the autonomy of executive bodies entrusted with discretionary powers. *Scheuer v. Rhodes* held that executive officials who have broad responsibilities must enjoy a "range of discretion [that is] comparably broad." Consequently, the immunities available under § 1983 [vary] directly with "the scope of discretion and responsibility of the office. . . . " Strict municipal liability can only undermine that discretion.[18] . . .

3

Today's decision also conflicts with the current law in 44 states and the District of Columbia. All of those jurisdictions provide municipal immunity at least analogous to a "good faith" defense against liability for constitutional torts. Thus, for municipalities in almost 90 per cent of our jurisdictions, the Court creates broader liability for constitutional deprivations than for state-law torts. . . .

C

The Court turns a blind eye to this overwhelming evidence that municipalities have enjoyed a qualified immunity and to the policy considerations that for the life of this republic have justified its retention. This disregard of precedent and policy is especially unfortunate because suits under § 1983 typically implicate evolving constitutional standards. A good-faith defense is much more important for those actions than in those involving ordinary tort liability. The duty not to run over a pedestrian with a municipal bus is far less likely to change than is the rule as to what process, if any, is due the bus driver if he claims the right to a hearing after discharge.

The right of a discharged government employee to a "name clearing" hearing was not recognized until our decision in *Board of Regents v. Roth*. That ruling was handed down 10 weeks after Owen was discharged and eight weeks after the city denied his request for a hearing. By stripping the city of any immunity, the Court punishes it for failing to predict our decision in *Roth*. As a result, local governments and their officials will face the unnerving prospect of crushing damages judgments whenever a policy valid under current law is later found to be unconstitutional. I can see no justice or wisdom in that outcome.

NOTES ON OWEN V. CITY OF INDEPENDENCE

1. THE DUE PROCESS ISSUE

In *Owen* the former police chief sought and received compensation for wrongful discharge. But why, exactly, was the discharge wrongful? The Court did not hold that Owen had a right to continued employment. As a discretion-

---

[18] The Court cannot wash away these extensive municipal immunities. It quotes [a 19th-century treatise] as referring to municipal liability for some torts. [The passage, however, refers] to exceptions to the existing immunity rules. The . . . treatise cited by the Court concedes, though deplores, the fact that many jurisdictions embraced the governmental/proprietary distinction. Thomas G. Shearman and Amasa A. Redfield, A Treatise on the Law of Negligence § 120, pp. 140–41 (1869). The same volume notes that local governments could not be sued for injury caused by discretionary acts, id., § 127, at p. 154, or for officers' acts beyond the powers of the municipal corporation, id., § 140, at p. 169. . . .

The Court takes some solace in the absence in the 19th century of a qualified immunity for local governments. That absence, of course, was due to the availability of absolute immunity for governmental and discretionary acts. . . .

ary employee, he was subject to termination for virtually any reason. The problem was apparently not the discharge itself, but rather the accompanying publicity. Of course, coverage by the media would have been beyond the city's power to control and in any event not the city's fault, so the crucial error seems to have been the public dissemination by city officials of statements harmful to Owen's reputation. Far and away the most injurious were the remarks of Councilman Roberts, remarks that even the dissent admitted were "neither measured nor benign."

Does the *Owen* decision suggest that the city should have prevented those communications? Would the necessity for a hearing have been avoided if the City Manager had refused to allow public disclosure of the charges in the investigative report? Or would it have been necessary as well to muzzle Councilman Roberts? Could this have been done? Is it desirable that the Constitution be construed to require it done?

Suppose that the offending statements had been withheld and that Owen had been discharged without adverse publicity. Suppose further that Owen then went to a neighboring town and applied for appointment as Chief of Police. If an officer of that town telephoned the City Manager of Independence and asked for a candid evaluation of Owen's character and abilities and for an explanation of the reasons for his dismissal, what would be the appropriate response? Should the City Manager give an opinion? Or would it be wiser to refuse to cooperate?

One answer might be that a municipality should make no effort to restrict the flow of information to the public but should simply be prepared to grant a "name-clearing hearing" to any employee whose reputation is injured as a result. This seems to be the Court's position in *Owen*. Presumably, after Councilman Roberts' remarks, the city should have held a hearing at which Owen would have had a chance to defend his record.

What would such a hearing look like? To what decision would it lead? Would the hearing officer attempt to adjudicate, whether, as Councilman Roberts alleged, narcotics and money had "mysteriously disappeared"? Or whether "inappropriate requests" to the police court had in fact been made by "high ranking police officials"? Or whether, as Councilman Roberts concluded, the investigative reports were "astoundingly shocking and virtually unbelievable"? By what standards would such issues be resolved? And if the determination were favorable to Owen, what relief would be given? Would he get his job back, or would he receive merely some sort of official certification of good character?

Perhaps the Court envisions that the "name-clearing hearing" would not lead to any decisional outcome but would merely present an opportunity for the airing of views. Suppose such a hearing is held, and Owen makes a wide-ranging defense of his conduct in office. What should the city officials do in response? Should they say anything? Does the hearing officer simply thank Owen for his time and allow the city to get on with the business of selecting a new Chief of Police? If so, the "name-clearing hearing" would be little more than a press conference. The value to Owen would depend on the willingness of the media to give coverage and sympathetic attention to his side of the story. Of course, the media could do that without an official proceeding, and the city's role in mediating between Owen and the press is at best obscure.

These issues did not surface in *Owen* because the time had already passed when the city might have attempted to restrain communication or to provide the required hearing. In the future, however, municipalities may be expected to attempt to structure their affairs so as to avoid civil liability and will have to choose among the possible inferences to be drawn from *Owen*.

2. THE IMMUNITY ISSUE

The *Owen* opinion illustrates the familiar amalgam of statutory language, legislative history, common-law background, and public policy. Which of these factors seems to have been the most influential in *Owen*? Which should have been? What are the appropriate inferences to be drawn from legislative silence on the subject of immunities? Should the answer hinge on the law of municipal immunity as it stood in 1871? If so, which side seems to have the better of the argument?

Within its sphere, *Owen* imposes strict enterprise liability on local governments. Yet if *Owen* is a step toward enterprise liability, it is only a small step. Absent congressional action, states and state agencies remain immune under the Eleventh Amendment. Individual officers at all levels have the defense of qualified immunity, which severely limits the indirect liability of the governments that employ them. And local governments, who alone among § 1983 defendants can be held strictly liable, can be sued only for acts done pursuant to an official policy or custom. *Owen* is, therefore, the exception rather than the rule. Should it be? Or should the whole scheme of individual, fault-based liability be discarded in favor of a much expanded strict liability imposed directly on government?

3. THE SIGNIFICANCE OF FAULT

The defense of qualified immunity means that liability under § 1983 generally is fault-based. *Owen* is exceptional in embracing a form of strict liability (if only for a limited class of cases).

This position is widely endorsed by academic commentators, many of whom favor strict liability either of the officer defendant or the government employer. See, e.g., Akhil Reed Amar, Of Sovereignty and Federalism, 96 Yale L.J. 1425 (1987) (insisting on the "remedial imperative" of governmental liability); George A. Bermann, Integrating Governmental and Officer Tort Liability, 77 Colum. L. Rev. 1175 (1977) (endorsing direct governmental liability with a right of indemnification against miscreant officials); Mark R. Brown, Correlating Municipal Liability and Official Immunity Under Section 1983, 1989 U. Ill. L. Rev. 625, 631 (arguing that governmental liability and officer immunity should be inversely correlated to eliminate any gap between right and remedy); Mark R. Brown, The Demise of Constitutional Prospectivity: New Life for *Owen*?, 79 Iowa L. Rev. 273, 311–12 (1994) (concluding that immunity is inappropriate even for violations of newly declared constitutional rights); Harold S. Lewis, Jr. & Theodore Y. Blumoff, Reshaping Section 1983,s Asymmetry, 140 U. Pa. L. Rev. 755, 756 (1992) (arguing for strict respondeat superior liability); Susanah M. Mead, 42 U.S.C. § 1983 Municipal Liability: The *Monell* Sketch Becomes a Distorted Picture, 65 N.C. L. Rev. 517, 538 (1987) (arguing for strict respondeat superior liability); Jon O. Newman, Suing the Lawbreakers: Proposals to Strengthen the Section 1983 Damage Remedy for Law Enforcers' Misconduct, 87 Yale L.J. 447

(1978) (calling for damages actions directly against state and federal governments); Laura Oren, Immunity and Accountability in Civil Rights Litigation: Who Should Pay?, 50 U. Pitt. L. Rev. 935, 1000–02 (1989) (arguing for strict respondeat superior liability); Peter H. Schuck, Suing Government: Citizen Remedies for Official Wrongs (1983) (arguing that enterprise liability would facilitate effective compensation).

The arguments for or against strict enterprise liability are generally instrumental in nature. That is, they turn on perceptions of efficient deterrence of constitutional violations, the fear of inhibiting the legitimate exercise of government power, and the like. Additionally, the issue has a noninstrumental aspect, concerned not with efficiency and deterrence but with fairness and justice. It is this latter aspect of the problem to which Justice Brennan referred when he found no "injustice" in imposing strict liability: "It hardly seems unjust to require a municipal defendant which has violated a citizen's constitutional rights to compensate him for the injury suffered thereby. . . . Elemental notions of fairness dictate that one who causes a loss should bear the loss."

This position has been attacked as a misunderstanding of the normative basis for compensation. See John C. Jeffries, Jr., Compensation for Constitutional Torts: Reflections on the Significance of Fault, 88 Mich. L. Rev. 82 (1989). Putting instrumental concerns to one side, Jeffries argues from principles of "corrective justice" that not only causation of injury, but also proof of fault should be required:

> Just as causation identifies why this plaintiff is entitled to recover, fault identifies why *this defendant* is obliged to pay. Causation itself is inadequate to this task, for there are, in the nature of things, many causes of any injury. The plaintiff's own conduct, for example, is usually, if not always, a but-for cause of plaintiff's injury. Other causal antecedents abound, and there is nothing inherent in the concept of causation (as distinct from external limitations imposed in the name of causation) to say which causes count. The showing of fault fills this gap. It identifies the causal antecedent that will be regarded as legally significant. It singles out a particular defendant—one whose *wrongful* act has caused the plaintiff's injury—to make good the plaintiff's loss.
>
> More simply, fault supplies the moral dimension to the causal relationship. While causation traces a physical connection between doer and sufferer, it provides in itself no moral basis for coercing compensation.

Whatever the merits of argument about the conceptual significance of fault in municipal liability under § 1983, it is clear that the issue has practical consequences only in some cases. Mostly, they involve situations where local government has failed to anticipate changes—or at least clarification—in the law. When governmental policy violates a settled rule of constitutional law, qualified immunity (even if it were available) would provide no defense. A qualified immunity defense (if available) could be made out only if it would have been reasonable at the time to regard the policy as consistent with constitutional limitations. The chief effect of *Owen*, therefore, is to impose additional liability on local governments in cases where uncertainties or ambiguities in the law make it reasonable for the locality not to foresee that its policy would be struck down. Do "[e]lemental notions of fairness" require compensation in that situation?

4. SUBSEQUENT RETROACTIVITY CASES

One way to look at *Owen* is that it imposed retroactive liability on the municipality for violating the requirement of a name-clearing hearing subsequently announced in Board of Regents v. Roth, 408 U.S. 564 (1972), and Perry v. Sindermann, 408 U.S. 593 (1972). In decisions since *Owen*, the Supreme Court first flirted with, then backed away from, an approach that would have made some constitutional decisions apply only prospectively.

American Trucking Associations, Inc. v. Smith, 496 U.S. 167 (1990), was a refund suit filed in state court by Arkansas taxpayers. They claimed that a highway use tax enacted in 1983 was unconstitutional. In 1987, the Supreme Court held in American Trucking Associations, Inc. v. Scheiner, 483 U.S. 266 (1987), that similar taxes imposed by Pennsylvania were unconstitutional. *Smith*, which was then pending in the Supreme Court, was remanded to the Arkansas Supreme Court for reconsideration in light of *Scheiner*. The Arkansas Supreme Court ruled that *Scheiner* should apply only prospectively. The case then came back to the Supreme Court. The judgment was for the most part affirmed, with the Court divided four-one-four.

Justice O'Connor wrote for a plurality of herself, Chief Justice Rehnquist, and Justices White, and Kennedy. Since *Scheiner* "established a new principle of law in the area of our dormant commerce clause jurisprudence" she thought it should not apply retroactively. Her analysis was a three-part inquiry derived from Chevron Oil Co. v. Huson, 404 U.S. 97 (1971):

> First, the decision to be applied nonretroactively must establish a new principle of law, either by overruling clear past precedent on which litigants may have relied, or by deciding an issue of first impression whose resolution was not clearly foreshadowed. Second, . . . we must . . . weigh the merits and demerits in each case by looking to the prior history of the rule in question, its purpose and effect, and whether retrospective operation will further or retard its operation. Finally, we [must] weig[h] the inequity imposed by retroactive application, for where a decision of this Court could produce substantial inequitable results if applied retroactively, there is ample basis in our cases for avoiding the injustice or hardship by a holding of nonretroactivity.

Justice O'Connor found inequity in applying *Scheiner* retroactively, since "the state promulgated and implemented its tax scheme in reliance" on the old law and a "refund, if required by state or federal law, could deplete the state treasury, thus threatening the state's current operations and future plans."

As to the seemingly contrary lesson of *Owen*, O'Connor said:

> Our delineation of the scope of liability under a statute designed to permit suit against government entities and officials provides little guidance for determining the fairest way to apply our own decisions. Indeed, the policy concerns involved are quite distinct. In *Owen*, we discerned that according municipalities a special immunity from liability for violations of constitutional rights would not best serve the goals of § 1983, even if those rights had not been clearly established when the violation occurred. Such a determination merely makes municipalities, like private individuals, responsible for anticipating developments in the law. We noted that such liability would motivate each of the city's elected officials to "consider whether his decision comports with constitutional mandates and . . . weigh the risk

that a violation might result in an award of damages from the public treasury." This analysis does not apply when a decision clearly breaks with precedent, a type of departure which, by definition, public officials could not anticipate nor have any responsibility to anticipate.

Justice Scalia concurred in the result. He thought prospective decisionmaking "incompatible with the judicial role," but concurred on the ground that *Scheiner* had been wrongly decided.

The dissenters, in an opinion by Justice Stevens, would have applied *Scheiner* to all cases then still pending on direct review. The dissent dealt with *Owen* in a footnote:

> Our decision in *Owen* is necessarily predicated upon the view that a court should apply the law in effect at the time of decision in considering whether the state has violated the Constitution. Although the plurality is technically correct that *Owen* did not hold that constitutional decisions should always apply "retroactively," that case, and the Congress that enacted § 1983, surely did not contemplate that state actors could achieve through the judicially crafted doctrine of retroactivity, the immunity not only from damages but also from liability denied them on the floors of Congress.

Three years later, the *Smith* plurality's suggestion that "new" constitutional rulings might apply only prospectively was rejected. In Harper v. Virginia Department of Taxation, 509 U.S. 86 (1993), the Court confronted another question of the effect a prior decision declaring state taxes invalid. This time the Court applied its prior ruling retroactively. Speaking through Justice Thomas, the majority seemed hostile to any notion of non-retroactivity in constitutional law: "When this Court applies a rule of federal law to the parties before it, that rule is the controlling interpretation of federal law and must be given full retroactive effect in all cases still open on direct review and as to all events, regardless of whether such events predate or postdate our announcement of the rule." Justice O'Connor, joined by Chief Justice Rehnquist, dissented.

The upshot of all this seems to be that *Owen* is restored to its apparent scope. Retroactive application of new constitutional rulings means, under *Owen*, that localities will be held liable for failing to anticipate such rulings, even in circumstances where individual defendants would have enjoyed the defense of qualified immunity.[a]

5. FEDERAL GOVERNMENTAL LIABILITY

An attempt to extend the rule of *Owen* to suits against the federal government was rejected in FDIC v. Meyer, 510 U.S. 471 (1994). Meyer was an executive in a savings and loan association. When the association failed, federal authorities took over and carried out their general policy of firing the senior management of failed thrifts. Meyer claimed that his termination without a hearing violated procedural due process and brought *Bivens* actions against both the official immediately responsible for his termination and the Federal Savings and Loan Insurance Corporation (FSLIC), whose duties were later assumed by the Federal Deposit Insurance Corporation (FDIC).

[a] For analysis of *Smith* and *Harper*, see Mark R. Brown, The Demise of Constitutional Prospectivity: New Life for *Owen*?, 79 Iowa L. Rev. 273 (1994).

The jury found in favor of the defendant official on grounds of qualified immunity but held the federal agency, which presumably had no such immunity, liable in the amount of $130,000. A unanimous Supreme Court ruled that *Bivens* actions would not lie against federal agencies. The effect is to remit *Bivens* plaintiffs to suits against federal officers, with the attendant limitations of qualified immunity. Direct governmental liability is limited to localities.

6. *CORRECTIONAL SERVICES CORP. V. MALESKO*

In Correctional Services Corp. v. Malesko, 534 U.S. 61 (2001), the court extended *Meyer* to private companies acting under color of federal law. Malesko was an inmate in a half-way house operated by Correctional Services Corp. (CSC) under contract with the Federal Bureau of Prisons. He had a heart condition and was given special permission to use the elevator to reach his room on the fifth floor. On one occasion, a CSC employee refused to let him do so. Malesko climbed the stairs and suffered a heart attack. His *Bivens* claims against various individual defendants were dismissed on statute-of-limitations grounds, but the action against the corporation was allowed to proceed as timely.

A divided Supreme Court extended the rule of *Meyer* to private corporations acting under color of federal law. Speaking for the Court, the Chief Justice described *Bivens* as an exception to the Court's general reluctance to find private rights of action in the absence of clear legislative authorization. He also noted that federal prisoners can bring *Bivens* actions only against individual officers and not against the United States or the Bureau of Prisons. The Court saw no reason to give Malesko broader federal remedies than he would have had if confined in a federal prison. Moreover, the Court noted that Malesko did not lack for alternative remedies, as the corporation could have been sued for negligence under state law.

Justice Stevens, joined by Justices Souter, Ginsburg, and Breyer, dissented. Stevens argued that the Court's exemption of corporate defendants would allow them to violate rights with impunity. He also argued that lawsuits against private prison corporations would have an important deterrent effect in preventing future Eighth Amendment violations. Whereas the majority compared Malesko to federal prisoners, Stevens compared him to state prisoners, who presumably can sue private prisons under § 1983. See Lugar v. Edmonson Oil Co., 457 U.S. 922 (1982) (permitting § 1983 suits against private corporations acting under color of state law). Unlike state prisoners, Malesko was left without a federal remedy.

INTRODUCTORY NOTES ON "OFFICIAL POLICY"

1. INTRODUCTION

Monell limited governmental liability to acts done pursuant to official policy or custom. This requirement has proved troublesome. The issue is clear where, as in *Monell,* the decision is taken pursuant to a rule or regulation of general applicability. More difficult questions arise when governmental liability is sought for a single act or decision by government officials. No one could contend that the Supreme Court's treatment of this issue has been clear.

The cases fall into two categories. The first concerns when the act of a government agent can properly be attributed to the agency itself. This issue is addressed in the note on *Pembaur* below and in the main case that follows, *City of St. Louis v. Praprotnik.* The second category concerns whether the government can be held liable for the omission of failing to train its officials properly. This issue is addressed in *City of Canton v. Harris,* which appears as a main case following *Praprotnik.*

2. *PEMBAUR V. CITY OF CINCINNATI*

Pembaur v. City of Cincinnati, 475 U.S. 469 (1986), arose from an investigation of alleged welfare fraud in Dr. Pembaur's medical clinic. A grand jury issued subpoenas for two of Pembaur's employees, both of whom failed to appear. The prosecutor then obtained warrants ordering their arrest.

When deputy sheriffs arrived at the clinic to execute the warrants, Pembaur locked the door separating the reception area from the rest of the clinic and refused to let them in. After consulting with the Cincinnati police, the deputies called their supervisor to ask for instructions. The supervisor told them to call William Whalen, assistant prosecutor of the county, and to follow his directions. Whalen conferred with his superior and relayed the instruction to "go in and get" the recalcitrant witnesses. When advised of these instructions, the city police officers on the scene obtained an axe and chopped down the door. The deputies then entered and searched for the witnesses. They arrested two individuals who fit the descriptions in the warrants but turned out to be the wrong persons.

Four years later, Steagald v. United States, 451 U.S. 204 (1981), ruled that, absent exigent circumstances, the police cannot enter an individual's home or business without a search warrant, merely because they are seeking to execute an arrest warrant for a third person. *Steagald* was conceded to apply retroactively, and thus became the basis for Pembaur's § 1983 action against all involved. The issue that ultimately came to the Supreme Court was the liability of the county for the actions of its officers.

At trial, the evidence showed no prior instance when the sheriff had been denied access to property in an attempt to arrest a third person. There was no written or general policy on the issue. The county's liability therefore turned on its responsibility for the decision of its officials on this particular occasion. Speaking for the Court, Justice Brennan said:

> The Deputy Sheriffs who attempted to serve the [arrest warrants] at petitioner's clinic found themselves in a difficult situation. Unsure of the proper course of action to follow, they sought instructions from their supervisors. The instructions they received were to follow the orders of the County Prosecutor. The prosecutor made a considered decision based on his understanding of the law and commanded the officers forcibly to enter petitioner's clinic. That decision directly caused the violation of petitioner's Fourth Amendment rights.
>
> Respondent argues that the County Prosecutor lacked authority to establish municipal policy respecting law enforcement practices because only the County Sheriff may establish policy respecting such practices. Respondent suggests that the County Prosecutor was merely rendering "legal advice" when he ordered the Deputy Sheriffs to "go in and get" the witnesses. Consequently, the argument concludes, the action of the individual

Deputy Sheriffs in following this advice and forcibly entering petitioner's clinic was not pursuant to a properly established municipal policy.

We might be inclined to agree with respondent if we thought that the prosecutor had only rendered "legal advice." However, the Court of Appeals concluded, based upon its examination of Ohio law, that both the County Sheriff and the County Prosecutor could establish county policy under appropriate circumstances, a conclusion that we do not question here. Ohio Rev.Code Ann. § 309.09 provides that county officers may "require . . . instructions from [the County Prosecutor] in matters connected with their official duties." Pursuant to standard office procedure, the Sheriff's office referred this matter to the Prosecutor and then followed his instructions. The Sheriff testified that his Department followed this practice under appropriate circumstances and that it was "the proper thing to do" in this case. We decline to accept respondent's invitation to overlook this delegation of authority by disingenuously labeling the prosecutor's clear command mere "legal advice." In ordering the Deputy Sheriffs to enter petitioner's clinic the County Prosecutor was acting as the final decisionmaker for the county, and the county may therefore be held liable under § 1983.

Justice White concurred to suggest that municipal liability was proper *only* because the search was not clearly illegal at the time it was made. If controlling law had plainly prohibited the search, he argued, the local officers could "not be said to have the authority to make contrary policy": "Had the sheriff or prosecutor in this case failed to follow an existing warrant requirement, it would be absurd to say that he was nevertheless executing county policy in authorizing the forceful entry. . . . " Here, however, the sheriff and the prosecutor exercised the discretion vested in them, and the decision they made therefore became "county policy." Justice O'Connor briefly endorsed these views in an opinion concurring in part and concurring in the judgment. Justice Stevens reiterated his belief that county liability could be based on respondeat superior.

Justice Powell, joined by Chief Justice Burger and Justice Rehnquist, dissented. He argued that "no official county policy could have been created solely by an off-hand telephone response from a busy County Prosecutor":

> Proper resolution of this case calls for identification of the applicable principles for determining when policy is created. The Court today does not do this, but instead focuses almost exclusively on the status of the decisionmaker. Its reasoning is circular: it contends that policy is what policymakers make, and policymakers are those who have authority to make policy. . . .
>
> In my view, the question whether official policy—in any normal sense of the term—has been made in a particular case is not answered by explaining who has final authority to make policy. The question here is not "*could* the County Prosecutor make policy?" but rather, "*did* he make policy?" By focusing on the authority granted to the official under state law, the Court's test fails to answer the key federal question presented. The Court instead turns the question into one of state law. . . . Here the Court of Appeals found that "both the County Sheriff and the County Prosecutor had authority under Ohio law to establish county policy under appropriate circumstances." Apparently that recitation of authority is all that is needed under the Court's test because no discussion is offered to

demonstrate that the sheriff or the prosecutor actually used that authority to establish official county policy in this case. . . .

In my view, proper resolution of the question whether official policy has been formed should focus on two factors: (i) the nature of the decision reached or the action taken, and (ii) the process by which the decision was reached or the action was taken.

Focusing on the nature of the decision distinguishes between policies and mere ad hoc decisions. Such a focus also reflects the fact that most policies embody a rule of general applicability. That is the tenor of the Court's statement in *Monell* that local government units are liable under § 1983 when the action that is alleged to be unconstitutional "implements or executes a policy statement, ordinance, regulation, or decision officially adopted and promulgated by the body's officers." The clear implication is that policy is created when a rule is formed that applies to all similar situations. . . . [6] When a rule of general applicability has been approved, the government has taken a position for which it can be held responsible.

Another factor indicating that policy has been formed is the process by which the decision at issue was reached. Formal procedures that involve, for example, voting by elected officials, prepared reports, extended deliberation or official records indicate that the resulting decisions taken "may fairly be said to represent official policy." Owen v. City of Independence, 445 U.S. 622 (1980), provides an example. . . .

Applying these factors to the instant case demonstrates that no official policy was formulated. Certainly, no rule of general applicability was adopted. The Court correctly notes that the sheriff "testified that the Department had no written policy respecting the serving of [arrest warrants] on the property of third persons and that the proper response in any given situation would depend upon the circumstances." Nor could he recall a specific instance in which entrance had been denied and forcibly gained. The Court's result today rests on the implicit conclusion that the prosecutor's response—"go in and get them"—altered the prior case-by-case approach of the Department and formed a new rule to apply in all similar cases. Nothing about the Prosecutor's response to the inquiry over the phone, nor the circumstances surrounding the response, indicates that such a rule of general applicability was formed.

Similarly, nothing about the way the decision was reached indicates that official policy was formed. The Prosecutor, without time for thoughtful consideration or consultation, simply gave an off-the-cuff answer to a single question. There was no *process* at all. The Court's holding undercuts the basic rationale of *Monell* and unfairly increases the risk of liability on the level of government least able to bear it. I dissent.

---

[6] The focus on a rule of general applicability does not mean that more than one instance of its application is required. The local government unit may be liable for the first application of a duly constituted unconstitutional policy.

City of St. Louis v. Praprotnik

Supreme Court of the United States, 1988.
485 U.S. 112.

■ JUSTICE O'CONNOR announced the judgment of the Court and delivered an opinion, in which CHIEF JUSTICE REHNQUIST, JUSTICE WHITE, and JUSTICE SCALIA join.

This case calls upon us to define the proper legal standard for determining when isolated decisions by municipal officials or employees may expose the municipality itself to liability under 42 U.S.C. § 1983.

I

The principal facts are not in dispute. Respondent James H. Praprotnik is an architect who began working for petitioner city of St. Louis in 1968. For several years, respondent consistently received favorable evaluations of his job performance, uncommonly quick promotions, and significant increases in salary. By 1980, he was serving in a management-level city planning position at petitioner's Community Development Agency (CDA).

The Director of CDA, Donald Spaid, had instituted a requirement that the agency's professional employees, including architects, obtain advance approval before taking on private clients. Respondent and other CDA employees objected to the requirement. In April 1980, respondent was suspended for 15 days by CDA's Director of Urban Design, Charles Kindleberger, for having accepted outside employment without prior approval. Respondent appealed to the city's Civil Service Commission, a body charged with reviewing employee grievances. Finding the penalty too harsh, the Commission reversed the suspension, awarded respondent back pay, and directed that he be reprimanded for having failed to secure a clear understanding of the rule.

The Commission's decision was not well received by respondent's supervisors at CDA. Kindleberger later testified that he believed respondent had lied to the Commission, and that Spaid was angry with respondent.

Respondent's next two annual job performance evaluations were markedly less favorable than those in previous years. In discussing one of these evaluations with respondent, Kindleberger apparently mentioned his displeasure with respondent's 1980 appeal to the Civil Service Commission. Respondent appealed both evaluations to the Department of Personnel. In each case, the Department ordered partial relief and was upheld by the city's Director of Personnel or the Civil Service Commission.

In April 1981, a new Mayor came into office, and Donald Spaid was replaced as Director of CDA by Frank Hamsher. As a result of budget cuts, a number of layoffs and transfers significantly reduced the size of CDA and of the planning section in which respondent worked. Respondent, however, was retained.

In the spring of 1982, a second round of layoffs and transfers occurred at CDA. At that time, the city's Heritage and Urban Design Division (Heritage) was seeking approval to hire someone who was qualified in architecture and urban planning. Hamsher arranged with the Director of Heritage, Henry Jackson, for certain functions to be transferred from CDA to Heritage. This arrangement, which made it possible for Heritage to employ a relatively high-level "city planning manager," was approved by Jackson's supervisor, Thomas Nash. Hamsher then transferred respondent to Heritage to fill this position.

Respondent objected to the transfer, and appealed to the Civil Service Commission. The Commission declined to hear the appeal because respondent had not suffered a reduction in his pay or grade. Respondent then filed suit in Federal District Court, alleging that the transfer was unconstitutional. The city was named as a defendant, along with Kindleberger, Hamsher, Jackson (whom respondent deleted from the list before trial), and Deborah Patterson, who had succeeded Hamsher at CDA.

At Heritage, respondent became embroiled in a series of disputes with Jackson and Jackson's successor, Robert Killen. Respondent was dissatisfied with the work he was assigned, which consisted of unchallenging clerical functions far below the level of responsibilities that he had previously enjoyed. At least one adverse personnel decision was taken against respondent, and he obtained partial relief after appealing that decision.

In December 1983, respondent was laid off from Heritage. The lay off was attributed to a lack of funds, and this apparently meant that respondent's supervisors had concluded that they could create two lower-level positions with the funds that were being used to pay respondent's salary. Respondent then amended the complaint in his lawsuit to include a challenge to the layoff. He also appealed to the Civil Service Commission, but proceedings in that forum were postponed because of the pending lawsuit and have never been completed.

The case went to trial on two theories: (1) that respondent's First Amendment rights had been violated through retaliatory actions taken in response to his appeal of his 1980 suspension; and (2) that respondent's layoff from Heritage was carried out for pretextual reasons in violation of due process. The jury returned special verdicts exonerating each of the three individual defendants, but finding the city liable under both theories. Judgment was entered on the verdicts, and the city appealed.

A panel of the Court of Appeals for the Eighth Circuit found that the due process claim had been submitted to the jury on an erroneous legal theory and vacated that portion of the judgment. With one judge dissenting, however, the panel affirmed the verdict holding the city liable for violating respondent's First Amendment rights. Only the second of these holdings is challenged here.

The Court of Appeals found that the jury had implicitly determined that respondent's layoff from Heritage was brought about by an unconstitutional city policy. Applying a test under which a "policymaker" is one whose employment decisions are "final" in the sense that they are not subjected to de novo review by higher-ranking officials, the Court of Appeals concluded that the city could be held liable for adverse personnel decisions taken by respondent's supervisors. In response to petitioner's contention that the city's personnel policies are actually set by the Civil Service Commission, the Court of Appeals concluded that the scope of review before that body was too "highly circumscribed" to allow it fairly to be said that the Commission, rather than the officials who initiated the actions leading to respondent's injury, were the "final authority" responsible for setting city policy.
. . .

We granted certiorari and we now reverse.

II

[Part II of Justice O'Connor's opinion concluded that the legal standard for municipal liability had been properly presented for review.]

III

A

. . . In the years since Monell v. N.Y. City Dept. of Social Services, 436 U.S. 658 (1978), was decided, the Court has considered several cases involving isolated acts by government officials and employees. We have assumed that an unconstitutional governmental policy could be inferred from a single decision taken by the highest officials responsible for setting policy in that area of the government's business. See Owen v. City of Independence, 445 U.S. 622 (1980); Newport v. Fact Concerts, Inc., 453 U.S. 247 (1981). At the other end of the spectrum, we have held that an unjustified shooting by a police officer cannot, without more, be thought to result from official policy. Oklahoma City v. Tuttle, 471 U.S. 808 (1985).

Two terms ago, in Pembaur v. Cincinnati, 475 U.S. 469 (1986), we undertook to define more precisely when a decision on a single occasion may be enough to establish an unconstitutional municipal policy. Although the Court was unable to settle on a general formulation, Justice Brennan's plurality opinion articulated several guiding principles. First, a majority of the Court agreed that municipalities may be held liable under § 1983 only for acts for which the municipality itself is actually responsible, "that is, acts which the municipality has officially sanctioned or ordered." Second, only those municipal officials who have "final policymaking authority" may by their actions subject the government to § 1983 liability. Third, whether a particular official has "final policymaking authority" is a question of *state law*. Fourth, the challenged action must have been taken pursuant to a policy adopted by the official or officials responsible under state law for making policy *in that area* of the city's business.

The Courts of Appeals have already diverged in their interpretation of these principles. Today, we set out again to clarify the issue that we last addressed in *Pembaur*.

B

We begin by reiterating that the identification of policymaking officials is a question of state law. "Authority to make municipal policy may be granted directly by a legislative enactment or may be delegated by an official who possesses such authority, and of course, whether an official had final policymaking authority is a question of state law." *Pembaur v. Cincinnati,* supra, at 483 (plurality opinion).[1] Thus, the identification of policymaking officials is not a question of federal law and it is not a question of fact in the usual sense. The states have extremely wide latitude in determining the form that local government takes, and local preferences have led to a profusion of distinct forms. . . . Without attempting to canvass the numberless factual scenarios that may come to light in litigation, we can be confident that state law (which may include valid local ordinances and regulations) will always direct a court to some official or body that has

---

[1] Unlike Justice Brennan, we would not replace this standard with a new approach in which state law becomes merely "an appropriate starting point" for an "assessment of a municipality's actual power structure." Municipalities cannot be expected to predict how courts or juries will assess their "actual power structures," and this uncertainty could easily lead to results that would be hard in practice to distinguish from the results of a regime governed by the doctrine of respondeat superior. It is one thing to charge a municipality with responsibility for the decisions of officials invested by law, or by a "custom or usage" having the force of law, with policymaking authority. It would be something else, and something inevitably more capricious, to hold a municipality responsible for every decision that is perceived as "final" through the lens of a particular factfinder's evaluation of the city's "actual power structure."

the responsibility for making law or setting policy in any given area of a local government's responsibility.[2]

We are not, of course, predicting that state law will always speak with perfect clarity. We have no reason to suppose, however, that federal courts will face greater difficulties here than those that they routinely address in other contexts. We are also aware that there will be cases in which policymaking responsibility is shared among more than one official or body. In the case before us, for example, it appears that the Mayor or aldermen are authorized to adopt such ordinances relating to personnel administration as are compatible with the City Charter. See St. Louis City Charter, art. XVIII, § 7(b). The Civil Service Commission, for its part, is required to "prescribe . . . rules for the administration and enforcement of the provisions of this article, and of any ordinance adopted in pursuance thereof, and not inconsistent therewith." § 7(a). Assuming that applicable law does not make the decisions of the Commission reviewable by the Mayor and Aldermen, or vice versa, one would have to conclude that policy decisions made either by the Mayor and Aldermen or by the Commission would be attributable to the city itself. In any event, however, a federal court would not be justified in assuming that municipal policymaking authority lies somewhere other than where the applicable law purports to put it. And certainly there can be no justification for giving a jury the discretion to determine which officials are high enough in the government that their actions can be said to represent a decision of the government itself.

As the plurality in *Pembaur* recognized, special difficulties can arise when it is contended that a municipal policymaker has delegated his policymaking authority to another official. If the mere exercise of discretion by an employee could give rise to a constitutional violation, the result would be indistinguishable from respondeat superior liability. If, however, a city's lawful policymakers could insulate the government from liability simply by delegating their policymaking authority to others, § 1983 could not serve its intended purpose. It may not be possible to draw an elegant line that will resolve this conundrum, but certain principles should provide useful guidance.

First, whatever analysis is used to identify municipal policymakers, egregious attempts by local governments to insulate themselves from liability for unconstitutional policies are precluded by a separate doctrine. Relying on the language of § 1983, the Court has long recognized that a plaintiff may be able to prove the existence of a widespread practice that, although not authorized by written law or express municipal policy, is "so permanent and well settled as to constitute a 'custom or usage' with the force of law." Adickes v. S.H. Kress & Co., 398 U.S. 144, 167–68 (1970). That principle, which has not been affected by *Monell* or subsequent cases, ensures that

[2] Justice Stevens, who believes that *Monell* incorrectly rejected the doctrine of respondeat superior, suggests a new theory that reflects his perceptions of the congressional purposes underlying § 1983. This theory would apparently ignore state law, and distinguish between "high" officials and "low" officials on the basis of an independent evaluation of the extent to which a particular official's actions have "the potential of controlling governmental decisionmaking," or are "perceived as the actions of the city itself." Whether this evaluation would be conducted by judges or juries, we think the legal test is too imprecise to hold much promise of consistent adjudication or principled analysis. We can see no reason, except perhaps a desire to come as close as possible to respondeat superior without expressly adopting that doctrine, that could justify introducing such unpredictability into a body of law that is already so difficult. . . .

most deliberate municipal evasions of the Constitution will be sharply limited.

Second, as the *Pembaur* plurality recognized, the authority to make municipal policy is necessarily the authority to make *final* policy. When an official's discretionary decisions are constrained by policies not of that official's making, those policies, rather than the subordinate's departures from them, are the act of the municipality. Similarly, when a subordinate's decision is subject to review by the municipality's authorized policymakers, they have retained the authority to measure the official's conduct for conformance with *their* policies. If the authorized policymakers approve a subordinate's decision and the basis for it, their ratification would be chargeable to the municipality because their decision is final.

C

Whatever refinements of these principles may be suggested in the future, we have little difficulty concluding that the Court of Appeals applied an incorrect legal standard in this case. In reaching this conclusion, we do not decide whether the First Amendment forbade the city from retaliating against respondent for having taken advantage of the grievance mechanism in 1980. . . .

The city cannot be held liable under § 1983 unless respondent proved the existence of an unconstitutional municipal policy. Respondent does not contend that anyone in city government ever promulgated, or even articulated, such a policy. Nor did he attempt to prove that such retaliation was ever directed against anyone other than himself. Respondent contends that the record can be read to establish that his supervisors were angered by his 1980 appeal to the Civil Service Commission; that new supervisors in a new administration chose, for reasons passed on through some informal means, to retaliate against respondent two years later by transferring him to another agency; and that this transfer was part of a scheme that led, another year and a half later, to his lay off. Even if one assumes that all this was true, it says nothing about the actions of those whom the law established as the makers of municipal policy in matters of personnel administration. The Mayor and Aldermen enacted no ordinance designed to retaliate against respondent or against similarly situated employees. On the contrary, the city established an independent Civil Service Commission and empowered it to review and correct improper personnel actions. Respondent does not deny that his repeated appeals from adverse personnel decisions repeatedly brought him at least partial relief, and the Civil Service Commission never so much as hinted that retaliatory transfers or lay offs were permissible. Respondent points to no evidence indicating that the Commission delegated to anyone its final authority to interpret and enforce the following policy set out in Article XVIII of the city's Charter, § 2(a):

> Merit and fitness. All appointments and promotions to positions in the service of the city and all measures for the control and regulation of employment in such positions, and separation therefrom, shall be on the sole basis of merit and fitness. . . .

The Court of Appeals concluded that "appointing authorities," like Hamsher and Killen were authorized to establish employment policy for the city with respect to transfers and layoffs. To the contrary, the City Charter expressly states that the Civil Service Commission has the power and the duty:

> To consider and determine any matter involved in the administration and enforcement of this [Civil Service] article and the rules and ordinances adopted in accordance therewith that may be referred to it for decision by the Director [of Personnel], or on appeal by any appointing authority, employee, or taxpayer of the city, from any act of the director of any appointing authority. The decision of the Commission in all such matters shall be final, subject, however, to any right of action under law of the State or of the United States.

This case therefore resembles the hypothetical example in *Pembaur*: "[I]f [city] employment policy was set by the [Mayor and Aldermen and by the Civil Service Commission], only [those] bod[ies'] decisions would provide a basis for [city] liability. This would be true even if the [Mayor and aldermen and the Commission] left the [appointing authorities] discretion to hire and fire employees and [they] exercised that discretion in an unconstitutional manner. . . . " A majority of the Court of Appeals panel determined that the Civil Service Commission's review of individual employment actions gave too much deference to the decisions of appointing authorities like Hamsher and Killen. Simply going along with discretionary decisions made by one's subordinates, however, is not a delegation to them of the authority to make policy. It is equally consistent with a presumption that the subordinates are faithfully attempting to comply with the policies that are supposed to guide them. It would be a different matter if a particular decision by a subordinate was cast in the form of a policy statement and expressly approved by the supervising policymaker. It would also be a different matter if a series of decisions by a subordinate official manifested a "custom or usage" of which the supervisor must have been aware. In both those cases, the supervisor could realistically be deemed to have adopted a policy that happened to have been formulated or initiated by a lower-ranking official. But the mere failure to investigate the basis of a subordinate's discretionary decisions does not amount to a delegation of policymaking authority, especially where (as here) the wrongfulness of the subordinate's decision arises from a retaliatory motive or other unstated rationale. In such circumstances, the purposes of § 1983 would not be served by treating a subordinate employee's decision as if it were a reflection of municipal policy.

Justice Brennan's opinion, concurring in the judgment, finds implications in our discussion that we do not think necessary or correct. We nowhere say or imply, for example, that "a municipal charter's precatory admonition against discrimination or any other employment practice not based on merit and fitness effectively insulates the municipality from any liability based on acts inconsistent with that policy." Rather, we would respect the decisions, embodied in state and local law, that allocate policymaking authority among particular individuals and bodies. Refusals to carry out stated policies could obviously help to show that a municipality's actual policies were different from the ones that had been announced. If such a showing were made, we would be confronted with a different case than the one we decide today.

Nor do we believe that we have left a "gaping" hole in § 1983 that needs to be filled with the vague concept of "de facto final policymaking authority." Except perhaps as a step towards overruling *Monell* and adopting the doctrine of respondeat superior, ad hoc searches for officials possessing such "de facto" authority would serve primarily to foster needless unpredictability in the application of § 1983.

IV

[T]he decision of the Court of Appeals is reversed, and the case is remanded for further proceedings consistent with this opinion.

It is so ordered.

■ JUSTICE KENNEDY took no part in the consideration or decision of this case.

■ JUSTICE BRENNAN, with whom JUSTICE MARSHALL and JUSTICE BLACKMUN join, concurring in the judgment.

[T]his case at bottom presents a relatively straightforward question: whether respondent's supervisor at the Community Development Agency, Frank Hamsher, possessed the authority to establish final employment policy for the city of St. Louis such that the city can be held liable under 42 U.S.C. § 1983 for Hamsher's allegedly unlawful decision to transfer respondent to a dead-end job. Applying the test set out two terms ago by the plurality in Pembaur v. Cincinnati, 475 U.S. 469 (1986), I conclude that Hamsher did not possess such authority and I therefore concur in the Court's judgment reversing the decision below. I write separately, however, because I believe that the commendable desire of today's plurality to "define more precisely when a decision on a single occasion may be enough" to subject a municipality to § 1983 liability has led it to embrace a theory of municipal liability that is both unduly narrow and unrealistic, and one that ultimately would permit municipalities to insulate themselves from liability for the acts of all but a small minority of actual city policymakers.

I

. . . The District Court instructed the jury that generally a city is not liable under § 1983 for the acts of its employees, but that it may be held to answer for constitutional wrongs "committed by an official high enough in the government so that his or her actions can be said to represent a government decision." . . . The Court of Appeals for the Eighth Circuit [affirmed, reasoning] that the city could be held accountable for an improperly motivated transfer and layoff if it had delegated to the responsible officials, either directly or indirectly, the authority to act on behalf of the city, and if the decisions made within the scope of this delegated authority were essentially final. Applying this test, the court noted that under the City Charter, "appointing authorities," or department heads, such as Hamsher could undertake transfers and layoffs subject only to the approval of the Director of Personnel, who undertook no substantive review of such decisions and simply conditioned his approval on formal compliance with city procedures. Moreover, because the Civil Service Commission engaged in highly circumscribed and deferential review of layoffs and, at least so far as this case reveals, no review whatever of lateral transfers, the court concluded that an appointing authority's transfer and layoff decisions were final.

Having found that Hamsher was a final policymaker whose acts could subject petitioner to § 1983 liability, the court determined that the jury had ample evidence from which it could find that Hamsher transferred respondent in retaliation for the latter's exercise of First Amendment rights, and that the transfer in turn precipitated respondent's layoff. . . .

II

. . . Municipalities, of course, conduct much of the business of governing through human agents. Where those agents act in accordance with formal policies, or pursuant to informal practices "so permanent and well settled as to constitute a 'custom or usage' with the force of law," Adickes v. S.H. Kress & Co., 398 U.S. 144, 167–68 (1970), we naturally ascribe their acts to the municipalities themselves and hold the latter responsible for any resulting constitutional deprivations. Monell v. N.Y. City Dept. of Social Services, 436 U.S. 658 (1978), which involved a challenge to a city-wide policy requiring all pregnant employees to take unpaid leave after their fifth month of pregnancy, was just such a case. Nor have we ever doubted that a single decision of a city's properly constituted legislative body is a municipal act capable of subjecting the city to liability. See, e.g., Newport v. Fact Concerts, Inc., 453 U.S. 247 (1981) (city council canceled concert permits for content-based reasons); Owen v. City of Independence, 445 U.S. 622 (1980) (city council passed resolution firing police chief without any pretermination hearing). In these cases we neither required, nor as the plurality suggests, assumed that these decisions reflected generally applicable "policies" as that term is commonly understood, because it was perfectly obvious that the actions of the municipalities' policymaking organs, whether isolated or not, were properly charged to the municipalities themselves. And, in *Pembaur* we recognized that "the power to establish policy is no more the exclusive province of the legislature at the local level than at the state or national level," and that the isolated decision of an executive municipal policymaker, therefore, could likewise give rise to municipal liability under § 1983.

In concluding that Frank Hamsher was a policymaker, the Court of Appeals relied on the fact that the city had delegated to him "the authority, either directly or indirectly, to act on [its] behalf," and that his actions within the scope of this delegated authority were effectively final. In *Pembaur,* however, we made clear that a municipality is not liable merely because the official who inflicted the constitutional injury had the final authority to *act* on its behalf; rather, as four of us explained, the official in question must possess "final authority to establish municipal policy with respect to the [challenged] action." Thus, we noted, "[t]he fact that a particular official—even a policymaking official—has discretion in the exercise of particular functions does not, without more, give rise to municipal liability based on an exercise of that discretion." [J]ust as in *Owen* and *Fact Concerts* we deemed it fair to hold municipalities liable for the isolated, unconstitutional acts of their legislative bodies, regardless of whether those acts were meant to establish generally applicable "policies," so too in *Pembaur* four of us concluded that it is equally appropriate to hold municipalities accountable for the isolated constitutional injury inflicted by an executive final municipal policymaker, even though the decision giving rise to the injury is not intended to govern future situations. In either case, as long as the contested decision is made in an area over which the official or legislative body *could* establish a final policy capable of governing future municipal conduct, it is both fair and consistent with the purposes of § 1983 to treat the decision as that of the municipality itself, and to hold it liable for the resulting constitutional deprivation.

In my view, *Pembaur* controls this case. As an "appointing authority," Hamsher was empowered under the City Charter to initiate lateral transfers such as the one challenged here, subject to the approval of both the Director of Personnel and the appointing authority of the transferee agency. The charter, however, nowhere confers upon agency heads any authority to establish city *policy,* final or otherwise, with respect to such transfers. Thus, for example, Hamsher was not authorized to promulgate binding guidelines or criteria governing how or when lateral transfers were to be accomplished. Nor does the record reveal that he in fact sought to exercise any such authority in these matters. There is no indication, for example, that Hamsher ever purported to institute or announce a practice of general applicability concerning transfers. Instead, the evidence discloses but one transfer decision—the one involving respondent—which Hamsher ostensibly undertook pursuant to a city-wide program of fiscal restraint and budgetary reductions. At most, then the record demonstrates that Hamsher had the authority to determine how best to *effectuate* a policy announced by his superiors, rather than the power to *establish* that policy. . . . Because the court identified only one unlawfully motivated municipal employee involved in respondent's transfer and layoff, and because that employee did not possess final policymaking authority with respect to the contested decision, the city may not be held accountable for any constitutional wrong respondent may have suffered.

III

These determinations, it seems to me, are sufficient to dispose of this case, and I therefore think it unnecessary to decide, as the plurality does, who the actual policymakers in St. Louis are. I question more than the mere necessity of these determinations, however, for I believe that in the course of passing on issues not before us, the plurality announces legal principles that are inconsistent with our earlier cases and unduly restrict the reach of § 1983 in cases involving municipalities.

The plurality begins its assessment of St. Louis' power structure by asserting that the identification of policymaking officials is a question of state law, by which it means that the question is neither one of federal law nor of fact, at least "not in the usual sense." Instead, the plurality explains, courts are to identify municipal policymakers by referring exclusively to applicable state statutory law. Not surprisingly, the plurality cites no authority for this startling proposition, nor could it, for we have never suggested that municipal liability should be determined in so formulaic and unrealistic a fashion. In any case in which the policymaking authority of a municipal tortfeasor is in doubt, state law will naturally be the appropriate starting point, but ultimately the factfinder must determine where such policymaking authority actually resides, and not simply "where the applicable law purports to put it." . . . Thus, although I agree with the plurality that juries should not be given open-ended "*discretion* to determine which officials are high enough in the government that their actions can be said to represent a decision of the government itself," (emphasis added), juries can and must find the predicate facts necessary to a determination of whether a given official possesses final policymaking authority. While the jury instructions in this case were regrettably vague, the plurality's solution tosses the baby out with the bath water. The identification of municipal policymakers is an essentially factual determination "in the usual sense," and is therefore rightly entrusted to a properly instructed jury.

Nor does the "custom or usage" doctrine adequately compensate for the inherent inflexibility of a rule that leaves the identification of policymakers exclusively to state statutory law. That doctrine, under which municipalities and states can be held liable for unconstitutional practices so well settled and permanent that they have the force of law has little if any bearing on the question whether a city has delegated de facto final policymaking authority to a given official. A city practice of delegating final policymaking authority to a subordinate or mid-level official would not be unconstitutional in and of itself, and an isolated unconstitutional act by an official entrusted with such authority would obviously not amount to a municipal "custom or usage." Under *Pembaur,* of course, such an isolated act *should* give rise to municipal liability. Yet a case such as this would fall through the gaping hole the plurality's construction leaves in § 1983, because state statutory law would not identify the municipal actor as a policymaking official, and a single constitutional deprivation, by definition, is not a well settled and permanent municipal practice carrying the force of law.

For these same reasons, I cannot subscribe to the plurality's narrow and overly rigid view of when a municipal official's policymaking authority is "final." Attempting to place a gloss on *Pembaur*'s finality requirement, the plurality suggests that whenever the decisions of an official are subject to some form of review—however limited—that official's decisions are nonfinal. Under the plurality's theory, therefore, even where an official wields policymaking authority with respect to a challenged decision, the city would not be liable for that official's policy decision unless *reviewing* officials affirmatively approved both the "decision and the basis for it." Reviewing officials, however, may as a matter of practice never invoke their plenary oversight authority, or their review powers may be highly circumscribed. Under such circumstances, the subordinate's decision is in effect the final municipal pronouncement on the subject. Certainly a § 1983 plaintiff is entitled to place such considerations before the jury, for the law is concerned not with the niceties of legislative draftsmanship but with the realities of municipal decisionmaking, and any assessment of a municipality's actual power structure is necessarily a factual and practical one.[7]

Accordingly, I cannot endorse the plurality's determination, based on nothing more than its own review of the City Charter, that the Mayor, the Aldermen, and the CSC are the only policymakers for the city of St. Louis. While these officials may well have policymaking authority, that hardly ends the matter; the question before us is whether the officials responsible for respondent's allegedly unlawful transfer were final policymakers. As I have previously indicated, I do not believe that CDA Director Frank Hamsher possessed any policymaking authority with respect to lateral transfers and thus I do not believe that his allegedly improper decision to transfer respondent could, without more, give rise to municipal liability. Although the plurality reaches the same result, it does so by reasoning that because others could have reviewed the decisions of Hamsher and Killen, the latter officials simply could not have been final policymakers.

This analysis, however, turns a blind eye to reality, for it ignores not only the lower court's determination, nowhere disputed, that CSC review was highly circumscribed and deferential, but that in this very case the Commission *refused* to judge the propriety of Hamsher's transfer decision

---

[7] The plurality also asserts that "[w]hen an official's discretionary decisions are constrained by policies not of that official's making, those policies, rather than the subordinate's departures from them, are the act of the municipality." While I have no quarrel with such a proposition in the abstract, I cannot accept the plurality's apparent view that a municipal charter's precatory admonition against discrimination or any other employment practice not based on merit and fitness effectively insulates the municipality from any liability based on acts inconsistent with that policy. Again, the relevant inquiry is whether the policy in question is actually and effectively enforced through the city's review mechanisms. Thus in this case, a policy prohibiting lateral transfers for unconstitutional or discriminatory reasons would not shield the city from liability if an official possessing final policymaking authority over such transfers acted in violation of the prohibition, because the CSC would lack jurisdiction to review the decision and thus could not enforce the policy. Where as here, however, the official merely possesses discretionary authority over transfers, the city policy is irrelevant, because the official's actions cannot subject the city to liability in any event.

because a lateral transfer was not an "adverse" employment action falling within its jurisdiction. Nor does the plurality account for the fact that Hamsher's predecessor, Donald Spaid, promulgated what the city readily acknowledges was a binding policy regarding secondary employment;[8] although the CSC ultimately modified the sanctions respondent suffered as a result of his apparent failure to comply with that policy, the record is devoid of any suggestion that the Commission reviewed the substance or validity of the policy itself. Under the plurality's analysis, therefore, even the hollowest promise of review is sufficient to divest all city officials save the Mayor and governing legislative body of final policymaking authority. . . . Because the plurality's mechanical "finality" test is fundamentally at odds with the pragmatic and factual inquiry contemplated by *Monell,* I cannot join what I perceive to be its unwarranted abandonment of the traditional factfinding process in § 1983 actions involving municipalities.

Finally, I think it necessary to emphasize that despite certain language in the plurality opinion suggesting otherwise, the Court today need not and therefore does not decide that a city can only be held liable under § 1983 where the plaintiff "prove[s] the existence of an unconstitutional municipal policy." . . . That question is certainly not presented by this case, and nothing we say today forecloses its future consideration. . . .

■ JUSTICE STEVENS, dissenting.

If this case involved nothing more than a personal vendetta between a municipal employee and his superiors, it would be quite wrong to impose liability on the City of St. Louis. In fact, however, the jury found the top officials in the city administration relying on pretextual grounds, had taken a series of retaliatory actions against respondent because he had testified truthfully on two occasions, one relating to personnel policy and the other involving a public controversy of importance to the Mayor and the members of his cabinet. No matter how narrowly the Court may define the standards for imposing liability upon municipalities in § 1983 litigation, the judgment entered by the District Court in this case should be affirmed.

In order to explain why I believe that affirmance is required by this Court's precedents,[1] it is necessary to begin with a more complete statement of the disputed factual issues that the jury resolved in respondent's favor. . . .

The City of St. Louis hired respondent as a licensed architect in 1968. During the ensuing decade, he was repeatedly promoted and consistently given "superior" performance ratings. In April of 1980, while serving as the Director of Urban Design in the Community Development Agency (CDA), he was recommended for a two-step salary increase by his immediate superior.

---

[8] Although the plurality is careful in its discussion of the facts to label Director Spaid's directive a "requirement" rather than a "policy," the city itself draws no such fine semantic distinctions. Rather, it states plainly that Spaid "promulgated a 'secondary employment' *policy* that sought to control outside employment by CDA architects," and that "[respondent] resented the policy. . . . "

[1] This would, of course, be an easy case if the Court disavowed its dicta in Part II of its opinion in Monell v. N.Y. City Dept. of Social Services, 436 U.S. 658, 691–95 (1978). Like many commentators who have confronted the question, I remain convinced that Congress intended the doctrine of respondeat superior to apply in § 1983 litigation. Given the Court's reiteration of the contrary ipse dixit in *Monell* and subsequent opinions, however, I shall join the Court's attempt to draw an intelligible boundary between municipal agents' actions that bind and those that do not. . . .

Thereafter, on two occasions he gave public testimony that was critical of official city policy. In 1980 he testified before the Civil Service Commission (CSC) in support of his successful appeal from a 15–day suspension. In that testimony he explained that he had received advance oral approval of his outside employment and voiced his objections to the requirement of prior written approval. The record demonstrates that this testimony offended his immediate superiors at the CDA.

In 1981 respondent testified before the Heritage and Urban Design Commission (HUD) in connection with a proposal to acquire a controversial rusting steel sculpture by Richard Serra. In his testimony he revealed the previously undisclosed fact that an earlier city administration had rejected an offer to acquire the same sculpture, and also explained that the erection of the sculpture would require the removal of structures on which the city had recently expended about $250,000. This testimony offended top officials of the city government, possibly including the Mayor, who supported the acquisition of the Serra sculpture, as well as respondent's agency superiors. They made it perfectly clear that they believed that respondent had violated a duty of loyalty to the Mayor by expressing his personal opinion about the sculpture. . . .

After this testimony respondent was the recipient of a series of adverse personnel actions that culminated in his transfer from an important management level professional position to a rather menial assignment for which he was "grossly overqualified" and his eventual layoff. [E]vidence in the record amply supports the conclusion that respondent was first transferred and then laid off, not for fiscal and administrative reasons, but in retaliation for his public testimony before the CSC and HUD. It is undisputed that respondent's right to testify in support of his civil service appeal and his right to testify in opposition to the city's acquisition of the Serra sculpture were protected by the First Amendment to the Federal Constitution. Given the jury's verdict, the case is therefore one in which a municipal employee's Federal Constitutional rights were violated by officials of the city government. . . .

In Monell v. N.Y. Dept. of Social Services, 436 U.S. 658 (1978), we held that municipal corporations are "persons" within the meaning of 42 U.S.C. § 1983. Since a corporation is incapable of doing anything except through the agency of human beings, that holding necessarily gave rise to the question of what human activity undertaken by agents of the corporation may create municipal liability in § 1983 litigation.

[In *Monell* and subsequent cases] the Court has permitted a municipality to be held liable for the unconstitutional actions of its agents when those agents: enforced a rule of general applicability, *Monell*; were of sufficiently high stature and acted through a formal process, Owen v. City of Independence, 445 U.S. 622 (1980); or were authorized to establish policy in the particular area of city government in which the tort was committed, Pembaur v. Cincinnati, 475 U.S. 469 (1986). Under these precedents, the City of St. Louis should be held liable in this case.

Both *Pembaur* and the plurality and concurring opinions today acknowledge that a high official who has ultimate control over a certain area of city government can bind the city through his unconstitutional actions even though those actions are not in the form of formal rules or regulations. Although the Court has explained its holdings by reference to the nonstatutory term "policy," it plainly has not embraced the standard understanding of that word as covering a rule of general applicability. Instead it has used that term to include isolated acts not intended to be binding over a class of situations. But when one remembers that the real question in cases such as this is not "what constitutes city policy?" but rather "when should a city be liable for the acts of its agents?", the inclusion of single acts by high officials makes sense, for those acts bind a municipality in a way that the misdeeds of low officials do not.

Every act of a high official constitutes a kind of "statement" about how similar decisions will be carried out; the assumption is that the same decision would have been made, and would again be made, across a class of cases. Lower officials do not control others in the same way. Since their actions do not dictate the responses of various subordinates, those actions lack the potential of controlling governmental decisionmaking; they are not perceived as the actions of the city itself. If a county police officer had broken down Dr. Pembaur's door on the officer's own initiative, this would have been seen as the action of an overanxious officer, and would not have sent a message to other officers that similar actions would be countenanced. . . . Here, the Mayor, those working for him, and the agency heads are high-ranking officials; accordingly, we must assume that their actions have city-wide ramifications, both through their similar response to a like class of situations, and through the response of subordinates who follow their lead.

Just as the actions of high-ranking and low-ranking municipal employees differ in nature, so do constitutional torts differ. An illegal search, *Pembaur,* or seizure, Oklahoma City v. Tuttle, 471 U.S. 808 (1985), is quite different from a firing without due process, *Owen*; the retaliatory personnel action involved in today's case is in still another category. One thing that the torts in *Pembaur, Tuttle,* and *Owen* had in common is that they occurred "in the open"; in each of those cases, the ultimate judgment of unconstitutionality was based on whether undisputed events (the breaking-in in *Pembaur,* the shooting in *Tuttle,* the firing in *Owen*) comported with accepted constitutional norms. But the typical retaliatory personnel action claim pits one story against another; although everyone admits that the transfer and discharge of respondent occurred, there is sharp, and ultimately central, dispute over the reasons—the motivation—behind the actions. *The very nature of the tort is to avoid a formal process. Owen*'s relevance should thus be clear. For if the Court is willing to recognize the existence of municipal policy in a non-rule case as long as high enough officials engaged in a formal enough process, it should not deny the existence of such a policy merely because those same officials act "underground," as it were. It would be a truly remarkable doctrine for this Court to recognize municipal liability in an employee discharge case when high officials are foolish enough to act through a "formal process," but not when similarly high officials attempt to avoid liability by acting on the pretext of budgetary concerns, which is what the jury found based on the evidence presented at trial.

Thus, holding St. Louis liable in this case is supported by both *Pembaur* and *Owen.* We hold a municipality liable for the decisions of its high officials in large part because those decisions, by definition, would be applied across a class of cases. Just as we assume in *Pembaur* that the County Prosecutor (or his subordinate) would issue the same break-down-the-door order in similar cases, and just as we assume in *Owen* that the City Council (or those following its lead) would fire an employee without notice of reasons or opportunity to be heard in similar cases, so too must we assume that whistleblowers like respondent would be dealt with in similar retaliatory fashion if they offend the Mayor, his staff, and relevant agency heads, or if they offend those lower-ranking officials who follow the example of their superiors. Furthermore, just as we hold a municipality liable for discharging an employee without due process when its City Council acts formally—for a due process violation is precisely the *type* of constitutional tort that a City Council might commit when it acts formally—so too must we hold a municipality liable for discharging an employee in retaliation against his public speech when similarly high officials act informally—for a First Amendment retaliation tort is precisely the *type* of constitutional tort that high officials might commit when they act in concert and informally.

Whatever difficulties the Court may have with binding municipalities on the basis of the unconstitutional conduct of individuals, it should have no such difficulties binding a city when many of its high officials—including officials directly under the Mayor, agency heads, and possibly the Mayor himself—cooperate to retaliate against a whistleblower for the exercise of his First Amendment rights.

I would affirm the judgment of the Court of Appeals.

NOTES ON OFFICIAL POLICY OR CUSTOM

1. QUESTIONS AND COMMENTS ON *PRAPROTNIK*

The opinions in *Praprotnik* suggest three ways of identifying acts that trigger municipal liability. Justice O'Connor looks to state law. Does that mean, as Justice Brennan charged, that a municipality could insulate itself against liability by "precatory statements" against unconstitutional policies? By providing adequate internal review of personnel decisions? How would—or should—a court distinguish between self-protective window dressing and genuine attempts to do the right thing?

Justice Brennan would distinguish between final authority to act on behalf of the municipality and final authority to make official policy with respect to that act. Is this distinction clear? Does it aim at something important, or is it mere characterization?

Finally, Justice Stevens suggests that municipalities should be liable for the acts of high-ranking officials. Why? Does the rank of the official necessarily correlate with the official status of that person's actions? Why should the decisive factor be the position held by the *person* who acted unlawfully rather than the relation between the government and the unlawful act?

2. ADDITIONAL COMMENTS ON *PRAPROTNIK*

The history of *Praprotnik* reveals something of a paradox: the jury exonerated each of the individual defendants, yet found the city liable. How could this be?

If no individual acted with an impermissible motive—that is, if the jury found that none of the individual defendants acted in retaliation for Praprotnik's exercise of his First Amendment rights—how could the city have committed a constitutional violation that requires such a motive? In any case where the underlying constitutional claim requires proof of a wrongful state of mind—for example, claims of racial discrimination under the Fourteenth Amendment, unconstitutional prison conditions under the Eighth Amendment, or retaliation under the First Amendment—it seems incontrovertible that the plaintiff must show that there is *someone* who acted with the requisite intent. Moreover, it should follow that the individuals who so acted would be liable for money damages. It would be highly unusual for actors motivated by an illicit objective to be protected by the defense of qualified immunity.

The fact that the jury found in favor of each of the individual defendants while finding against the city therefore suggests an inconsistency. The jury may have believed that there was impermissible retaliation, but was unwilling to impose monetary liability on individual officials. This possibility suggests that the jury may have undercompensated the plaintiff because they thought (often incorrectly, in light of indemnification practices) that it would be unfair to force public officials to pay for what seems to be the government's responsibility. Alternatively, the jury might have found no First Amendment violation, but felt sympathy for the plaintiff and saw the city as a deep pocket against whom liability could be imposed without fault. Does this suggest that the atmospherics of cases like *Praprotnik* may be driving some of the Court's attempts to limit governmental liability?

3. THE SIGNIFICANCE OF STATE LAW: *MCMILLIAN V. MONROE COUNTY*

The role of state law assumed center stage in McMillian v. Monroe County, 520 U.S. 781 (1997). Walter McMillian was convicted of murder and later released when the state courts found that the authorities had suppressed exculpatory evidence. McMillian then brought a § 1983 action against (among others) the sheriff of Monroe County and the county itself. The lower courts ruled that in matters of law enforcement, the sheriff was not a final policymaker for the county, and a divided Supreme Court affirmed.

The basis for this ruling was a detailed analysis of Alabama law, which revealed that, insofar as they were engaged in law enforcement, county sheriffs were in fact state officers. Speaking for the Court, Chief Justice Rehnquist examined a variety of state constitutional provisions (past and present) and state statutes dealing with sheriffs. The Chief Justice placed particular weight on the state Constitution, adopted in 1901, which added county sheriffs to a list of statewide officers constituting the "executive department" of the state. This action responded to reports that sheriffs were allowing mobs to abduct and lynch prisoners. The 1901 Constitution made such "neglect" by sheriffs an impeachable offense and moved the impeachment authority from the county courts (where sheriffs had much influence) to the state supreme court. Based on these provisions, the state supreme court had "held unequivocally that sheriffs are state officers, and that tort claims brought against sheriffs based on their official acts therefore constitute suits against the state, not against the sheriff's county." The Court was not concerned about the possibility that such conclusions could be manipulated to preclude liability, as the state constitutional provisions at issue long predated *Monell*.

Justice Ginsburg, joined by Justices Stevens, Souter, and Breyer, dissented. She focused on the facts that the county voters elected the sheriff, that county taxpayers paid his salary, and that the sheriff had broad authority to set law enforcement policy within the county. Nevertheless, she did not regard the majority's "Alabama-specific" approach as very consequential. In other states, sheriffs were still local policymakers, and the date of Alabama's constitutional provisions to the contrary "should discourage endeavors to insulate counties and municipalities from *Monell* liability by change-the-label devices."

4. APPEALABILITY OF POLICYMAKER STATUS

In Swint v. Chambers County Commission, 514 U.S. 35 (1995), a unanimous Court ruled that denial of summary judgment on whether an individual defendant was a "policymaker" for local government was not immediately appealable under the "collateral order" doctrine of Cohen v. Beneficial Industrial Loan Corp., 337 U.S. 541 (1949). The Court distinguished the denial of summary judgment on whether a defendant was protected by qualified immunity, which was held immediately appealable in Mitchell v. Forsyth, 472 U.S. 511 (1985).

City of Canton v. Harris

Supreme Court of the United States, 1989.
489 U.S. 378.

■ JUSTICE WHITE delivered the opinion of the Court.

In this case, we are asked to determine if a municipality can ever be liable under 42 U.S.C. § 1983 for constitutional violations resulting from its failure to train municipal employees. We hold that, under certain circumstances, such liability is permitted by the statute.

I

In April 1978, respondent Geraldine Harris was arrested by officers of the Canton Police Department. Harris was brought to the police station in a patrol wagon.

When she arrived at the station, Harris was found sitting on the floor of the wagon. She was asked if she needed medical attention, and responded with an incoherent remark. After she was brought inside the station for processing, Mrs. Harris slumped to the floor on two occasions. Eventually, the police officers left Mrs. Harris lying on the floor to prevent her from falling again. No medical attention was ever summoned for Mrs. Harris. After about an hour, Mrs. Harris was released from custody, and taken by an ambulance (provided by her family) to a nearby hospital. There, Mrs. Harris was diagnosed as suffering from several emotional ailments; she was hospitalized for one week, and received subsequent outpatient treatment for an additional year.

Some time later, Mrs. Harris commenced this action alleging many state law and constitutional claims against the city of Canton and its officials. Among these claims was one seeking to hold the city liable under 42 U.S.C. § 1983 for its violation of Mrs. Harris' right, under the Due Process Clause of the Fourteenth Amendment, to receive necessary medical attention while in police custody.

A jury trial was held on Mrs. Harris' claims. Evidence was presented that indicated that, pursuant to a municipal regulation,[2] shift commanders were authorized to determine, in their sole discretion, whether a detainee

[2] The city regulation in question provides that a police officer assigned to act as "jailer" at the city police station: "shall, when a prisoner is found to be unconscious or semi-unconscious, or when he or she is unable to explain his or her condition, or who complains of being ill, have such person taken to a hospital for medical treatment, with permission of his supervisor before admitting the person to city jail."

required medical care. In addition, testimony also suggested that Canton shift commanders were not provided with any special training (beyond first-aid training) to make a determination as to when to summon medical care for an injured detainee.

At the close of the evidence, the District Court submitted the case to the jury, which rejected all of Mrs. Harris' claims except one: her § 1983 claim against the city resulting from its failure to provide her with medical treatment while in custody. In rejecting the city's subsequent motion for judgment notwithstanding the verdict, the District Court explained the theory of liability as follows:

> The evidence construed in a manner most favorable to Mrs. Harris could be found by a jury to demonstrate that the city of Canton had a custom or policy of vesting complete authority with the police supervisor of when medical treatment would be administered to prisoners. Further, the jury could find from the evidence that the vesting of such carte blanche authority with the police supervisor without adequate training to recognize when medical treatment is needed was grossly negligent or so reckless that future police misconduct was almost inevitable or substantially certain to result.

On appeal, the Sixth Circuit affirmed this aspect of the District Court's analysis, holding that "a municipality is liable for failure to train its police force, [where] the plaintiff . . . prove[s] that the municipality acted recklessly, intentionally, or with gross negligence." The Court of Appeals also stated that an additional prerequisite of this theory of liability was that the plaintiff must prove "that the lack of training was so reckless or grossly negligent that deprivations of persons' constitutional rights were substantially certain to result." Thus, the Court of Appeals found that there had been no error in submitting Mrs. Harris' "failure to train" claim to the jury. However, the Court of Appeals reversed the judgment for respondent, and remanded this case for a new trial, because it found that certain aspects of the District Court's jury instructions might have led the jury to believe that it could find against the city on a mere respondeat superior theory. Because the jury's verdict did not state the basis on which it had ruled for Mrs. Harris on her § 1983 claim, a new trial was ordered.

The city petitioned for certiorari, arguing that the Sixth Circuit's holding represented an impermissible broadening of municipal liability under § 1983. We granted the petition.

II

[The Court considered and rejected an argument that the issues had not been properly preserved for review.]

III

In Monell v. New York City Dept. of Social Services, 436 U.S. 658 (1978), we decided that a municipality can be found liable under § 1983 only where the municipality *itself* causes the constitutional violation at issue. Respondeat superior or vicarious liability will not attach under § 1983. "It is only when the 'execution of the government's policy or custom . . . inflicts the injury' that the municipality may be held liable under § 1983." City of Springfield v. Kibbe, 480 U.S. 257, 267 (1987) (O'Connor, J., dissenting) (quoting *Monell*).

Thus, our first inquiry in any case alleging municipal liability under § 1983 is the question of whether there is a direct causal link between a municipal policy or custom, and the alleged constitutional deprivation. . . .

A

[P]etitioner urges us to adopt the rule that a municipality can be found liable under § 1983 only where "the policy in question [is] itself unconstitutional." Whether such a rule is a valid construction of § 1983 is a question the Court has left unresolved. See, e.g., City of St. Louis v. Praprotnik, 485 U.S. 112, 147 (1988) (Brennan, J., concurring in judgment). Under such an approach, the outcome here would be rather clear: we would have to reverse and remand the case with instructions that judgment be entered for petitioner.[5] There can be little doubt that on its face the city's policy regarding medical treatment for detainees is constitutional. The policy states that the City Jailer "shall . . . have [a person needing medical care] taken to a hospital for medical treatment, with permission of his supervisor. . . . " It is difficult to see what constitutional guarantees are violated by such a policy.

Nor, without more, would a city automatically be liable under § 1983 if one of its employees happened to apply the policy in an unconstitutional manner, for liability would then rest on respondeat superior. The claim in this case, however, is that if a concededly valid policy is unconstitutionally applied by a municipal employee, the city is liable if the employee has not been adequately trained and the constitutional wrong has been caused by that failure to train. For reasons explained below, we conclude . . . that there are limited circumstances in which an allegation of a "failure to train" can be the basis for liability under § 1983. Thus, we reject petitioner's contention that only unconstitutional policies are actionable under the statute.

B

Though we agree with the court below that a city can be liable under § 1983 for inadequate training of its employees, we cannot agree that the District Court's jury instructions on this issue were proper, for we conclude that the Court of Appeals provided an overly broad rule for when a municipality can be held liable under the "failure to train" theory. . . . We hold . . . that the inadequacy of police training may serve as the basis for § 1983 liability only where the failure to train amounts to deliberate indifference to the rights of persons with whom the police come into contact.[8]

---

5 In this Court, in addition to suggesting that the city's failure to train its officers amounted to a "policy" that resulted in the denial of medical care to detainees, respondent also contended the city had a "custom" of denying medical care to those detainees suffering from emotional or mental ailments. As respondent described it in her brief, and at argument, this claim of an unconstitutional "custom" appears to be little more than a restatement of her "failure-to-train as policy" claim.

However, to the extent that this claim poses a distinct basis for the city's liability under § 1983, we decline to determine whether respondent's contention that such a "custom" existed is an alternate grounds for affirmance. The "custom" claim was not passed on by the Court of Appeals—nor does it appear to have been presented to that court as a distinct ground for its decision. Thus, we will not consider it here.

8 The "deliberate indifference" standard we adopt for § 1983 "failure to train" claims does not turn upon the degree of fault (if any) that a plaintiff must show to make out an underlying claim of a constitutional violation. For example, this Court has never determined what degree of culpability must be shown before the particular constitutional deprivation asserted in this case—a denial of the due process right to medical care while in detention—is established. Indeed, in Revere v. Massachusetts General Hospital, 463 U.S. 239, 243–45 (1983), we reserved decision on the question of whether something less than [the] eighth amendment's "deliberate indifference" test may be applicable in claims by detainees asserting violations of their due process right to medical care while in custody.

This rule is most consistent with our admonition in *Monell* and Polk County v. Dodson, 454 U.S. 312, 326 (1981), that a municipality can be liable under § 1983 only where its policies are the "moving force [behind] the constitutional violation." Only where a municipality's failure to train its employees in a relevant respect evidences a "deliberate indifference" to the rights of its inhabitants can such a shortcoming be properly thought of as a city "policy or custom" that is actionable under § 1983. As Justice Brennan's opinion in Pembaur v. Cincinnati, 475 U.S. 469, 483–84 (1986) (plurality) put it: "[M]unicipal liability under § 1983 attaches where—and only where—a deliberate choice to follow a course of action is made from among various alternatives" by city policy makers. Only where a failure to train reflects a "deliberate" or "conscious" choice by a municipality—a "policy" as defined by our prior cases—can a city be liable for such a failure under § 1983.

Monell's rule that a city is not liable under § 1983 unless a municipal policy causes a constitutional deprivation will not be satisfied by merely alleging that the existing training program for a class of employees, such as police officers, represents a policy for which the city is responsible.[9] That much may be true. The issue in a case like this one, however, is whether that training program is adequate; and if it is not, the question becomes whether such inadequate training can justifiably be said to represent "city policy." It may seem contrary to common sense to assert that a municipality will actually have a policy of not taking reasonable steps to train its employees. But it may happen that in light of the duties assigned to specific officers or employees the need for more or different training is so obvious, and the inadequacy so likely to result in the violation of constitutional rights, that the policymakers of the city can reasonably be said to have been deliberately indifferent to the need.[10] In that event, the failure to provide proper training may fairly be said to represent a policy for which the city is responsible, and for which the city may be held liable if it actually causes injury.[11]

We need not resolve here the question left open in *Revere* for two reasons. First, petitioner has conceded that, as the case comes to us, we must assume that respondent's constitutional right to receive medical care was denied by city employees—whatever the nature of that right might be. Second, the proper standard for determining when a municipality will be liable under § 1983 for constitutional wrongs does not turn on any underlying culpability test that determines when such wrongs have occurred.

[9] The plurality opinion in Oklahoma City v. Tuttle, 471 U.S. 808 (1985), explained why this must be so:

> Obviously, if one retreats far enough from a constitutional violation some municipal "policy" can be identified behind almost any . . . harm inflicted by a municipal official; for example, [a police officer] would never have killed Tuttle if Oklahoma City did not have a "policy" of establishing a police force. But *Monell* must be taken to require proof of a city policy different in kind from this latter example before a claim can be sent to a jury on the theory that a particular violation was "caused" by the municipal "policy."

[10] For example, city policy makers know to a moral certainty that their police officers will be required to arrest fleeing felons. The city has armed its officers with firearms, in part to allow them to accomplish this task. Thus, the need to train officers in the constitutional limitations on the use of deadly force, see Tennessee v. Garner, 471 U.S. 1 (1985), can be said to be "so obvious," that failure to do so could properly be characterized as "deliberate indifference" to constitutional rights.

It could also be that the police, in exercising their discretion, so often violate constitutional rights that the need for further training must have been plainly obvious to the city policy makers, who, nevertheless, are "deliberately indifferent" to the need.

[11] The record indicates that city did train its officers and that its training included first-aid instruction. Petitioner argues that it could not have been obvious to the city that such

In resolving the issue of a city's liability, the focus must be on adequacy of the training program in relation to the tasks the particular officers must perform. That a particular officer may be unsatisfactorily trained will not alone suffice to fasten liability on the city, for the officer's shortcomings may have resulted from factors other than a faulty training program. It may be, for example, that an otherwise sound program has occasionally been negligently administered. Neither will it suffice to prove that an injury or accident could have been avoided if an officer had had better or more training, sufficient to equip him to avoid the particular injury-causing conduct. Such a claim could be made about almost any encounter resulting in injury, yet not condemn the adequacy of the program to enable officers to respond properly to the usual and recurring situations with which they must deal. And plainly, adequately trained officers occasionally make mistakes; the fact that they do says little about the training program or the legal basis for holding the city liable.

Moreover, for liability to attach in this circumstance the identified deficiency in a city's training program must be closely related to the ultimate injury. Thus in the case at hand, respondent must still prove that the deficiency in training actually caused the police officers' indifference to her medical needs. Would the injury have been avoided had the employee been trained under a program that was not deficient in the identified respect? Predicting how a hypothetically well trained officer would have acted under the circumstances may not be an easy task for the factfinder, particularly since matters of judgment may be involved, and since officers who are well trained are not free from error and perhaps might react very much like the untrained officer in similar circumstances. But judge and jury, doing their respective jobs, will be adequate to the task.

To adopt lesser standards of fault and causation would open municipalities to unprecedented liability under § 1983. In virtually every instance where a person has had his or her constitutional rights violated by a city employee, a § 1983 plaintiff will be able to point to something the city "could have done" to prevent the unfortunate incident. Thus, permitting cases against cities for their "failure to train" employees to go forward under § 1983 on a lesser standard of fault would result in de facto respondeat superior liability on municipalities—a result we rejected in *Monell.* It would also engage the federal courts in an endless exercise of second-guessing municipal employee-training programs. This is an exercise we believe the federal courts are ill-suited to undertake, as well as one that would implicate serious questions of federalism. Cf. Rizzo v. Goode, 423 U.S. 362, 378–80 (1976).

Consequently, while claims such as respondent's—alleging that the city's failure to provide training to municipal employees resulted in the constitutional deprivation she suffered—are cognizable under § 1983, they can only yield liability against a municipality where that city's failure to train reflects deliberate indifference to the constitutional rights of its inhabitants.

IV

The final question here is whether this case should be remanded for a new trial, or whether, as petitioner suggests, we should conclude that there are no possible grounds on which respondent can prevail. It is true that the

---

training was insufficient to administer the written policy, which was itself constitutional. This is a question to be resolved on remand.

evidence in the record now does not meet the standard of § 1983 liability we have set forth above. But, the standard of proof the District Court ultimately imposed on respondent (which was consistent with Sixth Circuit precedent) was a lesser one than the one we adopt today. Whether respondent should have an opportunity to prove her case under the "deliberate indifference" rule we have adopted is a matter for the Court of Appeals to deal with on remand.

V

Consequently, for the reasons given above, we vacate the judgment of the Court of Appeals and remand this case for further proceedings consistent with this opinion.

It is so ordered.

■ JUSTICE BRENNAN, concurring.

The Court's opinion, which I join, makes clear that the Court of Appeals is free to remand this case for a new trial.

■ JUSTICE O'CONNOR, with whom JUSTICE SCALIA and JUSTICE KENNEDY join, concurring in part and dissenting in part.

I join Parts I, II, and all of Part III of the Court's opinion except footnote 11. . . . My single point of disagreement with the majority is thus a small one. Because I believe, as the majority strongly hints, that respondent has not and could not satisfy the fault and causation requirements we adopt today, I think it unnecessary to remand this case to the Court of Appeals for further proceedings. . . .

Where, as here, a claim of municipal liability is predicated upon a failure to act, the requisite degree of fault must be shown by proof of a background of events and circumstances which establish that the "policy of inaction" is the functional equivalent of a decision by the city itself to violate the Constitution. Without some form of notice to the city, and the opportunity to conform to constitutional dictates both what it does and what it chooses not to do, the failure to train theory of liability could completely engulf *Monell,* imposing liability without regard to fault. Moreover, absent a requirement that the lack of training at issue bears a very close causal connection to the violation of constitutional rights, the failure to train theory of municipal liability could impose "prophylactic" duties on municipal governments only remotely connected to underlying constitutional requirements themselves. [Section] 1983 is not a "federal good government act" for municipalities. Rather it creates a federal cause of action against persons, including municipalities, who deprive citizens of the United States of their constitutional rights.

Sensitive to these concerns, the Court's opinion correctly requires a high degree of fault on the part of city officials before an omission that is not in itself unconstitutional can support liability as a municipal policy under *Monell.* As the Court indicates, "it may happen that . . . the need for more or different training is so obvious, and the inadequacy so likely to result in the violation of constitutional rights, that the policymakers of the city can reasonably be said to have been deliberately indifferent to the need." . . .

In my view, it could be shown that the need for training was obvious in one of two ways. First, a municipality could fail to train its employees concerning a clear constitutional duty implicated in recurrent situations that a particular employee is certain to face. As the majority notes, the constitutional limitations established by the Court on the use of deadly force by police officers present one such situation. . . . The claim in this case—that police officers were inadequately trained in diagnosing the symptoms of emotional illness—falls far short of the kind of "obvious" need for training that would support a finding of deliberate indifference to constitutional rights on the part of the city. . . .

Second, I think municipal liability for failure to train may be proper where it can be shown that policymakers were aware of, and acquiesced in, a pattern of constitutional violations involving the exercise of police discretion. In such cases, the need for training may not be obvious from the outset, but a pattern of constitutional violations could put the municipality on notice that its officers confront the particular situation on a regular basis, and that they often react in a manner contrary to constitutional requirements. . . . In fact, [however,] respondent presented no testimony from any witness indicating that there had been past incidents of "deliberate indifference" to the medical needs of emotionally disturbed detainees or that any other circumstance had put the city on actual or constructive notice of a need for additional training in this regard. There is quite simply nothing in this record to indicate that the city of Canton had any reason to suspect that failing to provide this kind of training would lead to injuries of any kind, let alone violations of the Due Process Clause. . . . Because respondent's evidence falls far short of establishing the high degree of fault on the part of the city required by our decision today, . . . I would reverse the judgment of the Court of Appeals and order entry of judgment for the city.

NOTES ON FAILURE TO TRAIN AS "OFFICIAL POLICY"

1. QUESTIONS AND COMMENTS ON *HARRIS*

The *Harris* Court apparently was unanimous about the *standards* that should govern municipal liability for failure to train, though the Justices disagreed about application of those standards to the facts of the case. Both opinions embraced the oxymoron "deliberate indifference" as the governing concept. Is the central feature of this inquiry subjective or objective? That is, is the inquiry one that seeks to determine what municipal policymakers were actually thinking about the constitutional rights at stake or what they *should have* thought based on external indicators? If the latter, what kinds of external indicators would be sufficient?

Recall that *Owen v. City of Independence* held, over the dissents of Justices Powell (replaced by Kennedy), Burger (replaced by Scalia), Stewart (replaced by O'Connor), and Rehnquist, that municipal government enjoys no qualified immunity from § 1983 liability and, in Justice Powell's words, "may be liable in damages for violating a constitutional right that was unknown when the events . . . occurred." To what extent do *Harris* and *Praprotnik* constitute the revenge of the *Owen* dissenters? Do the current standards for determining municipal liability differ greatly from the standards that would apply if municipal government were entitled to a qualified immunity defense?

2. *CONNICK V. THOMPSON*

City of Canton v. Harris contemplated that municipal liability for failure to train would ordinarily rest on a pattern of constitutional violations, which would make "the need for more or different training . . . so obvious, and the inadequacy so likely to result in the violation of constitutional rights, that the policymakers of the city can reasonably be said to have been deliberately indifferent to the need." *Harris*, however, preserved the possibility that deliberate indifference could be found without a pattern of violations. The example given in footnote 10 of that opinion was a failure to provide any training to police officers on the use of deadly force to arrest fleeing felons. In that situation, said the Court, the "need to train officers in the constitutional limitations on the use of deadly force can be said to be 'so obvious' that failure to do so could properly be characterized as 'deliberate indifference' to constitutional rights." 489 U.S. 378, 390 (1989).

Connick v. Thompson, 131 S.Ct. 1350, raised the question preserved in *Harris*: When, absent a pattern of similar violations, can the risk of a constitutional violation be so obvious that the failure to train for it amounts to deliberate indifference? John Thompson was charged with murder and an unrelated armed robbery. He was convicted of the robbery, despite exculpatory evidence that should have been, but was not, revealed by the prosecution as required by Brady v. Maryland, 373 U.S. 83 (1963). Because of the armed robbery conviction (which would have come out had he taken the stand), Thompson did not testify at his murder trial, where he was again convicted and sentenced to death. Some 18 years later, the *Brady* violation was discovered, the robbery conviction vacated, and the murder conviction reversed. Thompson was retried for murder but acquitted. He then sued Harry F. Connick, the Orleans Parish District Attorney, in his official capacity, claiming that the district attorney's office was responsible for the *Brady* violation based on a deliberately indifferent failure to train. He recovered $14 million, plus $1 million in attorney's fees.

The Supreme Court reversed. Speaking through Justice Thomas, the Court held that Connick was entitled to judgment as a matter of law because Thompson had not proved that the district attorney was "on actual or constructive notice of, and therefore deliberately indifferent to, a need for more or different *Brady* training":

> A pattern of similar constitutional violations by untrained employees is 'ordinarily necessary' to demonstrate deliberate indifference for purposes of failure to train. Bd of Comm'rs of Bryan County v. Brown, 520 U.S. 397, 409 (1997). . . . Without notice that a course of training is deficient in a particular respect, decisionmakers can hardly be said to have deliberately chosen a training program that will cause violations of constitutional rights.

The possibility of failure-to-train liability based on a single incident, as contemplated in *Harris*, did not apply:

> Failure to train prosecutors in their *Brady* obligations does not fall within the narrow range of [*City of Canton v. Harris*'s] hypothesized single-incident liability. The obvious need for specific legal training that was present in the *Canton* scenario is absent here. Armed police must sometimes make split-second decisions with life-or-death consequences. There is no reason to assume that police academy applicants are familiar with the constitutional constrains on the use of the deadly force. And, in the absence of training, there is no way for novice officers to obtain the legal knowledge they require. Under those circumstances, there is an obvious need for some form of training. In stark contrast, legal "[t]raining is what

differentiates attorneys from average public employees" [quoting from the opinion of Clement, J., in the Fifth Circuit].

> Attorneys are trained in the law and equipped with the tools to interpret and apply legal principles, understand constitutional limits, and exercise legal judgment. . . . In light of this regime of legal training and professional responsibility, recurring constitutional violations are not the "obvious consequence" of failing to provide prosecutors with formal in-house training about how to obey the law. Prosecutors are not only equipped but are also ethically bound to know what *Brady* entails and to perform legal research when they are uncertain. A district attorney is entitled to rely on prosecutors' professional training and ethical obligations in the absence of specific reason, such as a pattern of violations, to believe that those tools are insufficient to prevent future constitutional violations. . . . A licensed attorney making legal judgment, in his capacity as a prosecutor, about *Brady* material simply does nto present the same "highly predictable" constitutional violation as *Canton*'s untrained officer.

Justice Scalia, joined by Justice Alito, joined the opinion of the Court, but wrote separately to make an additional point. Scalia reviewed the instructions of the trial court, which basically required to jury to find (1) that Connick knew his prosecutors would confront *Brady* issues, (2) that compliance with *Brady* would involve difficult choices, and (3) that wrong choices would often result in deprivations of constitutional rights. Scalia said:

> That theory of deliberate indifference would repeal the law of *Monell* in favor of the Law of Large Numbers. *Brady* mistakes are inevitable. So are all species of error routinely confronted by prosecutors: authorizing a bad warrant; losing a *Batson* claim [Batson v. Kentucky, 476 U.S. 79 (1986)]; crossing the line in closing argument; or eliciting hearsay that violates the Confrontation Clause. Nevertheless, we do not have "de facto respondeat superior liability," *Canton*, 489 U.S. at 392, for each such violation under the rubric of failure-to-train simply because the municipality does not have a professional education program covering the specific violation in sufficient depth.

Justices Ginsburg, Breyer, Sotomayor, and Kagan dissented. Speaking through Justice Ginsburg, the dissenters challenged many aspects of the majority's understanding of the case. Justice Ginsburg recounted several *Brady* problems in Thompson's prosecutions (though not amounting to a pattern of similar violations), explored other instances of prosecutorial shoddiness, and identified "multiple shortfalls" in prosecutorial performance. Based on her detailed review of the record, Ginsburg found "abundant evidence" to support the jury's finding of deliberate indifference.

Much of the dispute between the majority and dissent in *Connick* is specific to, and indeed deeply embedded in, the facts of that case. Nonetheless, the opinions do reveal strongly divergent perspectives on failure to train. The majority appears preoccupied with the risk that liability for failure to train will degenerate into "de facto respondeat superior." The dissent is concerned with the evident injustice to this plaintiff and with the evidence of prosecutorial sloppiness or misconduct.

In this particular instance, the *Brady* violation seemed to have been the result of deliberate and unethical concealment by an individual prosecutor, who had since died. Even had he been alive, the individual prosecutor would have been absolutely immune. Thus, the plaintiff in *Connick* was defeated both by a restrictive understanding of "deliberate indifference" and by the rule of absolute immunity for individual officers. If change is needed, which would be the better route to a different result?

3. BIBLIOGRAPHY

The Court's decisions on the conditions for imposing governmental liability under § 1983 spawned an enormous literature in the 1980s.[a] Two more recent symposia address these issues from a variety of perspectives. The DePaul Law Review published a symposium on Municipal Liability in Civil Rights Litigation, with contents as follows: Susan Bandes, Introduction: The Emperor's New Clothes, 48 DePaul L. Rev. 619 (1999); Jack M. Beermann, Municipal Responsibility for Constitutional Torts, 48 DePaul L. Rev. 627 (1999); Michael J. Gerhardt, Institutional Analysis of Municipal Liability Under Section 1983, 48 DePaul L. Rev. 669 (1999); Karen M. Blum, Municipal Liability: Derivative or Direct? Statutory or Constitutional? Distinguishing the *Canton* Case from the *Collins* Case, 48 DePaul L. Rev. 687 (1999); David F. Hamilton, The Importance and Overuse of Policy and Custom Claims: A View from One Trench, 48 DePaul L. Rev. 723 (1999); G. Flint Taylor, A Litigator's View of Discovery and Proof in Police Misconduct Policy and Practice Cases, 48 DePaul L. Rev. 747 (1999). The Urban Lawyer published a symposium on Reconsidering *Monell's* Limitation on Municipal Liability for Civil

---

[a] See Susan Bandes, *Monell, Parratt, Daniels,* and *Davidson*: Distinguishing a Custom or Policy from a Random, Unauthorized Act, 72 Iowa L.Rev. 101 (1986) (distinguishing the general rule of *Monell* from the special case of *Parratt v. Taylor*, which focuses on the adequacy of state law); Karen M. Blum, Making Out the *Monell* Claim Under Section 1983, 25 Touro L. Rev. 829 (2009); George D. Brown, Municipal Liability under § 1983 and the Ambiguities of Burger Court Federalism; A Comment on *City of Oklahoma City v. Tuttle* and *Pembaur v. City of Cincinnati*—the "Official Policy" Cases, 27 B.C.L.Rev. 883 (1986); Mark R. Brown, Correlating Municipal Liability and Official Immunity Under Section 1983, 1989 U.Ill.L.Rev. 625 (1989) (arguing that governmental liability and the official immunity of individual officers should be inversely correlated so as to eliminate any gap in accountability for constitutional violations); Mark R. Brown, Accountability in Government and Section 1983, 25 U.Mich.J.L.Ref. 53 (1991) (arguing that high-ranking government officials should be liable for failure to control subordinates); Douglas L. Colbert, Bifurcation of Civil Rights Defendants: Undermining *Monell* in Police Brutality Cases, 44 Hastings L.J. 499 (1993) (focusing on severing the trial of individual and municipal defendants); Steven Stein Cushman, Municipal Liability under § 1983: Toward a New Definition of Municipal Policymaker, 34 B.C.L. Rev. 693 (1993) (offering a broader definition of de facto policymakers); Michael J. Gerhardt, The *Monell* Legacy: Balancing Federalism Concerns and Municipal Accountability under § 1983, 62 S.Cal.L.Rev. 539 (1989) (differentiating "policy" and "custom" and proposing resolution of various disputed issues in the law of municipal liability); Kit Kinports, The Buck Does Not Stop Here: Supervisory Liability in Section 1983 Cases, 1997 U. Ill. L. Rev. 147 (arguing that supervisory liability should be imposed for negligence in the supervision or training of subordinates); Barbara Kritchevsky, Making Sense of State of Mind: Determining Responsibility in Section 1983 Municipal Liability Litigation, 60 G.W.L.Rev. 417 (1992) (arguing that municipal liability should depend on the state of mind of municipal policymakers, not on that of the sometimes blameless municipal employees who directly cause the injury); Susanah M. Mead, 42 U.S.C. § 1983 Municipal Liability: The *Monell* Sketch Becomes a Distorted Picture, 65 N.C.L.Rev. 518 (1987) (urging reconsideration of respondeat superior); Solomon Oliver, Municipal Liability for Police Misconduct under 42 U.S.C. § 1983 after *City of Oklahoma City v. Tuttle,* 64 Wash.U.L.Q. 151 (1986) (analyzing failure-to-train liability after *Tuttle* but before *Harris*); Barbara Rook Snyder, The Final Authority Analysis: A Unified Approach to Municipal Liability under § 1983, 1986 Wis.L.Rev. 633 (arguing that municipalities should be held liable for the acts of an official or employee vested with "final authority" over the matter in question); Christina Whitman, Government Responsibility for Constitutional Torts, 85 Mich.L.Rev. 225 (1986) (calling for a closer focus on "how institutions can, as institutions, cause injuries").

Rights Violations, with an introduction by David M. Gelfand, 31 Urb. Law. 395 (1999), and the following articles: Robert J. Kaczorowski, Reflections on *Monell's* Analysis of the Legislative History of Section 1983, 31 Urb. Law. 407 (1999); Barbara Kritchevsky, Reexamining *Monell*: Basing Section 1983 Municipal Liability Doctrine on the Statutory Language, 31 Urb. Law. 437; Robert E. Manley, Effective But Messy, *Monell* Should Endure, 31 Urb. Law. 481 (1999); Oscar G. Chase and Arlo Monell Chase, *Monell*: The Story Behind the Landmark, 31 Urb. Law. 491 (1999); Ronald Turner, Employer Liability for Supervisory Hostile Environment Sexual Harassment: Comparing Title VII's and Section 1983's Regulatory Regimes, 31 Urb. Law. 503 (1999); Laura Oren, If *Monell* Were Reconsidered: Sexual Abuse and the Scope-of-Employment Doctrine in the Common Law, 31 Urb. Law. 527 (1999).

Finally, for an interesting article that calls for renewed attention to "custom" as a basis of municipal liability, see Myriam E. Gilles, Breaking the Code of Silence: Rediscovering "Custom" in Section 1983 Municipal Liability, 80 B.U. L. Rev. 17 (2000). Gilles focuses particularly on the "police code of silence" as a "custom" that "causes" constitutional violations.

Board of County Commissioners of Bryan County v. Brown

Supreme Court of the United States, 1997.
520 U.S. 397.

■ JUSTICE O'CONNOR delivered the opinion of the Court.

Respondent Jill Brown brought a claim for damages against petitioner Bryan County under 42 U.S.C. § 1983. She alleged that a county police officer used excessive force in arresting her, and that the county itself was liable for her injuries based on its sheriff's hiring and training decisions. She prevailed on her claims against the county following a jury trial, and the Court of Appeals for the Fifth Circuit affirmed the judgment against the county on the basis of the hiring claim alone. We granted certiorari. We conclude that the Court of Appeals' decision cannot be squared with our recognition that, in enacting § 1983, Congress did not intend to impose liability on a municipality unless deliberate action attributable to the municipality is the "moving force" behind the plaintiff's deprivation of federal rights. Monell v. New York City Dept. of Social Services, 436 U.S. 658, 694 (1978).

I

In the early morning hours of May 12, 1991, respondent Jill Brown and her husband were driving from Grayson County, Texas, to their home in Bryan County, Oklahoma. After crossing into Oklahoma, they approached a police checkpoint. Mr. Brown, who was driving, decided to avoid the checkpoint and return to Texas. After seeing the Browns' truck turn away from the checkpoint, Bryan County Deputy Sheriff Robert Morrison and Reserve Deputy Stacy Burns pursued the vehicle. Although the parties' version of event differ, at trial both deputies claimed that their patrol car reached speeds in excess of 100 miles per hour. Mr. Brown testified that he was unaware of the deputies' attempt to overtake him. The chase finally ended four miles south of the police checkpoint.

After he got out of the squad car, Deputy Sheriff Morrison pointed his gun toward the Browns' vehicle and ordered the Browns to raise their hands. Reserve Deputy Burns, who was unarmed, rounded the corner of the vehicle on the passenger's side. Burns twice ordered respondent Jill Brown from the vehicle. When she did not exit, he used an "arm bar" technique, grabbing respondent's arm at the wrist and elbow, pulling her from the vehicle, and spinning her to the ground. Respondent's knees were severely injured, and she later underwent corrective surgery. Ultimately, she may need knee replacements.

Respondent sought compensation for her injuries under 42 U.S.C. § 1983 and state law from Burns, Bryan County Sheriff B.J. Moore, and the county itself. Respondent claimed, among other things, that Bryan County was liable for Burns' alleged use of excessive force based on Sheriff Moore's decision to hire Burns, the son of his nephew. Specifically, respondent claimed that Sheriff Moore had failed to adequately review Burns' background. Burns had a record of driving infractions and had pleaded guilty to various driving-related and other misdemeanors, including assault and battery, resisting arrest, and public drunkenness. Oklahoma law does not preclude the hiring of an individual who has committed a misdemeanor to serve as a peace officer. At trial, Sheriff Moore testified that he had obtained Burns' driving record and a report on Burns from the National Crime Information Center, but had not closely reviewed either. Sheriff Moore authorized Burns to make arrests, but not to carry a weapon or to operate a patrol car.

In a ruling not at issue here, the District Court dismissed respondent's § 1983 claim against Sheriff Moore prior to trial. Counsel for Bryan County stipulated that Sheriff Moore "was the policy maker for Bryan County regarding the Sheriff's Department." At the close of respondent's case and again at the close of all the evidence, Bryan County moved for judgment as a matter of law. As to respondent's claim that Sheriff Moore's decision to hire Burns triggered municipal liability, the county argued that a single hiring decision by a municipal policymaker could not give rise to municipal liability under § 1983. The District Court denied the county's motions. The court also overruled the county's objections to jury instructions on the § 1983 claim against the county.

To resolve respondent's claims, the jury was asked to answer several interrogatories. The jury concluded that Stacy Burns had arrested respondent without probable cause and had used excessive force, and therefore found him liable for respondent's injuries. It also found that the "hiring policy" and the "training policy" of Bryan County "in the case of Stacy Burns as instituted by its policymaker, B.J. Moore," were each "so inadequate as to amount to deliberate indifference to the constitutional needs of the plaintiff." The District Court entered judgment for respondent on the issue of Bryan County's § 1983 liability. The county appealed on several grounds, and the Court of Appeals for the Fifth Circuit affirmed. The court held, among other things, that Bryan County was properly found liable under § 1983 based on Sheriff Moore's decision to hire Burns. The court addressed only those points that it thought merited review; it did not address the jury's determination of county liability based on inadequate training of Burns, nor do we. We granted certiorari to decide whether the county was properly held liable for respondent's injuries based on Sheriff Moore's single decision to hire Burns. We now reverse.

II

[I]n *Monell* and subsequent cases, we have required a plaintiff seeking to impose liability on a municipality under § 1983 to identify a municipal "policy" or "custom" that caused the plaintiff's injury. Locating a "policy" ensures that a municipality is held liable only for those deprivations resulting from the decisions of its duly constituted legislative body or of those officials whose acts may fairly be said to be those of the municipality. Similarly, an act performed pursuant to a "custom" that has not been formally approved by an appropriate decisionmaker may fairly subject a municipality to liability on the theory that the relevant practice is so widespread as to have the force of law.

The parties join issue on whether, under *Monell* and subsequent cases, a single hiring decision by a County Sheriff can be a "policy" that triggers municipal liability. Relying on our decision in Pembaur v. Cincinnati, 475 U.S. 469 (1986), respondent claims that a single act by a decisionmaker with final authority in the relevant area constitutes a "policy" attributable to the municipality itself. So long as a § 1983 plaintiff identifies a decision properly attributable to the municipality, respondent argues, there is no risk of imposing respondeat superior liability. Whether that decision was intended to govern only the situation at hand or to serve as a rule to be applied over time is immaterial. Rather, under respondent's theory, identification of an act of a proper municipal decisionmaker is all that is required to ensure that the municipality is held liable only for its own conduct. The Court of Appeals accepted respondent's approach.

As our § 1983 municipal liability jurisprudence illustrates, however, it is not enough for a § 1983 plaintiff merely to identify conduct properly attributable to the municipality. The plaintiff must also demonstrate that, through its deliberate conduct, the municipality was the "moving force" behind the injury alleged. That is, a plaintiff must show that the municipal action was taken with the requisite degree of culpability and must demonstrate a direct causal link between the municipal action and the deprivation of federal rights.

Where a plaintiff claims that a particular municipal action itself violates federal law, or directs an employee to do so, resolving these issues of fault and causation is straightforward. Section 1983 itself "contains no state-of-mind requirement independent of that necessary to state a violation" of the underlying federal right. Daniels v. Williams, 474 U.S. 327, 330 (1986). In any § 1983 suit, however, the plaintiff must establish the state of mind required to prove the underlying violation. Accordingly, proof that a municipality's legislative body or authorized decisionmaker has intentionally deprived a plaintiff of a federally protected right necessarily establishes that the municipality acted culpably. Similarly, the conclusion that the action taken or directed by the municipality or its authorized decisionmaker itself violates federal law will also determine that the municipal action was the moving force behind the injury of which the plaintiff complains.

Sheriff Moore's hiring decision was itself legal, and Sheriff Moore did not authorize Burns to use excessive force. Respondent's claim, rather, is that a single facially lawful hiring decision can launch a series of events that ultimately cause a violation of federal rights. Where a plaintiff claims that the municipality has not directly inflicted an injury, but nonetheless has caused an employee to do so, rigorous standards of culpability and causation must be applied to ensure that the municipality is not held liable solely for the actions of its employees. See Canton v. Harris, 489 U.S. 378,

391–92 (1989); Oklahoma City v. Tuttle, 471 U.S. 808, 824 (1985) (plurality opinion).

In relying heavily on *Pembaur*, respondent blurs the distinction between § 1983 cases that present no difficult questions of fault and causation and those that do. To the extent that we have recognized a cause of action under § 1983 based on a single decision attributable to a municipality, we have done so only where the evidence that the municipality had acted and that the plaintiff had suffered a deprivation of federal rights also proved fault and causation. For example, Owen v. Independence, 445 U.S. 622 (1980), and Newport v. Fact Concerts, Inc., 453 U.S. 247 (1981), involved formal decisions of municipal legislative bodies. In *Owen*, the City Council allegedly censured and discharged an employee without a hearing. In *Fact Concerts*, the City Council canceled a license permitting a concert following a dispute over the performance's content. Neither decision reflected implementation of a generally applicable rule. But we did not question that each decision, duly promulgated by city lawmakers, could trigger municipal liability if the decision itself were found to be unconstitutional. Because fault and causation were obvious in each case, proof that the municipality's decision was unconstitutional would suffice to establish that the municipality itself was liable for the plaintiff's constitutional injury.

Similarly, *Pembaur v. Cincinnati* concerned a decision by a County Prosecutor, acting as the county's final decisionmaker, to direct county deputies to forcibly enter petitioner's place of business to serve capiases upon third parties. Relying on *Owen* and *Newport*, we concluded that a final decisionmaker's adoption of a course of action "tailored to a particular situation and not intended to control decisions in later situations" may, in some circumstances, give rise to municipal liability under § 1983. In *Pembaur*, it was not disputed that the prosecutor had specifically directed the action resulting in the deprivation of petitioner's rights. The conclusion that the decision was that of a final municipal decisionmaker and was therefore properly attributable to the municipality established municipal liability. No questions of fault or causation arose.

Claims not involving an allegation that the municipal action itself violated federal law, or directed or authorized the deprivation of federal rights, present much more difficult problems of proof. That a plaintiff has suffered a deprivation of federal rights at the hands of a municipal employee will not alone permit an inference of municipal culpability and causation; the plaintiff will simply have shown that the employee acted culpably. We recognized these difficulties in *Canton v. Harris*, supra, where we considered a claim that inadequate training of shift supervisors at a city jail led to a deprivation of a detainee's constitutional rights. We held that, quite apart from the state of mind required to establish the underlying constitutional violation—in that case, a violation of due process—a plaintiff seeking to establish municipal liability on the theory that a facially lawful municipal action has led an employee to violate a plaintiff's rights must demonstrate that the municipal action was taken with "deliberate indifference" as to its known or obvious consequences. A showing of simple or even heightened negligence will not suffice.

We concluded in *Canton* that an "inadequate training" claim could be the basis for § 1983 liability in "limited circumstances." We spoke, however, of a deficient training "program," necessarily intended to apply over time to multiple employees. Existence of a "program" makes proof of fault and causation at least possible in an inadequate training case. If a program does not prevent constitutional violations, municipal decisionmakers may eventually be put on notice that a new program is called for. Their continued adherence to an approach that they know or should know has failed to prevent tortious conduct by employees may establish the conscious disregard for the consequences of their action—the "deliberate indifference"—necessary to trigger municipal liability. In addition, the existence of a pattern of tortious conduct by inadequately trained employees may tend to show that the lack of proper training, rather than a one-time negligent administration of the program or factors peculiar to the officer involved in a particular incident, is the "moving force" behind the plaintiff's injury.

Before trial, counsel for Bryan County stipulated that Sheriff Moore "was the policy maker for Bryan County regarding the Sheriff's Department." . . . Respondent does not claim that she can identify any pattern of injuries linked to Sheriff Moore's hiring practices. Indeed, respondent does not contend that Sheriff Moore's hiring practices are generally defective. The only evidence on this point at trial suggested that Sheriff Moore had adequately screened the backgrounds of all prior deputies he hired. Respondent instead seeks to trace liability to what can only be described as a deviation from Sheriff Moore's ordinary hiring practices. Where a claim of municipal liability rests on a single decision, not itself representing a violation of federal law and not directing such a violation, the danger that a municipality will be held liable without fault is high. Because the decision necessarily governs a single case, there can be no notice to the municipal decisionmaker, based on previous violations of federally protected rights, that his approach is inadequate. Nor will it be readily apparent that the municipality's action caused the injury in question, because the plaintiff can point to no other incident tending to make it more likely that the plaintiff's own injury flows from the municipality's action, rather than from some intervening cause.

In *Canton*, we did not foreclose the possibility that evidence of a single violation of federal rights, accompanied by a showing that a municipality has failed to train its employees to handle recurring situations presenting an obvious potential for such a violation, could trigger municipal liability. . . . Respondent purports to rely on *Canton*, arguing that Burns' use of excessive force was the plainly obvious consequence of Sheriff Moore's failure to screen Burns' record. In essence, respondent claims that this showing of "obviousness" would demonstrate both that Sheriff Moore acted with conscious disregard for the consequences of his action and that the Sheriff's action directly caused her injuries, and would thus substitute for the pattern of injuries ordinarily necessary to establish municipal culpability and causation.

The proffered analogy between failure-to-train cases and inadequate screening cases is not persuasive. In leaving open in *Canton* the possibility that a plaintiff might succeed in carrying a failure-to-train claim without showing a pattern of constitutional violations, we simply hypothesized that, in a narrow range of circumstances, a violation of federal rights may be a highly predictable consequence of a failure to equip law enforcement officers with specific tools to handle recurring situations. The likelihood that the situation will recur and the predictability that an officer lacking specific tools to handle that situation will violate citizens' rights could justify a finding that policymakers' decision not to train the officer reflected "deliberate indifference" to the obvious consequence of the policymakers' choice—namely, a violation of a specific constitutional or statutory right. The high degree of predictability may also support an inference of causation—that the municipality's indifference led directly to the very consequence that was so predictable.

Where a plaintiff presents a § 1983 claim premised upon the inadequacy of an official's review of a prospective applicant's record, however, there is a particular danger that a municipality will be held liable for an injury not directly caused by a deliberate action attributable to the municipality itself. Every injury suffered at the hands of a municipal employee can be traced to a hiring decision in a "but-for" sense: But for the municipality's decision to hire the employee, the plaintiff would not have suffered the injury. To prevent municipal liability for a hiring decision from collapsing into respondeat superior liability, a court must carefully test the link between the policymaker's inadequate decision and the particular injury alleged.

In attempting to import the reasoning of *Canton* into the hiring context, respondent ignores the fact that predicting the consequence of a single hiring decision, even one based on an inadequate assessment of a record, is far more difficult than predicting what might flow from the failure to train a single law enforcement officer as to a specific skill necessary to the discharge of his duties. . . .

We assume that a jury could properly find in this case that Sheriff Moore's assessment of Burns' background was inadequate. Sheriff Moore's own testimony indicated that he did not inquire into the underlying conduct or the disposition of any of the misdemeanor charges reflected on Burns' record before hiring him. But this showing of an instance of inadequate screening is not enough to establish "deliberate indifference." In layman's terms, inadequate screening of an applicant's record may reflect "indifference" to the applicant's background. For purposes of a legal inquiry into municipal liability under § 1983, however, that is not the relevant "indifference." A plaintiff must demonstrate that a municipal decision reflects deliberate indifference to the risk that a violation of a particular constitutional or statutory right will follow the decision. Only where adequate scrutiny of an applicant's background would lead a reasonable policymaker to conclude that the plainly obvious consequence of the decision to hire the applicant would be the deprivation of a third party's federally protected right can the official's failure to adequate scrutinize the applicant's background constitute "deliberate indifference."

[A] finding of culpability simply cannot depend on the mere probability that any officer inadequately screened will inflict any constitutional injury. Rather, it must depend on a finding that this officer was highly likely to inflict the particular injury suffered by the plaintiff. The connection between the background of the particular applicant and the specific constitutional violation alleged must be strong. What the District Court's instructions on culpability, and therefore the jury's finding of municipal liability, failed to capture is whether Burns' background made his use of excessive force in making an arrest a plainly obvious consequence of the hiring decision. . . .

Even assuming without deciding that proof of a single instance of inadequate screening could ever trigger municipal liability, the evidence in this case was insufficient to support a finding that, in hiring Burns, Sheriff Moore disregarded a known or obvious risk of injury. To test the link between Sheriff Moore's hiring decision and respondent's injury, we must ask whether a full review of Burns' record reveals that Sheriff Moore should have concluded that Burns' use of excessive force would be a plainly obvious consequence of the hiring decision. On this point, respondent's showing was inadequate. To be sure, Burns' record reflected various misdemeanor infractions. Respondent claims that the record demonstrated such a strong propensity for violence that Burns' application of excessive force was highly likely. The primary charges on which respondent relies, however, are those arising from a fight on a college campus where Burns was a student. In connection with this single incident, Burns was charged with assault and battery, resisting arrest, and public drunkenness. In January 1990, when he pleaded guilty to those charges, Burns also pleaded guilty to various driving-related offenses, including nine moving violations and a charge of driving with a suspended license. In addition, Burns had previously pleaded guilty to being in actual physical control of a vehicle while intoxicated.

The fact that Burns had pleaded guilty to traffic offenses and other misdemeanors may well have made him an extremely poor candidate for reserve deputy. Had Sheriff Moore fully reviewed Burn's record, he might have come to precisely that conclusion. But unless he would necessarily have reached that decision because Burns' use of excessive force would have been a plainly obvious consequence of the hiring decision, Sheriff Moore's inadequate scrutiny of Burns' record cannot constitute "deliberate indifference" to respondent's federally protected right to be free from a use of excessive force.

Justice Souter's reading of the case is that the jury believed that Sheriff Moore in fact read Burns' entire record. That is plausible, but it is also irrelevant. It is not sufficient for respondent to show that Sheriff Moore read Burns' record and therefore hired Burns with knowledge of his background. Such a decision may reflect indifference to Burns' record, but what is required is deliberate indifference to a plaintiff's constitutional right. That is, whether Sheriff Moore failed to examine Burns' record, partially examined it, or fully examined it, Sheriff Moore's hiring decision could not have been "deliberately indifferent" unless in light of that record Burns' use of excessive force would have been a plainly obvious consequence of the hiring decision. Because there was insufficient evidence on which a jury could base a finding that Sheriff Moore's decision to hire Burns reflected conscious disregard of an obvious risk that a use of excessive force would follow, the District Court erred in submitting respondent's inadequate screening claim to the jury.

III

Cases involving constitutional injuries allegedly traceable to an ill-considered hiring decision pose the greatest risk that a municipality will be held liable for an injury that it did not cause. In the broadest sense, every injury is traceable to a hiring decision. Where a court fails to adhere to rigorous requirements of culpability and causation, municipal liability collapses into respondeat superior liability. As we recognized in *Monell* and have repeatedly reaffirmed, Congress did not intend municipalities to be held liable unless deliberate action attributable to the municipality directly caused a deprivation of federal rights. A failure to apply stringent culpability and causation requirements raises serious federalism concerns, in that it risks constitutionalizing particular hiring requirements that states have themselves elected not to impose. Bryan County is not liable for Sheriff Moore's isolated decision to hire Burns without adequate screening, because respondent has not demonstrated that his decision reflected a conscious disregard for a high risk that Burns would use excessive force in violation of respondent's federally protected right. We therefore vacate the judgment of the Court of Appeals and remand this case for further proceedings consistent with this opinion.

■ JUSTICE SOUTER, with whom JUSTICE STEVENS and JUSTICE BREYER join, dissenting.

. . . Sheriff Moore's failure to screen out his 21–year–old great-nephew Burns on the basis of his criminal record, and the decision instead to authorize Burns to act as a Deputy Sheriff, constitutes a policy choice attributable to Bryan County under § 1983. There is no serious dispute that Sheriff Moore is the designated policymaker for implementing the Sheriff's law enforcement powers and recruiting officers to exercise them, or that he "has final authority to act for the municipality in hiring matters." As the authorized policymaker, Sheriff Moore is the county for purposes of § 1983 municipal liability arising from the Sheriffs Department's exercise of law enforcement authority. [I]t was open to the jury to find that the Sheriff knew of the record of his nephew's violent propensity, but hired him in deliberate indifference to the risk that he would use excessive force on the job, as in fact he later did. . . . The Sheriff's policy choice creating a substantial risk of a constitutional violation therefore could subject the county to liability under existing precedent. . . .

■ JUSTICE BREYER, with whom JUSTICE STEVENS and JUSTICE GINSBURG join, dissenting.

In Monell v. New York City Dept. of Social Servs., 436 U.S. 658 (1978), this Court said that municipalities cannot be held liable for constitutional torts under 42 U.S.C. § 1983 "on a respondeat superior theory," but they can be held liable "when execution of" a municipality's "policy or custom . . . inflicts the injury." That statement has produced a highly complex body of interpretive law. Today's decision exemplifies the law's complexity, for it distinguishes among a municipal action that "itself violates federal law," an action that "intentionally deprives a plaintiff of a federally protected right," and one that "has caused an employee to do so." It then elaborates this Court's requirement that a consequence be "so likely" to occur that a policymaker could "reasonably be said to have been *deliberately* indifferent" with respect to it, Canton v. Harris, 489 U.S. 378, 390 (1989) (emphasis added), with an admonition that the unconstitutional consequence must be "plainly obvious." The majority fears that a contrary view of prior precedent would undermine *Monell*'s basic distinction. That concern, however, rather than leading us to spin ever finer distinctions as we try to apply *Monell*'s basic distinction between liability that rests upon policy and liability that is vicarious, suggests that we should reexamine the legal soundness of that basic distinction itself.

I believe that the legal prerequisites for reexamination of an interpretation of an important statute are present here. The soundness of the original principle is doubtful. The original principle has generated a body of interpretive law that is so complex that the law has become difficult to apply. Factual and legal changes have divorced the law from the distinction's apparent original purposes. And there may be only a handful of individuals or groups that have significantly relied upon perpetuation of the original distinction. If all this is so, later law has made the original distinction, not simply wrong, but obsolete and a potential source of confusion. . . .

First, consider *Monell*'s original reasoning. The *Monell* "no vicarious liability" principle rested upon a historical analysis of § 1983 and upon

§ 1983's literal language—language that imposes liability upon (but only upon) any "person." Justice Stevens has clearly explained why neither of these rationales is sound. Oklahoma City v. Tuttle, 471 U.S. 808, 834–44 (1985) (Stevens, J., dissenting); Pembaur v. Cincinnati, 475 U.S. 469, 489–91 (1986) (Stevens, J., concurring in part and concurring in judgment). Essentially, the history on which *Monell* relied consists almost exclusively of the fact that the Congress that enacted § 1983 rejected an amendment (called the Sherman amendment) that would have made municipalities vicariously liable for the marauding acts of *private citizens*. That fact, as Justice Stevens and others have pointed out, does not argue against vicarious liability for the act of municipal *employees*. . . .

Without supporting history, it is difficult to find § 1983's words "every person" inconsistent with respondeat superior liability. In 1871 "bodies politic and corporate," such as municipalities were "persons." See Act of Feb. 25, ch. 71, § 2 (repealed 1939). Section 1983 requires that the "person" either "subject" or "cause" a different person "to be subjected" to a "deprivation" of a right. As a purely linguistic matter, a municipality, which can act only through its employees, might be said to have "subjected" a person or to have "caused" that person to have been "subjected" to a loss of rights when a municipality's employee acts within the scope of his or her employment.

Second, *Monell*'s basic effort to distinguish between vicarious liability and liability derived from "policy or custom" has produced a body of law that is neither readily understandable nor easy to apply. . . .

Finally, relevant legal and factual circumstances may have changed in a way that affects likely reliance upon *Monell*'s liability limitation. The legal complexity . . . makes it difficult for municipalities to predict just when they will be held liable based upon "policy or custom." Moreover, their potential liability is, in a sense, greater than that of individuals, for they cannot assert the "qualified immunity" defenses that individuals may raise. Owen v. Independence, 445 U.S. 622 (1980). Further, many states have statutes that appear to, in effect, mimic respondeat superior by authorizing indemnification of employees found liable under § 1983 for actions within the scope of their employment. [Citations omitted.] These statutes—valuable to government employees as well as to civil rights victims—can provide for payments from the government that are similar to those that would take place in the absence of *Monell*'s limitations. To the extent that they do so, municipal reliance upon the continuation of *Monell*'s "policy" limitation loses much of its significance.

Any statement about reliance, of course, must be tentative, as we have not heard argument on the matter. We do not know the pattern of indemnification: how often, and to what extent, states now indemnify their employees, and which of their employees they indemnify. I also realize that there may be other reasons, constitutional and otherwise, that I have not discussed that argue strongly for reaffirmation of *Monell*'s holding.

Nonetheless, for the reasons I have set forth, I believe the case for reexamination is a strong one. Today's decision underscores this need. Consequently, I would ask for further argument that would focus upon the continued viability of *Monell*'s distinction between vicarious municipal liability and municipal liability based upon policy and custom.

NOTES ON BRYAN COUNTY V. BROWN

1. THE FAILURE TO TRAIN CLAIM

The Court's opinion notes that Bryan County was held liable for Burns' violations of Brown's constitutional rights under two separate theories: that the county's "hiring policy" was "so inadequate as to amount to deliberate indifference to the constitutional needs of the plaintiff" *and* that the county's "training policy" was "so inadequate as to amount of deliberate indifference to the constitutional needs of the plaintiff." Only the former claim was addressed by either the Court of Appeals or the Supreme Court.

Initially, the Court of Appeals examined the failure-to-train claim and concluded that "we do not find the training practices inadequate." Brown v. Bryan County, 53 F.3d 1410, 1425 (5th Cir. 1995). In the view of the court, Brown's failure to present evidence of other similar incidents or of widespread misbehavior in the force precluded recovery under the inadequate training claim. On rehearing, however, the Court of Appeals expunged its analysis of the "inadequate training" claim and did not thereafter consider the issue. Brown v. Bryan County, 67 F.3d 1174, 1178 (5th Cir. 1995).

Given that the jury's verdict on the failure-to-train claim was thus left undisturbed, why did the Court of Appeals or the Supreme Court find it necessary to address the failure-to-screen claim? Presumably, there was no additional quantum of damages attributable solely to the failure to screen. Moreover, in light of the Court of Appeals' decision leaving the damages award undisturbed, why did the county seek Supreme Court review?

2. THE JURY CHARGE ON DELIBERATE INDIFFERENCE

The evidence at trial regarding the failure-to-screen claim consisted of an examination of Sheriff Moore, who revealed that he had obtained Burns' criminal record but had been quite cavalier about actually checking it, and the testimony of two experts. Brown's expert, Dr. Otto Schweizer, who had served as a field training officer, a police chief, and as a professor of criminal justice and police administration at the University of Central Oklahoma, testified that screening was necessary to weed out individuals who seek police employment for "the wrong reasons, for example, because 'they like to exert their power.' " Schweizer concluded that Burns' arrest record showed "blatant disregard for the law and problems that may show themselves in abusing the public or using excessive force." Even the county's expert acknowledged that it was "doubtful" he would have hired someone with Burns' record.

The District Court charged the jury that "Sheriff B.J. Moore would have acted with deliberate indifference in adopting an otherwise constitutional hiring policy for a deputy sheriff if the need for closer scrutiny of Stacy Burns' background was so obvious and the inadequacy of the scrutiny given so likely to result in violations of constitutional rights, that Sheriff B.J. Moore can be reasonably said to have been deliberately indifferent to the constitutional needs of the Plaintiff." *Brown*, 67 F.3d at 1185 n.21. In what way was this instruction inadequate? Was the problem the failure to specify the particular "constitutional needs" of the plaintiff? That is, would an instruction that identified Burns' use of excessive force as the violation of constitutional rights "so likely to result" from his hiring have been sufficient? Or is the problem here that the majority simply disagrees with the jury's assessment of the evidence and the probability of a constitutional violation? In any event, how likely is it that a change in the precise formulation of the liability standard given in a jury instruction would translate into a different outcome? If the jury in this case had been charged with language drawn directly out of Justice O'Connor's opinion, would it necessarily have declined to find liability?

3. THE INCREASING INCOHERENCE OF GOVERNMENTAL LIABILITY DOCTRINE

Justice Breyer's dissent raises the question whether the Court's incremental decisionmaking on questions of governmental liability has produced an overly complex and incoherent body of law that cuts finer and finer lines, creating increasingly meaningless distinctions. Is the current state of the law inherently unstable? If the Court were writing on a clean slate how would it recast the doctrine? Can the Court's inconsistent invocation of principles of tort liability—especially principles of fault and causation—be reconciled with some underlying theory of when governmental liability is appropriate? Is that theory consistent with *Monell*? With *Owen*?

6. FOR WHAT WRONGS?

SUBSECTION A: CONSTITUTIONAL RIGHTS ENFORCEABLE UNDER § 1983

INTRODUCTORY NOTE ON THE RELATIONSHIP OF RIGHTS AND REMEDIES

This book focuses primarily on enforcing the Constitution through § 1983 and related statutes. As the Supreme Court has repeatedly said, § 1983 "is not itself a source of substantive rights, but a method for vindicating federal rights elsewhere conferred by those parts of the United States Constitution and federal statutes that it describes." Baker v. McCollan, 443 U.S. 137, 144 n.3 (1979). For the most part, questions concerning the definition and scope of the underlying substantive rights being enforced in § 1983 actions have been set aside.

Nonetheless, the remedial context in which the Supreme Court is asked to define constitutional rights can influence the scope of the rights it recognizes.[a] In some areas of constitutional law, the potential availability of monetary damages under § 1983 has played a relatively small role in the evolution of the substantive rights. For example, the meaning of equal protection under the Fourteenth Amendment has been developed largely through lawsuits seeking declaratory or injunctive relief. Similarly, although the antecedents to the Fourth Amendment lay in common-law trespass actions against government officials, the contours of modern protections against unreasonable searches have been developed largely through motions to exclude evidence from use in criminal prosecution. In other areas, however, the potential of liability has significantly influenced the Court's decisionmaking.

[a] See generally Daryl J. Levinson, Rights Essentialism and Remedial Equilibration, 99 Colum. L. Rev. 857 (1999).

Broadly speaking, the Court has two ways of accommodating a concern that money damages may adversely affect the behavior of public officials and, through them, the quality of government operations. One is to adopt transsubstantive rules that limit the availability of damages as a *remedy*. The doctrines of absolute and qualified immunity are examples of this approach. So, too, is the rejection of respondeat superior liability in *Monell* cases. The other way, which is the broad topic of this Subsection, is to cabin the underlying substantive right. The Court's treatment of cases under the Due Process Clause of the Fourteenth Amendment offers the best illustration of remedial concerns that seem to have affected the delineation of substantive rights.

There are three sorts of § 1983 claims that might be brought under the due process. First, as a formal matter, the various guarantees of the Bill of Rights are made applicable to the states by way of incorporation in Fourteenth Amendment due process. Thus, a plaintiff might bring suit under § 1983 for violation by a state public official of rights to freedom of speech or freedom from unreasonable searches and seizures based on the First and Fourth Amendments, respectively, as incorporated in the Due Process Clause of the Fourteenth. Second, the Supreme Court has recognized a substantive component to due process that bars certain governmental actions "regardless of the fairness of the procedures used to implement them." Daniels v. Williams, 474 U.S. 327, 331 (1986). An example is the individual who is denied the substantive due process right to reproductive autonomy under Roe v. Wade, 410 U.S. 113 (1973). She too could bring suit under § 1983 to vindicate rights derived from the Fourteenth Amendment. Finally, due process provides a guarantee of fair procedures whenever a state deprives individuals of "life," "liberty," or "property." It is with respect to this last category—"procedural due process"—that the delineation of the right has become bound up especially closely with remedial concerns.

Doctrinally, the question whether a governmental actor has denied procedural due process can be divided into three separate concerns: First, has a cognizable "life," "liberty," or "property" interest been denied? Second, was the loss of that protected interest fairly attributable to the "state" as opposed to a private actor? Third, if the state did deprive an individual of life, liberty, or property, was it done "without due process of law"?

The Supreme Court's decision in *Paul v. Davis*, the next principal case, focuses on the definition of a constitutionally cognizable "liberty" interest. In reading the case, consider how much the Court's reasoning about the right was driven by concerns about the damages remedy.

Paul v. Davis

Supreme Court of the United States, 1976.
424 U.S. 693.

■ MR. JUSTICE REHNQUIST delivered the opinion of the Court.

We granted certiorari in this case to consider whether respondent's charge that petitioners' defamation of him, standing alone and apart from any other governmental action with respect to him, stated a claim for relief under 42 U.S.C. § 1983 and the Fourteenth Amendment. For the reasons hereinafter stated, we conclude that it does not.

Petitioner Paul is the Chief of Police of the Louisville, Ky., Division of Police, while petitioner McDaniel occupies the same position in the Jefferson County, Ky., Division of Police. In late 1972 they agreed to combine their efforts for the purpose of alerting local area merchants to possible shoplifters who might be operating during the Christmas season. In early December petitioners distributed to approximately 800 merchants in the Louisville metropolitan area a flyer, which began as follows:

> TO: BUSINESS MEN IN THE METROPOLITAN AREA
>
> The Chiefs of the Jefferson County and City of Louisville Police Departments, in an effort to keep their officers advised on shoplifting activity, have approved the attached alphabetically arranged flyer of subjects known to be active in this criminal field.
>
> This flyer is being distributed to you, the business man, so that you may inform your security personnel to watch for these subjects. These persons have been arrested during 1971 and 1972 or have been active in various criminal fields in high density shopping areas.
>
> Only the photograph and name of the subject is shown on this flyer, if additional information is desired, please forward a request in writing. . . .

The flyer consisted of five pages of "mug shot" photos, arranged alphabetically. Each page was headed:

NOVEMBER 1972
CITY OF LOUISVILLE
JEFFERSON COUNTY
POLICE DEPARTMENTS
ACTIVE SHOPLIFTERS

In approximately the center of page two there appeared photos and the name of the respondent, Edward Charles Davis III.

Respondent appeared on the flyer because on June 14, 1971, he had been arrested in Louisville on a charge of shoplifting. He had been arraigned on this charge in September 1971, and, upon his plea of not guilty, the charge had been "filed away with leave [to reinstate]," a disposition which left the charge outstanding. Thus, at the time petitioners caused the flyer to be prepared and circulated respondent had been charged with shoplifting but his guilt or innocence of that offense had never been resolved. Shortly after circulation of the flyer the charge against respondent was finally dismissed by a judge of the Louisville Police Court.

At the time the flyer was circulated respondent was employed as a photographer by the Louisville Courier–Journal and Times. The flyer, and respondent's inclusion therein, soon came to the attention of respondent's supervisor, the Executive Director of Photography for the two newspapers. This individual called respondent in to hear his version of the events leading to his appearing in the flyer. Following this discussion, the supervisor informed respondent that although he would not be fired, he "had best not find himself in a similar situation" in the future.

Respondent thereupon brought this § 1983 action in the District Court for the Western District of Kentucky, seeking redress for the alleged violation of rights guaranteed to him by the Constitution of the United States. [R]espondent sought damages as well as declaratory and injunctive relief. The District Court [dismissed the complaint], ruling that "[t]he facts alleged in this case do not establish that plaintiff has been deprived of any right secured to him by the Constitution of the United States."

Respondent appealed to the Court of Appeals for the Sixth Circuit which recognized that, under our decisions, for respondent to establish a claim cognizable under § 1983 he had to show that petitioners had deprived him of a right secured by the Constitution of the United States, and that any such deprivation was achieved under color of law. The Court of Appeals concluded that respondent had set forth a § 1983 claim "in that he has alleged facts that constitute a denial of due process of law." In its view our decision in Wisconsin v. Constantineau, 400 U.S. 433 (1971), mandated reversal of the District Court.

I

Respondent's due process claim is grounded upon his assertion that the flyer, and in particular the phrase "Active Shoplifters" appearing at the head of the page upon which his name and photograph appear, impermissibly deprived him of some "liberty" protected by the Fourteenth Amendment. His complaint asserted that the "active shoplifter" designation would inhibit him from entering business establishments for fear of being suspected of shoplifting and possibly apprehended, and would seriously impair his future employment opportunities. Accepting that such consequences may flow from the flyer in question, respondent's complaint would appear to state a classical claim for defamation actionable in the courts of virtually every state. Imputing criminal behavior to an individual is generally considered defamatory per se, and actionable without proof of special damages.

Respondent brought his action, however, not in the state courts of Kentucky, but in a United States District Court for that state. He asserted not a claim for defamation under the laws of Kentucky, but a claim that he had been deprived of rights secured to him by the Fourteenth Amendment of the United States Constitution. Concededly if the same allegations had been made about respondent by a private individual, he would have nothing more than a claim for defamation under state law. But, he contends, since petitioners are respectively an official of city and of county governments, his action is transmuted into one for deprivation by the state of rights secured under the Fourteenth Amendment. . . .

If respondent's view is to prevail, a person arrested by law enforcement officers who announce that they believe such person to be responsible for a particular crime in order to calm the fears of an aroused populace, presumably obtains a claim against such officers under § 1983. And since it is surely far more clear from the language of the Fourteenth Amendment that "life" is protected against state deprivation than it is that reputation is protected against state injury, it would be difficult to see why the survivors of an innocent bystander mistakenly shot by a policeman or negligently killed by a sheriff driving a government vehicle, would not have claims equally cognizable under § 1983.

It is hard to perceive any logical stopping place to such a line of reasoning. Respondent's construction would seem almost necessarily to result in every legally cognizable injury which may have been inflicted by a state official acting under "color of law" establishing a violation of the Fourteenth Amendment. We think it would come as a great surprise to those who drafted and shepherded the adoption of that amendment to learn that it worked such a result, and a study of our decisions convinces us they do not support the construction urged by respondent.

II

The result reached by the Court of Appeals, which respondent seeks to sustain here, must be bottomed on one of two premises. The first is that the Due Process Clause of the Fourteenth Amendment and § 1983 make actionable many wrongs inflicted by government employees which had heretofore been thought to give rise only to state-law tort claims. The second premise is that the infliction by state officials of a "stigma" to one's reputation is somehow different in kind from the infliction by the same official of harm or injury to other interests protected by state law, so that an injury to reputation is actionable under § 1983 and the Fourteenth Amendment even if other such harms are not. We examine each of these premises in turn.

A

The first premise would be contrary to pronouncements in our cases on more than one occasion with respect to the scope of § 1983 and of the Fourteenth Amendment. In the leading case of Screws v. United States, 325 U.S. 91 (1945), the Court considered the proper application of the criminal counterpart of § 1983, likewise intended by Congress to enforce the guarantees of the Fourteenth Amendment. In his opinion for the Court plurality in that case, Mr. Justice Douglas observed:

> Violation of local law does not necessarily mean that federal rights have been invaded. The fact that a prisoner is assaulted, injured, or even murdered by state officials does not necessarily mean that he is deprived of any right protected or secured by the Constitution or laws of the United States.

After recognizing that Congress' power to make criminal the conduct of state officials under the aegis of the Fourteenth Amendment was not unlimited because that amendment "did not alter the basic relations between the states and the national government," the plurality opinion observed that Congress should not be understood to have attempted

> to make all torts of state officials federal crimes. It brought within [the criminal provision] only specified actions done "under color" of law and then only those acts which deprived a person of some right secured by the Constitution or laws of the United States.

This understanding of the limited effect of the Fourteenth Amendment was not lost in the Court's decision in Monroe v. Pape, 365 U.S. 167 (1961). There the Court was careful to point out that the complaint stated a cause of action under the Fourteenth Amendment because it alleged an unreasonable search and seizure violative of the guarantee "contained in the Fourth Amendment [and] made applicable to the states by reason of the Due Process Clause of the Fourteenth Amendment." Respondent, however, has pointed to no specific constitutional guarantee safeguarding the interest he asserts has been invaded. Rather, he apparently believes that the Fourteenth Amendment's Due Process Clause should ex proprio vigore extend to him a right to be free of injury wherever the state may be characterized as the tortfeasor. But such a reading would make of the Fourteenth Amendment a font of tort law to be superimposed upon whatever systems may already be administered by the states. We have noted the "constitutional shoals" that confront any attempt to derive from congressional civil rights statutes a body of general federal tort law, Griffin v. Breckenridge, 403 U.S. 88, 101–02 (1971); a fortiori the procedural guarantees of the Due Process Clause cannot be the source for such law.

B

The second premise upon which the result reached by the Court of Appeals could be rested—that the infliction by state officials of a "stigma" to one's reputation is somehow different in kind from infliction by a state official of harm to other interests protected by state law—is equally untenable. The words "liberty" and "property" as used in the Fourteenth Amendment do not in terms single out reputation as a candidate for special protection over and above other interests that may be protected by state law. While we have in a number of our prior cases pointed out the frequently drastic effect of the "stigma" which may result from defamation by the government in a variety of contexts, this line of cases does not establish the proposition that reputation alone, apart from some more tangible interests such as employment, is either "liberty" or "property" by itself sufficient to invoke the procedural protection of the Due Process Clause. As we have said, the Court of Appeals, in reaching a contrary conclusion, relied primarily upon Wisconsin v. Constantineau, 400 U.S. 433 (1971). We think the correct import of that decision, however, must be derived from an examination of the precedents upon which it relied, as well as consideration of other decisions by this Court, before and after *Constantineau*, which bear upon the relationship between governmental defamation and the guarantees of the Constitution. While not uniform in their treatment of the subject, we think that the weight of our decisions establishes no constitutional doctrine converting every defamation by a public official into a deprivation of liberty within the meaning of the Due Process Clause of the Fifth or Fourteenth Amendment.

[At this point the Court reviewed pre-*Constantineau* decisions, focusing on Joint Anti–Fascist Refugee Committee v. McGrath, 341 U.S. 123 (1951), in which the Court "examined the validity of the Attorney General's designation of certain organizations as 'Communist' on a list which he furnished to the Civil Service." The *McGrath* Court was badly split and produced no majority opinion, but several Justices indicated that mere injury to reputation would not violate due process. For example, Justice Jackson noted that "the mere designation as subversive deprives the organizations themselves of no legal right or opportunity":

> By it they are not dissolved, subjected to any legal prosecution, punished, penalized or prohibited from carrying on any of their activities. Their claim of injury is that they cannot attract audiences, enlist members, or obtain contributions as readily as before. These, however, are sanctions applied by public disapproval, not by law.

Justice Jackson nevertheless concluded that, owing to the disqualification of their members from public employment, the organizations had stated a claim upon which relief could be granted.

[Three *McGrath* dissenters disagreed with that conclusion and would have held that the official listing of the organizations as "Communist" did not deprive them of property or liberty:

> It may be assumed that the listing is hurtful to their prestige, reputation and earning power. It may be such an injury as would entitle organizations to damages in a tort action against persons not protected by privilege. . . . This designation, however, does not prohibit any business of the organizations, subject them to any punishment, or deprive them of liberty of speech or other freedom.

[Justice Rehnquist summarized the various opinions in *McGrath* by saying that "at the least six of the eight Justices who participated in that case viewed any 'stigma' imposed by the official action of the Attorney General of the United States, divorced from its effect on the legal status of an organization or a person, such as loss of tax exemption or loss of government employment, as an insufficient basis for invoking the Due Process Clause of the Fifth Amendment." On this reading, *McGrath* and related cases supported two propositions:]

The Court has recognized the serious damage that could be inflicted by branding a government employee as "disloyal," and thereby stigmatizing his good name. But the Court has never held that the mere defamation of any individual, whether by branding him disloyal or otherwise, was sufficient to invoke the guarantees of procedural due process absent an accompanying loss of government employment.[4] . . .

It was against this backdrop that the Court in 1971 decided *Constantineau*. There the Court held that a Wisconsin statute authorizing the practice of "posting" was unconstitutional because it failed to provide procedural safeguards of notice and an opportunity to be heard, prior to an individual's being "posted." Under the statute "posting" consisted of forbidding in writing the sale or delivery of alcoholic beverages to certain persons who were determined to have become hazards to themselves, to their family, or to the community by reason of their "excessive drinking." The statute also made it a misdemeanor to sell or give liquor to any person so posted.

There is undoubtedly language in *Constantineau*, which is sufficiently ambiguous to justify the reliance upon it by the Court of Appeals:

> Yet certainly where the state attaches "a badge of infamy" to the citizen, due process comes into play. "[T]he right to be heard before being condemned to suffer grievous loss of any kind, even though it may not involve the stigma and hardships of a criminal conviction, is a principle basic to our society."
>
> Where a person's good name, reputation, honor, or integrity is at stake *because of what the government is doing to him*, notice and an opportunity to be heard are essential. [Emphasis supplied.]

The last paragraph of the quotation could be taken to mean that if a government official defames a person, without more, the procedural re-

---

[4] We cannot agree with the suggestion of our Brother Brennan, dissenting, that the actions of these two petitioner law enforcement officers come within the language used by Mr. Justice Harlan in his dissenting opinion in Jenkins v. McKeithen, 395 U.S. 411, 433 (1969). They are not by any conceivable stretch of the imagination, either separately or together, "an agency whose sole or predominant function, without serving any other public interest, is to expose and publicize the names of persons it finds guilty of wrongdoing." Indeed, the actions taken by these petitioners in this case fall far short of the more formalized proceedings of the Commission on Civil Rights established by Congress in 1957, the procedures of which were upheld against constitutional challenge by this Court in Hannah v. Larche, 363 U.S. 420 (1960). There the Court described the functions of the Commission in this language:

> It does not adjudicate. It does not hold trials or determine anyone's civil or criminal liability. It does not issue orders. Nor does it indict, punish, or impose any *legal sanctions*. It does not make determinations depriving anyone of his life, liberty, or property. In short, the Commission does not and cannot take any affirmative action which will affect an individual's *legal rights*. The only purpose of its existence is to find facts which may subsequently be used as the basis for legislative or executive action. (Emphasis supplied.)

Addressing itself to the question of whether the Commission's "proceedings might irreparably harm those being investigated by subjecting them to public opprobrium and scorn, the distinct likelihood of losing their jobs, and the possibility of criminal prosecutions," the Court said that "even if such collateral consequences were to flow from the Commission's investigations, they would not be the result of any affirmative determinations made by the Commission, and they would not affect the legitimacy of the Commission's investigative function."

quirements of the Due Process Clause of the Fourteenth Amendment are brought into play. If read that way, it would represent a significant broadening of the holdings of [*McGrath* and similar cases], relied upon by the *Constantineau* Court. We should not read this language as significantly broadening those holdings without in any way adverting to the fact if there is any other possible interpretation of *Constantineau*'s language. We believe there is.

We think that the italicized language in the last sentence quoted, "because of what the government is doing to him," referred to the fact that the government action taken in that case deprived the individual of a right previously held under state law—the right to purchase or obtain liquor in common with the rest of the citizenry. "Posting," therefore, significantly altered his status as a matter of state law, and it was alteration of legal status which, combined with the injury resulting from the defamation, justified the invocation of procedural safeguards. The "stigma" resulting from the defamatory character of the posting was doubtless an important factor in evaluating the extent of harm worked by that act, but we do not think that such defamation, standing alone, deprived Constantineau of any "liberty" protected by the procedural guarantees of the Fourteenth Amendment.

This conclusion is reinforced by our discussion of the subject a little over a year later in Board of Regents v. Roth, 408 U.S. 564 (1972). There we noted that "the range of interests protected by procedural due process is not infinite," and that with respect to property interests they are,

> of course, . . . not created by the Constitution. Rather, they are created and their dimensions are defined by existing rules or understandings that stem from an independent source such as state law—rules or understandings that secure certain benefits and that support claims of entitlement to those benefits.

While *Roth* recognized that governmental action defaming an individual in the course of declining to rehire him could entitle the person to notice and an opportunity to be heard as to the defamation, its language is quite inconsistent with any notion that a defamation perpetrated by a government official but unconnected with any refusal to rehire would be actionable under the Fourteenth Amendment:

> The state, *in declining to rehire the respondent*, did not make any charge against him that might seriously damage his standing and associations in his community. . . .
>
> Similarly, there is no suggestion that the state, *in declining to reemploy the respondent*, imposed on him a stigma or other disability that foreclosed his freedom to take advantage of other employment opportunities.

Thus it was not thought sufficient to establish a claim under § 1983 and the Fourteenth Amendment that there simply be defamation by a state official; the defamation had to occur in the course of the termination of employment. Certainly there is no suggestion in *Roth* to indicate that a hearing would be required each time the state in its capacity as employer might be considered responsible for a statement defaming an employee who continues to be an employee.

This conclusion is quite consistent with our most recent holding in this area, Goss v. Lopez, 419 U.S. 565 (1975), that suspension from school based upon charges of misconduct could trigger the procedural guarantees of the

Fourteenth Amendment. While the Court noted that charges of misconduct could seriously damage the student's reputation, it also took care to point out that Ohio law conferred a right upon all children to attend school, and that the act of the school officials suspending the student there involved resulted in a denial or deprivation of that right.

III

It is apparent from our decisions that there exists a variety of interests which are difficult of definition but are nevertheless comprehended within the meaning of either "liberty" or "property" as meant in the Due Process Clause. These interests attain this constitutional status by virtue of the fact that they have been initially recognized and protected by state law,[5] and we have repeatedly ruled that the procedural guarantees of the Fourteenth Amendment apply whenever the state seeks to remove or significantly alter that protected status. In Bell v. Burson, 402 U.S. 535 (1971), for example, the state by issuing drivers' licenses recognized in its citizens a right to operate a vehicle on the highways of the state. The Court held that the state could not withdraw this right without giving petitioner due process. In Morrissey v. Brewer, 408 U.S. 471 (1972), the state afforded parolees the right to remain at liberty as long as the conditions of their parole were not violated. Before the state could alter the status of a parolee because of alleged violations of these conditions, we held that the Fourteenth Amendment's guarantees of due process of law required certain procedural safeguards.

In each of these cases, as a result of the state action complained of, a right or status previously recognized by state law was distinctly altered or extinguished. It was this alteration, officially removing the interest from the recognition and protection previously afforded by the state, which we found sufficient to invoke the procedural guarantees contained in the Due Process Clause of the Fourteenth Amendment. But the interest in reputation alone which respondent seeks to vindicate in this action in federal court is quite different from the "liberty" and "property" recognized in those decisions. Kentucky law does not extend to respondent any legal guarantee of present enjoyment of reputation which has been altered as a result of petitioners' actions. Rather his interest in reputation is simply one of a number which the state may protect against injury by virtue of its tort law, providing a forum for vindication of those interests by means of damages actions. And any harm or injury to that interest, even where as here inflicted by an officer of the state, does not result in a deprivation of any "liberty" or "property" recognized by state or federal law, nor has it worked any change of respondent's status as theretofore recognized under the state's laws. For these reasons we hold that the interest in reputation asserted in this case is neither "liberty" nor "property" guaranteed against state deprivation without due process of law. . . .

---

[5] There are other interests, of course, protected not by virtue of their recognition by the law of a particular state, but because they are guaranteed in one of the provisions of the Bill of Rights which has been "incorporated" into the Fourteenth Amendment. Section 1983 makes a deprivation of such rights actionable independently of state law. See Monroe v. Pape, 365 U.S. 167 (1961).

Our discussion in Part III is limited to consideration of the procedural guarantees of the Due Process Clause and is not intended to describe those substantive limitations upon state action which may be encompassed within the concept of "liberty" expressed in the Fourteenth Amendment. Cf. Part IV, infra.

IV

Respondent's complaint also alleged a violation of a "right to privacy guaranteed by the First, Fourth, Fifth, Ninth, and Fourteenth Amendments." . . . While there is no "right of privacy" found in any specific guarantee of the Constitution, the Court has recognized that "zones of privacy" may be created by more specific constitutional guarantees and thereby impose limits upon government power. See Roe v. Wade, 410 U.S. 113, 152–53 (1973). Respondent's case, however, comes within none of these areas. . . . In *Roe* the Court pointed out that the personal rights found in this guarantee of personal privacy must be limited to those which are "fundamental" or "implicit in the concept of ordered liberty" as described in Palko v. Connecticut, 302 U.S. 319 (1937). The activities detailed as being within this definition were ones very different from that for which respondent claims constitutional protection—matters relating to marriage, procreation, contraception, family relationships, and child rearing and education. In these areas it has been held that there are limitations on the state's power to substantively regulate conduct.

Respondent's claim is far afield from this line of decisions. He claims constitutional protection against the disclosure of the fact of his arrest on a shoplifting charge. His claim is based, not upon any challenge to the state's ability to restrict his freedom of action in a sphere contended to be "private," but instead on a claim that the state may not publicize a record of an official act such as an arrest. None of our substantive privacy decisions hold this or anything like this, and we decline to enlarge them in this manner.

None of respondent's theories of recovery [was] based upon rights secured to him by the Fourteenth Amendment. Petitioners therefore were not liable to him under § 1983. The judgment of the Court of Appeals is reversed.

■ MR. JUSTICE STEVENS took no part in the consideration or decision of this case.

■ MR. JUSTICE BRENNAN with whom MR. JUSTICE MARSHALL concurs and MR. JUSTICE WHITE concurs in part, dissenting.

I dissent. The Court today holds that police officials, acting in their official capacities as law enforcers, may on their own initiative and without trial constitutionally condemn innocent individuals as criminals and thereby brand them with one of the most stigmatizing and debilitating labels in our society. If there are no constitutional restraints on such oppressive behavior, the safeguards constitutionally accorded an accused in a criminal trial are rendered a sham, and no individual can feel secure that he will not be arbitrarily singled out for similar ex parte punishment by those primarily charged with fair enforcement of the law. The Court accomplishes this result by excluding a person's interest in his good name and reputation from all constitutional protection, regardless of the character of or necessity for the government's actions. The result, which is demonstrably inconsistent with our prior case law and unduly restrictive in its construction of our precious bill of rights, is one in which I cannot concur. . . .

The stark fact is that the police here have officially imposed on respondent the stigmatizing label "criminal" without the salutary and constitutionally mandated safeguards of a criminal trial. The Court concedes that this action will have deleterious consequences for respondent [but finds] no infringement of constitutionally protected interests. This is because, the Court holds, neither a "liberty" nor a "property" interest was invaded by the injury done respondent's reputation and therefore no violation of § 1983 or the Fourteenth Amendment was alleged. I wholly disagree. . . .

There is no attempt by the Court to analyze the question as one of reconciliation of constitutionally protected personal rights and the exigencies of law enforcement. No effort is made to distinguish the "defamation" that occurs when a grand jury indicts an accused from the "defamation" that occurs when executive officials arbitrarily and without trial declare a person an "active criminal." Rather, the Court by mere fiat and with no analysis wholly excludes personal interest in reputation from the ambit of "life, liberty, or property" under the fifth and Fourteenth Amendments, thus rendering due process concerns *never* applicable to the official stigmatization, however arbitrary, of an individual. The logical and disturbing corollary of this holding is that no due process infirmities would inhere in a statute constituting a commission to conduct ex parte trials of individuals, so long as the only official judgment pronounced was limited to the public condemnation and branding of a person as a Communist, a traitor, an "active murderer," a homosexual, or any other mark that "merely" carries social opprobrium. The potential of today's decision is frightening for a free people.[9] That decision surely finds no support in our relevant constitutional jurisprudence.

"In a Constitution for a free people, there can be no doubt that the meaning of 'liberty' must be broad indeed." Board of Regents v. Roth, 408 U.S. 564, 572 (1972). "Without doubt, it denotes not merely freedom from bodily restraint but also the right of the individual . . . generally to enjoy those privileges long recognized . . . as essential to the orderly pursuit of happiness by free men." Meyer v. Nebraska, 262 U.S. 390, 399 (1923).[10] Certainly the enjoyment of one's good name and reputation has been recognized repeatedly in our cases as being among the most cherished of rights enjoyed by a free people, and therefore as falling within the concept of personal "liberty."

> [A]s Mr. Justice Stewart has reminded us, the individual's right to the protection of his own good name
>
> > "reflects no more than our basic concept of the essential dignity and worth of every human being—a concept at the root of any decent system of ordered liberty. The protection of private personality, like the protection of life itself, is left primarily to the individual states under the Ninth and Tenth Amendments. But this

[9] Today's holding places a vast and arbitrary power in the hands of federal and state officials. It is not difficult to conceive of a police department, dissatisfied with what it perceives to be the dilatory nature or lack of efficacy of the judicial system in dealing with criminal defendants, publishing periodic lists of "active rapists," "active larcenists," or other "known criminals." The hardships resulting from the official stigmatization—loss of employment and educational opportunities, creation of impediments to professional licensing, and the imposition of general obstacles to the right of all free men to the pursuit of happiness—will often be as severe as actual incarceration, and the Court today invites and condones such lawless action by those who wish to inflict punishment without compliance with the procedural safeguards constitutionally required of the criminal justice system.

[10] One of the more questionable assertions made by the Court suggests that "liberty" or "property" interests are protected only if they are recognized under state law or protected by one of the specific guarantees of the Bill of Rights. To be sure, the Court has held [in *Roth*] that "[p]roperty interests are not created by the Constitution. . . . " However, . . . we have never restricted "liberty" interests in the manner the Court today attempts to do. [T]he content of "liberty" . . . has never been thought to depend on recognition of an interest by the state or federal government, and has never been restricted to interests explicitly recognized by other provisions of the Bill of Rights. . . .

> does not mean that the right is entitled to any less recognition by this Court as a basic of our constitutional system." Rosenblatt v. Baer, 383 U.S. 75, 92 (1966) (concurring opinion).

Gertz v. Robert Welch, Inc., 418 U.S. 323, 341 (1974).

We have consistently held that

> "[W]here a person's good name, reputation, honor, or integrity is at stake because of what the government is doing to him, notice and an opportunity to be heard are essential." Wisconsin v. Constantineau, 400 U.S. 433 (1971).

Board of Regents v. Roth, 408 U.S. 564, 573 (1972). In the criminal justice system, this interest is given concrete protection through the presumption of innocence and the prohibition of state-imposed punishment unless the state can demonstrate beyond a reasonable doubt, at a public trial with the attendant constitutional safeguards, that a particular individual has engaged in proscribed criminal conduct. . . . [12]

Today's decision marks a clear retreat from Jenkins v. McKeithen, 395 U.S. 411 (1969), a case closely akin to the factual pattern of the instant case, and yet essentially ignored by the Court. *Jenkins*, which was also an action brought under § 1983, both recognized that the public branding of an individual implicates interests cognizable as either "liberty" or "property," and held that such public condemnation cannot be accomplished without procedural safeguards designed to eliminate arbitrary or capricious executive action. *Jenkins* involved the constitutionality of the Louisiana Labor–Management Commission of Inquiry, an executive agency whose "very purpose . . . is to find persons guilty of violating criminal laws without trial or procedural safeguards, and to publicize those findings."

> [T]he personal and economic consequences alleged to flow from such actions are sufficient to meet the requirement that appellant prove a legally redressable injury. . . . Appellant's allegations go beyond the normal publicity attending criminal prosecution; he alleges a concerted attempt publicly to brand him a criminal without trial.

. . . Although three Justices in dissent would have dismissed the complaint for lack of standing, since there were no allegations that the appellant would be investigated, called as a witness, or named in the Commission's findings, they nevertheless observed:

> [There is] a constitutionally significant distinction between two kinds of government bodies. The first is an agency whose sole or predominant function, without serving any other public interest, is to expose and publicize the names of persons it finds guilty of wrongdoing. To the extent that such a determination—whether called a "finding" or an "adjudication"—finally and directly affects the substantial personal interests, I do not doubt that the Due Process Clause may require that it be accompanied by many of the traditional adjudicatory procedural safeguards.

Thus, although the Court was divided on the particular procedural safeguards that would be necessary in particular circumstances, the common

---

[12] The Court's insensitivity to these constitutional dictates is particularly evident when it declares that because respondent had never been brought to trial, "his guilt or innocence of that offense [shoplifting] has never been resolved." It is hard to conceive of a more devastating flouting of the presumption of innocence. . . . Moreover, even if a person was once convicted of a crime, that does not mean that he is "actively engaged" in that activity now.

point of agreement, and the one that the Court today inexplicably rejects, was that the official characterization of an individual as a criminal affects a constitutional "liberty" interest.

The Court, however, relegates its discussion of *Jenkins* to a dissembling footnote. First, the Court ignores the fact that the Court in *Jenkins* clearly recognized a constitutional "liberty" or "property" interest in reputation sufficient to invoke the strictures of the Fourteenth Amendment. It baffles me how, in the face of that holding, the Court can come to today's conclusion by reliance on the fact that the conduct in question does not "come within the language" of the *dissent* in *Jenkins*. Second, and more important, the Court's footnote manifests the same confusion that pervades the remainder of its opinion; it simply fails to recognize the crucial difference between the question whether there is a personal interest in one's good name and reputation that is constitutionally cognizable as a "liberty" or "property" interest within the Fourteenth and Fifth Amendment Due Process Clauses, and the totally separate question whether particular government action with respect to that interest satisfies the mandates of due process. Although the dissenters in *Jenkins* thought that the Commission's procedures complied with due process, they clearly believed that there was a personal interest that had to be weighed in reaching that conclusion. The dissenters in *Jenkins*, like the Court in Hannah v. Larche, 363 U.S. 420 (1960), held the view that in the context of a *purely investigatory, factfinding agency*, full trial safeguards are not required to comply with due process. But that question would never have been reached unless there were some constitutionally cognizable personal interest making the inquiry necessary—the interest in reputation that is affected by public "exposure." The Court, by contrast, now implicitly repudiates a substantial body of case law and finds no such constitutionally cognizable interest in a person's reputation, thus foreclosing any inquiry into the procedural protections accorded that interest in a given situation. . . .

Moreover, Wisconsin v. Constantineau, 400 U.S. 433 (1971), which was relied on by the Court of Appeals in this case, did not rely at all on the fact asserted by the Court today as controlling—namely, upon the fact that "posting" denied Ms. Constantineau the right to purchase alcohol for a year. Rather, *Constantineau* stated: "The *only* issue present here is whether the label or characterization given a person by 'posting,' though a mark of serious illness to some, is to others such a stigma or badge of disgrace that procedural due process requires notice and an opportunity to be heard." (Emphasis supplied.) In addition to the statements quoted by the Court, the Court in *Constantineau* continued: " 'Posting' under the Wisconsin act may to some be merely the mark of an illness, to others it is a stigma, an official branding of a person. The label is a degrading one. Under the Wisconsin act, a resident of Hartford is given no process at all. This appellee was not afforded a chance to defend herself. She may have been the victim of an official's caprice. Only when the whole proceedings leading to the pinning of an unsavory label on a person are aired can oppressive results be prevented." " '[T]he right to be heard before being condemned to suffer grievous loss of any kind, *even though it may not involve the stigma and hardships of a criminal conviction*, is a principle basic to our society.' " Quoting Joint Anti–Fascist Refugee Committee v. McGrath, 341 U.S. 123, 168 (1951) (Frankfurter, J., concurring) (emphasis supplied). There again, the fact that governmental stigmatization of an individual implicates constitutionally protected interests was made plain.[15]

Thus, *Jenkins* and *Constantineau*, and the decisions upon which they relied, are cogent authority that a person's interest in his good name and reputation falls within the broad term "liberty" and clearly require that the government afford procedural protections before infringing that name and reputation by branding a person as a criminal. . . . The Court's approach . . . is to water down our prior precedents by reinterpreting them as confined to injury to reputation that affects an individual's employment prospects or, as "a right or status previously recognized by state law [that the state] distinctly altered or extinguished." The obvious answer is that such references in those cases (when there were such references) concerned the particular fact situations presented, and in nowise implied any limitation upon the application of the principles announced. Discussions of impact upon future employment opportunities were nothing more than recognition of the logical and natural consequences flowing from the stigma condemned.

Moreover, the analysis has a hollow ring in light of the Court's acceptance of the truth of the allegation that the "active shoplifter" label would "seriously impair [respondent's] future employment opportunities." This is clear recognition that an official "badge of infamy" affects tangible interests of the defamed individual and not merely an abstract interest in how people view him; for the "badge of infamy" has serious consequences in its impact on no less than the opportunities open to him to enjoy life, liberty, and the pursuit of happiness. It is inexplicable how the Court can say that a person's status is "altered" when the state suspends him from school, revokes his driver's license, fires him from a job, or denies him the right to purchase a drink of alcohol, but is in no way "altered" when it officially pins upon him the brand of a criminal, particularly since the Court recognizes how deleterious will be the consequences that inevitably flow from its official act. Our precedents clearly mandate that a person's interest in his good name and reputation is cognizable as a "liberty" interest within the meaning of the Due Process Clause, and the Court has simply failed to distinguish those precedents in any rational manner in holding that no invasion of a "liberty" interest was effected in the official stigmatizing without any "process" whatsoever.

---

[15] Even more recently in Goss v. Lopez, 419 U.S. 565 (1975), we recognized that students may not be suspended from school without being accorded due process safeguards. We explicitly referred to the "liberty interest in reputation" implicated by such suspensions based upon the fact that suspension for certain actions would stigmatize the student. . . . The Court states that today's holding is "quite consistent" with *Goss* because "Ohio law conferred a right upon all children to attend school, and . . . the act of the school officials suspending the student there involved resulted in a denial or deprivation of that right." However, that was only one-half of the holding in *Goss*. The Ohio law established a *property* interest which the Court held could not be deprived without according a student due process. However, the Court also specifically recognized that there was an independent *liberty* interest implicated in the case, not dependent upon the statutory right to attend school, but based . . . on the fact that suspension for certain conduct could affect a student's "good name, reputation, honor, or integrity."

Similarly, [t]he Court in *Roth* . . . was focusing on stigmatization as such. . . . The fact that a stigma is imposed by the government in terminating the employment of a government employee . . . does not detract from the fact that the operative "liberty" concept relates to the official stigmatization of the individual, whether imposed by the government in its status as an employer or otherwise.

I had always thought that one of this Court's most important roles is to provide a formidable bulwark against governmental violation of the constitutional safeguards securing in our free society the legitimate expectations of every person to innate human dignity and sense of worth. It is a regrettable abdication of that role and a saddening denigration of our majestic bill of rights when the Court tolerates arbitrary and capricious official conduct branding an individual as a criminal without compliance with constitutional procedures designed to ensure the fair and impartial ascertainment of criminal culpability. Today's decision must surely be a short-lived aberration.[18]

NOTES ON "LIBERTY" AND "PROPERTY" PROTECTED BY DUE PROCESS

1. INTRODUCTION

The Due Process Clause of the Fourteenth Amendment protects "life, liberty, or property" against deprivation without due process of law. This formulation covers a wide range of interests. At one time, the criterion for determining whether a particular interest was protected was simply its "importance" to the individual. See, e.g., Bell v. Burson, 402 U.S. 535 (1971). This approach proved so inclusive that, in the words of one authority, "there seems to have been an overriding consensus that every individual 'interest' worth talking about [was] encompassed within the 'liberty' and 'property' secured by the Due Process Clause and thus entitled to some constitutional protection. . . . " Henry Paul Monaghan, Of "Liberty" and "Property," 62 Corn.L.Rev. 405, 406–07 (1977).

Then the Supreme Court took a new approach. In Board of Regents v. Roth, 408 U.S. 564 (1972), the Court for the first time rejected a procedural due process claim on the ground that the interest at issue (continued employment as a non-tenured teacher) did not qualify as "life, liberty, or property." *Roth* emphasized the *nature* of the interest invaded, not simply its *importance* to the individual. This led to the development of a catalogue of "protectible interests." In subsequent years, the Court rejected several procedural due process claims under this rubric. *Paul v. Davis* is an early and controversial decision in that line.

The modern emphasis on defining "liberty" and "property" has led to some interesting interactions of state and federal law. On the one hand, the Due Process Clause of the Fourteenth Amendment is part of the federal Constitution, and it meaning is presumptively determined by federal law. On the other hand, the "liberty" and "property" interests that due process protects are defined, at least in part, by state law. Often, it is not clear which body of law determines the content of these terms.

---

[18] In light of my conviction that the state may not condemn an individual as a criminal without following the mandates of the trial process, I need not address the question whether there is an independent right of privacy which would yield the same result. Indeed, privacy notions appear to be inextricably interwoven with the considerations which require that a state not single out an individual for punishment outside the judicial process. Essentially, the core concept would be that a state cannot broadcast even such factual events as the occurrence of an arrest that does not culminate in a conviction when there are no legitimate law enforcement justifications for doing so. . . .

Mr. Justice White does not concur in this footnote.

The resulting inquiry is potentially circular. The federal Constitution overrides state law in requiring certain procedures for deprivation of "liberty" or "property." Yet the antecedent question of the existence of such interests is controlled, at least in the first instance, by state law. The risk is that states may define such interests so narrowly that the consequent federal procedural protection becomes, at least in certain contexts, unimportant.[a]

2. COMMENTS AND QUESTIONS ON *PAUL V. DAVIS*

The Court held that Davis had no cognizable "liberty interest" in his reputation. The Court's motivation for taking that position was clearly the desire to avoid "mak[ing] of the Fourteenth Amendment a font of tort law to be superimposed upon whatever systems may already be administered by the states."

But is the Court correct in saying that David lost neither liberty nor property? Is not one central idea of the tort of defamation the notion that individuals enjoy a property interest in their reputations?[b] If this is correct, was Davis's real problem that he alleged deprivation of liberty rather than property? This seems implausible, given the Court's articulated concern not to create a "font of tort law." In fact, most torts involve the deprivation of some "property" or "liberty" the plaintiff would otherwise enjoy. Is there any way for the Court to acknowledge that a plaintiff enjoys a liberty or property interest protected by tort law without finding that its impairment by a person acting under color of state law constitutes a violation of the Due Process Clause?

In this connection, it may be useful to consider how the Court would have responded to a lawsuit seeking only prospective relief. Suppose that § 1983 did not exist and that Davis had sought only an injunction removing his name from the list of "active shoplifters" on the grounds that he had never been adjudicated to be a shoplifter. Could he have obtained relief in federal court? Is it plausible that the Supreme Court would have dismissed the lawsuit on the ground that Davis suffered no cognizable injury from having his name on such a list? Other than the remedy sought, what is the difference between that hypothetical lawsuit and the case Davis actually brought?

Consider also the observation in Rodney Smolla, The Displacement of Federal Due Process Claims by State Tort Remedies: *Parratt v. Taylor* and *Logan v. Zimmerman Brush Co.*, 1982 U. Ill. L. Rev. 83, that "[t]he critics of *Paul v. Davis* have never explained satisfactorily how a § 1983 action is in any substantive law sense an improvement on the law of libel." Is such an explanation possible? Is it necessary?

---

[a] This prospect prompted one commentator to argue that "liberty" and "property" should be treated as federal common law, adopted by the federal courts to enforce federal rights and therefore subject to minimum federal standards. See Robert Jerome Glennon, Jr., Constitutional Liberty and Property: Federal Common Law and § 1983, 51 S.Cal.L.Rev. 355 (1978).

Due process is not the only context where specification of the underlying right limits § 1983 claims. Susan R. Klein, *Miranda* Deconstitutionalized: When the Self–Incrimination Clause and the Civil Rights Act Collide, 143 U. Pa. L. Rev. 417 (1994), reports that "[t]he vast majority of courts hearing the issue have held that a *Miranda* violation is not a proper basis for a § 1983 claim." The usual basis for this conclusion is that *Miranda* does not define a constitutional right but only states a prophylactic rule designed to protect one. In this reasoning, a violation of *Miranda* is not a violation of a constitutional right and is, therefore, also not a "deprivation of any rights, privileges, or immunities secured by the Constitution and laws"

[b] See Robert C. Post, The Social Foundations of Defamation Law: Reputation and the Constitution, 74 Calif. L. Rev. 691, 693–99 (1986) (collecting sources taking this view).

Academic reaction to the *Paul v. Davis* opinion has been largely hostile. In particular, the opinion has been criticized for its allegedly disingenuous treatment of precedent. See David Shapiro, Mr. Justice Rehnquist: A Preliminary View, 90 Harv.L.Rev. 293, 324–28 (1976) (concluding that it is "simply impossible" to reconcile *Paul* with prior decisions); Henry Paul Monaghan, Of "Liberty" and "Property," 62 Corn.L.Rev. 405, 423–29 (1977) (describing as "wholly startling" the Court's re-rationalization of its earlier cases).

Additionally, the decision has been criticized on the merits. Henry Monaghan, for example, found it "an unsettling conception of 'liberty' that protects an individual against state interference with his access to liquor but not with his reputation in the community." See also Frank McClellan and Phoebe Northcross, Remedies and Damages for Violations of Constitutional Rights, 18 Duq.L.Rev. 409, 422–33 (1980) (criticizing the blanket removal of reputation from protected liberty interests as "unwise and short-sighted").

Despite the widespread criticism of *Paul v. Davis*, there have been occasional indications of sympathy for the Court's concern to limit the intrusion of federal civil rights actions into state tort law. Commentators who have taken this position have looked for alternate rationales that might support the result in *Paul*. Of particular interest is the suggestion that *Paul* might have been based, not on a restrictive concept of protected "liberty" interests, but on a curtailment of the availability of remedies under § 1983.

The most prominent of these suggestions appears in Henry Paul Monaghan, supra. Monahan identified *Paul v. Davis* and other restrictive due process decisions as responses to the "staggering array of complaints" brought under § 1983. "Rightly or wrongly," he observed, "a majority of the present Court is struggling to place limits on the federal superintendence of the operations of state and local government, a struggle which has occurred largely in the context of '§ 1983' actions." In Monaghan's view, that effort was "understandable, if not acceptable," but the Court erred in addressing the problem by narrowing the scope of procedural due process. Instead, he speculated, perhaps it would have been better to read § 1983 "less than literally . . . so as not to embrace all the interests encompassed by the 'liberty' (and 'property') of the Due Process Clause."

This suggestion was echoed by Gerald Gunther, who noted that "a limiting statutory interpretation [of § 1983] would have made the Court's extensive discussion of constitutionally protected liberty interests unnecessary." Gerald Gunther, Cases and Materials on Constitutional Law 581 (11th ed. 1985).

What kind of limiting statutory construction did Monaghan and Gunther have in mind? One possibility was suggested by Melvyn Durchslag in Federalism and Constitutional Liberties: Varying the Remedy to Save the Right, 54 N.Y.U.L.Rev. 723, 734–48 (1979). Durchslag argued that the federalism concern vindicated in *Paul v. Davis* should have been handled through an elaboration of official immunity under § 1983 rather than by redefinition of the underlying constitutional right.[c]

[c] For a reinterpretation of *Paul*, see Barbara E. Armacost, Race and Reputation: The Real Legacy of *Paul v. Davis*, 85 Va. L. Rev. 569 (1999) (arguing that much of the "scholarly hand-wringing" is misdirected, because most of the claims excluded from due process by *Paul* are redirected to other constitutional "homes"). For commentary on an analogous problem, see Barbara Kritchevsky, The Availability of a Federal Remedy Under 42 U.S.C. § 1983 for Prose-

Of these several perspectives on *Paul v. Davis*, which is the most plausible? Is the decision simply wrong, or does it address a genuine problem? And if the latter, is the problem better addressed by a restrictive formulation of the underlying right or by a limiting construction of § 1983? And if the latter, what would that be?

3. *SIEGERT V. GILLEY*

Siegert v. Gilley, 500 U.S. 226 (1991). Siegert involved a clinical psychologist who resigned from a government hospital to avoid being fired. He then sought employment at a U.S. Army hospital in West Germany, but was turned down because of a bad recommendation from his former supervisor, who described the psychologist as "both inept and unethical, perhaps the least trustworthy individual I have supervised in my 13 years" on the job. Siegert filed a *Bivens* suit claiming that the supervisor had "maliciously and in bad faith published a defamatory per se statement . . . which [he] knew to be untrue, or with reckless disregard as to whether it was true or not."

The Supreme Court held that Siegert had not alleged any violation of constitutional rights. Speaking through Chief Justice Rehnquist, the majority cited *Paul* for the proposition that defamation was not a constitutional violation, even if the defendant, as was alleged here, acted with "malice." Justice Marshall, joined by Justices Blackmun and Stevens, argued that *Paul* was inapplicable, because Siegert had not suffered merely injury to reputation, but also loss of eligibility for future government employment. "It is a perverse jurisprudence," Marshall concluded, "that recognizes the loss of a 'legal' right to buy liquor as a significant deprivation but fails to accord equal significance to the foreclosure of opportunities for government employment."

4. *DESHANEY V. WINNEBAGO COUNTY DEPT. OF SOCIAL SERVICES*

The Court made another controversial determination of protected "liberty" interests in the "Poor Joshua" case,[d] DeShaney v. Winnebago County Dept. of Social Services, 489 U.S. 189 (1989). When four-year-old Joshua DeShaney was beaten by his father, he fell into a coma requiring brain surgery and was left with "brain damage so severe that he is expected to spend the rest of his life confined to an institution for the profoundly retarded." He had been the victim of repeated abuse following the time 26 months earlier when the county social service authorities were first contacted on his behalf. There were at least three hospitalizations and many other suspected injuries during this period and, though some efforts were made to create a more protective home environment, the authorities refused coercive intervention. Joshua and his mother[e] brought a § 1983 action against the county, its department of social services, and various department officials. The complaint "alleged that respondents had deprived Joshua of his liberty without due process of law, in violation of his rights under the Fourteenth Amendment, by failing to intervene to protect him against a

cution Under an Unconstitutional State Statute: The Sixth Circuit Struggles in *Richardson v. City of South Euclid*, 22 U.Tol.L.Rev. 303 (1991).

[d] The phrase comes from the last paragraph of Justice Blackmun's dissent, which begins: "Poor Joshua! Victim of repeated attacks by an irresponsible, bullying, cowardly, and intemperate father. . . . "

[e] Joshua's parents were divorced in Wyoming. Custody was awarded to the father, who later moved to Wisconsin, remarried, and was again divorced. The father was tried and convicted of child abuse.

risk of violence at his father's hands of which they knew or should have known." The District Court granted summary judgment for the defendants, and the Court of Appeals affirmed. The Supreme Court also affirmed.

In contrast to *Paul v. Davis*, where the Court held that the plaintiff had not experienced the impairment of a liberty interest in the first place, Joshua had undeniably been deprived of liberty. The *DeShaney* Court focused on the second component of the due process inquiry, whether the deprivation was properly chargeable to the *state* or whether it was only his father, a private actor, who was responsible for the deprivation.

Though describing the facts as "undeniably tragic," Chief Justice Rehnquist's opinion for the Court said:

> [N]othing in the language of the Due Process Clause itself requires the state to protect the life, liberty, and property of its citizens against invasion by private actors. The clause is phrased as a limitation on the state's power to act, not as a guarantee of certain minimum levels of safety and security. It forbids the state itself to deprive individuals of life, liberty, or property without "due process of law," but its language cannot fairly be extended to impose an affirmative obligation on the state to ensure that those interests do not come to harm through other means. . . . As a general matter, then, we conclude that a state's failure to protect an individual against private violence simply does not constitute a violation of the Due Process Clause.[f]

It was argued that a duty to protect "may arise out of certain 'special relationships' created or assumed by the state with respect to particular individuals." The Court granted as much. Prior cases had held, for example, that such duties arose with respect to persons in prison or involuntarily committed:

> But these cases afford petitioners no help. Taken together, they stand only for the proposition that when the state takes a person into its custody and holds him there against his will, the Constitution imposes upon it a corresponding duty to assume some responsibility for his safety and general well-being. The rationale for this principle is simple enough: when the state by the affirmative exercise of its power so restrains an individual's liberty that it renders him unable to care for himself, and at the same time fails to provide for his basic human needs—e.g., food, clothing, shelter, medical care, and reasonable safety—it transgresses the substantive limits on state action set by the eighth amendment and the Due Process Clause. The affirmative duty to protect arises not from the state's knowledge of the individual's predicament or from its expressions of intent to help him, but from the limitation which it has imposed on his freedom to act on his own behalf. In the substantive due process analysis, it is the state's affirmative act of restraining the individual's freedom to act on his own behalf—through incarceration, institutionalization, or other similar restraint of personal liberty—which is the "deprivation of liberty" triggering the protections of the Due Process Clause, not its failure to act to protect his liberty interests against harms inflicted by other means.

---

[f] The Chief Justice had previously noted that the claim was "one invoking the substantive rather than the procedural component of the Due Process Clause; petitioners do not claim that the state denied Joshua protection without according him appropriate procedural safeguards, but that it was categorically obligated to protect him in these circumstances."

The Chief Justice concluded:

> Judges and lawyers, like other humans, are moved by natural sympathy in a case like this to find a way for Joshua and his mother to receive adequate compensation for the grievous harm inflicted upon them. But before yielding to that impulse, it is well to remember once again that the harm was inflicted not by the state of Wisconsin, but by Joshua's father. The most that can be said of the state functionaries in this case is that they stood by and did nothing when suspicious circumstances dictated a more active role for them. In defense of them it must also be said that had they moved too soon to take custody of the son away from the father, they would likely have been met with charges of improperly intruding into the parent-child relationship, charges based on the same Due Process Clause that forms the basis for the present charge of failure to provide adequate protection.
>
> The people of Wisconsin may well prefer a system of liability which would place upon the state and its officials the responsibility for failure to act in situations such as the present one. They may create such a system, if they do not have it already, by changing the tort law of the state in accordance with the regular law-making process. But they should not have it thrust upon them by this Court's expansion of the Due Process Clause of the Fourteenth Amendment.[g]

Justice Brennan, joined by Justices Marshall and Blackmun, dissented. Justice Brennan stated that he "would focus first on the action that Wisconsin *has* taken with respect to Joshua and children like him, rather than on the actions that the state had failed to take." From this perspective, he extracted from the prison and involuntary commitment cases the principle that "if a state cuts off private sources of aid and then refuses aid itself, it cannot wash its hands of the harm that results from its inaction." Here the state had "cut off private sources of aid" by monopolizing the path of relief open to persons in Joshua's situation:

> In these circumstances, a private citizen, or even a person working in a government agency other than [the Department of Social Services (DSS)], would doubtless feel that her job was done as soon as she had reported her suspicions of child abuse to DSS. Through its child-welfare program, in other words, the state of Wisconsin has relieved ordinary citizens and governmental bodies other than the department of any sense of obligation to do anything more than report their suspicions of child abuse to DSS. If DSS ignores or dismisses these suspicions, no one will step in to fill the gap. Wisconsin's child-protection program thus effectively confined Joshua DeShaney within the walls of Randy DeShaney's violent home until such time as DSS took action to remove him. Conceivably, then, children like Joshua are made worse off by the existence of this program when the persons and entities charged with carrying it out fail to do their jobs.

---

[g] Petitioners also argue that the Wisconsin child protection statutes gave Joshua an 'entitlement' to receive protective services in accordance with the terms of the statute, an entitlement which would enjoy due process protection against state deprivation under our decision in Board of Regents v. Roth, 408 U.S. 564 (1972). But this argument is made for the first time in petitioners' brief to this Court: it was not pleaded in the complaint, argued to the Court of Appeals as a ground for reversing the District Court, or raised in the petition for certiorari. We therefore decline to consider it here.

> It simply belies reality, therefore, to contend that the state "stood by and did nothing" with respect to Joshua. Through its child-protection program, the state actively intervened in Joshua's life and, by virtue of this intervention, acquired even more certain knowledge that Joshua was in grave danger. These circumstances, in my view, plant this case solidly within the tradition of cases like [those governing prisons and involuntary commitments].

Justice Brennan added that liability could not be found in cases where the failure to intervene resulted from "the sound exercise of professional judgment," but required a level of "arbitrariness that we have in the past condemned." "Moreover," he continued, "that the Due Process Clause is not violated by merely negligent conduct, see Daniels v. Williams, 474 U.S. 327 (1986), and Davidson v. Cannon, 474 U.S. 344 (1986), means that a social worker who simply makes a mistake of judgment under what are admittedly complex and difficult conditions will not find herself liable in damages under § 1983."

5. THEORIES OF LIABILITY AFTER *DESHANEY*

After *DeShaney*, there remain two theories for holding governments or public officials liable for not preventing tortious acts by private parties. First, the government is responsible when the injury occurs while the plaintiff is in state custody or when the government has a special relationship with the plaintiff. See, e.g., Youngberg v. Romeo, 457 U.S. 307 (1982) (involuntarily committed mental patients have a substantive due process right to protection from harm); Farmer v. Brennan, 511 U.S. 825 (1994) (deliberate indifference to a known risk of injury to a prisoner can give rise to a claim under the Eighth Amendment). Lower courts have refused to extend this reasoning to children in schools, though some have argued that they are in custody because of compulsory school attendance laws. See generally Daniel B. Weddle, Bullying in Schools: The Disconnect Between Empirical Research and Constitutional, Statutory, and Tort Duties to Supervise, 77 Temp. L. Rev. 641 (2004).

Second, the state is liable when the danger of an injury at private hands is "state created." For examples of cases holding government officials liable under this theory, see Monfils v. Taylor, 165 F.3d 511 (7th Cir. 1998) (holding a police officer liable for the murder of a confidential informant when he released a tape recording of the victim's call to the police, despite the victim's repeated entreaties not to reveal his identity); Kniepp v. Tedder, 95 F.3d 1199 (3rd Cir. 1996) (holding that the plaintiff had a § 1983 claim for brain damage suffered in a fall after being abandoned by a police officer who had stopped her while she was intoxicated). Generally, courts have required a fairly tight causal nexus between the government action and the injury. See, e.g., Martinez v. California, 444 U.S. 277, 284–85 (1980) (refusing to hold state officials liable under § 1983 for the plaintiff's murder by a parolee five months after his release from prison). See generally Laura Oren, Safari Into the Snake Pit: The State–Created Danger Doctrine, 13 Wm. & Mary Bill of Rights J. 165 (2005).

6. *TOWN OF CASTLE ROCK V. GONZALES*

In *DeShaney*, the Court declined to consider whether Wisconsin's child-protection statutes had created a state-law entitlement to protective services, the denial of which could give rise to a procedural due process claim. That issue arose in Town of Castle Rock v. Gonzales, 545 U.S. 748 (2005).

A Colorado state court issued a restraining order against Ms. Gonzales' husband, requiring him to stay away from her and her children. Preprinted text on the back of the order directed law enforcement officials to "use every reasonable means to enforce this restraining order" and to "arrest, or, if an arrest would be impractical under the circumstances, seek a warrant for the arrest of the restrained person when you have information amounting to probable cause that the restrained person has violated or attempted to violate any provision of this order." The notice was designed to implement a parallel Colorado statute providing that "[a] peace officer shall arrest, or, if an arrest would be impractical under the circumstances, seek a warrant for the arrest of a restrained person when the peace officer has information amounting to probable cause that [t]he restrained person has violated or attempted to violate any provision of a [domestic violence-related] restraining order."

On the night in question, Ms. Gonzales's husband turned up at her house and took the couple's three daughters. After searching for them, she called the Castle Rock Police Department, which dispatched two officers (one-half of the town's night patrol force). She showed the officers the restraining order, but they said there was nothing that they could do about it and suggested she call the police again if the children did not return by 10:00 p.m. At about 8:30 p.m., the husband telephoned to say that he had the children at an amusement park in Denver. When she called the police department to ask that it "have someone check for" him and the children at the amusement park, the officer refused. Shortly after 10:00 p.m., Ms. Gonzales called the department again and was told to wait until midnight. At midnight, after another fruitless call to the police, she went to her husband's apartment, where she found no one. When she called, she was told to wait until an officer arrived. When no officer appeared in an hour, she went to the police station and submitted an incident report. Rather than then making an effort to locate the children, the officer on duty went to dinner. At 3:20 a.m., the husband arrived at the police station and opened fire with a semiautomatic weapon. Police returned the fire, killing him. Inside the cab of his pickup truck were the bodies of the three daughters, whom he had murdered.

Ms. Gonzales filed a § 1983 action against the town, asserting a property interest in police enforcement of the restraining order and alleging that the town had deprived her of that interest without due process by having a policy that tolerated nonenforcement of restraining orders. The lower court concluded that Colorado's domestic-violence statute created such a property interest but the Supreme Court, in an opinion by Justice Scalia, disagreed:

> We do not believe that these provisions of Colorado law truly made enforcement of restraining orders *mandatory*. A well established tradition of police discretion has long coexisted with apparently mandatory arrest statutes. . . .
>
> Against that backdrop, a true mandate of police action would require some stronger indication from the Colorado Legislature than "shall use every reasonable means to enforce a restraining order" (or even "shall arrest . . . or . . . seek a warrant"). That language is not perceptibly more mandatory than the Colorado statute which has long told municipal chiefs of police that they "shall pursue and arrest any person fleeing from justice in any part of the state" and that they "shall apprehend any person in the act of committing any offense . . . and, forthwith and without any war-

> rant, bring such person before a . . . competent authority for examination and trial." It is hard to imagine that a Colorado peace officer would not have some discretion to determine that—despite probable cause to believe a restraining order has been violated—the circumstances of the violation or the competing duties of that officer or his agency counsel decisively against enforcement in a particular instance. . . .
>
> Even if the statute could be said to have made enforcement of restraining orders "mandatory" because of the domestic-violence context of the underlying statute, that would not necessarily mean that state law gave *respondent* an entitlement to *enforcement* of the mandate. Making the actions of government employees obligatory can serve various legitimate ends other than the conferral of a benefit on a specific class of people. . . .

The Court went on to state that even if Colorado had created some sort of entitlement to enforcement of a restraining order, it was unclear whether that entitlement

> could constitute a "property" interest for purposes of the Due Process Clause. Such a right would not, of course, resemble any traditional conception of property. Although that alone does not disqualify it from due process protection, . . . the right to have a restraining order enforced does not "have some ascertainable monetary value," as even our "*Roth*-type property-as-entitlement" cases have implicitly required. Perhaps most radically, the alleged property interest here arises *incidentally,* not out of some new species of government benefit or service, but out of a function that government actors have always performed—to wit, arresting people who they have probable cause to believe have committed a criminal offense.
>
> [This] does not mean States are powerless to provide victims with personally enforceable remedies. Although the framers of the Fourteenth Amendment and the Civil Rights Act of 1871 did not create a system by which police departments are generally held financially accountable for crimes that better policing might have prevented, the people of Colorado are free to craft such a system under state law.

Justice Souter, joined by Justice Breyer, concurred. He focused on the nature of the claim. Ms. Gonzales asserted that Colorado law "promised a process by which her restraining order would be given vitality through careful and prompt consideration of an enforcement request" and asserted that the city's "[d]enial of that process" through its repeated demands that she call the department later, "drained all of the value from her property interest in the restraining order." Justice Souter termed her argument "unconventional because the state-law benefit for which it claims federal procedural protection is itself a variety of procedural regulation, a set of rules to be followed by officers exercising the State's executive power: use all reasonable means to enforce, arrest upon demonstrable probable cause, get a warrant, and so on."

> When her argument is understood as unconventional in this sense, a further reason appears for rejecting its call . . . , a reason that would apply even if the statutory mandates to the police were absolute, leaving the police with no discretion when the beneficiary of a protective order insists upon its enforcement. The Due Process Clause extends procedural protec-

> tion to guard against unfair deprivation by state officials of substantive state-law property rights or entitlements; the federal process protects the property created by state law. But Gonzales claims a property interest in a state-mandated process in and of itself. [A State does not] create a property right merely by ordaining beneficial procedure unconnected to some articulable substantive guarantee. This is not to say that state rules of executive procedure may not provide significant reasons to infer an articulable property right meant to be protected; but it is to say that we have not identified property with procedure as such. State rules of executive procedure, however important, may be nothing more than rules of executive procedure.
>
> Thus, in every instance of property recognized by this Court as calling for federal procedural protection, the property has been distinguishable from the procedural obligations imposed on state officials to protect it. Whether welfare benefits, Goldberg v. Kelly, 397 U.S. 254 (1970), attendance at public schools, Goss v. Lopez, 419 U.S. 565 (1975), utility services, Memphis Light, Gas & Water Div. v. Craft, 436 U.S. 1 (1978), public employment, Perry v. Sindermann, 408 U.S. 593 (1972), professional licenses, Barry v. Barchi, 443 U.S. 55 (1979), and so on, the property interest recognized in our cases has always existed apart from state procedural protection before the Court has recognized a constitutional claim to protection by federal process. To accede to Gonzales's argument would therefore work a sea change in the scope of federal due process, for she seeks federal process as a substitute simply for state process. . . . Gonzales's claim would . . . federalize every mandatory state-law direction to executive officers whose performance on the job can be vitally significant to individuals affected.

Justice Stevens, joined by Justice Ginsburg, dissented. He believed that Colorado law created an enforceable property interest:

> It is perfectly clear, on the one hand, that neither the Federal Constitution itself, nor any federal statute, granted respondent or her children any individual entitlement to police protection. Nor, I assume, does any Colorado statute create any such entitlement for the ordinary citizen. On the other hand, it is equally clear that federal law imposes no impediment to the creation of such an entitlement by Colorado law. Respondent certainly could have entered into a contract with a private security firm, obligating the firm to provide protection to respondent's family; respondent's interest in such a contract would unquestionably constitute "property" within the meaning of the Due Process Clause. If a Colorado statute enacted for her benefit, or a valid order entered by a Colorado judge, created the functional equivalent of such a private contract by granting respondent an entitlement to mandatory individual protection by the local police force, that state-created right would also qualify as "property" entitled to constitutional protection.

Justice Stevens recognized that state law generally accords police wide discretion. But he argued:

> [T]he Court gives short shrift to the unique case of "mandatory arrest" statutes in the domestic violence context; States passed a wave of these statutes in the 1980's and 1990's with the unmistakable goal of eliminating police discretion in this area. [The] Court's formalistic analysis

fails to take seriously the fact that the Colorado statute at issue in this case was enacted for the benefit of the narrow class of persons who are beneficiaries of domestic restraining orders, and that the order at issue in this case was specifically intended to provide protection to respondent and her children. [The] Court is simply wrong to assert that a citizen's interest in the government's commitment to provide police enforcement in certain defined circumstances does not resemble any "traditional conception of property"; in fact, a citizen's property interest in such a commitment is just as concrete and worthy of protection as her interest in any other important service the government or a private firm has undertaken to provide.

7. BIBLIOGRAPHY

A symposium published under the editorship of Sheldon Nahmod considers the boundary between constitutional tort law and ordinary tort. See Michael Wells, Constitutional Torts, Common Law Torts, and Due Process of Law, 72 Chi.–Kent L. Rev. 617 (1997) (seeking to ground constitutional tort decisions in a unifying principle of "abuse of power"); Christina Brooks Whitman, Emphasizing the Constitutional in Constitutional Torts, 72 Chi.–Kent L. Rev. 661 (1997) (arguing that ordinary tort law is a "distraction" when it comes to adjudicating constitutional tort claims); Jack M. Beermann, Common Law Elements of the Section 1983 Action, 72 Chi.–Kent L. Rev. 695 (1997) (arguing that common-law doctrines and concepts have been used unjustifiably to narrow the reach of § 1983); Laura Oren, Section 1983 and Sex Abuse in Schools: Making a Federal Case Out of It, 72 Chi.–Kent L. Rev. 747 (1997) (advocating "supervisory liability" for sexual abuse of children in public schools); Sheldon Nahmod, The Restructuring of Narrative and Empathy in Section 1983 Cases, 72 Chi.–Kent L. Rev. 819 (1997) (arguing that qualified-immunity doctrine has induced judges to empathize with officer defendants rather than with injured plaintiffs).

For commentary directly critical of the core holding of *DeShaney*, see Jack M. Beermann, Administrative Failure and Local Democracy: The Politics of *DeShaney*, 1990 Duke L.J. 1078 (1990); Steven J. Heyman, The First Duty of Government: Protection, Liberty and the Fourteenth Amendment, 41 Duke L.J. 507 (1991); Laura Oren, The State's Failure to Protect Children and Substantive Due Process: *DeShaney* in Context, 68 N.C.L.Rev. 659 (1990). For other critical commentary, see Karen M. Blum, Monell, DeShaney, and Zinermon: Official Policy, Affirmative Duty, Established State Procedure and Local Government Liability under Section 1983, 24 Creighton L.Rev. 1 (1990) (examining *DeShaney*'s impact on substantive due process claims against local governments); Thomas Eaton and Michael Wells, Government Inaction as a Constitutional Tort: DeShaney and its Aftermath, 66 Wash.L.Rev. 107 (1991) (inviting attention to the state's role in putting the individual at risk); (challenging "the reasoning at the core of *DeShaney*"); James T.R. Jones, Battered Spouses' Section 1983 Damage Actions Against the Unresponsive Police after *DeShaney*, 93 W.Va.L.Rev. 251 (1990–91) (discussing *DeShaney*'s impact on damage actions by abused spouses against the police); Sheldon H. Nahmod, State Constitutional Torts: *DeShaney*, Reverse–Federalisms and Community, 26 Rutgers L.J. 949 (1995) (noting that the federalism concerns in *Paul* and *DeShaney* are not applicable to state constitutional torts, which might be developed to deal with such situations); Julie

Shapiro, Snake Pits and Unseen Actors: Constitutional Liability for Indirect Harm, 62 U. Cinn. L. Rev. 883 (1994) (analyzing § 1983 liability in circumstances, such as *DeShaney*, where the state actor is not the immediate cause of the harm to the plaintiff). Finally, for a rare (if measured) defense of *DeShaney*, see Barbara E. Armacost, Affirmative Duties, Systemic Harms, and the Due Process Clause, 94 Mich. L. Rev. 982 (1996) (arguing that judicial refusal to impose governmental liability in other failure-to-protect cases reflects a reluctance to involve the courts in "second-guessing political decisions about the use of limited community resources").

SUBSECTION B: THE ROLE OF STATE LAW

INTRODUCTORY NOTES ON PARRATT V. TAYLOR *AND ITS PROGENY*

1. *PARRATT V. TAYLOR*

The plaintiff in Parratt v. Taylor, 451 U.S. 527 (1981), was a prison inmate who ordered $23.50 worth of hobby materials. When they arrived, he was in segregation and was not permitted to receive them. The materials were therefore signed for by two employees of the prison hobby center. When Taylor was released from segregation and able to resume his hobby, the packages were nowhere to be found.

Taylor filed a § 1983 damages action against the warden and the hobby manager of the prison. He claimed that the defendants had negligently deprived him of property without due process of law in violation of the Fourteenth Amendment. The District Court granted Taylor's motion for summary judgment and the Circuit Court affirmed. The Supreme Court granted certiorari and reversed.

Justice Rehnquist wrote for the Court. Three points merit attention:

(i) Mental Elements of § 1983

A preliminary issue was whether § 1983 required proof of intentional or reckless wrongdoing or allowed recovery for negligence. Justice Rehnquist's answer was that "[n]othing in the language of § 1983 or its legislative history limits the statute solely to intentional deprivations of constitutional rights." He noted that "§ 1983, unlike its criminal counterpart, 18 U.S.C. § 242, has never been found by this Court to contain a state-of-mind requirement."

This is not to say, it should be added, that state of mind never matters in a § 1983 case. The actor's culpability may still matter if the underlying constitutional violation requires proof of a particular state of mind. A good example is the Equal Protection Clause's guarantee against racial discrimination, which requires proof of a discriminatory purpose. See Village of Arlington Heights v. Metropolitan Housing Dev. Corp., 429 U.S. 252 (1977); Washington v. Davis, 426 U.S. 229 (1976). All *Parratt* decided was that proof of culpability was not required by § 1983 and that the plaintiff therefore has no obligation to establish the defendant's state of mind unless it is part of the underlying constitutional violation.

(ii) Negligent Deprivation

Given that § 1983 contains no state-of-mind requirement, it requires proof of two elements: first, that the defendant acted under color of state law; and second, that the action complained of "deprived a person of rights, privileges, or immunities secured by the Constitution or laws of the United States." In *Parratt* there was no question about state action. The case therefore turned on whether the defendants had "deprived" Taylor of a protected right. This raised the question whether negligent behavior by state officials could "deprive" Taylor of property without due process of law. Rehnquist's answer was brief and unelaborated:

> Unquestionably, respondent's claim satisfies three prerequisites of a valid due process claim: the petitioners acted under color of state law; the hobby kit falls within the definition of property; and the alleged loss, even though negligently caused, amounted to a deprivation.[a]

(iii) The Process Due

Rehnquist continued:

> Standing alone, however, these three elements do not establish a violation of the Fourteenth Amendment. Nothing in that amendment protects against all deprivations of life, liberty, or property by the state. The Fourteenth Amendment protects only against deprivations "without due process of law." Our inquiry therefore must focus on whether the respondent has suffered a deprivation of property without due process of law. In particular, we must decide whether the tort remedies which the state of Nebraska provides as a means of redress for property deprivations satisfy the requirements of procedural due process.

The case therefore turned on whether Nebraska's postdeprivation tort remedy satisfied the procedural demands of the Fourteenth Amendment. The Court found that remedy sufficient and that Taylor accordingly "has not alleged a violation of the Due Process Clause of the Fourteenth Amendment":

> The fundamental requirement of due process is the opportunity to be heard and it is an "opportunity which must be granted at a meaningful time and in a meaningful manner." Armstrong v. Manzo, 380 U.S. 545, 552 (1965). However, as many of the above cases recognize, we have rejected the proposition that "at a meaningful time and in a meaningful manner" *always* requires the state to provide a hearing prior to the initial deprivation of property. This rejection is based in part on the impracticability in some cases of providing any preseizure hearing under a state-

---

[a] This point prompted a dissent by Justice Powell:

> [T]he question is whether intent is required before there can be a "deprivation" of life, liberty, or property. . . . I would not hold that . . . a negligent act, causing unintended loss of or injury to property, works a deprivation in the constitutional sense. . . . A "deprivation" connotes an intentional act denying something to someone, or, at the very least, a deliberate decision not to act to prevent a loss. The most reasonable interpretation of the Fourteenth Amendment would limit due process claims to such active deprivations. [S]uch a rule would avoid trivializing the right of action provided in § 1983. That provision was enacted to deter real *abuses* by state officials in the exercise of governmental powers. It would make no sense to open the federal courts to lawsuits where there has been no affirmative abuse of power, merely a negligent deed by one who happens to be acting under color of state law.

authorized procedure, and the assumption that at some time a full and meaningful hearing will be available.

The justifications which we have found sufficient to uphold takings of property without any predeprivation process are applicable to a situation such as the present one involving a tortious loss of a prisoner's property as a result of a random and unauthorized act by a state employee. In such a case, the loss is not a result of some established state procedure and the state cannot predict precisely when the loss will occur. It is difficult to conceive of how the state could provide a meaningful hearing before the deprivation takes place. The loss of property, although attributable to the state as action under "color of law," is in almost all cases beyond the control of the state. Indeed, in most cases it is not only impracticable, but impossible, to provide a meaningful hearing before the deprivation. That does not mean, of course, that the state can take property without providing a meaningful postdeprivation hearing. The prior cases which have excused the prior-hearing requirement have rested in part on the availability of some meaningful opportunity subsequent to the initial taking for a determination of rights and liabilities.

Justice Rehnquist added these concluding remarks:

Our decision today is fully consistent with our prior cases. To accept respondent's argument that the conduct of the state officials in this case constituted a violation of the Fourteenth Amendment would almost necessarily result in turning every alleged injury which may have been inflicted by a state official acting under "color of law" into a violation of the Fourteenth Amendment cognizable under § 1983. It is hard to perceive any logical stopping place to such a line of reasoning. Presumably, under this rationale any party who is involved in nothing more than an automobile accident with a state official could allege a constitutional violation under § 1983. Such reasoning "would make of the Fourteenth Amendment a font of tort law to be superimposed upon whatever systems may already be administered by the states." Paul v. Davis, 424 U.S. 693, 701 (1976). We do not think that the drafters of the Fourteenth Amendment intended the amendment to play such a role in our society.[b]

2. NEGLIGENCE AS "DEPRIVATION" OF PROPERTY: *DANIELS V. WILLIAMS*

In Daniels v. Williams, 474 U.S. 327 (1986), the Court overruled that part of *Parratt* saying that negligent actions could constitute official "deprivations" within the meaning of the Due Process Clause. Daniels was a prisoner in a city jail. He tripped over a pillow allegedly left on a staircase by Williams, a

[b] Justices Stewart, White, and Blackmun wrote separately but concurred in the Court's opinion. Justice Powell concurred in the result on the rationale, as above in the preceding footnote, that no constitutional "deprivation" of property had occurred absent intent. Justice Marshall concurred in part and dissented in part. He agreed that "in cases involving claims of *negligent* deprivation of property without due process of law, the availability of an adequate postdeprivation cause of action for damages under state law may preclude a finding of a violation of the Fourteenth Amendment." But he thought that "prison officials have an affirmative obligation to inform a prisoner who claims that he is aggrieved by official action about the remedies available under state law" and that "[i]f they fail to do so, then they should not be permitted to rely on the existence of such remedies as adequate alternatives to a § 1983 action for wrongful deprivation of property."

corrections officer. Daniels asserted that the resulting injury was a "deprivation" of his "liberty" interest in freedom from bodily injury.

Speaking through Justice Rehnquist, the Court adopted Justice Powell's suggestion in *Parratt* that "the Due Process Clause is simply not implicated by a *negligent* act of an official causing unintended loss of or injury to life, liberty, or property." *Parratt v. Taylor* was explicitly overruled "to the extent that it states that mere lack of due care by a state official may 'deprive' an individual of life, liberty or property under the Fourteenth Amendment." The Court reasoned that the Due Process Clause was "intended to secure the individual from the arbitrary exercise of the powers of government":

> By requiring the government to follow appropriate procedures when its agents decide to "deprive any person of life, liberty, or property," the Due Process Clause promotes fairness in such decisions. And by barring certain government actions regardless of the fairness of the procedures used to implement them, it serves to prevent governmental power from being "used for purposes of oppression."
>
> We think that the actions of prison custodians in leaving a pillow on the prison stairs, or mislaying an inmate's property, are quite remote from the concerns just discussed. Far from an abuse of power, lack of due care suggests no more than a failure to measure up to the conduct of a reasonable person. To hold that injury caused by such conduct is a deprivation within the meaning of the Fourteenth Amendment would trivialize the centuries-old principle of due process of law.

Justice Rehnquist did reserve in a footnote, however, the possibility that something in between "negligence" and "intent" would suffice:

> [Daniels] concedes that [Williams] was at most negligent. Accordingly, this case affords us no occasion to consider whether something less than intentional conduct, such as recklessness or "gross negligence," is enough to trigger the protections of the Due Process Clause.

Justices Marshall, Blackmun, and Stevens concurred in the result.

3. NEGLIGENCE AS "DEPRIVATION" OF LIBERTY: *DAVIDSON V. CANNON*

In a companion case, Davidson v. Cannon, 474 U.S. 344 (1986), the Court extended the reasoning of *Daniels* to deprivations of liberty. Davidson sued state prison officials for failure to protect him from another inmate. Prior to the assault, the victim had sent a note to prison authorities warning of the risk, but they neglected to take timely action. The Court, with Justice Rehnquist again writing, rejected this claim on the authority of *Daniels*.

Justice Blackmun, joined by Justice Marshall, dissented. He agreed that mere negligence by government officials "*ordinarily*" would not be actionable under § 1983, but argued that the Court erred "in elevating this sensible rule of thumb to the status of inflexible constitutional dogma." In some cases, Blackmun concluded, governmental negligence was the kind of abuse of power at which the Due Process Clause was aimed. He thought this was such a case:

> It is one thing to hold that a commonplace slip and fall, or the loss of a $23.50 hobby kit, does not rise to the dignified level of a constitutional violation. It is a somewhat different thing to say that negligence that permits anticipated inmate violence resulting in injury, or perhaps leads to the ex-

> ecution of the wrong prisoner, does not implicate the Constitution's guarantee of due process. . . . It seems to me that when a state assumes sole responsibility for one's physical security and then ignores his call for help, the state cannot claim that it did not know a subsequent injury was likely to occur. [O]nce the state has taken away an inmate's means of protecting himself from attack by other inmates, a prison official's negligence in providing protection can amount to a deprivation of the inmate's liberty. . . .

Justice Blackmun also argued that the record might support a finding of recklessness, which in his view "must be sufficient" to cause a deprivation under the Fourteenth Amendment even if negligence is not. In a separate dissenting opinion, Justice Brennan agreed that "merely negligent conduct . . . does not constitute a deprivation of liberty under the Due Process Clause" but asserted that "official conduct which causes personal injury due to recklessness or deliberate indifference, does deprive the victim of liberty within the meaning of the Fourteenth Amendment."

4. *HUDSON V. PALMER*, INTENTIONAL WRONGDOING, AND THE ADEQUACY OF POST–DEPRIVATION PROCESS

In *Parratt v. Taylor,* Justice Blackmun suggested that postdeprivation remedies might not be adequate in cases of intentional wrongdoing. Hudson v. Palmer, 468 U.S. 517 (1984), addressed this question.

Hudson was an officer at a correctional institution. He conducted a "shakedown" search of inmate Palmer's cell, where he discovered a ripped pillowcase. Disciplinary proceedings were brought against Palmer, who was made to pay for the pillowcase. Subsequently, Palmer filed a § 1983 action claiming, inter alia, that Hudson himself had ripped the pillowcase—that is, that he had intentionally destroyed noncontraband personal property during the shakedown. Hudson denied the allegation and won a summary judgment, which in due course was affirmed by the Supreme Court. Indeed, on this issue, the decision was unanimous. Speaking through Chief Justice Burger, the Court said:

> While *Parratt* is necessarily limited by its facts to negligent deprivations of property, it is evident, as the Court of Appeals recognized, that its reasoning applies as well to intentional deprivations of property. The underlying rationale of *Parratt* is that when deprivations of property are effected through random and unauthorized conduct of a state employee, predeprivation procedures are simply "impracticable" since the state cannot know when such deprivations will occur. We can discern no logical distinction between negligent and intentional deprivations of property insofar as the "practicability" of affording pre-deprivation process is concerned. The state can no more anticipate and control in advance the random and unauthorized intentional conduct of its employees than it can anticipate similar negligent conduct. . . .
>
> Accordingly, we hold that an unauthorized intentional deprivation of property by a state employee does not constitute a violation of the procedural requirements of the Due Process Clause of the Fourteenth Amendment if a meaningful postdeprivation remedy for the loss is available. For intentional, as for negligent deprivations of property by state employees, the state's action is not complete until and unless it provides or refuses to provide a suitable postdeprivation remedy.

The Court was careful to note that the *Parratt* analysis does not apply to deprivations of property pursuant to established state procedures. Actions taken under established but constitutionally inadquate state procedures could violate due process regardless of the postdeprivation remedies that might be available. See Logan v. Zimmerman Brush Co., 455 U.S. 422 (1982).

5. THE ADEQUACY OF STATE–LAW REMEDIES

Parratt and *Hudson* gave rise to an interesting line of speculation about the continued viability of state sovereign immunity for garden-variety torts by state employees. Traditionally, states can claim sovereign immunity in their own courts when sued for torts committed by their employees. An attempt to evade this restriction by resort to federal court would be precluded by the Eleventh Amendment. As a result, garden-variety torts by government employees traditionally have been subject to compensation by the state only to the extent that the state has waived its right not to be sued.

Parratt and *Hudson* suggested a way around such restrictions. If a state were not to provide an adequate compensatory remedy for the tortious acts of its employees, then—under the rationale of those decisions—such acts would become procedural due process violations. The individuals injured thereby could bring suit under § 1983 by characterizing the tort claim as an instance of procedural inadequacy. Of course, the action would have to be brought against the employee rather than directly against the state, but that would not matter. Once the procedural due process right to adequate state procedures became "clearly established," presumably the defense of qualified immunity would become unavailable to the employee and the employee would be indemnified by the state for any adverse judgment. The possibility that *Parratt* and *Hudson* could lead to the erosion of the state's sovereign immunity for ordinary torts was narrowed by the *Daniels* limitation of deprivations to cases involving some culpable state of mind, but not entirely eliminated.

Justice Stevens squarely addressed this question in his concurrence in the judgments in *Daniels* and *Davidson*. He declined to join in overruling the *Parratt* holding that negligence could constitute a Fourteenth Amendment "deprivation" in the "procedural due process" cases. For him, the losses in both *Daniels* and *Davidson* were a "deprivation," forcing him to confront directly the question whether state sovereign immunity defense for official torts denied to the injured party the process that was due. He said it did not:

> *Davidson* puts the question whether a state policy of noncompensability for certain types of harm, in which state action may play a role, renders a state procedure constitutionally defective. In my judgment, a state policy that defeats recovery does not, in itself, carry that consequence. Those aspects of a state's tort regime that defeat recovery are not constitutionally invalid, so long as there is no fundamental unfairness in their operation. Thus, defenses such as contributory negligence or statutes of limitations may defeat recovery in particular cases without raising any question about the constitutionality of a state's procedures for disposing of tort litigation. Similarly, in my judgment, the mere fact that a state elects to provide some of its agents with a sovereign immunity defense in certain cases does not justify the conclusion that its remedial system is constitutionally inadequate. There is no reason to believe that the Due Process Clause of the Fourteenth Amendment and the legislation enacted pursuant to § 5 of that

amendment should be construed to suggest that the doctrine of sovereign immunity renders a state procedure fundamentally unfair.

6. *COUNTY OF SACRAMENTO V. LEWIS*

In other contexts as well, the availability of damages under § 1983 prompts special attention to the definition of the underlying right and, in particular, to the requisite mental state. At issue in County of Sacramento v. Lewis, 523 U.S. 833 (1998), was police liability for causing death in a high-speed automobile chase. The Supreme Court adopted a restrictive standard that effectively bars federal liability in such cases.

Sheriff's deputies encountered two boys on a motorcycle approaching at high speed. The deputies ordered the motorcycle to stop, but the boys evaded the patrol cars and drove away. Although the boys were suspected of nothing more serious than failure to stop, a deputy gave chase, following the motorcycle as close as 100 feet and reaching speeds as fast as 100 miles per hour. When the motorcycle tipped over, Philip Lewis, a 16–year–old boy who had been riding the motorcycle as a passenger, fell into the path of the patrol car and was killed. Lewis's parents sued the deputy and the county, alleging a violation of the boy's substantive due process right to life. Faced with these facts, the Ninth Circuit ruled that liability would be established on proof of "deliberate indifference to, or reckless disregard for, a person's right to life," but the Supreme Court disagreed and imposed a more stringent state of mind requirement.

Speaking through Justice Souter, the Court held that the proper standard for substantive due process analysis was not "deliberate indifference" but whether the deputy had been guilty of an abuse of power which "shocks the conscience." In the specific context of a high-speed automobile chase to apprehend suspected offenders, that standard required proof of an intent to harm the suspects. Justice Scalia, with whom Justice Thomas joined, agreed as to the result, but objected to the Court's resuscitation of the "ne plus ultra, the Napoleon Brandy, the Mahatma Ghandi, the Cellophane [citing Cole Porter] of subjectivity, th' ol' 'shocks the conscience' test." Justice Stevens also concurred in the judgment on the ground that, because of uncertainty as to the legal standard, the defendant was entitled to qualified immunity. There was no dissent.

7. QUESTIONS AND COMMENTS ON *PARRATT* AND ITS PROGENY

Parratt and its progeny have clarified some questions but not others. It is clear that the cause of action created by § 1983 does not contain a state-of-mind requirement. It is also settled that procedural due process does contain a state-of-mind requirement and is not violated by merely negligent actions. What is much less clear is the role of state law in determining whether due process has been violated. *Parratt* said that adequate state-law remedies could satisfy due process and thus cure any constitutional violation that might otherwise occur in the acts of individual government employees. Logan v. Zimmerman Brush Co., 455 U.S. 422 (1982), however, emphasized that deprivation of property pursuant to established state procedures would be treated very differently. Deprivation pursuant to established state procedures could violate due process regardless of available postdeprivation remedies. As the next main case suggests, the line between these propositions is not always bright.

Zinermon v. Burch

Supreme Court of the United States, 1990.
494 U.S. 113.

■ JUSTICE BLACKMUN delivered the opinion of the Court.

I

Respondent Darrell Burch brought this suit under 42 U.S.C. § 1983 against the 11 petitioners, who are physicians, administrators, and staff members at Florida State Hospital (FSH) in Chattahoochee, and others. Respondent alleges that petitioners deprived him of his liberty, without due process of law, by admitting him to FSH as a "voluntary" mental patient when he was incompetent to give informed consent to his admission. Burch contends that in his case petitioners should have afforded him procedural safeguards required by the Constitution before involuntary commitment of a mentally ill person, and that petitioners' failure to do so violated his due process rights.

Petitioners argue that Burch's complaint failed to state a claim under § 1983 because, in their view, it alleged only a random, unauthorized violation of the Florida statutes governing admission of mental patients. Their argument rests on Parratt v. Taylor, 451 U.S. 527 (1981), and Hudson v. Palmer, 468 U.S. 517 (1984), where this Court held that a deprivation of a constitutionally protected property interest caused by a state employee's random, unauthorized conduct does not give rise to a § 1983 procedural due process claim, unless the state fails to provide an adequate postdeprivation remedy. The Court in those two cases reasoned that in a situation where the state cannot predict and guard in advance against a deprivation, a postdeprivation tort remedy is all the process the state can be expected to provide, and is constitutionally sufficient.

[The District Court granted petitioners' motion to dismiss], pointing out that Burch did not contend that Florida's statutory procedure for mental health placement was inadequate to ensure due process, but only that petitioners failed to follow the state procedure. Since the state could not have anticipated or prevented this unauthorized deprivation of Burch's liberty, the District Court reasoned, there was no feasible predeprivation remedy, and, under *Parratt* and *Hudson,* the state's postdeprivation tort remedies provided Burch with all the process that was due him.

On appeal, an Eleventh Circuit panel affirmed the dismissal [but after a rehearing en banc the Court of Appeals] reversed the District Court, and remanded the case. . . . This Court granted certiorari to resolve the conflict—so evident in the divided views of the judges of the Eleventh Circuit—that has arisen in the Court of Appeals over the proper scope of the *Parratt* rule.

Because this case concerns the propriety of a [motion to dismiss], the question before us is a narrow one. We decide only whether the *Parratt* rule necessarily means that Burch's complaint fails to allege any deprivation of due process, because he was constitutionally entitled to nothing more than what he received—an opportunity to sue petitioners in tort for his allegedly unlawful confinement. The broader questions of what procedural safeguards the Due Process Clause requires in the context of an admission to a mental hospital, and whether Florida's statutes meet these constitutional requirements, are not presented in this case. Burch did not frame his action as a challenge to the constitutional adequacy of Florida's mental health statutes. Both before the Eleventh Circuit and in his brief here, he disavowed any challenge to the statutes themselves, and restricted his claim to the contention that petitioners' failure to provide constitutionally adequate safeguards in his case violated his due process rights.[3]

II

A

For purposes of review of a [motion to dismiss], the factual allegations of Burch's complaint are taken as true. Burch's complaint, and the medical records and forms attached to it as exhibits, provide the following factual background:

On December 7, 1981, Burch was found wandering along a Florida highway, appearing to be hurt and disoriented. He was taken to Apalachee Community Mental Health Services (ACMHS) in Tallahassee. ACMHS is a private mental health care facility designated by the state to receive patients suffering from mental illness. Its staff in their evaluation forms stated that, upon his arrival at ACMHS, Burch was hallucinating, confused, psychotic, and believed he was "in heaven." His face and chest were bruised and bloodied, suggesting that he had fallen or had been attacked. Burch was asked to sign forms giving his consent to admission and treatment. He did so. He remained at ACMHS for three days, during which time the facility's staff diagnosed his condition as paranoid schizophrenia and gave him psychotropic medication. On December 10, the staff found that Burch was "in need of longer-term stabilization" and referred him to FSH, a public hospital owned and operated by the state as a mental health treatment facility. Later that day, Burch signed forms requesting admission and authorizing treatment at FSH. He was then taken to FSH by a county sheriff.

Upon his arrival at FSH, Burch signed other forms for voluntary admission and treatment. One form, entitled "Request for Voluntary Admission," recited that the patient requests admission for "observation, diagnosis, care and treatment of [my] mental condition," and that the patient, if admitted, agrees "to accept such treatment as may be prescribed by members of the medical and psychiatric staff in accordance with the provisions of expressed and informed consent." Two of the petitioners, Janet V. Potter and Marjorie R. Parker, signed this form as witnesses. Potter is an accredited records technician; Parker's job title does not appear on the form.

On December 23, Burch signed a form entitled "Authorization for Treatment." This form stated that he authorized "the professional staff of [FSH] to administer treatment, except electroconvulsive treatment"; that he had been informed of "the purpose of treatment; common side effects thereof; alternative treatment modalities; approximate length of care," and of his power to revoke consent to treatment; and that he had read and fully

[3] Inasmuch as Burch does not claim that he was deprived of due process by an established state procedure, our decision in Logan v. Zimmerman Brush Co., 455 U.S. 422 (1982), is not controlling. In that case, the plaintiff challenged not a state official's error in implementing state law, but "the 'established state procedure' that destroys his entitlement without according him proper procedural safeguards."

Burch apparently concedes that, if Florida's statutes were strictly complied with, no deprivation of liberty without due process would occur. If only those patients who are competent to consent to admission are allowed to sign themselves in as "voluntary" patients, then they would not be deprived of any liberty interest at all. And if all other patients—those who are incompetent and those who are unwilling to consent to admission—are afforded the protections of Florida's involuntary placement procedures, they would be deprived of their liberty only after due process.

understood the authorization. Petitioner Zinermon, a staff physician at FSH, signed the form as the witness.

On December 10, Doctor Zinermon wrote a "progress note" indicating that Burch was "refusing to cooperate," would not answer questions, "appears distressed and confused," and "related that medication has been helpful." A nursing assessment form dated December 11 stated that Burch was confused and unable to state the reason for his hospitalization and still believed that "[t]his is heaven." Petitioner Zinermon on December 29 made a further report on Burch's condition, stating that, on admission, Burch had been "disoriented, semi-mute, confused and bizarre in appearance and thought . . . not cooperative to the initial interview," and "extremely psychotic, appeared to be paranoid and hallucinating." The doctor's report also stated that Burch remained disoriented, delusional, and psychotic.

Burch remained at FSH until May 7, 1982, five months after his initial admission to ACMHS. During that time, no hearing was held regarding his hospitalization and treatment.

After his release, Burch complained that he had been admitted inappropriately to FSH and did not remember signing a voluntary admission form. His complaint reached the Florida Human Rights Advocacy Committee of the state's Department of Health and Rehabilitation Services. The committee investigated and replied to Burch by letter dated April 4, 1984. The letter stated that Burch in fact had signed a voluntary admission form, but that there was "documentation that you were heavily medicated and disoriented on admission and . . . you were probably not competent to be signing legal documents." The letter also stated that, at a meeting of the committee with FSH staff on August 4, 1983, "hospital administration was made aware that they were very likely asking medicated clients to make decisions at a time when they were not mentally competent."

In February 1985, Burch filed a complaint in the United States District Court for the Northern District of Florida. He alleged, among other things, that ACMHS and the 11 individual petitioners, acting under color of Florida law, and "by and through the authority of their respective positions as employees at FSH . . . as part of their regular and official employment at FSH, took part in admitting plaintiff to FSH as a 'voluntary' patient." Specifically, he alleged:

> Defendants, and each of them, knew or should have known that plaintiff was incapable of voluntary, knowing, understanding and informed consent to admission and treatment at FSH. Nonetheless, defendants, and each of them, seized plaintiff and against plaintiff's will confined and imprisoned him and subjected him to involuntary commitment and treatment for the period from December 10, 1981, to May 7, 1982. For said period of 149 days, plaintiff was without the benefit of counsel and no hearing of any sort was held at which he could have challenged his involuntary admission and treatment at FSH.
>
> . . . Defendants, and each of them, deprived plaintiff of his liberty without due process of law in contravention of the Fourteenth Amendment to the United States Constitution. Defendants acted with willful, wanton and reckless disregard of and indifference to plaintiff's Constitutionally guaranteed right to due process of law.

B

Burch's complaint thus alleges that he was admitted and detained at FSH for five months under Florida's statutory provisions for "voluntary" admission. These provisions are part of a comprehensive statutory scheme under which a person may be admitted to a mental hospital in several different ways.

First, Florida provides for short-term emergency admission. If there is reason to believe that a person is mentally ill and likely "to injure himself or others" or is in "need of care or treatment and lacks sufficient capacity to make a responsible application on his own behalf," he may immediately be detained for up to 48 hours. A mental health professional, a law enforcement officer, or a judge may effect an emergency admission. After 48 hours, the patient is to be released unless he "voluntarily gives express and informed consent to evaluation or treatment," or a proceeding for court-ordered evaluation or involuntary placement is initiated.

Second, under a court order a person may be detained at a mental health facility for up to five days for evaluation, if he is likely "to injure himself or others" or if he is in "need of care or treatment which, if not provided, may result in neglect or refusal to care for himself and . . . such neglect or refusal poses a real and present threat of substantial harm to his well-being." Anyone may petition for a court-ordered evaluation of a person alleged to meet these criteria. After five days, the patient is to be released unless he gives "express and informed consent" to admission and treatment, or unless involuntary placement proceedings are initiated.

Third, a person may be detained as an involuntary patient, if he meets the same criteria as for evaluation, and if the facility administrator and two mental health professionals recommend involuntary placement. Before involuntary placement, the patient has a right to notice, a judicial hearing, appointed counsel, access to medical records and personnel, and an independent expert examination. If the court determines that the patient meets the criteria for involuntary placement, it then decides whether the patient is competent to consent to treatment. If not, the court appoints a guardian advocate to make treatment decisions. After six months, the facility must either release the patient, or seek a court order for continued placement by stating the reasons therefor, summarizing the patient's treatment to that point, and submitting a plan for future treatment.

Finally, a person may be admitted as a voluntary patient. Mental hospitals may admit for treatment any adult "making application by express and informed consent," if he is "found to show evidence of mental illness and to be suitable for treatment." "Express and informed consent" is defined as "consent voluntarily given in writing after sufficient explanation and disclosure . . . to enable the person . . . to make a knowing and willful decision without any element of force, fraud, deceit, duress, or other form of constraint or coercion." A voluntary patient may request discharge at any time. If he does, the facility administrator must either release him within three days, or initiate the involuntary placement process. At the time of his admission and each six months thereafter, a voluntary patient and his legal guardian or representatives must be notified in writing of the right to apply for a discharge.

Burch, in apparent compliance with [the Florida statutes], was admitted by signing forms applying for voluntary admission. He alleges, however, that petitioners violated this statute in admitting him as a voluntary patient, because they knew or should have known that he was incapable of making an informed decision as to his admission. He claims that he was entitled to receive the procedural safeguards provided by Florida's involuntary placement procedure, and that petitioners violated his due process rights by failing to initiate this procedure. The question presented is whether these allegations suffice to state a claim under § 1983, in light of *Parratt* and *Hudson.*

III

A

To understand the background against which this question arises, we return to the interpretation of § 1983 articulated in Monroe v. Pape, 365 U.S. 167 (1961). In *Monroe,* this Court . . . explained that § 1983 was intended not only to "override" discriminatory or otherwise unconstitutional state laws, and to provide a remedy for violations of civil rights "where state law was inadequate," but also to provide a federal remedy "where the state remedy, though adequate in theory, was not available in practice." The Court said:

> It is no answer that the state has a law which if enforced would give relief. The federal remedy is supplementary to the state remedy, and the latter need not be first sought and refused before the federal one is invoked.

Thus, overlapping state remedies are generally irrelevant to the question of the existence of a cause of action under § 1983. . . .

This general rule applies in a straightforward way to two of the three kinds of § 1983 claims that may be brought against the state under the Due Process Clause of the Fourteenth Amendment. First, the clause incorporates many of the specific protections defined in the Bill of Rights. A plaintiff may bring suit under § 1983 for state officials' violation of his rights to, e.g., freedom of speech or freedom from unreasonable searches and seizures. Second, the Due Process Clause contains a substantive component that bars certain arbitrary, wrongful government actions "regardless of the fairness of the procedures used to implement them." Daniels v. Williams, 474 U.S. 327, 331 (1986). As to these two types of claims, the constitutional violation actionable under § 1983 is complete when the wrongful action is taken. A plaintiff, under *Monroe v. Pape,* may invoke § 1983 regardless of any state-tort remedy that might be available to compensate him for the deprivation of these rights.

The Due Process Clause also encompasses a third type of protection, a guarantee of fair procedure. A § 1983 action may be brought for a violation of procedural due process, but here the existence of state remedies is relevant in a special sense. In procedural due process claims, the deprivation by state action of a constitutionally protected interest in "life, liberty, or property" is not in itself unconstitutional; what is unconstitutional is the deprivation of such an interest *without due process of law.* The constitutional violation actionable under § 1983 is not complete when the deprivation occurs; it is not complete unless and until the state fails to provide due process. Therefore, to determine whether a constitutional violation has occurred, it is necessary to ask what process the state provided, and whether it was constitutionally adequate. This inquiry would examine the procedural safeguards built into the statutory or administrative procedure of effecting the deprivation, and any remedies for erroneous deprivations provided by statute or tort law.

In this case, Burch does not claim that his confinement at FSH violated any of the specific guarantees of the Bill of Rights. Burch's complaint could be read to include a substantive due process claim, but that issue was not raised in the petition for certiorari, and we express no view on whether the facts Burch alleges could give rise to such a claim. The claim at issue falls within the third, or procedural, category of § 1983 claims based on the Due Process Clause.

B

Due process, as this Court often has said, is a flexible concept that varies with the particular situation. To determine what procedural protections the Constitution requires in a particular case, we weigh several factors:

> First, the private interest that will be affected by the official action; second, the risk of an erroneous deprivation of such interest through the procedures used, and the probable value, if any, of additional or substitute procedural safeguards; and finally, the government's interest, including the function involved and the fiscal and administrative burdens that the additional or substitute procedural requirement would entail.

Mathews v. Eldridge, 424 U.S. 319, 335 (1976).

Applying this test, the Court usually has held that the Constitution requires some kind of a hearing *before* the state deprives a person of liberty or property. . . . In some circumstances, however, the Court has held that a statutory provision for a postdeprivation hearing, or a common-law tort remedy for erroneous deprivation, satisfies due process.

This is where the *Parratt* rule comes into play. *Parratt* and *Hudson* represent a special case of the general *Mathews v. Eldridge* analysis, in which postdeprivation tort remedies are all the process that is due, simply because they are the only remedies the state could be expected to provide. In *Parratt,* a state prisoner brought a § 1983 action because prison employees negligently had lost materials he had ordered by mail.[14] The prisoner did not dispute that he had a postdeprivation remedy. Under state law, a tort-claim procedure was available by which he could have recovered the value of the materials. This Court ruled that the tort remedy was all the process the prisoner was due. . . . The Court explained:

> The justifications which we have found sufficient to uphold takings of property without any predeprivation process are applicable to a situation such as the present one involving a tortious loss of a prisoner's property as a result of a random and unauthorized act by a state employee. In such a case, the loss is not a result of some established state procedure and the state cannot predict precisely when the loss will occur. It is difficult to conceive of how the state could provide a meaningful hearing before the deprivation takes place.

Given these special circumstances, it was clear that the state, by making available a tort remedy that could adequately redress the loss, had given the prisoner the process he was due. Thus, *Parratt* is not an exception to the *Mathews* balancing test, but rather an application of that test to the unusual case in which one of the variables in the *Mathews* equation—the value of predeprivation safeguards—is negligible in preventing the kind of deprivation at issue. Therefore, no matter how significant the private interest at stake and the risk of its erroneous deprivation, the state cannot be required constitutionally to do the impossible by providing predeprivation process.

---

[14] *Parratt* was decided before this Court ruled, in Daniels v. Williams, 474 U.S. 327, 336 (1986), that a negligent act by a state official does not give rise to § 1983 liability.

In *Hudson,* the Court extended this reasoning to an intentional deprivation of property. A prisoner alleged that, during a search of his prison cell, a guard deliberately and maliciously destroyed some of his property, including legal papers. Again, there was a tort remedy by which the prisoner could have been compensated. In *Hudson,* as in *Parratt,* the state official was not acting pursuant to any established state procedure, but, instead, was apparently pursuing a random, unauthorized personal vendetta against the prisoner. The Court pointed out: "The state can no more anticipate and control in advance the random and unauthorized intentional conduct of its employees than it can anticipate similar negligent conduct." . . .

C

Petitioners argue that the dismissal [of the complaint] was proper because, as in *Parratt* and *Hudson,* the state could not possibly have provided predeprivation process to prevent the kind of "random, unauthorized" wrongful deprivation of liberty Burch alleges, so the postdeprivation remedies provided by Florida's statutory and common law necessarily are all the process Burch was due.[15]

Before turning to that issue, however, we must address a threshold question raised by Burch. He argues that *Parratt* and *Hudson* cannot apply to his situation, because those cases are limited to deprivations of property, not liberty.

Burch alleges that he was deprived of his liberty interest in avoiding confinement in a mental hospital without either informed consent or the procedural safeguards of the involuntary placement process. Petitioners do not seriously dispute that there is a substantial liberty interest in avoiding confinement in a mental hospital. Burch's confinement at FSH for five months without a hearing or any other procedure to determine either that he validly had consented to admission, or that he met the statutory standard for involuntary placement, clearly infringes on this liberty interest.

Burch argues that postdeprivation tort remedies are *never* constitutionally adequate for a deprivation of liberty, as opposed to property, so the *Parratt* rule cannot apply to this case. We, however, do not find support in precedent for a categorical distinction between a deprivation of liberty and one of property. . . .

It is true that *Parratt* and *Hudson* concerned deprivations of property. It is also true that Burch's interest in avoiding six months' confinement is of an order different from inmate Parratt's interest in mail-order materials valued at $23.50. But the reasoning of *Parratt* and *Hudson* emphasizes the state's inability to provide predeprivation process because of the random and unpredictable nature of the deprivation, not the fact that only property losses were at stake. In situations where the state feasibly can provide a predeprivation hearing before taking property, it generally must do so regardless of the adequacy of a postdeprivation tort remedy to compensate for the taking. Conversely, in situations where a predeprivation hearing is unduly burdensome in proportion to the liberty interest at stake, or where the state is truly unable to anticipate and prevent a random deprivation of a

[15] Burch does not dispute that he had remedies under Florida law for unlawful confinement. Florida's mental health statutes provide that a patient confined unlawfully may sue for damages. . . . Also, a mental patient detained at a mental health facility, or a person acting on his behalf, may seek a writ of habeas corpus to "question the cause and legality of such detention and request . . . release." Finally, Florida recognizes the common-law tort of false imprisonment.

liberty interest, postdeprivation remedies might satisfy due process. Thus, the fact that a deprivation of liberty is involved in this case does not automatically preclude application of the *Parratt* rule.

To determine whether, as petitioners contend, the *Parratt* rule necessarily precludes § 1983 liability in this case, we must ask whether predeprivation procedural safeguards could address the risk of deprivations of the kind Burch alleges. To do this, we examine the risk involved. The risk is that some persons who come into Florida's mental health facilities will apparently be willing to sign forms authorizing admission and treatment, but will be incompetent to give the "express and informed consent" required for voluntary placement. . . . Indeed, the very nature of mental illness makes it foreseeable that a person needing mental health care will be unable to understand any proffered "explanation and disclosure of the subject matter" of the forms that person is asked to sign, and will be unable "to make a knowing and willful decision" whether to consent to admission. A person who is willing to sign forms but is incapable of making an informed decision is, by the same token, unlikely to benefit from the voluntary patient's statutory right to request discharge. Such a person thus is in danger of being confined indefinitely without benefit of the procedural safeguards of the involuntary placement process, a process specifically designed to protect persons incapable of looking after their own interests.

Persons who are mentally ill and incapable of giving informed consent to admission would not necessarily meet the statutory standard for involuntary placement, which requires either that they are likely to injure themselves or others, or that their neglect or refusal to care for themselves threatens their well-being. The involuntary placement process serves to guard against the confinement of a person who, though mentally ill, is harmless and can live safely outside an institution. Confinement of such a person not only violates Florida law, but also is unconstitutional. O'Connor v. Donaldson, 422 U.S. 563, 575 (1975) (there is no constitutional basis for confining mentally ill persons involuntarily "if they are dangerous to no one and can live safely in freedom"). Thus, it is at least possible that if Burch had had an involuntary placement hearing, he would not have been found to meet the statutory standard for involuntary placement, and would not have been confined at FSH. Moreover, even assuming that Burch would have met the statutory requirements for involuntary placement, he still could have been harmed by being deprived of other protections built into the involuntary placement procedure, such as the appointment of a guardian advocate to make treatment decisions, and periodic judicial review of placement.

The very risks created by the application of the informed-consent requirement to the special context of mental health care are borne out by the facts alleged in this case. It appears from the exhibits accompanying Burch's complaint that he was simply given admission forms to sign by clerical workers, and, after he signed, was considered a voluntary patient. Burch alleges that petitioners knew or should have known that he was incapable of informed consent. [T]he way in which Burch allegedly was admitted to FSH certainly did not ensure compliance with the statutory standard for voluntary admission.

We now consider whether predeprivation safeguards would have any value in guarding against the kind of deprivation Burch allegedly suffered. Petitioners urge that here, as in *Parratt* and *Hudson,* such procedures could have no value at all, because the state cannot prevent its officials from making random and unauthorized errors in the admission process. We disagree.

The Florida statutes, of course, do not allow incompetent persons to be admitted as "voluntary" patients. But the statutes do not direct any member of the facility staff to determine whether a person is competent to give consent, nor to initiate the involuntary placement procedure for every incompetent patient. A patient who is willing to sign forms but incapable of informed consent certainly cannot be relied on to protest his "voluntary" admission and demand that the involuntary placement procedure be followed. The staff are the only persons in a position to take notice of any misuse of the voluntary admission process, and to ensure that the proper procedure is followed.

Florida chose to delegate to petitioners a broad power to admit patients to FSH, i.e., to effect what, in the absence of informed consent, is a substantial deprivation of liberty. Because petitioners had state authority to deprive persons of liberty, the Constitution imposed on them the state's concomitant duty to see that no deprivation occur without adequate procedural protections.

It may be permissible constitutionally for a state to have a statutory scheme like Florida's, which gives state officials broad power and little guidance in admitting mental patients. But when those officials fail to provide constitutionally required procedural safeguards to a person whom they deprive of liberty, the state officials cannot then escape liability by invoking *Parratt* and *Hudson.* It is immaterial whether the due process violation Burch alleges is best described as arising from petitioners' failure to comply with state procedures for admitting involuntary patients, or from the absence of a specific requirement that petitioners determine whether a patient is competent to consent to voluntary admission. Burch's suit is neither an action challenging the facial adequacy of a state's statutory procedures, nor an action based only on state officials' random and unauthorized violation of state laws. Burch is not simply attempting to blame the state for misconduct by its employees. He seeks to hold state officials accountable for their abuse of their broadly delegated, uncircumscribed power to effect the deprivation at issue.

This case, therefore, is not controlled by *Parratt* and *Hudson,* for three basic reasons:

First, petitioners cannot claim that the deprivation of Burch's liberty was unpredictable. Under Florida's statutory scheme, only a person competent to give informed consent may be admitted as a voluntary patient. There is, however, no specified way of determining, before a patient is asked to sign admission forms, whether he is competent. It is hardly unforeseeable that a person requesting treatment for mental illness might be incapable of informed consent, and that state officials with the power to admit patients might take their apparent willingness to be admitted at face value and not initiate involuntary placement procedures. Any erroneous deprivation will occur, if at all, at a specific, predictable point in the admission process—when a patient is given admission forms to sign.

This situation differs from the state's predicament in *Parratt.* While it could anticipate that prison employees would occasionally lose property through negligence, it certainly "cannot predict precisely when the loss will occur." Likewise, in *Hudson*, the state might be able to predict that guards occasionally will harass or persecute prisoners they dislike, but cannot "know when such deprivations will occur."

Second, we cannot say that predeprivation process was impossible here. Florida already has an established procedure for involuntary placement. The problem is only to ensure that this procedure is afforded to all patients who cannot be admitted voluntarily, both those who are unwilling and those who are unable to give consent.

In *Parratt*, the very nature of the deprivation made predeprivation process "impossible." It would do no good for the state to have a rule telling its employees not to lose mail by mistake, and it "borders on the absurd to suggest that a state must provide a hearing to determine whether or not a corrections officer should engage in negligent conduct." *Daniels*, supra, at 342 n. 19 (Stevens, J., concurring in judgments). In *Hudson*, the errant employee himself could anticipate the deprivation since he intended to effect it, but the state still was not in a position to provide predeprivation process, since it could not anticipate or control such random and unauthorized intentional conduct. Again, a rule forbidding a prison guard from maliciously destroying a prisoner's property would not have done any good; it would be absurd to suggest that the state hold a hearing to determine whether a guard should engage in such conduct.

Here, in contrast, there is nothing absurd in suggesting that, had the state limited and guided petitioners' power to admit patients, the deprivation might have been averted. Burch's complaint alleges that petitioners "knew or should have known" that he was incompetent, and nonetheless admitted him as a voluntary patient in "willful, wanton, and reckless disregard" of his constitutional rights. Understood in context, the allegation means only that petitioners disregarded their duty to ensure that the proper procedures were followed, not that they, like the prison guard in *Hudson*, were bent upon effecting the substantive deprivation and would have done so despite any and all predeprivation safeguards. Moreover, it would indeed be strange to allow state officials to escape § 1983 liability for failing to provide constitutionally required procedural protections, by assuming that those procedures would be futile because the same state officials would find a way to subvert them.

Third, petitioners cannot characterize their conduct as "unauthorized" in the sense the term is used in *Parratt* and *Hudson*. The state delegated to them the power and authority to effect the very deprivation complained of here, Burch's confinement in a mental hospital, and also delegated to them the concomitant duty to initiate the procedural safeguards set up by state law to guard against unlawful confinement. In *Parratt* and *Hudson,* the state employees had no similar broad authority to deprive prisoners of their personal property, and no similar duty to initiate (for persons unable to protect their own interests) the procedural safeguards required before deprivations occur. The deprivation here is "unauthorized" only in the sense that it was not an act sanctioned by state law, but, instead, was a "depriv[ation] of constitutional rights . . . by an official's abuse of his position." *Monroe,* supra, at 172.

We conclude that petitioners cannot escape § 1983 liability by characterizing their conduct as a "random, unauthorized" violation of Florida law which the state was not in a position to predict or avert, so that all the process Burch could possibly be due is a postdeprivation damages remedy. Burch, according to the allegations of his complaint, was deprived of a substantial liberty interest without either valid consent or an involuntary placement hearing, by the very state officials charged with the power to deprive mental patients of their liberty and the duty to implement procedural safeguards. Such a deprivation is foreseeable, due to the nature of mental illness, and will occur, if at all, at a predictable point in the admission process. Unlike *Parratt* and *Hudson,* this case does not represent the special instance of the *Mathews* due process analysis where postdeprivation process is all that is due because no predeprivation safeguards would be of use in preventing the kind of deprivation alleged.

We express no view on the ultimate merits of Burch's claim; we hold only that his complaint was sufficient to state a claim under § 1983 for violation of his procedural due process rights.

The judgment of the Court of Appeals is affirmed.

It is so ordered.

■ JUSTICE O'CONNOR, with whom THE CHIEF JUSTICE, JUSTICE SCALIA, and JUSTICE KENNEDY join, dissenting.

Without doubt, respondent Burch alleges a serious deprivation of liberty, yet equally clearly he alleges no violation of the Fourteenth Amendment. The Court concludes that an allegation of state actors' wanton, unauthorized departure from a state's established policies and procedures, working a deprivation of liberty, suffices to support a procedural due process claim even though the state provides adequate post-deprivation remedies for that deprivation. The Court's opinion unnecessarily transforms well-established procedural due process doctrine and departs from controlling precedent. I respectfully dissent.

Parratt v. Taylor, 451 U.S. 527 (1981), and Hudson v. Palmer, 468 U.S. 517 (1984), should govern this case. Only by disregarding the gist of Burch's complaint—that state actors' wanton and unauthorized departure from established practice worked the deprivation—and by transforming the allegations into a challenge to the adequacy of Florida's admissions procedures can the Court attempt to distinguish this case from *Parratt* and *Hudson.*

Burch alleges a deprivation occasioned by petitioners' contravention of Florida's established procedures. Florida allows the voluntary admission process to be employed to admit to its mental hospitals only patients who have made "application by express and informed consent for admission," and requires that the elaborate involuntary admission process be used to admit patients requiring treatment and incapable of giving such consent. Burch explicitly disavows any challenge to the adequacy of those established procedural safeguards accompanying Florida's two avenues of admission to mental hospitals. . . .

Parratt and *Hudson* should readily govern procedural due process claims such as respondent's. Taken together, the decisions indicate that for deprivations worked by such random and unauthorized departures from otherwise unimpugned and established state procedures the state provides the process due by making available adequate postdeprivation remedies. . . .

Application of *Parratt* and *Hudson* indicates that respondent has failed to state a claim allowing recovery under 42 U.S.C. § 1983. Petitioners' actions were unauthorized: they are alleged to have wrongly and without license departed from established state practices. Florida officials in a position to establish safeguards commanded that the voluntary admission process be employed only for consenting patients and that the involuntary hearing procedures be used to admit unconsenting patients. Yet it is alleged that petitioners "with willful, wanton and reckless disregard of and indifference to" Burch's rights contravened both commands. As in *Parratt,* the deprivation "occurred as a result of the unauthorized failure of agents of the state to follow established state procedure." The wanton or reckless nature of the failure indicates it to be random. The state could not foresee the particular contravention and was hardly "in a position to provide for predeprivation process," *Hudson,* supra, at 534, to ensure that officials bent upon subverting the state's requirements would in fact follow those procedures. For this wrongful deprivation resulting from an unauthorized departure from established state practice, Florida provides adequate postdeprivation remedies, as two courts below concluded, and which the Court and respondent do not dispute. *Parratt* and *Hudson* thus should govern this case and indicate that respondent has failed to allege a violation of the Fourteenth Amendment.

The allegedly wanton nature of the subversion of the state procedures underscores why the state cannot in any relevant sense anticipate and meaningfully guard against the random and unauthorized actions alleged in this case. The Court suggests that the state could foresee "that a person requesting treatment for mental illness might be incapable of informed consent." While foreseeability of that routine difficulty in evaluating prospective patients is relevant in considering the general adequacy of Florida's voluntary admission procedures, *Parratt* and *Hudson* address whether the state can foresee and thus be required to forestall the deliberate or reckless departure from established state practice. Florida may be able to predict that over time some state actors will subvert its clearly implicated requirements. Indeed, that is one reason that the state must implement an adequate remedial scheme. But Florida "cannot predict precisely when the loss will occur," *Parratt,* supra, at 541, and the Due Process Clause does not require the state to do more than establish appropriate remedies for any wrongful departure from its prescribed practices.

The Court attempts to avert the force of *Parratt* and *Hudson* by characterizing petitioners' alleged failures as only the routine but erroneous application of the admissions process. . . . The Court's characterization omits petitioners' alleged wrongful state of mind and thus the nature and source of the wrongful deprivation.

A claim of negligence will not support a procedural due process claim, see Daniels v. Williams, 474 U.S. 327 (1986), and it is an unresolved issue whether an allegation of gross negligence or recklessness suffices. Ibid., at 334 n. 3. Respondent, if not the Court, avoids these pitfalls. According to Burch, petitioners "knew" him to be incompetent or were presented with such clear evidence of his incompetence that they should be charged with such knowledge. Petitioners also knew that Florida law required them to provide an incompetent prospective patient with elaborate procedural safeguards. Far from alleging inadvertent or negligent disregard of duty, respondent alleges that petitioners "acted with willful, wanton and reckless disregard of and indifference" to his rights by treating him without providing the hearing that Florida requires. That is, petitioners did not bumble or commit "errors" by taking Burch's "apparent willingness to be admitted at face value." Rather, they deliberately or recklessly subverted his rights and contravened state requirements.

The unauthorized and wrongful character of the departure from established state practice makes additional procedures an "impracticable" means of preventing the deprivation. "The underlying rationale of *Parratt* is that when deprivations of property are effected through random and unauthorized conduct of a state employee, predeprivation procedures are simply 'impracticable' since the state cannot know when such deprivations will occur." *Hudson,* supra, at 533. The Court suggests that additional safeguards surrounding the voluntary admission process would have quite possibly reduced the risk of deprivation. This reasoning conflates the value of procedures for preventing error in the repeated and usual case (evaluated according to the test set forth in Mathews v. Eldridge, 424 U.S. 319 (1976)) with the value of additional predeprivation procedures to forestall deprivations by state actors bent upon departing from or indifferent to complying with established practices. . . . Burch alleges that, presented with the clearest evidence of his incompetence, petitioners nonetheless wantonly or recklessly denied him the protections of the state's admission procedures and requirements. The state actor so indifferent to guaranteed protections would be no more prevented from working the deprivation by additional procedural requirements than would the mail handler in *Parratt* or the prison guard in *Hudson.* In those cases, the state could have, and no doubt did, provide a range of predeprivation requirements and safeguards guiding both prison searches and care of packages. . . . In all three cases, the unpredictable, wrongful departure is beyond the state's reasonable control. Additional safeguards designed to secure correct results in the usual case do not practicably forestall state actors who flout the state's command and established practice.

Even indulging the Court's belief that the proffered safeguards would provide "some" benefit, *Parratt* and *Hudson* extend beyond circumstances in which procedural safeguards would have had "negligible" value. In *Parratt* and *Hudson* additional measures would conceivably have had some benefit in preventing the alleged deprivations. A practice of barring individual or unsupervised shakedown searches, a procedure of always pairing or monitoring guards, or a requirement that searches be conducted according to "an established policy" (the proposed measure rejected as unnecessary in *Hudson*) might possibly have helped to prevent the type of deprivation considered in *Hudson.* More sensible staffing practices, better training, or a more rigorous tracking procedure may have averted the deprivation at issue in *Parratt.* In those cases, like this one, the state knew the exact context in which the wrongful deprivation would occur. Yet the possibility of implementing such marginally beneficial measures, in light of the type of alleged deprivation, did not alter the analysis. The state's inability to foresee and to forestall the wrongful departure from established procedures renders additional predeprivation measures "impracticable" and not required by the dictates of due process. . . .

The suggestion that the state delegated to petitioners insufficiently trammeled discretion conflicts with positions that the Court ostensibly embraces. The issue whether petitioners possessed undue discretion is bound with and more properly analyzed as an aspect of the adequacy of the state's procedural safeguards, yet the Court claims Burch did not present this issue and purports not to decide it. By suggesting that petitioners' acts are attributable to the state, the Court either abandons its position that "Burch does not claim that he was deprived of due process by an established state procedure" or abandons *Parratt* and *Hudson*'s distinction between established procedures and unauthorized departures from those practices. Petitioners were not charged with formulating policy, and the complaint does not allege widespread and common departure from required procedures. Neither do the Court's passing reflections that a hearing is constitutionally required in the usual case of treatment of an incompetent patient advance the argument. That claim either states the conclusion that the state's combined admission procedures are generally inadequate, or repudiates *Parratt* and *Hudson*'s focus upon random and unauthorized acts and upon the state's ability to formulate safeguards. To the extent that a liberty interest exists in the application of the involuntary admission procedures whenever appropriate, it is the random and unauthorized action of state actors that effected the deprivation, one for which Florida also provides adequate post-deprivation process. . . .

The Court's reliance upon the state's inappropriate delegation of duty also creates enormous line-drawing problems. Today's decision applies to deprivations occasioned by state actors given "little guidance" and "broadly delegated, uncircumscribed power" to initiate required procedures. At some undefined point, the breadth of the delegation of power requires officials to channel the exercise of that power or become liable for its misapplications. When guidance is provided and the power to effect the deprivation circumscribed, no liability arises. And routine exercise of the power must be sufficiently fraught with the danger of "erroneous deprivation." In the absence of this broadly delegated power that carries with it pervasive risk of wrongful deprivation, *Parratt* and *Hudson* still govern. In essence, the Court's rationale applies when state officials are loosely charged with fashioning effective procedures or ensuring that required procedures are not routinely evaded. In a roundabout way, this rationale states the unexceptional conclusion that liability exists when officials' actions amount to the established state practice, a rationale unasserted in this case and, otherwise, appropriately analyzed under the *Mathews* test.

The Court's decision also undermines two of this Court's established and delicately related doctrines, one articulated in *Mathews* and the other articulated in *Parratt*. As the Court acknowledges, the procedural component of the Due Process Clause requires the state to formulate procedural safeguards and adequate postdeprivation process sufficient to satisfy the dictates of fundamental fairness and the Due Process Clause. Until today, the reasoning embodied in *Mathews* largely determined that standard and the measures a state must establish to prevent a deprivation of a protected interest from amounting to a constitutional violation. *Mathews* employed the now familiar three-part test (considering the nature of the private interest, efficacy of additional procedures, and governmental interests) to determine what predeprivation procedural safeguards were required of the state. That test reflects a carefully crafted accommodation of conflicting interests, weighed and evaluated in light of what fundamental fairness requires. *Parratt* drew upon concerns similar to those embodied in the *Mathews* test. For deprivations occasioned by wrongful departures from unchallenged and established state practices, *Parratt* concluded that adequate postdeprivation process meets the requirements of the Due Process Clause because additional predeprivation procedural safeguards would be "impracticable" to forestall these deprivations. The *Mathews* and *Parratt* doctrines work in tandem. State officials able to formulate safeguards must discharge the duty to establish sufficient predeprivation procedures, as well as adequate postdeprivation remedies to provide process in the event of wrongful departures from established state practice. The doctrines together define the procedural measures that fundamental fairness and the Constitution demand of the state.

The Court today discovers an additional realm of required procedural safeguards. Now, all procedure is divided into three parts. In place of the border clearly dividing the duties required by *Mathews* from those required by *Parratt,* the Court marks out a vast terra incognita of unknowable duties and expansive liability of constitutional dimension. The *Mathews* test, we are told, does not determine the state's obligation to provide predeprivation procedural safeguards. Rather, to avoid the constitutional violation a state must have fully circumscribed and guided officials' exercise of power and provided additional safeguards, without regard to their efficacy or the nature of the governmental interests. Even if the validity of the state's procedures is not directly challenged, the burden is apparently on certain state actors to demonstrate that the state sufficiently constrained their powers. Despite the many cases of this Court applying and affirming *Mathews,* it is unclear what now remains of the test. And the *Parratt* doctrine no longer reflects a general interpretation of the Due Process Clause or the complement of the principles contained in *Mathews.* It is, instead, displaced when the state delegates certain types of duties in certain inappropriate ways. This resulting "no-man's land" has no apparent boundaries. We are provided almost no guidance regarding what the Due Process Clause requires, how that requirement is to be deduced, or why fundamental fairness imposes upon the states the obligation to provide additional safeguards of nearly any conceivable value. We are left only with the implication that where doubt exists, liability of constitutional dimension will be found. Without so much as suggesting that our prior cases have warned against such a result, the Court has gone some measure to " 'make of the Fourteenth Amendment a font of tort law to be superimposed upon whatever systems may already be administered by the states.' " *Parratt,* supra, at 544 (quoting Paul v. Davis, 424 U.S. 693, 701 (1976)). . . .

The Court believes that Florida's statutory scheme contains a particular flaw. That statutory omission involves the determination of competence in the course of the voluntary admission process, and the Court signals that it believes that these suggested additional safeguards would not be greatly burdensome. The Court further believes that Burch's complaint and argument properly raise these issues and that adopting the additional safeguards would provide relevant benefit to one in Burch's position. The traditional *Mathews* test was designed and, until today, has been employed to evaluate and accommodate these concerns. . . . That test holds Florida to the appropriate standard and, given the Court's beliefs set out above, would perhaps have yielded a result favoring respondent. While this approach, if made explicit, would have required a strained reading of respondent's complaint and arguments, that course would have been far preferable to the strained reading of controlling procedural due process law that the Court today adopts. Ordinarily, a complaint must state a legal cause of action, but here it may be said that the Court has stated a novel cause of action to support a complaint.

I respectfully dissent.[a]

[a] For commentary on *Zinermon,* see Larry Alexander, Constitutional Torts, The Supreme Court, and the Law of Noncontradiction: An Essay on *Zinermon v. Burch,* 87 Nw.U.L.Rev. 576 (1993); Jose Robert Juarez, Jr., The Supreme Court as the Cheshire Cat: Escaping the Section 1983 Wonderland, 25 St. Mary's L.J. 1 (1993).—[Footnote by eds.]

NOTES ON THE ROLE OF STATE LAW

1. QUESTIONS AND COMMENTS ON *ZINERMON*

Why did the plaintiff in *Zinermon* disclaim the argument that Florida's statutory commitment procedures provided constitutionally inadequate safeguards? Consider the implications of such a claim for a damages remedy.

As a state entity, the Florida State Hospital was immune from suit under Edelman v. Jordan, 415 U.S. 651 (1974), and Will v. Michigan Department of State Police, 491 U.S. 58 (1989). Thus, the plaintiff could not seek money damages from the state. Given the unavailability of the state as a defendant, the plaintiff might have worried that claiming that the individual defendants acted pursuant to an unconstitutional state policy would set the stage for a successful assertion of qualified immunity: the individual defendants would claim that they conformed to a state policy that they reasonably could have believed to be lawful. Thus, the plaintiff had a strong practical incentive to allege instead that the individual defendants acted in an unauthorized fashion.

What would a sensible plaintiff's lawyer have done if the hospital been a municipal, rather than a state institution? Would the case have evolved differently?

2. QUESTIONS AND COMMENTS ON THE ADEQUACY OF STATE LAW

Zinermon makes clear that *Parratt* did not signal a general return to the position advocated by Justice Frankfurter in *Monroe v. Pape.* As Justice Blackmun says, "for two of the three kinds of § 1983 claims that may be brought . . . under the Due Process Clause of the Fourteenth Amendment," the presence or absence of a state remedy is irrelevant. Specifically, for violations of the Bill of Rights or of the "substantive components" of the Due Process Clause, § 1983 provides remedial protection quite irrespective of any "process" provided by the state. It is only the third kind of claim—generalized interferences with liberty or property not covered by these more specific provisions—with which *Parratt* and its progeny are concerned. For these kinds of claims, once a person has been "deprived" of an identifiable "liberty" or "property" interest by state action, § 1983 will provide a remedy if the state has not provided adequate procedural protections.

If *Parratt* and *Hudson* were right in looking to the adequacy of state law remedies to determine whether there has been a due process violation, should the same approach be applied in *Zinermon*? Are the Court's grounds for distinguishing the earlier precedents persuasive? Would *Parratt* and *Hudson* come out differently if they were re-analyzed in the terms suggested by *Zinermon*?

Finally, is it possible that the approach of *Parratt* and *Hudson* should have been applied in *Paul v. Davis*? This question has been raised in Rodney Smolla, The Displacement of Federal Due Process Claims by State Tort Remedies: *Parratt v. Taylor* and *Logan v. Zimmerman Brush Co.,* 1982 U. Ill. L. Rev. 831. Under Smolla's analysis, the state's provision of an adequate post-deprivation remedy would satisfy due process, and leave the injured plaintiff with no federal claim to pursue. Is this analysis persuasive? What would be its application to *DeShaney*?

SUBSECTION C: NON–CONSTITUTIONAL RIGHTS ENFORCEABLE UNDER § 1983

Maine v. Thiboutot

Supreme Court of the United States, 16980.
448 U.S. 1.

■ MR. JUSTICE BRENNAN delivered the opinion of the Court.

This case presents two related questions arising under 42 U.S.C. §§ 1983 and 1988. Respondents brought this suit in the Maine Superior Court alleging that petitioners, the state of Maine and its Commissioner of Human Services, violated § 1983 by depriving respondents of welfare benefits to which they were entitled under the federal Social Security Act, specifically 42 U.S.C. § 602(a)(7). The petitioners present two issues: (1) whether § 1983 encompasses claims based on purely statutory violations of federal law, and (2) if so, whether attorney's fees under § 1988 may be awarded to the prevailing party in such an action.[1]

I

Respondents, Lionel and Joline Thiboutot, are married and have eight children, three of whom are Lionel's by a previous marriage. The Maine Department of Human Services notified Lionel that, in computing the aid to families with dependent children (AFDC) benefits to which he was entitled for the three children exclusively his, it would no longer make allowance for the money spent to support the other five children, even though Lionel is legally obligated to support them. Respondents, challenging the state's interpretation of 42 U.S.C. § 602(a)(7), exhausted their state administrative remedies and then sought judicial review of the administrative action in the state Superior Court. By amended complaint, respondents also claimed relief under § 1983 for themselves and others similarly situated. The Superior Court's judgment enjoined petitioners from enforcing the challenged rule and ordered them to adopt new regulations, to notify class members of the new regulations, and to pay the correct amounts retroactively to eligible class members.[2] The court, however, denied respondents' motion for attorney's fees. The Supreme Judicial Court of Maine concluded that respondents had no entitlement to attorney's fees under state law, but were eligible for attorney's fees pursuant to the Civil Rights Attorneys' Fees Awards Act of 1976. We granted certiorari. We affirm.

II

Section 1983 provides:

> Every person who, under color of any statute, ordinance, regulation, custom, or usage, of any state or territory, subjects, or causes to be subjected, any citizen of the United States or other person within the jurisdiction thereof to the deprivation of any rights, privileges, or immunities secured by the Constitution *and laws*, shall be liable to the

---

[1] Petitioners also argue that jurisdiction to hear § 1983 claims rests exclusively with the federal courts. Any doubt that state courts may also entertain such actions was dispelled by Martinez v. California, 444 U.S. 277, 283–84 n.7 (1980). There, while reserving the question whether state courts are *obligated* to entertain § 1983 actions, we held that Congress has not barred them from doing so.

[2] The state did not appeal the judgment against it.

> party injured in an action at law, suit in equity, or other proper proceeding for redress. [Emphasis added.]

The question before us is whether the phrase "and laws," as used in § 1983, means what it says, or whether it should be limited to some subset of laws. Given that Congress attached no modifiers to the phrase, the plain language of the statute undoubtedly embraces respondents' claim that petitioners violated the Social Security Act.

Even were the language ambiguous, however, any doubt as to its meaning has been resolved by our several cases suggesting, explicitly or implicitly, that the § 1983 remedy broadly encompasses violations of federal statutory as well as constitutional law. Rosado v. Wyman, 397 U.S. 397 (1970), for example, "held that suits in federal court under § 1983 are proper to secure compliance with the provisions of the Social Security Act on the part of participating states." Edelman v. Jordan, 415 U.S. 651, 675 (1974). Monell v. New York City Dept. of Social Services, 436 U.S. 658 (1978), as support for its conclusion that municipalities are "persons" under § 1983, reasoned that "there can be no doubt that § 1 of the Civil Rights Act [of 1871] was intended to provide a remedy, to be broadly construed, against all forms of official violation of federally protected rights." Similarly, Owen v. City of Independence, 445 U.S. 622 (1980), in holding that the common-law immunity for discretionary functions provided no basis for according municipalities a good-faith immunity under § 1983, noted that a court "looks only to whether the municipality has conformed to the requirements of the federal Constitution and statutes." . . . Greenwood v. Peacock, 384 U.S. 808, 829–30 (1966), observed that under § 1983 state "officers may be made to respond in damages not only for violations of rights conferred by federal equal civil rights laws, but for violations of other federal constitutional and statutory rights as well." . . .

While some might dismiss as dictum the foregoing statements, numerous and specific as they are, our analysis in several § 1983 cases involving Social Security Act claims has relied on the availability of a § 1983 cause of action for statutory claims. Constitutional claims were also raised in these cases, providing a jurisdiction base, but the statutory claims were allowed to go forward, and were decided on the merits, under the court's pendent jurisdiction. In each of the following cases § 1983 was necessarily the exclusive statutory cause of action because, as the Court held in *Edelman v. Jordan*, the Social Security Act affords no private right of action against a state. [Citations omitted.]

In the face of the plain language of § 1983 and our consistent treatment of that provision, petitioners nevertheless persist in suggesting that the phrase "and laws" should be read as limited to civil rights or equal protection laws. Petitioners suggest that when § 1 of the Civil Rights Act of 1871, which accorded jurisdiction and a remedy for deprivations of rights secured by "the Constitution of the United States" was divided by the 1874 statutory revision into a remedial section, Rev. Stat. § 1979, and jurisdictional sections, Rev. Stat. §§ 563(12) and 629(16), Congress intended that the same change made in § 629(16) be made as to each of the new sections as well. Section 629(16), the jurisdictional provision for the circuit courts and the model for the current jurisdictional provision, 28 U.S.C. § 1343(3), applied to the deprivation of rights secured by "the Constitution of the United States, or of any right secured by any law providing for equal rights." On the other hand, the remedial provision, the predecessor of § 1983, was expanded to apply to deprivations of rights secured by "the

Constitution and laws" and § 563(12), the provision granting jurisdiction to the district courts, to deprivations of rights secured by "the Constitution of the United States, or of any right secured by any law of the United States."

We need not repeat at length the detailed debate over the meaning of the scanty legislative history concerning the addition of the phrase "and laws." See Chapman v. Houston Welfare Rights Org., 441 U.S. 600 (1979). One conclusion which emerges clearly is that the legislative history does not permit a definitive answer. There is no express explanation offered for the insertion of the phrase "and laws." On the one hand, a principal purpose of the added language was to "ensure that federal legislation providing specifically for equality of rights would be brought within the ambit of the civil action authorized by that statute." Id. at 637 (Powell, J., concurring). On the other hand, there are no indications that that was the only purpose, and Congress' attention was specifically directed to this new language. Representative Lawrence, in a speech to the House of Representatives that began by observing that the revisers had very often changed the meaning of existing statutes, referred to the civil rights statutes as "possibly [showing] verbal modifications bordering on legislation." He went on to read to Congress the original and revised versions. In short, Congress was aware of what it was doing, and the legislative history does not demonstrate that the plain language was not intended.[5] Petitioners' arguments amount to the claim that had Congress been more careful, and had it fully thought out the relationships among the various sections,[6] it might have acted differently. That argument, however, can best be addressed to Congress, which, it is important to note, has remained quiet in the face of our many pronouncements on the scope of § 1983.

III

Petitioners next argue that, even if this claim is within § 1983, Congress did not intend statutory claims to be covered by the Civil Rights Attorneys' Fees Awards Act of 1976, which added the following sentence to 42 U.S.C. § 1988 (emphasis added):

> In *any action* or proceeding *to enforce* a provision of §§ 1981, 1982, 1983, 1985, and 1986 of this Title . . . , the court, in its discretion, may allow the prevailing party, other than the United States, a reasonable attorney's fee as part of the costs."

Once again, given our holding in Part II, supra, the plain language provides an answer. The statute states that fees are available in *any* § 1983 action. Since we hold that this statutory action is properly brought under § 1983,

---

5 In his concurring opinion in Chapman v. Houston Welfare Rights Org., 441 U.S. 600 (1979), Mr. Justice Powell's argument proceeds on the basis of the flawed premise that Congress did not intend to change the meaning of existing laws when it revised the statutes in 1874. He assumed that Congress had instructed the revisers not to make changes, and that the revisers had obeyed those instructions. In fact, the second section of the statute creating the revision commission mandated that the commissioners "mak[e] such alterations as may be necessary to reconcile the contradictions, supply the omissions, and amend the imperfections of the original text." Furthermore, it is clear that Congress understood this mandate to authorize the commission to do more than merely "copy and arrange in proper order, and classify in heads the actual text of statutes in force." . . .

6 There is no inherent illogic in construing § 1983 more broadly than § 1343(3) was construed in *Chapman v. Houston Welfare Rights Org.*, supra. It would only mean that there are statutory rights which Congress has decided cannot be enforced in the federal courts unless 28 U.S.C. § 1331(a)'s $10,000 jurisdictional amount is satisfied. [The jurisdictional minimum for § 1331 was repealed on December 1, 1980—addition to footnote by eds.]

and since § 1988 makes no exception for statutory § 1983 actions, § 1988 plainly applies to this suit.

The legislative history is entirely consistent with the plain language. As was true with § 1983, a major purpose of the Civil Rights Attorneys' Fees Act was to benefit those claiming deprivations of constitutional and civil rights. Principal sponsors of the measure in both the House and the Senate, however, explicitly stated during the floor debate that the statute would make fees available more broadly. Representative Drinan explained that the act would apply to § 1983 and that § 1983 "authorizes suits against state and local officials based upon federal statutory as well as constitutional rights. . . . " Senator Kennedy also included a Social Security Act case as an example of the cases "enforc[ing] the rights promised by Congress or the Constitution" which the act would embrace. In short, there can be no question that Congress passed the Fees Act anticipating that it would apply to statutory § 1983 claims.

Several states, participating as amicus curiae, argue that even if § 1988 applies to § 1983 claims alleging deprivations of statutory rights, it does not apply in state courts. There is no merit to this argument. [We have] held that § 1983 actions may be brought in state courts. Representative Drinan described the purpose of the Civil Rights Attorneys' Fees Act as "authoriz[ing] the award of a reasonable attorney's fee in actions brought in state or federal courts." And Congress viewed the fees authorized by § 1988 as "an integral part of the remedies necessary to obtain" compliance with § 1983. It follows from this history and from the Supremacy Clause that the fee provision is part of the § 1983 remedy whether the action is brought in federal or state court.

Affirmed.

■ MR. JUSTICE POWELL, with whom the CHIEF JUSTICE and MR. JUSTICE REHNQUIST join, dissenting.

The Court holds today, almost casually, that 42 U.S.C. § 1983 creates a cause of action for deprivations under color of state law of any federal statutory right. Having transformed purely statutory claims into "civil rights" actions under § 1983, the Court concludes that 42 U.S.C. § 1988 permits the "prevailing party" to recover his attorney's fees. These two holdings dramatically expand the liability of state and local officials and may virtually eliminate the "American rule" in suits against those officials.

The Court's opinion reflects little consideration of the consequences of its judgment. It relies upon the "plain" meaning of the phrase "and laws" in § 1983 and upon this Court's assertedly "consistent treatment" of that statute. But the reading adopted today is anything but "plain" when the statutory language is placed in historical context. Moreover, until today this Court never had held that § 1983 encompasses all purely statutory claims. Past treatment of the subject has been incidental and far from consistent. The only firm basis for decision is the historical evidence, which convincingly shows that the phrase the Court now finds so clear was—and remains—nothing more than a shorthand reference to equal rights legislation enacted by Congress. To read "and laws" more broadly is to ignore the lessons of history, logic, and policy. . . .

I

Section 1983 provides in relevant part that "[e]very person who, under color of [state law] subjects . . . any . . . person . . . to the deprivation of any rights, privileges, or immunities secured by the Constitution and laws, shall be liable to the party injured. . . . " The Court asserts that "the phrase "and laws' . . . means what it says," because "Congress attached no modifiers to the phrase. . . . " Finding no "definitive" contrary indications in the legislative history of § 1983, the Court concludes that that statute provides a remedy for violations of the Social Security Act. The Court suggests that those who would read the phrase "and laws" more narrowly should address their arguments to Congress.

If we were forbidden to look behind the language in legislative enactments, there might be some force to the suggestion that "and laws" must be read to include all federal statutes.[1] But the "plain meaning" rule is not as inflexible as the Court imagines. . . . We have recognized consistently that statutes are to be interpreted " 'not only by a consideration of the words themselves, but by considering, as well, the context, the purposes of the law, and the circumstances under which the words were employed.' " . . .

Blind reliance on plain meaning is particularly inappropriate where, as here, Congress inserted the critical language without explicit discussion when it revised the statutes in 1874. Indeed, not a single shred of evidence in the legislative history of the adoption of the 1874 revision mentions this change. Since the legislative history also shows that the revision generally was not intended to alter the meaning of existing law, this Court previously has insisted that apparent changes be scrutinized with some care. . . .

II

The origins of the phrase "and laws" in § 1983 were discussed in detail in two concurring opinions last term. Compare Chapman v. Houston Welfare Rights Org., 441 U.S. 600, 623 (1979) (Powell, J., concurring) with id. at 646 (White, J., concurring in judgment). I shall not recount the full historical evidence presented in my *Chapman* opinion. Nevertheless, the Court's abrupt dismissal of the proposition that "Congress did not intend to change the meaning of existing laws when it revised the statutes in 1874" reflects a misconception so fundamental as to require a summary of the historical record.

A

Section 1983 derives from § 1 of the Civil Rights Act of 1871, which provided a cause of action for deprivation of constitutional rights only. "Laws" were not mentioned. The phrase "and laws" was added in 1874, when Congress consolidated the laws of the United States into a single volume under a new subject-matter arrangement. Consequently, the intent of Congress in 1874 is central to this case.

In addition to creating a cause of action, § 1 of the 1871 Act conferred concurrent jurisdiction upon "the district or circuit courts of the United States. . . . " In the 1874 revision, the remedial portion of § 1 was codified as § 1979 of the Revised Statutes, which provided for a cause of action in terms identical to the present § 1983. The jurisdictional portion of § 1 was divided into § 563(12), conferring district court jurisdiction, and § 629(16),

---

[1] The "plain meaning" of "and laws" may be more elusive than the Court admits. One might expect that a statute referring to all rights secured either by the Constitution or by the laws would employ the disjunctive "or." . . .

In contrast, a natural reading of the conjunctive "and" in § 1983 would require that the right at issue be secured both by the Constitution and by the laws. In 1874, this would have included the rights set out in the Civil Rights Act of 1866, which had been incorporated in the Fourteenth Amendment and re-enacted in the Civil Rights Act of 1870. . . .

conferring circuit court jurisdiction. Although §§ 1979, 563(12), and 629(16) came from the same source, each was worded differently. Section 1979 referred to deprivations of rights "secured by the Constitution and laws"; § 563(12) described rights secured "by the Constitution of the United States, or . . . by any law of the United States"; and § 629(16) encompassed rights secured "by the Constitution of the United States, or . . . by any law providing for equal rights of citizens of the United States." When Congress merged the jurisdiction of circuit and district courts in 1911, the narrower language of § 629(16) was adopted and ultimately became the present 28 U.S.C. § 1343(3).

B

In my view, the legislative history unmistakably shows that the variations in phrasing were inadvertent, and that each section was intended to have precisely the same scope. Moreover, the only defensible interpretation of the contemporaneous legislative record is that the reference to "laws" in each section was intended "to do no more than ensure that federal legislation providing specifically for equality of rights would be brought within the ambit of the civil action authorized by [§ 1979]." Careful study of the available materials leaves no serious doubt that the Court's contrary conclusion is completely at odds with the intent of Congress in 1874.

The Court holds today that the foregoing reasoning is based on a "flawed premise," because Congress instructed the revision commission to change the statutes in certain respects. But it is the Court's premise that is flawed. The revision commission, which worked for six years on the project, submitted to Congress a draft that did contain substantive changes. But a joint congressional committee, which was appointed in early 1873 to transform the draft into a bill, concluded that it would be "utterly impossible to carry the measure through, if it was understood that it contained new legislation." Therefore, the committee employed Thomas Jefferson Durant to "strike out . . . modifications of the existing law" "wherever the meaning of the law had been changed." On December 10, 1873 Durant's completed work was introduced in the House with the solemn assurance that the bill "embodies the law as it is."

The House met in a series of evening sessions to review the bill and to restore original meaning where necessary. During one of these sessions, Representative Lawrence delivered the speech upon which the Court now relies. Lawrence explained that the revisers often had separated existing statutes into substantive, remedial, and criminal sections to accord with the new organization of the statutes by topic. He read both the original and revised versions of the civil rights statutes to illustrate the arrangement, and "possibly [to] show verbal modifications bordering on legislation." After reading § 1979 without mentioning the addition of "and laws," Lawrence stated that "[a] comparison of all these will present a fair specimen of the manner in which the work has been done, and from these all can judge of the accuracy of the translation." Observing that "[t]his mode of classifying . . . to some extent duplicates in the revision portions of statutes" that previously were one, Lawrence praised "the general accuracy" of the revision. Nothing in this sequence of remarks supports the decision of the Court today. There was no mention of the addition of "and laws" nor any hint that the reach of § 1983 was to be extended. If Lawrence had any such intention, his statement to the House was a singularly disingenuous way of proposing a major piece of legislation.

In context, it is plain that Representative Lawrence did not mention changes "bordering on legislation" as a way of introducing substantive changes in § 1 of the 1871 Act. Rather, he was emphasizing that the revision was not intended to modify existing statutes, and that his reading might reveal errors that should be eliminated. No doubt Congress "was aware of what it was doing." It was meeting specially in one last attempt to detect and strike out legislative changes that may have remained in the proposed revision despite the best efforts of Durant and the joint committee. No representative challenged those sections of the revised statutes that derived from § 1 of the Civil Rights Act of 1871. That silence reflected the understanding of those present that "and laws" did not alter the original meaning of the statute.[6] The members of Congress who participated in the year long effort to expunge all substantive alterations from the revised statutes evince no intent whatever to enact a far-reaching modification of § 1 of the Civil Rights Act of 1871. The relevant evidence, largely ignored by the Court today, shows that Congress painstakingly sought to avoid just such changes.

III

The legislative history alone refutes the Court's assertion that the 43rd Congress intended to alter the meaning of § 1983. But there are other compelling reasons to reject the Court's interpretation of the phrase "and laws." First, by reading those words to encompass every federal enactment, the Court extends § 1983 beyond the reach of its jurisdictional counterpart. Second, that reading creates a broad program for enforcing federal legislation that departs significantly from the purposes of § 1983. Such unexpected and plainly unintended consequences should be avoided whenever a statute reasonably may be given an interpretation that is consistent with the legislative purpose.

A

The Court acknowledges that its construction of § 1983 creates federal "civil rights" for which 28 U.S.C. § 1343(3) supplies no federal jurisdiction. The Court finds no "inherent illogic" in this view. But the gap in the Court's logic is wide indeed in light of the history and purpose of the civil rights legislation we consider today. Sections 1983 and 1343(3) derive from the same section of the same act. As originally enacted the two sections were necessarily coextensive. And this Court has emphasized repeatedly that the right to a federal forum in every case was viewed as a crucial ingredient in the federal remedy afforded by § 1983. . . . Since § 1343(3) covers statutory claims only when they arise under laws providing for the equal rights of citizens, the same limitation necessarily is implicit in § 1983. The Court's decision to apply that statute without regard to the scope of its jurisdictional counterpart is at war with the plainly expressed intent of Congress.

B

The Court's opinion does not consider the nature or scope of the litigation it has authorized. In practical effect, today's decision means that state and local governments, officers, and employees now face liability whenever a person believes he has been injured by the administration of *any* federal-

---

[6] The addition of "and laws" did not change the meaning of § 1 because Congress assumed that that phrase referred only to federal equal rights legislation. In 1874, the only such legislation was contained in the 1866 and 1870 Civil Rights Acts, which conferred rights also secured by the recently adopted Fourteenth Amendment.

state cooperative program, whether or not that program is related to equal or civil rights. . . .

Even a cursory survey of the United States code reveals that literally hundreds of cooperative regulatory and social welfare enactments may be affected. The states now participate in the enforcement of federal laws governing migrant labor, noxious weeds, historic preservation, wildlife conservation, anadromous fisheries, scenic trails, and strip mining. Various statutes authorize federal-state cooperative agreements in most aspects of federal land management. In addition, federal grants administered by state and local governments now are available in virtually every area of public administration. Unemployment, Medicaid, school lunch subsidies, food stamps, and other welfare benefits may provide particularly inviting subjects of litigation. Federal assistance also includes a variety of subsidies for education, housing, health care, transportation, public works, and law enforcement. Those who might benefit from these grants now will be potential § 1983 plaintiffs.

No one can predict the extent to which litigation arising from today's decision will harass state and local officials; nor can one foresee the number of new filings in our already overburdened courts. But no one can doubt that these consequences will be substantial. And the Court advances no reason to believe that any Congress—from 1874 to the present day—intended this expansion of federally imposed liability on state defendants.

Moreover, state and local governments will bear the entire burden of liability for violations of statutory "civil rights" even when federal officials are involved equally in the administration of the affected program. Section 1983 grants no right of action against the United States, and few of the foregoing cooperative programs provide expressly for private actions to enforce their terms. Thus, private litigants may sue responsible federal officials only in the relatively rare case in which a cause of action may be implied from the governing substantive statute. Cf. Transamerica Mtg. Advisors v. Lewis, 444 U.S. 11 (1979); Touche Ross & Co. v. Redington, 442 U.S. 560 (1979). It defies reason to believe that Congress intended—without discussion—to impose such a burden only upon state defendants.

Even when a cause of action against federal officials is available, litigants are likely to focus efforts upon state defendants in order to obtain attorney's fees under the liberal standard of 42 U.S.C. § 1988. There is some evidence that § 1983 claims already are being appended to complaints solely for the purpose of obtaining fees in actions where "civil rights" of any kind are at best an afterthought. . . .

IV

The Court finally insists that its interpretation of § 1983 is foreordained by a line of precedent so strong that further analysis is unnecessary. It is true that suits against state officials alleging violations of the Social Security Act have become commonplace in the last decade. The instant action follows that pattern. Thus, the Court implies, today's decision is a largely inconsequential reaffirmation of a statutory interpretation that has been settled authoritatively for many years.

This is a tempting way to avoid confronting the serious issues presented by this case. But the attempt does not withstand analysis. Far from being a long-accepted fact, purely statutory § 1983 actions are an invention of the last 20 years. And the Court's seesaw approach to § 1983 over the last century leaves little room for certainty on any question that has not been discussed fully and resolved explicitly by this Court. Yet, until last term, neither this Court nor any justice ever had undertaken—directly and thoroughly—a consideration of the question presented in this case. . . .

The issue did not arise with any frequency until the late 1960's, when challenges to state administration of federal social welfare legislation became commonplace. The lower courts responded to these suits with conflicting conclusions. Some found § 1983 applicable to all federal statutory claims. Others refused to apply it to statutory rights. Yet others believed that § 1983 covered some but not all rights derived from nonconstitutional sources. Numerous scholarly comments discussed the possible solutions, without reaching a consensus. . . .

The Court quotes the statement in Edelman v. Jordan, 415 U.S. 651, 675 (1974), that Rosado v. Wyman, 397 U.S. 397 (1970), " 'held that suits in federal court under § 1983 are proper to secure compliance with the provisions of the Social Security Act on the part of participating states.' " If that statement were true, the confusion remaining after *Rosado* is simply inexplicable. In fact, of course, *Rosado* established no such proposition of law. The plaintiffs in that case challenged a state welfare provision on constitutional grounds premising jurisdiction upon § 1343(3), and added a pendent statutory claim. This Court held first that the District Court retained its power to adjudicate the statutory claim even after the constitutional claim, on which § 1343(3) jurisdiction was based, became moot. The opinion then considered the merits of the plaintiffs' argument that New York law did not comport with the Social Security Act. Although the Court had to assume the existence of a private right of action to enforce that act, the opinion did not discuss or purport to decide whether § 1983 applies to statutory claims.

Rosado is not the only case to have assumed sub silentio that welfare claimants have a cause of action to challenge the adequacy of state programs under the Social Security Act. As the Court observes, many of our recent decisions construing the act made the same unspoken assumption. It does not necessarily follow that the Court in those cases assumed that the cause of action was provided by § 1983 rather than the Social Security Act itself. But even if it did, these cases provide no support for the Court's ruling today. "[W]hen questions of jurisdiction have been passed on in prior decisions sub silentio, this Court has never considered itself bound when a subsequent case finally brings the jurisdictional issue before us." Hagans v. Lavine, 415 U.S. 528, 535 n.5 (1974). This rule applies with even greater force to questions involving the availability of a cause of action, because the question whether a cause of action exists—unlike the existence of federal jurisdiction—may be assumed without being decided. Thus, the Court's ruling finds no support in past cases in which the issue was not squarely raised. . . .

The Court also relies upon "numerous and specific" dicta in prior decisions. But none of the cited cases contains anything more than a bare assertion of the proposition that is to be proved. Most say much less than that. For example, the Court occasionally has referred to § 1983 as a remedy for violations of "federally protected rights" or of "the federal Constitution and statutes," Monell v. New York City Dept. of Social Services, 436 U.S. 658, 700–01 (1978); Owen v. City of Independence, 445 U.S. 622, 649, 650 (1980). These generalized references merely restate the language of the statute. They shed no light on the question whether all or only some statutory rights are protected. To the extent they have any relevance to the issue at hand, they could be countered by the frequent occasions on which the

Court has referred to § 1983 as a remedy for constitutional violations without mentioning statutes. But the debate would be meaningless, for none of these offhand remarks provides the remotest support for the positions taken in this case.

The only remaining decisions in the Court's "consistent" line of precedents are Greenwood v. Peacock, 384 U.S. 808, 829–30 (1966), and Edelman v. Jordan, 415 U.S. 651, 675 (1974). In each case, the Court asserted—without discussion and in the course of disposing of other issues—that § 1983's coverage of statutory rights extended beyond federal equal rights laws. Neither contains any discussion of the question; neither cites relevant authority. Nor has this Court always uncritically assumed the proposition for which *Greenwood* and *Edelman* now are said to stand. On the same day the Court decided *Edelman*, it refused to express a view on the question whether § 1983 creates a cause of action for purely statutory claims. Hagans v. Lavine, 415 U.S. 528, 534 n.5 (1974). The point was reserved again in Southeastern Community College v. Davis, 442 U.S. 397, 404–05 n.5 (1979).

To rest a landmark decision of this Court on two statements made in dictum without critical examination would be extraordinary in any case. In the context of § 1983, it is unprecedented. Our decisions construing the civil rights legislation of the Reconstruction era have repudiated "blind adherence to the principle of stare decisis. . . . " As Mr. Justice Frankfurter once observed, the issues raised under § 1983 concern "a basic problem of American federalism" that "has significance approximating constitutional dimension." *Monroe v. Pape*, supra, at 222 (dissenting opinion). Although Mr. Justice Frankfurter's view did not prevail in *Monroe*, we have heeded consistently his admonition that the ordinary concerns of stare decisis apply less forcefully in this than in other areas of the law. E.g., *Monell v. New York City Dept. of Social Services*, supra. Against this backdrop, there is no justification for the Court's reliance on unexamined dicta as the principal support for a major extension of liability under § 1983.

V

In my view, the Court's decision today significantly expands the concept of "civil rights" and creates a major new intrusion into state sovereignty under our federal system. There is no probative evidence that Congress intended to authorize the pervasive judicial oversight of state officials that will flow from the Court's construction of § 1983. Although today's decision makes new law with far-reaching consequences, the Court brushes aside the critical issues of congressional intent, national policy, and the force of past decisions as precedent. I would reverse the judgment of the Supreme Judicial Court of Maine.

NOTES ON NON–CONSTITUTIONAL RIGHTS ENFORCEABLE UNDER § 1983

1. *CHAPMAN V. HOUSTON WELFARE RIGHTS ORG.*

As the *Thiboutot* opinions mention, the issue before the Court was first extensively examined in Chapman v. Houston Welfare Rights Org., 441 U.S. 600 (1979). That case involved claims that state welfare regulations violated the Social Security Act. The question was whether federal courts had jurisdiction over such claims under the jurisdictional counterpart to § 1983, 28 U.S.C.

§ 1343(3).[a] Section 1343(3) confers subject matter jurisdiction on federal district courts over actions to redress the deprivation under color of law "of any right, privilege or immunity secured by the Constitution of the United States or by any Act of Congress *providing for equal rights* of citizens or of all persons within the jurisdiction of the United States" (emphasis added). The Court held that this statute did not include claims of incompatibility between state welfare regulations and the Social Security Act.[b]

Speaking for the Court, Justice Stevens's opinion was joined by Chief Justice Burger, and Justices Blackmun, Powell, and Rehnquist. The majority considered and rejected several theories for bringing such claims within the coverage of § 1343(3). First, the Court held that "secured by the Constitution," as these words are used in § 1343(3), did not include rights secured by the Supremacy Clause of Article VI. To hold otherwise would go too far, for every federal right is "secured" against state interference by the Supremacy Clause. If that suffices, every conceivable federal claim against a state agent would be "secured by the Constitution" within the meaning of § 1343(3) and the additional language providing for jurisdiction over claims "secured . . . by any Act of Congress providing for equal rights" would be rendered superfluous and without meaning.

Second, the Court also held that the Social Security Act was not itself a law "providing for equal rights" within the meaning of § 1343(3). Third, the Court found that § 1983 was also not a law "providing for equal rights" within the meaning of § 1434(3). If it were, then § 1343(3) would indirectly be given the broader scope of the "and laws" language of § 1983. The Court rejected this construction, noting that § 1983 does not secure any rights, equal or otherwise, but merely provides a cause of action for rights secured elsewhere. The Court found it unnecessary to decide whether §§ 1983 and 1343(3) covered the same behavior, but concluded that the limiting language in the latter could not be ignored.

In a dissent joined by Justices Brennan and Marshall, Justice Stewart argued that § 1983 was in fact an "Act of Congress providing for equal rights" and therefore that § 1343(3) created federal jurisdiction for every claim brought under § 1983. Stewart pointed to *Rosado v. Wyman* and other cases treating § 1983 as the source of a cause of action to enforce the Social Security Act and rejected as anomalous the "conclusion that Congress intended § 1983 to create some causes of action which could not be heard in a federal court under § 1343(3)." That conclusion would be contrary to the Court's understanding that "the common origin of §§ 1983 and 1343(3) in § 1 of the 1871 Act suggests that the two provisions were meant to be, and are, complementary." The correct result, he argued, would be to bring the two provisions into alignment by reading § 1983 as a law "providing for equal rights" under § 1343(3):

---

[a] Today, any claim based on federal law could be brought under 28 U.S.C. § 1331, but at the time of *Chapman* that statute required a minimum jurisdictional amount of more than $10,000, which this claim did not satisfy. The alternative jurisdictional basis of § 1343(3) therefore mattered.

[b] The Court also found no jurisdiction under 28 U.S.C. § 1343(4), a provision which originated in the Civil Rights Act of 1957 and which gives the district courts jurisdiction over actions to enforce "any Act of Congress providing for the protection of civil rights, including the right to vote." Because of its different origin, the meaning of § 1343(4) has no relevance to the interpretation of § 1983.

> The Court's reasoning to the contrary seems to rely solely on the fact that § 1983 does not create any rights. Section 1343(3) does not require, however, that the act create rights. Nor does it require that the act "provide" them. It refers to any act of Congress that provides "for" equal rights. Section 1983 provides for rights when it creates a cause of action for deprivation of those rights under color of state law. It is, therefore, one of the statutes for which § 1343(3), by its terms, confers jurisdiction upon the federal district courts.

The most elaborate opinions in *Chapman* were the concurrences of Justices Powell and White. Powell, who was joined by Chief Justice Burger and Justice Rehnquist, wrote separately to say that §§ 1983 and 1343(3) should be read as having the same scope and that the better interpretation would be to limit § 1983 to the reach of its jurisdictional counterpart. Powell supported this claim by an extensive review of the legislative history, the highlights of which are restated in his *Thiboutot* dissent.

Justice White concurred in the result. He wrote separately to argue that §§ 1983 and 1343(3) were in fact not coextensive. White began by saying that the majority's construction of § 1343(3) was "compelled" by the "plain terms of that statute and the absence of any overriding indication in the legislative history that these plain terms should be ignored." At the same time, White found nothing in the history of § 1983 indicating that its equally "plain terms" should not also be given effect. White argued that the history of revision and recodification of various civil rights statutes yielded so many "ambiguities, contradictions, and uncertainties" that there was "no satisfactory basis" for overriding the literal terms of these laws. He concluded, therefore, that §§ 1983 and 1343(3) "cannot be read as though they were but one statute," but that each should be accorded the meaning indicated by its language. Ironically, although Justice White was alone in finding that §§ 1983 and 1343(3) could be read independently, it was his position that ultimately prevailed in *Thiboutot.*

2. QUESTIONS AND COMMENTS ON *MAINE V. THIBOUTOT*

Note that *Thiboutot* was decided before Will v. Michigan Department of State Police, 491 U.S. 58 (1989), and Alden v. Maine, 527 U.S.706 (1999). Given *Will*'s holding that a state is not a "person" for purposes of § 1983, Maine would not be an appropriate party in a § 1983 suit.

The potential reach of *Thiboutot* is suggested by an appendix to Justice Powell's dissent. The appendix lists a number of federal statutes that do not provide for private enforcement and that typically involve state and local officials in their administration. The examples fall into three broad categories: (1) joint federal-state regulatory programs—e.g., the Historic Sites, Buildings, and Antiquities Act, the Fish and Wildlife Coordination Act, and the Surface Mining Control and Reclamation Act; (2) resource management programs administered cooperatively by federal and state agencies—e.g., laws involving the administration of national parks and forest lands, the construction and management of water projects, and oil leasing; and (3) federal grant programs that either subsidize state or local activities or provide matching funds for state and local programs that meet federal standards.

Of these categories, the last is most important. It includes not only the welfare, unemployment, and medical assistance programs administered under the Social Security Act, but also grant programs under the Food Stamp Act, the

Small Business Investment Act, the National School Lunch Act, the Public Works and Economic Development Act, the Energy Conservation and Production Act, the Developmentally Disabled Assistance and Bill of Rights Act, and the Urban Mass Transportation Act, among others. These statutes typically provide only for enforcement by federal agencies, but *Thiboutot* says that they may also be enforced by private damage actions under § 1983. The potential significance is hard to overstate. As noted in Richard B. Cappalli, Federal Grants and the New Statutory Tort: State and Local Officials Beware!, 12 Urb.Law. 445, 446 (1980):

> [W]hen state and local officials act (and many hospital, university, and nonprofit organization officials), the likelihood of finding an applicable federal standard of conduct is great. The officials are involved in a program activity which is aided by the federal government. The aid carries a series of standards imposed by the grant statute and its implementing regulations. While these standards are usually expressed at a high level of generality, they are readily usable in evaluating the "legality" of the officials' conduct in a wide variety of circumstances.

The enforcement of grant-in-aid standards by private damage actions raises a number of potential problems. See generally Cass R. Sunstein, Section 1983 and the Private Enforcement of Federal Law, 49 U.Chi.L.Rev. 394, 416–18 (1982). In some instances, Congress may have intended that the specified enforcement mechanism be exclusive. The addition of a private right of action may lead to over-enforcement of the federal standards. In some cases, the provision of a judicial remedy may invade agency specialization in the elaboration of statutory standards. Judicial enforcement, which tends to be decentralized and which depends on the agenda of private litigants, may also impair an agency's ability to devise a consistent and coordinated policy of enforcement. And finally, judicial supervision may diminish the political accountability of those who administer federal programs.

For all of these reasons, judicial enforcement of federal statutes under § 1983 may provide needed judicial oversight of state compliance with federal statutes, but may in other instances be disruptive of federal regulatory objectives. The question therefore arose whether and to what extent the courts would attempt to integrate *Thiboutot*'s recognition of a comprehensive private right of action with the enforcement structures and underlying policies of the particular statutes being enforced. The Supreme Court's reactions to such issues are revealed in the cases that follow.

3. *NATIONAL SEA CLAMMERS*

In Middlesex County Sewerage Authority v. National Sea Clammers Association, 453 U.S. 1 (1981), an organization of commercial fisherman sued various governmental authorities to stop the discharge of sewage and other pollutants into New York Harbor and the Hudson River. The plaintiffs sought damages, as well as injunctive and declaratory relief. Plaintiffs alleged that the pollution violated the Federal Water Pollution Control Act and the Marine Protection, Research, and Sanctuaries Act. Both statutes authorized "citizen suits," but only after 60–days' notice to both federal and state authorities and to the alleged violators. Additionally, the statutes authorized only prospective relief.

Plaintiffs failed to give the required notice, and the District Court entered summary judgment on that ground. The Court of Appeals reversed on the theory that the statutorily authorized citizen suits were not the only causes of action available to these plaintiffs. Both statutes had "savings clauses" that preserved "any right which any person (or class of persons) may have under any statute or common law." The Court of Appeals reasoned that the savings clauses preserved implied rights of action that were not burdened by procedural requirements.

The Supreme Court reversed. Speaking through Justice Powell, the Court reiterated the now established doctrine that the existence of a private right of action to enforce the provisions of a federal regulatory statute turns chiefly on legislative intent. The Court examined the statutes in question and concluded that the legislative provision of "unusually elaborate enforcement mechanisms," including citizen suits for injunctive relief, rather plainly meant that the legislature had not also silently authorized additional and inconsistent remedies. The Court then turned to the question whether an "*express* congressional authorization of private suits under these acts" might be found in § 1983. The analysis of this issue did not follow *Maine v. Thiboutot* but closely tracked the earlier rejection of implied private rights of action in the underlying statutes:

> When the remedial devices provided in a particular act are sufficiently comprehensive, they may suffice to demonstrate congressional intent to preclude the remedy of suits under § 1983. . . . As discussed above, the Federal Water Pollution Control Act and the Marine Protection, Research, and Sanctuaries Act do provide quite comprehensive enforcement mechanisms. It is hard to believe that Congress intended to preserve the § 1983 right of action when it created so many specific statutory remedies including the two citizen-suit provisions. We therefore conclude that the existence of these express remedies demonstrates not only that Congress intended to foreclose implied private actions but also that it intended to supplant any remedy that otherwise would be available under § 1983.

Justice Stevens, joined by Justice Blackmun, dissented. Stevens argued that the limited remedies in these regulatory statutes should not preclude resort to § 1983. In Stevens' view, the savings clauses and the legislative history indicated a congressional desire to preserve all otherwise available remedies, including § 1983. More fundamentally, he asserted that question was "not whether Congress 'intended to preserve the § 1983 right of action,' but rather whether Congress intended to withdraw that right of action." As he explained in a footnote, the difference between the two formulations was not merely semantic:

> As the Court formulates the inquiry, the burden is placed on the § 1983 plaintiff to show an explicit or implicit congressional intention that violations of the substantive statute at issue be redressed in private § 1983 actions. The correct formulation, however, places the burden on the defendant to show that Congress intended to foreclose access to the § 1983 remedy as a means of enforcing the substantive statute. Because the § 1983 plaintiff is invoking an express private remedy that is, on its face, applicable any time a violation of a federal statute is alleged, see *Maine v. Thiboutot*, the burden is properly placed on the defendant to show that Congress, in enacting the particular substantive statute at issue, intended an exception to the general rule of § 1983. A defendant may carry this burden by identifying express statutory language or legislative history re-

vealing Congress' intent to foreclose the § 1983 remedy, or by establishing that Congress intended that the remedies provided in the substantive statute itself be exclusive.

The Court responded that "contrary to Justice Stevens' argument, we do not suggest that the burden is on a plaintiff to demonstrate congressional intent to preserve § 1983." No further explanation was forthcoming. In particular, the Court did not say what kind of showing would be required to establish the continuing availability of a § 1983 remedy.

4. *WRIGHT V. ROANOKE REDEVELOPMENT AND HOUSING AUTHORITY*

The Court returned to the *Sea Clammers* problem in Wright v. Roanoke Redevelopment and Housing Authority, 479 U.S. 418 (1987). The case involved a suit against a public housing authority by low-income tenants, who alleged that they had been overbilled for utilities in violation of a federal rent ceiling. The question was whether the federal rent ceiling could be enforced by § 1983.

Justice White's opinion for the Court recharacterized *Sea Clammers*. He read that case to say that, "if there is a state deprivation of a 'right' secured by a federal statute, § 1983 provides a remedial cause of action unless the state actor demonstrates by express provision or other specific evidence from the statute itself that Congress intended to foreclose such private enforcement." Applying this standard, the Court held that "the remedial mechanisms provided [are not] sufficiently comprehensive and effective to raise a clear inference that Congress intended to foreclose a § 1983 cause of action for the enforcement of tenants' rights secured by federal law." Justice O'Connor, joined by Chief Justice Rehnquist and Justices Powell and Scalia, dissented.[c]

Note the *Wright* Court's insistence on "express provision or other specific evidence from the statute itself that Congress intended to foreclose . . . private enforcement." Would the statutes in *Sea Clammers* meet that test?

5. *SMITH V. ROBINSON*

Smith v. Robinson, 468 U.S. 992 (1984), involved the right of a handicapped child to a "free appropriate public education." The plaintiffs advanced an equal protection argument but prevailed under the federal Education of the Handicapped Act (EHA), which provides an express remedy, enforceable in federal court, for the rights it protects.

The question then arose whether the plaintiffs were entitled to attorney's fees. The EHA does not authorize attorney's fees. But the plaintiffs had also asserted their constitutional claim under § 1983, and plaintiffs who prevail in § 1983 actions—or who assert a "substantial but unaddressed" § 1983 claim and who prevail on other grounds, see Maher v. Gagne, 448 U.S. 122 (1980)—are entitled to attorney's fees under 42 U.S.C. § 1988.

---

[c] For a decision similar in analysis and outcome, see Wilder v. Virginia Hospital Association, 496 U.S. 498 (1990). The Court held that a provision of the Medicaid Act requiring states to reimburse hospitals according to rates "reasonable and adequate to meet the costs" was enforceable in a private cause of action under § 1983. The majority followed *Wright* and distinguished *Sea Clammers*. Chief Justice Rehnquist and Justices O'Connor, Scalia, and Kennedy dissented.

In an opinion by Justice Blackmun, the Court had "little difficulty concluding that Congress intended the EHA to be the exclusive avenue through which a plaintiff may assert an equal protection claim to a publicly financed education." The "crucial consideration" was what Congress intended, and here Congress clearly intended to make the EHA remedy exclusive. It followed that attorney's fees were not available. Justice Brennan, joined by Justices Marshall and Stevens, dissented.

The issue in *Smith v. Robinson* was whether the EHA was intended by Congress to provide an exclusive mechanism for the assertion of the plaintiffs' constitutional rights and thereby to displace their ability to assert these rights under § 1983. Is there a case to be made that the standard by which to judge whether a *constitutional* right can be asserted under § 1983 should be different from the standard that should control whether a *statutory* right can be asserted?

6. *BLESSING V. FREESTONE*

The Court considered another attempt at private enforcement of the Social Security Act in Blessing v. Freestone, 520 U.S. 329 (1999). Five mothers in Arizona had children eligible to receive child support services from the state pursuant to Title IV–D of the Social Security Act. They sued the director of Arizona's child support agency, claiming that they had enforceable individual rights to require "substantial compliance" with the requirements of Title IV–D, which included helping to establish paternity, locate absent parents, obtain support orders, and collect overdue child support. In addition, Title IV–D required state agencies to be staffed at particular levels, to set up various information systems, and to keep certain records.

The Social Security Act provided no private remedy. Under the statute, the Secretary of Health and Human Services was authorized to reduce a state's AFDC grant if it did not "substantially comply" with the requirements of Title IV–D. Federal audits revealed that Arizona had fallen short on essentially every measure of compliance, but the Secretary had not reduced the state's AFDC grant. The *Freestone* plaintiffs claimed that the state's shortcomings violated their federal rights under Title IV–D and sought broad declaratory and injunctive relief under § 1983. The District Court granted summary judgment in favor of the defendants, but the Ninth Circuit reversed. Relying on Wilder v. Virginia Hospital Association, 496 U.S. 498 (1990) (see footnote c, supra), the Court of Appeals found that "needy families with children" were the intended beneficiaries of Title IV–D, that the plaintiffs' interest was "sufficiently concrete to be judicially enforceable," and that Title IV–D imposed binding obligations on each state to satisfy all of the requirements for AFDC funding.

The Supreme Court unanimously reversed. Speaking through Justice O'Connor, it held that the Court of Appeals had failed to identify with requisite specificity the "rights" created by federal law:

> As best we can tell, the Court of Appeals seemed to think that respondents had a right to require the director of Arizona's child support agency to bring the state's program into substantial compliance with Title IV–D. But the requirement that a state operate its child support program in "substantial compliance" with Title IV–D was not intended to benefit individual children and custodial parents, and therefore it does not constitute a federal right. Far from creating an individual entitlement to services, the

standard is simply a yardstick for the Secretary to measure the systemwide performance of a state's Title IV–D program. Thus, the Secretary must look to the aggregate services provided by the state, not to whether the needs of any particular person have been satisfied. [Under Health and Human Services regulations, a] state substantially complies with Title IV–D when it provides most mandated services (such as enforcement of support obligations) in only 75 percent of the cases reviewed during the federal audit period. States must aim to establish paternity in 90 percent of all eligible cases, but may satisfy considerably lower targets so long as their efforts are steadily improving. It is clear, then, that even when a state is in "substantial compliance" with Title IV–D, any individual plaintiff might still be among the 10 or 25 percent of persons whose needs ultimately go unmet. Moreover, even upon a finding of substantial noncompliance, the Secretary can merely reduce the state's AFDC grant by up to five percent; she cannot, by force of her own authority, command the state to take any particular action or to provide any services to certain individuals. In short, the substantial compliance standard is designed simply to trigger penalty provisions that increase the frequency of audits and reduce the state's AFDC grant by a maximum of five percent. As such, it does not give rise to individual rights.

The Court of Appeals erred not only in finding that individuals have an enforceable right to substantial compliance, but also in taking a blanket approach to determining whether Title IV–D creates rights. It is readily apparent that many other provisions of that multifaceted statutory scheme do not fit our traditional three criteria for identifying statutory rights. . . . For example, Title IV–D lays out detailed requirements for the State's data processing system. . . . Obviously, these complex standards do not give rise to individualized rights to computer services. They are simply intended to improve the overall efficiency of the States' child support enforcement scheme. The same reasoning applies to the staffing levels of the state agency, which respondents seem to claim are inadequate. . . . These mandates do not, however, give rise to federal rights. For one thing, the link between increased staffing and the services provided to any particular individual is far too tenuous to support the notion that Congress meant to give each and every Arizonan who is eligible for Title IV–D the right to have the State Department of Economic Security staffed at a "sufficient" level. . . . We do not foreclose the possibility that some provisions of Title IV–D give rise to individual rights. The lower court did not separate out the particular rights it believed arise from the statutory scheme, and we think the complaint is less than clear in this regard. . . .

At the same time, the Court rejected the Director's argument that *any* § 1983 suit would be barred by Title IV–D's remedial scheme. The Court emphasized that *Sea Clammers* and *Smith v. Robinson* had been the only occasions where it had found remedial schemes sufficiently comprehensive to supplant § 1983. In each case, the Court had identified unusually elaborate private enforcement provisions that made it "hard to believe that Congress intended to preserve the § 1983 right of action." Unlike the federal programs in *Sea Clammers* and *Smith v. Robinson*, Title IV–D contained no private remedy, either judicial or administrative. The limited powers to audit and cut federal funding were "not comprehensive enough to close the door on § 1983 liability" altogether.

Does this analysis clarify *Sea Clammers* and *Smith v. Robinson*?

7. COMMENTARY AND BIBLIOGRAPHY

Thiboutot and its progeny have prompted much comment. Most commentators argue that the § 1983 remedy should be presumptively available, absent "clear evidence" of a congressional intent to withdraw it. See, e.g., Paul Wartelle and Jeffrey Hadley Louden, Private Enforcement of Federal Statutes: The Role of the Section 1983 Remedy, 9 Hast.Con.L.Q. 487, 543 (1982). In practice, this approach would read *Thiboutot* very broadly, for it would be rare indeed to find express indication of a legislative intent to preclude enforcement under § 1983.

A radically different position is taken in George D. Brown, Whither *Thiboutot*?: Section 1983, Private Enforcement, and the Damages Dilemma, 33 DePaul L.Rev. 31 (1983), which argues that "the Supreme Court's decision to apply, in a cursory fashion, a plain meaning approach to an exceedingly complex area was doomed from the start."

A case-by-case approach is advanced by Cass Sunstein in Section 1983 and the Private Enforcement of Federal Law, 49 U.Chi.L.Rev. 394 (1982). Sunstein is reluctant either to apply § 1983 across the board or readily to infer its repeal by implication. The appropriate test, he suggests, is whether there is "manifest inconsistency" between the statutory enforcement scheme and a private right of action. If so, the § 1983 remedy should be precluded, notwithstanding the absence of explicit legislative intent to accomplish that result. Manifest inconsistency is likely to exist, he added, when underlying statute create independent private causes of action against state officers, when they involve open-ended substantive standards that require agency interpretation, and when they demand consistent and coordinated enforcement that can only be achieved through administrative agencies.

8. INTERACTION OF § 1983 AND IMPLIED PRIVATE RIGHTS OF ACTION

In functional terms, *Thiboutot* is in many ways comparable to a separate line of cases dealing with "implied" private rights of action. In these cases, federal courts have been asked to supplement administrative remedies in regulatory statutes by with "implied" but not explicitly authorized private rights of action. Over time the Court has grown increasingly reluctant to do so.

(i) Alexander v. Sandoval

The intersection of this increasingly restrictive line of cases and the broad reach of *Maine v. Thiboutot* arose in the aftermath of Alexander v. Sandoval, 532 U.S. 275 (2001). The case involved a private action to enforce disparate-impact regulations promulgated by the Department of Justice under § 602 of Title VI of the 1964 Civil Rights Act. In Cannon v. University of Chicago, 441 U.S. 677 (1979), the Court had held that § 601 of the Act, a provision forbidding racial discrimination in programs receiving federal funds, created an implied right of action in favor of private parties. In *Sandoval*, however, the Court held that § 602 of the Act, authorizing federal agencies to promulgate regulations to "effectuate" the rights guaranteed by Title VI, does *not* create an implied right of action. Enforcement of regulations promulgated under § 602 was therefore limited to the statutorily-specified remedy of defunding the offending program. The Court therefore barred a private lawsuit challenging the decision of the Alabama Department of Public Safety to offer drivers' license examinations only in English, on grounds of its disparate impact on Spanish-speaking applicants.

In dissent, Justice Stevens, joined by Justices Souter, Ginsburg, and Breyer suggested plaintiffs could circumvent the lack of a private right of action under § 602 of Title VI by using § 1983:

> [T]o the extent that the majority denies relief to the respondents merely because they neglected to mention 42 U.S.C. § 1983 in framing their Title VI claim, this case is something of a sport. Litigants who in the future wish to enforce the Title VI regulations against state actors in all likelihood must only reference § 1983 to obtain relief; indeed, the plaintiffs in this case (or other similarly situated individuals) presumably retain the option of re-challenging Alabama's English-only policy in a complaint that invokes § 1983 even after today's decision.

(ii) Gonzaga University v. Doe

The Supreme Court sought to align the tests for implied private rights of action and statutory enforcement through § 1983 in Gonzaga University v. Doe, 536 U.S. 273 (2002). The case concerned the Family Educational Rights and Privacy Act of 1974 (FERPA), 20 U.S.C. § 1232g, which prohibits federal funding of schools that permit the release of students' records without written consent. Doe alleged that Gonzaga, a private university in Washington state, violated FERPA by revealing allegations of sexual misconduct by an employee to state officials involved in teacher certification. The employee sued in state court under § 1983, and the state courts agreed that Gonzaga had acted under color of state law in helping the state officials. A jury awarded both compensatory and punitive damages, and the Washington Supreme Court upheld the verdict.

The United States Supreme Court reversed. The Court recognized that *Thiboutot* and private right of action cases had caused "uncertainty" in the lower courts. Some decisions allowed plaintiffs to enforce statutory rights under § 1983 so long as they fell "within the general zone of interest that the statute is intended to protect; something less than what is required for a statute to create rights enforceable directly from the statute itself under an implied private right of action." *Gonzaga University* rejected this approach:

> We now reject the notion that our cases permit anything short of an unambiguously conferred right to support a cause of action brought under § 1983. Section 1983 provides a remedy only for the deprivation of "rights, privileges, or immunities secured by the Constitution and laws" of the United States. Accordingly, only "rights," not "benefits" or "interests," may be enforced under that section. This being so, we further reject the notion that our implied right of action cases are separate and distinct from our § 1983 cases. To the contrary, our implied right of action cases should guide the determination of whether a statute confers rights enforceable under § 1983.

> We have recognized that whether a statutory violation may be enforced through § 1983 "is a different inquiry than that involved in determining whether a private right of action can be implied from a particular statute." Wilder v. Virginia Hospital Association, 496 U.S. 498, 508 n.9 (1990). But the inquiries overlap in one meaningful respect—in either case we must first determine whether Congress intended to create a federal right. Thus we have held that "the question whether Congress . . . intended to create a private right of action [is] definitively answered in the negative" where "a statute by its terms grants no private rights to any identifiable class." Touche Ross & Co. v. Redington, 442 U.S. 560, 576 (1979). For a statute to create such private rights, its text must be "phrased in terms of the persons benefited." Cannon v. University of Chicago, 441 U.S. 677, 692 n.13 (1979). . . . But even where a statute is phrased in such explicit rights-creating terms, a plaintiff suing under an implied right of action still must show that the statute manifests an intent "to create not just a private right but also a private remedy." Alexander v. Sandoval, 532 U.S. 275, 286 (2001).
>
> Plaintiffs suing under § 1983 do not have the burden of showing an intent to create a private remedy because § 1983 generally supplies a remedy for the vindication of rights secured by federal statutes. Once a plaintiff demonstrates that a statute confers an individual right, the right is presumptively enforceable by § 1983. But the initial inquiry—determining whether a statute confers any right at all—is no different from the initial inquiry in an implied right of action case, the express purpose of which is to determine whether or not a statute "confers rights on a particular class of persons." California v. Sierra Club, 451 U.S. 287, 294 (1981). . . .
>
> A court's role in discerning whether personal rights exist in the § 1983 context should therefore not differ from its role in discerning whether personal rights exist in the implied right of action context. . . . Both inquiries simply require a determination as to whether or not Congress intended to confer individual rights upon a class of beneficiaries. . . . Accordingly, where the text and structure of a statute provide no indication that Congress intends to create new individual rights, there is no basis for a private suit, whether under § 1983 or under an implied right of action.

The Court found that FERPA did not contain the kind of rights-creating language that could support a § 1983 claim. It did not contain "individually focused terminology"—for example, that "no person shall be subjected to" violations of FERPA. Instead, FERPA, like the provisions at issue in *Blessing*, had an "aggregate focus," referring to institutional policies and requiring that funds recipients "comply substantially." The conclusion that FERPA's nondisclosure provisions do not confer enforceable rights was "buttressed by the mechanism that Congress chose to provide for enforcing those provisions." The Court noted Congress' express direction to the Secretary of Education to "deal with violations" and the extensive administrative complaint structure the Secretary had created and found that "[t]hese administrative procedures squarely distinguish this case from *Wright* and *Wilder*, where an aggrieved individual lacked any federal review mechanism." Finally, the Court pointed to statutory language providing that "except for the conduct of hearings, none of the functions of the Secretary under this section shall be carried out in any of the regional offices" of the Department of Education. 20 U.S.C. § 1232g(g). The legislative history showed that Congress had provided for "centralized review" because of concern that "regionalizing the enforcement of [FERPA] may lead to multiple interpretations. . . . " 120 Cong. Rec. 39863 (1974) (joint statement). "It is implausible," the Court concluded, "to presume that the same Congress nonetheless intended private suits to be brought before thousands of federal-and state-court judges, which could only result in the sort of 'multiple interpretations' the Act explicitly sought to avoid."

Justice Breyer, joined by Justice Souter, concurred in the judgment. They agreed that congressional intent was the key issue in determining whether an individual could bring suit under § 1983, and that FERPA manifested no such intent, but would not have adopted a presumption that Congress intended to create a right only if the text or structure of a statute showed an "unambiguous" intent.

Justice Stevens, joined by Justice Ginsburg, dissented. They argued that the FERPA did contain rights-creating language and satisfied the *Blessing* test. They also disagreed with what they saw as the Court's "needlessly borrowing from cases involving implied rights of action":

> [O]ur implied right of action cases "reflect a concern, grounded in separation of powers, that Congress rather than the courts controls the availability of remedies for violations of statutes." Wilder v. Virginia Hospital Association, 496 U.S. 498, 509 n. 9 (1990). However, imposing the implied right of action framework upon the § 1983 inquiry is not necessary: The separation-of-powers concerns present in the implied right of action context "are not present in a § 1983 case," because Congress expressly authorized private suits in § 1983 itself. Id.

(iii) City of Rancho Palos Verdes v. Abrams

The restrictive approach of *Gonzaga University* was reaffirmed in City of Rancho Palos Verdes v. Abrams, 544 U.S. 113 (2005). Plaintiff Abrams sued his locality, claiming that the denial of a zoning permit for a radio antenna on his property violated restrictions imposed on localities by the Telecommunications Act of 1996. Writing for a nearly unanimous Court, Justice Scalia began with the familiar admonition that the statute must create individually enforceable rights in the class of beneficiaries to which the plaintiff belongs. That showing, however, creates only a rebuttable presumption that the right is enforceable under § 1983. The presumption is rebutted if the defendant shows that Congress "did not intend" that the newly created right be enforceable under § 1983, and a lack of congressional intent is the "ordinary inference" from a different statutory enforcement scheme. In the case of the Telecommunications Act, individual enforcement is explicitly authorized but on a shorter timetable, arguably without compensatory damages, and certainly without attorneys fees. These differences in remedy precluded application of § 1983, absent legislation indication of a purpose to provide that relief. Justice Breyer, joined by Justices O'Connor, Souter, and Ginsburg, concurred to say that context would sometimes be important in determining whether Congress intended to exclude enforcement under § 1983. Only Justice Stevens dissented.

(iv) Commentary

For discussion of the implications of these cases, see Brian D. Galle, Can Federal Agencies Authorize Private Suits Under Section 1983?: A Theoretical Approach, 69 Brooklyn L. Rev. 163 (2003); Pamela S. Karlan, Disarming the Private Attorney General, 2003 U. Ill. L. Rev. 183; Bradford C. Mank, Can Administrative Regulations Interpret Rights Enforceable Under Section 1983?: Why *Chevron* Deference Survives *Sandoval* and *Gonzaga*, 32 F.S.U.L. Rev. 843 (2005); Bradford C. Mank, Suing Under Section 1983: The Future After *Gonzaga University v. Doe*, 39 Hous. L. Rev. 1417 (2003); Ralph D. Mawdsley, A Section 1983 Cause of Action Under IDEA? Measuring the Effect of *Gonzaga University v. Doe*, 170 Ed. L. Rep. 425 (2002).

NOTES ON § 1983 ACTIONS TO ENFORCE PREEMPTION

1. GOLDEN STATE TRANSIT CORP. V. LOS ANGELES: § 1983 ACTIONS TO ENFORCE FEDERAL PREEMPTION OF STATE LAW

Can § 1983 be used to recover damages for state regulation that is unlawful only because it is preempted by federal law? The answer, it seems, is "It depends."

In 1986 the Supreme Court ruled that Los Angeles could not condition renewal of a taxi franchise on settlement of a labor dispute between the cab company and its union. Golden State Transit Corp. v. City of Los Angeles, 475 U.S. 608 (1986). That condition, said the Court, interfered with the company's right under the National Labor Relations Act to use economic weapons in collective bargaining. The company then sued the city for money damages under § 1983. A divided Supreme Court upheld the company's claim, but in terms that did not comprehend all damages actions for enforcement of preempted state law. Golden State Transit Corp. v. City of Los Angeles, 493 U.S. 103 (1989).

Speaking through Justice Stevens, the majority reasoned that the cab company was "the intended beneficiary of a statutory scheme that prevents governmental interference with the collective-bargaining process." Because the NLRA created rights in both labor and management, not only against each other but also against the state, the cab company could enforce those rights by a damages action under § 1983. In other cases, however, a private party might be only an incidental beneficiary of a federal scheme intended to benefit the general public. In that circumstance, damages under § 1983 would not be available, although the litigant may have the right to enjoin the preempted state regulation under the general equitable powers of the federal courts.

Justice Kennedy, joined by Chief Justice Rehnquist and Justice O'Connor, dissented. They argued that § 1983 should not be interpreted to authorize money damages "when the only wrong committed by the state or its local entities is misapprehending the precise location of the boundaries between state and federal power."[a]

---

[a] See also Livadas v. Bradshaw, 512 U.S. 107 (1994), which followed *Golden State* in saying that state conduct preempted by the National Labor Relations Act is actionable under § 1983. For analysis of this issue, see Henry Paul Monaghan, Federal Statutory Review under Section 1983 and the APA, 91 Colum.L.Rev. 233 (1991).

2. *DENNIS V. HIGGINS*: § 1983 ACTIONS TO ENFORCE DORMANT COMMERCE CLAUSE CLAIMS

Golden State was followed in Dennis v. Higgins, 498 U.S. 439 (1991). Dennis was the owner of a motor carrier. He filed suit in a Nebraska state court against the Director of the Nebraska Department of Motor Vehicles, arguing that a particular tax on motor carriers violated the dormant (or negative) Commerce Clause. One claim was based on § 1983. The trial court held the tax unconstitutional on the asserted ground and enjoined future collection, but dismissed the § 1983 claim. The state Supreme Court affirmed the dismissal of the § 1983 claim on the ground, inter alia, that "the Commerce Clause does not establish individual rights against government, but instead allocates power between the state and federal governments."

The Supreme Court reversed in an opinion by Justice White. He put the issue as whether the Commerce Clause served only the abstract goals of promoting national economic and political unity or whether it was also designed to benefit individuals. The Court held that the clause "of its own force imposes limitations on state regulation of commerce, and is the source of a right of action in those injured by regulations that exceed such limitations" and that it therefore confers "rights, privileges, or immunities" within the meaning of those words as used in § 1983. Justice Kennedy, joined by Chief Justice Rehnquist, dissented, arguing that the majority had "compound[ed] the error of *Golden State*."

7. DAMAGES

Memphis Community School District v. Stachura

Supreme Court of the United States, 1986.
477 U.S. 299.

■ JUSTICE POWELL delivered the opinion of the Court.

This case requires us to decide whether 42 U.S.C. § 1983 authorizes an award of compensatory damages based on the factfinder's assessment of the value or importance of a substantive constitutional right.

I

Respondent Edward Stachura is a tenured teacher in the Memphis, Michigan, public schools. When the events that led to this case occurred, respondent taught seventh-grade life science, using a textbook that had been approved by the School Board. The textbook included a chapter on human reproduction. During the 1978–79 school year, respondent spent six weeks on this chapter. As part of their instruction, students were shown pictures of respondent's wife during her pregnancy. Respondent also showed the students two films concerning human growth and sexuality. These films were provided by the County Health Department, and the Principal of respondent's school had approved their use. Both films had been shown in past school years without incident.

After the showing of the pictures and the films, a number of parents complained to school officials about respondent's teaching methods. These complaints, which appear to have been based largely on inaccurate rumors about the allegedly sexually explicit nature of the pictures and films, were discussed at an open School Board meeting held on April 23, 1979. Following the advice of the School Superintendent, respondent did not attend the meeting, during which a number of parents expressed the view that respondent should not be allowed to teach in the Memphis school system.[1] The day after the meeting, respondent was suspended with pay. The School Board later confirmed the suspension, and notified respondent that an "administrative evaluation" of his teaching methods was underway. No such evaluation was ever made. Respondent was reinstated the next fall, after filing this lawsuit.

Respondent sued the School District, the Board of Education, various Board members and school administrators, and two parents who had participated in the April 29 School Board meeting. The complaint alleged that respondent's suspension deprived him of liberty and property without due process of law and violated his First Amendment right to academic freedom. Respondent sought compensatory and punitive damages under 42 U.S.C. § 1983 for these constitutional violations.

At the close of the trial on these claims, the District Court instructed the jury as to the law governing the asserted bases for liability. Turning to damages, the court instructed the jury that on finding liability it should award a sufficient amount to compensate respondent for the injury caused by petitioners' unlawful actions:

> You should consider in this regard any lost earnings; loss of earning capacity; out-of-pocket expenses; and any mental anguish or emotional distress that you find the Plaintiff to have suffered as a result of conduct by the defendant depriving him of his civil rights.

In addition to this instruction on the standard elements of compensatory damages, the court explained that punitive damages could be awarded, and described the standards governing the punitive awards.[2] Finally, at respondent's request and over petitioners' objection, the court charged that damages also could be awarded based on the value or importance of the constitutional rights that were violated:

> If you find that the Plaintiff has been deprived of a Constitutional right, you may award damages to compensate him for the deprivation. Damages for this type of injury are more difficult to measure than damages for a physical injury or injury to one's property. There are no medical bills or other expenses by which you can judge how much compensation is appropriate. In one sense, no monetary value we place upon Constitutional rights can measure their importance in our society or compensate a citizen adequately for their deprivation. However, just because these rights are not capable of precise evaluation does not mean that an appropriate monetary amount should not be awarded.
>
> The precise value you place upon any Constitutional right which you find was denied to Plaintiff is within your discretion. You may wish to consider the importance of the right in our system of govern-

---

1 One member of the School Board described the meeting as follows:

At this time, the public was in a total uproar and completely out of control. . . . People were hollering and shouting and the statement was made from the public that if Mr. Stachura was allowed to return in the morning, they would be there to picket the school.

At this point of total panic, [the School Superintendent] stated in order to maintain peace in our School District, we would suspend Mr. Stachura with full pay and get this mess straightened out.

2 Petitioners do not challenge the award of punitive damages in this Court.

ment, the role which this right has played in the history of our republic, [and] the significance of the right in the context of the activities which the Plaintiff was engaged in at the time of the violation of the right.

The jury found petitioners liable, and awarded a total of $275,000 in compensatory damages and $46,000 in punitive damages. The District Court entered judgment notwithstanding the verdict as to one of the defendants, reducing the total award to $266,750 in compensatory damages and $36,000 in punitive damages.

[The Court of Appeals affirmed.] We reverse, and remand for a new trial limited to the issue of compensatory damages.

II

. . . [T]he damages instructions plainly authorized—in addition to punitive damages—two distinct types of "compensatory" damages: one based on respondent's actual injury according to ordinary tort law standards, and another based on the "value" of certain rights. We therefore consider whether the latter category of damages was properly before the jury.

III

A

We have repeatedly noted that 42 U.S.C. § 1983 creates " 'a species of tort liability' in favor of persons who are deprived of 'rights, privileges, or immunities secured' to them by the Constitution." Carey v. Piphus, 435 U.S. 247, 253 (1978). Accordingly, when § 1983 plaintiffs seek damages for violations of constitutional rights, the level of damages is ordinarily determined according to principles derived from the common law of torts. See Smith v. Wade, 461 U.S. 30 (1983).

Punitive damages aside, damages in tort cases are designed to provide "*compensation* for the injury caused to plaintiff by defendant's breach of duty." 2 F. Harper, F. James & O. Gray, Law of Torts § 25.1, p. 490 (2d ed. 1986) (emphasis in original). To that end, compensatory damages may include not only out-of-pocket loss and other monetary harms, but also such injuries as "impairment of reputation . . . , personal humiliation, and mental anguish and suffering." Gertz v. Robert Welch, Inc., 418 U.S. 323, 350 (1974). Deterrence is also an important purpose of this system, but it operates through the mechanism of damages that are *compensatory*—damages grounded in determinations of plaintiffs' actual losses. Congress adopted this common-law system of recovery when it established liability for "constitutional torts." Consequently, "the basic purpose" of § 1983 damages is "to *compensate persons for injuries* that are caused by the deprivation of constitutional rights." *Carey v. Piphus*, supra, at 254 (emphasis added).

Carey v. Piphus represents a straightforward application of these principles. *Carey* involved a suit by a high school student suspended for smoking marijuana; the student claimed he was denied procedural due process because he was suspended without an opportunity to respond to the charges against him. The Court of Appeals for the Seventh Circuit held that even if the suspension was justified, the student could recover substantial compensatory damages simply because of the insufficient procedures used to suspend him from school. We reversed, and held that the student could recover compensatory damages only if he proved actual injury caused by the denial of his constitutional rights. We noted: "Rights, constitutional and otherwise, do not exist in a vacuum. Their purpose is to protect persons from injuries to particular interests." Where no injury was present, no "compensatory" damages could be awarded.

The instructions at issue here cannot be squared with *Carey*, or with the principles of tort damages on which *Carey* and § 1983 are grounded. The jurors in this case were told that, in determining how much was necessary to "compensate [respondent] for the deprivation" of his constitutional rights, they should place a money value on the "rights" themselves by considering such factors as the particular right's "importance . . . in our system of government," its role in American history, and its "significance . . . in the context of the activities" in which respondent was engaged. These factors focus, not on compensation for provable injury, but on the jury's subjective perception of the importance of constitutional rights as an abstract matter. *Carey* establishes that such an approach is impermissible. The constitutional right transgressed in *Carey*—the right to due process of law—is central to our system of ordered liberty. We nevertheless held that *no* compensatory damages could be awarded for violation of that right absent proof of actual injury. *Carey* thus makes clear that the abstract value of a constitutional right may not form the basis for § 1983 damages.[11]

Respondent nevertheless argues that *Carey* does not control here, because in this case a *substantive* constitutional right—respondent's First Amendment right to academic freedom—was infringed. The argument misperceives our analysis in *Carey*. That case does not establish a two-tiered system of constitutional rights, with substantive rights afforded greater protection than "mere" procedural safeguards. . . . [W]hatever the constitutional basis for § 1983 liability, such damages must always be designed "to *compensate injuries* caused by the [constitutional] deprivation." Id. at 265 (emphasis added).[13] That conclusion simply leaves no room for noncompensatory damages measured by the jury's perception of the abstract "importance" of a constitutional right.

Nor do we find such damages necessary to vindicate the constitutional rights that § 1983 protects. Section 1983 presupposes that damages that compensate for actual harm ordinarily suffice to deter constitutional violations. Moreover, damages based on the "value" of constitutional rights are

---

[11] We did approve an award of nominal damages for the deprivation of due process in *Carey*. Our discussion of that issue makes clear that nominal damages, and not damages based on some undefinable "value" of infringed rights, are the appropriate means of "vindicating" rights whose deprivation has not caused actual, provable injury:

> Common-law courts traditionally have vindicated deprivations of certain "absolute" rights that are not shown to have caused actual injury through the award of a nominal sum of money. By making the deprivation of such rights actionable for nominal damages without proof of actual injury, the law recognizes the importance to organized society that those rights be scrupulously observed; but at the same time, it remains true to the principle that substantial damages should be awarded only to compensate actual injury or, in the case of exemplary or punitive damages, to deter or punish malicious deprivations of rights.

[13] *Carey* recognized that "the task . . . of adapting common-law rules of damages to provide fair compensation for injuries caused by the deprivation of a constitutional right" is one "of some delicacy." We also noted that "the elements and prerequisites for recovery of damages appropriate to compensate injuries caused by the deprivation of one constitutional right are not necessarily appropriate to compensate injuries caused by the deprivation of another." This "delicate" task need not be undertaken here. None of the parties challenges the portion of the jury instructions that permitted recovery for actual harm to respondent, and the instructions that *are* challenged simply do not authorize compensation for injury. We therefore hold only that damages based on the "value" or "importance" of constitutional rights are not authorized by § 1983, because they are not truly compensatory.

an unwieldy tool for ensuring compliance with the Constitution. History and tradition do not afford any sound guidance concerning the precise value that juries should place on constitutional protections. Accordingly, were such damages available, juries would be free to award arbitrary amounts without any evidentiary basis, or to use their unbounded discretion to punish unpopular defendants. Such damages would be too uncertain to be of any great value to plaintiffs, and would inject caprice into determinations of damages in § 1983 cases. We therefore hold that damages based on the abstract "value" or "importance" of constitutional rights are not a permissible element of compensatory damages in such cases.

B

Respondent further argues that the challenged instructions authorized a form of "presumed" damages—a remedy that is both compensatory in nature and traditionally part of the range of tort law remedies. Alternatively, respondent argues that the erroneous instructions were at worst harmless error.

Neither argument has merit. Presumed damages are a *substitute* for ordinary compensatory damages, not a *supplement* for an award that fully compensates the alleged injury. When a plaintiff seeks compensation for an injury that is likely to have occurred but difficult to establish, some form of presumed damages may possibly be appropriate. In these circumstances, presumed damages may roughly approximate the harm that the plaintiff suffered and thereby compensate for harms that may be impossible to measure. [T]he instructions at issue in this case did not serve this purpose, but instead called on the jury to measure damages based on a subjective evaluation of the importance of particular constitutional values. Since such damages are wholly divorced from any compensatory purpose, they cannot be justified as presumed damages.[14] Moreover, no rough substitute for compensatory damages was required in this case, since the jury was fully authorized to compensate respondent for both monetary and nonmonetary harms caused by petitioners' conduct.

Nor can we find that the erroneous instructions were harmless. . . . It is likely, although not certain, that a major part of these damages was intended to "compensate" respondent for the abstract "value" of his due process and First Amendment rights. For these reasons, the case must be remanded for a new trial on compensatory damages. . . .

It is so ordered.

■ JUSTICE BRENNAN and JUSTICE STEVENS join the opinion of the Court and also join JUSTICE MARSHALL's opinion concurring in the judgment.

---

[14] For the same reason, Nixon v. Herndon, 273 U.S. 536 (1927), and similar cases do not support the challenged instructions. In *Nixon*, the Court held that a plaintiff who was illegally prevented from voting in a state primary election suffered compensable injury. This holding did not rest on the "value" of the right to vote as an abstract matter; rather, the Court recognized that the plaintiff had suffered a particular injury—his inability to vote in a particular election—that might be compensated through substantial money damages.

Nixon followed a long line of cases. . . . Although these decisions sometimes speak of damages for the value of the right to vote, their analysis shows that they involve nothing more than an award of presumed damages for a nonmonetary harm that cannot easily be quantified . . .

The "value of the right" in the context of these decisions is the money value of the particular loss that the plaintiff suffered—a loss of which "each member of the jury has personal knowledge." It is *not* the value of the right to vote as an general, abstract matter, based on its role in our history or system of government . . . . .

■ JUSTICE MARSHALL, with whom JUSTICE BRENNAN, JUSTICE BLACKMUN, and JUSTICE STEVENS join, concurring in the judgment.

I agree with the Court that this case must be remanded for a new trial on damages. Certain portions of the Court's opinion, however, can be read to suggest that damages in § 1983 cases are necessarily limited to "out-of-pocket loss," "other monetary harms," and "such injuries as 'impairment of reputation . . . , personal humiliation, and mental anguish and suffering.' " I do not understand the Court to so hold, and I write separately to emphasize that the violation of a constitutional right, in a proper case, may itself constitute a compensable injury.

The appropriate starting point of any analysis in this area is this Court's opinion in Carey v. Piphus, 435 U.S. 247 (1978). In *Carey* we recognized that "the basic purpose of a § 1983 damages award should be to compensate persons for injuries caused by the deprivation of constitutional rights." We explained, however, that application of that principle to concrete cases was not a simple matter. "It is not clear," we stated, "that common-law tort rules of damages will provide a complete solution to the damages issue in every § 1983 case." Rather, "the rules governing compensation for injuries caused by the deprivation of constitutional rights should be tailored to the interests protected by the particular right in question—just as the common-law rules of damages themselves were defined by the interests protected in various branches of tort law."

Applying these principles, we held in *Carey* that substantial damages should not be awarded where a plaintiff has been denied procedural due process but has made no further showing of compensable damage. We repeated, however, that "the elements and prerequisites for recovery of damages appropriate to compensate injuries caused by the deprivation of one constitutional right are not necessarily appropriate to compensate injuries caused by the deprivation of another." We referred to cases that support the award of substantial damages simply upon a showing that a plaintiff was wrongfully deprived of the right to vote, without requiring any further demonstration of damages.

Following *Carey*, the courts of appeals have recognized that invasions of constitutional rights sometimes cause injuries that cannot be redressed by a wooden application of common-law damages rules. In Hobson v. Wilson, 737 F.2d 1 (D.C.Cir.1984), . . . plaintiffs claimed that defendant Federal Bureau of Investigation agents had invaded their First Amendment rights to assemble for peaceable political protest, to associate with others to engage in political expression, and to speak on public issues free of unreasonable government interference. The District Court found that the defendants had succeeded in diverting plaintiffs from, and impeding them in, their protest activities. The Court of Appeals for the District of Columbia Circuit held that injury to a First Amendment protected interest could itself constitute compensable injury wholly apart from any "emotional distress, humiliation and personal indignity, emotional pain, embarrassment, fear, anxiety and anguish" suffered by plaintiffs. The court warned, however, that the injury could be compensated with substantial damages only to the extent that it was "reasonably quantifiable"; damages should not be based on "the so-called inherent value of the rights violated."

I believe that the *Hobson* court correctly stated the law. When a plaintiff is deprived, for example, of the opportunity to engage in a demonstration to express his political views, "[i]t is facile to suggest that no damage is done." Dellums v. Powell, 566 F.2d 167, 195 (D.C. Cir. 1977). . . . There is no reason why such an injury should not be compensable in damages. At the same time, however, the award must be proportional to the actual loss sustained.

The instructions given the jury in this case were improper because they did not require the jury to focus on the loss actually sustained by the respondent. . . . These instructions invited the jury to speculate on matters wholly detached from the real injury occasioned respondent by the deprivation of the right. Further, the instructions might have led the jury to grant respondent damages based on the "abstract value" of the right to procedural due process—a course directly barred by our decision in *Carey*.

The Court therefore properly remands for a new trial on damages. I do not understand the Court, however, to hold that deprivations of constitutional rights can never themselves constitute compensable injuries. Such a rule would be inconsistent with the logic of *Carey*, and would defeat the purpose of § 1983 by denying compensation for genuine injuries caused by the deprivation of constitutional rights.

NOTES ON COMPENSATORY DAMAGES IN CIVIL RIGHTS ACTIONS

1. BACKGROUND

After *Monroe v. Pape*, both the Court and the commentators assumed that damages for "constitutional torts" would be the same as those for ordinary torts. Compensation would be paid for the plaintiff's out-of-pocket loss and for such intangible harms as injury to reputation, personal humiliation, and pain and suffering. Subsequently, some began to wonder whether additional damages should be available to take account of the value of the constitutional right. The rationale was deterrence. "To ensure that awards of compensatory damages would be large enough to have the desired deterrent effect, these commentators recommended the recognition of 'presumed general damages' in the form of 'quasi-punitive damages' for the 'inherent value of a constitutional right.' " Jean C. Love, Presumed General Compensatory Damages in Constitutional Tort Litigation: A Corrective Justice Perspective, 49 W. & L. L.Rev. 67, 71 (1992).

Carey v. Piphus, 435 U.S. 247 (1978), rejected this suggestion. The Court held that absent proof of some sort of actual injury, students who were improperly suspended from school without procedural due process, were entitled only to nominal damages of one dollar. *Stachura* affirms this position. Consequently, civil rights plaintiffs may recover only the kinds of damages traditionally available in tort. There is no additional award to vindicate the abstract value of the constitutional right in question.

Although neither opinion mentioned the point, the Justices' refusal to allow such damages may have something to do with the Civil Rights Attorneys' Fees Award Act of 1976. This statute, which is examined in detail in Chapter II, authorizes prevailing civil rights plaintiffs to recover compensation for their attorneys. The objective was to recruit lawyers to bring civil rights cases. Of particular concern were uneconomic cases where plaintiff's injury had a low dollar value. Of course, requiring the defendant to pay the plaintiff's lawyer means not only that more plaintiffs will find lawyers but also that the judgments against defendants will be higher, often much higher, than would otherwise be the case. Vindication and deterrence are accordingly increased, although the "compensation" goes to the lawyer and not the client.

2. QUESTIONS AND COMMENTS ON *STACHURA*

Although the Justices were unanimous in disapproving the instruction given by the trial court, they may not have agreed on the instruction that should have been given. Justice Marshall emphasized that the denial of a constitutional right is itself a compensable injury, quite apart from any other harms, but that "the award must be proportional to the actual loss sustained." Does the majority disagree? Is the trial court's instruction faulted only for a certain looseness of phrasing, or does the Supreme Court have a more fundamental objection?

Note also that the *Stachura* Court apparently accepted at least some uses of presumed damages, though only "as a *substitute* for ordinary compensatory damages, not a *supplement* for an award that fully compensates the alleged injury." Does this mean that a civil rights plaintiff could recover large damages without proof of actual harm so long as they are described as "presumed" compensation for intangible injuries? Is there a difference between such presumed damages and the overtly non-compensatory damages authorized by the trial court's instruction in *Stachura*? If not, should either be allowed?

3. THE RELATION OF RISK TO INJURY IN CONSTITUTIONAL TORTS

A different and more surprising objection to conventional tort recoveries in § 1983 cases is advanced in John C. Jeffries, Jr., Damages for Constitutional Violations: The Relation of Risk to Injury in Constitutional Torts, 75 Va. L. Rev. 1461 (1989). The article argues that compensation for violations of constitutional rights should encompass only "constitutionally relevant injuries—that is, injuries within the risks that the constitutional prohibition seeks to avoid." The idea is that the violation of some constitutional doctrines—especially those that are essentially prophylactic in rationale—produces harms far removed from the purposes of awarding damages under § 1983.

A search-and-seizure violation is used to make the point:

> Suppose, for example, that a police officer conducts an unlawful search and finds nothing. This is an actionable wrong, and the person searched would have a claim for damages to the extent of his or her injury. The injury, however, would likely be insignificant. A search that uncovers nothing (unless accompanied by some additional wrong such as assault) is likely to be little more than an inconvenience. Of course, consequential damages would be available if the victim suffers "pain and suffering" from the invasion of privacy, but the unsuccessful search ordinarily does modest harm.
>
> Compare the case of the unlawful search that uncovers incriminating evidence. The wrong is the same, but the injury is considerably more severe. The person searched would face the prospect of criminal charge, trial, conviction, and punishment. In some circumstances the exclusionary rule would bar use of the illegally obtained evidence, but that is not invariably so, and in any event the accusation is in itself injurious. Harms associated with criminal accusation and trial would certainly be foreseeable (indeed, desired) consequences of an unlawful search. If all such injury were compensable, however, the result would be a radical disparity between the kind of harm against which protection is desired (unreasonable invasion of privacy) and the kind of harm for which compensation would

be sought (criminal prosecution and trial). A regime compensating individuals for all injury caused by government unconstitutionality would end up awarding money damages to offset losses that should be attributed to (and that are also 'but for' caused by) the claimant's own misconduct. The result would be a wealth transfer from society generally to those guilty of criminal wrongdoing. The prospect is peculiar, if not perverse.

The correct approach, says Jeffries, is to limit compensation for constitutional violations to the kinds of injuries the constitutional prohibition was designed to avoid. Under this scheme, the victim of an unconstitutional search could recover damages for the invasion of privacy but not for harms flowing from the discovery of incriminating evidence.[a]

4. VALUING CONSTITUTIONAL RIGHTS: *NIXON V. HERNDON*

In contrast to the Fourth Amendment rights discussed in the prior note, some constitutional rights do not have common-law analogs. Under such circumstances, how ought the rights to be valued?

In Nixon v. Herndon, 273 U.S. 536 (1927), cited in footnote 14 of *Stachura*, the plaintiff was an African American voter. A Texas statute provided that "in no event shall a negro be eligible to participate in a Democratic party primary election held in the State of Texas." He sued the Judges of Elections who refused to provide him with a ballot, claiming damages of $5,000. The Court recognized the long historical roots of damages actions for denials of the right to vote and cited its prior decision in Wiley v. Sinkler, 179 U.S. 58 (1900), in which the Court unanimously recognized a qualified voter's right to sue for damages and said that the "amount of damages the plaintiff shall recover in such an action is peculiarly appropriate for the determination of a jury."

How ought a jury to determine the appropriate measure of damages? Is the way in which a plaintiff's rights have been denied relevant? Some denials—such as those based on intentional racial discrimination—may inflict greater dignitary harms than others. Should the damages be greater if the election is close and the vote of the plaintiff (or, more plausibly, a group of similarly situated plaintiffs) might have affected the outcome?

5. VALUING CONSTITUTIONAL RIGHTS: *CAREY V. PIPHUS*

Consider also denials of procedural due process. In Carey v. Piphus, 435 U.S. 247 (1978), students had been improperly suspended from school without first receiving the constitutionally mandated hearing. The Court held that if the school officials could show that the students "would have been suspended even if a proper hearing had been held," then the students could not recover compensatory damages for injuries caused by the suspensions. They could recover for the feelings of mental and emotional distress they suffered from not having been treated fairly, though the Supreme Court limited how such injury should be assessed:

---

[a] For criticism of these views, see Sheldon Nahmod, Constitutional Damages and Corrective Justice: A Different View, 76 Va. L. Rev. 997 (1990) (arguing that constitutional violations are analogous to intentional torts and that no limitation of compensatory damages is appropriate, as the intentional wrongdoer ought to bear all the costs of his or her misconduct).

> [The school officials] do not deny that a purpose of procedural due process is to convey to the individual a feeling that the government has dealt with him fairly, as well as to minimize the risk of mistaken deprivations of protected interests. They go so far as to concede that, in a proper case, persons in respondents' position might well recover damages for mental and emotional distress caused by the denial of procedural due process. [Their] argument is the more limited one that such injury cannot be presumed to occur, and that plaintiffs at least should be put to their proof on the issue, as plaintiffs are in most tort actions.
>
> We agree with [the officials] in this respect. . . . First, it is not reasonable to assume that every departure from procedural due process, no matter what the circumstances or how minor, inherently is . . . likely to cause distress. . . . [W]here a deprivation is justified but procedures are deficient, whatever distress a person feels may be attributable to the justified deprivation rather than to deficiencies in procedure. . . .
>
> Finally, we foresee no particular difficulty in producing evidence that mental and emotional distress actually was caused by the denial of procedural due process itself. Distress is a personal injury familiar to the law, customarily proved by showing the nature and circumstances of the wrong and its effect on the plaintiff.

In a footnote, the Court observed: "We use the term 'distress' to include mental suffering or emotional anguish. Although essentially subjective, genuine injury in this respect may be evidenced by one's conduct and observed by others. Juries must be guided by appropriate instructions, and an award of damages must be supported by competent evidence concerning the injury."[b]

6. SPECIAL RULES FOR PRISONER LAWSUITS

The Prison Litigation Reform Act of 1995 provides that "[n]o Federal civil action may be brought by a prisoner confined in a jail, prison, or other correctional facility, for mental or emotional injury suffered while in custody without a prior showing of physical injury." 42 U.S.C. § 1997e(e). The Supreme Court has characterized § 1997e(e) as "prohibiting claims for emotional injury without prior showing of physical injury." Woodford v. Ngo, 548 U.S. 81 (2006).

In cases where the constitutional provision at issue is designed at least in part to prevent physical injury—for example, the Fourth and Eighth Amendment prohibitions on the use of excessive force and even Eighth Amendment prison conditions cases—the operation of § 1997e(e) may be fairly straightforward. For example, even if a prison guard used unreasonable force to subdue a prisoner, the prisoner cannot recover for emotional distress unless he can prove physical injury. Courts have required such plaintiffs to show an injury that "need not be significant but must be more than de minimis." Oliver v. Keller, 289 F.3d 623 (9th Cir. 2002) (a canker sore and some discomfort from the conditions in a jail holding cell do not qualify).

---

[b] For an example of recovery of substantial damages for denial of due process, see Merritt v. Mackey, 932 F.2d 1317 (9th Cir. 1991) (upholding the district court's award of $35,000 compensatory damages for failure to provide a hearing before the plaintiff was terminated from his job even though the court found that he would have been terminated even if the hearing had been held).

By contrast, the courts of appeals have divided on the availability of damages in § 1983 suits alleging violations of constitutional provisions not generally thought to protect physical well-being. See, e.g., Canell v. Lightner, 143 F.3d 1210 (9th Cir. 1998) (refusing to apply § 1997e(e) to a claim raising Free Exercise and Establishment Clause claims because "deprivation of First Amendment rights entitles a plaintiff to judicial relief wholly aside from the physical injury he can show"); Mason v. Schriro, 45 F. Supp. 2d 709, 715–21 (W.D. Mo. 1999) (allowing an equal protection suit alleging damages from racial segregation within a prison to proceed). The Department of Justice has taken the position that punitive damages may be proper if they are "based solely on an alleged constitutional violation, and not on any mental or emotional injury caused by the violation." See Searles v. Van Bebber, 251 F.3d 869 (10th Cir. 2001) (describing this position). In Geiger v. Jowers, 404 F.3d 371 (5th Cir. 2005), however, the court held that § 1997e(e) barred the claims of a prisoner who alleged tampering with his mail in violation of the First Amendment, holding he could not recover for mental anguish, emotional distress, psychological harm, and insomnia.

Smith v. Wade

Supreme Court of the United States, 1983.
461 U.S. 30.

■ JUSTICE BRENNAN delivered the opinion of the Court.

We granted certiorari in this case to decide whether the District Court for the Western District of Missouri applied the correct legal standard in instructing the jury that it might award punitive damages under 42 U.S.C. § 1983. The Court of Appeals for the Eighth Circuit sustained the award of punitive damages. We affirm.

I

The petitioner, William H. Smith, is a guard at Algoa Reformatory, a unit of the Missouri Division of Corrections for youthful first offenders. The respondent, Daniel R. Wade, was assigned to Algoa as an inmate in 1976. In the summer of 1976 Wade voluntarily checked into Algoa's protective custody unit. Because of disciplinary violations during his stay in protective custody, Wade was given a short term in punitive segregation and then transferred to administrative segregation. On the evening of Wade's first day in administrative segregation, he was placed in a cell with another inmate. Later, when Smith came on duty in Wade's dormitory, he placed a third inmate in Wade's cell. According to Wade's testimony, his cellmates harassed, beat, and sexually assaulted him.

Wade brought suit under 42 U.S.C. § 1983 . . . alleging that his Eighth Amendment rights had been violated. At trial his evidence showed that he had placed himself in protective custody because of prior violence against him by other inmates. The third prisoner whom Smith added to the cell had been placed in administrative segregation for fighting. Smith had made no effort to find out whether another cell was available; in fact there was another cell in the same dormitory with only one occupant. Further, only a few weeks earlier, another inmate had been beaten to death in the same dormitory during the same shift, while Smith had been on duty. Wade asserted that Smith . . . knew or should have known that an assault against him was likely under the circumstances.

[T]he district judge . . . instructed the jury that Wade could make out an Eighth Amendment violation only by showing "physical abuse of such base, inhumane and barbaric proportions as to shock the sensibilities." Further, because of Smith's qualified immunity as a prison guard, see Procunier v. Navarette, 434 U.S. 555 (1978), the judge instructed the jury that Wade could recover only if [Smith was] guilty of "gross negligence" (defined as "a callous indifference or a thoughtless disregard for the consequences of one's act or failure to act") or "[e]gregious failure to protect" (defined as "a flagrant or remarkably bad failure to protect") Wade. He reiterated that Wade could not recover on a showing of simple negligence.

The district judge also charged the jury that it could award punitive damages on a proper showing:

> In addition to actual damages, the law permits the jury, under certain circumstances, to award the injured person punitive and exemplary damages, in order to punish the wrongdoer for some extraordinary misconduct, and to serve as an example or warning to others not to engage in such conduct.
>
> If you find the issues in favor of the plaintiff, and if the conduct of . . . the [defendant] is shown to be *a reckless or callous disregard of, or indifference to, the rights or safety of others*, then you may assess punitive or exemplary damages in addition to any award of actual damages.
>
> . . . The amount of punitive or exemplary damages assessed against [the] defendant may be such sum as you believe will serve to punish [him] and to deter him and others from like conduct. [Emphasis added.]

The jury . . . found Smith liable . . . and awarded $25,000 in compensatory and $5,000 in punitive damages. The District Court entered judgment on the verdict, and the Court of Appeals affirmed.

In this Court, Smith attacks only the award of punitive damages. He does not challenge the correctness of the instructions on liability or qualified immunity, nor does he question the adequacy of the evidence to support the verdict of liability for compensatory damages.

II

Section 1983 is derived from § 1 of the Civil Rights Act of 1871. It was intended to create "a species of tort liability" in favor of persons deprived of federally secured rights. Carey v. Piphus, 435 U.S. 247, 253 (1978). We noted in *Carey* that there was little in the section's legislative history concerning the damages recoverable for this tort liability. In the absence of more specific guidance, we looked first to the common law of torts (both modern and as of 1871), with such modification or adaptation as might be necessary to carry out the purpose and policy of the statute. We have done the same in other contexts arising under § 1983, especially the recurring problem of common-law immunities.[2]

---

[2] Justice Rehnquist's dissent faults us for referring to modern tort decisions in construing § 1983. Its argument rests on the unstated and unsupported premise the Congress necessarily intended to freeze into permanent law whatever principles were correct in 1871, rather than to incorporate applicable general legal principles as they evolve. See also O'Connor, J., dissenting. The dissents are correct, of course, that when the language of the section and its legislative history provide no clear answer, we have found guidance in the law prevailing at the time when § 1983 was enacted; but it does not follow that that law is absolutely controlling, or that current law is irrelevant. On the contrary, if the prevailing view on some point of

Smith correctly concedes that "punitive damages are available in a 'proper' § 1983 action. . . . " Although there was debate about the theoretical correctness of the punitive damages doctrine in the latter part of the last century, the doctrine was accepted as settled law by nearly all state and federal courts, including this Court. It was likewise generally established that individual public officers were liable for punitive damages for their misconduct on the same basis as other individual defendants. Further, although the precise issue of the availability of punitive damages under § 1983 has never come squarely before us, we have had occasion more than once to make clear our view that they are available; indeed, we have rested decisions on related questions on the premise of such availability.[5]

Smith argues, nonetheless, that this was not a "proper" case in which to award punitive damages. More particularly, he attacks the instruction that punitive damages could be awarded on a finding of reckless or callous disregard of or indifference to Wade's rights or safety. Instead, he contends that the proper test is one of actual malicious intent—"ill will, spite, or intent to injure."[6] He offers two arguments for this position: first, that actual intent is the proper standard for punitive damages in all cases under § 1983; and second, that even if intent is not always required, it should be required here because the threshold for punitive damages should always be higher than that for liability in the first instance. We address these in turn.

III

Smith does not argue that the common law, either in 1871 or now, required or requires a showing of actual malicious intent for recovery of punitive damages.

Perhaps not surprisingly, there was significant variation (both terminological and substantive) among American jurisdictions in the latter 19th century on the precise standard to be applied in awarding punitive damages—variation that was exacerbated by the ambiguity and slipperiness of

---

general tort law had changed substantially in the intervening century (which is not the case here), we might be highly reluctant to assume that Congress intended to perpetuate a now-obsolete doctrine. . . .

[5] In Newport v. Fact Concerts, Inc., 453 U.S. 247 (1981), for example, we held that a municipality (as opposed to an individual defendant) is immune from liability for punitive damages under § 1983. A significant part of our reasoning was that deterrence of constitutional violations would be adequately accomplished by allowing punitive damages awards directly against the responsible individuals. . . . Similarly, in Carlson v. Green, 446 U.S. 14 (1980), we stated that punitive damages would be available in an action against federal officials directly under the Eighth Amendment, partly on the reasoning that since such damages are available under § 1983, it would be anomalous to allow punitive awards against state officers but not federal ones.

Justice Rehnquist's dissent, without squarely denying that punitive damages are available under § 1983, does its best to cast doubt on the proposition. It argues that the phrase "for redress" at the end of the section means that Congress intended to limit recovery to compensatory damages. This novel construction is strained; a more plausible reading of the statute is that the phrase "or other proper proceeding for redress" is simply an expansive alternative to the preceding phrases "action at law" and "suit in equity," intended to avoid any unwanted technical limitations that might lurk in the other phrases. . . .

[6] . . . We note in passing that it appears quite uncertain whether even Justice Rehnquist's dissent ultimately agrees with Smith's view that "ill will, spite, or intent to injure" should be required to allow punitive damages awards. Justice Rehnquist consistently confuses, and attempts to blend together, the quite distinct concepts of *intent to cause* injury, on the one hand, and *subjective consciousness* of risk of injury (or of unlawfulness) on the other. . . . If Justice Rehnquist does indeed mean to propose a standard reaching subjective consciousness as well as actual injurious intent, one wonders why the instructions given in this case do not meet his standard. It is hard to see how Smith could have disregarded or been indifferent to the danger to Wade unless he was subjectively conscious of that danger. . . .

such common terms as "malice" and "gross negligence." Most of the confusion, however, seems to have been over the degree of negligence, recklessness, carelessness, or culpable indifference that should be required—not over whether actual intent was essential. On the contrary, the rule in a large majority of jurisdictions was that punitive damages (also called exemplary damages, vindictive damages, or smart money) could be awarded without a showing of actual ill will, spite, or intent to injure.

This Court so stated on several occasions, before and shortly after 1871. In Philadelphia, W. & B.R. Co. v. Quigley, 62 U.S. (21 How.) 202, 214 (1859), a diversity libel suit, the Court held erroneous an instruction that authorized the jury to return a punitive award but gave the jury virtually no substantive guidance as to the proper threshold. We described the standard thus:

> Whenever the injury complained of has been inflicted maliciously or wantonly, and with circumstances of contumely or indignity, the jury are not limited to the ascertainment of a simple compensation for the wrong committed against the aggrieved person. But the malice spoken of in this rule is not merely the doing of an unlawful or injurious act. The word implies that the act complained of was conceived in the spirit of mischief, *or of criminal indifference to civil obligations*. (Emphasis added.)

The Court further explained the standard for punitive damages in Milwaukee & St. Paul R. Co. v. Arms, 91 U.S. 489, 495 (1876), a diversity railroad collision case:

> Redress commensurate to such [personal] injuries should be afforded. In ascertaining its extent, the jury may consider all the facts which relate to the wrongful act of the defendant, and its consequences to the plaintiff; but they are not at liberty to go farther, unless it was done wilfully, *or was the result of that reckless indifference to the rights of others which is equivalent to an intentional violation of them*. In that case the jury are authorized, for the sake of public example, to give such additional damages as the circumstances require. The tort is aggravated by the evil motive, and on this rests the rule of exemplary damages.
>
> . . . To [assess punitive damages], there must have been some wilful misconduct, *or that entire want of care which would raise the presumption of a conscious indifference to consequences*. (Emphasis added.)

The Court therefore held erroneous a jury instruction allowing a punitive award on "gross negligence"; it concluded that the latter term was too vague, and too likely to be confused with mere ordinary negligence, to provide a fair standard. It remanded for a new trial.[10]

The large majority of state and lower federal courts were in agreement that punitive damages awards did not require a showing of actual malicious intent; they permitted punitive awards on variously stated standards

[10] . . . Justice Rehnquist's dissent reads this case as imposing a requirement of actual malicious intent, on the assumption that when the Court said "indifference to consequences" it really meant "intent to cause consequences," and when it said "recklessness" it really meant "bad motive or intent to injure." [But] the *Milwaukee* Court did not say, or come close to saying, that recklessness is *identical* to intent, or that it is material only as *evidence* of intent; rather, it said that recklessness is "*equivalent*" to intent, meaning that the two are equally culpable and deserving of punishment and deterrence. . . .

of negligence, recklessness, or other culpable conduct short of actual malicious intent.

The same rule applies today. The Restatement (Second) of Torts § 908(2) (1977), for example, states: "Punitive damages may be awarded for conduct that is outrageous, because of the defendant's evil motive *or his reckless indifference to the rights of others.*" (Emphasis added.) Most cases under state common law, although varying in their precise terminology, have adopted more or less the same rule, recognizing that punitive damages in tort cases may be awarded not only for actual intent to injure or evil motive, but also for recklessness, serious indifference to or disregard for the rights of others, or even gross negligence.

The remaining question is whether the policies and purposes of § 1983 itself require a departure from the rules of tort common law. As a general matter, we discern no reason why a person whose federally guaranteed rights have been violated should be granted a more restrictive remedy than a person asserting an ordinary tort cause of action. Smith offers us no persuasive reason to the contrary.

Smith's argument, which he offers in several forms, is that an actual-intent standard is preferable to a recklessness standard because it is less vague. He points out that punitive damages, by their very nature, are not awarded to compensate the injured party. He concedes, of course, that deterrence of future egregious conduct is a primary purpose of both § 1983 and of punitive damages. But deterrence, he contends, cannot be achieved unless the standard of conduct sought to be deterred is stated with sufficient clarity to enable potential defendants to conform to the law and to avoid the proposed sanction. Recklessness or callous indifference, he argues, is too uncertain a standard to achieve deterrence rationally and fairly. A prison guard, for example, can be expected to know whether he is acting with actual ill will or intent to injure, but not whether he is being reckless or callously indifferent.

Smith's argument, if valid, would apply to ordinary tort cases as easily as to § 1983 suits; hence, it hardly presents an argument for adopting a different rule under § 1983. In any event, the argument is unpersuasive. While . . . an intent standard may be easier to understand and apply to particular situations than a recklessness standard, we are not persuaded that a recklessness standard is too vague to be fair or useful. . . .

More fundamentally, Smith's argument for certainty in the interest of deterrence overlooks the distinction between a standard for punitive damages and a standard of liability in the first instance. Smith seems to assume that prison guards and other state officials look mainly to the standard for punitive damages in shaping their conduct. We question the premise; we assume, and hope, that most officials are guided primarily by the underlying standards of federal substantive law—both out of devotion to duty, and in the interest of avoiding liability for compensatory damages. At any rate, the conscientious officer who desires clear guidance on how to do his job and avoid lawsuits can and should look to the standard for actionability in the first instance. . . .

In this case, the jury was instructed to apply a high standard of constitutional right ("physical abuse of such base, inhumane and barbaric proportions as to shock the sensibilities"). It was also instructed, under the principle of qualified immunity, that Smith could not be held liable at all unless he was guilty of "a callous indifference or a thoughtless disregard for the consequences of [his] act or failure to act," or of "a flagrant or remarkably bad failure to protect" Wade. These instructions were not challenged in this Court, nor were they challenged on grounds of vagueness in the lower courts. Smith's contention that this recklessness standard is too vague to provide clear guidance and reasonable deterrence might more properly be reserved for a challenge seeking different standards of liability in the first instance. As for punitive damages, however, in the absence of any persuasive argument to the contrary based on the policies of § 1983, we are content to adopt the policy judgment of the common law—that reckless or callous disregard for the plaintiff's rights, as well as intentional violations of federal law, should be sufficient to trigger a jury's consideration of the appropriateness of punitive damages.

IV

Smith contends that even if § 1983 does not ordinarily require a showing of actual malicious intent for an award of punitive damages, such a showing should be required in this case. He argues that the deterrent and punitive purposes of punitive damages are served only if the threshold for punitive damages is higher in every case than the underlying standard for liability in the first instance. In this case, while the district judge did not use the same precise terms to explain the standards of liability for compensatory and punitive damages, the parties agree that there is no substantial difference between the showings required by the two instructions; both apply a standard of reckless or callous indifference to Wade's rights. Hence, Smith argues, the district judge erred in not requiring a higher standard for punitive damages, namely, actual malicious intent.

This argument incorrectly assumes that, simply because the instructions specified the same *threshold* of liability for punitive and compensatory damages, the two forms of damages were equally available to the plaintiff. The argument overlooks a key feature of punitive damages—that they are never awarded as of right, no matter how egregious the defendant's conduct. . . . To make its punitive award, the jury was required to find not only that Smith's conduct met the recklessness threshold (a question of ultimate fact), but *also* that his conduct merited a punitive award of $5,000 in addition to the compensatory award (a discretionary moral judgment).

Moreover, the rules of ordinary tort law are once more against Smith's argument. There has never been any general common-law rule that the threshold for punitive damages must always be higher than that for compensatory liability. On the contrary, both the First and Second Restatements of Torts have pointed out that "in torts like malicious prosecution that require a particular antisocial state of mind, the improper motive of the tortfeasor is both a necessary element in the cause of action and a reason for awarding punitive damages." . . .

This common-law rule makes sense in terms of the purposes of punitive damages. Punitive damages are awarded in the jury's discretion "to punish [the defendant] for his outrageous conduct and to deter him and others like him from similar conduct in the future." Restatement (Second) of Torts § 908(1) (1977). The focus is on the character of the tortfeasor's conduct—whether it is of the sort that calls for deterrence and punishment over and above that provided by compensatory awards. If it is of such a character, then it is appropriate to allow a jury to assess punitive damages; and that assessment does not become less appropriate simply because the plaintiff in the case faces a more demanding standard of actionability. . . .

V

We hold that a jury may be permitted to assess punitive damages in an action under § 1983 when the defendant's conduct is shown to be motivated by evil motive or intent, or when it involves reckless or callous indifference to the federally protected rights of others. We further hold that this threshold applies even when the underlying standard of liability for compensatory damages is one of recklessness. Because the jury instructions in this case are in accord with this rule, the judgment of the Court of Appeals is affirmed.

■ JUSTICE REHNQUIST, with whom THE CHIEF JUSTICE and JUSTICE POWELL join, dissenting.

This case requires us to determine what degree of culpability on the part of a defendant in an action under § 1983 will permit an award of punitive damages. The District Court instructed the jury that it could award punitive damages in favor of the plaintiff if it concluded that the defendant's conduct constituted "reckless or callous disregard of, or indifference to, the rights or safety of others." In my view, a forthright inquiry into the intent of the 42d Congress and a balanced consideration of the public policies at issue compel the conclusion that the proper standard for an award of punitive damages under § 1983 requires at least some degree of bad faith or improper motive on the part of the defendant. . . .

I

[At the outset] it is useful to consider briefly the purposes of punitive damages. A fundamental premise of our legal system is the notion that damages are awarded to *compensate* the victim—to redress the injuries that he or she *actually* has suffered. In sharp contrast to this principle, the doctrine of punitive damages permits the award of "damages" beyond even the most generous and expansive conception of actual injury to the plaintiff. This anomaly is rationalized principally on three grounds. First, punitive damages "are assessed for the avowed purpose of visiting *a punishment* upon the defendant." Second, the doctrine is rationalized on the ground that it deters persons from violating the rights of others. Third, punitive damages are justified as a "bounty" that encourages private lawsuits seeking to assert legal rights.

Despite these attempted justifications, the doctrine of punitive damages has been vigorously criticized throughout the nation's history. Countless cases remark that such damages have never been "a favorite of the law." The year after § 1983 was enacted, the New Hampshire Supreme Court declared: "The idea of [punitive damages] is wrong. It is a monstrous heresy. It is an unsightly and unhealthy excrescence, deforming the symmetry of the body of the law." Fay v. Parker, 53 N.H. 342, 382 (1872). Such remarks reflect a number of deeply held reservations regarding punitive damages, which can only be briefly summarized here.

Punitive damages are generally seen as a windfall to plaintiffs, who are entitled to receive full compensation for their injuries—but no more. Even assuming that a punitive "fine" should be imposed after a civil trial, the penalty should go to the state, not to the plaintiff—who by hypothesis is fully compensated. Moreover, although punitive damages are "quasi-criminal," their imposition is unaccompanied by the types of safeguards present in criminal proceedings. This absence of safeguards is exacerbated by the fact that punitive damages are frequently based upon the caprice and prejudice of jurors. We observed in Electrical Workers v. Foust, 442

U.S. 42, 50–51 n.14 (1979), that "punitive damages may be employed to punish unpopular defendants," and noted elsewhere that "juries assess punitive damages in wholly unpredictable amounts bearing no necessary relation to the actual harm caused." Gertz v. Robert Welch, Inc., 418 U.S. 323, 350 (1974). Finally, the alleged deterrence achieved by punitive damage awards is likely outweighed by the costs—such as the encouragement of unnecessary litigation and the chilling of desirable conduct—flowing from the rule, at least when the standards on which the awards are based are ill-defined.

Because of these considerations, a significant number of American jurisdictions refuse to condone punitive damages awards. . . . Nonetheless, a number of states do permit juries to award punitive damages in certain circumstances. Historically, however, there has been little uniformity among the standards applied in these states for determining on what basis a jury might award punitive damages.

One fundamental distinction is essential to an understanding of the differences among the various standards for punitive damages. Many jurisdictions have required some sort of wrongful motive, actual intention to inflict harm or intentional doing of an act known to be unlawful—"express malice," "actual malice," "bad faith," "wilful wrong" or "ill will."[3] Other states, however, have permitted punitive damage awards merely upon a showing of very careless or negligent conduct by the defendant—"gross negligence," "recklessness," or "extreme carelessness." In sharp contrast to the first set of terms noted above, which connote a requirement of actual ill will towards the plaintiff, these latter phrases import only a degree of negligence. The distinction between acts that are intentionally harmful and those that are very negligent, or unreasonable, involves a basic difference of kind, not just a variation of degree. The former typically demands inquiry into the actor's subjective motive and purpose, while the latter ordinarily requires only an objective determination of the relative risks and advantages accruing to society from particular behavior. . . .

It is illuminating to examine the Court's reasoning with this distinction in mind.

II

At bottom, this case requires the Court to decide when a particular remedy is available under § 1983. Until today, the Court has adhered, with some fidelity, to the scarcely controversial principle that its proper role in interpreting § 1983 is determining what the 42d Congress intended. . . . The reason our earlier decisions interpreting § 1983 have relied upon common-law decisions is simple: Members of the 42d Congress were lawyers, familiar with the law of their time. In resolving ambiguities in the enactments of that Congress, as with other Congresses, it is useful to consider the legal principles and rules that shaped the thinking of its members. The decisions of state courts decided well after 1871, while of some academic interest, are largely irrelevant to what the members of the 42d Congress intended by way of a standard for punitive damages. . . .

---

[3] Decisions handed down at the time the 42d Congress deliberated leave little question that when a court required a showing of malice in order to recover punitive damages, an inquiry into the actual mental state of the defendant—his motives, intentions, knowledge, or design—was required. [Justice Rehnquist's lengthy examination of the various 19th-century uses of "actual malice," "implied malice," and associated terms is omitted.—Addition to footnote by eds.]

III

The Court also purports to rely on decisions, handed down in the second half of the last century by this Court, in drawing up its rule that mere recklessness will support an award of punitive damages. In fact, these decisions unambiguously support an actual-malice standard. The Court rests primarily on Philadelphia, W. & B.R. Co. v. Quigley, 62 U.S. (21 How.) 202 (1859), a diversity tort action against a railroad. There, we initially observed that in "certain actions of tort," punitive damages might be awarded, and then described those actions as "[w]henever the injury complained of has been inflicted maliciously or wantonly, and with circumstances of contumely or indignity." As discussed previously, it was relatively clear at the time that "malice" required a showing of actual ill will or intent to injure. Perhaps foreseeing future efforts to expand the rule, however, we hastened to specify the type of malice that would warrant punitive damages: "the malice spoken of in this rule is not merely the doing of an unlawful or injurious act. The word implies that the act complained of *was conceived in the spirit of mischief, or of criminal indifference to civil obligations*." (Emphasis added.) It would have been difficult to have more clearly expressed the "actual malice" standard. We explicitly rejected an "implied malice" formulation, and then mandated inquiry into the "spirit" in which a defendant's act was "conceived." . . .

Our decisions following 1871 indicate yet more clearly that we adhered to an actual-malice or intent-to-injure requirement in punitive damages actions. In Milwaukee & St. Paul R. Co. v. Arms, 91 U.S. 489 (1876), a verdict against a railroad in a diversity action was reversed because the jury was erroneously charged that it might award punitive damages on a finding of "gross negligence." . . . After quoting the passage in *Quigley*, discussed above, rejecting an implied-malice and adopting an actual-intent-to-injure standard, the Court said:

> [The rule permitting punitive damages is] applicable to suits for personal injuries received through the negligence of others. Redress commensurate to such injuries should be afforded. In ascertaining its extent, the jury may consider all the facts which relate to the wrongful act of the defendant, and its consequences to the plaintiff; but they are not at liberty to go farther, unless *it was done wilfully, or was the result of that reckless indifference to the rights of others which is equivalent to an intentional violation of them*. . . . The tort is aggravated by the *evil motive, and on this rests the rule of exemplary damages*. (Emphasis added.)

Read in context, this language strongly suggests that an actual-malice standard was intended. The rule of exemplary damages "rests" on a defendant's "evil motive," and, while "reckless indifference" may justify some awards of punitive damages, it may do so only in "that" class of "reckless indifference . . . which is equivalent to an *intentional violation*" of the plaintiff's rights. (Emphasis added.)

This interpretation of the opinion in *Arms* is the only reading that can be squared with the holding in that case. The Court held that it was error to give an instruction that "gross negligence" would support a finding of punitive damages. This instruction was condemned because "gross negligence" is "a relative term," and "a word of description, and not of definition." The Court regarded "gross negligence" as too imprecise and ill-defined a standard to support the extraordinary remedy of punitive damages. Given this, it is more than a little peculiar to read the *Arms* opinion as supporting the recklessness standard embraced by the Court. . . .

Perhaps, by minute dissection of stray clauses in a few of the foregoing decisions, combined with a studied refusal to confront the plain intent underlying phrases like "evil motive," "design and intention," and "intentional wrong," one could discern some shadowy rule of liability resting on recklessness. Ninety years ago, however, the Court, after an exhaustive analysis of the foregoing decisions, explicitly and unambiguously reached the opposite conclusion. In Lake Shore & M.S.R. Co. v. Prentice, 147 U.S. 101 (1893), the Court considered whether punitive damages were properly awarded against a railroad in a diversity action. The Court noted that the law on the subject was "well-settled" and paraphrased the *Quigley* standard: The jury may award punitive damages "if the defendant has acted wantonly, or oppressively, or with such malice as implies a spirit of mischief or criminal indifference to civil obligations." Then, as it had in [earlier cases], the Court explained this formulation, observing that a "*guilty intention* on the part of the defendant is *required* in order to charge him with exemplary or punitive damages." (Emphasis added.) . . . The Court went on to note that "criminal intent [is] necessary to warrant the imposition of [punitive] damages," and elsewhere wrote that "wanton, malicious or oppressive intent" and "unlawful and criminal intent," were required for the award of such damages. *Prentice* simply leaves no question that actual wrongful intent, not just recklessness, was required for a recovery of punitive damages, and, in addition, that this was what "well-settled" law always had required. . . .

In addition, the decisions rendered by state courts in the years preceding and immediately following the enactment of § 1983 attest to the fact that a solid majority of jurisdictions took the view that the standard for an award of punitive damages included a requirement of ill will. . . .

While a few jurisdictions may have adopted a more lenient, if less precise, standard of recklessness, the majority's claim that the prevailing standard in 1871 was one of recklessness simply cannot be sustained. The decisions of this Court, which were likely well known to federal legislators, supported an animus requirement. . . . Among the states, there were many approaches to the imposition of punitive damages, with a variety of standards prevailing throughout the nation. Nonetheless, a solid majority of jurisdictions followed the rule that punitive damages require some element of "evil motive," "wickedness," or "formed design to injure and oppress." Thus, if we are to adhere to the principle, consistently followed in our previous decisions, that the members of the 42d Congress intended § 1983 to reflect existing common-law rules, it is very likely that wrongful animus was a prerequisite for an award of punitive damages.

IV

Even apart from this historical background, I am persuaded by a variety of additional facts that the 42d Congress intended a "wrongful intent" requirement. . . .

[I]t is useful to consider the language of § 1983 itself—which should, of course, be the starting point for any inquiry into legislative intent. Section 1983 provides:

> Every person who, under color of any statute, ordinance, regulation, custom, or usage, of any State . . . subjects, or causes to be subjected, any citizen of the United States or other person within the ju-

risdiction thereof to the deprivation of any rights, privileges, or immunities secured by the Constitution and laws, shall be liable to the party *injured* in an action at law, suit in equity, or other proper proceeding *for redress*. (Emphasis added.)

Plainly, the statutory language itself provides absolutely no support for the cause of action for punitive damages that the Court reads into the provision. Indeed, it merely creates "liab[ility] to the party injured . . . for redress." "Redress" means "[r]eparation of, satisfaction or compensation for, a wrong sustained or the loss resulting from this." 8 Oxford English Dictionary 310 (1933). And, as the Court concedes, punitive damages are not "reparation" or "compensation"; their very purpose is to punish, not to compensate. If Congress meant to create a right to recover punitive damages, then it chose singularly inappropriate words: both the reference to injured parties and to redress suggests compensation, and not punishment. . . .

[I]t is accurate to say that the foundation upon which the right to punitive damages under § 1983 rests is precarious, at the best. . . . Given the legislative ambiguity, the sensible approach to the problem would be an honest recognition that, if we are to infer a right to punitive damages, it should be a restrained one. . . . An intent requirement, unlike a recklessness standard, is logically consistent with the underlying justification for *punitive* damages. It is a fundamental principle of American law that penal consequences generally ought to be imposed only where there has been some sort of wrongful animus creating the type of culpability warranting this treatment. . . . Given that punitive damages are meant to punish, it is difficult to believe that Congress would have departed from the "instinctive," "universal and persistent" linkage in our law between punishment and wrongful intent.

V

Finally, even if the evidence of congressional intent were less clearcut, I would be persuaded to resolve any ambiguity in favor of an actual-malice standard. It scarcely needs repeating that punitive damages are not a "favorite of the law," owing to the numerous persuasive criticisms that have been leveled against the doctrine. The majority reasons that these arguments apply to all awards of punitive damages, not just to those under § 1983; while this is of course correct, it does little to reduce the strength of the arguments, and, if they are persuasive, we should not blindly follow the mistakes other courts have made.

. . . It is anomalous, and counter to deep-rooted legal principles and common-sense notions, to punish persons who meant no harm, and to award a windfall, in the form of punitive damages, to someone who already has been fully compensated. These peculiarities ought to be carefully limited—not expanded to every case where a jury may think a defendant was too careless, particularly where a vaguely defined, elastic standard like "reckless indifference" gives free reign to the biases and prejudices of juries. In short, there are persuasive reasons not to create a new punitive damages remedy unless it is clear that Congress so intended.

The argument is particularly powerful in a case like this, where the uncertainty resulting from largely random awards of punitive damages will have serious effects upon the performance by state and local officers of their official duties. One of the principal themes of our immunity decisions is that the threat of liability must not deter an official's "willingness to execute his office with the decisiveness and the judgment required by the public good." Scheuer v. Rhodes, 416 U.S. 232, 240 (1974). To avoid stifling the types of initiative and decisiveness necessary for the "government to govern," we have held that officials will be liable for compensatory damages only for certain types of conduct. Precisely the same reasoning applies to liability for punitive damages. Because punitive damages generally are not subject to any relation to actual harm suffered, and because the recklessness standard is so imprecise, the remedy poses an even greater threat to the ability of officials to take decisive, efficient action. . . .

Moreover, notwithstanding the Court's inability to discern them, there are important distinctions between a right to damages under § 1983 and a similar right under state tort law. A leading rationale seized upon by proponents of punitive damages to justify the doctrine is that "the award is . . . a covert response to the legal system's overt refusal to provide financing for litigation." D. Dobbs, Law of Remedies 221 (1973). Yet, 42 U.S.C. § 1988 provides not just a "covert response" to plaintiffs' litigation expenses but an explicit provision for an award to the prevailing party in a § 1983 action of "a reasonable attorney's fee as part of the costs." . . . This difference between the incentives that are present in state tort actions, and those in § 1983 actions, makes the Court's reliance upon the standard for punitive damages in the former entirely inapposite: in fashioning a new financial lure to litigate under § 1983 the Court does not act in a vacuum, but, by adding to existing incentives, creates an imbalance of inducements to litigate that may have serious consequences.

The staggering effect of § 1983 claims upon the workload of the federal courts has been decried time and again. The torrent of frivolous claims under that section threatens to incapacitate the judicial system's resolution of claims where true injustice is involved; those claims which truly warrant redress are in a very real danger of being lost in a sea of meritless disputes. Yet, apparently oblivious to this, the Court today reads into the silent, inhospitable terms of § 1983 a remedy that is designed to serve as a "bounty" to encourage private litigation. In a time when the courts are flooded with suits that do not raise colorable claims, in large part because of the existing incentives for litigation under § 1983, it is regrettable that the Court should take upon itself, in apparent disregard for the likely intent of the 42d Congress, the legislative task of encouraging yet more litigation. There is a limit to what the federal judicial system can bear.

Finally, by unquestioningly transferring the standard of punitive damages in *state* tort actions to *federal* § 1983 actions, the Court utterly fails to recognize the fundamental difference that exists between an award of punitive damages by a federal court, acting under § 1983, and a similar award by a state court acting under prevailing local laws. While state courts may choose to adopt such measures as they deem appropriate to punish officers of the jurisdiction in which they sit, the standards they choose to adopt can scarcely be taken as evidence of what it is appropriate for a federal court to do. When federal courts enforce punitive damages awards against local officials they intrude into sensitive areas of sovereignty of coordinate branches of our nation, thus implicating the most basic values of our system of federalism. Moreover, by yet further distorting the incentives that exist for litigating claims against local officials in federal court, as opposed to state courts, the Court's decision makes it even more difficult for state courts to attempt to conform the conduct of state officials to the Constitution.

I dissent.

■ JUSTICE O'CONNOR, dissenting.

Although I agree with the result reached in Justice Rehnquist's dissent, I write separately because I cannot agree with the approach taken by either the Court or Justice Rehnquist. Both opinions engage in exhaustive but ultimately unilluminating, exegesis of the common law of the availability of punitive damages in 1871. Although both the Court and Justice Rehnquist display admirable skills in legal research and analysis of great numbers of musty cases, the results do not significantly further the goal of the inquiry: to establish the intent of the 42d Congress. In interpreting § 1983, we have often looked to the common law as it existed in 1871, in the belief that, when Congress was silent on a point, it intended to adopt the principles of the common law with which it was familiar. See, e.g., Newport v. Fact Concerts, Inc., 453 U.S. 247, 258 (1981); Carey v. Piphus, 435 U.S. 247, 255 (1978). This approach makes sense when there was a generally prevailing rule of common law, for then it is reasonable to assume that Congressmen were familiar with that rule and imagined that it would cover the cause of action that they were creating. But when a significant split of authority existed, it strains credulity to argue that Congress simply assumed that one view rather than the other would govern. Particularly . . . in an area in which the courts of an earlier period frequently used inexact and contradictory language, we cannot safely infer anything about congressional intent from the divided contemporaneous judicial opinions. The battle of the string citations can have no winner.

Once it is established that the common law of 1871 provides us with no real guidance on this question, we should turn to the policies under § 1983 to determine which rule best accords with those policies. In *Fact Concerts*, we identified the purposes of § 1983 as pre-eminently to compensate victims of constitutional violations and to deter further violations. The conceded availability of compensatory damages, particularly when coupled with the availability of attorney's fees under § 1988, completely fulfills the goal of compensation, leaving only deterrence to be served by awards of punitive damages. We must then confront the close question whether a standard permitting an award of unlimited punitive damages on the basis of recklessness will chill public officials in the performance of their duties more than it will deter violations of the Constitution, and whether the availability of punitive damages for reckless violations of the Constitution in addition to attorney's fees will create an incentive to bring an ever-increasing flood of § 1983 claims, threatening the ability of the federal courts to handle those that are meritorious. Although I cannot concur in Justice Rehnquist's wholesale condemnation of awards of punitive damages in any context or with the suggestion that punitive damages should not be available even for intentional or malicious violations of constitutional rights, I do agree with the discussion in Part V of his opinion of the special problems of permitting awards of punitive damages for the recklessness of public officials. Since awards of compensatory damages and attorney's fees already provide significant deterrence, I am persuaded that the policies counseling against awarding punitive damages for the recklessness of public officials outweigh the desirability of any incremental deterrent effect that such awards may have. Consequently, I dissent.

NOTES ON PUNITIVE DAMAGES IN CIVIL RIGHTS ACTIONS

1. BACKGROUND

Lower courts had long assumed that punitive damages are available in § 1983 actions. In Carlson v. Green, 446 U.S. 14 (1980), the Court said that punitive damages may be awarded in a *Bivens* action against federal officials. Given the generally parallel development of *Bivens* and § 1983, the availability of punitive damages in statutory civil rights actions seemed clear. Any lingering doubt was laid to rest in Newport v. Fact Concerts, Inc., 453 U.S. 247 (1981), in which the Court relied on the availability of punitive damages against individual § 1983 defendants as a reason for precluding such awards against municipalities.

Presumably, the constitutional limits on punitive damages, whatever they may prove to be, apply straightforwardly to actions under § 1983. In Browning–Ferris Industries v. Kelco Disposal, Inc., 492 U.S. 257 (1989), the Court found that the Excessive Fines Clause of the Eighth Amendment did not limit punitive damages awarded in litigation between private parties. Subsequently, however, the Court has held that grossly excessive punitive damages violate the Due Process Clause, though it is by no means easy to determine how much is too much.[a] On one important point, however, the law is now clear. The question whether punitive damages are unconstitutionally excessive should be reviewed de novo by Courts of Appeals. Cooper Industries, Inc. v. Leatherman Tool Group, Inc., 532 U.S. 424 (2001).

2. QUESTIONS AND COMMENTS ON *SMITH V. WADE*

Punitive damages have become increasingly controversial. One aspect of the debate concerns the substantive standard for their imposition. This issue is analogous to the question of appropriate mens rea for criminal liability, and it suffers from the same history of terminological confusion. Insofar as they rely on historical precedents, both Justice Brennan and Justice Rehnquist are burdened by what Brennan called "the ambiguity and slipperiness" of traditional mens rea language.

Reduced to its essentials, the issue is whether punitive damages should be reserved for cases where the defendant's motive for acting was highly culpable or whether it should also extend to some cases of indifference or inattention. Consider, for example, the facts of *Smith*. Should the jury have been permitted to consider punitive damages if Smith should have known, but did not in fact know, that it was dangerous to put the third inmate into Wade's cell? Or should the jury have been required to find that Smith knew that there was a substantial risk that the cellmates would injure Wade but did not care?

3. BIBLIOGRAPHY

The general literature on punitive damages is voluminous, but scholarship specifically addressed to civil rights cases is fairly limited. For an early analysis, see Jean C. Love, Damages: A Remedy for the Violation of Constitution-

---

[a] See, e.g., BMW v. Gore, 517 U.S. 559 (1996) (requiring a reasonable relationship between compensatory and punitive damages); TXO Production Corp. v. Alliance Resources Corp., 509 U.S. 443 (1993) (upholding punitive damages that exceeded compensatory damages by a greater percentage than in *BMW v. Gore*).

al Rights, 67 Cal.L.Rev. 1242, 1274–81 (1979). And for criticism of *Smith* and the next main case, *Fact Concerts,* see Michael Wells, Punitive Damages for Constitutional Torts, 56 La. L. Rev. 841 (1996).

City of Newport v. Fact Concerts, Inc.

Supreme Court of the United States, 1981.
453 U.S. 247.

■ JUSTICE BLACKMUN delivered the opinion of the Court.

In Monell v. New York City Dept. of Social Services, 436 U.S. 658 (1978), this Court for the first time held that a local government was subject to suit as a "person" within the meaning of 42 U.S.C. § 1983. Aside from concluding that a municipal body was not wholly immune from civil liability, the Court had no occasion to explore the nature or scope of any particular municipal immunity under the statute. The question presented by this case is whether a municipality may be held liable for punitive damages under § 1983.

I

A

Respondent Fact Concerts, Inc., is a Rhode Island corporation organized for the purpose of promoting musical concerts. In 1975, it received permission from the Rhode Island Department of Natural Resources to present several summer concerts at Fort Adams, a state park located in the city of Newport. In securing approval for the final concerts, to be held August 30 and 31, respondent sought and obtained an entertainment license from petitioner city of Newport. Under their written contract, respondent retained control over the choice of performers and the type of music to be played while the city reserved the right to cancel the license without liability if "in the opinion of the City the interests of public safety demand."

Respondent engaged a number of well-known jazz music acts to perform during the final August concerts. Shortly before the dates were specified, the group Blood, Sweat and Tears was hired as a replacement for a previously engaged performer who was unable to appear. Members of the Newport City Council, including the Mayor, became concerned that Blood, Sweat and Tears, which they characterized as a rock group rather than as a jazz band, would attract a rowdy and undesirable audience to Newport. Based on this concern, the Council attempted to have Blood, Sweat and Tears removed from the program.

On Monday, August 25, Mayor Donnelly informed respondent by telephone that he considered Blood, Sweat and Tears to be a rock group, and that they would not be permitted to perform because the city had experienced crowd disturbances at previous rock concerts. Officials of respondent appeared before the City Council at a special meeting the next day, and explained that Blood, Sweat and Tears in fact were a jazz band that had performed at Carnegie Hall in New York City and at similar symphony hall facilities throughout the world. Speaking for the Council, the Mayor reiterated that the city did not condone rock festivals. Without attempting to investigate either the nature of the group's music or the representations made by respondent, the Council voted to cancel the license for both days unless Blood, Sweat and Tears were removed from the program. The vote received considerable publicity, and this adversely affected ticket sales.

Later in the same week, respondent was informed by the City Solicitor that the Council had changed its position and would allow Blood, Sweat and Tears to perform if they did not play rock music. On Thursday, August 28, respondent agreed to attend a second special Council meeting the following day.

The second Council session convened on the afternoon of August 29, the day before the first scheduled performance. Mayor Donnelly informed the Council members that the city had two options—it could either allow Blood, Sweat and Tears to perform subject to the prohibition against rock music, or cancel the concert altogether. Although the City Solicitor advocated the first alternative and advised that the cancellation would be unlawful, the Council did not offer the first option to respondent. Instead, one of the Council members inquired whether all provisions of the contract had been fulfilled. The City Manager, who had just returned from the concert site, reported that the wiring-together of the spectator seats was not fully completed by 3 p.m., and that the auxiliary electric generator was not in place. Under the contract, respondent had agreed to fulfill these two conditions as part of the overall safety procedures.[4] The Council then voted to cancel the contract because respondent had not "lived up to all phases" of the agreement. The Council offered respondent a new contract for the same dates, specifically excluding Blood, Sweat and Tears. Respondent, however, indicated that it would take legal action if the original contract was not honored. After the meeting adjourned at 9:30 p.m., the decision to revoke respondent's license was broadcast extensively over the local media.

On Saturday morning, August 30, respondent obtained in state court a restraining order enjoining the Mayor, the City Council, and the city from interfering with the performance of the concerts. The two-day event, including the appearance of Blood, Sweat and Tears, took place without incident. Fewer than half the available tickets were sold.

B

Respondent instituted the present action in the United States District Court for the District of Rhode Island, naming the city, its Mayor, and the six other Council members as defendants. Alleging, inter alia, that the license cancellation amounted to content-based censorship, and that its constitutional rights to free expression and due process had been violated under color of state law, respondent sought compensatory and punitive damages against the city and its officials under § 1983 and under two pendent state-law counts, including tortious interference with contractual relationships. At the conclusion of six days of trial, the District Court charged the jury with respect to the § 1983 and tortious interference counts. Included in its charge was an instruction, given without objection, that authorized the jury to award punitive damages against each defendant individually, "based on the degree of culpability of the individual defendant." The jury returned verdicts for respondent on both counts, awarding compensatory damages of $72,910 and punitive damages of $275,000; of the punitive

[4] Testimony at the trial indicated that in fact substantial compliance had been achieved. The director of the Rhode Island Department of Natural Resources, who also visited the site on Friday afternoon, stated that respondent's preparations were satisfactory for health and safety purposes. He said that he informed the City Manager that the criticisms offered were "picayune" (although this characterization, upon objection, was stricken by the trial judge) and "frivolous." The director offered to attend the second Council meeting to assist in any way possible, but was told by the Mayor and the City Manager that he was not needed.

damages, $75,000 was spread among the seven individual officials and $200,000 was awarded against the city.[6]

Petitioner moved for a new trial, arguing that punitive damages cannot be awarded under § 1983 against a municipality, and that even if they can, the award was excessive. Because petitioner challenged the punitive damages instruction to which it had not objected at trial, the District Court noted that the challenge was untimely under Federal Rule of Civil Procedure 51. But the court was determined not to "rest its decision on this procedural ground alone." Reasoning that "a careful resolution of this novel question is critical to a just verdict in this case," the court proceeded to consider petitioner's substantive legal arguments on the merits.

. . . Although noting that the burden imposed upon tax-paying citizens warranted judicial caution in this area, the court concluded that in appropriate circumstances municipalities could be held liable for punitive damages in a § 1983 action.[8]

The United States Court of Appeals for the First Circuit affirmed. That court noted, as an initial matter, that the challenge to the punitive damages award was flawed due to petitioner's failure to object to the charge at trial. . . . The Court of Appeals also expressed a belief that the challenged instruction might well not have been error at all. . . .

Because of the importance of the issue, we granted certiorari.

II

At the outset, respondent asserts that the punitive damages issue was not properly preserved for review before this Court. In light of Rule 51's uncompromising language[9] and the policies of fairness and judicial efficiency incorporated therein, respondent claims that petitioner's failure to object to the charge at trial should foreclose any further challenge to that instruction. The problem with respondent's argument is that the District Court in the first instance declined to accept it. Although the punitive damages question perhaps could have been avoided simply by a reliance, under Rule 51, upon petitioner's procedural default, the judge concluded that the interests of justice required careful consideration of this "novel question" of federal law. Because the District Court reached and fully adjudicated the merits, and the Court of Appeals did not disagree with that adjudication, no interests in fair and effective trial administration advanced by Rule 51 would be served if we refused now to reach the merits ourselves. . . .

III

It is by now well settled that the tort liability created by § 1983 cannot be understood in a historical vacuum. In the Civil Rights Act of 1871, Congress created a federal remedy against a person who, acting under color of state law, deprives another of constitutional rights. Congress, however, expressed no intention to do away with the immunities afforded state officials at common law, and the Court consistently has declined to construe the

---

[6] The jury assessed 75 per cent of the punitive damages upon the § 1983 claim and 25 per cent upon the state-law claim. We do not address the propriety of the punitive damages awarded against the petitioner under Rhode Island law.

[8] The court, however, went on to rule that the $200,000 award against petitioner was excessive and unjust. It ordered a remittitur, reducing the punitive damages award to $75,000. Respondent accepted the remittitur without objection.

[9] Rule 51 reads in pertinent part: "No party may assign as error the giving or the failure to give an instruction unless he objects thereto before the jury retires to consider its verdict, stating distinctly the matter to which he objects and the grounds of his objection."

general language of § 1983 as automatically abolishing such traditional immunities by implication. Instead, the Court has recognized immunities of varying scope applicable to different officials sued under the statute. One important assumption underlying the Court's decisions in this area is that members of the 42d Congress were familiar with common-law principles, including defenses previously recognized in ordinary tort litigation, and that they likely intended these common-law principles to obtain, absent specific provisions to the contrary.

At the same time, the Court's willingness to recognize certain traditional immunities as affirmative defenses has not led it to conclude that Congress incorporated *all* immunities existing at common law. See Scheuer v. Rhodes, 416 U.S. 232, 243 (1974). Indeed, because the 1871 Act was designed to expose state and local officials to a new form of liability, it would defeat the promise of the statute to recognize any pre-existing immunity without determining both the policies that it serves and its compatibility with the purposes of § 1983. See Imbler v. Pachtman, 424 U.S. 409, 424 (1976); Owen v. City of Independence, 445 U.S. 622, 638 (1980). Only after careful inquiry into considerations of both history and policy has the Court construed § 1983 to incorporate a particular immunity defense.

Since *Monell* was decided three years ago, the Court has applied this two-part approach when scrutinizing a claim of immunity proffered by a municipality. In *Owen v. City of Independence*, supra, the Court held that neither history nor policy supported a construction of § 1983 that would allow a municipality to assert the good faith of its officers or agents as a defense to liability for damages. *Owen*, however, concerned only compensatory damages, and petitioner contends that with respect to a municipality's liability for punitive damages, an examination of the common-law background and policy considerations yields a very different result.

A

By the time Congress enacted what is now § 1983, the immunity of a municipal corporation from punitive damages at common law was not open to serious question. It was generally understood by 1871 that a municipality, like a private corporation, was to be treated as a natural person subject to suit for a wide range of tortious activity, but this understanding did not extend to the award of punitive or exemplary damages. Indeed, the courts that had considered the issue prior to 1871 were virtually unanimous in denying such damages against a municipal corporation. Judicial disinclination to award punitive damages against a municipality has persisted to the present day in the vast majority of jurisdictions. . . .

In general, courts viewed punitive damages as contrary to sound public policy, because such awards would burden the very taxpayers and citizens for whose benefit the wrongdoer was being chastised. The courts readily distinguished between liability to compensate for injuries inflicted by a municipality's officers and agents, and vindictive damages appropriate as punishment for the bad-faith conduct of those same officers and agents. Compensation was an obligation properly shared by the municipality itself, whereas punishment properly applied only to the actual wrongdoers. The courts thus protected the public from unjust punishment, and the municipalities from undue fiscal constraints.

Given that municipal immunity from punitive damages was well established at common law by 1871, we proceed on the familiar assumption that "Congress would have specifically so provided had it wished to abolish the doctrine." Pierson v. Ray, 386 U.S. 547, 555 (1967). Nothing in the legislative debates suggests that, in enacting § 1 of the Civil Rights Act, the 42d Congress intended any such abolition. Indeed, the limited legislative history relevant to this issue suggests the opposite.

Because there was virtually no debate on § 1 of the Act, the Court has looked to Congress' treatment of the amendment to the Act introduced by Senator Sherman as indicative of congressional attitudes toward the nature and scope of municipal liability.[24] Initially, it is significant that the Sherman amendment as proposed contemplated the award of no more than compensatory damages for injuries inflicted by mob violence. The amendment would not have exposed municipal government to punitive damages; rather, it proposed that municipalities "shall be liable *to pay full compensation* to the person or persons damnified" by mob violence (emphasis added). That the exclusion of punitive damages was no oversight was confirmed by Representative Butler, one of the amendment's chief supporters, when he responded to a critical inquiry on the floor of the House:

> The invalidity of the gentleman's argument is that he looks upon [the amendment] as a punishment for the county. Now, we do not look upon it as a punishment at all. It is a mutual insurance. We are there a community, and if there is any wrong done by our community, or by the inhabitants of our community, we will indemnify the injured party for that wrong. . . .

We doubt that a Congress having no intention of permitting punitive awards against municipalities in the explicit context of the Sherman amendment would have meant to expose municipal bodies to such novel liability sub silentio under § 1 of the Act.

Notwithstanding the compensatory focus of the amendment, its proposed extension of municipal liability met substantial resistance in Congress, resulting in its defeat on two separate occasions. In addition to the constitutional reservations broached by legislators, which the Court has discussed at some length in *Monell*, members of both chambers also expressed more practical objections. Notably, supporters as well as opponents of § 1 voiced concern that this extension of public liability might place an unmanageable financial burden on local governments. Legislators also expressed apprehension that innocent taxpayers would be unfairly punished for the deeds of persons over whom they had neither knowledge nor control. Admittedly, both these objections were raised with particular reference to the threat of expansive municipal liability embodied in the Sherman amendment. The two concerns are not without relevance to the present inquiry, however, in that they reflect policy considerations similar to those relied upon by the common-law courts in rejecting punitive damages awards. We see no reason to believe that Congress' opposition to punishing innocent taxpayers and bankrupting local governments would have been less applicable with regard to the novel specter of punitive damages against municipalities.

B

Finding no evidence that Congress intended to disturb the settled common-law immunity, we now must determine whether considerations of public policy dictate a contrary result. In doing so, we examine the objectives underlying punitive damages in general, and their relationship to the goals of § 1983 in particular.

---

[24] The legislative background of § 1983 is exhaustively addressed in *Monell*. . . .

Punitive damages by definition are not intended to compensate the injured party, but rather to punish the tortfeasor whose wrongful action was intentional or malicious, and to deter him and others from similar extreme conduct. Regarding retribution, it remains true that an award of punitive damages against a municipality "punishes" only the taxpayers, who took no part in the commission of the tort. These damages are assessed over and above the amount necessary to compensate the injured party. Thus, there is no question here of equitably distributing the losses resulting from official misconduct. Cf. *Owen v. City of Independence*, supra. Indeed, punitive damages imposed on a municipality are in effect a windfall to a fully compensated plaintiff, and are likely accompanied by an increase in taxes or a reduction of public services for the citizens footing the bill. Neither reason nor justice suggests that such retribution should be visited upon the shoulders of blameless or unknowing taxpayers.[29]

Under ordinary principles of retribution, it is the wrongdoer himself who is made to suffer for his unlawful conduct. If a government official acts knowingly and maliciously to deprive others of their civil rights, he may become the appropriate object of the community's vindictive sentiments. A municipality, however, can have no malice independent of the malice of its officials. Damages awarded for *punitive* purposes, therefore, are not sensibly assessed against the governmental entity itself. . . .

The other major objective of punitive damages awards is to prevent future misconduct. Respondent argues vigorously that deterrence is a primary purpose of § 1983, and that because punitive awards against municipalities for the malicious conduct of their policymaking officials will induce voters to condemn official misconduct through the electoral process, the threat of such awards will deter future constitutional violations. Respondent is correct in asserting that the deterrence of future abuses of power by persons acting under color of state law is an important purpose of § 1983. It is in this context that the Court's prior statements contemplating punitive damages "in 'a proper' § 1983 action" should be understood. Carlson v. Green, 446 U.S. 14, 22 (1980); Carey v. Piphus, 435 U.S. 247, 257 n. 11 (1978). For several reasons, however, we conclude that the deterrence rationale of § 1983 does not justify making punitive damages available against municipalities.

First, it is far from clear that municipal officials, including those at the policymaking level, would be deterred from wrongdoing by the knowledge that large punitive awards could be assessed based on the wealth of their municipality. Indemnification may not be available to the municipality under local law, and even if it were, officials likely will not be able themselves to pay such sizable awards. Thus, assuming, arguendo, that the responsible official is not impervious to shame and humiliation, the impact on the individual tortfeasor of this deterrence in the air is at best uncertain.

There also is no reason to suppose that corrective action, such as the discharge of offending officials who were appointed and the public excoriation of those who were elected, will not occur unless punitive damages are awarded against the municipality. The Court recently observed in a related context: "The more reasonable assumption is that responsible superiors are motivated not only by concern for the public fisc but also by concern for the

---

[29] It is perhaps possible to imagine an extreme situation where the taxpayers are directly responsible for perpetrating an outrageous abuse of constitutional rights. Nothing of that kind is presented by this case. Moreover, such an occurrence is sufficiently unlikely that we need not anticipate it here.

government's integrity. *Carlson v. Green*, supra, at 21. This assumption is no less applicable to the electorate at large. And if additional protection is needed, the compensatory damages that are available against a municipality may themselves induce the public to vote the wrongdoers out of office.

Moreover, there is available a more effective means of deterrence. By allowing juries and courts to assess punitive damages in appropriate circumstances against the offending official, based on his personal financial resources, the statute directly advances the public's interest in preventing repeated constitutional deprivations. In our view, this provides sufficient protection against the prospect that a public official may commit recurrent constitutional violations by reason of his office. The Court previously has found, with respect to such violations, that a damages remedy recoverable against individuals is more effective as a deterrent than the threat of damages against a government employer. *Carlson v. Green*, supra, at 21. We see no reason to depart from that conclusion here, especially since the imposition of additional penalties would most likely fall upon the citizen-taxpayer.

Finally, although the benefits associated with awarding punitive damages against municipalities under § 1983 are of doubtful character, the costs may be very real. In light of the Court's decision last term in Maine v. Thiboutot, 448 U.S. 1 (1980), the § 1983 damages remedy may now be available for violations of federal statutory as well as constitutional law. Under this expanded liability, municipalities and other units of state and local government face the possibility of having to assure compensation for persons harmed by abuses of governmental authority covering a large range of activity in everyday life. To add the burden of exposure for the malicious conduct of individual government employee may create a serious risk to the financial integrity of these governmental entities.

The Court has remarked elsewhere on the broad discretion traditionally accorded to juries in assessing the amount of punitive damages. Electrical Workers v. Foust, 442 U.S. 42, 50–51 (1979); Gertz v. Robert Welch, Inc., 418 U.S. 323, 349–50 (1974). Because evidence of a tortfeasor's wealth is traditionally admissible as a measure of the amount of punitive damages that should be awarded, the unlimited taxing power of a municipality may have a prejudicial impact on the jury, in effect encouraging it to impose a sizable award. The impact of such a windfall recovery is likely to be both unpredictable and, at times, substantial, and we are sensitive to the possible strain on local treasuries and therefore on services available to the public at large. Absent a compelling reason for approving such an award, not present here, we deem it unwise to inflict the risk.

IV

In sum, we find that considerations of history and policy do not support exposing a municipality to punitive damages for the bad-faith actions of its officials. Because absolute immunity from such damages obtained at common law and was undisturbed by the 42d Congress, and because that immunity is compatible with both the purposes of § 1983 and general principles of public policy, we hold that a municipality is immune from punitive damages under 42 U.S.C. § 1983. Accordingly, the judgment of the Court of Appeals is vacated, and the case is remanded for further proceedings consistent with this opinion.

■ JUSTICE BRENNAN, with whom JUSTICE MARSHALL and JUSTICE STEVENS join, dissenting.

The Court today considers and decides a challenge to the District Court's jury instructions, even though petitioners failed to object to the instructions in a timely manner, as required by Rule 51 of the Federal Rules of Civil Procedure. Because this departure from Rule 51 is unprecedented and unwarranted, I respectfully dissent. . . .

Rule 51 could not be expressed more clearly. Cases too numerous to list have held that failure to object to proposed jury instructions in a timely manner in accordance with Rule 51 precludes appellate review. Rule 51 serves an important function in ensuring orderly judicial administration and fairness to the parties. The trial judge is thereby informed in precise terms of any objections to proposed instructions, and thus is given "an opportunity upon second thought, and before it is too late, to correct any inadvertent or erroneous failure to charge." Moreover, the rule prevents litigants from making the tactical decision not to object to instructions at trial in order to preserve a ground for appeal. In light of the significant purposes and "uncompromising language" of Rule 51, courts should not depart lightly from its structures. . . .

I consider this a peculiarly *inapt* case to disregard petitioners' procedural default. There would be no injustice whatsoever in adhering to the rule in this case. Petitioners were given clear notice that punitive damages would be an issue in the case; the jury instructions were unambiguous; petitioners had ample opportunity to object; they failed to do so, without offering any reason or excuse. Whether their default was negligent or tactical, they have no cause to complain. If these petitioners' default is to be excused, whose should not? If Rule 51 is to be disregarded in this case, when should it be enforced?

I dissent.

NOTES ON GOVERNMENTAL LIABILITY FOR PUNITIVE DAMAGES

1. *WEBSTER V. CITY OF HOUSTON*

The reasoning of *Fact Concerts* was extensively criticized in Webster v. Houston, 689 F.2d 1220 (5th Cir. 1982). Randy Webster, age 17, stole a van. The police gave chase and eventually stopped the vehicle. Although Webster was unarmed and apparently made no resistance, he was thrown to the ground and shot in the head. One of the officers on the scene provided a "throw down" weapon, which was placed in Webster's hand. The officers then reported that Webster had emerged armed from the vehicle and was immediately shot.

Although several police officers knew that Webster had in fact been unarmed, the subsequent police investigation failed to uncover that fact. Testimony of a civilian eyewitness was disregarded, and routine physical evidence was ignored.

The truth came to light only after Webster's parents filed a § 1983 action. Eventually, a jury returned a verdict against two of the officers and the city of Houston. Compensatory damages were set at only $2,548.75, apparently to pay for funeral expenses. Punitive awards of $1 million and $200,000 were made against the two officers, and an additional $200,000 was awarded against the city of Houston.

On appeal, the Fifth Circuit approved the finding of compensatory liability.[a] The record supported the jury's determination that use of a "throw down" gun had the "covert approval" of the Houston Police Department and therefore constituted a "policy or custom" within the meaning of *Monell*. This conclusion was bolstered by the "cover-up," which "gave credence to the idea that a throw down was a tactic acceptable to the police hierarchy."

The punitive award against the city was set aside on the authority of *Fact Concerts*. Judge Goldberg concurred specially. He agreed, "with considerable grief," that *Fact Concerts* presented "an impenetrable barrier" to punitive liability. Goldberg then launched into a lengthy review of *Fact Concerts*. He agreed with both the rationale and the result in that case, but thought the decision "sweeps more broadly than its rationale would justify." His critique followed the sequence of the analysis in *Fact Concerts*.

First, he examined the reliance on history. Whereas *Fact Concerts* had involved liability for a proprietary activity, this case involved the quintessential governmental activity. Traditionally, municipal corporations had been totally immune from liability, whether compensatory or punitive, for governmental acts. But, as *Monell* indicated, § 1983 had been intended to change all that. That Congress might disallow punitive damages for proprietary acts but allow punitive liability for governmental acts (traditionally the more protected) might seem anomalous, but was not. It was consistent with "the core purposes of § 1983—prevention of governmental misconduct caused by aiding and abetting violence through failure to exercise the machineries of justice."

Goldberg then turned to the policy arguments advanced in *Fact Concerts* and found them inapplicable to the instant case:

> The great factual differences between *Newport* and the case before me . . . make *Newport*'s arguments against punitive damages inapplicable here. The primary factual difference making *Newport*'s arguments inapplicable is that *Newport* involved the wrongful acts of individual officials, whereas this case deals with a wrongful policy of concealing police murder, not traceable to any single individual, but rather the outgrowth of the collective inaction of the entire police department.
>
> Thus, while the Court in *Newport* argued that punitive damages against the municipality would not deter *individual* misconduct, here we have *municipal* or *group* misconduct. Second, whereas in *Newport* the Court relied on sanctions from superiors as a sufficient deterrent, in this case, the bad policy actually exists due to the collective inaction of the superiors. . . . Third, in *Newport* the Court suggested that damages assessed directly against the offending official were a better deterrent. But while damages assessed directly against an individual might deter individual misconduct, at whom do we point the finger of guilt in the case of tragic collective apathy? All the individual police officers who knew of the policy but did nothing? The instructors at the police academy who allowed this horrible technique to be inculcated at the very time adherence to law and the constitutional and fundamental human morality should have been taught? The police chief? The City Council? The citizens snug in their

[a] The majority concluded, however, that the jury had acted improperly in awarding no damages for Webster's pain and suffering or for his parents' mental anguish. As the court put it, "We believe that the jury, in awarding punitive damages, thought it had covered all the bases." The court therefore remanded for a new trial on the issue of damages.

beds, oblivious to the fact that young men were being shot down by their "protectors"? Finally, the Court in *Newport* argued that punitive damages for lost ticket sales might deprive the citizens of other services because of financial burdens from increased liability. But in this *core* § 1983 case, that is exactly what Congress wanted. It is necessary that the threatened damages cause some deprivation for the populace so that they will be nudged out of their blissful ignorance, "and the effect will be most wholesome."

Having disputed the applicability of the Supreme Court's arguments *against* punitive damages, Judge Goldberg then sought to show that, on the facts presented here, punitive damages would affirmatively "help to deter the conduct § 1983 was designed to prevent." This contention led to an economic analysis of the case for awarding punitive damages:

> [T]he key datum is that every action has social costs and social benefits. The correctness of a decision is judged by whether the social costs are less than the social benefits. Problems arise, however, when the decisionmaker will receive the benefits but other parties bear the cost. In that case the decisionmaker will decide to follow the course bringing benefits, regardless whether that course is socially correct. The function of damages is to force the decisionmaker to consider the costs of his or her actions as well as the benefits and promote socially correct decisionmaking. The point of damages, then, is to "internalize" costs to the decisionmaker.
>
> The choice between compensatory and punitive damages should be made based on whether one or the other will properly internalize the social costs and produce socially correct decisions. If all the parties bearing all the costs and enjoying all the benefits are before the court, then compensatory damages will properly account for all costs and benefits. . . .
>
> If, however, the situation is such that not all of the costs will come before the court, then compensatory damages will be inadequate to internalize the costs and punitive damages are needed. This is much more likely to happen when the relevant decision is one promulgating a policy, as in the present case, rather than one regarding a discrete event, as in *Newport*. The full costs of a policy might not come before the courts for several reasons.
>
> The full costs of a policy might not be before a court because not all instances of the policy's application are known. For example, if a policy results in ten citizens suffering a cost of $10, but only one of those instances is discovered, compensatory damages would not internalize all the costs. If a court can tell that nine instances of application are likely to remain undiscovered, when one *does* come before it, the court should assess $90 punitive damages to internalize the costs of the undiscovered applications. [In this case] it is hard to avoid the inference that some cases are not coming before the courts.
>
> Another instance in which punitive damages are needed to internalize social costs is if some social costs are known but are diffused widely through society. This point highlights the key difference between *Newport* and this case, the reason it would be an injustice to award punitive damages in *Newport* and a greater injustice not to award them here. In *Newport* the total social damages from the incident are summed up in the lost

profits of the promoters and some minor dissatisfaction of those music lovers who would have bought tickets but for the City Council's actions. This case, however, produces social costs of the gravest nature. Without trivializing the most grievous injury done to the Webster family, it makes a travesty of the most fundamental values of our society to ignore the damages done to *them* by Houston's policy. The most primal reason for banding together in social groups is protection from violence. When members of the very institution created to protect us from violence instead inflict it, the social fabric is torn. This is but a tear, however, because we can all understand the possibility of uncontrollable renegades. But when the crime is concealed in accordance with the tacit policy of that institution, the social fabric is ripped into tattered rags.

It is only by threat of punitive damages that we can be sure policymakers will be cognizant of this grave social cost. It is only by threat of punitive damages that we can arouse policymakers from their dozing to eradicate policies such as this. If ever there were a need for punitive damages to encourage sound decisionmaking, this is it. It is time the courts have a showdown with the "throw-down."

2. FOOTNOTE 29

Footnote 29 of the *Fact Concerts* opinion states that "It is perhaps possible to imagine an extreme situation where the taxpayers are directly responsible for perpetrating an outrageous abuse of constitutional rights." Does this footnote perhaps leave the door ajar for imposition of punitive liability on appropriate facts?

The *Webster* court referred to footnote 29, but concluded that it was not applicable: "The plight of Randy Webster, however reprehensible, however tragic, does not rise to the level of outrageous conduct to which Justice Blackmun referred." If the facts of *Webster* do not attain the necessary level of outrageousness, what facts would? Or is the problem that the taxpayers of Houston were not "directly responsible" for the misconduct? Was Judge Goldberg right in reading *Fact Concerts* to preclude punitive awards against municipalities no matter what the facts?

3. CORPORATE PUNITIVE LIABILITY: AN ANALOGY

Outside the civil rights context, the most controversial application of punitive damages is against large corporations. The traditional rule is that a defendant's wealth may be taken into account in determining how great a penalty is needed to make it hurt. As a consequence, punitive awards against large corporate defendants may register in the millions. This trend is especially evident in products liability cases, where very large punitive awards for design or marketing of defective products are increasingly common.

In *Fact Concerts* the Court found that punitive damages were inappropriate for municipalities. One reason was the perceived unwisdom and unfairness of visiting retribution "upon the shoulders of blameless or unknowing taxpayers." Another was the Court's belief that punitive awards against individual officials were in any event "a more effective means of deterrence."

Arguably, both of these reasons apply to corporate defendants as well. The burden of punitive awards will ultimately fall on the shareholders. Although they may have benefitted from management's misconduct, they are likely to be "blameless" in the same sense as citizens of a municipality. Similarly, denial of punitive liability against corporations would leave intact the "more effective" deterrent of judgments against individual corporate officers.

Given the similarities of the two contexts, it is ironic that punitive liability flourishes in one area but is precluded in the other. Does the reasoning in *Fact Concerts* suggest that punitive damages should not be available against private corporations? Or does the availability of punitive damages against private corporations suggest that *Fact Concerts* was wrongly decided? Or are the two situations sufficiently different to justify different outcomes?

CHAPTER 2

ATTORNEY'S FEES

1. ENTITLEMENT TO FEES

INTRODUCTORY NOTES ON THE CIVIL RIGHTS ATTORNEYS' FEES AWARDS ACT

1. BACKGROUND ON LEGAL REPRESENTATION IN CIVIL RIGHTS CASES

The cost of litigating a constitutional claim can be substantial, requiring significant fact development, legal research, trial time, and briefing on appeal. In many cases, the potential plaintiff will be an individual or group of modest means who cannot afford to retain a private attorney through the regular market, in which attorneys charge by the hour or set a fixed fee based for handling the case. There are several alternative means of providing counsel.

First, the government might provide lawyers for civil rights claimants the same way that it does for indigent criminal defendants. In Lassiter v. Department of Social Services, 452 U.S. 18 (1981), however, the Supreme Court held that the Constitution does not require the government to provided appointed counsel in civil cases: it found a "presumption that there is a right to appointed counsel only where the indigent, if he is unsuccessful, may lose his personal freedom." The Court observed that the three-part test of Mathews v. Eldridge, 424 U.S. 319 (1976)—a test that assesses due process by looking at the nature of the private interests at stake, the government's interest, and the risk that the procedures used will lead to erroneous decisions—might occasionally require the appointment of counsel, but said that such determinations should usually be made on a case-by-case basis. More recently, in Turner v. Rogers, 131 S.Ct. 2507, the Court held that due process does not automatically require the appointment of counsel in civil cases where an individual faces incarceration. The case before the Court involved a civil contempt proceeding brought by one parent against the other for child support.

Thus, while the government funds various legal services programs that provide aid to indigent individuals, for the most part there is no constitutional requirement that it do so. In fact, legal services programs are statutorily precluded from filing some forms of civil rights litigation. See, e.g., 42 U.S.C. § 2996f(b)(9) (forbidding legal services organizations from using federal legal services funds to litigate any case involving school desegregation). But see Legal Services Corp. v. Velasquez, 531 U.S. 533 (2001) (holding that a federal funding restriction that prevented attorneys representing clients in welfare-related proceedings from challenging the constitutionality of state or federal violates the First Amendment).

Second, one might rely on private attorneys, either voluntarily or through judicial appointment as a condition of admission to the bar, to provide services free of charge or at reduced rates. In Mallard v. United States District Court, 490 U.S. 296 (1989), a federal district court directed Mallard, a recently admitted attorney, to represent indigent inmates in a § 1983 lawsuit against prison officials. Mallard objected to the appointment, and the Supreme Court held that 28 U.S.C. § 1915(d) (now codified as § 1915(e)(1)), which provides that a district court may "request an attorney to represent any person unable to afford counsel," did not authorize it to require an unwilling attorney to represent an indigent litigant in a civil case. While many state rules of professional responsibility follow the American Bar Association's recommendation that attorneys provide some number of hours of pro bono service, see ABA Model Rules of Professional Conduct Rule 6.1 (2004) (suggesting fifty hours of service per year), this recommendation is not an enforceable obligation. See Deborah L. Rhode, Access to Justice 16–18 (2004) (discussing various proposals for mandatory pro bono representation); Esther F. Lardent, Mandatory Pro Bono in Civil Cases: The Wrong Answer to the Right Question, 49 Md. L. Rev. 78 (1990). Whatever the actual amount of pro bono representation, unmet legal needs remain. See Erwin Chemerinsky, Closing the Courthouse Doors to Civil Rights Litigants, 5 U. Pa. J. Const. L. 537 (2003).

Third, civil rights plaintiffs might enter into contingent fee agreements, under which the attorney agrees to represent the plaintiff in return for receiving a portion of any judgment the plaintiff recovers. Contingent-fee arrangements are usual for plaintiffs in a variety of personal-injury cases. Thus, to the extent that civil rights claims involve constitutional torts, civil rights litigation might also be financed this way. The appropriateness of this analogy is discussed later in this Chapter. For now, it is worth observing that many civil rights cases will either produce no monetary recovery (e.g., suits for injunctive relief) or will produce monetary recoveries too small to attract competent counsel given the number of hours of work required to win the case.

Fourth, one might adopt a fee-shifting regime in which the litigation expenses of the winning party are paid by the losing party (whether plaintiff or defendant). This is the so-called "English Rule." While the English Rule might make meritorious civil rights claims more attractive to potential attorneys, it also increases the riskiness of such lawsuits: a plaintiff must consider the costs he or she will be assessed if the lawsuit fails. Particularly in light of the distinctive defenses available in § 1983 lawsuits that may result in plaintiffs losing even if they establish the unconstitutionality of the defendants' conduct (such as qualified immunity), the English Rule might deter, rather than enable, such litigation. Cf. Fleischmann Distilling Co. v. Maier Brewing Co., 386 U.S. 714, 718 (1967) ("In support of the American rule, it has been argued that since litigation is at best uncertain one should not be penalized for merely defending or prosecuting a lawsuit, and that the poor might be unjustly discouraged from instituting actions to vindicate their rights if the penalty for losing included the fees of their opponents' counsel.").

In contrast to the English Rule, the "American Rule" generally requires each party, win or lose, to pay its own attorney. Over time, courts have developed a number of exceptions to the American Rule. Of particular significance, courts began to award prevailing plaintiffs their attorney's fees in cases where the plaintiffs were performing the services of a "private attorney general." The phrase was coined by Judge Jerome Frank in Associated Industries v. Ickes, 134 F.2d 694, 704 (2d Cir. 1943), and courts came to view plaintiffs who established important constitutional principles in the course of vindicating their own legal rights as "having rendered substantial service . . . to the community at large by securing for it the benefits assumed to flow" from the defendant's "compliance with its constitutional mandate." Bradley v. School Bd., 416 U.S. 696, 718 (1974).

Many modern civil rights statutes explicitly authorize attorneys' fees, but courts sometimes awarded fees even without express statutory authorization, relying on their inherent equitable powers. In Alyeska Pipeline Service Co. v. Wildnerness Society, 421 U.S. 240 (1975), the Supreme Court put a stop to this practice, stating that, in light of the traditional reliance on the American Rule, "it would be inappropriate for the judiciary, without legislative guidance, to reallocate the burdens of litigation."

2. THE CIVIL RIGHTS ATTORNEYS' FEES AWARDS ACT

The chief consequence of the *Alyeska Pipeline* was to preclude award of attorney's fees in § 1983 actions. Since attorney's fees were specifically authorized by modern civil rights laws, the disparity seemed anomalous. Congress responded by passing the Civil Rights Attorneys' Fees Awards Act of 1976, now codified in 42 U.S.C. § 1988(b):

> In any action or proceeding to enforce a provision of §§ 1981, 1982, 1983, 1985, and 1986 of this Title, Title IX of Public Law 92–318 [the Education Amendments of 1972, 20 U.S.C. § 1681 et seq.], or Title VI of the Civil Rights Act of 1964 [42 U.S.C. § 2000d et seq.], the court, in its discretion, may allow the prevailing party, other than the United States, a reasonable attorney's fee as part of the costs.

Congress based this statute on analogous provisions in Titles II and VII of the 1964 Civil Rights Act. The legislative history indicates that Congress intended that the standard for awarding fees under these provisions "be generally the same." S. Rep. No. 1011, 94th Cong., 2d Sess., at 3 (1976). This history accounts for two important glosses on the text of the statute.

3. "IN ITS DISCRETION"

The text of § 1988(b) seems to make fee awards discretionary with the court. In fact, award of fees to the successful civil rights plaintiff is required, absent "special circumstances [that] would render such an award unjust." This interpretation comes from Newman v. Piggie Park Enterprises, Inc., 390 U.S. 400 (1968), which found in the 1964 Civil Rights Act a legislative intention routinely to award attorney's fees to prevailing plaintiffs in order to encourage and reward private enforcement of civil rights. *Piggie Park* was specially cited in the legislative history of § 1988(b), and its limitation of judicial discretion is taken to control the application of § 1988(b).

The "special circumstances" that might justify denial of fees to a prevailing plaintiff are not entirely settled, but it is clear that the category is extremely narrow. A survey of Fifth Circuit cases found that none of the following circumstances justified a denial of fees:

> A prevailing party's independent ability to pay counsel; a defendant's good faith; the fact that ultimate responsibility for payment falls on innocent taxpayers or a public or private entity with a limited budget which has already incurred substantial legal expenses; the fact that plaintiff's counsel is court appointed or a salaried attorney with a public interest organization; the fact that more time was spent litigating the issue of fees than the merits; and the fact that the claim is essentially one sounding in tort for

> private monetary damages or outside the ambit of seeking relief for discrimination based on race, sex, or other inherently offensive criteria.

George C. Cochran, Section 1988 Attorney Fee Awards in the Fifth Circuit, 15 Tex. Tech. L. Rev. 1, 19–20 (1984). There seem to be only two circumstances found to justify denial of fees. First, a pro se litigant is not entitled to fees, even if the litigant is also a lawyer. See Kay v. Ehrler, 499 U.S. 432 (1991). The Justices reasoned there that the statutory policy of ensuring successful prosecution of meritorious claims would be enhanced by maintaining the incentive for all plaintiffs, including members of the bar, to retain counsel. Second, there are some cases in which, even though a plaintiff formally prevails, the judgment is so limited relative to the relief originally sought that a court may nonetheless deny the plaintiff fees. See Farrar v. Hobby, 506 U.S. 103 (1992), discussed later in this Chapter. Otherwise, prevailing plaintiffs recover their fees.

4. "PREVAILING PARTY"

Section 1988(b) seems to say that plaintiffs and defendants would be equally entitled to recover fees as a "prevailing party." Such balanced incentives, however, presumably would do little to encourage private enforcement of the civil rights acts. (Indeed, they might actually discourage such enforcement by increasing the risks plaintiffs face.) The literal reading of the statute has therefore been rejected in favor of a differentiation between plaintiffs and defendants. A prevailing plaintiff "should ordinarily recover an attorney's fee unless special circumstances would render such an award unjust." Newman v. Piggie Park Enterprises, Inc., 390 U.S. 400, 402 (1968). A prevailing defendant, by contrast, may recover fees only when the litigation is unreasonable, frivolous, meritless, or vexatious. The term "meritless" has been construed by the Court to mean "groundless or without foundation, rather than [that] the plaintiff has ultimately lost his case." Christiansburg Garment Co. v. Equal Employment Opportunity Commission, 434 U.S. 412, 421 (1978) (involving an unsuccessful charge of racial discrimination in employment in violation of Title VII of the 1964 Civil Rights Act).

The *Christiansburg Garment Co.* opinion explains the basis for distinguishing plaintiffs from defendants under the attorney's fees provision of Title VII:

> [A] moment's reflection reveals that there are at least two strong equitable considerations counseling an attorney's fee award to a prevailing Title VII plaintiff that are wholly absent in the case of a prevailing Title VII defendant.
>
> First as emphasized so forcefully in *Piggie Park,* the plaintiff is the chosen instrument of Congress to vindicate "a policy that Congress considered of the highest priority." Second, when a district court awards counsel fees to a prevailing plaintiff, it is awarding them against a violator of federal law. As the Court of Appeals clearly perceived, "these policy considerations which support the award of fees to a prevailing plaintiff are not present in the case of a prevailing defendant."

This reasoning was adopted for § 1988(b) in Hughes v. Rowe, 449 U.S. 5 (1980).[a] In Fox v. Vice, 131 S.Ct. 2205 (2011), the Court held that in cases involving a mix of frivolous and non-frivolous claims by the plaintiff, § 1988 "allows a defendant to recover reasonable attorney's fees incurred because of, but only because of, a frivolous claim. Or what is the same thing stated as a but-for test: Section 1988 permits the defendant to receive only the portion of his fees that he would not have paid but for the frivolous claim." Thus, "if a frivolous claim occasioned the attorney's fees at issue, a court may decide that the defendant should not have to pay them. But if the defendant would have incurred those fees anyway, to defend against *non*-frivolous claims, then a court has no basis for transferring the expense to the plaintiff."

5. LITIGATION AGAINST FEDERAL DEFENDANTS

Section 1988(b) by its terms applies to lawsuits brought under § 1983 and other specified statutes. None of them covers suits against the United States or federal officers. Attorney's fees in such actions are provided under a different statute, the Equal Access to Justice Act (EAJA), 28 U.S.C. § 2412(d)(1)(A), which authorizes attorney's fees to prevailing parties "other than the United States" in "any civil action (other than cases sounding in tort) . . . brought by or against the United States in any court having jurisdiction of that action. . . . " That provision, however, precludes fee award when "the court finds that the position of the United States was substantially justified or that special circumstances make an award unjust." The standard for awarding fees in cases against the United States is thus more restrictive than the standard for awarding fees under § 1983. The United States has waived its sovereign immunity with respect to claims "seeking relief other than money damages," 5 U.S.C. § 702, and permits actions for declaratory or injunctive relief to be brought either against the United States or against federal officers in their official capacity. Thus, in a lawsuit seeking declaratory or injunctive relief against federal officials, there is a mechanism for prevailing plaintiffs to obtain attorney's fees. But federal courts of appeals have refused to award fees to prevailing plaintiffs in *Bivens* actions—the analogous common-law damages actions against individuals acting under color of federal law—under either the EAJA or § 1988(b) to obtain attorney's fees. See, e.g., Kreines v. United States, 33 F.3d 1105, 1109 (9th Cir. 1994) (explaining that because "Federal agents are sued in their

[a] For a window on the complexities to which the requirement of a "prevailing party" can occasionally give rise, see Hewitt v. Helms, 482 U.S. 755 (1987). Plaintiff was a prisoner who sought damages for allegedly unlawful disciplinary confinement. Ultimately, he was denied monetary relief because of the defendants' immunity, but the court agreed with plaintiff's interpretation of the Constitution. Because the plaintiff had been released from prison in the meantime, however, his claim for prospective relief was dismissed as moot. The state corrections authority nonetheless revised its regulations to cure the defect found by the trial court. Plaintiff then sought attorney's fees, presenting, in the words of Justice Scalia, "the peculiar-sounding question whether a party who litigates to judgment and loses on all of his claims can nonetheless be a 'prevailing party' for purposes of an award of attorney's fees." The Court determined that he could not. Justice Marshall dissented, in an opinion joined by Justices Brennan, Blackmun, and Stevens

For even stranger facts, see Rhodes v. Stewart, 488 U.S. 1 (1988). Two prisoners brought a § 1983 action to gain access to a magazine. The District Court entered a declaratory judgment in their favor, even though one prisoner had died and the other had been released, and then awarded attorney's fees. The Supreme Court reversed, holding that a judgment moot when entered could not create a "prevailing party" for purposes of attorney's fees. Rather, a judgment would "constitute relief, for purposes of § 1988(b), if, and only if, it affects the behavior of the defendant toward the plaintiff." Justices Marshall and Blackmun, joined by Brennan, dissented.

individual capacities rather than their official capacities in *Bivens* actions," these cases are not "civil action[s] . . . against the United States" that trigger an eligibility for fees under the EAJA).

Plainly, a plaintiff who litigates all his or her claims to judgment and wins on all is a prevailing party within the meaning of § 1988(b). The question of who else qualifies as a prevailing party is substantially more complicated.

Buckhannon Board and Care Home v. West Virginia Department of Health and Human Resources

Supreme Court of the United States, 2001.
532 U.S. 598.

■ CHIEF JUSTICE REHNQUIST delivered the opinion of the Court.

Numerous federal statutes allow courts to award attorney's fees and costs to the "prevailing party." The question presented here is whether this term includes a party that has failed to secure a judgment on the merits or a court-ordered consent decree, but has nonetheless achieved the desired result because the lawsuit brought about a voluntary change in the defendant's conduct. We hold that it does not.

Buckhannon Board and Care Home, Inc., which operates care homes that provide assisted living to their residents, failed an inspection by the West Virginia Office of the State Fire Marshal because some of the residents were incapable of "self-preservation" as defined under state law . . . On October 28, 1997, after receiving cease and desist orders requiring the closure of its residential care facilities within 30 days, Buckhannon Board and Care Home, Inc., on behalf of itself and other similarly situated homes and residents (hereinafter petitioners), brought suit in the United States District Court for the Northern District of West Virginia against the State of West Virginia, two of its agencies, and 18 individuals (hereinafter respondents), seeking declaratory and injunctive relief that the "self-preservation" requirement violated the Fair Housing Amendments Act of 1988 (FHAA), 42 U.S.C. §§ 3601 et seq., and the Americans with Disabilities Act of 1990 (ADA), 42 U.S.C. §§ 12101 et seq.

Respondents agreed to stay enforcement of the cease and desist orders pending resolution of the case and the parties began discovery. In 1998, the West Virginia Legislature enacted two bills eliminating the "self-preservation" requirement, and respondents moved to dismiss the case as moot. The District Court granted the motion, finding that the 1998 legislation had eliminated the allegedly offensive provisions and that there was no indication that the West Virginia Legislature would repeal the amendments.

Petitioners requested attorney's fees as the "prevailing party" under the FHAA, 42 U.S.C. § 3613(c)(2) ("The court, in its discretion, may allow the prevailing party . . . a reasonable attorney's fee and costs"), and ADA, 42 U.S.C. § 12205 ("The court . . . , in its discretion, may allow the prevailing party . . . a reasonable attorney's fee, including litigation expenses, and costs"). Petitioners argued that they were entitled to attorney's fees under the "catalyst theory," which posits that a plaintiff is a "prevailing party" if it achieves the desired result because the lawsuit brought about a voluntary change in the defendant's conduct. Although most Courts of Appeals recognize the "catalyst theory," the Court of Appeals for the Fourth Circuit had rejected it [in an earlier case] . . . To resolve the disagreement amongst the Courts of Appeals, we granted certiorari, and now affirm.

In the United States, parties are ordinarily required to bear their own attorney's fees—the prevailing party is not entitled to collect from the loser. See Alyeska Pipeline Service Co. v. Wilderness Society, 421 U.S. 240, 247 (1975). Under this "American Rule," we follow "a general practice of not awarding fees to a prevailing party absent explicit statutory authority." Key Tronic Corp. v. United States, 511 U.S. 809, 819 (1994). Congress, however, has authorized the award of attorney's fees to the "prevailing party" in numerous statutes in addition to those at issue here, such as the Civil Rights Act of 1964, 42 U.S.C. § 2000e–5(k), the Voting Rights Act Amendments of 1975, 42 U.S.C. § 1973l(e), and the Civil Rights Attorney's fees Awards Act of 1976, 42 U.S.C. § 1988.[4]

In designating those parties eligible for an award of litigation costs, Congress employed the term "prevailing party," a legal term of art. Black's Law Dictionary 1145 (7th ed. 1999) defines "prevailing party" as "[a] party in whose favor a judgment is rendered, regardless of the amount of damages awarded. . . . –Also termed *successful party*." This view that a "prevailing party" is one who has been awarded some relief by the court can be distilled from our prior cases.

In Hanrahan v. Hampton, 446 U.S. 754, 758 (1980) (per curiam), we reviewed the legislative history of § 1988 and found that "Congress intended to permit the interim award of counsel fees only when a party has prevailed on the merits of at least some of his claims." Our "respect for ordinary language requires that a plaintiff receive at least some relief on the merits of his claim before he can be said to prevail." Hewitt v. Helms, 482 U.S. 755, 760 (1987). We have held that even an award of nominal damages suffices under this test. See Farrar v. Hobby, 506 U.S. 103 (1992).[6]

In addition to judgments on the merits, we have held that settlement agreements enforced through a consent decree may serve as the basis for an award of attorney's fees. See Maher v. Gagne, 448 U.S. 122 (1980). Although a consent decree does not always include an admission of liability by the defendant, it nonetheless is a court-ordered "change [in] the legal relationship between [the plaintiff] and the defendant." Texas State Teachers Assn. v. Garland Independent School Dist., 489 U.S. 782, 792 (1989).[7] These decisions, taken together, establish that enforceable judgments on the merits and court-ordered consent decrees create the "material alteration of the legal relationship of the parties" necessary to permit an award of attorney's fees. Id. at 792–93.

---

[4] We have interpreted these fee-shifting provisions consistently, see Hensley v. Eckerhart, 461 U.S. 424, 433, n.7 (1983), and so approach the nearly identical provisions at issue here.

[6] However, in some circumstances such a "prevailing party" should still not receive an award of attorney's fees. See *Farrar v. Hobby*, supra, at 115–16.

[7] We have subsequently characterized the *Maher* opinion as also allowing for an award of attorney's fees for private settlements. See *Farrar v. Hobby*, supra, at 111; *Hewitt v. Helms*, supra, at 760. But this dicta ignores that *Maher* only "held that fees *may* be assessed . . . after a case has been settled by the entry of a consent decree." Evans v. Jeff D., 475 U.S. 717, 720 (1986). Private settlements do not entail the judicial approval and oversight involved in consent decrees. And federal jurisdiction to enforce a private contractual settlement will often be lacking unless the terms of the agreement are incorporated into the order of dismissal.

We think, however, the "catalyst theory" falls on the other side of the line from these examples. It allows an award where there is no judicially sanctioned change in the legal relationship of the parties. Even under a limited form of the "catalyst theory," a plaintiff could recover attorney's fees if it established that the "complaint had sufficient merit to withstand a motion to dismiss for lack of jurisdiction or failure to state a claim on which relief may be granted." Brief for United States as Amicus Curiae 27. This is not the type of legal merit that our prior decisions, based upon plain language and congressional intent, have found necessary. . . . A defendant's voluntary change in conduct, although perhaps accomplishing what the plaintiff sought to achieve by the lawsuit, lacks the necessary judicial imprimatur on the change. Our precedents thus counsel against holding that the term "prevailing party" authorizes an award of attorney's fees without a corresponding alteration in the legal relationship of the parties.

. . . We have only awarded attorney's fees where the plaintiff has received a judgment on the merits, see, e.g., *Farrar*, supra, at 112, or obtained a court-ordered consent decree, *Maher*, supra, at 129–30—we have not awarded attorney's fees where the plaintiff has secured the reversal of a directed verdict, see *Hanrahan*, supra, at 759, or acquired a judicial pronouncement that the defendant has violated the Constitution unaccompanied by "*judicial* relief," *Hewitt*, supra, at 760 (emphasis added). Never have we awarded attorney's fees for a nonjudicial "alteration of actual circumstances." While urging an expansion of our precedents on this front, the dissenters would simultaneously abrogate the "merit" requirement of our prior cases and award attorney's fees where the plaintiff's claim "was at least colorable" and "not . . . groundless." We cannot agree that the term "prevailing party" authorizes federal courts to award attorney's fees to a plaintiff who, by simply filing a nonfrivolous but nonetheless potentially meritless lawsuit (it will never be determined), has reached the "sought-after destination" without obtaining any judicial relief.

Petitioners nonetheless argue that the legislative history of the Civil Rights Attorney's Fees Awards Act supports a broad reading of "prevailing party" which includes the "catalyst theory." We doubt that legislative history could overcome what we think is the rather clear meaning of "prevailing party"—the term actually used in the statute. Since we resorted to such history in *Garland*, 489 U.S. at 790, *Maher,* 448 U.S. at 129, and *Hanrahan*, 446 U.S. at 756–57, however, we do likewise here.

The House Report to § 1988 states that "the phrase 'prevailing party' is not intended to be limited to the victor only after entry of a final judgment following a full trial on the merits," H. R. Rep. No. 94–1558, p. 7 (1976), while the Senate Report explains that "parties may be considered to have prevailed when they vindicate rights through a consent judgment or without formally obtaining relief," S. Rep. No. 94–1011, p. 5 (1976). Petitioners argue that these Reports and their reference to a 1970 decision from the Court of Appeals for the Eighth Circuit, Parham v. Southwestern Bell Telephone Co., 433 F.2d 421 (1970), indicate Congress' intent to adopt the "catalyst theory."[9] We think the legislative history cited by petitioners is at

[9] Although the Court of Appeals in *Parham* awarded attorney's fees to the plaintiff because his "lawsuit acted as a catalyst which prompted the [defendant] to take action . . . seeking compliance with the requirements of Title VII," 433 F.2d at 429–30, it did so only after finding that the defendant had acted unlawfully, see id. at 426 ("We hold as a matter of law that [plaintiff's evidence] established a violation of Title VII"). Thus, consistent with our holding in *Farrar*, *Parham* stands for the proposition that an enforceable judgment permits an award of attorney's fees. And like the consent decree in *Maher v. Gagne*, supra, the Court of

best ambiguous as to the availability of the "catalyst theory" for awarding attorney's fees. Particularly in view of the "American Rule" that attorney's fees will not be awarded absent "explicit statutory authority," such legislative history is clearly insufficient to alter the accepted meaning of the statutory term.

Petitioners finally assert that the "catalyst theory" is necessary to prevent defendants from unilaterally mooting an action before judgment in an effort to avoid an award of attorney's fees. They also claim that the rejection of the "catalyst theory" will deter plaintiffs with meritorious but expensive cases from bringing suit. We are skeptical of these assertions, which are entirely speculative and unsupported by any empirical evidence (e.g., whether the number of suits brought in the Fourth Circuit has declined, in relation to other Circuits, since [that court rejected the catalyst theory.]

Petitioners discount the disincentive that the "catalyst theory" may have upon a defendant's decision to voluntarily change its conduct, conduct that may not be illegal. "The defendants' potential liability for fees in this kind of litigation can be as significant as, and sometimes even more significant than, their potential liability on the merits," Evans v. Jeff D., 475 U.S. 717, 734 (1986), and the possibility of being assessed attorney's fees may well deter a defendant from altering its conduct.

And petitioners' fear of mischievous defendants only materializes in claims for equitable relief, for so long as the plaintiff has a cause of action for damages, a defendant's change in conduct will not moot the case. Even then, it is not clear how often courts will find a case mooted: "It is well settled that a defendant's voluntary cessation of a challenged practice does not deprive a federal court of its power to determine the legality of the practice" unless it is "absolutely clear that the allegedly wrongful behavior could not reasonably be expected to recur." Friends of Earth, Inc. v. Laidlaw Environmental Services (TOC), Inc., 528 U.S. 167, 189 (2000). If a case is not found to be moot, and the plaintiff later procures an enforceable judgment, the court may of course award attorney's fees. Given this possibility, a defendant has a strong incentive to enter a settlement agreement, where it can negotiate attorney's fees and costs.

We have also stated that "[a] request for attorney's fees should not result in a second major litigation," Hensley v. Eckerhart, 461 U.S. 424, 437 (1983), and have accordingly avoided an interpretation of the fee-shifting statutes that would have "spawned a second litigation of significant dimension," *Garland*, 489 U.S. at 791. Among other things, a "catalyst theory" hearing would require analysis of the defendant's subjective motivations in changing its conduct, an analysis that "will likely depend on a highly fact-bound inquiry and may turn on reasonable inferences from the nature and timing of the defendant's change in conduct." Brief for United States as Amicus Curiae 28. Although we do not doubt the ability of district courts to perform the nuanced "three thresholds" test required by the "catalyst theory"—whether the claim was colorable rather than groundless; whether the lawsuit was a substantial rather than an insubstantial cause of the defendant's change in conduct; whether the defendant's change in conduct was

---

Appeals in *Parham* ordered the District Court to "retain jurisdiction over the matter for a reasonable period of time to insure the continued implementation of the appellee's policy of equal employment opportunities." 433 F.2d at 429. Clearly *Parham* does not support a theory of fee shifting untethered to a material alteration in the legal relationship of the parties as defined by our precedents.

motivated by the plaintiff's threat of victory rather than threat of expense—it is clearly not a formula for "ready administrability." Burlington v. Dague, 505 U.S. 557, 566 (1992).

Given the clear meaning of "prevailing party" in the fee-shifting statutes, we need not determine which way these various policy arguments cut. In *Alyeska*, 421 U.S. at 260, we said that Congress had not "extended any roving authority to the Judiciary to allow counsel fees as costs or otherwise whenever the courts might deem them warranted." To disregard the clear legislative language and the holdings of our prior cases on the basis of such policy arguments would be a similar assumption of a "roving authority." For the reasons stated above, we hold that the "catalyst theory" is not a permissible basis for the award of attorney's fees under the FHAA, 42 U.S.C. § 3613(c)(2), and ADA, 42 U.S.C. § 12205.

■ JUSTICE SCALIA with whom JUSTICE THOMAS joins, concurring.

I join the opinion of the Court in its entirety, and write to respond at greater length to the contentions of the dissent.

I

"Prevailing party" is not some newfangled legal term invented for use in late–20th–century fee-shifting statutes. . . .

At the time 42 U.S.C. § 1988 was enacted, I know of no case, state or federal, in which—either under a statutory invocation of "prevailing party," or under the common-law rule—the "catalyst theory" was enunciated as the basis for awarding costs. . . . While . . . costs were awarded in actions at law to the "prevailing party," an equity court could award costs "as the equities of the case might require." The other state or state-law cases the dissent cites as awarding costs despite the absence of a judgment all involve a judicial finding—or its equivalent, an acknowledgment by the defendant—of the merits of plaintiff's case. Moreover, the dissent cites not a single case in which this Court—or even any other federal court applying federal law prior to enactment of the fee-shifting statutes at issue here—has regarded as the "prevailing party" a litigant who left the courthouse emptyhanded. If the term means what the dissent contends, that is a remarkable absence of authority.

That a judicial finding of liability was an understood requirement of "prevailing" is confirmed by many statutes that use the phrase in a context that *presumes* the existence of a judicial ruling. See, e.g., 5 U.S.C. § 1221(g)(2) ("if an employee . . . is the prevailing party . . . and the decision is based on a finding of a prohibited personnel practice"); 8 U.S.C. § 1324b(h) (permitting the administrative law judge to award an attorney's fee to the prevailing party "if the losing party's argument is without reasonable foundation in law and fact").

The dissent points out that the Prison Litigation Reform Act of 1995 limits attorney's fees to an amount " 'proportionately related to the court ordered relief for the violation.' " This shows that *sometimes* Congress *does* explicitly "tightly bind fees to judgments," inviting (the dissent believes) the conclusion that "prevailing party" does *not* fasten fees to judgments. That conclusion does not follow from the premise. What this statutory provision demonstrates, *at most*, is that use of the phrase "prevailing party" is not the *only* way to impose a requirement of court-ordered relief. That is assuredly true. But it would be no more rational to reject the normal meaning of "prevailing party" because some statutes produce the same result with different language, than it would be to conclude that, since there are many synonyms for the word "jump," the word "jump" must mean something else.

[W]hen "prevailing party" is used by courts or legislatures in the context of a lawsuit, it is a term of art. It has traditionally—and to my knowledge, prior to enactment of the first of the statutes at issue here, *invariably*—meant the party that wins the suit or obtains a finding (or an admission) of liability. Not the party that ultimately gets his way because his adversary dies before the suit comes to judgment; not the party that gets his way because circumstances so change that a victory on the legal point for the other side turns out to be a practical victory for him; and not the party that gets his way because the other side ceases (for whatever reason) its offensive conduct. If a nuisance suit is mooted because the defendant asphalt plant has gone bankrupt and ceased operations, one would not normally call the plaintiff the prevailing party. And it would make no difference, as far as the propriety of that characterization is concerned, if the plant did not go bankrupt but moved to a new location to avoid the expense of litigation. In one sense the plaintiff would have "prevailed"; but he would not be the prevailing party in the lawsuit. . . .

II

The dissent distorts the term "prevailing party" beyond its normal meaning for policy reasons, but even those seem to me misguided. They rest upon the presumption that the catalyst theory applies when "*the suit's merit* led the defendant to abandon the fray, to switch rather than fight on, to accord plaintiff sooner rather than later the principal redress sought in the complaint," (emphasis added). What the dissent's stretching of the term produces is . . . an award of attorney's fees when the merits of plaintiff's case remain unresolved—when, for all one knows, the defendant only "abandoned the fray" because the cost of litigation—either financial or in terms of public relations—would be too great. In such a case, the plaintiff may have "prevailed" as Webster's defines that term—"gained victory by virtue of strength or superiority." But I doubt it was greater strength in financial resources, or superiority in media manipulation, rather than *superiority in legal merit*, that Congress intended to reward. . . .

It could be argued, perhaps, that insofar as abstract justice is concerned, there is little to choose between the dissent's outcome and the Court's: If the former sometimes rewards the plaintiff with a phony claim (there is no way of knowing), the latter sometimes denies fees to the plaintiff with a solid case whose adversary slinks away on the eve of judgment. But it seems to me the evil of the former far outweighs the evil of the latter. There is all the difference in the world between a rule that denies the extraordinary boon of attorney's fees to some plaintiffs who are no less "deserving" of them than others who receive them, and a rule that causes the law to be the very instrument of wrong—exacting the payment of attorney's fees to the extortionist.

It is true that monetary settlements and consent decrees can be extorted as well, and we have approved the award of attorney's fees in cases resolved through such mechanisms. Our decision that the statute makes plaintiff a "prevailing party" under such circumstances was based entirely on language in a House Report, see *Maher v. Gagne*, 448 U.S. at 129, and if this issue were to arise for the first time today, I doubt whether I would agree with that result. But in the case of court-approved settlements and consent decrees, even if there has been no judicial determination of the merits, the outcome is at least the product of, and bears the sanction of, judicial action *in the lawsuit*. There is at least *some* basis for saying that the party favored by the settlement or decree prevailed *in the suit*. Extending the holding of *Maher* to a case in which no judicial action whatever has been taken stretches the term "prevailing party" (and the potential injustice that *Maher* produces) beyond what the normal meaning of that term in the litigation context can conceivably support. . . .

III

. . . The Court today concludes that a party cannot be deemed to have prevailed, for purposes of fee-shifting statutes such as 42 U.S.C. §§ 1988, 3613(c)(2), unless there has been an enforceable "alteration of the legal relationship of the parties." That is the normal meaning of "prevailing party" in litigation, and there is no proper basis for departing from that normal meaning. Congress is free, of course, to revise these provisions—but it is my guess that if it does so it will not create the sort of inequity that the catalyst theory invites, but will require the court to determine that there was at least a substantial likelihood that the party requesting fees would have prevailed.

■ JUSTICE GINSBURG, with whom JUSTICE STEVENS, JUSTICE SOUTER, and JUSTICE BREYER, join, dissenting.

. . . The Court's insistence that there be a document filed in court—a litigated judgment or court-endorsed settlement—upsets long-prevailing Circuit precedent applicable to scores of federal fee-shifting statutes. The decision allows a defendant to escape a statutory obligation to pay a plaintiff's counsel fees, even though the suit's merit led the defendant to abandon the fray, to switch rather than fight on, to accord plaintiff sooner rather than later the principal redress sought in the complaint. Concomitantly, the Court's constricted definition of "prevailing party," and consequent rejection of the "catalyst theory,"impede access to court for the less well-heeled, and shrink the incentive Congress created for the enforcement of federal law by private attorneys general. . . .

I

[Petitioners' original complaint] sought an immediate order stopping defendants from closing Buckhannon' facilities, injunctive relief permanently barring enforcement of the self-preservation requirement, damages, and attorney's fees. . . .

Less than a month after the District Court found that plaintiffs were entitled to a trial, the West Virginia Legislature repealed the [challenged rule]. Plaintiffs still allege, and seek to prove, that their suit triggered the statutory repeal. After the rule's demise, defendants moved to dismiss the case as moot, and plaintiffs sought attorney's fees as "prevailing parties" under the FHAA, 42 U.S.C. § 613(c)(2), and the ADA, 42 U.S.C. § 2205. . . .

Prior to 1994, every Federal Court of Appeals (except the Federal Circuit, which had not addressed the issue) concluded that plaintiffs in situations like Buckhannon's . . . could obtain a fee award if their suit acted as a "catalyst" for the change they sought, even if they did not obtain a judgment or consent decree. . . .

In 1994, the Fourth Circuit en banc, dividing 6–to–5, broke ranks with its sister courts. The court declared that, in light of Farrar v. Hobby, 506 U.S. 103 (1992), a plaintiff could not become a "prevailing party" without "an enforceable judgment, consent decree, or settlement." As the Court today acknowledges, and as we have previously observed, the language on which the Fourth Circuit relied was dictum: *Farrar* "involved no catalytic effect"; the issue plainly "was not presented for this Court's decision in *Farrar*." Friends of Earth, Inc. v. Laidlaw Environmental Services (TOC), Inc., 528 U.S. 167, 194 (2000). . . .

The array of federal court decisions applying the catalyst rule suggested three conditions necessary to a party's qualification as "prevailing" short of a favorable final judgment or consent decree. A plaintiff first had to show that the defendant provided "some of the benefit sought" by the lawsuit. Under most Circuits' precedents, a plaintiff had to demonstrate as well that the suit stated a genuine claim, i.e., one that was at least "colorable," not "frivolous, unreasonable, or groundless." Plaintiff finally had to establish that her suit was a "substantial" or "significant" cause of defendant's action providing relief. In some Circuits, to make this causation showing, plaintiff had to satisfy the trial court that the suit achieved results "by threat of victory," not "by dint of nuisance and threat of expense.". . . .

II

. . . The Court today detects a "clear meaning" of the term prevailing party that has heretofore eluded the large majority of courts construing those words. "Prevailing party," today's opinion announces, means "one who has been awarded some relief by the court." The Court derives this "clear meaning" principally from Black's Law Dictionary, which defines a "prevailing party," in critical part, as one "in whose favor a judgment is rendered" (quoting Black's Law Dictionary 1145 (7th ed. 1999)).

One can entirely agree with Black's Law Dictionary that a party "in whose favor a judgment is rendered" prevails, and at the same time resist, as most Courts of Appeals have, any implication that *only* such a party may prevail. . . . Notably, this Court did not refer to Black's Law Dictionary in Maher v. Gagne, 448 U.S. 122 (1980), which held that a consent decree could qualify a plaintiff as "prevailing." The Court explained:

> The fact that [plaintiff] prevailed through a settlement rather than through litigation does not weaken her claim to fees. Nothing in the language of [42 U.S.C.] § 1988 conditions the District Court's power to award fees on full litigation of the issues or on a judicial determination that the plaintiff's rights have been violated.

The spare "prevailing party" language of the fee-shifting provision applicable in *Maher*, and the similar wording of the fee-shifting provisions now before the Court, contrast with prescriptions that so tightly bind fees to judgments as to exclude the application of a catalyst concept. The Prison Litigation Reform Act of 1995, for example, directs that fee awards to prisoners under § 1988 be "proportionately related to the *court ordered relief* for the violation." 42 U.S.C. § 1997e(d)(1)(B)(i) (1994 ed., Supp. IV) (emphasis added). That statute, by its express terms, forecloses an award to a prisoner on a catalyst theory. But the FHAA and ADA fee-shifting prescriptions, modeled on 42 U.S.C. § 1988 unmodified, do not similarly staple fee awards to "court ordered relief." Their very terms do not foreclose a catalyst theory.

. . .

Recognizing that no practice set in stone, statute, rule, or precedent dictates the proper construction of modern civil rights fee-shifting prescriptions, I would "assume . . . that Congress intends the words in its enactments to carry 'their ordinary, contemporary, common meaning.' " In everyday use, "prevail" means "gain victory by virtue of strength or superiority: win mastery: triumph." Webster's Third New International Dictionary 1797 (1976). There are undoubtedly situations in which an individual's goal is to obtain approval of a judge, and in those situations, one cannot "prevail" short of a judge's formal declaration. In a piano competition or a figure skating contest, for example, the person who prevails is the person declared winner by the judges. However, where the ultimate goal is not an arbiter's approval, but a favorable alteration of actual circumstances, a formal declaration is not essential. Western democracies, for instance, "prevailed" in the Cold War even though the Soviet Union never formally surrendered. Among television viewers, John F. Kennedy "prevailed" in the first debate with Richard M. Nixon during the 1960 Presidential contest, even though moderator Howard K. Smith never declared a winner. See T. White, The Making of the President 1960, pp. 293–94 (1961).

A lawsuit's ultimate purpose is to achieve actual relief from an opponent. Favorable judgment may be instrumental in gaining that relief. Generally, however, "the judicial decree is not the end but the means. At the end of the rainbow lies not a judgment, but some action (or cessation of action) by the defendant. . . . " Hewitt v. Helms, 482 U.S. 755, 761 (1987). On this common understanding, if a party reaches the "sought-after destination," then the party "prevails" regardless of the "route taken." Hennigan v. Ouachita Parish School Bd., 749 F.2d 1148, 1153 (5th Cir. 1985).

Under a fair reading of the FHAA and ADA provisions in point, I would hold that a party "prevails" in "a true and proper sense" when she achieves, by instituting litigation, the practical relief sought in her complaint. . . .

III

As the Courts of Appeals have long recognized, the catalyst rule suitably advances Congress' endeavor to place private actions, in civil rights and other legislatively defined areas, securely within the federal law enforcement arsenal. . . .

Under the catalyst rule that held sway until today, plaintiffs who obtained the relief they sought through suit on genuine claims ordinarily qualified as "prevailing parties," so that courts had discretion to award them their costs and fees. Persons with limited resources were not impelled to "wage total law" in order to assure that their counsel fees would be paid. They could accept relief, in money or of another kind, voluntarily proffered by a defendant who sought to avoid a recorded decree. And they could rely on a judge then to determine, in her equitable discretion, whether counsel fees were warranted and, if so, in what amount.[10]

Congress appears to have envisioned that very prospect. The Senate Report on the 1976 Civil Rights Attorney's Fees Awards Act states: "For purposes of the award of counsel fees, parties may be considered to have prevailed when they vindicate rights through a consent judgment or *without formally obtaining relief.*" S. Rep. No. 94–1011, at 5 (emphasis added).

---

[10] Given the protection furnished by the catalyst rule, aggrieved individuals were not left to worry, and wrongdoers were not led to believe, that strategic maneuvers by defendants might succeed in averting a fee award. Apt here is Judge Friendly's observation construing a fee-shifting statute kin to the provisions before us: "Congress clearly did not mean that where a [Freedom of Information Act] suit had gone to trial and developments have made it apparent that the judge was about to rule for the plaintiff, the Government could abort any award of attorney fees by an eleventh hour tender of information." Vermont Low Income Advocacy Council v. Usery, 546 F.2d 509, 513 (2d Cir. 1976) (interpreting 5 U.S.C. § 552(a)(4)(E), allowing a complainant who "substantially prevails" to earn an attorney's fee).

In support, the Report cites cases in which parties recovered fees in the absence of any court-conferred relief. The House Report corroborates: "After a complaint is filed, a defendant might voluntarily cease the unlawful practice. *A court should still award fees* even though it might conclude, as a matter of equity, that *no formal relief*, such as an injunction, is needed." H. R. Rep. No. 94–1558, at 7 (emphases added). These Reports . . . are hardly ambiguous. . . . Congress, I am convinced, understood that " 'victory' in a civil rights suit is typically a practical, rather than a strictly legal matter." Exeter–West Greenwich Regional School Dist. v. Pontarelli, 788 F.2d 47, 51 (1st Cir. 1986) (citation omitted).

The Court features a case cited by the House as well as the Senate in the Reports on § 1988, Parham v. Southwestern Bell Tel. Co., 433 F.2d 421 (8th Cir. 1970). The Court deems *Parham* consistent with its rejection of the catalyst rule, alternately because the Eighth Circuit made a "finding that the defendant had acted unlawfully," and because that court ordered the District Court to " 'retain jurisdiction over the matter . . . to insure the continued implementation of the [defendant's] policy of equal employment opportunities.' " Congress did not fix on those factors, however: Nothing in either Report suggests that judicial findings or retention of jurisdiction is essential to an award of fees. . . .

IV

The Court identifies several "policy arguments" that might warrant rejection of the catalyst rule. A defendant might refrain from altering its conduct, fearing liability for fees as the price of voluntary action. Moreover, rejection of the catalyst rule has limited impact: Desisting from the challenged conduct will not render a case moot where damages are sought, and even when the plaintiff seeks only equitable relief, a defendant's voluntary cessation of a challenged practice does not render the case moot "unless it is 'absolutely clear that the allegedly wrongful behavior could not reasonably be expected to recur' " (quoting *Friends of Earth, Inc.*, 528 U.S. at 189). Because a mootness dismissal is not easily achieved, the defendant may be impelled to settle, negotiating fees less generous than a court might award. Finally, a catalyst rule would "require analysis of the defendant's subjective motivations," and thus protract the litigation.

The Court declines to look beneath the surface of these arguments, placing its reliance, instead, on a meaning of "prevailing party" that other jurists would scarcely recognize as plain. Had the Court inspected the "policy arguments" listed in its opinion, I doubt it would have found them impressive.

In opposition to the argument that defendants will resist change in order to stave off an award of fees, one could urge that the catalyst rule may lead defendants promptly to comply with the law's requirements: the longer the litigation, the larger the fees. Indeed, one who knows noncompliance will be expensive might be encouraged to conform his conduct to the legal requirements before litigation is threatened. No doubt, a mootness dismissal is unlikely when recurrence of the controversy is under the defendant's control. But, as earlier observed, why should this Court's fee-shifting rulings drive a plaintiff prepared to accept adequate relief, though out-of-court and unrecorded, to litigate on and on? And if the catalyst rule leads defendants to negotiate not only settlement terms but also allied counsel fees, is that not a consummation to applaud, not deplore?

As to the burden on the court, is it not the norm for the judge to whom the case has been assigned to resolve fee disputes (deciding whether an award is in order, and if it is, the amount due), thereby clearing the case from the calendar? If factfinding becomes necessary under the catalyst rule, is it not the sort that "the district courts, in their factfinding expertise, deal with on a regular basis"? Might not one conclude overall, as Courts of Appeals have suggested, that the catalyst rule "saves judicial resources," by encouraging "plaintiffs to discontinue litigation after receiving through the defendant's acquiescence the remedy initially sought"?

The concurring opinion adds another argument against the catalyst rule: That opinion sees the rule as accommodating the "extortionist" who obtains relief because of "greater strength in financial resources, or superiority in media manipulation, rather than superiority in legal merit." This concern overlooks both the character of the rule and the judicial superintendence Congress ordered for all fee allowances. The catalyst rule was auxiliary to fee-shifting statutes whose primary purpose is "to promote the vigorous enforcement" of the civil rights laws. *Christiansburg Garment Co.*, 434 U.S. at 422. To that end, courts deemed the conduct-altering catalyst that counted to be the substance of the case, not merely the plaintiff's atypically superior financial resources, media ties, or political clout. And Congress assigned responsibility for awarding fees not to automatons unable to recognize extoritionists, but to judges expected and instructed to exercise "discretion." So viewed, the catalyst rule provided no berth for nuisance suits or "thinly disguised forms of extortion," Tyler v. Corner Constr. Corp., 167 F.3d 1202, 1206 (8th Cir. 1999) (citation omitted).[12]

V

As to our attorney fee precedents, the Court correctly observes, "we have never had occasion to decide whether the term 'prevailing party' allows an award of fees under the 'catalyst theory,' " and "there is language in our cases supporting both petitioners and respondents." It bears emphasis, however, that in determining whether fee shifting is in order, the Court in the past has placed greatest weight not on any "judicial *imprimatur*," but on the practical impact of the lawsuit.[13] In *Maher v. Gagne*, supra, in which the Court held fees could be awarded on the basis of a consent decree, the opinion nowhere relied on the presence of a formal judgment. Some years later, in *Hewitt v. Helms*, supra, the Court suggested that fees might be awarded the plaintiff who "obtained relief without [the] benefit of a formal judgment." 482 U.S. at 760. The Court explained: "If the defendant, under the pressure of the lawsuit, pays over a money claim before the judicial judgment is pronounced," or "if the defendant, under pressure of [a suit for declaratory judgment], alters his conduct (or threatened conduct) towards

[12] . . . The concurring opinion . . . states that a prevailing party must obtain relief "*in the lawsuit*." One can demur to that elaboration of the statutory text and still adhere to the catalyst rule. Under the rule, plaintiff's suit raising genuine issues must trigger the defendant's voluntary action; plaintiff will not prevail under the rule if defendant "ceases . . . [his] offensive conduct" by dying or going bankrupt. A behavior-altering event like dying or bankruptcy occurs outside the lawsuit; a change precipitated by the lawsuit's claims and demand for relief is an occurrence brought about "through" or "in" the suit.

[13] To qualify for fees in any case, we have held, relief must be real. See Rhodes v. Stewart, 488 U.S. 1, 4 (1988) (per curiam) (a plaintiff who obtains a formal declaratory judgment, but gains no real "relief whatsoever," is not a "prevailing party" eligible for fees); *Hewitt v. Helms*, 482 U.S. at 761 (an interlocutory decision reversing a dismissal for failure to state a claim, although stating that plaintiff's rights were violated, does not entitle plaintiff to fees; to "prevail," plaintiff must gain relief of "substance," i.e., more than a favorable "judicial statement that does not affect the relationship between the plaintiff and the defendant").

the plaintiff," i.e., conduct "that was the basis for the suit, the plaintiff will have prevailed." I agree, and would apply that analysis to this case.

The Court posits a " 'merit' requirement of our prior cases." *Maher*, however, affirmed an award of attorney's fees based on a consent decree that "did not purport to adjudicate [plaintiff's] statutory or constitutional claims." 448 U.S. at 126 n.8. The decree in *Maher* "explicitly stated that 'nothing [therein was] intended to constitute an admission of fault by either party.' " Ibid. The catalyst rule, in short, conflicts with none of "our prior *holdings*."[14]

* * *

The Court states that the term "prevailing party" in fee-shifting statutes has an "accepted meaning." If that is so, the "accepted meaning" is not the one the Court today announces. It is, instead, the meaning accepted by every Court of Appeals to address the catalyst issue before our 1987 decision in *Hewitt*, and disavowed since then only by the Fourth Circuit. A plaintiff prevails, federal judges have overwhelmingly agreed, when a litigated judgment, consent decree, out-of-court settlement, or the defendant's voluntary, postcomplaint payment or change in conduct in fact affords redress for the plaintiff's substantial grievances.

When this Court rejects the considered judgment prevailing in the Circuits, respect for our colleagues demands a cogent explanation. Today's decision does not provide one. The Court's narrow construction of the words "prevailing party" is unsupported by precedent and unaided by history or logic. Congress prescribed fee-shifting provisions like those included in the FHAA and ADA to encourage private enforcement of laws designed to advance civil rights. Fidelity to that purpose calls for court-awarded fees when a private party's lawsuit, whether or not its settlement is registered

---

[14] The Court repeatedly quotes passages from *Hanrahan v. Hampton*, 446 U.S. at 757–58, stating that to "prevail," plaintiffs must receive relief "on the merits." Nothing in *Hanrahan*, however, declares that relief "on the merits" requires a "judicial imprimatur." As the Court acknowledges, *Hanrahan* concerned an interim award of fees, after plaintiff succeeded in obtaining nothing more than reversal of a directed verdict. At that juncture, plaintiff had obtained no change in defendant's behavior, and the suit's ultimate winner remained undetermined. There is simply no inconsistency between *Hanrahan*, denying fees when a plaintiff might yet obtain no real benefit, and the catalyst rule, allowing fees when a plaintiff obtains the practical result she sought in suing. Indeed, the harmony between the catalyst rule and *Hanrahan* is suggested by *Hanrahan* itself; like Maher v. Gagne, 448 U.S. 122, 129 (1980), *Hanrahan* quoted the Senate Report recognizing that parties may prevail "through a consent judgment *or* without formally obtaining relief." 446 U.S. at 757 (quoting S. Rep. No. 94–1011, at 5) (emphasis added). *Hanrahan* also selected for citation the influential elaboration of the catalyst rule in *Nadeau v. Helgemoe*, 581 F.2d at 279–81. See 446 U.S. at 757.

The Court additionally cites Texas State Teachers Assn. v. Garland Independent School Dist., 489 U.S. 782 (1989), which held, unanimously, that a plaintiff could become a "prevailing party" without obtaining relief on the "central issue in the suit." Id. at 790. *Texas State Teachers* linked fee awards to a "material alteration of the legal relationship of the parties," id. at 792–93, but did not say, as the Court does today, that the change must be "court-ordered." The parties' legal relationship does change when the defendant stops engaging in the conduct that furnishes the basis for plaintiff's civil action, and that action, which both parties would otherwise have litigated, is dismissed.

The decision with language most unfavorable to the catalyst rule, Farrar v. Hobby, 506 U.S. 103 (1992), does not figure prominently in the Court's opinion—and for good reason, for *Farrar* "involved no catalytic effect." *Farrar* held that a plaintiff who sought damages of $17 million, but received damages of $1, was a "prevailing party" nonetheless not entitled to fees. 506 U.S. at 113–16. In reinforcing the link between the right to a fee award and the "degree of success obtained," id. at 114 (quoting *Hensley v. Eckerhart*, 461 U.S. at 436), *Farrar*'s holding is consistent with the catalyst rule.

in court, vindicates rights Congress sought to secure. I would so hold and therefore dissent from the judgment and opinion of the Court.

NOTES ON THE MEANING OF "PREVAILING PARTY"

1. QUESTIONS AND COMMENTS ON *BUCKHANNON HOME*

Prior to the Court's decision in *Buckhannon Home*, every court of appeals except the Fourth Circuit had approved the award of fees based on a catalyst theory, beginning with the First Circuit in Nadeau v. Helgemoe, 581 F.2d 275 (1st Cir. 1978). See Robin Stanley, Note, *Buckhannon Board* and *Care Home, Inc. v. West Virginia Department of Health and Human Resources*: To the Prevailing Party Goes the Spoils . . . and the Attorney's Fees!, 36 Akron L. Rev. 363, 376–77 (2003) (collecting cases). *Buckhannon Home* thus marked a major change in the law regarding attorney's fees.

The Supreme Court's opinion leaves unsettled precisely what constitutes sufficient judicial imprimatur to entitle a plaintiff to attorneys' fees, and the lower courts have differed on that subject. At one end of the spectrum, the Ninth Circuit held that a paraplegic athletic coach who challenged the defendants' refusal to allow him to perform his coaching duties and who voluntarily dismissed his case as part of a settlement agreement allowing him to resume coaching, was a prevailing party entitled to fees. See Barrios v. California Interscholastic Federation, 277 F.3d 1128 (9th Cir. 2002). The Ninth Circuit distinguished *Buckhannon* on the ground that Barrios "does not claim to be a 'prevailing party' simply by virtue of his being a catalyst of policy change; rather, his settlement agreement affords him a legally enforceable instrument." It described *Buckhannon Home*'s reference to court-supervised consent decrees as "dictum." See also Carbonell v. INS, 429 F.3d 894 (9th Cir. 2005) (holding that as long as a plaintiff's lawsuit achieves some change in the legal relationship between the parties, he may be entitled to fees, even if that legal change is not embodied in a formal consent decree). By contrast, the Eighth Circuit stated in Christina A. v. Bloomberg, 315 F.3d 990 (8th Cir. 2003), that if the agreement between the plaintiff and the defendant is a "private settlement" rather than a "settlement agreement[] enforced through a consent decree," it is "clear from *Buckhannon*" that the plaintiff "is not a 'prevailing party' entitled to attorney's fees under 42 U.S.C. 1988." A number of other courts have taken a middle position, undertaking a case-specific analysis of whether the settlement agreement bears sufficient judicial imprimatur. See Matthew B. Tenney, Comment, When Does a Party Prevail?: A Proposed "Third Circuit–Plus" Test for Judicial Imprimatur, 2005 B.Y.U. L. Rev. 429, 453–55. The Supreme Court has reaffirmed that even an injunction that "merely 'order[s] [d]efendants to comply with the law' " in situations where their past conduct violated the Constitution normally will have "worked the requisite material alteration in the parties' relationship" that triggers an entitlement to fees. Lefemine v. Wideman, 133 S.Ct. 9 (per curiam).

2. PLAINTIFFS WHO OBTAIN PRELIMINARY SUCCESS: *SOLE V. WYNER*

For a plaintiff to be a prevailing party, the plaintiff must do more than obtain success at some stage of the litigation. Thus, for example, although a § 1983 plaintiff seeking damages may successfully establish the unconstitutionality of a government official's conduct, thereby creating precedent that will change official behavior, she will not be entitled to attorney's fees in a damages action if the defendant is protected against award of damages by qualified immunity. Compare Pamela S. Karlan, The Paradoxical Structure of Constitutional Litigation, 75 Fordham L. Rev. 1913, 1926 (2007) (suggesting that perhaps "qualified immunity doctrine should be recast" to enable plaintiffs who prevail on the first issue but lose on the second to receive attorney's fees as prevailing parties), with James E. Pfander, Resolving the Qualified Immunity Dilemma: Constitutional Tort Claims for Nominal Damages, 111 Colum. L. Rev. 1601, 1607 (2011) (suggesting the creation of a nominal damages action free of immunity and attorney's fees to obtain determination of constitutional claims) and Camreta v. Greene, 131 S.Ct. 2020 (2011) (Kennedy, J., dissenting) (raising a similar suggestion).

In Sole v. Wyner, 551 U.S. 74 (2007), the Court clarified that a litigant "who achieves a transient victory at the threshold of an action can gain no award under [§ 1988] if, at the end of the litigation, her initial success is undone and she leaves the courthouse emptyhanded." The plaintiff in that case sued Florida state park officials who threatened to prevent her from creating an antiwar artwork consisting of naked people "assembled into a peace sign" on a state beach for Valentine's Day. The day after her complaint seeking preliminary and permanent injunctive relief was filed, the District Court granted a preliminary injunction suggesting that a curtain or screen, rather than an outright ban on public nudity, would be sufficient. The peace symbol display took place the next day. A year later, after discovery and a hearing, the District Court refused to issue a permanent injunction and granted the defendants' motion for summary final judgment. Nonetheless, the District Court held that because the plaintiff had obtained a preliminary injunction whose issuance could not be revisited, she qualified as a prevailing party entitled to fees for the first phase of the litigation. The Court of Appeals affirmed, reasoning that the plaintiff had obtained the ability to create her artwork.

The Supreme Court unanimously reversed. The plaintiff's "fleeting success" in obtaining a preliminary injunction was inadequate because prevailing party status "does not attend achievement of a preliminary injunction that is reversed, dissolved, or otherwise undone by the final decision in the same case." In this case, "the eventual ruling on the merits for defendants, after both sides considered the case fit for final adjudication, superseded the preliminary ruling. . . . At the end of the fray, Florida's Bathing Suit Rule remained intact, and Wyner had gained no enduring 'chang[e] [in] the legal relationship' between herself and the state officials she sued." The Court "express[ed] no view on whether, in the absence of a final decision on the merits of a claim for permanent injunctive relief, success in gaining a preliminary injunction may sometimes warrant an award of counsel fees." Courts of appeals have addressed that question and come to varying conclusions based on the circumstances of the individual case. See, e.g., Singer Mgmt. Consultants, Inc. v. Milgram, 650 F.3d 223, 224 (3d Cir.) (en banc) (holding that a party that obtains a temporary restraining order but gets no additional relief "because the opposing party's voluntary change of position moots the case" is not a prevailing party for purpose of fees); Dearmore v. City of Garland, 519 F.3d 517, 524 (5th Cir. 2008) (holding that plaintiffs can be entitled to fees when they (1) "win a preliminary injunction, (2) based upon an unambiguous indication of probable success on the merits of the plaintiff's claims as opposed to a mere balancing of the equities in favor of the plaintiff, (3) that causes the defendant to moot the action, which prevents the plaintiff from obtaining final relief on the merits"; under those circumstances, *Buckhannon* poses no obstacle because "this test grants prevailing party status only when the defendant moots the plaintiff's action in response to a court order, not just in response to the filing of a lawsuit").

3. PLAINTIFFS WHO OBTAIN SUCCESS PRIOR TO FORMAL LITIGATION: NORTH CAROLINA DEPT. OF TRANSPORTATION V. CREST ST. COMMUNITY COUNCIL

Sometimes, an attorney will best represent his or her client by pursuing various administrative avenues before filing suit, even though § 1983 does not require administrative exhaustion. Suppose the desired relief is obtained in the administrative process. Is the client then entitled to attorneys' fees?

In North Carolina Dept. of Transportation v. Crest St. Community Council, Inc., 479 U.S. 6 (1986), the Supreme Court said "no." The case involved a proposed highway through a black neighborhood in Durham, North Carolina. A community group claimed that the routing decision violated Title VI of the 1964 Civil Rights Act, 42 U.S.C. § 2000d. That statute forbids racial discrimination in any federally funded program or activity and authorizes the cut-off of federal funds as a sanction. The statute also has been construed to create a private right of action, and such lawsuits are among the civil rights actions for which attorney's fees are authorized under 42 U.S.C. § 1988(b).

The community group took their complaint to the United States Department of Transportation, which, after investigation, advised the North Carolina agency that there was "reasonable cause" to believe that the proposed highway location would violate Title VI. Ensuing discussions resulted in modification of the plan and a settlement accepted by all parties.

The dispute lasted for some five years, and the lawyer for the community group spent more than 12,000 hours on the project. According to the Supreme Court, "[t]he result of this diligent labor was both substantial and concrete." Nonetheless, the Court barred the group's effort to collect attorney's fees. Speaking through Justice O'Connor, the Court reasoned that § 1988(b) authorized fees only in an "action or proceeding to enforce" the listed civil rights laws. Here there had been no judicial complaint filed on the underlying civil rights claim; the independent action brought to collect the fees did not qualify.

The Court recognized that dicta in some earlier decisions had suggested that it would be anomalous to award fees only when the dispute leads to litigation, but concluded that "the paradoxical nature of this result may have been exaggerated":

> There are many types of behavior that may lead others to comply with civil rights laws. For example, an employee, after talking to his lawyer, may choose to discuss hiring or promotion practices with an employer, and as a result of this discussion the employer may alter those practices to comply more fully with employment discrimination laws. In some sense it may be considered anomalous that this employee's initiative would not be awarded with attorney's fees. But an award of attorney's fees under § 1988(b) depends not only on results obtained, but also on what actions were needed to obtain those results. It is entirely reasonable to limit the award of attorney's fees to those parties who, in order to obtain relief, found it necessary to file a complaint in court.

The Court also rejected the suggestion that "today's holding would create an incentive to file protective lawsuits in order to obtain attorney's fees":

> [W]e think that the better view was expressed by our conclusion in Webb v. Dyer County Board of Education, 471 U.S. 234 (1985), that "competent counsel will be motivated by the interests of the client to pursue . . . administrative remedies when they are available and counsel believes that they may prove successful." An interpretation of § 1988(b) cannot be based on the assumption that "an attorney would advise the client to forgo an available avenue of relief solely because § 1988(b) does not provide for attorney fees. . . . " Moreover, our holding creates a legitimate incentive for potential civil rights defendants to resolve disputes expeditiously, rather than risk the attorney's fees liability connected to civil rights litigation.

Justice Brennan, joined by Justices Marshall and Blackmun, dissented. "What today's holding ensures," he said, "is that no challenge brought under a statute covered by § 1988(b) will ever be settled without a court action." Brennan also spelled out the extent to which *Crest St. Council* had gone beyond *Webb:*

> In Webb v. Dyer County Board of Education, 471 U.S. 234 (1985), the Court held that § 1988(b) does not mandate an automatic award of fees to a civil rights claimant who prevails in an administrative proceeding. Specifically, the Court required that the proceeding involved be one "to enforce" the underlying civil rights statute. But here the Court has not determined whether the administrative scheme promulgated by the United States Department of Transportation is a "proceeding to enforce . . . Title VI." Instead, the Court sweeps aside the possibility of fees in *any* administrative proceeding—whether mandatory or optional, whether integral or peripheral to an enforcement scheme—unless the complainant files a concurrent lawsuit alleging the same civil rights violations. Unless such a complaint is filed in court, success at the administrative level automatically precludes any subsequent action for fees.

The lesson for civil rights lawyers, said Brennan, was "that they must file a civil lawsuit to have any hope of obtaining attorney's fees upon prevailing in an administrative enforcement proceeding." This, he said, will place a "pointless burden" on federal district courts, particularly in cases where claimants are "unfettered by a requirement that they exhaust administrative remedies" prior to filing such a suit.

4. NOMINAL SUCCESS: *FARRAR V. HOBBY*

There may be some cases in which, even though a plaintiff formally prevails, the judgment is so limited relative to the relief originally sought that a court may nonetheless deny the plaintiff fees. In Farrar v. Hobby, 506 U.S. 103 (1992), the Supreme Court confronted such a case.

Joseph Farrar ran a school for delinquent, disabled, and disturbed teens. When one of his students died, he was indicted for willful failure to provide medical care, and his school was shut down by the state of Texas. Farrar then sued several state officials, including Lieutenant Governor William P. Hobby, Jr., for conspiring to deprive him of liberty and property without due process of law. He sought $17 million in damages.

After ten years of litigation, a jury determined that the defendants had acted unlawfully but that their acts had not been the proximate cause of any injury to Farrar. Accordingly, the court entered an order that the plaintiffs, who by this time were the administrators of Farrar's estate, "take nothing, that the action be dismissed on the merits, and that the parties bear their own costs." The Fifth Circuit reversed that ruling as to Hobby, holding that under Carey v. Piphus, 435 U.S. 247 (1978), the plaintiffs were entitled to nominal damages ($1) for any violation of due process rights, even without proof of actual injury. Armed with this "victory," plaintiffs then sought attorney's fees under § 1988(b) and were awarded more than $300,000 in fees and expenses.

In reviewing this award, the Supreme Court reached seemingly contradictory conclusions. On the one hand, the Court said the plaintiffs were "prevailing parties" under § 1988(b). Speaking through Justice Thomas, the Court decided that even nominal damages worked a "material alteration of the legal relationship of the parties," since they could be enforced in court. On the other hand, the Court decided that the only appropriate fee award in this case was nothing:

> Once civil rights litigation materially alters the legal relationship between the parties, "the degree of the plaintiff's overall success goes to the reasonableness" of a fee award under Hensley v. Eckerhart, 461 U.S. 424 (1983). Indeed, "the most critical factor" in determining the reasonableness of a fee award "is the degree of success obtained." *Hensley*, supra, at 436. In this case, petitioners received nominal damages instead of the $17 million in compensatory damages that they sought. . . .
>
> In some circumstances, even a plaintiff who formally "prevails" under § 1988(b) should receive no attorney's fees at all. A plaintiff who seeks compensatory damages but receives no more than nominal damages is often such a prevailing party. As we have held, a nominal damages award does render a plaintiff a prevailing party by allowing him to vindicate his "absolute" right to procedural due process through enforcement of a judgment against the defendant. *Carey v. Piphus*, supra, at 266. In a civil rights suit for damages, however, the awarding of nominal damages also highlights the plaintiff's failure to prove actual, compensable injury. . . . When a plaintiff recovers only nominal damages because of his failure to prove an essential element of his claim for monetary relief, the only reasonable fee is usually no fee at all.

Justice O'Connor concurred. She saw the plaintiff's success as "purely technical or de minimis." She argued that the litigation had served no public purpose and recovering one dollar from one defendant after ten years of litigation was "simply not the type of victory that merits an award of attorney's fees."

Justice White, joined by Justices Blackmun, Stevens, and Souter, dissented in part. He agreed with the Court that Farrar was a "prevailing party" under § 1988(b) but implied that the award of more than $300,000 in fees and expenses might be error "as a matter of law." White argued, however, that the issue of the amount of a reasonable fee under these circumstances should be remanded for reconsideration by the District Court.[a]

---

[a] On the aftermath of this decision, see Note, The Catalyst Theory of Civil Rights Fee Shifting After *Farrar v. Hobby*, 80 Va. L. Rev. 1429 (1994).

The broader question whether the degree of a prevailing party's success should influence the amount of fee awards generally is considered more fully in the next section.

2. DETERMINING FEE AWARDS

City of Riverside v. Rivera

Supreme Court of the United States, 1986.
477 U.S. 561.

■ JUSTICE BRENNAN announced the judgment of the Court and delivered an opinion in which JUSTICE MARSHALL, JUSTICE BLACKMUN, and JUSTICE STEVENS join.

The issue presented in this case is whether an award of attorney's fees under 42 U.S.C. § 1988[a] is per se "unreasonable" within the meaning of the statute if it exceeds the amount of damages recovered by the plaintiff in the underlying civil rights action.

I

Respondents, eight Chicano individuals, attended a party on the evening of August 1, 1975, at the Riverside, California, home of respondents Santos and Jennie Rivera. A large number of unidentified police officers, acting without a warrant, broke up the party using tear gas and, as found by the District Court, "unnecessary physical force." Many of the guests, including four of the respondents, were arrested. The District Court later found that "[t]he party was not creating a disturbance in the community at the time of the break-in." Criminal charges against the arrestees were ultimately dismissed for lack of probable cause.

On June 4, 1976, respondents sued the City of Riverside, its chief of police, and 30 individual police officers under 42 U.S.C. §§ 1981, 1983, 1985(3), and 1986 for allegedly violating their First, Fourth, and Fourteenth Amendment rights. The complaint, which also alleged numerous state-law claims, sought damages, and declaratory and injunctive relief. On August 5, 1977, 23 of the individual police officers moved for summary judgment; the District Court granted summary judgment in favor of 17 of these officers. The case against the remaining defendants proceeded to trial in September 1980. The jury returned a total of 37 individual verdicts in favor of the respondents and against the city and five individual officers, finding 11 violations of § 1983, four instances of false arrest and imprisonment, and 22 instances of negligence. Respondents were awarded $33,350 in compensatory and punitive damages: $13,300 for their federal claims, and $20,050 for their state-law claims.[1]

---

[a] The Court's reference was to the portion of 42 U.S.C. § 1988 that has since been renumbered as § 1988(b). Subsequent citations by the Court to § 1988 have been replaced by § 1988(b).—[Footnote by eds.]

[1] Counsel for respondents explained to the District Court that respondents had not pursued their request for injunctive relief because "the bottom line of what we would ask for is that the police officers obey the law. And that is virtually always denied by a court because a court properly, I think, says that for the future we will assume that all police officers will abide by the law, including the Constitution." The District Court's response to this explanation is significant: "[I]f you [respondents] had asked for [injunctive relief] against some of the officers I think I would have granted it. . . . I would agree with you that there is a problem about telling the officers that they have to obey the law. But if you want to know what the court thought about some of the behavior, it was—it would have warranted an injunction."

Respondents also sought attorney's fees and costs under § 1988(b). They requested compensation for 1,946.75 hours expended by their two attorneys at a rate of $125 per hour, and for 84.5 hours expended by law clerks at a rate of $25.00 per hour, a total of $245,456.25. The District Court found both the hours and rates reasonable, and awarded respondents $245,456.25 in fees. The court rejected respondents' request for certain additional expenses, and for a multiplier sought by respondents to reflect the contingent nature of their success and the high quality of their attorneys' efforts.

Petitioners appealed only the attorney's fees award, which the Court of Appeals for the Ninth Circuit affirmed. Petitioners sought a writ of certiorari from this Court. We granted the writ, vacated the Court of Appeals' judgment, and remanded the case for reconsideration in light of Hensley v. Eckerhart, 461 U.S. 424 (1983). On remand, the District Court held two additional hearings, reviewed additional briefing, and reexamined the record as a whole. The court made extensive findings of fact and conclusions of law, and again concluded that respondents were entitled to an award of $245,456.25 in attorney's fees, based on the same total number of hours expended on the case and the same hourly rates. The court again denied respondents' request for certain expenses and for a multiplier.

Petitioners again appealed the fee award. And again, the Court of Appeals affirmed, finding that "the District Court correctly reconsidered the case in light of *Hensley*. . . . "

Petitioners again sought a writ of certiorari from this Court, alleging that the District Court's fee award was not "reasonable" within the meaning of § 1988(b), because it was disproportionate to the amount of damages recovered by respondents. We granted the writ, and now affirm the Court of Appeals.

II

A

In Alyeska Pipeline Service Co. v. Wilderness Society, 421 U.S. 240 (1975), the Court reaffirmed the "American rule" that, at least absent express statutory authorization to the contrary, each party to a lawsuit ordinarily shall bear its own attorney's fees. In response to *Alyeska*, Congress enacted the Civil Rights Attorneys' Fees Awards Act of 1976, 42 U.S.C. § 1988(b), which authorized the district courts to award reasonable attorney's fees to prevailing parties in specified civil rights litigation. While the statute itself does not explain what constitutes a reasonable fee, both the House and Senate Reports accompanying § 1988(b) expressly endorse the analysis set forth in Johnson v. Georgia Highway Express, Inc., 488 F.2d 714 (5th Cir. 1974). See S. Rep. No. 94–1011, p. 6 (1976) (hereafter Senate Report); H.R.Rep. No. 94–1558, p. 8 (1976) (hereafter House Report). *Johnson* identifies 12 factors to be considered in calculating a reasonable attorney's fee.[3]

[3] These factors are: (1) the time and labor required; (2) the novelty and difficulty of the questions; (3) the skill requisite to perform the legal service properly; (4) the preclusion of employment by the attorney due to acceptance of the case; (5) the customary fee; (6) whether the fee is fixed or contingent; (7) time limitations imposed by the client or the circumstances; (8) the amount involved and the results obtained; (9) the experience, reputation, and ability of the attorneys; (10) the "undesirability" of the case; (11) the nature and length of the professional relationship with the client; and (12) awards in similar cases.

Hensley v. Eckerhart, 461 U.S. 424 (1983), announced certain guidelines for calculating a reasonable attorney's fee under § 1988(b). *Hensley* stated that "[t]he most useful starting point for determining the amount of a reasonable fee is the number of hours reasonably expended on the litigation multiplied by a reasonable hourly rate." This figure, commonly referred to as the "lodestar," is presumed to be the reasonable fee contemplated by § 1988(b). The opinion cautioned that "[t]he district court . . . should exclude from this initial fee calculation hours that were not 'reasonably expended' " on the litigation.

Hensley then discussed other considerations that might lead the district court to adjust the lodestar figure upward or downward, including the "important factor of the 'results obtained.' " The opinion noted that where a prevailing plaintiff has succeeded on only some of his claims, an award of fees for time expended on unsuccessful claims may not be appropriate. In these situations, the Court held that the judge should consider whether or not the plaintiff's unsuccessful claims were related to the claims on which he succeeded, and whether the plaintiff achieved a level of success that makes it appropriate to award attorney's fees for hours reasonably expended on unsuccessful claims:

> In [some] cases the plaintiff's claims for relief will involve a common core of facts or will be based on related legal theories. Much of counsel's time will be devoted generally to the litigation as a whole, making it difficult to divide the hours expended on a claim-by-claim basis. Such a lawsuit cannot be viewed as a series of discrete claims. Instead the district court should focus on the significance of the overall relief obtained by the plaintiff in relation to the hours reasonably expended on the litigation.

Accordingly, *Hensley* emphasized that "[w]here a plaintiff has obtained excellent results, his attorney should recover a fully compensatory fee," and that "the fee award should not be reduced simply because the plaintiff failed to prevail on every contention raised in the lawsuit."

B

Petitioners argue that the District Court failed properly to follow *Hensley* in calculating respondents' fee award. We disagree. The District Court carefully considered the results obtained by respondents pursuant to the instructions set forth in *Hensley*, and concluded that respondents were entitled to recover attorney's fees for all hours expended on the litigation. First, the court found that "[t]he amount of time expended by counsel in conducting this litigation was reasonable and reflected sound legal judgment under the circumstances."[4] The court also determined that counsels' excellent performances in this case entitled them to be compensated at prevailing market rates, even though they were relatively young when this litigation began.

---

[4] *Hensley* stated that a fee applicant should "exercise 'billing judgment' with respect to hours worked." Petitioners maintain that respondents failed to exercise "billing judgment" in this case, since they sought compensation for all time spent litigating this case. We think this argument misreads the mandate of *Hensley*. *Hensley* requires a fee applicant to exercise "billing judgment" not because he should necessarily be compensated for less than the actual number of hours spent litigating a case, but because the hours he does seek compensation for must be reasonable. "Counsel for the prevailing party should make a good-faith effort to exclude from a fee request hours that are excessive, redundant, or otherwise unnecessary. . . . " In this case, the District Court found that the number of hours expended by respondents' counsel was reasonable. Thus, counsel did, in fact, exercise the "billing judgment" recommended in *Hensley*. . . .

The District Court then concluded that it was inappropriate to adjust respondents' fee award downward to account for the fact that respondents had prevailed only on some of their claims, and against only some of the defendants. The court first determined that "it was never actually clear what officer did what until we had gotten through with the whole trial," so that "[u]nder the circumstances of this case, it was reasonable for plaintiffs initially to name 31 individual defendants . . . as well as the City of Riverside as defendants in this action." The court remarked:

> I think every one of the claims that were made were related and if you look at the common core of facts that we had here that you had total success. . . . There was a problem about who was responsible for what and that problem was there all the way through to the time that we concluded the case. Some of the officers couldn't agree about who did what and it is not at all surprising that it would, in my opinion, have been wrong for you not to join all those officers since you yourself did not know precisely who were the officers that were responsible.

The court then found that the lawsuit could not "be viewed as a series of discrete claims," *Hensley*, supra, at 435:

> All claims made by plaintiffs were based on a common core of facts. The claims on which plaintiffs did not prevail were closely related to the claims on which they did prevail. The time devoted to claims on which plaintiffs did not prevail cannot reasonably be separated from time devoted to claims on which plaintiffs did prevail.

The District Court also considered the amount of damages recovered, and determined that the size of the damages award did not imply that respondent's success was limited:

> [T]he size of the jury award resulted from (a) the general reluctance of jurors to make large awards against police officers, and (b) the dignified restraint which the plaintiffs exercised in describing their injuries to the jury. For example, although some of the actions of the police would clearly have been insulting and humiliating to even the most insensitive person and were, in the opinion of the court, intentionally so, plaintiffs did not attempt to play up this aspect of the case.[5]

The court paid particular attention to the fact that the case "presented complex and interrelated issues of fact and law," and that "[a] fee award in this civil rights action will . . . advance the public interest":

> Counsel for plaintiffs . . . served the public interest by vindicating important constitutional rights. Defendants had engaged in lawless, unconstitutional conduct, and the litigation of plaintiffs' case was necessary to remedy defendants' misconduct. Indeed, the court was shocked at some of the acts of the police officers in this case and was convinced from the testimony that these acts were motivated by a general hostility to the Chicano community in the area where the incident occurred. The amount of time expended by plaintiffs' counsel in conducting this litigation was clearly reasonable and necessary to serve

---

5 At the second hearing on remand, the court also remarked: "I have tried several civil rights violation cases in which police officers have figured and in the main they prevailed because juries do not bring in verdicts against police officers very readily nor against cities. The size of the verdicts against the individuals is not at all surprising because juries are very reluctant to bring in large verdicts against police officers who don't have the resources to answer those verdicts. The relief here I think was absolutely complete."

> the public interest as well as the interests of plaintiffs in the vindication of their constitutional rights.

Finally, the District Court "focus[ed] on the significance of the overall relief obtained by [respondents] in relation to the hours reasonably expended on the litigation." *Hensley*, supra, at 435. The court concluded that respondents had "achieved a level of success in this case that makes the total number of hours expended by counsel a proper basis for making the fee award":

> Counsel for plaintiffs achieved excellent results for their clients, and their accomplishment in this case was outstanding. The amount of time expended by counsel in conducting this litigation was reasonable and reflected sound legal judgment under the circumstances.

Based on our review of the record, we agree with the Court of Appeals that the District Court's findings were not clearly erroneous. We conclude that the District Court correctly applied the factors announced in *Hensley* in calculating respondents' fee award, and that the court did not abuse its discretion in awarding attorney's fees for all time reasonably spent litigating the case.

III

Petitioners, joined by the Solicitor General as amicus curiae, maintain that *Hensley*'s lodestar approach is inappropriate in civil rights cases where a plaintiff recovers only monetary damages. In these cases, so the argument goes, use of the lodestar may result in fees that exceed the amount of damages recovered and that are therefore unreasonable. Likening such cases to private tort actions, petitioners and the Solicitor General submit that attorney's fees in such cases should be proportionate to the amount of damages a plaintiff recovers. Specifically, they suggest that fee awards in damages cases should be modeled upon the contingent fee arrangements commonly used in personal injury litigation. In this case, assuming a 33 percent contingency rate, this would entitle respondents to recover approximately $11,000 in attorney's fees.

The amount of damages a plaintiff recovers is certainly relevant to the amount of attorney's fees to be awarded under § 1988(b). It is, however, only one of many factors that a court should consider in calculating an award of attorney's fees. We reject the proposition that fee awards under § 1988(b) should necessarily be proportionate to the amount of damages a civil rights plaintiff actually recovers.

A

As an initial matter, we reject the notion that a civil rights action for damages constitutes nothing more than a private tort suit benefitting only the individual plaintiffs whose rights were violated. Unlike most private tort litigants, a civil rights plaintiff seeks to vindicate important civil and constitutional rights that cannot be valued solely in monetary terms. See Carey v. Piphus, 435 U.S. 247, 266 (1978). And, Congress has determined that "the public as a whole has an interest in the vindication of the rights conferred by the statutes enumerated in § 1988(b), over and above the value of a civil rights remedy to a particular plaintiff. . . . " *Hensley*, supra, at 444 n. 4 (Brennan, J., concurring in part and dissenting in part). Regardless of the form of relief he actually obtains, a successful civil rights plaintiff often secures important social benefits that are not reflected in nominal or relatively small damages awards. In this case, for example, the District Court found that many of petitioners' unlawful acts were "motivated by a general hostility to the Chicano community," and that this litigation therefore served the public interest:

> The institutional behavior involved here . . . had to be stopped and . . . nothing short of having a lawsuit like this would have stopped it. [T]he improper motivation which appeared as a result of all of this seemed to me to have pervaded a very broad segment of police officers in the department.

In addition, the damages a plaintiff recovers [contribute] significantly to the deterrence of civil rights violations in the future. This deterrent effect is particularly evident in the area of individual police misconduct, where injunctive relief generally is unavailable.

Congress expressly recognized that a plaintiff who obtains relief in a civil rights lawsuit " 'does so not for himself alone but also as a "private attorney general," vindicating a policy that Congress considered of the highest importance.' " House Report, at 2 (quoting Newman v. Piggie Park Enterprises, Inc., 390 U.S. 400, 402 (1968)). "If the citizen does not have the resources, his day in court is denied him; the congressional policy which he seeks to assert and vindicate goes unvindicated; and the entire nation, not just the individual citizen, suffers." 122 Cong.Rec. 33313 (1976) (remarks of Sen. Tunney).

Because damages awards do not reflect fully the public benefit advanced by civil rights litigation, Congress did not intend for fees in civil rights cases, unlike most private law cases, to depend on obtaining substantial monetary relief. Rather, Congress made clear that it "intended that the amount of fees awarded under [§ 1988(b)] be governed by the same standards which prevail in other types of equally complex federal litigation, such as antitrust cases and *not be reduced because the rights involved may be nonpecuniary in nature*." Senate Report, at 6 (emphasis added). . . . The Senate report specifically approves of the fee awards made in cases such as Stanford Daily v. Zurcher, 64 F.R.D. 680 (N.D.Cal.1974); and Swann v. Charlotte–Mecklenburg Board of Education, 66 F.R.D. 483 (W.D.N.C.1975). In each of these cases, counsel received substantial attorney's fees despite the fact the plaintiffs sought no monetary damages. Thus, Congress recognized that reasonable attorney's fees under § 1988(b) are not conditioned upon and need not be proportionate to an award of money damages. The lower courts have generally eschewed such a requirement.

B

A rule that limits attorney's fees in civil rights cases to a proportion of the damages awarded would seriously undermine Congress' purpose in enacting § 1988(b). Congress enacted § 1988(b) specifically because it found that the private market for legal services failed to provide many victims of civil rights violations with effective access to the judicial process. These victims ordinarily cannot afford to purchase legal services at the rates set by the private market. Moreover, the contingent fee arrangements that make legal services available to many victims of personal injuries would often not encourage lawyers to accept civil rights cases, which frequently involve substantial expenditures of time and effort but produce only small monetary recoveries. As the House Report states:

> [W]hile damages are theoretically available under the statutes covered by [§ 1988(b)], it should be observed that, in some cases, immunity doctrines and special defenses, available only to public officials, preclude *or severely limit the damage remedy*. Consequently, awarding

counsel fees to prevailing plaintiffs in such litigation is particularly important and necessary if federal civil and constitutional rights are to be adequately protected.

House Report, at 9 (emphasis added; footnote omitted). Congress enacted § 1988(b) specifically to enable plaintiffs to enforce the civil rights laws even where the amount of damages at stake would not otherwise make it feasible for them to do so. . . .

A rule of proportionality would make it difficult, if not impossible, for individuals with meritorious civil rights claims but relatively small potential damages to obtain redress from the courts. This is totally inconsistent with the Congress' purpose in enacting § 1988(b). Congress recognized that private-sector fee arrangements were inadequate to ensure sufficiently vigorous enforcement of civil rights. In order to ensure that lawyers would be willing to represent persons with legitimate civil rights grievances, Congress determined that it would be necessary to compensate lawyers for all time reasonably expended on a case.

This case illustrates why the enforcement of civil rights laws cannot be entrusted to private-sector fee arrangements. The District Court observed that "[g]iven the nature of this lawsuit and the type of defense presented, many attorneys in the community would have been reluctant to institute and to continue to prosecute this action." The court concluded, moreover, that "[c]ounsel for plaintiffs achieved excellent results for their clients, and their accomplishment in this case was outstanding. The amount of time expended by counsel in conducting this litigation was reasonable and reflected sound legal judgment under the circumstances." Nevertheless, petitioners suggest that respondents' counsel should be compensated for only a small fraction of the actual time spent litigating the case. In light of the difficult nature of the issues presented by this lawsuit and the low pecuniary value of . . . the rights respondents sought to vindicate, it is highly unlikely that the prospect of a fee equal to a fraction of the damages respondents might recover would have been sufficient to attract competent counsel.[10] Moreover, since counsel might not have found it economically feasible to expend the amount of time respondents' counsel found necessary to litigate the case properly, it is even less likely that counsel would have achieved the excellent results that respondents' counsel obtained here. Thus, had respondents had to rely on private-sector fee arrangements, they might well have been unable to obtain redress for their grievances. It is precisely for this reason that Congress enacted § 1988(b).

IV

We agree with petitioners that Congress intended that statutory fee awards be "adequate to attract competent counsel, but . . . not produce windfalls to attorneys." Senate Report, at 6. However, we find no evidence that Congress intended that, in order to avoid "windfalls to attorneys," attorney's fees be proportionate to the amount of damages a civil rights plaintiff might recover. Rather, there already exists a wide range of safeguards

[10] The Solicitor General suggests that "[t]he prospect of recovering $11,000 for representing [respondents] in a damages suit (assuming a contingency rate of 33 percent) is likely to attract a substantial number of attorneys." Brief for United States as Amicus Curiae 22–23. However, the District Court found that the 1,946.75 hours respondents' counsel spent litigating the case was reasonable and that "[t]here was not any possible way that you could have avoided putting in that amount of time. . . . " We reject the Solicitor General's suggestion that the prospect of working nearly 2,000 hours at a rate of $5.65 an hour, to be paid more than 10 years after the work began, is "likely to attract a substantial number of attorneys."

designed to protect civil rights defendants against the possibility of excessive fee awards. Both the House and Senate Reports identify standards for courts to follow in awarding and calculating attorney's fees; these standards are designed to insure that attorneys are compensated only for time *reasonably expended* on a case. The district court has the discretion to deny fees to prevailing plaintiffs under special circumstances, see *Hensley*, supra, at 429 (citing Senate Report, at 4), and to award attorney's fees against plaintiffs who litigate frivolous or vexatious claims. See Christiansburg Garment Co. v. EEOC, 434 U.S. 412, 416–17 (1978); Hughes v. Rowe, 449 U.S. 5, 14–16 (1980) (per curiam); House Report, at 6–7. Furthermore, we have held that a civil rights defendant is not liable for attorneys' fees incurred after a pretrial settlement offer, where the judgment recovered by the plaintiff is less than the offer. Marek v. Chesny, 473 U.S. 1 (1985).[11] We believe that these safeguards adequately protect against the possibility that § 1988(b) might produce a "windfall" to civil rights attorneys.

In the absence of any indication that Congress intended to adopt a strict rule that attorney's fees under § 1988(b) be proportionate to damages recovered, we decline to adopt such a rule ourselves.[12] The judgment of the Court of Appeals is hereby

Affirmed.

■ JUSTICE POWELL, concurring in the judgment.

I join only the Court's judgment. The plurality opinion reads our decision in Hensley v. Eckerhart, 461 U.S. 424 (1983), more expansively than I would, and more expansively than is necessary to decide this case. For me affirmance—quite simply—is required by the District Court's detailed findings of fact, which were approved by the Court of Appeals. On its face, the fee award seems unreasonable. But I find no basis for this Court to reject the findings made and approved by the courts below.

I

. . . On remand [for reconsideration of the fee award in light of *Hensley*], the District Court heard oral argument and "reconsidered the memoranda, affidavits, and exhibits previously filed by the parties, as well the record as a whole." That court then made explicit findings of fact, including the following that are relevant to the fee award:

1. "All claims made by plaintiffs were based on a common core of facts. The claims on which plaintiffs did not prevail were closely related to the claims on which they did prevail. The time devoted to claims on which plaintiffs did not prevail cannot reasonably be separated from time devoted to claims on which plaintiffs did prevail."

2. "Counsel demonstrated outstanding skill and experience in handling this case."

3. "[M]any attorneys in the community would have been reluctant to institute and to continue to prosecute this action."

---

[11] Thus, petitioners could have avoided liability for the bulk of the attorney's fees for which they now find themselves liable by making a reasonable settlement offer in a timely manner. . . .

[12] We note that Congress has been urged to amend § 1988(b) to prohibit the award of attorney's fees that are disproportionate to monetary damages recovered. See, e.g., The Legal Fees Equity Act, S. 2802, 98th Cong., 2d Sess. (1984); S. 1580, 99th Cong., 1st Sess. (1985). These efforts have thus far not been persuasive.

4. The number of hours claimed to have been expended by the two lawyers was "fair and reasonable."

5. "Counsel for plaintiffs achieved excellent results for their clients, and their accomplishment in this case was outstanding. The amount of time expended by counsel . . . was reasonable and reflected sound legal judgment under the circumstances."

6. Counsel "also served the public interest by vindicating important constitutional rights."

7. The "hourly rate [of $125 per hour is] typical of the prevailing market rate for similar services by lawyers of comparable skill, experience and reputation within the Central District at the time these services were performed."

8. Finally, in view of the level of success attained in this case, "the total number of hours expended by counsel [is] a proper basis for making the fee award."

Federal Rule of Civil Procedure 52(a) provides that "[f]indings of fact [by a district court] shall not be set aside unless clearly erroneous. . . . " The Court of Appeals did not disagree with any of the foregoing findings by the District Court. I see no basis on which this Court now could hold that these findings are clearly erroneous. To be sure, some of the findings fairly can be viewed as conclusions or matters of opinion, but the findings that are critical to the judgments of the courts below are objective facts. Justice Rehnquist's arguments in dissent suggest that the District Court may have been mistaken. But . . . "a reviewing court [may not] reverse the finding of the trier of fact simply because it is convinced that it would have decided the case differently." . . .

II

. . . Petitioners argue for a rule of proportionality between the fee awarded and the damages recovered in a civil rights case. Neither the decisions of this Court nor the legislative history of § 1988(b) support such a "rule." The facts and circumstances of litigation are infinitely variable. Under *Hensley*, of course, "the most critical factor [in the final determination of fee awards] is the degree of success obtained." Where recovery of private damages is the purpose of a civil rights litigation, a district court, in fixing fees, is obligated to give primary consideration to the amount of damages awarded as compared to the amount sought. In some civil rights cases, however, the court may consider the vindication of constitutional rights in addition to the amount of damages recovered. In this case, for example, the District Court made an explicit finding that the "public interest" had been served by the jury's verdict that the warrantless entry was lawless and unconstitutional. Although the finding of a Fourth Amendment violation hardly can be considered a new constitutional ruling, in the special circumstances of this case, the vindication of the asserted Fourth Amendment right may well have served a public interest, supporting the amount of the fees awarded. As the District Court put it, there were allegations that the police misconduct was "motivated by a general hostility to the Chicano community in the area. . . . " The record also contained evidence of racial slurs by some of the police.

Finally, petitioners also contend that in determining a proper fee under § 1988(b) in a suit for damages the court should consider the prevailing contingent fee rate charged by counsel in personal injury cases. The use of contingent fee arrangements in many types of tort cases was customary long before Congress enacted § 1988(b). It is clear from the legislative history that § 1988(b) was enacted because existing fee arrangements were thought not to provide an adequate incentive to lawyers particularly to represent plaintiffs in unpopular civil rights cases. I therefore find petitioners' asserted analogy to personal injury claims unpersuasive in this context.

III

In sum, despite serious doubts as to the fairness of the fees awarded in this case, I cannot conclude that the detailed findings made by the District Court, and accepted by the Court of Appeals, were clearly erroneous, or that the District Court abused its discretion in making this fee award.

■ CHIEF JUSTICE BURGER, dissenting.

I join Justice Rehnquist's dissenting opinion. I write only to add that it would be difficult to find a better example of legal nonsense than the fixing of attorney's fees by a judge at $245,456.25 for the recovery of $33,350 damages.

The two attorneys receiving this nearly quarter-million dollar fee graduated from law school in 1973 and 1974; they brought this action in 1975, which resulted in the $33,350 jury award in 1980. Their total professional experience when this litigation began consisted of Gerald Lopez' one-year service as a law clerk to a judge and Roy Cazares' two years' experience as a trial attorney in the Defenders' Program of San Diego County. For their services the District Court found that an hourly rate of $125 per hour was reasonable.

Can anyone doubt that no private party would ever have dreamed of paying these two novice attorneys $125 per hour in 1975, which, considering inflation, would represent perhaps something more nearly a $250 per hour rate today? For example, as Justice Rehnquist points out, would any private litigant be willing to pay a total of $17,875 simply for preparation of a pretrial order?

This fee award plainly constitutes a grave abuse of discretion which should be rejected by this Court—particularly when we have already vacated and remanded this identical fee award previously—rather than simply affirming the District Court's findings as not being either "clearly erroneous" or an "abuse of discretion." The Court's result will unfortunately only add fuel to the fires of public indignation over the costs of litigation.

■ JUSTICE REHNQUIST, with whom THE CHIEF JUSTICE, JUSTICE WHITE, and JUSTICE O'CONNOR join, dissenting.

In Hensley v. Eckerhart, 461 U.S. 424, 433 (1983), our leading case dealing with attorney's fees awarded pursuant to 42 U.S.C. § 1988(b), we said that "[t]he most useful starting point for determining the amount of a reasonable fee is the number of hours reasonably expended on the litigation multiplied by a reasonable hourly rate." As if we had foreseen the case now before us, we went on the emphasize that "[t]he district court . . . should exclude from this initial fee calculation hours that were not 'reasonably expended' " on the litigation. Id. at 434, quoting S. Rep. No. 94–1011, p. 6 (1976). Today, despite its adoption of a revisionist interpretation of *Hensley*, the plurality nonetheless acknowledges that "*Hensley* requires a fee applicant to exercise 'billing judgment' not because he should necessarily be compensated for less than the actual number of hours spent litigating a case, but because the hours he does seek compensation for must be *reasonable*." (Emphasis in original.) I see no escape from the conclusion that the

District Court's finding that respondents' attorneys "reasonably" spent 1,946.75 hours to recover a money judgment of $33,350 is clearly erroneous, and that therefore the District Court's award of $245,456.25 in attorney's fees to respondents should be reversed. The Court's affirmance of the fee award emasculates the principles laid down in *Hensley*, and turns § 1988(b) into a relief act for lawyers.

A brief look at the history of this case reveals just how "unreasonable" it was for respondents' lawyers to spend so much time on it. Respondents filed their initial complaint in 1976, seeking injunctive and declaratory relief and compensatory and punitive damages from the City of Riverside, its chief of police, and 30 police officers, based on 256 separate claims allegedly arising out of the police breakup of a single party. Prior to trial, 17 of the police officers were dismissed from the case on motions for summary judgment, and respondents dropped their requests for injunctive and declaratory relief. More significantly, respondents also dropped their original allegation that the police had acted with discriminatory intent. The action proceeded to trial, and the jury completely exonerated nine additional police officers. Respondents ultimately prevailed against only the city and five police officers on various § 1983, false arrest and imprisonment, and common negligence claims. No restraining orders or injunctions were ever issued against petitioners, nor was the city ever compelled to change a single practice or policy as a result of respondents' suit. The jury awarded respondents a total of $33,350 in compensatory and punitive damages. Only about one-third of this total, or $13,300 was awarded to respondents based on violations of their federal constitutional rights.

Respondents then filed a request for $495,713.51 in attorney's fees, representing approximately 15 times the amount of the underlying money judgment. In April 1981, the District Court made its initial fee award of $245,456.25, declining to apply respondents' requested "multiplier," but awarding, to the penny, the entire "lodestar" claimed by respondents and their attorneys. The Ninth Circuit affirmed. We granted certiorari, vacated, and remanded, in light of *Hensley*, supra. On remand, the District Court convened a hearing, at which the court promptly announced, "I tell you now that I will not change the award. I will simply go back and be more specific about it." The court ultimately proved true to its word. After reviewing the record and the submissions of the parties, the court convened a second hearing, at which it approved exactly the same award as before: $245,456.25 in attorney's fees. The only noticeable change was that, the second time around, the court created a better "paper trail" by including in its order a discussion of those factors in *Hensley* and Johnson v. Georgia Highway Express, Inc., 488 F.2d 714 (5th Cir. 1974), which it believed supported such a huge fee award. The Ninth Circuit again affirmed.

It is obvious to me that the District Court viewed *Hensley* not as a constraint on its discretion, but instead as a blueprint for justifying, in an after-the-fact fashion, a fee award it had already decided to enter solely on the basis of the "lodestar." In fact, the District Court failed at almost every turn to apply any kind of "billing judgment," or to seriously consider the "results obtained," which we described in *Hensley* as "the important factor" in determining a "reasonable" fee award. A few examples should suffice: (1) The court approved almost 209 hours of "prelitigation time," for a total of $26,118.75. (2) The court approved some 197 hours of time spent in conversations between respondents' two attorneys, for a total of $24,625. (3) The court approved 143 hours for preparation of a pre-trial order, for a total of

$17,875.00. (4) Perhaps most egregiously, the court approved 45.50 hours of "stand-by time," or time spent by one of respondents' attorneys, who was then based in San Diego, to wait in a Los Angeles hotel room for a jury verdict to be rendered in Los Angeles, where his co-counsel was then employed by the U.C.L.A. School of Law, less than 40 minutes' driving time from the courthouse. The award for "stand-by-time" totaled $5,687.50. I find it hard to understand how any attorney can be said to have exercised "billing judgment" in spending such huge amounts of time on a case ultimately worth only $33,350.

Indeed, on the basis of some of the statements made by the District Court in this case, I reluctantly conclude that the court may have attempted to make up to respondents in attorney's fees what it felt the jury had wrongfully withheld from them in damages. As the court noted in its opinion, apparently believing that the observation supported the entry of a huge award of attorney's fees:

> [T]he size of the jury award resulted from (a) the general reluctance of jurors to make large awards against police officers, and (b) the dignified restraint which the plaintiffs exercised in describing their injuries to the jury. For example, although some of the actions of the police would clearly have been insulting and humiliating to even the most insensitive person and were, in the opinion of the court, intentionally so, plaintiffs did not attempt to play up this aspect of the case.

But a District Court, in awarding attorney's fees under § 1988(b), does not sit to retry questions submitted to and decided by the jury. If jurors are reluctant to make large awards against police officers, this is a fact of life that plaintiffs, defendants, and district courts must live with, and a district court simply has no business trying to correct what it regards as an unfortunate tendency in the award of damages by granting inflated attorney's fees.

The analysis of whether the extraordinary number of hours put in by respondents' attorneys in this case was "reasonable" must be made in light of both the traditional billing practices in the profession, and the fundamental principle that the award of a "reasonable" attorney's fee under § 1988(b) means a fee that would have been deemed reasonable if billed to affluent plaintiffs by their own attorneys. This latter principle was stressed in the legislative history of § 1988(b), and by this Court in *Hensley*:

> Counsel for the prevailing party should make a good faith effort to exclude from a fee request hours that are excessive, redundant, or otherwise unnecessary, just as a lawyer in private practice ethically is obligated to exclude such hours from his fee submission. "In the private sector, 'billing judgment' is an important component in fee setting. It is no less important here. Hours that are not properly billed to one's *client* also are not properly billed to one's *adversary* pursuant to statutory authority."

I think that this analysis, which appears nowhere in the plurality's opinion, leads inexorably to the conclusion that the District Court's fee award of $245,456.25, based on a prevailing hourly rate of $125 multiplied by the number of hours which respondents' attorneys claim to have spent on the case, is not a "reasonable" attorney's fee under § 1988(b).

Suppose that A offers to sell Blackacre to B for $10,000. It is commonly known and accepted that Blackacre has a fair market value of $10,000. B consults an attorney and requests a determination whether A can convey good title to Blackacre. The attorney writes an elaborate memorandum concluding that A's title to Blackacre is defective, and submits a bill to B for $25,000. B refuses to pay the bill, the attorney sues, and the parties stipulate that the attorney spent 200 hours researching the title issue because of an extraordinarily complex legal and factual situation, and that the prevailing rate at which the attorney billed, which was also a "reasonable" rate, was $125. Does anyone seriously think that a court should award the attorney the full $25,000 which he claims? Surely a court would start from the proposition that, unless special arrangements were made between the client and the attorney, a "reasonable" attorney's fee for researching the title to a piece of property worth $10,000 could not exceed the value of the property. Otherwise the client would have been far better off never going to an attorney in the first place, and simply giving A $10,000 for a worthless deed. The client thereby would have saved himself $15,000.

Obviously the billing situation in a typical litigated case is more complex than in this bedrock example of a defective title claim, but some of the same principles are surely applicable. If A has a claim for contract damages in the amount of $10,000 against B, and retains an attorney to prosecute the claim, it would be both extraordinary and unjustifiable, in the absence of any special arrangement, for the attorney to put in 200 hours on the case and send the client a bill for $25,000. Such a bill would be "unreasonable," regardless of whether A obtained a judgment against B for $10,000 or obtained a take-nothing judgment. And in such a case, where the prospective recovery is limited, it is exactly this "billing judgment" which enables the parties to achieve a settlement; any competent attorney, whether prosecuting or defending a contract action for $10,000, would realize that the case simply cannot justify a fee in excess of the potential recovery on the part of either the plaintiff's or the defendant's attorney. All of these examples illuminate the point made in *Hensley* that "the important factor" in determining a "reasonable" fee is the "results obtained." The very "reasonableness" of the hours expended on a case by a plaintiff's attorney necessarily will depend, to a large extent, on the amount that may reasonably be expected to be recovered if the plaintiff prevails.

The amount of damages which a jury is likely to award in a tort case is of course more difficult to predict than the amount it is likely to award in a contract case. But even in a tort case some measure of the kind of "billing judgment" previously described must be brought to bear in computing a "reasonable" attorney's fee. Again, a hypothetical example will illustrate the point. If, at the time respondents filed their lawsuit in 1976, there had been in the Central District of California a widely publicized survey of jury verdicts in this type of civil rights action which showed that successful plaintiffs recovered between $10,000 and $75,000 in damages, could it possibly be said that it would have been "reasonable" for respondents' attorneys to put in on the case hours which, when multiplied by the attorneys' prevailing hourly rate, would result in an attorney's fee of over $245,000? In the absence of such a survey, it might be more difficult for a plaintiff's attorney to accurately estimate the amount of damages likely to be recovered, but this does not absolve the attorney of the responsibility for making such an estimate and using it as a guide in the exercise of "billing judgment."

In the context of § 1988(b), there would obviously be some exceptions to the general rules of "billing judgment" which I have been discussing, but none of these exceptions [is] applicable here. If the litigation is unnecessarily prolonged by the bad-faith conduct of the defendants, or if the litigation produces significant, identifiable benefits for persons other than the plaintiffs, then the purpose of Congress in authorizing attorney's fees under § 1988(b) should allow a larger award of attorney's fees than would be "reasonable" where the only relief is the recovery of monetary damages by individual plaintiffs. Nor do we deal with a case such as Carey v. Piphus, 435 U.S. 247, 266 (1978), in which the deprivation of a constitutional right necessarily results in only nominal pecuniary damages. Here, respondents successfully claimed both compensatory and punitive damages for false arrest and imprisonment, negligence, and violations of their constitutional rights under the Fourth and Fourteenth Amendments, and the jury assessed damages as juries do in such cases. In short, this case shares none of the special aspects of certain civil rights litigation which the plurality suggests, in Part III of its opinion, would justify an award of attorney's fees totally divorced from the amount of damages awarded by the jury.

The plurality explains the position advanced by petitioner and the Solicitor General concerning fee awards in a case such as this, and then goes on to "reject the proposition that fee awards under § 1988(b) should necessarily be proportionate to the amount of damages a civil rights plaintiff actually recovers." I agree with the plurality that the importation of the contingent-fee model to govern fee awards under § 1988(b) is not warranted by the terms and legislative history of the statute. But I do not agree with the plurality if it means to reject the kind of "proportionality" that I have previously described. Nearly 2,000 attorney-hours spent on a case in which the total recovery was only $33,000, in which only $13,300 of that amount was recovered for the federal claims, and in which the District Court expressed the view that, in such cases, juries typically were reluctant to award substantial damages against police officers, is simply not a "reasonable" expenditure of time. The snippets of legislative history which the plurality relies upon to dismiss *any* relationship between the amount of time put in on a case and the amount of damages awarded are wholly unconvincing. One may agree with all of the glowing rhetoric contained in the plurality's opinion about Congress' noble purpose in authorizing attorney's fees under § 1988(b) without concluding that Congress intended to turn attorneys loose to spend as many hours as possible to prepare and try a case that could reasonably be expected to result only in a relatively minor award of monetary damages.

In *Hensley*, we noted that "complex civil rights litigation involving numerous challenges to institutional practices or conditions" might well require "many hours of lawyers' services," and thus justify a large award of attorney's fee. This case is a far cry from the situation we referred to in *Hensley*. I would reverse the judgment of the Ninth Circuit affirming the District Court's award of attorney's fees, and remand the case to the District Court for recomputation of the fee award in light of both *Hensley* and the principles set forth in this opinion.

NOTES ON DETERMINING FEE AWARDS

1. QUESTIONS AND COMMENTS ON *CITY OF RIVERSIDE*

Of the several issues that have arisen since passage of the 1976 act, none is more important than the question of proportionality. Under the statute, a party may recover fees only by prevailing on the merits. The question is: Should the size of the fee be limited by the value of the victory? Should plaintiff's recovery of attorney's fees include all time validly spent in litigating the claim, no matter how trivial, or should there be some implicit deflator of the fee to match the size or importance of the judgment obtained?

In *City of Riverside,* the Solicitor General proposed that fee awards in damage actions be conformed to the model of a contingent fee. Under this approach, where plaintiff obtained only monetary damages, the maximum fee award would be some fraction (often one-third) of the amount of judgment. None of the Justices endorsed this view. Is the Court's unanimity on this point surprising?

Given the Court's rejection of the contingent-fee model, the question then becomes whether some looser notion of proportionality controls. Consider the facts of *City of Riverside.* The dissenters thought that the 197 hours of conversation between plaintiffs' attorneys and the $5,687.50 of hotel "stand-by time" were not reasonable in view of the judgment obtained. Would these expenses have been (more nearly?) reasonable had the jury returned a larger verdict? Does the answer depend on the degree to which the dollar value of the lawsuit could have been predicted? Does it depend on the judge's assessment of the public interest served by the litigation? Recall that the *City of Riverside* trial judge would have issued an injunction had he been asked, and that he apparently would have preferred a larger verdict. Are these appropriate considerations in determining a reasonable attorney's fee?

2. APPLYING THE LODESTAR: REASONABLE HOURS

As *City of Riverside* noted, the presumptive starting point for determining the appropriate fee award is the "lodestar," described in Hensley v. Eckerhart, 461 U.S. 424, 433 (1983), as "the number of hours reasonably expended on the litigation multiplied by a reasonable hourly rate." How are these two numbers to be calculated?

The starting point for calculating the number of hours reasonably expended is to look at the hours spent on the claims on which the plaintiff prevailed. This can be potentially complicated if the plaintiff wins on less than all of the claims advanced in the complaint.

Where a successful claim and an unsuccessful claim are essentially unrelated, the result is obvious. The unsuccessful claim is treated as if it had been raised in a separate lawsuit, and no fees are awarded for that effort. See Hensley v. Eckerhart, 461 U.S. 424, 435 (1983). Where successful and unsuccessful claims arise from the same facts, the problem is more difficult. In such cases, the "most critical factor is the degree of success obtained." Id. at 436. Trial courts apparently are left to their own discretion in determining what fee is reasonable in light of the success obtained.

This approach led to a split in the lower courts as to the threshold level of success needed for an award of fees. The more demanding test required that the plaintiff prevail on the "central issue" in the litigation and achieve the "primary relief sought." In Texas State Teachers Association v. Garland Independent School District, 489 U.S. 782 (1989), the Supreme Court rejected this standard. Instead, the Court adopted the more permissive view that fees should be awarded where plaintiff succeeds on "any significant issue" in the litigation and achieves "some of the benefit" sought in bringing suit. "Purely technical or de minimis" success does not count, but a fee award is appropriate whenever the plaintiff achieves a "material alteration of the legal relationship of the parties." At that point, the degree of overall success goes only to the amount of the award, not to its availability vel non.

For those hours attributable to claims on which the plaintiff prevailed, courts have required plaintiffs to exercise "billing judgment," subtracting hours which are duplicative, unproductive, excessive, or otherwise unnecessary. See *Hensley*, 461 U.S. at 434 ("Hours that are not properly billed to one's client are not properly billed to one's adversary pursuant to statutory authority.") For an example of this principle in action, see Grendel's Den v. Larkin, 749 F.2d 945, 953–54 (1st Cir. 1984) (refusing to award compensation for 66 hours of preparation for a half-hour oral argument in the Supreme Court because the expenditure of so much time reflected an "assumption . . . that the standard of service to be rendered and compensated is one of perfection, the best that illimitable expenditures of time can achieve. But just as a criminal defendant is entitled to a fair trial and not a perfect one, a litigant is entitled to attorney's fees under 42 U.S.C. § 1988 for an effective and completely competitive representation but not one of supererogation.") And courts generally require contemporaneous time records if a dispute arises as to how many hours the plaintiff's attorney actually spent. Id. at 951.

3. APPLYING THE LODESTAR: REASONABLE RATES

With respect to the reasonable hourly rate, the Supreme Court stated in Blum v. Stenson, 465 U.S. 886, 895 (1984), that "the statute and legislative history establish that 'reasonable fees' under § 1988 are to be calculated according to the prevailing market rates in the relevant community." Lower courts have taken different approaches to determining this figure. The usual starting point is the attorney's actual billing rate for paying clients. See, e.g., Mathur v. Board of Trustees, 317 F.3d 738 (7th Cir. 2003). But some attorneys will have no such billing rate, either because they do not bill their paying clients by the hour (charging either a flat or a contingent fee instead) or because they have no paying clients (because they work for a nonprofit public interest law firm or a legal services organization). In such cases, courts look at the hourly rates charged by other lawyers of comparable expertise and experience. Complications can arise when there is a significant disparity between an attorney's actual billing rate and the local market rate if the attorney normally practices elsewhere. For example, in *Mathur*, the case was litigated in the Southern District of Illinois, where attorneys' hourly rates are substantially lower than in Chicago, where the plaintiff's lawyer practiced. The Court of Appeals held that the District Court could adjust the hourly rate downward only if it was clear that local lawyers were both willing and able to represent the plaintiff. Similarly, in Brian A. v. Hattaway, 83 Fed. Appx. 692 (6th Cir. 2003), the Court of Appeals affirmed an award of fees for out-of-town public interest lawyers at an hourly rate far higher than the local rate because the plaintiff showed that these lawyers had special expertise unavailable in the local jurisdiction and their rates were reasonable for attorneys of their degree of skill, experience, and reputation. Otherwise, courts often limit a lawyer's hourly rate to the rate generally charged in the forum jurisdiction, rather than the attorney's home jurisdiction. See, e.g., Farbotko v. Clinton County, 433 F.3d 204 (2nd Cir. 2005); Interfaith Community Org. v. Honeywell Int'l, Inc., 426 F. 3d 694 (3rd Cir. 2005).

4. SURVIVAL OF THE CONTINGENT FEE

Riverside makes plain that statutory attorney's fees are not limited by the model of the contingent fee. This view was confirmed in Blanchard v. Bergeron, 489 U.S. 87 (1989), where the plaintiff entered into a contingent fee arrangement which entitled his lawyer to 40 percent of the $10,000 judgment that plaintiff eventually received. The Court of Appeals took the position that the appropriate fee award was therefore $4,000, rather than the $7,500 indicated by the lodestar, but the Supreme Court unanimously disagreed, saying that the lodestar was the appropriate starting point for determining the fee despite the contingency agreement.

It is equally true, however, that a contingent fee is not limited to the statutory award. In Venegas v. Mitchell, 495 U.S. 82 (1990), the client agreed to pay his lawyer a 40 percent contingency. Judgment was entered for over $2,000,000, to which the court added $117,000 in attorney's fees. The client then claimed that the statutory calculation of a reasonable fee barred his lawyer from collecting the much larger contingency fee. The Supreme Court unanimously disagreed: "[Section] 1983 controls what the losing defendant must pay, not what the prevailing plaintiff must pay his lawyer." Depriving plaintiffs of the option of agreeing to pay more than the statutory fee "if that is necessary to secure counsel of their choice would not further § 1988(b)'s general purpose of enabling such plaintiffs in civil rights cases to secure competent counsel."

5. FEE AWARDS FOR TIME SPENT IN ADMINISTRATIVE PROCEEDINGS

Section 1983 actions lie against persons acting "under color of" state law, chiefly state officers. Often state law provides administrative remedies for official misconduct. Where a claimant successfully invokes such a remedy, can attorney's fees be awarded under § 1988(b) for time spent in the agency proceedings?

In New York Gaslight Club, Inc. v. Carey, 447 U.S. 54 (1980), the Court held that the provision authorizing attorney's fees in an "action or proceeding" under Title VII of the 1964 Civil Rights Act covered state administrative hearings. Under Title VII, however, a claimant *must* resort to available state remedies before seeking federal relief. Under § 1983, by contrast, exhaustion of state remedies normally is not required. Patsy v. Board of Regents of the State of Florida, 457 U.S. 496 (1982). A § 1983 claimant usually can by-pass state administrative opportunities and go directly to federal court.

In Webb v. Board of Education, 471 U.S. 234 (1985), this difference was found decisive. A black school teacher sought and obtained local administrative review of his dismissal. When the school board eventually decided to adhere to its decision, the teacher brought a federal civil rights action. A partial record of the administrative hearing was filed with the District Court. After some litigation, a consent order was entered granting the plaintiff some $15,400 in damages. The issue of attorney's fees was reserved for later resolution. In subsequent negotiations, plaintiff claimed a fee of $21,000, but the school board would offer only $5,000. Plaintiff then filed a motion for award of fees under § 1988(b). One of the disputed issues was whether the fee should include time spent in the state administrative proceedings. The trial court decided to exclude such time, but accepted plaintiff's representations on all other points and awarded a fee of nearly $10,000. The Court of Appeals affirmed, and the Supreme Court granted certiorari to determine whether state administrative proceedings should be covered under § 1988(b).

Speaking through Justice Stevens, the Court ruled that since a § 1983 claimant could go straight to federal court, a state administrative hearing did not qualify as an "action or proceeding to enforce [§ 1983]," as specified in § 1988(b). The Court noted, however, that some services performed by an attorney before filing a complaint might be compensable as time spent on the litigation. Thus, if a "discrete portion" of work done in the administrative proceeding were "both useful and of a type ordinarily necessary to advance the civil rights litigation," it would be covered by the fee award.[a] In this case, the District Court's decision to deny fees for time spent in the administrative process was found to be reasonable.

Justice Brennan, with whom Justice Blackmun joined, wrote separately. He argued that the case called for a remand to the trial court to consider whether some of the time spent in the administrative hearing contributed directly to the success in federal court. Justice Marshall did not participate.[b]

6. REIMBURSEMENT FOR EXPERT WITNESSES AND RELATED EXPENSES

Section 1988(b) refers to a "reasonable attorney's fee." Courts have construed this phrase to include the attorney's expenses as well. But what about fees for expert witnesses? Their participation may be necessary to prove a plaintiff's case. For example, a plaintiff who brings an excessive use of force claim under § 1983 may need expert testimony regarding police practices; a plaintiff seeking to prove unconstitutional discrimination may need a statistician.

In West Virginia University Hospitals, Inc. v. Casey, 499 U.S. 83 (1991), a hospital successfully challenged state medicaid reimbursements and was awarded more than $100,000 in fees for expert witnesses. The experts were found to be essential to the presentation of the case, but the Supreme Court nevertheless denied recovery. Decisive for the majority was the pre-existing tradition, evident in other federal statutes, of treating fees for expert witnesses as something separate and apart from attorney's fees. The suggestion that the Court should adopt a contrary interpretation to aid the purposes of the attorney's fees act was rejected. "That argument," said Justice Scalia, "profoundly mistakes our role." Read in context, the statute was clear and could not be enlarged by judicial decision. That Congress might well have included experts had it come to mind did not matter, for it was not a judicial responsibility to correct legislative "forgetfulness."

---

[a] For implementation of this approach in the context of the attorney fee provisions of the Clean Air Act, see Pennsylvania v. Delaware Valley Citizens' Council for Clear Air, 478 U.S. 546 (1986).

[b] For pre-*Webb* criticism of the denial of § 1988(b) attorney's fees for time spent in state administrative proceedings, see Jeffrey Parness and Gigi Woodruff, Federal District Court Proceedings to Recover Attorney's Fees for Prevailing Parties on Section 1983 Claims in State Administrative Agencies, 18 Ga. L. Rev. 83 (1983). The authors argue that allowing such fees would encourage resort to available state remedies, thus taking advantage of the expertise of state agencies, relieving some of the caseload of the federal courts, and contributing to good federal-state relations.

Justices Marshall, Blackmun, and Stevens dissented. Marshall accused the majority of using "the implements of literalism to wound, rather than to minister to, congressional intent. . . . "[c]

7. SPECIAL RULES FOR PRISONERS' RIGHTS LAWSUITS

In 1996, as part of the Prison Litigation Reform Act, Congress amended 42 U.S.C. § 1997e, substantially limiting the attorney's fees in lawsuits challenging prison conditions. Section 1997e(d)(1)(B)(i) requires that "the amount of the fee [be] proportionally related to the court ordered relief for the violation." How ought that to be assessed in cases seeking declaratory or injunctive relief? In cases involving monetary judgments, § 1997e(d)(2) provides that "a portion of the judgment (not to exceed 25 percent) shall be applied to satisfy the amount of attorney's fees awarded against the defendant. If the award of attorney's fees is not greater than 150 percent of the judgment, the excess shall be paid by the defendant." Does this provision cap the available amount of fees? Finally, § 1997e(d)(3) limits the hourly rate in prisoners' rights litigation to 150 percent of the hourly rate established by the Criminal Justice Act for court-appointed counsel for indigent defendants in federal criminal cases. In Martin v. Haddix, 527 U.S. 343 (1999), the Supreme Court held that the PLRA's provisions applied to all work performed after the act's effective date, including monitoring work under a consent decree which had provided for a higher hourly rate.

8. BIBLIOGRAPHY

Several treatises cover attorney's fees issues. See, e.g., Alan Hirsch and Diane Sheehey, Awarding Attorneys' Fees and Managing Fee Litigation (1994); E. Richard Larson, Federal Court Awards of Attorney's Fees (1981); Robert L. Rossi, Attorneys' Fees (1995); Herbert B. Newberg, Attorney Fee Awards (1986); Civil Rights Litigation Attorneys Fees Annual Handbook (1985).

There have also been symposia addressing attorney's fees issues. See, e.g., Symposium on Fee Shifting, 71 Chi.–Kent L. Rev. 415 (1995), with articles by David Anderson and Thomas Rowe, Bruce Hay, Keith Hylton, Harold Krent, Susan Olson, Richard Painter, Mark Stein, and Eric Talley. See also Symposium on Attorney Fee Shifting, 47 Law & Contemp. Probs. 1 (Winter 1984), which features a bibliography, see Kathryn M. Christie, Attorney Fee Shifting: A Bibliography, 47 Law & Contemp. Prob. 347 (1984), and articles by Murray L. Schwartz; John Leubsdorf; Werner Pfenningstorf; Herbert M. Kritzer; Thomas D. Rowe, Jr.; Ronald Braeutigam, Bruce Owen, and John Panzar; Frances Zemans; Bruce E. Fein; Robert V. Percival and Geoffrey P. Miller; Marshall J. Breger; Alfred P. Conard; and Charles W. Wolfram.

See also Samuel R. Berger, Court Awarded Attorney's Fees: What is "Reasonable"?, 126 U.Pa.L.Rev. 281 (1977) (discussing practical problems in implementing fee awards); Jeffrey S. Brand, The Second Front in the Fight for Civil Rights: The Supreme Court, Congress, and Statutory Fees, 69 Tex.L.Rev. 291 (1990) (concluding that the policies behind the fees act have been undercut by recent decisions); Robert Diamond, The Firestorm Over Attorney Fees Awards, 69 A.B.A.J. 1420 (1983) (focusing on fee awards to non-profit organizations); Kenneth R. Feinberg and John S. Gomperts, Attorney's

---

[c] Congress subsequently amended § 1988 to authorize the award of expert fees in § 1981 cases. See 42 U.S.C. §§ 1988(c), 2000e–5(k). The change did not affect § 1983. See Webster Greenthumb Co. v. Fulton County, Ga., 112 F. Supp. 2d 1339, 1380 (N.D. Ga. 2000).

Fees in the Agent Orange Litigation: Modifying the Lodestar Analysis for Mass Tort Cases, 14 N.Y.U.L.Rev. of Law & Soc. Change 613 (1986) (recounting the experience of a special master in the Agent Orange litigation); E. Richard Larson, Current Proposals in Congress to Limit and to Bar Court–Awarded Attorney's Fees in Public Interest Litigation, 14 N.Y.U.Rev. of Law & Soc. Change 523 (1986) (reviewing legislative proposals); Thomas D. Rowe, Jr., The Legal Theory of Attorney Fee Shifting: A Critical Overview, 1982 Duke L.J. 651 (analyzing rationales); Thomas D. Rowe, Jr., The Supreme Court on Attorney Fee Awards, 1985 and 1986 Terms: Economics, Ethics, and Ex Ante Analysis, 1 Geo.J.Legal Ethics 621 (1988) (analyzing the economic reasoning in recent cases); Stewart Schwab and Theodore Eisenberg, Explaining Constitutional Tort Litigation: The Influence of the Attorney Fees Statutes and the Government as Defendant, 73 Corn.L.Rev. 719 (1988) (assessing the impact of attorney's fees on litigation and success rates); and Charles Silver, Unloading the Lodestar: Toward a New Fee Award Procedure, 70 Tex.L.Rev. 865 (1992) (proposing an alternative to the lodestar).

3. FEE ENHANCEMENT

INTRODUCTORY NOTE ON RISK ENHANCEMENT

One of the most controversial issues in the law of attorney's fees is the question of risk enhancement. Is it proper to enhance the lodestar to account for the risk of not prevailing? In other words, may a court make an award beyond the sum of hours reasonably expended times reasonable hourly rate in order to compensate the plaintiff's attorney for having run of risk of recovering no fee award in the event of an adverse judgment?[a]

For many years, most lower courts said yes. As a result, the practice grew up of applying a "multiplier" to enhance the lodestar in risky cases. The issue reached the Supreme Court (for the second time, an earlier case of the same name having proved inconclusive) in Pennsylvania v. Delaware Valley Citizens' Council for Clean Air, 483 U.S. 711 (1987) (*Delaware Valley II*). In that case, a citizens group sued to force the state of Pennsylvania to comply with provisions of the Clean Air Act. In awarding attorney's fees under that statute, the lower courts doubled the lodestar calculation for certain phases of the litigation to compensate for the risks of contingency. The Supreme Court disapproved this result, but on grounds that left the general permissibility of risk enhancement in much doubt.

Justice White spoke for himself, Chief Justice Rehnquist, and Justices Powell and Scalia. They said risk enhancement should never be allowed. They saw risk enhancement as a way of forcing losing defendants to compensate plaintiffs' lawyers for not prevailing in other cases. Justices Blackmun, Brennan, Marshall, and Stevens disagreed. They argued that an upward adjustment in the lodestar was necessary to make fee awards competitive with the private market for legal services, which takes account of the risk of contingency.

The decisive vote was that of Justice O'Connor, who voted with the majority to overturn the fee award but wrote separately to explain her view that a premium for contingency should be allowed in some circumstances. It should be

---

[a] The availability of enhancement for delay in payment, as distinct from risk of nonpayment, was affirmed in Missouri v. Jenkins, 491 U.S. 274 (1989).

based, she said, not on the novelty or complexity of the issues in a particular case but on a general determination of how a relevant market compensates lawyers for the risk of contingency. Just how this determination was to be made was not spelled out.

Delaware Valley II provided no clear answers. By the time the issue returned to the Supreme Court, the composition of that body had changed. The result was a much clearer, though surely no less controversial, decision.

City of Burlington v. Dague

Supreme Court of the United States, 1992.
505 U.S. 557.

■ JUSTICE SCALIA delivered the opinion of the Court.

This case presents the question whether a court, in determining an award of reasonable attorney's fees under § 7002(e) of the Solid Waste Disposal Act (SWDA), as amended, 42 U.S.C. § 6972(e), or § 505(d) of the Federal Water Pollution Control Act (Clean Water Act (CWA)), as amended, 33 U.S.C. § 1365(d), may enhance the fee award above the "lodestar" amount in order to reflect the fact that the party's attorneys were retained on a contingent-fee basis and thus assumed the risk of receiving no payment at all for their services. Although different fee-shifting statutes are involved, the question is essentially identical to the one we addressed, but did not resolve, in Pennsylvania v. Delaware Valley Citizens' Council for Clean Air, 483 U.S. 711 (1987) (*Delaware Valley II*).

I

Respondent Dague (whom we will refer to in place of all the respondents) owns land in Vermont adjacent to a landfill that was owned and operated by petitioner City of Burlington. Represented by attorneys retained on a contingent-fee basis, he sued Burlington over its operation of the landfill. The District Court ruled, inter alia, that Burlington had violated provisions of the SWDA and the CWA, and ordered Burlington to close the landfill by January 1, 1990. It also determined that Dague was a "substantially prevailing party" entitled to an award of attorney's fees under the acts.

In calculating the attorney's fees award, the District Court first found reasonable the figures advanced by Dague for his attorneys' hourly rates and for the number of hours expended by them, producing a resulting "lodestar" attorney's fee of $198,027.50. . . . Addressing Dague's request for a contingency enhancement, the court . . . declared that Dague's "risk of not prevailing was substantial" and that "absent an opportunity for enhancement, [Dague] would have faced substantial difficulty in obtaining counsel of reasonable skill and competence in this complicated field of law." It concluded that "a 25 percent enhancement is appropriate, but anything more would be a windfall to the attorneys." It therefore enhanced the lodestar amount by 25 percent—$49,506.87.

The Court of Appeals affirmed in all respects. Reviewing the various opinions in *Delaware Valley II,* the court concluded that the issue whether and when a contingency enhancement is warranted remained open. . . . We granted certiorari only with respect to the propriety of the contingency enhancement.

II

We first provide some background to the issue before us. Fees for legal services in litigation may be either "certain" or "contingent" (or some hybrid of the two). A fee is certain if it is payable without regard to the outcome of the suit; it is contingent if the obligation to pay depends on a particular result's being obtained. Under the most common contingent-fee contract for litigation, the attorney receives no payment for his services if his client loses. Under this arrangement, the attorney bears a contingent risk of nonpayment that is the inverse of the case's prospects of success: if his client has an 80 percent chance of winning, the attorney's contingent risk is 20 percent.

In *Delaware Valley II,* we reversed a judgment that had affirmed enhancement of a fee award to reflect the contingent risk of nonpayment. In the process, we addressed whether the typical federal fee-shifting statute (there, § 304(d) of the Clean Air Act, 42 U.S.C. § 7604(d)) permits an attorney's fees award to be enhanced on account of contingency. In the principal opinion, Justice White, joined on this point by three other Justices, determined that such enhancement is not permitted. Justice O'Connor, in an opinion concurring in part and concurring in the judgment, concluded that no enhancement for contingency is appropriate "unless the applicant can establish that without an adjustment for risk the prevailing party would have faced substantial difficulties in finding counsel in the local or other relevant market" (internal quotations omitted), and that any enhancement "must be based on the difference in market treatment of contingent fee cases *as a class,* rather than on an assessment of the 'riskiness' of any particular case" (emphasis in original). Justice Blackmun's dissenting opinion, joined by three other Justices, concluded that enhancement for contingency is always statutorily required.

We turn again to this same issue.

III

Section 7002(e) of the SWDA and § 505(d) of the CWA authorize a court to "award costs of litigation (including *reasonable attorney . . . fees*)" (emphasis added). This language is similar to that of many other federal fee-shifting statutes, see, e.g., 42 U.S.C. § 1988(b); our case law construing what is a "reasonable" fee applies uniformly to all of them.

The "lodestar" figure has, as its name suggests, become the guiding light of our fee-shifting jurisprudence. We have established a "strong presumption" that the lodestar represents the "reasonable" fee, Pennsylvania v. Delaware Valley Citizens' Council for Clean Air, 478 U.S. 546, 565 (1986) (*Delaware Valley I*), and have placed upon the fee applicant who seeks more than that the burden of showing that "such an adjustment is *necessary* to the determination of a reasonable fee." Blum v. Stenson, 465 U.S. 886, 898 (1984) (emphasis added). The Court of Appeals held, and Dague argues here, that a "reasonable" fee for attorneys who have been retained on a contingency-fee basis must go beyond the lodestar, to compensate for risk of loss and of consequent nonpayment. Fee-shifting statutes should be construed, he contends, to replicate the economic incentives that operate in the private legal market, where attorneys working on a contingency-fee basis can be expected to charge some premium over their ordinary hourly rates. Petitioner Burlington argues, by contrast, that the lodestar fee may not be enhanced for contingency.

We note at the outset that an enhancement for contingency would likely duplicate in substantial part factors already subsumed in the lodestar. The risk of loss in a particular case (and, therefore, the attorney's contingent risk) is the product of two factors: (1) the legal and factual merits of the claim, and (2) the difficulty of establishing those merits. The second factor, however, is ordinarily reflected in the lodestar—either in the higher number of hours expended to overcome the difficulty, or in the higher hourly rate of the attorney skilled and experienced enough to do so. Taking account of it again through lodestar enhancement amounts to double-counting.

The first factor (relative merits of the claim) is not reflected in the lodestar, but there are good reasons why it should play no part in the calculation of the award. It is, of course, a factor that always exists (no claim has a 100 percent chance of success), so that computation of the lodestar would never end the court's inquiry in contingent-fee cases. Moreover, the consequences of awarding contingency enhancement to take account of this "merits" factor would be to provide attorneys with the same incentive to bring relatively meritless claims as relatively meritorious ones. Assume, for example, two claims, one with underlying merit of 20 percent, the other of 80 percent. Absent any contingency enhancement, a contingent-fee attorney would prefer to take the latter, since he is four times more likely to be paid. But with a contingency enhancement, this preference will disappear: the enhancement for the 20 percent claim would be a multiplier of 5 (100/20), which is quadruple the 1.25 multiplier (100/80) that would attach to the 80 percent claim. Thus, enhancement for the contingency risk posed by each case would encourage meritorious claims to be brought, but only at the social cost of indiscriminately encouraging nonmeritorious claims to be brought as well. We think that an unlikely objective of the "reasonable fees" provisions. "These statutes were not designed as a form of economic relief to improve the financial lot of lawyers." *Delaware Valley I,* supra, at 565.

Instead of enhancement based upon the contingency risk posed by each case, Dague urges that we adopt the approach set forth in the *Delaware Valley II* concurrence. We decline to do so, first and foremost because we do not see how it can intelligibly be applied. On the one hand, it would require the party seeking contingency enhancement to "establish that without the adjustment for risk [he] 'would have faced substantial difficulties in finding counsel in the local or other relevant market.' " 483 U.S., at 733. On the other hand, it would forbid enhancement based "on an assessment of the 'riskiness' of any particular case." 483 U.S., at 731; see id., at 734 (no enhancement "based on 'legal' risks or risks peculiar to the case"). But since the predominant reason that a contingent-fee claimant has difficulty finding counsel in any legal market where the winner's attorney's fees will be paid by the loser is that attorneys view his case as too risky (i.e., too unlikely to succeed), these two propositions, as a practical matter, collide.

A second difficulty with the approach taken by the concurrence in *Delaware Valley II* is that it would base the contingency enhancement on "the difference in market treatment of contingent fee cases *as a class.*" To begin with, for a very large proportion of contingency-fee cases—those seeking not monetary damages but injunctive or other equitable relief—there is no "market treatment." Such cases scarcely exist, except to the extent Congress has created an artificial "market" for them by fee-shifting—and looking to that "market" for the meaning of fee-shifting is obviously circular. Our decrees would follow the "market," which in turn is based on our decrees. But even apart from that difficulty, any approach that applies uniform treatment to the entire class of contingent-fee cases, or to any conceivable subject-matter-based subclass, cannot possibly achieve the supposed goal of mirroring market incentives. As discussed above, the contingent risk of a case (and hence the difficulty of getting contingent-fee lawyers to take it) depends principally upon its particular merits. Contingency enhancement calculated on *any* class-wide basis, therefore, guarantees *at best* (leaving aside the double-counting problem described earlier) that those cases within the class that have the class-average chance of success will be compensated according to what the "market" requires to produce the services, and that *all cases* having above-class-average chance of success will be overcompensated.

Looking beyond the *Delaware Valley II* concurrence's approach, we perceive no other basis, fairly derivable from the fee-shifting statutes, by which contingency enhancement, if adopted, could be restricted to fewer than all contingent-fee cases. And we see a number of reasons for concluding that no contingency enhancement whatever is compatible with the fee-shifting statutes at issue. First, just as the statutory language limiting fees to prevailing (or substantially prevailing) parties bars a prevailing plaintiff from recovering fees relating to claims on which he lost, Hensley v. Eckerhart, 461 U.S. 424 (1983), so should it bar a prevailing plaintiff from recovering for the risk of loss. See *Delaware Valley II,* supra, 483 U.S., at 719–20 (principal opinion). An attorney operating on a contingency-fee basis pools the risks presented by his various cases: cases that turn out to be successful pay for the time he gambled on those that did not. To award a contingency enhancement under a fee-shifting statute would in effect pay for the attorney's time (or anticipated time) in cases where his client does not prevail.

Second, both before and since *Delaware Valley II,* "we have generally turned away from the contingent-fee model"—which would make the fee award a percentage of the value of the relief awarded in the primary action—"to the lodestar model." Venegas v. Mitchell, 495 U.S. 82, 87 (1990). We have done so, it must be noted, even though the lodestar model often (perhaps, generally) results in a larger fee award than the contingent-fee model. See, e.g., Report of the Federal Courts Study Committee 104 (Apr. 2, 1990) (lodestar method may "give lawyers incentives to run up hours unnecessarily, which can lead to overcompensation"). For example, in Blanchard v. Bergeron, 489 U.S. 87 (1989), we held that the lodestar governed, even though it produced a fee that substantially exceeded the amount provided in the contingent-fee agreement between plaintiff and his counsel (which was self-evidently an amount adequate to attract the needed legal services). Contingency enhancement is a feature inherent in the contingent-fee model (since attorneys factor in the particular risks of a case in negotiating their fee and in deciding whether to accept the case). To engraft this feature onto the lodestar model would be to concoct a hybrid scheme that resorts to the contingent-fee model to increase a fee award but not to reduce it. Contingency enhancement is therefore not consistent with our general rejection of the contingent-fee model for fee awards, nor is it necessary to the determination of a reasonable fee.

And finally, the interest in ready administrability that has underlain our adoption of the lodestar approach and the related interest in avoiding burdensome satellite litigation (the fee application "should not result in a second major litigation," *Hensley,* supra, at 437), counsel strongly against adoption of contingency enhancement. Contingency enhancement would make the setting of fees more complex and arbitrary, hence more unpredictable, and hence more litigable. It is neither necessary nor even possible for application of the fee-shifting statutes to mimic the intricacies of the fee-paying market in every respect. See *Delaware Valley I,* supra, at 565.

Adopting the position set forth in Justice White's opinion in *Delaware Valley II,* we hold that enhancement for contingency is not permitted under the fee-shifting statutes at issue. We reverse the Court of Appeals' judgment insofar as it affirmed the 25 percent enhancement of the lodestar.

It is so ordered.

■ JUSTICE BLACKMUN, with whom JUSTICE STEVENS joined, dissenting.

In language typical of most federal fee-shifting provisions, the statutes involved in this case authorize courts to award the prevailing party a "reasonable" attorney's fee. Two principles, in my view, require the conclusion that the "enhanced" fee awarded to respondents was reasonable. First, this Court consistently has recognized that a "reasonable" fee is to be a "fully compensatory fee," Hensley v. Eckerhart, 461 U.S. 424, 435 (1983), and is to be "calculated on the basis of rates and practices prevailing in the relevant market." Missouri v. Jenkins, 491 U.S. 274, 286 (1989). Second, it is a fact of the market that an attorney who is paid only when his client prevails will tend to charge a higher fee than one who is paid regardless of outcome, and relevant professional standards long have recognized that this practice is reasonable.

The Court does not deny these principles. It simply refuses to draw the conclusion that follows ineluctably: If a statutory fee consistent with market practices is "reasonable," and if in the private market an attorney who assumes the risk of nonpayment can expect additional compensation, then it follows that a statutory fee may include additional compensation for contingency and still qualify as reasonable. The Court's decision to the contrary violates the principles we have applied consistently in prior cases and will seriously weaken the enforcement of those statutes for which Congress has authorized fee awards—notably, many of our nation's civil rights laws and environmental laws.

I

Congress' purpose in adopting fee-shifting provisions was to strengthen the enforcement of selected federal laws by ensuring that private persons seeking to enforce those laws could retain competent counsel. In particular, federal fee-shifting provisions have been designed to address two related difficulties that otherwise would prevent private persons from obtaining counsel. First, many potential plaintiffs lack sufficient resources to hire attorneys. Second, many of the statutes to which Congress attached fee-shifting provisions typically will generate either no damages or only small recoveries; accordingly, plaintiffs bringing cases under these statutes cannot offer attorneys a share of a recovery sufficient to justify a standard contingent fee arrangement. See Pennsylvania v. Delaware Valley Citizens' Council for Clean Air (*Delaware Valley II*), 483 U.S. 711, 749 (dissenting opinion). The strategy of the fee-shifting provisions is to attract competent counsel to selected federal cases by ensuring that if they prevail, counsel will receive fees commensurable with what they could obtain in other litigation. If federal fee-bearing litigation is less remunerative than private litigation, then the only attorneys who will take such cases will be underemployed lawyers—who likely will be less competent than the successful, busy lawyers who would shun federal fee-bearing litigation—and public interest lawyers who, by any measure, are insufficiently numerous to handle all the cases for which other competent attorneys cannot be found. See *Delaware Valley II,* supra, at 742–43 (dissenting opinion).

In many cases brought under federal statutes that authorize fee-shifting, plaintiffs will be unable to ensure that their attorneys will be compensated for the risk that they might not prevail. This will be true in precisely those situations targeted by the fee-shifting statutes—where plaintiffs lack sufficient funds to hire an attorney on a win-or-lose basis and where potential damage awards are insufficient to justify a standard contingent fee arrangement. In these situations, unless the fee-shifting statutes are construed to compensate attorneys for the risk of nonpayment associated with loss, the expected return from cases brought under federal fee-shifting provisions will be less than could be obtained in otherwise comparable private litigation offering guaranteed, win-or-lose compensation. Prudent counsel, under these conditions, would tend to avoid federal fee-bearing claims in favor of private litigation, even in the very situations for which the attorney's fee statutes were designed. This will be true even if the fee-bearing claim is more likely meritorious than the competing private claim.

In *Delaware Valley II,* five Justices of this Court concluded that for these reasons the broad statutory term "reasonable attorney's fee" must be construed to permit, in some circumstances, compensation above the hourly win-or-lose rate generally borrowed to compute the lodestar fee. Together with the three Justices who joined my dissenting opinion in that case, I would have allowed enhancement where, and to the extent that, the attorney's compensation is contingent upon prevailing and receiving a statutory award. I indicated that if, by contrast, the attorney and client have been able to mitigate the risk of nonpayment—either in full, by agreeing to win-or-lose compensation or to a contingent share of a substantial damage recovery, or in part, by arranging for partial payment—then to that extent enhancement should be unavailable. I made clear that the "risk" for which enhancement might be available is not the particular factual and legal riskiness of an individual case, but the risk of nonpayment associated with contingent cases considered as a class. Congress, I concluded, did not intend to prohibit district courts from considering contingency in calculating a "reasonable" attorney's fee.[4]

Justice O'Connor's concurring opinion agreed that "Congress did not intend to foreclose consideration of contingency in setting a reasonable fee" and that "compensation for contingency must be based on the difference in market treatment of contingent fee cases *as a class,* rather than on an assessment of the 'riskiness' of any particular case" (emphasis in original). As I understand her opinion, Justice O'Connor further agreed that a court considering an enhancement must determine whether and to what extent the attorney's compensation was contingent, as well as whether and to what

[4] A number of bills introduced in Congress would have done just this, by prohibiting "bonuses and multipliers" where a suit is against the United States, a state, or a local government. These bills failed to receive congressional approval. See *Delaware Valley II,* supra, at 739, n. 3 (dissenting opinion). Moreover, in some instances Congress explicitly has prohibited enhancements, as in the 1986 amendments to the Education of the Handicapped Act. See 20 U.S.C. § 1415(e)(4)(C) ("[n]o bonus or multiplier may be used in calculating the fees awarded under this subsection"). Congress' express prohibition on enhancement in this statute suggests that it did not understand the standard fee-shifting language used elsewhere to bar enhancement.

extent that contingency was, or could have been, mitigated. Her concurrence added, however, an additional inquiry designed to make the market-based approach "not merely justifiable in theory but also objective and nonarbitrary in practice." She suggested two additional "constraints on a court's discretion" in determining whether, and how much, enhancement is warranted. First, "district courts and courts of appeals should treat a determination of how a particular market compensates for contingency as controlling future cases involving the same market," and varying rates of enhancement among markets must be justifiable by reference to real differences in those markets. Second, the applicant bears the burden of demonstrating that without an adjustment for risk "the prevailing party would have faced substantial difficulties in finding counsel in the local or other relevant market" (internal quotations omitted).

II

After criticizing at some length an approach it admits respondents and their amici do not advocate and after rejecting the approach of the *Delaware Valley II* concurrence, the Court states that it "see[s] a number of reasons for concluding that no contingency enhancement whatever is compatible with the fee-shifting statutes at issue." I do not find any of these arguments persuasive.

The Court argues, first, that "[a]n attorney operating on a contingency-fee basis pools the risks presented by his various cases" and uses the cases that were successful to subsidize those that were not. "To award a contingency enhancement under a fee-shifting statute," the Court concludes, would "in effect" contravene the prevailing-party limitation, by allowing the attorney to recover fees for cases in which his client does not prevail. What the words "in effect" conceal, however, is the Court's inattention to the language of the statutes: The provisions at issue in this case, like fee-shifting provisions generally, authorize fee awards to prevailing parties, not their attorneys. Respondents simply do not advocate awarding fees to any party who has not prevailed. Moreover, the Court's reliance on the "prevailing party" limitation is somewhat misleading: the Court's real objection to contingency enhancement is that the amount of an enhanced award would be excessive, not that parties receiving enhanced fee awards are not prevailing parties entitled to an award. . . .

Second, the Court suggests that "both before and since *Delaware Valley II*, 'we have generally turned away from the contingent-fee model'—which would make the fee award a percentage of the value of the relief awarded in the primary action—'to the lodestar model.' " This argument simply plays on two meanings of "contingency." Most assuredly, respondents—who received no damages for their fee-bearing claims—do not advocate "mak[ing] the fee award a percentage" of that amount. Rather, they argue that the lodestar figure must be enhanced because their attorneys' compensation was contingent on prevailing, and because their attorneys could not otherwise be compensated for assuming the risk of nonpayment.

Third, the Court suggests that allowing for contingency enhancement "would make the setting of fees more complex and arbitrary" and would likely lead to "burdensome satellite litigation" that this Court has said should be avoided. The present case is an odd one in which to make this point: the issue of enhancement hardly occupied center stage in the fees portion of this litigation, and it became a time-consuming matter only after the Court granted certiorari, limited to this question alone. Moreover, if Justice O'Connor's standard were adopted, the matter of the amount by which fees should be increased would quickly become settled in the various district courts and courts of appeals for the different kinds of federal litigation. And in any event, speculation that enhancement determinations would be "burdensome" does not speak to the issue whether they are required by the fee-shifting statutes.

The final objection to be considered is the Court's contention that any approach that treats contingent-fee cases as a class is doomed to failure. The Court's argument on this score has two parts. First, the Court opines that "for a very large proportion of contingency-fee cases"—cases in which only equitable relief is sought—"there is no 'market treatment,' " except insofar as Congress has created an "artificial" market with the fee-shifting statutes themselves. It is circular, the Court contends, to "loo[k] to *that* 'market' for the meaning of fee-shifting." And even leaving that difficulty aside, the Court continues, the real "risk" to which lawyers respond is the riskiness of particular cases. Because under a class-based contingency enhancement system the same enhancement will be awarded whether the chance of prevailing was 80 percent or 20 percent, "*all cases* having above-class-average chance of success will be overcompensated" (emphasis in original).

Both parts of this argument are mistaken. The circularity objection overlooks the fact that even under the Court's unenhanced lodestar approach, the district court must find a relevant private market from which to select a fee. The Court offers no reason why this market disappears only when the inquiry turns to enhancement. The second part of the Court's argument is mistaken so far as it assumes the only relevant incentive to which attorneys respond is the risk of losing particular cases. As explained above, a proper system of contingency enhancement addresses a different kind of incentive: the common incentive of all lawyers to avoid *any* fee-bearing claim in which the plaintiff cannot guarantee the lawyer's compensation if he does not prevail. Because, as the Court observes, "no claim has a 100 percent chance of success," *any* such case under a pure lodestar system will offer a lower prospective return per hour than one in which the lawyer will be paid at the same lodestar rate, win or lose. Even the *least* meritorious case in which the attorney is guaranteed compensation whether he wins or loses will be economically preferable to the *most* meritorious fee-bearing claim in which the attorney will be paid only if he prevails, so long as the cases require the same amount of time. Yet as noted above, this latter kind of case—in which potential plaintiffs can neither afford to hire attorneys on a straight hourly basis nor offer a percentage of a substantial damage recovery—is exactly the kind of case for which the fee-shifting statutes were designed.

III

Preventing attorneys who bring actions under fee-shifting statutes from receiving fully compensatory fees will harm far more than the legal profession. Congress intended the fee-shifting statutes to serve as an integral enforcement mechanism in a variety of federal statutes—most notably, civil rights and environmental statutes. The amicus briefs filed in this case make clear that we can expect many meritorious actions will not be filed, or, if filed, will be prosecuted by less experienced and able counsel. Today's decision weakens the protections we afford important federal rights.

I dissent.

■ JUSTICE O'CONNOR, dissenting.

I continue to be of the view that in certain circumstances a "reasonable" attorney's fee should not be computed by the purely retrospective lodestar figure, but also must incorporate a reasonable incentive to an attorney contemplating whether or not to take a case in the first place. See Pennsylvania v. Delaware Valley Citizens' Council for Clean Air, 483 U.S. 711, 731–34 (1987) (*Delaware Valley II*) (O'Connor, J., concurring in part and concurring in judgment). As Justice Blackmun cogently explains, when an attorney must choose between two cases—one with a client who will pay the attorney's fees win or lose and the other who can only promise the statutory compensation if the case is successful—the attorney will choose the fee-paying client, unless the contingency-client can promise an enhancement of sufficient magnitude to justify the extra risk of nonpayment. Thus, a reasonable fee should be one that would "attract competent counsel," and in some markets this must include the assurance of a contingency enhancement if the plaintiff should prevail. I therefore dissent from the Court's holding that a "reasonable" attorney's fee can never include an enhancement for cases taken on contingency.

In my view the promised enhancement should be "based on the difference in market treatment of contingent fee cases as a class, rather than on an assessment of the 'riskiness' of any particular case" (emphasis omitted). As Justice Blackmun has shown, the Court's reasons for rejecting a market-based approach do not stand up to scrutiny. Admittedly, the courts called upon to determine the enhancements appropriate for various markets would be required to make economic calculations based on less-than-perfect data. Yet that is also the case, for example, in inverse condemnation and antitrust cases, and the Court has never suggested that the difficulty of the task or possible inexactitude of the result justifies forgoing those calculations altogether. As Justice Blackmun notes, these initial hurdles would be overcome as the enhancements appropriate to various markets became settled in the district courts and courts of appeals.

In this case, the District Court determined that a 25 percent contingency enhancement was appropriate by reliance on the likelihood of success in the individual case. The Court of Appeals affirmed on the basis of its holding in Friends of the Earth v. Eastman Kodak Co., 834 F.2d 295 (2d Cir. 1987), which asks simply whether, without the possibility of a fee enhancement, the prevailing party would not have been able to obtain competent counsel. Although I believe that inquiry is part of the contingency enhancement determination, I also believe that it was error to base the degree of enhancement on case-specific factors. Because I can find no market-specific support for the 25 percent enhancement figure in the affidavits submitted by respondents in support of the fee request, I would vacate the judgment affirming the fee award and remand for a market-based assessment of a suitable enhancement for contingency.

NOTE ON RISK ENHANCEMENT

The impact of *Dague* is assessed in Julie Davies, Federal Civil Rights Practice in the 1990's: The Dichotomy Between Reality and Practice, 48 Hastings L.J. 197 (1997). Davies reports that the reactions of civil rights lawyers are surprisingly mixed. Plaintiffs' lawyers generally agreed that *Dague* had lowered their leverage in settlement negotiations, but many viewed the loss of multipliers as relatively insignificant. Several "stated that under the lodestar formulation, they are paid at a high hourly rate, and that courts have adjusted for the lack of a multiplier by awarding them a greater percentage of the hours billed." Davies finds, however, that the lack of fee enhancement does affect lawyers bringing class actions, especially in cases requiring expert witnesses. (Recall that expert witness fees are not recoverable under § 1988(b).)

Dague notes that there are two kinds of fee arrangements—"certain" and "contingent." One difficulty in determining fees may arise from the fact that most market hourly rates are set in the context of "certain" fee arrangements: that is, the hourly rate charged in a given market by lawyers with a particular degree of experience may be set in cases where payment is certain. Most contingent-fee arrangements, by contrast, do not specify an hourly rate. The "effective hourly rate" of contingent-fee practitioners, however, may be quite high indeed, and is likely to be higher than the rate of equivalent lawyers who face no risk of nonpayment. See generally Herbert M. Kritzer, The Wages of Risk: The Returns of Contingency Fee Legal Practice, 47 DePaul L. Rev. 267 (1998) (describing the effective hourly rates earned by contingent fee practitioners). Ought the reasonable hourly rate itself be adjusted by taking into account how the market prices cases?

For a sophisticated economic analysis of the question of multipliers, see Peter H. Huang, A New Options Theory for Risk Multipliers of Attorney's Fees in Federal Civil Rights Litigation, 73 N.Y.U.L. Rev. 1943 (1998), which uses options theory to argue that fee enhancement should be allowed but that multipliers should be set at "less than the initial reciprocal of the probability of the plaintiff prevailing in the lawsuit." For another sophisticated economic analysis of risk enhancement and alternatives, see Richard Craswell, Deterrence and Damages: The Multiplier Principle and Its Alternatives, 97 Mich. L. Rev. 2185 (1999) (concluding that the traditional multiplier can achieve optimal deterrence "only if the multiplier is calculated on a case-by-case basis" and undertaking analysis of more plausible alternatives).

INTRODUCTORY NOTE ON RESULT ENHANCEMENT

After *Dague*, courts can no longer enhance the lodestar to take into account the contingency of civil rights actions. But *Dague* did not address other potential justifications for upward adjustments to the lodestar amount. In Hensley v. Eckerhart, 461 U.S. 424 (1983), the Court had intimated that an enhanced award might be justifiable "in some cases of exceptional success." What results might qualify for such adjustment?

Perdue v. Kenny A.

Supreme Court of the United States, 2010.
130 S.Ct. 1662.

■ JUSTICE ALITO delivered the opinion of the Court.

This case presents the question whether the calculation of an attorney's fee, under federal fee-shifting statutes, based on the "lodestar," i.e., the number of hours worked multiplied by the prevailing hourly rates, may be increased due to superior performance and results.[1] We have stated in

[1] Justice Breyer would have us answer this question "Yes" and then end the opinion. Such an opinion would be of little use to the bench or bar and would pointlessly invite an additional round of litigation. The issue of the standards to be applied in granting an enhancement is fairly subsumed within the question that we agreed to decide and has been extensively discussed in the briefs filed in this case.

previous cases that such an increase is permitted in extraordinary circumstances, and we reaffirm that rule. But as we have also said in prior cases, there is a strong presumption that the lodestar is sufficient; factors subsumed in the lodestar calculation cannot be used as a ground for increasing an award above the lodestar; and a party seeking fees has the burden of identifying a factor that the lodestar does not adequately take into account and proving with specificity that an enhanced fee is justified. Because the District Court did not apply these standards, we reverse the decision below and remand for further proceedings consistent with this opinion.

I

A

Respondents (plaintiffs below) are children in the Georgia foster-care system and their next friends. They filed this class action on behalf of 3,000 children in foster care and named as defendants the Governor of Georgia and various state officials (petitioners in this case). Claiming that deficiencies in the foster-care system in two counties near Atlanta violated their federal and state constitutional and statutory rights, respondents sought injunctive and declaratory relief, as well as attorney's fees and expenses.

The United States District Court for the Northern District of Georgia eventually referred the case to mediation, where the parties entered into a consent decree, which the District Court approved. The consent decree resolved all pending issues other than the fees that respondents' attorneys were entitled to receive under 42 U.S.C. § 1988.

B

Respondents submitted a request for more than $14 million in attorney's fees. Half of that amount was based on their calculation of the lodestar—roughly 30,000 hours multiplied by hourly rates of $200 to $495 for attorneys and $75 to $150 for non-attorneys. In support of their fee request, respondents submitted affidavits asserting that these rates were within the range of prevailing market rates for legal services in the relevant market.

The other half of the amount that respondents sought represented a fee enhancement for superior work and results. Affidavits submitted in support of this request claimed that the lodestar amount "would be generally insufficient to induce lawyers of comparable skill, judgment, professional representation and experience" to litigate this case. Petitioners objected to the fee request, contending that some of the proposed hourly rates were too high, that the hours claimed were excessive, and that the enhancement would duplicate factors that were reflected in the lodestar amount.

The District Court awarded fees of approximately $10.5 million. 454 F. Supp.2d 1260 (N.D. Ga. 2006). The District Court found that the hourly rates proposed by respondents were "fair and reasonable," but that some of the entries on counsel's billing records were vague and that the hours claimed for many of the billing categories were excessive. The court therefore cut the non-travel hours by 15 percent and halved the hourly rate for travel hours. This resulted in a lodestar calculation of approximately $6 million.

The court then enhanced this award by 75 percent, concluding that the lodestar calculation did not take into account "(1) the fact that class counsel were required to advance case expenses of $1.7 million over a three-year period with no on[-]going reimbursement, (2) the fact that class counsel were not paid on an on-going basis as the work was being performed, and

(3) the fact that class counsel's ability to recover a fee and expense reimbursement were completely contingent on the outcome of the case." Id. at 1288. The court stated that respondents' attorneys had exhibited "a higher degree of skill, commitment, dedication, and professionalism . . . than the Court has seen displayed by the attorneys in any other case during its 27 years on the bench." Id. at 1289. The court also commented that the results obtained were " 'extraordinary' " and added that "[a]fter 58 years as a practicing attorney and federal judge, the Court is unaware of any other case in which a plaintiff class has achieved such a favorable result on such a comprehensive scale." Id. at 1290. The enhancement resulted in an additional $4.5 million fee award.

Relying on prior Circuit precedent, a panel of the Eleventh Circuit affirmed, 532 F.3d 1209 (2008), [and] denied rehearing en banc over the dissent of three judges. 547 U.S. 1319 (2008). . . .

II

The general rule in our legal system is that each party must pay its own attorney's fees and expenses, see Hensley v. Eckerhart, 461 U.S. 424, 429 (1983), but Congress enacted 42 U.S.C. § 1988 in order to ensure that federal rights are adequately enforced. Section 1988 provides that a prevailing party in certain civil rights actions may recover "a reasonable attorney's fee as part of the costs."[3] Unfortunately, the statute does not explain what Congress meant by a "reasonable" fee, and therefore the task of identifying an appropriate methodology for determining a "reasonable" fee was left for the courts.

One possible method was set out in Johnson v. Georgia Highway Express, Inc., 488 F.2d 714, 717–19 (5th Cir. 1974), which listed 12 factors that a court should consider in determining a reasonable fee.[4] This method, however, "gave very little actual guidance to district courts. Setting attorney's fees by reference to a series of sometimes subjective factors placed unlimited discretion in trial judges and produced disparate results." Pennsylvania v. Delaware Valley Citizens' Council for Clean Air, 478 U.S. 546, 563 (1986) (*Delaware Valley I*).

An alternative, the lodestar approach, was pioneered by the Third Circuit in Lindy Bros. Builders, Inc. of Philadelphia v. American Radiator & Standard Sanitary Corp., 487 F. 2d 161 (1973), and "achieved dominance in the federal courts" after our decision in *Hensley*. Gisbrecht v. Barnhart, 535 U. S. 789, 801 (2002). "Since that time, '[t]he "lodestar" figure has, as its name suggests, become the guiding light of our fee-shifting jurisprudence' " (quoting Burlington v. Dague, 505 U.S. 557, 562 (1992)).

Although the lodestar method is not perfect, it has several important virtues. First, in accordance with our understanding of the aim of fee-shifting statutes, the lodestar looks to "the prevailing market rates in the relevant community." Blum v. Stenson, 465 U.S. 886, 895 (1984). Developed

---

3 Virtually identical language appears in many of the federal fee-shifting statutes. See Burlington v. Dague, 505 U.S. 557, 562 (1992).

4 These factors were: "(1) the time and labor required; (2) the novelty and difficulty of the questions; (3) the skill requisite to perform the legal service properly; (4) the preclusion of employment by the attorney due to the acceptance of the case; (5) the customary fee; (6) whether the fee is fixed or contingent; (7) time limitations imposed by the client or the circumstances; (8) the amount involved and the results obtained; (9) the experience, reputation, and ability of the attorneys; (10) the 'undesirability' of the case; (11) the nature and length of the professional relationship with the client; and (12) awards in similar cases." Hensley v. Eckerhart, 461 U.S. 424, n.3 (1983).

after the practice of hourly billing had become widespread, the lodestar method produces an award that *roughly* approximates the fee that the prevailing attorney would have received if he or she had been representing a paying client who was billed by the hour in a comparable case. Second, the lodestar method is readily administrable, see *Dague*, 505 U.S., at 566; see also Buckhannon Board & Care Home, Inc. v. West Virginia Dept. of Health and Human Resources, 532 U.S. 598, 609 (2001); and unlike the *Johnson* approach, the lodestar calculation is "objective," *Hensley*, 461 U.S., at 433, and thus cabins the discretion of trial judges, permits meaningful judicial review, and produces reasonably predictable results.

III

Our prior decisions concerning the federal fee-shifting statutes have established six important rules that lead to our decision in this case.

First, a "reasonable" fee is a fee that is sufficient to induce a capable attorney to undertake the representation of a meritorious civil rights case. Section 1988's aim is to enforce the covered civil rights statutes, not to provide "a form of economic relief to improve the financial lot of attorneys." *Delaware Valley I*, 478 U.S., at 565.

Second, the lodestar method yields a fee that is presumptively sufficient to achieve this objective. See *Dague*, 505 U.S., at 562; *Delaware Valley I*, 478 U.S., at 565. Indeed, we have said that the presumption is a "strong" one. *Dague*, 505 U.S., at 562; *Delaware Valley I*, 478 U.S., at 565.

Third, although we have never sustained an enhancement of a lodestar amount for performance, we have repeatedly said that enhancements may be awarded in " 'rare' " and " 'exceptional' " circumstances. *Delaware Valley I*, 478 U.S., at 565; *Blum*, 465 U.S., at 897; *Hensley*, 461 U.S., at 435.

Fourth, we have noted that "the lodestar figure includes most, if not all, of the relevant factors constituting a 'reasonable' attorney's fee," *Delaware Valley I*, 478 U.S., at 566, and have held that an enhancement may not be awarded based on a factor that is subsumed in the lodestar calculation, see *Dague*, 505 U.S., at 562–63; Pennsylvania v. Delaware Valley Citizens' Council for Clean Air, 483 U.S. 711, 726–27 (1987) (*Delaware Valley II*) (plurality opinion); *Blum,* 465 U.S., at 898. We have thus held that the novelty and complexity of a case generally may not be used as a ground for an enhancement because these factors "presumably [are] fully reflected in the number of billable hours recorded by counsel." Ibid. We have also held that the quality of an attorney's performance generally should not be used to adjust the lodestar "[b]ecause considerations concerning the quality of a prevailing party's counsel's representation normally are reflected in the reasonable hourly rate." *Delaware Valley I*, 478 U.S., at 566.

Fifth, the burden of proving that an enhancement is necessary must be borne by the fee applicant. *Dague*, 505 U.S., at 561; *Blum,* 465 U.S., at 901–02.

Finally, a fee applicant seeking an enhancement must produce "specific evidence" that supports the award. Id., at 899, 901. This requirement is essential if the lodestar method is to realize one of its chief virtues, i.e., providing a calculation that is objective and capable of being reviewed on appeal.

IV

A

In light of what we have said in prior cases, we reject any contention that a fee determined by the lodestar method may not be enhanced in any situation. The lodestar method was never intended to be conclusive in all circumstances. Instead, there is a "strong presumption" that the lodestar figure is reasonable, but that presumption may be overcome in those rare circumstances in which the lodestar does not adequately take into account a factor that may properly be considered in determining a reasonable fee.

B

In this case, we are asked to decide whether either the quality of an attorney's performance or the results obtained are factors that may properly provide a basis for an enhancement. We treat these two factors as one. When a plaintiff's attorney achieves results that are more favorable than would have been predicted based on the governing law and the available evidence, the outcome may be attributable to superior performance and commitment of resources by plaintiff's counsel. Or the outcome may result from inferior performance by defense counsel, unanticipated defense concessions, unexpectedly favorable rulings by the court, an unexpectedly sympathetic jury, or simple luck. Since none of these latter causes can justify an enhanced award, superior results are relevant only to the extent it can be shown that they are the result of superior attorney performance. Thus, we need only consider whether superior attorney performance can justify an enhancement. And in light of the principles derived from our prior cases, we inquire whether there are circumstances in which superior attorney performance is not adequately taken into account in the lodestar calculation. We conclude that there are a few such circumstances but that these circumstances are indeed "rare" and "exceptional," and require specific evidence that the lodestar fee would not have been "adequate to attract competent counsel." *Blum*, 465 U.S., at 897 (internal quotation marks omitted).

First, an enhancement may be appropriate where the method used in determining the hourly rate employed in the lodestar calculation does not adequately measure the attorney's true market value, as demonstrated in part during the litigation.[5] This may occur if the hourly rate is determined by a formula that takes into account only a single factor (such as years since admission to the bar) or perhaps only a few similar factors. In such a case, an enhancement may be appropriate so that an attorney is compensated at the rate that the attorney would receive in cases not governed by the federal fee-shifting statutes. But in order to provide a calculation that is objective and reviewable, the trial judge should adjust the attorney's hourly rate in accordance with specific proof linking the attorney's ability to a prevailing market rate.

Second, an enhancement may be appropriate if the attorney's performance includes an extraordinary outlay of expenses and the litigation is exceptionally protracted. . . . [W]hen an attorney agrees to represent a civil rights plaintiff who cannot afford to pay the attorney, the attorney presumably understands that no reimbursement is likely to be received

---

[5] Respondents correctly note that an attorney's "brilliant insights and critical maneuvers sometimes matter far more than hours worked or years of experience." But as we said in *Blum*, supra, at 898, "[i]n those cases, the special skill and experience of counsel should be reflected in the reasonableness of the hourly rates."

until the successful resolution of the case, and therefore enhancements to compensate for delay in reimbursement for expenses must be reserved for unusual cases. In such exceptional cases, however, an enhancement may be allowed, but the amount of the enhancement must be calculated using a method that is reasonable, objective, and capable of being reviewed on appeal, such as by applying a standard rate of interest to the qualifying outlays of expenses.

Third, there may be extraordinary circumstances in which an attorney's performance involves exceptional delay in the payment of fees. An attorney who expects to be compensated under § 1988 presumably understands that payment of fees will generally not come until the end of the case, if at all. Compensation for this delay is generally made "either by basing the award on current rates or by adjusting the fee based on historical rates to reflect its present value." Missouri v. Jenkins, 491 U.S. 274, 282 (1989) (internal quotation marks omitted). But we do not rule out the possibility that an enhancement may be appropriate where an attorney assumes these costs in the face of unanticipated delay, particularly where the delay is unjustifiably caused by the defense. In such a case, however, the enhancement should be calculated by applying a method similar to that described above in connection with exceptional delay in obtaining reimbursement for expenses.

We reject the suggestion that it is appropriate to grant performance enhancements on the ground that departures from hourly billing are becoming more common. As we have noted, the lodestar was adopted in part because it provides a rough approximation of general billing practices, and accordingly, if hourly billing becomes unusual, an alternative to the lodestar method may have to be found. However, neither respondents nor their amici contend that that day has arrived. Nor have they shown that permitting the award of enhancements on top of the lodestar figure corresponds to prevailing practice in the general run of cases.

We are told that, under an increasingly popular arrangement, attorneys are paid at a reduced hourly rate but receive a bonus if certain specified results are obtained, and this practice is analogized to the award of an enhancement such as the one in this case. The analogy, however, is flawed. An attorney who agrees, at the outset of the representation, to a *reduced hourly rate* in exchange for the opportunity to earn a performance bonus is in a position far different from an attorney in a § 1988 case who is compensated at the *full prevailing rate* and then seeks a performance enhancement in addition to the lodestar amount after the litigation has concluded. Reliance on these comparisons for the purposes of administering enhancements, therefore, is not appropriate.

V

In the present case, the District Court did not provide proper justification for the large enhancement that it awarded. The court increased the lodestar award by 75 percent but, as far as the court's opinion reveals, this figure appears to have been essentially arbitrary. Why, for example, did the court grant a 75 percent enhancement instead of the 100 percent increase that respondents sought? And why 75 percent rather than 50 percent or 25 percent or 10 percent?

The District Court commented that the enhancement was the "minimum enhancement of the lodestar necessary to reasonably compensate [respondents'] counsel." But the effect of the enhancement was to increase the top rate for the attorneys to more than $866 per hour,[7] and the District Court did not point to anything in the record that shows that this is an appropriate figure for the relevant market.

The District Court pointed to the fact that respondents' counsel had to make extraordinary outlays for expenses and had to wait for reimbursement, but the court did not calculate the amount of the enhancement that is attributable to this factor. Similarly, the District Court noted that respondents' counsel did not receive fees on an ongoing basis while the case was pending, but the court did not sufficiently link this factor to proof in the record that the delay here was outside the normal range expected by attorneys who rely on § 1988 for the payment of their fees or quantify the disparity. Nor did the court provide a calculation of the cost to counsel of any extraordinary and unwarranted delay. And the court's reliance on the contingency of the outcome contravenes our holding in *Dague*. See 505 U. S., at 565.

Finally, insofar as the District Court relied on a comparison of the performance of counsel in this case with the performance of counsel in unnamed prior cases, the District Court did not employ a methodology that permitted meaningful appellate review. Needless to say, we do not question the sincerity of the District Court's observations, and we are in no position to assess their accuracy. But when a trial judge awards an enhancement on an impressionistic basis, a major purpose of the lodestar method—providing an objective and reviewable basis for fees—is undermined.

Determining a "reasonable attorney's fee" is a matter that is committed to the sound discretion of a trial judge, but the judge's discretion is not unlimited. It is essential that the judge provide a reasonably specific explanation for all aspects of a fee determination, including any award of an enhancement. Unless such an explanation is given, adequate appellate review is not feasible, and without such review, widely disparate awards may be made, and awards may be influenced (or at least, may appear to be influenced) by a judge's subjective opinion regarding particular attorneys or the importance of the case. In addition, in future cases, defendants contemplating the possibility of settlement will have no way to estimate the likelihood of having to pay a potentially huge enhancement. See Marek v. Chesny, 473 U.S. 1, 7 (1985) (" '[M]any a defendant would be unwilling to make a binding settlement offer on terms that left it exposed to liability for attorney's fees in whatever amount the court might fix on motion of the plaintiff' ").

Section 1988 serves an important public purpose by making it possible for persons without means to bring suit to vindicate their rights. But unjustified enhancements that serve only to enrich attorneys are not consistent with the statute's aim.[8] In many cases, attorney's fees awarded under

---

7 Justice Breyer's reliance on the average hourly rate for all of respondents' attorneys is highly misleading. In calculating the lodestar, the District Court found that the hourly rate for each of these attorneys was "eminently fair and reasonable" and "consistent with the prevailing market rates in Atlanta for comparable work." Justice Breyer's calculation of an average hourly rate for all attorney hours reflects nothing more than the fact that much of the work was performed by attorneys whose "fair and reasonable" market rate was below the market average. There is nothing unfair about compensating these attorneys at the very rate that they requested.

8 Justice Breyer's opinion dramatically illustrates the danger of allowing a trial judge to award a huge enhancement not supported by any discernible methodology. That approach would retain the $4.5 million enhancement here so that respondents' attorneys would earn as much as the attorneys at some of the richest law firms in the country. These fees would be

§ 1988 are not paid by the individuals responsible for the constitutional or statutory violations on which the judgment is based. Instead, the fees are paid in effect by state and local taxpayers, and because state and local governments have limited budgets, money that is used to pay attorney's fees is money that cannot be used for programs that provide vital public services.

* * *

For all these reasons, the judgment of the Court of Appeals is reversed, and the case is remanded for proceedings consistent with this opinion.

It is so ordered.

■ JUSTICE KENNEDY, concurring.

If one were to ask an attorney or a judge to name the significant cases of his or her career, it would be unsurprising to find the list includes a case then being argued or just decided. When immersed in a case, lawyers and judges find within it a fascination, an intricacy, an importance that transcends what the detached observer sees. So the pending or just completed case will often seem extraordinary to its participants. That is the dynamic of the adversary system, the system that so well serves the law.

It is proper for the Court today to reject the proposition that all enhancements are barred; still, it must be understood that extraordinary cases are presented only in the rarest circumstances.

With these comments, I join in full the opinion of the Court.

■ JUSTICE THOMAS, concurring.

Nearly 30 years ago, a group of attorneys sought a fee award under 42 U.S.C. § 1988 after "achiev[ing] only limited success" litigating their clients' constitutional claims. Hensley v. Eckerhart, 461 U.S. 424, 431 (1983). This Court's opinion resolving their claim for fees observed that "in some cases of *exceptional* success an enhanced award" of attorney's fees under § 1988 "may be justified." Id., at 435 (emphasis added). That observation plainly was dicta, but one year later this Court relied on it to reject the "argument that an 'upward adjustment' " to the lodestar calculation "is never permissible." Blum v. Stenson, 465 U.S. 886, 897 (1984). Yet "we have never sustained an enhancement of a lodestar amount for performance," and our jurisprudence since *Blum* has charted "a decisional arc that bends decidedly against enhancements," 532 F.3d 1209, 1221 (11th Cir. 2008) (Carnes, J.).

Today the Court holds, consistent with *Hensley* and *Blum*, that a lodestar fee award under § 1988 may be enhanced for attorney performance in a "few" circumstances that "are indeed 'rare' and 'exceptional.' " But careful readers will observe the precise limitations that the Court imposes on the availability of such enhancements. These limitations preserve our prior cases and advance our attorney's fees jurisprudence further along the decisional arc that Judge Carnes described. I agree with the Court's approach and its conclusion because, as the Court emphasizes, the lodestar calcula-

paid by the taxpayers of Georgia, where the annual per capita income is less than $34,000, see Dept. of Commerce, Bureau of Census, Statistical Abstract of the United States: 2010, p. 437 (2009) (Table 665) (figures for 2008), and the annual salaries of attorneys employed by the State range from $48,000 for entry-level lawyers to $118,000 for the highest paid division chief, see Brief for State of Alabama et al. as Amici Curiae, 10, and n.3 (citing National Association of Attorneys General, Statistics on the Office of the Attorney General, Fiscal Year 2006, pp. 37–39). Section 1988 was enacted to ensure that civil rights plaintiffs are adequately represented, not to provide such a windfall.

tion will in virtually every case already reflect all indicia of attorney performance relevant to a fee award.

■ JUSTICE BREYER, with whom JUSTICE STEVENS, JUSTICE GINSBURG, and JUSTICE SOTOMAYOR join, concurring in part and dissenting in part.

We granted certiorari in this case to consider "whether the calculation of an attorney's fee" that is "based on the 'lodestar' " can "*ever* be enhanced based solely on [the] quality of [the lawyers'] performance and [the] results obtained," Pet. for Cert. i (emphasis added). The Court answers that question in the affirmative. As our prior precedents make clear, the lodestar calculation "does not end the [fee] inquiry" because there "remain other considerations that may lead the district court to adjust the fee upward." Hensley v. Eckerhart, 461 U.S. 424, 434 (1983). For that reason, "[t]he lodestar method was never intended to be conclusive in all circumstances." Instead, as the Court today reaffirms, when "superior attorney performance" leads to "exceptional success an enhanced award may be justified," *Hensley*, 461 U.S., at 435; see also Pennsylvania v. Delaware Valley Citizens' Council for Clean Air, 478 U.S. 546, 565 (1986); Blum v. Stenson, 465 U.S. 886, 896–900 (1984). I agree with that conclusion.

Where the majority and I part ways is with respect to a question that is not presented, but that the Court obliquely, and in my view inappropriately, appears to consider nonetheless—namely, whether the lower courts correctly determined *in this case* that exceptional circumstances justify a lodestar enhancement. I would not reach that issue, which lies beyond the narrow question that we agreed to consider. See 556 U.S. ___ (2009) (limiting review to the first question presented); Pet. for Cert. i (stating question). Nor do I believe that this Court, which is twice removed from the litigation underlying the fee determination, is properly suited to resolve the fact-intensive inquiry that 42 U.S.C. § 1988 demands. But even were I to engage in that inquiry, I would hold that the District Court did not abuse its discretion in awarding an enhancement. And I would therefore affirm the judgment of the Court of Appeals.

As the Court explains, the basic question that must be resolved when considering an enhancement to the lodestar is whether the lodestar calculation "adequately measure[s]" an attorney's "value," as "demonstrated" by his performance "during the litigation." While I understand the need for answering that question through the application of standards, I also believe that the answer inevitably involves an element of judgment. Moreover, when reviewing a district court's answer to that question, an appellate court must inevitably give weight to the fact that a district court is better situated to provide that answer. For it is the district judge, and only the district judge, who will have read all of the motions filed in the case, witnessed the proceedings, and been able to evaluate the attorneys' overall performance in light of the objectives, context, legal difficulty, and practical obstacles present in the case. In a word, the district judge will have observed the attorney's true "value, *as demonstrated . . . during the litigation*." By contrast, a court of appeals, faced with a cold and perhaps lengthy record, will inevitably have less time and opportunity to determine whether the lawyers have done an exceptionally fine job. And this Court is yet less suited to performing that inquiry. Accordingly, determining whether a fee enhancement is warranted in a given case "is a matter that is committed to the sound discretion of a trial judge," and the function of appellate courts is to review that judge's determination for an abuse of such discretion.

This case well illustrates why our tiered and functionally specialized judicial system places the task of determining an attorney's fee award primarily in the district court's hands. The plaintiffs' lawyers spent eight years investigating the underlying facts, developing the initial complaint, conducting court proceedings, and working out final relief. The District Court's docket, with over 600 entries, consists of more than 18,000 pages. Transcripts of hearings and depositions, along with other documents, have produced a record that fills 20 large boxes. Neither we, nor an appellate panel, can easily read that entire record. Nor should we attempt to second-guess a district judge who is aware of the many intangible matters that the written page cannot reflect.

My own review of this expansive record cannot possibly be exhaustive. But those portions of the record I have reviewed lead me to conclude, like the Court of Appeals, that the District Judge did not abuse his discretion when awarding an enhanced fee. I reach this conclusion based on four considerations.

First, the record indicates that the lawyers' objective in this case was unusually important and fully consistent with the central objectives of the basic federal civil-rights statute, 42 U.S.C. § 1983. Moreover, the problem the attorneys faced demanded an exceptionally high degree of skill and effort. Specifically, these lawyers and their clients sought to have the State of Georgia reform its entire foster-care system—a system that much in the record describes as well below the level of minimal constitutional acceptability. The record contains investigative reports, mostly prepared by Georgia's own Office of the Child Advocate, which show, for example, the following:

- The State's foster-care system was unable to provide essential medical and mental health services; children consequently and unnecessarily suffered illness and life long medical disabilities, such as permanent hearing loss, due to failures on the part of the State to administer basic care and antibiotics.
- Understaffing and improper staffing placed children in the care of individuals with dangerous criminal records; children were physically assaulted by the staff, locked outside of the shelters at night as punishment, and abused in other ways.
- The shelters themselves were "unsanitary and dilapidated," "unclean," infested with rats, "overcrowded," unsafe, and " 'out of control.' "
- Due to improper supervision and other deficiencies at the shelters, 20 percent of the children abused drugs; some also became victims of child prostitution.
- Systemic failures also caused vulnerable children to suffer regular beatings and sexual abuse, including rape, at the hands of more aggressive shelter residents.
- Not surprisingly, many children—upwards of 5 per day and over 750 per year—tried to escape these conditions; others tried to commit suicide.

The State's Office of the Child Advocate, whose reports provide much of the basis for the foregoing description, concluded that the system was "operating in crisis mode" and that any private operator who ran such a system "would never be licensed to care for children." The advocate noted that neither her investigative reports nor national news publicity (including a television program that highlighted a 5–year–old foster child's death from beatings) had prompted corrective action by the State.

The advocate further stated that litigation was necessary to force reform. And she repeatedly asked the State to give her office the authority to conduct that litigation. But the State did not grant the Child Advocate's office the litigating authority she sought.

The upshot is that the plaintiffs' attorneys did what the child advocate could not do: They initiated this lawsuit. They thereby assumed the role of "a 'private attorney general' " by filling an enforcement void in the State's own legal system, a function "that Congress considered of the highest priority," Newman v. Piggie Park Enterprises, Inc., 390 U.S. 400, 402 (1968) (per curiam), and "meant to promote in enacting § 1988," Texas State Teachers Assn. v. Garland Independent School Dist., 489 U.S. 782, 793 (1989).

Second, the course of the lawsuit was lengthy and arduous. The plaintiffs and their lawyers began with factual investigations beyond those which the child advocate had already conducted. They then filed suit. And the State met the plaintiffs' efforts with a host of complex procedural, as well as substantive, objections. The State, for example, argued that the law forbade the plaintiffs to investigate the shelters; on the eve of a state-court decision that might have approved the investigations, the State then removed the case to federal court; the State then sought protective orders preventing the attorneys from speaking to the shelters' staff; and, after losing its motions, the State delayed to the point where the District Court "was forced to admonish [the] State Defendants for 'relying on technical legal objections to discovery requests in order to delay and hinder the discovery process.' " 454 F. Supp.2d. 1260, 1268 (N.D. Ga. 2006).

In the meantime, the State moved for dismissal, basing the motion on complex legal doctrines such as *Younger* abstention and the *Rooker–Feldman* doctrine, which the District Court found inapplicable. See Younger v. Harris, 401 U.S. 37 (1971); Rooker v. Fidelity Trust Co., 363 U.S. 413 (1923). The State also opposed the petitioners' request to certify a class of the 3,000 children in foster care, but the District Court again rejected the State's argument. And, after that, the State filed a lengthy motion for summary judgment, which plaintiffs' attorneys opposed in thorough briefing supported by comprehensive exhibits. After losing that motion and eventually agreeing to mediation, the State forced protracted litigation as to who should be the mediator. All told, in opposing the plaintiffs' efforts to have the foster-care system reformed, the State spent $2.4 million on outside counsel (who, because they charge the State reduced rates, worked significantly more hours than that figure alone indicates) and tapped its own law department for an additional 5,200 hours of work.

Third, in the face of this opposition, the results obtained by the plaintiffs' attorneys appear to have been exceptional. The 47–page consent decree negotiated over the course of the mediation sets forth 31 specific steps that the State will take in order to address the specific deficiencies of the sort that I described above. And it establishes a reporting and oversight mechanism that is backed up by the District Court's enforcement authority. As a result of the decree, the State agreed to comprehensive reforms of its foster-care system, to the benefit of children in many different communities. . . .

Fourth and finally, the District Judge, who supervised these proceedings, who saw the plaintiffs amass, process, compile, and convincingly present vast amounts of factual information, who witnessed their defeat of numerous state procedural and substantive motions, and who was in a position to evaluate the ultimate mediation effort, said:

1. the "mediation effort in this case went far beyond anything that this Court has seen in any previous case," 454 F. Supp. 2d, at 1282;
2. "based on its personal observation of plaintiffs' counsel's performance throughout this litigation, the Court finds that . . . counsel brought a higher degree of skill, commitment, dedication, and professionalism to this litigation than the Court has seen displayed by the attorneys in any other case during its 27 years on the bench," id., at 1288–90;
3. the Consent Decree "provided extraordinary benefits to the plaintiff class. . . . " Id., at 1282. "[T]he settlement achieved by plaintiffs' counsel is comprehensive in its scope and detailed in its coverage.
   . . . After 58 years as a practicing attorney and federal judge, the Court is unaware of any other case in which a plaintiff class has achieved such a favorable result on such a comprehensive scale," id., at 1289–90.

Based on these observations and on its assessment of the attorneys' performance during the course of the litigation, the District Court concluded that "the evidence establishes that the quality of service rendered by class counsel . . . was far superior to what consumers of legal services in the legal marketplace . . . could reasonably expect to receive for the rates used in the lodestar calculation." Id., at 1288.

On the basis of what I have read, I believe that assessment was correct. I recognize that the ordinary lodestar calculation yields a large fee award. But by my assessment, the lodestar calculation in this case translates to an average hourly fee per attorney of $249. See id., at 1287 (lodestar calculation and attorney hours). (The majority's reference to an hourly fee of $866 refers to the rate associated with the *single highest* paid of the 17 attorneys under the *enhanced* fee, not the *average* hourly rate under the *lodestar*. . . .)

At $249 per hour, the lodestar would compensate this group of attorneys—whom the District Court described as extraordinary—at a rate *lower* than the *average* rate charged by attorneys practicing law in the State of Georgia, where the average hourly rate is $268. See id., at 89. Accordingly, even the majority would seem to acknowledge that some form of an enhancement is appropriate in this case. ("[A]n enhancement may be appropriate where the method used in determining the hourly rate employed in the lodestar calculation does not adequately measure the attorney's true market value, as demonstrated in part during the litigation"). Indeed, the fact that these exceptional results were achieved in a case where "much of the work," performed by relatively inexperienced attorneys (who, accordingly, would be compensated by the lodestar "below the market average") is all the more reason to think that their service rendered their outstanding performance worthy of an enhancement. By comparison, the District Court's enhanced award—a special one-time adjustment unique to this exceptional case—would compensate these attorneys, on this one occasion, at an average hourly rate of $435, which is comparable to the rates charged by the

Nation's leading law firms on average on every occasion. Thus, it would appear that the enhanced award is wholly consistent with the purpose of § 1988, which was enacted to ensure that "counsel for prevailing parties [are] paid as is traditional with attorneys compensated by a fee-paying client." S. Rep. No. 94–1011, p. 6 (1976); see H.R. Rep. No. 94–1558, p. 9 (1976) ("[C]ivil rights plaintiffs should not be singled out for different and less favorable treatment"); see also *Blum,* 465 U.S., at 893, 897.

In any event, the circumstances I have listed likely make this a "rare" or "exceptional" case warranting an enhanced fee award. And they certainly make clear that it was neither unreasonable nor an abuse of discretion for the District Court to reach that conclusion. Indeed, if the facts and circumstances that I have described are even roughly correct, then it is fair to ask: If this is not an exceptional case, what is?

* * *

My disagreement with the Court is limited. As I stated at the outset, we are in complete agreement with respect to the answer to the question presented: "[A]n increase" to the lodestar "due to superior performance and results" "is permitted in extraordinary circumstances." Unlike Justice Thomas, I do not read the Court's opinion to "advance our attorney's fees jurisprudence further along the decisional arc" toward a point where enhancements are "virtually" barred in all cases. Our prior cases make clear that enhancements are permitted in " 'exceptional' cases," *Delaware Valley,* 478 U.S., at 565, where the attorney achieves "exceptional success," *Hensley,* 461 U.S., at 435. By definition, such exceptional circumstances occur only rarely. See Kennedy, J., concurring). I do not see how the Court could "advance" our fee enhancement jurisprudence so as to further discourage lodestar enhancements without overruling the precedents I have just cited, which the Court has not done. To the contrary, today the Court "reaffirm[s]" those precedents, which allow enhancements for exceptional performance. And with respect to that central holding we are unanimous.

Nor is my disagreement with the Court absolute with respect to the proper resolution of the case before us, for the Court does not purport to prohibit the District Court from awarding an enhanced fee on remand if that court provides more detailed reasoning supporting its decision. But the majority and I do disagree in this respect: I would not disturb the judgment below. "A request for attorney's fees should not result in a second major litigation." *Hensley*, 461 U.S., at 437. Nor should it lead to years of protracted appellate review. We did not grant certiorari in this case to consider the fact-intensive dispute over whether this is, in fact, an exceptional case that merits a lodestar enhancement. The District Court has already resolved that question and the Court of Appeals affirmed its judgment, having found no abuse of discretion. I would have been content to resolve no more than the question presented. But, even were I to follow the Court's inclination to say more, I would hold that the principles upon which we agree—including the applicability of abuse-of-discretion review to a District Court's fee determination—require us to affirm the judgment below.

NOTE ON RESULT ENHANCEMENT

The Court's opinion in *Kenny A.* suggests two justifications for the Court's earlier decision to adopt the lodestar approach in preference to the twelve-factor standard laid out in Johnson v. Georgia Highway Express, Inc., 488

F.2d 714 (5th Cir. 1974), and endorsed by both the House and Senate Reports accompanying § 1988(b), which expressly directed courts to consider the "novelty and difficulty of the questions" and the "amount involved and the results obtained" along with the number of hours spent and the attorney's usual rate. One justification for focusing on the lodestar concerns administrability and objectivity. The other is that the lodestar method does a reasonably good job of mirroring the fee an attorney would receive from paying clients. In this regard, consider the observations of former Solicitor General Clement, who served as Kenny A.'s lawyer before the Supreme Court, while the case was still pending:

> The fee award in Kenny A. seems large and probably attracted the Supreme Court's attention because of its size. The total award after enhancement was ten million dollars. But to offer some perspective, within a couple of weeks of the Supreme Court argument in the Kenny A. case, there was a settlement of the Fen-phen litigation, which was a long-standing products liability litigation. There was a class action and a common fund in that case, so the court in the common fund situation had to award attorney's fees. . . . What were the "reasonable" attorney's fees in the Fen-phen litigation? Five hundred sixty-seven million dollars.
>
> Now my point is not to criticize that award. But the size of the award highlights a fundamental asymmetry here in the system. These common fund cases are typically securities cases and similar complex civil litigation. Courts in making these large awards as a percentage of the common fund will do what they call the "Lodestar cross check." They check the total common fund award by comparing it to the fees generated by a Lodestar approach that multiplies the hours expended by the prevailing rates. . . . If the Lodestar was nine million and the award based on a percentage of the common fund was forty-five million, that yields a multiplier of five. The question then becomes whether that multiplier is reasonable. And the courts that perform this "cross check" routinely approve as reasonable multipliers two and three times the Lodestar amount. I do not know whether the current Congress has the same intent as the 1976 Congress. But to the extent that Congress in 1976 was trying to get rough parity between the incentives to take on civil rights plaintiff's work and the incentives to take on complex civil litigation, the system does not seem to accomplish Congress's goal.
>
> To be clear, my point here is not that if this decision does not come out my clients' way that civil rights work will dry up and go away. But the reason that civil rights work will not dry up is because there are lawyers . . . who are dedicated to this kind of work as an absolute matter of commitment and principle. That is admirable, but the Congress that passed § 1988 did not want to rely on that kind of public-mindedness alone, and Congress appears to have been very interested in making civil rights work the practice, not just of specialized advocacy groups, but of the bar as a whole. Accordingly, it is worth thinking about the kind of asymmetry that exists and how the incentives may cause civil rights work to shift away from generalist lawyers in the private bar and towards specialized public interest groups. That may be a good trend or a bad trend, but it is the effect of the current system of incentives.

4. ATTORNEY'S FEES AND SETTLEMENT NEGOTIATIONS

Evans v. Jeff D.

Supreme Court of the United States, 1986.
475 U.S. 717.

■ JUSTICE STEVENS delivered the opinion of the Court.

The Civil Rights Attorneys' Fees Awards Act of 1976 (Fees Act) provides that "the court, in its discretion, may allow the prevailing party . . . a reasonable attorney's fee" in enumerated civil rights actions. 42 U.S.C. § 1988.[a] In Maher v. Gagne, 448 U.S. 122 (1980), we held that fees *may* be assessed against state officials after a case has been settled by the entry of a consent decree. In this case, we consider the question whether attorney's fees *must* be assessed when the case has been settled by a consent decree granting prospective relief to the plaintiff class but providing that the defendants shall not pay any part of the prevailing party's fees or costs. We hold that the District Court has the power, in its sound discretion, to refuse to award fees.

I

The petitioners are the governor and other public officials of the State of Idaho responsible for the education and treatment of children who suffer from emotional and mental handicaps. Respondents are a class of such children who have been or will be placed in petitioners' care.

On August 4, 1980, respondents commenced this action by filing a complaint against petitioners in the United States District Court for the District of Idaho. The factual allegations in the complaint described deficiencies in both the education programs and the health care services provided respondents. These deficiencies allegedly violated the United States Constitution, the Idaho Constitution, four federal statutes, and certain provisions of the Idaho Code. The complaint prayed for injunctive relief and for an award of costs and attorney's fees, but it did not seek damages.

On the day the complaint was filed, the District Court entered two orders, one granting the respondents leave to proceed in forma pauperis, and a second appointing Charles Johnson as their next friend for the sole purpose of instituting and prosecuting the action. At that time Johnson was employed by the Idaho Legal Aid Society, Inc., a private, non-profit corporation that provides free legal services to qualified low-income persons. Because the Idaho Legal Aid Society is prohibited from representing clients who are capable of paying their own fees,[3] it made no agreement requiring any of the respondents to pay for the costs of litigation or the legal services it provided through Johnson. Moreover, the special character of both the class and its attorney-client relationship with Johnson explains why it did not enter into any agreement covering the various contingencies that might arise during the course of settlement negotiations of a class action of this kind.

[a] The Court's reference was to the portion of 42 U.S.C. § 1988 that has since been renumbered to § 1988(b). Subsequent citations by the Court to § 1988 have been replaced by § 1988(b).—[Footnote by eds.]

[3] Idaho Legal Aid receives grants under the Legal Services Corporation Act, 42 U.S.C. §§ 2996–29961, and is not allowed to represent clients who are capable of paying their own legal fees, see § 2996(b)(1); 45 C.F.R. § 1609 (1984).

Shortly after petitioners filed their answer, and before substantial work had been done on the case, the parties entered into settlement negotiations. They were able to reach agreement concerning that part of the complaint relating to education services with relative ease, and, on October 14, 1981, entered into a stipulation disposing of that part of the case. The stipulation provided that each party would bear its "own attorney's fees and costs thus far incurred." The District Court promptly entered an order approving the partial settlement.

Negotiations concerning the treatment claims broke down, however, and the parties filed cross-motions for summary judgment. Although the District Court dismissed several of respondents' claims, it held that the federal constitutional claims raised genuine issues of fact to be resolved at trial. Thereafter, the parties stipulated to the entry of a class certification order, engaged in discovery, and otherwise prepared to try the case in the spring of 1983.

In March 1983, one week before trial, petitioners presented respondents with a new settlement proposal. As respondents themselves characterize it, the proposal "offered virtually all of the injunctive relief [they] had sought in their complaint." The Court of Appeals agreed with this characterization, and further noted that the proposed relief was "more than the District Court in earlier hearings had indicated it was willing to grant." As was true of the earlier partial settlement, however, petitioners' offer included a provision for a waiver by respondents of any claim to fees or costs. Originally, this waiver was unacceptable to the Idaho Legal Aid Society, which had instructed Johnson to reject any settlement offer conditional upon a waiver of fees, but Johnson ultimately determined that his ethical obligation to his clients mandated acceptance of the proposal. The parties conditioned the waiver on approval by the District Court.

After a stipulation was signed, Johnson filed a written motion requesting the District Court to approve the settlement "except for the provision on costs and attorney's fees," and to allow the respondents to present a bill of costs and fees for consideration by the court. At the oral argument on that motion, Johnson contended that petitioners' offer had exploited his ethical duty to his clients—that he was "forced," by an offer giving his clients "the best result [they] could have gotten in this court or any other court," to waive his attorney's fees. The District Court, however, evaluated the waiver in the context of the entire settlement and rejected the ethical underpinnings of Johnson's argument. Explaining that although petitioners were "not willing to concede that they were obligated to [make the changes in their practices required by the stipulation], . . . they were willing to do them as long as their costs were outlined and they didn't face additional costs," it concluded that "it doesn't violate any ethical considerations for an attorney to give up his attorney fees in the interest of getting a better bargain for his client[s]." Accordingly, the District Court approved the settlement and denied the motion to submit a costs bill.

[A]fter ordering preliminary relief, the Court of Appeals invalidated the fee waiver and left standing the remainder of the settlement; it then instructed the District Court to "make its own determination of the fees that are reasonable" and remanded for that limited purpose. . . . We now reverse.

II

The disagreement between the parties and amici as to what exactly is at issue in this case makes it appropriate to put certain aspects of the case to one side in order to state precisely the question that the case does present.

To begin with, the Court of Appeals' decision rested on an erroneous view of the District Court's power to approve settlements in class actions. Rule 23(e) wisely requires court approval of the terms of any settlement of a class action, but the power to approve or reject a settlement negotiated by the parties before trial does not authorize the court to require the parties to accept a settlement to which they have not agreed. . . . The District Court could not enforce the settlement on the merits and award attorney's fees any more than it could, in a situation in which the attorney had negotiated a large fee at the expense of the plaintiff class, preserve the fee award and order greater relief on the merits. The question we must decide, therefore, is whether the District Court had a duty to reject the proposed settlement because it included a waiver of statutorily authorized attorney's fees.

That duty, whether it takes the form of a general prophylactic rule or arises out of the special circumstances of this case, derives ultimately from the Fees Act rather than from the strictures of professional ethics. . . . Plainly, Johnson had no *ethical* obligation to seek a statutory fee award. His ethical duty was to serve his clients loyally and competently. Since the proposal to settle the merits was more favorable than the probable outcome of the trial, Johnson's decision to recommend acceptance was consistent with the highest standards of our profession. The District Court, therefore, correctly concluded that approval of the settlement involved no breach of ethics in this case.

The defect, if any, in the negotiated fee waiver must be traced not to the rules of ethics but to the Fees Act. Following this tack, respondents argue that the statute must be construed to forbid a fee waiver that is the product of "coercion." They submit that a "coercive waiver" results when the defendant in a civil rights action (1) offers a settlement on the merits of equal or greater value than that which plaintiffs could reasonably expect to achieve at trial but (2) conditions the offer on a waiver of plaintiffs' statutory eligibility for attorney's fees. Such an offer, they claim, exploits the ethical obligation of plaintiffs' counsel to recommend settlement in order to avoid defendant's statutory liability for its opponents' fees and costs.

The question this case presents, then, is whether the Fees Act requires a district court to disapprove a stipulation seeking to settle a civil rights class action under Rule 23 when the offered relief equals or exceeds the probable outcome at trial but is expressly conditioned on waiver of statutory eligibility for attorney's fees. For reasons set out below, we are not persuaded that Congress has commanded that all such settlements must be rejected by the District Court. Moreover, on the facts of record in this case, we are satisfied that the District Court did not abuse its discretion by approving the fee waiver.

III

The text of the Fees Act provides no support for the proposition that Congress intended to ban all fee waivers offered in connection with substantial relief on the merits. On the contrary, the language of the act, as well as its legislative history, indicates that Congress bestowed on the "prevailing *party*" (generally plaintiffs) a statutory eligibility for a discretionary award of attorney's fees in specified civil rights actions. It did not prevent the party from waiving this eligibility any more than it legislated against assignment of this right to an attorney, such as effectively occurred here. Instead, Congress enacted the fee-shifting provision as "an integral party of the remedies necessary to obtain" compliance with civil rights laws, to further the same general purpose—promotion of respect for civil rights—that led it to provide damages and injunctive relief. The statute and its legislative history nowhere suggest that Congress intended to forbid *all* waivers of attorney's fees—even those insisted upon by a civil rights plaintiff in exchange for some other relief to which he is indisputably not entitled—any more than it intended to bar a concession on damages to secure broader injunctive relief. Thus, while it is undoubtedly true that Congress expected fee-shifting to attract competent counsel to represent citizens deprived of their civil rights, it neither bestowed fee awards upon attorneys nor rendered them nonwaivable or nonnegotiable; instead, it added them to the arsenal of remedies available to combat violations of civil rights, a goal not invariably inconsistent with conditioning settlement on the merits of a waiver of statutory attorney's fees.

In fact, we believe that a general proscription against negotiated waiver of attorney's fees in exchange for a settlement on the merits would itself impede vindication of civil rights, at least in some cases, by reducing the attractiveness of settlement. . . . Most defendants are unlikely to settle unless the cost of the predicted judgment, discounted by its probability, plus the transaction costs of further litigation, are greater than the cost of the settlement package. If fee waivers cannot be negotiated, the settlement package must either contain an attorney's fee component of potentially large and typically uncertain magnitude, or else the parties must agree to have the fee fixed by the court. Although either of these alternatives may well be acceptable in many cases, there surely is a significant number in which neither alternative will be as satisfactory as a decision to try the entire case.

The adverse impact of removing attorney's fees and costs from bargaining might be tolerable if the uncertainty introduced into settlement negotiations were small. But it is not. The defendants' potential liability for fees in this kind of litigation can be as significant as, and sometimes even more significant than, their potential liability on the merits. . . .

The unpredictability of attorney's fees may be just as important as their magnitude when a defendant is striving to fix its liability. Unlike a determination of costs, which ordinarily involve smaller outlays and are more susceptible of calculation, "[t]here is no precise rule or formula" for determining attorney's fees. Hensley v. Eckerhart, 461 U.S. 424, 436 (1983). Among other considerations, the district court must determine what hours were reasonably expended on what claims, whether that expenditure was reasonable in light of the success obtained, and what is an appropriate hourly rate for the services rendered. Some district courts have also considered whether a "multiplier" or other adjustment is appropriate. The consequence of this succession of necessarily judgmental decisions for the ultimate fee award is inescapable: a defendant's liability for his opponent's attorney's fees in a civil rights action cannot be fixed with a sufficient degree of confidence to make defendants indifferent to their exclusion from negotiation. It is therefore not implausible to anticipate that parties to a significant number of civil rights cases will refuse to settle if liability for attorney's fees remains open, thereby forcing more cases to trial, unnecessarily burdening the judicial system, and disserving civil rights litigants. Respondents' own waiver of attorney's fees and costs to obtain settlement of their educational claims is eloquent testimony to the utility of fee waivers in vindicating civil rights claims. We conclude, therefore, that it is not necessary to construe the Fees Act as embodying a general rule prohibiting settlements conditioned on the waiver of fees in order to be faithful to the purposes of that act.[30]

IV

The question remains whether the District Court abused its discretion in this case by approving a settlement which included a complete fee waiver. . . .

The Court of Appeals, respondents, and various amici supporting their position . . . suggest that the court's authority to pass on settlements, typically invoked to ensure fair treatment of class members, must be exercised in accordance with the Fees Act to promote the availability of attorneys in civil rights cases. Specifically, respondents assert that the State of Idaho could not pass a valid statute precluding the payment of attorney's fees in settlements of civil rights cases to which the Fees Act applies. From this they reason that the Fees Act must equally preclude the adoption of a uniform statewide policy that serves the same end, and accordingly contend that a consistent practice of insisting on a fee waiver as a condition of settlement in civil rights litigation is in conflict with the federal statute authorizing fees for prevailing parties, including those who prevail by way of settlement. Remarkably, there seems little disagreement on these points. Petitioners and the amici who support them never suggest that the district court is obligated to place its stamp of approval on every settlement in which the plaintiffs' attorneys have agreed to a fee waiver. The Solicitor General, for example, has suggested that a fee waiver need not be approved when the defendant had "no realistic defense on the merits," or if the waiver was part of a "vindictive effort . . . to teach counsel that they had better not bring such cases."

We find it unnecessary to evaluate this argument, however, because the record in this case does not indicate that Idaho has adopted such a statute, policy, or practice. Nor does the record support the narrower proposition that petitioners' request to waive fees was a vindictive effort to deter attorneys from representing plaintiffs in civil rights suits against Idaho. . . .

---

[30] The Court is unanimous in concluding that the Fees Act should not be interpreted to prohibit all simultaneous negotiations of a defendant's liability on the merits and his liability for his opponent's attorney's fees. . . .

Although the dissent would allow simultaneous negotiations, it would require that "whatever fee the parties agree to" be "found by the court to be a 'reasonable' one under the Fees Act." The dissent's proposal is imaginative, but not very practical. Of the 10,757 "other civil rights" cases filed in federal court last year—most of which were § 1983 actions for which § 1988(b) authorizes an award of fees—only 111 sought class relief. Assuming that of the approximately 99 percent of these civil rights actions that are not class actions, a further 90 percent would settle rather than go to trial, the dissent's proposal would require district courts to evaluate the reasonableness of fee agreements in several thousand civil rights cases annually while they make that determination in slightly over 100 civil rights class actions now. Moreover, if this novel procedure really is necessary to carry out the purposes of the Fees Act, presumably it should be applied to all cases arising under federal statutes that provide for fee-shifting.

In light of the record, respondents must—to sustain the judgment in their favor—confront the District Court's finding that the extensive structural relief they obtained constituted an adequate quid pro quo for their waiver of attorney's fees. The Court of Appeals did not overturn this finding. . . . Only by making the unsupported assumption that the respondent class was entitled to retain the favorable portions of the settlement while rejecting the fee waiver could the Court of Appeals conclude that the District Court had acted unwisely.

What the outcome of this settlement illustrates is that the Fees Act has given the victims of civil rights violations a powerful weapon that improves their ability to employ counsel, to obtain access to the courts, and thereafter to vindicate their rights by means of settlement or trial. For aught that appears, it was the "coercive" effect of respondents' statutory right to seek a fee award that motivated petitioners' exceptionally generous offer. Whether this weapon might be even more powerful if fee waivers were prohibited in cases like this is another question,[34] but it is in any event a question Congress is best equipped to answer. Thus far, the legislature has not commanded that fees be paid whenever a case is settled. Unless it issues such a command, we shall rely primarily on the sound discretion of the district courts to appraise the reasonableness of particular class-action settlements on a case-by-case basis, in the light of all the relevant circumstances. In this case, the District Court did not abuse its discretion in upholding a fee waiver which secured broad injunctive relief, relief greater than that which plaintiffs could reasonably have expected to achieve at trial.

The judgment of the Court of Appeals is reversed.

■ JUSTICE BRENNAN, with whom JUSTICE MARSHALL and JUSTICE BLACKMUN join, dissenting.

Ultimately, enforcement of the laws is what really counts. It was with this in mind that Congress enacted the Civil Rights Attorneys' Fees Awards Act of 1976, 42 U.S.C. § 1988(b). Congress authorized fee-shifting to improve enforcement of civil rights legislation by making it easier for victims of civil rights violations to find lawyers willing to take their cases. Because today's decision will make it more difficult for civil rights plaintiffs to obtain legal assistance, a result plainly contrary to Congress' purpose, I dissent.

I

The Court begins its analysis by emphasizing that neither the language nor the legislative history of the Fees Act supports "the proposition that Congress intended to ban all fee waivers offered in connection with substantial relief on the merits." I agree. There is no evidence that Congress gave the question of fee waivers any thought at all. However, the Court mistakenly assumes that this omission somehow supports the conclusion that fee waivers are permissible. On the contrary, that Congress did

---

[34] We are cognizant of the possibility that decisions by individual clients to bargain away fee awards may, in the aggregate and in the long run, diminish lawyers' expectations of statutory fees in civil rights cases. If this occurred, the pool of lawyers willing to represent plaintiffs in such cases might shrink, constricting the "effective access to the judicial process" for persons with civil rights grievances which the Fees Act was intended to provide. That the "tyranny of small decisions" may operate in this fashion is not to say that there is any reason or documentation to support such a concern at the present time. Comment on this issue is therefore premature at this juncture. We believe, however, that as a practical matter the likelihood of this circumstance arising is remote.

not specifically consider the issue of fee waivers tells us absolutely nothing about whether such waivers ought to be permitted. It is blackletter law that "[i]n the absence of specific evidence of Congressional intent, it becomes necessary to resort to a broader consideration of the legislative policy behind th[e] provision." . . . Accordingly, the first and most important question to be asked is what Congress' purpose was in enacting the Fees Act. We must then determine whether conditional fee waivers are consistent with this purpose.

II

The Court asserts that Congress authorized fee awards "to further the same general purpose—promotion of respect for civil rights—that led it to provide damages and injunctive relief." The attorney's fee made available by the act, we are told, is simply an addition to "the arsenal of remedies available to combat violations of civil rights."

Obviously, the Fees Act is intended to "promote respect for civil rights." Congress would hardly have authorized fee awards in civil rights cases to promote respect for the securities laws. But discourse at such a level of generality is deceptive. The question is *how* did Congress envision that awarding attorney's fees would promote respect for civil rights? Without a clear understanding of the way in which Congress intended for the Fees Act to operate, we cannot even begin responsibly to go about the task of interpreting it. In theory, Congress might have awarded attorney's fees as simply an additional form of make-whole relief, the threat of which would "promote respect for civil rights" by deterring potential civil rights violators. If this were the case, the Court's equation of attorney's fees with damages would not be wholly inaccurate. However, the legislative history of the Fees Act discloses that this is not the case. Rather, Congress provided fee awards to ensure that there would be lawyers available to plaintiffs who could not otherwise afford counsel, so that these plaintiffs could fulfill their role in the federal enforcement scheme as "private attorneys general," vindicating the public interest. . . .

In the wake of Alyeska Pipeline Service Co. v. Wilderness Society, 421 U.S. 240 (1975), Congress acted to correct "anomalous gaps" in the availability of attorney's fees to enforce civil rights laws. Testimony at hearings on the proposed legislation disclosed that civil rights plaintiffs, "a vast majority of [whom] cannot afford legal counsel," were suffering "very severe hardships because of the *Alyeska* decision." The unavailability of fee-shifting made it impossible for legal aid services, "already short of resources," to bring many lawsuits, and, without much possibility of compensation, private attorneys were refusing to take civil rights cases. Congress found that *Alyeska* had a "devastating" impact on civil rights litigation, and it concluded that the need for corrective legislation was "compelling."

Accepting this Court's invitation, see *Alyeska*, supra, at 269–71, Congress passed the Fees Act . . . under which attorney's fees were awarded as a means of securing enforcement of civil rights laws by ensuring that lawyers would be willing to take civil rights cases. The legislative history manifests this purpose with monotonous clarity. . . .

III

As this review of the legislative history makes clear, then, by awarding attorney's fees Congress sought to attract competent counsel to represent victims of civil rights violations. Congress' primary purpose was to enable "private attorneys general" to protect the public interest by creating economic incentives for lawyers to represent them. The Court's assertion that the Fees Act was intended to do nothing more than give individual victims of civil rights violations another remedy is thus at odds with the whole thrust of the legislation. . . .

I have gone to great lengths to show how the Court mischaracterizes the purpose of the Fees Act because the Court's error leads it to ask the wrong question. Having concluded that the Fees Act merely creates another remedy to vindicate the rights of individual plaintiffs, the Court asks whether negotiated waivers of statutory attorney's fees are "invariably inconsistent" with the availability of such fees as a remedy for individual plaintiffs. Not surprisingly, the Court has little difficulty knocking down this frail straw man. But the *proper* question is whether permitting negotiated fee waivers is consistent with Congress' goal of attracting competent counsel. It is therefore necessary to consider the effect on *this* goal of allowing individual plaintiffs to negotiate fee waivers.

A

Permitting plaintiffs to negotiate fee waivers in exchange for relief on the merits actually raises two related but distinct questions. First, is it permissible under the Fees Act to negotiate a settlement of attorney's fees simultaneously with the merits? Second, can the "reasonable attorney's fee" guaranteed in the act be waived? . . .

[S]ince simultaneous negotiation and waiver may have different effects on the congressional policy of encouraging counsel to accept civil rights cases, each practice must be analyzed independently to determine whether or not it is consistent with the Fees Act. [My] examination leads me to conclude: (1) that plaintiffs should not be permitted to waive the "reasonable fee" provided by the Fees Act; but (2) that parties may undertake to negotiate their fee claims simultaneously with the merits so long as whatever fee the parties agree to is found by the court to be a "reasonable" one under the Fees Act.

B

1

It seems obvious that allowing defendants in civil rights cases to condition settlement of the merits on a waiver of statutory attorney's fees will diminish lawyers' expectations of receiving fees and decrease the willingness of lawyers to accept civil rights cases. Even the Court acknowledges "the possibility that decisions by individual clients to bargain away fee awards may, in the aggregate and in the long run, diminish lawyers' expectations of statutory fees in civil rights cases." See n. 34, supra. The Court tells us, however, that "[c]omment on this issue" is "premature at this juncture" because there is not yet supporting "documentation." The Court then goes on anyway to observe that "as a practical matter the likelihood of this circumstance arising is remote." . . .

But it does not require a sociological study to see that permitting fee waivers will make it more difficult for civil rights plaintiffs to obtain legal assistance. It requires only common sense. Assume that a civil rights defendant makes a settlement offer that includes a demand for waiver of statutory attorney's fees. The decision whether to accept or reject the offer is the plaintiff's alone, and the lawyer must abide by the plaintiff's decision. See, e.g., ABA, Model Rules of Professional Conduct 1.2(a) (1984); ABA, Model Code of Professional Responsibility EC 7–7 to EC 7–9 (1982). As a formal matter, of course, the statutory fee belongs to the plaintiff, and thus technically the decision to waive entails a sacrifice only by the plaintiff. As a practical matter, however, waiver affects only the lawyer. Because "a vast majority of the victims of civil rights violations" have no resources to pay attorney's fees, lawyers cannot hope to recover fees from the plaintiff and must depend entirely on the Fees Act for compensation. The plaintiff has no real stake in the statutory fee and is unaffected by its waiver. Consequently, plaintiffs will readily agree to waive fees if this will help them to obtain other relief they desire. . . .

Of course, from the lawyer's standpoint, things could scarcely have turned out worse. He or she invested considerable time and effort in the case, won, and has exactly nothing to show for it. Is the Court really serious in suggesting that it takes a study to prove that this lawyer will be reluctant when, the following week, another civil rights plaintiff enters his office and asks for representation? Does it truly require that somebody conduct a test to see that legal aid services, having invested scarce resources on a case, will feel the pinch when they do not recover the statutory fee?

And, of course, once fee waivers are permitted, defendants will seek them as a matter of course, since this is a logical way to minimize liability. . . . The cumulative effect this practice will have on the civil rights bar is evident. It does not denigrate the high ideals that motivate many civil rights practitioners to recognize that lawyers are in the business of practicing law, and that, like other business people, they are and must be concerned with earning a living. The conclusion that permitting fee waivers will seriously impair the ability of civil rights plaintiffs to obtain legal assistance is embarrassingly obvious.

Because making it more difficult for civil rights plaintiffs to obtain legal assistance is precisely the opposite of what Congress sought to achieve by enacting the Fees Act, fee waivers should be prohibited. . . .

2

This all seems so obvious that it is puzzling that the Court reaches a different result. The Court's rationale is that, unless fee waivers are permitted, "parties to a significant number of civil rights cases will refuse to settle. . . . " This is a wholly inadequate justification for the Court's result.

First, the effect of prohibiting fee waivers on settlement offers is just not an important concern in the context of the Fees Act. I agree with the Court that encouraging settlements is desirable policy. But it is *judicially* created policy, applicable to litigation of any kind and having no special force in the context of civil rights cases. The *congressional* policy underlying the Fees Act is, as I have argued throughout, to create incentives for lawyers to devote time to civil rights cases by making it economically feasible for them to do so. As explained above, permitting fee waivers significantly undercuts this policy. Thus, even if prohibiting fee waivers does discourage some settlements, a *judicial* policy favoring settlement cannot possibly take precedence over this express *congressional* policy. We must implement Congress' agenda, not our own. . . .

The Fees Act was designed to help civil rights plaintiffs in a particular way—by ensuring that there will be lawyers willing to represent them. The fact that fee waivers may produce some settlement offers that are beneficial to a few individual plaintiffs is hardly "consistent with the purposes of the Fees Act" if permitting fee waivers fundamentally undermines what Congress sought to achieve. Each individual plaintiff who waives his right to statutory fees in order to obtain additional relief for himself makes it that much more difficult for the next victim of a civil rights violation to find a lawyer willing or able to bring *his* case. As obtaining legal assistance becomes more difficult, the "benefit" the Court so magnanimously preserves for civil rights plaintiffs becomes available to fewer and fewer individuals, exactly the opposite result from that intended by Congress. . . .

Second, even assuming that settlement practices are relevant, the Court greatly exaggerates the effect that prohibiting fee waivers will have on defendants' willingness to make settlement offers. This is largely due to the Court's failure to distinguish the fee waiver issue from the issue of simultaneous negotiation of fees and merits claims. The Court's discussion mixes concerns over a defendant's reluctance to settle because total liability remains uncertain with reluctance to settle because the cost of settling is too high. However, it is a prohibition on simultaneous negotiation, not a prohibition on fee waivers, that makes it difficult for the defendant to ascertain his total liability at the time he agrees to settle the merits. Thus, while prohibiting fee waivers may deter settlement offers simply because requiring the defendant to pay a "reasonable attorney's fee" increases the total cost of settlement, this is a separate issue altogether, and the Court's numerous arguments about why defendants will not settle unless they can determine their total liability at the time of settlement are simply beside the point. . . .

I believe that the Court overstates the extent to which prohibiting fee waivers will deter defendants from making settlement offers. Because the parties can negotiate a fee (or a range of fees) that is not unduly high and condition their settlement on the court's approval of this fee, the magnitude of a defendant's liability for fees in the settlement context need be neither uncertain nor particularly great. Against this, the defendant must weigh the risk of a non-negotiated fee to be fixed by the court after a trial; as the Court reminds us, fee awards in *this* context may be very uncertain and, potentially, of very great magnitude. Thus, powerful incentives remain for defendants to seek settlement. Moreover, the Court's decision last term in Marek v. Chesny, 473 U.S. 1 (1985), provides an additional incentive for defendants to make settlement offers, namely, the opportunity to limit liability for attorney's fees if the plaintiff refuses the offer and proceeds to trial.[b]

All of which is not to deny that prohibiting fee waivers will deter some settlements; any increase in the costs of settling will have this effect. However, by exaggerating the size and the importance of fee awards, and by ignoring the options available to the parties in settlement negotiations, the Court makes predictions that are inflated. An actual disincentive to settling exists only where three things are true: (1) the defendant feels he is likely to win if he goes to trial, in which case the plaintiff will recover no fees; (2) the plaintiff will agree to relief on the merits that is less costly to the defendant than litigating the case; and (3) adding the cost of a negotiated attorney's fee makes it less costly for the defendant to litigate. I believe that this describes a very small class of cases—although, like the Court, I cannot "document" the assertion.

---

[b] *Marek v. Chesny* is covered in the notes following this case. It concerned Fed. Rule Civ. Proc. 68, which the Court interpreted to disallow recovery of § 1988(b) attorney's fees for work done after defendant made a settlement offer, where the offer turned out to be higher than the plaintiff's ultimate recovery.—[Footnote by eds.]

C

I would, on the other hand, permit simultaneous negotiation of fees and merits claims, since this would not contravene the purposes of the Fees Act. Congress determined that awarding prevailing parties a "reasonable" fee would create necessary—and sufficient—incentives for attorney's to work on civil rights cases. Prohibiting plaintiffs from waiving statutory fees ensures that lawyers will receive this "reasonable" statutory fee. Thus, if fee waivers are prohibited, permitting simultaneous fees and merits negotiations will not interfere with the act; the lawyer will still be entitled to and will still receive a reasonable attorney's fee. . . .

IV

Although today's decision will undoubtedly impair the effectiveness of the private enforcement scheme Congress established for civil rights legislation, I do not believe that it will bring about the total disappearance of "private attorneys general." It is to be hoped the Congress will repair this Court's mistake. In the meantime, other avenues of relief are available. The Court's decision in no way limits the power of state and local bar associations to regulate the ethical conduct of lawyers. Indeed, several bar associations have already declared it unethical for defense counsel to seek fee waivers. See Committee on Professional Ethics of the Association of the Bar of the City of New York Op. No. 82–80 (1985); District of Columbia Legal Ethics Committee Op. No. 147. Such efforts are to be commended and, it is to be hoped, will be followed by other state and local organizations concerned with respecting the intent of Congress and with protecting civil rights.

In addition, it may be that civil rights attorneys can obtain agreements from their clients not to waive attorney's fees. Such agreements simply replicate the private market for legal services (in which attorneys are not ordinarily required to contribute to their client's recovery), and thus will enable civil rights practitioners to make it economically feasible—as Congress hoped—to expend time and effort litigating civil rights claims.

* * *

During the floor debates over passage of the Fees Act, Senator Hugh Scott reminded the Congress in terms that might well have been addressed to the Court today that "we must bear in mind at all times that rights that cannot be enforced through the legal process are valueless; such a situation breeds cynicism about the basic fairness of our judicial system. [We] must be vigilant to insure that our legal rights are not hollow ones."

NOTES ON NEGOTIATED FEE WAIVERS

1. QUESTIONS AND COMMENTS ON *EVANS V. JEFF D.*

In his dissent, Justice Brennan drew a line between simultaneous negotiation of fees and merits, which he would allow, and waiver of fees, which he would forbid. Are the two really separable? How could a fee settlement be negotiated if plaintiff were not allowed to waive the right to a "reasonable" attorney's fee? Would not an agreed fee be a waiver of any claim to a greater amount? Brennan's answer is that the parties should be permitted to negotiate about the fee "so long as whatever fee the parties agree to is found by the court to be a 'reasonable' one under the Fees Act." Is this workable? What kinds of negotiating incentives would it create?

Note also Brennan's suggestion that civil rights lawyers have their clients agree not to waive attorney's fees. Would that work? Is there an ethical problem with a lawyer limiting the client's right to settle? Would there have been an ethical problem if, on the facts of *Jeff D.*, Charles Johnson had followed the direction of the Legal Aid Society and refused the settlement offer on the ground that it omitted his compensation?

Even if some civil rights lawyers can negotiate retainer agreements that restrain their clients from waiving attorney's fees, such a practice is not feasible in cases such as *Jeff D.* which involve class action litigation—where the attorney cannot effectively negotiate with the entire class, most of whose members have no actual relationship to the lawyer—or which involve clients who are not competent to negotiate retainer agreements in any case. But the lawyer in such situations is likely to be effectively in control of the client as well as the litigation. Will the class-action counsel be able to protect his or her own interests? Or will the possibility of avoiding fee waivers only in individual-plaintiff damages actions skew civil rights attorneys' choices of which kinds of cases to pursue? If lawyers pursue an intermediate position—in which any settlement offer from the defendant, however denominated, is treated as a common pool a portion of which goes to the lawyer—how will this affect attorneys' behavior? Will it induce them to trade off some measure of injunctive relief for more monetary relief since the latter can be a source of compensation?

2. ETHICAL PROHIBITIONS ON DEMANDING FEE WAIVER

Prior to the decision in *Jeff D.*, several state ethics committees had taken a position against allowing defendant's attorney to negotiate for waiver of fees in civil rights cases. Perhaps the most influential was the opinion of the Ethics Committee of the Association of the Bar of the City of New York.[a] The New York opinion took a strict position against conditioning settlement on fee waiver or trying to negotiate fees and merits simultaneously. The District of Columbia bar took a less restrictive position, allowing a lump sum settlement offer for both merits and fees but forbidding bargaining for complete waiver of fees.[b] Finally, some states have expressly approved both simultaneous negotiation and negotiation for fee waiver.[c]

The restrictive opinions were based chiefly on the perceived incompatibility between negotiating for fee waiver and the purposes of the Civil Rights Attorneys' Fees Award Act. On that view, such negotiating practices were condemned as "prejudicial to the administration of justice" under DR 1–102(A)(5) of the Code of Professional Responsibility. Although other reasons have also been given, concern for effective enforcement of the civil rights acts seems to have been dominant. Certainly, that is the understanding reflected in Justice Brennan's encouragement of restrictive rulings "by other state and local organ-

[a] Op. 80–94 (1981), reaffirmed Op. 82–80 (1982). Substantially the same position was taken in Maine. See Grievance Comm'n of the Bd. of Overseers of the Bar of Maine, Op. 17 (1981).

[b] See District of Columbia Bar Legal Ethics Comm., Op. 147 (1985).

[c] Connecticut Comm. on Professional Ethics, Informal Op. 98–19 (1985); State Bar of New Mexico, Op. 1985–3 (1985); Virginia State Bar, Op. 536 (1983). Additionally, the Georgia bar approved simultaneous negotiation of merits and fees without taking a clear position on negotiating for fee waiver. Georgia State Bar Disciplinary Bd., Op. 39 (1984).

izations concerned with respecting the intent of Congress and with protecting civil rights."

In light of the ruling in *Jeff D.*, Brennan's invitation raises an interesting question: What is the propriety of state and local bar organizations undertaking an independent assessment of the intent of Congress and the ways of protecting civil rights? Is it appropriate for bar ethics committees to seek to implement Justice Brennan's dissent, or should they feel bound, insofar as the question turns on the policies underlying § 1988(b), to accept the contrary understanding of the Supreme Court?[d]

The New York committee evidently took the latter view, for after the Court's decision in *Jeff D.* the committee withdrew its restrictive rulings. The committee reported that its earlier opinions "were based in large part on the Committee's interpretation of the legislative policies underlying the civil rights and civil liberties statutes" and that "the principal underpinning" of those rulings had been "removed" by the decision in *Jeff D.*

Nevertheless, the committee admonished against the inference that "conduct previously deemed unethical by the Committee is now necessarily being sanctioned." Instead, the committee held open the possibility that an ethical problem might arise if a settlement offer conditioned on waiver of fees were "coercive" and perhaps in other circumstances as well. This possibility was left to future consideration "in concrete factual settings."

3. ETHICAL PROHIBITIONS ON RESISTING FEE WAIVER

This removal of the ethical prohibition against demanding fee waiver prompted reconsideration of the position of the attorney who is the target of such a demand. Does the civil rights plaintiff's attorney have an ethical obligation to accept waiver of fees in order to secure a settlement in the client's "best interests"?

The New York committee left this question to future consideration, but several members filed a separate minority statement to express their views. They wanted to rule that civil rights plaintiffs' lawyers had no ethical obligation to waive a reasonable fee. Devotion to the client's "best interests" did not extend so far. As the minority reasoned, the prospects of any settlement negotiation would be improved if the lawyers involved agreed to forego their fees. Waiver of fees would decrease the defendant's cost of settlement, while increasing its value to the plaintiff. But lawyers were entitled to charge for their services even though clients would be better off not having to pay for them.

This reasoning extended to civil rights cases, including suits for injunctive relief:

> In public interest cases where only injunctive relief is sought and the defendant offers to settle by agreeing to that relief provided the plaintiff's lawyer waives any fee, the argument is made that the plaintiff's attorney

---

[d] This issue is addressed in R. Hewitt Pate, Comment, *Evans v. Jeff D.* and the Proper Scope of State Ethics Decisions, 73 Va.L.Rev. 783 (1987). Pate takes the view that implementing § 1988(b) is not a proper function of state ethics committees: "In the absence of a definitive construction of [§ 1988(b)], it may or may not [have been] reasonable for the ethics committees to issue opinions based on their understanding of what measures are necessary to protect congressional goals. Once the Supreme Court has addressed the matter and come to a different conclusion, however, respect for the Court's interpretation would seem to demand that the committees reconsider their views."

> has a special ethical duty to do so because he cannot be permitted to block the client or class from obtaining all that was sought. That argument, however, cannot withstand analysis. All that was sought was not merely injunctive relief, but a lawyer from start to finish of the case willing to perform services in pursuit of that relief, with an expectation and opportunity to obtain compensation by judicial award only if the suit were successful. Nothing in legal ethics allows a client to reap the benefits of that success, and at the same time, to defeat the lawyer's opportunity to seek and obtain such compensation.

For these reasons, the minority concluded that: "(a) it is ethically permissible for a lawyer to seek a court award and obtain the payment of reasonable fees (assuming the lawyer has a statutory, contractual or other legal right to do so . . .) and (b) the lawyer has no duty to relinquish or waive any right he may possess to seek such an award and payment, even if it would be in the client's best interest to do so or the client were to so direct, and even assuming it were ethical for the adverse attorney to propose settlement conditioned on such relinquishment or waiver."

The views expressed in the minority statement were in turn disputed in a separate concurrence. The concurring members emphasized that the client, not the lawyer, has the statutory right to collect attorney's fees. The lawyer could include in a retainer agreement a covenant barring waiver of fees, but that would create only a contractual right against the client, not an independent legal interest in the lawsuit. Hence, the decision whether to settle would remain with the client, even if the practical effect of settlement would be to diminish or eliminate the likelihood of payment of fees. "In short," the concurrence concluded, "we doubt that an attorney can ever ethically force a client to the hazards of trial in order to preserve the attorney's prospects of recovering a fee."

4. SETTLEMENT OFFERS AS A MEANS FOR LIMITING ATTORNEY'S FEES: *MAREK V. CHESNY*

Federal Rule of Civil Procedure 68(a) sets out a process for defendants, prior to trial, to make a formal offer "to allow judgment on specified terms, with the costs then accrued." Rule 68(d) provides that if the plaintiff offeree rejects the offer, and "the judgment that the offeree finally obtains is not more favorable than the unaccepted offer, the offeree must pay the costs incurred after the offer was made." In Marek v. Chesny, 473 U.S. 1 (1985), the Supreme Court considered how Rule 68 offers of judgment interact with attorney's fees awards under § 1988. The case involved a lawsuit over a police shooting that resulted in the death of respondent's son. Prior to trial, the police officers made a timely offer of judgment "for a sum, including costs now accrued and attorney's fees, of one hundred thousand ($100,000) dollars." Respondent turned down the offer. At trial, respondent obtained a verdict for $60,000. He then requested roughly $171,000 in costs, including attorney's fees. Only $32,000 of that amount reflected costs and fees accrued prior to the offer of judgment.

The Court's opinion began by approving the practice of making an offer of judgment that lumps together both damages and costs:

> If an offer recites that costs are included or specifies an amount for costs, and the plaintiff accepts the offer, the judgment will necessarily include costs; if the offer does not state that costs are included and an

amount for costs is not specified, the court will be obliged by the terms of the rule to include in its judgment an additional amount which in its discretion it determines to be sufficient to cover the costs. In either case, however, the offer has allowed judgment to be entered against the defendant both for damages caused by the challenged conduct and for costs. Accordingly, it is immaterial whether the offer recites that costs are included, whether it specifies the amount the defendant is allowing for costs, or for that matter, whether it refers to costs at all. As long as the offer does not implicitly or explicitly provide that the judgment *not* include costs, a timely offer will be valid.

The Court then held that the "costs" referred to in Rule 68 include attorney's fees in fee-shifting cases. The upshot was that § 1983 plaintiffs who turn down an offer of judgment equal to or more favorable than the judgment they receive at trial will be foreclosed from receiving fees for work after the offer was made:

> Rule 68's policy of encouraging settlements is neutral, favoring neither plaintiffs nor defendants; it expresses a clear policy of favoring settlement of all lawsuits. Civil rights plaintiffs—along with other plaintiffs—who reject an offer more favorable than what is thereafter recovered at trial will not recover attorney's fees for services performed after the offer is rejected. But, since the rule is neutral, many civil rights plaintiffs will benefit from the offers of settlement encouraged by Rule 68. Some plaintiffs will receive compensation in settlement where, on trial, they might not have recovered, or would have recovered less than what was offered. And, even for those who would prevail at trial, settlement will provide them with compensation at an earlier date without the burdens, stress, and time of litigation. In short, settlements rather than litigation will serve the interests of plaintiffs as well as defendants.
>
> To be sure, application of Rule 68 will require plaintiffs to "think very hard" about whether continued litigation is worthwhile; that is precisely what Rule 68 contemplates. The effect of Rule 68, however, is in no sense inconsistent with the congressional policies underlying § 1983 and § 1988(b). Section 1988(b) authorizes courts to award only "reasonable" attorney's fees to prevailing parties. . . . This case presents a good example: the $139,692 in post-offer legal services resulted in a recovery of $8,000 less than petitioner's settlement offer. Given Congress' focus on the success achieved, we are not persuaded that shifting the post-offer costs to respondent in these circumstances would in any sense thwart its intent under § 1988(b).

Justices Powell and Rehnquist filed concurring opinions.

Justice Brennan, joined by Justice Marshall, dissented. He argued that the "costs" referred to in Rule 68 should include only the relatively limited costs taxable in every case (such as filing fees and other expenses listed in 28 U.S.C. § 1920 and Federal Rule of Civil Procedure 54(d)). He further argued that a mechanical application of Rule 68 undercut the totality-of-the-circumstances reasonableness standard for fee awards under § 1988.

> Rule 68, on the other hand, is not "sensitive" at all to the merits of an action and to antidiscrimination policy. It is a mechanical per se provision

> automatically shifting "costs" incurred after an offer is rejected, and it deprives a district court of *all* discretion with respect to the matter. . . . The conflict between § 1988(b) and Rule 68 could not be more apparent.
>
> Of course, a civil-rights plaintiff who *unreasonably* fails to accept a settlement offer, and who thereafter recovers less than the proffered amount in settlement, is barred under § 1988(b) itself from recovering fees for unproductive work performed in the wake of the rejection. This is because "the extent of a plaintiff's success is *a* crucial factor in determining the proper amount of attorney's fees"; hours that are "excessive, redundant, or otherwise unnecessary" must be excluded from that calculus. To this extent, the results might sometimes be the same under either § 1988(b)'s reasonableness inquiry or the Court's wooden application of Rule 68. . . .

He also warned that application of Rule 68 might undercut plaintiffs' rights by "encouraging defendants who know they have violated the law to make 'low-ball' offers immediately after suit is filed and before plaintiffs have been able to obtain the information they are entitled to by way of discovery to assess the strength of their claims and the reasonableness of the offers." And he pointed to difficulties that might arise from the distinctive nature of civil rights suits:

> Other difficulties will follow from the Court's decision. For example, if a plaintiff recovers less money than was offered before trial but obtains potentially far-reaching injunctive or declaratory relief, it is altogether unclear how the Court intends judges to go about quantifying the "value" of the plaintiff's success. And the Court's decision raises additional problems concerning representation and conflicts of interest in the context of civil-rights class actions. These are difficult policy questions, and I do not mean to suggest that stronger settlement incentives would necessarily conflict with the effective enforcement of the civil-rights laws. But contrary to the Court's four-paragraph discussion, the policy considerations do not all point in one direction. . . .

For analysis of *Marek* see Roy D. Simon, Jr., The New Meaning of Rule 68: *Marek v. Chesny* and Beyond, 14 N.Y.U. Rev. of Law & Social Change 475 (1986) (providing practical guidance about the operation of Rule 68 in light of *Marek*, with particular reference to cases involving injunctive relief). A general analysis of the administration of Rule 68, including special attention to the problem of attorney's fees and proposals for reform, may be found in Lynn Sanders Branham, Offer of Judgment and Rule 68: A Response to the Chief Justice, 18 John Marshall L.Rev. 341 (1985). For criticism of *Marek* and other incentives to settlement, see Laura Macklin, Promoting Settlement, Foregoing the Facts, 14 N.Y.U. Rev. of Law & Social Change 575 (1986) (emphasizing the value of judicial fact-finding as a "source of tested information" for the public at large).

For assessment of the practical impact of *Marek v. Chesny*, see Julie Davies, Federal Civil Rights Practice in the 1990's: The Dichotomy Between Reality and Theory, 48 Hastings L.J. 197, 222–25 (1997). Davies interviewed civil rights lawyers, who reported that they rarely encountered Rule 68 offers. One factor, Davies believes, is that "it is often difficult for defense counsel to evaluate a case, including plaintiffs' attorney's fees, to derive an offer that is serious enough to get the plaintiff's attorney's attention." Another factor is the difficulty of persuading the defendant to authorize a realistic settlement offer at an early date.

For additional discussion of the reluctance to use Rule 68 in fee-generating cases, see Harold S. Lewis, Jr. and Thomas A. Eaton, Of Offers Not (Frequently) Made and Rarely Accepted: The Mystery of Federal Rule 68, 57 Mercer L. Rev. 723 (2006), and the other articles in FRCP 68: Can Offers of Judgment Provide Adequate Incentives for Fair, Early Settlement of Fee–Recovery Cases, 57 Mercer L. Rev. 717–855 (2006).

5. BIBLIOGRAPHY

For analysis of a variety of ethical problems than can arise in settlement negotiations in civil rights cases, see Emily Calhoun, Attorney–Client Conflicts of Interest and the Concept of Non–Negotiable Fee Awards Under 42 U.S.C. § 1988, 55 U.Colo.L.Rev. 341 (1984). Calhoun surveys the potential problems and discusses a number of attempted palliatives, including retainer agreements, judicial scrutiny of civil rights settlements, and bifurcated negotiation of fees and merits. She concludes that none of these solutions is satisfactory and therefore urges that civil rights attorney's fees should be made non-negotiable. Otherwise, the implicit conflict of interest between attorney and client will be subject to various forms of exploitation in the settlement process.

Another treatment of these issues may be found in Charles Wolfram, The Second Set of Players: Lawyers, Fee Shifting, and the Limits of Professional Discipline, 47 Law & Contemp. Prob. 293 (1984). Wolfram suggests that a ban against conditioning settlement on waiver of fees is supported by strictly "ethical" considerations—that is, by policies unrelated to interpretation of the Fees Act. He offers two rationales. First, he characterizes the kind of settlement offer made in *Jeff D.* as "extortionate" and says that "extortion is wrongful duress impermissible to both lawyers and nonlawyers." Second, he says that "lawyers and nonlawyers alike are prohibited by law from creating a conflict of interest that carries a substantial risk of harming the interests of the represented opponent." Are these remarks persuasive? Do they adequately take account of the extent to which the lawyer's ethical obligations are shaped by the primary responsibility to his or her own client?

For an attempt to assess the impact of *Evans v. Jeff D.*, see Julie Davies, Federal Civil Rights Practice in the 1990's: The Dichotomy Between Reality and Theory, 48 Hastings L.J. 197 (1997). Davies interviewed civil rights lawyers, who reported that they rarely encountered requests for fee waivers and that such requests are typically refused. The lawyers nevertheless believed that *Jeff D.* had tilted settlement behavior in favor of defendants by allowing lump-sum offers, which the lawyers felt were less likely to be fully compensatory of their time than bifurcated negotiations of fees and merits.

NOTE ON TAXATION OF ATTORNEY'S FEES

Section 1988(b) provides, in pertinent part, that courts may "allow the prevailing party . . . a reasonable attorney's fee." As the opinion in *Jeff D.* suggests, the entitlement to fees is vested in the litigant, not in the attorney. In the 1990s, an issue arose concerning the tax consequences of this allocation. Is the portion of an award payable as attorney's fees included in the litigant's adjusted gross income? In many cases, the additional income would in any event be offset by a miscellaneous itemized deduction, but such deductions are not available under the Alternative Minimum Tax. For taxpayers subject to the AMT, inclusion of attorney's fees in the litigant's taxable income can have a major impact on tax liability.

In Commissioner of Internal Revenue v. Banks, 543 U.S. 426 (2005), the Supreme Court confronted the closely analogous question of a litigant's tax liability for the portion of a settlement or judgment paid to the attorney as a contingent fee. The Court held that, "as a general rule, when a litigant's recovery constitutes income, the litigant's income includes the portion of the recovery paid to the attorney as a contingent fee." The Court, however, noted at least a possibility that court-ordered fee awards might be treated differently.

In any event, the issue is not likely to have continuing significance. The American Jobs Creation Act of 2004 added § 62(a)(19) to the Internal Revenue Code. That amendment allows a taxpayer, whether or not subject to the AMT, to deduct "attorney's fees and court costs paid by, or on behalf of, the taxpayer in connection with any action involving a claim of unlawful discrimination." Elsewhere, "unlawful discrimination" is defined to include any law "providing for the enforcement of civil rights." It seems likely that this provision covers all, or almost all, cases of attorney's fees under § 1988. The statute is not retroactive and therefore had no application to *Banks*.

CHAPTER 3

ADMINISTRATION OF THE CIVIL RIGHTS ACTS

1. STATE SOVEREIGN IMMUNITY AND THE ELEVENTH AMENDMENT

[This Section provides detailed coverage of the Eleventh Amendment and state sovereign immunity. Those who wish may substitute these materials (including *Edelman v. Jordan* and the notes following) for the Introductory Notes on the Eleventh Amendment that begin Chapter I, Section 3. At the conclusion of these materials, the reader should return to Chapter I, Section 3, for the Introductory Note on *Hafer v. Melo* and the Importance of Officer Suits, the main case of *Hafer v. Melo*, and the subsequent Notes on Personal vs. Official Capacity.]

INTRODUCTORY NOTES ON THE ELEVENTH AMENDMENT

1. INTRODUCTION

Much of the structure of constitutional tort law reflects the influence of the Eleventh Amendment and state sovereign immunity. Only to a very limited extent is this a matter of constitutional compulsion. Of far greater moment is the pattern of the law of state sovereign immunity, a pattern that has strongly influenced the construction of § 1983. In a sense, the subconstitutional law of § 1983 and *Bivens* echoes the constitutionally-based law of the Eleventh Amendment. How and why this is so requires a brief recapitulation of the origins and history of that provision.

2. *CHISHOLM V. GEORGIA*

The only thing about the Eleventh Amendment that is indisputably clear is that it was intended to overrule the Supreme Court's decision in Chisholm v. Georgia, 2 U.S. (2 Dall.) 419 (1793). In *Chisholm*, the executor of a South Carolina merchant sued the state of Georgia to recover for supplies furnished under a contract. Under § 13 of the Judiciary Act of 1789,[a] the Supreme Court had original jurisdiction in diversity actions between a state and a citizen of another state. The Court held that the suit could go forward despite Georgia's claim of sovereign immunity.

In the manner of the time, each Justice wrote separately. Justices Blair and Cushing thought the suit authorized by the language of Article III, which extends the federal judicial power to "Controversies . . . between a State and

[a] "[T]he supreme court shall have exclusive jurisdiction of all controversies of a civil nature, where a state is a party, except between a state and its citizens; and except also, between a state and citizens of other states, or aliens, in which latter case it shall have original, but not exclusive jurisdiction."

Citizens of another State." Justice Wilson added that by creating the national government and vesting in its courts the power to hear controversies involving states, the people bound the states to answer legal claims as would any individual. Wilson made particular reference to the Art. I, § 10, prohibition against laws impairing the obligation of contracts: "What good purpose could this Constitutional provision secure, if a State might pass a law impairing the obligation of its own contracts; and be amenable, for such a violation of right, to no controlling judiciary power?" Chief Justice Jay agreed with Wilson.

Justice Iredell was the sole dissenter. He interpreted § 13 of the Judiciary Act to confer jurisdiction only over such controversies as were recognized at common law. As there was no precedent for an action of assumpsit against a state, Iredell concluded that the Court lacked statutory jurisdiction.[b]

3. REACTION TO *CHISHOLM*

The reaction to *Chisholm* was swift and hostile. The concern was not merely the affront to state sovereignty but a practical fear of exhausting state treasuries: "In the crucial condition of the finances of most of the states at that time, only disaster was to be expected if suits could be successfully maintained by holders of state issues of paper and other credits, or by Loyalist refugees to recover property confiscated or sequestered by the states; and that this was no theoretical danger was shown by the immediate institution of such suits against the states in South Carolina, Georgia, Virginia and Massachusetts." 1 Charles Warren, The Supreme Court in United States History 99 (1922). The Commonwealth of Massachusetts adopted a resolution calling for the overturn of *Chisholm*, and the Georgia House of Representatives passed a bill to the effect that any persons attempting to execute process in the *Chisholm* case should be hanged. Id. at 100–01.

Constitutional amendments were proposed in the House of Representatives on the second and third days after *Chisholm* was announced. The proposal adopted by Congress in the next session and ultimately ratified as the Eleventh Amendment to the Constitution reads as follows:

> The Judicial power of the United States shall not be construed to extend to any suit in law or equity, commenced or prosecuted against one of the United States by Citizens of another State, or by Citizens or Subjects of any Foreign State.

4. THE NEXT HUNDRED YEARS

For three-quarters of a century, the Eleventh Amendment was of little consequence. In Osborn v. Bank of the United States, 22 U.S. (9 Wheat.) 738 (1824), Chief Justice Marshall said that the amendment applied only when a state was "party of record." Thus, the amendment could be avoided simply by suing an appropriate state officer rather than the state itself.

This convenient evasion survived until the end of Reconstruction. The Civil War had left the southern states economically destitute, yet saddled with debt. As the northern armies withdrew, one of the first goals of the restored

---

[b] Contrary to Justice Iredell's view, today it is widely accepted that the Article III provisions on the original jurisdiction of the Supreme Court are self-executing and do not require legislative authorization. Under the modern view, a case would either fall the Supreme Court's original jurisdiction or not, without regard to statutory provisions.

local leadership was to repudiate public bonds. The bondholders sought to hold the states to their obligations by suit in federal court. Given the similar history of *Chisholm,* the Eleventh Amendment was an obvious problem, and the bondholders tried a variety of ways to avoid it. These included mandamus actions against state officials, Louisiana ex rel. Elliott v. Jumel, 107 U.S. 711 (1883); suits by other states, New Hampshire v. Louisiana and New York v. Louisiana, 108 U.S. 76 (1883); attachment of state property, Christian v. Atlantic & North Carolina R., 133 U.S. 233 (1890); and suit against a state by one of its own citizens, Hans v. Louisiana, 134 U.S. 1 (1890). None of these strategies worked. With some significant (and difficult to explain) exceptions, the Supreme Court refurbished and extended the Eleventh Amendment to defeat recovery.

5. *HANS V. LOUISIANA*

In Hans v. Louisiana, 134 U.S. 1 (1890), a citizen of Louisiana sued to recover unpaid interest on state bonds. Hans claimed that a state constitutional amendment disavowing the obligation to pay interest was a "Law impairing the Obligation of Contracts" in violation of Art. I, § 10, of the federal Constitution. His case was not a diversity action, as *Chisholm* had been, but a claim arising under the Constitution or laws of the United States. The Court found that the Eleventh Amendment nevertheless barred recovery. Speaking through Justice Bradley, the Court said:

> In the present case [Hans] contends that he, being a citizen of Louisiana, is not embarrassed by the obstacle of the Eleventh Amendment, inasmuch as that amendment only prohibits suits against a State which are brought by the citizens of another State, or by citizens or subjects of a foreign State. It is true, the amendment does so read: and if there were no other reason or ground for abating his suit, it might be maintainable; and then we should have this anomalous result, that in cases arising under the Constitution or laws of the United States, a State may be sued in the federal courts by its own citizens, though it cannot be sued for a like cause of action by the citizens of other States, or of a foreign state; and may be thus sued in the federal courts, although not allowing itself to be sued in its own courts. If this is the necessary consequence of the language of the Constitution and the law, the result is no less startling and unexpected than was the original decision of this court [in] Chisholm v. Georgia, 2 U.S. (2 Dall.) 419 (1793), [which] created such a shock of surprise throughout the country that, at the first meeting of Congress thereafter, the Eleventh Amendment to the constitution was almost unanimously proposed, and was in due course adopted by the legislatures of the States. This amendment . . . did not in terms prohibit suits by individuals against the States, but declared that the Constitution should not be construed to import any power to authorize the bringing of such suits. The language of the amendment is that "the judicial power of the United States shall *not be construed to extend* to any suit in law or equity, commenced or prosecuted against one of the United States by citizens of another state, or by citizens or subjects of any foreign state." The Supreme Court had construed the judicial power as extending to such a suit, and its decision was thus overruled.

Bradley quoted Hamilton, Madison, and Marshall to the effect that it is "inherent in the nature of sovereignty" that the state cannot be sued without its consent. He continued:

> It seems to us that these views of those great advocates and defenders of the Constitution were most sensible and just. . . . [The argument by Hans] is an attempt to strain the Constitution and the law to a construction never imagined or dreamed of. Can we suppose that, when the Eleventh Amendment was adopted, it was understood to be left open for citizens of a State to sue their own state in the federal courts, whilst the idea of suits by citizens of other states, or of foreign states, was indignantly repelled? Suppose that Congress, when proposing the Eleventh Amendment, had appended to it a proviso that nothing therein contained should prevent a State from being sued by its own citizens in cases arising under the Constitution or laws of the United States: can we imagine that it would have been adopted by the States? The supposition that it would is almost an absurdity on its face.

6. LOCAL GOVERNMENTS

On the same day it decided *Hans v. Louisiana,* the Supreme Court held in Lincoln County v. Luning, 133 U.S. 529 (1890), that the Eleventh Amendment did not protect a county from suit in federal court. Subsequent cases have extended this holding to other units of local government.[c]

Today, the disparity between states and their political subdivisions may seem anomalous, but it appears to have a foundation in history. At the time the Eleventh Amendment was adopted, municipal corporations were analogized to private corporations and were deemed to lack the attributes of sovereignty possessed by states. By the time that the municipal corporation came to be seen as a distinct legal form exercising governmental powers delegated by the state, the amenability of local governments to suit in federal court had long been established. It was perhaps that in recognition of that tradition that the Court construed § 1983 to authorize (in limited circumstances) damages actions against localities, even though such actions are not permitted against states. See Monell v. New York City Department of Social Serivces, 436 U.S. 658 (1978).

7. THE DIVERSITY INTERPRETATION

Hans read the Eleventh Amendment as constitutionalizing state sovereign immunity, even in suits by citizens of the defendant state. Although the text refers only to suits by citizens of other states or foreign countries, the Court read the amendment as evidencing a comprehensive policy of state sovereign immunity in federal court, except for suits by the United States or by another state.[d]

The chief alternative to *Hans* is the "diversity" interpretation of the Eleventh Amendment. This approach reads the amendment as a restriction on the federal courts only when jurisdiction is based on diversity of citizenship. The

---

[c] See, e.g., Workman v. New York, 179 U.S. 552 (1900) (cities); Mount Healthy City School District v. Doyle, 429 U.S. 274 (1977) (school boards).

[d] Rhode Island v. Massachusetts, 37 U.S. (12 Pet.) 657 (1838) (Eleventh Amendment does not bar suit by another state); United States v. Texas, 143 U.S. 621, 645 (1892) (Eleventh Amendment does not bar suit by the United States).

diversity interpretation sees the error of *Chisholm* as its treatment of the mere fact of diversity jurisdiction as an abrogation of state sovereign immunity *for a claim based on state law*. In this view, the Eleventh Amendment did not constitutionalize state sovereign immunity but merely repudiated the idea that state sovereign immunity had been abrogated by Article III diversity jurisdiction. Suits arising under federal law would be unaffected.

On this reading, the failure of the amendment to prohibit suits by a state's own citizens is perfectly understandable, as such suits would not in any event have come within the state-citizen diversity provision of Article III. Note, however, that the text of the amendment is not limited to diversity cases. Taken literally, it would preclude *all* suits against a state by a citizen of another state, even those based on federal law. The usual response to this observation is that the failure to distinguish federal question cases is not surprising, given that there was at the time no statute generally authorizing the federal courts to hear cases arising under federal law and no disposition by the national legislature to impose federal liability upon the states. The question whether a suit based on federal law should be prohibited by the Eleventh Amendment, so the argument goes, was simply not in view.

Practically speaking, the diversity interpretation would read the Eleventh Amendment to mean nothing at all for the enforcement of federal law. The only cases it would cover would be suits brought by out-of-state plaintiffs to enforce state-law obligations. Perhaps for this reason, no Justice of the Supreme Court wholly accepted the diversity interpretation until Justice Brennan's dissent, joined by Justices Marshall, Blackmun, and Stevens, in Atascadero State Hospital v. Scanlon, 473 U.S. 234, 289–90 (1985). Since then, the diversity interpretation has repeatedly been accepted by four Justices, but never five. See, e.g., Welch v. State Dept. of Highways and Public Transportation, 483 U.S. 468, 496 (1987) (Brennan, J., dissenting, joined by Marshall, Blackmun, and Stevens, JJ.); Seminole Tribe v. Florida, 517 U.S. 44, 76 (1996) (Stevens, J., dissenting), and 100 (Souter, J., dissenting, joined by Ginsburg and Breyer, JJ.). For a bare but persistent majority of the Justices, some version of *Hans* remains good law.

8. *EX PARTE YOUNG*

Hans prohibited private damage actions against states in federal court, absent state consent. It might be thought that state immunity would also bar suits for declaratory and injunctive relief. The well-settled rule to the contrary dates at least from Ex parte Young, 209 U.S. 123 (1908).

Young was a suit brought by railroad shareholders who claimed that Minnesota legislation setting railroad rates was unconstitutional. They sued Edward T. Young, the Attorney General of Minnesota, seeking to enjoin enforcement of the state statute. The federal court issued an injunction and, when Young nevertheless moved to enforce the state law, found him in content. The case came to the Supreme Court on Young's original application for writs of habeas corpus and certiorari.

In the Supreme Court, the chief question was whether enjoining enforcement of a state statute contravened the Eleventh Amendment. In dissent, Justice Harlan argued that the suit was really against the state and therefore barred by the Eleventh Amendment:

> Let it be observed that the suit instituted . . . in the Circuit Court of the United States was, as to the defendant Young, one against him *as, and only because he was,* Attorney General of Minnesota. No relief was sought against him individually but only in his capacity *as* Attorney General. And the manifest, indeed the avowed and admitted, object of seeking such relief was *to tie the hands* of the *State.* . . . It would therefore seem clear that within the true meaning of the Eleventh Amendment the suit brought in the Federal court was one, in legal effect, against the State—as much so as if the State had been formally named on the record as a party—and therefore it was a suit to which, under the Amendment, so far as the State or its Attorney General was concerned, the judicial power of the United States did not and could not extend. . . .

The majority disagreed. Speaking through Justice Peckham, the Court explained why the Eleventh Amendment was no bar to an injunction against the Attorney General:

> It is contended that the complainants do not complain and they care nothing about any action which Mr. Young might take or bring as an ordinary individual, but that he was complained of as an officer, to whose discretion is confided the use of the name of the State of Minnesota so far as litigation is concerned, and that when or how he shall use it is a matter resting in his discretion and cannot be controlled by any court.
>
> The answer to all this is the same as made in every case where an official claims to be acting under the authority of the State. The act to be enforced is alleged to be unconstitutional, and if it be so, the use of the name of the State to enforce an unconstitutional act to the injury of complainants is a proceeding without the authority of and one which does not affect the State in its sovereign or governmental capacity. It is simply an illegal act upon the part of a state official in attempting by the use of the name of the State to enforce a legislative enactment which is void because unconstitutional. *If the act which the state Attorney General seeks to enforce be a violation of the Federal Constitution, the officer in proceeding under such enactment comes into conflict with the superior authority of the Constitution, and he is in that case stripped of his official or representative character and is subjected in his person to the consequences of his individual conduct.* The State has no power to impart to him any immunity from responsibility to the supreme authority of the United States. . . . [Emphasis added.]

The italicized sentence states what is often described as the "fiction" of *Ex parte Young.* The approval of injunctions against state officers created (or at least confirmed) a substantial exception to state sovereign immunity. For most purposes, a state can be sued in federal court for prospective relief by the simple expedient of naming the appropriate state officer as the defendant.

Note also that the complainants in *Ex parte Young* sued to prevent violation of their constitutional rights without the aid of any statute specifically authorizing such an action. Where did the cause of action come from? Though the answer to this question is not entirely clear, *Ex parte Young* has come to be cited for the proposition that a cause of action for equitable relief to prevent violation of constitutional rights exists independent of explicit congressional authorization. For that reason, the revivification of § 1983 in *Monroe v. Pape* did not change the law with respect to injunctive relief. The importance of

Monroe lay rather in its recognition of a statutorily authorized cause of action for money damages.

Obviously, *Hans* and *Ex parte Young* create radically different legal regimes. In *Hans*, state sovereign immunity blocks private enforcement of federal law. In *Young*, that enforcement is freely authorized. The boundary between these conflicting doctrines is the subject of the next main case.

Edelman v. Jordan

Supreme Court of the United States, 1974.
415 U.S. 651.

[Respondent Jordan brought a class action to challenge the practices of certain Illinois officials in administering federal-state programs under the Aid to the Aged, Blind, or Disabled Act (AABD). The District Court found that the defendant officials had failed to process AABD applications within applicable time limits and had failed to make the benefits retroactive to the date of initial eligibility, as required by federal regulations issued by the Department of Health, Education and Welfare under the Social Security Act. The court enjoined any future violations and ordered the state officials to refund all wrongfully withheld past benefits. The Seventh Circuit affirmed over the defendants' objection that the Eleventh Amendment barred the award of retroactive benefits. The Supreme Court granted certiorari.]

■ MR. JUSTICE REHNQUIST delivered the opinion of the Court. . . .

While the [Eleventh] Amendment by its terms does not bar suits against a State by its own citizens, this Court has consistently held that an unconsenting State is immune from suits brought in federal courts by her own citizens as well as by citizens of another State. Hans v. Louisiana, 134 U.S. 1 (1890). It is also well established that even though a State is not named a party to the action, the suit may nonetheless be barred by the Eleventh Amendment. In Ford Motor Co. v. Department of Treasury, 323 U.S. 459, 464 (1945), the Court said:

> [W]hen the action is in essence one for the recovery of money from the state, the state is the real, substantial party in interest and is entitled to invoke its sovereign immunity from suit even though individual officials are nominal defendants.

Thus the rule has evolved that a suit by private parties seeking to impose a liability which must be paid from public funds in the state treasury is barred by the Eleventh Amendment.

The Court of Appeals in this case, while recognizing that the *Hans* line of cases permitted the state to raise the Eleventh Amendment as a defense to suit by its own citizens, nevertheless concluded that the Amendment did not bar the award of retroactive payments of the statutory benefits found to have been wrongfully withheld. The Court of Appeals held that the above-cited cases, when read in light of this Court's landmark decision in Ex parte Young, 209 U.S. 123 (1908), do not preclude the grant of such a monetary award in the nature of equitable restitution. . . .

Ex parte Young was a watershed case in which this Court held that the Eleventh Amendment did not bar an action in the federal courts seeking to enjoin the Attorney General of Minnesota from enforcing a statute claimed to violate the Fourteenth Amendment of the United States Constitution. This holding has permitted the Civil War Amendments to the Constitution to serve as a sword, rather than merely as a shield, for those whom they were designed to protect. But the relief awarded in *Ex parte Young* was prospective only; the Attorney General of Minnesota was enjoined to conform his future conduct of that office to the requirement of the Fourteenth Amendment. Such relief is analogous to that awarded by the District Court in the prospective portion of its order under review in this case.

But the retroactive portion of the District Court's order here, which requires the payment of a very substantial amount of money which that court held should have been paid, but was not, stands on quite a different footing. These funds will obviously not be paid out of the pocket of petitioner Edelman. Addressing himself to a similar situation in Rothstein v. Wyman, 467 F.2d 226 (2d Cir.1972), Judge McGowan observed for the court:

> It is not pretended that these payments are to come from the personal resources of these appellants. Appellees expressly contemplate that they will, rather, involve substantial expenditures from the public funds of the state. . . .
>
> It is one thing to tell the Commissioner of Social Services that he must comply with the federal standards for the future if the state is to have the benefit of federal funds in the programs he administers. It is quite another thing to order the Commissioner to use state funds to make reparation for the past. The latter would appear to us to fall afoul of the Eleventh Amendment if that basic constitutional provision is to be conceived of as having any present force.

We agree with Judge McGowan's observations. The funds to satisfy the award in this case must inevitably come from the general revenues of the State of Illinois, and thus the award resembles far more closely the monetary award against the state itself, *Ford Motor Co. v. Department of Treasury*, supra, than it does the prospective injunctive relief awarded in *Ex parte Young*. . . .

As in most areas of the law, the difference between the type of relief barred by the Eleventh Amendment and that permitted under *Ex parte Young* will not in many instances be that between day and night. The injunction issued in *Ex parte Young* was not totally without effect on the State's revenues, since the state law which the Attorney General was enjoined from enforcing provided substantial monetary penalties against railroads which did not conform to its provisions. Later cases from this Court have authorized equitable relief which has probably had greater impact on state treasuries than did that awarded in *Ex parte Young*. . . . But the fiscal consequences to state treasuries in these cases were the necessary result of compliance with decrees which by their terms were prospective in nature. State officials, in order to shape their official conduct to the mandate of the Court's decrees, would more likely have to spend money from the state treasury than if they had been left free to pursue their previous course of conduct. Such an ancillary effect on the state treasury is a permissible and often an inevitable consequence of the principle announced in *Ex parte Young*, supra.

But that portion of the District Court's decree which petitioner challenges on Eleventh Amendment grounds goes much further than any of the cases cited. It requires payment of state funds, not as a necessary consequence of compliance in the future with a substantive federal-question determination, but as a form of compensation to those whose applications were processed on the slower time schedule at a time when petitioner was under no court-imposed obligation to conform to a different standard. While the Court of Appeals described this retroactive award of monetary relief as a form of "equitable restitution," it is in practical effect indistinguishable in many aspects from an award of damages against the State. . . .

The Court of Appeals held in the alternative that even if the Eleventh Amendment be deemed a bar to the retroactive relief awarded respondent in this case, the State of Illinois had waived its Eleventh Amendment immunity and consented to the bringing of such a suit by participating in the federal AABD program. . . . The Court of Appeals held that as a matter of federal law Illinois had "constructively consented" to this suit by participating in the federal AABD program and agreeing to administer federal and state funds in compliance with federal law. Constructive consent is not a doctrine commonly associated with the surrender of constitutional rights, and we see no place for it here. In deciding whether a State has waived its constitutional protection under the Eleventh Amendment, we will find waiver only where stated "by the most express language or by such overwhelming implications from the text as [will] leave no room for any other reasonable construction." Murray v. Wilson Distilling Co., 213 U.S. 151, 171 (1909). . . . The mere fact that a State participates in a program through which the Federal Government provides assistance for the operation by the State of a system of public aid is not sufficient to establish consent on the part of the State to be sued in the federal courts. . . .

For the foregoing reasons we decide that the Court of Appeals was wrong in holding that the Eleventh Amendment did not constitute a bar to that portion of the District Court decree which ordered retroactive payment of benefits found to have been wrongfully withheld. The judgment of the Court of Appeals is therefore reversed and the cause remanded for further proceedings consistent with this opinion.

So ordered.

■ MR. JUSTICE DOUGLAS, dissenting. . . .

As the complaint in the instant case alleges violations by officials of Illinois of the Equal Protection Clause of the Fourteenth Amendment, it seems that the case is governed by *Ex parte Young* so far as injunctive relief is concerned. The main thrust of the argument is that the instant case asks for relief which if granted would affect the treasury of the State.

Most welfare decisions by federal courts have a financial impact on the States. . . . Whether the decree is prospective only or requires payments for the weeks or months wrongfully skipped over by the state officials, the nature of the impact on the state treasury is precisely the same. . . .

It is said however, that the Eleventh Amendment is concerned, not with immunity of States from suit, but with the jurisdiction of the federal courts to entertain the suit. The Eleventh Amendment does not speak of "jurisdiction"; it withholds the "judicial power" of federal courts "to any suit in law or equity . . . against one of the United States. . . . " If that "judicial power," or "jurisdiction" if one prefers that concept, may not be exercised even in "any suit in . . . equity" then *Ex parte Young* should be overruled. But there is none eager to take the step. Where a State has consented to join a federal-state cooperative project, it is realistic to conclude that the State has agreed to assume its obligations under that legislation. There is nothing in the Eleventh Amendment to suggest a difference between suits at law and suits in equity, for it treats the two without distinction. If common sense has any role to play in constitutional adjudication, once there is a waiver of immunity it must be true that it is complete so far as effective operation of the state-federal joint welfare program is concerned.

. . . I would affirm the judgment of the Court of Appeals.

■ MR. JUSTICE BRENNAN, dissenting.

This suit is brought by Illinois citizens against Illinois officials. In that circumstance, Illinois may not invoke the Eleventh Amendment, since that amendment bars only federal court suits against States by citizens of other States. Rather, the question is whether Illinois may avail itself of the nonconstitutional but ancient doctrine of sovereign immunity as a bar to respondent's claim for retroactive AABD payments. In my view Illinois may not assert sovereign immunity for the reason I expressed in dissent in Employees v. Department of Public Health and Welfare, 411 U.S. 279, 298 (1973): the States surrendered that immunity in Hamilton's words, "in the plan of the Convention," that formed the Union, at least insofar as the States granted Congress specifically enumerated powers. Congressional authority to enact the Social Security Act, of which AABD is a part, is to be found in Art. I, § 8, cl. 1, one of the enumerated powers granted Congress by the States in the Constitution. I remain of the opinion that "because of its surrender, no immunity exists that can be the subject of a congressional declaration or a voluntary waiver," 911 U.S. at 300, and thus have no occasion to inquire whether or not Congress authorized an action for AABD retroactive benefits, or whether or not Illinois voluntarily waived the immunity by its continued participation in the program against the background of precedents which sustained judgments ordering retroactive payments.

I would affirm the judgment of the Court of Appeals.

■ MR. JUSTICE MARSHALL, with whom MR. JUSTICE BLACKMUN joins, dissenting.

The Social Security Act's categorical assistance programs, including the Aid to the Aged, Blind, or Disabled (AABD) program involved here, are fundamentally different from most federal legislation. Unlike the Fair Labor Standards Act involved in last Term's decision in Employees v. Department of Public Health and Welfare, 411 U.S. 279 (1973), or the Federal Employers' Liability Act at issue in Parden v. Terminal R. Co., 377 U.S. 184 (1964), the Social Security Act does not impose federal standards and liability upon all who engage in certain regulated activities, including often unwilling state agencies. Instead, the Act seeks to induce state participation in the federal welfare programs by offering federal matching funds in exchange for the State's voluntary assumption of the Act's requirements. I find this basic distinction crucial: it leads me to conclude that by participation in the programs, the States waive whatever immunity they might otherwise have from federal court orders requiring retroactive payment of welfare benefits.[1] . . . I respectfully dissent.

---

1 In view of my conclusion on this issue, I find it unnecessary to consider whether the Court correctly treats this suit as one against the State rather than as a suit against a state officer permissible under the rationale of Ex parte Young, 209 U.S. 123 (1908).

NOTES ON ATTEMPTED CIRCUMVENTIONS OF STATE SOVEREIGN IMMUNITY

1. INTRODUCTION

Basically, *Edelman v. Jordan* reaffirmed *Hans* within the area, described as retrospective relief, which is not controlled by *Ex parte Young*. As a result, the Eleventh Amendment (or the principle of state sovereign immunity it is said to reflect) generally bars the award of money damages against states and state agencies, though not against units of local government.

In the years since *Edelman*, this understanding of the constitutional status of state sovereign immunity has repeatedly been attacked by those who subscribe to the "diversity" interpretation of the Eleventh Amendment. Additionally, opponents of state sovereign immunity have sought ways to circumvent *Hans* without necessarily overruling it. Three strategies have predominated. First, as in *Edelman*, opponents of state sovereign immunity advanced a notion of waiver or consent that would deprive a state of immunity if it voluntarily participated in an activity (at least a non-core activity) subject to federal regulation. Second, they argued that even if a state did not waive its immunity or consent to suit, Congress could override state immunity by appropriate legislation. Third, they claimed that, whatever immunity states enjoyed in federal court, they had to submit to suit for money damages in state court for violations of federal law. Each of these contentions is examined below.

2. WAIVER OR CONSENT

It is well settled that a state can waive its Eleventh Amendment immunity and consent to suit in federal court. Consent (although apparently revocable during the course of the litigation) may be given by the state's legal representative or by statute. Such statutes, however, will be narrowly construed, and the state is free to consent to suit only in its own courts. This rule is consistent with the tradition of sovereign immunity, which the sovereign may choose to waive.

Opponents of state sovereign immunity have advanced a broader notion of implied waiver or constructive consent that would deprive a state of its immunity if it voluntarily subjected itself to federal regulation. This was the basis of Justice Marshall's dissent in *Edelman*, where he argued that, by voluntarily participating in federal welfare programs and accepting federal funds, Illinois had waived whatever immunity it might otherwise have possessed against liability for not following federal requirements. The *Edelman* majority responded that the mere fact of state participation in a federal program was "not sufficient" to establish consent to be sued.

That position has been repeated, emphatically, in College Savings Bank v. Florida Prepaid Postsecondary Education Expense Board, 527 U.S. 666 (1999). That case involved the Trademark Remedy Clarification Act (TRCA), federal legislation that expressly subjects states to damage actions under the Lanham Act for false and misleading advertising. The state of Florida allegedly engaged in such advertising in connection with a tuition prepayment program. The plaintiff was a commercial competitor who had allegedly been injured by Florida's false and misleading statements. The plaintiff's theory, in the words of Justice Scalia, was that Florida has "constructively waived its immunity from suit by engaging in the voluntary and nonessential activity of selling and advertising a for-profit educational investment vehicle in interstate commerce after being put on notice by the clear language of the TRCA that it would be subject to Lanham Act liability for doing so." The Court, however, categorically rejected the idea of constructive waiver, reiterating the position in *Edelman* that "constructive consent is not a doctrine commonly associated with the surrender of constitutional rights."

3. CONGRESSIONAL ABROGATION

Arguments based on constructive waiver or consent sometimes edged toward the idea of a federal legislative power to abrogate state sovereign immunity, with or without the state's consent. In Fitzpatrick v. Bitzer, 427 U.S. 445 (1976), the Court unequivocally embraced this idea, at least for federal legislation passed pursuant to the power to enforce Fourteenth Amendment rights. *Fitzpatrick* involved a 1972 amendment to Title VII of the Civil Rights Act of 1964. The amendment explicitly authorized federal courts to award money damages against a state found to have engaged in employment discrimination by reason of "race, color, religion, sex, or national origin." Plaintiffs sued to recover retroactive retirement benefits of the sort precluded in *Edelman v. Jordan*. The Court nevertheless ruled in their favor.

Writing for the Court, Justice Rehnquist observed that the Fourteenth Amendment "quite clearly contemplates limitations on [state] authority" and represents a "shift in the federal-state balance." He continued:

> [Our cases have] sanctioned intrusions by Congress, acting under the Civil War Amendments, into the judicial, executive, and legislative spheres of autonomy previously reserved to the States. . . . It is true that none of [our] previous cases presented the question of the relationship between the Eleventh Amendment and the enforcement power granted to Congress under § 5 of the Fourteenth Amendment. But we think that the Eleventh Amendment, and the principle of state sovereignty which it embodies, are necessarily limited by the enforcement provisions of § 5 of the Fourteenth Amendment. In that section Congress is expressly granted authority to enforce "by appropriate legislation" the substantive provisions of the Fourteenth Amendment, which themselves embody significant limitations on state authority. When Congress acts pursuant to § 5, not only is it exercising legislative authority that is plenary within the terms of the constitutional grant, it is exercising that authority under one section of a constitutional Amendment whose other sections by their own terms embody limitations on state authority. We think that Congress may, in determining what is "appropriate legislation" for the purpose of enforcing the provisions of the Fourteenth Amendment, provide for private suits against States or state officials which are constitutionally impermissible in other contexts.

After *Fitzpatrick*, the question remained whether Congress could abrogate state sovereign immunity under the Commerce Clause and other Article I powers, as well as under the enforcement provisions of the Civil War amendments. In Seminole Tribe v. Florida, 517 U.S. 44 (1996), the Court said "no." The *Seminole Tribe* majority (consisting of Chief Justice Rehnquist and Justices O'Connor, Scalia, Kennedy, and Thomas) reaffirmed their allegiance to *Hans* and to the idea of a constitutionally grounded doctrine of state sovereign immunity. Whatever Congress could do under the subsequently enacted provisions of the Civil War amendments, it could not abrogate state immunity in the exercise of its powers under Article I. Justice Stevens dissented in *Seminole Tribe*, and so did Justice Souter, with whom Justices Ginsburg and Breyer joined. In a wide-ranging opinion, Souter argued that *Hans* was wrongly decided and that the majority had compounded "already serious error" by investing state sovereign immunity with "constitutional inviolability against the considered judgment of Congress to abrogate it."

The decisions in *Seminole Tribe* and *Fitzpatrick* make it important which source of congressional authority undergirds a particular statute. While Congress can create similar rights and duties under both the Commerce Clause and the Fourteenth Amendment, the mechanisms available to enforce those obligations differ significantly. Only in cases when Congress exercises its authority under the Fourteenth Amendment (or one of the other post-Reconstruction Amendments) can it provide individuals with the right to sue states.

4. THE REQUIREMENT OF CLEAR STATEMENT

The Court has never retreated from *Fitzpatrick*, but it has repeatedly emphasized a requirement of "clear statement" for federal abrogation of state sovereign immunity. In Atascadero State Hospital v. Scanlon, 473 U.S. 234, 242 (1985), the Court declared that legislative abrogation of state sovereign immunity could occur only where Congress made that intention "unmistakably clear in the language of the statute."

This requirement was confirmed in Sossamon v. Texas, 131 S.Ct. 1651 (2011). The Religious Land use and Institutionalized Persons Act of 2000 (RLUIPA), 42 U.S. C. § 2000cc et seq., prohibits states and localities from imposing any "substantial burden on the religious exercise" of an institutionalized person in any program receiving federal funds, absent a compelling government interest. The effect of this statute is to require affirmative accommodation of religious exercise by prisoners and other institutionalized persons. RLUIPA not only imposes this obligation but expressly provides a private right of action: "A person may assert a violation of [RLUIPA] as a claim or defense in a judicial proceeding and obtain appropriate relief against a government." § 2000cc–2(a). There seems to be little doubt that Congress could require state consent to private damages actions as a condition for receiving federal funds, but the Court found that Congress had not done so. Speaking through Justice Thomas, the majority said that "appropriate relief" was "open-ended and ambiguous" and did not "expressly and unambiguously" require a waiver of sovereign immunity. Justices Kagan and Breyer dissented.

5. STATE IMMUNITY IN STATE COURT

The Eleventh Amendment speaks only to the "Judicial power of the United States." From time to time, the Court has said that the amendment does not apply in state court. In Nevada v. Hall, 440 U.S. 410 (1979), for example, an employee of the state of Nevada was involved in an automobile accident while on official business in California. Persons injured in the accident sued Nevada (and the estate of the deceased driver) in California state court. The Supreme Court held that although Nevada could invoke state-law sovereign immunity in its own courts and Eleventh Amendment immunity in federal court, it had no federal entitlement to immunity from suit in the courts of another state.[a]

After *Edelman v. Jordan* and *Seminole Tribe*, opponents of state sovereign immunity began to wonder whether the problem could be avoided by resort to state court. The Supremacy Clause, they reasoned, requires state courts to enforce federal law, "any Thing in the Constitution or Laws of any State to the Contrary notwithstanding." If federal law directs states to pay money damages, state courts would have to do so, state sovereign immunity notwithstanding. The superior authority of the Eleventh Amendment might limit Congress's power to authorize suit in federal court but would have no application to damage actions in state court.

This argument came to the Supreme Court in Alden v. Maine, 527 U.S. 706 (1999). Probation officers claimed that Maine had violated the overtime provisions of the Fair Labor Standards Act and sued the state for additional compensation, as the federal statute explicitly authorized them to do. They went first to federal court, but their case was dismissed after *Seminole Tribe* made clear that Congress could override Eleventh Amendment immunity only to enforce the Civil War amendments, not as part of its power to regulate interstate commerce. The plaintiffs then went to state court, arguing that the Eleventh Amendment was inapplicable and that the federal statute gave them the right to money damages from the state.

The Supreme Court rejected this argument by a vote of five to four. Speaking for the majority, Justice Kennedy announced that "the powers delegated to Congress under Article I of the United States Constitution do not include the power to subject nonconsenting States to private suits for damages in state courts." Justice Souter filed a lengthy dissent, which Justices Stevens, Ginsburg, and Breyer joined. After *Seminole* Tribe and *Alden*, state sovereign immunity against federal claims is the same in both state and federal court.

6. *WILL V. MICHIGAN DEPARTMENT OF STATE POLICE*

Despite these restrictive precedents, room could still be found for damages actions directly against state governments under § 1983. The reason is that, generally speaking, § 1983 is used to enforce individual rights derived from the Fourteenth Amendment (including both rights defined in the Fourteenth Amendment rights incorporated by that Amendment and made applicable to the states). One could argue, therefore, that § 1983 triggers the rule of *Fitzpatrick v. Bitzer*. That is, § 1983 could be seen to fall within Congress's Fourteenth Amendment power to abrogate the immunity of states and make them pay money damages.

Whether § 1983 should be so construed was raised in *Edelman*, where the Court held that § 1983 was not intended to override state immunity. A few years later, this conclusion was reconfirmed in Quern v. Jordan, 440 U.S. 332 (1979), where the Court said that § 1983 "does not explicitly and by clear language indicate on its face an intent to sweep away the immunity of the States. . . . " Together *Edelman* and *Quern* settled that § 1983 does not authorize

[a] See also Franchise Tax Board v. Hyatt, 538 U.S. 488 (2003) (holding that Nevada state courts were not required to give a California state agency the same immunity that would have provided in California's own courts).

damage actions against states as such, even though it clearly would have been within Congress's power for it to have given the statute that effect.[b]

Even after these decisions, the idea nevertheless persisted that perhaps § 1983 might authorize damage actions against states in *state* court, where the Eleventh Amendment in terms does not apply. This would have created the bizarre situation of a federal statute enforceable *only* in state court. That oddity was avoided in Will v. Michigan Department of State Police, 491 U.S. 58 (1989), where the Court held that, "neither a State or its officials acting in their official capacities are 'persons' under § 1983." Speaking for the Court, Justice White argued that the intent to make states directly liable had not been shown with the clarity required to alter the "usual constitutional balance" between the states and the national government.

7. CONCLUSION

The upshot of all this is nearly exact alignment between constitutional doctrine and § 1983. The Eleventh Amendment forbids damage actions against states and state agencies. Edelman v. Jordan, 415 U.S. 651 (1974). Section 1983 (at least insofar as it is used to enforce constitutional rights) could have been construed to override state immunity, Fitzpatrick v. Bitzer, 427 U.S. 445 (1976), but it has not been. Quern v. Jordan, 440 U.S. 332 (1979). And owing to the decision in Will v. Michigan Department of State Police, 491, U.S. 58 (1989), state sovereign immunity operates alike in state and federal court.

Localities are treated differently. The Eleventh Amendment does not protect local governments from private actions for money damages, Lincoln County v. Luning, 133 U.S. 529 (1890), and § 1983 has been read to authorize such actions. Monell v. New York City Department of Social Services, 436 U.S. 658 (1978). At both state and local levels, therefore, the subconstitutional law of § 1983 has been construed to replicate the constitutional law of the Eleventh Amendment.

NOTE ON EDELMAN V. JORDAN *AND IMMUNITY FROM RETROSPECTIVE RELIEF*

Justice Douglas argued in his *Edelman* dissent that the financial impact of an *Ex parte Young* injunction was in principle indistinguishable from an award of monetary relief. Even the *Edelman* majority admitted that "the difference between the type of relief barred by the Eleventh Amendment and that permitted under *Ex parte Young* will not in many instances be that between day and night." But in the end, the Court felt constrained by principle and precedent to draw a line between *Ford*-type relief and *Ex parte Young*-type relief.

Just how shadowy that line can become is suggested in Milliken v. Bradley (II), 433 U.S. 267 (1977), where the Court upheld a school desegregation order requiring the expenditure of state (as well as local) funds for several educational components of the desegregation decree, including remedial reading programs. The Court disposed of the state's Eleventh Amendment objection as follows:

---

[b] See United States v. Georgia, 546 U.S. 151 (2006) (stating that "no one doubts" that § 5 of the Fourteenth Amendment grants Congress the power to abrogate state sovereign immunity and impose damages liability for Fourteenth Amendment violations).

> The decree to share the future costs of educational components in this case fits squarely within the prospective-compliance exception reaffirmed by *Edelman*. That exception, which had its genesis in *Ex parte Young*, permits federal courts to enjoin state officials to conform their conduct to requirements of federal law, notwithstanding a direct and substantial impact on the state treasury. The order challenged here does no more than that. The decree requires state officials, held responsible for unconstitutional conduct, in findings which are not challenged, to eliminate a de jure segregated school system. . . . The educational components, which the District Court ordered into effect *prospectively*, are plainly designed to wipe out continuing conditions of inequality produced by the inherently unequal dual school system long maintained by Detroit. . . . That the programs are also 'compensatory' in nature does not change the fact that they are part of a plan that operates *prospectively* to bring about the delayed benefits of a unitary school system. We therefore hold that such prospective relief is not barred by the Eleventh Amendment.

Could the award of past payments at issue in *Edelman* be fairly described as "part of a plan that operates *prospectively* to bring about the delayed benefits of" the federally required payment schedule? Is there a meaningful distinction between the two cases?

2. EXHAUSTION OF REMEDIES IN § 1983 SUITS

INTRODUCTORY NOTES ON EXHAUSTION OF REMEDIES IN § 1983 SUITS

1. *PATSY V. BOARD OF REGENTS*

Monroe v. Pape established that state *judicial* remedies need not be exhausted prior to filing a federal suit under § 1983: "The federal remedy is supplementary to the state remedy, and the latter need not be first sought and refused before the federal one is invoked." The Court has applied the same principle to the exhaustion of state *administrative* remedies, notwithstanding the well-recognized rule that administrative remedies normally must be pursued before going to court. In a long series of cases beginning with McNeese v. Board of Education, 373 U.S. 668 (1963), the Court declined to require dismissal of § 1983 suits for failure to exhaust state administrative remedies. It addressed the issue fully in Patsy v. Board of Regents, 457 U.S. 496 (1982), holding explicitly that "exhaustion of state administrative remedies should not be required as a prerequisite to bringing an action pursuant to § 1983."

The *Patsy* Court justified its holding chiefly by invoking *McNeese* and other precedents. The decision was also based on the enactment in 1980 of the Civil Rights of Institutionalized Persons Act, 42 U.S.C. § 1997 et seq. (1976 ed., Supp. IV). The Court argued:

> In § 1997e, Congress also created a specific, limited exhaustion requirement for adult prisoners bringing actions pursuant to § 1983. Section 1997e and its legislative history demonstrate that Congress understood that exhaustion is not generally required in § 1983 actions, and that it decided to carve out only a narrow exception to this rule. A judicially imposed exhaustion requirement would be inconsistent with Congress' decision to adopt § 1997e and would usurp policy judgments that Congress has

> reserved for itself. In considering whether an exhaustion requirement should be incorporated into the bill, Congress clearly expressed its belief that a decision to require exhaustion for certain § 1983 actions would work a change in the law.

The Court acknowledged various policy arguments in favor of requiring exhaustion of administrative remedies:

> [A]n exhaustion requirement would lessen the perceived burden that § 1983 actions impose on federal courts; would further the goal of comity and improve federal-state relations by postponing federal-court review until after the state administrative agency had passed on the issue; and would enable the agency, which presumably has expertise in the area at issue, to enlighten the federal court's ultimate decision.

But it found the arguments unpersuasive:

> [P]olicy considerations alone cannot justify judicially imposed exhaustion unless exhaustion is consistent with congressional intent. Furthermore, as the debates over incorporating the exhaustion requirement in § 1997e demonstrate, the relevant policy considerations do not invariably point in one direction, and there is vehement disagreement over the validity of the assumptions underlying many of them. The very difficulty of these policy considerations, and Congress' superior institutional competence to pursue this debate, suggest that legislative not judicial solutions are preferable.
>
> Beyond the policy issues that must be resolved in deciding *whether* to require exhaustion, there are equally difficult questions concerning the design and scope of an exhaustion requirement. These questions include how to define those categories of § 1983 claims in which exhaustion might be desirable; how to unify and centralize the standards for judging the kinds of administrative procedures that should be exhausted; what tolling requirements and time limitations should be adopted; what is the res judicata and collateral estoppel effect of particular administrative determinations; what consequences should attach to the failure to comply with procedural requirements of administrative proceedings; and whether federal courts could grant necessary interim injunctive relief and hold the action pending exhaustion, or proceed to judgment without requiring exhaustion even though exhaustion might otherwise be required, where the relevant administrative agency is either powerless or not inclined to grant such interim relief. These and similar questions might be answered swiftly and surely by legislation, but would create costly, remedy-delaying, and court-burdening litigation if answered incrementally by the judiciary in the context of diverse constitutional claims relating to thousands of different state agencies.
>
> The very variety of claims, claimants, and state agencies involved in § 1983 cases argues for congressional consideration of the myriad of policy considerations, and may explain why Congress, in deciding whether to require exhaustion in certain § 1983 actions brought by adult prisoners, carved out such a narrow, detailed exception to the no-exhaustion rule.

2. FEDERAL HABEAS CORPUS FOR STATE PRISONERS: EXHAUSTION OF REMEDIES

Habeas corpus is the traditional remedy by which federal district courts review the constitutionality of state criminal convictions. Interesting questions can arise about the relationship between federal habeas corpus and certain kinds of § 1983 suits. This is the topic of Section 1, Subsection B of this Chapter, infra. But it needs to be noted at the outset that the rules for exhaustion of state *judicial* remedies are different in federal habeas corpus litigation.

The obligation to exhaust state judicial remedies prior to seeking federal habeas was established in Ex parte Royall, 117 U.S. 241 (1886). The principle was codified in 1948, and has become a prominent and complex feature of the modern writ. Today, each issue sought to be presented to a federal habeas court must first be presented to a state court, either in the trial and appellate proceedings leading to the conviction or in state habeas corpus or some analogous procedure for post-conviction review. The Court held in Rose v. Lundy, 455 U.S. 509 (1982), that a petition for federal habeas corpus must be dismissed if it contains *any* claims that have not been exhausted, even if other claims are ready for federal review. Only if state law provides no present opportunity to raise a claim—*and has provided no such opportunity in the past*—is exhaustion not required. Given the available avenues for litigation of claims under every state's law today, this is not likely to happen.

3. ABSTENTION: *YOUNGER V. HARRIS*

Closely related to the habeas corpus exhaustion requirement is the obligation of federal courts to abstain from deciding cases brought by plaintiffs who are attempting to interfere with state criminal proceedings already begun against them. Younger v. Harris, 401 U.S. 37 (1971), held that a federal § 1983 action cannot be used to derail a state criminal prosecution once it is pending. A subsequent decision extended *Younger* to state criminal prosecutions begun after a federal suit is filed but before substantial proceedings on the merits. Hicks v. Miranda, 422 U.S. 332 (1975). In general, therefore, federal courts have no power to enjoin pending state criminal proceedings on the ground that the statutes being enforced are unconstitutional or that the prosecution will or may violate constitutional rights. Federal courts cannot, for example, use § 1983 to enjoin the admission of evidence in pending state criminal trials on the ground that its admission would violate the *Miranda* rules or the Fourth Amendment. All such claims must be presented in state trial and appellate venues prior to any proceeding in federal court. And if a criminal conviction is upheld by the state courts, habeas corpus is the only federal remedy by which the conviction can be attacked.

SUBSECTION A: EXHAUSTION OF REMEDIES IN PLRA SUITS

INTRODUCTORY NOTES ON IMPROPER HABEAS EXHAUSTION

1. THE PLRA

The exhaustion requirement adopted for prisoner litigation in 1980 in the Civil Rights of Institutionalized Persons Act figured prominently in the holding in Patsy v. Board of Regents, 457 U.S. 496 (1982), that administrative remedies need not in general be exhausted in § 1983 suits. The 1980 statute was amended in the Prison Litigation Reform Act of 1995 (PLRA). The consequence of improper exhaustion under the PLRA is the subject of the next main case, *Woodford v. Ngo*. Background on the habeas consequences of improper exhaustion will aid understanding of that case.

2. *DANIELS V. ALLEN*

Daniels was convicted of murder and sentenced to death. His challenge to the conviction on federal constitutional grounds was rejected by the state Supreme Court without consideration of the merits because Daniels' lawyer failed to perfect a timely appeal. On review of Daniels' federal habeas petition, the United States Supreme Court held that his claims could not be heard because he failed to follow available state procedures. Daniels v. Allen, 344 U.S. 443 (1953). The doctrinal basis for this ruling was not clear, but the result was: if the state courts relied on the failure to follow reasonable procedures as the reason for declining to consider the merits of a federal claim, federal habeas review was not available. In the jargon of habeas corpus law of the day, the defendant's claim was "procedurally foreclosed."

3. *FAY V. NOIA*

Daniels was overturned in Fay v. Noia, 372 U.S. 391 (1963). *Fay* held that the exhaustion requirement was not a doctrine of forfeitures. State remedies were required to be exhausted only if currently available. Federal habeas petitioners were not barred from relief by failing to pursue a state remedy that was no longer available.

Fay also held that a federal habeas petitioner's failure to raise a claim in state court ordinarily did not amount to a waiver of the claim. Claims could be waived by failing to raise them in state court, but only if the standard of Johnson v. Zerbst, 304 U.S. 458 (1938), was met—the intentional relinquishment of a known right. Under *Fay*, therefore, most claims not heard in state court were open to review in federal habeas proceedings. Federal courts could refuse to hear claims that were procedurally foreclosed in state court only if a conscious decision was made to "deliberately bypass" state procedures.

4. *WAINRIGHT V. SYKES*

The *Fay v. Noia* approach to state procedural foreclosures was significantly curtailed in Wainwright v. Sykes, 433 U.S. 72 (1977). Sykes sought federal habeas relief based on the admission of inculpatory statements in his murder trial. The state courts denied relief because his lawyer had not made a contemporaneous objection at the time the statements were offered in evidence. The Supreme Court rejected the *Fay* "deliberate bypass" formula in favor of a more demanding "cause and prejudice" inquiry. If the state courts refuse to hear a federal claim because the habeas petitioner failed to follow state procedures, the federal courts will hear the claim only if the petitioner can show good "cause" for not raising the claim and "prejudice" in the sense that the evidence made a critical difference on the question of guilt or innocence.

The *Sykes* "cause and prejudice" standard significantly expanded the range of procedural missteps that will result in the denial of federal habeas corpus. There are two situations, however, where the habeas petitioner is not required to meet the "cause and prejudice" standard. The first is where the state procedure on which foreclosure is based does not constitute an "adequate and independent" state ground. See Lee v. Kemna, 534 U.S. 362 (2002). The state procedure, in other words, must provide a fair opportunity for consideration of the federal claim on the merits. The second exception to the "cause and prejudice" standard is triggered by a claim of "actual innocence." As explained in Murray v. Carrier, 477 U.S. 478, 495–96 (1986):

> We remain confident that, for the most part, "victims of a fundamental miscarriage of justice will meet the cause-and-prejudice standard." But we do not pretend that this will always be true. Accordingly, we think that in an extraordinary case, where a constitutional violation has probably resulted in the conviction of one who is actually innocent, a federal habeas court may grant the writ even in the absence of a showing of cause for the procedural default.

Woodford v. Ngo

Supreme Court of the United States, 2006.
548 U.S. 81.

■ JUSTICE ALITO delivered the opinion of the Court.

This case presents the question whether a prisoner can satisfy the Prison Litigation Reform Act's exhaustion requirement, 42 U.S.C. § 1997e(a), by filing an untimely or otherwise procedurally defective administrative grievance or appeal. We hold that proper exhaustion of administrative remedies is necessary.

I

A

Congress enacted the Prison Litigation Reform Act of 1995 (PLRA), 42 U.S.C. § 1997e et seq., in 1996 in the wake of a sharp rise in prisoner litigation in the federal courts. The PLRA contains a variety of provisions designed to bring this litigation under control. See, e.g., § 1997e(c) (requiring district courts to weed out prisoner claims that clearly lack merit); § 1997e(e) (prohibiting claims for emotional injury without prior showing of physical injury); § 1997e(d) (restricting attorney's fees). A centerpiece of the PLRA's effort "to reduce the quantity . . . of prisoner suits" is an "invigorated" exhaustion provision, § 1997e(a). Before 1980, prisoners asserting constitutional claims had no obligation to exhaust administrative remedies. In the Civil Rights of Institutionalized Persons Act, Congress enacted a weak exhaustion provision, which authorized district courts to stay actions under § 1983, for a limited time while a prisoner exhausted "such plain, speedy, and effective administrative remedies as are available." 42 U.S.C. § 1997e(a)(1) (1994 ed.). "Exhaustion under the 1980 prescription was in large part discretionary; it could be ordered only if the State's prison grievance system met specified federal standards, and even then, only if, in the particular case, the court believed the requirement 'appropriate and in the interests of justice.' " Porter v. Nussle, 534 U.S. 516, 523 (2002) (quoting § 1997e). In addition, this provision did not require exhaustion if the prisoner sought only money damages and such relief was not available under the relevant administrative scheme.

The PLRA strengthened this exhaustion provision in several ways. Exhaustion is no longer left to the discretion of the district court, but is mandatory. See Booth v. Churner, 532 U.S. 731, 739 (2001). Prisoners must now exhaust all "available" remedies, not just those that meet federal standards. Indeed, as we held in *Booth,* a prisoner must now exhaust administrative remedies even where the relief sought—monetary damages—cannot be granted by the administrative process. Finally, exhaustion of available administrative remedies is required for any suit challenging prison conditions, not just for suits under § 1983. *Nussle*, 534 U.S., at 524.

B

California has a grievance system for prisoners who seek to challenge their conditions of confinement. To initiate the process, an inmate must fill out a simple form, Dept. of Corrections, Inmate/Parolee Appeal Form, CDC 602 (12/87) (hereinafter Form 602), that is made "readily available to all inmates." The inmate must fill out two parts of the form: part A, which is labeled "Describe Problem," and part B, which is labeled "Action Requested." Then, as explained on Form 602 itself, the prisoner "must first informally seek relief through discussion with the appropriate staff member." The staff member fills in part C of Form 602 under the heading "Staff Response" and then returns the form to the inmate. If the prisoner is dissatisfied with the result of the informal review, or if informal review is waived by the State, the inmate may pursue a three-step review process. Although California labels this "formal" review (apparently to distinguish this process from the prior step), the three-step process is relatively simple. At the first level, the prisoner must fill in part D of Form 602, which states: "If you are dissatisfied, explain below." The inmate then must submit the form, together with a few other documents, to the appeals coordinator within 15 working days—three weeks—of the action taken. This level may be bypassed by the appeals coordinator in certain circumstances. Within 15 working days after an inmate submits an appeal, the reviewer must inform the inmate of the outcome by completing part E of Form 602 and returning the form to the inmate.

If the prisoner receives an adverse determination at this first level, or if this level is bypassed, the inmate may proceed to the second level of review conducted by the warden. The inmate does this by filling in part F of Form 602 and submitting the form within 15 working days of the prior decision. Within 10 working days thereafter, the reviewer provides a decision on a letter that is attached to the form. If the prisoner's claim is again denied or the prisoner otherwise is dissatisfied with the result, the prisoner must explain the basis for his or her dissatisfaction on part H of the form and mail the form to the Director of the California Department of Corrections and Rehabilitation within 15 working days. An inmate's appeal may be rejected where "[t]ime limits for submitting the appeal are exceeded and the appellant had the opportunity to file within the prescribed time constraints."

C

Respondent is a prisoner who was convicted for murder and is serving a life sentence in the California prison system. In October 2000, respondent was placed in administrative segregation for allegedly engaging in "inappropriate activity" in the prison chapel. Two months later, respondent was returned to the general population, but respondent claims that he was prohibited from participating in "special programs," including a variety of religious activities. Approximately six months after that restriction was imposed, respondent filed a grievance with prison officials challenging that action. That grievance was rejected as untimely because it was not filed within 15 working days of the action being challenged. Respondent appealed that decision internally without success, and subsequently sued petitioners—California correctional officials—under 42 U.S.C. § 1983 in Federal District Court. The District Court granted petitioners' motion to dismiss because respondent had not fully exhausted his administrative remedies as required by § 1997e(a).

The Court of Appeals for the Ninth Circuit reversed and held that respondent had exhausted administrative remedies simply because no such remedies remained available to him. The Ninth Circuit's decision, while consistent with the decision of a divided panel of the Sixth Circuit . . . , conflicts with decisions of four other Courts of Appeals. We granted certiorari to address this conflict, and we now reverse.

II

A

The PLRA provides as follows:

> No action shall be brought with respect to prison conditions under section 1983 of this title, or any other Federal law, by a prisoner confined in any jail, prison, or other correctional facility *until such administrative remedies as are available are exhausted*." § 1997e(a) (2000 ed.) (emphasis added).

There is no dispute that this language requires a prisoner to "exhaust" administrative remedies, but the parties differ sharply in their understanding of the meaning of this requirement. Petitioners argue that this provision requires proper exhaustion. This means, according to petitioners, that a prisoner must complete the administrative review process in accordance with the applicable procedural rules, including deadlines, as a precondition to bringing suit in federal court. Respondent, on the other hand, argues that this provision demands what he terms "exhaustion simpliciter." In his view, § 1997e(a) simply means that a prisoner may not bring suit in federal court until administrative remedies are no longer available. Under this interpretation, the reason why administrative remedies are no longer available is irrelevant. Bare unavailability suffices even if this results from a prisoner's deliberate strategy of refraining from filing a timely grievance so that the litigation of the prisoner's claim can begin in federal court.

The key for determining which of these interpretations of § 1997e(a) is correct lies in the term of art "exhausted." Exhaustion is an important doctrine in both administrative and habeas law, and we therefore look to those bodies of law for guidance.

B

"The doctrine of exhaustion of administrative remedies is well established in the jurisprudence of administrative law." McKart v. United States, 395 U.S. 185, 193 (1969). "The doctrine provides 'that no one is entitled to judicial relief for a supposed or threatened injury until the prescribed administrative remedy has been exhausted.' " Ibid. Exhaustion of administrative remedies serves two main purposes. McCarthy v. Madigan, 503 U.S. 140, 145 (1992).

First, exhaustion protects "administrative agency authority." Ibid. Exhaustion gives an agency "an opportunity to correct its own mistakes with respect to the programs it administers before it is haled into federal court," and it discourages "disregard of [the agency's] procedures." Ibid.

Second, exhaustion promotes efficiency. Claims generally can be resolved much more quickly and economically in proceedings before an agency than in litigation in federal court. In some cases, claims are settled at the administrative level, and in others, the proceedings before the agency convince the losing party not to pursue the matter in federal court. "And even where a controversy survives administrative review, exhaustion of the administrative procedure may produce a useful record for subsequent judicial consideration." Ibid. . . .

Because exhaustion requirements are designed to deal with parties who do not want to exhaust, administrative law creates an incentive for these parties to do what they would otherwise prefer not to do, namely, to give the agency a fair and full opportunity to adjudicate their claims. Administrative law does this by requiring proper exhaustion of administrative remedies, which "means using all steps that the agency holds out, and doing so *properly* (so that the agency addresses the issues on the merits)." Pozo v. McCaughtry, 286 F.3d 1022, 1024 (7th Cir. 2002) (emphasis in original). . . . Proper exhaustion demands compliance with an agency's deadlines and other critical procedural rules because no adjudicative system can function effectively without imposing some orderly structure on the course of its proceedings.

C

The law of habeas corpus has rules that are substantively similar to those described above. The habeas statute generally requires a state prisoner to exhaust state remedies before filing a habeas petition in federal court. "This rule of comity reduces friction between the state and federal court systems by avoiding the 'unseem[liness]' of a federal district court's overturning a state-court conviction without the state courts having had an opportunity to correct the constitutional violation in the first instance." O'Sullivan v. Boerckel, 526 U.S. 838, 845 (1999) (alteration in original). A state prisoner is generally barred from obtaining federal habeas relief unless the prisoner has properly presented his or her claims through one "complete round of the State's established appellate review process." Ibid. In practical terms, the law of habeas, like administrative law, requires proper exhaustion, and we have described this feature of habeas law as follows: "To . . . 'protect the integrity' of the federal exhaustion rule, we ask not only whether a prisoner has exhausted his state remedies, but also whether he has *properly* exhausted those remedies. . . . " Id., at 848 (emphasis in original).

The law of habeas, however, uses terminology that differs from that of administrative law. In habeas, the sanction for failing to exhaust properly (preclusion of review in federal court) is given the separate name of procedural default, although the habeas doctrines of exhaustion and procedural default "are similar in purpose and design and implicate similar concerns," Keeney v. Tamayo–Reyes, 504 U.S. 1, 7 (1992). In habeas, state-court remedies are described as having been "exhausted" when they are no longer available, regardless of the reason for their unavailability. Thus, if state-court remedies are no longer available because the prisoner failed to comply with the deadline for seeking state-court review or for taking an appeal, those remedies are technically exhausted, but exhaustion in this sense does not automatically entitle the habeas petitioner to litigate his or her claims in federal court. Instead, if the petitioner procedurally defaulted those claims, the prisoner generally is barred from asserting those claims in a federal habeas proceeding.

III

With this background in mind, we are persuaded that the PLRA exhaustion requirement requires proper exhaustion.

A

The text of 42 U.S.C. § 1997e(a) strongly suggests that the PLRA uses the term "exhausted" to mean what the term means in administrative law, where exhaustion means proper exhaustion. Section 1997e(a) refers to "such administrative remedies as are available," and thus points to the doctrine of exhaustion in administrative law.

B

Construing § 1997e(a) to require proper exhaustion also fits with the general scheme of the PLRA. . . . The PLRA attempts to eliminate unwarranted federal-court interference with the administration of prisons, and thus seeks to "affor[d] corrections officials time and opportunity to address complaints internally before allowing the initiation of a federal case." *Nussle,* 534 U.S., at 525. The PLRA also was intended to "reduce the quantity and improve the quality of prisoner suits." Id. at 524.

Requiring proper exhaustion serves all of these goals. It gives prisoners an effective incentive to make full use of the prison grievance process and accordingly provides prisons with a fair opportunity to correct their own errors. This is particularly important in relation to state corrections systems because it is "difficult to imagine an activity in which a State has a stronger interest, or one that is more intricately bound up with state laws, regulations, and procedures, than the administration of its prisons." Preiser v. Rodriguez, 411 U.S. 475, 491–92 (1973).

Proper exhaustion reduces the quantity of prisoner suits because some prisoners are successful in the administrative process, and others are persuaded by the proceedings not to file an action in federal court. Finally, proper exhaustion improves the quality of those prisoner suits that are eventually filed because proper exhaustion often results in the creation of an administrative record that is helpful to the court. When a grievance is filed shortly after the event giving rise to the grievance, witnesses can be identified and questioned while memories are still fresh, and evidence can be gathered and preserved.

While requiring proper exhaustion serves the purposes of the PLRA, respondent's interpretation of § 1997e(a) would make the PLRA exhaustion scheme wholly ineffective. The benefits of exhaustion can be realized only if the prison grievance system is given a fair opportunity to consider the grievance. The prison grievance system will not have such an opportunity unless the grievant complies with the system's critical procedural rules. A prisoner who does not want to participate in the prison grievance system will have little incentive to comply with the system's procedural rules unless noncompliance carries a sanction, and under respondent's interpretation of the PLRA noncompliance carries no significant sanction. . . .

C

Finally, as interpreted by respondent, the PLRA exhaustion requirement would be unprecedented. Respondent has not pointed to any statute or case that purports to require exhaustion while at the same time allowing a party to bypass deliberately the administrative process by flouting the agency's procedural rules. It is most unlikely that the PLRA, which was intended to deal with what was perceived as a disruptive tide of frivolous prisoner litigation, adopted an exhaustion requirement that goes further than any other model that has been called to our attention in permitting the wholesale bypassing of administrative remedies. . . .

Apparently recognizing that such an interpretation neither has a statutory basis nor refers to a concept of exhaustion from an existing body of law, respondent does not contend that § 1997e(a) prohibits deliberate bypass; in his view, all that § 1997e(a) demands is that a prisoner wait until any opportunity for administrative review has evaporated. But in making this argument, respondent asks us to hold that the PLRA was meant to adopt an exhaustion scheme that stands in sharp contrast to both current and past habeas law and is unlike any other exhaustion scheme that has been called to our attention. . . .

IV

. . . Respondent contends that requiring proper exhaustion will lead prison administrators to devise procedural requirements that are designed to trap unwary prisoners and thus to defeat their claims. Respondent does not contend, however, that anything like this occurred in his case, and it is speculative that this will occur in the future. Corrections officials concerned about maintaining order in their institutions have a reason for creating and retaining grievance systems that provide—and that are perceived by prisoners as providing—a meaningful opportunity for prisoners to raise meritorious grievances. And with respect to the possibility that prisons might create procedural requirements for the purpose of tripping up all but the most skillful prisoners, while Congress repealed the "plain, speedy, and effective" standard, see 42 U.S.C. § 1997e(a)(1) (1994 ed.) (repealed 1996), we have no occasion here to decide how such situations might be addressed.

Respondent argues that requiring proper exhaustion is harsh for prisoners, who generally are untrained in the law and are often poorly educated. This argument overlooks the informality and relative simplicity of prison grievance systems like California's, as well as the fact that prisoners who litigate in federal court generally proceed pro se and are forced to comply with numerous unforgiving deadlines and other procedural requirements.

* * *

For these reasons, we reverse the judgment of the Court of Appeals for the Ninth Circuit and remand the case for proceedings consistent with this opinion.

It is so ordered.

■ JUSTICE BREYER, concurring in the judgment.

I agree with the Court that, in enacting the Prison Litigation Reform Act (PLRA), 42 U.S.C. § 1997e(a), Congress intended the term "exhausted" to "mean what the term means in administrative law, where exhaustion means proper exhaustion." I do not believe that Congress desired a system in which prisoners could elect to bypass prison grievance systems without consequences. Administrative law, however, contains well-established exceptions to exhaustion [citing cases that recognized exceptions for constitutional claims, futility, hardship, and inadequate or unavailable administrative remedies]. Moreover, habeas corpus law, which contains an exhaustion requirement that is "substantively similar" to administrative law's and which informs the Court's opinion, also permits a number of exceptions [citing the dissent by Justice Stevens, which noted that habeas corpus law permits "petitioners to overcome procedural defaults if they can show that the procedural rule is not firmly established and regularly followed, if they can demonstrate cause and prejudice to overcome a procedural default, or if enforcing the procedural default rule would result in a miscarriage of justice"].

At least two Circuits that have interpreted the statute in a manner similar to that which the Court today adopts have concluded that the PLRA's proper exhaustion requirement is not absolute. In my view, on remand, the lower court should similarly consider any challenges that respondent may have concerning whether his case falls into a traditional exception that the statute implicitly incorporates.

▪ JUSTICE STEVENS, with whom JUSTICE SOUTER and JUSTICE GINSBURG join, dissenting.

The citizen's right to access an impartial tribunal to seek redress for official grievances is so fundamental and so well established that it is sometimes taken for granted. A state statute that purported to impose a 15–day period of limitations on the right of a discrete class of litigants to sue a state official for violation of a federal right would obviously be unenforceable in a federal court. The question in this case is whether, by enacting the exhaustion requirement in the Prison Litigation Reform Act of 1995 (PLRA), Congress intended to authorize state correction officials to impose a comparable limitation on prisoners' constitutionally protected right of access to the federal courts. The text of the statute, particularly when read in the light of our well-settled jurisprudence, provides us with the same unambiguous negative answer that common sense would dictate.

I

[Section 1997e(a)] requires prisoners to exhaust informal remedies before filing a lawsuit under federal law. They must file an administrative grievance and, if the resolution of that grievance is unsatisfactory to them, they must exhaust available administrative appeals. The statute, however, says nothing about the reasons why a grievance may have been denied; it does not distinguish between a denial on the merits and a denial based on a procedural error. It does not attach any significance to a prison official's decision that a prisoner has made procedural missteps in exhausting administrative remedies. In the words of federal courts jurisprudence, the text of the PLRA does not impose a sanction of waiver or procedural default upon those prisoners who make such procedural errors. . . . [1] The plain text of the PLRA simply requires that "such administrative remedies as are available" be exhausted before the prisoner can take the serious step of filing a federal lawsuit against the officials who hold him in custody.

Today, however, the Court concludes that the "PLRA exhaustion requirement requires proper exhaustion." The absence of textual support for that conclusion is a sufficient reason for rejecting it. . . .

II

. . . The majority's disregard of the plain text of the PLRA is especially unjustified in light of the backdrop against which the statute was enacted. . . . As the Solicitor General correctly points out in his brief

[1] Because we have used the term "waiver" in referring to this sanction in the habeas corpus context, I use that term in this opinion. Strictly speaking, it would be more accurate to characterize this sanction as a "forfeiture" sanction, as there is no question that prisoners do not, by making a procedural error in the course of exhausting administrative remedies, purposefully relinquish their right to bring constitutional claims in federal court.

supporting petitioners, "the PLRA's exhaustion provision is essentially identical to that of the habeas corpus statute." . . . [W]e have held that state-court remedies are "exhausted" for the purposes of the federal habeas statute so long as "they are no longer available, regardless of the reason for their unavailability." In other words, the exhaustion requirement in the federal habeas statute does *not* incorporate a procedural default sanction.[5] . . .

The Court [cites McKart v. United States, 395 U.S. 185, 193 (1969), for the proposition that] "no one is entitled to judicial relief for a supposed or threatened injury until the prescribed administrative remedy has been exhausted." [This] language . . . is indeed similar to the language of the PLRA (and the habeas corpus statute). But this provides no help to the majority: We clearly used this language to describe only an exhaustion requirement, not a procedural default sanction.

The quoted language originally appeared in Justice Brandeis' opinion in Myers v. Bethlehem Shipbuilding Corp., 303 U.S. 41, 50–51 (1938). *Myers* is a simple exhaustion case: The question presented was whether an employer could seek the immediate intervention of federal courts in response to a complaint filed with the National Labor Relations Board that it had engaged in unfair labor practices, or whether it had to await the conclusion of the Board's proceedings to avail itself of judicial review. The case was purely about timing—there was no discussion whatever of procedural default. . . .

In sum, the language the majority quotes from *McKart* further supports the [conclusion] that Congress intended the exhaustion requirement in the PLRA to be read in conformity with our decisions interpreting the exhaustion requirement in the federal habeas statute—that is, to require exhaustion, but not to impose a waiver sanction for procedural errors made in the course of exhaustion.

III

Absent any support for a procedural default sanction in the text of the PLRA, the Court turns to background principles of administrative law in an effort to justify its holding. The Court's discussion of these background administrative law principles misapprehends our precedent. [W]e have never suggested that the word "exhaustion," standing alone, imposes a . . .

---

[5] In habeas law it is a separate judge-made doctrine of procedural default, stemming from our decision in Wainwright v. Sykes, 433 U.S. 72 (1977), that may bar relief even though a claim has been exhausted. This procedural default doctrine is based on unique considerations of comity in the habeas context, including the need to ensure that the state criminal trial remains the "main event" rather than a "tryout on the road" for a later federal habeas proceeding. Moreover, procedural default in habeas is closely related to the principle that this Court lacks certiorari jurisdiction to review a state-court judgment that rests on an adequate and independent state procedural ground. It is undisputed that these unique considerations do not apply in the context of § 1983 suits, because the "very purpose of § 1983 was to interpose the federal courts between the States and the people, as guardians of the people's federal rights." Mitchum v. Foster, 407 U.S. 225, 242 (1972). Accordingly, the majority correctly does not suggest that we incorporate our procedural default jurisprudence from the federal habeas context into prison conditions suits under § 1983.

Nonetheless, I fear that the majority's analysis may actually create a harsher procedural default regime under the PLRA than the judge-made procedural default doctrine in habeas law. . . . Our habeas jurisprudence allows petitioners to overcome procedural defaults if they can show that the procedural rule is not firmly established and regularly followed, see James v. Kentucky, 466 U.S. 341, 348 (1984), if they can demonstrate cause and prejudice to overcome a procedural default, or if enforcing the procedural default rule would result in a miscarriage of justice, see Murray v. Carrier, 477 U.S. 478 (1986).

waiver requirement. Accordingly, the Court's claim that a procedural default sanction is mandated by simply "interpreting and applying the statutory requirement set out in the PLRA exhaustion provision" is patently erroneous.

[O]rdinary principles of administrative law do not justify engrafting procedural default into the PLRA. The purpose of a § 1983 action such as that filed by respondent is not to obtain direct review of an order entered in the grievance procedure, but to obtain redress for an alleged violation of federal law committed by state corrections officials. It is undisputed that the PLRA does nothing to change the nature of the federal action under § 1983; prisoners who bring such actions after exhausting their administrative remedies are entitled to de novo proceedings in the federal district court without any deference (on issues of law or fact) to any ruling in the administrative grievance proceedings. In sum, because federal district court proceedings in prison condition litigation bear no resemblance to appellate review of lower court decisions, the administrative law precedent cited by the majority makes clear that we should not engraft a judge-made procedural default sanction into the PLRA. The majority's misapprehension of our precedent is especially troubling because, as the American Bar Association points out, we should be particularly hesitant to impose "judicially-created procedural technicalities . . . 'in a statutory scheme in which laymen, unassisted by trained lawyers, initiate the process.' " . . .

IV

The principal arguments offered by the Court in support of its holding are policy arguments that, in its view, are grounded in the purposes of the PLRA.[9] The majority correctly identifies two of the principal purposes of the PLRA: (1) affording corrections officials time and opportunity to address complaints internally before the initiation of a federal lawsuit; and (2) reducing the quantity, and improving the quality, of prison litigation. Both of these purposes would be served by the PLRA, even if the Court did not engraft a procedural default sanction into the statute.

The first policy concern identified by the majority does not even arguably justify either a timeliness requirement or a procedural default sanction. Prison officials certainly have the opportunity to address claims that were filed in some procedurally defective manner; indeed, California, like the vast majority of state prison systems, explicitly gives prison administrators an opportunity to hear untimely or otherwise procedurally defective grievances. See generally Kermit Roosevelt III, Exhaustion Under the Prison Litigation Reform Act: The Consequence of Procedural Error, 52 Emory L.J. 1771, 1810, and n. 192 (2003) (hereinafter Roosevelt). Because it is undisputed that the PLRA mandates that prisoners exhaust their administrative remedies before filing a federal lawsuit, prison officials will have the opportunity to address prisoners' claims before a suit is filed.

Second, . . . [o]rdinary exhaustion also improves the quality of prisoner suits. By giving prison officials an opportunity to address a prisoner's grievance before the initiation of the lawsuit, ordinary exhaustion "often results in the creation of an administrative record that is helpful to the court." I acknowledge, of course, that the majority's creation of a waiver sanction for procedural missteps during the course of exhaustion will have

[9] Of course, if the majority were serious that "what matters is not whether proper exhaustion was necessary to reach [policy goals], but whether proper exhaustion was mandated by Congress," its opinion would not rest almost entirely on policy arguments.

[a] significant effect in reducing the number of lawsuits filed by prisoners. [However, the] competing values that Congress sought to effectuate by enacting the PLRA were reducing the number of frivolous filings, on one hand, while preserving prisoners' capacity to file meritorious claims, on the other. As explained by Senator Hatch when he introduced the legislation on the Senate floor, the PLRA was needed because the quantity of frivolous suits filed by prisoners was, in Senator Hatch's view, making it difficult for "courts to consider meritorious claims." 141 Cong. Rec. 27042 (1995). He continued: "Indeed, I do not want to prevent inmates from raising legitimate claims. This legislation will not prevent those claims from being raised." Ibid. Similarly, as Senator Thurmond, a cosponsor of the bill, stated: "[The PLRA] will allow meritorious claims to be filed, but gives the judge broader discretion to prevent frivolous and malicious lawsuits filed by prison inmates." Id., at 27044.

But the procedural default sanction created by this Court, unlike the exhaustion requirement created by Congress, bars litigation at random, irrespective of whether a claim is meritorious or frivolous. Consider, for example, an inmate who has been raped while in prison. . . . [I]nmates who are sexually assaulted by guards, or whose sexual assaults by other inmates are facilitated by guards, have suffered grave deprivations of their Eighth Amendment rights. Yet, the Court's engraftment of a procedural default sanction into the PLRA's exhaustion requirement risks barring such claims when a prisoner fails, inter alia, to file her grievance (perhaps because she correctly fears retaliation) within strict time requirements that are generally no more than 15 days, and that, in nine States, are between two and five days.

Much of the majority opinion seems to assume that, absent the creation of a waiver sanction, prisoners will purposely circumvent prison grievance proceedings. However, prisoners generally lack both the incentive and the capacity to engage in such evasive tactics. Because federal courts do not provide any deference to administrative decisions by prison officials and any later federal suit is de novo, prisoners—even prisoners who are acting in bad faith—lack an incentive to avoid filing an administrative grievance unless they fear retaliation. Moreover, because prisoners must exhaust administrative remedies, prison officials can always thwart efforts by prisoners to avoid the grievance process by simply exercising their discretion to excuse any procedural defect in the presentation of the prisoners' claims.

At any rate, there is a simple solution that would allow courts to punish prisoners who seek to deliberately bypass state administrative remedies, but that would not impose the Draconian punishment of procedural default on prisoners who make reasonable, good-faith efforts to comply with relevant administrative rules but, out of fear of retaliation, a reasonable mistake of law, or simple inadvertence, make some procedural misstep along the way. Federal courts could simply exercise their discretion to dismiss suits brought by the former group of litigants but not those brought by the latter.

The majority argues that imposing a sanction against prisoners who deliberately bypass administrative remedies "neither has a statutory basis nor refers to a concept of exhaustion from an existing body of law." In fact, this criticism applies to the majority's engraftment of an overinclusive procedural default sanction into the PLRA. If this Court insists upon rewriting § 1997e(a) in light of its understanding of the statute's purposes, surely the majority should add to the statute no harsher a sanction for making a procedural error during exhaustion than is necessary to accomplish its policy goals. . . . Applying such a deliberate bypass sanction to the PLRA would ensure that prisoners who act in bad faith are penalized, while not interfering with the capacity of other inmates to litigate meritorious constitutional claims.

In sum, the version of the PLRA Congress actually enacted, which includes an exhaustion requirement but not a procedural default sanction, is plainly sufficient to advance the policy values identified by the Court. Moreover, if, as the Court worries, there are many prisoners who act in bad faith and purposely eschew administrative remedies, the imposition of a deliberate bypass standard would resolve that problem, without depriving litigants who act in good faith but nonetheless make a procedural error from obtaining judicial relief relating to their valid constitutional claims. The majority's holding is as unsupported by the policy concerns it discusses as it is by the text of the statute.

V

The majority leaves open the question whether a prisoner's failure to comply properly with procedural requirements that do not provide a "meaningful opportunity for prisoners to raise meritorious grievances" would bar the later filing of a suit in federal court. What the majority has in mind by a "meaningful opportunity" is unclear, and this question is sure to breed a great deal of litigation in federal courts in the years to come. For example, in this case, respondent filed a second grievance after his first grievance was rejected, arguing that his first grievance was in fact timely because he was challenging petitioners' continuing prohibition on his capacity to participate in Catholic observances, such as Confession, Holy Week services, and Bible study. The prison again rejected this second grievance on timeliness grounds, even though the denial of respondent's capacity to engage in religious activities was clearly ongoing, and thus had occurred within the prison's 15–day statute of limitations. Assuming respondent explicitly requested the restoration of his right to engage in religious activities within 15 days of the filing of his second grievance and prison officials denied the request, did petitioners' grievance procedures fail to provide respondent with a "meaningful opportunity" to raise his claim, because, in light of the continuing nature of the injury respondent is challenging, his grievance was in fact timely?

What about cases involving other types of procedural missteps? Does a 48–hour limitations period furnish a meaningful opportunity for a prisoner to raise meritorious grievances in the context of a juvenile who has been raped and repeatedly assaulted, with the knowledge and assistance of guards, while in detention? Does a prison grievance system provide such a meaningful opportunity when women prisoners fail to file timely grievances relating to a pattern of rape and sexual harassment throughout a city's prisons, because they correctly fear retaliation if they file such complaints? Are such remedies meaningful when a prisoner files a grievance concerning a prison official having encouraged him to commit suicide, which the prisoner reasonably thinks raises one claim, but which prison officials interpret to raise two separate claims—one related to the guard's comments and one related to the prisoner's failure to receive health care—and thus dismiss for violating a prison regulation against including more than one claim in a single grievance? What if prison officials dismiss a timely filed appeal because the prisoner explains that the prison will take two weeks to finish making certain copies of relevant documents by sending a letter to the Secretary of the Department of Corrections, rather than to the Secretary of Inmate Grievances and Appeals, as he should have under the prison regulations?[a] More generally, are remedies meaningful when prison officials refuse to hear a claim simply because a prisoner makes some hypertechnical procedural error?[b]

Depending on the answer to questions like these, the majority's interpretation of the PLRA may cause the statute to be vulnerable to constitutional challenges. "[T]he right of access to the courts is an aspect of the First Amendment right to petition the Government for redress of grievances." Bill Johnson's Restaurants, Inc. v. NLRB, 461 U.S. 731, 741 (1983). Accordingly, the Constitution guarantees that prisoners, like all citizens, have a reasonably adequate opportunity to raise constitutional claims before impartial judges, see, e.g., Lewis v. Casey, 518 U.S. 343, 351 (1996). Moreover, because access to the courts is a fundamental right, government-drawn classifications that impose substantial burdens on the capacity of a group of citizens to exercise that right require searching judicial examination under the Equal Protection Clause, see, e.g., Lyng v. Automobile Workers, 485 U.S. 360, 370 (1988).

The correct interpretation of the PLRA would obviate the need for litigation over any of these issues. More importantly, the correct interpretation of the statute would recognize that, in enacting the PLRA, Members of Congress created a rational regime designed to reduce the quantity of frivolous prison litigation while adhering to their constitutional duty "to respect the dignity of all persons," even "those convicted of heinous crimes." Roper v. Simmons, 543 U.S. 551, 560 (2005). Because today's decision ignores that duty, I respectfully dissent.

NOTES ON THE PLRA EXHAUSTION REQUIREMENT

1. *BOOTH V. CHURNER* AND *PORTER V. NUSSLE*

The Court decided two PLRA cases prior to *Woodford*. As stated in *Woodford*, the question in Booth v. Churner, 532 U.S. 731 (2001), was "whether an inmate seeking only money damages must complete a prison administrative process that could provide some sort of relief on the complaint stated, but no money." The Court's answer was unanimous, based largely on a textual analysis of the statute: "We hold that he must."

Porter v. Nussle, 534 U.S. 516 (2002), was filed by a prisoner who claimed that corrections officers singled him out for a severe beating. The statute requires exhaustion of administrative remedies prior to filing an action "brought with respect to prison conditions." Nussel's argument was that his claim of excessive force did not address "prison conditions" and hence did not require exhaustion. The Court, again unanimously, rejected the argument, holding that the PLRA's "exhaustion requirement applies to all prisoners seeking redress for prison circumstances or occurrences." The Court relied on several precedents in other contexts, as well as its general sense of the Congression-

[a] Citations by Justice Stevens to lower court filings for each of these claims have been omitted.—[Footnote by eds.]

[b] Here Justice Stevens cited two Circuit cases, one of which said that "substantial" compliance with prison grievance procedures should suffice and the other of which he described as saying that "failure to comply with procedural requirements in grievance proceedings may be excused based on special circumstances, such as a prisoner's reasonable, but mistaken, understanding of prison regulations."—[Footnote by eds.]

al goal: "Why should a prisoner have immediate access to court when a guard assaults him on one occasion, but not when beatings are widespread or routine? . . . Do prison authorities have an interest in receiving prompt notice of, and opportunity to take action against, guard brutality that is somehow less compelling than their interest in receiving notice and an opportunity to stop other types of staff wrongdoing?"

2. QUESTIONS AND COMMENTS ON *WOODFORD*

A case for the result embraced by the *Woodford* dissenters was made before that decision in Kermit Roosevelt III, Exhaustion Under the Prison Litigation Reform Act: The Consequence of Procedural Error, 52 Emory L.J. 1771, 1814 (2003). In his introductory comments, Roosevelt observed:

> Let us be candid. There is no denying that frivolous suits make up a large number—and even a fairly large percentage—of the claims brought by inmates under § 1983. But there are also real abuses that take place within the prison system. Prisoners have, among other things, been raped, shot, and beaten to death by guards. For those wrongs, there should be remedies. A rule that controls access to courts not by examining the merits of a claim but by shutting the door on uncounseled inmates who fail to navigate a procedural minefield is not a good one.

He concluded that construing the PLRA exhaustion requirement as a bar "would be extremely effective in reducing the number of such suits that courts must decide on the merits," that "[p]rison administrative procedures are difficult to comply with as things stand," and that "if prison administrators can use them to defeat § 1983 suits before they are filed, we should expect the procedures to become even more complex and unforgiving." There is little reason, he argued, to think that a foreclosure rule would eliminate only frivolous suits. Since Congress did not clearly make the choice to deter prisoner suits "wholesale, without any reference to their merits," the courts should not "lightly" take this solution "upon themselves."

What explains the Court's rejection of these arguments?

3. *JONES V. BOCK*

Jones v. Bock, 549 U.S. 199 (2007), reached the Court after *Woodford*. The issues were stated by the Court as follows:

> The [court below] adopted several procedural rules designed to implement [the PLRA] exhaustion requirement and facilitate early judicial screening. These rules require a prisoner to allege and demonstrate exhaustion in his complaint, permit suit only against defendants who were identified by the prisoner in his grievance, and require courts to dismiss the entire action if the prisoner fails to satisfy the exhaustion requirement as to any single claim in his complaint.

(i) Enhanced Pleading

Chief Justice Roberts wrote for a unanimous Court. On the question on pleading and demonstrating exhaustion in the complaint, he said: "Federal Rule of Civil Procedure 8(a) requires simply a 'short and plain statement of the claim' in a complaint, while Rule 8(c) identifies a nonexhaustive list of affirmative defenses that must be pleaded in response. The PLRA itself is not a source of a prisoner's claim; claims covered by the PLRA are typically brought under 42 U.S.C. § 1983, which does not require exhaustion at all." The Court said that "courts should generally not depart from the usual practice under the Federal Rules on the basis of perceived policy concerns," and concluded that "failure to exhaust is an affirmative defense under the PLRA. . . . [I]nmates are not required to specially plead or demonstrate exhaustion in their complaints."

(ii) Identification of Defendants

The Court's response to the limitation of prisoner suits to defendants identified in the grievance was similar:

> Here again the lower court's procedural rule lacks a textual basis in the PLRA. The PLRA requires exhaustion of "such administrative remedies as are available," but nothing in the statute imposes a "name all defendants" requirement along the lines of the Sixth Circuit's judicially created rule. . . . The level of detail necessary in a grievance to comply with the grievance procedures will vary from system to system and claim to claim, but it is the prison's requirements, and not the PLRA, that define the boundaries of proper exhaustion. As [the prison's] procedures make no mention of naming particular officials, the [lower court's] rule imposing such a prerequisite to proper exhaustion is unwarranted.

(iii) Total Exhaustion Requirement

The Court stated the third issue and its answer as follows:

> The final issue concerns how courts should address complaints in which the prisoner has failed to exhaust some, but not all, of the claims asserted in the complaint. All agree that no unexhausted claim may be considered. The issue is whether the court should proceed with the exhausted claims, or instead . . . dismiss the entire action if any one claim is not properly exhausted. . . .
>
> As a general matter, if a complaint contains both good and bad claims, the court proceeds with the good and leaves the bad. . . . Respondents note an exception to this general rule, the total exhaustion rule in habeas corpus. In Rose v. Lundy, 455 U.S. 509, 522 (1982), we held that "mixed" habeas petitions—containing both exhausted and unexhausted claims—cannot be adjudicated. This total exhaustion rule applied in habeas was initially derived from considerations of "comity and federalism," not any statutory command. Rhines v. Weber, 544 U.S. 269, 273 (2005). . . . Separate claims in a single habeas petition generally seek the same relief from custody, and success on one is often as good as success on another. In such a case it makes sense to require exhaustion of all claims in state court before allowing the federal action to proceed. A typical PLRA suit with multiple claims, on the other hand, may combine a wide variety of discrete complaints, about interactions with guards, prison conditions, generally applicable rules, and so on, seeking different relief on each claim. There is no reason failure to exhaust on one necessarily affects any other. . . .

The Court added that the further practical point that "the effect of a total exhaustion rule could be that inmates will file various claims in separate suits, to avoid the possibility of an unexhausted claim tainting the others. That would certainly not comport with the purpose of the PLRA to reduce the quantity of inmate suits." In addition, district judges may spend substantial time on a prisoner complaint before they realize that an unexhausted claim is concluded. If "dismissal of the entire complaint [is required] under the total exhaustion rule, [the judges] will often have to begin the process all over again when the prisoner refiles."

In conclusion as to all three issues, the Court added the following:

> We are not insensitive to the challenges faced by the lower federal courts in managing their dockets and attempting to separate, when it comes to prisoner suits, not so much wheat from chaff as needles from haystacks. We once again reiterate, however, . . . that adopting different and more onerous pleading rules to deal with particular categories of cases should be done through established rulemaking procedures, and not on a case-by-case basis by the courts.

Given *Woodford*, is unanimity in *Jones* surprising?

SUBSECTION B: THE RELATION OF § 1983 TO HABEAS CORPUS

Preiser v. Rodriguez

United States Supreme Court, 1973.
411 U.S. 475.

■ MR. JUSTICE STEWART delivered the opinion of the Court.

The respondents in this case were state prisoners who were deprived of good-conduct-time credits by the New York State Department of Correctional Services as a result of disciplinary proceedings. They then brought actions in a federal district court, pursuant to the Civil Rights Act of 1871, 42 U.S.C. § 1983. Alleging that the department had acted unconstitutionally in depriving them of the credits, they sought injunctive relief to compel restoration of the credits, which in each case would result in their immediate release from confinement in prison. [The District Court granted the requested relief, the Court of Appeals affirmed, and the Supreme Court granted certiorari.] The question before us is whether state prisoners seeking such redress may obtain equitable relief under the Civil Rights Act, even though the federal habeas corpus statute, 28 U.S.C. § 2254, clearly provides a specific federal remedy.

The question is of considerable practical importance. For if a remedy under the Civil Rights Act is available, a plaintiff need not first seek redress in a state forum. If, on the other hand, habeas corpus is the exclusive federal remedy in these circumstances, then a plaintiff cannot seek the intervention of a federal court until he has first sought and been denied relief in the state courts, if a state remedy is available and adequate. 28 U.S.C. § 2254(b). . . .

The problem involves the interrelationship of two important federal laws. The relevant habeas corpus statutes are 28 U.S.C. §§ 2241 and 2254. . . . Section 2254 provides in pertinent part:

> (a) [A] district court shall entertain an application for a writ of habeas corpus in behalf of a person in custody pursuant to the judg-

ment of a State court only on the ground that he is in custody in violation of the Constitution or laws or treaties of the United States.

(b) An application for a writ of habeas corpus in behalf of a person in custody pursuant to the judgment of a state court shall not be granted unless it appears that the applicant has exhausted the remedies available in the courts of the State, or that there is either an absence of available state corrective process or the existence of circumstances rendering such process ineffective to protect the rights of the prisoner.

(c) An applicant shall not be deemed to have exhausted the remedies available in the courts of the State, within the meaning of this section, if he has the right under the law of the State to raise, by any available procedure, the question presented.

[T]he essence of habeas corpus is an attack by a person in custody upon the legality of that custody, and that the traditional function of the writ is to secure release from illegal custody. . . .

By the time the American colonies achieved independence, the use of habeas corpus to secure release from unlawful physical confinement . . . was . . . an integral part of our common-law heritage. The writ was given explicit recognition in the Suspension Clause of the Constitution, art. I, § 9, cl. 2; was incorporated in the first congressional grant of jurisdiction to the federal courts; and was early recognized by this Court as a "great constitutional privilege."

The original view of a habeas corpus attack upon detention under a judicial order was a limited one. The relevant inquiry was confined to determining simply whether or not the committing court had been possessed of jurisdiction. But, over the years, the writ of habeas corpus evolved as a remedy available to effect discharge from any confinement contrary to the Constitution or fundamental law, even though imposed pursuant to conviction by a court of competent jurisdiction. Thus, whether the petitioner's challenge to his custody is that the statute under which he stands convicted is unconstitutional; that he has been imprisoned prior to trial on account of a defective indictment against him; that he is unlawfully confined in the wrong institution; that he was denied his constitutional rights at trial; that his guilty plea was invalid; that he is being unlawfully detained by the executive or the military; or that his parole was unlawfully revoked, causing him to be reincarcerated in prison—in each case his grievance is that he is being unlawfully subjected to physical restraint, and in each case habeas corpus has been accepted as the specific instrument to obtain release from such confinement.

In the case before us, the respondents' suits in the District Court fell squarely within this traditional scope of habeas corpus. They alleged that the deprivation of their good-conduct-time credits was causing or would cause them to be in illegal physical confinement, i.e., that once their conditional-release date had passed, any further detention of them in prison was unlawful; and they sought restoration of those good-time credits, which, by the time the District Court ruled on their petitions, meant their immediate release from physical custody.

[R]ecent cases have established that habeas corpus relief is not limited to immediate release from illegal custody, but that the writ is available as well to attack future confinement and obtain future releases. . . . So, even if restoration of respondents' good-time credits had merely shortened the length of their confinement, rather than required immediate discharge from that confinement, their suits would still have been within the core of habeas corpus in attacking the very duration of their physical confinement itself. It is beyond doubt, then, that the respondents could have sought and obtained fully effective relief through federal habeas corpus proceedings.

Although conceding that they could have proceeded by way of habeas corpus, the respondents argue that the Court of Appeals was correct in holding that they were nonetheless entitled to bring their suits under § 1983 so as to avoid the necessity of first seeking relief in a state forum. Pointing to the broad language of § 1983, they argue that since their complaints plainly came within the literal terms of that statute, there is no justifiable reason to exclude them from the broad remedial protection provided by that law. . . .

The broad language of § 1983, however, is not conclusive of the issue before us. The statute is a general one, and, despite the literal applicability of its terms, the question remains whether the specific federal habeas corpus statute, explicitly and historically designed to provide the means for a state prisoner to attack the validity of his confinement, must be understood to be the exclusive remedy available in a situation like this where it so clearly applies. The respondents' counsel acknowledged at oral argument that a state prisoner challenging his underlying conviction and sentence on federal constitutional grounds in a federal court is limited to habeas corpus. It was conceded that he cannot bring a § 1983 action, even though the literal terms of § 1983 might seem to cover such a challenge, because Congress has passed a more specific act to cover that situation, and, in doing so, has provided that a state prisoner challenging his conviction must first seek relief in a state forum, if a state remedy is available. It is clear to us that the result must be the same in the case of a state prisoner's challenge to the fact or duration of his confinement, based, as here, upon the alleged unconstitutionality of state administrative action. Such a challenge is just as close to the core of habeas corpus as an attack on the prisoner's conviction, for it goes directly to the constitutionality of his physical confinement itself and seeks either immediate release from that confinement or the shortening of its duration.

. . . Congress clearly required exhaustion of adequate state remedies as a condition precedent to the invocation of federal judicial relief under those laws. It would wholly frustrate explicit congressional intent to hold that the respondents in the present case could evade this requirement by the simple expedient of putting a different label on their pleadings. In short, Congress has determined that habeas corpus is the appropriate remedy for state prisoners attacking the validity of the fact or length of their confinement, and that specific determination must override the general terms of § 1983.

The policy reasons underlying the habeas corpus statute support this conclusion. The respondents concede that the reason why only habeas corpus can be used to challenge a state prisoner's underlying conviction is the strong policy requiring exhaustion of state remedies in that situation—to avoid the unnecessary friction between the federal and state court systems that would result if a lower federal court upset a state court conviction without first giving the state court system an opportunity to correct its own constitutional errors. But they argue that this concern applies only to federal interference with state court convictions; and to support this argument, they quote from Ex parte Royall, 117 U.S. 241 (1886), the case that first mandated exhaustion of state remedies as a precondition to federal habeas corpus:

> The injunction to hear the case summarily, and thereupon "to dispose of the party as law and justice require" does not deprive the court of discretion as to the time and mode in which it will exert the powers conferred upon it. That discretion should be exercised in the light of the relations existing, under our system of government, *between the judicial tribunals of the Union and of the States,* and in recognition of the fact that the public good requires that those relations be not disturbed by *unnecessary conflict between courts* equally bound to guard and protect rights secured by the Constitution. (Emphasis added.)

In the respondents' view, the whole purpose of the exhaustion requirement, now codified in § 2254(b), is to give state *courts* the first chance at remedying *their own* mistakes, and thereby to avoid "the unseemly spectacle of federal district courts trying the regularity of proceedings had in *courts* of coordinate jurisdiction." This policy, the respondents contend, does not apply when the challenge is not to the action of a state court, but, as here, to the action of a state administrative body. In that situation, they say, the concern with avoiding unnecessary interference by one court with the courts of another sovereignty with concurrent powers, and the importance of giving state courts the first opportunity to correct constitutional errors made by them, do not apply; and hence the purpose of the exhaustion requirement of the habeas corpus statute is inapplicable.

We cannot agree. The respondents, we think, view the reasons for the exhaustion requirement of § 2254(b) far too narrowly. The rule of exhaustion in federal habeas corpus actions is rooted in considerations of federal-state comity. That principle was defined in Younger v. Harris, 401 U.S. 37, 44 (1971), as "a proper respect for state functions," and it has as much relevance in areas of particular state administrative concern as it does where state judicial action is being attacked. . . .

It is difficult to imagine an activity in which a State has a stronger interest, or one that is more intricately bound up with state laws, regulations, and procedures, than the administration of its prisoners. The relationship of state prisoners and the state officers who supervise their confinement is far more intimate than that of a State and a private citizen. For state prisoners, eating, sleeping, dressing, washing, working, and playing are all done under the watchful eye of the State, and so the possibilities for litigation under the Fourteenth Amendment are boundless. What for a private citizen would be a dispute with his landlord, with his employer, with his tailor, with his neighbor, or with his banker becomes, for the prisoner, a dispute with the State. Since these internal problems of state prisons involve issues so peculiarly within state authority and expertise, the States have an important interest in not being bypassed in the correction of these problems. Moreover, because most potential litigation involving state prisoners arises on a day-to-day basis, it is most efficiently and properly handled by the state administrative bodies and state courts, which are, for the most part, familiar with the grievances of state prisoners and in a better physical and practical position to deal with those grievances. In New York, for example, state judges sit on a regular basis at all but one of the State's correctional facilities, and thus inmates may present their grievances to a court at the place of their confinement, where the relevant records are available and where potential witnesses are located. The strong considerations of comity that require giving a state court system that has convicted a defendant the first opportunity to correct its own errors thus also require giving the States the first opportunity to correct the errors made in the internal administration of their prisons.[10]

[T]he respondents contend that confining state prisoners to federal habeas corpus, after first exhausting state remedies, could deprive those prisoners of any damages remedy to which they might be entitled for their mistreatment, since damages are not available in federal habeas corpus proceedings, and New York provides no damages remedy at all for state prisoners. In the respondents' view, if habeas corpus is the exclusive federal remedy for a state prisoner attacking his confinement, damages might never be obtained, at least where the State makes no provision for them. They argue that even if such a prisoner were to bring a subsequent federal civil rights action for damages, that action could be barred by principles of res judicata where the state courts had previously made an adverse determination of his underlying claim, even though a federal habeas court had later granted him relief on habeas corpus.

The answer to this contention is that the respondents here sought no damages, but only equitable relief—restoration of their good-time credits—and our holding today is limited to that situation. If a state prisoner is seeking damages, he is attacking something other than the fact or length of his confinement, and he is seeking something other than immediate or more speedy release—the traditional purpose of habeas corpus. In the case of a damages claim, habeas corpus is *not* an appropriate or available federal remedy. Accordingly, as the State itself concedes, a damages action by a state prisoner could be brought under the Civil Rights Act in federal court without any requirement of prior exhaustion of state remedies. . . .

Principles of res judicata are, of course, not wholly applicable to habeas corpus proceedings. 28 U.S.C. § 2254(d). Hence, a state prisoner in the respondents' situation who has been denied relief in the state courts is not precluded from seeking habeas relief on the same claims in federal court. On the other hand, res judicata has been held to be fully applicable to a civil rights action brought under § 1983. Accordingly, there would be an inevitable incentive for a state prisoner to proceed at once in federal court by way of a civil rights action, lest he lose his right to do so. This would have the unfortunate dual effect of denying the state prison administration and the state courts the opportunity to correct the errors committed in the State's own prisons, and of isolating those bodies from an understanding of and hospitality to the federal claims of state prisoners in situations such as those before us. Federal habeas corpus, on the other hand, serves the important function of allowing the State to deal with these peculiarly local problems on its own, while preserving for the state prisoner an expeditious federal forum for the vindication of his federally protected rights, if the State has denied redress.

---

[10] The dissent argues that the respondents' attacks on the actions of the prison administration here are no different, in terms of the potential for exacerbating federal-state relations, from the attacks made by the petitioners in McNeese v. Board of Education, 373 U.S. 668 (1963), Damico v. California, 389 U.S. 416 (1967), and Monroe v. Pape, 365 U.S. 167 (1961), on the various state administrative actions there. Thus, it is said, since exhaustion of state remedies was not required in those cases, it is anomalous to require it here. The answer, of course, is that in those cases, brought pursuant to § 1983, no other, more specific federal statute was involved that might have reflected a different congressional intent. In the present case, however, the respondents' actions fell squarely within the traditional purpose of federal habeas corpus, and Congress has made the specific determination in § 2254(b) that requiring the exhaustion of adequate state remedies in such cases will best serve the policies of federalism.

The respondents place a great deal of reliance on our recent decisions upholding the right of state prisoners to bring federal civil rights actions to challenge the conditions of their confinement. Cooper v. Pate, 378 U.S. 546 (1964); Houghton v. Shafer, 392 U.S. 639 (1968); Wilwording v. Swenson, 404 U.S. 249 (1971); Haines v. Kerner, 404 U.S. 519 (1972). But none of the state prisoners in those cases was challenging the fact or duration of his physical confinement itself, and none was seeking immediate release or a speedier release from that confinement—the heart of habeas corpus. In *Cooper,* the prisoner alleged that, solely because of his religious beliefs, he had been denied permission to purchase certain religious publications and had been denied other privileges enjoyed by his fellow prisoners. In *Houghton,* the prisoner's contention was that prison authorities had violated the Constitution by confiscating legal materials which he had acquired for pursuing his appeal, but which, in violation of prison rules, had been found in the possession of another prisoner. In *Wilwording,* the prisoners' complaints related solely to their living conditions and disciplinary measures while confined in maximum security. And in *Haines,* the prisoner claimed that prison officials had acted unconstitutionally by placing him in solitary confinement as a disciplinary measure, and he sought damages for claimed physical injuries sustained while so segregated. It is clear then, that in all those cases, the prisoners' claims related solely to the States' alleged unconstitutional treatment of them while in confinement. None sought, as did the respondents here, to challenge the very fact or duration of the confinement itself. Those cases, therefore, merely establish that a § 1983 action is a proper remedy for a state prisoner who is making a constitutional challenge to the conditions of his prison life, but not to the fact or length of his custody. Upon that understanding, we reaffirm those holdings.[14]

This is not to say that habeas corpus may not also be available to challenge such prison conditions. See Johnson v. Avery, 393 U.S. 483 (1969); *Wilwording v. Swenson,* supra. When a prisoner is put under additional and unconstitutional restraints during his lawful custody, it is arguable that habeas corpus will lie to remove the restraints making the custody illegal.

But we need not in this case explore the appropriate limits of habeas corpus as an alternative remedy to a proper action under § 1983. That question is not before us. What is involved here is the extent to which § 1983 is a permissible alternative to the traditional remedy of habeas corpus. Upon that question, we hold today that when a state prisoner is challenging the very fact or duration of his physical imprisonment, and the relief he seeks is a determination that he is entitled to immediate release or a speedier release from that imprisonment, his sole federal remedy is a writ of habeas corpus. Accordingly, we reverse the judgment before us.

It is so ordered.

■ MR. JUSTICE BRENNAN with whom MR. JUSTICE DOUGLAS and MR. JUSTICE MARSHALL join, dissenting.

The question presented by this case is one that I, like the Court of Appeals, had thought already resolved by our decision last Term in Wilword-

[14] If a prisoner seeks to attack both the conditions of his confinement and the fact or length of that confinement, his latter claim, under our decision today, is cognizable only in federal habeas corpus, with its attendant requirement of exhaustion of state remedies. But, consistent with our prior decisions, that holding in no way precludes him from simultaneously litigating in federal court, under § 1983, his claim relating to the conditions of his confinement.

ing v. Swenson, 404 U.S. 249 (1971). We held there that the Ku Klux Klan Act of 1871, 42 U.S.C. § 1983; 28 U.S.C. § 1343(3), confers jurisdiction on the United States district courts to entertain a state prisoner's application for injunctive relief against allegedly unconstitutional conditions of confinement. At the same time, we held that "[t]he remedy provided by these acts 'is supplementary to the state remedy, and the latter need not be first sought and refused before the federal one is invoked.' State prisoners are not held to any stricter standard of exhaustion than other civil rights plaintiffs."

Regrettably, the Court today eviscerates that proposition by drawing a distinction that is both analytically unsound and, I fear, unworkable in practice. The net effect of the distinction is to preclude respondents from maintaining these actions under § 1983, leaving a petition for writ of habeas corpus the only available federal remedy. As a result, respondents must exhaust state remedies before their claims can be heard in a federal district court. I remain committed to the principles set forth in *Wilwording v. Swenson* and I therefore respectfully dissent. . . .

The Court's conclusion that *Wilwording* is not controlling is assertedly justified by invocation of a concept, newly invented by the Court today, variously termed the "core of habeas corpus," the "heart of habeas corpus," and the "essence of habeas corpus." In the Court's view, an action lying at the "core of habeas corpus" is one that "goes directly to the constitutionality of [the prisoner's] physical confinement itself and seeks either immediate release from that confinement or the shortening of its duration." With regard to such actions, habeas corpus is now considered the prisoner's exclusive remedy. . . .

At bottom, the Court's holding today rests on an understandable apprehension that the no-exhaustion rule of § 1983 might, in the absence of some limitation, devour the exhaustion rule of the habeas corpus statute. The problem arises because the two statutes necessarily overlap. Indeed, every application by the state prisoner for federal habeas corpus relief against his jailers could, as a matter of logic and semantics, be viewed as an action under the Ku Klux Klan Act to obtain injunctive relief against "the deprivation," by one acting under color of state law, "of any rights, privileges, or immunities secured by the Constitution and laws" of the United States. 42 U.S.C. § 1983. To prevent state prisoners from nullifying the habeas corpus exhaustion requirement by invariably styling their petitions as pleas for relief under § 1983, the Court today devises an ungainly and irrational scheme that permits some prisoners to sue under § 1983, while others may proceed only by way of petition for habeas corpus. And the entire scheme operates in defiance of the purposes underlying both the exhaustion requirement of habeas corpus and the absence of a comparable requirement under § 1983.

I

[In Part I of his opinion, Justice Brennan noted that the majority left *Wilwording* "unimpaired" where the challenge is merely to the conditions of confinement.]

II

Putting momentarily to one side the grave analytic shortcomings of the Court's approach, it seems clear that the scheme's unmanageability is sufficient reason to condemn it. For the unfortunate but inevitable legacy of today's opinion is a perplexing set of uncertainties and anomalies. And the nub of the problem is the definition of the Court's new-found and essentially ethereal concept, the "core of habeas corpus." . . .

Between a suit for damages and an attack on the conviction itself or on the deprivation of good-time credits are cases where habeas corpus is an appropriate and available remedy, but where the action falls outside the "core of habeas corpus" because the attack is directed at the conditions of confinement, not at its fact or duration. Notwithstanding today's decision, a prisoner may challenge, by suit under § 1983, prison living conditions and disciplinary measures, or confiscation of legal materials, or impairment of the right to free exercise of religion, even though federal habeas corpus is available as an alternative remedy. It should be plain enough that serious difficulties will arise whenever a prisoner seeks to attack in a single proceeding both the conditions of his confinement and the deprivation of good-time credits. And the addition of a plea for monetary damages exacerbates the problem.

If a prisoner's sole claim is that he was placed in solitary confinement pursuant to an unconstitutional disciplinary procedure, he can obtain federal injunctive relief and monetary damages in an action under § 1983. The unanswered question is whether he loses the right to proceed under § 1983 if, as punishment for his alleged misconduct, his jailers have not only subjected him to unlawful segregation and thereby inflicted an injury that is compensable in damages, but have compounded the wrong by improperly depriving him of good-time credits. Three different approaches are possible.

First, we might conclude that jurisdiction under § 1983 is lost whenever good-time credits are involved, even where the action is based primarily on the need for monetary relief or an injunction against continued segregation. If that is the logic of the Court's opinion, then the scheme creates an undeniable, and in all likelihood irresistible, incentive for state prison officials to defeat the jurisdiction of the federal courts by adding the deprivation of good-time credits to whatever other punishment is imposed. And if all of the federal claims must be held in abeyance pending exhaustion of state remedies, a prisoner's subsequent effort to assert a damages claim under § 1983 might arguably be barred by principles of res judicata. To avoid the loss of his damages claim, a prisoner might conclude that he should make no mention of the good-time issue and instead seek only damages in a § 1983 action. That approach (assuming it would not be disallowed as a subterfuge to circumvent the exhaustion requirement) creates its own distressing possibilities. For, having obtained decision in federal court on the issue of damages, the prisoner would presumably be required to repair to state court in search of his lost good-time credits, returning once again to federal court if his state court efforts should prove unavailing.

Moreover, a determination that no federal claim can be raised where good-time credits are at stake would give rise to a further anomaly. If the prisoner is confined in an institution that does not offer good-time credits, and therefore cannot withdraw them, his prison-conditions claims could always be raised in a suit under § 1983. On the other hand, an inmate in an institution that uses good-time credits as reward and punishment, who seeks a federal hearing on the identical legal and factual claims, would normally be required to exhaust state remedies and then proceed by way of federal habeas corpus. The rationality of that difference in treatment is certainly obscure. Yet that is the price of permitting the availability of a federal forum to be controlled by the happenstance (or stratagem) that good-time credits are at stake.

As an alternative, we might reject outright the premises of the first approach and conclude that a plea for money damages or for an injunction against continued segregation is sufficient to bring all related claims, including the question of good-time credits, under the umbrella of § 1983. That approach would, of course, simplify matters considerably. And it would make unnecessary the fractionation of the prisoner's claims into a number of different issues to be resolved in duplicative proceedings in state and federal courts. Nevertheless, the approach would seem to afford a convenient means of sidestepping the basic thrust of the Court's opinion, and we could surely expect state prisoners routinely to add to their other claims a plea for monetary relief. So long as the prisoner could formulate at least a colorable damages claim, he would be entitled to litigate all issues in federal court without first exhausting state remedies.

In any event, the Court today rejects, perhaps for the reasons suggested above, both of the foregoing positions. Instead, it holds that insofar as a prisoner's claim relates to good-time credits, he is required to exhaust state remedies; but he is not precluded from simultaneously litigating in federal court, under § 1983, his claim for monetary damages or an injunction against continued segregation. Under that approach, state correctional authorities have no added incentive to withdraw goodtime credits, since that action cannot, standing alone, keep the prisoner out of federal court. And, at the same time, it does not encourage a prisoner to assert an unnecessary claim for damages or injunctive relief as a means of bringing his good-time claim under the purview of § 1983. Nevertheless, this approach entails substantial difficulties—perhaps the greatest difficulties of the three. In the first place, its extreme inefficiency is readily apparent. For in many instances a prisoner's claims will be under simultaneous consideration in two distinct forums, even though the identical legal and factual questions are involved in both proceedings. Thus, if a prisoner's punishment for some alleged misconduct is both a term in solitary and the deprivation of good-time credits, and if he believes that the punishment was imposed pursuant to unconstitutional disciplinary procedures, he can now litigate the legality of those procedures simultaneously in state court (where he seeks restoration of good-time credits) and in federal court (where he seeks damages or an injunction against continued segregation). Moreover, if the federal court is the first to reach decision, and if that court concludes that the procedures are, in fact, unlawful, then the entire state proceeding must be immediately aborted, even though the state court may have devoted substantial time and effort to its consideration of the case. By the same token, if traditional principles of res judicata are applicable to suits under § 1983, the prior conclusion of the state court suit would effectively set at naught the entire federal court proceeding. This is plainly a curious prescription for improving relations between state and federal courts.

Since some of the ramifications of this new approach are still unclear, the unfortunate outcome of today's decision—an outcome that might not be immediately surmised from the seeming simplicity of the basic concept, the "core of habeas corpus"—is almost certain to be the further complication of prison-conditions litigation. In itself that is disquieting enough. But it is especially distressing that the remaining questions will have to be resolved on the basis of pleadings, whether in habeas corpus or suit under § 1983, submitted by state prisoners, who will often have to cope with these questions without even minimal assistance of counsel.

III

. . . The concern that § 1983 not be used to nullify the habeas corpus exhaustion doctrine is, of course, legitimate. But our effort to preserve the integrity of the doctrine must rest on an understanding of the purposes that underlie it. In my view, the Court misapprehends these fundamental purposes and compounds the problem by paying insufficient attention to the reasons why exhaustion of state remedies is not required in suits under § 1983. As a result, the Court mistakenly concludes that allowing suit under § 1983 would jeopardize the purposes of the exhaustion rule.

By enactment of the Ku Klux Klan Act in 1871, and again by the grant in 1875 of original federal-question jurisdiction to the United State District Courts, Congress recognized important interests in permitting a plaintiff to choose a federal forum in cases arising under federal law. . . .

This grant of jurisdiction was designed to preserve and enhance the expertise of federal courts in applying federal law; to achieve greater uniformity of results; and, since federal courts are "more likely to apply federal law sympathetically and understandingly than are state courts," to minimize misapplications of federal law. . . .

These considerations, applicable generally in cases arising under federal law, have special force in the context of the Ku Klux Klan Act of 1871. In a suit to enforce fundamental constitutional rights, the plaintiff's choice of a federal forum has singular urgency. The statutory predecessor to § 1983 was, after all, designed "to afford a federal right in federal courts because, by reason of prejudice, passion, neglect, intolerance or otherwise, state laws might not be enforced and the claims of citizens to the rights, privileges, and immunities guaranteed by the Fourteenth Amendment might be denied by the state agencies." Monroe v. Pape, 365 U.S. 167, 180 (1961). And the statute's legislative history

> makes evident that Congress clearly conceived that it was altering the relationship between the States and the Nation with respect to the protection of federally created rights; it was concerned that state instrumentalities could not protect those rights; it realized that state officers might, in fact, be antipathetic to the vindication of those rights; and it believed that these failings extended to the state courts. . . . The very purpose of § 1983 was to interpose the federal courts between the States and the people, as guardians of the people's federal rights—to protect the people from unconstitutional action under color of state law, "whether that action be executive, legislative or judicial." Mitchum v. Foster, 407 U.S. 225, 242 (1972).

It is against this background that we have refused to require exhaustion of state remedies by civil rights plaintiffs. [T]he absence of an exhaustion requirement in § 1983 is not an accident of history or the result of careless oversight by Congress or this Court. On the contrary, the no-exhaustion rule is an integral feature of the statutory scheme. Exhaustion of state remedies is not required precisely because such a requirement would jeopardize the purposes of the act. For that reason, the imposition of such a requirement, even if done indirectly by means of a determination that jurisdiction under § 1983 is displaced by an alternative remedial device, must be justified by a clear statement of congressional intent, or, at the very least, by the presence of the most persuasive considerations of policy. In my view, no such justification can be found.

Crucial to the Court's analysis of the case before us is its understanding of the purposes that underlie the habeas corpus exhaustion requirement. But just as the Court pays too little attention to the reasons for a no-exhaustion rule in actions under § 1983, it also misconceives the purposes of the exhaustion requirement in habeas corpus. As a result, the Court reaches what seems to me the erroneous conclusion that the purposes of the exhaustion requirement are fully implicated in respondents' actions, even though respondents sought to bring these actions under § 1983.

"The rule of exhaustion in federal habeas corpus actions is," according to today's opinion, "rooted in considerations of federal-state comity. That principle was defined in Younger v. Harris, 401 U.S. 37, 44 (1971), as 'a proper respect for state functions,' and it has as much relevance in areas of particular state administrative concern as it does where state judicial action is being attacked." Moreover, the Court reasons that since the relationship between state prisoners and state officers is especially intimate, and since prison issues are peculiarly within state authority and expertise, "the States have an important interest in not being bypassed in the correction of those problems." With all respect, I cannot accept either the premises or the reasoning that lead to the Court's conclusion.

Although codified in the habeas corpus statute in 1948, the exhaustion requirement is a "judicially crafted instrument which reflects a careful balance between important interests of federalism and the need to preserve the writ of habeas corpus as a 'swift and imperative remedy in all cases of illegal restraint or confinement.'" Braden v. 30th Judicial Circuit, 410 U.S. 484, 490 (1973). The indisputable concern of all our decisions concerning the doctrine has been the relationship "between the *judicial tribunals* of the union and of the States. [T]he public good requires that those relations be not disturbed by unnecessary conflict between *courts* equally bound to guard and protect rights secured by the Constitution." *Ex parte Royall,* supra, at 251 (emphasis added). . . .

That is not to say, however, that the purposes of the doctrine are implicated only where an attack is directed at a state court conviction or sentence. *Ex parte Royall* itself did not involve a challenge to a state conviction, but rather an effort to secure a prisoner's release on habeas corpus "in advance of his trial in the [state] court in which he [was] indicted." But there, too, the focus was on relations between the state and federal *judiciaries.* It is a fundamental purpose of the exhaustion doctrine to preserve the "orderly administration of state judicial business, preventing the interruption of state adjudication by federal habeas proceedings. It is important that petitioners reach state appellate courts, which can develop and correct errors of state and federal law and most effectively supervise and impose uniformity on trial courts." . . .

With these considerations in mind, it becomes clear that the Court's decision does not serve the fundamental purposes behind the exhaustion doctrine. For although respondents were confined pursuant to the judgment of a state judicial tribunal, their claims do not relate to their convictions or sentences, but only to the administrative action of prison officials who subjected them to allegedly unconstitutional treatment, including the deprivation of good-time credits. This is not a case, in other words, where federal intervention would interrupt a state proceeding or jeopardize the orderly administration of state judicial business. Nor is it a case where an action in federal court might imperil the relationship between state and federal courts. The "regularity of proceedings had in courts of coordinate jurisdiction" is not in any sense at issue.

To be sure, respondents do call into question the constitutional validity of action by state officials, and friction between those officials and the federal court is by no means an inconceivable result. But standing alone, that possibility is simply not enough to warrant application of an exhaustion requirement. First, while we spoke in Younger v. Harris, 401 U.S. 37, 44 (1971), of the need for federal courts to maintain a "proper respect for state functions," neither that statement nor our holding there supports the instant application of the exhaustion doctrine. Our concern in *Younger* was the "longstanding public policy against federal court interference with *state court proceedings*" by means of a federal injunction against the continuation of those proceedings. *Younger* is thus an instructive illustration of the very proposition that the Court regrettably misconstrues. It does not in any sense demand, or even counsel, today's decision.

Second, the situation that exists in the case before us—an attack on state administrative rather than judicial action—is the stereotypical situation in which relief under § 1983 is authorized. See, e.g., McNeese v. Board of Education, 373 U.S. 668 (1963) (attack on school districting scheme); Damico v. California, 389 U.S. 416 (1967) (attack on welfare requirements); Monroe v. Pape, 365 U.S., at 183 (attack on police conduct). In each of these cases the exercise of federal jurisdiction was potentially offensive to the state and its officials. In each of these cases the attack was directed at an important state function in an area in which the state has wide powers of regulation. Yet in each of these cases we explicitly held that exhaustion of state remedies was not required. And in comparable cases we have taken pains to insure that the abstention doctrine is not used to defeat the plaintiff's initial choice of a federal forum, even though the plaintiff could reserve the right to litigate the federal claim in federal court at the conclusion of the state proceeding. England v. Louisiana State Board of Medical Examiners, 375 U.S. 411 (1964). Like Judge Kaufman, who concurred in the affirmance of the cases now before us, "I cannot believe that federal jurisdiction in cases involving prisoner rights is any more offensive to the state than federal jurisdiction in the areas" where the exhaustion requirement has been explicitly ruled inapplicable.

Third, if the Court is correct in assuming that the exhaustion requirement must be applied whenever federal jurisdiction might be a source of substantial friction with the State, then I simply do not understand why the Court stops where it does in rolling back the district courts' jurisdiction under § 1983. Application of the exhaustion doctrine now turns on whether or not the action is directed at the fact or duration of the prisoner's confinement. It seems highly doubtful to me that a constitutional attack on prison conditions is any less disruptive of federal-state relations than an attack on prison conditions joined with a plea for restoration of good-time credits. . . . Yet the Court holds today that exhaustion is required where a prisoner attacks the deprivation of good-time credits, but not where he challenges only the conditions of his confinement. It seems obvious to me that both of those propositions cannot be correct.

Finally, the Court's decision may have the ironic effect of turning a situation where state and federal courts are not initially in conflict into a situation where precisely such conflict does result. Since respondents' actions would neither interrupt a state judicial proceeding nor, even if successful, require the invalidation of a state judicial decision, "[t]he question is simply whether one court or another is going to decide the case." Note, Exhaustion of State Remedies Under the Civil Rights Act, 68 Colum. L. Rev. 1201, 1205–06 (1968). If we had held, consistently with our prior cases, that the plaintiff has the right to choose a federal forum, the exercise of that right would not offend or embarrass a state court with concurrent jurisdiction. Now, however, a prisoner who seeks restoration of good-time credits must proceed first in state court, although he has the option of petitioning the federal court for relief if his state suit is unsuccessful. If the prisoner does resort to a federal habeas corpus action, the potential for friction with the State is certain to increase. The State is likely, after all, to derive little pleasure from the federal court's effort to determine whether there was "either an absence of available State corrective process or the existence of circumstances rendering such process ineffective to protect the rights of the prisoner." 28 U.S.C. § 2254(b). And since it is the validity of the state court's decision that is placed in issue, the State will have to endure a federal court inquiry into whether the State's factfinding process was adequate to afford a full and fair hearing, 28 U.S.C. § 2254(d)(2), whether the petitioner was denied due process of law in the state court proceeding, § 2254(d)(7), and whether the state court's factual determinations were fairly supported by the record, § 2254(d)(8). Cf. Townsend v. Sain, 372 U.S. 293 (1963). Since none of these questions would even arise if the Court had held these actions properly brought under § 1983, it seems a good deal premature to proclaim today's decision a major victory in our continuing effort to achieve a harmonious and healthy federal-state system.

IV

In short, I see no basis for concluding that jurisdiction under § 1983 is, in this instance, pre-empted by the habeas corpus remedy. Respondents' effort to bring these suits under the provisions of the Ku Klux Klan Act should not be viewed as an attempted circumvention of the exhaustion requirement of the habeas corpus statute, for the effort does not in any sense conflict with the policies underlying that requirement. By means of these suits, they demand an immediate end to action under color of state law that has the alleged effect of violating fundamental rights guaranteed by the Federal Constitution. The Ku Klux Klan Act was designed to afford an expeditious federal hearing for the resolution of precisely such claims as these. Since I share the Court's view that exhaustion of state judicial remedies is not required in any suit properly brought in federal court under § 1983 and since I am convinced that respondents have properly invoked the jurisdictional grant of § 1983, I would affirm the judgment of the Court of Appeals.

NOTES ON THE RELATION OF § 1983 TO HABEAS CORPUS

1. RES JUDICATA

If a state court is first to judgment on the merits of a question of federal constitutional law by virtue of the exhaustion of state remedies or an abstention doctrine, is that the end of the matter? Is subsequent federal-court consideration foreclosed by res judicata?

The answer is "yes," and "no." As illustrated by Allen v. McCurry, 449 U.S. 90 (1980), which appears together with accompanying notes as a main case in Section 3 below, normal res judicata principles are applicable in § 1983 litigation. Thus, a prior state-court judgment can foreclose federal court resolution of a constitutional issue in a § 1983 suit if the conditions for invoking the doctrine of res judicata are fully met.

But, as *Preiser* says, "[p]rinciples of res judicata are not wholly applicable to habeas corpus proceedings." Among the complexities of federal habeas corpus are special rules governing when an issue that was or could have been litigated in state court can be raised in a subsequent federal habeas proceeding. Doctrines addressing this issue have been developed independently of the law of res judicata, and so it is accurate to say that res judicata, as such, is not "wholly applicable to habeas proceedings." Thus the mere fact of exhaustion of state remedies is not an automatic foreclosure of federal habeas relief.

2. QUESTIONS AND COMMENTS ON THE RELATION OF § 1983 TO HABEAS CORPUS

There is an obvious tension between § 1983 and habeas corpus. Consider, for example, a claim based on evidence discovered after conviction that a state prosecutor knowingly used perjured testimony. It is likely that such a claim could be presented to the state courts for adjudication. Every state has a post-conviction process in which this kind of claim could be presented.

But § 1983 does not require exhaustion of state remedies and *Younger v. Harris* does not require abstention once the state criminal proceedings are over. Does this mean that a convicted defendant could go directly to federal court under § 1983 and seek an injunction to prevent enforcement of the state criminal sentence?

As *Preiser* says, it is the major function of modern federal habeas to provide an avenue for such relief. And habeas has an exhaustion requirement. If § 1983 is available in such a case, the habeas exhaustion requirement would become a dead letter and, indeed, federal habeas as the avenue of relief for such cases would become obsolete. If the two remedies are to retain independent functions, therefore, it is clear that some line must be drawn between them. Does *Preiser* draw the right line? Should it be drawn elsewhere?[a]

3. RELATION OF *PREISER* TO § 1983 ACTIONS FOR DAMAGES

Preiser contemplates the possibility of a prisoner seeking state court relief from the terms and conditions of confinement and simultaneously seeking money damages in a federal court under § 1983. It also raises the possibility of a federal § 1983 suit for money damages involving issues that could be raised in a pending state criminal trial or appeal. *Younger*, recall, precluded only suits for declaratory judgment or injunction. It did not address damage claims.

The disposition of § 1983 suits for damages involving issues relevant to pending or completed state criminal proceedings was addressed by the Supreme Court in the next main case.

[a] For extensive analysis of the considerable body of decisional law that emerged following *Preiser* and some proposed solutions to issues it left open, see Martin Schwartz, The *Preiser* Puzzle: Continued Frustrating Conflict Between the Civil Rights and Habeas Corpus Remedies for State Prisoners, 37 De Paul L. Rev. 85 (1988). The administration of the *Preiser* holding after the Antiterrorism and Effective Death Penalty Act (AEDPA) is explored and proposed reforms suggested in Nancy J. King & Suzanna Sherry, Habeas Corpus and State Sentencing Reform: A Story of Unintended Consequences, 58 Duke L.J. 1 (2008).

Heck v. Humphrey

Supreme Court of the United States, 1994.
512 U.S. 477.

■ JUSTICE SCALIA delivered the opinion of the Court.

This case presents the question whether a state prisoner may challenge the constitutionality of his conviction in a suit for damages under 42 U.S.C. § 1983.

I

Petitioner Roy Heck was convicted in Indiana state court of voluntary manslaughter for the killing of Rickie Heck, his wife, and is serving a 15–year sentence in an Indiana prison. While the appeal from his conviction was pending, petitioner . . . filed this suit in federal district court under 42 U.S.C. § 1983, naming as defendants respondents James Humphrey and Robert Ewbank, Dearborn County prosecutors, and Michael Krinoph, an investigator with the Indiana State Police. The complaint alleged that respondents, acting under color of state law, had engaged in an "unlawful, unreasonable, and arbitrary investigation" leading to petitioner's arrest; "knowingly destroyed" evidence "which was exculpatory in nature and could have proved [petitioner's] innocence"; and caused "an illegal and unlawful voice identification procedure" to be used at petitioner's trial. The complaint sought, among other things, compensatory and punitive monetary damages. It did not ask for injunctive relief, and petitioner has not sought release from custody in this action.

The District Court dismissed the action without prejudice, because the issues it raised "directly implicate the legality of [petitioner's] confinement." While petitioner's appeal to the Seventh Circuit was pending, the Indiana Supreme Court upheld his conviction and sentence on direct appeal; his first petition for a writ of habeas corpus in Federal District Court was dismissed because it contained unexhausted claims; and his second federal habeas petition was denied, and the denial affirmed by the Seventh Circuit.

When the Seventh Circuit reached petitioner's appeal from dismissal of his § 1983 complaint, it affirmed the judgment and approved the reasoning of the District Court: "If, regardless of the relief sought, the plaintiff [in a federal civil rights action] is challenging the legality of his conviction,[2] so that if he won his case the state would be obliged to release him even if he hadn't sought that relief, the suit is classified as an application for habeas corpus and the plaintiff must exhaust his state remedies, on pain of dismissal if he fails to do so." Heck filed a petition for certiorari, which we granted.

---

[2] Neither in his petition for certiorari nor in his principal brief on the merits did petitioner contest the description of his monetary claims (by both the District Court and the Court of Appeals) as challenging the legality of his conviction. Thus, the question we understood to be before us was whether money damages premised on an unlawful conviction could be pursued under § 1983. Petitioner sought to challenge this premise in his reply brief, contending that findings validating his damages claims would not invalidate his conviction. That argument comes too late. We did not take this case to review such a fact-bound issue, and we accept the characterization of the lower courts.

We also decline to pursue, without implying the nonexistence of, another issue, suggested by the Court of Appeals' statement that, if petitioner's "conviction were proper, this suit would in all likelihood be barred by res judicata." The res judicata effect of state-court decisions in § 1983 actions is a matter of state law. See Migra v. Warren City School Dist. Bd. of Ed., 465 U.S. 75 (1984).

II

This case lies at the intersection of the two most fertile sources of federal-court prisoner litigation—the Civil Rights Act of 1871, 42 U.S.C. § 1983, and the federal habeas corpus statute, 28 U.S.C. § 2254. Both of these provide access to a federal forum for claims of unconstitutional treatment at the hands of state officials, but they differ in their scope and operation. In general, exhaustion of state remedies "is *not* a prerequisite to an action under § 1983," Patsy v. Board of Regents of Fla., 457 U.S. 496, 501 (1982) (emphasis added), even an action by a state prisoner. The federal habeas corpus statute, by contrast, requires that state prisoners first seek redress in a state forum. See Rose v. Lundy, 455 U.S. 509 (1982).

Preiser v. Rodriguez, 411 U.S. 475 (1973), considered the potential overlap between these two provisions, and held that habeas corpus is the exclusive remedy for a state prisoner who challenges the fact or duration of his confinement and seeks immediate or speedier release, even though such a claim may come within the literal terms of § 1983. We emphasize that *Preiser* did *not* create an exception to the "no exhaustion" rule of § 1983; it merely held that certain claims by state prisoners are not *cognizable* under that provision, and must be brought in habeas corpus proceedings, which do contain an exhaustion requirement.

This case is clearly not covered by the holding of *Preiser*, for petitioner seeks not immediate or speedier release, but monetary damages, as to which he could not "have sought and obtained fully effective relief through federal habeas corpus proceedings." Id., at 488. In dictum, however, *Preiser* asserted that since a state prisoner seeking only damages "is attacking something other than the fact or length of . . . confinement, and . . . is seeking something other than immediate or more speedy release[,] . . . a damages action by a state prisoner could be brought under [§ 1983] in federal court without any requirement of prior exhaustion of state remedies." That statement may not be true, however, when establishing the basis for the damages claim necessarily demonstrates the invalidity of the conviction. In that situation, the claimant *can* be said to be "attacking the fact or length of confinement," bringing the suit within the other dictum of *Preiser*: "Congress has determined that habeas corpus is the appropriate remedy for state prisoners attacking the validity of the fact or length of their confinement, and that specific determination must override the general terms of § 1983." In the last analysis, we think the dicta of *Preiser* to be an unreliable, if not an unintelligible, guide: that opinion had no cause to address, and did not carefully consider, the damages question before us today.

. . . To answer that question correctly, we see no need to abandon, as the Seventh Circuit and those courts in agreement with it have done, our teaching that § 1983 contains no exhaustion requirement beyond what Congress has provided. The issue with respect to monetary damages challenging conviction is not, it seems to us, exhaustion; but rather, the same as the issue was with respect to injunctive relief challenging conviction in *Preiser*: whether the claim is cognizable under § 1983 at all. We conclude that it is not.

"We have repeatedly noted that 42 U.S.C. § 1983 creates a species of tort liability." Memphis Community School Dist. v. Stachura, 477 U.S. 299, 305 (1986). "[O]ver the centuries the common law of torts has developed a set of rules to implement the principle that a person should be compensated fairly for injuries caused by the violation of his legal rights. These rules, defining the elements of damages and the prerequisites for their recovery, provide the appropriate starting point for the inquiry under § 1983 as well." Carey v. Piphus, 435 U.S. 247, 257–58 (1978). Thus, to determine whether there is any bar to the present suit, we look first to the common law of torts.

The common-law cause of action for malicious prosecution provides the closest analogy to claims of the type considered here because, unlike the related cause of action for false arrest or imprisonment, it permits damages for confinement imposed pursuant to legal process. "If there is a false arrest claim, damages for that claim cover the time of detention up until issuance of process or arraignment, but not more." W. Keeton, D. Dobbs, R. Keeton, & D. Owen, Prosser and Keeton on Law of Torts 888 (5th ed. 1984). But a successful malicious prosecution plaintiff may recover, in addition to general damages, "compensation for any arrest or imprisonment, including damages for discomfort or injury to his health, or loss of time and deprivation of the society." Id., at 887–88 (footnotes omitted).

One element that must be alleged and proved in a malicious prosecution action is termination of the prior criminal proceeding in favor of the accused. Prosser and Keeton, supra, at 874. This requirement "avoids parallel litigation over the issues of probable cause and guilt . . . and it precludes the possibility of the claimant [sic] succeeding in the tort action after having been convicted in the underlying criminal prosecution, in contravention of a strong judicial policy against the creation of two conflicting resolutions arising out of the same or identical transaction." 8 S. Speiser, C. Krause, & A. Gans, American Law of Torts § 28:5, p. 24 (1991). Furthermore, "to permit a convicted criminal defendant to proceed with a malicious prosecution claim would permit a collateral attack on the conviction through the vehicle of a civil suit." Ibid.[4] This Court has long expressed similar concerns for finality and consistency and has generally declined to expand opportunities for collateral attack, see Parke v. Raley, 506 U.S. 20 (1992); Teague v. Lane, 489 U.S. 288, 308 (1989). We think the hoary principle that civil tort actions are not appropriate vehicles for challenging the validity of outstanding criminal judgments applies to § 1983 damages actions that necessarily require the plaintiff to prove the unlawfulness of his

[4] Justice Souter criticizes our reliance on malicious prosecution's favorable termination requirement as illustrative of the common-law principle barring tort plaintiffs from mounting collateral attacks on their outstanding criminal convictions. Malicious prosecution is an inapt analogy, he says, because "[a] defendant's conviction, under Reconstruction-era common law, dissolved his claim for malicious prosecution because the conviction was regarded as irrebuttable evidence that the prosecution never lacked probable cause," citing T. Cooley, Law of Torts 185 (1879). Chief Justice Cooley no doubt intended merely to set forth the general rule that a conviction defeated the malicious prosecution plaintiff's allegation (essential to his cause of action) that the prior proceeding was without probable cause. But this was not an absolute rule in all jurisdictions, and early on it was recognized that there must be exceptions to the rule in cases involving circumstances such as fraud, perjury, or mistake of law [Citations omitted.] Some cases even held that a "conviction, although it be afterwards reversed, is prima facie evidence—and that only—of the existence of probable cause." Neher v. Dobbs, 47 Neb. 863, 868, 66 N.W. 864, 865 (1896) (collecting cases). . . . Yet even if Justice Souter were correct in asserting that a prior conviction, although reversed, "dissolved [a] claim for malicious prosecution," our analysis would be unaffected. It would simply demonstrate that no common-law action, not even malicious prosecution, would permit a criminal proceeding to be impugned in a tort action, even after the conviction had been reversed. That would, if anything, strengthen our belief that § 1983, which borrowed general tort principles, was not meant to permit such collateral attack.

conviction or confinement, just as it has always applied to actions for malicious prosecution.[5]

We hold that, in order to recover damages for allegedly unconstitutional conviction or imprisonment, or for other harm caused by actions whose unlawfulness would render a conviction or sentence invalid,[6] a § 1983 plaintiff must prove that the conviction or sentence has been reversed on direct appeal, expunged by executive order, declared invalid by a state tribunal authorized to make such determination, or called into question by a federal court's issuance of a writ of habeas corpus, 28 U.S.C. § 2254. A claim for damages bearing that relationship to a conviction or sentence that has not been so invalidated is not cognizable under § 1983. Thus, when a state prisoner seeks damages in a § 1983 suit, the district court must consider whether a judgment in favor of the plaintiff would necessarily imply the invalidity of his conviction or sentence; if it would, the complaint must be dismissed unless the plaintiff can demonstrate that the conviction or sentence has already been invalidated. But if the district court determines that the plaintiff's action, even if successful, will not demonstrate the invalidity of any outstanding criminal judgment against the plaintiff, the action should be allowed to proceed,[7] in the absence of some other bar to the suit.[8]

---

[5] Justice Souter's discussion of abuse of process does not undermine this principle. It is true that favorable termination of prior proceedings is not an element of that cause of action—but neither is an impugning of those proceedings one of its consequences. The gravamen of that tort is not the wrongfulness of the prosecution, but some extortionate perversion of lawfully initiated process to illegitimate ends. [Citations omitted.] Cognizable injury for abuse of process is limited to the harm caused by the misuse of process, and does not include harm (such as conviction and confinement) resulting from that process's being carried through to its lawful conclusion. Thus, one could no more seek compensatory damages for an outstanding criminal conviction in an action for abuse of process than in one for malicious prosecution. . . .

[6] An example of this latter category—a § 1983 action that does not seek damages directly attributable to conviction or confinement but whose successful prosecution would necessarily imply that the plaintiff's criminal conviction was wrongful—would be the following: A state defendant is convicted of and sentenced for the crime of resisting arrest, defined as intentionally preventing a peace officer from effecting a lawful arrest. . . . He then brings a § 1983 action against the arresting officer, seeking damages for violation of his Fourth Amendment right to be free from unreasonable seizures. In order to prevail in this § 1983 action, he would have to negate an element of the offense of which he has been convicted. Regardless of the state law concerning res judicata, the § 1983 action will not lie.

[7] For example, a suit for damages attributable to an allegedly unreasonable search may lie even if the challenged search produced evidence that was introduced in a state criminal trial resulting in the § 1983 plaintiff's still-outstanding conviction. Because of doctrines like independent source and inevitable discovery, see Murray v. United States, 487 U.S. 533, 539 (1988), and especially harmless error, see Arizona v. Fulminante, 499 U.S. 279, 307–08 (1991), such a § 1983 action, even if successful, would not *necessarily* imply that the plaintiff's conviction was unlawful. In order to recover compensatory damages, however, the § 1983 plaintiff must prove not only that the search was unlawful, but that it caused him actual, compensable injury, see Memphis Community School Dist. v. Stachura, 477 U.S. 299, 308 (1986), which, we hold today, does *not* encompass the "injury" of being convicted and imprisoned (until his conviction has been overturned).

[8] For example, if a state criminal defendant brings a federal civil-rights lawsuit during the pendency of his criminal trial, appeal, or state habeas action, abstention may be an appropriate response to the parallel state-court proceedings. See Colorado River Water Conservation Dist. v. United States, 424 U.S. 800 (1976).

Moreover, we do not decide whether abstention might be appropriate in cases where a state prisoner brings a § 1983 damages suit raising an issue that also could be grounds for relief in a state-court challenge to his conviction or sentence. Cf. Tower v. Glover, 467 U.S. 914, 923 (1984).

Respondents had urged us to adopt a rule that was in one respect broader than this: exhaustion of state remedies should be required, they contended, not just when success in the § 1983 damages suit would necessarily show a conviction or sentence to be unlawful, but whenever "judgment in a § 1983 action would resolve a necessary element to a likely challenge to a conviction, even if the § 1983 court [need] not determine that the conviction is invalid." Brief for Respondent 26, n.10. Such a broad sweep was needed, respondents contended, lest a judgment in a prisoner's favor in a federal-court § 1983 damage action claiming, for example, a Fourth Amendment violation, be given preclusive effect as to that sub-issue in a subsequent state-court postconviction proceeding. Preclusion might result, they asserted, if the state exercised sufficient control over the officials' defense in the § 1983 action. While we have no occasion to rule on the matter at this time, it is at least plain that preclusion will not necessarily be an automatic, or even a permissible, effect.[9]

In another respect, however, our holding sweeps more broadly than the approach respondents had urged. We do not engraft an exhaustion requirement upon § 1983, but rather deny the existence of a cause of action. Even a prisoner who has fully exhausted available state remedies has no cause of action under § 1983 unless and until the conviction or sentence is reversed, expunged, invalidated, or impugned by the grant of a writ of habeas corpus. That makes it unnecessary for us to address the statute-of-limitations issue wrestled with by the Court of Appeals, which concluded that a federal doctrine of equitable tolling would apply to the § 1983 cause of action while state challenges to the conviction or sentence were being exhausted. (The court distinguished our cases holding that state, not federal, tolling provisions apply in § 1983 actions, see Board of Regents v. Tomanio, 446 U.S. 478 (1980); Hardin v. Straub, 490 U.S. 536 (1989), on the ground that petitioner's claim was "in part one for habeas corpus.") Under our analysis the statute of limitations poses no difficulty while the state challenges are being pursued, since the § 1983 claim has not yet arisen. Just as a cause of action for malicious prosecution does not accrue until the criminal proceedings have terminated in the plaintiff's favor, 1 C. Corman, Limitation of Actions § 7.4.1, p. 532 (1991), so also a § 1983 cause of action for damages attributable to an unconstitutional conviction or sentence does not accrue until the conviction or sentence has been invalidated.[10]

---

[9] State courts are bound to apply federal rules in determining the preclusive effect of federal-court decisions on issues of federal law. . . . The federal rules on the subject of issue and claim preclusion, unlike those relating to exhaustion of state remedies, are [almost entirely judge-made.] And in developing them the courts can, and indeed should, be guided by the federal policies reflected in congressional enactments. . . . Thus, the court-made preclusion rules may, as judicial application of the categorical mandate of § 1983 may *not*, take account of the policy embodied in § 2254(b)'s exhaustion requirement that state courts be given the first opportunity to review constitutional claims bearing upon state prisoners' release from custody.

[10] Justice Souter also adopts the common-law principle that one cannot use the device of a civil tort action to challenge the validity of an outstanding criminal conviction, but thinks it necessary to abandon that principle in those cases (of which no real-life example comes to mind) involving former state prisoners who, because they are no longer in custody, cannot bring postconviction challenges. We think the principle barring collateral attacks—a longstanding and deeply rooted feature of both the common law and our own jurisprudence—is not rendered inapplicable by the fortuity that a convicted criminal is no longer incarcerated. Justice Souter opines that disallowing a damages suit for a former state prisoner framed by Ku Klux Klan-dominated state officials is "hard indeed to reconcile . . . with the purpose of § 1983." But if, as Justice Souter appears to suggest, the goal of our interpretive enterprise under § 1983 were to provide a remedy for all conceivable invasions of federal rights that freedmen may have suffered at the hands of officials of the former States of the Confederacy, the entire landscape of our § 1983 jurisprudence would look very different. We would not, for

Applying these principles to the present action, in which both courts below found that the damage claims challenged the legality of the conviction, we find that the dismissal of the action was correct. The judgment of the Court of Appeals for the Seventh Circuit is

Affirmed.

■ JUSTICE THOMAS, concurring.

The Court and Justice Souter correctly begin their analyses with the realization that "[t]his case lies at the intersection of . . . the Civil Rights Act of 1871, 42 U.S.C. § 1983, and the federal habeas corpus statute, 28 U.S.C. § 2254." One need only read the respective opinions in this case to understand the difficulty of the task before the Court today. Both the Court and Justice Souter embark on a similar enterprise—harmonizing "[t]he broad language of § 1983," a "general" statute, with "the specific federal habeas corpus statute." Preiser v. Rodriguez, 411 U.S. 475, 489 (1973).

I write separately to note that it is we who have put § 1983 and the habeas statute on what Justice Souter appropriately terms a "collision course." It has long been recognized that we have expanded the prerogative writ of habeas corpus and § 1983 far beyond the limited scope either was originally intended to have. Expanding the two historic statutes brought them squarely into conflict in the context of suits by state prisoners, as we made clear in *Preiser*.

Given that the Court created the tension between the two statutes, it is proper for the Court to devise limitations aimed at ameliorating the conflict, provided that it does so in a principled fashion. Because the Court today limits the scope of § 1983 in a manner consistent both with the federalism concerns undergirding the explicit exhaustion requirement of the habeas statute and with the state of the common law at the time § 1983 was enacted, I join the Court's opinion.

■ JUSTICE SOUTER, with whom JUSTICE BLACKMUN, JUSTICE STEVENS, and JUSTICE O'CONNOR join, concurring in the judgment.

The Court begins its analysis as I would, by observing that "[t]his case lies at the intersection of the two most fertile sources of federal-court prisoner litigation—the Civil Rights Act of 1871, 42 U.S.C. § 1983, and the federal habeas corpus statute, 28 U.S.C. § 2254," two statutes that "provide access to a federal forum for claims of unconstitutional treatment at the hands of state officials," while "differ[ing] in their scope and operation." But instead of analyzing the statutes to determine which should yield to the other at this intersection, the Court appears to take the position that the statutes were never on a collision course in the first place because, like the common-law tort of malicious prosecution, § 1983 requires (and, presumably, has always required) plaintiffs seeking damages for unconstitutional conviction or confinement to show the favorable termination of the underlying proceeding.

While I do not object to referring to the common law when resolving the question this case presents, I do not think that the existence of the tort of malicious prosecution alone provides the answer. Common-law tort rules can provide a "starting point for the inquiry under § 1983," Carey v. Piphus, 435 U.S. 247, 258 (1978), but we have relied on the common law in

example, have adopted the rule that judicial officers have absolute immunity from liability for damages under § 1983, a rule that would prevent recovery by a former slave who had been tried and convicted before a corrupt state judge in league with the Ku Klux Klan.

§ 1983 cases only when doing so was thought to be consistent with ordinary rules of statutory construction, as when common-law principles have textual support in other provisions of the Civil Rights Act of 1871, see, e.g., id., at 255–56 (damages under § 1983), or when those principles were so fundamental and widely understood at the time § 1983 was enacted that the 42d Congress could not be presumed to have abrogated them silently, see, e.g., Tenney v. Brandhove, 341 U.S. 367, 376 (1951) (immunity under § 1983); Pierson v. Ray, 386 U.S. 547, 553–54 (1967) (same). At the same time, we have consistently refused to allow common-law analogies to displace statutory analysis, declining to import even well-settled common-law rules into § 1983 "if [the statute's] history or purpose counsel against applying [such rules] in § 1983 actions." Wyatt v. Cole, 504 U.S. 158, 164 (1992). Cf. Anderson v. Creighton, 483 U.S. 635, 645 (1987) ("[W]e have never suggested that the precise contours of official immunity [under § 1983] can and should be slavishly derived from the often arcane rules of the common law").

An examination of common-law sources arguably relevant in this case confirms the soundness of our hierarchy of principles for resolving questions concerning § 1983. If the common law were not merely a "starting point" for the analysis under § 1983, but its destination, then (unless we were to have some authority to choose common-law requirements we like and discard the others) principle would compel us to accept as elements of the § 1983 cause of action not only the malicious-prosecution tort's favorable-termination requirement, but other elements of the tort that cannot coherently be transplanted. In addition to proving favorable termination, a plaintiff in a malicious prosecution action, according to the same sources the Court relies upon, must prove the "[a]bsence of probable cause for the proceeding" as well as " '[m]alice,' or a primary purpose other than that of bringing an offender to justice." W. Keeton, D. Dobbs, R. Keeton, & D. Owen, Prosser and Keeton on the Law of Torts 871 (5th ed. 1984); see also 8 S. Speiser, C. Krause, & A. Gans, American Law of Torts § 28:7, p. 38, § 28:11, p. 61 (1991). As § 1983 requirements, however, these elements would mean that even a § 1983 plaintiff whose conviction was invalidated as unconstitutional (premised, for example, on a confession coerced by an interrogation-room beating) could not obtain damages for the unconstitutional conviction and ensuing confinement if the defendant police officials (or perhaps the prosecutor) had probable cause to believe the plaintiff was guilty and intended to bring him to justice. Absent an independent statutory basis for doing so, importing into § 1983 the malicious-prosecution tort's favorable-termination requirement but not its probable-cause requirement would be particularly odd since it is from the latter that the former derives. See Prosser and Keeton, supra, at 874 ("The requirement that the criminal prosecution terminate in favor of the malicious prosecution plaintiff . . . is primarily important not as an independent element of the malicious prosecution action but only for what it shows about probable cause or guilt-in-fact"); M. Bigelow, Leading Cases on the Law of Torts 196 (1875) ("The action for a malicious prosecution cannot be maintained until the prosecution has terminated; for otherwise the plaintiff might obtain judgment in the one case and yet be convicted in the other, which would of course disprove the averment of a want of probable cause.").

If, in addition, the common law were the master of statutory analysis, not the servant (to switch metaphors), we would find ourselves with two masters to contend with here, for we would be subject not only to the tort of malicious prosecution but to the tort of abuse of process as well, see *Wyatt v. Cole*, supra, at 164 (calling these two actions "the most closely analogous torts" to § 1983), the latter making it "unnecessary for the plaintiff to prove that the proceeding has terminated in his favor." Prosser and Keeton, supra, at 897. The Court suggests that the tort of malicious prosecution provides "the closest analogy to claims of the type considered here" because "it permits damages for confinement imposed pursuant to legal process." But the same appears to be true for the tort of abuse of process. See Restatement (Second) of Torts § 682, Illustration 1 (1977). . . . [2]

Furthermore, even if the tort of malicious prosecution were today marginally more analogous than other torts to the type of § 1983 claim in the class of cases before us (because it alone may permit damages for unlawful conviction or postconviction confinement, see n.3, infra), the Court overlooks a significant historical incongruity that calls into question the utility of the analogy to the tort of malicious prosecution insofar as it is used exclusively to determine the scope of § 1983: the damages sought in the type of § 1983 claim involved here, damages for unlawful conviction or postconviction confinement, were not available at all in an action for malicious prosecution at the time of § 1983's enactment. A defendant's conviction, under Reconstruction-era common law, dissolved his claim for malicious prosecution because the conviction was regarded as irrebuttable evidence that the prosecution never lacked probable cause. See T. Cooley, Law of Torts 185 (1879) ("If the defendant is convicted in the first instance and appeals, and is acquitted in the appellate court, the conviction below is conclusive of probable cause"). Thus the definition of "favorable termination" with which the framers of § 1983 were aware (if they were aware of any definition) included none of the events relevant to the type of § 1983 claim involved in this case ("revers[al] on direct appeal, expunge[ment] by executive order, [a] declar[ation] [of] invalid[ity] by a state tribunal authorized to make such determination, or [the] call[ing] into question by a federal court's issuance of a writ of habeas corpus"), and it is easy to see why the analogy to the tort of malicious prosecution in this context has escaped the collective wisdom of the many courts and commentators to have previously addressed the issue, as well as the parties to this case. Indeed, relying on the tort of malicious prosecution to dictate the outcome of this case would logically drive one to the position, untenable as a matter of statutory interpretation (and, to be clear, disclaimed by the Court), that conviction of a crime wipes out a person's § 1983 claim for damages for unconstitutional conviction or postconviction confinement.[3]

---

[2] As the Court observes, there are differences between the tort of abuse of process and that of malicious prosecution. While "the gist of the tort [of malicious prosecution] is . . . commencing an action or causing process to issue without justification," abuse of process involves "misusing, or misapplying process justified in itself for an end other than that which it was designed to accomplish." Prosser and Keeton, supra, at 897. Neither common-law tort, however, precisely matches the statutory § 1983 claim for damages for unlawful conviction or confinement; and, depending on the nature of the underlying right alleged to have been violated (consider, for example, the right not to be selected for prosecution solely because of one's race), the tort of abuse of process might provide a better analogy to a § 1983 claim for unconstitutional conviction or confinement than the malicious-prosecution tort.

[3] Some of the traditional common-law requirements appear to have liberalized over the years, see Prosser and Keeton, supra, at 882 ("[t]here is a considerable minority view which regards the conviction as creating only a presumption, which may be rebutted by any competent evidence showing that probable cause for the prosecution did not in fact exist"), strengthening the analogy the Court draws. But surely the Court is not of the view that a single tort in its late 20th-century form can conclusively (and retroactively) dictate the requirements of a 19th-century statute for a discrete category of cases. Defending the historical analogy, the Court suggests that Chief Justice Cooley did not mean what he clearly said and that, despite

We are not, however, in any such strait, for our enquiry in this case may follow the interpretive methodology employed in Preiser v. Rodriguez, 411 U.S. 475 (1973). . . . In *Preiser*, we read the "general" § 1983 statute in light of the "specific federal habeas corpus statute," which applies only to "person[s] in custody," 28 U.S.C. § 2254(a), and the habeas statute's policy, embodied in its exhaustion requirement, § 2254(b), that state courts be given the first opportunity to review constitutional claims bearing upon a state prisoner's release from custody. Though in contrast to *Preiser* the state prisoner here seeks damages, not release from custody, the distinction makes no difference when the damages sought are for unconstitutional conviction or confinement. (As the Court explains, nothing in *Preiser* . . . is properly read as holding that the relief sought in a § 1983 action dictates whether a state prisoner can proceed immediately to federal court.) Whether or not a federal-court § 1983 damages judgment against state officials in such an action would have preclusive effect in later litigation against the state, mounting damages against the defendant-officials for unlawful confinement (damages almost certainly to be paid by state indemnification) would, practically, compel the state to release the prisoner. Because allowing a state prisoner to proceed directly with a federal-court § 1983 attack on his conviction or sentence "would wholly frustrate explicit congressional intent" as declared in the habeas exhaustion requirement, the statutory scheme must be read as precluding such attacks. This conclusion flows not from a preference about how the habeas and § 1983 statutes ought to have been written, but from a recognition that "Congress has determined that habeas corpus is the appropriate remedy for state prisoners attacking the validity of the fact or length of their confinement, [a] specific determination [that] must override the general terms of § 1983." *Preiser*, supra, at 490.

That leaves the question of how to implement what statutory analysis requires. It is at this point that the malicious-prosecution tort's favorable-termination requirement becomes helpful, not in dictating the elements of a § 1983 cause of action, but in suggesting a relatively simple way to avoid collisions at the intersection of habeas and § 1983. A state prisoner may seek federal-court § 1983 damages for unconstitutional conviction or confinement, but only if he has previously established the unlawfulness of his conviction or confinement, as on appeal or on habeas. This has the effect of requiring a state prisoner challenging the lawfulness of his confinement to follow habeas's rules before seeking § 1983 damages for unlawful confinement in federal court, and it is ultimately the Court's holding today. It neatly resolves a problem that has bedeviled lower courts and law students (some of whom doubtless have run up against a case like this in law-school exams). The favorable-termination requirement avoids the knotty statute-of-limitations problem that arises if federal courts dismiss § 1983 suits filed before an inmate pursues federal habeas, and (because the statute-of-limitations clock does not start ticking until an inmate's conviction is set

the Cooley treatise, the Reconstruction-era common-law recognized a limited exception to the rule denying a malicious-prosecution plaintiff the benefit of the invalidation of his conviction: an exception for convictions "obtained by some type of fraud." Even if such a narrow exception existed, however, the tort of malicious prosecution as it stood during the mid–19th century would still make for a weak analogy to a statutory action under which, as even the Court accepts, defendants whose convictions were reversed as violating "any righ[t] . . . secured by the Constitution," 42 U.S.C. § 1983, may obtain damages for the unlawful confinement associated with the conviction (assuming, of course, no immunity bar). Nor, of course, would the existence of such an exception explain how one element of a malicious-prosecution action may be imported into § 1983, but not the others.

aside) it does so without requiring federal courts to stay, and therefore to retain on their dockets, prematurely filed § 1983 suits.[4]

It may be that the Court's analysis takes it no further than I would thus go, and that any objection I may have to the Court's opinion is to style, not substance. The Court acknowledges the habeas exhaustion requirement and explains that it is the reason that the habeas statute "intersect[s]" in this case with § 1983, which does not require exhaustion; it describes the issue it faces as "the same" as that in *Preiser*; it recites the principle that common-law tort rules " 'provide the appropriate starting point for the inquiry under § 1983' "; and it does not transpose onto § 1983 elements of the malicious-prosecution tort that are incompatible with the policies of § 1983 and the habeas statute as relevant to claims by state prisoners. The Court's opinion can be read as saying nothing more than that now, after enactment of the habeas statute and because of it, prison inmates seeking § 1983 damages in federal court for unconstitutional conviction or confinement must satisfy a requirement analogous to the malicious-prosecution tort's favorable-termination requirement.

That would be a sensible way to read the opinion, in part because the alternative would needlessly place at risk the rights of those outside the intersection of § 1983 and the habeas statute, individuals not "in custody" for habeas purposes. If these individuals (people who were merely fined, for example, or who have completed short terms of imprisonment, probation or parole, or who discover (through no fault of their own) a constitutional violation after full expiration of their sentences), like state prisoners, were required to show the prior invalidation of their convictions or sentences in order to obtain § 1983 damages for unconstitutional conviction or imprisonment, the result would be to deny any federal forum for claiming a deprivation of federal rights to those who cannot first obtain a favorable state ruling. The reason, of course, is that individuals not "in custody" cannot invoke federal habeas jurisdiction, the only statutory mechanism besides § 1983 by which individuals may sue state officials in federal court for violating federal rights. That would be an untoward result.

It is one thing to adopt a rule that forces prison inmates to follow the federal habeas route with claims that fall within the plain language of § 1983 when that is necessary to prevent a requirement of the habeas statute from being undermined. That is what the Court did in *Preiser*, and that is what the Court's rule would do for state prisoners. Harmonizing § 1983 and the habeas statute by requiring a state prisoner seeking damages for

[4] The requirement that a state prisoner seeking § 1983 damages for unlawful conviction or confinement be successful in state court or on federal habeas strikes me as soundly rooted in the statutory scheme. Because "Congress has determined that habeas corpus is the appropriate remedy for state prisoners attacking the validity of the fact or length of their confinement, [a] specific determination [that] override[s] the general terms of § 1983," *Preiser*, supra, at 490, a state prisoner whose constitutional attacks on his confinement have been rejected by state courts cannot be said to be unlawfully confined unless a federal habeas court declares his "custody [to be] in violation of the Constitution or laws or treaties of the United States," 28 U.S.C. § 2254(a). An unsuccessful federal habeas petitioner cannot, therefore, consistently with the habeas statute, receive § 1983 damages for unlawful confinement. That is not to say, however, that a state prisoner whose request for release has been (or would be) rejected by state courts or by a federal habeas court is necessarily barred from seeking any § 1983 damages for violations of his constitutional rights. If a § 1983 judgment in his favor would not demonstrate the invalidity of his confinement he is outside the habeas statute and may seek damages for a constitutional violation even without showing "favorable termination." A state prisoner may, for example, seek damages for an unreasonable search that produced evidence lawfully or harmlessly admitted at trial, or even nominal damages for, say, a violation of his right to procedural due process.

unconstitutional conviction to establish the previous invalidation of his conviction does not run afoul of what we have called, repeatedly, "[t]he very purpose of" § 1983: "to interpose the federal courts between the States and the people, as guardians of the people's federal rights." Mitchum v. Foster, 407 U.S. 225, 242 (1972). A prisoner caught at the intersection of § 1983 and the habeas statute can still have his attack on the lawfulness of his conviction or confinement heard in federal court, albeit one sitting as a habeas court; and, depending on the circumstances, he may be able to obtain § 1983 damages.

It would be an entirely different matter, however, to shut off federal courts altogether to claims that fall within the plain language of § 1983. "[I]rrespective of the common law support" for a general rule disfavoring collateral attacks, the Court lacks the authority to do any such thing absent unambiguous congressional direction where, as here, reading § 1983 to exclude claims from federal court would run counter to "§ 1983's history" and defeat the statute's "purpose." *Wyatt v. Cole*, supra. Consider the case of a former slave framed by Ku Klux Klan-controlled law-enforcement officers and convicted by a Klan-controlled state court of, for example, raping a white woman; and suppose that the unjustly convicted defendant did not (and could not) discover the proof of unconstitutionality until after his release from state custody. If it were correct to say that § 1983 independently requires a person not in custody to establish the prior invalidation of his conviction, it would have been equally right to tell the former slave that he could not seek federal relief even against the law-enforcement officers who framed him unless he first managed to convince the state courts that his conviction was unlawful. That would be a result hard indeed to reconcile either with the purpose of § 1983 or with the origins of what was "popularly known as the Ku Klux Act," Collins v. Hardyman, 341 U.S. 651, 657 (1951), the statute having been enacted in part out of concern that many state courts were "in league with those who were bent upon abrogation of federally protected rights," *Mitchum v. Foster*, supra, at 240. . . . It would also be a result unjustified by the habeas statute or any other post-§ 1983 enactment.

Nor do I see any policy reflected in a congressional enactment that would justify denying to an individual today federal damages (a significantly less disruptive remedy than an order compelling release from custody) merely because he was unconstitutionally fined by a state, or to a person who discovers after his release from prison that, for example, state officials deliberately withheld exculpatory material. And absent such a statutory policy, surely the common law can give us no authority to narrow the "broad language" of § 1983, which speaks of deprivations of "any" constitutional rights, privileges or immunities, by "[e]very" person acting under color of state law, and to which "we have given full effect [by] recognizing that [§ 1983] 'provide[s] a remedy to be broadly construed, against all forms of official violation of federally protected rights.' " Dennis v. Higgins, 498 U.S. 439, 443, 445 (1991).

In sum, while the malicious-prosecution analogy provides a useful mechanism for implementing what statutory analysis requires, congressional policy as reflected in enacted statutes must ultimately be the guide. I would thus be clear that the proper resolution of this case (involving, of course, a state prisoner) is to construe § 1983 in light of the habeas statute and its explicit policy of exhaustion. I would not cast doubt on the ability of an individual unaffected by the habeas statute to take advantage of the broad reach of § 1983.[a]

NOTES ON DAMAGES SUITS AND STATE CRIMINAL PROCEEDINGS

1. QUESTIONS AND COMMENTS

Joseph L. Hoffmann and Lauren K. Robel, Federal Court Supervision of State Criminal Justice Administration, 543 Annals Am. Acad. Pol. & Soc. 154 (1996), concludes that the "apparent breadth" of the holding in *Heck v. Humphrey* is misleading and that *Heck* actually "does very little to restrict § 1983 actions that might interfere with the policies of habeas law." As is suggested by the examples in Justice Scalia's footnote 7 and by his repeated use of the word "necessarily" when describing § 1983 as potentially undermining state conviction, there are many situations where § 1983 damages claims can proceed, even though they involve issues that in some sense were part of state criminal prosecutions. Simultaneous litigation will still be possible "so long as the plaintiff seeks to recover not for imprisonment, but instead only for those damages resulting directly from the unconstitutional conduct." As Justice Scalia implies in footnote 7, it may be difficult for the plaintiff to show an "actual, compensable injury" in some such cases, but there will be situations where physical injuries are alleged and there is always the possibility of punitive damages against individual defendants.

Are these big holes? Should the Court have gone further? Hoffmann and Robel say "yes." They argue that the issue should be whether the criminal defendant had a meaningful opportunity to get a merits resolution of the federal claim in a habeas proceeding. If so (and even if the opportunity was not pursued), they think that a § 1983 action should be barred.

By contrast, Justice Souter argues that the Court went too far. He believes that there is a class of criminal convictions where federal habeas corpus is unavailable and where it would therefore not be appropriate to limit the scope of § 1983. Justice Souter may be suggesting (and Justice Scalia rejecting) that § 1983 should be available as a form of collateral attack on state court judgments whenever they are immune from habeas review. Would this involve a significant class of cases?

Consider also the statute of limitations issues that will arise under *Heck*. Is Justice Scalia right that "the statute of limitations poses no difficulty"? Would a prudent lawyer wait until after the state criminal proceedings have concluded before filing a § 1983 claim in federal court?

Note finally that another aspect of *Heck* involves res judicata. Will cases arise after *Heck* in which a cause of action for damages can be asserted under § 1983 even though a state court has rejected the same claim on the merits in a prior criminal case? If so, what res judicata principles will be applied in the § 1983 action? One dimension of this issue was considered in *Allen v. McCurry*, which is considered in Section 3, infra.

---

[a] For sustained criticism of *Heck* as improperly making the § 1983 remedy depend on the existence of a common-law claim, see Jack M. Beermann, Common Law Elements of the Section 1983 Action, 72 Chi.–Kent L. Rev. 695 (1997).—[Footnote by eds.]

2. ABSTENTION: *DEAKINS V. MONAGHAN*

Justice Scalia anticipated that in some situations the § 1983 action "will not demonstrate the invalidity of any outstanding criminal judgment" and that in such cases, "the action should be allowed to proceed, in the absence of some other bar to the suit." He speculates in footnote 8 about what that other "bar" might be.

Deakins v. Monaghan, 484 U.S. 193 (1988), involved an eight-hour search of business premises during which hundreds of documents were seized. Various proceedings ensued before the state judge who had issued a warrant for the search in connection with grand jury proceedings. A § 1983 action was brought in federal court, seeking damages, an injunction, and attorney's fees on the ground that the search was unconstitititional, but the claim for injunctive relief was later withdrawn. The District Court dismissed the remaining damages claim in deference to the pending state grand jury proceedings. The Court of Appeals found dismissal inappropriate, but said that the District Court should have stayed its hand until the grand jury proceedings concluded. An indictment was then returned (without reliance on the disputed materials) against the § 1983 plaintiffs. After the indictment, the state trial court took jurisdiction over the question whether the disputed documents should be returned or whether they would be available for use in the pending criminal trial. The question decided by the Supreme Court was whether the District Court had properly dismissed the § 1983 complaint.

(i) Justice Blackmun's Opinion

Justice Blackmun wrote for the Court:

> Petitioners argue that the *Younger* doctrine—which requires a federal court to abstain where a plaintiff's federal claims could be adjudicated in a pending state judicial proceeding—applies to complaints seeking only monetary relief. Petitioners further argue that it is within the district court's discretion to dismiss rather than stay a federal complaint for damages and fees where abstention is required. We need not decide the extent to which the *Younger* doctrine applies to a federal action seeking only monetary relief, however, because even if the *Younger* doctrine requires abstention here, the District Court had no discretion to dismiss rather than to stay claims for monetary relief that cannot be redressed in the state proceeding.

In reversing the District Court's dismissal of the claims for damages and attorney's fees, the Court of Appeals applied the Third Circuit rule that requires a district court to stay rather than dismiss claims that are not cognizable in the parallel state proceeding. The Third Circuit rule is sound. It allows a parallel state proceeding to go forward without interference from its federal sibling, while enforcing the duty of federal courts "to assume jurisdiction where jurisdiction properly exists."[7] This Court repeatedly has stated that the federal courts have a "virtually unflagging obligation" to exercise their jurisdiction except in those extraordinary circumstances " 'where the order to the parties to

[7] In [prior decisions], the Court of Appeals recognized that unless it retained jurisdiction during the pendency of the state proceeding, a plaintiff could be barred permanently from asserting his claims in the federal forum by the running of the applicable statute of limitations.

repair to the state court would clearly serve an important countervailing interest.' " Colorado River Water Conservation District v. United States, 424 U.S. 800 (1976). . . .

> [P]etitioners argue that allowing the District Court to dismiss the complaint will prevent the piecemeal litigation of the dispute between the parties. But the involvement of the federal courts cannot be blamed for the fragmentary nature of the proceedings in this litigation. Because the state criminal proceeding can provide only equitable relief, any action for damages would necessarily be separate. Indeed, the state forum in which petitioners invite respondents to pursue their claims for monetary relief clearly would require the initiation of a separate action. Piecemeal litigation of the issues involved in this case is thus inevitable.

(ii) Justice White's Concurrence

Justice White, joined by Justice O'Connor, concurred. He agreed that dismissal of the damages claim was inappropriate, but faulted the Court for not adequately explaining "why the federal courts must or may stay, rather than proceed to adjudicate, the federal constitutional claims for damages." "After all," he continued, "the Court's opinion cites the 'virtually unflagging obligation' of the federal courts to adjudicate claims within their jurisdiction absent extraordinary circumstances. . . . Why, then, stay the § 1983 damages claim asserting a violation of federal constitutional rights? Why does not the District Court's 'unflagging obligation' require it to proceed on that claim?"

Justice White's answer to these questions was that "*Younger* requires, not only dismissal of the equitable claim in the case, but also that the damages action should not go forward":

> The reasons for such an approach are obvious. As the *Younger* decision itself recognized, it has long been the rule that the federal courts should not interfere with or pre-empt the progress of state criminal proceedings. A judgment in the federal damages action may decide several questions at issue in the state criminal proceeding. . . . If the claims the Court remands today were disposed of on the merits by the District Court, this decision would presumably be owed res judicata effect in the forthcoming state criminal trial of respondents. "[T]he potential for federal-state friction is obvious." Guerro v. Mulhearn, 498 F.2d 1249, 1253 (1st Cir. 1974).
>
> It was for these same reasons that we held that a federal court should not entertain a declaratory judgment action aimed at adjudicating a federal issue involved in a state criminal proceeding. See Samuels v. Mackell, 401 U.S. 66 (1971) [a companion of *Younger*]. As was true in *Samuels*, here, "the practical effect of the two forms of relief [here, damages and injunction] will be virtually identical, and the basic policy against federal interference with pending state criminal prosecutions will be frustrated as much by a declaratory judgment [or, I believe, a damage award] as it would be by an injunction." See id., at 73. Under *Samuels*, for example, if a state criminal prosecution is ongoing, a federal court cannot adjudicate a plaintiff's request for a declaration that evidence being used in that prosecution was seized contrary to the Fourth Amendment. Yet if *Younger* does not apply to damages claims, that same court in the same circumstances *could* rule the search unconstitutional as long as the federal plaintiff was

seeking damages *in addition to* a determination of the unconstitutionality of the seizure—a prerequisite of any damages award. Why the latter action should be considered *less* problematic for purposes of comity or "Our Federalism" escapes me. If anything, I would have thought just the opposite to be true.

In light of . . . our decisions in *Younger* and *Samuels*, it is clear that the District Court should not dismiss the damages claims, yet must not proceed to judgment on them either. Consequently, I would couple our remand of this case with a holding that, pursuant to *Younger*, the lower courts *may not* adjudicate respondents' damages claims until the conclusion of the pending state criminal proceedings.[5]

The majority answered White's argument in a footnote. It would be inappropriate to decide whether *Younger* abstention applies to damage actions, it concluded, in part because the issue had not been considered below. Additionally, this had not been the subject of the grant of certiorari, which had originally been issued to consider whether *Younger* abstention applied to grand jury proceedings. That issue had been rendered moot by the subsequent indictment of some of the § 1983 plaintiffs and by the decision to drop a claim for equitable relief.

(iii) Questions and Comments

What did Justice Blackmun mean when he said that the Court was not deciding whether *Younger* applied, but then approved the Third Circuit rule requiring a stay of the District Court proceedings? Is there any practical difference between these two bases for deferring to the state court litigation? In Moses H. Cone Memorial Hospital v. Mercury Constr. Corp., 460 U.S. 1 (1983), Justice Brennan observed that "a stay is just as much a refusal to exercise jurisdiction as a dismissal." The point of the remark was to explain the *Moses H. Cone* holding that neither a stay nor a dismissal of federal proceedings is appropriate unless the case meets the *Colorado River* "extraordinary circumstances" exception to the "unflagging obligation" of district courts to exercise their jurisdiction. In light of *Moses H. Cone*, how can the Court's decision in *Deakins* be justified? On the merits of the *Younger* question, does Justice White reach the right result?

3. *EDWARDS V. BALISOK*

The Supreme Court reaffirmed and perhaps extended *Heck* in Edwards v. Balisok, 520 U.S. 641 (1997). Balisok, a state prisoner, did not contest or seek redress for his loss of good-time credits, but he did seek damages for the allegedly unconstitutional proceedings used to take them away. The Ninth Circuit found *Heck* inapplicable on the ground that a claim challenging only the procedures used in a disciplinary hearing could always be brought under § 1983, but the Supreme Court unanimously reversed. Speaking through Justice Scalia, the Court said that the Ninth Circuit's reasoning "disregards the possibility, clearly envisioned by *Heck*, that the nature of the challenge to the procedures

---

[5] While three of the respondents have been indicted, three others have not. Even if *Younger* does not apply to their claims for damages, the District Court would be prudent, under Colorado River Water Conservation District v. United States, 424 U.S. 800 (1976), to stay the adjudication of these claims—virtually indistinguishable from the substance of the ongoing state criminal proceedings involving the other respondents—as well.

could be such as necessarily to imply the invalidity of the judgment." Here, for example, Balisok had alleged deceit and bias by the prison hearing officer, allegations that, if proved, would imply the invalidity of the disciplinary action taken against him. *Heck* therefore controlled.

4. *WILKINSON V. DOTSON*

William Dotson and Rogerico Johnson were serving lengthy prison sentences in Ohio state prisons. Dotson was sentenced to life in 1981. He sought parole in 2000. The parole board denied relief and postponed further consideration for five years. Johnson began a 10–30 year term in 1992. He was considered and rejected for parole in 1999.

In both cases the parole board applied standards that were adopted in 1998, well after the two prisoners were convicted and sentenced. Both sought an injunction under § 1983 on the ground that retroactive application of the 1998 guidelines denied them due process and violated the Ex Post Facto clause. The District Court held the case cognizable only under habeas. The Court of Appeals disagreed. In an opinion by Justice Breyer, the Supreme Court agreed with the Circuit Court. Wilkinson v. Dotson, 544 U.S. 74 (2005).

In the course of holding that the suit could proceed under § 1983, Justice Breyer summarized the prior cases and applied their principles:

> Throughout the legal journey from *Preiser* to *Balisok*, the Court has focused on the need to ensure that state prisoners use only habeas corpus (or similar state) remedies when they seek to invalidate the duration of their confinement—either directly through an injunction compelling speedier release or indirectly through a judicial determination that necessarily implies the unlawfulness of the State's custody. Thus, *Preiser* found an implied exception to § 1983's coverage where the claim seeks—not where it simply "relates to"—"core" habeas corpus relief, i.e., where a state prisoner requests present or future release. . . . *Heck* specifies that a prisoner cannot use § 1983 to obtain damages where success would necessarily imply the unlawfulness of a (not previously invalidated) conviction or sentence. And *Balisok* . . . demonstrates that habeas remedies do not displace § 1983 actions where success in the civil rights suit would not necessarily vitiate the legality of (not previously invalidated) state confinement. These cases, taken together, indicate that a state prisoner's § 1983 action is barred (absent prior invalidation)—no matter the relief sought (damages or equitable relief), no matter the target of the prisoner's suit (state conduct leading to conviction or internal prison proceedings)—if success in that action would necessarily demonstrate the invalidity of confinement or its duration.
>
> Applying these principles to the present case, we conclude that respondents' claims are cognizable under § 1983, i.e., they do not fall within the implicit habeas exception. Dotson and Johnson seek relief that will render invalid the state procedures used to deny parole eligibility (Dotson) and parole suitability (Johnson). Neither respondent seeks an injunction ordering his immediate or speedier release into the community. And . . . a favorable judgment will not "necessarily imply the invalidity of [their] conviction[s] or sentence[s]." *Heck*, 512 U.S., at 487. Success for Dotson does not mean immediate release from confinement or a shorter stay in prison; it means at most new eligibility review, which at most will speed

> consideration of a new parole application. Success for Johnson means at most a new parole hearing at which Ohio parole authorities may, in their discretion, decline to shorten his prison term. Because neither prisoner's claim would necessarily spell speedier release, neither lies at "the core of habeas corpus." *Preiser*, 411 U.S., at 489. Finally, the prisoners' claims for future relief (which, if successful, will not necessarily imply the invalidity of confinement or shorten its duration) are yet more distant from that core.

Justice Scalia joined the Court's opinion but wrote separately "to note that a contrary holding would require us to broaden the scope of habeas relief beyond recognition." He continued:

> It is one thing to say that permissible habeas relief, as our cases interpret the statute, includes ordering a "quantum change in the level of custody," Graham v. Broglin, 922 F.2d 379, 381 (7th Cir. 1991) (Posner, J.), such as release from incarceration to parole. It is quite another to say that the habeas statute authorizes federal courts to order relief that neither terminates custody, accelerates the future date of release from custody, nor reduces the level of custody. That is what is sought here: the mandating of a new parole hearing that may or may not result in release, prescription of the composition of the hearing panel, and specification of the procedures to be followed. A holding that this sort of judicial immersion in the administration of discretionary parole lies at the "core of habeas" would utterly sever the writ from its common-law roots. The dissent suggests that because a habeas court may issue a conditional writ ordering a prisoner released unless the State conducts a new sentencing proceeding, the court may also issue a conditional writ ordering release absent a new parole proceeding. But the prisoner who shows that his sentencing was unconstitutional is actually entitled to release, because the judgment pursuant to which he is confined has been invalidated; the conditional writ serves only to "delay the release . . . in order to provide the State an opportunity to correct the constitutional violation." Hilton v. Braunskill, 481 U.S. 770, 775 (1987). By contrast, the validly sentenced prisoner who shows only that the State made a procedural error in denying discretionary parole has not established a right to release, and so cannot obtain habeas relief—conditional or otherwise. Conditional writs enable habeas courts to give States time to replace an invalid judgment with a valid one, and the consequence when they fail to do so is always release. Conditional writs are not an all-purpose weapon with which federal habeas courts can extort from the respondent custodian forms of relief short of release, whether a new parole hearing or a new mattress in the applicant's cell.

Justice Thomas joined the Scalia opinion. Justice Kennedy was the lone dissenter.

5. ACCESS TO DNA EVIDENCE

In District Attorney's Office v. Osborne, 557 U.S. 52 (2009), the Court deferred decision on whether § 1983 or habeas was the correct remedial route for assertion of a constitutional right of post-conviction access to DNA testing. It could do so, the Court held, because the plaintiff's due process claim lacked merit in any event. Joined by Justice Kennedy, Justice Alito wrote a separate concurrence in which he concluded that the § 1983 remedy could not be used for this purpose:

> It is no answer to say, as respondent does, that he simply wants to use § 1983 as a discovery tool to lay the foundation for a future state post-conviction application, a state clemency petition, or a request for relief by means of "prosecutorial consent." Such tactics implicate precisely the same federalism and comity concerns that motivated our decisions (and Congress') to impose exhaustion requirements and discovery limits in federal habeas proceedings. If a petitioner can evade the habeas statute's exhaustion requirements in this way, I see no reason why a state prisoner asserting an ordinary *Brady* claim—i.e., a state prisoner who claims that the prosecution failed to turn over exculpatory evidence prior to trial—could not follow the same course.
>
> What respondent seeks was accurately described in his complaint—the discovery of evidence that has a material bearing on his conviction. Such a claim falls within "the core" of habeas. Preiser v. Rodriguez, 411 U.S. 475, 489 (1973). Recognition of a constitutional right to postconviction scientific testing of evidence in the possession of the prosecution would represent an expansion of *Brady* and a broadening of the discovery rights now available to habeas petitioners. We have never previously held that a state prisoner may seek discovery by means of a § 1983 action, and we should not take that step here. I would hold that respondent's claim (like all other *Brady* claims) should be brought in habeas.[b]

The issue returned in Skinner v. Switzer, 131 S.Ct. 1289 (2011). Skinner was sentenced to death in 1995 for murdering his live-in girlfriend and her two sons. A significant amount of biological evidence was collected and preserved by the police, but was untested at the time of trial.[c] The state enacted a statute in 2001 allowing postconviction testing on application by prisoners in limited circumstances. Skinner moved for testing under these procedures in 2001 and again in 2007, but both motions were denied. He then filed a § 1983 suit for injunctive relief against the local prosecutor who had custody of the biological evidence. His claim was that the state statute denied him procedural due process because it had been construed completely to foreclose postconviction DNA testing in cases where the prisoner could have sought testing prior to trial but did not.

In an opinion by Justice Ginsburg, the Court declined to address the merits of Skinner's due process claim, but did hold that it was cognizable under § 1983. After summarizing *Heck* and *Dotson*, the Court's opinion continued:

> Measured against our prior holdings, Skinner has properly invoked § 1983. Success in his suit for DNA testing would not "necessarily imply" the invalidity of his conviction. While test results might prove exculpatory, that outcome is hardly inevitable; . . . results might prove inconclusive

[b] In a prior footnote, Alito said: "This case is quite different from *Dotson*. In that case, two state prisoners filed § 1983 actions challenging the constitutionality of Ohio's parole procedures and seeking 'a new parole hearing that may or may not result in release, prescription of the composition of the hearing panel, and specification of the procedures to be followed.' Regardless of whether such remedies fall outside the authority of federal habeas judges, there is no question that the relief respondent seeks in this case—'exculpatory' evidence that tends to prove his innocence—lies 'within the core of habeas corpus.' "—[Footnote by eds.]

[c] His lawyer testified during state post-conviction proceedings that he had not asked for testing prior to trial because he was afraid the results would implicate Skinner.

or they might further incriminate Skinner. . . . Although Skinner's *immediate* plea is simply for an order requiring DNA testing, his ultimate aim, Switzer urges, is to use the test results as a platform for attacking his conviction. It suffices to point out that Switzer has found no case, nor has the dissent, in which the Court has recognized habeas as the sole remedy, or even an available one, where the relief sought would "neither terminat[e] custody, accelerat[e] the future date of release from custody, nor reduc[e] the level of custody." Wilkinson v. Dotson, 544 U. S. 74, 86 (Scalia, J., concurring).

Switzer argued that allowing § 1983 suits in this context would lead to a "vast expansion" of federal jurisdiction seeking discovery and other relief associated with prior convictions. The Court responded that there was no evidence in Circuits that allowed § 1983 DNA suits "of any litigation flood or even rainfall." Two reasons for this were the rejection in *Osborne* of substantive due process as the basis for DNA testing claims and significant limitations on prisoner litigation contained in the Prison Litigation Reform Act of 1995. Finally, the Court responded to the argument that its holding would open the doors to § 1983 suits for *Brady* claims:

> Unlike DNA testing, which may yield exculpatory, incriminating, or inconclusive results, a *Brady* claim, when successful postconviction, necessarily yields evidence undermining a conviction: *Brady* evidence is, by definition, always favorable to the defendant and material to his guilt or punishment. And parties asserting *Brady* violations postconviction generally do seek a judgment qualifying them for "immediate or speedier release" from imprisonment. Accordingly, *Brady* claims have ranked within the traditional core of habeas corpus and outside the province of § 1983.

Joined by Justices Kennedy and Alito, Justice Thomas dissented. He did not attempt to bring the situation into precise analytic alignment with *Preiser v. Rodriguez*'s focus on the fact or duration of custody. Rather, he described the case as a due process challenge to state collateral review procedures (under which DNA testing had been denied), and concluded that post-conviction challenges to such procedures should proceed under habeas corpus: "Challenges to all state procedures for reviewing the validity of a conviction should be treated the same as challenges to state trial procedures, which we have already recognized may not be brought under § 1983. . . . For purposes of deciding which claims fall within the bounds of § 1983, I think it makes sense to treat similarly all constitutional challenges to procedures concerning the validity of a conviction." *Wilkinson v. Dotson* was distinguished on the ground that the due process attack on state parole procedures involved in that case did not impeach the validity of the underlying criminal conviction or sentence. Justice Thomas added:

> In truth, the majority provides a roadmap for any unsuccessful state habeas petitioner to relitigate his claim under § 1983: After state habeas is denied, file a § 1983 suit challenging the state habeas process rather than the result.[3]. . .

---

[3] Nor is there any reason to believe that the Court's holding will be cabined to collateral review procedures. . . . Just as any unsuccessful state habeas petitioner will now resort to § 1983 and challenge state collateral review procedures, so, too, will unsuccessful appellants turn to § 1983 to challenge the state appellate procedures.

> This Court has struggled to limit § 1983 and prevent it from intruding into the boundaries of habeas corpus. In crafting these limits, we have recognized that suits seeking "immediate or speedier release" from confinement fall outside its scope. *Dotson*, at 82. We found another limit when faced with a civil action in which "a judgment in favor of the plaintiff would necessarily imply the invalidity of his conviction or sentence." *Heck*, at 487. This case calls for yet another: due process challenges to state procedures used to review the validity of a conviction or sentence. Under that rule, Skinner's claim is not cognizable under § 1983. . . .

Which side has the better of this argument? Does *Heck v. Humphrey* suggest an answer?

6. *NELSON V. CAMPBELL*

Nelson v. Campbell, 541 U.S. 637 (2004), involved the following problem:

> Three days before his scheduled execution by lethal injection, petitioner David Nelson filed a civil rights action in District Court, pursuant to 42 U.S.C. § 1983, alleging that the use of a "cut-down" procedure to access his veins would violate the Eighth Amendment. Petitioner, who had already filed one unsuccessful federal habeas application, sought a stay of execution so that the District Court could consider the merits of his constitutional claim. The question before us is whether § 1983 is an appropriate vehicle for petitioner's Eighth Amendment claim seeking a temporary stay and permanent injunctive relief.

The Circuit Court held that the claim sounded in habeas, and dismissed because it was a repetitive application that fit no exception allowing it to go forward. "Thus," the Supreme Court noted, "the 11th Circuit held that petitioner was without recourse to challenge the constitutionality of the cut-down procedure in Federal District Court."

In an opinion by Justice O'Connor, the Supreme Court held unanimously that the petitioner's § 1983 claim could go forward. Because petitioner had compromised veins due to years of drug abuse, unusual medical procedures were necessary in order to carry out the execution. Petitioner's claim carefully stated that he was not objecting to the fact of execution by legal injection, but only to the particular "cut-down" procedure by which it was proposed to be administered.[d] The Court responded:

> We have not yet had occasion to consider whether civil rights suits seeking to enjoin the use of a particular method of execution—e.g., lethal injection or electrocution—fall within the core of federal habeas corpus or, rather, whether they are properly viewed as challenges to the conditions of

---

[d] At one point, petitioner was told that "prison personnel would . . . make a 2–inch incision in petitioner's arm or leg; the procedure would take place one hour before the scheduled execution; and only local anesthesia would be used. There was no assurance that a physician would perform or even be present for the procedure." By contrast, petitioner submitted an affidavit from a reputable physician to the effect that "the cut-down is a dangerous and antiquated medical procedure to be performed only by a trained physician in a clinical environment with the patient under deep sedation. In light of safer and less-invasive contemporary means of venous access, [the Doctor] concluded that 'there is no comprehensible reason for the State of Alabama to be planning to employ the cut-down procedure to obtain intravenous access, unless there exists an intent to render the procedure more painful and risky than it otherwise needs to be.' "

a condemned inmate's death sentence. Neither the "conditions" nor the "fact or duration" label is particularly apt. A suit seeking to enjoin a particular means of effectuating a sentence of death does not directly call into question the "fact" or "validity" of the sentence itself—by simply altering its method of execution, the State can go forward with the sentence. On the other hand, imposition of the death penalty presupposes a means of carrying it out. In a State such as Alabama, where the legislature has established lethal injection as the preferred method of execution, a constitutional challenge seeking to permanently enjoin the use of lethal injection may amount to a challenge to the fact of the sentence itself. A finding of unconstitutionality would require statutory amendment or variance, imposing significant costs on the State and the administration of its penal system. And while it makes little sense to talk of the "duration" of a death sentence, a State retains a significant interest in meting out a sentence of death in a timely fashion.

We need not reach here the difficult question of how to categorize method-of-execution claims generally. Respondents at oral argument conceded that § 1983 would be an appropriate vehicle for an inmate who is not facing execution to bring a "deliberate indifference" challenge to the constitutionality of the cut-down procedure if used to gain venous access for purposes of providing medical treatment. . . . We see no reason on the face of the complaint to treat petitioner's claim differently solely because he has been condemned to die.

Respondents counter that, because the cut-down is part of the execution procedure, petitioner's challenge is, in fact, a challenge to the fact of his execution. They offer the following argument: A challenge to the use of lethal injection as a method of execution sounds in habeas; venous access is a necessary prerequisite to, and thus an indispensable part of, any lethal injection procedure; therefore, a challenge to the State's means of achieving venous access must be brought in a federal habeas application. Even were we to accept as given respondents' premise that a challenge to lethal injection sounds in habeas, the conclusion does not follow. That venous access is a necessary prerequisite does not imply that a particular means of gaining such access is likewise necessary. Indeed, the gravamen of petitioner's entire claim is that use of the cut-down would be *gratuitous*. Merely labeling something as part of an execution procedure is insufficient to insulate it from a § 1983 attack.

If as a legal matter the cut-down were a statutorily mandated part of the lethal injection protocol, or if as a factual matter petitioner were unable or unwilling to concede acceptable alternatives for gaining venous access, respondents might have a stronger argument that success on the merits, coupled with injunctive relief, would call into question the death sentence itself. But petitioner has been careful throughout these proceedings, in his complaint and at oral argument, to assert that the cut-down, as well as the warden's refusal to provide reliable information regarding the cut-down protocol, are *wholly unnecessary* to gaining venous access. Petitioner has alleged alternatives that, if they had been used, would have allowed the State to proceed with the execution as scheduled. . . .

We note that our holding here is consistent with our approach to civil rights damages actions, which, like method-of-execution challenges, fall at

> the margins of habeas. Although damages are not an available habeas remedy, we have previously concluded that a § 1983 suit for damages that would "necessarily imply" the invalidity of the fact of an inmate's conviction, or "necessarily imply" the invalidity of the length of an inmate's sentence, is not cognizable under § 1983 unless and until the inmate obtains favorable termination of a state, or federal habeas, challenge to his conviction or sentence. Heck v. Humphrey, 512 U.S. 477, 487 (1994); Edwards v. Balisok, 520 U.S. 641, 648 (1997). . . . In the present context, focusing attention on whether petitioner's challenge to the cut-down procedure would *necessarily* prevent Alabama from carrying out its execution both protects against the use of § 1983 to circumvent any limits imposed by the habeas statute and minimizes the extent to which the fact of a prisoner's imminent execution will require differential treatment of his otherwise cognizable § 1983 claims.

The Court also addressed the propriety of a stay of execution in contexts such as this, and emphasized the narrowness of its holding:

> Respondents argue that a decision to reverse the judgment of the Eleventh Circuit would open the floodgates to all manner of method-of-execution challenges, as well as last minute stay requests. But, because we do not here resolve the question of how to treat method-of-execution claims generally, our holding is extremely limited.
>
> Moreover, as our previous decision in Gomez v. United States Dist. Court for Northern Dist. of Cal., 503 U.S. 653 (1992) (per curiam), makes clear, the mere fact that an inmate states a cognizable § 1983 claim does not warrant the entry of a stay as a matter of right. *Gomez* came to us on a motion by the State to vacate a stay entered by an en banc panel of the Court of Appeals for the Ninth Circuit that would have allowed the District Court time to consider the merits of a condemned inmate's last-minute § 1983 action challenging the constitutionality of California's use of the gas chamber. We left open the question whether the inmate's claim was cognizable under § 1983, but vacated the stay nonetheless. The inmate, Robert Alton Harris, who had already filed four unsuccessful federal habeas applications, waited until the 11th hour to file his challenge despite the fact that California's method of execution had been in place for years: "This claim could have been brought more than a decade ago. There is no good reason for this abusive delay, which has been compounded by last-minute attempts to manipulate the judicial process. A court may consider the last-minute nature of an application to stay execution in deciding whether to grant equitable relief."
>
> A stay is an equitable remedy, and "[e]quity must take into consideration the State's strong interest in proceeding with its judgment and . . . attempt[s] at manipulation." Thus, before granting a stay, a district court must consider not only the likelihood of success on the merits and the relative harms to the parties, but also the extent to which the inmate has delayed unnecessarily in bringing the claim. Given the State's significant interest in enforcing its criminal judgments, there is a strong equitable presumption against the grant of a stay where a claim could have been brought at such a time as to allow consideration of the merits without requiring entry of a stay.

Finally, the ability to bring a § 1983 claim, rather than a habeas application, does not entirely free inmates from substantive or procedural limitations. The Prison Litigation Reform Act of 1995 (Act) imposes limits on the scope and duration of preliminary and permanent injunctive relief, including a requirement that, before issuing such relief, "[a] court shall give substantial weight to any adverse impact on . . . the operation of a criminal justice system caused by the relief." 18 U.S.C. § 3626(a)(1); accord, § 3626(a)(2). It requires that inmates exhaust available state administrative remedies before bringing a § 1983 action challenging the conditions of their confinement. 42 U.S.C. § 1997e(a) ("No action shall be brought with respect to prison conditions under section 1983 of this title, or any other Federal law, by a prisoner confined in any jail, prison, or other correctional facility until such administrative remedies as are available are exhausted"). The Act mandates that a district court "shall," on its own motion, dismiss "any action brought with respect to prison conditions under section 1983 of this title . . . if the court is satisfied that the action is frivolous, malicious, fails to state a claim upon which relief can be granted, or seeks monetary relief from a defendant who is immune from relief." § 1997e(c)(1). Indeed, if the claim is frivolous on its face, a district court may dismiss the suit before the plaintiff has exhausted his state remedies. § 1997e(c)(2).

7. *HILL V. MCDONOUGH*

Hill v. McDonough, 547 U.S. 573 (2006), raised the *Nelson* issue in a different context. Hill's challenge, filed four days before his scheduled execution for a 1983 murder conviction, was to the particular three-drug sequence used in Florida's lethal injection protocol. In particular, he "alleged that the first drug injected, sodium pentothal, would not be a sufficient anesthetic to render painless the administration of the second and third drugs, pancuronium bromide and potassium chloride. There was an ensuing risk, Hill alleged, that he could remain conscious and suffer severe pain as the pancuronium paralyzed his lungs and body and the potassium chloride caused muscle cramping and a fatal heart attack."

The District Court treated his § 1983 claim as a habeas petition, and dismissed it because it did not comply with the limitations on successive petitions. The Circuit Court affirmed on the day of the scheduled execution. The Supreme Court granted a stay, and later granted certiorari. In a unanimous opinion by Justice Kennedy, it held the case controlled by *Nelson* and therefore appropriate as a § 1983 action:

> Here, as in *Nelson,* Hill's action if successful would not necessarily prevent the State from executing him by lethal injection. The complaint does not challenge the lethal injection sentence as a general matter but seeks instead only to enjoin the respondents "from executing [Hill] in the manner they currently intend." The specific objection is that the anticipated protocol allegedly causes "a foreseeable risk of . . . gratuitous and unnecessary" pain. Hill concedes that "other methods of lethal injection the Department could choose to use would be constitutional," and respondents do not contend, at least to this point in the litigation, that granting Hill's injunction would leave the State without any other practicable, legal method of executing Hill by lethal injection. Florida law, moreover, does not require the Department of Corrections to use the challenged procedure. See

Fla. Stat. §§ 922.105(1), (7) (prescribing lethal injection and leaving implementation to the Department of Corrections). Hill's challenge appears to leave the State free to use an alternative lethal injection procedure. Under these circumstances a grant of injunctive relief could not be seen as barring the execution of Hill's sentence.

One difference between the present case and *Nelson,* of course, is that Hill challenges the chemical injection sequence rather than a surgical procedure preliminary to the lethal injection. In *Nelson,* however, the State argued that the invasive procedure was not a medical operation separable from the lethal injection but rather a "necessary prerequisite to, and thus an indispensable part of, any lethal injection procedure." The Court reasoned that although venous access was necessary for lethal injection, it did not follow that the State's chosen means of access were necessary; "the gravamen of petitioner's entire claim" was that the procedure was "gratuitous." The same is true here. Although the injection of lethal chemicals is an obvious necessity for the execution, Hill alleges that the challenged procedure presents a risk of pain the State can avoid while still being able to enforce the sentence ordering a lethal injection.

One concern is that the foregoing analysis may be more theoretical than real based on the practicalities of the case. A procedure that avoids the harms Hill alleges, for instance, may be susceptible to attack for other purported risks of its own. Respondents and their supporting amici thus contend that the legal distinction between habeas corpus and § 1983 actions must account for the practical reality of capital litigation tactics: Inmates file these actions intending to forestall execution, and *Nelson's* emphasis on whether a suit challenges something "necessary" to the execution provides no endpoint to piecemeal litigation aimed at delaying the execution. Viewed in isolation, no single component of a given execution procedure may be strictly necessary, the argument goes, and a capital litigant may put off execution by challenging one aspect of a procedure after another. The amici States point to *Nelson's* aftermath as a cautionary example, contending that on remand the District Court allowed Nelson to amend his complaint and that litigation over the constitutionality of Alabama's adopted alternative—one that Nelson had previously proposed—continues to this day.

Respondents and their supporting amici conclude that two different rules should follow from these practical considerations. The United States as amicus curiae contends that a capital litigant's § 1983 action can proceed if, as in Nelson, the prisoner identifies an alternative, authorized method of execution. A suit like Hill's that fails to do so, the United States maintains, is more like a claim challenging the imposition of any method of execution—which is to say, the execution itself—because it shows the complainant is unable or unwilling to concede acceptable alternatives "[e]xcept in the abstract."

Although we agree courts should not tolerate abusive litigation tactics, even if the United States' proposed limitation were likely to be effective we could not accept it. It is true that the *Nelson* plaintiff's affirmative identification of an acceptable alternative supported our conclusion that the suit need not proceed as a habeas action. That fact, however, was not decisive. *Nelson* did not change the traditional pleading requirements for

§ 1983 actions. If the relief sought would foreclose execution, recharacterizing a complaint as an action for habeas corpus might be proper. Imposition of heightened pleading requirements, however, is quite a different matter. Specific pleading requirements are mandated by the Federal Rules of Civil Procedure, and not, as a general rule, through case-by-case determinations of the federal courts.

Respondents and the States as amici frame their argument differently. While not asking the Court in explicit terms to overrule *Nelson,* they contend a challenge to a procedure implicating the direct administration of an execution must proceed as a habeas action. They rely on cases barring § 1983 damages actions that, if successful, would imply the invalidation of an existing sentence or confinement. Those cases, they contend, demonstrate that the test of whether an action would undermine a sentence must "be applied functionally." By the same logic, it is said, a suit should be brought in habeas if it would frustrate the execution as a practical matter.

This argument cannot be squared with *Nelson's* observation that its criterion—whether a grant of relief to the inmate would necessarily bar the execution—is consistent with [our] approach to damages actions that implicate habeas relief. In those cases the question is whether "the nature of the challenge to the procedures could be such as necessarily to imply the invalidity" of the confinement or sentence. As discussed above, and at this stage of the litigation, the injunction Hill seeks would not necessarily foreclose the State from implementing the lethal injection sentence under present law, and thus it could not be said that the suit seeks to establish "unlawfulness [that] would render a conviction or sentence invalid." Any incidental delay caused by allowing Hill to file suit does not cast on his sentence the kind of negative legal implication that would require him to proceed in a habeas action.

3. RES JUDICATA

Allen v. McCurry

Supreme Court of the United States, 1980.
449 U.S. 90.

■ JUSTICE STEWART delivered the opinion of the Court.

At a hearing before his criminal trial in a Missouri court, the respondent, Willie McCurry, invoked the Fourth and Fourteenth Amendments to suppress evidence that had been seized by the police. The trial court denied the suppression motion in part, and McCurry was subsequently convicted after a jury trial. The conviction was later affirmed on appeal. Because he did not assert that the state courts had denied him a "full and fair opportunity" to litigate his search and seizure claim, McCurry was barred by this Court's decision in Stone v. Powell, 428 U.S. 465 (1976), from seeking a writ of habeas corpus in a federal district court. Nevertheless, he sought federal-court redress for the alleged constitutional violation by bringing a damages suit under 42 U.S.C. § 1983 against the officers who had entered his home and seized the evidence in question. We granted certiorari to consider whether the unavailability of federal habeas corpus prevented the police officers from raising the state courts' partial rejection of McCurry's constitutional claim as a collateral estoppel defense to the § 1983 suit against them for damages.

I

In April 1977, several undercover police officers, following an informant's tip that McCurry was dealing in heroin, went to his house in St. Louis, Mo., to attempt a purchase. Two officers, petitioners Allen and Jacobsmeyer, knocked on the front door, while the other officers hid nearby. When McCurry opened the door, the two officers asked to buy some heroin "caps." McCurry went back into the house and returned soon thereafter, firing a pistol at and seriously wounding Allen and Jacobsmeyer. After a gun battle with the other officers and their reinforcements, McCurry retreated into the house; he emerged again when the police demanded that he surrender. Several officers then entered the house without a warrant, purportedly to search for other persons inside. One of the officers seized drugs and other contraband that lay in plain view, as well as additional contraband found in dresser drawers and in auto tires on the porch.

McCurry was charged with possession of heroin and assaults with intent to kill. At the pretrial suppression hearing, the trial judge excluded the evidence seized from the dresser drawers and tires, but denied suppression of the evidence found in plain view. McCurry was convicted of both the heroin and assault offenses.

McCurry subsequently filed the present § 1983 action for $1 million in damages against petitioners Allen and Jacobsmeyer, other unnamed individual police officers, and the city of St. Louis and its police department. The complaint alleged a conspiracy to violate McCurry's Fourth Amendment rights, an unconstitutional search and seizure of his house, and an assault on him by unknown police officers after he had been arrested and handcuffed. The petitioners moved for summary judgment. The District Court apparently understood the gist of the complaint to be the allegedly unconstitutional search and seizure and granted summary judgment, holding that collateral estoppel prevented McCurry from relitigating the search-and-seizure question already decided against him in the state courts.[2]

The Court of Appeals reversed the judgment and remanded the case for trial. The appellate court said it was not holding that collateral estoppel was generally inapplicable in a § 1983 suit raising issues determined against the federal plaintiff in a state criminal trial. But noting that *Stone v. Powell*, supra, barred McCurry from federal habeas corpus relief, and invoking "the special role of the federal courts in protecting civil rights," the court concluded that the § 1983 suit was McCurry's only route to a federal

---

[2] The merits of the Fourth Amendment claim are discussed in the opinion of the Missouri Court of Appeals. State v. McCurry, 587 S.W.2d 337 (1979). The state courts upheld the entry of the house as a reasonable response to emergency circumstances, but held illegal the seizure of any evidence discovered as a result of that entry except what was in plain view. McCurry therefore argues here that even if the doctrine of collateral estoppel generally applies to this case, he should be able to proceed to trial to obtain damages for the part of the seizure declared illegal by the state courts. The petitioners contend, on the other hand, that the complaint alleged essentially an illegal entry, adding that only the entry could possibly justify the $1 million prayer. Since the state courts upheld the entry, the petitioners argue that if collateral estoppel applies here at all, it removes from trial all issues except the alleged assault. The United States Court of Appeals, however, addressed only the broad question of the applicability of collateral estoppel to § 1983 suits brought by plaintiffs in McCurry's circumstances, and questions as to the scope of collateral estoppel with respect to the particular issues in this case are not now before us.

forum for his constitutional claim and directed the trial court to allow him to proceed to trial unencumbered by collateral estoppel.

II

The federal courts have traditionally adhered to the related doctrines of res judicata and collateral estoppel. Under res judicata, a final judgment on the merits of an action precludes the parties or their privies from relitigating issues that were or could have been raised in that action. Under collateral estoppel, once a court has decided an issue of fact or law necessary to its judgment, that decision may preclude relitigation of the issue in a suit on a different cause of action involving a party to the first case.[5] As this Court and other courts have often recognized, res judicata and collateral estoppel relieve parties of the cost and vexation of multiple lawsuits, conserve judicial resources, and, by preventing inconsistent decisions, encourage reliance on adjudication.

In recent years, this Court has reaffirmed the benefits of collateral estoppel in particular, finding the policies underlying it to apply in contexts not formerly recognized at common law. Thus, the Court has eliminated the requirement of mutuality in applying collateral estoppel to bar relitigation of issues decided earlier in federal-court suits, Blonder–Tongue Laboratories, Inc. v. University of Illinois Foundation, 402 U.S. 313 (1971), and has allowed a litigant who was not a party to a federal case to use collateral estoppel "offensively" in a new federal suit against the party who lost on the decided issue in the first case. Parklane Hosiery Co. v. Shore, 439 U.S. 322 (1979). But one general limitation the Court has repeatedly recognized is that the concept of collateral estoppel cannot apply when the party against whom the earlier decision is asserted did not have a "full and fair opportunity" to litigate that issue in the earlier case. Montana v. United States, 440 U.S. 147, 153 (1979).[7]

The federal courts generally have also consistently accorded preclusive effect to issues decided by state courts. Thus, res judicata and collateral estoppel not only reduce unnecessary litigation and foster reliance on adjudication, but also promote the comity between state and federal courts that has been recognized as a bulwark of the federal system. See Younger v. Harris, 401 U.S. 37, 43–45 (1971).

Indeed, though the federal courts may look to the common law or to the policies supporting res judicata and collateral estoppel in assessing the preclusive effect of decisions of other federal courts, Congress has specifi-

---

[5] The Restatement of Judgments now speaks of res judicata as "claim preclusion" and collateral estoppel as "issue preclusion." Restatement (2d) of Judgments § 74 (Tent. Draft No. 3, April 1976). Some courts and commentators use "res judicata" as generally meaning both forms of preclusion.

Contrary to a suggestion in the dissenting opinion, this case does not involve the question whether a § 1983 claimant can litigate in federal court an issue he might have raised but did not raise in previous litigation.

[7] Other factors, of course, may require an exception to the normal rules of collateral estoppel in particular cases.

Contrary to the suggestion of the dissent, our decision today does not "fashion" any new, more stringent doctrine of collateral estoppel, nor does it hold that the collateral-estoppel effect of a state-court decision turns on the single factor of whether the state gave the federal claimant a full and fair opportunity to litigate a federal question. Our decision does not "fashion" any doctrine of collateral estoppel at all. Rather, it construes § 1983 to determine whether the conventional doctrine of collateral estoppel applies to the case at hand. It must be emphasized that the question whether any exceptions or qualifications within the bounds of that doctrine might ultimately defeat a collateral-estoppel defense in this case is not before us.

cally required all federal courts to give preclusive effect to state-court judgments whenever the courts of the State from which the judgments emerged would do so:

> [J]udicial proceedings [of any court of any state] shall have the same full faith and credit in every court within the United States and its Territories and Possessions as they have by law or usage in the courts of such State. . . . 28 U.S.C. § 1738.

It is against this background that we examine the relationship of § 1983 and collateral estoppel, and the decision of the Court of Appeals in this case.

III

This Court has never directly decided whether the rules of res judicata and collateral estoppel are generally applicable to § 1983 actions. But in Preiser v. Rodriguez, 411 U.S. 475, 497 (1973), the Court noted with implicit approval the view of other federal courts that res judicata principles fully apply to civil rights suits brought under that statute. And the virtually unanimous view of the courts of appeals since *Preiser* has been that § 1983 presents no categorical bar to the application of res judicata and collateral estoppel concepts.[10] These federal appellate court decisions have spoken with little explanation or citation in assuming the compatibility of § 1983 and rules of preclusion, but the statute and its legislative history clearly support the courts' decisions.

Because the requirement of mutuality of estoppel was still alive in the federal courts until well into this century, the drafters of the 1871 Civil Rights Act, of which § 1983 is a part, may have had less reason to concern themselves with rules of preclusion than a modern Congress would. Nevertheless, in 1871 res judicata and collateral estoppel could certainly have applied in federal suits following state-court litigation between the same parties or their privies, and nothing in the language of § 1983 remotely expresses any congressional intent to contravene the common-law rules of preclusion or to repeal the express statutory requirements of the predecessor of 28 U.S.C. § 1738. Section 1983 creates a new federal cause of action. It says nothing about the preclusive effect of state-court judgments.[12]

Moreover, the legislative history of § 1983 does not in any clear way suggest that Congress intended to repeal or restrict the traditional doctrines of preclusion. The main goal of the act was to override the corrupting influence of the Ku Klux Klan and its sympathizers on the governments and law enforcement agencies of the Southern States, see Monroe v. Pape, 365 U.S. 167, 174 (1961), and of course the debates show that one strong motive behind its enactment was grave congressional concern that the state courts had been deficient in protecting federal rights. But in the context of

---

[10] A very few courts have suggested that the normal rules of claim preclusion should not apply in § 1983 suits in one peculiar circumstance: Where a § 1983 plaintiff seeks to litigate in federal court a federal issue which he could have raised but did not raise in an earlier state-court suit against the same adverse party. These cases present a narrow question not now before us, and we intimate no view as to whether they were correctly decided.

[12] By contrast, the roughly contemporaneous statute extending the federal writ of habeas corpus to state prisoners expressly rendered "null and void" any state-court proceeding inconsistent with the decision of a federal habeas court, Act of Feb. 5, 1867, ch. 28 (current version at 28 U.S.C. § 2254). . . . In any event the traditional exception to res judicata for habeas corpus review provides no analogy to § 1983 cases, since that exception finds its source in the unique purpose of habeas corpus—to release the applicant for the writ from unlawful confinement.

the legislative history as a whole, this congressional concern lends only the most equivocal support to any argument that, in cases where the state courts have recognized the constitutional claims asserted and provided fair procedures for determining them, Congress intended to override § 1738 or the common-law rules of collateral estoppel and res judicata. Since repeals by implication are disfavored, much clearer support than this would be required to hold that § 1738 and the traditional rules of preclusion are not applicable to § 1983 suits.

As the Court has understood the history of the legislation, Congress realized that in enacting § 1983 it was altering the balance of judicial power between the state and federal courts. See Mitchum v. Foster, 407 U.S. 225, 241 (1972). But in doing so, Congress was adding to the jurisdiction of the federal courts, not subtracting from that of the state courts. See *Monroe v. Pape*, supra, at 183 ("The federal remedy is supplementary to the state remedy . . . "). The debates contain several references to the concurrent jurisdiction of the state courts over federal questions, and numerous suggestions that the state courts would retain their established jurisdiction so that they could, when the then current political passions abated, demonstrate a new sensitivity to federal rights.

To the extent that it did intend to change the balance of power over federal questions between the state and federal courts, the 42d Congress was acting in a way thoroughly consistent with the doctrines of preclusion. In reviewing the legislative history of § 1983 in *Monroe v. Pape*, the Court inferred that Congress had intended a federal remedy in three circumstances: where state substantive law was facially unconstitutional, where state procedural law was inadequate to allow full litigation of a constitutional claim, and where state procedural law, though adequate in theory, was inadequate in practice. In short, the federal courts could step in where the state courts were unable or unwilling to protect federal rights. This understanding of § 1983 might well support an exception to res judicata and collateral estoppel where state law did not provide fair procedures for the litigation of constitutional claims, or where a state court failed to even acknowledge the existence of the constitutional principle on which a litigant based his claim. Such an exception, however, would be essentially the same as the important general limit on rules of preclusion that already exists: Collateral estoppel does not apply where the party against whom an earlier court decision is asserted did not have a full and fair opportunity to litigate the claim or issue decided by the first court. But the Court's view of § 1983 in *Monroe* lends no strength to any argument that Congress intended to allow relitigation of federal issues decided after a full and fair hearing in a state court simply because the state court's decision may have been erroneous.[17]

[17] The dissent suggests that the Court's decision in England v. Medical Examiners, 375 U.S. 411 (1964), demonstrates the impropriety of affording preclusive effect to the state-court decision in this case. The *England* decision is inapposite to the question before us. In the *England* case, a party first submitted to a federal court his claim that a state statute violated his constitutional rights. The federal court abstained and remitted the plaintiff to the state courts, holding that a state-court decision that the statute did not apply to the plaintiff would moot the federal question. The plaintiff submitted both the state-and federal-law questions to the state courts, which decided both questions adversely to him. This Court held that in such a circumstance, a plaintiff who properly reserved the federal issue by informing the state court of his intention to return to federal court, if necessary, was not precluded from litigating the federal question in federal court. The holding in *England* depended entirely on this Court's view of the purpose of abstention in such a case: Where a plaintiff properly invokes federal-court jurisdiction in the first instance on a federal claim, the federal court has a duty to accept

The Court of Appeals in this case acknowledged that every court of appeals that has squarely decided the question has held that collateral estoppel applies when § 1983 plaintiffs attempt to relitigate in federal court issues decided against them in state criminal proceedings. But the court noted that the only two federal appellate decisions invoking collateral estoppel to bar relitigation of Fourth Amendment claims decided adversely to the § 1983 plaintiffs in state courts came before this Court's decision in Stone v. Powell, 428 U.S. 465 (1976). It also noted that some of the decisions holding collateral estoppel applicable to § 1983 actions were based at least in part on the estopped party's access to another federal forum through habeas corpus. The Court of Appeals thus concluded that since *Stone v. Powell* had removed McCurry's right to a hearing of his Fourth Amendment claim in federal habeas court, collateral estoppel should not deprive him of a federal judicial hearing of that claim in a § 1983 suit.

Stone v. Powell does not provide a logical doctrinal source for the court's ruling. This Court in *Stone* assessed the costs and benefits of the judge-made exclusionary rule within the boundaries of the federal courts' statutory power to issue writs of habeas corpus, and decided that the incremental deterrent effect that the issuance of the writ in Fourth Amendment cases might have on police conduct did not justify the cost the writ imposed upon the fair administration of criminal justice. The *Stone* decision concerns only the prudent exercise of federal-court jurisdiction under 28 U.S.C. § 2254. It has no bearing on § 1983 suits or on the question of the preclusive effect of state-court judgments.

The actual basis of the Court of Appeals' holding appears to be a generally framed principle that every person asserting a federal right is entitled to one unencumbered opportunity to litigate that right in a federal district court, regardless of the legal posture in which the federal claim arises. But the authority for this principle is difficult to discern. It cannot lie in the Constitution, which makes no such guarantee, but leaves the scope of the jurisdiction of the federal district courts to the wisdom of Congress. And no such authority is to be found in § 1983 itself. For reasons already discussed at length, nothing in the language or legislative history of § 1983 proves any congressional intent to deny binding effect to a state-court judgment or decision when the state court, acting within its proper jurisdiction, has given the parties a full and fair opportunity to litigate federal claims, and thereby has shown itself willing and able to protect federal rights. And nothing in the legislative history of § 1983 reveals any purpose to afford less deference to judgments in state criminal proceedings than to those in state civil proceedings. There is, in short, no reason to believe that Congress intended to provide a person claiming a federal right an unrestricted opportunity to relitigate an issue already decided in a state court simply because the issue arose in a state proceeding in which he would rather not have been engaged at all.

Through § 1983, the 42d Congress intended to afford an opportunity for legal and equitable relief in a federal court for certain types of injuries. It is difficult to believe that the drafters of the act considered it a substitute for a federal writ of habeas corpus, the purpose of which is not to redress civil injury, but to release the applicant from unlawful physical confine-

---

that jurisdiction. Abstention may serve only to postpone, rather than to abdicate, jurisdiction, since its purpose is to determine whether resolution of the federal question is even necessary, or to obviate the risk of a federal court's erroneous construction of state law. These concerns have no bearing whatsoever on the present case.

ment, Preiser v. Rodriguez, 411 U.S. 475, 484 (1973); Fay v. Noia, 372 U.S. 391, 399 n.5 (1963), particularly in light of the extremely narrow scope of federal habeas relief for state prisoners in 1871.

The only other conceivable basis for finding a universal right to litigate a federal claim in a federal district court is hardly a legal basis at all, but rather a general distrust of the capacity of state courts to render correct decisions on constitutional issues. It is ironic that *Stone v. Powell* provided the occasion for the expression of such an attitude in the present litigation, in view of this Court's emphatic reaffirmation in that case of the constitutional obligation of the state courts to uphold federal law, and its expression of confidence in their ability to do so.

The Court of Appeals erred in holding that McCurry's inability to obtain federal habeas corpus relief upon his Fourth Amendment claim renders the doctrine of collateral estoppel inapplicable to his § 1983 suit.[25] Accordingly, the judgment is reversed, and the case is remanded to the Court of Appeals for proceedings consistent with this opinion.

■ JUSTICE BLACKMUN, with whom JUSTICE BRENNAN and JUSTICE MARSHALL join, dissenting.

The legal principles with which the Court is concerned in this civil case obviously far transcend the ugly facts of respondent's criminal convictions in the courts of Missouri for heroin possession and assault.

The Court today holds that notions of collateral estoppel apply with full force to this suit brought under 42 U.S.C. § 1983. In my view, the Court, in so ruling, ignores the clear import of the legislative history of that statute and disregards the important federal policies that underlie its enforcement. It also shows itself insensitive both to the significant differences between the § 1983 remedy and the exclusionary rule, and to the pressures upon a criminal defendant that make a free choice of forum illusory. I do not doubt that principles of preclusion are to be given such effect as is appropriate in a § 1983 action. In many cases, the denial of res judicata or collateral estoppel effect would serve no purpose and would harm relations between federal and state tribunals. Nonetheless, the Court's analysis in this particular case is unacceptable to me. It works injustice on this § 1983 plaintiff, and it makes more difficult the consistent protection of constitutional rights, a consideration that was at the core of the enactors' intent. Accordingly, I dissent.

In deciding whether a common-law doctrine is to apply to § 1983 when the statute itself is silent, prior cases uniformly have accorded the intent of the legislators great weight. . . . In the present case, however, the Court minimizes the significance of the legislative history and discounts its own prior explicit interpretations of the statute. Its discussion is limited to articulating what it terms the single fundamental principle of res judicata and collateral estoppel.

Respondent's position merits a quite different analysis. Although the legislators of the 42d Congress did not expressly state whether the then existing common-law doctrine of preclusion would survive enactment of § 1983, they plainly anticipated more than the creation of a federal statutory remedy to be administered indifferently by either a state or a federal court. The legislative intent, as expressed by supporters and understood by

[25] We do not decide *how* the body of collateral-estoppel doctrine of 28 U.S.C. § 1738 should apply in this case.

opponents, was to restructure relations between the state and federal courts. Congress deliberately opened the federal courts to individual citizens in response to the States' failure to provide justice in their own courts. Contrary to the view presently expressed by the Court, the 42d Congress was not concerned solely with procedural regularity. Even where there was procedural regularity, which the Court today so stresses, Congress believed that substantive justice was unobtainable. The availability of the federal forum was not meant to turn on whether, in an individual case, the state procedures were adequate. Assessing the state of affairs as a whole, Congress specifically made a determination that federal oversight of constitutional determinations through the federal courts was necessary to ensure the effective enforcement of constitutional rights.

That the new federal jurisdiction was conceived of as concurrent with state jurisdiction does not alter the significance of Congress' opening the federal courts to these claims. Congress consciously acted in the broadest manner possible. The legislators perceived that justice was not being done in the States then dominated by the Klan, and it seems senseless to suppose that they would have intended the federal courts to give full preclusive effect to prior state adjudications. That supposition would contradict their obvious aim to right the wrongs perpetuated in those same courts.

I agree that the legislative history is capable of alternative interpretations. I would have thought, however, that our prior decisions made very clear which reading is required. The Court repeatedly has recognized that § 1983 embodies a strong congressional policy in favor of federal courts' acting as the primary and final arbiters of constitutional rights. In Monroe v. Pape, 365 U.S. 167, 180 (1961), the Court held that Congress passed the legislation in order to substitute a federal forum for the ineffective, although plainly available, state remedies:

> It is abundantly clear that one reason the legislation was passed was to afford a federal right in federal courts because, by reason of prejudice, passion, neglect, intolerance or otherwise, state laws might not be enforced and the claims of citizens to the enjoyment of rights, privileges, and immunities guaranteed by the Fourteenth Amendment might be denied by the state agencies.[10]

The Court appears to me to misconstrue the plain meaning of *Monroe*. It states that in that case "the Court inferred that Congress had intended a federal remedy in three circumstances: where state substantive law was facially unconstitutional, where state procedural law was inadequate to allow full litigation of a constitutional claim, and where state procedural law, though adequate in theory, was inadequate in practice." It is true that the Court in *Monroe* described those three circumstances as the "three main aims" of the legislation. Yet in that case, the Court's recounting of the legislative history and its articulation of these three purposes were intended only as illustrative of *why* the 42d Congress chose to establish a federal remedy in federal court, not as a delineation of *when* the remedy would be available. The Court's conclusion was that this remedy was to be available no matter what the circumstances of state law:

---

[10] To the extent that *Monroe v. Pape* held that a municipality was not a "person" within the meaning of § 1983, it was overruled by the Court in Monell v. New York City Dept. of Social Services, 436 U.S. 658, 664–89 (1978). That ruling, of course, does not affect *Monroe*'s authoritative pronouncement of the legislative purposes of § 1983.

> It is no answer that the State has a law which if enforced would give relief. The federal remedy is supplementary to the state remedy, and the latter need not be first sought and refused before the federal one is invoked. Hence the fact that Illinois by its constitution and laws outlaws unreasonable searches and seizures is no barrier to the present suit in the federal court.

In Mitchum v. Foster, 407 U.S. 225, 242 (1972), the Court reiterated its understanding of the effect of § 1983 upon state and federal relations:

> Section 1983 was thus a product of a vast transformation from the concepts of federalism that had prevailed in the late 18th century. . . . The very purpose of § 1983 was to interpose the federal courts between the States and the people, as guardians of the people's federal rights—to protect the people from unconstitutional action under color of state law, "where that action be executive, legislative, or judicial."

At the very least, it is inconsistent now to narrow, if not repudiate, the meaning of *Monroe* and *Mitchum* and to alter our prior understanding of the distribution of power between the state and federal courts.

One should note also that in England v. Medical Examiners, 375 U.S. 411 (1964), the Court had affirmed the federal courts' special role in protecting constitutional rights under § 1983. In that case it held that a plaintiff required by the abstention doctrine to submit his constitutional claim first to a state court could not be precluded entirely from having the federal court, in which he initially had sought relief, pass on his constitutional claim. The Court relied on "the unqualified terms in which Congress, pursuant to constitutional authorization, has conferred specific categories of jurisdiction upon the federal courts," and on its "fundamental objections to any conclusion that a litigant who has properly invoked the jurisdiction of a federal district court to consider federal constitutional claims can be compelled, without his consent and through no fault of his own, to accept instead a state court's determination of those claims." The Court set out its understanding as to when a litigant in a § 1983 case might be precluded by prior litigation, holding that "if a party freely and without reservation submits his federal claims for decision by the state courts, litigates them there, and has them decided there, then—whether or not he seeks direct review of the state decision in this Court—he has elected to forgo his right to return to the district court." I do not understand why the Court today should abandon this approach.

The Court now fashions a new doctrine of preclusion, applicable only to actions brought under § 1983, that is more strict and more confining than the federal rules of preclusion applied in other cases. In Montana v. United States, 440 U.S. 147, 155 (1979), the Court pronounced three major factors to be considered in determining whether collateral estoppel serves as a barrier in the federal court:

> [W]hether the issues presented . . . are in substance the same . . . ; whether controlling facts or legal principles have changed significantly since the state-court judgment; and finally, whether other special circumstances warrant an exception to the normal rules of preclusion.

But now the Court states that the collateral-estoppel effect of prior state adjudication should turn on only one factor, namely, what it considers the "one general limitation" inherent in the doctrine of preclusion: "that the concept of collateral estoppel cannot apply when the party against whom the earlier decision is asserted did not have a 'full and fair opportunity' to litigate that issue in the earlier case." If that one factor is present, the Court asserts, the litigant properly should be barred from relitigating the issue in federal court.[12] One cannot deny that this factor is an important one. I do not believe, however, that the doctrine of preclusion requires the inquiry to be so narrow, and my understanding of the policies underlying § 1983 would lead me to consider all relevant factors in each case before concluding that the preclusion was warranted.

In this case, the police officers seek to prevent a criminal defendant from relitigating the constitutionality of their conduct in searching his house, after the state trial court had found that conduct in part violative of the defendant's Fourth Amendment rights and in part justified by the circumstances. I doubt that the police officers, now defendants in this § 1983 action, can be considered to have been in privity with the State in its role as prosecutor. Therefore, only "issue preclusion" is at stake.

The following factors persuade me to conclude that this respondent should not be precluded from asserting his claim in federal court. First, at the time § 1983 was passed, a non-party's ability, as a practical matter, to invoke collateral estoppel was non-existent. One could not preclude an opponent from relitigating an issue in a new cause of action, though that issue had been determined conclusively in a prior proceeding, unless there was "mutuality." Additionally, the definitions of "cause of action" and "issue" were narrow. As a result, and obviously, no preclusive effect could arise out of a criminal proceeding that would affect subsequent *civil* litigation. Thus, the 42d Congress could not have anticipated or approved that a criminal defendant, tried and convicted in state court, would be precluded from raising against police officers a constitutional claim arising out of his arrest.

Also, the process of deciding in a state criminal trial whether to exclude or admit evidence is not at all the equivalent of a § 1983 proceeding. The remedy sought in the latter is utterly different. In bringing the civil suit the criminal defendant does not seek to challenge his conviction collaterally. At most, he wins damages. In contrast, the exclusion of evidence may prevent a criminal conviction. A trial court, faced with the decision whether to exclude relevant evidence, confronts institutional pressures that may cause it to give a different shape to the Fourth Amendment right from what would result in civil litigation of a damages claim. Also, the issue whether to exclude evidence is subsidiary to the purpose of a criminal trial, which is to determine the guilt or innocence of the defendant, and a trial court, at least subconsciously, must weigh the potential damage to the truth-seeking process caused by excluding relevant evidence. See Stone v. Powell, 428 U.S. 465, 489–95 (1976).

A state criminal defendant cannot be held to have chosen "voluntarily" to litigate his Fourth Amendment claim in the state court. The risk of conviction puts pressure upon him to raise all possible defenses. He also faces uncertainty about the wisdom of foregoing litigation on *any* issue, for there is the possibility that he will be held to have waived his right to appeal on that issue. The "deliberate bypass" of state procedures, which the imposition of collateral estoppel under these circumstances encourages, surely is not a preferred goal. To hold that a criminal defendant who raises a Fourth

[12] This articulation of the preclusion doctrine of course would bar a § 1983 litigant from relitigating any issue he *might* have raised, as well as any issue he actually litigated in his criminal trial.

Amendment claim at his criminal trial "freely and without reservation submits his federal claims for decision by the state courts," *England v. Medical Examiners*, supra, at 419, is to deny reality. The criminal defendant is an involuntary litigant in the state tribunal, and against him all the forces of the State are arrayed. To force him to a choice between foregoing either a potential defense or a federal forum for hearing his constitutional civil claim is fundamentally unfair.

I would affirm the judgment of the Court of Appeals.

NOTES ON RES JUDICATA IN CIVIL RIGHTS ACTIONS

1. QUESTIONS AND COMMENTS

Even the *McCurry* dissenters agreed that state-court judgments should be given preclusive effect in some § 1983 actions. The easiest case is where a civil plaintiff submits a § 1983 claim to state court, loses, and then attempts to relitigate that same claim in federal court. If state law would foreclose a second suit in state court, there would be no reason to allow a federal bite at the apple. The plaintiff made a choice to submit the claim to state court and should be bound by the consequences.

A less obvious case would be where the plaintiff litigates a state-law claim in state court and loses on an issue of fact that proves relevant in a later federal court action. Here again, the usual application of issue preclusion (or collateral estoppel) presumably should be followed if state law so provides. The plaintiff controlled the choice of forum and could anticipate, or perhaps should be required to anticipate, the consequences of choosing state court.

The issue presented in *McCurry* is more difficult because the federal claimant was an involuntary litigant in the state criminal prosecution. Of course, McCurry could have elected not to raise the Fourth Amendment issue in state court, but the cost of doing so would have been to forego a potential defense to the criminal charges. Realistically, McCurry did not have "a free choice of forum" in which to litigate his federal claim.

It is this denial of access to a federal forum that underlies the argument against applying ordinary preclusion principles in McCurry's case. Which way does *Stone v. Powell* cut? Is it more plausible to regard *Stone* as supporting the position of the Court of Appeals in *McCurry* or the Supreme Court's position?

One way of thinking about these questions is to ask what would have happened to *Stone* had *McCurry* gone the other way. In that event, a defendant who lost in state court could nonetheless vindicate the underlying values of the Fourth Amendment through de novo consideration of the claim in federal court via § 1983. If the federal court agreed with the federal claimant in a § 1983 suit, what should the court do in a subsequent habeas proceeding? Should it continue to regard the state-court judgment as determinative of the legality of confinement, even though the conviction was based on a search or seizure now found by a federal court to have been unconstitutional? One commentator has suggested that the answer to this question is "yes," because "continued incarceration even in the light of a proven Fourth Amendment violation can, if one accepts the holding of *Stone v. Powell*, no longer be considered unjust." Comment, The Collateral–Estoppel Effect to be Given State–Court Judgments in Federal § 1983 Damage Suits, 128 U.Pa.L.Rev. 1471, 1502 (1980). Is this right? If so, does *Stone* mean that a Fourth Amendment damages claim in federal court under § 1983 is never an effort "to recover damages for allegedly unconstitutional conviction or imprisonment, or for other harm caused by actions whose unlawfulness would render a conviction or sentence invalid"? The quote is from *Heck v. Humphrey*, supra. Does *Heck* itself (apart from usual notions of res judicata) stand in the way of a § 1983 damages action in the *McCurry* situation?

Finally, consider how principles of res judicata ought to be applied in the *McCurry* situation. If the state court excludes evidence in a criminal trial on the ground that the Fourth Amendment was violated, is it likely that a federal court would be free to re-examine that conclusion in a subsequent § 1983 damages action against the police officers who conducted the search? If the state court holds that the Fourth Amendment was not violated and admits the evidence, is it likely that this would be the end of the matter in a subsequent § 1983 damages action? How should these situations be analyzed?

2. *MIGRA V. BOARD OF EDUCATION*

Allen v. McCurry involved issue preclusion. The operation of claim preclusion in § 1983 actions arose a few years later in Migra v. Warren City School District Board of Education, 465 U.S. 75 (1984).

(i) Claim vs. Issue Preclusion

Ethel Migra worked under successive annual contracts as supervisor of elementary schools in Warren City, Ohio. She accepted an offer of re-employment for a given year, but the school board subsequently reversed itself and decided not to renew her contract. Migra brought suit in state court, claiming breach of contract by the board and wrongful interference with her contract of employment by the board members who voted against her. She won that suit and was awarded reinstatement and compensatory damages.

Migra then filed a § 1983 action in federal court. She alleged that the non-renewal was in retaliation for a desegregation plan she had authored and a social studies curriculum she had designed. She claimed that the non-renewal was intended to punish her for the exercise of her right of free speech and also claimed violations of due process and equal protection. She sought injunctive relief, plus compensatory and punitive damages. The District Court dismissed the complaint, and the Court of Appeals affirmed.

Speaking for a unanimous Supreme Court, Justice Blackmun reviewed *Allen v. McCurry* and concluded that the same approach should apply to claims that were or could have been raised in a prior state court proceeding. "It is difficult," he said, "to see how the policy concerns underlying § 1983 would justify a distinction between the issue preclusive and claim preclusive effects of state-court judgments." The argument that § 1983 should be an exception to the usual principles of preclusion was based on "concern over the adequacy of state courts as protectors of federal rights." Any such distrust, however, "would presumably apply equally to issues that actually were decided in a state court as well as to those that could have been." Nor were arguments based on the relative expertise of state and federal courts persuasive:

> Petitioner suggests that to give state court judgments full issue preclusive effect but no claim preclusive effect would enable litigants to bring their state claims in state court and their federal claims in federal court,

thereby taking advantage of the relative expertise of both forums. Although such a division may seem attractive from a plaintiff's perspective, it is not the system established by § 1738. That statute embodies the view that it is more important to give full faith and credit to state court judgments than to ensure separate forums for federal and state claims. This reflects a variety of concerns, including notions of comity, the need to prevent vexatious litigation, and a desire to conserve judicial resources.

In the present litigation, petitioner does not claim that the state court would not have adjudicated her federal claims had she presented them in her original suit in state court. Alternatively, petitioner could have obtained a federal forum for her federal claim by litigating it first in a federal court. Section 1983, however, does not override state preclusion law and guarantee petitioner a right to proceed to judgment in state court on her state claims and then turn to federal court for adjudication of her federal claims. We hold, therefore, that petitioner's state court judgment in this litigation has the same preclusive effect in federal court that the judgment would have had in the Ohio state courts.

Is this reasoning sound? Consider the contrary argument in Stephen J. Shapiro, The Application of State Claim Preclusion Rules in a Federal Civil Rights Action, 10 Ohio Northern L.Rev. 223 (1983). Shapiro suggested that there are good reasons to differentiate issue from claim preclusion and to allow an exception for the latter. First, allowing relitigation of issues already adjudicated in state court "calls the correctness of the state court decision into question" and thereby offends the interest in comity between state and federal courts. Allowing a claimant to present a federal claim not heard in state court, by contrast, "not only shows no disrespect for the state court decision, but actually furthers the principles of comity by encouraging litigants to bring state claims in the state courts." As a corollary, an exception for claim preclusion would reduce the burden on the federal courts by allowing litigants to present their state claims to state court without risking loss of access to a federal forum. Finally, issue and claim preclusion were thought to have different benefits: Whereas issue preclusion "avoids duplicative legal effort and therefore conserves judicial resources," claim preclusion, "although reducing the number of lawsuits, does not usually reduce the total judicial effort expended by the parties or the court."

Is this reasoning persuasive? In a footnote in *Migra*, Justice Blackmun noted that he had dissented in *McCurry*, but explained that the "rationale of that dissent . . . was based largely on the fact that the § 1983 plaintiff in that case first litigated his constitutional claim in state court in the posture of his being a *defendant* in a criminal proceeding." Here, by contrast, "petitioner was in an offensive posture in her state court proceeding, and could have proceeded first in federal court had she wanted to litigate her federal claim in a federal forum." Under this reasoning, was *Migra* a better case for preclusion than *McCurry*?

(ii) The Significance of State Law

In *Migra* the Court quoted another case to the effect that "§ 1738 requires federal courts to give the same preclusive effect to state court judgments that those judgments would be given in the courts of the State from which the judgments emerged." It was not clear, however, whether Ohio law would have regarded Migra's breach of contract suit and her later § 1983 action as based on the same "claim" or "cause of action" for purposes of preclusion. The lower courts seemed to have resolved that question according to general preclusion principles rather than by specific reference to Ohio law. The Supreme Court said that Ohio law should govern and remanded the case for further inquiry into the controlling state law.

This point prompted an interesting concurrence by Justice White, with whom Chief Justice Burger and Justice Powell joined. Justice White noted that § 1738 had long been construed to mean that a federal court could accord a state-court judgment "no greater efficacy" than would a court of the rendering state, but found that construction nevertheless "unfortunate":

> In terms of the purpose of that section, which is to require federal courts to give effect to state-court judgments, there is no reason to hold that a federal court may not give preclusive effect to a state judgment simply because the judgment would not bar relitigation in the state courts. If the federal courts have developed rules of res judicata and collateral estoppel that prevent relitigation in circumstances that would not be preclusive in state courts, the federal courts should be free to apply them, the parties then being free to relitigate in the state courts. The contrary construction of § 1738 is nevertheless one of long standing, and Congress has not seen fit to disturb it, however justified such an action might have been.

Is White's suggestion sound? Stephen Shapiro thinks not. He suggested that according greater preclusive effect than would a state court might be unfair to the plaintiff, who may have relied on state preclusion law in bringing the original suit. Additionally, he thought that White's approach "may interfere with state substantive policies by giving too great a preclusive effect" to state-court judgments. 10 Ohio Northern L.Rev., at 237–38. Are these arguments persuasive? Are they adequately answered by White's observation that the litigant would remain free to return to state court?

3. *HARING V. PROSISE*

Consider also the facts of Haring v. Prosise, 462 U.S. 306 (1983). After pleading guilty to a charge of manufacturing a controlled substance, Prosise filed a § 1983 action against the police officers who had searched his apartment. The District Court held this claim barred, but the Supreme Court disagreed. Speaking through Justice Marshall, a unanimous Court held that the issue under § 1738 was whether state law would regard the conviction as preclusive. Here it would not, because the Fourth Amendment claim was not litigated or resolved in the state criminal prosecution. The only issue determined by the guilty plea was whether Prosise had manufactured a controlled substance, and "[t]his question is simply irrelevant to the legality of the search under the Fourth Amendment or to Prosise's right to compensation from state officials under § 1983."

The Court refused to embrace any notion of waiver. True, a defendant who pleads guilty cannot later raise claims about the admissibility of evidence in a habeas proceeding. The guilty plea is a "break in the chain of events," Tollett v. Henderson, 411 U.S. 258, 267 (1973), and renders alleged evidentiary violations irrelevant to the legality of the conviction. In such a case, the conviction rests on the defendant's plea of guilty and not on any evidence that may have been unlawfully acquired. By contrast, the § 1983 action does not test the validity of the conviction, but "challenges directly the legality of police conduct." Therefore, issues associated with the underlying police behavior are open to litigation in a civil rights action, even though barred from consideration on habeas by a valid guilty plea.

Haring v. Prosise was decided a decade before *Heck v. Humphrey*. Does it survive that decision? If so, does *Haring* reinforce the conclusion that *Heck* does not require *McCurry* suits to be dismissed for failure to state a claim?

4. *KREMER V. CHEMICAL CONSTRUCTION CORP.*

Two years after *McCurry*, the Supreme Court applied the same approach to the rather complicated facts of Kremer v. Chemical Construction Corp., 456 U.S. 461 (1982). Kremer filed a charge with the Equal Employment Opportunity Commission, alleging employment discrimination in violation of Title VII of the Civil Rights Act of 1964. That statute prohibits EEOC action until any comparable state agency has had at least 60 days to resolve the matter. Kremer's complaint was therefore referred to the New York State Division of Human Rights, which in due course concluded that the charge was unfounded. Kremer then returned to the EEOC, but simultaneously sought judicial review in state court of the state agency's action. The EEOC found that there was no reasonable cause to believe that Kremer's charge was true and issued a right-to-sue notice, after which Kremer brought a Title VII action in federal court. By this time, however, the New York agency determination had been affirmed in the state courts. The District Court dismissed the Title VII complaint on grounds of res judicata.

The Supreme Court, speaking through Justice White, found § 1738 fully applicable to Title VII cases: "Section 1738 requires federal courts to give the same preclusive effect to state court judgments that those judgments would be given in the courts of the state from which the judgments emerged." Under Title VII neither EEOC action nor a determination by any state agency would bar de novo trial in federal court. But Kremer had sought *judicial* review of the state agency's action, and the judgment of that reviewing court was entitled to full faith and credit under § 1738. The fact that the state court was reviewing an administrative determination did not matter, for "[t]here is no requirement that judicial review must proceed de novo if it is to be preclusive." Justice Blackmun, joined by Justices Brennan and Marshall, dissented.

5. *MCDONALD V. CITY OF WEST BRANCH*

All of the preceding cases involved the preclusive effect of judgments by state courts. The preclusive effect of an arbitration award was considered in McDonald v. City of West Branch, Michigan, 466 U.S. 284 (1984). There a discharged police officer filed a grievance under a collective bargaining agreement. The dispute went to arbitration, and the arbitrator found just cause for the discharge. The officer did not appeal the arbitrator's decision, but instead filed a § 1983 action in federal district court. Speaking through Justice Brennan, the Supreme Court held unanimously that § 1738 did not apply. The Court also declined to fashion any judicial rule of preclusion for arbitration awards. The Court reasoned that, "although arbitration is well suited to resolving contractual disputes, . . . it cannot provide an adequate substitute for a judicial proceeding in protecting the federal statutory and constitutional rights that § 1983 was designed to safeguard."

6. BIBLIOGRAPHY

The issue of the preclusive effect of state-court judgments in subsequent § 1983 actions has spawned a considerable literature. In addition to the sources already cited, see the comprehensive survey of this subject in Robert H. Smith, Full Faith and Credit and § 1983: A Reappraisal, 63 N.C.L.Rev. 59 (1984). Smith argues that the preclusive effect of state-court judgments in § 1983 suits should be subject to some exceptions, and he suggests consideration of five variables to determine whether an exception is warranted. These variables include: (i) whether the party facing preclusion had a choice of forum in the first instance; (ii) whether the federal action would relitigate claims or issues already determined by the state court and thus risk inconsistent rulings; (iii) whether the state court's consideration was limited in scope or procedure or tangential to the federal claim; (iv) whether allowing relitigation would unduly burden other litigants; and (v) whether specially important federal policies are at stake.

See also Barbara Ann Atwood, State Court Judgments in Federal Litigation: Mapping the Contours of Full Faith and Credit, 58 Ind.L.J. 59 (1982) (analyzing the cases with particular reference to the impact of exclusive federal jurisdiction on issue and claim preclusion under § 1738); Stephen B. Burbank, Interjurisdictional Preclusion: A General Approach, 71 Corn. L.Rev. 733, 817–22 (1986) (suggesting an approach to problems of preclusion in the federal-state context and applying it to § 1983 litigation); William V. Luneburg, The Opportunity to be Heard and the Doctrines of Preclusion: Federal Limits on State Law, 31 Vill.L.Rev. 81 (1986) (considering the role of federal law in the context of an extensive discussion of issue and claim preclusion); and Joan Mahoney, A Sword as Well as a Shield: The Offensive Use of Collateral Estoppel in Civil Rights Litigation, 69 Iowa L.Rev. 469 (1984) (suggesting that resort to federal court may be encouraged in order to take advantage of success by the offensive assertion of collateral estoppel in subsequent state-court actions).

Many of the problems dealt with in the subsequent cases were anticipated in J.W. Torke, Res Judicata in Federal Civil Rights Actions Following State Litigation, 9 Ind.L.Rev. 543 (1976). Also of interest are the provocative comments in David P. Currie, Res Judicata: The Neglected Defense, 45 U.Chi.L.Rev. 317 (1978). See also the still useful, though inevitably dated, discussions in William H. Theis, Res Judicata in Civil Rights Act Cases: An Introduction to the Problem, 70 Nw.U.L.Rev. 859 (1976); Allan D. Vestal, State Court Judgment as Preclusive in § 1983 Litigation in a Federal Court, 27 Okla.L.Rev. 185 (1974); and the excellent early treatment in Wayne McCormack, Federalism and § 1983: Limitations on Judicial Enforcement of Constitutional Claims, Part II, 60 Va.L.Rev. 250 (1974).

A correlative problem is the extent to which state claims that have a factual relationship to a federal civil rights action can be brought in federal court (and might be regarded as precluded in subsequent state-court litigation if they are not). Congress broadened the jurisdiction of federal courts to hear such claims in 28 U.S.C. § 1367, which brings ancillary jurisdiction and both pendent claim and pendant party jurisdiction under the single heading of "supplemental jurisdiction." For an analysis of the applicability of this statute to claims under § 1983 and other federal civil rights statutes, see Steven H.

Steinglass, Pendent Jurisdiction and Civil Rights Litigation, 7 Civil Rights Litigation and Attorney Fees Annual Handbook 31 (1991).

4. STATUTES OF LIMITATIONS

Wilson v. Garcia

Supreme Court of the United States, 1985.
471 U.S. 261.

■ JUSTICE STEVENS delivered the opinion of the Court.

In this case we must determine the most appropriate state statute of limitations to apply to claims enforceable under § 1 of the Civil Rights Act of 1871, which is codified in its present form as 42 U.S.C. § 1983.

On January 28, 1982, respondent brought this § 1983 action in the United States District Court for the District of New Mexico seeking "money damages to compensate him for the deprivation of his civil rights guaranteed by the Fourth, Fifth, and Fourteenth Amendments to the United States Constitution and for the personal injuries he suffered which were caused by the acts and omissions of the [petitioners] acting under color of law." The complaint alleged that on April 27, 1979, petitioner Wilson, a New Mexico State Police Officer, unlawfully arrested the respondent, "brutally and viciously" beat him, and sprayed his face with tear gas; that petitioner Vigil, the Chief of the New Mexico State Police, had notice of Officer Wilson's allegedly "violent propensities," and had failed to reprimand him for committing other unprovoked attacks on citizens; and that Vigil's training and supervision of Wilson were seriously deficient.

The respondent's complaint was filed two years and nine months after the claim purportedly arose. Petitioners moved to dismiss on the ground that the action was barred by the two-year statute of limitations contained in § 41–4–15(A) of the New Mexico Tort Claims Act. The petitioners' motion was supported by a decision of the New Mexico Supreme Court which squarely held that the Tort Claims Act provides "the most closely analogous state cause of action" to § 1983, and that its two-year statute of limitations is therefore applicable to actions commenced under § 1983 in the state courts. DeVargas v. New Mexico, 97 N.M. 563, 642 P.2d 166 (1982). In addition to the two-year statute of limitations in the Tort Claims Act, two other New Mexico statutes conceivably could apply to § 1983 claims: § 37–1–8, which provides a three-year limitation period for actions "for an injury to the person or reputation of any person"; and § 37–1–4, which provides a four-year limitation period for "all other actions not herein otherwise provided for." If either of these longer statutes applies to the respondent's § 1983 claim, the complaint was timely filed.

[The District Court ruled that *DeVargas* was not controlling and that § 1983 suits were best characterized as actions based on a statute. As New Mexico had no statute specifically addressed to such actions, the District Court applied the residual four-year statute of limitations for all claims not otherwise provided for. The Court of Appeals for the Tenth Circuit affirmed in a unanimous en banc opinion, but on the ground that all § 1983 actions should be characterized as personal injury actions. That court therefore applied the three-year statute of limitations provided for such claims.]

I

The Reconstruction Civil Rights Acts do not contain a specific statute of limitations governing § 1983 actions. . . . When Congress has not established a time limitation for a federal cause of action, the settled practice has been to adopt a local time limitation as federal law if it is not inconsistent with federal law or policy to do so. In 42 U.S.C. § 1988(a),[a] Congress has implicitly endorsed this approach with respect to claims enforceable under the Reconstruction Civil Rights Acts.

The language of § 1988(a),[13] directs the courts to follow "a three-step process" in determining the rules of decision applicable to civil rights claims:

> First, courts are to look to the laws of the United States "so far as such laws are suitable to carry [the civil and criminal civil rights statutes] into effect." If no suitable federal rule exists, courts undertake the second step by considering application of state "common law, as modified and changed by the constitution and statutes" of the forum state. A third step asserts the predominance of the federal interests: courts are to apply state law only if not "inconsistent with the Constitution and laws of the United States." Burnett v. Grattan, 468 U.S. 42, 47–48 (1984).

This case principally involves the second step in the process: the selection of "the most appropriate," Johnson v. Railway Express Agency, Inc., 421 U.S. 454, 462 (1975), or "the most analogous," Board of Regents v. Tomanio, 446 U.S. 478, 488 (1980), state statute of limitations to apply to this § 1983 claim.

In order to determine the "most appropriate" or "most analogous" New Mexico statute to apply to the respondent's claim, we must answer three questions. We must first consider whether state law or federal law governs the characterization of a § 1983 claim for statute of limitations purposes. If federal law applies, we must next decide whether all § 1983 claims should be characterized in the same way, or whether they should be evaluated differently depending upon the varying factual circumstances and legal theories presented in each individual case. Finally, we must characterize the essence of the claim in the pending case, and decide which state statute provides the most appropriate limiting principle. Although the text of neither § 1983, nor § 1988(a), provides a pellucid answer to any of these questions, all three parts of the inquiry are, in final analysis, questions of statutory construction.

---

[a] The Court's reference was to 42 U.S.C. § 1988, which has since been renumbered to § 1988(a). Subsequent citations by the Court to § 1988 have been replaced by § 1988(a).—[Footnote by eds.]

[13] Title 42 U.S.C. § 1988(a) provides, in relevant part: "The jurisdiction in civil and criminal matters conferred on the district courts by the provisions of this [chapter and title 18], for the protection of all persons in the United States in their civil rights and for their vindication, shall be exercised and enforced in conformity with the laws of the United States, so far as such laws are suitable to carry the same into effect; but in all cases where they are not adapted to the object, or are deficient in the provisions necessary to furnish suitable remedies and punish offenses against law, the common law, as modified and changed by the constitution and statutes of the State wherein the court having jurisdiction of such civil or criminal cause is held, so far as the same is not inconsistent with the Constitution and laws of the United States, shall be extended to and govern the said courts in the trial and disposition of the cause."

II

Our identification of the correct source of law properly begins with the text of § 1988(a). Congress' first instruction in the statute is that the law to be applied in adjudicating civil rights claims shall be in "conformity with the laws of the United States, so far as such laws are suitable." 42 U.S.C. § 1988(a). This mandate implies that resort to state law—the second step in the process—should not be undertaken before principles of federal law are exhausted. The characterization of § 1983 for statute of limitations purposes is derived from the elements of the cause of action, and Congress' purpose in providing it. These, of course, are matters of federal law. Since federal law is available to decide the question, the language of § 1988(a) directs that the matter of characterization should be treated as a federal question. Only the length of the limitations period, and closely related questions of tolling and application, are to be governed by state law.

This interpretation is also supported by Congress' third instruction in § 1988(a): state law shall only apply "so far as the same is not inconsistent with" federal law. This requirement emphasizes "the predominance of the federal interest" in the borrowing process, taken as a whole. *Burnett v. Grattan*, supra. Even when principles of state law are borrowed to assist in the enforcement of this federal remedy, the state rule is adopted as "a federal rule responsive to the need whenever a federal right is impaired." Sullivan v. Little Hunting Park, Inc., 396 U.S. 229, 240 (1969). The importation of the policies and purposes of the States on matters of civil rights is not the primary office of the borrowing provision in § 1988(a); rather, the statute is designed to assure that neutral rules of decision will be available to enforce the civil rights actions, among them § 1983. Congress surely did not intend to assign to state courts and legislatures a conclusive role in the formative function of defining and characterizing the essential elements of a federal cause of action.

. . . The Court of Appeals was therefore correct in concluding that it was not bound by the New Mexico Supreme Court's holding in *DeVargas*.

III

. . . The borrowing of statutes of limitations for § 1983 claims serves . . . policies of repose. Of course, the application of *any* statute of limitations would promote repose. By adopting the statute governing an analogous cause of action under state law, federal law incorporates the State's judgment on the proper balance between the policies of repose and the substantive policies of enforcement embodied in the state cause of action. However, when the federal claim differs from the state cause of action in fundamental respects, the State's choice of a specific period of limitation is, at best, only a rough approximation of "the point at which the interests in favor of protecting valid claims are outweighed by the interests in prohibiting the prosecution of stale ones." Johnson v. Railway Express Agency, Inc., 421 U.S. 454, 463–64 (1975).

Thus, in considering whether all § 1983 claims should be characterized in the same way for limitations purposes, it is useful to recall that § 1983 provides "a uniquely federal remedy against incursions under the claimed authority of state law upon rights secured by the Constitution and laws of the nation." Mitchum v. Foster, 407 U.S. 225, 239 (1972). . . . Therefore, it is "the purest coincidence" when state statutes or common law provide[s] for equivalent remedies; any analogies to those causes of action are bound to be imperfect.

In this light, practical considerations help to explain why a simple, broad characterization of all § 1983 claims best fits the statute's remedial purpose. The experience of the courts that have predicated their choice of the correct statute of limitations on an analysis of the particular facts of each claim demonstrates that their approach inevitably breeds uncertainty and time-consuming litigation that is foreign to the central purposes of § 1983. Almost every § 1983 claim can be favorably analogized to more than one of the ancient common-law forms of action, each of which may be governed by a different statute of limitations. In the case before us, for example, the respondent alleges that he was injured by a New Mexico state police officer who used excessive force to carry out an unlawful arrest. This § 1983 claim is arguably analogous to distinct state tort claims for false arrest, assault and battery, or personal injuries. Moreover, the claim could also be characterized as one arising under a statute, or as governed by the special New Mexico statute authorizing recovery against the State for the torts of its agents.

A catalog of other constitutional claims that have been alleged under § 1983 would encompass numerous and diverse topics and subtopics: discrimination in public employment on the basis of race or the exercise of First Amendment rights, discharge or demotion without procedural due process, mistreatment of school children, deliberate indifference to the medical needs of prison inmates, the seizure of chattels without advance notice or sufficient opportunity to be heard—to identify only a few. If the choice of the statute of limitations were to depend upon the particular facts or the precise legal theory of each claim, counsel could almost always argue, with considerable force, that two or more periods of limitations should apply to each § 1983 claim. Moreover, under such an approach different statutes of limitations would be applied to the various § 1983 claims arising in the same state, and multiple periods of limitations would often apply to the same case.[33] There is no reason to believe that Congress would have sanctioned this interpretation of its statute.

When § 1983 was enacted, it is unlikely that Congress actually foresaw the wide diversity of claims that the new remedy would ultimately embrace. The simplicity of the admonition in § 1988(a) is consistent with the assumption that Congress intended the identification of the appropriate statute of limitations to be an uncomplicated task for judges, lawyers and litigants, rather than a source of uncertainty, and unproductive and ever increasing litigation. Moreover, the legislative purpose to create an effective remedy for the enforcement of federal civil rights is obstructed by uncertainty in the applicable statute of limitations, for scarce resources must be dissipated by useless litigation on collateral matters.

Although the need for national uniformity "has not been held to warrant the displacement of state statutes of limitations for civil rights actions," uniformity within each State is entirely consistent with the borrowing principle contained in § 1988(a). We conclude that the statute is fairly construed as a directive to select, in each state, the one most appropriate statute of limitations for all § 1983 claims. The federal interests in uni-

---

[33] For example, in Polite v. Diehl, 507 F.2d 119 (3d Cir. 1974) (en banc), the plaintiff alleged that police officers unlawfully arrested him, beat him and sprayed him with mace, coerced him into pleading guilty to various offenses, and had his automobile towed away. The court held that a one-year false arrest statute of limitations applied to the arrest claim, a two-year personal injuries statute applied to the beating and coerced-plea claims, and a six-year statute for actions seeking the recovery of goods applied to the towing claim.

formity, certainty, and the minimization of unnecessary litigation all support the conclusion that Congress favored this simple approach.

IV

After exhaustively reviewing the different ways that § 1983 claims have been characterized in every federal circuit, the Court of Appeals concluded that the tort action for the recovery of damages for personal injuries is the best alternative available. We agree that this choice is supported by the nature of the § 1983 remedy, and by the federal interest in ensuring that the borrowed period of limitations not discriminate against the federal civil rights remedy.

The specific historical catalyst for the Civil Rights Act of 1871 was the campaign of violence and deception in the South, fomented by the Ku Klux Klan, which was denying decent citizens their civil and political rights. . . .

The atrocities that concerned Congress in 1871 plainly sounded in tort. Relying on this premise we have found tort analogies compelling in establishing the elements of a cause of action under § 1983 and in identifying the immunities available to defendants. As we have noted, however, the § 1983 remedy encompasses a broad range of potential tort analogies, from injuries to property to infringements of individual liberties.

Among the potential analogies, Congress unquestionably would have considered the remedies established in the Civil Rights Act to be more analogous to tort claims for personal injury than, for example, to claims for damages to property or breach of contract. The unifying theme of the Civil Rights Act of 1871 is reflected in the language of the Fourteenth Amendment that unequivocally recognizes the equal status of every "*person*" subject to the jurisdiction of any of the several States. The Constitution's command is that all "*persons*" shall be accorded the full privileges of citizens; no *person* shall be deprived of life, liberty, or property without due process of law or be denied the equal protection of the laws. A violation of that command is an injury to the individual rights of the person.

. . . Had the 42d Congress expressly focused on the issue decided today, we believe it would have characterized § 1983 as conferring a general remedy for injuries to personal rights.

The relative scarcity of statutory claims when § 1983 was enacted makes it unlikely that Congress would have intended to apply the catchall periods of limitations for statutory claims that were later enacted by many States. Section 1983, of course, is a statute, but it only provides a remedy and does not itself create any substantive rights. . . .

Finally, we are satisfied that Congress would not have characterized § 1983 as providing a cause of action analogous to state remedies for wrongs committed by public officials. It was the very ineffectiveness of state remedies that led Congress to enact the Civil Rights Act in the first place. Congress therefore intended that the remedy provided in § 1983 be independently enforceable whether or not it duplicates a state remedy. The characterization of all § 1983 actions as involving claims for personal injuries minimizes the risk that the choice of a state statute of limitations would not fairly serve the federal interests vindicated by § 1983. General personal injury actions, sounding in tort, constitute a major part of the total volume of civil litigation in the state courts today, and probably did in 1871 when § 1983 was enacted. It is most unlikely that the period of limitations applicable to such claims ever was, or ever would be, fixed in a way that would discriminate against federal claims, or be inconsistent with federal law in any respect.

V

In view of our holding that § 1983 claims are best characterized as personal injury actions, the Court of Appeals correctly applied the three-year statute of limitations governing actions "for an injury to the person or reputation of any person." N.Mex.Stat.Ann. § 37–1–8. The judgment of the Court of Appeals is affirmed.

■ JUSTICE POWELL took no part in the consideration or decision of this case.

■ JUSTICE O'CONNOR, dissenting.

Citing "practical considerations," the Court today decides to jettison a rule of venerable application and adopt instead one "simple, broad characterization of all § 1983 claims." Characterization of § 1983 claims is, I agree, a matter of federal law. But I see no justification, given our longstanding interpretation of 42 U.S.C. § 1988(a) and Congress' awareness of it, for abandoning the rule that courts must identify and apply the statute of limitations of the state claim most closely analogous to the particular § 1983 claim. In declaring that all § 1983 claims, regardless of differences in their essential characteristics, shall be considered most closely analogous to one narrow class of tort, the Court, though purporting to conform to the letter of § 1988(a), abandons the policies § 1988(a) embodies. I respectfully dissent.

I

. . . This Court has consistently interpreted § 1988(a) as instructing that the rule applicable to the analogous state claim shall furnish the rule of decision "so far as the same is not inconsistent with the Constitution and laws of the United States." See, e.g., Board of Regents v. Tomanio, 446 U.S. 478 (1980); Robertson v. Wegmann, 436 U.S. 584 (1978); Johnson v. Railway Express Agency, Inc., 421 U.S. 454 (1975). . . .

Despite vocal criticism of the "confusion" created by individualized statutes of limitation, most federal courts of appeal and state courts have continued the settled practice of seeking appropriate factual analogies for each genus of § 1983 claim. [Citing cases.] These courts have recognized that:

> [t]he variety of possible claims that might be brought under § 1983 is unlimited, ranging from simple police brutality to school desegregation cases. To impose one statute of limitations for actions so diverse would be to disregard the unanimous judgments of the States that periods of limitations should vary with the subject matter of the claim. While the present system of reference to these many state limits is not perfect in operation, it surely preserves some of the judgments that have been made about what appropriate periods of limitation should be for causes of actions diverse in nature. Note, Choice of Law Under § 1983, 37 U.Chi.L.Rev. 494, 504 (1970).

II

The majority concedes that "[b]y adopting the statute governing an analogous cause of action under state law, federal law incorporates the State's judgment on the proper balance between the policies of repose and the substantive policies of enforcement embodied in the state cause of action." Yet the Court posits, without any serious attempt at explanation, that a § 1983 claim differs so fundamentally from a state law cause of action that "any analogies to those causes of action are bound to be imperfect." . . .

Thus, with hardly a backward look, the majority leaves behind a century of precedent. Inspired by "the federal interests in uniformity, certainty, and the minimization of unnecessary litigation," the Court suddenly discovers that § 1988(a) "is fairly construed as a directive to select, in each state, the one most appropriate statute of limitations for all § 1983 claims." This fact, of course, escaped the drafters of the Civil Rights Acts, who referred the courts only to general state law principles. Groping to discern what the 42d Congress would have done had it "expressly focused on the issue decided today," the Court "believes" that "the 42d Congress . . . would have characterized § 1983 as conferring a general remedy for injuries to personal rights."

The Court's all-purpose analogy is appealing; after all, every compensable injury, whether to constitutional or statutory rights, through violence, deception or broken promises, to the person's pocketbook, person or dignity, might plausibly be described as a "personal injury." But so sweeping an analogy is no analogy at all. In all candor, the Court has perceived a need for uniformity and has simply seized this opportunity to legislate it. The Court takes this step even though a number of bills proposed to recent Congresses to standardize § 1983 limitations period have failed of enactment, a fact that the Court would normally interpret as a persuasive indication that Congress does not agree that concerns for uniformity dictate a unitary rule.

As well as coopting federal legislation, the Court's decision effectively forecloses legislative creativity on the part of the States. Were a State now to formulate a detailed statutory scheme setting individualized limitations periods for various § 1983 claims, drawing upon policies regarding the timeliness of suits for assault, libel, written contract, employment disputes, and so on, the Supremacy Clause would dictate that the blunt instrument announced today must supersede such legislative fine-tuning. . . .

In exchange for the accrued, collective wisdom of many legislatures, the Court gains only a half-measure of uniformity. . . . True, the Court's decision means that all § 1983 claims in a given State must be brought within a single set period. Yet even the promise of uniformity within each State is illusory. In achieving state-wide symmetry among civil rights claims the Court creates fresh problems of asymmetry that are of far greater moment to the local practitioner. Any lawyer knows that § 1983 claims do not occur in splendid isolation; they are usually joined with claims under state tort or contract law arising out of the same facts. In the end, today's decision saves neither judges nor local practitioners any headaches, since for 150 years characterization of the state law claims with reference to the relevant facts has been a routine prerequisite to establishing the applicable statute of limitations. As one state high court noted:

> We do not believe that it was the intent of Congress in enacting § 1983 to establish a cause of action with a different statute of limitations than that provided by the State for common law or state statutory action on the identical set of facts. Miller v. City of Overland Park, 231 Kan. 557, 560–62, 646 P.2d 1114, 1116–18 (1982).

Such will be the inevitable result of the Court's decision. For example, under the newly revised Pennsylvania statutory scheme at issue in [a companion case], a state law claim for libel or slander will be stale in one year, but a § 1983 claim based on the same facts can still be filed after two years. More puzzling still, a § 1983 claim for violation of constitutional rights arising out of a breach of contract will be foreclosed in two years but its state law counterpart based on the identical breach will remain fresh and litigable at six years. This sort of half-baked uniformity is a poor substitute for the careful selection of the appropriate state law analogy. . . .

As Professor Mishkin remarked regarding federal choice-of-law rules, often "the call for 'uniformity' " is not so much grounded in any practical necessity as in a "desire for symmetry of abstract legal principles and a revolt against the complexities of a federated system." Paul J. Mishkin, The Variousness of "Federal Law": Competence and Discretion in the Choice of National and State Rules for Decision, 105 U.Pa.L.Rev. 797, 813 (1957). Though the task of characterization is admittedly not "uncomplicated," it is nevertheless a routine feature of state procedural law, a task that is handled daily by the same judges, lawyers and litigants as rely on § 1983, often in the same actions. It was Congress' choice in 1866, when it incorporated by reference "the common law, as modified [by] the statutes of the [forum] state," to forgo legislating a simplistic rule and to entrust judges with the task of integrating a federal remedy into a federal system.

Therefore, I would reverse the Court of Appeals' scholarly but ultimately flawed attempt to impose a single state limitations period for all § 1983 claims. Because I would apply the statute of limitations New Mexico applies to state claims directly analogous to the operative facts of this case, I respectfully dissent.

NOTES ON STATUTES OF LIMITATIONS IN CIVIL RIGHTS ACTIONS

1. CHOOSING AN ANALOGOUS STATE STATUTE

Before *Wilson v. Garcia*, federal courts had to select among competing analogies to determine the limitations period for civil rights actions. The possibilities included: (1) provisions applicable to various tort and contract actions; (2) provisions governing all suits for injury to the person; (3) provisions governing liability based on a statute; (4) provisions specifically applicable to civil rights actions; and (5) "catch-all" provisions for actions not governed by a more specific statute. The approach varied from state to state and from circuit to circuit, and sometimes led to involved disputes about the interaction of state and federal law.[a]

The decision in *Wilson v. Garcia* obviously sought to simplify this process. Did it succeed? What about O'Connor's contention that the majority has introduced a new disuniformity between § 1983 actions and the state tort or contract actions available on the same facts? Which disuniformity is less tolerable?[b]

---

[a] See, e.g., John R. Pagan, Civil Rights and "Personal Injuries": Virginia's Statute of Limitations for § 1983 Suits, 26 Wm. & Mary L.Rev. 199 (1985). For a post-*Wilson* sequel by the same author, see Virginia's Statute of Limitations for Section 1983 Claims After *Wilson v. Garcia*, 19 U.Rich.L.Rev. 257 (1985).

[b] For analysis of the effect of *Wilson v. Garcia*, see Julie A. Davies, In Search of the "Paradigmatic Wrong"?: Selecting a Limitations Period for Section 1983, 36 Kan.L.Rev. 133 (1987); Stephen J. Shapiro, Choosing the Appropriate State Statute of Limitations for Section 1983 Claims After *Wilson v. Garcia*: A Theory Applied to Maryland Law, 16 U.Balt.L.Rev. 242 (1987). For an argument that *Wilson* should be abandoned in favor of a laches doctrine, see Robert Jarvis and Judith Anne Jarvis, The Continuing Problem of Statutes of Limitations in Section 1983 Cases: Is the Answer Out at Sea?, 22 John Marshall L.Rev. 285 (1988) .

2. *OWENS V. OKURE*: CHOICE BETWEEN PERSONAL INJURY STATUTES

Wilson holds that the state statute of limitations for tort suits "for the recovery of damages for personal injuries" is the best choice for § 1983 actions. What happens if the state has several statutes of limitation for personal injury actions?

This situation arose in Owens v. Okure, 488 U.S. 235 (1989). New York had a one-year statute of limitations for intentional torts and a three-year residual statute for personal injury claims not otherwise covered by a specific provision. The plaintiff's action was filed 22 months after the allegedly unlawful arrest that provided the basis for his complaint. The District Court denied a motion to dismiss, but certified the question for interlocutory appeal. The Circuit Court and the Supreme Court affirmed. For a unanimous Court, Justice Marshall noted that "[e]very state has multiple intentional tort limitations provisions, carving up the universe of intentional torts into different configurations." By contrast, "every state has one general or residual statute of limitations governing personal injury actions [which are] easily identifiable by language or application." Because "our task today is to provide courts with a rule for determining the appropriate personal injury limitations statute that can be applied with ease and predictability in all 50 States, [w]e . . . hold that where state law provides multiple statutes of limitations for personal injury actions, courts considering § 1983 claims should borrow the general or residual statute for personal injury actions."

3. REJECTING AN INAPPROPRIATE STATE STATUTE

Before *Wilson*, it was sometimes contended that a state statute of limitations, although designed for or analogous to a § 1983 action, was nevertheless inappropriate because it was inconsistent with federal policy. The easy case arose where a state imposed a shorter limit on § 1983 actions than would be applied to analogous claims under state law. See, e.g., Johnson v. Davis, 582 F.2d 1316 (4th Cir. 1978), where the Fourth Circuit rejected a Virginia statute imposing a one-year limitation on § 1983 actions even though analogous state-law actions generally would have been timely within two years. Even where state law did not overtly discriminate against federal claims, however, questions of compatibility with federal policy sometimes arose.

An example is Burnett v. Grattan, 468 U.S. 42 (1984). Two white employees discharged from a predominantly black Maryland college alleged racial discrimination in violation of 42 U.S.C. §§ 1981, 1983, 1985(3), and 1986. The District Court dismissed these claims as time-barred under a six-month statute of limitations applicable to employment discrimination complaints filed with the Maryland Human Affairs Commission. The Supreme Court rejected that standard, in part because of practical differences between an administrative proceeding before the Maryland commission and a civil action in federal court and in part because of a divergence between the objectives of the two regimes. The Maryland statute was designed for prompt identification and resolution of employment disputes, chiefly through conciliation and private settlement. The federal civil rights statutes were intended to provide compensation and to prevent abuses of state power. That the six-month limitation might protect against "the seemingly endless stream of unfounded, and often stale, lawsuits" against public officers did not matter, for elevating that concern was "manifestly inconsistent" with the central objective of the federal civil rights statutes to provide a remedy for deprivation of federal rights.[c]

4. DETERMINING WHEN A STATUTE IS TOLLED

Federal borrowing of state law to determine the timeliness of federal civil rights actions has not been limited to selection of the most appropriate state statute. Federal courts have also looked to state law to determine the circumstances that will suspend or toll the running of the applicable limitation period. Sometimes, this produces a curious interaction of state and federal law.

In Johnson v. Railway Express Agency, Inc., 421 U.S. 454 (1975), Willie Johnson alleged racial discrimination by his employer and his union with respect to seniority rules and job assignments. He filed a complaint with the Equal Employment Opportunity Commission pursuant to Title VII of the 1964 Civil Rights Act. The Commission has authority to investigate such claims, to seek voluntary compliance, and, in appropriate cases, to bring civil actions. Independent action by the claimant is barred for 180 days. After that time, the claimant can demand a "right-to-sue" letter and institute a Title VII action without waiting for completion of the conciliation process. If the claim is proved, the court may award backpay and affirmative relief, but the backpay cannot begin earlier than two years prior to filing of the complaint.

In Johnson's case the Commission's investigation and attempted conciliation took more than two years. Eventually, the Commission found that there was reasonable cause to believe the charges and gave Johnson notice of his right to sue. He then brought suit in federal court, claiming racial discrimination in violation of both Title VII and 42 U.S.C. § 1981. The latter statute provides that all persons "shall have the same right . . . to make and enforce contracts . . . as is enjoyed by white citizens," and has been construed to reach racial discrimination in employment. The statute was derived from the 1866 and 1870 Civil Rights Acts and contains no limitation provision. The federal court therefore looked to state law. The applicable one-year period had long since passed, but Johnson argued that the running of the statute should be tolled during the pendency of his timely EEOC complaint. The Supreme Court disagreed.

Speaking through Justice Blackmun, the Court noted first that the Title VII and § 1981 remedies were "separate, distinct, and independent." Johnson was therefore entitled to make both claims. But the timeliness of the § 1981 claim would depend on the length of the applicable state statute and on state law as to tolling:

> Any period of limitation, including the one-year period specified by [Tennessee law], is understood fully only in the context of the various circumstances that suspend it from running against a particular cause of action. Although any statute of limitations is necessarily arbitrary, the length of the period allowed for instituting suit inevitably reflects a value judgment concerning the point at which the interests in favor of protecting valid claims are outweighed by the interests in prohibiting prosecution of stale ones. In virtually all statutes of limitations the chronological length of the limitation period is interrelated with provisions regarding tolling,

---

[c] Justice Powell concurred in the judgment on narrower grounds, as did Justice Rehnquist, who was joined by Chief Justice Burger and Justice O'Connor.

> revival, and questions of application. In borrowing a state period of limitation for application to a federal cause of action, a federal court is relying on the State's wisdom in setting a limit, and exceptions thereto, on the prosecution of a closely analogous claim.

State law specified a number of circumstances during which a limitation period would be tolled, but none applied to this case. Therefore, Johnson's § 1981 claim had become time-barred during the pendency of his EEOC complaint.

Justice Marshall, joined by Justices Douglas and Brennan, dissented:

> In my judgment, following the antitolling position of the Court to its logical conclusion produces an inequitable result. Aggrieved employees will be forced into simultaneously prosecuting premature § 1981 actions in the federal courts. In essence, the litigant who first explores conciliation prior to resort to litigation must file a duplicative claim in the district court on which the court will either take no action until the Title VII proceedings are concluded or proceed in frustration of the EEOC attempts to conciliate. No federal policy considerations warrant this waste of judicial time and derogation of the conciliation process.

Does *Wilson v. Garcia* undermine *Johnson* ? Are the federal interests in "uniformity, certainty, and the minimization of unnecessary litigation," found important in *Wilson*, also relevant to determining the circumstances under which a statute of limitations will be tolled? Or is the *Johnson* Court right in thinking that tolling is too integrally related to the duration of the limitations period to be disentangled?

5. FEDERAL LAW IN STATE COURT

INTRODUCTORY NOTE ON FEDERAL LAW IN STATE COURT

It has long been settled that state courts have the power to hear federal claims, absent provision by Congress of exclusive federal jurisdiction. Gulf Offshore Co. v. Mobil Oil Corp., 453 U.S. 473 (1981). A more difficult question is whether state courts also have a duty to hear federal claims. The law on that question is surprisingly complicated. The next main case, *Haywood v. Drown*, addresses that question in the context of § 1983.

A related question is whether state courts that choose to hear federal claims (or that are required to do so) are required to follow federal procedures. In general, the answer is "no." State courts follow state procedures in adjudicating federal claims, just as federal courts follow federal procedures in adjudicating state claims. See Hanna v. Plumer, 380 U.S. 460 (1965). There are exceptions to this rule and, more importantly, difficult questions concerning whether particular state laws are fairly described as procedural or are more closely bound up with the substantive rights on which federal law is supreme. The second main case reprinted below, *Felder v. Casey*, addressed that issue, again in the specific context of § 1983.

Haywood v. Drown

Supreme Court of the United States, 2009.
556 U.S. 729.

■ JUSTICE STEVENS delivered the opinion of the Court.

In our federal system of government, state as well as federal courts have jurisdiction over suits brought pursuant to 42 U.S.C. § 1983, the statute that creates a remedy for violations of federal rights committed by persons acting under color of state law. While that rule is generally applicable to New York's supreme courts—the State's trial courts of general jurisdiction—New York's Correction Law § 24 divests those courts of jurisdiction over § 1983 suits that seek money damages from correction officers. New York thus prohibits the trial courts that generally exercise jurisdiction over § 1983 suits brought against other state officials from hearing virtually all such suits brought against state correction officers. The question presented is whether that exceptional treatment of a limited category of § 1983 claims is consistent with the Supremacy Clause of the United States Constitution.

I

Petitioner, an inmate in New York's Attica Correctional Facility, commenced two § 1983 actions against several correction employees alleging that they violated his civil rights in connection with three prisoner disciplinary proceedings and an altercation. Proceeding pro se, petitioner filed his claims in State Supreme Court and sought punitive damages and attorney's fees. The trial court dismissed the actions on the ground that, under N. Y. Correct. Law Ann. § 24 (West 1987) (hereinafter Correction Law § 24), it lacked jurisdiction to entertain any suit arising under state or federal law seeking money damages from correction officers for actions taken in the scope of their employment. The intermediate appellate court summarily affirmed the trial court. The New York Court of Appeals, by a 4–to–3 vote, also affirmed. . . . [W]e granted certiorari [and] now reverse.

II

Motivated by the belief that damages suits filed by prisoners against state correction officers were by and large frivolous and vexatious, New York passed Correction Law § 24. The statute employs a two-step process to strip its courts of jurisdiction over such damages claims and to replace those claims with the State's preferred alternative. The provision states in full:

> 1. No civil action shall be brought in any court of the state, except by the attorney general on behalf of the state, against any officer or employee of the department, in his personal capacity, for damages arising out of any act done or the failure to perform any act within the scope of employment and in the discharge of the duties by such officer or employee.
>
> 2. Any claim for damages arising out of any act done or the failure to perform any act within the scope of employment and in the discharge of the duties of any officer or employee of the department shall be brought and maintained in the court of claims as a claim against the state.

Thus, under this scheme, a prisoner seeking damages from a correction officer will have his claim dismissed for want of jurisdiction and will be left, instead, to pursue a claim for damages against an entirely different party (the State) in the Court of Claims—a court of limited jurisdiction.[1]

For prisoners seeking redress, pursuing the Court of Claims alternative comes with strict conditions. In addition to facing a different defendant, plaintiffs in that Court are not provided with the same relief, or the same procedural protections, made available in § 1983 actions brought in state courts of general jurisdiction. Specifically, under New York law, plaintiffs in the Court of Claims must comply with a 90–day notice requirement; are not entitled to a jury trial; have no right to attorney's fees; and may not seek punitive damages or injunctive relief.

We must decide whether Correction Law § 24, as applied to § 1983 claims, violates the Supremacy Clause.

III

This Court has long made clear that federal law is as much the law of the several States as are the laws passed by their legislatures. Federal and state law "together form one system of jurisprudence, which constitutes the law of the land for the State; and the courts of the two jurisdictions are not foreign to each other, nor to be treated by each other as such, but as courts of the same country, having jurisdiction partly different and partly concurrent." Claflin v. Houseman, 93 U.S. 130, 136–37 (1876). Although § 1983, a Reconstruction-era statute, was passed "to interpose the federal courts between the States and the people, as guardians of the people's federal rights," Mitchum v. Foster, 407 U.S. 225, 242 (1972), state courts as well as federal courts are entrusted with providing a forum for the vindication of federal rights violated by state or local officials acting under color of state law.

So strong is the presumption of concurrency that it is defeated only in two narrowly defined circumstances: first, when Congress expressly ousts state courts of jurisdiction; and second, "[w]hen a state court refuses jurisdiction because of a neutral state rule regarding the administration of the courts," Howlett v. Rose, 496 U.S. 356, 372 (1990). Focusing on the latter circumstance, we have emphasized that only a neutral jurisdictional rule will be deemed a "valid excuse" for departing from the default assumption that "state courts have inherent authority, and are thus presumptively competent, to adjudicate claims arising under the laws of the United States." Tafflin v. Levitt, 493 U.S. 455, 458 (1990).

In determining whether a state law qualifies as a neutral rule of judicial administration, our cases have established that a State cannot employ a jurisdictional rule "to dissociate [itself] from federal law because of disagreement with its content or a refusal to recognize the superior authority of its source." *Howlett*, 496 U.S., at 371. In other words, although States retain substantial leeway to establish the contours of their judicial systems, they lack authority to nullify a federal right or cause of action they believe is inconsistent with their local policies. . . .

---

[1] Although the State has waived its sovereign immunity from liability by allowing itself to be sued in the Court of Claims, a plaintiff seeking damages against the State in that court cannot use § 1983 as a vehicle for redress because a State is not a "person" under § 1983. See Will v. Michigan Dept. of State Police, 491 U.S. 58, 66 (1989). [Thus, although state-law tort claims could be brought directly against the state, federal § 1983 damages actions (which include the availability of attorney's fees) could be brought only in federal court.]—[Addition to footnote by eds.]

It is principally on this basis that Correction Law § 24 violates the Supremacy Clause. In passing Correction Law § 24, New York made the judgment that correction officers should not be burdened with suits for damages arising out of conduct performed in the scope of their employment. Because it regards these suits as too numerous or too frivolous (or both), the State's longstanding policy has been to shield this narrow class of defendants from liability when sued for damages.[2] The State's policy, whatever its merits, is contrary to Congress' judgment that *all* persons who violate federal rights while acting under color of state law shall be held liable for damages. As we have unanimously recognized, "[a] State may not . . . relieve congestion in its courts by declaring a whole category of federal claims to be frivolous. Until it has been proved that the claim has no merit, that judgment is not up to the States to make." *Howlett*, 496 U.S., at 380. . . . That New York strongly favors a rule shielding correction officers from personal damages liability and substituting the State as the party responsible for compensating individual victims is irrelevant. The State cannot condition its enforcement of federal law on the demand that those individuals whose conduct federal law seeks to regulate must nevertheless escape liability.

IV

While our cases have uniformly applied the principle that a State cannot simply refuse to entertain a federal claim based on a policy disagreement, we have yet to confront a statute like New York's that registers its dissent by divesting its courts of jurisdiction over a disfavored federal claim in addition to an identical state claim. The New York Court of Appeals' holding was based on the misunderstanding that this equal treatment of federal and state claims rendered Correction Law § 24 constitutional. To the extent our cases have created this misperception, we now make clear that equality of treatment does not ensure that a state law will be deemed a neutral rule of judicial administration and therefore a valid excuse for refusing to entertain a federal cause of action.

Respondents correctly observe that, in the handful of cases in which this Court has found a valid excuse, the state rule at issue treated state and federal claims equally. In Douglas v. New York, N. H. & H. R. Co., 279 U.S. 377 (1929), we upheld a state law that granted state courts discretion to decline jurisdiction over state and federal claims alike when neither party was a resident of the State. Later, in Herb v. Pitcairn, 324 U.S. 117 (1945), a city court dismissed an action brought under the Federal Employers' Liability Act (FELA), 45 U.S.C. § 51 et seq., for want of jurisdiction because the cause of action arose outside the court's territorial jurisdiction. We upheld the dismissal on the ground that the State's venue laws were not being applied in a way that discriminated against the federal claim. In a third case, Missouri ex rel. Southern R. Co. v. Mayfield, 340 U.S. 1 (1950), we held that a State's application of the forum non conveniens doctrine to

---

[2] In many respects, Correction Law § 24 operates more as an immunity-from-damages provision than as a jurisdictional rule. . . . In Howlett v. Rose, 496 U.S. 356 (1990), we considered the question whether a Florida school board could assert a state-law immunity defense in a § 1983 action brought in state court when the defense would not have been available if the action had been brought in federal court. We unanimously held that the State's decision to extend immunity "over and above [that which is] already provided in § 1983 . . . directly violates federal law," and explained that the "elements of, and the defenses to, a federal cause of action are defined by federal law." Thus, if Correction Law § 24 were understood as offering an immunity defense, *Howlett* would compel the conclusion that it violates the Supremacy Clause.

bar adjudication of a FELA case brought by nonresidents was constitutionally sound as long as the policy was enforced impartially. And our most recent decision finding a valid excuse, Johnson v. Fankell, 520 U.S. 911 (1997), rested largely on the fact that Idaho's rule limiting interlocutory jurisdiction did not discriminate against § 1983 actions.

Although the absence of discrimination is necessary to our finding a state law neutral, it is not sufficient. A jurisdictional rule cannot be used as a device to undermine federal law, no matter how evenhanded it may appear. As we made clear in *Howlett*, "[t]he fact that a rule is denominated jurisdictional does not provide a court an excuse to avoid the obligation to enforce federal law if the rule does not reflect the concerns of power over the person and competence over the subject matter that jurisdictional rules are designed to protect." Ensuring equality of treatment is thus the beginning, not the end, of the Supremacy Clause analysis.

In addition to giving too much weight to equality of treatment, respondents mistakenly treat this case as implicating the "great latitude [States enjoy] to establish the structure and jurisdiction of their own courts." *Howlett*, at 372. Although Correction Law § 24 denies state courts authority to entertain damages actions against correction officers, this case does not require us to decide whether Congress may compel a State to offer a forum, otherwise unavailable under state law, to hear suits brought pursuant to § 1983. The State of New York has made this inquiry unnecessary by creating courts of general jurisdiction that routinely sit to hear analogous § 1983 actions. . . . For instance, if petitioner had attempted to sue a police officer for damages under § 1983, the suit would be properly adjudicated by a state supreme court. Similarly, if petitioner had sought declaratory or injunctive relief against a correction officer, that suit would be heard in a state supreme court. It is only a particular species of suits—those seeking damages relief against correction officers—that the State deems inappropriate for its trial courts.[3]

We therefore hold that, having made the decision to create courts of general jurisdiction that regularly sit to entertain analogous suits, New York is not at liberty to shut the courthouse door to federal claims that it considers at odds with its local policy. A State's authority to organize its courts, while considerable, remains subject to the strictures of the Constitution. We have never treated a State's invocation of "jurisdiction" as a trump that ends the Supremacy Clause inquiry, and we decline to do so in this case. Because New York's supreme courts generally have personal jurisdiction over the parties in § 1983 suits brought by prisoners against correction officers and because they hear the lion's share of all other § 1983 actions, we find little concerning "power over the person and competence over the subject matter" in Correction Law § 24.[5]

---

[3] While we have looked to a State's "common-law tort analogues" in deciding whether a state procedural rule is neutral, see Felder v. Casey, 487 U.S. 131, 146, n. 3 (1988), we have never equated "analogous claims" with "identical claims." Instead, we have searched for a similar claim under state law to determine whether a State has established courts of adequate and appropriate jurisdiction capable of hearing a § 1983 suit. See Testa v. Katt, 330 U.S. 386, 388, 394 (1947); Martinez v. California, 444 U.S. 277, 283–84, n.7 (1980) ("[W]here the same *type* of claim, if arising under state law, would be enforced in the state courts, the state courts are generally not free to refuse enforcement of the federal claim" (emphasis added)). Section 1983 damages claims against other state officials and equitable claims against correction officers are both sufficiently analogous to petitioner's § 1983 claims.

[5] The dissent's proposed solution would create a blind spot in the Supremacy Clause. If New York had decided to employ a procedural rule to burden the enforcement of federal law,

Accordingly, the dissent's fear that "no state jurisdictional rule will be upheld as constitutional" is entirely unfounded. Our holding addresses only the unique scheme adopted by the State of New York—a law designed to shield a particular class of defendants (correction officers) from a particular type of liability (damages) brought by a particular class of plaintiffs (prisoners). Based on the belief that damages suits against correction officers are frivolous and vexatious, Correction Law § 24 is effectively an immunity statute cloaked in jurisdictional garb. Finding this scheme unconstitutional merely confirms that the Supremacy Clause cannot be evaded by formalism.

V

The judgment of the New York Court of Appeals is reversed, and the case is remanded to that court for further proceedings not inconsistent with this opinion. . . .

▪ JUSTICE THOMAS, with whom THE CHIEF JUSTICE, JUSTICE SCALIA, and JUSTICE ALITO join as to Part III, dissenting.

The Court holds that New York Correction Law Annotated § 24, which divests New York's state courts of subject-matter jurisdiction over suits seeking money damages from correction officers, violates the Supremacy Clause of the Constitution because it requires the dismissal of federal actions brought in state court under 42 U.S.C. § 1983. I disagree. Because neither the Constitution nor our precedent requires New York to open its courts to § 1983 federal actions, I respectfully dissent.

I

Although the majority decides this case on the basis of the Supremacy Clause, the proper starting point is Article III of the Constitution. Article III, § 1, provides that "[t]he judicial Power of the United States, shall be vested in one supreme Court, and in such inferior Courts as the Congress may from time to time ordain and establish." The history of the drafting and ratification of this Article establishes that it leaves untouched the States' plenary authority to decide whether their local courts will have subject-matter jurisdiction over federal causes of action.

The text of Article III reflects the Framers' agreement that the National Government needed a Supreme Court. There was sharp disagreement at the Philadelphia Convention, however, over the need for lower federal courts. Several of the Framers, most notably James Madison, favored a strong central government that included lower federal tribunals. Under the Virginia Plan, the Constitution would have established a "National Judiciary . . . to consist of one or more supreme tribunals, and of inferior tribunals to be chosen by the National Legislature." 1 Records of the Federal Convention of 1787, p. 21 (M. Farrand ed. 1911) (hereinafter Farrand). A revised version of the proposal, which stated that the National Judiciary would " 'consist of One supreme tribunal, and of one or more inferior tribunals,' " was approved on June 4, 1787. Id., at 95.

---

the dissent would find the scheme unconstitutional. Yet simply because New York has decided to impose an even greater burden on a federal cause of action by selectively withdrawing the jurisdiction of its courts, the dissent detects no constitutional violation. Thus, in the dissent's conception of the Supremacy Clause, a State could express its disagreement with (and even open hostility to) a federal cause of action, declare a desire to thwart its enforcement, and achieve that goal by removing the disfavored category of claims from its courts' jurisdiction. If this view were adopted, the lesson of our precedents would be that other States with unconstitutionally burdensome procedural rules did not go far enough "to avoid the obligation to enforce federal law." *Howlett*, 469 U.S., at 381.

The following day, however, John Rutledge raised an objection to "establishing any national tribunal except a single supreme one." Id., at 119. He proposed striking the language providing for the creation of lower federal courts because state courts were "most proper" for deciding "all cases in the first instance." According to Rutledge, "the right of appeal to the supreme national tribunal [was] sufficient to secure the national rights [and] uniformity of Judgm[en]ts," and the lower federal courts were thus an "unnecessary encroachment" on the sovereign prerogative of the States to adjudicate federal claims. Madison nonetheless defended the Virginia Plan. He countered that "inferior [federal] tribunals . . . dispersed throughout the Republic" were necessary to meet the needs of the newly formed government: "An effective Judiciary establishment commensurate to the legislative authority [is] essential. A Government without a proper Executive [and] Judiciary would be the mere trunk of a body without arms or legs to act or move." But despite Madison's objections, Rutledge's motion prevailed.

Madison and James Wilson soon thereafter proposed alternative language that " 'empowered [Congress] to institute inferior tribunals.' " This version moderated the original Virginia Plan because of the "distinction between establishing such tribunals absolutely, and giving a discretion to the Legislature to establish or not establish [inferior federal courts]." Over continued objections that such courts were an unnecessary expense and an affront to the States, the scaled-back version of the Virginia Plan passed.

On June 15, 1787, however, the New Jersey Plan was introduced. Although it did not directly challenge the decision to permit Congress to "institute" inferior federal courts, the plan, among other things, required state courts to adjudicate federal claims. . . .

The introduction of the New Jersey Plan reignited the debate over the need for lower federal courts. . . . At the conclusion of this debate, the New Jersey Plan, including its component requiring state-court consideration of federal claims, was defeated and the Madison–Wilson proposal was delivered to the Committee of Detail. The Committee amended the proposal's language to its current form in Article III, which gives Congress the power to "ordain and establish" inferior federal courts. The delegates to the Constitutional Convention unanimously adopted this revised version and it was ultimately ratified by the States.

This so-called Madisonian Compromise bridged the divide "between those who thought that the establishment of lower federal courts should be constitutionally mandatory and those who thought there should be no federal courts at all except for a Supreme Court with, inter alia, appellate jurisdiction to review state court judgments." R. Fallon, D. Meltzer, & D. Shapiro, Hart and Wechsler's The Federal Courts and the Federal System 348 (4th ed. 1996). In so doing, the compromise left to the wisdom of Congress the creation of lower federal courts. . . .

The assumption that state courts would continue to exercise concurrent jurisdiction over federal claims was essential to this compromise. See The Federalist No. 82, pp. 130, 132 (E. Bourne ed. 1947) (A. Hamilton) ("[T]he inference seems to be conclusive, that the State courts would have a concurrent jurisdiction in all cases arising under the laws of the Union, where it was not expressly prohibited"). In light of that historical understanding, this Court has held that, absent an Act of Congress providing for exclusive jurisdiction in the lower federal courts, the "state courts have inherent authority, and are thus presumptively competent, to adjudicate claims arising under the laws of the United States." Tafflin v. Levitt, 493

U.S. 455, 458–59 (1990). As a result, "if exclusive jurisdiction [in the federal courts] be neither express nor implied, the State courts have concurrent jurisdiction whenever, by their own constitution, they are competent to take it." Claflin v. Houseman, 93 U.S. 130, 136 (1876).

The Constitution's implicit preservation of state authority to entertain federal claims, however, did not impose a duty on state courts to do so. As discussed above, there was at least one proposal to expressly require state courts to take original jurisdiction over federal claims (subject to appeal in federal court) that was introduced in an attempt to forestall the creation of lower federal courts. But in light of the failure of this proposal—which was offered before the adoption of the Madisonian Compromise—the assertions by its supporters that state courts would ordinarily entertain federal causes of action cannot reasonably be viewed as an assurance that the States would never alter the subject-matter jurisdiction of their courts. The Framers' decision to empower Congress to create federal courts that could either supplement or displace state-court review of federal claims, as well as the exclusion of any affirmative command requiring the States to consider federal claims in the text of Article III, confirm this understanding.

The earliest decisions addressing this question, written by then-serving and future Supreme Court Justices, confirm that state courts remain "tribunals over which the government of the Union has no adequate control, and which may be closed to any claim asserted under a law of the United States." Osborn v. Bank of United States, 9 Wheat. 738, 821 (1824). "The states, in providing their own judicial tribunals, have a right to limit, control, and restrict their judicial functions, and jurisdiction, according to their own mere pleasure." Mitchell v. Great Works Milling & Mfg. Co., 17 F. Cas. 496, 499 (No. 9,662) (CCD Me. 1843) (Story, J.). In short, there was "a very clear intimation given by the judges of the Supreme Court, that the state courts were not bound in consequence of any act of Congress, to assume and exercise jurisdiction in such cases. It was merely permitted to them to do so as far, as was compatible with their state obligations." 1 J. Kent, Commentaries on American Law 375 (1826).

Under our federal system, therefore, the States have unfettered authority to determine whether their local courts may entertain a federal cause of action. Once a State exercises its sovereign prerogative to deprive its courts of subject-matter jurisdiction over a federal cause of action, it is the end of the matter as far as the Constitution is concerned.

The present case can be resolved under this principle alone. New York Correction Law § 24 (NYCLA) provides that "[n]o civil action shall be brought in any court of the state, except by the attorney general on behalf of the state, against any officer or employee of the department, in his personal capacity, for damages arising out of any act done or the failure to perform any act within the scope of the employment and in the discharge of the duties by such officer or employee." The majority and petitioner agree that this statute erects a jurisdictional bar that prevents the state courts from entertaining petitioner's claim for damages under § 1983. Because New York's decision to withdraw jurisdiction over § 1983 damages actions—or indeed, over any claims—does not offend the Constitution, the judgment below should be affirmed.

II

The Court has evaded Article III's limitations by finding that the Supremacy Clause constrains the States' authority to define the subject-matter jurisdiction of their own courts. In particular, the Court has held that "the Federal Constitution prohibits state courts of general jurisdiction from refusing" to entertain a federal claim "solely because the suit is brought under a federal law" as a "state may not discriminate against rights arising under federal laws." McKnett v. St. Louis & San Francisco R. Co., 292 U.S. 230, 233–34 (1934). There is no textual or historical support for the Court's incorporation of this antidiscrimination principle into the Supremacy Clause.

A

1

The Supremacy Clause provides that "[t]his Constitution, and the Laws of the United States which shall be made in Pursuance thereof . . . shall be the supreme Law of the Land; and the Judges in every State shall be bound thereby, any Thing in the Constitution or Laws of any State to the Contrary notwithstanding." Under this provision, "[t]he laws of the United States are laws in the several States, and just as much binding on the citizens and courts thereof as the State laws are. . . . The two together form one system of jurisprudence, which constitutes the law of the land for the State." *Claflin*, 93 U.S., at 136–37. Thus, a valid federal law is substantively superior to a state law; "if a state measure conflicts with a federal requirement, the state provision must give way." Swift & Co. v. Wickham, 382 U.S. 111, 120 (1965). As a textual matter, however, the Supremacy Clause does not address whether a state court must entertain a federal cause of action; it provides only a rule of decision that the state court must follow if it adjudicates the claim.

The Supremacy Clause's path to adoption at the Convention confirms this focus. Its precursor was introduced as part of the New Jersey Plan. But, as explained above, the New Jersey Plan also included an entirely separate provision that addressed state-court jurisdiction, which would have required all federal questions to "b[e] determined in the first instance in the courts of the respective states." 3 Farrand 287. These two provisions of the New Jersey Plan worked in tandem to require state courts to entertain federal claims and to decide the substantive dispute in favor of federal law if a conflict between the two arose.

After the adoption of the Madisonian Compromise and the defeat of the New Jersey Plan, the Framers returned to the question of federal supremacy. A proposal was introduced granting Congress the power to " 'negative all laws passed by the several States (contravening in the opinion of [Congress] the articles of Union, or any treaties subsisting under the authority of [Congress]).' " 2 id., at 27. James Madison believed the proposal "essential to the efficacy [and] security of the [federal] Gov[ernmen]t." But others at the Convention, including Roger Sherman, "thought it unnecessary, as the Courts of the States would not consider as valid any law contravening the Authority of the Union, and which the legislature would wish to be negatived." In the end, Madison's proposal was defeated. But as a substitute for that rejected proposal, Luther Martin resurrected the Supremacy Clause provision from the New Jersey Plan and it was unanimously approved.

This historical record makes clear that the Supremacy Clause's exclusive function is to disable state laws that are substantively inconsistent with federal law—not to require state courts to hear federal claims over which the courts lack jurisdiction. This was necessarily the case when the clause was first introduced as part of the New Jersey Plan, as it included a separate provision to confront the jurisdictional question. Had that plan prevailed and been ratified by the States, construing the Supremacy Clause to address state-court jurisdiction would have rendered the separate jurisdictional component of the New Jersey Plan mere surplusage.

The Supremacy Clause's exclusive focus on substantive state law is also evident from the context in which it was revived. First, the Clause was not adopted until after the New Jersey Plan's rejection, as part of the entirely separate debate over Madison's proposal to grant Congress the power to "negative" the laws of the States. By then, the Framers had already adopted Article III, thereby ending the fight over state-court jurisdiction. The question before the Convention thus was not which courts (state or federal) were best suited to adjudicate federal claims, but which branch of government (Congress or the courts) would be most effective in vindicating the substantive superiority of federal law. The Supremacy Clause was directly responsive to that question.

Second, the timing of the Clause's adoption suggests that the Framers viewed it as achieving the same end as Madison's congressional "negative" proposal. Although Madison believed that Congress could most effectively countermand inconsistent state laws, the Framers decided that the Judiciary could adequately perform that function. There is no evidence that the Framers envisioned the Supremacy Clause as having a substantively broader sweep than the proposal it replaced. And, there can be no question that Madison's congressional "negative" proposal was entirely unconcerned with the dispute over whether state courts should be required to exercise jurisdiction over federal claims. Indeed, Madison's proposal did not require the States to become enmeshed in any federal business at all; it merely provided that state laws could be directly nullified if Congress found them to be inconsistent with the Constitution or laws of the United States. The role of the Supremacy Clause is no different. It does not require state courts to entertain federal causes of action. Rather, it only requires that in reaching the merits of such claims, state courts must decide the legal question in favor of the "law of the Land." . . .

The supremacy of federal law, therefore, is not impugned by a State's decision to strip its local courts of subject-matter jurisdiction to hear certain federal claims. Subject-matter jurisdiction determines only whether a court has the power to entertain a particular claim—a condition precedent to reaching the merits of a legal dispute. Although the line between subject-matter jurisdiction over a claim and the merits of that claim can at times prove difficult to draw, the distinction is crucial in the Supremacy Clause context. If the state court does not reach the merits of the dispute for lack of statutory or constitutional jurisdiction, the preeminence of federal law remains undiminished. . . .

2

The Court was originally faithful to this conception of federal supremacy. In *Claflin*, the Court concluded that because the federal statute under consideration did not deprive the state court of jurisdiction, the state court was competent to resolve the claim. But the Court was careful to also explain that the Constitution did not impose an obligation on the States to accept jurisdiction over such claims. See 93 U.S., at 137 (explaining that there "is no reason why the State courts should not be open for the prosecution of rights growing out of the laws of the United States, to which their jurisdiction is competent, and not denied"). The Constitution instead left the States with the choice—but not the obligation—to entertain federal actions.

Then in Second Employers' Liability Cases, 223 U.S. 1 (1912), the Court applied the rule set forth in *Claflin* and correctly rejected a Connecticut court's refusal to enforce the 1908 Federal Employers' Liability Act (FELA), 45 U.S.C. § 51 et seq. FELA neither provided for exclusive federal jurisdiction nor attempted to require state courts to entertain claims brought under it. Therefore, the statute was enforceable "as of right, in the courts of the States *when their jurisdiction, as prescribed by local laws, is adequate to the occasion*." 223 U.S., at 55 (emphasis added). Connecticut had not deprived its courts of subject-matter jurisdiction over FELA claims; thus, the state court's refusal to hear the claim was "not because the ordinary jurisdiction of the Superior Courts, as defined by the constitution and laws of the State, was deemed inadequate or not adapted to the adjudication of such a case." Rather, the state court took the position that "it would be inconvenient and confusing for the same court, in dealing with cases of the same general class, to apply in some the standards of right established by the congressional act and in others the different standards recognized by the laws of the State."

The Court's reversal of such a decision is compatible with the original understanding of Article III and the Supremacy Clause. Because there was no question that the state court had subject-matter jurisdiction under state law to adjudicate the federal claim, the Court correctly observed that the state court's refusal to decide the case amounted to a policy dispute with federal law: "When Congress, in the exertion of the power confided to it by the Constitution, adopted that [federal] act, it spoke for all the people and all the States, and thereby established a policy for all. That policy is as much the policy of Connecticut as if the act had emanated from its own legislature, and should be respected accordingly in the courts of the State." It was for this specific reason, then, that the Court rejected Connecticut's refusal to adjudicate the federal claim. As the Court correctly noted, the "existence of the jurisdiction creates an implication of duty to exercise it, and that its exercise may be onerous does not militate against that implication."

But nothing in *Second Employers'* suggested that the Supremacy Clause could pre-empt a state law that deprived the local court of subject-matter jurisdiction over the federal claim. Instead, the *Second Employers'* Court took exactly the opposite position on this question: "[W]e deem it well to observe that there is not here involved any attempt by Congress to enlarge or regulate the jurisdiction of state courts . . . but only a question of the duty of such a court, when its ordinary jurisdiction as prescribed by local laws is appropriate to the occasion."

The Court again confronted this issue in Douglas v. New York, N. H. & H. R. Co., 279 U.S. 377 (1929). There, the Court considered whether a New York court was required to hear a claim brought under FELA. Unlike the Connecticut court in *Second Employers'*, however, the New York court did not have jurisdiction under state law to entertain the federal cause of action. As a result, this Court upheld the state-court ruling that dismissed the claim. . . . [B]ecause the New York court lacked subject-matter jurisdiction under state law, it was not "otherwise competent" to adjudicate the federal claim.

In sum, *Claflin*, *Second Employers'*, and *Douglas* together establish that a state courts inability to entertain a federal claim because of a lack of state-law jurisdiction is an "otherwise valid excuse" that in no way denies the superiority of federal substantive law. It simply disables the state court from adjudicating a claim brought under that federal law.

3

It was not until five years after *Douglas* that the Court used the Supremacy Clause to strike down a state jurisdictional statute for its failure to permit state-court adjudication of federal claims. See McKnett v. St. Louis & San Francisco R. Co., 292 U.S. 230 (1934). The Court started by correctly noting that it "was settled" in *Second Employers'* "that a state court whose ordinary jurisdiction as prescribed by local laws is appropriate to the occasion, may not refuse to entertain suits under [FELA]." Yet, even though the Alabama court *lacked* such jurisdiction over the relevant federal claim pursuant to a state statute, the *McKnett* Court held that the state court had improperly dismissed the federal claim.

According to the Court, "[w]hile Congress has not attempted to compel states to provide courts for the enforcement of [FELA], the Federal Constitution prohibits state courts of general jurisdiction from refusing to do so solely because the suit is brought under a federal law. The denial of jurisdiction by the Alabama court is based solely upon the source of law sought to be enforced. The plaintiff is cast out because he is suing to enforce a federal act. A state may not discriminate against rights arising under federal laws."

For all the reasons identified above, *McKnett* cannot be reconciled with the decisions of this Court that preceded it. Unlike the Connecticut court in *Second Employers'*, the Alabama Supreme Court did not indulge its own bias against adjudication of federal claims in state court by refusing to hear a federal claim over which it had subject-matter jurisdiction. Rather, like the New York court decision affirmed in *Douglas*, the Alabama court's dismissal merely respected a jurisdictional barrier to adjudication of the federal claim imposed by state law. The fact that Alabama courts were competent to hear similar state-law claims should have been immaterial. Alabama had exercised its sovereign right to establish the subject-matter jurisdiction of its courts. Under *Claflin* and its progeny, that legislative judgment should have been upheld.

Despite *McKnett*'s infidelity to the Constitution and more than a century of Supreme Court jurisprudence, the Court's later decisions have repeated *McKnett*'s declaration that state jurisdictional statutes must be policed for antifederal discrimination. See, e.g., Testa v. Katt, 330 U.S. 386, 394 (1947) ("It is conceded that this same type of claim arising under Rhode Island law would be enforced by that State's courts. . . . Under these circumstances the State courts are not free to refuse enforcement of petitioners' claim"); Howlett v. Rose, 496 U.S. 356, 375 (1990) ("[W]hether the question is framed in pre-emption terms, as petitioner would have it, or in the obligation to assume jurisdiction over a 'federal' cause of action, . . . the Florida court's refusal to entertain one discrete category of § 1983 claims, when the court entertains similar state-law actions against state defendants, violates the Supremacy Clause"). The outcome in these cases, however, can be reconciled with first principles notwithstanding the Court's stated reliance on *McKnett*'s flawed interpretation of the Supremacy Clause.

In *Testa*, the Court struck down the Rhode Island Supreme Court's refusal to entertain a claim under the federal Emergency Price Control Act. There was no dispute that "the Rhode Island courts [had] jurisdiction adequate and appropriate under established local law to adjudicate this action." The Rhode Island court nevertheless declined to exercise that jurisdiction under its decision in Robinson v. Norato, 71 R. I. 256, 258, 43 A.2d 467, 468 (1945), which had relied on a "universally acknowledged" doctrine "of private international law" as a basis for refusing to adjudicate federal "penal" claims. Because the Rhode Island Supreme Court had invoked this common-law doctrine despite the existence of state-law statutory jurisdiction over the federal claims, this Court correctly ruled that the state court's "policy against enforcement . . . of statutes of other states and the United States which it deems penal, [could not] be accepted as a 'valid excuse.' "

Testa thus represents a routine application of the rule of law set forth in *Second Employers'*: As long as jurisdiction over a federal claim exists as a matter of state law, state-court judges cannot sua sponte refuse to enforce federal law because they disagree with Congress' decision to allow for adjudication of certain federal claims in state court.

In *Howlett*, the Court likewise correctly struck down a Florida Supreme Court decision affirming the dismissal of a § 1983 suit on state-law sovereign immunity grounds. The Florida court had interpreted the State's statutory "waiver of sovereign immunity" not to extend to federal claims brought in state court. According to the state court, absent a statutory waiver, Florida's pre-existing common-law sovereign immunity rule provided a "blanket immunity on [state] governmental entities from federal civil rights actions under § 1983" brought in Florida courts. Based on this rule, the Florida Supreme Court affirmed the dismissal with prejudice of the § 1983 suit against the state officials.

No antidiscrimination rule was required to strike down the Florida Supreme Court's decision. Even though several Florida courts had concluded that the defense of sovereign immunity was jurisdictional, "[t]he force of the Supremacy Clause is not so weak that it can be evaded by mere mention of the word 'jurisdiction.' " That is, state courts cannot evade their obligation to enforce federal law by simply characterizing a statute or common-law rule as "jurisdictional"; the state law must in fact operate in a jurisdictional manner. No matter where the line between subject-matter jurisdiction and the merits is drawn, Florida's "common law immunity" rule crossed it.

First, because the Florida Supreme Court had dismissed the § 1983 lawsuit with prejudice, its decision was on the merits. Second, Florida's sovereign immunity rule violated the Supremacy Clause by operating as a state-law defense to a federal law. Resolving a federal claim with preclusive effect based on a state-law defense is far different from simply closing the door of the state courthouse to that federal claim. The first changes federal law by denying relief on the merits; the second merely dictates the forum in which the federal claim will be heard.

In the end, of course, "the ultimate touchstone of constitutionality is the Constitution itself and not what we have said about it." Graves v. New York ex rel. O'Keefe, 306 U.S. 466, 491–92 (1939) (Frankfurter, J., concurring). And contrary to *McKnett*, the Constitution does not require state courts to give equal billing to state and federal claims. To read the Supremacy Clause to include an anti-discrimination principle undermines the compromise that shaped Article III and contradicts the original understanding of Constitution. There is no justification for preserving such a principle. But even if the Court chooses to adhere to the antidiscrimination rule as part of the Supremacy Clause inquiry, the rule's infidelity to the text, structure, and history of the Constitution counsels against extending the principle any further than our precedent requires.

B

Although the Supremacy Clause does not, on its own force, pre-empt state jurisdictional statutes of any kind, it may still pre-empt state law once Congress has acted. Federal law must prevail when Congress validly enacts a statute that expressly supersedes state law, or when the state law conflicts with a federal statute. NYCLA § 24 does not fall prey to either category of pre-emption.

First, federal law does not expressly require New York courts to accept jurisdiction over § 1983 suits. Under § 1983, any state official who denies "any citizen of the United States or other person within the jurisdiction thereof . . . any rights, privileges, or immunities secured by the Constitution and laws, shall be liable to the party injured in an action at law, suit in equity, or other proper proceeding for redress." The statute addresses who may sue and be sued for violations of federal law. But it includes no substantive command requiring New York to provide a state judicial forum to a § 1983 plaintiff. . . .

Second, NYCLA § 24 does not conflict with § 1983. As explained above, Congress did not grant § 1983 plaintiffs a "right" to bring their claims in state court or "guarantee" that the state forum would remain open to their suits. Moreover, Congress has created inferior federal courts that have the power to adjudicate all § 1983 actions. And this Court has expressly determined that § 1983 plaintiffs do not have to exhaust state-court remedies before proceeding in federal court. See Patsy v. Bd of Regents of State of Fla., 457 U.S. 496, 516 (1982).

Therefore, even if every state court closed its doors to § 1983 plaintiffs, the plaintiffs could proceed with their claims in the federal forum. And because the dismissal of § 1983 claims from state court pursuant to NYCLA § 24 is for lack of subject-matter jurisdiction, it has no preclusive effect on claims refiled in federal court, see Allen v. McCurry, 449 U.S. 90, 94, 105 (1980) (requiring "a final judgment on the merits" before a § 1983 would be barred in federal court under the doctrine of claim preclusion), and thus does not alter the substance of the federal claim. Any contention that NYCLA § 24 conflicts with § 1983 therefore would be misplaced.

The Court nevertheless has relied on an expansive brand of "conflict" pre-emption to strike down state-court procedural rules that are perceived to "burde[n] the exercise of the federal right" in state court. Felder v. Casey, 487 U.S. 131, 141 (1988). In such cases, the Court has asked if the state-law rule, when applied "to § 1983 actions brought in state courts [is] consistent with the goals of the federal civil rights laws, or does the enforcement of such a requirement instead 'stand as an obstacle to the accomplishment and execution of the full purposes and objectives of Congress'?" See id., at 138 (quoting Hines v. Davidowitz, 312 U.S. 52, 67 (1941)). There has been no suggestion in this case, however, that NYCLA § 24 is a procedural rule that must be satisfied in order to bring the § 1983 action in state court. As explained above, petitioner's claim was not procedurally deficient; the state court simply lacked the power to adjudicate the claim. Thus, the *Felder* line of cases is inapplicable to this case.

But even if there were such a claim made in this case, the Supremacy Clause supplies this Court with no authority to pre-empt a state procedural law merely because it "burdens the exercise" of a federal right in state court. "Under the Supremacy Clause, state law is pre-empted only by federal law 'made in Pursuance' of the Constitution, Art. VI, cl. 2—not by extratextual considerations of the purposes underlying congressional inaction," such as a desire to ensure that federal law is not burdened by state-law procedural obligations. Wyeth v. Levine, 555 U.S. 555, 603 (2009). (Thomas, J., concurring in judgment). A sweeping approach to pre-emption based on perceived congressional purposes "leads to the illegitimate—and thus, unconstitutional—invalidation of state laws." Id., at 604. I cannot agree with the approach employed in *Felder* "that pre-empts state laws merely because they 'stand as an obstacle to the accomplishment and execution of the full purposes and objectives' of federal law . . . as perceived by this Court." 555 U.S., at 604.

III

Even accepting the entirety of the Court's precedent in this area of the law, however, I still could not join the majority's resolution of this case as it mischaracterizes and broadens this Court's decisions. The majority concedes not only that NYCLA § 24 is jurisdictional, but that the statute is neutral with respect to federal and state claims. Nevertheless, it concludes that the statute violates the Supremacy Clause because it finds that "equality of treatment does not ensure that a state law will be deemed a neutral rule of judicial administration and therefore a valid excuse for refusing to entertain a federal cause of action." This conclusion is incorrect in light of Court precedent for several reasons.

A

The majority mischaracterizes this Court's precedent when it asserts that jurisdictional neutrality is "the beginning, not the end, of the Supremacy Clause analysis." As explained above, "subject to only one limitation, each State of the Union may establish its own judicature, distribute judicial power among the courts of its choice, [and] define the conditions for the exercise of their jurisdiction and the modes of their proceeding, to the same extent as Congress is empowered to establish a system of inferior federal courts within the limits of federal judicial power." Brown v. Gerdes, 321 U.S. 178, 188 (1944) (Frankfurter, J., concurring). That "one limitation" is the neutrality principle that the Court has found in the Supremacy Clause. Here, it is conceded that New York has deprived its courts of subject-matter jurisdiction over a particular class of claims on terms that treat federal and state actions equally. That is all this Court's precedent requires.

The majority's assertion that jurisdictional neutrality is not the touchstone because "[a] jurisdictional rule cannot be used as a device to undermine federal law, no matter how even-handed it may appear," reflects a misunderstanding of the law. A jurisdictional statute simply deprives the relevant court of the power to decide the case altogether. Such a statute necessarily operates without prejudice to the adjudication of the matter in a competent forum. Jurisdictional statutes therefore by definition are incapable of undermining federal law. NYCLA § 24 no more undermines § 1983 than the amount-in-controversy requirement for federal diversity jurisdiction undermines state law. The relevant law (state or federal) remains fully operative in both circumstances. The sole consequence of the jurisdictional barrier is that the law cannot be enforced in one particular judicial forum.[10]

---

[10] If by asserting that state law is not permitted to "undermine federal law," the majority instead is arguing that NYCLA § 24 is a procedural rule that too heavily "burdens the exercise of the federal right" in state court, see *Felder*, 487 U.S., at 141, its argument is equally mis-

As a result, the majority's focus on New York's reasons for enacting this jurisdictional statute is entirely misplaced. The States "remain independent and autonomous within their proper sphere of authority." Printz v. United States, 521 U.S. 898, 928 (1997). New York has the organic authority, therefore, to tailor the jurisdiction of state courts to meet its policy goals.

It may be true that it was "Congress' judgment that *all* persons who violate federal rights while acting under color of state law shall be held liable for damages." But Congress has not enforced that judgment by statutorily requiring the States to open their courts to *all* § 1983 claims. And this Court has "never held that state courts must entertain § 1983 suits." National Private Truck Council, Inc. v. Oklahoma Tax Comm'n, 515 U.S. 582, 587, n.4 (1995). Our decisions have held only that the States cannot use jurisdictional statutes to discriminate against federal claims. Because NYCLA § 24 does not violate this command, any policy-driven reasons for depriving jurisdiction over a "federal claim in addition to an identical state claim" are irrelevant for purposes of the Supremacy Clause.

This Court's decision in *Howlett* is not to the contrary. Despite the majority's assertion, *Howlett* does not stand for the proposition "that a State cannot employ a jurisdictional rule 'to dissociate itself from federal law because of disagreement with its content or a refusal to recognize the superior authority of its source.'" As an initial matter, the majority lifts the above quotation—which was merely part of a passage explaining that a "State may not discriminate against federal causes of action"—entirely out of context. *Howlett's* reiteration of *McKnett's* neutrality command, which is all the selected quotation reflects, offers no refuge to the majority in light of its concession that NYCLA § 24 affords "equal treatment" to "federal and state claims."

Howlett instead stands for the unremarkable proposition that States may not add immunity defenses to § 1983. A state law is not jurisdictional just because the legislature has "denominated" it as such. As the majority observes, the State's "invocation of 'jurisdiction' " cannot "trump" the "Supremacy Clause inquiry." The majority, therefore, is correct that a state court's decision "to nullify a federal right or cause of action [that it] believe[s] is inconsistent with [its] local policies" cannot evade the Supremacy Clause by hiding behind a jurisdictional label, because "the Supremacy Clause cannot be evaded by formalism." Rather, a state statute must in fact *operate* jurisdictionally: It must deprive the court of the power to hear the claim and it must not preclude relitigation of the action in a proper forum. *Howlett* proved the point by striking down a state-law immunity rule that

placed. First, the majority concedes that NYCLA § 24 is not a state procedural rule. Second, applying the reasoning of *Felder* to a jurisdictional statute like NYCLA § 24 would overrule all of the Court s decisions upholding state laws that decline jurisdiction over federal claims, and would virtually ensure that in future cases, no state jurisdictional rule will be upheld as constitutional. By simply rendering a federal claim noncognizable in state court, a statute depriving a state court of subject-matter jurisdiction (even under the terms and conditions permitted by this Court's precedent) will always violate *Felder's* command that a state rule must not undermine the "remedial objectives" of a federal claim. The jurisdictional statute also will unavoidably implicate *Felder's* concern that a state rule should not inevitably produce a different outcome depending on whether a claim is asserted in state or federal court. A state jurisdictional statute necessarily will result in a different outcome in state court, where it will cause dismissal of the federal claim, than in federal court, where that claim will be heard. It is for this reason that the Court has been careful to keep its examination of state jurisdictional statutes and state procedural rules in different categories.

bore the jurisdictional label but operated as a defense on the merits and provided for the dismissal of the state court action with prejudice.

. . . Unlike the Florida immunity rule in *Howlett*, NYCLA § 24 is not a defense to a federal claim and the dismissal it authorizes is without prejudice. For this reason, NYCLA § 24 is not merely "denominated" as jurisdictional—it actually is jurisdictional. The New York courts, therefore, have not declared a "category" of § 1983 claims to be " 'frivolous' " or to have " 'no merit' " in order to " 'relieve congestion' " in the state-court system (quoting *Howlett*, at 380). These courts have simply recognized that they lack the power to adjudicate this category of claims regardless of their merit.

The majority's failure to grapple with the clear differences between the immunity rule at issue in *Howlett* and NYCLA § 24 proves that its decision is untethered from precedent. And more broadly, the majority's failure to account for the important role of claim preclusion in evaluating whether a statute is jurisdictional undermines the important line drawn by this Court's decisions between subject-matter jurisdiction and the merits. See Marrese v. American Academy of Orthopaedic Surgeons, 470 U.S. 373, 382 (1985) ("With respect to matters that were not decided in the state proceedings . . . claim preclusion generally does not apply where 'the plaintiff was unable to . . . seek a remedy because of the limitations on the subject matter jurisdiction of the courts' " (quoting Restatement (Second) of Judgments § 26(1)(c)(1982))).

The majority's principal response is that NYCLA § 24 "is effectively an immunity statute cloaked in jurisdictional garb." But this curious rejoinder resurrects an argument that the majority abandons earlier in its own opinion. The majority needs to choose. Either it should definitively commit to making the impossible case that a statute denying state courts the power to entertain a claim without prejudice to its reassertion in federal court is an immunity defense in disguise, or it should clearly explain why some other aspect of *Howlett* controls the outcome of this case. This Court has required Congress to speak clearly when it intends to "upset the usual constitutional balance of federal and state powers." Gregory v. Ashcroft, 501 U.S. 452, 460 (1991). It should require no less of itself.

At bottom, the majority's warning that upholding New York's law "would permit a State to withhold a forum for the adjudication of any federal cause of action with which it disagreed as long as the policy took the form of a jurisdictional rule" is without any basis in fact. This Court's jurisdictional neutrality command already guards against antifederal discrimination. A decision upholding NYCLA § 24, which fully adheres to that rule, would not "circumvent our prior decisions." It simply would adhere to them.[11]

[11] The majority also suggests that allowing jurisdictional neutrality to be the test "would create a blind spot in the Supremacy Clause" because a procedural rule that too heavily burdens a federal cause of action would be struck down as unconstitutional while "a State could express its disagreement with (and even open hostility to) a federal cause of action, declare a desire to thwart its enforcement, and achieve that goal by removing the disfavored category of claims from its courts' jurisdiction." This is incorrect for at least two reasons. First, as explained above, a State may permissibly register its hostility to federal law only by subjecting analogous state-law claims to equally disfavored treatment. Hostility to federal law is thus irrelevant under this Court's precedent—the Supremacy Clause is concerned only with whether there is antifederal discrimination. Second, the majority obscures important differences between procedural rules, like the notice-of-claim rule at issue in *Felder*, and neutral jurisdictional statutes like NYCLA § 24. Unlike a neutral jurisdictional statute, which merely pre-

B

The majority also incorrectly concludes that NYCLA § 24 is not a neutral jurisdictional statute because it applies to a "narrow class of defendants" and because New York courts "hear the lion's share of all other § 1983 actions." A statute's jurisdictional status does not turn on its narrowness or on its breadth. Rather, as explained above, a statute's jurisdictional status turns on the grounds on which the state-law dismissal rests and the consequences that follow from such rulings. No matter how narrow the majority perceives NYCLA § 24 to be, it easily qualifies as jurisdictional under this established standard. Accordingly, it is immaterial that New York has chosen to allow its courts of general jurisdiction to entertain § 1983 actions against certain categories of defendants but not others (such as correction officers), or to entertain § 1983 actions against particular defendants for only certain types of relief.

Building on its assumption that a statute's jurisdictional status turns on its scope, the majority further holds that "having made the decision to create courts of general jurisdiction that regularly sit to entertain analogous suits, New York is not at liberty to shut the courthouse door to federal claims that it considers at odds with its local policy." But whether two claims are "analogous" is relevant only for purposes of determining whether a state jurisdictional statute discriminates against federal law. This inquiry necessarily requires an evaluation of the similarities between *federal* and *state* law claims to assess whether state-court jurisdiction is being denied to a federal claim simply because of its federal character.

In contrast, the majority limits its analysis to state-law claims, finding discrimination based solely on the fact that state law provides jurisdiction in state court for claims against state officials who serve in "analogous" roles to the correction officers. The majority's inquiry is not probative of antifederal discrimination, which is the concern that first led this Court in *McKnett* to find a Supremacy Clause limitation on state-court jurisdictional autonomy. Consequently, there is no support for the majority's assertion that New York's decision to treat police officers differently from correction officers for purposes of civil litigation somehow violates the Constitution.

Worse still, the majority concludes that § 1983 claims for damages against "other state officials" are "sufficiently analogous to petitioner's § 1983 claims" to trigger a Supremacy Clause violation. Under this reasoning, if a State grants its trial courts jurisdiction to hear § 1983 claims for damages against *any* state official, the State's decision to deny those courts the power to entertain some narrower species of § 1983 claims—even on jurisdictionally neutral terms—a fortiori violates the Supremacy Clause. The majority's assurance that its holding is applicable only to New York's "unique scheme" thus rings hollow. The majority is forcing States into an all-or-nothing choice that neither the Constitution nor this Court's decisions require.

---

vents a state court from entertaining a federal claim, failure to comply with a state procedural rule will result in dismissal of a federal claim with prejudice. Contrary to the majority's assertion, therefore, it is not that state courts with "unconstitutionally burdensome procedural rules did not go far enough"—it is instead that they went too far by placing an insurmountable procedural hurdle in the plaintiff's path that led to a judgment against him on the merits. As a result, the Court's assessment of whether a state procedural rule too heavily burdens a federal right does not have any bearing on the Court's continued adherence to the neutrality principle as the sole determinant in evaluating state-law jurisdictional statutes.

Indeed, the majority's novel approach breaks the promise that the States still enjoy " 'great latitude . . . to establish the structure and jurisdiction of their own courts' " (quoting *Howlett*, 496 U.S., at 372). It cannot be that New York has forsaken the right to withdraw a particular class of claims from its courts' purview simply because it has created courts of general jurisdiction that would otherwise have the power to hear suits for damages against correction officers. The Supremacy Clause does not fossilize the jurisdiction of state courts in their original form. Under this Court's precedent, States remain free to alter the structure of their judicial system even if that means certain federal causes of action will no longer be heard in state court, so long as States do so on nondiscriminatory terms. Today's decision thus represents a dramatic and unwarranted expansion of this Court's precedent.

IV

"[I]n order to protect the delicate balance of power mandated by the Constitution, the Supremacy Clause must operate only in accordance with its terms." *Wyeth*, 555 U.S., at 585) (Thomas, J., concurring in judgment). By imposing on state courts a duty to accept subject-matter jurisdiction over federal § 1983 actions, the Court has stretched the Supremacy Clause beyond all reasonable bounds and upended a compromise struck by the Framers in Article III of the Constitution. Furthermore, by declaring unconstitutional even those laws that divest state courts of jurisdiction over federal claims on a non-discriminatory basis, the majority has silently overturned this Court's unbroken line of decisions upholding state statutes that are materially indistinguishable from the New York law under review. And it has transformed a single exception to the rule of state judicial autonomy into a virtually ironclad obligation to entertain federal business. I respectfully dissent.

NOTES ON THE DUTY OF STATE COURTS TO HEAR FEDERAL QUESTIONS

1. *HOWLETT V. ROSE*

Before *Haywood*, the most prominent decision on the duty of state courts to hear § 1983 cases was Howlett v. Rose, 496 U.S. 356 (1990). The plaintiff in *Howlett* was a former high school student who sued the school board (and three officials) for an allegedly illegal search of his car and the resulting suspension. School boards and other local governments are proper defendants under § 1983, Monell v. Dept. of Social Services, 436 U.S. 658 (1978), though states and state agencies are not. Will v. Michigan Dept. of State Police, 491 U.S. 58 (1989). Thus, so far as federal law was concerned, Howell was entitled to bring a § 1983 action (as well as related state-law claims) against the school board in either state or federal court. The Florida courts, however, concluded that Florida's statutory waiver of sovereign immunity applied only to state-law claims and thus barred suit against the school board on federal claims in state court.

So phrased, the ruling of the Florida courts that the school board enjoyed an immunity not recognized by federal law seems a straightforward violation of the Supremacy Clause, and perhaps that is all that need have been said. The Supreme Court, however, wrote more elaborately to review the principles applicable in the area. The Court concluded: (1) that federal claims ordinarily are enforceable in state court; (2) that a "valid excuse" for declining to hear federal claims cannot violate or be inconsistent with federal law; but (3) that a state court ordinarily can refuse jurisdiction under "a neutral state rule regarding the administration of the courts." The attempt to characterize Florida's position as a neutral jurisdictional rule of this sort was unanimously rejected:

> The state of Florida has constituted the Circuit Court for Pinellas County as a court of general jurisdiction. It exercises jurisdiction over tort claims by private citizens against state entities (including school boards), of the size and type of petitioner's claim here, and it can enter judgment against them. That court also exercises jurisdiction over § 1983 actions against individual officers and is fully competent to provide the remedies the federal statute requires. Petitioner has complied with all the state law procedures for invoking the jurisdiction of that court.

The fact that the state called its immunity rule "jurisdictional" was of no consequence: "The force of the Supremacy Clause is not so weak that it can be evaded by mere mention of the word 'jurisdiction.' "

2. QUESTIONS AND COMMENTS ON *HAYWOOD*

As the *Haywood* opinions reveal, the propositions for which the precedents stand may be formulated in at least three ways. Most broadly, *Testa, Howlett,* and *Haywood* may be taken to stand for the proposition that state courts with general jurisdiction cannot decline to adjudicate federal claims for reasons reflecting disagreement with federal policy. Under this reading, *Haywood* was correctly decided, because New York's reasons for redirecting damages actions against corrections officers were contrary to the federal policy embodied in § 1983.

A second reading is slightly narrower. It would take the true principle to be only that state courts with jurisdiction to hear "analogous" state claims cannot discriminate against federal claims by excluding them from state-court jurisdiction. This formulation explains *Howlett* but arguably not *Haywood.* As Justice Thomas pointed out in Part III of his dissent (joined by Roberts, Scalia, and Alito), New York's law treated damage actions against corrections officers the same, whether they were state or federal. Thus, if discrimination against federal claims were the only issue, *Haywood* arguably should have gone the other way.

The most narrow reading is apparently endorsed only by Justice Thomas. He argued in Parts I and II of his dissent that states should be free to discriminate against federal claims so long as the approach is genuinely jurisdictional. Put differently, Thomas believes that states should be free to exclude federal claims from state court so long as (1) Congress has not commanded otherwise (in a valid exercise of its constitutional authority) and (2) the resulting judgments are jurisdictional only, do not resolve the merits, and therefore do not preclude vindication of federal claims in federal court. Even this narrowest statement of the governing principles is sufficient to explain *Howlett*, which is perhaps why that decision was unanimous.

3. THE OCCASIONAL OBLIGATION OF STATE COURTS TO FOLLOW FEDERAL PROCEDURES IN ADJUDICATING FEDERAL CLAIMS

As noted, state courts are generally free to follow state procedures in the adjudication of federal claims. Questions arise, however, when a state "procedure" burdens a federal right. That issue is addressed in the next main case. Is it essentially the same issue as was presented in *Haywood*? Or are limitations on jurisdiction and burdensome procedures importantly different? Is it sufficient that in all events, § 1983 plaintiffs have the option of suing in federal court?

Felder v. Casey

Supreme Court of the United States, 1988.
487 U.S. 131.

■ JUSTICE BRENNAN delivered the opinion of the Court.

A Wisconsin statute provides that before suit may be brought in state court against a state or local governmental entity or officer, the plaintiff must notify the governmental defendant of the circumstances giving rise to the claim, the amount of the claim, and his or her intent to hold the named defendant liable. The statute further requires that, in order to afford the defendant an opportunity to consider the requested relief, the claimant must refrain from filing suit for 120 days after providing such notice. Failure to comply with these requirements constitutes grounds for dismissal of the action. In the present case, the Supreme Court of Wisconsin held that this notice-of-claim statute applies to federal civil rights actions brought in state court under 42 U.S.C. § 1983. Because we conclude that these requirements are pre-empted as inconsistent with federal law, we reverse.

I

On July 4, 1981, Milwaukee police officers stopped petitioner Bobby Felder for questioning while searching his neighborhood for an armed suspect. The interrogation proved to be hostile and apparently loud, attracting the attention of petitioner's family and neighbors, who succeeded in convincing the police that petitioner was not the man they sought. According to police reports, the officers then directed petitioner to return home, but he continued to argue and allegedly pushed one of them, thereby precipitating his arrest for disorderly conduct. Petitioner alleges that in the course of this arrest the officers beat him about the head and face with batons, dragged him across the ground, and threw him, partially unconscious, into the back of a paddy wagon face first, all in full view of his family and neighbors. Shortly afterwards, in response to complaints from these neighbors, a local city alderman and members of the Milwaukee Police Department arrived on the scene and began interviewing witnesses to the arrest. Three days later, the local alderman wrote directly to the chief of police requesting a full investigation into the incident. Petitioner, who is black, alleges that various members of the police department responded to this request by conspiring to cover up the misconduct of the arresting officers, all of whom are white. The department took no disciplinary action against any of the officers, and the city attorney subsequently dropped the disorderly conduct charge against petitioner.

Nine months after the incident, petitioner filed this action in the Milwaukee County Circuit Court against the city of Milwaukee and certain of its police officers, alleging that the beating and arrest were unprovoked and racially motivated, and violated his rights under the Fourth and Fourteenth Amendments to the United States Constitution. He sought redress under 42 U.S.C. § 1983, as well as attorneys fees pursuant to § 1988. The officers moved to dismiss the suit based on petitioner's failure to comply with the State's notice-of-claim statute. That statute provides that no action may be brought or maintained against any state governmental subdivision, agency, or officer unless the claimant either provides written notice of the claim within 120 days of the alleged injury, or demonstrates that the relevant subdivision, agency, or officer had actual notice of the claim and was not prejudiced by the lack of written notice. Wis.Stat. § 893.80(1)(a) (1983 and Supp. 1987).[2] The statute further provides that the party seeking redress must also submit an itemized statement of the relief sought to the governmental subdivision or agency, which then has 120 days to grant or disallow the requested relief. Finally, claimants must bring suit within six months of receiving notice that their claim has been disallowed.

The trial court . . . denied the motion. . . . The Wisconsin Supreme Court . . . reversed. [T]he court reasoned that while Congress may establish the procedural framework under which claims are heard in federal courts, States retain the authority under the Constitution to prescribe the rules and procedures that govern actions in their own tribunals. Accordingly, a party who chooses to vindicate a congressionally created right in state court must abide by the State's procedures. Requiring compliance with the notice-of-claim statute, the court determined, does not frustrate the remedial and deterrent purposes of the federal civil rights laws because the statute neither limits the amount a plaintiff may recover for violation of his or her civil rights, nor precludes the possibility of such recovery altogether. Rather, the court reasoned, the notice requirement advances the State's legitimate interests in protecting against stale or fraudulent claims, facilitating prompt settlement of valid claims, and identifying and correcting inappropriate conduct by governmental employees and officials. Turning to the question of compliance in this case, the court concluded that the

---

[2] Section 893.80 provides in relevant part:

(1) Except as provided in sub. (1m), no action may be brought or maintained against any . . . governmental subdivision or agency thereof nor against any officer, official, agent or employee of the . . . subdivision or agency for acts done in their official capacity or in the course of their agency or employment upon a claim or cause of action unless:

> (a) Within 120 days after the happening of the event giving rise to the claim, written notice of the circumstances of the claim signed by the party, agent or attorney is served on the . . . governmental subdivision or agency and on the officer, official, agent or employee. . . . Failure to give the requisite notice shall not bar action on the claim if the . . . governmental subdivision or agency had actual notice of the claim and the claimant shows to the satisfaction of the court that the delay or failure to give the requisite notice has not been prejudicial to the defendant . . . subdivision or agency or to the defendant officer, official, agent or employee; and
>
> (b) A claim containing the address of the claimant and an itemized statement of the relief sought is presented to the appropriate clerk or person who performs the duties of a clerk or secretary for the defendant . . . subdivision or agency and the claim is disallowed. Failure of the appropriate body to disallow within 120 days after presentation is a disallowance. Notice of disallowance shall be served on the claimant by registered or certified mail and the receipt therefor, signed by the claimant, or the returned registered letter, shall be proof of service. No action on a claim against any defendant . . . subdivision or agency nor against any defendant officer, official, agent or employee may be brought after 6 months from the date of service of the notice, and the notice shall contain a statement to that effect.

Many States have adopted similar provisions. See generally Civil Actions Against State Government, Its Divisions, Agencies, and Officers 559–69 (W. Winborne ed. 1982).

complaints lodged with the local police by petitioner's neighbors and the letter submitted to the police chief by the local alderman failed to satisfy the statute's actual notice standard, because these communications neither recited the facts giving rise to the alleged injuries nor revealed petitioner's intent to hold the defendants responsible for those injuries.

We granted certiorari and now reverse.

II

No one disputes the general and unassailable proposition relied upon by the Wisconsin Supreme Court below that States may establish the rules of procedure governing litigation in their own courts. By the same token, however, where state courts entertain a federally created cause of action, the "federal right cannot be defeated by the forms of local practice." Brown v. Western Ry. of Alabama, 338 U.S. 294, 296 (1949). The question before us today, therefore, is essentially one of pre-emption: is the application of the State's notice-of-claim provision to § 1983 actions brought in state courts consistent with the goals of the federal civil rights laws[?] . . . Because the notice-of-claim statute at issue here conflicts both in its purpose and effects with the remedial objectives of § 1983, and because its enforcement in such actions will frequently and predictably produce different outcomes in § 1983 litigation based solely on whether the claim is asserted in state or federal court, we conclude that the state law is pre-empted when the § 1983 action is brought in a state court.

A

. . . Although we have never passed on the question, the lower federal courts have all, with but one exception, concluded that notice-of-claim provisions are inapplicable to § 1983 actions brought in federal court. These courts have reasoned that, unlike the lack of statutes of limitations in the federal civil rights laws, the absence of any notice-of-claim provision is not a deficiency requiring the importation of such statutes into the federal civil rights scheme. Because statutes of limitation are among the universally familiar aspects of litigation considered indispensable to any scheme of justice, it is entirely reasonable to assume that Congress did not intend to create a right enforceable in perpetuity. Notice-of-claim provisions, by contrast, are neither universally familiar nor in any sense indispensable prerequisites to litigation, and there is thus no reason to suppose that Congress intended federal courts to apply such rules, which "significantly inhibit the ability to bring federal actions." Brown v. United States, 742 F.2d 1498, 1507 (D.C. Cir. 1984).

While we fully agree with this near unanimous consensus of the federal courts, that judgment is not dispositive here, where the question is not one of adoption but of pre-emption. Nevertheless, this determination that notice-of-claim statutes are inapplicable to federal-court § 1983 litigation informs our analysis in two crucial respects. First, it demonstrates that the application of the notice requirement burdens the exercise of the federal right by forcing civil rights victims who seek redress in state courts to comply with a requirement that is entirely absent from civil rights litigation in federal courts. This burden, as we explain below, is inconsistent in both design and effect with the compensatory aims of the federal civil rights laws. Second, it reveals that the enforcement of such statutes in § 1983 actions brought in state court will frequently and predictably produce different outcomes in federal civil rights litigation based solely on whether that litigation takes place in state or federal court. States may not apply such an outcome-determinative law when entertaining substantive federal rights in their courts.

B

[T]he central purpose of the Reconstruction–Era laws is to provide compensatory relief to those deprived of their federal rights by state actors. Section 1983 accomplishes this goal by creating a form of liability that, by its very nature, runs only against a specific class of defendants: government bodies and their officials. Wisconsin's notice-of-claim statute undermines this "uniquely federal remedy" in several interrelated ways. First, it conditions the right of recovery that Congress has authorized, and does so for a reason manifestly inconsistent with the purposes of the federal statute: to minimize governmental liability. Nor is this condition a neutral and uniformly applicable rule of procedure; rather, it is a substantive burden imposed only upon those who seek redress for injuries resulting from the use or misuse of governmental authority. Second, the notice provision discriminates against the federal right. While the State affords the victim of an intentional tort two years to recognize the compensable nature of his or her injury, the civil rights victim is given only four months to appreciate that he or she has been deprived of [federal constitutional or] statutory rights. Finally, the notice provision operates, in part, as an exhaustion requirement, in that it forces claimants to seek satisfaction in the first instance from the governmental defendant. We think it plain that Congress never intended that those injured by governmental wrongdoers could be required, as a condition of recovery, to submit their claims to the government responsible for their injuries.

(1)

[Notice of claim statutes] "are enacted primarily for the benefit of governmental defendants" and enable those defendants to "investigate early, prepare a stronger case, and perhaps reach an early settlement." Moreover, where the defendant is unable to obtain a satisfactory settlement, the Wisconsin statute forces claimants to bring suit within a relatively short period after the local governing body disallows the claim, in order to "assure prompt initiation of litigation." To be sure, the notice requirement serves the additional purpose of notifying the proper public officials of dangerous physical conditions or inappropriate and unlawful governmental conduct, which allows for prompt corrective measures. This interest, however, is clearly not the predominant objective of the statute. Indeed, the Wisconsin Supreme Court has emphasized that the requisite notice must spell out both the amount of damages the claimant seeks and his or her intent to hold the governing body responsible for those damages precisely because these requirements further the State's interest in minimizing liability and the expenses associated with it.

In sum, as respondents explain, the State has chosen to expose its subdivisions to large liability and defense costs, and, in light of that choice, has made the concomitant decision to impose conditions that "assis[t] municipalities in controlling those costs." The decision to subject state subdivisions to liability for violations of federal rights, however, was a choice that Congress, not the Wisconsin legislature, made, and it is a decision that the State has no authority to override. Thus, however understandable or laudable the State's interest in controlling liability expenses might otherwise be, it is patently incompatible with the compensatory goals of the federal legislation, as are the means the State has chosen to effectuate it.

This incompatibility is revealed by the design of the notice-of-claim statute itself, which operates as a condition precedent to recovery in all actions brought in state court against governmental entities or officers. "Congress," we have previously noted, "surely did not intend to assign to state courts and legislatures a conclusive role in the formative function of defining and characterizing the essential elements of a federal cause of action." Wilson v. Garcia, 471 U.S. 261, 269 (1985). Yet that is precisely the consequence of what Wisconsin has done here: although a party bringing suit against a local governmental unit need not allege compliance with the notice statute as part of his or her complaint, the statute confers on governmental defendants an affirmative defense that obligates the plaintiff to demonstrate compliance with the notice requirement before he or she may recover at all, a showing altogether unnecessary when such an action is brought in federal court. States, however, may no more condition the federal right to recover for violations of civil rights than bar that right altogether, particularly where those conditions grow out of a waiver of immunity which, however necessary to the assertion of state-created rights against local governments, is entirely irrelevant insofar as the assertion of the federal right is concerned, and where the purpose and effect of those conditions, when applied in § 1983 actions, is to control the expense associated with the very litigation Congress has authorized.

This burdening of a federal right, moreover, is not the natural or permissible consequence of an otherwise neutral, uniformly applicable state rule. Although it is true that the notice-of-claim statute does not discriminate between state and federal causes of action against local governments, the fact remains that the law's protection extends only to governmental defendants and thus conditions the right to bring suit against the very persons and entities Congress intended to subject to liability. We therefore cannot accept the suggestion [in an amicus brief] that this requirement is simply part of "the vast body of procedural rules, rooted in policies unrelated to the definition of any particular substantive cause of action, that forms no essential part of 'the cause of action' as applied to any given plaintiff." On the contrary, the notice-of-claim provision is imposed only upon a specific class of plaintiffs—those who sue governmental defendants—and, as we have seen, is firmly rooted in policies very much related to, and to a large extent directly contrary to, the substantive cause of action provided those plaintiffs. This defendant-specific focus of the notice requirement serves to distinguish it, rather starkly, from rules uniformly applicable to all suits, such as rules governing service of process or substitution of parties, which respondents cite as examples of procedural requirements that penalize noncompliance through dismissal. That state courts will hear the entire § 1983 cause of action once a plaintiff complies with the notice-of-claim statute, therefore, in no way alters the fact that the statute discriminates against the precise type of claim Congress has created.

(2)

While respondents and amici suggest that prompt investigation of claims inures to the benefit of claimants and local governments alike, by providing both with an accurate factual picture of the incident, such statutes "are enacted primarily for the benefit of governmental defendants" and are intended to afford such defendants an opportunity to prepare a stronger case. Sound notions of public administration may support the prompt notice requirement, but those policies necessarily clash with the remedial purposes of the federal civil rights laws. In *Wilson v. Garcia,* supra, we held that, for purposes of choosing a limitations period for § 1983 actions, federal courts must apply the state statute of limitations governing personal injury claims because it is highly unlikely that States would ever fix the limitations period applicable to such claims in a manner that would discriminate against the federal right. Here, the notice-of-claim provision most emphatically does discriminate in a manner detrimental to the federal right: only those persons who wish to sue governmental defendants are required to provide notice within such an abbreviated time period. Many civil rights victims, however, will fail to appreciate the compensable nature of their injuries within the four-month window provided by the notice-of-claim provision, and will thus be barred from asserting their federal right to recovery in state court unless they can show that the defendant had actual notice of the injury, the circumstances giving rise to it, and the claimant's intent to hold the defendant responsible—a showing which, as the facts of this vividly demonstrate, is not easily made in Wisconsin.

(3)

Finally, the notice provision imposes an exhaustion requirement on persons who choose to assert their federal right in state courts, inasmuch as the § 1983 plaintiff must provide the requisite notice of injury within 120 days of the civil rights violation, then wait an additional 120 days while the governmental defendant investigates the claim and attempts to settle it. In Patsy v. Board of Regents of Florida, 457 U.S. 496 (1982), we held that plaintiffs need not exhaust state administrative remedies before instituting § 1983 suits in federal court. The Wisconsin Supreme Court, however, deemed that decision inapplicable to this state-court suit on the theory that States retain the authority to prescribe the rules and procedures governing suits in their courts. As we have just explained, however, that authority does not extend so far as to permit States to place conditions on the vindication of a federal right. Moreover, as we noted in *Patsy,* Congress enacted § 1983 in response to the widespread deprivations of civil rights in the Southern States and the inability or unwillingness of authorities in those States to protect those rights or punish wrongdoers. Although it is true that the principal remedy Congress chose to provide injured persons was immediate access to *federal* courts, it did not leave the protection of such rights exclusively in the hands of the federal judiciary, and instead conferred concurrent jurisdiction on state courts as well. Given the evil at which the federal civil rights legislation was aimed, there is simply no reason to suppose that Congress meant "to provide these individuals immediate access to the federal courts notwithstanding any provision of state law to the contrary," *Patsy,* supra, at 504, yet contemplated that those who sought to vindicate their federal rights in state courts could be required to seek redress in the first instance from the very state officials whose hostility to those rights precipitated their injuries.

Respondents nevertheless argue that any exhaustion requirement imposed by the notice-of-claim statute is essentially de minimis because the statutory settlement period entails none of the additional expense or undue delay typically associated with administrative remedies, and indeed does not alter a claimant's right to seek full compensation through suit. This argument fails for two reasons. First, it ignores our prior assessment of "the dominant characteristic of civil rights actions: *they belong in court.*" Burnett v. Grattan, 468 U.S. 42, 50 (1984) (emphasis added). "These causes of action," we have explained, "exist independent of any other legal or administrative relief that may be available as a matter of federal or state law.

They are judicially enforceable *in the first instance*." Ibid. (emphasis added). The dominant characteristic of a § 1983 action, of course, does not vary depending upon whether it is litigated in state or federal court, and States therefore may not adulterate or dilute the predominant feature of the federal right by imposing mandatory settlement periods, no matter how reasonable the administrative waiting period or the interests it is designed to serve may appear.

Second, our decision in *Patsy* rested not only on the legislative history of § 1983 itself, but also on the fact that in the Civil Rights of Institutionalized Persons Act of 1980, 42 U.S.C. § 1997e, Congress established an exhaustion requirement for a specific class of § 1983 actions—those brought by adult prisoners challenging the conditions of their confinement—and that in so doing, Congress expressly recognized that it was working a change in the law. Accordingly, we refused to engraft an exhaustion requirement onto another type of § 1983 action where Congress had not provided for one, not only because the judicial imposition of such a requirement would be inconsistent with Congress' recognition that § 1983 plaintiffs normally need not exhaust administrative remedies, but also because decisions concerning both the desirability and the scope and design of any exhaustion requirement turn on a host of policy considerations which "do not invariably point in one direction," and which, for that very reason, are best left to "Congress' superior institutional competence." "[P]olicy considerations alone," we concluded, "cannot justify judicially imposed exhaustion unless exhaustion is consistent with congressional intent." While the exhaustion required by Wisconsin's notice-of-claim statute does not involve lengthy or expensive administrative proceedings, it forces injured persons to seek satisfaction from those alleged to have caused the injury in the first place. Such a dispute resolution system may have much to commend it, but that is a judgment the current Congress must make, for we think it plain that the Congress which enacted § 1983 over 100 years ago would have rejected as utterly inconsistent with the remedial purposes of its broad statute the notion that a State could require civil rights victims to seek compensation from offending state officials before they could assert a federal action in state court.

Finally, to the extent the exhaustion requirement is designed to sift out "specious claims" from the stream of complaints that can inundate local governments in the absence of immunity, we have rejected such a policy as inconsistent with the aims of the federal legislation. In *Burnett,* state officials urged the adoption of a six-month limitations period in a § 1983 action in order that they might enjoy "some reasonable protection from the seemingly endless stream of unfounded, and often stale, lawsuits brought against them." Such a contention, we noted, "reflects in part a judgment that factors such as minimizing the diversion of state officials' attention from their duties outweigh the interest in providing [claimants] ready access to a forum to resolve valid claims." As we explained there, and reaffirm today, "[t]hat policy is manifestly inconsistent with the central objective of the Reconstruction–Era civil rights statutes."

C

Respondents and their supporting amici urge that we approve the application of the notice-of-claim statute to § 1983 actions brought in state court as a matter of equitable federalism. They note that " '[t]he general rule, bottomed deeply in belief in the importance of state control of state judicial procedure, is that federal law takes the state courts as it finds them.' " Litigants who chose to bring their civil rights actions in state courts presumably do so in order to obtain the benefit of certain procedural advantages in those courts, or to draw their juries from urban populations. Having availed themselves of these benefits, civil rights litigants must comply as well with those state rules they find less to their liking.

However equitable this bitter-with-the-sweet argument may appear in the abstract, it has no place under our Supremacy Clause analysis. Federal law takes state courts as it finds them only insofar as those courts employ rules that do not "impose unnecessary burdens upon rights of recovery authorized by federal laws." *Brown v. Western Ry. of Alabama,* supra, at 298–299. States may make the litigation of federal rights as congenial as they see fit—not as a quid pro quo for compliance with other, uncongenial rules, but because such congeniality does not stand as an obstacle to the accomplishment of Congress' goals. As we have seen, enforcement of the notice-of-claim statute in § 1983 actions brought in state court so interferes with and frustrates the substantive right Congress created that, under the Supremacy Clause, it must yield to the federal interest. This interference, however, is not the only consequence of the statute that renders its application in § 1983 cases invalid. In a State that demands compliance with such a statute before a § 1983 action may be brought or maintained in its courts, the outcome of federal civil rights litigation will frequently and predictably depend on whether it is brought in state or federal court. Thus, the very notions of federalism upon which respondents rely dictate that the State's outcome determinative law must give way when a party asserts a federal right in state court.

Under Erie R. Co. v. Tompkins, 304 U.S. 64 (1938), when a federal court exercises diversity or pendent jurisdiction over state-law claims, "the outcome of the litigation in the federal court should be substantially the same, so far as legal rules determine the outcome of a litigation, as it would be if tried in a state court." Guaranty Trust Co. v. York, 326 U.S. 99, 109 (1945). Accordingly, federal courts entertaining state-law claims against Wisconsin municipalities are obligated to apply the notice-of-claim provision. Just as federal courts are constitutionally obligated to apply state law to state claims, see *Erie,* supra, at 78–79, so too the Supremacy Clause imposes on state courts a constitutional duty "to proceed in such manner that all the substantial rights of the parties under controlling federal law [are] protected."

Civil rights victims often do not appreciate the constitutional nature of their injuries and thus will fail to file a notice of injury or claim within the requisite time period, which in Wisconsin is a mere four months. Unless such claimants can prove that the governmental defendant had actual notice of the claim, which, as we have already noted, is by no means a simple task in Wisconsin, and unless they also file an itemized claim for damages, they must bring their § 1983 suits in federal court or not at all. Wisconsin, however, may not alter the outcome of federal claims it chooses to entertain in its courts by demanding compliance with outcome-determinative rules that are inapplicable when such claims are brought in federal court, for " '[w]hatever spring[s] the State may set for those who are endeavoring to assert rights that the State confers, the assertion of federal rights, when plainly and reasonably made, is not to be defeated under the name of local practice.' " *Brown v. Western Ry. of Alabama,* supra, at 299. The state notice-of-claim statute is more than a mere rule of procedure: as we discussed above, the statute is a substantive condition on the right to sue governmental officials and entities, and the federal courts have therefore correctly recognized that the notice statute governs the adjudication of state-law claims in diversity actions. In *Guaranty Trust,* supra, we held that, in order to give effect to a State's statute of limitations, a federal court could not hear a state-law action that a state court would deem time-barred. Conversely, a state court may not decline to hear an otherwise properly presented federal claim because that claim would be barred under a state law requiring timely filing of notice. State courts simply are not free to vindicate the substantive interests underlying a state rule of decision at the expense of the federal right.

Finally, in *Wilson v. Garcia,* we characterized § 1983 suits as claims for personal injuries because such an approach ensured that the same limitations period would govern all § 1983 actions brought in any given state, and thus comported with Congress' desire that the federal civil rights laws be given a uniform application within each state. A law that predictably alters the outcome of § 1983 claims depending solely on whether they are brought in state or federal court within the same State is obviously inconsistent with this federal interest in intra-state uniformity.

III

In enacting § 1983, Congress entitled those deprived of their civil rights to recover full compensation from the governmental officials responsible for those deprivations. A state law that conditions that right of recovery upon compliance with a rule designed to minimize governmental liability, and that directs injured persons to seek redress in the first instance from the very targets of the federal legislation, is inconsistent in both purpose and effect with the remedial objectives of the federal civil rights law. Principles of federalism, as well as the Supremacy Clause, dictate that such a state law must give way to vindication of the federal right when that right is asserted in state court.

Accordingly, the judgment of the Supreme Court of Wisconsin is reversed, and the case is remanded for further proceedings not inconsistent with this opinion.

It is so ordered.

■ JUSTICE WHITE, concurring.

It cannot be disputed that, if Congress had included a statute of limitations in 42 U.S.C. § 1983, any state court that entertained a § 1983 suit would have to apply that statute of limitations. . . . Similarly, where the Court has determined that a particular state statute of limitations ought to be borrowed in order to effectuate the congressional intent underlying a federal cause of action that contains no statute of limitations of its own, any state court that entertains the same federal cause of action must apply the same state statute of limitations. We made such a determination in Wilson v. Garcia, 471 U.S. 261 (1985), which held that § 1983 suits must as a matter of federal law be governed by the state statute of limitations applicable to tort suits for the recovery of damages for personal injuries. . . . It has since been assumed that *Wilson v. Garcia* governs the timeliness of § 1983 suits brought in state as well as federal court. [citations omitted]

The Wisconsin Supreme Court likewise assumed that *Wilson v. Garcia* governed which statute of limitations should apply to petitioner's § 1983 claim. The court then effectively truncated the applicable limitations period, however, by dismissing petitioner's § 1983 suit for failure to file a notice of claim within 120 days of the events at issue as required by Wis.Stat.

§ 893.80.[3] Hence, petitioner was allowed only about four months in which to investigate whether the facts and the law would support any claim against respondents (or retain a lawyer who would do so), and to notify respondents of his claim, rather than the two or three years that he would have been allowed under Wisconsin law had he sought to assert a similar personal-injury claim against a private party. It is also unlikely that any other State would apply a 120–day limitations period—or, indeed, a limitations period of less than one year—to such a personal-injury claim.[4] This reflects a generally accepted belief among state policymakers that individuals who have suffered injuries to their personal rights cannot fairly be expected to seek redress within so short a period of time.

The application of the Wisconsin notice-of-claim statute to bar petitioner's § 1983 suit—which is "in reality, 'an action for injury to personal rights' "—thus undermines the purposes of *Wilson v. Garcia* to promote "[t]he federal interests in uniformity, certainty, and the minimization of unnecessary litigation," and assure that state procedural rules do not "discriminate against the federal civil rights remedy." I therefore agree that in view of the adverse impact of Wisconsin's notice-of-claim statute on the federal policies articulated in *Wilson v. Garcia,* the Supremacy Clause proscribes the statute's application to § 1983 suits brought in Wisconsin state courts.

■ JUSTICE O'CONNOR, with whom CHIEF JUSTICE REHNQUIST joins, dissenting.

"A state statute cannot be considered 'inconsistent' with federal law merely because the statute causes the plaintiff to lose the litigation." Robertson v. Wegmann, 436 U.S. 584, 593 (1978). Disregarding this self-evident principle, the Court today holds that Wisconsin's notice of claim statute is pre-empted by federal law as to actions under 42 U.S.C. § 1983 filed in state court. This holding is not supported by the statute whose pre-emptive force it purports to invoke, or by our precedents. Relying only on its own intuitions about "the goals of the federal civil rights laws," the Court fashions a new theory of pre-emption that unnecessarily and improperly suspends a perfectly valid state statute. . . .

Wisconsin's notice of claim statute, which imposes a limited exhaustion of remedies requirement on those with claims against municipal governments and their officials, serves at least two important purposes apart from providing municipal defendants with a special affirmative defense in litigation. First, the statute helps ensure that public officials will receive prompt notice of wrongful conditions or practices, and thus enables them to take prompt corrective action. Second, it enables officials to investigate claims in a timely fashion, thereby making it easier to ascertain the facts accurately and to settle meritorious claims without litigation. These important aspects of the Wisconsin statute bring benefits to governments and

---

3 To be sure, § 893.80 provides that failure to file a notice of claim within the initial 120–day period "shall not bar an action on the claim if the [governmental] subdivision or agency had actual notice of the claim and the claimant shows to the satisfaction of the court that the delay or failure to give the requisite notice has not been prejudicial to the defendant." The facts of this case demonstrate, however, that the "actual notice" requirement is difficult to satisfy. For example, the Wisconsin Supreme Court held that respondents had not received "actual notice" of petitioner's claim even though the local alderman had written directly to the chief of police requesting an investigation of the incident only three days after its occurrence.

4 See Stephen J. Shapiro, Choosing the Appropriate State Statute of Limitations for Section 1983 Claims After *Wilson v. Garcia:* A Theory Applied to Maryland Law, 16 U.Balt.L.Rev. 242, 245–46 (1987).

claimants alike, and it should come as no surprise that 37 other States have apparently adopted similar notice of claim requirements. Without some compellingly clear indication that Congress has forbidden the States to apply such statutes in their own courts, there is no reason to conclude that they are "preempted" by federal law. Allusions to such vague concepts as "the compensatory aims of the federal civil rights laws," which are all that the Court actually relies on, do not provide an adequate substitute for the statutory analysis that we customarily require of ourselves before we reach out to find statutory pre-emption of legitimate procedures used by the States in their own courts.

Section 1983, it is worth recalling, creates no substantive law. It merely provides one vehicle by which certain provisions of the Constitution and other federal laws may be judicially enforced. Its purpose, as we have repeatedly said, " 'was to interpose the *federal courts* between the States and the people, as guardians of the people's federal rights. . . . ' " Patsy v. Board of Regents of Florida, 457 U.S. 496, 503 (1982) (quoting Mitchum v. Foster, 407 U.S. 225, 242 (1972)) (emphasis added). For that reason, the original version of § 1983 provided that the federal courts would have exclusive jurisdiction of actions arising under it. See Civil Rights Act of 1871, ch. 22, § 1, 17 Stat. 13. This fact is conclusive proof that the "Congress which enacted § 1983 over 100 years ago," could not possibly have meant thereby to alter the operation of state courts in any way or to "pre-empt" them from using procedural statutes like the one at issue today.

State courts may now entertain § 1983 actions if a plaintiff chooses a state court over the federal forum that is always available as a matter of right. See, e.g., Martinez v. California, 444 U.S. 277, 283 and n.7 (1980). Abandoning the rule of exclusive federal jurisdiction over § 1983 actions, and thus restoring the tradition of concurrent jurisdiction, however, "did not leave behind a pre-emptive grin without a statutory cat." Congress has never given the slightest indication that § 1983 was meant to replace state procedural rules with those that apply in the federal courts. The majority does not, because it cannot, cite any evidence to the contrary.

In an effort to remedy this fatal defect in its position, the majority engages in an extended discussion of *Patsy v. Board of Regents of Florida,* supra. *Patsy,* however, actually undermines the majority's conclusion. In that case, the Court concluded that state exhaustion of remedies requirements were not to be applied in § 1983 actions brought in *federal court.* The Court relied on legislative history indicating that § 1983 was meant to provide a federal forum with characteristics *different* from those in the state courts, and it came only to the limited and hesitant conclusion that "it seems fair to infer that the 1871 Congress did not intend that an individual be compelled *in every case* to exhaust state administrative remedies before filing an action under [§ 1983]." [Emphasis added.] Even this limited conclusion, the Court admitted, was "somewhat precarious," which would have made no sense if the Court had been able to rely on the more general proposition—from which the holding in *Patsy* follows a fortiori—that it adopts today.

Patsy also relied on the Civil Rights of Institutionalized Persons Act of 1980, § 7, 42 U.S.C. § 1997e, which ordinarily requires exhaustion of state remedies before an adult prisoner can bring a § 1983 action in federal court. The Court concluded that the "legislative history of § 1997e demonstrates that Congress has taken the approach of carving out specific exceptions to the general rule that *federal courts* cannot require exhaustion under § 1983." [Emphasis added.] This finding lends further support to the proposition that Congress has never concerned itself with the application of exhaustion requirements in *state* courts, and § 1997e conclusively shows that Congress does not believe that such requirements are somehow inherently incompatible with the nature of actions under § 1983.

For similar reasons, Brown v. Western Ry. of Alabama, 338 U.S. 294 (1949), which is repeatedly quoted by the majority, does not control the present case. In *Brown,* which arose under the Federal Employers' Liability Act (FELA), this Court refused to accept a state court's interpretation of allegations in a complaint asserting a federal statutory right. Concluding that the state court's interpretation of the complaint operated to "detract from 'substantive rights' granted by Congress in FELA cases," the Court "simply h[e]ld that under the facts alleged it was error to dismiss the complaint and that [the claimant] should be allowed to try his case." In the case before us today, by contrast, the statute at issue does not diminish or alter any substantive right cognizable under § 1983. As the majority concedes, the Wisconsin courts "will hear the entire § 1983 cause of action once a plaintiff complies with the notice-of-claim statute."

Unable to find support for its position in § 1983 itself, or in its legislative history, the majority suggests that the Wisconsin statute somehow "discriminates against the federal right." The Wisconsin statute, however, applies to all actions against municipal defendants, whether brought under state or federal law. The majority is therefore compelled to adopt a new theory of discrimination, under which the challenged statute is said to "conditio[n] the right to bring suit against the very persons and entities [viz. local governments and officials] Congress intended to subject to liability." This theory, however, is untenable. First, the statute erects no barrier at all to a plaintiff's right to bring a § 1983 suit against anyone. Every plaintiff has the option of proceeding in federal court, and the Wisconsin statute has not the slightest effect on that right. Second, if a plaintiff chooses to proceed in the Wisconsin state courts, those courts stand ready to hear the entire federal cause of action, as the majority concedes. Thus, the Wisconsin statute "discriminates" only against a right that Congress has never created: the right of a plaintiff to have the benefit of selected federal court procedures after the plaintiff has rejected the federal forum and chosen a state forum instead. The majority's "discrimination" theory is just another version of its unsupported conclusion that Congress intended to force the state courts to adopt procedural rules from the federal courts.

The Court also suggests that there is some parallel between this case and cases that are tried in federal court under the doctrine of Erie R. Co. v. Tompkins, 304 U.S. 64 (1938). Quoting the "outcome-determinative" test of Guaranty Trust Co. v. York, 326 U.S. 99, 109 (1945), the Court opines today that state courts hearing federal suits are obliged to mirror federal procedures to the same extent that federal courts are obliged to mirror state procedures in diversity suits. This suggestion seems to be based on a sort of upside-down theory of federalism, which the Court attributes to Congress on the basis of no evidence at all. Nor are the implications of this "reverse-*Erie*" theory quite clear. If the Court means the theory to be taken seriously, it should follow that defendants, as well as plaintiffs, are entitled to the benefit of all federal court procedural rules that are "outcome determinative." If, however, the Court means to create a rule that benefits only plaintiffs, then the discussion of *Erie* principles is simply an unsuccessful effort to find some analogy, no matter how attenuated, to today's unprecedented holding.

"Borrowing" cases under 42 U.S.C. § 1988(a), which the Court cites several times, have little more to do with today's decision than does *Erie*. Under that statute and those cases, we are sometimes called upon to fill in gaps in federal law by choosing a state procedural rule for application in § 1983 actions brought in federal court. See, e.g., Wilson v. Garcia, 471 U.S. 261 (1985); Burnett v. Grattan, 468 U.S. 42 (1984). The congressionally imposed necessity of *supplementing* federal law with state procedural rules might well caution us against *supplanting* state procedural rules with federal gaps, but it certainly offers no support for what the Court does today.

Finally Justice White's concurrence argues that Wisconsin's notice of claim statute is in the nature of a statute of limitations, and that the principles articulated in *Wilson v. Garcia* preclude its application to any action under § 1983. Assuming, arguendo, that state courts must apply the same statutes of limitations that federal courts borrow under § 1988(a), the concurrence is mistaken in treating this notice of claim requirement as a statute of limitations. As the concurrence acknowledges, the 120–day claim period established by the Wisconsin statute does not apply if the local government had actual notice of the claim and has not been prejudiced by the plaintiff's delay. The concurrence suggests that the Wisconsin statute nonetheless is equivalent to a statute of limitations because the present case demonstrates "that the 'actual notice' requirement is difficult to satisfy." I agree that a sufficiently burdensome notice of claim requirement could effectively act as a statute of limitations. The facts of this case, however, will not support such a characterization of the Wisconsin law. The court below said that no "Detailed claim for damages" need be submitted; rather, the injured party need only "recit[e] the facts giving rise to the injury and [indicate] an intent . . . to hold the city responsible for any damages resulting from the injury." It has not been suggested that petitioner tried to comply with this requirement but encountered difficulties in doing so. Indeed, it would have been easier to file the required notice of claim than to file this lawsuit, which petitioner proved himself quite capable of doing. Far from encountering "difficulties" in complying with the notice of claim statute, petitioner never tried.

As I noted at the outset, the majority correctly characterizes the issue before us as one of statutory pre-emption. In order to arrive at the result it has chosen, however, the Court is forced to search for "inconsistencies" between Wisconsin's notice of claim statute and some ill-defined federal policy that Congress has never articulated, implied, or suggested, let alone enacted. Nor is there any difficulty in explaining the absence of congressional attention to the problem that the Court wrongly imagines it is solving. A plaintiff who chooses to bring a § 1983 action in state court necessarily rejects the federal courts that Congress has provided. Virtually the only conceivable reason for doing so is to benefit from procedural advantages available exclusively in state court. Having voted with their feet for state procedural systems, such plaintiffs would hardly be in a position to ask Congress for a new type of forum that combines the advantages that Congress gave them in the federal system with those that Congress did not give them, and which are only available in state courts. Fortunately for these plaintiffs, however, Congress need not be consulted. The concept of statutory pre-emption takes on new meaning today, and it is one from which I respectfully dissent.

NOTE ON FELDER V. CASEY

In *Felder v. Casey*, Justice Brennan identified at least four reasons for rejecting Wisconsin's application of its notice-of-claim statute: it burdened federal rights; it discriminated against federal rights; it wrongly required exhaustion of remedies; and it applied an outcome-determinative state procedure in a manner that undermined the federal substantive interests.

The first, second, and fourth of these arguments would seem to be different ways of saying the same thing: Each is premised on the Court's belief that the notice-of-claim provision placed an intolerable burden on the assertion of the plaintiff's federal rights. Exactly what is this burden? Why should a plaintiff who chooses a state court not be required to take the bitter with the sweet?

The third argument—focusing on the exhaustion-of-state-remedies aspect of the notice-of-claim statute—would seem amenable to the same retort: If federal courts are open without requiring the plaintiff to exhaust state administrative remedies, why does it undermine the federal right if the state courts impose such a requirement? Why not the bitter with the sweet here too?

Justice White has a completely different analysis. He starts with the premise that "[i]t cannot be disputed that, if Congress had included a statute of limitations in 42 U.S.C. § 1983, any state court that entertained a § 1983 suit would have to apply that statute of limitations." See McAllister v. Magnolia Petroleum Co., 357 U.S. 221 (1958); Engel v. Davenport, 271 U.S. 33 (1926); cf. Atlantic Coast Line R. Co. v. General Burnett, 239 U.S. 199 (1915). Given this premise, it followed that the state courts could not apply a shorter statute of limitations than would have been applied by a federal court.

Justice O'Connor's response was a confession-and-avoidance: She agreed with the prior case law, but argued that the notice-of-claim statute was not really a statute of limitations. Was this her strongest response? Why should it be impermissible for a state court to apply a shorter or a longer statute of limitations to a federal claim than would a federal court?

In the end, do all of these arguments come down to the same thing? Justice Brennan identifies, as he puts it, a "federal interest in intra-state uniformity." He is surely right that *if* there is such a federal interest, the Supremacy Clause requires states to respect it, and the notice-of-claim statute fails because it is inconsistent with that interest. Justice O'Connor, in effect, disputes the existence of such a federal interest. Who is right?

6. RIGHT TO A JURY TRIAL

City of Monterey v. Del Monte Dunes at Monterey

Supreme Court of the United States, 1999.
526 U.S. 687.

■ JUSTICE KENNEDY delivered the opinion of the Court, except as to part IV–A–2.

This case began with attempts by the respondent, Del Monte Dunes, and its predecessor in interest to develop a parcel of land within the jurisdiction of the petitioner, the city of Monterey. The city, in a series of repeated rejections, denied proposals to develop the property, each time imposing more rigorous demands on the developers. Del Monte Dunes brought suit in the United States District Court for the Northern District of California, under 42 U.S.C. § 1983. After protracted litigation, the case was submitted to the jury on Del Monte Dunes' theory that the city effected a regulatory taking or otherwise injured the property by unlawful acts, without paying compensation or providing an adequate postdeprivation remedy for the loss. The jury found for Del Monte Dunes, and the Court of Appeals affirmed.

The petitioner contends that the regulatory takings claim should not have been decided by the jury. . . .

IV

. . . As the Court of Appeals recognized, the answer [to this question] depends on whether Del Monte Dunes had a statutory or constitutional right to a jury trial, and, if it did, the nature and extent of the right. Del Monte Dunes asserts the right to a jury trial is conferred by § 1983 and by the Seventh Amendment. . . .

The character of § 1983 is vital to our Seventh Amendment analysis, but the statute does not itself confer the jury right. Section 1983 authorizes a party who has been deprived of a federal right under the color of state law to seek relief through "an action at law, suit in equity, or other proper proceeding for redress." Del Monte Dunes contends that the phrase "action at law" is a term of art implying a right to a jury trial. We disagree, for this is not a necessary implication. . . .

As a consequence, we must reach the constitutional question. The Seventh Amendment provides that "in Suits at common law, where the value in controversy shall exceed twenty dollars, the right of trial by jury shall be preserved. . . . " Consistent with the textual mandate that the jury right be preserved, our interpretation of the Amendment has been guided by historical analysis comprising two principal inquiries. "We ask, first, whether we are dealing with a cause of action that either was tried at law at the time of the founding or is at least analogous to one that was." Markman v. Westview Instruments, Inc., 517 U.S. 370, 376 (1996). "If the action in question belongs in the law category, we then ask whether the particular trial decision must fall to the jury in order to preserve the substance of the common-law right as it existed in 1791."

A

With respect to the first inquiry, we have recognized that "suits at common law" include "not merely suits, which the common law recognized among its old and settled proceedings, but [also] suits in which legal rights were to be ascertained and determined, in contradistinction to those where equitable rights alone were recognized, and equitable remedies were administered." Parsons v. Bedford, 3 Peters 433, 447 (1830). The Seventh Amendment thus applies not only to common-law causes of action but also to statutory causes of action " 'analogous to common-law causes of action ordinarily decided in English law courts in the late 18th century, as opposed to those customarily heard by courts of equity or admiralty.' "

1

. . . It is undisputed that when the Seventh Amendment was adopted there was no action equivalent to § 1983, framed in specific terms for vindicating constitutional rights. It is settled law, however, that the Seventh Amendment jury guarantee extends to statutory claims unknown to the common law, so long as the claims can be said to "sound basically in tort," and seek legal relief. Curtis v. Loether, 415 U.S. 189, 195–96 (1974).

As Justice Scalia explains, there can be no doubt that claims brought pursuant to § 1983 sound in tort. Just as common-law tort actions provide redress for interference with protected personal or property interests, § 1983 provides relief for invasions of rights protected under federal law. Recognizing the essential character of the statute, " 'we have repeatedly noted that 42 U.S.C. § 1983 creates a species of tort liability,' " Heck v. Humphrey, 512 U.S. 477, 483 (1994) (quoting Memphis Community School Dist. v. Stachura, 477 U.S. 299, 305 (1986)), and have interpreted the statute in light of the "background of tort liability," Monroe v. Pape, 365 U.S. 167, 187 (1961). . . .

Here Del Monte Dunes sought legal relief. It was entitled to proceed in federal court under § 1983 because, at the time of the city's actions, the State of California did not provide a compensatory remedy for temporary regulatory takings. The constitutional injury alleged, therefore, is not that property was taken but that it was taken without just compensation. Had the city paid for the property or had an adequate postdeprivation remedy been available, Del Monte Dunes would have suffered no constitutional injury from the taking alone. Because its statutory action did not accrue until it was denied just compensation, in a strict sense Del Monte Dunes sought not just compensation per se but rather damages for the unconstitutional denial of such compensation. Damages for a constitutional violation are a legal remedy. . . . See, e.g., Teamsters v. Terry, 494 U.S. 558, 570 (1990) ("Generally, an action for money damages was 'the traditional form of relief offered in the courts of law' ") (quoting *Curtis v. Loether*, supra, at 196).

Even when viewed as a simple suit for just compensation, we believe Del Monte Dunes' action sought essentially legal relief. "We have recognized the 'general rule' that monetary relief is legal." Feltner v. Columbia Pictures Television, Inc., 523 U.S. 340, 352 (1998) (quoting *Teamsters v. Terry*, supra, at 570). Just compensation, moreover, differs from equitable restitution and other monetary remedies available in equity, for in determining just compensation, "the question is what has the owner lost, not what has the taker gained." Boston Chamber of Commerce v. Boston, 217 U.S. 189, 195 (1910). As its name suggests, then, just compensation is, like ordinary money damages, a compensatory remedy. . . . Because Del Monte Dunes' statutory suit sounded in tort and sought legal relief, it was an action at law.

2

In attempt to avoid the force of this conclusion, the city urges us to look not to the statutory basis of Del Monte Dunes' claim but rather to the underlying constitutional right asserted. . . . Because the jury's role in estimating just compensation in condemnation proceedings was inconsistent and unclear at the time the Seventh Amendment was adopted, this Court has said "that there is no constitutional right to a jury in eminent domain proceedings." United States v. Reynolds, 397 U.S. 14, 18 (1970); accord, Bauman v. Ross, 167 U.S. 548, 593 (1897). The city submits that the analogy to formal condemnation proceedings is controlling, so that there is no jury right here.

As Justice Scalia notes, we have declined in other contexts to classify § 1983 actions based on the nature of the underlying right asserted, and the city provides no persuasive justification for adopting a different rule for

Seventh Amendment purposes. Even when analyzed not as a § 1983 action simpliciter, however, but as a § 1983 action seeking redress for an uncompensated taking, Del Monte Dunes' suit remains an action at law.

Although condemnation proceedings spring from the same Fifth Amendment right to compensation which, as incorporated by the Fourteenth Amendment, is applicable here, a condemnation action differs in important respects from a § 1983 action to redress an uncompensated taking. Most important, when the government initiates condemnation proceedings, it concedes the landowner's right to receive just compensation and seeks a mere determination of the amount of compensation due. Liability simply is not an issue. As a result, even if condemnation proceedings were an appropriate analogy, condemnation practice would provide little guidance on the specific question whether Del Monte Dunes was entitled to a jury determination of liability.

This difference renders the analogy to condemnation proceedings not only unhelpful but also inapposite. When the government takes property without initiating condemnation proceedings, it "shifts to the landowner the burden to discover the encroachment and to take affirmative action to recover just compensation." United States v. Clarke, 445 U.S. 253, 257 (1980). Even when the government does not dispute its seizure of the property or its obligation to pay for it, the mere "shifting of the initiative from the condemning authority to the condemnee" can place the landowner "at a significant disadvantage.". . . .

Condemnation proceedings differ from the instant cause of action in another fundamental respect as well. When the government condemns property for public use, it provides the landowner a forum for seeking just compensation, as is required by the Constitution. If the condemnation proceedings do not, in fact, deny the landowner just compensation, the government's actions are neither unconstitutional nor unlawful. Even when the government takes property without initiating condemnation proceedings, there is no constitutional violation " 'unless or until the State fails to provide an adequate postdeprivation remedy for the property loss.' ". . . .

Consistent with this understanding, and as a matter of historical practice, when the government has taken property without providing an adequate means for obtaining redress, suits to recover just compensation have been framed as common-law tort actions. Tort actions of these descriptions lay at common law, 3 W. Blackstone, Commentaries on the Laws of England, ch. 12 (1768) (trespass; trespass on the case); id., ch. 13 (trespass on the case for nuisance), and in these actions, as in other suits at common law, there was a right to trial by jury. . . .

V

For the reasons stated, the judgment of the Court of Appeals is affirmed.

It is so ordered.

■ JUSTICE SCALIA, concurring in part and concurring in the judgment.

I join all except part IV–A–2 of Justice Kennedy's opinion. In my view, all § 1983 actions must be treated alike insofar as the Seventh Amendment right to jury trial is concerned; [and] that right exists when monetary damages are sought. . . .

I

. . . The fundamental difference between my view of this case and Justice Souter's is that I believe § 1983 establishes a unique, or at least distinctive, cause of action, in that the legal duty which is the basis for relief is ultimately defined not by the claim-creating statute itself, but by an extrinsic body of law to which the statute refers, namely "federal rights elsewhere conferred." Baker v. McCollan, 443 U.S. 137, 144, n. 3 (1979). In this respect § 1983 is, so to speak, a prism through which many different lights may pass. Unlike Justice Souter, I believe that, in analyzing this cause of action for Seventh Amendment purposes, the proper focus is on the prism itself, not on the particular ray that happens to be passing through in the present case.

The Seventh Amendment inquiry looks first to the "nature of the statutory action." Feltner v. Columbia Pictures Television, Inc., 523 U.S. 340, 348 (1998). The only "statutory action" here is a § 1983 suit. The question before us, therefore, is not what common-law action is most analogous to some generic suit seeking compensation for a Fifth Amendment taking, but what common-law action is most analogous to a § 1983 claim. The fact that the breach of duty which underlies the particular § 1983 claim at issue here—a Fifth Amendment takings violation—may give rise to another cause of action besides a § 1983 claim, namely a so-called inverse condemnation suit, which is (according to part IV–A–2 of Justice Kennedy's opinion) or is not (according to Justice Souter's opinion) entitled to be tried before a jury, seems to me irrelevant. The central question remains whether a § 1983 suit is entitled to a jury. The fortuitous existence of an inverse-condemnation cause of action is surely not essential to the existence of the § 1983 claim. Indeed, for almost all § 1983 claims arising out of constitutional violations, no alternative private cause of action does exist—which makes it practically useful, in addition to being theoretically sound, to focus on the prism instead of the refracted light.

This is exactly the approach we took in Wilson v. Garcia, 471 U.S. 261 (1985)—an opinion whose analysis is so precisely in point that it gives this case a distinct quality of deja vu. *Wilson* required us to analogize § 1983 actions to common-law suits for a different purpose: not to determine applicability of the jury-trial right, but to identify the relevant statute of limitations. Since no federal limitations period was provided, the Court had to apply 42 U.S.C. § 1988(a), which stated that, in the event a federal civil rights statute is "deficient in the provisions necessary to furnish suitable remedies and punish offenses against law, the common law, as modified and changed by the constitution and statutes of the State wherein the court having jurisdiction of such civil or criminal cause is held, so far as the same is not inconsistent with the Constitution and laws of the United States, shall be extended to and govern the [federal] courts in the trial and disposition of the cause. . . . " In applying this provision, the Court identified as one of the steps necessary for its analysis resolution of precisely the question I have been discussing here: "We must . . . decide whether all § 1983 claims should be characterized in the same way, or whether they should be evaluated differently depending upon the varying factual circumstances and legal theories presented in each individual case." The Court concluded (as I do here) that all § 1983 claims should be characterized in the same way. It said (as I have) that § 1983 was "a uniquely federal remedy," and that it is "the purest coincidence . . . when state statutes or the common law provide for equivalent remedies; any analogies to those causes of action are bound to be imperfect." And the Court was affected (as I am here) by the practical difficulties of the other course, which it described as follows:

> Almost every § 1983 claim can be favorably analogized to more than one of the ancient common-law forms of action, each of which may be governed by a different statute of limitations. . . .
>
> A catalog of . . . constitutional claims that have been alleged under § 1983 would encompass numerous and diverse topics and subtopics: discrimination in public employment on the basis of race or the exercise of First Amendment rights, discharge or demotion without procedural due process, mistreatment of schoolchildren, deliberate indifference to the medical needs of prison inmates, the seizure of chattels without advance notice or sufficient opportunity to be heard—to identify only a few.

For these reasons the Court concluded that all § 1983 actions should be characterized as "tort actions for the recovery of damages for personal injuries."

To be sure, § 1988 is not the Seventh Amendment. It is entirely possible to analogize § 1983 to the "common law" in one fashion for purposes of that statute, and in another fashion for purposes of the constitutional guarantee. But I cannot imagine why one would want to do that. For both purposes it is a "unique federal remedy" whose character is determined by the federal cause of action, and not by the innumerable constitutional and statutory violations upon which that cause of action is dependent. And for both purposes the search for (often nonexistent) common-law analogues to remedies for those particular violations is a major headache. . . . I adhere to the approach of *Wilson*, reaffirmed and refined in Owens v. Okure, 488 U.S. 235 (1989), that a § 1983 action is a § 1983 action.

II

To apply this methodology to the present case: There is no doubt that the cause of action created by § 1983 is, and was always regarded as, a tort claim. Thomas Cooley's treatise on tort law, which was published roughly contemporaneously with the enactment of § 1983, tracked Blackstone's view, see 3 W. Blackstone, Commentaries on the Laws of England 115–19 (1768), that torts are remedies for invasions of certain rights, such as the rights to personal security, personal liberty, and property. T. Cooley, Law of Torts 2–3 (1880). Section 1983 assuredly fits that description. Like other tort causes of action, it is designed to provide compensation for injuries arising from the violation of legal duties, see Carey v. Piphus, 435 U.S. 247, 254 (1978), and thereby, of course, to deter future violations.

This Court has confirmed in countless cases that a § 1983 cause of action sounds in tort. . . . We have commonly described it as creating a "constitutional tort," since violations of constitutional rights have been the most frequently litigated claims. In Wilson v. Garcia, we explicitly identified § 1983 as a personal-injury tort, stating that "[a] violation of [§ 1983] is an injury to the individual rights of the person," and that "Congress unquestionably would have considered the remedies established in the Civil Rights Act [of 1871] to be more analogous to tort claims for personal injury than, for example, to claims for damages to property or breach of contract."

As described earlier, we used § 1983's identity as a personal-injury tort to determine the relevant statute of limitations under 42 U.S.C. § 1988(a). We have also used § 1983's character as a tort cause of action to determine the scope of immunity, Kalina v. Fletcher, 522 U.S. 118, 124–25 (1997), the recoverable damages, *Heck*, supra, at 483; *Memphis Community School Dist.*, 477 U.S., at 305–06, and the scope of liability, Monroe v. Pape, 365 U.S. 167, 187 (1961). In Owen v. City of Independence, 445 U.S. 622, 657 (1980), we even asserted that the attributes of § 1983 could change to keep up with modern developments in the law of torts: "Doctrines of tort law have changed significantly over the past century, and our notions of governmental responsibility should properly reflect that evolution. . . . The principle of equitable loss-spreading has joined fault as a factor in distributing the costs of official misconduct." . . .

In sum, it seems to me entirely clear that a § 1983 cause of action for damages is a tort action for which jury trial would have been provided at common law. The right of jury trial is not eliminated, of course, by virtue of the fact that, under our modern unified system, the equitable relief of an injunction is also sought. Nor—to revert to the point made in part I of this discussion—is the tort nature of the cause of action, and its entitlement to jury trial, altered by the fact that another cause of action was available (an inverse condemnation suit) to obtain the same relief. Even if that were an equitable cause of action . . . the nature of the § 1983 suit would no more be transformed by it than, for example, a common-law fraud action would be deprived of the right to jury trial by the fact that the defendant was a trustee who could, instead, have been sued for an equitable accounting. . . .

■ JUSTICE SOUTER, with whom JUSTICE O'CONNOR, JUSTICE GINSBURG, and JUSTICE BREYER join, concurring in part and dissenting in part. . . .

II

The city's proposed analogy of inverse condemnation proceedings to direct ones is intuitively sensible, given their common Fifth Amendment constitutional source and link to the sovereign's power of eminent domain. . . .

The strength of the analogy is fatal to respondents' claim to a jury trial as a matter of right. Reaffirming what was already a well-established principle, the Court explained over a century ago that "the estimate of the just compensation for property taken for the public use, under the right of eminent domain, is not required to be made by a jury," Bauman v. Ross, 167 U.S. 548, 593 (1897), and we have since then thought it "long . . . settled that there is no constitutional right to a jury in eminent domain proceedings." United States v. Reynolds, 397 U.S. 14, 18 (1970). . . .

There is no jury right . . . because condemnation proceedings carried "no uniform and established right to a common law jury trial in England or the colonies at the time . . . the Seventh Amendment was adopted." [A]t the time of the framing the notion of regulatory taking or inverse condemnation was yet to be derived, the closest analogue to the then-unborn claim was that of direct condemnation, and the right to compensation for such direct takings carried with it no right to a jury trial, just as the jury right is foreign to it in the modern era. On accepted Seventh Amendment analysis, then, there is no reason to find a jury right either by direct analogy or for the sake of preserving the substance of any jury practice known to the law at the crucial time. Indeed, the analogy with direct condemnation actions is so strong that there is every reason to conclude that inverse condemnation should implicate no jury right.

III

The plurality avoids this obvious conclusion [in part] by endorsing the course followed by Justice Scalia in his separate opinion, by selecting an analogy not to tort actions as such, but to tort-like § 1983 actions. This alternative, however, is ultimately found wanting, for it prefers a statutory analogy to a constitutional one. . . .

[Section 1983 actions for money damages have] been treated as tort-like in character and thus as much entitled to jury trial as tort actions have been at common law. For two independent reasons, however, I think the analogy with § 1983 actions, either as a class or as a subclass of damages actions, is inadequate.

1

First, the analogy to all § 1983 actions does not serve any unified field theory of jury rights under § 1983. While the statute is indeed a prism through which rights originating elsewhere may pass on their way to a federal jury trial, trial by jury is not a uniform feature of § 1983 actions. The statute provides not only for actions at law with damages remedies where appropriate, but for "suits in equity, or other proper proceedings for redress." 42 U.S.C. § 1983. Accordingly, rights passing through the § 1983 prism may in proper cases be vindicated by injunction, orders of restitution, and by declaratory judgments, none of which implicate, or always implicate, a right to jury trial. . . .

Nor . . . is there a sound basis for treating inverse condemnation as providing damages for a tort. A State's untoward refusal to provide an adequate remedy to obtain compensation, the sine qua non of an inverse condemnation remedy under § 1983, is not itself the independent subject of an award of damages (and respondents do not claim otherwise); the remedy is not damages for tortious behavior, but just compensation for the value of the property taken.

2

Even if an argument for § 1983 simplicity and uniformity were sustainable, however, it would necessarily be weaker than the analogy with direct condemnation actions. That analogy rests on two elements that are present in each of the two varieties of condemnation actions: a Fifth Amendment constitutional right and a remedy specifically mandated by that same amendment. Because constitutional values are superior to statutory values, uniformity as between different applications of a given constitutional guarantee is more important than uniformity as between different applications of a given statute. If one accepts that proposition as I do, a close analogy between direct and inverse condemnation proceedings is necessarily stronger than even a comparably close resemblance between two statutory actions. . . .

NOTE ON THE RIGHT TO A JURY TRIAL IN § 1983 ACTIONS

The decision that the Seventh Amendment confers the right to trial by jury does not completely answer the question of *which* issues must be determined by the jury rather than by the judge. In a garden-variety § 1983 damages action, which plainly falls within the jury trial requirement of the Seventh Amendment, questions such as the availability of a qualified immunity defense are often, indeed usually, decided by the court as questions of law. In the *Monterey* case, in addition to holding that respondents were entitled to a trial by jury, the Court also affirmed the Court of Appeals' decision that the questions whether respondents had been denied all economically viable use of their property and whether the city's denial of a permit substantially advanced legitimate public interests were questions of fact properly determined by the jury. The Court recognized that the latter question was "best understood as a mixed question of fact and law," but held that in this case the question had been so narrowed as to be "fact-bound," and therefore appropriate for resolution by the jury. But it cautioned that in the case of a more sweeping challenge to the constitutionality of a city's general land-use ordinances or policies, determining whether the statutory purposes were legitimate or whether the purposes were furthered by the law or policy might fall within the province of the judge.

The allocation of authority between judge and jury may have a series of practical consequences. The Federal Rules of Civil Procedure require trial by jury when, in an appropriate case, any party makes a timely demand. Fed. R. Civ. P. 38(b). Consider when and why particular litigants will demand a jury trial. When, for example, will plaintiffs ask for a jury trial? When will government officers or municipal entities?

Note also that under Beacon Theatres v. Westover, 359 U.S. 500 (1959), and Dairy Queen, Inc. v. Wood, 369 U.S. 469 (1962), if equitable and legal claims are joined in the same lawsuit, the Seventh Amendment requires that the trial court allow the jury to determine the factual issues in the legal claims before it decides identical issues regarding the equitable claims.

7. RELEASE–DISMISSAL AGREEMENTS

Newton v. Rumery

Supreme Court of the United States, 1987.
480 U.S. 386.

■ JUSTICE POWELL announced the judgment of the Court and delivered the opinion of the Court with respect to Parts I, II, III–A, IV, and V, and an opinion with respect to Part III–B in which THE CHIEF JUSTICE, JUSTICE WHITE, and JUSTICE SCALIA join.

The question in this case is whether a court properly may enforce an agreement in which a criminal defendant releases his right to file a § 1983 action in return for a prosecutor's dismissal of pending criminal charges.

I

In 1983, a grand jury in Rockingham County, New Hampshire, indicted David Champy for aggravated felonious sexual assault. Respondent Bernard Rumery, a friend of Champy's, read about the charges in a local newspaper. Seeking information about the charges, he telephoned Mary Deary, who was acquainted with both Rumery and Champy. Coincidentally, Deary had been the victim of the assault in question and was expected to be the principal witness against Champy. The record does not reveal directly the date or substance of this conversation between Rumery and Deary, but Deary apparently was disturbed by the call. On March 12, according to police records, she called David Barrett, the Chief of Police for the town of Newton. She told him that Rumery was trying to force her to drop the charges against Champy. Rumery talked to Deary again on May 11. The substance of this conversation also is disputed. Rumery claims that Deary called him and that she raised the subject of Champy's difficulties.

According to the police records, however, Deary told Chief Barrett that Rumery had threatened that, if Deary went forward on the Champy case, she would "end up like" two women who recently had been murdered in Lowell, Massachusetts. Barrett arrested Rumery and accused him of tampering with a witness . . . , a Class B felony.

Rumery promptly retained Stephen Woods, an experienced criminal defense attorney. Woods contacted Brian Graf, the Deputy County Attorney for Rockingham County. He warned Graf that he "had better [dismiss] these charges, because we're going to win them and after that we're going to sue." After further discussions, Graf and Woods reached an agreement, under which Graf would dismiss the charges against Rumery if Rumery would agree not to sue the town, its officials, or Deary for any harm caused by the arrest. All parties agreed that one factor in Graf's decision not to prosecute Rumery was Graf's desire to protect Deary from the trauma she would suffer if she were forced to testify. As the prosecutor explained in the District Court:

> I had been advised by Chief Barrett that Mary Deary did not want to testify against Mr. Rumery. The witness tampering charge would have required Mary Deary to testify. . . .
>
> I think that was a particularly sensitive type of case where you are dealing with a victim of an alleged aggravated felonious sexual assault.

Woods drafted an agreement in which Rumery agreed to release any claims he might have against the town, its officials, or Deary if Graf agreed to dismiss the criminal charges (the release-dismissal agreement). After Graf approved the form of the agreement, Woods presented it to Rumery. Although Rumery's recollection of the events was quite different, the District Court found that Woods discussed the agreement with Rumery in his office for about an hour and explained to Rumery that he would forgo all civil actions if he signed the agreement. Three days later, on June 6, 1983, Rumery returned to Woods' office and signed the agreement. The criminal charges were dropped.

Ten months later, on April 13, 1984, Rumery filed an action under 42 U.S.C. § 1983 in the federal District Court for the District of New Hampshire. He alleged that the town and its officers had violated his constitutional rights by arresting him, defaming him, and imprisoning him falsely. The defendants filed a motion to dismiss, relying on the release-dismissal agreement as an affirmative defense. Rumery argued that the agreement was unenforceable because it violated public policy. The court rejected Rumery's argument and concluded that a "release of claims under § 1983 is valid . . . if it results from a decision that is voluntary, deliberate and informed." The court found that Rumery

> is a knowledgeable, industrious individual with vast experience in the business world. [H]e intelligently and carefully, after weighing all the factors, concluded that it would be in his best interest and welfare to sign the covenant. He was also represented by a very competent attorney with more than ordinary expertise in the sometimes complex area of criminal law.

The court then dismissed Rumery's suit.

On appeal, the Court of Appeals for the First Circuit reversed. It adopted a per se rule invalidating release-dismissal agreements. [W]e granted the town's petition for a writ of certiorari. We reverse.

II

We begin by noting the source of the law that governs this case. The agreement purported to waive a right to sue conferred by a federal statute. The question whether the policies underlying that statute may in some circumstances render that waiver unenforceable is a question of federal law. We resolve this question by reference to traditional common-law principles, as we have resolved other questions about the principles governing § 1983 actions. E.g., Pulliam v. Allen, 466 U.S. 522, 539–40 (1984). The relevant principle is well-established: a promise is unenforceable if the interest in its enforcement is outweighed in the circumstances by a public policy harmed by enforcement of the agreement.

III

The Court of Appeals concluded that the public interests related to release-dismissal agreements justified a per se rule of invalidity. We think the court overstated the perceived problems and also failed to credit the significant public interests that such agreements can further. Most importantly, the Court of Appeals did not consider the wide variety of factual situations that can result in release-dismissal agreements. Thus, although we agree that in some cases these agreements may infringe important interests of the criminal defendant and of society as a whole, we do not believe that the mere possibility of harm to these interests calls for a per se rule.

A

Rumery's first objection to release-dismissal agreements is that they are inherently coercive. He argues that it is unfair to present a criminal defendant with a choice between facing criminal charges and waiving his right to sue under § 1983. We agree that some release-dismissal agreements may not be the product of an informed and voluntary decision. The risk, publicity, and expense of a criminal trial may intimidate a defendant, even if he believes his defense is meritorious. But this possibility does not justify invalidating all such agreements. In other contexts criminal defendants are required to make difficult choices that effectively waive constitutional rights. For example, it is well settled that plea bargaining does not violate the Constitution even though a guilty plea waives important constitutional rights.[3] See Brady v. United States, 397 U.S. 742, 752–53 (1970); Santobello v. New York, 404 U.S. 257, 264 (1971) (Douglas, J. concurring). We see no reason to believe that release-dismissal agreements pose a more coercive choice than other situations we have accepted. E.g., Corbitt v. New Jersey, 439 U.S. 212 (1978) (upholding a statute that imposed higher sentences on defendants who went to trial than on those who entered guilty pleas). . . .

In many cases a defendant's choice to enter into a release-dismissal agreement will reflect a highly rational judgment that the certain benefits of escaping criminal prosecution exceed the speculative benefits of prevailing in a civil action. Rumery's voluntary decision to enter this agreement

[3] We recognize that the analogy between plea bargains and release-dismissal agreements is not complete. The former are subject to judicial oversight. Moreover, when the State enters a plea bargain with a criminal defendant, it receives immediate and tangible benefits, such as promptly imposed punishment without the expenditure of prosecutorial resources. Also, the defendant's agreement to plead to some crime tends to ensure some satisfaction of the public interest in the prosecution of crime and confirms that the prosecutor's charges have a basis in fact. The benefits the State may realize in particular cases from release-dismissal agreements may not be as tangible, but they are not insignificant.

exemplifies such a judgment. Rumery is a sophisticated businessman. He was not in jail and was represented by an experienced criminal lawyer, who drafted the agreement. Rumery considered the agreement for three days before signing it. The benefits of the agreement to Rumery are obvious: he gained immunity from criminal prosecution in consideration of abandoning a civil suit that he may well have lost.

Because Rumery voluntarily waived his right to sue under § 1983, the public interest opposing involuntary waiver of constitutional rights is no reason to hold this agreement invalid. Moreover, we find that the possibility of coercion in the making of similar agreements insufficient by itself to justify a per se rule against release-dismissal bargains. If there is such a reason, it must lie in some external public interest necessarily injured by release-dismissal agreements.

B

[T]he Court of Appeals held that all release-dismissal agreements offend public policy because it believed these agreements "tempt prosecutors to trump up charges in reaction to a defendant's civil rights claim, suppress evidence of police misconduct, and leave unremedied deprivations of constitutional rights." We can agree that in some cases there may be a substantial basis for this concern. It is true, of course, that § 1983 actions to vindicate civil rights may further significant public interests. But it is important to remember that Rumery had no public duty to institute a § 1983 action merely to further the public's interest in revealing police misconduct. Congress has confided the decision to bring such actions to the injured individuals, not to the public at large. Thus, we hesitate to elevate more diffused public interests above Rumery's considered decision that he would benefit personally from the agreement.

We also believe the Court of Appeals misapprehended the range of public interests arguably affected by a release-dismissal agreement. The availability of such agreements may threaten important public interests. They may tempt prosecutors to bring frivolous charges, or to dismiss meritorious charges, to protect the interests of other officials.[4] But a per se rule of invalidity fails to credit other relevant public interests and improperly assumes prosecutorial misconduct.[5]

The vindication of constitutional rights and the exposure of official misconduct are not the only concerns implicated by § 1983 suits. No one suggests that all such suits are meritorious. Many are marginal and some are frivolous. Yet even when the risk of ultimate liability is negligible, the burden of defending such lawsuits is substantial. Counsel may be retained by the official, as well as the governmental entity. Preparation for trial, and the trial itself, will require the time and attention of the defendant officials, to the detriment of their public duties. In some cases litigation will extend over a period of years. This diversion of officials from their normal duties and the inevitable expense of defending even unjust claims is distinctly not

[4] Actions taken for these reasons properly have been recognized as unethical. See Model Code of Professional Responsibility, Disciplinary Rule 7–105 (1980).

[5] Prosecutors themselves rarely are held liable in § 1983 actions. See Imbler v. Pachtman, 424 U.S. 409 (1976) (discussing prosecutorial immunity). Also, in many States and municipalities—perhaps in most—prosecutors are elected officials and are entirely independent of the civil authorities likely to be defendants in § 1983 suits. There may be situations, of course, when a prosecutor is motivated to protect the interests of such officials or of police. But the constituency of an elected prosecutor is the public, and such a prosecutor is likely to be influenced primarily by the general public interest.

in the public interest. To the extent release-dismissal agreements protect public officials from the burdens of defending such unjust claims, they further this important public interest.

A per se rule invalidating release-dismissal agreements also assumes that prosecutors will seize the opportunity for wrongdoing. In recent years the Court has considered a number of claims that prosecutors have acted improperly. E.g., Wayte v. United States, 470 U.S. 598 (1985); United States v. Goodwin, 457 U.S. 368 (1982); Bordenkircher v. Hayes, 434 U.S. 357 (1978). Our decisions in those cases uniformly have recognized that courts normally must defer to prosecutorial decisions as to whom to prosecute. The reasons for judicial deference are well-known. Prosecutorial charging decisions are rarely simple. In addition to assessing the strength and importance of a case, prosecutors also must consider other tangible and intangible factors, such as government enforcement priorities. Finally, they also must decide how best to allocate the scarce resources of a criminal justice system that simply cannot accommodate the litigation of every serious charge. . . .

Against this background of discretion, the mere opportunity to act improperly does not compel an assumption that all—or even a significant number of—release-dismissal agreements stem from the prosecutors abandoning "the independence of judgment required by [their] public trust," Imbler v. Pachtman, 424 U.S. 409, 423 (1976).[7] Rather, tradition and experience justify our belief that the great majority of prosecutors will be faithful to their duty. Indeed, the merit of this view is illustrated by this case, where the only evidence of prosecutorial misconduct is the agreement itself.

Because release-dismissal agreements may further legitimate prosecutorial and public interests, we reject the Court of Appeals' holding that all such agreements are invalid per se.[8]

IV

Turning to the agreement presented by this case, we conclude that the District Court's decision to enforce the agreement was correct. As we have noted, it is clear that Rumery voluntarily entered the agreement. Moreover, in this case the prosecutor had an independent, legitimate reason to make this agreement directly related to his prosecutorial responsibilities. The agreement foreclosed both the civil and criminal trials concerning Rumery, in which Deary would have been a key witness. She therefore was spared the public scrutiny and embarrassment she would have endured if she had to testify in either of those cases. Both the prosecutor and the defense at-

---

7 Of course, the Court has found that certain actions are so likely to result from prosecutorial misconduct that it has " 'presume[d]' an improper vindictive motive," United States v. Goodwin, 457 U.S. 368, 373 (1982). E.g., Blackledge v. Perry, 417 U.S. 21 (1974) (holding that it violates the due process clause for a prosecutor to increase charges in response to a defendant's exercise of his right to appeal). But the complexity of pretrial decisions by prosecutors suggests that judicial evaluation of those decisions should be especially deferential. Thus, the Court has never accepted such a blanket claim with respect to pretrial decisions. See *United States v. Goodwin*, supra; Bordenkircher v. Hayes, 434 U.S. 357 (1978).

8 Justice Stevens' evaluation of the public interests associated with release-dismissal agreements relies heavily on his view that Rumery is a completely innocent man. He rests this conclusion on the testimony Rumery and his attorney presented to the District Court, but fails to acknowledge that the District Court's factual findings gave little credence to this testimony. Justice Stevens also gives great weight to the fact that Rumery "must be presumed to be innocent." But this is not a criminal case. This is a civil case, in which Rumery bears the ultimate burden of proof.

torney testified in the District Court that this was a significant consideration in the prosecutor's decision.

In sum, we conclude that this agreement was voluntary, that there is no evidence of prosecutorial misconduct, and that enforcement of this agreement would not adversely affect the relevant public interests.[10]

V

We reverse the judgment of the Court of Appeals and remand the case to the District Court for dismissal of the complaint.

It is so ordered.

■ JUSTICE O'CONNOR, concurring in part and in the judgment.

I join in parts I, II, III–A, IV, and V of the Court's opinion. More particularly, I join the Court in disapproving the Court of Appeal's broad holding that a criminal defendant's promise not to sue local governments and officials for constitutional violations arising out of his arrest and prosecution, given in exchange for the prosecutor's agreement to dismiss pending criminal charges, is void, as against public policy under all circumstances. I agree with the Court that a case-by-case approach appropriately balances the important interests on both sides of the question of the enforceability of these agreements, and that on the facts of this particular case Bernard Rumery's covenant not to sue is enforceable. I write separately, however, in order to set out the factors that lead me to conclude that this covenant should be enforced and to emphasize that it is the burden of those relying upon such covenants to establish that the agreement is neither involuntary nor the product of an abuse of the criminal process.

As the Court shows, there are substantial policy reasons for permitting release-dismissal bargains to be struck in appropriate cases. Certainly some § 1983 litigation is meritless, and the inconvenience and distraction of public officials caused by such suits is not inconsiderable. Moreover, particular release-dismissal agreements may serve bona fide criminal justice goals. Here, for example, the protection of Mary Deary, the complaining witness in an aggravated sexual assault case, was an important, legitimate criminal justice objective served by the release-dismissal agreement. Similarly, prosecutors may legitimately believe that, though the police properly defused a volatile situation by arresting a minor misdemeanant, the public interest in further prosecution is outweighed by the cost of litigation. Sparing the local community the expense of litigation associated with some minor crimes for which there is little or no public interest in prosecution may be a legitimate objective of a release-dismissal agreement.

On the other hand, as the Court acknowledges, release-dismissal agreements potentially threaten the integrity of the criminal process and preclude vindication of federal civil rights. Permitting such releases may tempt public officials to bring frivolous criminal charges in order to deter meritorious civil complaints. The risk and expense of a criminal trial can easily intimidate even an innocent person whose civil and constitutional rights have been violated. The coercive power of criminal process may be twisted to serve the end of suppressing complaints against official abuse, to

[10] . . . We have no occasion in this case to determine whether an inquiry into voluntariness alone is sufficient to determine the enforceability of release-dismissal agreements. We also note that it would be helpful to conclude release-dismissal agreements under judicial supervision. Although such supervision is not essential to the validity of an otherwise proper agreement, it would help ensure that the agreements did not result from prosecutorial misconduct.

the detriment not only of the victim of such abuse, but also of society as a whole.

In addition, the availability of the release option may tempt officials to ignore their public duty by dropping meritorious criminal prosecutions in order to avoid the risk, expense and publicity of a § 1983 suit. The public has an interest in seeing its laws faithfully executed. But, officials may give more weight to the private interest in seeing a civil claim settled than to the public interest in seeing the guilty convicted. By introducing extraneous considerations into the criminal process, the legitimacy of that process may be compromised. Release-dismissal bargains risk undermining faith in the fairness of those who administer the criminal process. Finally, the execution of release-dismissal agreements may result in having to determine whether the prosecutor violated any of his ethical obligations as a lawyer.

As the Court indicates, a release-dismissal agreement is not directly analogous to a plea-bargain. The legitimacy of plea bargaining depends in large measure upon eliminating extraneous considerations from the process. See Santobello v. New York, 404 U.S. 257, 260–61 (1971); Brady v. United States, 397 U.S. 742, 753 (1970); ALI, Model Code of Pre–Arraignment Procedure § 350.5(2) (1975). No court would knowingly permit a prosecutor to agree to accept a defendant's plea to a lesser charge in exchange for the defendant's cash payment to the police officers who arrested him. Rather, the prosecutor is permitted to consider only legitimate criminal justice concerns in striking his bargain—concerns such as rehabilitation, allocation of criminal justice resources, the strength of the evidence against the defendant, and the extent of his cooperation with the authorities. The central problem with the release-dismissal agreement is that public criminal justice interests are explicitly traded against the private financial interest of the individuals involved in the arrest and prosecution. Moreover, plea bargaining takes place only under judicial supervision, an important check against abuse. Release-dismissal agreements are often reached between the prosecutor and defendant with little or no judicial oversight.

Nevertheless, the dangers of the release-dismissal agreement do not preclude its enforcement in all cases. The defendants in a § 1983 suit may establish that a particular release executed in exchange for the dismissal of criminal charges was voluntarily made, not the product of prosecutorial overreaching, and in the public interest. But they must prove that this is so; the courts should not presume it as I fear portions of part III–B of the Court's opinion may imply.

Many factors may bear on whether a release was voluntary and not the product of overreaching, some of which come readily to mind. The knowledge and experience of the criminal defendant and the circumstances of the execution of the release, including, importantly, whether the defendant was counseled, are clearly relevant. The nature of the criminal charges that are pending is also important, for the greater the charge, the greater the coercive effect. The existence of a legitimate criminal justice objective for obtaining the release will support its validity. And, importantly, the possibility of abuse is clearly mitigated if the release-dismissal agreement is executed under judicial supervision.

Close examination of all the factors in this case leads me to concur in the Court's decision that this covenant not to sue is enforceable. There is ample evidence in the record concerning the circumstances of the execution of this agreement. Testimony of the prosecutor, defense counsel and Rumery himself leave little doubt that the agreement was entered into voluntarily. While the charge pending against Rumery was serious—subjecting him to up to seven years in prison—it is one of the lesser felonies under New Hampshire law, and a long prison term was probably unlikely given the absence of any prior criminal record and the weaknesses in the case against Rumery. Finally, as the Court correctly notes, the prosecutor had a legitimate reason to enter into this agreement directly related to his criminal justice function. The prosecutor testified that:

> I had been advised by Chief Barrett that Mary Deary did not want to testify against Mr. Rumery. The witness tampering charge would have required Mary Deary to testify. She would have been the primary source of evidence against Mr. Rumery. There was still considerable concern about Mary Deary because the David Champy case was still pending.
>
> I think that was a particular sensitive type of case where you are dealing with a victim of an alleged aggravated felonious sexual assault. And I think I was taking into consideration the fact that I had her as a victim of one case, and now, the State was in a position of perhaps having to force her to testify against her will perhaps causing more trauma or upset to her forcing her to go through more things than what I felt comfortable with doing. So that was one of the considerations I was taking into play at that time, that I had been informed that Mary Deary did not want to go forward with the prosecution, that she felt she had gone through enough.

Thus, Mary Deary's emotional distress, her unwillingness to testify against Rumery, presumably in later civil as well as criminal proceedings, and the necessity of her testimony in the pending sexual assault case against David Champy all support the prosecutor's judgment that the charges against Rumery should be dropped if further injury to Deary, and therefore the Champy case, could thereby be avoided.

Against the convincing evidence that Rumery voluntarily entered into the agreement and that it served the public interest, there is only Rumery's blanket claim that agreements such as this one are inherently coercive. While it would have been preferable, and made this an easier case, had the release-dismissal agreement been concluded under some form of judicial supervision, I concur in the Court's judgment, and all but part III–B of its opinion, that Rumery's § 1983 suit is barred by his valid, voluntary release.

■ JUSTICE STEVENS, with whom JUSTICE BRENNAN, JUSTICE MARSHALL, and JUSTICE BLACKMUN join, dissenting.

The question whether the release-dismissal agreement signed by the respondent is unenforceable is much more complex than the Court's opinion indicates. A complete analysis of the question presented by this case cannot end with the observation that respondent made a knowing and voluntary choice to sign a settlement agreement. Even an intelligent and informed, but completely innocent, person accused of crime should not be required to choose between a threatened indictment and trial, with their attendant publicity and the omnipresent possibility of wrongful conviction, and surrendering the right to a civil remedy against individuals who have violated his or her constitutional rights. Moreover, the prosecutor's representation of competing and possibly conflicting interests compounds the dangerous potential of release-dismissal agreements. To explain my disagreement with the majority, I shall first discuss the dilemma confronted by respondent at the time his lawyer advised him to sign the agreement, then comment on the three different interests the prosecutor represented, and finally discuss the plurality's evaluation of the relevant public interests in this case.

I

Respondent is an innocent man. As a matter of law, he must be presumed to be innocent. As a matter of fact, the uncontradicted sworn testimony of respondent, and his lawyer, buttressed by the circumstantial evidence, overwhelmingly attest to his innocence. There was no written statement by the alleged victim, sworn or unsworn, implicating respondent in any criminal activity. The charge that respondent had threatened the victim was reported to the police by the victim's daughter, and the substance of the conversation as summarized in Chief Barrett's report was based in part on conversations between another police officer and the victim, and in part on his own conversation with the victim when she was in a state of extreme emotional distress. Respondent was never indicted, and the warrant for his arrest was issued on the basis of a sketchy statement by Chief Barrett. Even the assistant prosecutor who was in charge of the case was surprised to learn that Chief Barrett had arrested respondent on the basis of the information in the police report. Thus, when the Newton police officers arrested respondent in his home they had not even obtained a written statement from the complaining witness. Prior to the arrest, and prior to the police chief's press conference concerning it, respondent was a respected member of a small community who had never been arrested, even for a traffic offense.

A few days before respondent was scheduled for a probable cause hearing on the charge of witness tampering, respondent's attorney advised him to sign a covenant not to sue the town of Newton, its police officers or the witness Deary in exchange for dismissal of the charge against him. The advice was predicated on the lawyer's judgment that the value of a dismissal outweighed the harmful consequences of an almost certain indictment on a felony charge together with the risk of conviction in a case in which the outcome would depend on the jury's assessment of the relative credibility of respondent and his alleged victim. The lawyer correctly advised respondent that even if he was completely innocent, there could be no guarantee of acquittal. He therefore placed a higher value on his client's interest in terminating the criminal proceeding promptly than on the uncertain benefits of pursuing a civil remedy against the town and its police department.[9] After delaying a decision for three days, respondent reluctantly followed his lawyer's advice.

From respondent's point of view, it is unquestionably true that the decision to sign the release-dismissal agreement was, as the Court emphasizes, "voluntary, deliberate, and informed." It reflected "a highly rational judgment that the certain benefits of escaping criminal prosecution exceed the speculative benefits of prevailing in a civil action." As the plurality iterates and reiterates, respondent made a "considered decision that he would benefit personally from the agreement." I submit, however, that the deliberate and rational character of respondent's decision is not a sufficient reason for concluding that the agreement is enforceable. Otherwise, a promise to pay a state trooper $20 for not issuing a ticket for a traffic viola-

[9] Although the witness Deary was a covenantee, she was not named as a defendant in the civil case.

tion, or a promise to contribute to the police department's retirement fund in exchange for the dismissal of a felony charge, would be enforceable. Indeed, I would suppose that virtually all contracts that courts refuse to enforce nevertheless reflect perfectly rational decisions by the parties who entered into them. There is nothing irrational about an agreement to bribe a police officer, to enter into a wagering arrangement, to pay usurious rates of interests, or to threaten to indict an innocent man in order to induce him to surrender something of value.

The "voluntary, deliberate, and informed" character of a defendant's decision generally provides an acceptable basis for upholding the validity of a plea bargain. But it is inappropriate to assume that the same standard determines the validity of a quite different agreement to forego a civil remedy for the violation of the defendant's constitutional rights in exchange for complete abandonment of a criminal charge.

The net result of every plea bargain is an admission of wrongdoing by the defendant and the imposition of a criminal sanction with its attendant stigma. Although there may be some cases in which an innocent person pleads guilty to a minor offense to avoid the risk of conviction on a more serious charge, it is reasonable to presume that such cases are rare and represent the exception rather than the rule. See Fed.Rule Crim.Procedure 11(f) (court may not enter judgment on a guilty plea unless it is satisfied the plea has a factual basis). Like a plea bargain, an agreement by the suspect to drop § 1983 charges and to pay restitution to the victim in exchange for the prosecutor's termination of criminal proceedings involves an admission of wrongdoing by the defendant. The same cannot be said about an agreement that completely exonerates the defendant. Not only is such a person presumptively innocent as a matter of law; as a factual matter the prosecutor's interest in obtaining a covenant not to sue will be strongest in those cases in which he realizes that the defendant was innocent and was wrongfully accused. Moreover, the prosecutor will be most willing—indeed, he is ethically obligated—to drop charges when he believes that probable cause as established by the available, admissible evidence is lacking.

The plea bargain represents a practical compromise between the prosecutor and the defendant that takes into account the burdens of litigation and its probable outcome, as well as society's interest in imposing appropriate punishment upon an admitted wrongdoer. The defendant admits wrongdoing for conduct upon which the guilty plea is based and avoids further prosecution; the prosecutor need not go to trial; and an admitted wrongdoer is punished, all under close judicial supervision. By simultaneously establishing and limiting the defendant's criminal liability, plea bargains strike a delicate balance of individual and social advantage. This mutuality of advantage does not exist in release-dismissal agreements. A defendant entering a release-dismissal agreement is forced to waive claims based on official conduct under color of state law, in exchange merely for the assurance that the State will not prosecute him for conduct for which he has made no admission of wrongdoing. The State is spared the necessity of going to trial, but its willingness to drop the charge completely indicates that it might not have proceeded with the prosecution in any event. No social interest in the punishment of wrongdoers is satisfied; the only interest vindicated is that of resolving once and for all the question of § 1983 liability.

Achieving this result has no connection with the give-and-take over the defendant's wrongdoing that is the essence of the plea-bargaining process, and thus cannot be justified by reference to the principles of mutual advantage that support plea bargaining. Although the outcome of a criminal proceeding may affect the value of the civil claim, as a matter of law the claims are quite distinct. Even a guilty defendant may be entitled to receive damages for physical abuse, and conversely, the fact that a defendant is ultimately acquitted is entirely consistent with the possibility that the police had probable cause to arrest him and did not violate any of his constitutional rights.

The plurality assumes that many § 1983 suits "are marginal and some are frivolous." Whether that assumption is correct or incorrect, the validity of each ought to be tested by the adversary process. Experience teaches us that some § 1983 suits in which release-dismissal agreements are sought are meritorious. Whatever the true value of a § 1983 claim may be, a defendant who is required to give up such a claim in exchange for a dismissal of a criminal charge is being forced to pay a price that is unrelated to his possible wrongdoing as reflected in that charge. Indeed, if the defendant is forced to abandon a claim that has a value of $1000, the price that he pays is the functional equivalent of a $1000 payment to a police department's retirement benefit fund.

Thus, even though respondent's decision in this case was deliberate, informed, and voluntary, this observation does not address two distinct objections to enforcement of the release-dismissal agreement. The prosecutor's offer to drop charges if the defendant accedes to the agreement is inherently coercive; moreover, the agreement exacts a price unrelated to the character of the defendant's own conduct.

II

When the prosecutor negotiated the agreement with respondent, he represented three potentially conflicting interests. His primary duty, of course, was to represent the sovereign's interests in the evenhanded and effective enforcement of its criminal laws. In addition, as the covenant demonstrates, he sought to represent the interests of the town of Newton and its police department in connection with their possible civil liability to respondent. Finally, as the inclusion of Mary Deary as a covenantee indicates, the prosecutor also represented the interest of a potential witness who allegedly accused both respondent and a mutual friend of separate instances of wrongdoing.

If we view the problem from the standpoint of the prosecutor's principal client, the State of New Hampshire, it is perfectly clear that the release-dismissal agreement was both unnecessary and unjustified. For both the prosecutor and the State of New Hampshire enjoy absolute immunity from common-law and § 1983 liability arising out of a prosecutor's decision to initiate criminal proceedings. See Imbler v. Pachtman, 424 U.S. 409, 427 (1976). The agreement thus gave the State and the prosecutor no protection that the law did not already provide.

The record in this case indicates that an important reason for obtaining the covenant was "[t]o protect the police department." There is, however, an obvious potential conflict between the prosecutor's duty to enforce the law and his objective of protecting members of the police department who are accused of unlawful conduct. The public is entitled to have the prosecutor's decision to go forward with a criminal case, or to dismiss it, made independently of his concerns about the potential damages liability of the police department. It is equally clear that this separation of functions cannot be achieved if the prosecutor may use the threat of criminal prosecution as a weapon to obtain a favorable termination of a civil claim against the police.

In negotiating a release-dismissal agreement, the prosecutor inevitably represents both the public and the police. When release agreements are enforceable, consideration of the police interest in avoiding damages liability severely hampers the prosecutor's ability to conform to the strictures of professional responsibility in deciding whether to prosecute. In particular, the possibility that the suspect will execute a covenant not to sue in exchange for a decision not to prosecute may well encourage a prosecutor to bring or to continue prosecutions in violation of his or her duty to "refrain from prosecuting a charge that the prosecutor knows is not supported by probable cause." ABA Model Rules of Professional Conduct, Rule 3.8(a) (1984).

This ethical obligation of every prosecutor is consistent with the general and fundamental rule that "[a] lawyer should exercise independent professional judgment on behalf of a client." ABA Model Code of Professional Responsibility, Canon 5 (1980). Every attorney should avoid situations in which he is representing potentially conflicting interests. As we noted in *Imbler v. Pachtman*, prosecutorial immunity from § 1983 lawsuits "does not leave the public powerless to deter misconduct or to punish that which occurs," in large part because "a prosecutor stands perhaps unique, among officials whose acts could deprive persons of constitutional rights, in his amenability to professional discipline by an association of his peers."

The prosecutor's potential conflict of interest increases in magnitude in direct proportion to the seriousness of the charges of police wrongdoing. Yet a rule that determines the enforceability of a release-dismissal agreement by focusing entirely on the quality of the defendant's decision to sign the agreement cannot detect the seriousness of this conflict of interest because it cannot distinguish the meritorious § 1983 claims from the frivolous ones. On the other hand, if the merits of the claim must be evaluated in each case in order to decide whether the agreement should be enforced, the agreement would not serve the goal of saving the litigation costs associated with a trial of the claim itself. The efficiency argument on behalf of enforcing a release-dismissal agreement thus requires inattention to conflicts of interest in precisely those circumstances in which the agreement to be enforced is most likely to have been exacted by a prosecutor serving the interests of more than one constituency.

At bottom, the Court's holding in this case seems to rest on concerns related to the potential witness, Mary Deary.[18] As is true with the prosecutor's concerns for police liability, there is a potential conflict between the public interest represented by the prosecutor and the private interests of a recalcitrant witness. As a general matter there is no reason to fashion a rule that either requires or permits a prosecutor always to defer to the interests of a witness. The prosecutor's law enforcement responsibilities will sometimes diverge from those interests; there will be cases in which the prosecutor has a plain duty to obtain critical testimony despite the desire of the witness to remain anonymous or to avoid a courtroom confrontation

---

[18] Despite a good deal of unfortunate language in its opinion, in the final analysis the Court merely rejects a per se rule invalidating all release-dismissal agreements and holds that this particular agreement is enforceable. If the interest in protecting the potential witness were not present, presumably the author of the Court's opinion would adhere to the views he expressed in Bordenkircher v. Hayes, 434 U.S. 357, 372–73 (1978) (Powell, J., dissenting).

with an offender. There may be other cases in which a witness has given false or exaggerated testimony for malicious reasons. It would plainly be unwise for the Court to hold that a release-dismissal agreement is enforceable simply because it affords protection to a potential witness.

Arguably a special rule should be fashioned for witnesses who are victims of sexual assaults. The trauma associated with such an assault leaves scars that may make it especially difficult for a victim to press charges or to testify publicly about the event. It remains true, however, that uncorroborated, unsworn statements by persons who claim to have been victims of any crime, including such an assault, may be inaccurate, exaggerated or incomplete—and sometimes even malicious. It is even more clear that hearsay descriptions of statements by such persons may be unreliable. Rather than adopting a general rule that upholds a release-dismissal agreement whenever the criminal charge was based on a statement by the alleged victim of a sexual assault, I believe the Court should insist upon a "close examination" of the facts that purportedly justified the agreement.

Thus, in this case Justice O'Connor has suggested that three special facts support the conclusion that the prosecutor was legitimately interested in protecting the witness Deary from "further injury": (1) her "emotional distress"; (2) her unwillingness to testify against Rumery; and (3) the necessity of her testimony in the pending sexual assault case against Champy. Each of these facts merits a brief comment.

The only evidence of Deary's emotional distress in the record is found in Chief Barrett's report of his telephone conversation on the afternoon of May 11, 1983. While he was talking to Deary's daughter he "could hear an intense argument and sobbing in the background"; after he was finally able to talk to Deary herself, he characterized her conversation as "hysterical, distra[u]ght, and terrified." It is, of course, reasonable to assume that Deary's emotional distress may have affected her unwillingness to testify against either Champy or Rumery, and thereby influenced the prosecutor's decision to dismiss the witness tampering charge. But the testimony of the prosecutor, who appears only to have talked to her about the sexual assault charge, does not even mention the possibility that she might have to testify in any civil litigation.

Deary's unwillingness to testify against Rumery is perfectly obvious.[19] That fact unquestionably supports the prosecutor's decision to dismiss the charge against respondent, but it is not a sufficient reason for exonerating police officers from the consequences of actions that they took when they must have known that Deary was unwilling to testify. For it was the precipitous character of the police decision to make an arrest without first obtaining a written statement from the witness and contrary to the expectations—and presumably the advice—of the prosecutor that created the risk that the victim might have to testify in open court.[20]

---

[19] Indeed, that fact must have been obvious to the police before they arrested respondent. For it was Deary's daughter, not Deary herself, who advised the police of Deary's call to respondent on May 11. Since the allegedly incriminating version of that call is based on two police officers' summary of what they had been told by Deary and her daughter—rather than a coherent statement by Deary herself—it is reasonable to assume that Deary was unwilling to provide the police with a statement of her recollection of exactly what was said in her conversation with respondent.

[20] Moreover, it is by no means apparent that testimony in a § 1983 action arising out of Rumery's telephone conversations with Deary would require any inquiry about the facts of the underlying assault or about the victim's relationship with Champy, the alleged assailant.

The need for Deary's testimony in the pending sexual assault case against Champy simply cannot justify denying this respondent a remedy for a violation of his Fourth Amendment rights. Presumably, if there had been an actual trial of the pending charge against Champy,[21] that trial would have concluded long before Deary would have been required to testify in any § 1983 litigation.

It may well be true that a full development of all the relevant facts would provide a legitimate justification for enforcing the release-dismissal agreement. In my opinion, however, the burden of developing those facts rested on the defendants in the § 1983 litigation, and that burden has not been met by mere conjecture and speculation concerning the emotional distress of one reluctant witness.

III

Because this is the first case of this kind that the Court has reviewed, I am hesitant to adopt an absolute rule invalidating all such agreements.[22] I am, however, persuaded that the federal policies reflected in the enactment and enforcement of § 1983 mandate a strong presumption against the enforceability of such agreements and that the presumption is not overcome in this case by the facts or by any of the policy concerns discussed by the plurality.[23] The very existence of the statute identifies the important federal interests in providing a remedy for the violation of constitutional

---

[21] Champy pleaded guilty to a lesser included offense and the felony charge against him was dismissed without a trial.

[22] It seems likely, however, that the costs of having courts determine the validity of release-dismissal agreements will outweigh the benefits that most agreements can be expected to provide. A court may enforce such an agreement only after a careful inquiry into the circumstances under which the plaintiff signed the agreement and into the legitimacy of the prosecutor's objective in entering into the agreement. This inquiry will occupy a significant amount of the court's and the parties' time, and will subject prosecutorial decisionmaking to judicial review. But the only benefit most of these agreements will provide is another line of defense for prosecutors and police in § 1983 actions. This extra protection is unnecessary because prosecutors already enjoy absolute immunity and because police have been afforded qualified immunity, see Harlow v. Fitzgerald, 457 U.S. 800 (1982). Thus, the vast majority of "marginal or frivolous" § 1983 suits can be dismissed under existing standards with little more burden on the defendants than is entailed in defending a release-dismissal agreement. Moreover, there is an oddly suspect quality to this extra protection; the agreement is one that a public official signs, presumably in good faith, but that a court must conclude is invalid unless that official proves otherwise. In most cases, if social and judicial resources are to be expended at all, they would seem better spent on an evaluation of the merits of the § 1983 claim rather than on a detour into the enforceability of a release-dismissal agreement.

[23] The Courts of Appeals which have found agreements not to sue void as against public policy demonstrate, in my view, much more sensitivity to the possibility of prosecutorial abuse than does the Court's opinion today. As the Seventh Circuit has held:

> [W]e think that the release is void as against public policy. . . . As well stated in Dixon v. District of Columbia, 394 F.2d 966, 968–69 (D.C. Cir. 1968), a case where the arrestee violated his 'tacit' agreement not to sue and the prosecutor retaliated by filing the traffic charges, which had been held in abeyance pursuant to the tacit agreement:
>
> > The government may not prosecute for the purpose of deterring people from exercising their right to protest official misconduct and petition for redress of grievances. . . .
> >
> > The major evil of these agreements is not that charges are sometimes dropped against people who probably should be prosecuted. Much more important, these agreements suppress complaints against police misconduct which should be thoroughly aired in a free society. And they tempt the prosecutor to trump up charges for use in bargaining for suppression of the complaint. The danger of concocted charges is particularly great because complaints against the police usually arise in connection with arrests for extremely vague offenses such as disorderly conduct or resisting arrest.
>
> Boyd v. Adams, 513 F.2d 83, 88–89 (7th Cir. 1975).

rights and in having the merits of such claims resolved openly by an impartial adjudicator rather than sub silentio by a prosecutor whose primary objective in entering release-dismissal agreements is definitely not to ensure that all meritorious § 1983 claims prevail. The interest in vindication of constitutional violations unquestionably outweighs the interest in avoiding the expense and inconvenience of defending unmeritorious claims. Paradoxically, the plurality seems more sensitive to that burden than to the cost to the public and the individual of denying relief in meritorious cases. In short, the plurality's decision seems to rest on the unstated premise that § 1983 litigation imposes a net burden on society. If that were a correct assessment of the statute, it should be repealed. Unless that is done, however, we should respect the congressional decision to attach greater importance to the benefits associated with access to a federal remedy than to the burdens of defending these cases.[24]

The plurality also suggests that these agreements must be enforced in order to give proper respect to the prosecutor's exercise of discretion. I must confess that I do not understand this suggestion. The prosecutor is adequately protected by the shield of absolute immunity. Moreover, in this case it is police misconduct—not that of the prosecutor—that is challenged in the § 1983 litigation. A holding that the agreement is unenforceable need not rest on an assumption that "prosecutors will seize the opportunity for wrongdoing." On the contrary, it would merely respect the wholly unrelated premise that undergirds § 1983 itself—that law enforcement officers sometimes violate the constitutional rights of individual citizens. The public interest in identifying and redressing such violations is, in my judgment, paramount to the prosecutor's interest in using the threat of a felony indictment and trial as a means of avoiding an independent appraisal of the merits of a § 1983 claim.

Accordingly, although I am not prepared to endorse all of the reasoning of the Court of Appeals, I would affirm its judgment.

NOTES ON NEWTON V. RUMERY

1. THE LEGITIMACY OF RELEASE–DISMISSAL AGREEMENTS

Should release-dismissal agreements be tolerated? The following comments may help to identify the relevant issues.

(i) Unequal Bargaining Power: The Analogy of Plea Bargains

Rumery contended, and the dissenters agreed, that release-dismissal agreements are "inherently coercive" and should for that reason be disallowed. The underpinning of this view is a perception of unequal bargaining power between the authorities and the accused. As the Court said, "[t]he risk, publicity,

[24] Justice O'Connor suggests that these agreements might serve a legitimate purpose when the charges dismissed are misdemeanors rather than felonies. "Sparing the local community the expense of litigation associated with some minor crimes for which there is little or no public interest in prosecution may be a legitimate objective of a release-dismissal agreement." Implicit in this reasoning, I think, is the assumption that the court has independently determined that the arrest was proper. Otherwise, a valid § 1983 claim could be barred under this reasoning because of a factor wholly unrelated to the merits of the claim—the public's lack of interest in prosecuting the misdemeanor charges that were dismissed. These agreements could then be routinely upheld in circumstances where they were improperly employed. For example, one would expect that an officer attempting to cover up an illegal arrest would find it easier to trump up misdemeanor charges (such as resisting arrest) than felony charges.

and expense of a criminal trial may intimidate a defendant, even if he believes his defense is meritorious." If, as seems plausible, the defendant's threat to bring a civil rights action is not comparably intimidating to the public official, there may be a systemic inequality of bargaining power that renders release-dismissal agreements inherently suspect.

Consider in this respect the analogy of the plea bargain. For better or for worse, the great majority of criminal prosecutions are resolved by plea bargains. While many distrust this practice, the judicial attitude has been largely supportive, and the constitutionality of such agreements is well established. At least at first blush, the negotiations underlying the plea bargain would seem to feature the same inequality of bargaining power that arguably infects release-dismissal agreements. And to the extent that such inequality yields "wrong" results, the evil is arguably worse where the defendant agrees to plead guilty to a charge of crime rather than merely to forego a civil remedy. The question, therefore, is why the "inherently coercive" aspect of release-dismissal agreements should be a matter of concern to a system that tolerates, indeed encourages, plea bargains.

One answer is that the plea bargain is subject to judicial supervision. Typically, the judge inquires whether the defendant understands the nature of the charge, the penalties associated with that offense, and the rights waived by a plea of guilty. See Boykin v. Alabama, 395 U.S. 238 (1969). The judge further seeks to determine that the plea is voluntary. The cases are clear, however, that a plea is voluntary if it results from an informed choice among known alternatives, no matter how unpleasant the alternatives or how difficult the choice between them. See, e.g., Brady v. United States, 397 U.S. 742 (1970). Additionally, at least in the federal system, the judge must determine that there is a sufficient factual basis to support a finding of guilt. See Fed. Rule of Crim. Proc. 11(f).[a]

No doubt procedures of this sort are helpful in identifying pleas based on ignorance, confusion, or prosecutorial overreaching. One may wonder, however, whether they are equally relevant to the problem of unequal bargaining power. The prosecutorial threat used to produce a plea bargain seems fundamentally similar to that involved in release-dismissal agreements. Whether the "inherently coercive" nature of that threat is significantly reduced by judicial supervision may perhaps be doubted.

In dissent, Justice Stevens suggested other reasons for distinguishing plea bargains. Among other things he focused on "the principles of mutual advantage that support plea bargaining" and argued that this "mutuality of advantage" is lacking in release-dismissal agreements. Why is this so? Is it not clear that each side has something to gain (as well as something to lose) by concluding such an agreement?

(ii) The Nature of the Government's Interest

Perhaps Stevens means to say that the government's objective in obtaining release-dismissal agreements is not legitimate—that is, that the defendant's willingness to forego a § 1983 claim is not the kind of benefit for which the prosecutor can validly bargain. Under this view, the problem with release-

[a] Procedures of this sort were probably what the Court and Justice O'Connor had in mind when they suggested judicial supervision of release-dismissal agreements.

dismissal agreements is not so much the process of their negotiation, but rather that the government is pursuing an interest that does not deserve vindication. Is this right? Are the government's interests in plea bargains substantially different from those involved in release-dismissal agreements?

At other points, Stevens approaches the same idea somewhat differently. The problem, he says, with the release-dismissal agreement is that it "exacts a price unrelated to the character of the defendant's own conduct." In plea bargaining, the terms of the bargain are presumably related to the strength of each side's position. Of course, the same is true in a release-dismissal agreement. The difference lies in the relation between the two sides. In a plea bargain, the strength of the prosecution's position and the strength of the defendant's position are inversely related; both sides cannot have a strong case on the same facts. In a release-dismissal agreement, however, the strength of the two claims may be entirely unrelated; the civil rights claim may be based on police misconduct having no bearing on the defendant's guilt or innocence. Thus, in Stevens' words, the defendant who relinquishes a § 1983 claim in return for dismissal of a criminal charge is "forced to pay a price that is unrelated to the possible wrongdoing as reflected in that charge."

Does this line of reasoning show that the government's interest in concluding release-dismissal agreements is illegitimate? Does it explain why plea bargaining and release-dismissal agreements should be treated differently?

(iii) Prosecutorial Misconduct

Finally, Justice Stevens says that release-dismissal agreements create, or exacerbate, prosecutorial conflicts of interest. "There is," said Stevens, "an obvious potential conflict between the prosecutor's duty to enforce the law and his objective of protecting members of the police department who are accused of unlawful conduct." "In negotiating a release-dismissal agreement, the prosecutor inevitably represents both the public and the police," a duality of interest that "severely hampers" the prosecutor's conformance to ethical obligations. Moreover, in this case, the prosecutor's loyalties were further divided by a concern for the complaining witness.

Are these concerns persuasive? Is it unethical for a prosecutor to consider the interests of both the public at large and the law enforcement community? What is the role of the Supreme Court in monitoring such ethical conflicts?

2. STANDARDS FOR THE ACCEPTANCE OF RELEASE–DISMISSAL AGREEMENTS

Newton v. Rumery was the Supreme Court's first encounter with release-dismissal agreements in civil rights actions. The Court rejected a per se rule against the practice, but it stopped short of a blanket acceptance of all such agreements. Instead, it adopted an intermediate position allowing enforcement of release-dismissal agreements in some circumstances. Further litigation will doubtless be required to spell out what those circumstances may be.

The Court emphasized that the agreement was voluntary—at least in the sense that Rumery had a meaningful choice and that he exercised that choice in a rational and informed manner. Relevant to that conclusion were the facts that Rumery was a sophisticated businessman, that he was represented by experienced counsel, and that he took time to consider the decision.

What if these factors are missing? If they are critical to the validity of an agreement, then *Rumery* may have a very limited application. Presumably this would mean that a valid agreement could not be made with an unrepresented arrestee. In that event, the utility to the authorities of concluding such agreements would be greatly reduced, as would the prospect of systematic avoidance of civil rights actions by routinely inducing arrestees to release their claims.

On the other hand, it is far from clear that individual sophistication and advice of counsel are prerequisites to voluntary choice. Under *Miranda*, for example, a suspect who has been told of the options may validly waive both the right to counsel during interrogation *and* the Fifth Amendment privilege against self-incrimination. Such waivers must be informed and voluntary, but they are not deemed involuntary simply because the suspect was not a sophisticated individual with an experienced lawyer and ample time to consider the matter. Should the same standard of voluntariness be adopted for release-dismissal agreements? Or does *Rumery* imply a different inquiry?

3. BIBLIOGRAPHY

For commentary on *Rumery,* see Seth F. Kreimer, Releases, Redress, and Police Misconduct: Reflections on Agreements to Waive Civil Rights Actions in Exchange for Dismissal of Criminal Charges, 136 U.Pa.L.Rev. 851 (1988). Kreimer emphasizes the unusual facts of *Rumery* (including the role of counsel and the sophistication of the accused) and argues that enforcing release-dismissal agreements in other contexts would have substantial costs. Prominent among them is the threat to prosecutorial integrity that would be posed by "a continuing incentive to modify criminal prosecution decisions in the interests of goals extraneous to the criminal process," such as protecting the police. Kreimer reports interviews with several prosecutors, most of whom disapprove release-dismissal agreements as a matter of policy. He also argues that release-dismissal agreements could undermine the role of § 1983 in deterring official misconduct and vindicating constitutional rights.

See also Michael E. Solimine, Enforcement and Interpretation of Settlements of Federal Civil Rights Actions, 19 Rutgers L.J. 295 (1988). Solimine criticizes *Rumery* on choice-of-law grounds. He argues that the validity of the release-dismissal agreement should have been determined under the contract law of New Hampshire. Solimine argues that a federal common law rule is unnecessary since this is not, in his view, an issue requiring a uniform solution.

8. REMEDYING "DEFICIENCIES" IN FEDERAL LAW

Robertson v. Wegmann

Supreme Court of the United States, 1978.
436 U.S. 584.

■ MR. JUSTICE MARSHALL delivered the opinion of the Court.

In early 1970, Clay L. Shaw filed a civil rights action under 42 U.S.C. § 1983 in the United States District Court for the Eastern District of Louisiana. Four years later, before trial had commenced, Shaw died. The question presented is whether the District Court was required to adopt as federal law a Louisiana survivorship statute, which would have caused this action to abate, or was free instead to create a federal common-law rule allowing the action to survive. Resolution of this question turns on whether the state statute is "inconsistent with the Constitution and laws of the United States." 42 U.S.C. § 1988.[1]

I

In 1969, Shaw was tried in a Louisiana state court on charges of having participated in a conspiracy to assassinate President John F. Kennedy. He was acquitted by a jury but within days was arrested on charges of having committed perjury in his testimony at the conspiracy trial. Alleging that these prosecutions were undertaken in bad faith, Shaw's § 1983 complaint named as defendants the then District Attorney of Orleans Parish, Jim Garrison, and five other persons, including petitioner Willard E. Robertson, who was alleged to have lent financial support to Garrison's investigation of Shaw through an organization known as "Truth or Consequences." On Shaw's application, the District Court enjoined prosecution of the perjury action, and the Court of Appeals affirmed.[2]

Since Shaw had filed an action seeking damages, the parties continued with discovery after the injunction issued. Trial was set for November 1974, but in August 1974 Shaw died. The executor of his estate, respondent Edward F. Wegmann (hereafter respondent), moved to be substituted as plaintiff, and the District Court granted the motion. Petitioner and other defendants then moved to dismiss the action on the ground that it had abated on Shaw's death.

The District Court denied the motion to dismiss. It began its analysis by referring to 42 U.S.C. § 1988(a); this statute provides that, when federal law is "deficient" with regard to "suitable remedies" in federal civil rights actions, federal courts are to be governed by

> the common law, as modified and changed by the constitution and statutes of the State wherein the court having jurisdiction of [the] civil . . . cause is held, so far as the same is not inconsistent with the Constitution and laws of the United States. . . .

The court found the federal civil rights laws to be "deficient in not providing for survival." It then held that, under Louisiana law, an action like Shaw's would survive only in favor of a spouse, children, parents, or siblings. Since no person with the requisite relationship to Shaw was alive at the time of his death, his action would have abated had state law been adopted as the federal rule. But the court refused to apply state law, find-

---

[1] Title 42 U.S.C. § 1988 provides in pertinent part:

> The jurisdiction in civil and criminal matters conferred on the district courts by the provisions of this [chapter and title 18], for the protection of all persons in the United States in their civil rights, and for their vindication, shall be exercised and enforced in conformity with the laws of the United States, so far as such laws are suitable to carry the same into effect; but in all cases where they are not adapted to the object, or are deficient in the provisions necessary to furnish suitable remedies and punish offenses against law, the common law, as modified and changed by the constitution and statutes of the State wherein the court having jurisdiction of such civil or criminal cause is held, so far as the same is not inconsistent with the Constitution and laws of the United States, shall be extended to and govern the said courts in the trial and disposition of the cause, and, if it is of a criminal nature, in the infliction of punishment on the party found guilty.

[This provision has since been renumbered to § 1988(a). Subsequent citations by the Court to § 1988 have been replaced by § 1988(a)—Addition to footnote by eds.]

[2] The Court of Appeals held that this Court's decision in Younger v. Harris, 401 U.S. 37 (1971), did not bar the enjoining of the state perjury prosecution, since the District Court's "finding of a bad faith prosecution establishes irreparable injury both great and immediate for purposes of the comity restraints discussed in *Younger*."

ing it inconsistent with federal law, and in its place created "a federal common law of survival in civil rights actions in favor of the personal representative of the deceased."

On an interlocutory appeal taken pursuant to 28 U.S.C. § 1292(b), the United States Court of Appeals for the Fifth Circuit affirmed. The court first noted that all parties agreed that, "if Louisiana law applies, Shaw's § 1983 claim abates." Like the District Court, the Court of Appeals applied 42 U.S.C. § 1988(a), found federal law "deficient" with regard to survivorship, and held Louisiana law "inconsistent with the broad remedial purposes embodied in the Civil Rights Acts." It offered a number of justifications for creating a federal common-law rule allowing respondent to continue Shaw's action: Such a rule would better further the policies underlying § 1983; would "foste[r] the uniform application of the civil rights laws"; and would be consistent with "[t]he marked tendency of the federal courts to allow actions to survive in other areas of particular federal concern." The court concluded that, "as a matter of federal common law, a § 1983 action instituted by a plaintiff prior to his death survives in favor of his estate."

We granted certiorari, and we now reverse.

II

As both courts below held, and as both parties here have assumed, the decision as to the applicable survivorship rule is governed by 42 U.S.C. § 1988(a). This statute recognizes that in certain areas "federal law is unsuited or insufficient 'to furnish suitable remedies' "; federal law simply does not "cover every issue that may arise in the context of a federal civil rights action." Moor v. County of Alameda, 411 U.S. 693, 701 (1973). When federal law is thus "deficient," § 1988(a) instructs us to turn to "the common law, as modified and changed by the constitution and statutes of the [forum] State," as long as these are "not inconsistent with the Constitution and laws of the United States." Regardless of the source of the law applied in a particular case, however, it is clear that the ultimate rule adopted under § 1988(a) " 'is a federal rule responsive to the need whenever a federal right is impaired.' " *Moor v. County of Alameda*, supra, at 703, quoting Sullivan v. Little Hunting Park, Inc., 396 U.S. 229, 240 (1969).

As we noted in *Moor v. County of Alameda*, and as was recognized by both courts below, one specific area not covered by federal law is that relating to "the survival of civil rights actions under § 1983 upon the death of either the plaintiff or defendant." State statutes governing the survival of state actions do exist, however. These statutes, which vary widely with regard to both the types of claims that survive and the parties as to whom survivorship is allowed, were intended to modify the simple, if harsh, 19th century common-law rule: "[A]n injured party's personal claim was [always] extinguished . . . upon the death of either the injured party himself or the alleged wrongdoer." *Moor v. County of Alameda*, supra, at 702 n.14. Under § 1988(a), this state statutory law, modifying the common law,[5] provides the principal reference point in determining survival of civil rights actions,

[5] Section 1988(a)'s reference to "the common law" might be interpreted as a reference to the decision law of the forum state, or as a reference to the kind of general common law that was an established part of our federal jurisprudence by the time of § 1988(a)'s passage in 1866, see Swift v. Tyson, 41 U.S. (16 Pet.) 1 (1842). The latter interpretation has received some judicial and scholarly support. See, e.g., William H. Theis, *Shaw v. Garrison*: Some Observations on 42 U.S.C. § 1988(a) and Federal Common Law, 36 La.L.Rev. 681, 684–85 (1976). It makes no difference for our purposes which interpretation is the correct one, because Louisiana has a survivorship statute that, under the terms of § 1988(a), plainly governs this case.

subject to the important proviso that state law may not be applied when it is "inconsistent with the Constitution and laws of the United States." Because of this proviso, the courts below refused to adopt as federal law the Louisiana survivorship statute and in its place created a federal common-law rule.

III

In resolving questions of inconsistency between state and federal law raised under § 1988(a), courts must look not only at particular federal statutes and constitutional provisions, but also at "the policies expressed in [them]." *Sullivan v. Little Hunting Park, Inc.*, supra, at 240. Of particular importance is whether application of state law "would be inconsistent with the federal policy underlying the cause of action under consideration." Johnson v. Railway Express Agency, Inc., 421 U.S. 454, 465 (1975). The instant cause of action arises under 42 U.S.C. § 1983, one of the "Reconstruction civil rights statutes" that this Court has accorded " 'a sweep as broad as [their] language.' " Griffin v. Breckenridge, 403 U.S. 88, 97 (1971), quoting United States v. Price, 383 U.S. 787, 801 (1966).

Despite the broad sweep of § 1983, we can find nothing in the statute or its underlying policies to indicate that a state law causing abatement of a particular action should invariably be ignored in favor of a rule of absolute survivorship. The policies underlying § 1983 include compensation of persons injured by deprivation of federal rights and prevention of abuses of power by those acting under color of state law. No claim is made here that Louisiana's survivorship laws are in general inconsistent with these policies, and indeed most Louisiana actions survive the plaintiff's death. Moreover, certain types of actions that would abate automatically on the plaintiff's death in many States—for example, actions for defamation and malicious prosecution—would apparently survive in Louisiana. In actions other than those for damage to property, however, Louisiana does not allow the deceased's personal representative to be substituted as plaintiff; rather, the action survives only in favor of a spouse, children, parents, or siblings.[6] But surely few persons are not survived by one of these close relatives, and in any event no contention is made here that Louisiana's decision to restrict certain survivorship rights in this manner is an unreasonable one.

It is therefore difficult to see how any of § 1983's policies would be undermined if Shaw's action were to abate. The goal of compensating those injured by a deprivation of rights provides no basis for requiring compensation of one who is merely suing as the executor of the deceased's estate. And, given that most Louisiana actions survive the plaintiff's death, the fact that a particular action might abate surely would not adversely affect § 1983's role in preventing official illegality, at least in situations in which there is no claim that the illegality caused the plaintiff's death. A state official contemplating illegal activity must always be prepared to face the prospect of a § 1983 action being filed against him. In light of this prospect, even an official aware of the intricacies of Louisiana survivorship law would hardly be influenced in his behavior by its provisions.[10]

---

[6] For those actions that do not abate automatically on the plaintiff's death, most States apparently allow the personal representative of the deceased to be substituted as plaintiff.

[10] In order to find even a marginal influence on behavior as a result of Louisiana's survivorship provisions, one would have to make the rather farfetched assumptions that a state official had both the desire and the ability deliberately to select as victims only those persons who would die before conclusion of the § 1983 suit (for reasons entirely unconnected with the official illegality) and who would not be survived by any close relatives.

It is true that § 1983 provides "a uniquely federal remedy against incursions under the claimed authority of state law upon rights secured by the Constitution and laws of the nation." Mitchum v. Foster, 407 U.S. 225, 239 (1972). That a federal remedy should be available, however, does not mean that a § 1983 plaintiff (or his representative) must be allowed to continue an action in disregard of the state law to which § 1988(a) refers us. A state statute cannot be considered "inconsistent" with federal law merely because the statute causes the plaintiff to lose the litigation. If success of the § 1983 action were the only benchmark, there would be no reason at all to look to state law, for the appropriate rule would then always be the one favoring the plaintiff, and its source would be essentially irrelevant. But § 1988(a) quite clearly instructs us to refer to state statutes; it does not say that state law is to be accepted or rejected solely on which side is advantaged thereby. Under the circumstances presented here, the fact that Shaw was not survived by one of several close relatives should not itself be sufficient to cause the Louisiana survivorship provisions to be deemed "inconsistent with the Constitution and laws of the United States."

IV

Our holding today is a narrow one, limited to situations in which no claim is made that state law generally is inhospitable to survival of § 1983 actions and in which the particular application of state survivorship law, while it may cause abatement of the action, has no independent adverse effect on the policies underlying § 1983. A different situation might well be presented, as the District Court noted, if state law "did not provide for survival of any tort actions," or if it significantly restricted the types of actions that survive. We intimate no view, moreover, about whether abatement based on state law could be allowed in a situation in which deprivation of federal rights caused death.

Here it is agreed that Shaw's death was not caused by the deprivation of rights for which he sued under § 1983, and Louisiana law provides for the survival of most tort actions. Respondent's only complaint about Louisiana law is that it would cause Shaw's action to abate. We conclude that the mere fact of abatement of a particular lawsuit is not sufficient ground to declare state law "inconsistent" with federal law.

Accordingly, the judgment of the Court of Appeals is reversed.

■ MR. JUSTICE BLACKMUN, with whom MR. JUSTICE BRENNAN and MR. JUSTICE WHITE join, dissenting.

It is disturbing to see the Court, in this decision, although almost apologetically self-described as "a narrow one," cut back on what is acknowledged to be the "broad sweep" of 42 U.S.C. § 1983. Accordingly, I dissent.

I do not read the emphasis of § 1988(a), as the Court does, to the effect that the federal District Court "was required to adopt" the Louisiana statute, and was free to look to federal common law only as a secondary matter. It seems to me that this places the cart before the horse. Section 1988(a) requires the utilization of federal law ("shall be exercised and enforced in conformity with the laws of the United States"). It authorizes resort to the state statute only if the federal laws "are not adapted to the object" of "protection of all persons in the United States in their civil rights, and for their vindication" or are "deficient in the provisions necessary to furnish suitable remedies and punish offenses against law." Even then, state statutes are an alternative source of law only if "not inconsistent with the Constitution and laws of the United States." Surely, federal law is the rule and not the exception.

Accepting this as the proper starting point, it necessarily follows, it seems to me, that the judgment of the Court of Appeals must be affirmed, not reversed. To be sure, survivorship of a civil rights action under § 1983 upon the death of either party is not specifically covered by the federal statute. But that does not mean that "the laws of the United States" are not "suitable" or are "not adapted to the object" or are "deficient in the provisions necessary." The federal law and the underlying federal policy stand bright and clear. And in the light of that brightness and that clarity, I see no need to resort to the myriad of state rules governing the survival of state actions.

First. In Sullivan v. Little Hunting Park, Inc., 396 U.S. 229 (1969), a case that concerned the availability of compensatory damages for a violation of § 1982, a remedial question, as here, not governed explicitly by any federal statute other than § 1988(a). Mr. Justice Douglas, writing for the Court, painted with a broad brush the scope of the federal court's choice-of-law authority:

> As we read § 1988(a), . . . both federal and state rules on damages may be utilized, *whichever better serves the policies expressed in the federal statutes*. . . . The rule of damages, whether drawn from federal or state sources, is a federal rule responsive to the need whenever a federal right is impaired. (Emphasis added.)

The Court's present reading of § 1988(a) seems to me to be hyperlogical and sadly out of line with the precept set forth in that quoted material. The statute was intended to give courts flexibility to shape their procedures and remedies in accord with the underlying policies of the Civil Rights Acts, choosing whichever rule "*better* serves" those policies. I do not understand the Court to deny a federal court's authority under § 1988(a) to reject state law when, to apply it, seriously undermines substantial federal concerns. But I do not accept the Court's apparent conclusion that, absent such an extreme inconsistency, § 1988(a) restricts courts to state law on matters of procedure and remedy. That conclusion too often would interfere with the efficient redress of constitutional rights.

Second. The Court's reading of § 1988(a) cannot easily be squared with its treatment of the problems of immunity and damages under the Civil Rights Acts. Only this term, in Carey v. Piphus, 435 U.S. 247 (1978), the Court set a rule for the award of damages under § 1983 for deprivation of procedural due process by resort to "federal common law." Though the case arose from Illinois, the Court did not feel compelled to inquire into Illinois' statutory or decisional law of damages, nor to test that law for possible "inconsistency" with the federal scheme, before embracing a federal common-law rule. Instead, the Court fashioned a federal damages rule, from common-law sources and its view of the type of injury, to govern such cases uniformly state-to-state.

Similarly, in constructing immunities under § 1983, the Court has consistently relied on federal common-law rules. As *Carey v. Piphus* recognized, in attributing immunity to prosecutors, Imbler v. Pachtman, 424 U.S. 409, 417–19 (1976); to judges, Pierson v. Ray, 386 U.S. 547, 554–55 (1967); and to other officials, matters on which the language of § 1983 is silent, we have not felt bound by the tort immunities recognized in the particular forum State and, only after finding an "inconsistency" with federal standards, then considered a uniform federal rule. Instead, the immunities have been fashioned in light of historic common-law concerns and the policies of the Civil Rights Acts.

Third. A flexible reading of § 1988(a), permitting resort to a federal rule of survival because it "better serves" the policies of the Civil Rights Acts, would be consistent with the methodology employed in the other major choice-of-law provision in the federal structure, namely the Rules of Decision Act. 28 U.S.C. § 1652. That act provides that state law is to govern a civil trial in a federal court "except where the Constitution or treaties of the United States or acts of Congress otherwise require or provide." The exception has not been interpreted in a crabbed or wooden fashion, but, instead, has been used to give expression to important federal interests. Thus, for example, the exception has been used to apply a federal common law of labor contracts in suits under § 301(a) of the Labor Management Relations Act, Textile Workers v. Lincoln Mills, 353 U.S. 448 (1957); to apply federal common law to transactions in commercial paper issued by the United States where the United States is a party, Clearfield Trust Co. v. United States, 318 U.S. 363 (1943); and to avoid application of governing state law to the reservation of mineral rights in a land acquisition agreement to which the United States was a party and that bore heavily upon a federal wildlife regulatory program. United States v. Little Lake Misere Land Co., 412 U.S. 580 (1973).

Just as the Rules of Decision Act cases disregard state law where there is conflict with federal *policy*, even though no explicit conflict with the terms of a federal statute, so, too, state remedial and procedural law must be disregarded under § 1988(a) where the law fails to give adequate expression to important federal concerns. The opponents of the 1866 Act were distinctly aware that the legislation that became § 1988(a) would give the federal courts power to shape federal common-law rules. See, for example, the protesting remarks of Congressman Kerr relative to § 3 of the 1866 Act (which contained the predecessor version of § 1988(a)):

> I might go on and in this manner illustrate the practical working of this extraordinary measure. [T]he authors of this bill feared, very properly too, that the system of laws heretofore administered in the federal courts might fail to supply any precedent to guide the courts in the enforcement of the strange provisions of this bill, and not to be thwarted by this difficulty, they confer upon the courts the power of judicial legislation, the power to make such other laws as they may think necessary. Such is the practical effect of the last clause of the third section [of § 1988(a)]. That is to say, the federal courts may, in such cases, make such rules and apply such law as they please, and call it *common law* (emphasis in original). Cong. Globe, 39th Cong., 1st Sess., 1271 (1866).

Fourth. Section 1983's critical concerns are compensation of the victims of unconstitutional action, and deterrence of like misconduct in the future. Any crabbed rule of survivorship obviously interferes directly with the second critical interest and may well interfere with the first.

The unsuitability of Louisiana's law is shown by the very case at hand. It will happen not infrequently that a decedent's only survivor or survivors are non-relatives or collateral relatives who do not fit within the four named classes of Louisiana statutory survivors. Though the Court surmises that "surely few persons are not survived" by a spouse, children, parents, or siblings, any lawyer who has had experience in estate planning or in probating estates knows that situation is frequently encountered. The Louisiana survivorship rule applies no matter how malicious or ill-intentioned a defendant's action was. In this case, as the Court acknowledges, the District Court found that defendant Garrison brought state perjury charges against plaintiff Shaw "in bad faith and for purposes of harassment," a finding that the Court of Appeals affirmed as not clearly erroneous. The federal interest in specific deterrence, when there was malicious intention to deprive a person of his constitutional rights, is particularly strong, as *Carey v. Piphus* intimates, supra, at 257 n.11. Insuring a specific deterrent under federal law gains importance from the very premise of the Civil Rights Act that state tort policy often is inadequate to deter violations of the constitutional rights of disfavored groups.

The Louisiana rule requiring abatement appears to apply even where the death was intentional and caused, say, by a beating delivered by a defendant. The Court does not deny this result, merely declaiming that in such a case it might reconsider the applicability of the Louisiana survivorship statute. But the Court does not explain how either certainty or federalism is served by such a variegated application of the Louisiana statute, nor how an abatement rule would be workable when made to depend on a fact of causation often requiring an entire trial to prove.

It makes no sense to me to make even a passing reference to behavioral influence. The Court opines that no official aware of the intricacies of Louisiana survivorship law would "be influenced in his behavior by its provisions." But defendants in Shaw's litigation obviously have been "sweating it out" through the several years of proceedings and litigation in this case. One can imagine the relief occasioned when the realization dawned that Shaw's death might—just might—abate the action. To that extent, the deterrent against behavior such as that attributed to the defendants in this case surely has been lessened.

As to compensation, it is no answer to intimate, as the Court does, that Shaw's particular survivors were not personally injured, for obviously had Shaw been survived by parents or siblings, the cause of action would exist despite the absence in them of so deep and personal an affront, or any at all, as Shaw himself was alleged to have sustained. The Court propounds the unreasoned conclusion that the "goal of compensating those injured by a deprivation of rights provides no basis for requiring compensation of one who is merely suing as the executor of the deceased's estate." But the Court does not purport to explain why it is consistent with the purposes of § 1983 to recognize a derivative or independent interest in a brother or parent, while denying similar interest to a nephew, grandparent, or legatee.

Fifth. The Court regards the Louisiana system's structuring of survivorship rights as not unreasonable. The observation, of course, is a gratuitous one, for as the Court immediately observes, it does not resolve the issue that confronts us here. We are not concerned with the reasonableness of the Louisiana survivorship statute in allocating tort recoveries. We are concerned with its application in the face of a claim of civil rights guaranteed the decedent by federal law. . . .

The Court acknowledges "the broad sweep of § 1983," but seeks to justify the application of a rule of non-survivorship here because it feels that Louisiana is comparatively generous as to survivorship anyway. This grudging allowance of what the Louisiana statute does not give, just because it gives in part, seems to me to grind adversely against the statute's "broad sweep." Would the Court's decision be otherwise if actions for defamation and malicious prosecution in fact did not survive at all in Louisiana? . . .

Sixth. A federal rule of survivorship allows uniformity, and counsel immediately know the answer. Litigants identically aggrieved in their federal civil rights, residing in geographically adjacent States, will not have differing results due to the vagaries of state law. Litigants need not engage in uncertain characterization of a § 1983 action in terms of its nearest tort cousin, a questionable procedure to begin with, since the interests protected by tort law and constitutional law may be quite different. Nor will federal rights depend on the arcane intricacies of state survival law—which differs in Louisiana according to whether the right is "strictly personal," whether the action concerns property damage, or concerns "other damages."

The policies favoring so-called "absolute" survivorship, viz., survivorship in favor of a decedent's non-related legatees in the absence of familial legatees, are the simple goals of uniformity, deterrence, and perhaps compensation. A defendant who has violated someone's constitutional rights has no legitimate interest in a windfall release upon the death of the victim. A plaintiff's interest in certainty, in an equal remedy, and in deterrence supports such an absolute rule. I regard as unanswered the justifications advanced by the District Court and the Court of Appeals: uniformity of decisions and fulfillment of the great purposes of § 1983.

Seventh. Rejecting Louisiana's survivorship limitations does not mean that state procedure and state remedies will cease to serve as important sources of civil rights laws. State law, for instance, may well be a suitable source of statutes of limitation, since that is a rule for which litigants prudently can plan. Rejecting Louisiana's survivorship limitations means only that state rules are subject to some scrutiny for suitability. Here the deterrent purpose of § 1983 is disserved by Louisiana's rule of abatement.

It is unfortunate that the Court restricts the reach of § 1983 by today's decision construing § 1988(a). Congress now must act again if the gap in remedy is to be filled.

NOTES ON 42 U.S.C. § 1988(A)

1. INTRODUCTION

In 1880 Justice Clifford dismissed the predecessor version of 42 U.S.C. § 1988(a) as "a mere jumble of federal law, common law, and state law, consisting of incongruous and irreconcilable regulations" and giving no effective guidance for choosing among them. Tennessee v. Davis, 100 U.S. 257, 299 (1880) (Clifford, J., dissenting). Subsequent attempts to interpret the statute have not been quite so despairing, but § 1988(a) is by any reckoning opaque.

The statute was originally enacted as § 3 of the Civil Rights Act of 1866. Section 1 of that statute guaranteed certain rights against denial on the basis of race; its successor provisions are now codified as 42 U.S.C. §§ 1981 and 1982. Section 2 of the act authorized criminal penalties for "any person who, under color of any law, statute, ordinance, regulation, or custom, shall subject, or cause to be subjected, any inhabitant of any State or Territory to the deprivation of any right secured or protected by this act." This section served as the model for § 1 of the Civil Rights Act of 1871, which eventually became 42 U.S.C. § 1983. The successor to the criminal provision now appears at 18 U.S.C. § 242. Section 3 of the 1866 Act contained the language now codified as

§ 1988(a). All of these statutes were reorganized in the general codification of 1875, but have remained substantially unchanged since that time.

Section 1988(a) is worth reproducing in full in order, as one commentator put it, "to remind readers of the full scope of its obscurity":[a]

> The jurisdiction in civil and criminal matters conferred on the district courts by the provisions of this [chapter and title 18], for the protection of all persons in the United States in their civil rights, and for their vindication, shall be exercised and enforced in conformity with the laws of the United States, so far as such laws are suitable to carry the same into effect; but in all cases where they are not adapted to the object, or are deficient in the provisions necessary to furnish suitable remedies and punish offenses against the law, the common law, as modified and changed by the constitution and statutes of the State wherein the court having jurisdiction of such civil or criminal cause is held, so far as the same is not inconsistent with the Constitution and laws of the United States, shall be extended to and govern the said courts in the trial and disposition of the cause, and, if it is of a criminal nature, in the infliction of punishment on the party found guilty.

For a long time, this language was largely ignored, but as *Robertson v. Wegmann* illustrates, the Supreme Court has held that it requires federal incorporation of state law to resolve certain aspects of civil rights actions brought under Reconstruction-era statutes, including § 1983. This holding is at once familiar and controversial. In order to understand the arguments, it is necessary to delve into the complexities of § 1988(a).

2. IDENTIFYING DEFICIENCIES IN FEDERAL LAW

Section 1988(a) requires adjudication "in conformity with the laws of the United States," except "where they are not adapted to the object, or are deficient in the provisions necessary to furnish suitable remedies." Thus, the first step is to determine when federal law is "not adapted" or "deficient." Under the approach of *Robertson v. Wegmann*, that seems simple enough: Federal law is deficient where the statute is silent. But consider the implications of this view. The statutes of the Reconstruction era, including § 1983, are typically not very detailed. If state law were applied to every issue not explicitly dealt with in the statutes, then the enforcement of federal civil rights would depend importantly and pervasively on the vagaries of state law.

In fact, however, no wholesale incorporation of state law has occurred. On the contrary, many of the statutory blanks in § 1983 have been filled in without reference to state law. Thus, for example, in a long and growing line of cases, the Supreme Court has developed a body of law governing official immunity from damages liability under § 1983. The early cases tended to emphasize the assumption that the Congress in 1871 must have intended to limit liability under § 1983 by the various concepts of official immunity then recognized at common law. The later cases speak more frankly of the needs of federal policy. But the common ground among all the cases is that official immunity is governed by a uniform rule of federal law and does not vary with the local law of the place where the action is brought. The question is "why not"? Why is § 1983

[a] The phrase is from Seth F. Kreimer, The Source of Law in Civil Rights Actions: Some Old Light on § 1988, 133 U.Pa.L.Rev. 601, 613 (1985).

not deficient with respect to official immunity in the same way that it is deficient with respect to survivorship? Is there an intelligible way to reconcile these cases on this issue?

A very different approach is suggested by Justice Blackmun's dissent. Blackmun argues that statutory silence does not make federal law deficient. Instead, § 1988(a) "was intended to give courts flexibility to shape their procedures and remedies in accord with the underlying policies of the Civil Rights Acts." But if federal courts are authorized to make up the law as they go along, why would it ever be "not adapted" or "deficient" within the meaning of § 1988(a)? Has Justice Blackmun simply read § 1988(a) out of existence?

3. AVOIDING INCONSISTENCY WITH FEDERAL LAW

Once a deficiency in federal law is identified, § 1988(a) directs the federal court to apply the "common law," as modified and changed by state statutes, "so far as the same is not inconsistent with the Constitution and laws of the United States." How is such inconsistency to be ascertained? The answer would be simple enough if the inconsistency clause were taken to refer only to state rules or statutes that are in themselves unconstitutional. In that event, the inconsistency clause would be both straightforward and meaningless, for even without statutory direction a federal court would not apply an unconstitutional state law.

The *Robertson* majority seemed to envision a much broader role for the inconsistency clause. The Court observed that Louisiana's abatement rules were in some respects more liberal than those of other States and were in any event not unreasonable. Additionally, the Court noted that a "different situation might well be presented . . . if state law 'did not provide for survival of any tort actions,' or if it significantly restricted the types of actions that survive." Why would that situation be different? Would significant restrictions on survivorship of tort actions be unconstitutional? Or is the Court suggesting that some lesser "inconsistency" would suffice to disallow incorporation of state law under § 1988(a)? If the latter is meant, with what federal law would the state rule be "inconsistent"?

Note that the questions of deficiency and inconsistency are perplexingly linked. At least under one reading, § 1988(a) seems to say that a federal statute might be deficient in failing to speak to a point, but might nevertheless adopt a position or policy that would render some state statutes inconsistent with it. Is that plausible? Is it troublesome to think of § 1983 as at once silent with respect to survivorship, yet articulating a position that would make some state laws inconsistent?

4. THE EISENBERG THESIS

These and other questions about § 1988(a) are meticulously explored by Theodore Eisenberg in State Law in Federal Civil Rights Cases: The Proper Scope of § 1988, 128 U.Pa.L.Rev. 499 (1980). Eisenberg attempted to make sense of § 1988(a) by returning to the original text of the Civil Rights Act of 1866 and reading § 3 in the context of the other provisions. He came up with a radically different interpretation, one that suggests that § 1988(a) is simply not applicable to the issue presented in *Robertson v. Wegmann*.

Specifically, Eisenberg argues that the predecessor of § 1988(a) was originally intended to apply only where a federal court tries a case arising under state law. That situation would occur chiefly where a state criminal defendant, confronted with some denial of civil rights by a state court, exercises the right to remove the prosecution to federal court. The right to remove such cases was originally provided in § 3 of the Civil Rights Act of 1866, along with the language of the current § 1988(a). The removal provision, however, was modified in the recodification of 1874, and the successor provision now appears at 28 U.S.C. § 1443. Eisenberg's thesis is that the language now found in § 1988(a) merely meant to say that trial of such cases (and a few others) in federal courts should be governed by state substantive law, except insofar as such law is itself inconsistent with the civil rights guaranteed by the act of 1866. Eisenberg argues that this interpretation solves a number of puzzles about the meaning of § 1988(a) (only some of which have been explored in the preceding notes), and that it "draws modest but important support from the legislative histories of the 1866 act and of later relevant provisions."

Note that this interpretation would leave scant contemporary significance for § 1988(a), for today the situations in which civil rights removal would give rise to a federal court trial of a state cause of action are rare.[b] And what to do with the silences of § 1983 and the other Reconstruction-era civil rights statutes? "The answer," says Eisenberg, "is not surprising. Federal courts should fill out the federal civil rights program by the same techniques used to fill out other federal programs"—that is, by the techniques of federal common law.

Eisenberg develops his thesis in far more detail than can be recounted here. Informed assessment of its merit would require careful study, but it is perhaps worth noting that this interpretation is far easier to square with the original text and structure of the Civil Rights Act of 1866 than with the terms of the statutes as they have progressed through successive revisions. Perhaps that is why the Eisenberg thesis has not been favored by the Supreme Court.

5. THE KREIMER THESIS

Another interesting interpretation of § 1988(a) is advanced by Seth F. Kreimer in The Source of Law in Civil Rights Actions: Some Old Light on § 1988, 133 U.Pa.L.Rev. 601 (1985). Kreimer focuses on the "common law" to which § 1988(a) directs reference. He suggests that this phrase be read in light of the then-prevailing view of *Swift v. Tyson* equating "laws" with "statutes." Under this reading, federal law is "deficient" whenever no statute controls, and in that event the court should apply general "common law," except as modified by local statutes. This reading suggests that the "norm is uniformity." Federal courts should apply a uniform body of federal civil rights law except as to those issues that are specifically governed by state statutes. This explains the tradition of incorporating state law on limitation of actions and survivorship, both matters typically covered by statute. It also explains the tradition with respect to immunities, where no state statute applies and the federal courts have developed federal common law.

Kreimer terms this interpretation "consistent with the words of [§ 1988(a)], current practice under § 1983, and the statute's historical context." He also finds it supported on balance by the "decidedly mixed" historical record.

---

[b] See Georgia v. Rachel, 384 U.S. 780 (1966); City of Greenwood v. Peacock, 384 U.S. 808 (1966).

Perhaps most important, Kreimer's interpretation has "the advantage of leaving opportunities for federal courts to craft sensible and uniform solutions to contemporary problems based on contemporary values." Specifically, Kreimer suggests that, given the demise of "general" common law as contemplated in *Swift v. Tyson*, federal courts should take § 1988(a) as a directive to establish a federal common law of civil rights actions. But, Kreimer argues, state law cannot be ignored. Section 1988(a) establishes a congressional intention to incorporate applicable state statutes, and the federal courts must therefore "be on the lookout" for such statutes. In this way, the courts can continue to elaborate a federal common law of civil rights actions with only minor interferences from state law. This approach, says Kreimer, is "preferable to either willfully ignoring an apparently applicable statute or finding oneself adrift in a raging sea of state law. Until Congress decides to remedy the predicament, it is the best we can do."

9. THE TAX INJUNCTION ACT AS A LIMIT ON § 1983 SUITS

Hibbs v. Winn

Supreme Court of the United States, 2004.
542 U.S. 88.

■ JUSTICE GINSBURG delivered the opinion of the Court.

Arizona law authorizes income-tax credits for payments to organizations that award educational scholarships and tuition grants to children attending private schools. See Ariz.Rev.Stat. Ann. § 43–1089 (West Supp.2003). Plaintiffs below, respondents here, brought an action in federal court challenging § 43–1089, and seeking to enjoin its operation, on Establishment Clause grounds. The question presented is whether the Tax Injunction Act (TIA or Act), 28 U.S.C. § 1341, which prohibits a lower federal court from restraining "the assessment, levy or collection of any tax under State law," bars the suit. Plaintiffs-respondents do not contest their own tax liability. Nor do they seek to impede Arizona's receipt of tax revenues. Their suit, we hold, is not the kind § 1341 proscribes.

In decisions spanning a near half century, courts in the federal system, including this Court, have entertained challenges to tax credits authorized by state law, without conceiving of § 1341 as a jurisdictional barrier. On this first occasion squarely to confront the issue, we confirm the authority federal courts exercised in those cases.

It is hardly ancient history that States, once bent on maintaining racial segregation in public schools, and allocating resources disproportionately to benefit white students to the detriment of black students, fastened on tuition grants and tax credits as a promising means to circumvent Brown v. Board of Education, 347 U.S. 483 (1954). The federal courts, this Court among them, adjudicated the ensuing challenges, instituted under 42 U.S.C. § 1983, and upheld the Constitution's equal protection requirement. [Citations omitted.]

In the instant case, petitioner Hibbs, Director of Arizona's Department of Revenue, argues, in effect, that we and other federal courts were wrong in those civil-rights cases. The TIA, petitioner maintains, trumps § 1983; the Act, according to petitioner, bars all lower federal-court interference with state tax systems, even when the challengers are not endeavoring to avoid a tax imposed on them, and no matter whether the State's revenues would be raised or lowered should the plaintiffs prevail. The alleged jurisdictional bar, which petitioner asserts has existed since the TIA's enactment in 1937, was not even imagined by the jurists in the pathmarking civil-rights cases just cited, or by the defendants in those cases, litigants with every interest in defeating federal-court adjudicatory authority. Our prior decisions command no respect, petitioner urges, because they constitute mere "sub silentio holdings." We reject that assessment.

We examine in this opinion both the scope of the term "assessment" as used in the TIA, and the question whether the Act was intended to insulate state tax laws from constitutional challenge in lower federal courts even when the suit would have no negative impact on tax collection. Concluding that this suit implicates neither § 1341's conception of assessment nor any of the statute's underlying purposes, we affirm the judgment of the Court of Appeals.

I

Plaintiffs-respondents, Arizona taxpayers, filed suit in the United States District Court for the District of Arizona, challenging Ariz.Rev.Stat. Ann. § 43–1089 (West Supp.2003) as incompatible with the Establishment Clause. Section 43–1089 provides a credit to taxpayers who contribute money to "school tuition organizations" (STOs). An STO is a nonprofit organization that directs moneys, in the form of scholarship grants, to students enrolled in private elementary or secondary schools. STOs must disburse as scholarship grants at least 90 percent of contributions received, may allow donors to direct scholarships to individual students, may not allow donors to name their own dependents, must designate at least two schools whose students will receive funds, and must not designate schools that "discriminate on the basis of race, color, handicap, familial status or national origin." STOs are not precluded by Arizona's statute from designating schools that provide religious instruction or that give admissions preference on the basis of religion or religious affiliation. When taxpayers donate money to a qualified STO, § 43–1089 allows them, in calculating their Arizona tax liability, to credit up to $500 of their donation (or $625 for a married couple filing jointly).

In effect, § 43–1089 gives Arizona taxpayers an election. They may direct $500 (or, for joint-return filers, $625) to an STO, or to the Arizona Department of Revenue. As long as donors do not give STOs more than their total tax liability, their $500 or $625 contributions are costless.

The Arizona Supreme Court, by a 3–to–2 vote, rejected a facial challenge to § 43–1089 before the statute went into effect. That case took the form of a special discretionary action invoking the court's original jurisdiction. [This decision], it is undisputed, has no preclusive effect on the instant as-applied challenge to § 43–1089 brought by different plaintiffs.

Respondents' federal-court complaint against the Director of Arizona's Department of Revenue (Director) alleged that § 43–1089 "authorizes the formation of agencies that have as their sole purpose the distribution of State funds to children of a particular religious denomination or to children attending schools of a particular religious denomination." Respondents sought injunctive and declaratory relief, and an order requiring STOs to pay funds still in their possession "into the state general fund."

The Director moved to dismiss the action, relying on the TIA, which reads in its entirety:

> The district courts shall not enjoin, suspend or restrain the assessment, levy or collection of any tax under State law where a plain, speedy and efficient remedy may be had in the courts of such State.

The Director did not assert that a federal-court order enjoining § 43–1089 would interfere with the State's tax levy or collection efforts. He urged only that a federal injunction would restrain the "assessment" of taxes "under State law." Agreeing with the Director, the District Court held that the TIA required dismissal of the suit.

The Court of Appeals for the Ninth Circuit reversed. . . . We granted certiorari in view of the division of opinion on whether the TIA bars constitutional challenges to state tax credits in federal court. We now affirm the judgment of the Ninth Circuit.

II

Before reaching the merits of this case, we must address respondents' contention that the Director's petition for certiorari was jurisdictionally untimely under 28 U.S.C. § 2101(c) and our Rules. [The Court held the petition timely.]

III

To determine whether this litigation falls within the TIA's prohibition, it is appropriate, first, to identify the relief sought. Respondents seek prospective relief only. Specifically, their complaint requests "injunctive relief prohibiting [the Director] from allowing taxpayers to utilize the tax credit authorized by A.R.S. § 43–1089 for payments made to STOs that make tuition grants to children attending religious schools, to children attending schools of only one religious denomination, or to children selected on the basis of their religion." Respondents further ask for a "declaration that A.R.S. § 43–1089, on its face and as applied," violates the Establishment Clause "by affirmatively authorizing STOs to use State income-tax revenues to pay tuition for students attending religious schools or schools that discriminate on the basis of religion." Finally, respondents seek "[a]n order that [the Director] inform all [such] STOs that . . . all funds in their possession as of the date of this Court's order must be paid into the state general fund." Taking account of the prospective nature of the relief requested, does respondents' suit, in 28 U.S.C. § 1341's words, seek to "enjoin, suspend or restrain the assessment, levy or collection of any tax under State law"? The answer to that question turns on the meaning of the term "assessment" as employed in the TIA.[1]

As used in the Internal Revenue Code (IRC), the term "assessment" involves a "recording" of the amount the taxpayer owes the Government. 26 U.S.C. § 6203. The "assessment" is "essentially a bookkeeping notation." Laing v. United States, 423 U.S. 161, 170 n.13 (1976). Section 6201(a) of the IRC authorizes the Secretary of the Treasury "to make . . . assessments of all taxes . . . imposed by this title." An assessment is made "by recording the liability of the taxpayer in the office of the Secretary in accordance with rules or regulations prescribed by the Secretary." § 6203.[3]

---

[1] State taxation, for § 1341 purposes, includes local taxation.

[3] The term "assessment" is used in a variety of ways in tax law. In the property-tax setting, the word usually refers to the process by which the taxing authority assigns a taxable value to real or personal property. To calculate the amount of property taxes owed, the tax

We do not focus on the word "assessment" in isolation, however. Instead, we follow "the cardinal rule that statutory language must be read in context [since] a phrase gathers meaning from the words around it." General Dynamics Land Systems, Inc. v. Cline, 540 U.S. 581, 596 (2004). In § 1341 and tax law generally, an assessment is closely tied to the collection of a tax, i.e., the assessment is the official recording of liability that triggers levy and collection efforts.

The rule against superfluities complements the principle that courts are to interpret the words of a statute in context. See 2A N. Singer, Statutes and Statutory Construction § 46.06, pp. 181–86 (rev. 6th ed. 2000) ("A statute should be construed so that effect is given to all its provisions, so that no part will be inoperative or superfluous, void or insignificant. . . ."). If, as the Director asserts, the term "assessment," by itself, signified "[t]he entire plan or scheme fixed upon for charging or taxing," the TIA would not need the words "levy" or "collection"; the term "assessment," alone, would do all the necessary work.

Earlier this Term, in United States v. Galletti, 541 U.S. 114 (2004), the Government identified "two important consequences" that follow from the IRS' timely tax assessment: "[T]he IRS may employ administrative enforcement methods such as tax liens and levies to collect the outstanding tax"; and "the time within which the IRS may collect the tax either administratively *or* by a 'proceeding in court' is extended [from 3 years] to 10 years after the date of assessment." The Government . . . made clear in briefing *Galletti* that, under the IRC definition, the tax "assessment" serves as the trigger for levy and collection efforts. The Government did not describe the term as synonymous with the entire plan of taxation. Nor did it disassociate the word "assessment" from the company ("levy or collection") that word keeps.[4] Instead, and in accord with our understanding, the Government related "assessment" to the term's collection-propelling function.

IV

Congress modeled § 1341 upon earlier federal "statutes of similar import," laws that, in turn, paralleled state provisions proscribing "actions in State courts to enjoin the collection of State and county taxes." S.Rep. No. 1035, 75th Cong., 1st Sess., 1 (1937) (hereinafter S. Rep.). In composing the TIA's text, Congress drew particularly on an 1867 measure, sometimes called the Anti–Injunction Act (AIA), which bars "any court" from entertaining a suit brought "for the purpose of restraining the assessment or collection of any [federal] tax." Act of Mar. 2, 1867, ch. 169, § 10, 14 Stat. 475, now codified at 26 U.S.C. § 7421(a). See Jefferson County v. Acker, 527 U.S. 423, 434–35 (1999). While § 7421(a) "apparently has no recorded legislative history," Bob Jones Univ. v. Simon, 416 U.S. 725, 736 (1974), the Court has recognized, from the AIA's text, that the measure serves twin purposes: It responds to "the Government's need to assess and collect taxes as expeditiously as possible with a minimum of preenforcement judicial interfer-

assessor multiplies the assessed value by the appropriate tax rate. Income taxes, by contrast, are typically self-assessed in the United States. As anyone who has filed a tax return is unlikely to forget, the taxpayer, not the taxing authority, is the first party to make the relevant calculation of income taxes owed. The word "self-assessment," however, is not a technical term; as IRC § 6201(a) indicates, the Internal Revenue Service executes the formal act of income-tax assessment.

4 The dissent is of two minds in this regard. On the one hand, it twice suggests that a proper definition of the term "assessment," for § 1341 purposes, is "the entire plan or scheme fixed upon for charging or taxing." On the other hand, the dissent would disconnect the word from the enforcement process ("levy or collection") that "assessment" sets in motion.

ence"; and it " 'require[s] that the legal right to the disputed sums be determined in a suit for refund,' " ibid.[5] Lower federal courts have similarly comprehended § 7421(a). See, e.g., McGlotten v. Connally, 338 F.Supp. 448, 453–454 (D.D.C. 1972) (three-judge court) (§ 7421(a) does not bar action seeking to enjoin income-tax exemptions to fraternal orders that exclude nonwhites from membership, for in such an action, plaintiff "does not contest the amount of his own tax, nor does he seek to limit the amount of tax revenue collectible by the United States"); Tax Analysts and Advocates v. Shultz, 376 F.Supp. 889, 892 (D.D.C.1974) (§ 7421(a) does not bar challenge to IRS revenue ruling allowing contributors to political candidate committees to avoid federal gift tax on contributions in excess of $3,000 ceiling; while § 7421(a) "precludes suits to restrain the assessment or collection of taxes," the proscription does not apply when "plaintiffs seek not to restrain the Commissioner from collecting taxes, but rather to *require* him to collect *additional* taxes according to the mandates of the law." (emphases in original)).

Just as the AIA shields federal tax collections from federal-court injunctions, so the TIA shields state tax collections from federal-court restraints. In both 26 U.S.C. § 7421(a) and 28 U.S.C. § 1341, Congress directed taxpayers to pursue refund suits instead of attempting to restrain collections. Third-party suits not seeking to stop the collection (or contest the validity) of a tax *imposed on plaintiffs,* as *McGlotten* and *Tax Analysts* explained, were outside Congress' purview. The TIA's legislative history is not silent in this regard. The Act was designed expressly to restrict "the jurisdiction of the district courts of the United States over suits relating to the collection of State taxes." S. Rep., p. 1.

Specifically, the Senate Report commented that the Act had two closely related, state-revenue-protective objectives: (1) to eliminate disparities between taxpayers who could seek injunctive relief in federal court—usually out-of-state corporations asserting diversity jurisdiction—and taxpayers with recourse only to state courts, which generally required taxpayers to pay first and litigate later; and (2) to stop taxpayers, with the aid of a federal injunction, from withholding large sums, thereby disrupting state government finances. In short, in enacting the TIA, Congress trained its attention on taxpayers who sought to avoid paying their tax bill by pursuing a challenge route other than the one specified by the taxing authority. Nowhere does the legislative history announce a sweeping congressional direction to prevent "federal-court interference with all aspects of state tax administration." Brief for Petitioner 20.[7]

The understanding of the Act's purposes and legislative history set out above underpins this Court's previous applications of the TIA. In California v. Grace Brethren Church, 457 U.S. 393 (1982), for example, we recognized that the principal purpose of the TIA was to "limit drastically" federal-court interference with "the collection of [state] taxes." True, the Court referred

[5] That Congress had in mind challenges to assessments triggering collections, i.e., attempts to prevent the collection of revenue, is borne out by the final clause of 26 U.S.C. § 7421(a), added in 1966: "whether or not such person is the person *against whom* such tax was assessed" (emphasis added).

[7] The language of the TIA differs significantly from that of the Johnson Act, which provides in part: "The district courts shall not enjoin, suspend or restrain *the operation of, or compliance with,*" public-utility rate orders made by state regulatory bodies. 28 U.S.C. § 1342 (emphasis added). The TIA does not prohibit interference with "the operation of, or compliance with" state tax laws; rather, § 1341 proscribes interference only with those aspects of state tax regimes that are needed to produce revenue—i.e., assessment, levy, and collection.

to the disruption of "state tax administration," but it did so specifically in relation to the "the collection of revenue." The complainants in *Grace Brethren Church* were several California churches and religious schools. They sought federal-court relief from an unemployment compensation tax that state law imposed on them. Their federal action, which bypassed state remedies, was exactly what the TIA was designed to ward off. The Director and the dissent endeavor to reconstruct *Grace Brethren Church* as precedent for the proposition that the TIA totally immunizes from lower federal-court review "all aspects of state tax administration, and not just interference with the collection of revenue." The endeavor is unavailing given the issue before the Court in *Grace Brethren Church* and the context in which the words "state tax administration" appear.

The Director invokes several other decisions alleged to keep matters of "state tax administration" entirely free from lower federal-court "interference." Like *Grace Brethren Church,* all of them fall within § 1341's undisputed compass: All involved plaintiffs who mounted federal litigation to avoid paying state taxes (or to gain a refund of such taxes). Federal-court relief, therefore, would have operated to reduce the flow of state tax revenue. See Arkansas v. Farm Credit Servs. of Central Ark., 520 U.S. 821, 824 (1997) (corporations chartered under federal law claimed exemption from Arkansas sales and income taxation); National Private Truck Council, Inc. v. Oklahoma Tax Comm'n, 515 U.S. 582, 584 (1995) (action seeking to prevent Oklahoma from collecting taxes State imposed on nonresident motor carriers); Fair Assessment in Real Estate Assn., Inc. v. McNary, 454 U.S. 100, 105–06 (1981) (taxpayers, alleging unequal taxation of real property, sought, inter alia, damages measured by alleged tax overassessments); Rosewell v. LaSalle National Bank, 450 U.S. 503, 510 (1981) (state taxpayer, alleging her property was inequitably assessed, refused to pay state taxes).[8]

Our prior decisions are not fairly portrayed cut loose from their secure, state-revenue-protective moorings. See, e.g., *Grace Brethren Church,* 457 U.S., at 410 ("If federal declaratory relief were available to test state tax assessments, state tax administration might be thrown into disarray, and *taxpayers might escape the ordinary procedural requirements imposed by state law.* During the pendency of the federal suit *the collection of revenue under the challenged law might be obstructed, with consequent damage to the State's budget, and perhaps a shift to the State of the risk of taxpayer insolvency.*") (emphases added).[9]

In sum, this Court has interpreted and applied the TIA only in cases Congress wrote the Act to address, i.e., cases in which state taxpayers seek federal-court orders enabling them to avoid paying state taxes. We have read harmoniously the § 1341 instruction conditioning the jurisdictional

---

[8] Petitioner urges, and the dissent agrees, that the TIA safeguards another vital state interest: the authority of state courts to determine what state law means. Respondents, however, have not asked the District Court to interpret any state law—there is no disagreement as to the meaning of Ariz.Rev.Stat. Ann. § 43–1089 (West Supp.2003), only about whether, as applied, the State's law violates the Federal Constitution. That is a question federal courts are no doubt equipped to adjudicate.

[9] We note, furthermore, that this Court has relied upon "principles of comity," Brief for Petitioner 26, to preclude original federal-court jurisdiction only when plaintiffs have sought district-court aid in order to arrest or countermand state tax collection. See Fair Assessment in Real Estate Assn., Inc. v. McNary, 454 U.S. 100, 107–08 (1981) (Missouri taxpayers sought damages for increased taxes caused by alleged overassessments); Great Lakes Dredge & Dock Co. v. Huffman, 319 U.S. 293, 296–99 (1943) (plaintiffs challenged Louisiana's unemployment compensation tax).

bar on the availability of "a plain, speedy and efficient remedy" in state court. The remedy inspected in our decisions was not one designed for the universe of plaintiffs who sue the State. Rather, it was a remedy tailor-made for taxpayers. See, *e.g., Rosewell,* 450 U.S., at 528 ("Illinois' legal remedy that provides property owners paying property taxes under protest a refund without interest in two years is a 'plain, speedy and efficient remedy' under the [TIA]"); *Grace Brethren Church,* 457 U.S., at 411 ("[A] state-court remedy is 'plain, speedy and efficient' "only if it "provides the taxpayer with a 'full hearing and judicial determination' at which she may raise any and all constitutional objections to the tax.").[10]

V

In other federal courts as well, § 1341 has been read to restrain state taxpayers from instituting federal actions to contest their liability for state taxes, but not to stop third parties from pursuing constitutional challenges to tax benefits in a federal forum. Relevant to the distinction between taxpayer claims that would reduce state revenues and third-party claims that would enlarge state receipts, Seventh Circuit Judge Easterbrook wrote trenchantly:

> Although the district court concluded that § 1341 applies to any federal litigation touching on the subject of state taxes, neither the language nor the legislative history of the statute supports this interpretation. The text of § 1341 does not suggest that federal courts should tread lightly in issuing orders that might allow local governments to raise additional taxes. The legislative history . . . shows that § 1341 is designed to ensure that federal courts do not interfere with states' collection of taxes, so long as the taxpayers have an opportunity to present to a court federal defenses to the imposition and collection of the taxes. The legislative history is filled with concern that federal judgments were emptying state coffers and that corporations with access to the diversity jurisdiction could obtain remedies unavailable to resident taxpayers. *There was no articulated concern about federal courts' flogging state and local governments to collect additional taxes.* Dunn v. Carey, 808 F.2d 555, 558 (7th Cir. 1986) (emphasis added).

[Discussion of other lower federal court decisions has been omitted. Also omitted is discussion of "numerous federal-court decisions—including decisions of this Court reviewing lower federal-court judgments—[that] have reached the merits of third-party constitutional challenges to tax benefits without mentioning the TIA."][12]

* * *

[10] Far from "ignor[ing]" the "plain, speedy and efficient remedy" proviso, as the dissent charges, we agree that this "codified exception" is key to a proper understanding of the Act. The statute requires the State to provide *taxpayers* with a swift and certain remedy when they resist tax collections. An action dependent on a court's discretion, for example, would not qualify as a fitting taxpayer's remedy.

[12] In school desegregation cases, as a last resort, federal courts have asserted authority to direct the imposition of, or increase in, local tax levies, even in amounts exceeding the ceiling set by state law. See Missouri v. Jenkins, 495 U.S. 33, 57 (1990); Liddell v. Missouri, 731 F.2d 1294, 1320 (8th Cir. 1984) (en banc); cf. Griffin v. School Bd. of Prince Edward Cty., 377 U.S. 218, 233 (1964). Controversial as such a measure may be, see *Jenkins,* 495 U.S., at 65–81 (Kennedy, J., concurring in part and concurring in judgment), it is noteworthy that § 1341 was not raised in those cases by counsel, lower courts, or this Court on its own motion.

In a procession of cases not rationally distinguishable from this one, no Justice or member of the bar of this Court ever raised a § 1341 objection that, according to the petitioner in this case, should have caused us to order dismissal of the action for want of jurisdiction. [Citations omitted,] Consistent with the decades-long understanding prevailing on this issue, respondents' suit may proceed without any TIA impediment.[13]

For the reasons stated, the judgment of the United States Court of Appeals for the Ninth Circuit is

Affirmed.

■ JUSTICE STEVENS, concurring.

In Part IV of his dissent, Justice Kennedy observes that "years of unexamined habit by litigants and the courts" do not lessen this Court's obligation correctly to interpret a statute. It merits emphasis, however, that prolonged congressional silence in response to a settled interpretation of a federal statute provides powerful support for maintaining the status quo. In statutory matters, judicial restraint strongly counsels waiting for Congress to take the initiative in modifying rules on which judges and litigants have relied. In a contest between the dictionary and the doctrine of stare decisis, the latter clearly wins. The Court's fine opinion, which I join without reservation, is consistent with these views.

■ JUSTICE KENNEDY, with whom THE CHIEF JUSTICE, JUSTICE SCALIA, and JUSTICE THOMAS join, dissenting.

In this case, the Court shows great skepticism for the state courts' ability to vindicate constitutional wrongs. Two points make clear that the Court treats States as diminished and disfavored powers, rather than merely applies statutory text. First, the Court's analysis of the Tax Injunction Act (TIA or Act), 28 U.S.C. § 1341, contrasts with a literal reading of its terms. Second, the Court's assertion that legislative histories support the conclusion that "[t]hird-party suits not seeking to stop the collection (or contest the validity) of a tax *imposed on plaintiffs* . . . were outside Congress' purview" in enacting the TIA and the anti-injunction provision on which the TIA was modeled is not borne out by those sources, as previously recognized by the Court. In light of these points, today's holding should probably be attributed to the concern the Court candidly shows animates it. See [passages] noting it was the federal courts that "upheld the Constitution's equal protection requirement" when States circumvented Brown v. Board of Education, 347 U.S. 483 (1954), by manipulating their tax laws. The concern, it seems, is that state courts are second rate constitutional arbiters, unequal to their federal counterparts. State courts are due more respect than this. Dismissive treatment of state courts is particularly unjustified since the TIA, by express terms, provides a federal safeguard: The Act lifts its bar on federal court intervention when state courts fail to provide "a plain, speedy, and efficient remedy." § 1341.

In view of the TIA's text, the congressional judgment that state courts are qualified constitutional arbiters, and the respect state courts deserve, I disagree with the majority's superseding the balance the Act strikes between federal and state court adjudication. I agree with the majority that

[13] In confirming that cases of this order may be brought in federal court, we do not suggest that "state courts are second rate constitutional arbiters." Instead, we underscore that adjudications of great moment discerning no § 1341 barrier cannot be written off as reflecting nothing more than "unexamined custom" or unthinking "habit."

the petition for certiorari was timely under 28 U.S.C. § 2101(c), and so submit this respectful dissent on the merits of the decision.

I

Today is the first time the Court has considered whether the TIA bars federal district courts from granting injunctive relief that would prevent States from giving citizens statutorily mandated state tax credits. There are cases, some dating back almost 50 years, which proceeded as if the jurisdictional bar did not apply to tax credit challenges; but some more recent decisions have said the bar is applicable. Compare, e.g., Mueller v. Allen, 463 U.S. 388 (1983); Committee for Public Ed. & Religious Liberty v. Nyquist, 413 U.S. 756 (1973); Griffin v. School Bd. of Prince Edward Cty., 377 U.S. 218 (1964), with, e.g., ACLU Foundation of LA. v. Bridges, 334 F.3d 416 (5th Cir. 2003); In re Gillis, 836 F.2d 1001 (6th Cir. 1988). While unexamined custom favors the first position, the statutory text favors the latter. In these circumstances a careful explanation for the conclusion is necessary; but in the end the scope and purpose of the Act should be understood from its terms alone.

The question presented—whether the TIA bars the District Court from granting injunctive relief against the tax credit—requires two inquiries. First, the term assessment, as used in § 1341, must be defined. Second, we must determine if an injunction prohibiting the Director from allowing the credit would enjoin, suspend, or restrain an assessment.

The word assessment in the TIA is not isolated from its use in another federal statute. The TIA was modeled on the anti-injunction provision of the Internal Revenue Code (Code), 26 U.S.C. § 7421(a). That provision specifies, and has specified since 1867, that federal courts may not restrain or enjoin an "assessment or collection of any [federal] tax." The meaning of the term assessment in this Code provision is discernible by reference to other Code sections.

Chapter 63 of Title 26 addresses the subject of assessments and sheds light on the meaning of the term in the Code. Section 6201(a) first instructs that "[t]he Secretary [of the Internal Revenue Service] is . . . required to make the . . . assessments of all taxes . . . imposed by this title . . . " Further it provides, "[t]he Secretary shall assess all taxes determined by the taxpayer or by the Secretary . . . " Section 6203 in turn sets forth a method for making an assessment: "The assessment shall be made by recording the liability of the taxpayer in the office of the Secretary."

Taken together, the provisions of Title 26 establish that an assessment, as that term is used in § 7421(a), must at the least encompass the recording of a taxpayer's ultimate tax liability. This is what the taxpayer owes the Government. See also Laing v. United States, 423 U.S. 161, 170 n.13 (1976) ("The 'assessment,' essentially a bookkeeping notation, is made when the Secretary or his delegate establishes an account against the taxpayer on the tax rolls"). Whether the Secretary or his delegate (today, the Commissioner) makes the recording on the basis of a taxpayer's self-reported filing form or instead chooses to rely on his own calculation of the taxpayer's liability (*e.g.*, via an audit) is irrelevant. The recording of the liability on the Government's tax rolls is itself an assessment.

The TIA was modeled on the anti-injunction provision; it incorporates the same terminology employed by the provision; and it employs that terminology for the same purpose. It is sensible, then, to interpret the TIA's terms by reference to the Code's use of the term. Cf. Lorillard v. Pons, 434

U.S. 575, 581 (1978) ("[W]here, as here, Congress adopts a new law incorporating sections of a prior law, Congress normally can be presumed to have had knowledge of the interpretation given to the incorporated law, at least insofar as it affects the new statute"). The Court of Appeals, which concluded that an assessment was the official estimate of the value of income or property used to calculate a tax or the imposition of a tax on someone, placed principal reliance for its interpretation on a dictionary definition. That was not entirely misplaced; but unless the definition is considered in the context of the prior statute, the advantage of that statute's interpretive guidance is lost.

Furthermore, the court defined the term in an unusual way. It relied on a dictionary that was unavailable when the TIA was enacted; it relied not on the definition of the term under consideration, "assessment," but on the definition of the term's related verb form, "assess"; and it examined only a portion of that terms' definition. In the dictionary used by the Court of Appeals, the verb is defined in two ways not noted by the court. One of the alternative definitions is quite relevant—"(2) to fix or determine the amount of (damages, a tax, a fine, etc.)." Further,

> Had [the panel] looked in a different lay dictionary, [it] would have found a definition contrary to the one it preferred, such as "the entire plan or scheme fixed upon for charging or taxing." . . . Had the panel considered tax treatises and law dictionaries . . . it would have found much in accord with this broader definition. . . . Even the federal income tax code supports a broad reading of "assessment." Winn v. Killian, 321 F.3d 911, 912 (9th Cir. 2003) (Kleinfeld, J., dissenting from denial of rehearing en banc).

Guided first by the Internal Revenue Code, an assessment under § 1341, at a minimum, is the recording of taxpayers' liability on the State's tax rolls. The TIA, though a federal statute that must be interpreted as a matter of federal law, operates in a state-law context. In this respect, the Act must be interpreted so as to apply evenly to the 50 various state-law regimes and to the various recording schemes States employ. It is therefore irrelevant whether state officials record taxpayer liabilities with their own pen in a specified location, by collecting and maintaining taxpayers' self-reported filing forms, or in some other manner. The recordkeeping that equates to the determination of taxpayer liability on the State's tax rolls is the assessment, whatever the method. The Court seems to agree with this.

The dictionary definition of assessment provides further relevant information. Contemporaneous dictionaries from the time of the TIA's enactment define assessment in expansive terms. They would broaden any understanding of the term, and so the Act's bar. See, e.g., Webster's New International Dictionary 139 (1927) (providing three context relevant definitions for the term assessment: It is the act of apportioning or determining an amount to be paid; a valuation of property for the purpose of taxation; or the entire plan or scheme fixed upon for charging or taxing). See also United States v. Galletti, 541 U.S.114, 122 (2004) (noting that under the Code the term assessment refers not only to recordings of tax liability but also to "the calculation . . . of a tax liability," including self-calculation done by the taxpayer). The Court need not decide the full scope of the term assessment in the TIA, however. For present purposes, a narrow definition of the term suffices. Applying the narrowest definition, the TIA's literal text bars district courts from enjoining, suspending, or restraining a State's recording of taxpayer liability on its tax rolls, whether the recordings are made by self-reported taxpayer filing forms or by a State's calculation of taxpayer liability.

The terms "enjoin, suspend, or restrain" require little scrutiny. No doubt, they have discrete purposes in the context of the TIA; but they also have a common meaning. They refer to actions that restrict assessments to varying degrees. It is noteworthy that the term "enjoin" has not just its meaning in the restrictive sense but also has meaning in an affirmative sense. The Black's Law Dictionary current at the TIA's enactment gives as a definition of the term, "to require; command; positively direct." Black's Law Dictionary 663 (3d ed.1933). That definition may well be implicated here, since an order invalidating a tax credit would seem to command States to collect taxes they otherwise would not collect. The parties, however, proceed on the assumption that enjoin means to bar. It is unobjectionable for the Court to make the assumption too, leaving the broader definition for later consideration.

Respondents argue the TIA does not bar the injunction they seek because even after the credit is enjoined, the Director will be able to record and enforce taxpayers' liabilities. In fact, respondents say, with the credit out of the way the Director will be able to record and enforce a higher level of liability and so profit the State. ("The amount of tax payable by some taxpayers would increase, but that can hardly be characterized as an injunction or restraint of the assessment process"). The argument, however, ignores an important part of the Act: "under State law." 28 U.S.C. § 1341 ("The district courts shall not enjoin, suspend or restrain the assessment . . . of any tax under State law"). The Act not only bars district courts from enjoining, suspending, or restraining a State's recording of taxpayer liabilities altogether; but it also bars them from enjoining, suspending, or restraining a State from recording the taxpayer liability that state law mandates.

Section 43–1089 is state law. It is an integral part of the State's tax statute; it is reflected on state tax forms; and the State Supreme Court has held that it is part of the calculus necessary to determine tax liability. A recording of a taxpayer's liability under state law must be made in accordance with § 43–1089. The same can be said with respect to each and every provision of the State's tax law. To order the Director not to record on the State's tax rolls taxpayer liability that reflects the operation of § 43–1089 (or any other state tax law provision for that matter) would be to bar the Director from recording the correct taxpayer liability. The TIA's language bars this relief and so bars this suit.

The Court tries to avoid this conclusion by saying that the recordings that constitute assessments under § 1341 must have a "collection-propelling function" and that the recordings at issue here do not have such a function. See also footnote 4 ("[T]he dissent would disconnect the word [assessment] from the enforcement process"). That is wrong. A recording of taxpayer liability on the State's tax rolls of course propels collection. In most cases the taxpayer's payment will accompany his filing, and thus will accompany the assessment so that no literal collection of moneys is necessary. As anyone who has paid taxes must know, however, if owed payment were not included with the tax filing, the State's recording of one's liability on the State's rolls would certainly cause subsequent collection efforts, for the filing's recording (i.e., the assessment) would propel collection by establishing the State's legal right to the taxpayer's moneys.

II

The majority offers prior judicial interpretations of the Code's similarly worded anti-injunction provision to support its contrary conclusions about the statutory text. That this Court and other federal courts have allowed nontaxpayer suits challenging tax credits to proceed in the face of the anti-injunction provision is not at all controlling. Those cases are quite distinguishable. Had the plaintiffs in those cases been barred from suit, there would have been no available forum at all for their claims. See McGlotten v. Connally, 338 F.Supp. 448, 453–54 (D.D.C.1972) (three-judge court) ("The preferred course of raising [such tax exemption and deduction] objections in a suit for refund is not available. In this situation we cannot read the statute to bar the present suit"). See also Tax Analysts and Advocates v. Shultz, 376 F.Supp. 889, 892 (D.D.C.1974) ("Since plaintiffs are not seeking to restrain the collection of taxes, and since they cannot obtain relief through a refund suit, [26 U.S.C.] § 7421(a) does not bar the injunctive relief they seek"). The Court ratified those decisions only insofar as they relied on this limited rationale as the basis for an exception to the statutory bar on adjudication. . . .

In contrast to the anti-injunction provision, the TIA on its own terms ensures an adequate forum for claims it bars. The TIA specially exempts actions that could not be heard in state courts by providing an exception for instances "where a plain, speedy, and efficient remedy may [not] be had in the courts of [the] State." 28 U.S.C. § 1341. . . . The practical effect is that a literal reading of the TIA provides for federal district courts to stand at the ready where litigants encounter legal or practical obstacles to challenging state tax credits in state courts. And this Court, of course, stands at the ready to review decisions by state courts on these matters.

The Court does not discuss this codified exception, yet the clause is crucial. It represents a congressional judgment about the balance that should exist between the respect due to the States (for both their administration of tax schemes and their courts' interpretation of tax laws) and the need for constitutional vindication. To ignore the provision is to ignore that Congress has already balanced these interests.

Respondents admit they would be heard in state court. Indeed a quite similar action previously was heard there. As a result, the TIA's exception does not apply. To proceed as if it does is to replace Congress' balancing of the noted interests with the Court's.

III

The Court and respondents further argue that the TIA's policy purposes and relatedly the federal anti-injunction provision's policy purposes (as discerned from legislative histories) justify today's holding. The two Acts, they say, reflect a unitary purpose: "In both . . . Congress directed taxpayers to pursue refund suits instead of attempting to restrain [tax] collections." See also [the Court's statement] that the Act's underlying purpose is to bar suits by "taxpayers who sought to avoid paying their tax bill." This purpose, the Court and respondents say, shows that the Act was not intended to foreclose relief in challenges to tax credits. The proposition rests on the premise that the TIA's sole purpose is to prevent district court orders that would decrease the moneys in state fiscs. Because the legislative histories of the Acts are not carefully limited in the manner that this reading suggests, the policy argument against a literal application of the Act's terms fails.

Taking the federal anti-injunction provision first, as has been noted before, "[its] history expressly reflects the congressional desire that all injunctive suits against the tax collector be prohibited." South Carolina v. Regan, 465 U.S. 367, 387 (1984) (O'Connor, J., concurring in judgment). The provision responded to "the grave dangers which accompany intrusion of the injunctive power of the courts into the administration of the revenue." Id., at 388. It "generally precludes judicial resolution of all abstract tax controversies," whether brought by a taxpayer or a nontaxpayer. Id., at 392. Thus, the provision's object is not just to bar suits that might "interrupt 'the process of collecting . . . taxes,' " but "[s]imilarly, the language and history evidence a congressional desire to prohibit courts from restraining any aspect of the tax laws' administration." Id., at 399.

The majority's reading of the TIA's legislative history is also inconsistent with the interpretation of this same history in the Court's earlier cases. The Court has made clear that the TIA's purpose is not only to protect the fisc but also to protect the State's tax system administration and tax policy implementation. California v. Grace Brethren Church, 457 U.S. 393 (1982), is a prime example.

In *Grace Brethren Church* the Court held that the TIA not only bars actions by individuals to stop tax collectors from collecting moneys (i.e., injunctive suits) but also bars declaratory suits. The Court explained that permitting declaratory suits to proceed would "defea[t] the principal purpose of the Tax Injunction Act: 'to limit drastically federal district court jurisdiction to interfere with so important a local concern as the collection of taxes.' " It continued:

> If federal declaratory relief were available to test state tax assessments, state tax administration might be thrown into disarray, and taxpayers might escape the ordinary procedural requirements imposed by state law. During the pendency of the federal suit the collection of revenue under the challenged law might be obstructed, with consequent damage to the State's budget, and perhaps a shift to the State of the risk of taxpayer insolvency. Moreover, federal constitutional issues are likely to turn on questions of state tax law, which, like issues of state regulatory law, are more properly heard in the state courts.

While this, of course, demonstrates that protecting the state fisc from damage is part of the TIA's purpose, it equally shows that actions that would throw the "state tax administration . . . into disarray" also implicate the Act and its purpose. The Court's concern with preventing administrative disarray puts in context its explanation that the TIA's principal concern is to limit federal district court interference with the "collection of taxes." The phrase, in this context, refers to the operation of the whole tax collection system and the implementation of entire tax policy, not just a part of it. While an order interfering with a specific collection suit disrupts one of the most essential aspects of a State's tax system, it is not the only way in which federal courts can disrupt the State's tax system:

> [T]he legislative history of the Tax Injunction Act demonstrates that Congress worried not so much about the form of relief available in the federal courts, as about divesting the federal courts of jurisdiction to interfere with state tax administration. *Grace Brethren Church*, supra, at 409 n.22.

The Court's decisions in Fair Assessment in Real Estate Assn., Inc. v. McNary, 454 U.S. 100 (1981), National Private Truck Council, Inc. v. Oklahoma Tax Comm'n, 515 U.S. 582 (1995) *(NPTC)*, and *Rosewell*, supra, make the same point. Though the majority says these cases support its holding because they "involved plaintiffs who mounted federal litigation to avoid paying state taxes," the language of these cases is too clear to be ignored and is contrary to the Court's holding today. In *Fair Assessment,* the Court observed that "[t]he [TIA] 'has its roots in equity practice, in principles of federalism, and in recognition of the imperative need of a State to administer its own fiscal operations.' This last consideration was [its] principal motivating force." In *NPTC*, the Court said, "Congress and this Court repeatedly have shown an aversion to federal interference with state tax administration. The passage of the [TIA] in 1937 is one manifestation of this aversion." [*NPTC* also summed] up this aversion, generated also from principles of comity and federalism, as creating a "background presumption that federal law generally will not interfere with administration of state taxes." In *Rosewell,* the Court described the Act's language as "broad" and "prophylactic" [and also said that] the TIA was "passed to limit federal-court interference in state tax matters."

The Act is designed to respect not only the administration of state tax systems but also state court authority to say what state law means. "[F]ederal constitutional issues are likely to turn on questions of state tax law, which, like issues of state regulatory law, are more properly heard in the state courts." *Grace Brethren Church*, supra, at 410. This too establishes that the TIA's purpose is not solely to ensure that the State's fisc is not decreased. There would be only a diminished interest in allowing state courts to say what the State's tax statutes mean if the Act protected just the state fisc. The TIA protects the responsibility of the States and their courts to administer their own tax systems and to be accountable to the citizens of the State for their policies and decisions. The majority objects that "there is no disagreement to the meaning of" state law in this case. As an initial matter, it is not clear that this is a fair conclusion. The litigation in large part turns on what state law requires and whether the product of those requirements violates the Constitution. More to the point, however, even if there were no controversy about the statutory framework the Arizona tax provision creates, the majority's ruling has implications far beyond this case and will most certainly result in federal courts in other States and in other cases being required to interpret state tax law in order to complete their review of challenges to state tax statutes.

Our heretofore consistent interpretation of the Act's legislative history to prohibit interference with state tax systems and their administration accords with the direct, broad, and unqualified language of the statute. The Act bars all orders that enjoin, suspend, or restrain the assessment of any tax under state law. In effecting congressional intent we should give full force to simple and broad proscriptions in the statutory language.

Because the TIA's language and purpose are comprehensive, arguments based on congressional silence on the question whether the TIA applies to actions that increase moneys a state tax system collects are of no moment. Whatever weight one gives to legislative histories, silence in the legislative record is irrelevant when a plain congressional declaration exists on a matter. "[W]hen terms are unambiguous we may not speculate on probabilities of intention." Insurance Co. v. Ritchie, 72 U.S. (5 Wall.) 541, 545 (1867). Here, Congress has said district courts are barred from disrupting the State's tax operations. It is immaterial whether the State's collection is raised or lowered. A court order will thwart and replace the State's chosen tax policy if it causes either result. No authority supports the proposition that a State lacks an interest in reducing its citizens' tax burden. It is a troubling proposition for this Court to proceed on the assumption that the State's interest in limiting the tax burden on its citizens to that for which its law provides is a secondary policy, deserving of little respect from us.

IV

The final basis on which both the majority and respondents rest is that years of unexamined habit by litigants and the courts alike have resulted in federal courts' entertaining challenges to state tax credits. While we should not reverse the course of our unexamined practice lightly, our obligation is to give a correct interpretation of the statute. We are not obliged to maintain the status quo when the status quo is unfounded. The exercise of federal jurisdiction does not and cannot establish jurisdiction. See United States v. L.A. Tucker Truck Lines, Inc., 344 U.S. 33, 37–38 (1952): "[T]his Court is not bound by a prior exercise of jurisdiction in a case where it was not questioned and it was passed sub silentio." In this respect, the present case is no different than Federal Election Comm'n v. NRA Political Victory Fund, 513 U.S. 88 (1994). The case presented the question whether we had jurisdiction to consider a certiorari petition filed by the Federal Election Commission (FEC), and not by the Solicitor General on behalf of the FEC. The Court held that it lacked jurisdiction. Though that answer seemed to contradict the Court's prior practices, the Court said:

> Nor are we impressed by the FEC's argument that it has represented itself before this Court on several occasions in the past without any question having been raised about its authority to do so. . . . The jurisdiction of this Court was challenged in none of these actions, and therefore the question is an open one before us.

See also Will v. Michigan Dept. of State Police, 491 U.S. 58, 63 n.4 (1989) (" '[T]his Court has never considered itself bound when a subsequent case finally brings the jurisdictional issue before us.' Hagans v. Lavine, 415 U.S. 528, 535 n.5 (1974)"). These cases make clear that our failure to consider a question hardly equates to a thing's being decided. As a consequence, I would follow the statutory language.

* * *

After today's decision, "[n]ontaxpaying associations of taxpayers, and most other nontaxpayers, will now be allowed to sidestep Congress' policy against [federal] judicial resolution of abstract [state] tax controversies." *Regan,* 465 U.S., at 394 (O'Connor, J., concurring in judgment). This unfortunate result deprives state courts of the first opportunity to hear such cases and to grant the relief the Constitution requires.

For the foregoing reasons, with respect, I dissent.

CHAPTER 4

ADDITIONAL RECONSTRUCTION LEGISLATION

1. 42 U.S.C. § 1982

Jones v. Alfred H. Mayer Co.

Supreme Court of the United States, 1968.
392 U.S. 409.

■ MR. JUSTICE STEWART delivered the opinion of the Court.

In this case we are called upon to determine the scope and the constitutionality of an act of Congress, 42 U.S.C. § 1982, which provides that:

> All citizens of the United States shall have the same right, in every State and Territory, as is enjoyed by white citizens thereof to inherit, purchase, lease, sell, hold, and convey real and personal property.

On September 2, 1965, the petitioners filed a complaint in the District Court for the Eastern District of Missouri, alleging that the respondents had refused to sell them a home in the Paddock Woods community of St. Louis County for the sole reason that petitioner Joseph Lee Jones is a Negro. Relying in part upon § 1982, the petitioners sought injunctive and other relief. The District Court sustained the respondents' motion to dismiss the complaint, and the Court of Appeals for the Eighth Circuit affirmed, concluding that § 1982 applies only to state action and does not reach private refusals to sell. We granted certiorari to consider the questions thus presented. For the reasons that follow, we reverse the judgment of the Court of Appeals. We hold that § 1982 bars *all* racial discrimination, private as well as public, in the sale or rental of property, and that the statute, thus construed, is a valid exercise of the power of Congress to enforce the Thirteenth Amendment.[5]

I

At the outset, it is important to make clear precisely what this case does *not* involve. Whatever else it may be, 42 U.S.C. § 1982 is not a comprehensive open housing law. In sharp contrast to the Fair Housing Title (Title VIII) of the Civil Rights Act of 1968, the statute in this case deals only with racial discrimination and does not address itself to discrimination on grounds of religion or national origin. It does not deal specifically with discrimination in the provision of services or facilities in connection with

---

[5] Because we have concluded that the discrimination alleged in the petitioners' complaint violated a federal statute that Congress had the power to enact under the Thirteenth Amendment, we find it unnecessary to decide whether that discrimination also violated the Equal Protection Clause of the Fourteenth Amendment.

the sale or rental of a dwelling. It does not prohibit advertising or other representations that indicate discriminatory preferences. It does not refer explicitly to discrimination in financing arrangements or in the provision of brokerage services. It does not empower a federal administrative agency to assist aggrieved parties. It makes no provision for intervention by the Attorney General. And, although it can be enforced by injunction,[13] it contains no provision expressly authorizing a federal court to order the payment of damages.[14]

Thus, although § 1982 contains none of the exemptions that Congress included in the Civil Rights Act of 1968, it would be a serious mistake to suppose that § 1982 in any way diminishes the significance of the law recently enacted by Congress. Indeed, the Senate Subcommittee on Housing and Urban Affairs was informed in hearings held after the Court of Appeals had rendered its decision in this case that § 1982 might well be "a presently valid federal statutory ban against discrimination by private persons in the sale or lease of real property." The Subcommittee was told, however, that even if this Court should so construe § 1982, the existence of that statute would not "eliminate the need for congressional action" to spell out "responsibility on the part of the federal government to enforce the rights it protects." The point was made that, in light of the many difficulties confronted by private litigants seeking to enforce such rights on their own, "legislation is needed to establish federal machinery for enforcement of the rights guaranteed under § 1982 of Title 42 even if the plaintiffs in *Jones v. Alfred H. Mayer Co.* should prevail in the United States Supreme Court."

On April 10, 1968, Representative Kelly of New York focused the attention of the House upon the present case and its possible significance.[a] She described the background of this litigation, recited the text of § 1982, and then added:

> When the Attorney General was asked in court about the effect of the old law [§ 1982] as compared with the pending legislation which is being considered on the House floor today, he said that the scope was somewhat different, the remedies and procedures were different, and that the new law was still quite necessary.

Later the same day, the House passed the Civil Rights Act of 1968. Its enactment had no effect upon § 1982[20] and no effect upon this litigation,[21] but

[13] . . . The fact that § 1982 . . . provides no explicit method of enforcement does not, of course, prevent a federal court from fashioning an effective equitable remedy. Cf. Ex parte Young, 209 U.S. 123 (1908).

[14] The complaint in this case alleged that the petitioners had "suffered actual damages in the amount of $50,000," but no facts were stated to support or explain that allegation. Upon receiving the injunctive relief to which they are entitled, the petitioners will presumably be able to purchase a home from the respondents at the price prevailing at the time of the wrongful refusal in 1965—substantially less, the petitioners concede, than the current market value of the property in question. Since it does not appear that the petitioners will then have suffered any uncompensated injury, we need not decide here whether, in some circumstances, a party aggrieved by a violation of § 1982 might properly assert an implied right to compensatory damages. In no event, on the facts alleged in the present complaint, would the petitioners be entitled to punitive damages. We intimate no view, however, as to what damages might be awarded in a case of this sort arising in the future under the Civil Rights Act of 1968.

[a] The case had been argued in the Supreme Court on April 1–2, 1968. It was decided on June 17. The Attorney General argued for reversal as an amicus curiae for the United States.—[Footnote by eds.]

[20] At oral argument, the Attorney General expressed the view that, if Congress should enact the pending bill, § 1982 would not be affected in any way but "would stand independent-

it underscored the vast differences between, on the one hand, a general statute applicable only to racial discrimination in the rental and sale of property and enforceable only by private parties acting on their own initiative, and, on the other hand, a detailed housing law, applicable to a broad range of discriminatory practices and enforceable by a complete arsenal of federal authority. Having noted these differences, we turn to a consideration of § 1982 itself.

II

This Court last had occasion to consider the scope of § 1982 in 1948, in Hurd v. Hodge, 334 U.S. 24 (1948). That case arose when property owners in the District of Columbia sought to enforce racially restrictive covenants against the Negro purchasers of several homes on their block. A federal District Court enforced the restrictive agreements by declaring void the deeds of the Negro purchasers. It enjoined further attempts to sell or lease them the properties in question and directed them to "remove themselves and all of their personal belongings" from the premises within 60 days. The Court of Appeals for the District of Columbia Circuit affirmed, and this Court granted certiorari to decide whether [the predecessor of] § 1982 barred enforcement of the racially restrictive agreements in that case.

The agreements in *Hurd* covered only two-thirds of the lots of a single city block, and preventing Negroes from buying or renting homes in that specific area would not have rendered them ineligible to do so elsewhere in the city. Thus, if § 1982 had been thought to do no more than grant Negro citizens the legal capacity to buy and rent property free of prohibitions that wholly disabled them because of their race, judicial enforcement of the restrictive covenants at issue would not have violated § 1982. But this Court took a broader view of the statute. Although the covenants could have been enforced without denying the general right of Negroes to purchase or lease real estate, the enforcement of those covenants would nonetheless have denied the Negro purchasers "the same right 'as is enjoyed by white citizens . . . to inherit, purchase, lease, sell, hold, and convey real and personal property.' " 334 U.S., at 34. That result, this Court concluded, was prohibited by § 1982. To suggest otherwise, the Court said, "is to reject the plain meaning of language." Ibid.

---

ly." That is, of course, correct. The Civil Rights Act of 1968 does not mention 42 U.S.C. § 1982, and we cannot assume that Congress intended to effect any change, either substantive or procedural, in the prior statute. See also § 815 of the 1968 Act: "Nothing in this title shall be construed to invalidate or limit any law of . . . any . . . jurisdiction in which this title shall be effective, that grants, guarantees, or protects the . . . rights . . . granted by this title. . . ."

[21] On April 22, 1968, we requested the views of the parties as to what effect, if any, the enactment of the Civil Rights Act of 1968 had upon this litigation. The parties and the Attorney General, representing the United States as amicus curiae, have informed us that the respondents' housing development will not be covered by the 1968 act until January 1, 1969; that, even then, the act will have no application to cases where, as here, the alleged discrimination occurred prior to April 11, 1968, the date on which the act became law; and that, if the act were deemed applicable to such cases, the petitioners' claim under it would nonetheless be barred by the 180–day limitation period of [the 1968 statute].

Nor did the passage of the 1968 act after oral argument in this case furnish a basis for dismissing the writ of certiorari as improvidently granted. Rice v. Sioux City Cemetery, 349 U.S. 70 (1955), relied upon in dissent, was quite unlike this case, for the statute that belatedly came to the Court's attention in *Rice* reached precisely the same situations that would have been covered by a decision in this Court sustaining the petitioner's claim on the merits. The coverage of § 1982, however, is markedly different from that of the Civil Rights Act of 1968.

Hurd v. Hodge squarely held, therefore, that a Negro citizen who is denied the opportunity to purchase the home he wants "[s]olely because of [his] race and color," 334 U.S., at 34, has suffered the kind of injury that § 1982 was designed to prevent. The basic source of the injury in *Hurd* was, of course, the action of private individuals—white citizens who had agreed to exclude Negroes from a residential area. But an arm of the government—in that case, a federal court—had assisted in the enforcement of that agreement.[24] Thus *Hurd v. Hodge* did not present the question whether *purely* private discrimination, unaided by any action on the part of government, would violate § 1982 if its effect were to deny a citizen the right to rent or buy property solely because of his race or color.. . . . It is true that a dictum in *Hurd* said that § 1982 was directed only toward "governmental action," 334 U.S., at 31, but neither *Hurd* nor any other case before or since has presented that precise issue for adjudication in this Court. Today we face that issue for the first time.

III

We begin with language of the statute itself. In plain and unambiguous terms, § 1982 grants to all citizens, without regard to race or color, "the same right" to purchase and lease property "as is enjoyed by white citizens." As the Court of Appeals in this case evidently recognized, that right can be impaired as effectively by "those who place property on the market" as by the state itself. For, [as that court said,] even if the state and its agents lend no support to those who wish to exclude persons from their communities on racial grounds, the fact remains that, whenever property "is placed on the market for whites only, whites have a right denied to Negroes." So long as a Negro citizen who wants to buy or rent a home can be turned away simply because he is not white, he cannot be said to enjoy "the *same* right . . . as is enjoyed by white citizens . . . to . . . purchase [and] lease . . . real and personal property." 42 U.S.C. § 1982. (Emphasis added.)

On its face, therefore, § 1982 appears to prohibit *all* discrimination against Negroes in the sale or rental of property—discrimination by private owners as well as discrimination by public authorities. Indeed, even the respondents seem to concede that, if § 1982 "means what it says"—to use the words of the respondents' brief—then it must encompass every racially motivated refusal to sell or rent and cannot be confined to officially sanctioned segregation in housing. Stressing what they consider to be the revolutionary implications of so literal a reading of § 1982, the respondents argue that Congress cannot possibly have intended any such result. Our examination of the relevant history, however, persuades us that Congress meant exactly what it said.

IV

[Justice Stewart extensively examined the legislative history of the statute in this section of his opinion. His views are summarized in the Notes on the Legislative History of § 1982, following this case. Justice Stewart concluded:]

In light of the concerns that led Congress to adopt it and the contents of the debates that preceded its passage, it is clear that the act was designed to do just what its terms suggest: to prohibit all racial discrimination, whether or not under color of law, with respect to the rights enumerated therein—including the right to purchase or lease property. . . .

---

[24] . . . See Shelley v. Kraemer, 334 U.S. 1, 12 (1948).

As we said in a somewhat different setting two terms ago, "We think that history leaves no doubt that, if we are to give [the law] the scope that its origins dictate, we must accord it a sweep as broad as its language." United States v. Price, 383 U.S. 787, 801 (1966). "We are not at liberty to seek ingenious analytical instruments," ibid., to carve from § 1982 an exception for private conduct—even though its application to such conduct in the present context is without established precedent. And, as the Attorney General of the United States said at the oral argument of this case, "[t]he fact that the statute lay partially dormant for many years cannot be held to diminish its force today."

V

The remaining question is whether Congress has power under the Constitution to do what § 1982 purports to do: to prohibit all racial discrimination, private and public, in the sale and rental of property. Our starting point is the Thirteenth Amendment, for it was pursuant to that constitutional provision that Congress originally enacted what is now § 1982. The amendment consists of two parts. Section 1 states:

> Neither slavery nor involuntary servitude, except as a punishment for crime whereof the party shall have been duly convicted, shall exist within the United States, or any place subject to their jurisdiction.

Section 2 provides:

> Congress shall have power to enforce this article by appropriate legislation.

As its text reveals, the Thirteenth Amendment "is not a mere prohibition of state laws establishing or upholding slavery, but an absolute declaration that slavery or involuntary servitude shall not exist in any part of the United States." Civil Rights Cases, 109 U.S. 3, 20 (1883). It has never been doubted, therefore, "that the power vested in Congress to enforce the article by appropriate legislation," ibid., includes the power to enact laws "direct and primary, operating upon the acts of individuals, whether sanctioned by state legislation or not." Id., at 23.

Thus, the fact that § 1982 operates upon the unofficial acts of private individuals, whether or not sanctioned by state law, presents no constitutional problem. If Congress has power under the Thirteenth Amendment to eradicate conditions that prevent Negroes from buying and renting property because of their race or color, then no federal statute calculated to achieve that objective can be thought to exceed the constitutional power of Congress simply because it reaches beyond state action to regulate the conduct of private individuals. The constitutional question in this case, therefore, comes to this: Does the authority of Congress to enforce the Thirteenth Amendment "by appropriate legislation" include the power to eliminate all racial barriers to the acquisition of real and personal property? We think the answer to that question is plainly yes.

By its own unaided force and effect, "the Thirteenth Amendment abolished slavery, and established universal freedom." *Civil Rights Cases*, supra, at 20. Whether or not the amendment *itself* did any more than that—a question not involved in this case—it is at least clear that the enabling clause of that amendment empowered Congress to do much more. For that clause clothed "Congress with power to pass *all laws necessary and proper for abolishing all badges and incidents of slavery in the United States*." Ibid. (Emphasis added.). . .

Congress has the power under the Thirteenth Amendment rationally to determine what are the badges and the incidents of slavery, and the authority to translate that determination into effective legislation. Nor can we say that the determination Congress has made is an irrational one. For this Court recognized long ago that, whatever else they may have encompassed, the badges and incidents of slavery—its "burdens and disabilities"—included restraints upon "those fundamental rights which are the essence of civil freedom, namely, the same right . . . to inherit, purchase, lease, sell and convey property, as is enjoyed by white citizens." *Civil Rights Cases*, supra, at 22. Just as the Black Codes, enacted after the Civil War to restrict the free exercise of those rights, were substitutes for the slave system, so the exclusion of Negroes from white communities became a substitute for the Black Codes. And when racial discrimination herds men into ghettos and makes their ability to buy property turn on the color of their skin, then it too is a relic of slavery.

Negro citizens, North and South, who saw in the Thirteenth Amendment a promise of freedom—freedom to "go and come at pleasure" and to "buy and sell when they please"—would be left with "a mere paper guarantee" if Congress were powerless to assure that a dollar in the hands of a Negro will purchase the same thing as a dollar in the hands of a white man. At the very least, the freedom that Congress is empowered to secure under the Thirteenth Amendment includes the freedom to buy whatever a white man can buy, the right to live wherever a white man can live. If Congress cannot say that being a free man means at least this much, then the Thirteenth Amendment made a promise the nation cannot keep. . . . The judgment is

Reversed.

■ [The concurring opinion of JUSTICE DOUGLAS has been omitted.]

■ MR. JUSTICE HARLAN, whom MR. JUSTICE WHITE joins, dissenting.

The decision in this case appears to me to be most ill-considered and ill-advised. . . .

For reasons which follow, I believe that the Court's construction of § 1982 as applying to purely private action is almost surely wrong, and at the least is open to serious doubt. [T]he political processes of our own era have, since the date of oral argument in this case, given birth to a civil rights statute embodying "fair housing" provisions which would at the end of this year make available to others, though apparently not to the petitioners themselves, the type of relief which the petitioners now seek. It seems to me that this latter factor so diminishes the public importance of this case that by far the wisest course would be for this Court to refrain from decision and to dismiss the writ as improvidently granted.

I

I shall deal first with the Court's construction of § 1982, which lies at the heart of its opinion. That construction is that the statute applies to purely private as well as to state-authorized discrimination.

A

The Court's opinion focuses upon the statute's legislative history, but it is worthy of note that the precedents in this Court are distinctly opposed to the Court's view of the statute.

[For example, in] Hurd v. Hodge, 334 U.S. 24 (1948), the issue was . . . whether the courts of the District [of Columbia] might enforce racially restrictive covenants. At the outset of the process of reasoning by which it held that judicial enforcement of such a covenant would violate the predecessor of § 1982, the Court said:

> We may start with the proposition that the statute does not invalidate private restrictive agreements so long as the purposes of those agreements are achieved by the parties through voluntary adherence to the terms. The action toward which the provisions of the statute under consideration is [sic] directed is governmental action. . . . [8]

B

Like the Court, I begin analysis of § 1982 by examining its language. In its present form, the section provides:

> All citizens of the United States shall have the same right, in every State and Territory, as is enjoyed by white citizens thereof to inherit, purchase, lease, sell, hold, and convey real and personal property.

The Court finds it "plain and unambiguous," that this language forbids purely private as well as state-authorized discrimination. With all respect, I do not find it so. For me, there is an inherent ambiguity in the term "right," as used in § 1982. The "right" referred to may either be a right to equal status under the law, in which case the statute operates only against state-sanctioned discrimination, or it may be an "absolute" right enforceable against private individuals. To me, the words of the statute, taken alone, suggest the former interpretation, not the latter. . . .

C

The Court rests its opinion chiefly upon the legislative history of the Civil Rights Act of 1866. I shall endeavor to show that those debates do not, as the Court would have it, overwhelmingly support the result reached by the Court, and in fact that a contrary conclusion may equally well be drawn. [Justice Harlan's lengthy discussion of the legislative history has been omitted here, but is summarized in the Notes on the Legislative History of § 1982, infra.]

D

The foregoing analysis of the language, structure, and legislative history of the 1866 Civil Rights Act shows, I believe, that the Court's thesis that the Act was meant to extend to purely private action is open to the most serious doubt, if indeed it does not render that thesis wholly untenable. Another, albeit less tangible, consideration points in the same direction. Many of the legislators who took part in the congressional debates inevitably must have shared the individualistic ethic of their time, which emphasized personal freedom and embodied a distaste for governmental interference which was soon to culminate in the era of laissez-faire. It seems to me that most of these men would have regarded it as a great intrusion on individual liberty for the government to take from a man the power to refuse for personal reasons to enter into a purely private transaction involving the disposition of property, albeit those personal reasons might reflect racial bias. It should be remembered that racial prejudice was not uncommon in 1866, even outside the South. Although Massachusetts had recently enacted the nation's first law prohibiting racial discrimination in public accommodations, Negroes could not ride within Philadelphia streetcars or

---

[8] It seems to me that this passage is not dictum, as the Court terms it, but a holding. For if the Court had held the covenants in question invalid as between the parties, then it would not have had to rely upon a finding of "state action."

attend public schools with white children in New York City. Only five states accorded equal voting rights to Negroes, and it appears that Negroes were allowed to serve on juries only in Massachusetts. Residential segregation was the prevailing pattern almost everywhere in the North. There were no state "fair housing" laws in 1866, and it appears that none had ever been proposed. In this historical context, I cannot conceive that a bill thought to prohibit purely private discrimination not only in the sale or rental of housing but in *all* property transactions would not have received a great deal of criticism explicitly directed to this feature. The fact that the 1866 Act received *no* criticism of this kind is for me strong additional evidence that it was not regarded as extending so far.

In sum, the most which can be said with assurance about the intended impact of the 1866 Civil Rights Act upon purely private discrimination is that the Act probably was envisioned by most members of Congress as prohibiting official, community-sanctioned discrimination in the South, engaged in pursuant to local "customs" which in the recent time of slavery probably were embodied in laws or regulations. . . .

II

The foregoing, I think, amply demonstrates that the Court has chosen to resolve this case by according to a loosely worded statute a meaning which is open to the strongest challenge in light of the statute's legislative history. In holding that the Thirteenth Amendment is sufficient constitutional authority for § 1982 as interpreted, the Court also decides a question of great importance. Even contemporary supporters of the aims of the 1866 Civil Rights Act doubted that those goals could constitutionally be achieved under the Thirteenth Amendment. [I]t is plain that the course of decision followed by the Court today entails the resolution of important and difficult issues. . . .

The fact that a case is "hard" does not, of course, relieve a judge of his duty to decide it. Since, the Court did vote to hear this case, I normally would consider myself obligated to decide whether the petitioners are entitled to relief. . . . After mature reflection, however, I have concluded that this is one of those rare instances in which an event which occurs after the hearing of argument so diminishes a case's public significance, when viewed in light of the difficulty of the questions presented, as to justify this Court in dismissing the writ as improvidently granted.

The occurrence to which I refer is the recent enactment of the Civil Rights Act of 1968. Title VIII of that act contains comprehensive "fair housing" provisions, which . . . will become applicable on January 1, 1969, to persons who, like the petitioners, attempt to buy houses from developers. Under those provisions, such persons will be entitled to injunctive relief and damages from developers who refuse to sell to them on account of race or color, unless the parties are able to resolve their dispute by other means. Thus, the type of relief which the petitioners seek will be available within seven months' time under the terms of a presumptively constitutional act of Congress. In these circumstances, it seems obvious that the case has lost most of its public importance, and I believe that it would be much the wiser course for this Court to refrain from deciding it. I think it particularly unfortunate for the Court to persist in deciding this case on the basis of a highly questionable interpretation of a sweeping, century-old statute which, as the Court acknowledges, contains none of the exemptions which the Congress of our own time found it necessary to include in a statute regulating relationships so personal in nature. In effect, this Court, by its construction of § 1982, has extended the coverage of federal "fair housing" laws far beyond that which Congress in its wisdom chose to provide in the Civil Rights Act of 1968. The political process now having taken hold again in this very field, I am at a loss to understand why the Court should have deemed it appropriate or, in the circumstances of this case, necessary to proceed with such precipitate and insecure strides.

I am not dissuaded from my view by the circumstances that the 1968 Act was enacted after oral argument in this case, at a time when the parties and amici curiae had invested time and money in anticipation of a decision on the merits, or by the fact that the 1968 Act apparently will not entitle these petitioners to the relief which they seek. For the certiorari jurisdiction was not conferred upon this Court "merely to give the defeated party in the . . . Court of Appeals another hearing," or "for the benefit of the particular litigants," but to decide issues, "the settlement of which is of importance to the public as distinguished from . . . the parties." I deem it far more important that this Court should avoid, if possible, the decision of constitutional and unusually difficult statutory questions than that we fulfill the expectations of every litigant who appears before us. . . .

[I]f the petition for a writ of certiorari in this case had been filed a few months after, rather than a few months before, the passage of the 1968 Civil Rights Act, I venture to say that the case would have been deemed to possess such "isolated significance," in comparison with its difficulties, that the petition would not have been granted.

For these reasons, I would dismiss the writ of certiorari as improvidently granted.

NOTES ON THE SIGNIFICANCE AND HISTORY OF § 1982

1. THE SIGNIFICANCE OF § 1982

Jones v. Alfred H. Mayer Co. plays the same role in interpretation of § 1982 as *Monroe v. Pape* plays for § 1983. Both decisions gave new life to statutes enacted during Reconstruction but largely neglected for a century thereafter. Both were handed down at the height of the power and influence of the Warren Court, and both expanded federal power at the expense of the states. Both also spawned developing bodies of case law implementing and defining causes of action grounded in broadly worded statutes.

As interpreted in *Jones*, § 1982 carries these expansive tendencies even further than § 1983. Section 1982 entirely dispenses with the requirement of action "under color of" state law, as it is phrased in § 1983, or the parallel requirement of "state action" under the Fourteenth Amendment. As interpreted in *Jones*, § 1982 reaches purely private discrimination in the absence of involvement of the state or state assistance. This assertion of federal power covers any and all transactions involving property, whether real or personal, and the companion provision, 42 U.S.C. § 1981, covers contracts. Between them, §§ 1981 and 1982 prohibit racial discrimination in virtually every economic transaction. Moreover, they do so in areas of law—property and contract—which have traditionally been regulated primarily by the states. Despite this broad reach, §§ 1981 and 1982 have a very specific focus, dealing exclusively with racial discrimination, which has long been an area of federal concern.

2. TEXT OF THE ORIGINAL STATUTE

Both § 1982 and § 1981 derive from § 1 of the Civil Rights Act of 1866, which provided as follows:

> *Be it enacted by the Senate and House of Representatives of the United States of America in Congress assembled*, That all persons born in the United States and not subject to any foreign power, . . . are hereby declared to be citizens of the United States; and such citizens, of every race and color, without regard to any previous condition of slavery or involuntary servitude, . . . shall have the same right, in every State and Territory in the United States, to make and enforce contracts, to sue, be parties, and give evidence, to inherit, purchase, lease, sell, hold, and convey real and personal property, and to full and equal benefit of all laws and proceedings for the security of person and property, as is enjoyed by white citizens, and shall be subject to like punishment, pains, and penalties, and to none other, any law, statute, ordinance, regulation, or custom, to the contrary notwithstanding.

Another modern statute, 18 U.S.C. § 242, derives from § 2 of the 1866 Act. Section 2 read:

> That any person who, under color of any law, statute, ordinance, regulation, or custom, shall subject, or cause to be subjected, any inhabitant of any State or Territory to the deprivation of any right secured or protected by this act, or to different punishment, pains, or penalties on account of such person having at any time been held in a condition of slavery or involuntary servitude, except as a punishment for crime whereof the party shall have been duly convicted, or by reason of his color or race, than is prescribed for the punishment of white persons, shall be deemed guilty of a misdemeanor, and, on conviction, shall be punished by fine not exceeding one thousand dollars, or imprisonment not exceeding one year, or both, in the discretion of the court.

3. JUSTICE STEWART'S READING OF THE HISTORY

Justice Stewart began his analysis of the legislative history of § 1982 by observing that it was clear to the Congress of 1866 that the right to purchase real estate "might be infringed not only by 'State or local law' but also by 'custom, or prejudice.' " The reference to "custom, or prejudice" was based on a bill passed by the Congress to enlarge the military powers of the Freedmen's Bureau. As Justice Stewart explained, the Freedman's Bureau statute extended "military jurisdiction over certain areas in the South where, 'in consequence of any state or local law, . . . *custom, or prejudice*, any of the civil rights belonging to white persons (including the right . . . to inherit, purchase, lease, sell, hold, and convey real and personal property . . .) are refused or denied to Negroes . . . on account of race, color, or any previous condition of slavery or involuntary servitude. . . . ' " (Emphasis supplied by Justice Stewart.)

That bill was vetoed by President Johnson and never became law. Justice Stewart pointed out, however, that several legislators observed that the coverage of § 1 of the 1866 Act "would duplicate the substantive scope" of the Freedmen's Bureau bill. Such remarks led Justice Stewart to conclude that, "when Congress provided in § 1 of the Civil Rights Act [of 1866] that the right to purchase and lease property was to be enjoyed equally throughout the United

States by Negro and white citizens alike, it plainly meant to secure that right against interference from any source whatever, whether governmental or private."

To buttress this conclusion, Justice Stewart cited references in the legislative record to the "imposing body of evidence pointing to the mistreatment of Negroes by private individuals and unofficial groups, mistreatment unrelated to any hostile state legislation." In particular, he emphasized a "comprehensive stud[y]" before the Congress that reported the existence of some laws in the South that prohibited blacks from owning property, but referred to such laws as "mere isolated cases." The report concluded, as Justice Stewart summarized it, that even if such statutes were repealed, "equal treatment for the Negro would not yet be secured."

Justice Stewart also quoted from statements made in the House and Senate. For example, while the ratification of the Thirteenth Amendment was pending, Senator Wilson of Massachusetts introduced a bill to strike down all racially discriminatory laws in the South. Senator Trumbull responded:

> . . . I hold that under [§ 2 of the Thirteenth Amendment] Congress will have the authority, when the constitutional amendment is adopted, *not only to pass the bill of the Senator from Massachusetts, but a bill that will be much more efficient to protect the freedman in his rights. . . . It is idle to say that a man is free who cannot go and come at pleasure, who cannot buy and sell, who cannot enforce his rights.* [So] when the constitutional amendment is adopted, I trust we may pass a bill . . . that will be *much more sweeping and efficient than the bill under consideration.* (Emphasis supplied by Justice Stewart.)

The Thirteenth Amendment was ratified five days after this statement, and the next day Senator Trumbull said that the "more sweeping and efficient" bill to which he had referred ought to be enacted "at an early day for the purpose of quieting apprehensions in the minds of many friends of freedom lest by local legislation *or a prevailing public sentiment* in some of the states persons of the African race should continue to be oppressed and in fact deprived of their freedom. . . . " (Emphasis supplied by Justice Stewart.) The bill that later became the Civil Rights Act of 1866 was introduced by Senator Trumbull two weeks later.

Justice Stewart attached no limiting significance to the fact that the 1866 statute was reenacted after the adoption of the Fourteenth Amendment:

> Nor was the scope of the 1866 Act altered when it was re-enacted in 1870, some two years after the ratification of the Fourteenth Amendment. It is quite true that some members of Congress supported the Fourteenth Amendment "in order to eliminate doubt as to the constitutional validity of the Civil Rights Act as applied to the states." Hurd v. Hodge, 334 U.S. 24, 32–33 (1948). But it certainly does not follow that the adoption of the Fourteenth Amendment or the subsequent readoption of the Civil Rights Act were meant somehow to *limit* its application to state action. The legislative history furnishes not the slightest factual basis for any such speculation, and the conditions prevailing in 1870 make it highly implausible. For by that time, most, if not all, of the former Confederate states, then under the control of "reconstructed" legislatures, had formally repudiated racial discrimination, and the focus of congressional concern had clearly

> shifted from hostile statutes to the activities of groups like the Ku Klux Klan, operating wholly outside the law. . . . All Congress said in 1870 was that the 1866 law "is hereby re-enacted." That is all Congress meant.

Two other points about Justice Stewart's reading of the 1866 legislation should be noted. The first relates to the last clause of § 1 of the original statute ("any law, statute, ordinance, regulation, or custom, to the contrary notwithstanding"). This clause could be read to modify all of § 1. This reading would indicate that § 1 was aimed only at eradicating discriminatory laws or customs, and therefore that § 1 was aimed only at forms of "state action" that resulted in the prohibited discrimination. Justice Stewart responded to this possibility in a footnote:

> It is, of course, immaterial that § 1 ended with the words "any law, statute, ordinance, regulation, or custom, to the contrary notwithstanding." The phrase was obviously inserted to qualify the reference to "like punishment, pains, and penalties, and to none other," thus emphasizing the supremacy of the 1866 statute over inconsistent state or local laws, if any. It was deleted, presumably as surplusage, in § 1978 of the Revised Statutes of 1874.

Second, Justice Stewart saw an informative relationship between § 1 of the 1866 statute and § 2, the criminal provision now codified at 18 U.S.C. § 242:

> [I]f § 1 had been intended to grant nothing more than an immunity from *governmental* interference, then much of § 2 would have made no sense at all. For that section, which provided fines and prison terms for certain individuals who deprived others of rights "secured or protected" by § 1, was carefully drafted to exempt private violations of § 1 from the criminal sanctions it imposed. There would, of course, have been no private violations to exempt if the only "right" granted by § 1 had been a right to be free of discrimination by public officials. Hence the structure of the 1866 Act, as well as its language, points to the conclusion . . . that § 1 was meant to prohibit *all* racially motivated deprivations of the rights enumerated in the statute, although only those deprivations perpetrated "under color of law" were to be criminally punishable under § 2.

4. JUSTICE HARLAN'S READING OF THE HISTORY

Justice Harlan read the history differently. He started by observing that "since intervening revisions have not been meant to alter substance, the intended meaning of § 1982 must be drawn from the words in which it was originally enacted." As to the text of the original, he said:

> It seems to me that this original wording indicates even more strongly than the present language that § 1 of the act (as well as § 2, which is explicitly so limited) was intended to apply only to action taken pursuant to state or community authority, in the form of a "law, statute, ordinance, regulation, or custom." And with deference I suggest that the language of § 2, taken alone, no more implies that § 2 "was carefully drafted to exempt private violations of § 1 from the criminal sanctions it imposed," than it does that § 2 was carefully drafted to enforce all of the rights secured by § 1.

Harlan then examined the legislative history chronologically, extracting excerpts that supported a "state action" reading of the statute and offering a contrasting interpretation of the excerpts quoted by the majority. In support of a "state action" construction, for example, he offered the following statements by Senator Trumbull:

> [This bill] may be assailed as drawing to the federal government powers that properly belong to "states"; but I apprehend, rightly considered, it is not obnoxious to that objection. *It will have no operation in any state where the laws are equal, where all persons have the same civil rights without regard to color or race. It will have no operation in the state of Kentucky when her slave code and all her laws discriminating between persons on account of race or color shall be abolished.* [Emphasis supplied by Justice Harlan.]

A few days later, Senator Trumbull said:

> *[I]f the state of Kentucky makes no discrimination in civil rights between its citizens, this bill has no operation whatever in the state of Kentucky.* Are all the rights of the people of Kentucky gone because they cannot discriminate and punish one man for doing a thing that they do not punish another for doing? The bill draws to the federal government no power whatever if the states will perform their constitutional obligations. [Emphasis supplied by Justice Harlan.]

And two months later Senator Trumbull observed:

> This bill in no manner interferes with the municipal regulations of any state which protects all alike in their rights of person and property. *It could have no operation in Massachusetts, New York, Illinois, or most of the states of the Union.* [Emphasis supplied by Justice Harlan.]

Of the latter statement, Justice Harlan observed that "[t]he remarks just quoted constitute the plainest possible statement that the civil rights bill was intended to apply only to state-sanctioned conduct and not to purely private action."

Illustrative of Justice Harlan's response to the passages relied on by the majority is his treatment of the exchange between Senators Wilson and Trumbull while the Thirteenth Amendment was pending. Harlan quoted a different part of their discussion. Senator Trumbull said that Senator Wilson's bill to strike down racially discriminatory laws in the South did "not go far enough." "[U]ntil [the Thirteenth Amendment] is adopted," Trumbull continued, "there may be some question . . . as to the authority of Congress to pass such a bill as this, but after the adoption of the constitutional amendment, there can be none. The second clause of that amendment was inserted for some purpose, and I would like to know . . . for what purpose? Sir, for the purpose, and none other, of preventing state legislatures from enslaving, under any pretense, those whom the first clause declared should be free."

Harlan assessed the significance of this passage as follows:

> Senator Trumbull then indicated that he would introduce [a bill] to secure the freedmen in their civil rights, [the bill] in his view being authorized by the second clause of the Thirteenth Amendment. Since he had just stated that the purpose of that clause was to enable Congress to nulli-

fy acts of the state legislatures, it seems inferable that this was also to be the aim of the promised [bill].

At another point, Harlan observed that "virtually all" of the statements quoted by the majority "appear to be either irrelevant or equally consistent with a 'state action' interpretation" of the statute. For example, as to Senator Trumbull's reference to discrimination resulting from "a prevailing public sentiment," Justice Harlan said that the comment "is also consistent with a 'state action' reading of the bill, for the bill explicitly prohibited actions done under color of 'custom' as well as of formal laws."

5. REACTIONS IN THE LITERATURE

Scholarly reaction to the debate in *Jones* about the meaning of the legislative history has been mixed. Robert L. Kohl, The Civil Rights Act of 1866, Its Hour Come Round at Last: *Jones v. Alfred H. Mayer Co.*, 55 Va.L.Rev. 272, 299 (1969), concludes that "[w]hile statements from the congressional debates may be cited to support both sides of the question, on balance the legislative history clearly justifies the Court's application of the act to private land developers." In particular, Kohl reports that evidence before the Congress of 1866 indicated that the South "was covertly attempting to reintroduce a new, privately enforced slave system. [W]itness after witness . . . testified to the fact that whites in the South simply would not sell land to black people." The "real problem" before the Congress, Kohl concludes, "was not the existence of negative legislation but private opposition." Id. at 276–83. Another author has reached a similar conclusion based on an examination of the entire history surrounding the adoption of the Thirteenth and Fourteenth Amendments and the enactment of the 1866 Civil Rights Act. Robert J. Kaczorowski, Revolutionary Constitutionalism in the Era of the Civil War and Reconstruction, 61 N.Y.U.L.Rev. 863 (1986).

Other authors have been far more critical of *Jones*. Gerhard Casper in *Jones v. Mayer*: Clio, Bemused and Confused Muse, 1968 Supreme Court Rev. 89, 100, 122, called Justice Stewart's treatment of the history "creation by authoritative revelation" and concluded that "[t]he Civil Rights Act, interpreted historically, does not address itself to the problem [of fair housing]." And in his History of the Supreme Court of the United States: Reconstruction and Reunion, 1864–88, Part One 1117–1260 (1971), Charles Fairman rebutted the majority's interpretation of history, noting that his "critique has been carried no further than was needed to disembarrass the field of history." See also Barry Sullivan, Historical Reconstruction, Reconstruction History, and the Proper Scope of Section 1981, 98 Yale L.J. 541 (1989); Theodore Eisenberg & Stewart Schwab, The Importance of Section 1981, 73 Cornell L. Rev. 596 (1988).

For a reassessment of the entire history of the Civil Rights Act of 1866, from its initial enactment to its latest amendment in 1991, see George Rutherglen, The Improbable History of Section 1981: Clio Still Bemused and Confused, 2003 Sup. Ct. Rev. 303. This study concludes that the Act was originally intended to protect the right to full participation in public life regardless of race and that it prohibits any systematic form of discrimination that denies this right, whether by government or by private individuals. The Act was therefore correctly interpreted in *Jones v. Mayer* to reach some forms of private discrimination that do not involve state action under the Fourteenth Amendment.

Although *Jones v. Mayer* may have gone too far in interpreting the Act to prohibit all forms of private discrimination, no matter how isolated or insignificant, this interpretation of the Act was adopted by Congress in the Civil Rights Act of 1991. The author has placed the debate over the historical reasoning in *Jones v. Mayer* in the larger perspective of constitutional history:

> Before 1866, civil rights existed only as an uncertain implication of state citizenship. After 1866, they became the foundation of an entirely new field of law, elaborated in great detail and with great controversy in the years since then. Where civil rights previously were dependent upon a shared understanding of the common law rights of citizens, the Civil Rights Act of 1866 elevated them to the status of binding federal law. The Privileges and Immunities Clause had previously been limited to an indefinite range of rights . . . and subject to pervasive racial classifications under federal and state law. Most constitutional rights, such as those enumerated in the Bill of Rights, ran only against the federal government. The Thirteenth Amendment added freedom from slavery to the list of constitutionally protected rights, but did not elaborate further on what that entailed. The rights historically protected by the common law remained in the background, with only such force as state law chose to give to them—until Congress selected some as fundamental and enumerated them in the Civil Rights Act of 1866.

George Rutherglen, Civil Rights in the Shadow of Slavery: The Constitution, Common Law, and the Civil Rights Act of 1866 159 (2013).

NOTES ON JONES V. ALFRED H. MAYER CO.

1. THE HOUSING PROVISIONS OF THE CIVIL RIGHTS ACT OF 1968

The majority opinion begins and the dissent ends by discussing the Civil Rights Act of 1968, which was passed by Congress after oral argument but before the decision in *Jones*. The main features of that statute, now codified in 42 U.S.C. §§ 3601–19, are summarized in Justice Stewart's opinion and briefly elaborated below.

The Civil Rights Act of 1968 makes it unlawful "to refuse to sell or rent after the making of a bona fide offer . . . a dwelling to any person because of race, color, religion, sex, family status, or national origin." 42 U.S.C. § 3604(a). Insofar as this prohibition applies to racial discrimination, its coverage overlaps with § 1982 as interpreted in *Jones*. This makes the *Jones* decision, although in theory very broad, in practice rather narrow. What looks like a broad expansion of federal power to prohibit private discrimination turns out, on examination, to be a modest addition to a statute just recently passed by Congress. Does the limited immediate practical effect of the decision in *Jones* make it more or less justifiable?

Section 1982, as interpreted in *Jones*, nevertheless reached some forms of discrimination not prohibited by the Civil Rights Act of 1968. Important exemptions to the prohibition in the latter are found in § 3603(b), which states:

> Nothing in § 3604 [except the prohibition on discriminatory advertising] shall apply to—
>
> > (1) any single-family house sold or rented by an owner [with numerous provisos the thrust of which were to exclude those in the

business of selling houses from the exemption and to preclude the discriminatory use of brokers or advertising], or

(2) rooms or units in dwellings containing living quarters occupied or intended to be occupied by no more than four families living independently of each other, if the owner actually maintains and occupies one of such living quarters as his residence.

Section 3607(a) also contains an exception for religious organizations and private clubs "not in fact open to the public." What implications should these exceptions have for interpretation of § 1982, which contains no similar provisions?

The procedures for enforcing the Civil Rights Act of 1968 also are more complicated than those under § 1982.[a] These procedures have been substantially revised since the enactment of the statute, but they have always provided two independent remedies for persons who claim to be victims of housing discrimination. The first is by filing a complaint with the Secretary of Housing and Urban Development (HUD) within one year of the alleged discrimination. HUD then investigates the complaint and tries to resolve it by conciliation. If that fails, HUD determines whether there is reasonable cause to find a violation. A finding of reasonable cause leads to a referral to an appropriate state or local agency or, in the absence of such an agency, to an administrative hearing by HUD to determine whether the statute has been violated and to order "such relief as may be appropriate," including civil penalties. The Attorney General also has authority to sue to enforce the statute in a variety of circumstances. As an alternative to this complex network of administrative remedies and public actions, persons who claim to be victims of housing discrimination have a second remedy. They can decide to go to court directly and sue. They must do so within two years of the alleged violation, and if a violation ultimately is found, actual and punitive damages can be awarded, as well as injunctive relief.

Under § 1982, only the second of these alternatives is available. Section 1982 contains no provisions for administrative remedies or, for that matter, for judicial remedies either. The statute is simply declaratory and, as *Jones v. Alfred H. Mayer Co.* holds, is enforced according to the remedies typically available in federal court.

Note should also be made of § 3615 of the 1968 legislation, which appears under the title "Effect on State Laws":

> Nothing in this title shall be construed to invalidate or limit any law of a State or political subdivision of a State, or of any other jurisdiction in which this title shall be effective, that grants, guarantees, or protects the same rights as are granted by this title; but any law of a State, a political subdivision or other such jurisdiction that purports to require or permit any action that would be a discriminatory housing practice under this title shall to that extent be invalid.

What effect, if any, should the enactment of this statute have had on the Court's interpretation of § 1982? Compare Justice Stewart's edited quotation from this provision in footnote 20 of his opinion in *Jones*.

---

[a] For a description of both the original and revised procedures under the act, see Leland B. Ware, New Weapons for an Old Battle: The Enforcement Provisions of the 1988 Amendments to the Fair Housing Act, 7 Admin. L.J. 59, 68–96 (1993).

2. PRIOR DECISIONS ON RESTRICTIVE COVENANTS

Jones v. Alfred H. Mayer Co. involved a variation of a problem that had been before the Court in a pair of cases decided in 1948. In both cases, blacks had purchased from willing white sellers lands that were subject to restrictive covenants forbidding sale to blacks. White owners of adjacent parcels brought suit to enjoin the black purchasers from taking possession. The lower courts issued the injunctions. The Supreme Court granted certiorari and, with three Justices not participating, unanimously reversed.

(i) Shelley v. Kraemer

Shelley v. Kraemer, 334 U.S. 1 (1948), involved two injunctions issued by a state court. The Supreme Court noted that the restrictions in the deeds before the Court "could not be squared with the requirements of the Fourteenth Amendment if imposed by state statute or local ordinance," and continued:

> But the present cases . . . do not involve action by state legislatures or city councils. Here the particular patterns of discrimination and the areas in which the restrictions are to operate, are determined, in the first instance, by the terms of agreements among private individuals. Participation of the state consists in the enforcement of the restrictions so defined. The crucial issue with which we are here confronted is whether this distinction removes these cases from the operation of the prohibitory provisions of the Fourteenth Amendment.
>
> Since the decision of this Court in the Civil Rights Cases, 109 U.S. 3 (1883), the principle has become firmly embedded in our constitutional law that the action inhibited by the first section of the Fourteenth Amendment is only such action as may fairly be said to be that of the states. That amendment erects no shield against merely private conduct, however discriminatory or wrongful.
>
> We conclude, therefore, that the restrictive agreements standing alone cannot be regarded as violative of any rights guaranteed to petitioners by the Fourteenth Amendment. So long as the purposes of those agreements are effectuated by voluntary adherence to their terms, it would appear clear that there has been no action by the state and the provisions of the amendment have not been violated.

The Court then turned to whether "state action" could be found in judicial enforcement of the restrictive covenants:

> We have no doubt that there has been state action in these cases in the full and complete sense of the phrase. The undisputed facts disclose that petitioners were willing purchasers of properties upon which they desired to establish homes. The owners of the properties were willing sellers; and contracts of sale were accordingly consummated. It is clear that but for the active intervention of the state courts, supported by the full panoply of state power, petitioners would have been free to occupy the properties in question without restraint.
>
> These are not cases . . . in which the states have merely abstained from action, leaving private individuals free to impose such discriminations as they see fit. Rather, these are cases in which the states have made available to such individuals the full coercive power of government to deny

petitioners, on the grounds of race or color, the enjoyment of property rights in premises which petitioners are willing and financially able to acquire and which the grantors are willing to sell. The difference between judicial enforcement and non-enforcement of the restrictive covenants is the difference to petitioners between being denied rights of property available to other members of the community and being accorded full enjoyment of those rights on an equal footing. . . .

We hold that in granting judicial enforcement of the restrictive agreements in these cases, the states have denied petitioners the equal protection of the laws and that, therefore, the action of the state courts cannot stand. We have noted that freedom from discrimination by the states in the enjoyment of property rights was among the basic objectives sought to be effectuated by the framers of the Fourteenth Amendment. That such discrimination has occurred in these cases is clear. Because of the race or color of these petitioners they have been denied rights of ownership or occupancy enjoyed as a matter of course by other citizens of different race or color. . . .

The historical context in which the Fourteenth Amendment became a part of the Constitution should not be forgotten. Whatever else the framers sought to achieve, it is clear that the matter of primary concern was the establishment of equality in the enjoyment of basic civil and political rights and the preservation of those rights from discriminatory action on the part of the states based on considerations of race or color. . . . Upon full consideration, we have concluded that in these cases the states have acted to deny petitioners the equal protection of the laws guaranteed by the Fourteenth Amendment.

(ii) Hurd v. Hodge

The companion case, Hurd v. Hodge, 334 U.S. 24 (1948), involved an injunction issued by a federal court in the District of Columbia. At the time, the Supreme Court had not yet held that the Due Process Clause of the Fifth Amendment requires the federal government to adhere to the same standards of equal protection that the Fourteenth Amendment requires of the states.[b] Thus, the Court could not simply cite *Shelley* and reverse. It was argued that the Court should nonetheless hold that the Due Process Clause of the Fifth Amendment was violated by the lower court's order. The Court found it unnecessary to resolve the constitutional issue and decided the case under the predecessor to § 1982:

We may start with the proposition that [§ 1982] does not invalidate private restrictive agreements so long as the purposes of those agreements are achieved by the parties through voluntary adherence to the terms. The action toward which the provisions of the statute under consideration [are] directed is governmental action. . . .

In considering whether judicial enforcement of restrictive covenants is the kind of governmental action which the first section of the Civil Rights Act of 1866 was intended to prohibit, reference must be made to the

---

[b] That step was taken in Bolling v. Sharpe, 347 U.S. 497 (1954), a companion case to Brown v. Board of Education, 347 U.S. 483 (1954). *Bolling* held that racial segregation in the District of Columbia public schools violated what has come to be known as the "equal protection component" of the Fifth Amendment Due Process Clause.

scope and purposes of the Fourteenth Amendment; for that statute and the amendment were closely related both in inception and in the objectives which Congress sought to achieve.

Both the Civil Rights Act of 1866 and the joint resolution which was later adopted as the Fourteenth Amendment were passed in the first session of the 39th Congress. Frequent references to the Civil Rights Act are to be found in the record of the legislative debates on the adoption of the amendment. It is clear that in many significant respects the statute and the amendment were expressions of the same general congressional policy. Indeed, as the legislative debates reveal, one of the primary purposes of many members of Congress in supporting the Fourteenth Amendment was to incorporate the guarantees of the Civil Rights Act of 1866 in the organic law of the land. Others supported the adoption of the amendment in order to eliminate doubt as to the constitutional validity of the Civil Rights Act as applied to the states. . . .

. . . In *Shelley v. Kraemer*, we have held that the Fourteenth Amendment . . . forbids . . . discrimination where imposed by state courts in the enforcement of restrictive covenants. That holding is clearly indicative of the construction to be given to the relevant provisions of the Civil Rights Act in their application to the courts of the District of Columbia.[c]

Moreover, the explicit language employed by Congress to effectuate its purposes leaves no doubt that judicial enforcement of the restrictive covenants by the courts of the District of Columbia is prohibited by the Civil Rights Act. That statute, by its terms, requires that all citizens of the United States shall have the same right "as is enjoyed by white citizens . . . to inherit, purchase, lease, sell, hold, and convey real and personal property." That the Negro petitioners have been denied that right by virtue of the action of the federal courts of the District is clear. The Negro petitioners entered into contracts of sale with willing sellers for the purchase of properties upon which they desired to establish homes. Solely because of their race and color they are confronted with orders of court divesting their titles in the properties and ordering that the premises be vacated. White sellers, one of whom is a petitioner here, have been enjoined from selling the properties to any Negro or colored person. Under such circumstances, to suggest that the Negro petitioners have been accorded the same rights as white citizens to purchase, hold, and convey real property is to reject the plain meaning of language. We hold that the action of the District Court directed against the Negro purchasers and the white sellers denies rights intended by Congress to be protected by the Civil Rights Act and that, consequently, the action cannot stand.

Alternatively, the Court held:

Even in the absence of the [civil rights] statute, there are other considerations which would indicate that enforcement of restrictive covenants in these cases is judicial action contrary to the public policy of the United

---

[c] The Court had previously held that "the District of Columbia is included within the phrase 'every State and Territory' " as used in the predecessor to § 1982. "Nor can there be any doubt," the Court added, "of the constitutional power of Congress to enact such legislation with reference to the District of Columbia."—[Footnote by eds.]

States, and as such should be corrected by this Court in the exercise of its supervisory powers over the courts of the District of Columbia. . . .

We are here concerned with action of federal courts of such a nature that if taken by the courts of a state would violate the prohibitory provisions of the Fourteenth Amendment. It is not consistent with the public policy of the United States to permit federal courts in the nation's capital to exercise general equitable powers to compel action denied the state courts where such state action has been held to be violative of the guaranty of the equal protection of the laws. We cannot presume that the public policy of the United States manifests a lesser concern for the protection of such basic rights against discriminatory action of federal courts than against such action taken by the courts of the states.

3. THE NATURE OF THE RIGHTS CREATED BY § 1982

By its literal terms, § 1982 prohibits government from limiting the right to purchase property on the basis of race. It may be thought to follow, as the Court held in *Hurd v. Hodge*, that § 1982 prohibits a court from preventing the sale of property from a willing seller to a willing buyer because a non-party to the sale objects on racial grounds. But is it clear, as Justice Stewart thought, that § 1982 was meant to permit a buyer to compel a sale from an unwilling seller?

This issue is usually analyzed as whether the statute requires "state action"—that is, whether § 1982 prohibits only racial discrimination that can be attributed to government or whether it also prohibits racial discrimination by an individual citizen. In Justice Harlan's view, § 1982 required "state action," although his reliance on the word "custom" in both sections of the Civil Rights Act of 1866 indicated that for him the statute did not require the formal sanction of state law. Harlan's position was that § 1982 imposed no duty on individual citizens to disregard race in their decisions to sell or not to sell to a particular purchaser.

Of course, the refusal of the Alfred H. Mayer Co. to sell to blacks was not exactly like a decision by an isolated individual. Mayer was a real estate developer which exercised "continuing authority over a suburban housing complex with about 1,000 inhabitants." Racial discrimination by such a company is quite different in its impact from a decision by a single individual. Note, however, that this factor is irrelevant to the rationale of the majority, which chose to analyze the case as though it involved any private choice about the sale of property.

Consider in this respect the comments of Louis Henkin in Foreword: On Drawing Lines, The Supreme Court, 1967 Term, 82 Harv.L.Rev. 63, 85 (1968). He concludes that "even those deeply sympathetic with the petitioner's claim must be troubled by the Court's reading of [the statutory] text." Whether black or white, most people ordinarily have no assurance that one private person will sell to another; most are not protected "from the seller's capricious discrimination." Compare the comments of Gerhard Casper in *Jones v. Mayer*: Clio, Bemused and Confused Muse, 1968 Sup. Ct. Rev. 89, 99: "On its face, the statute is ambiguous, since it might also be read to say the following . . . : 'All citizens of the United States shall have the same privilege . . . as is enjoyed by white citizens . . . to purchase real property from anybody who is willing to sell to them. Negro *A* is a citizen. Therefore, *A* shall have the same privilege . . . as is enjoyed by white citizens . . . to purchase real property from anybody who is willing to sell to him.' "

Consider also the impact of the precedents prior to *Jones*. Why was enforcement of the restrictive covenant in *Shelley v. Kraemer* held to violate the Fourteenth Amendment rather than § 1982? Is *Hurd v. Hodge* precedent for or against the decision in *Jones*? The Court has struggled over the years with the state action concept, and *Shelley v. Kraemer* has been a particularly troublesome precedent. Could one of the motives of the *Jones* Court have been to put *Shelley* behind it? To resolve the problem of housing discrimination without continuing involvement in a particularly unsatisfactory branch of the state action controversy? In this respect, consider the precedential effect of *Jones* as compared to the precedential effect of *Shelley*. Can *Jones* be confined to housing discrimination? Should it be?

4. THE CONSTITUTIONAL QUESTION

Today, few would criticize the Court's holding that § 1982 as construed was a constitutional exercise of congressional power. The Court reasoned that the Thirteenth Amendment abolished the institution of slavery, and that the congressional authority under § 2 contains not only the power to implement this conclusion but also the power "rationally to determine what are the badges and incidents of slavery" and to legislate against their perpetuation.

The Court did not suggest that the Thirteenth Amendment itself forbids housing discrimination by a private party. Rather, Congress may advance its own "rational" definition of "the badges and incidents of slavery" and may prohibit private as well as governmental behavior that is "rationally related" to the eradication of the incidents of slavery as so defined. In other words, Congress is not limited to prohibiting forms of discrimination that the Thirteenth Amendment itself forbids. Congress can go beyond the self-executing terms of the amendment and identify for itself the kinds of racial discrimination it wishes to prohibit.

Note the breadth of this interpretation. Congress struggled long and hard in debating its constitutional authority for enactment of the public accommodations provisions of the Civil Rights Act of 1964. Eventually, it took an extremely energetic reading of the Commerce Clause to uphold the congressional action.[d] Yet it is clear, is it not, that the refusal of a restaurant to seat a black customer or the refusal of a motel to rent a room on racial grounds can "rationally" be regarded as a "badge or incident of slavery" that Congress could prohibit under the Thirteenth Amendment? Note that *Jones* was the first decision by the Supreme Court in the modern civil rights era to address congressional power under the Thirteenth Amendment. Could this have been the Court's objective, that is, to establish a broad basis for congressional authority to deal with problems of racial discrimination?

For discussions of the general power of Congress to enforce the Thirteenth Amendment, see Alexander Tsesis, The Thirteenth Amendment and American Freedom (2004); Symposium, The Thirteenth Amendment 71 Md. L. Rev. 12 (2011); The Promises of Liberty: The History and Contemporary Relevance of the Thirteenth Amendment (Alexander Tsesis, ed. 2010); Jack M. Balkin, The

---

[d] See Heart of Atlanta Motel v. United States, 379 U.S. 241 (1964); Katzenbach v. McClung, 379 U.S. 294 (1964).

Reconstruction Power, 85 N.Y.U. L. Rev. 1801 (2010); William M. Carter, Jr., Race, Rights, and the Thirteenth Amendment: Defining the Badges and Incidents of Slavery,40 UC Davis L. Rev. 1311 (2007); Jennifer Mason McAward, The Scope of Congress's Thirteenth Amendment Enforcement Power After *City of Boerne v. Flores*, 88 Wash. U. L. Rev. 77 (2010); James Gray Pope, Contract, Race, and Freedom of Labor in the Constitutional Law of "Involuntary Servitude." 119 Yale L.J. 1474 (2010); George Rutherglen, State Action, Private Action, and the Thirteenth Amendment, 94 Va. L. Rev. 1367 (2008); Alexander Tsesis, A Civil Rights Approach: Achieving Revolutionary Abolitionism Through the Thirteenth Amendment, 39 UC Davis L. Rev. 1773 (2006).

2. 42 U.S.C. § 1981

Runyon v. McCrary

Supreme Court of the United States, 1976.
427 U.S. 160.

■ MR. JUSTICE STEWART delivered the opinion of the Court.

The principal issue presented by these consolidated cases is whether a federal law, namely 42 U.S.C. § 1981, prohibits private schools from excluding qualified children solely because they are Negroes.

I

. . . Michael McCrary and Colin Gonzales, are Negro children. By their parents, they filed a class action against . . . Russell and Katheryne Runyon, who are the proprietors of Bobbe's School in Arlington, Va. Their complaint alleged that they had been prevented from attending the school because of the [Runyon's] policy of denying admission to Negroes, in violation of 42 U.S.C. § 1981.[1] . . . They sought declaratory and injunctive relief and damages. On the same day Colin Gonzales . . . filed a complaint by his parents against the . . . Fairfax–Brewster School, Inc., located in Fairfax County, Va. The . . . Southern Independent School Association, sought and was granted permission to intervene as a party defendant in the suit against the Runyons. That organization is a nonprofit association composed of six state private school associations, and represents 395 private schools. It is stipulated that many of these schools deny admission to Negroes.

The suits were consolidated for trial. The findings of the District Court, which were left undisturbed by the Court of Appeals, were as follows. Bobbe's School opened in 1958 and grew from an initial enrollment of five students to 200 in 1972. A day camp was begun in 1967 and has averaged 100 children per year. The Fairfax–Brewster School commenced operations in 1955 and opened a summer day camp in 1956. A total of 223 students were enrolled at the school during the 1972–73 academic year, and 236 attended the day camp in the summer of 1972. Neither school has ever accepted a Negro child for any of its programs.

[1] Title 42 U.S.C. § 1981 provides: "All persons within the jurisdiction of the United States shall have the same right in every State and Territory to make and enforce contracts, to sue, be parties, give evidence, and to the full and equal benefit of all laws and proceedings for the security of persons and property as is enjoyed by white citizens, and shall be subject to like punishment, pains, penalties, taxes, licenses, and exactions of every kind, and to no other."

In response to a mailed brochure addressed "resident" and an advertisement in the "Yellow Pages" of the telephone directory, Mr. and Mrs. Gonzales telephoned and then visited the Fairfax–Brewster School in May 1969. After the visit, they submitted an application for Colin's admission to the day camp. The school responded with a form letter, which stated that the school was "unable to accommodate [Colin's] application." Mr. Gonzales telephoned the school. Fairfax–Brewster's Chairman of the Board explained that the reason for Colin's rejection was that the school was not integrated. Mr. Gonzales then telephoned Bobbe's School, from which the family had also received in the mail a brochure addressed to "resident." In response to a question concerning that school's admissions policies, he was told that only members of the Caucasian race were accepted. In August 1972, Mrs. McCrary telephoned Bobbe's School in response to an advertisement in the telephone book. She inquired about nursery school facilities for her son, Michael. She also asked if the school was integrated. The answer was no.

Upon these facts, the District Court found that the Fairfax–Brewster School had rejected Colin Gonzales' application on account of his race and that Bobbe's School had denied both children admission on racial grounds. The court held that 42 U.S.C. § 1981 makes illegal the schools' racially discriminatory admissions policies. It therefore enjoined Fairfax–Brewster School and Bobbe's School and the member schools of the Southern Independent School Association from discriminating against applicants for admission on the basis of race. . . .

The Court of Appeals for the Fourth Circuit, sitting en banc, affirmed the District Court's grant of equitable [relief]. We granted the petitions for certiorari . . . to consider whether 42 U.S.C. § 1981 prevents private schools from discriminating racially among applicants. . . .

II

It is worth noting at the outset some of the questions that these cases do not present. They do not present any question of the right of a private social organization to limit its membership on racial or any other grounds. They do not present any question of the right of a private school to limit its student body to boys, to girls, or to adherents of a particular religious faith, since 42 U.S.C. § 1981 is in no way addressed to such categories of selectivity. They do not even present the application of § 1981 to private sectarian schools that practice *racial* exclusion on religious grounds.[6] Rather, these cases present only two basic questions: whether § 1981 prohibits private, commercially operated, nonsectarian schools from denying admission to prospective students because they are Negroes and, if so, whether that federal law is constitutional as so applied.

A. Applicability of § 1981

It is now well established that § 1 of the Civil Rights Act of 1866, 42 U.S.C. § 1981, prohibits racial discrimination in the making and enforcement of private contracts.

In Jones v. Alfred H. Mayer Co., 392 U.S. 409 (1968), the Court held that the portion of § 1 of the Civil Rights Act of 1866 presently codified as 42 U.S.C. § 1982 prohibits private racial discrimination in the sale or rental

---

[6] Nothing in this record suggests that either the Fairfax–Brewster School or Bobbe's Private School excludes applicants on religious grounds, and the Free Exercise Clause of the First Amendment is thus in no way here involved.

of real or personal property. Relying on the legislative history of § 1, from which both § 1981 and § 1982 derive, the Court concluded that Congress intended to prohibit "all racial discrimination, private and public, in the sale . . . of property" and that this prohibition was within Congress' power under § 2 of the Thirteenth Amendment "rationally to determine what are the badges and the incidents of slavery, and . . . to translate that determination into effective legislation."

[T]hat holding necessarily implied that the portion of § 1 of the 1866 Act presently codified as 42 U.S.C. § 1981 likewise reaches purely private acts of racial discrimination. The statutory holding in *Jones* was that the "[1866] Act was designed to do just what its terms suggest: to prohibit all racial discrimination, whether or not under color of law, with respect to the rights enumerated therein—including the right to purchase or lease property." One of the "rights enumerated" in § 1 is "the same right . . . to make and enforce contracts . . . as is enjoyed by white citizens. . . . " Just as in *Jones* a Negro's § 1 right to purchase property on equal terms with whites was violated when a private person refused to sell to the prospective purchaser solely because he was a Negro, so also a Negro's § 1 right to "make and enforce contracts" is violated if a private offeror refuses to extend to a Negro, solely because he is a Negro, the same opportunity to enter into contracts as he extends to white offerees.

The applicability of the holding in *Jones* to § 1981 was confirmed by this Court's decisions in Tillman v. Wheaton–Haven Recreation Assn., 410 U.S. 431, 439–40 (1973), and Johnson v. Railway Express Agency, Inc., 421 U.S. 454, 459–60 (1975). In *Tillman* the petitioner urged that a private swimming club had violated 42 U.S.C. §§ 1981, 1982, and 2000a et seq. by enforcing a guest policy that discriminated against Negroes. The Court noted that "[t]he operative language of both § 1981 and § 1982 is traceable to the [Civil Rights Act of] 1866." Referring to its earlier rejection of the respondents' contention that Wheaton–Haven was exempt from § 1982 under the private-club exception of the Civil Rights Act of 1964, the Court concluded: "In light of the historical interrelationship between § 1981 and § 1982 [there is] no reason to construe these sections differently when applied, on these facts, to the claim of Wheaton–Haven that it is a private club." Accordingly the Court remanded the case to the District Court for further proceedings "free of the misconception that Wheaton–Haven is exempt from §§ 1981, 1982, and 2000a." In *Johnson v. Railway Express Agency*, the Court noted that § 1981 "relates primarily to racial discrimination in the making and enforcement of contracts" and held unequivocally "that § 1981 affords a federal remedy against discrimination in private employment on the basis of race."

It is apparent that the racial exclusion practiced by the Fairfax–Brewster School and Bobbe's Private School amounts to a classic violation of § 1981. The parents of Colin Gonzales and Michael McCrary sought to enter into contractual relationships with Bobbe's School for educational services. Colin Gonzales' parents sought to enter into a similar relationship with the Fairfax–Brewster School. Under those contractual relationships, the schools would have received payments for services rendered, and the prospective students would have received instruction in return for those payments. The educational services of Bobbe's School and the Fairfax–Brewster School were advertised and offered to members of the general public.[10] But neither school offered services on an equal basis to white and nonwhite students. As the Court of Appeals held, "there is ample evidence in the record to support the trial judge's factual determinations [that] Colin [Gonzales] and Michael [McCrary] were denied admission to the schools because of their race." The Court of Appeals' conclusion that § 1981 was thereby violated follows inexorably from the language of that statute, as construed in *Jones, Tillman*, and *Johnson*.

The . . . schools and school association argue principally that § 1981 does not reach private acts of racial discrimination. That view is wholly inconsistent with *Jones*' interpretation of the legislative history of § 1 of the Civil Rights Act of 1866, an interpretation that was reaffirmed in Sullivan v. Little Hunting Park, Inc., 396 U.S. 229 (1969), and again in *Tillman v. Wheaton–Haven Recreation Assn.* And this consistent interpretation of the law necessarily requires the conclusion that § 1981, like § 1982, reaches private conduct.

It is noteworthy that Congress in enacting the Equal Employment Opportunity Act of 1972, as amended, 42 U.S.C. § 2000e et seq., specifically considered and rejected an amendment that would have repealed the Civil Rights Act of 1866, as interpreted by this Court in *Jones*, insofar as it affords private-sector employees a right of action based on racial discrimination in employment.[11] There could hardly be a clearer indication of congressional agreement with the view that § 1981 *does* reach private acts of racial discrimination. In these circumstances there is no basis for deviating from the well-settled principles of stare decisis applicable to this Court's construction of federal statutes.

---

[10] These cases do not raise the issue of whether the "private club or other [private] establishment" exemption in § 201(e) of the Civil Rights Act of 1964, 42 U.S.C. § 2000a(e), operates to narrow § 1 of the Civil Rights Act of 1866. As the Court of Appeals implied, that exemption, if applicable at all, comes into play only if the establishment is "not in fact open to the public. . . . " 42 U.S.C. § 2000a(e). Both Bobbe's School and the Fairfax–Brewster School advertised in the "Yellow Pages" of the telephone directory and both used mass mailings in attempting to attract students. As the Court of Appeals observed, these "schools are private only in the sense that they are managed by private persons and they are not direct recipients of public funds. Their actual and potential constituency, however, is more public than private. They appeal to the parents of all children in the area who can meet their academic and other admission requirements. This is clearly demonstrated in this case by the public advertisements."

The pattern of exclusion is thus directly analogous to that at issue in Sullivan v. Little Hunting Park, Inc., 396 U.S. 229 (1969), and Tillman v. Wheaton–Haven Recreation Assn., 410 U.S. 431 (1973), where the so-called private clubs were open to all objectively qualified whites—i.e., those living within a specified geographic area.

Moreover, it is doubtful that a plausible "implied repeal" argument could be made in this context in any event. Implied repeals occur if two acts are in irreconcilable conflict. Title II of the Civil Rights Act of 1964, of which the "private club" exemption is a part, does not by its terms reach private schools. Since there would appear to be no potential for overlapping application of § 1981 and Title II of the 1964 Act with respect to racial discrimination practiced by private schools, there would also appear to be no potential for conflict between § 1981 and Title II's "private club" exemption in this context.

[11] Senator Hruska proposed an amendment which would have made Title VII of the Civil Rights Act of 1964 and the Equal Pay Act the exclusive sources of federal relief for employment discrimination. Senator Williams, the floor manager of the pending bill and one of its original sponsors, argued against the proposed amendment. [Among other things, he referred explicitly to *Jones* and said:] "Mr. President, the amendment of the Senator from Nebraska will repeal the first major piece of civil rights legislation in this Nation's history. We cannot do that." The Senate was persuaded by Senator Williams entreaty that it not "strip from [the] individual his rights that have been established, going back to the first civil rights law of 1866," and Senator Hruska's proposed amendment was rejected.

B. Constitutionality of § 1981 as Applied

The question remains whether § 1981, as applied, violates constitutionally protected rights of free association and privacy, or a parent's right to direct the education of his children.[12]

1. Freedom of Association

In NAACP v. Alabama, 357 U.S. 449, 460 (1958), and similar decisions, the Court has recognized a First Amendment right "to engage in association for the advancement of beliefs and ideas. . . . " That right is protected because it promotes and may well be essential to the "[e]ffective advocacy of both public and private points of view, particularly controversial ones" that the First Amendment is designed to foster.

From this principle it may be assumed that parents have a First Amendment right to send their children to educational institutions that promote the belief that racial segregation is desirable, and that the children have an equal right to attend such institutions. But it does not follow that the *practice* of excluding racial minorities from such institutions is also protected by the same principle. As the Court stated in Norwood v. Harrison, 413 U.S. 455, 469–70 (1973), "the Constitution . . . places no value on discrimination," and while "[i]nvidious private discrimination may be characterized as a form of exercising freedom of association protected by the First Amendment . . . it has never been accorded affirmative constitutional protections. And even some private discrimination is subject to special remedial legislation in certain circumstances under § 2 of the Thirteenth Amendment; Congress has made such discrimination unlawful in other significant contexts." In any event, as the Court of Appeals noted, "there is no showing that discontinuance of [the] discriminatory admission practices would inhibit in any way the teaching in these schools of any ideas or dogma."

2. Parental Rights

In Meyer v. Nebraska, 262 U.S. 390, 399 (1923), the Court held that the liberty protected by the Due Process Clause of the Fourteenth Amendment includes the right "to acquire useful knowledge, to marry, establish a home and bring up children," and, concomitantly, the right to send one's children to a private school that offers specialized training—in that case, instruction in the German language. In Pierce v. Society of Sisters, 268 U.S. 510, 534 (1925), the Court applied "the doctrine of *Meyer v. Nebraska*" to hold unconstitutional an Oregon law requiring the parent, guardian, or other person having custody of a child between eight and 16 years of age to send that child to public school on pain of criminal liability. The Court thought it "entirely plain that the [statute] unreasonably interferes with the liberty of parents and guardians to direct the upbringing and education of children under their control." In Wisconsin v. Yoder, 406 U.S. 205 (1972), the Court stressed the limited scope of *Pierce*, pointing out that it lent "no support to the contention that parents may replace state educational requirements with their own idiosyncratic views of what knowledge a child needs to be a productive and happy member of society" but rather "held simply that while a state may posit [educational] standards, it may not preempt the educational process by requiring children to attend public schools." Id., at 239 (White, J. concurring). And in Norwood v. Harrison, 413 U.S. 455, 461–63 (1973), the Court once again stressed the "limited

[12] It is clear that the schools have standing to assert these arguments on behalf of their patrons. See Pierce v. Society of Sisters, 268 U.S. 510, 535–36 (1925).

scope of *Pierce*," which simply "affirmed the right of private schools to exist and to operate. . . . "

It is clear that the present application of § 1981 infringes no parental right recognized in *Meyer, Pierce, Yoder*, or *Norwood*. No challenge is made to the . . . schools' right to operate or the right of parents to send their children to a particular private school rather than a public school. Nor do these cases involve a challenge to the subject matter which is taught at any private school. Thus, the Fairfax–Brewster School and Bobbe's School and members of the intervenor association remain presumptively free to inculcate whatever values and standards they deem desirable. *Meyer* and its progeny entitle them to no more.

3. The Right of Privacy

The Court has held that in some situations the Constitution confers a right of privacy. See Roe v. Wade, 410 U.S. 113, 152–53 (1973); Eisenstadt v. Baird, 405 U.S. 438, 453 (1972); Stanley v. Georgia, 394 U.S. 557, 564–65 (1969); Griswold v. Connecticut, 381 U.S. 479, 484–85 (1965).

While the application of § 1981 to the conduct at issue here—a private school's adherence to a racially discriminatory admission policy—does not represent governmental intrusion into the privacy of the home or a similarly intimate setting, it does implicate parental interests. These interests are related to the procreative rights protected in *Roe v. Wade* and *Griswold v. Connecticut*. A person's decision whether to bear a child and a parent's decision concerning the manner in which his child is to be educated may fairly be characterized as exercises of familial rights and responsibilities. But it does not follow that because government is largely or even entirely precluded from regulating the child-bearing decision, it is similarly restricted by the Constitution from regulating the implementation of parental decisions concerning a child's education.

The Court has repeatedly stressed that while parents have a constitutional right to send their children to private schools and a constitutional right to select private schools that offer specialized instruction, they have no constitutional right to provide their children with private school education unfettered by reasonable government regulation.[15] Indeed, the Court in *Pierce* expressly acknowledged "the power of the state reasonably to regulate all schools, to inspect, supervise and examine them, their teachers and pupils. . . . "

Section 1981, as applied to the conduct at issue here, constitutes an exercise of federal legislative power under § 2 of the Thirteenth Amendment fully consistent with *Meyer, Pierce*, and the cases that followed in their wake. As the Court held in *Jones v. Alfred H. Mayer Co.*: "It has never been doubted . . . 'that the power vested in Congress to enforce [the Thirteenth Amendment] by appropriate legislation' . . . includes the power to enact laws 'direct and primary, operating upon the acts of individuals, whether sanctioned by state legislation or not.' " The prohibition of racial discrimination that interferes with the making and enforcement of contracts for private educational services furthers goals closely analogous to those served by § 1981's elimination of racial discrimination in the making

---

[15] The *Meyer–Pierce–Yoder* "parental" right and the privacy right, while dealt with separately in this opinion, may be no more than verbal variations of a single constitutional right.

of private employment contracts[16] and, more generally, by § 1982's guarantee that "a dollar in the hands of a Negro will purchase the same thing as a dollar in the hands of a white man." . . .

For the reasons stated in this opinion, the judgment of the Court of Appeals is . . . affirmed.

It is so ordered.

■ MR. JUSTICE POWELL, concurring.

If the slate were clean I might well be inclined to agree with Mr. Justice White that § 1981 was not intended to restrict private contractual choices. Much of the review of the history and purpose of this statute set forth in his dissenting opinion is quite persuasive. It seems to me, however, that it comes too late.

The applicability of § 1981 to private contracts has been considered maturely and recently, and I do not feel free to disregard these precedents. As they are reviewed in the Court's opinion, I merely cite them: Johnson v. Railway Express Agency, 421 U.S. 454 (1975), an opinion in which I joined; Tillman v. Wheaton–Haven Recreation Assn, 410 U.S. 431 (1973), another opinion in which I joined; Sullivan v. Little Hunting Park, Inc., 396 U.S. 229 (1969); and particularly and primarily, Jones v. Alfred H. Mayer Co., 392 U.S. 409 (1968). Although the latter two cases involved § 1982, rather than § 1981, I agree that their considered holdings with respect to the purpose and meaning of § 1982 necessarily apply to both statutes in view of their common derivation.

Although the range of consequences suggested by the dissenting opinion goes far beyond what we hold today, I am concerned that our decision not be construed more broadly than would be justified.

By its terms § 1981 necessarily imposes some restrictions on those who would refuse to extend to Negroes "the same right . . . to make and enforce contracts . . . as is enjoyed by white citizens." But our holding that this restriction extends to certain actions by private individuals does not imply the intrusive investigation into the motives of every refusal to contract by a private citizen that is suggested by the dissent. As the Court of Appeals suggested, some contracts are so personal "as to have a discernible rule of exclusivity which is inoffensive to § 1981."

. . . In certain personal contractual relationships, . . . such as those where the offeror selects those with whom he desires to bargain on an individualized basis, or where the contract is the foundation of a close association (such as, for example, that between an employer and a private tutor, babysitter, or housekeeper), there is reason to assume that, although the choice made by the offeror is selective, it reflects "a purpose of exclusiveness" other than the desire to bar members of the Negro race. Such a purpose, certainly in most cases, would invoke associational rights long respected.

The case presented on the record before us does not involve this type of personal contractual relationship. As the Court of Appeals said, the . . . "schools are private only in the sense that they are managed by private persons and they are not direct recipients of public funds. Their actual and potential constituency, however, is more public than private." The schools

[16] The Court has recognized in similar contexts the link between equality of opportunity to obtain an education and equality of employment opportunity. See McLaurin v. Oklahoma State Regents, 339 U.S. 637 (1950); Sweatt v. Painter, 339 U.S. 629 (1950).

extended a public offer open, on its face, to any child meeting certain minimum qualifications who chose to accept. They advertised in the "Yellow Pages" of the telephone directories and engaged extensively in general mail solicitations to attract students. The schools are operated strictly on a commercial basis, and one fairly could construe their open-end invitations as offers that matured into binding contracts when accepted by those who met the academic, financial, and other racially neutral specified conditions as to qualifications for entrance. There is no reason to assume that the schools had any special reason for exercising an option of personal choice among those who responded to their public offers. A small kindergarten or music class, operated on the basis of personal invitations extended to a limited number of preidentified students, for example, would present a far different case.

I do not suggest that a "bright line" can be drawn that easily separates the type of contract offer within the reach of § 1981 from the type without. The case before us is clearly on one side of the line, however defined, and the kindergarten and music school examples are clearly on the other side. Close questions undoubtedly will arise in the gray area that necessarily exists in between. But some of the applicable principles and considerations, for the most part identified by the Court's opinion, are clear: § 1981, as interpreted by our prior decisions, does reach certain acts of racial discrimination that are "private" in the sense that they involve no *state* action. But choices, including those involved in entering into a contract, that are "private" in the sense that they are not part of a commercial relationship offered generally or widely, and that reflect the selectivity exercised by an individual entering into a personal relationship, certainly were never intended to be restricted by the 19th century Civil Rights Acts. The open offer to the public generally involved in the cases before us is simply not a "private" contract in this sense. Accordingly, I join the opinion of the Court.

■ MR. JUSTICE STEVENS, concurring.

For me the problem in these cases is whether to follow a line of authority which I firmly believe to have been incorrectly decided.

Jones v. Alfred H. Mayer Co., 392 U.S. 409 (1968), and its progeny have unequivocally held that § 1 of the Civil Rights Act of 1866 prohibits private racial discrimination. There is no doubt in my mind that that construction of the statute would have amazed the legislators who voted for it. Both its language and the historical setting in which it was enacted convince me that Congress intended only to guarantee all citizens the same legal capacity to make and enforce contracts, to obtain, own, and convey property, and to litigate and give evidence. Moreover, since the legislative history discloses an intent not to outlaw segregated public schools at that time, it is quite unrealistic to assume that Congress intended the broader result of prohibiting segregated private schools. Were we writing on a clean slate, I would therefore vote to reverse.

But *Jones* has been decided and is now an important part of the fabric of our law. Although I recognize the force of Mr. Justice White's argument that the construction of § 1982 does not control § 1981, it would be most incongruous to give those two sections a fundamentally different construction. . . . I am persuaded, therefore, that we must either apply the rationale of *Jones* or overrule that decision.

There are two reasons which favor overruling. First, as I have already stated, my conviction that *Jones* was wrongly decided is firm. Second, it is extremely unlikely that reliance upon *Jones* has been so extensive that this Court is foreclosed from overruling it. There are, however, opposing arguments of greater force.

The first is the interest in stability and orderly development of the law. As Mr. Justice Cardozo remarked, with respect to the routine work of the judiciary: "The labor of judges would be increased almost to the breaking point if every past decision could be reopened in every case, and one could not lay one's own course of bricks on the secure foundation of the courses laid by others who had gone before him."[2] Turning to the exceptional case, Mr. Justice Cardozo noted: "[W]hen a rule, after it has been duly tested by experience, has been found to be inconsistent with the sense of justice or with the social welfare, there should be less hesitation in frank avowal and full abandonment. . . . If judges have woefully misinterpreted the mores of their day, or if the mores of their day are no longer those of ours, they ought not to tie, in helpless submission, the hands of their successors."[3] In this case, those admonitions favor adherence to, rather than departure from, precedent. For even if *Jones* did not accurately reflect the sentiments of the Reconstruction Congress, it surely accords with the prevailing sense of justice today.

The policy of the nation as formulated by the Congress in recent years has moved constantly in the direction of eliminating racial segregation in all sectors of society. This Court has given a sympathetic and liberal construction to such legislation. For the Court now to overrule *Jones* would be a significant step backwards, with effects that would not have arisen from a correct decision in the first instance. Such a step would be so clearly contrary to my understanding of the mores of today that I think the Court is entirely correct in adhering to *Jones*.

With this explanation, I join the opinion of the Court.

■ MR. JUSTICE WHITE, with whom MR. JUSTICE REHNQUIST joins, dissenting.

We are urged here to extend the meaning and reach of 42 U.S.C. § 1981 so as to establish a general prohibition against a private individual's or institution's refusing to enter into a contract with another person because of the person's race. Section 1981 has been on the books since 1870 and to so hold for the first time would be contrary to the language of the section [and] to its legislative history . . . The majority's belated discovery of a congressional purpose . . . which escaped all . . . federal courts for almost 100 years is singularly unpersuasive.[2] I therefore respectfully dissent.

I

. . . On its face the statute gives "[a]ll persons" (plainly including Negroes) the "*same right* . . . to make . . . contracts . . . as is enjoyed by white citizens." (Emphasis added.) The words "right . . . enjoyed by white citizens" clearly refer to rights existing apart from this statute. Whites had at the time when § 1981 was first enacted, and have (with a few exceptions . . .), no right to make a contract with an unwilling private person, no matter what that person's motivation for refusing to contract.

---

[2] Benjamin Cardozo, The Nature of the Judicial Process 149 (1921).

[3] Id., at 150–52.

[2] I do not question at this point the power of Congress or a state legislature to ban racial discrimination in private school admissions decisions. But as I see it Congress has not yet chosen to exercise that power.

Indeed it is and always has been central to the very concept of a "contract" that there be "assent by the parties who form the contract to the terms thereof," Restatement of Contracts § 19(b) (1932). The right to make contracts, enjoyed by white citizens, was therefore always a right to enter into binding agreements only with willing second parties. Since the statute only gives Negroes the "same rights" to contract as is enjoyed by whites, the language of the statute confers no right on Negroes to enter into a contract with an unwilling person no matter what that person's motivation for refusing to contract. What is conferred by 42 U.S.C. § 1981 is the *right*—which was enjoyed by whites—"to make contracts" with other willing parties and to "enforce" those contracts in court. Section 1981 would thus invalidate any state statute or court-made rule of law which would have the effect of disabling Negroes or any other class of persons from making contracts or enforcing contractual obligations or otherwise giving less weight to their obligations than is given to contractual obligations running to whites. The statute by its terms does not require any private individual or institution to enter into a contract or perform any other act under any circumstances; and it consequently fails to supply a cause of action by . . . students against . . . schools based on the latter's racially motivated decision not to contract with them.[5]

II

The legislative history of 42 U.S.C. § 1981 confirms that the statute means what it says and no more, i.e., that it outlaws any legal rule disabling any person from making or enforcing a contract, but does not prohibit private racially motivated refusals to contract. [Justice White's discussion of the legislative history is omitted. His reading of the history is summarized in the Notes on the Legislative History of § 1981, infra. He concluded:]

Thus the legislative history of § 1981 unequivocally confirms that Congress' purpose in enacting that statute was solely to grant to all persons equal capacity to contract as is enjoyed by whites and included no purpose to prevent private refusals to contract, however motivated.

III

[After further discussion of the legislative history, Justice White observed:]

[A]s a matter of common sense, it would seem extremely unlikely that Congress would have intended—without a word in the legislative history addressed to the precise issue—to pass a statute prohibiting every racially

[5] One of the major issues in this case plainly is whether the construction in Jones v. Alfred H. Mayer Co., 392 U.S. 409 (1968), placed on similar language contained in 42 U.S.C. § 1982 granting all citizens the "same rights to . . . purchase . . . real . . . property" as is enjoyed by white citizens prevents this Court from independently construing the language in 42 U.S.C. § 1981 . . . *Jones v. Alfred H. Mayer Co.* does not so constrict this Court. First, the legislative history of § 1981 is very different from the legislative history of § 1982 so heavily relied on by the Court in *Jones v. Alfred H. Mayer Co.* Second, notwithstanding the dictum in *Jones v. Alfred H. Mayer Co.*, quoted by the majority, even the majority does not contend that the grant of the other rights enumerated in § 1981, i.e., the rights "to sue, be parties, give evidence," and "*enforce* contracts" accomplishes anything other than the removal of *legal* disabilities to sue, be a party, testify or enforce a contract. Indeed it is impossible to give such language any other meaning. Thus, even accepting the *Jones v. Alfred H. Mayer Co.* dictum as applicable to § 1981, the question still would remain whether the right to "make contracts" is to be construed in the same vein as the other "right[s]" included in § 1981 or rather in the same vein as the right to "purchase . . . real property" under § 1982 involved in *Jones v. Alfred H. Mayer Co.*

motivated refusal to contract by a private individual. It is doubtful that all such refusals could be considered badges or incidents of slavery within Congress' proscriptive power under the Thirteenth Amendment. A racially motivated refusal to hire a Negro or a white babysitter or to admit a Negro or a white to a private association cannot be called a badge of slavery—and yet the construction given by the majority to the . . . statute attributes to Congress an intent to proscribe them.

IV

The majority's holding that 42 U.S.C. § 1981 prohibits all racially motivated contractual decisions . . . threatens to embark the judiciary on a treacherous course. Whether such conduct should be condoned or not, whites and blacks will undoubtedly choose to form a variety of associational relationships pursuant to contracts which exclude members of the other race. Social clubs, black and white, and associations designed to further the interests of blacks or whites are but two examples. Lawsuits by members of the other race attempting to gain admittance to such an association are not pleasant to contemplate. As the associational or contractual relationships become more private, the pressures to hold § 1981 inapplicable to them will increase. Imaginative judicial construction of the word "contract" is foreseeable; Thirteenth Amendment limitations on Congress' power to ban "badges and incidents of slavery" may be discovered; the doctrine of the right to association may be bent to cover a given situation. In any event, courts will be called upon to balance sensitive policy considerations against each other—considerations which have never been addressed by any Congress—all under the guise of "construing" a statute. This is a task appropriate for the legislature, not for the judiciary.

Such balancing of considerations as has been done by Congress in the area of racially motivated decisions not to contract with a member of the other race has led it to ban private racial discrimination in most of the job market and most of the housing market and to go no further. The judiciary should not undertake the political task of trying to decide what other areas are appropriate ones for a similar rule. . . .

Accordingly, I would reverse.

NOTES ON THE LEGISLATIVE HISTORY OF § 1981

1. JUSTICE STEWART'S READING OF THE HISTORY

Justice Stewart did not engage in an extensive examination of the legislative history of § 1981 in *Runyon* because he regarded both § 1981 and § 1982 as originating in the language of § 1 of the Civil Rights Act of 1866. This is the conventional view. For Stewart, therefore, *Jones v. Alfred H. Mayer Co.* settled the "state action" issue as to both statutes. Moreover, subsequent decisions by the Supreme Court, as detailed in Stewart's opinion, confirmed this conclusion.

2. JUSTICE WHITE'S READING OF THE HISTORY

Justice White's contrary reading of the history was based on the complicated process of reenacting and codifying §§ 1981 and 1982. Essentially, he would have preserved the holding in *Jones* because § 1982 was reenacted under the Thirteenth Amendment—preserving its coverage of private action—while § 1981 was reenacted under the Fourteenth Amendment—limiting it to state action. This would have allowed him to acknowledge *Jones* as a precedent for property cases, where it did not make much difference, while limiting its implications for contract cases like *Runyon*, where it did. In Justice White's mind, the basis for distinguishing the coverage of the two, otherwise indistinguishable, statutes rested on a marginal note to the Revised Statutes of 1874. How persuasive could an appeal to such a dim source of authority be? By relying upon such marginalia, did Justice White only show how desperate he was to limit the implications of *Jones* by any means, whether plausible or not? Was he right to be alarmed by the implications of *Jones* for later cases like *Runyon*?

3. THE PRACTICAL SIGNIFICANCE OF *JONES* IN *RUNYON*

The practical effects of interpreting § 1981 and § 1982 to reach private discrimination are different. On the facts of *Runyon*, there is no other federal statute, analogous to the Civil Rights Act of 1968 in *Jones*, that prohibits racial discrimination in private schools. Constitutional decisions on school desegregation are confined to public schools because of the state action requirement and, as Justice Stewart acknowledges, other constitutional decisions protect some autonomy interests in private education. After *Runyon*, § 1981 stands alone as the sole federal prohibition against purely private discrimination in private education.

In any event, the scope of § 1981 extends more broadly than § 1982. Section 1981 reaches discrimination in all forms of contracting, not just transactions involving property. Moreover, any contract appears to be covered by the statute, no matter how personal and private, from hiring a babysitter to joining a private club.[a] By far the most important application of § 1981, however, has been to employment, which is the topic of the next principal case.

Johnson v. Railway Express Agency, Inc.

Supreme Court of the United States, 1975.
421 U.S. 454.

■ MR. JUSTICE BLACKMUN delivered the opinion of the Court.

This case presents the issue whether the timely filing of a charge of employment discrimination with the Equal Employment Opportunity Commission (EEOC), pursuant to § 706 of Title VII of the Civil Rights Act of 1964 tolls the running of the period of limitation applicable to an action based on the same facts, instituted under 42 U.S.C. § 1981.

I

Petitioner, Willie Johnson, Jr., is a Negro. He started to work for respondent Railway Express Agency, Inc., now, by change of name, REA Express, Inc. (REA), in Memphis, Tenn., in the spring of 1964 as an express handler. On May 31, 1967, while still employed by REA, but now as a driver rather than as a handler, petitioner, with others, timely filed with the EEOC a charge that REA was discriminating against its Negro employees with respect to seniority rules and job assignments. He also charged the respondent unions, Brotherhood of Railway Clerks Tri–State Local and Brotherhood of Railway Clerks Lily of the Valley Local, with maintaining racially segregated memberships (white and Negro respectively). Three weeks later, on June 20, REA terminated petitioner's employment. Peti-

[a] The application of § 1981 to private clubs has been a continuing source of litigation. See, e.g., Graham v. Leavenworth Country Club, 15 F. Supp. 2d 1062 (D. Kan. 1998).

tioner then amended his charge to include an allegation that he had been discharged because of his race.

The EEOC issued its "Final Investigation Report" on December 22, 1967. The report generally supported petitioner's claims of racial discrimination. It was not until more than two years later, however, on March 31, 1970, that the Commission rendered its decision finding reasonable cause to believe petitioner's charges. And 9½ more months went by before the EEOC, on January 15, 1971, pursuant to 42 U.S.C. § 2000e–5(e) as it then read, gave petitioner notice of his right to institute a Title VII civil action against the respondents within 30 days.

The District Court dismissed the § 1981 claims as barred by Tennessee's one-year statute of limitations. Petitioner's remaining claims were dismissed on other grounds.

In his appeal to the United States Court of Appeals for the Sixth Circuit, petitioner, with respect to his § 1981 claims, argued that the running of the one-year period of limitation was suspended during the pendency of his timely filed administrative complaint with the EEOC under Title VII. The Court of Appeals rejected this argument. [W]e granted certiorari restricted to the limitation issue. . . .

II

A. Title VII of the Civil Rights Act of 1964 was enacted "to assure equality of employment opportunities by eliminating those practices and devices that discriminate on the basis of race, color, religion, sex, or national origin." Alexander v. Gardner–Denver Co., 415 U.S. 36, 44 (1974). It creates statutory rights against invidious discrimination in employment and establishes a comprehensive scheme for the vindication of those rights.

Anyone aggrieved by employment discrimination may lodge a charge with the EEOC. That Commission is vested with the "authority to investigate individual charges of discrimination, to promote voluntary compliance with the requirements of Title VII, and to institute civil actions against employers or unions named in a discrimination charge." Ibid. Thus, the Commission itself may institute a civil action. If, however, the EEOC is not successful in obtaining "voluntary compliance" and, for one reason or another, chooses not to sue on the claimant's behalf, the claimant, after the passage of 180 days, may demand a right-to-sue letter and institute the Title VII action himself without waiting for the completion of the conciliation procedures. . . .

Despite Title VII's range and its design as a comprehensive solution for the problem of invidious discrimination in employment, the aggrieved individual clearly is not deprived of other remedies he possesses and is not limited to Title VII in his search for relief. "[T]he legislative history of Title VII manifests a congressional intent to allow an individual to pursue independently his rights under both Title VII and other applicable state and federal statutes." *Alexander v. Gardner–Denver Co.*, 415 U.S. at 48. In particular, Congress noted "that the remedies available to the individual under Title VII are co-extensive with the individual's right to sue under the provisions of § 1981, and that the two procedures augment each other and are not mutually exclusive." H.R. Rep. No. 92–238, p.19 (1971), U.S. Code Cong. & Admin. News, 1972 at 2137, 2154. Later, in considering the Equal Employment Opportunity Act of 1972, the Senate rejected an amendment that would have deprived a claimant of any right to sue under § 1981. 118 Cong. Rec. 3371–73 (1972).

B. Title 42 U.S.C. § 1981, being the present codification of § 16 of the century-old Civil Rights Act of 1870, on the other hand, on its face relates primarily to racial discrimination in the making and enforcement of contracts. Although this Court has not specifically so held, it is well settled among the federal Courts of Appeals—and we now join them—that § 1981 affords a federal remedy against discrimination in private employment on the basis of race. An individual who establishes a cause of action under § 1981 is entitled to both equitable and legal relief, including compensatory and, under certain circumstances, punitive damages. And a backpay award under § 1981 is not restricted to the two years specified for backpay recovery under Title VII.

Section 1981 is not coextensive in its coverage with Title VII. The latter is made inapplicable to certain employers. Also, Title VII offers assistance in investigation, conciliation, counsel, waiver of court costs, and attorneys' fees, items that are unavailable at least under the specific terms of § 1981.[a]

III

Petitioner, and the United States as amicus curiae, concede, as they must, the independence of the avenues of relief respectively available under Title VII and the older § 1981. See Jones v. Alfred H. Mayer Co., 392 U.S. 409, 416. Further, it has been noted that the filing of a Title VII charge and resort to Title VII's administrative machinery are not prerequisites for the institution of a § 1981 action. [Citations to lower court cases omitted.]

We are satisfied, also, that Congress did not expect that a § 1981 court action usually would be resorted to only upon completion of Title VII procedures and the Commission's efforts to obtain voluntary compliance. Conciliation and persuasion through the administrative process, to be sure, often constitute a desirable approach to settlement of disputes based on sensitive and emotional charges of invidious employment discrimination. We recognize, too, that the filing of a lawsuit might tend to deter efforts at conciliation, that lack of success in the legal action could weaken the Commission's efforts to induce voluntary compliance, and that a suit is privately oriented and narrow, rather than broad, in application, as successful conciliation tends to be. But these are the natural effects of the choice Congress has made available to the claimant by its conferring upon him independent administrative and judicial remedies. The choice is a valuable one. Under some circumstances, the administrative route may be highly preferred over the litigatory; under others the reverse may be true. We are disinclined, in the face of congressional emphasis upon the existence and independence of the two remedies, to infer any positive preference for one over the other, without a more definite expression in the legislation Congress has enacted, as, for example, a proscription of a § 1981 action while an EEOC claim is pending.

We generally conclude, therefore, that the remedies available under Title VII and under § 1981, although related, and although directed to most of the same ends, are separate, distinct, and independent. With this base established, we turn to the limitation issue.

[a] Attorneys' fees first became available in § 1981 suits in the Civil Rights Attorneys' Fees Award Act of 1976.—[Footnote by eds.]

IV

A. Since there is no specifically stated or otherwise relevant federal statute of limitations for a cause of action under § 1981, the controlling period would ordinarily be the most appropriate one provided by state law. For purposes of this case, the one-year limitation period in Tenn. Code Ann. § 28–304 (Supp.1974) clearly and specifically has application. The cause of action asserted by petitioner accrued if at all, not later than June 20, 1967, the date of his discharge. Therefore, in the absence of some circumstance that suspended the running of the limitation period, petitioner's cause of action under § 1981 was time barred after June 20, 1968, over 2½ years before petitioner filed his complaint.

B. Respondents argue that the only circumstances that would suspend or toll the running of the limitation period under § 28–304 are those expressly provided under state law. Petitioner concedes, at least implicitly, that no tolling circumstance described in the State's statutes was present to toll the period for his § 1981 claim. . . .

C. Although state law is our primary guide in this area, it is not, to be sure, our exclusive guide. [C]onsiderations of state law may be displaced where their application would be inconsistent with the federal policy underlying the cause of action under consideration.

Petitioner argues that a failure to toll the limitation period in this case will conflict seriously with the broad remedial and humane purposes of Title VII. Specifically, he urges that Title VII embodies a strong federal policy in support of conciliation and voluntary compliance as a means of achieving the statutory mandate of equal employment opportunity. He suggests that failure to toll the statute on a § 1981 claim during the pendency of an administrative complaint in the EEOC would force a plaintiff into premature and expensive litigation that would destroy all chances for administrative conciliation and voluntary compliance.

[I]t is conceivable, and perhaps almost to be expected, that failure to toll will have the effect of pressing a civil rights complainant who values his § 1981 claim into court before the EEOC has completed its administrative proceeding. One answer to this, although perhaps not a highly satisfactory one, is that the plaintiff in his § 1981 suit may ask the court to stay proceedings until the administrative efforts at conciliation and voluntary compliance have been completed. But the fundamental answer to petitioner's argument lies in the fact—presumably a happy one for the civil rights claimant—that Congress clearly has retained § 1981 as a remedy against private employment discrimination separate from and independent of the more elaborate and time-consuming procedures of Title VII. Petitioner freely concedes that he could have filed his § 1981 action at any time after his cause of action accrued; in fact, we understand him to claim an unfettered right so to do. Thus, in a very real sense, petitioner has slept on his § 1981 rights. The fact that his slumber may have been induced by faith in the adequacy of his Title VII remedy is of little relevance inasmuch as the two remedies are truly independent. Moreover, since petitioner's Title VII court action now also appears to be time barred because of the peculiar procedural history of this case, petitioner, in effect, would have us extend the § 1981 cause of action well beyond the life of even his Title VII cause of action. We find no policy reason that excuses petitioner's failure to take the minimal steps necessary to preserve each claim independently. . . .

The judgment of the Court of Appeals is affirmed. . . .

■ MR. JUSTICE MARSHALL, with whom MR. JUSTICE DOUGLAS and MR. JUSTICE BRENNAN join, concurring in part and dissenting in part.

In recognizing that Congress intended to supply aggrieved employees with independent but related avenues of relief under Title VII of the Civil Rights Act of 1964 and § 1981, the Court emphasizes the importance of a full arsenal of weapons to combat unlawful employment discrimination in the private as well as the public sector. The majority stands on firm ground in recognizing that both remedies are available to victims of discriminatory practices. Accordingly, I concur in Parts I–III of the Court's opinion.

But, the Court stumbles in its analysis of the relation between the two statutes on the tolling question. The majority concludes that the filing of a Title VII charge with the Equal Employment Opportunity Commission (EEOC) does not toll the applicable statute of limitations. It relies exclusively on state law for the period and effect of the limitation and discounts the importance of the federal policies of conciliation and avoidance of unnecessary litigation in this area. The majority recognizes these policies but concludes that tolling the statute of limitations for a § 1981 suit during the pendency of Title VII proceedings is not an appropriate means of furthering them. I disagree. The congressional purpose of discouraging premature judicial intervention and the absence of any real risk of reviving stale claims suggest the propriety of tolling here. On balance, I view the failure to apply the tolling principle as undermining the foundation of Title VII and frustrating the congressional policy of providing alternative remedies. I must, therefore, dissent from [the remainder] of the opinion. . . .

Simply stated, we must determine whether the national policy considerations favoring the continued availability of the § 1981 cause of action outweigh the interests protected by the State's statute of limitations.

I

. . . Forced compliance with a short statute of limitations during the pendency of a charge before the EEOC would discourage and/or frustrate recourse to the congressionally favored policy of conciliation. . . . [The] EEOC's ability to conciliate complaints is frustrated by the majority's requirement that an employee file the § 1981 action prior to the conclusion of the Title VII conciliation efforts in order to avoid the bar of the statute of limitations. Legislative pains to avoid unnecessary and costly litigation by making the informal investigatory and conciliatory offices of the EEOC readily available to victims of unlawful discrimination cannot be squared with the formal mechanistic requirement of early filing for the technical purpose of tolling a limitations statute. In sum, the federal policies weigh strongly in favor of tolling.

II

Examination of the purposes served by the statute of limitations indicates that they would not be frustrated by adoption of the tolling rule. Statutes of limitations are designed to insure fairness to defendants by preventing the revival of stale claims in which the defense is hampered by lost evidence, faded memories, and disappearing witnesses, and to avoid unfair surprise. None of these factors exists here.

Respondents were informed of the petitioner's grievances through the complaint filed with the Commission and conciliation negotiations. The charge filed with the EEOC and the § 1981 claim arise out of the same factual circumstances. The petitioner in this case diligently pursued the informal procedures before the Commission and adhered to the congressional preference for conciliation prior to litigation. Now, when Johnson asserts his right to proceed with litigation under § 1981 after his good-faith, albeit unnecessary, compliance with Title VII procedures, the majority interposes the bar of the Tennessee statute of limitations which clearly was not designed to include such cases.

In my judgment, following the antitolling position of the Court to its logical conclusion produces an inequitable result. Aggrieved employees will be forced into simultaneously prosecuting premature § 1981 actions in the federal courts. In essence, the litigant who first explores conciliation prior to resort to litigation must file a duplicative claim in the district court on which the court will either take no action until the Title VII proceedings are concluded or proceed in frustration of the EEOC attempts to conciliate. No federal policy considerations warrant this waste of judicial time and derogation of the conciliation process.

Adoption of the tolling principle, however, protects the federal interest in both preserving multiple remedies for employment discrimination and in the proper function of the limitations statute. As a normal consequence tolling works to suspend the operation of a statute of limitations during the pendency of an event or condition. . . . The federal policy in favor of continuing availability of multiple remedies for persons subject to employment discrimination is inconsistent with the majority's decision not to suspend the operation of the statute. As long as the claim arising under § 1981 is essentially limited to the Title VII claim, staleness and unfair surprise disappear as justification for applying the statute.[3] Additionally, the difference in statutory origin for the right asserted under the EEOC charge and the subsequent § 1981 suit is of no consequence since the claims are essentially equivalent in substance. Since the EEOC charge gives notice that petitioner also has a grievance under § 1981, that filing . . . satisfied the equitable policies underlying the limitation provision.

Neither the legislative history of these acts nor the avowed purposes of statutes of limitations foreclose good-faith resort to the administrative procedures of the EEOC. Adoption of the tolling theory avoids the Draconian choice of losing the benefits of conciliation or giving up the right to sue, yet preserves the independent nature of the § 1981 action. Accordingly, I would reverse the court below on this point.

NOTES ON JOHNSON V. RAILWAY EXPRESS AGENCY, INC.

1. THE DECISION AND ITS ASSUMPTIONS

In its broadest terms, *Johnson v. Railway Express Agency, Inc.* concerns the question of how § 1981 is related to Title VII of the Civil Rights Act of 1964. On this broad question, the Court's opinion is more important for what it assumes than for what it decides. Title VII (codified in 42 U.S.C. §§ 2000e et seq.) is the principal modern civil rights statute prohibiting discrimination in employment. It covers both public and private employment and prohibits discrimination on the basis of race, national origin, sex, and religion. In *Johnson*, the Court assumed that § 1981 provides a cause of action for employment discrimination entirely independent of Title VII. This assumption was not strictly necessary to the Court's decision, since the Court denied any relief to the plain-

[3] Where there are differences between the § 1981 claim and the Title VII complaint, the district courts could easily limit the tolling to those portions of the § 1981 claim that overlapped the Title VII allegations.

tiff under § 1981. The actual decision in the case is therefore confined to the statute of limitations under § 1981 and, in particular, to the narrow question whether the running of the statute of limitations is tolled while a charge of discrimination is pending under Title VII.

2. TITLE VII OF THE CIVIL RIGHTS ACT OF 1964

Despite the seeming technicality of the statute of limitations question actually decided in *Johnson*, the case raises fundamental issues about the relationship between Reconstruction legislation and modern civil rights acts. These issues first appeared in *Jones v. Alfred H. Mayer Co.*, where the relationship between § 1982 and the Civil Rights Act of 1968 formed the background to the decision, but have proved far more significant in the relationship between § 1981 and Title VII. In order to appreciate the relationship between these two statutes, it is first necessary to understand the basic provisions of Title VII.

In contrast to § 1981, Title VII is an elaborate and complicated statute with provisions defining what it prohibits and specifying how it is enforced. These diverge at many points from the law under § 1981. As a matter of substantive law, Title VII is both broader and narrower than § 1981. It is broader in that it extends to grounds of discrimination not covered by § 1981, such as sex and religion, and it extends to some practices, such as advertising and training programs, that need not involve enforceable contracts. In addition, Title VII prohibits practices with discriminatory effects, not just those with discriminatory intent.[a] Under the theory of disparate impact, Title VII prohibits neutral employment practices with a disproportionate adverse impact upon groups, such as a racial minorities, when those practices cannot be justified as "job related for the position in question and consistent with business necessity." 42 U.S.C. § 2000e–2(k)(1). In other respects, Title VII is narrower than § 1981. It covers employers only with 15 or more employees and it has various exceptions and special provisions for employment practices such as seniority systems, tests, and affirmative action plans.

As a matter of procedure and remedies, Title VII creates a far more complicated scheme than the simple private action for damages and equitable relief available under § 1981. A plaintiff must first exhaust administrative remedies in order to sue under Title VII. This requires filing a charge with the Equal Employment Opportunity Commission (EEOC), and if an appropriate state or local agency enforces a law against employment discrimination, with that agency as well. In a typical case, the plaintiff's charge must be filed with the EEOC within 300 days of the alleged discrimination and the EEOC must then defer action on the charge for 60 days to give a state or local agency an opportunity to act. After this period expires, the EEOC investigates the charge, and if it finds reasonable cause to support it, engages in efforts at conciliation to resolve the charge. The EEOC and the Department of Justice also have authority to sue. In any case in which they do not, an individual can take the case to court, whether or not the EEOC has found reasonable cause to support the charge of discrimination. All actions must be filed within 90 days of the individual's receipt of a "right-to-sue letter" from the EEOC. Once in court, a plaintiff can seek equitable relief in the form of an injunction and recovery of back-

[a] General Building Contractors Association, Inc. v. Pennsylvania, 458 U.S. 375 (1982), which is discussed in the notes following the next main case, held that § 1981 requires a finding of discriminatory intent and does not base liability only on proof of discriminatory effects.

pay. Compensatory damages are not available and the parties are not entitled to a jury trial in a pure Title VII case.

Johnson v. Railway Express Agency, Inc. addresses both the procedural and the remedial restrictions on Title VII claims. The Court assumes that damages and the attendant right to jury trial are available under § 1981 despite their absence under Title VII. Although the Court passes over these issues briefly, they proved to be very important in the development of remedies for sex discrimination. This form of discrimination is not covered by § 1981, so that plaintiffs alleging sex discrimination in employment originally were restricted to the equitable remedies under Title VII and could not recover damages. This discrepancy in the treatment of sex-and race-based discrimination was eliminated with passage of the Civil Rights Act of 1991, summarized in a set of notes after the next main case.

3. THE STATUTE OF LIMITATIONS ISSUE

The precise holding in *Johnson v. Railway Express Agency, Inc.* was that the statute of limitations applicable to a § 1981 claim was not tolled while the plaintiff exhausted administrative remedies under Title VII. The Court's rationale was that "Congress clearly has retained § 1981 as a remedy against private employment discrimination separate from and independent of the more elaborate and time-consuming procedures of Title VII." Does this make sense? Should each statute be interpreted and applied without regard to the other?

As applied to the statute of limitations, the Court's principle of independence of remedies left the normally applicable state law in place because Title VII supplied no overriding federal policy. Justice Marshall argues in dissent that tolling the statute of limitations under § 1981 is necessary to preserve the policies favoring administrative resolution of claims through investigation and conciliation under Title VII. Otherwise, plaintiffs are forced to file their § 1981 claims before they have exhausted their administrative remedies under Title VII. Do policies favoring administrative resolution of claims have any place in the interpretation of § 1981? Is tolling the statute of limitations the best way to implement these policies? Would it be better to stay the litigation of § 1981 claims in appropriate cases? Or should the two remedies be allowed to proceed with complete independence? Bear in mind that the statute of limitations under Title VII, involving time limits for exhausting state and federal administrative remedies and then for filing in court, already is exceedingly complex.

Does it matter to the debate between the Court and Justice Marshall that Congress enacted Title VII before *Jones v. Alfred H. Mayer Co.* interpreted § 1982, and by implication § 1981, to prohibit private discrimination? Of what relevance is the Court's observation that Congress later considered and rejected an amendment that would have prevented Title VII plaintiffs from suing under § 1981? The choice presented to Congress was all-or-nothing: either preserve § 1981 as a remedy for employment discrimination or repeal it. The question presented in *Johnson* was different: whether to interpret the statutes independently or to integrate their procedures. Is the Congressional inaction therefore irrelevant to the issues before the Court?

Legislation subsequent to *Johnson v. Railway Express Agency, Inc.* has complicated the analysis of the appropriate statute of limitations applicable to claims under § 1981. A new federal catch-all statute of limitations, 28 U.S.C. § 1658, creates a four-year limitation period for claims under federal statutes enacted after 1990 if those statutes do not themselves contain a limitation period. In Jones v. R.R. Donnelley & Sons Co., 541 U.S. 369 (2004), the Supreme Court held that some, but not all, claims under § 1981 were governed by this new four-year limitation period. In particular, this new limitation period applies to claims for "performance, modification, and termination of contracts" that were not recognized before a new § 1981(b) was added to the statute by the Civil Rights Act of 1991. These claims arise under a statute enacted after 1990 and so are governed by the new federal statute of limitations, but previously recognized claims under § 1981 continue to be governed by the appropriate state statute of limitations.

NOTES ON PATTERSON V. MCLEAN CREDIT UNION *AND THE CIVIL RIGHTS ACT OF 1991*

1. *PATTERSON V. MCLEAN CREDIT UNION*

Brenda Patterson, an African–American woman, was employed by the McLean Credit Union as a teller and file coordinator for 10 years. After she was laid off, she sued McLean under § 1981, alleging that because of her race she had been harassed on the job, refused a promotion, and finally discharged. The District Court held that racial harassment was not actionable under § 1981. The failure-to-promote and discharge allegations were tried to a jury, which found for McLean.

The Court of Appeals affirmed and the Supreme Court granted certiorari. After oral argument on the issues decided by the lower courts, the Court requested that the parties brief and argue an additional question: "Whether or not the interpretation of 42 U.S.C. § 1981 adopted by this Court in Runyon v. McCrary, 427 U.S. 160 (1976), should be reconsidered." The decision to order reargument on this additional question created considerable controversy within the Court, prompting four justices to dissent in two separate opinions. Patterson v. McLean Credit Union, 485 U.S. 617, 619 (1988) (Blackmun, J., dissenting); id. at 621 (Stevens, J., dissenting). However, in the end, the Court was unanimous that *Runyon* should not be overruled. Justice Kennedy wrote the majority opinion, reasoning that "[c]onsiderations of stare decisis have special force in the area of statutory interpretation, for here, unlike in the context of constitutional interpretation, the legislative power is implicated, and Congress remains free to alter what we have done." Patterson v. McLean Credit Union, 491 U.S. 164 (1989).

Although the Court was unanimous on the continued vitality of *Runyon*, it divided sharply over the question whether Patterson's harassment claim fell within the scope of § 1981. Justice Kennedy pointed out that the statute spoke to the right to "make and enforce contracts" free of racial discrimination. The issue was whether harassment on the job affected the "making" and "enforcing" of contracts of employment. He said that it did not because making a contract "extends only to the formation of a contract" and enforcing a contract covers only "protection of a legal process and of a right of access to legal process." Harassment in performing a contract fell between these two endpoints and therefore outside the coverage of the statute. Justice Brennan, joined by three other justices, dissented from this holding.

Justice Kennedy noted, however, that Patterson's promotion claim was "a different matter" because "it involved the opportunity to enter into a new contract with the employer." Justice Kennedy also addressed the allocation of the burden of proof. The Court was again unanimous on this issue, concluding that the District Court erred in instructing the jury "that petitioner could carry her burden of persuasion only by showing that she was in fact better qualified than the white applicant who got the job." In an employment discrimination case, a plaintiff can carry the burden of proving that the defendant's offered reason is a pretext for racial discrimination by presenting a variety of different kinds of evidence, including evidence of past racial harassment. Although, as the Court had previously held, such evidence would not itself support an independent claim under § 1981, it could be used to support an inference of discrimination in promotions.

2. THE CIVIL RIGHTS ACT OF 1991

The Civil Rights Act of 1991 contained a comprehensive set of amendments to the laws against employment discrimination, including both § 1981 and Title VII. In amending § 1981, the act moved the pre-existing statute to subsection (a) and added two new subsections, (b) and (c).[a] Section 1981(b) was designed to overrule the holding in *Patterson* that claims of racial harassment fell outside the scope of the statute. It states that the phrase "make and enforce contracts" includes "the making, performance, modification, and termination of contracts, and the enjoyment of all benefits, privileges, terms, and conditions of the contractual relationship." This change was intended to extend the statutory bar beyond discrimination in hiring to on-the-job racial harassment.[b]

Section 1981(c) addressed another holding in *Patterson*, but by ratifying it instead of overruling it. This subsection was intended to settle, once and for all, the question whether § 1981 covers private discrimination. It declares that "[t]he rights protected by this section are protected against impairment by nongovernmental discrimination and impairment under color of State law."

On balance, do these amendments vindicate the Court's interpretation of § 1981 and § 1982, stretching back to the original decision in *Jones v. Alfred H. Mayer Co.*? Note that the Civil Rights Act of 1991 did not make any change in § 1982. Does the application of that statute to private discrimination now stand on weaker ground than the application of § 1981? Did the Court just guess right about what Congress would subsequently do in considering § 1981 as a prohibition against private discrimination?

On the narrower question of coverage of racial harassment, the Court in *Patterson* did not anticipate the reaction of Congress, which overruled its decision in this respect. And, in fact, the Civil Rights Act of 1991 overruled several other decisions of the Supreme Court that had offered a narrow interpretation of Title VII. Does this mixed record indicate that the Supreme Court should just ignore the likely reaction of Congress to its decisions? Or does it confirm the position of those justices who consistently argued for a broad interpretation of the civil rights laws? What does this tell us about the interaction between judicial interpretation of statutes and subsequent legislative amendments? One

---

[a] In a somewhat confusing exercise in codification, the act also added an entirely new statute, § 1981a, which expanded the remedies available under Title VII and other statutes prohibiting employment discrimination. Section 1981a is discussed in the next chapter of this book, but its provisions must be sharply distinguished from those of § 1981(a).

[b] In Rivers v. Roadway Express, Inc., 511 U.S. 298 (1994), the Court held that the changes made to § 1981 were not retroactive and therefore did not apply to cases that arose before its enactment.

leading scholar, now a federal judge, has argued that courts should take the opportunity for statutory interpretation to initiate a dialogue with the legislature about the proper meaning and application of statutes previously enacted. Guido Calabresi, A Common Law for the Age of Statutes (1982). Has this process improved and clarified the scope of § 1981? How should it influence future decisions on the scope of the statute?

The Civil Rights Act of 1991 also raised other questions about the scope of § 1981. Some courts have suggested that a contract of employment terminable-at-will does not support a claim for discriminatory discharge under § 1981, because it does not impose any restriction on either party's power to terminate the employment relationship while others have rejected this reasoning on the common-sense ground that a contract terminable at will is still a contract. See Harry Hutchinson, The Collision of Employment-at-Will, Section 1981 & *Gonzalez*: Discharge, Consent and Contract Sufficiency, 3 U. Pa. J. Lab. & Empl. L. 207 (2001); Joanna L. Grossman, Making a Federal Case Out of It: Section 1981 and At–Will Employment, 67 Brook. L. Rev. 329 (2001).

Another unresolved issue is whether the Civil Rights Acts of 1991 creates a cause of action for private violations of the "equal benefit clause" in the original version of § 1981. This clause was a statutory predecessor of the Equal Protection Clause of the Fourteenth Amendment. It is now found in § 1981(a) and it is now protected from "impairment by nongovernmental discrimination" by § 1981(c). Does this mean that Congress has effectively repealed the state action requirement as it applies to some aspects of the Equal Protection Clause? Does it have the power to do so? See George Rutherglen, The Improbable History of Section 1981: Clio Still Bemused and Confused, 2003 Sup. Ct. Rev. 303, 303–04, 347–48; Jeremy Deese, Case Note: Civil Rights—42 U.S.C. Section 1981—Scope of the Equal Benefit Clause, 71 Tenn. L. Rev. 199 (2003).

For other discussion of the scope of private action prohibited by § 1981, see Anne–Marie G. Harris, Shopping While Black: Applying 42 U.S.C. Section 1981 to Cases of Consumer Racial Profiling, 23 B.C. Third World L.J. 1 (2003); Florence Wagman Roisman, The Impact of the Civil Rights Act of 1866 on Racially Discriminatory Donative Transfers, 53 Ala. L. Rev. 463 (2002).

3. *CBOCS V. HUMPHRIES*

In CBOCS v. Humphries, 553 U.S. 442 (2008), the Supreme Court recognized claims of retaliation under § 1981, relying upon a "well-embedded interpretation" of the statute. The plaintiff alleged that he had been dismissed because of his race and because he had complained about racial discrimination against another employee. Addressing only the second of these claims, the Court held that claims of retaliation had been recognized under § 1982, the companion statute to § 1981, in Sullivan v. Little Hunting Park, Inc., 396 U.S. 229 (1969). These two statutes are construed similarly because they share a common origin in the Civil Rights Act of 1866. Although *Patterson* cast doubt on the application of § 1981 to claims of discrimination in the course of employment, that decision was superseded by the Civil Rights Act of 1991. That act added subsection (b) to § 1981, which provides for coverage of discrimination in the "making, performance, modification, and termination of contracts, and the enjoyment of all benefits, privileges, terms, and conditions of the contractual relationship." The Court took this statutory language to reinstate the law as it existed before *Patterson* and to cover claims of retaliation that arose in the course of the employment relationship. Justices Thomas and Scalia dissented on the ground that the literal terms of § 1981 still do not contain an explicit prohibition against retaliation, as does Title VII.

4. BIBLIOGRAPHY

The prospect that *Runyon* might be overruled provoked numerous contributions to the literature. For a sample, see Theodore Eisenberg and Stewart Schwab, The Importance of Section 1981, 73 Corn. L. Rev. 596 (1988); Robert Kaczorowski, The Enforcement Provisions of the Civil Rights Act of 1866: A Legislative History in Light of *Runyon v. McCrary,* 98 Yale L.J. 565 (1989); Barry Sullivan, Historical Reconstruction, Reconstruction History, and the Proper Scope of Section 1981, 98 Yale L.J. 541 (1989); Symposium: *Patterson v. McLean,* 87 Mich.L.Rev. 1 (1988) (containing a series of articles focusing on the stare decisis issue).

By contrast, the amendments to § 1981 made by the Civil Rights Act of 1991 have not been specifically discussed, but assimilated to the overall effect of the act on changing doctrine also under Title VII. See The Civil Rights Act of 1991: A Symposium, 54 La. L. Rev. 1459 (1994) (with articles by Roger Clegg, Glen D. Nager, Julia M. Broas, C. Boyden Gray, John O. McGinnis, R. Gaull Silberman, Susan E. Murphy, Susan P. Adams, and Nelson Lund); Symposium: The Civil Rights Act of 1991: Unraveling the Controversy, 45 Rutgers L. Rev. 887 (1993) (with articles by Alfred A. Slocum, Alfred W. Blumrosen, Robert Belton, Jerome McCristal Culp, Jr., Rosemary Alito, Peter M. Leibold, Stephen A. Sola, and Reginald E. Jones); Symposium: The Civil Rights Act of 1991: Theory and Practice, 68 Notre Dame L. Rev. 911 (1993) (with articles by Douglas W. Kmiec, Ronald D. Rotunda, Neal Devins, Jules B. Gerard, Marian C. Haney, Glen D. Nager, Eric Schnapper, and Michael Carvin).

McDonald v. Santa Fe Trail Transportation Co.

Supreme Court of the United States, 1976.
427 U.S. 273.

■ MR. JUSTICE MARSHALL delivered the opinion of the Court.

Petitioners, L. N. McDonald and Raymond L. Laird, brought this action in the United States District Court for the Southern District of Texas seeking relief against Santa Fe Trail Transportation Co. (Santa Fe) . . . for alleged violations of the Civil Rights Act of 1866, 42 U.S.C. § 1981, and of Title VII of the Civil Rights Act of 1964, 42 U.S.C. § 2000e Et seq., in connection with their discharge from Santa Fe's employment. [W]e must decide, first, whether a complaint alleging that white employees charged with misappropriating property from their employer were dismissed from employment, while a black employee similarly charged was not dismissed, states a claim under Title VII. Second, we must decide whether § 1981, which provides that "[a]ll persons . . . shall have the same right . . . to make and enforce contracts . . . as is enjoyed by white citizens" affords protection from racial discrimination in private employment to white persons as well as nonwhites.

I

Because the District Court dismissed this case on the pleadings, we take as true the material facts alleged in petitioners' complaint. On September 26, 1970, petitioners, both white, and Charles Jackson, a Negro employee of Santa Fe, were jointly and severally charged with misappropriating 60 one-gallon cans of antifreeze which was part of a shipment Santa Fe was carrying for one of its customers. Six days later, petitioners were fired by Santa Fe, while Jackson was retained. . . . The following April, complaints were filed with the Equal Employment Opportunity Commission (EEOC) charging that Santa Fe had discriminated against both petitioners on the basis of their race in firing them . . . in violation of Title VII of the Civil Rights Act of 1964. Agency process proved . . . unavailing for petitioners, however, and the EEOC notified them in July 1971 of their right under the Act to initiate a civil action in district court within 30 days. This suit followed, petitioners joining their § 1981 claim to their Title VII allegations.

[T]he District Court [dismissed] petitioners' claims under both Title VII and § 1981. . . . [T]he District Court determined that § 1981 is wholly inapplicable to racial discrimination against white persons, and dismissed the claim for want of jurisdiction. Turning . . . to petitioners' claims under Title VII, the District Court concluded . . . that "the dismissal of white employees charged with misappropriating company property while not dismissing a similarly charged Negro employee does not raise a claim upon which Title VII relief may be granted."

The Court of Appeals affirmed the dismissal. . . . We granted certiorari. We reverse.

II

Title VII of the Civil Rights Act of 1964 prohibits the discharge of "any individual" because of "such individual's race," § 703(a)(1), 42 U.S.C. § 2000e–2(a)(1). Its terms are not limited to discrimination against members of any particular race. Thus, although we were not there confronted with racial discrimination against whites, we described the Act in Griggs v. Duke Power Co., 401 U.S. 424, 431 (1971), as prohibiting "[d]iscriminatory preference for any [racial] group, *minority or majority*" (emphasis added). Similarly the EEOC, whose interpretations are entitled to great deference, has consistently interpreted Title VII to proscribe racial discrimination in private employment against whites on the same terms as racial discrimination against nonwhites, holding that to proceed otherwise would "constitute a derogation of the Commission's Congressional mandate to eliminate all practices which operate to disadvantage the employment opportunities of any group protected by Title VII, including Caucasians." EEOC Decision No. 74–31, 7 FEP 1326, 1328 (1973). This conclusion is in accord with uncontradicted legislative history to the effect that Title VII was intended to "cover white men and white women and all Americans," 110 Cong. Rec. 2578 (1964) (remarks of Rep. Celler), and create an "obligation not to discriminate against whites," id. at 7218 (memorandum of Sen. Clark). We therefore hold today that Title VII prohibits racial discrimination against the white petitioners in this case upon the same standards as would be applicable were they Negroes and Jackson white[8]. . . .

---

[8] . . . Santa Fe disclaims that the actions challenged here were any part of an affirmative action program and we emphasize that we do not consider here the permissibility of such a program, whether judicially required or otherwise prompted.

Respondents contend that, even though generally applicable to white persons, Title VII affords petitioners no protection in this case, because their dismissal was based upon their commission of a serious criminal offense against their employer. . . . Fairly read, the complaint asserted that petitioners were discharged for their alleged participation in a misappropriation of cargo entrusted to Santa Fe, but that a fellow employee, likewise implicated, was not so disciplined, and that the reason for the discrepancy in discipline was that the favored employee is Negro while petitioners are white. While Santa Fe may decide that participation in a theft of cargo may render an employee unqualified for employment, this criterion must be "applied, alike to members of all races," and Title VII is violated if, as petitioners alleged, it was not.

. . . The Act prohibits *all* racial discrimination in employment, without exception for any group of particular employees, and while crime or other misconduct may be a legitimate basis for discharge, it is hardly one for racial discrimination. . . . It may be that theft of property . . . is a . . . compelling basis for discharge . . . but this does not diminish the illogic in retaining guilty employees of one color while discharging those of another color. . . .

III

Title 42 U.S.C. § 1981 provides in pertinent part: "All persons within the jurisdiction of the United States shall have the same right in every State and Territory to make and enforce contracts . . . as is enjoyed by white citizens." We have previously held, where discrimination against Negroes was in question, that § 1981 affords a federal remedy against discrimination in private employment on the basis of race, and respondents do not contend otherwise. The question here is whether § 1981 prohibits racial discrimination in private employment against whites as well as nonwhites.

While neither of the courts below elaborated its reasons for not applying § 1981 to racial discrimination against white persons, respondents suggest two lines of argument to support that judgment. First, they argue that by operation of the phrase "as is enjoyed by white citizens," § 1981 unambiguously limits itself to the protection of nonwhite persons against racial discrimination. Second, they contend that such a reading is consistent with the legislative history of the provision, which derives its operative language from § 1 of the Civil Rights Act of 1866. The 1866 statute, they assert, was concerned predominantly with assuring specified civil rights to the former Negro slaves freed by virtue of the Thirteenth Amendment, and not at all with protecting the corresponding civil rights of white persons.

We find neither argument persuasive. Rather, our examination of the language and history of § 1981 convinces us that § 1981 is applicable to racial discrimination in private employment against white persons.

First, we cannot accept the view that the terms of § 1981 exclude its application to racial discrimination against white persons. On the contrary, the statute explicitly applies to "*all* persons" (emphasis added), including white persons. While a mechanical reading of the phrase "as is enjoyed by white citizens" would seem to lend support to respondents' reading of the statute, we have previously described this phrase simply as emphasizing "the racial character of the rights being protected," Georgia v. Rachel, 384 U.S. 780, 791 (1966). In any event, whatever ambiguity there may be in the language of § 1981, is clarified by an examination of the legislative history of § 1981's language as it was originally forged in the Civil Rights Act of 1866. It is to this subject that we now turn.

The bill ultimately enacted as the Civil Rights Act of 1866 was introduced by Senator Trumbull of Illinois as a "bill . . . to protect *all* persons in the United States in their civil rights" (emphasis added), and was initially described by him as applying to "every race and color." Cong. Globe, 39th Cong., 1st Sess., 211 (1866) (hereinafter Cong. Globe). Consistent with the views of its draftsman,[17] and the prevailing view in the Congress as to the reach of its powers under the enforcement section of the Thirteenth Amendment, the terms of the bill prohibited any racial discrimination in the making and enforcement of contracts against whites as well as nonwhites. Its first section provided:

> That there shall be no discrimination in civil rights or immunities among the inhabitants of any State or Territory of the United States on account of race, color, or previous condition of slavery, but the inhabitants of every race and color, without regard to any previous condition of slavery or involuntary servitude, . . . shall have the same right to make and enforce contracts, to sue, be parties, and give evidence, to inherit, purchase, lease, sell, hold, and convey real and personal property, and to full and equal benefit of all laws and proceedings for the security of person and property, and shall be subject to like punishment, pains, and penalties, and to none other, any law, statute, ordinance, regulation, or custom, to the contrary notwithstanding.

Cong. Globe, p. 211. While it is, of course, true that the immediate impetus for the bill was the necessity for further relief of the constitutionally emancipated former Negro slaves, the general discussion of the scope of the bill did not circumscribe its broad language to that limited goal. On the contrary, the bill was routinely viewed, by its opponents and supporters alike, as applying to the civil rights of whites as well as nonwhites.[20] The point was most directly focused on in the closing debate in the Senate. During that debate, in response to the argument of Senator Davis of Kentucky that by providing for the punishment of racial discrimination in its enforcement section, § 2, the bill extended to Negroes a protection never afforded whites, Senator Trumbull said:

> Sir, *this bill applies to white men as well as black men.* It declares that all persons in the United States shall be entitled to the same civil rights, the right to the fruit of their own labor, the right to make contracts, the right to buy and sell, and enjoy liberty and happiness; and

---

[17] Cf. Cong. Globe 474:

> I take it that any statute which is not equal to all, and which deprives any citizen of civil rights which are secured to other citizens, is an unjust encroachment upon his liberty; and is, in fact, a badge of servitude which, by the Constitution, is prohibited.

[20] See, e.g., Cong. Globe, p. 504 (remarks of Sen. Howard, a supporter: "[The bill] simply gives to persons who are of different races or colors the same civil rights"); p. 505 (remarks of Sen. Johnson, an opponent: "[T]he white as well as the black is included in this first section . . . "); p. 601 (remarks of Sen. Hendricks, an opponent: "[The bill] provides, in the first place, that the civil rights of *all* men, without regard to color, shall be equal." (Emphasis added.)

Respondents reasonably assert that references to the bill's placing Negroes' and whites' civil rights "upon precisely the same footing," p. 604 (remarks of Sen. Cowan, an opponent), and similar remarks might be read consistently either with the position that the measure was solely for relief of nonwhites, or with the position that it applies to protect whites as well. Respondents are unable, however, to summon any congressional debate from any stage in the bill's consideration to contradict the plain language of the bill as introduced and the explicit statements of Senator Trumbull, and others, that the bill, as introduced, did comprehend the prohibition of antiwhite discrimination.

> that is abominable and iniquitous and unconstitutional! Could anything be more monstrous or more abominable than for a member of the Senate to rise in his place and denounce with such epithets as these a bill, the only object of which is to secure equal rights to all the citizens of the country, *a bill that protects a white man just as much as a black man?* With what consistency and with what face can a Senator in his place here say to the Senate and the country that this is a bill for the benefit of black men exclusively when there is no such distinction in it, and when *the very object of the bill is to break down all discrimination between black men and white men?*

Cong. Globe, p. 599 (emphasis supplied). So advised, the Senate passed the bill shortly thereafter. Cong. Globe, p. 606–07.

It is clear, thus, that the bill, as it passed the Senate, was not limited in scope to discrimination against nonwhites. Accordingly, respondents pitch their legislative history argument largely upon the House's amendment of the Senate bill to add the "as is enjoyed by white citizens" phrase. But the statutory history is equally clear that that phrase was not intended to have the effect of eliminating from the bill the prohibition of racial discrimination against whites.

Representative Wilson of Iowa, Chairman of the Judiciary Committee and the bill's floor manager in the House, proposed the addition of the quoted phrase immediately upon the introduction of the bill. The change was offered explicitly to technically "perfect" the bill, and was accepted as such without objection or debate. Cong. Globe, p. 1115.

That Wilson's amendment was viewed simply as a technical adjustment without substantive effect is corroborated by the structure of the bill as it then stood. Even as amended the bill still provided that "there shall be no discrimination in civil rights or immunities among citizens of the United States in any State or Territory of the United States on account of race, color, or previous condition of slavery." To read Wilson's amendment as excluding white persons from the particularly enumerated civil rights guarantees of the Act would contradict this more general language; and we would be unwilling to conclude, without further evidence, that in adopting the amendment without debate or discussion, the House so regarded it.

Moreover, Representative Wilson's initial elaboration on the meaning of Senator Trumbull's bill, which immediately followed his securing passage of the foregoing amendment, fortifies our view that the amended bill was intended to protect whites as well as nonwhites. As Wilson described it, the purpose of the measure was to provide "for the equality of citizens . . . in the enjoyment of 'civil rights and immunities.' " Cong. Globe, p. 1117. Then, speaking in particular of "immunities" as " 'freedom or exemption from obligation,' " he made clear that the bill "secures to citizens of the United States equality in the exemptions of the law. . . . Whatever exemptions there may be shall apply to all citizens alike. One race shall not be more favored in this respect than another," ibid. Finally, in later dialogue Wilson made quite clear that the purpose of his amendment was not to affect the Act's protection of white persons. Rather, he stated, "the reason for offering [the amendment] was this: it was thought by some persons that unless these qualifying words were incorporated in the bill, those rights might be extended to all citizens, whether male or female, majors or minors." Cong. Globe, House App., p. 157. Thus, the purpose of the amendment was simply "to emphasize the racial character of the rights being protected," Georgia v. Rachel, 384 U.S. at 791, not to limit its application to nonwhite persons.

The Senate debate on the House version of the bill likewise emphasizes that Representative Wilson's amendment was not viewed as limiting the bill's prohibition of racial discrimination against white persons. Senator Trumbull, still managing the bill on the floor of the Senate, was asked whether there was not an inconsistency between the application of the bill to all "citizens of every race and color" and the statement that they shall have "the same right to make and enforce contracts . . . *as is enjoyed by white persons*," and it was suggested that the emphasized words were superfluous. Cong. Globe, p. 1413. Senator Trumbull responded in agreement with the view that the words were merely "superfluous. I do not think they alter the bill. . . . [A]nd as in the opinion of the [Senate Judiciary] [C]ommittee which examined this matter they did not alter the meaning of the bill, the committee thought proper to recommend a concurrence." Ibid.

Finally, after the Senate's acquiescence in the House version of the bill and the subsequent veto by President Johnson, the debate in both the Senate and the House again reflected the proponents' views that the bill did not favor nonwhites. Senator Trumbull once more rejected the view that the bill "discriminates in favor of colored persons," Cong. Globe, p. 1758, and in a similar vein, Representative Lawrence observed in the House that its "broad and comprehensive philanthropy which regards all men in their civil rights as equal before the law, is not made for any . . . race or color . . . but . . . will, if it become[s] a law, protect every citizen. . . . " Cong. Globe, p. 1833. On these notes, both Houses passed the bill by the prescribed margins, and the veto was overridden. Cong. Globe, pp. 1802, 1861.

This cumulative evidence of congressional intent makes clear, we think, that the 1866 statute, designed to protect the "same right . . . to make and enforce contracts" of "citizens of every race and color" was not understood or intended to be reduced by Representative Wilson's amendment, or any other provision, to the protection solely of nonwhites. Rather, the Act was meant, by its broad terms, to proscribe discrimination in the making or enforcement of contracts against, or in favor of, any race. Unlikely as it might have appeared in 1866 that white citizens would encounter substantial racial discrimination of the sort proscribed under the Act, the statutory structure and legislative history persuade us that the 39th Congress was intent upon establishing in the federal law a broader principle than would have been necessary simply to meet the particular and immediate plight of the newly freed Negro slaves. And while the statutory language has been somewhat streamlined in re-enactment and codification, there is no indication that § 1981 is intended to provide any less than the Congress enacted in 1866 regarding racial discrimination against white persons. Thus, we conclude that the District Court erred in dismissing petitioners' claims under § 1981 on the ground that the protections of that provision are unavailable to white persons.

The judgment of the Court of Appeals for the Fifth Circuit is reversed, and the case is remanded for further proceedings consistent with this opinion.

■ [The dissenting opinion of JUSTICE WHITE, joined by JUSTICE REHNQUIST, has been omitted. JUSTICE WHITE dissented for the reasons stated in his dissent in *Runyon v. McCrary*, namely that § 1981 did not apply to discrimination by private parties.]

NOTES ON MCDONALD V. SANTA FE TRAIL TRANSPORTATION CO.

1. CONGRUENCE BETWEEN TITLE VII AND § 1981

The Court held in *McDonald* that both Title VII and § 1981 prohibit discrimination against whites. Is this consistent with the principle of *Johnson v. Railway Express Agency, Inc.* that these statutes are "separate, distinct, and independent"? The holding that Title VII protects whites follows directly from the statutory language in Title VII protecting "any individual" from discrimination. Section 1981, although it protects "all persons" from discrimination, only confers on them "the same right . . . as is enjoyed by white citizens." So phrased, what right could § 1981 have conferred on "white citizens" that they did not already enjoy?

2. THE EFFECT OF CONSTITUTIONAL LAW

When *McDonald* was decided, the constitutionality of affirmative action was completely unresolved, and even today it remains controversial. Should the uncertainty surrounding this constitutional question affect the interpretation of Title VII and § 1981? Should it have the same effect on both statutes? Recall that no affirmative action plan was involved in *McDonald* but simply an allegation of disparate treatment of white employees. Does that make the case harder or easier? Also, no public employer was involved in the case, so the that the Constitution did not apply directly to the disputed employment decisions because of the absence of "state action." Instead, the Constitution could have applied only to state action in the form of a judicial interpretation of Title VII or § 1981 allowing minority employees, but not white employees, to sue. Would such an interpretation of one or both statutes be constitutionally suspect?

3. DISCRIMINATION ON THE BASIS OF NATIONAL ORIGIN

In two decisions, the Supreme Court extended the scope of § 1981 and § 1982 to most instances of discrimination on the basis of national origin. Saint Francis College v. Al–Khazraji, 481 U.S. 604 (1987); Shaare Tefila Congregation v. Cobb, 481 U.S. 615 (1987). These cases involved discrimination, respectively, against Arabs and Jews. The Supreme Court's reasoning in both cases depended upon historical conceptions of race that were current when the Civil Rights Act of 1866 was passed.

In *Saint Francis College*, the Court quoted at length from dictionaries and encyclopedias of the day and reached the following conclusion:

> These dictionary and encyclopedic sources are somewhat diverse, but it is clear that they do not support the claim that for the purposes of § 1981, Arabs, Englishmen, Germans and certain other ethnic groups are to be considered a single race. We would expect the legislative history of § 1981, which the Court held in *Runyon v. McCrary* had its source in the Civil Rights Act of 1866 as well as the Voting Rights Act of 1870, to reflect this common understanding, which it surely does. The debates are replete with references to the Scandinavian races, as well as the Chinese, Latin, Spanish, and Anglo–Saxon races. Jews, Mexicans, and Mongolians were similarly categorized. . . .
>
> Based on the history of § 1981, we have little trouble in concluding that Congress intended to protect from discrimination identifiable classes

> of persons who are subjected to intentional discrimination solely because of their ancestry or ethnic characteristics. Such discrimination is racial discrimination that Congress intended § 1981 to forbid, whether or not it would be classified as racial in terms of modern scientific theory. The Court of Appeals was thus quite right in holding that § 1981, "at a minimum," reaches discrimination against an individual "because he or she is genetically part of an ethnically and physiognomically distinctive subgrouping of homo sapiens." It is clear from our holding, however, that a distinctive physiognomy is not essential to qualify for § 1981 protection. If respondent on remand can prove that he was subjected to intentional discrimination based on the fact that he was born an Arab, rather than solely on the place or nation or his origin, or his religion, he will have made out a case under § 1981.

The Court relied upon exactly the same reasoning in *Shaare Tefila*, framing the question presented in the following terms:

> As *St. Francis* makes clear, the question before us is not whether Jews are considered to be a separate race by today's standards, but whether, at the time § 1982 was adopted, Jews constituted a group of people that Congress intended to protect. It is evident from the legislative history of the section reviewed in Saint Francis College, a review that we need not repeat here, that Jews and Arabs were among the peoples then considered to be distinct races and hence within the protection of the statute. Jews are not foreclosed from stating a cause of action against other members of what today is considered to be part of the Caucasian race.

The Court's reliance on contemporary views of race when §§ 1981 and 1982 were first enacted has some appeal. In interpreting an old statute, it is necessary to appreciate the historical and cultural context in which it was passed. But does the Court carry this concern too far? What if the contemporary views of race excluded Arabs and Jews from the category of discrimination prohibited by these statutes? Would the Court have followed that history? Under the Constitution, national origin is treated the same as race, making both classifications subject to strict scrutiny. E.g., Grutter v. Bollinger, 539 U.S. 306, 329–30 (2003); Gratz v. Bollinger, 539 U.S. 244, 270–71 (2003). Given this interpretation of the Constitution, would it have made sense to exclude claims based on national origin from the coverage of §§ 1981 and 1982? See Eileen R. Kaufman & Martin Schwartz, Civil Rights in Transition: Sections 1981 and 1982 Cover Discrimination on the Basis of Ancestry and Ethnicity, 4 Touro L. Rev. 183 (1988).

4. *GENERAL BUILDING CONTRACTORS V. PENNSYLVANIA*

The relationship between § 1981, the Fourteenth Amendment, and Title VII also figured in General Building Contractors Ass'n, Inc. v. Pennsylvania, 458 U.S. 375 (1982). The case held that § 1981 requires a finding of discriminatory intent and does not prohibit discrimination based only on proof of discriminatory effects. That holding followed the Fourteenth Amendment, which also prohibits only intentional discrimination. Title VII, by contrast, also prohibits employment practices with discriminatory effects. If employment practices have "a disparate impact on the basis of race, color, religion, sex, or national origin," then the employer must justify the practices as "job related for the position in question and consistent with business necessity." 42 U.S.C. 2000e–2(k)(1)(A)(i).

The case involved an action under § 1981 to correct racial discrimination in an apprentice system and in the operation of a union hiring hall that was the exclusive source of jobs in the construction industry in Philadelphia. The defendants were a local union, various trade associations, and a class of approximately 1400 construction industry employers. The hiring hall system was facially neutral; indeed the relevant contracts contained a non-discrimination clause at the time the suit was filed. The District Court found, however, that the local union "practiced a pattern of intentional discrimination" in administering the system and that "substantial racial disparities" resulted. Similar findings were made about the administration of the apprentice system. But the court found insufficient evidence that the trade associations and employers were even aware of the union discrimination and held that the plaintiffs had failed to prove an "intent to discriminate by the employers as a class." The court nonetheless entered an injunction against the trade associations and the employers (as well as the union and the operators of the apprentice system) requiring a series of remedial steps. The District Court ruled explicitly that § 1981 "requires no proof of purposeful conduct on the part of any of the defendants," that "proof of disparate impact alone" was sufficient, and that the trade unions and employers were liable on a theory of respondeat superior because they had delegated hiring authority to persons who had intentionally discriminated. The trade associations and the employers appealed.

The Court of Appeals affirmed, but the Supreme Court reversed. Writing for the Court, Justice Rehnquist said:

> In determining whether § 1981 reaches practices that merely result in a disproportionate impact on a particular class, or instead is limited to conduct motivated by a discriminatory purpose, we must be mindful of the "events and passions of the time" in which the law was forged. . . . The principal object of the legislation was to eradicate the Black Codes, laws enacted by Southern legislatures imposing a range of civil disabilities on freedmen. Most of these laws embodied express racial classifications and although others, such as those penalizing vagrancy, were facially neutral, Congress plainly perceived all of them as consciously conceived methods of resurrecting the incidents of slavery. . . .
>
> The immediate evils with which the 39th Congress was concerned simply did not include practices that were "neutral on their face, and even neutral in terms of intent," Griggs v. Duke Power Co., 401 U.S. 424, 430 (1971), but that had the incidental effect of disadvantaging blacks to a greater degree than whites. Congress instead acted to protect the freedmen from intentional discrimination. . . . The supporters of the bill repeatedly emphasized that the legislation was designed to eradicate blatant deprivations of civil rights, clearly fashioned with the purpose of oppressing the former slaves. To infer that Congress sought to accomplish more than this would require stronger evidence in the legislative record than we have been able to discern. . . .
>
> Our conclusion that § 1981 reaches only purposeful discrimination is supported by one final observation about its legislative history. As noted earlier, the origins of the law can be traced to both the Civil Rights Act of 1866 and the Enforcement Act of 1870. Both of these laws, in turn, were

legislative cousins of the Fourteenth Amendment. The 1866 Act represented Congress' first attempt to ensure equal rights for the freedmen following the formal abolition of slavery effected by the Thirteenth Amendment. As such, it constituted an initial blueprint of the Fourteenth Amendment, which Congress proposed in part as a means of "incorporat[ing] the guaranties of the Civil Rights Act of 1866 in the organic law of the land." Hurd v. Hodge, 334 U.S. 24, 32 (1948). The 1870 Act, which contained the language that now appears in § 1981, was enacted as a means of enforcing the recently ratified amendment. In light of the close connection between these acts and the amendment, it would be incongruous to construe the principal object of their successor, § 1981, in a manner markedly different from that of the amendment itself.[17]

With respect to the latter, "official action will not be held unconstitutional solely because it results in a racially disproportionate impact," Village of Arlington Heights v. Metropolitan Housing Dev. Corp., 429 U.S. 252, 264–65 (1977). "[E]ven if a neutral law has a disproportionately adverse impact upon a racial minority, it is unconstitutional under the Equal Protection Clause only if that impact can be traced to a discriminatory purpose." Personnel Administrator of Mass. v. Feeney, 442 U.S. 256, 272 (1979). See Washington v. Davis, 426 U.S. 229 (1976). The same Congress that proposed the Fourteenth Amendment also passed the Civil Rights Act of 1866, and the ratification of that amendment paved the way for the Enforcement Act of 1870. These measures were all products of the same milieu and were directed against the same evils. Although Congress might have charted a different course in enacting the predecessors to § 1981 than it did in proposing the Fourteenth Amendment, we have found no convincing evidence that it did so.

Justice Rehnquist went on to say that even "[o]n the assumption that respondeat superior applies to suits based on § 1981, there is no basis for holding either the employers or the associations liable under that doctrine" because no "agency relationship" between the trade associations and employers on the one hand and those who intentionally discriminated on the other had been shown on the facts. Consequently, injunctive relief against the trade associations and employers was inappropriate, although the Court did leave open the possibility that "minor and ancillary provisions" of the decree against the union and the administrators of the apprentice program might affect these defendants.

---

[17] It is true that § 1981, because it is derived in part from the 1866 Act, has roots in the Thirteenth as well as the Fourteenth Amendment. Indeed, we relied on that heritage in holding that Congress could constitutionally enact § 1982, which is also traceable to the 1866 Act, without limiting its reach to "state action." See Jones v. Alfred H. Mayer Co., 392 U.S. 409, 438 (1968). As we have already intimated, however, the fact that Congress acted in the shadow of the Thirteenth Amendment does not demonstrate that Congress sought to eradicate more than purposeful discrimination when it passed the 1866 Act. For example, Congress also enacted 42 U.S.C. § 1985(3) in part to implement the commands of the Thirteenth Amendment. See Griffin v. Breckenridge, 403 U.S. 88, 104–05 (1971). While holding that § 1985(3) does not require state action but also reaches private conspiracies, we have emphasized that a violation of the statute requires "some racial, or perhaps otherwise class-based, invidiously discriminatory animus behind the conspirators' action."

We need not decide whether the Thirteenth Amendment itself reaches practices with a disproportionate effect as well as those motivated by discriminatory purpose, or indeed whether it accomplished anything more than the abolition of slavery. We conclude only that the existence of that amendment, and the fact that it authorized Congress to enact legislation abolishing the "badges and incidents of slavery" do not evidence congressional intent to reach disparate effects in enacting § 1981.

Justice Stevens wrote separately to disassociate himself from the Court's reasoning on the intentional discrimination issue:

> As I noted in my separate opinion in Runyon v. McCrary, 427 U.S. 160, 189 (1976), the Congress that enacted § 1 of the Civil Rights Act of 1866 "intended only to guarantee all citizens the same legal capacity to make and enforce contracts, to obtain, own, and convey property, and to litigate and give evidence." Any violation of that guarantee—whether deliberate, negligent, or purely accidental—would, in my opinion, violate 42 U.S.C. § 1981. The statute itself contains no requirement that an intent to discriminate must be proved.
>
> The Court has broadened the coverage of § 1981 far beyond the scope actually intended by its authors; in essence, the Court has converted a statutory guarantee of equal rights into a grant of equal opportunities. See Jones v. Alfred H. Mayer Co., 392 U.S. 409 (1968); *Runyon v. McCrary*. Whether or not those decisions faithfully reflect the intent of Congress, the enlarged coverage of the statute "is now an important part of the fabric of our law." *Runyon*, supra, at 190 (Stevens, J., concurring).
>
> Since I do not believe Congress intended § 1981 to have any application at all in the area of employment discrimination generally covered by Title VII of the Civil Rights Act of 1964, an analysis of the motives and intent of the Reconstruction Congress cannot be expected to tell us whether proof of intentional discrimination should be required in the judicially created portion of the statute's coverage. Since Congress required no such proof in the statute it actually enacted, a logician would be comfortable in concluding that no such proof should ever be required. Nevertheless, since that requirement tends to define the entire coverage of § 1981 in a way that better reflects the basic intent of Congress than would a contrary holding, I concur in the conclusion reached by the Court . . . insofar as it relates to the statutory protection of equal opportunity but, perhaps illogically, would reach a different conclusion in a case challenging a denial of a citizen's civil rights.

Justice Marshall, joined by Justice Brennan, dissented. On the intentional discrimination issue, he said:

> The fallacy in the Court's approach is that, in construing § 1981 and its legislative history, the Court virtually ignores Congress' broad remedial purposes and our paramount national policy of eradicating racial discrimination and its pernicious effects. When viewed in this light, it is clear that proof of intentional discrimination should not be required in order to find a violation of § 1981.
>
> [T]he 1866 Civil Rights Act was not an isolated technical statute dealing with only a narrow subject. Instead, it was an integral part of a broad congressional scheme intended to work a major revolution in the prevailing social order. It is inconceivable that the Congress which enacted this statute would permit this purpose to be thwarted by excluding from the statute private action that concededly creates serious obstacles to the pursuit of job opportunities by Negroes solely because the aggrieved persons could not prove that the actors deliberately intended such a result. . . . Racial discrimination in all areas, and particularly in the areas of educa-

tion and employment, is a devastating and reprehensible policy that must be vigilantly pursued and eliminated from our society. . . .

Quite apart from this issue, however, Justice Marshall thought that injunctive relief against the trade associations and the employers was appropriate:

> Even if I agreed with the Court that intent must be proved in a § 1981 action, I could not agree with its conclusion that the . . . contracting associations should be immunized, even from injunctive liability, for the intentional discrimination practiced by the union hall to which they delegated a major portion of their hiring decisions. Under § 1981, minorities have an unqualified right to enter into employment contracts on the same basis as white persons. It is undisputed that in these cases, the [plaintiff] class was denied this right through intentional discrimination. The fact that the associations chose to delegate a large part of the hiring process to the local union hiring hall, which then engaged in intentional discrimination, does not alter the fact that respondents were denied the right to enter into employment contracts with the associations on the same basis as white persons.

5. QUESTIONS AND COMMENTS ON *GENERAL BUILDING CONTRACTORS*

In *General Building Contractors*, Justice Rehnquist relied on the relationship between the Fourteenth Amendment and the predecessors of § 1981 to support his conclusion that § 1981 required intentional discrimination. Yet this relationship was insufficient in *Runyon* to require that "state action" be proved in order to make out a violation of § 1981. Is there an explanation for this differential impact of the Fourteenth Amendment on the meaning of § 1981? Note that the difference cannot be explained by intervening shifts in the Court's personnel. Rehnquist was joined in the *General Building Contractors* majority by three Justices—Burger, Blackmun, and Powell—who were in the majority in *Runyon*. Is the answer that such cases are not in the end controlled by historical considerations? If so, what policies support the extension of § 1981 to private employers but its limitation to intentional discrimination? At the end of the day, given that Title VIII prohibits employment practices with discriminatory effects, does the decision in *General Building Contractors* make all that much difference?

At the time that *General Building Contractors* was decided, liability for practices with disparate impact had not yet been codified in Title VII but was based solely on judicial interpretation. Justice Stevens and Justice Marshall pointed out in their separate opinions that the literal terms of § 1981 allowed a similar interpretation of that statute. Does it matter that § 1981 supports an award of damages, but that Title VII allows the award only of equitable relief, mainly in the form of back pay and injunctions? Congress has since codified liability for disparate impact under Title VII but not under § 1981. The statute which accomplished this codification, the Civil Rights Act of 1991, made extensive changes to both statutes, but left the holding of *General Building Contractors* intact. Does that finally settle the issue?

Justice Marshall also argued that the employers and trade associations should have been subject at least to injunctive relief even if § 1981 requires intentional discrimination. It was plain here, after all, that intentional discrimination had occurred and that jobs had been denied as a result. Would it have been inconsistent with the Court's holding that § 1981 requires intentional discrimination for it nonetheless to have held that the employers and trade associations should bear some of the costs of remedying the impact of a clear violation of § 1981? What showing should be required in order to impose a share of the remedial costs on the employers and associations? That they actively encouraged the intentional discrimination? That they knew of the discrimination and looked the other way? That they should have known of the discrimination, or would have if they had paid any attention to the composition of the work force?

6. BIBLIOGRAPHY

An important premise of the decision in *General Building Contractors* is the limitation of the Equal Protection Clause of the Fourteenth Amendment to intentional discrimination. This position is well established in the cases—see Washington v. Davis, 426 U.S. 229 (1976); Village of Arlington Heights v. Metropolitan Housing Dev. Corp., 429 U.S. 252 (1977)—but is nonetheless controversial. See David Strauss, Discriminatory Intent and the Taming of *Brown*, 56 U. Chi. L. Rev. 935 (1989); Symposium, Legislative Motivation, 15 San Diego L. Rev. 925 (1978) (with articles by J. Morris Clark, Scott H. Bice, Paul Brest, Theodore Eisenberg, John Hart Ely, Kenneth L. Karst, Arthur S. Miller, Michael Perry, and Larry G. Simon). Of special interest among the many subsequent works on the subject is Charles R. Lawrence III, The Id, the Ego, and Equal Protection: Reckoning with Unconscious Racism, 39 Stan.L.Rev. 317 (1987), which argues for extension of equal protection scrutiny to situations where government action is race-dependent but where the racial ingredient is unconscious rather than purposeful. Such claims have recently been revived as psychologically based theories of "implicit bias," supported by studies revealing instantaneous adverse reactions to members of minority groups. For contrasting views of these theories, see Samual R. Bagenstos, Implicit Bias, Science, and Antidiscrimnation Law, 1 Harv. L. & Pol'y Rev. 477 (2007) (favorable); Gregory Mitchell & Philip E. Tetlock, Facts Do Matter: A Reply to Bagenstos, 37 Hofstra L. Rev. 737 (2009) (critical).

Jett v. Dallas Independent School District

Supreme Court of the United States, 1989.
491 U.S. 701.

■ JUSTICE O'CONNOR delivered the opinion of the Court.

The question before us in these cases is whether 42 U.S.C. § 1981 provides an independent federal cause of action for damages against local governmental entities, and whether that cause of action is broader than the damage remedy available under 42 U.S.C. § 1983, such that a municipality may be held liable for its employees' violations of § 1981 under a theory of respondeat superior.

I

Petitioner Norman Jett, a white male, was employed by respondent Dallas Independent School District (DISD) as a teacher, athletic director, and head football coach at South Oak Cliff High School (South Oak) until his reassignment to another DISD school in 1983. Petitioner was hired by the DISD in 1957, was assigned to assistant coaching duties at South Oak in 1962, and was promoted to athletic director and head football coach of

South Oak in 1970. During petitioner's lengthy tenure at South Oak, the racial composition of the school changed from predominantly white to predominantly black. In 1975, the DISD assigned Dr. Fredrick Todd, a black, as principal of South Oak. Petitioner and Todd clashed repeatedly over school policies, and in particular over petitioner's handling of the school's football program. These conflicts came to a head following a November 19, 1982, football game between South Oak and the predominantly white Plano High School. Todd objected to petitioner's comparison of the South Oak team with professional teams before the match, and to the fact that petitioner entered the official's locker room after South Oak lost the game and told two black officials that he would never allow black officials to work another South Oak game. Todd also objected to petitioner's statements, reported in a local newspaper, to the effect that the majority of South Oak players could not meet proposed NCAA academic requirements for collegiate athletes.

On March 15, 1983, Todd informed petitioner that he intended to recommend that petitioner be relieved of his duties as athletic director and head football coach at South Oak. On March 17, 1983, Todd sent a letter to John Kincaide, the director of athletics for DISD, recommending that petitioner be removed based on poor leadership and planning skills and petitioner's comportment before and after the Plano game. Petitioner subsequently met with John Santillo, director of personnel for DISD, who suggested that petitioner should transfer schools because any remaining professional relationship with Principal Todd had been shattered. Petitioner then met with Linus Wright, the superintendent of the DISD. At this meeting, petitioner informed Superintendent Wright that he believed that Todd's criticisms of his performance as head coach were unfounded and that in fact Todd was motivated by racial animus and wished to replace petitioner with a black head coach. Superintendent Wright suggested that the difficulties between Todd and petitioner might preclude petitioner from remaining in his coaching position at South Oak, but assured petitioner that another position in the DISD would be secured for him.

On March 25, 1983, Superintendent Wright met with Kincaide, Santillo, Todd and two other DISD officials to determine whether petitioner should remain at South Oak. After the meeting, Superintendent Wright officially affirmed Todd's recommendation to remove petitioner from his duties as coach and athletic director at South Oak. Wright indicated that he felt compelled to follow the recommendation of the school principal. Soon after this meeting, petitioner was informed by Santillo that effective August 4, 1983, he was reassigned as a teacher at the DISD Business Magnet School, a position that did not include any coaching duties. Petitioner's attendance and performance at the Business Magnet School were poor, and on May 5, 1983, Santillo wrote petitioner indicating that he was being placed on "unassigned personnel budget" and being reassigned to a temporary position in the DISD security department. Upon receiving Santillo's letter, petitioner filed this lawsuit in the District Court for Northern District of Texas. The DISD subsequently offered petitioner a position as a teacher and freshman football and track coach at Jefferson High School. Petitioner did not accept this assignment, and on August 19, 1983, he sent his formal letter of resignation to the DISD.

Petitioner brought this action against the DISD and Principal Todd in his personal and official capacities, under 42 U.S.C. §§ 1981 and 1983, alleging due process, First Amendment, and equal protection violations. Petitioner's due process claim alleged that he had a constitutionally protected property interest in his coaching position at South Oak, of which he was deprived without due process of law. Petitioner's First Amendment claim was based on the allegation that his removal and subsequent transfer were actions taken in retaliation for his statements to the press regarding the sports program at South Oak. His equal protection and § 1981 causes of action were based on the allegation that his removal from the athletic director and head coaching positions at South Oak was motivated by the fact that he was white, and that Principal Todd, and through him the DISD, were responsible for the racially discriminatory diminution in his employment status. Petitioner also claimed that his resignation was in fact the product of racial harassment and retaliation for the exercise of his First Amendment rights and thus amounted to a constructive discharge. These claims were tried to a jury, which found for petitioner on all counts. The jury awarded petitioner $650,000 against the DISD, $150,000 against Principal Todd and the DISD jointly and severally, and $50,000 in punitive damages against Todd in his personal capacity.

On motion for judgment notwithstanding the verdict respondents argued that liability against the DISD was improper because there was no showing that petitioner's injuries were sustained pursuant to a policy or custom of the school district. The District Court rejected this argument, finding that the DISD Board of Trustees had delegated final and unreviewable authority to Superintendent Wright to reassign personnel as he saw fit. In any event, the trial court found that petitioner's claim of racial discrimination was cognizable under § 1981 as well as § 1983, and indicated that "liability is permitted on solely a basis of respondeat superior when the claim is one of racial discrimination under § 1981." The District Court set aside the punitive damage award against Principal Todd as unsupported by the evidence, found the damage award against the DISD excessive and ordered a remittitur of $200,000, but otherwise denied respondents' motions for judgment n.o.v. and a new trial and upheld the jury's verdict in all respects. Principal Todd has reached a settlement with petitioner and is no longer a party to this action.

On appeal, the Court of Appeals for the Fifth Circuit reversed in part and remanded. Initially, the court found that petitioner had no constitutionally protected property interest "in the intangible, noneconomic benefits of his assignment as coach." Since petitioner had received both his teacher and coach's salary after his reassignment, the change in duties did not deprive him of any state law entitlement protected by the due process clause. The Court of Appeals also set aside the jury's finding that petitioner was constructively discharged from his teaching position within the DISD. The court found the evidence insufficient to sustain the claim that petitioner's loss of coaching duties and subsequent offer of reassignment to a lesser coaching position were so humiliating or unpleasant that a reasonable employee would have felt compelled to resign. While finding the question "very close," the Court of Appeals concluded that there was sufficient evidence from which a reasonable jury could conclude that Principal Todd's recommendation that petitioner be transferred from his coaching duties at South Oak was motivated by impermissible racial animus. The court noted that Todd had replaced petitioner with a black coach, that there had been racial overtones in the tension between Todd and petitioner before the Plano game, that Todd's explanation of his unsatisfactory rating of petitioner was questionable and was not supported by the testimony of other DISD officials who spoke of petitioner's performance in laudatory terms. The court also affirmed the jury's finding that Todd's recommendation that petitioner be relieved of his coaching duties was motivated in substantial part by petitioner's protected statements to the press concerning the academic standing of athletes at South Oak. These remarks addressed matters of public concern, and Todd admitted that they were a substantial consideration in his decision to recommend that petitioner be relieved of his coaching duties.

The Court of Appeals then turned to the DISD's claim that there was insufficient evidence to support a finding of municipal liability under 42 U.S.C. § 1983. The Court of Appeals found that the District Court's instructions as to the school district's liability were deficient in two respects. First, the District Court's instruction did not make clear that the school district could be held liable for the actions of Principal Todd or Superintendent Wright only if those officials were delegated policymaking authority by the school district or acted pursuant to a well settled custom that represented official policy. Second, even if Superintendent Wright could be considered a policymaker for purposes of the transfer of school district personnel, the jury made no finding that Superintendent Wright's decision to transfer petitioner was either improperly motivated, or consciously indifferent to the improper motivations of Principal Todd.

The Court of Appeals also rejected the District Court's conclusion that the DISD's liability for Principal Todd's actions could be predicated on a theory of respondeat superior under § 1981. The court noted that in Monell v. New York City Dept. of Social Services, 436 U.S. 658 (1978), this Court held that Congress did not intend municipalities to be subject to vicarious liability for the federal constitutional or statutory violations of their employees. The Court of Appeals reasoned that "[t]o impose such vicarious liability for only certain wrongs based on § 1981 apparently would contravene the congressional intent behind § 1983."

[W]e granted Norman Jett's petition for certiorari. . . . We also granted the DISD's cross-petition for certiorari . . . to clarify the application of our decisions in St. Louis v. Praprotnik, 485 U.S. 112 (1988) (plurality opinion), and Pembaur v. Cincinnati, 475 U.S. 469 (1986) (plurality opinion), to the school district's potential liability for the discriminatory actions of Principal Todd.

[T]he school district has argued that the limitations on municipal liability under § 1983 are applicable to violations of the rights protected by § 1981. Because petitioner has obtained a jury verdict to the effect that Dr. Todd violated his rights under § 1981, and the school district has never contested the judgment below on the ground that § 1981 does not reach petitioner's employment injury, we assume for purposes of these cases, without deciding, that petitioner's rights under § 1981 have been violated by his removal and reassignment.

II

. . . In essence, petitioner argues that in 1866 the 39th Congress intended to create a cause of action for damages against municipal actors and others who violated the rights now enumerated in § 1981. While petitioner concedes that the text of the 1866 Act itself is completely silent on this score, petitioner contends that a civil remedy was nonetheless intended for the violation of the rights contained in § 1 of the 1866 Act. Petitioner argues that Congress wished to adopt the prevailing approach to municipal liability to effectuate this damages remedy, which was respondeat superior. Petitioner concludes that with this federal damages remedy in place in

1866, it was not the intent of the 42nd Congress, which passed present day § 1983, to narrow the more sweeping remedy against local governments which Congress had created five years earlier. Since "repeals by implication are not favored," petitioner concludes that § 1981 must provide an independent cause of action for racial discrimination against local governmental entities, and that this broader remedy is unaffected by the constraints on municipal liability announced in *Monell.* In the alternative, petitioner argues that even if § 1981 does not create an express cause of action for damages against local governmental entities, 42 U.S.C. § 1988 invites this Court to craft a remedy by looking to common law principles, which again point to a rule of respondeat superior. To examine these contentions, we must consider the text and history of both the Civil Rights Act of 1866 and Civil Rights Act of 1871, the precursors of §§ 1981 and 1983 respectively. . . .

A

[At this point, Justice O'Connor undertook a lengthy examination of the legislative history of § 1981 and related civil rights statutes originally proposed in 1865 and ultimately enacted over President Johnson's veto in 1866. She then concluded:]

Several points relevant to our present inquiry emerge from the history surrounding the adoption of the Civil Rights Act of 1866. First, nowhere did the Act provide for an express damages remedy for violation of the provisions [that became § 1981.] Second, no original federal jurisdiction was created by the 1866 Act which could support a federal damages remedy against state actors. Finally, the penal provision [now 18 U.S.C. § 242], the only provision explicitly directed at state officials, was, in Senator Trumbull's words, designed to punish the "person who, under the color of the law, does the act," not "the community where the custom prevails." Cong.Globe, 39th Cong., 1st Sess., 1758 (1866).

Two events subsequent to the passage of the 1866 Act bear on the relationship between §§ 1981 and 1983. First, on June 13, 1866, just over two months after the passage of the 1866 Act, a joint resolution was passed sending the Fourteenth Amendment to the states for ratification. As we have noted in the past, the first section of the 1866 Act, "constituted an initial blueprint of the Fourteenth Amendment." General Building Contractors Assn., Inc. v. Pennsylvania, 458 U.S. 375, 389 (1982). Many of the members of the 39th Congress viewed § 1 of the Fourteenth Amendment as "constitutionalizing" and expanding the protections of the 1866 Act and viewed what became § 5 of the amendment as laying to rest doubts shared by both sides of the aisle concerning the constitutionality of that measure. See . . . Hurd v. Hodge, 334 U.S. 24, 32 (1948) ("[A]s the legislative debates reveal, one of the primary purposes of many members of Congress in supporting the adoption of the Fourteenth Amendment was to incorporate the guaranties of the Civil Rights Act of 1866 in the organic law of the land").

Second, the 41st Congress reenacted the substance of the 1866 Act in a Fourteenth Amendment statute, the Enforcement Act of 1870. Section 16 of the 1870 Act was modeled after § 1 of the 1866 Act. Section 17 reenacted with some modification the criminal provisions of § 2 of the earlier civil rights law, and § 18 of the 1870 Act provided that the entire 1866 [Act] was reenacted. We have thus recognized that present day 42 U.S.C. § 1981 is both a Thirteenth and a Fourteenth Amendment statute. *General Building Contractors,* supra, at 383–86.

B

What is now § 1983 was enacted as § 1 of "An Act to Enforce the Provisions of the Fourteenth Amendment to the Constitution of the United States and For other Purposes," Act of April 20, 1871. The immediate impetus for the bill was evidence of widespread acts of violence perpetrated against the freedmen and loyal white citizens by groups such as the Ku Klux Klan. On March 23, 1871, President Grant sent a message to Congress indicating that the Klan's reign of terror in the Southern states had "render[ed] life and property insecure," and that "the power to correct these evils [was] beyond the control of state authorities." Cong.Globe, 42nd Cong., 1st Sess., 244 (1871). A special joint committee consisting of 10 distinguished Republicans, five from each House of Congress, was formed in response to President Grant's call for legislation, and drafted the bill that became what is now known as the Ku Klux Klan Act of 1871. As enacted, sections 2 through 6 of the bill specifically addressed the problem of the private acts of violence perpetrated by groups like the Klan.

Unlike the rest of the bill, § 1 is not specifically addressed to the activities of the Klan. As passed by the 42nd Congress, § 1 provided . . . :

> That any person who, under color of any law, statute, ordinance, regulation, custom, or usage of any State, shall subject, or cause to be subjected, any person within the jurisdiction of the United States to the deprivation of any rights, privileges, or immunities secured by the Constitution of the United States, shall, any such law, statute, ordinance, regulation, custom, or usage of the State to the contrary notwithstanding, be liable to the party injured in any action at law, suit in equity, or other proper proceeding for redress; such proceeding to be prosecuted in the several district or circuit courts of the United States, with and subject to the same rights of appeal, review upon error, and other remedies provided in like cases in such courts. . . .

Three points are immediately clear from the face of the act itself. First, unlike any portion of the 1866 Act, this statute explicitly ordained that any "person" acting under color of state law or custom who was responsible for a deprivation of constitutional rights would "be liable to the party injured in any action at law." Thus, "the 1871 Act was designed to expose state and local officials to a new form of liability." Newport v. Fact Concerts, Inc., 453 U.S. 247, 259 (1981). Second, the 1871 Act explicitly provided original federal jurisdiction for prosecution of these civil actions against state actors. See Will v. Michigan Dept. of State Police, 491 U.S. 58, 66 (1989) ("[A] principle purpose behind the enactment of § 1983 was to provide a federal forum for civil rights claims"). Third, the first section of the 1871 Act was explicitly modeled on § 2 of the 1866 Act, and was seen by both opponents and proponents as amending and enhancing the protections of the 1866 Act by providing a new civil remedy for its enforcement against state actors. See Chapman v. Houston Welfare Rights Org., 441 U.S. 600, 610–11, n.25 (1979) ("Section 1 of the [1871] Act generated the least concern; it merely added civil remedies to the criminal penalties imposed by the 1866 Civil Rights Act").

Even a cursory glance at the House and Senate debates on the 1871 Act makes these three points clear. In introducing the bill to the House, Representative Shellabarger, who served on the joint committee which drafted the bill, stated:

> The model for it will be found in the second section of the act of April 9, 1866, known as the "Civil Rights Act." That section provides a criminal proceeding in identically the same case as this one provides a civil remedy for, except that the deprivation under color of state law must, under the civil rights act, have been on account of race, color or former slavery. Cong.Globe, 42 Cong., 1st Sess., App. 68 (1871).

Representative Shellabarger added that § 1 provided a civil remedy "on the same state of facts" as § 2 of the Civil Rights Act of 1866. Obviously Representative Shellabarger's introduction of § 1 of the bill to his colleagues would have been altogether different if he had been of the view that the 39th Congress, of which he had been a member, had *already* created a *broader* federal damages remedy against state actors in 1866. The view that § 1 of the 1871 Act was an amendment of or supplement to the 1866 Act designed to create new civil remedy against state actors was echoed throughout the debates in the House.

Both proponents and opponents in the House viewed § 1 as working an *expansion* of federal jurisdiction. Supporters continually referred to the failure of the state courts to enforce federal law designed for the protection of the freedman, and saw § 1 as remedying this situation by interposing the federal courts between the state and citizens of the United States. See id., at 376 (Rep. Lowe) ("The case has arisen . . . when the federal government must resort to its own agencies to carry its own authority into execution. Hence this bill throws open the doors of the United States courts to those whose rights under the Constitution are denied or impaired"). Opponents recognized the expansion of original jurisdiction and railed against it on policy and constitutional grounds. See id., at 429 (Rep. McHenry) ("The first section of the bill . . . vests in the federal courts jurisdiction to determine the individual rights of citizens of the same state; a jurisdiction which of right belongs only to the state tribunals").

The Senate debates on § 1 of the 1871 Act are of a similar tenor. . . . Senators addressed § 1 of the act as creating a new civil remedy and expanding federal jurisdiction to accommodate it in terms incompatible with the supposition that the 1866 Act had already created such a cause of action against state actors. . . .

The final aspect of the history behind the adoption of present day § 1983 relevant to the question before us is the rejection by the 42nd Congress of the Sherman Amendment, which specifically proposed the imposition of a form of vicarious liability on municipal governments. This history was thoroughly canvassed in the Court's opinion in *Monell,* and only its broadest outlines need be traced here. [Justice O'Connor's treatment of this history is omitted.]

The strong adverse reaction to the Sherman Amendment, and continued references to its complete novelty in the law of the United States, make it difficult to entertain petitioner's contention that the 1866 Act had already created a form of vicarious liability against municipal governments. Equally important is the basis for opposition. As we noted in *Monell,* a large number of those who objected to the principle of vicarious liability embodied in the Sherman Amendment were of the view that Congress did not have the power to assign the duty to enforce federal law to state instrumentalities by making them liable for the constitutional violations of others. [Prior] decisions of this Court lent direct support to the constitutional arguments of the opponents. . . . In *Monell,* we concluded that it was this constitutional objection which was the driving force behind the eventual rejection of the Sherman Amendment.

Although the debate surrounding the constitutional [objection] occurred in the context of the Sherman Amendment and not § 1 of the 1871 Act, in *Monell* we found it quite inconceivable that the same legislators who opposed vicarious liability on constitutional grounds in the Sherman Amendment debates would have silently adopted the same principle in § 1. Because the "creation of a federal law of respondeat superior would have raised all the constitutional problems associated with the obligation to keep the peace" embodied in the Sherman Amendment, we held that the existence of the constitutional background "compell[ed] the conclusion that Congress did not intend municipalities to be held liable [under § 1] unless action pursuant to official municipal policy of some nature caused a constitutional tort." *Monell,* supra, at 691.

[The decisions leading to the constitutional concerns that led to the defeat of the Sherman Amendment] were on the books when the 39th Congress enacted § 1 of the 1866 Act. Supporters of the 1866 Act were clearly aware of [them], and cited [them] for the proposition that the federal government could use its *own* instrumentalities to effectuate its laws. There was, however, no suggestion in the debates surrounding the 1866 Act that the statute violated [the constitutional principle] that federal duties could not be imposed on state instrumentalities by rendering them vicariously liable for the violations of others. Just as it affected our interpretation of § 1 of the 1871 Act in *Monell,* we think the complete silence on this score in the face of a constitutional background known to those who enacted the 1866 Act militates against imputing to Congress an intent to silently impose vicarious liability on municipalities under the earlier statute.

As originally enacted, the text of § 1983 referred only to the deprivation "of any rights, privileges, or immunities secured by the Constitution of the United States." In 1874, Congress enacted the Revised Statutes of the United States. The words "and laws" were added to the remedial provision of § 1 of the 1871 Act. . . .

There is no commentary or other information surrounding the addition of the phrase "and laws" to the remedial provisions of present day § 1983. . . .

We have noted in the past that the addition of the phrase "and laws" to the text of what is now § 1983, although not without its ambiguities as to intended scope, was *at least* intended to make clear that the guarantees contained in § 1 of the 1866 Act and § 16 of the Enforcement Act of 1870, were to be enforced against state actors through the express remedy for damages contained in § 1983. See *Chapman,* supra, at 617 (§ 1 of the 1871 Act "served only to ensure that an individual had a cause of action for violations of the Constitution, which in the Fourteenth Amendment embodied and extended to all individuals as against state action the substantive protections afforded by § 1 of the 1866 Act"). See also Maine v. Thiboutot, 448 U.S. 1, 7 (1980) ("There is no express explanation offered for the insertion of the phrase 'and laws.' On the one hand, a principal purpose of the added language was to ensure that federal legislation providing specifically for equality of rights would be brought within the ambit of the civil action authorized by that statute").

III

We think the history of the 1866 Act and the 1871 Act recounted above indicates that Congress intended that the explicit remedial provisions of § 1983 be controlling in the context of damages actions brought against state actors alleging violation of the rights declared in § 1981. That we have read § 1 of the 1866 Act to reach private action and have implied a damages remedy to effectuate the declaration of rights contained in that provision does not authorize us to do so in the context of the "state action" portion of § 1981, where Congress has established its own remedial scheme. In the context of the application of § 1981 and § 1982 to private actors, we "had little choice but to hold that aggrieved individuals could enforce this prohibition, *for there existed no other remedy to address such violations of the statute.*" Cannon v. University of Chicago, 441 U.S. 677, 728 (1979) (White, J., dissenting) (emphasis added). That is manifestly not the case here, and whatever the limits of the judicial power to imply or create remedies, it has long been the law that such power should not be exercised in the face of an express decision by Congress concerning the scope of remedies available under a particular statute. See National Railroad Passenger Corp. v. National Assn. of Railroad Passengers, 414 U.S. 453, 458 (1974) ("A frequently stated principle of statutory construction is that when legislation expressly provides a particular remedy or remedies, courts should not expand the coverage of the statute to subsume other remedies").

Petitioner cites 42 U.S.C. § 1988, and argues that provision "compels adoption of a respondeat superior standard." That section, as amended, provides in pertinent part:

> The jurisdiction in civil . . . matters conferred on the district courts by the provisions of this [chapter and Title 18], for the protection of all persons in the United States in their civil rights, and for their vindication, shall be exercised and enforced in conformity with the laws of the United States, so far as such laws are suitable to carry the same into effect; but in all cases where they are not adapted by the object, or are deficient in the provisions necessary to furnish suitable remedies and punish offenses against law, the common law, as modified and changed by the constitution and the statutes of the State wherein the court having jurisdiction of such civil or criminal cause is held, so far as the same is not inconsistent with the Constitution and laws of the United States, shall be extended to and govern the said courts in the trial and disposition of the cause. . . .

Far from supporting petitioner's call for the creation or implication of a damages remedy broader than that provided by § 1983, we think the plain language of § 1988 supports the result we reach here. As we noted in Moor v. County of Alameda, 411 U.S. 693, 706 (1973), in rejecting an argument similar to petitioner's contention here, "[§ 1988] expressly limits the authority granted federal courts to look to the common law, as modified by state law, to instances in which that law 'is not inconsistent with the Constitution and laws of the United States.' " As we indicated in *Moor,* "Congress did not intend, *as a matter of federal law,* to impose vicarious liability on municipalities for violations of federal civil rights by their employees." Section 1983 provides an explicit remedy in damages which, with its limitations on municipal liability, Congress thought "suitable to carry . . . into effect" the rights guaranteed by § 1981 as against state actors. Thus, if anything, § 1988 points us in the direction of the express federal damages remedy for enforcement of the rights contained in § 1981, not state common law principles.

Our conclusion that the express cause of action for damages created by § 1983 constitutes the exclusive federal remedy for violation of the rights guaranteed in § 1981 by state governmental units finds support in our decision in Brown v. GSA, 425 U.S. 820 (1976). In *Brown,* we dealt with the interaction of § 1981 and the provisions of § 717 of Title VII, 42 U.S.C. § 2000e–16, which proscribe discrimination in federal employment and establish an administrative and judicial enforcement scheme. The petitioner in *Brown* had been passed over for federal promotion on two occasions, and after the second occasion he filed a complaint with his agency alleging that he was denied promotion because of his race. The agency's Director of Civil Rights concluded after investigation that race had not entered into the promotional process, and informed Brown by letter of his right under § 717(c) to bring an action in federal district court within 30 days of the agency's final decision. Forty-two days later Brown filed suit in federal court, alleging violations of both Title VII and § 1981. The lower courts dismissed Brown's complaint as untimely under § 717(c), and this Court affirmed, holding that § 717 of Title VII constituted the exclusive remedy for allegations of racial discrimination in federal employment.

The Court began its analysis by noting that "Congress simply failed explicitly to describe § 717's position in the constellation of antidiscrimination law." We noted that in 1972, when Congress extended the strictures of Title VII to federal employment, the availability of an implied damages remedy under § 1981 for employment discrimination was not yet clear. The Court found that this perception on the part of Congress, "seems to indicate that the congressional intent in 1972 was to create an exclusive, pre-emptive administrative and judicial scheme for the redress of federal employment discrimination." The Court bolstered its holding by invoking the general principle that "a precisely drawn, detailed statute pre-empts more general remedies."

In *Brown,* as here, while Congress has not definitively spoken as to the relationship of § 1981 and § 1983, there is very strong evidence that the 42nd Congress which enacted the precursor of § 1983 thought that it was enacting the first, and at that time the only, federal damages remedy for the violation of federal constitutional and statutory rights by state governmental actors. The historical evidence surrounding the revision of 1874 further indicates that Congress thought that the declaration of rights in § 1981 would be enforced against state actors through the remedial provisions of § 1983. That remedial scheme embodies certain limitations on the liability of local governmental entities based on federalism concerns which had very real constitutional underpinnings for the Reconstruction Congresses. As petitioner here would have it, the careful balance drawn by the 42nd Congress between local autonomy and fiscal integrity and the vindication of federal rights could be completely upset by an artifice of pleading.

Since our decision in *Monell,* the Courts of Appeals have unanimously rejected the contention, analogous to petitioner's argument here, that the doctrine of respondeat superior is available against a municipal entity under a *Bivens*-type action implied directly from the Fourteenth Amendment. Given our repeated recognition that the Fourteenth Amendment was intended in large part to embody and expand the protections of the 1866 Act as against state actors, we believe that the logic of these decisions applies with equal force to petitioner's invitation to this Court to create a damages remedy broader than § 1983 from the declaration of rights now found in § 1981. We hold that the express "action at law" provided by § 1983 for the "deprivation of any rights, privileges, or immunities secured by the Constitution and laws," provides the exclusive federal damages remedy for the violation of the rights guaranteed by § 1981 when the claim is pressed against a state actor. Thus to prevail on his claim for damages against the school district, petitioner must show that the violation of his "right to make contracts" protected by § 1981 was caused by a custom or policy within the meaning of *Monell* and subsequent cases.

IV

. . . Last term in St. Louis v. Praprotnik, 485 U.S. 112 (1988) (plurality opinion), we attempted a clarification of tools a federal court should employ in determining where policymaking authority lies for purposes of § 1983. In *Praprotnik,* the plurality reaffirmed the teachings of our prior cases to the effect that "whether a particular official has 'final policymaking authority' is a question of *state law.*" As with other questions of state law relevant to the application of federal law, the identification of those officials whose decisions represent the official policy of the local governmental unit is itself a legal question to be resolved by the trial judge *before* the case is submitted to the jury. Reviewing the relevant legal materials, including state and local positive law, as well as " 'custom or usage' having the force of law," *Praprotnik,* supra, at 124, n.1, the trial judge must identify those officials or governmental bodies who speak with final policymaking authority for the local governmental actor concerning the action alleged to have caused the particular constitutional or statutory violation at issue. Once those officials who have the power to make official policy on a particular issue have been identified, it is for the jury to determine whether *their* decisions have caused the deprivation of rights at issue by policies which affirmatively command that it occur or by acquiescence in a longstanding practice or custom which constitutes the "standard operating procedure" of the local governmental entity.

. . . Pursuant to its cross-petition . . . , the school district urges us to review Texas law and determine that neither Principal Todd nor Superintendent Wright possessed the authority to make final policy decisions concerning the transfer of school district personnel. Petitioner Jett seems to concede that Principal Todd did not have policymaking authority as to employee transfers, but argues that Superintendent Wright had been delegated authority to make school district policy concerning employee transfers and that his decisions in this area were final and unreviewable.

We decline to resolve this issue on the record before us. We think the Court of Appeals, whose expertise in interpreting Texas law is greater than our own, is in a better position to determine whether Superintendent Wright possessed final policymaking authority in the area of employee transfers, and if so whether a new trial is required to determine the responsibility of the school district for the actions of Principal Todd in light of this determination. We thus affirm the judgment of the Court of Appeals to the extent it holds that the school district may not be held liable for its employees' violation of the rights enumerated in § 1981 under a theory of respondeat superior. We remand the case to the Court of Appeals for it to determine where final policymaking authority as to employee transfers lay in light of the principles enunciated by the plurality opinion in *Praprotnik* outlined above.

It is so ordered.

■ JUSTICE SCALIA, concurring in part and concurring in the judgment.

I join Parts I and IV of the Court's opinion, and Part III except insofar as it relies upon legislative history. To hold that the more general provisions of 42 U.S.C. § 1981 establish a mode of liability for a particular category of offense by municipalities that is excluded from the closely related statute (42 U.S.C. § 1983) which deals more specifically with that precise category of offense would violate the rudimentary principles of construction that the specific governs the general and that, where text permits, statutes dealing with similar subjects should be interpreted harmoniously.

■ JUSTICE BRENNAN, with whom JUSTICE MARSHALL, JUSTICE BLACKMUN, and JUSTICE STEVENS join, dissenting. . . .

Because I would conclude that § 1981 itself affords a cause of action in damages on the basis of governmental conduct violating its terms, and because I would conclude that such an action may be predicated on a theory of respondeat superior, I dissent.

I

. . . The question is whether [§ 1981] permits a cause of action in damages against those who violate its terms.

The Court approaches this issue as though it were new to us, recounting in lengthy and methodical detail the introduction, debate, passage, veto, and enactment of the 1866 Act. The story should by now be familiar to anyone with even a passing acquaintance with this statute. This is so because we have reviewed this history in the course of deciding—and reaffirming the answer to—the very question that the Court deems so novel today. An essential aspect of the holding in each of [our prior § 1981] cases was the principle that a person injured by a violation of § 1 of the 1866 Act (now 42 U.S.C. §§ 1981 and 1982) may bring an action for damages under that statute against the person who violated it.

We have had good reason for concluding that § 1981 itself affords a cause of action against those who violate its terms. The statute does not explicitly furnish a cause of action for the conduct it prohibits, but this fact was of relatively little moment at the time the law was passed. During the period when § 1 of the 1866 Act was enacted, and for over 100 years thereafter, the federal courts routinely concluded that a statute setting forth substantive rights without specifying remedy contained an implied cause of action for damages incurred in violation of the statute's terms. The classic statement of this principle comes from Texas & Pacific R. Co. v. Rigsby, 241 U.S. 33, 39–40 (1916), in which we observed: "A disregard of the command of the statute is a wrongful act, and where it results in damage to one of the class for whose especial benefit the statute was enacted, the right to recover the damages from the party in default is implied, according to a doctrine of the common law." This case fits comfortably within *Rigsby*'s framework. It is of small consequence, therefore, that the 39th Congress established no explicit damages remedy in § 1 of the 1866 Act.[2]

---

[2] During the 1970s, we modified our approach to determining whether a statute contains an implied cause of action, announcing [a] four-part test [in Cort v. Ash, 422 U.S. 66 (1975).] It would make no sense, however, to apply a test first enunciated in 1975 to a statute enacted in 1866. An inquiry into Congress' actual intent must take account of the interpretive principles in place at the time. Thus, I would interpret § 1981 in light of the principle described in *Rigsby,* rather than the one described in *Cort.*

Application even of the test fashioned in *Cort,* however, would lead to the conclusion that Jett may bring a cause of action in damages against respondent under § 1981. Jett belongs to

Indeed, the debates on § 1 demonstrate that the legislators' worry was not that their actions would do too much, but that they would do too little. In introducing the bill that became the 1866 Act, Senator Trumbull explained that the statute was necessary because "[t]here is very little importance in the general declaration of abstract truths and principles [contained in the Thirteenth Amendment] unless they can be carried into effect, *unless the persons who are to be affected by them have some means of availing themselves of their benefits.*" Cong. Globe, 39th Cong., 1st Sess., 474 (1866) (emphasis added). Representative Thayer of Pennsylvania echoed this theme: "When I voted for the amendment to abolish slavery . . . I did not suppose that I was offering . . . a mere paper guarantee. . . . The bill which now engages the attention of the House has for its object to carry out and guaranty the reality of that great measure. It is to give to it practical effect and force. It is to prevent that great measure from remaining a dead letter upon the constitutional page of this country."

In these circumstances, it would be unreasonable to conclude that inferring a private cause of action from § 1981 is incompatible with Congress' intent. Yet in suggesting that § 2 of the 1866 Act demonstrates Congress' intent that criminal penalties serve as the only remedy for violations of § 1, this is exactly the conclusion that the Court apparently would have us draw. Not only, however, is this argument contrary to legislative intent, but we have already squarely rejected it. In Jones v. Alfred H. Mayer Co., 392 U.S. 409 (1968), respondent argued that because § 2 furnished criminal penalties for violations of § 1 occurring "under color of law," § 1 could not be read to provide a civil remedy for violations of the statute by private persons. Dismissing this argument, we explained: "[Section] 1 was meant to prohibit *all* racially motivated deprivations of the rights enumerated in the statute, although only those deprivations perpetrated 'under color of law' were to be criminally punishable under § 2."[3]

The only way that the Court can distinguish *Jones,* and the cases following it, from this case is to argue that our recognition of an implied cause of action against private persons did not include recognition of an action against local governments and government officials. But before today, no one had questioned that a person could sue a government official for damages due to a violation of § 1981. . . . The lower courts have heeded well the message from our cases: they unanimously agree that suit may be brought directly under § 1981 against government officials who violate the statute's terms.

Perhaps recognizing how odd it would be to argue that one may infer from § 1 of the 1866 Act a cause of action against private persons, but not one against government officials, the Court appears to claim that the 1871 Act erased whatever action against government officials previously existed under the 1866 Act. The Court explains:

---

the special class of persons (those who have been discriminated against in the making of contracts) for whom the statute was created; all of the indicators of legislative intent point in the direction of an implied cause of action; such an action is completely consistent with the statute's purposes; and, in view of the fact, that this Civil War-era legislation was in part designed to curtail the authority of the states, it would be unreasonable to conclude that this cause of action is one relegated to state law.

[3] . . . The Court's assertion that the 1866 Act created no original federal jurisdiction for civil actions based on the statute is similarly unavailing. [T]he Court's argument confuses the question of which courts (state or federal) will enforce a cause of action with whether a cause of action exists.

> That we have read § 1 of the 1866 Act to reach private action and have implied a damages remedy to effectuate the declaration of rights contained in that provision does not authorize us to do so in the context of the "state action" portion of § 1981, where Congress has established its own remedial scheme. In the context of the application of § 1981 and § 1982 to private actors, we "had little choice but to hold that aggrieved individuals could enforce this prohibition, *for there existed no other remedy to address such violations of the statute.*" That is manifestly not the case here, and whatever the limits of the judicial power to imply or create remedies, it has long been the law that such power should not be exercised in the face of an express decision by Congress concerning the scope of remedies available under a particular statute.

This argument became available only after § 1983 was passed, and thus suggests that § 1983 changed the cause of action implicitly afforded by § 1981. However, not only do we generally disfavor repeals by implication, but we should be particularly hostile to them when the allegedly repealing statute specifically rules them out. In this regard, § 7 of the 1871 Act is highly significant; it provided "[t]hat nothing herein contained shall be construed to supersede or repeal any former act or law except so far as the same may be repugnant thereto."[4]

The Court's argument fails for other reasons as well. Its essential point appears to be that, in § 1983, "Congress has established its own remedial scheme" for the " 'state action' portion of § 1981."[5] For this argument, the Court may not rely, as it attempts to do, on the principle that " 'when legislation expressly provides a particular remedy or remedies, courts should not expand the coverage of the statute to subsume other remedies.' " That principle limits the inference of a remedy for the violation of a statute only when *that same statute* already sets forth specific remedies. It cannot be used to support the argument that the provision of particular remedies in § 1983 tells us whether we should infer a damages remedy for violations of § 1981.

The suggestion, moreover, that today's holding "finds support in" Brown v. GSA, 425 U.S. 820 (1976), is audacious. Section 1983—which, for example, specifies no exhaustion requirement, no damages limitation, no defenses, and no statute of limitations—can hardly be compared with § 717 of the Civil Rights of 1964, at issue in *Brown,* with its many detailed requirements and remedies. Indeed, in Preiser v. Rodriguez, 411 U.S. 475, 489 (1973), we emphasized the "general" nature of § 1983 in refusing to allow former prisoners to challenge a prison's withholding of good-time credits under § 1983 rather than under the federal habeas corpus statute, 28 U.S.C. § 2254. We never before have suggested that § 1983's remedial scheme is so thorough that it pre-empts the remedies that might otherwise

---

[4] Several amici argue that we need not conclude that § 1983 impliedly repealed the cause of action furnished by § 1981 in order to decide that § 1983 provides the sole remedy for violations of § 1981. Their theory is that an implied cause of action did not exist when the 1871 Act was passed, and that therefore one may argue that the 1871 Act furnished the only remedy for the 1866 Act without arguing that the later statute in any way repealed the earlier one. To support their premise, they observe, first, that it was not until the 1960s that courts recognized a private cause of action under § 1 of the 1866 Act. [T]he relevance of the date on which we expressly recognized that one could bring a suit for damages directly under § 1 escapes me; that we did so in the 1960s does not suggest that we would not have done so had we faced the question in the 1860s. . .

[5] The one bright spot in today's decision is its reaffirmation of our holding in Maine v. Thiboutot, 448 U.S. 1 (1980).

be available under other statutes; indeed, all of our intimations have been to the contrary.

According to the Court, to allow an action complaining of government conduct to be brought directly under § 1981 would circumvent our holding in Monell v. New York City Dept. of Social Services, 436 U.S. 658 (1978), that liability under § 1983 may not be based on a theory of respondeat superior. Not only am I unconvinced that we should narrow a statute as important as § 1981 on the basis of something so vague and inconclusive as "federalism concerns which had very real constitutional underpinnings for the Reconstruction Congress," but I am also unable to understand how *Monell's* limitation on § 1983 liability begins to tell us whether the same restriction exists under § 1981, enacted five years earlier than § 1983 and covering a far narrower range of conduct. It is difficult to comprehend, in any case, why the Court is worried that construing § 1981 to create a cause of action based on governmental conduct would render local governments vicariously liable for the delicts of their employees, since it elsewhere goes to great lengths to suggest that liability under § 1981 may not be vicarious.

The Court's primary reason for distinguishing between private and governmental conduct under § 1981 appears to be its impression that, because private conduct is not actionable under § 1983, we "had little choice" but to hold that private individuals who violated § 1981 could be sued directly under § 1981. This claim, however, suggests that whether a cause of action in damages exists under § 1981 depends on the scope of § 1983. In deciding whether a particular statute includes an implied cause of action, however, we have not in the past suggested that the answer will turn on the reach of a different statute. . . .

The Court's approach not only departs from our prior analysis of implied causes of action, but also attributes an intent to the 39th Congress that fluctuates depending on the state of the law with regard to § 1983. On the Court's theory, if this case had arisen during the period between our decisions in Monroe v. Pape, 365 U.S. 167 (1961), and *Monell,* when we believed that local governments were not "persons" within the meaning of § 1983, we would apparently have been required to decide that a cause of action could be brought against local governments and their official directly under § 1981. . . . In other words, on the Court's view, a change in the scope of § 1983 alters the reach of § 1981. I cannot endorse such a bizarre conception of congressional intent.

II

I thus would hold that Jett properly brought his suit against respondent directly under § 1981. It remains to consider whether that statute permits recovery against a local government body on a theory of respondeat superior.

Because § 1981 does not explicitly create a cause of action in damages, we would look in vain for an express statement that the statute contemplates liability based on the doctrine of respondeat superior. In *Monell,* however, our background assumption appears to have been that unless a statute subjecting institutions (such as municipalities) to liability evidences an intent not to impose liability on them based on respondeat superior, such liability will be assumed. The absolute language of § 1981 therefore is significant: "All persons within the jurisdiction of the United States shall have the same right in every State and Territory to make and enforce contracts . . . as is enjoyed by white citizens." Certainly nothing in this wording refutes the argument that vicarious liability may be imposed under this law.

Section 1983, in contrast, forbids a person to "subjec[t], or caus[e] to be subjected" another person to a deprivation of the rights protected by the statute. It is telling that § 1981 does not contain this explicit language of causation. In holding in *Monell* that liability under § 1983 may not be predicated on a theory of respondeat superior, we emphasized that § 1983 "plainly imposes liability on a government that, under color of some official policy, 'causes' an employee to violate another's constitutional rights. . . . Indeed, the fact that Congress did specifically provide that *A*'s tort became *B*'s liability if *B* 'caused' *A* to subject another to a tort suggests that Congress did not intend § 1983 liability to attach where such a causation was absent." The absence of this language in § 1 of the 1866 Act, now § 1981, argues against the claim that liability under this statute may not be vicarious.

While it acknowledged that § 1 of the 1866 Act did not contain the "subjects, or causes to be subjected" language of § 1983, the Court of Appeals nevertheless emphasized that § 2 of the 1866 Act did contain this language. There is not the least inconsistency, however, in arguing that the *criminal* penalties under the 1866 Act may not be imposed on the basis of respondeat superior, but that the civil penalties may be. Indeed, it is no surprise that the history surrounding the enactment of § 2 . . . indicates that Congress envisioned criminal penalties only for those who by their own conduct violated the statute, since vicarious criminal liability would be extraordinary. The same cannot be said of vicarious civil liability.

Nor does anything in the history of § 1981 cast doubt on the argument that liability under the statute may be vicarious. The Court of Appeals placed heavy reliance on Congress' rejection of the Sherman Amendment, which would have imposed a dramatic form of vicarious liability on municipalities, five years after passing the 1866 Act. That the Court appears to accept this argument is curious, given our frequent reminder that " 'the views of a subsequent Congress form a hazardous basis for inferring the intent of an earlier one.' " Consumer Product Safety Comm'n v. GTE Sylvania, Inc., 447 U.S. 102, 117 (1980). I do not understand how Congress' rejection of an amendment imposing a very new kind of vicarious liability on municipalities can tell us what a different and earlier Congress intended with respect to conventional vicarious liability.

According to the Court, the history of the Sherman Amendment is relevant to the interpretation of § 1981 because it reveals Congress' impression that it had no authority to subject municipalities to the kind of liability encompassed by the amendment. The Court fails to recognize, however, that the circumstances in which municipalities would be vicariously liable under the Sherman Amendment are very different from those in which they would be liable under § 1981. [Had the Sherman Amendment been enacted, it] would have forced municipalities to ensure that private citizens did not violate the rights of others. . . . To hold a local government body liable for the discriminatory cancellation of a contract entered into by that local body itself, however, is a very different matter. Even assuming that the 39th Congress had the same constitutional concerns as the 42nd, therefore, those concerns cast no doubt on Congress' authority to hold local government bodies vicariously liable under § 1 of the 1866 Act in circumstances such as those present here.

I thus would conclude that liability under § 1981 may be predicated on a theory of respondeat superior.

III

No one doubts that § 1983 was an unprecedented federal statute. The question is not whether § 1983 wrought a change in the law, but whether it did so in such a way as to withdraw a remedy that § 1 of the 1866 Act had implicitly afforded. Unlike the Court, I would conclude that it did not.

■ [JUSTICE STEVENS' separate dissent is omitted.]

NOTES ON JETT V. DALLAS INDEPENDENT SCHOOL DISTRICT

1. BACKGROUND

The decision in *Jett* implicates at least three lines of prior decisions. The first concerns when it is appropriate for the courts to enforce a private damages action for violations of the Constitution. The leading case is Bivens v. Six Unknown Named Agents of Federal Bureau of Narcotics, 403 U.S. 388 (1971), where the Court held that damages could be sought from federal law enforcement officials for violation of the Fourth Amendment. The decisions since *Bivens* have varied and have turned chiefly on whether the Court has been able to find, in the language of *Bivens,* "special factors counseling hesitation in the absence of affirmative action by Congress" or an alternative remedy which Congress explicitly declared to be a substitute for judicially implied relief.

The second line of cases involves the implication of a private damages action from a federal statute that does not explicitly authorize such relief. The cases in this context have gone through three stages: (i) the suggestion of J.I. Case v. Borak, 377 U.S. 426 (1964), that private remedies would be freely available; (ii) the adoption in Cort v. Ash, 422 U.S. 66 (1975), of a four-part inquiry to determine when a private remedy should be implied; and (iii) the statement in Touche Ross & Co. v. Redington, 442 U.S. 560 (1979), that such remedies would not be recognized unless "Congress intended to create the private right of action asserted."

The third line of cases concerns the meaning of the words "and laws" in 42 U.S.C. § 1983. The Court indicated in Maine v. Thiboutot, 448 U.S. 1 (1980), that § 1983 supplied a private cause of action for damages against any state official who violated rights created by any federal statute. Subsequent cases have cast doubt on the breadth of this proposition, but it still remains clear that *some* federal statutes are enforceable against state officials through damage actions based on § 1983. The important question is the starting point for analysis: whether a § 1983 remedy is available *unless* Congress appears to have directed otherwise, or whether it is available only *if* Congress appears to have so intended.

2. QUESTIONS AND COMMENTS

The Court holds in *Jett* that a remedy cannot be implied from § 1981 against a unit of local government whose officials deny the substantive rights it creates. Instead, § 1981 is to be regarded in this context as the origin of rights that are enforceable only through the cause of action created by § 1983. The plaintiff can recover against a unit of local government, therefore, only if the conditions established for § 1983 can be satisfied. In cases where *private* actors are sued under § 1981, by contrast, the remedy appears to be implied from § 1981 itself. Section 1983 is irrelevant because of its limitation to actions taken under color of state law.

Which line of cases summarized above is most relevant to the Court's decision? Is the Court's holding consistent with analogous precedents? Would it have been better (and more consistent with cases against *private* actors) for the Court to have reached its result by recognizing that a *cause of action* can be implied from § 1981, but that § 1981, like § 1983, does not embrace the doctrine of respondeat superior in cases of governmental liability? Would this rationale have been more consistent with the prior § 1981 precedents? Are there reasons for restricting the liability of government actors based on respondeat superior that do not apply to private actors?

Under Title VII, all employers—whether public or private—are usually liable for acts of their subordinates under the doctrine of respondeat superior. As the next chapter discusses in more detail, liability for sexual harassment constitutes a limited exception to this rule, but it is limited. The claim in *Jett* for discriminatory dismissal falls squarely under the general rule. Plaintiffs who sue their public employers can therefore easily get around this decision simply by adding a Title VII claim to their claims under § 1981 and § 1983. Given this result, why did the Court interpret § 1981 to conform to the more limited liability under § 1983 rather than the broader liability under Title VII? Is *Jett* just another example of the principle, illustrated by *General Building Contractors*, that § 1981 follows constitutional law rather than Title VII when the two diverge? The decision treats liability of public employers under § 1981 under the narrower principles applicable to constitutional torts under § 1983 instead of the broader principles governing liability of employers under Title VII. Is the best argument for this conclusion the same argument advanced in *General Building Contractors*: that if it makes a difference, § 1981 should be interpreted according to statutes and constitutional provisions also enacted during Reconstruction rather than a statute enacted almost a century later?

How is the result in *Jett* affected by the Civil Rights Act of 1991? The new provisions in § 1981(c) recognize that there are "rights protected by this section," but it does not address the question of remedies. On the other hand, these rights are protected equally "against impairment by nongovernmental discrimination and impairment under color of State law." *Jett*, unlike *Patterson v. McLean Credit Union*, was not overruled, even in part, by the Civil Rights Act of 1991. Does this congressional silence amount to acquiescence in or ratification of the decision?

3. 42 U.S.C. § 1985(3)

Griffin v. Breckenridge

Supreme Court of the United States, 1971.
403 U.S. 88.

■ MR. JUSTICE STEWART delivered the opinion of the Court.

This litigation began when the petitioners filed a complaint in the United States District Court for the Southern District of Mississippi, seeking compensatory and punitive damages and alleging, in substantial part, as follows:

2. The plaintiffs are Negro citizens of the United States and residents of Kemper County, Mississippi. . . .

3. The defendants, Lavon Breckenridge and James Calvin Breckenridge, are white adult citizens of the United States residing in DeKalb, Kemper County, Mississippi.

4. On July 2, 1966, the . . . plaintiffs . . . were passengers in an automobile belonging to and operated by R. G. Grady of Memphis, Tennessee. They were traveling upon the federal, state and local highways in and about DeKalb, Mississippi, performing various errands and visiting friends.

5. On July 2, 1966 defendants, acting under a mistaken belief that R. G. Grady was a worker for civil rights for Negroes, wilfully and maliciously conspired, planned, and agreed to block the passage of said plaintiffs in said automobile upon the public highways, to stop and detain them and to assault, beat and injure them with deadly weapons. Their purpose was to prevent said plaintiffs and other Negro–Americans, through such force, violence and intimidation, from seeking the equal protection of the laws and from enjoying the equal rights, privileges and immunities of citizens under the laws of the United States and the state of Mississippi, including but not limited to their rights to freedom of speech, movement, association and assembly; their right to petition their government for redress of their grievances; their rights to be secure in their persons and their homes; and their rights not to be enslaved nor deprived of life and liberty other than by due process of law.

6. Pursuant to their conspiracy, defendants drove their truck into the path of Grady's automobile and blocked its passage over the public road. Both defendants then forced Grady and said plaintiffs to get out of Grady's automobile and prevented said plaintiffs from escaping while defendant James Calvin Breckenridge clubbed Grady with a blackjack, pipe or other kind of club by pointing firearms at said plaintiffs and uttering threats to kill and injure them if defendants' orders were not obeyed, thereby terrorizing them to the utmost degree and depriving them of their liberty.

7. Pursuant to their conspiracy, defendants wilfully, intentionally, and maliciously menaced and assaulted each of the said plaintiffs by pointing firearms and wielding deadly blackjacks, pipes or other kinds of clubs, while uttering threats to kill and injure said plaintiffs, causing them to become stricken with fear of immediate injury and death and to suffer extreme terror, mental anguish and emotional and physical distress.

8. Pursuant to defendants' conspiracy, defendant James Calvin Breckenridge then wilfully, intentionally and maliciously clubbed each of said plaintiffs on and about the head, severely injuring all of them, while both defendants continued to assault said plaintiffs and prevent their escape by pointing their firearms at them. . . .

12. By their conspiracy and acts pursuant thereto, the defendants have wilfully and maliciously, directly and indirectly, intimidated and prevented the . . . plaintiffs . . . and other Negro–Americans from enjoying and exercising their rights, privileges and immunities as citizens of the United States and the State of Mississippi, including but not limited to, their rights to freedom of speech, movement, associ-

ation and assembly, the right to petition their government for redress of grievances; their right to be secure in their person; their right not to be enslaved nor deprived of life, liberty or property other than by due process of law, and their rights to travel the public highways without restraint in the same terms as white citizens in Kemper County, Mississippi. . . .

The jurisdiction of the federal court was invoked under the language of 42 U.S.C. § 1985(3), which provides:

> If two or more persons in any State or Territory conspire or go in disguise on the highway or on the premises of another, for the purpose of depriving, either directly or indirectly, any person or class of persons of the equal protection of the laws, or of equal privileges and immunities under the laws [and] in any case of conspiracy set forth in this section, if one or more persons engaged therein do, or cause to be done, any act in furtherance of the object of such conspiracy, whereby another is injured in his person or property, or deprived of having and exercising any right or privilege of a citizen of the United States, the party so injured or deprived may have an action for the recovery of damages, occasioned by such injury or deprivation, against any one or more of the conspirators.

The District Court dismissed the complaint for failure to state a cause of action, relying on the authority of this Court's opinion in Collins v. Hardyman, 341 U.S. 651 (1951), which in effect construed the above language of § 1985(3) as reaching only conspiracies under color of state law. The Court of Appeals for the Fifth Circuit affirmed the judgment of dismissal. Judge Goldberg's thorough opinion for that court expressed "serious doubts" as to the "continued vitality" of *Collins v. Hardyman*, and stated that "it would not surprise us if *Collins v. Hardyman* were disapproved and if § 1985(3) were held to embrace private conspiracies to interfere with rights of national citizenship," but concluded that "[s]ince we may not adopt what the Supreme Court has expressly rejected, we obediently abide the mandate in *Collins*." We granted certiorari to consider questions going to the scope and constitutionality of 42 U.S.C. § 1985(3).

I

Collins v. Hardyman was decided 20 years ago. The complaint in that case alleged that the plaintiffs were members of a political club that had scheduled a meeting to adopt a resolution opposing the Marshall Plan, and to send copies of the resolution to appropriate federal officials; that the defendants conspired to deprive the plaintiffs of their rights as citizens of the United States peaceably to assemble and to equal privileges and immunities under the laws of the United States; that, in furtherance of the conspiracy, the defendants proceeded to the meeting site and, by threats and violence, broke up the meeting, thus interfering with the right of the plaintiffs to petition the government for the redress of grievances; and that the defendants did not interfere or conspire to interfere with the meetings of other political groups with whose opinions the defendants agreed. The Court held that this complaint did not state a cause of action under § 1985(3):

> The complaint makes no claim that the conspiracy or the overt acts involved any action by state officials, or that defendants even pretended to act under color of state law. It is not shown that defendants had or claimed any protection or immunity from the law of the state,

> or that they in fact enjoyed such because of any act or omission by state authorities.
>
> What we have here is not a conspiracy to affect in any way these plaintiffs' equality of protection by the law, or their equality of privileges and immunities under the law. There is not the slightest allegation that defendants were conscious of or trying to influence the law, or were endeavoring to obstruct or interfere with it. . . . Such private discrimination is not inequality before the law unless there is some manipulation of the law or its agencies to give sanction or sanctuary for doing so.

The Court was careful to make clear that it was deciding no constitutional question, but simply construing the language of the statute, or more precisely, determining the applicability of the statute to the facts alleged in the complaint:[2]

> We say nothing of the power of Congress to authorize such civil actions as respondents have commenced or otherwise to redress such grievances as they assert. We think that Congress has not, in the narrow class of conspiracies defined by this statute, included the conspiracy charged here. We therefore reach no constitutional questions.

Nonetheless, the Court made equally clear that the construction it gave to the statute was influenced by the constitutional problems that it thought would have otherwise been engendered:

> It is apparent that, if this complaint meets the requirements of this act, it raises constitutional problems of the first magnitude that, in the light of history, are not without difficulty. These would include issues as to congressional power under and apart from the Fourteenth Amendment, the reserved power of the states, the content of rights derived from national as distinguished from state citizenship, and the question of separability of the act in its application to those two classes of rights.

Mr. Justice Burton filed a dissenting opinion, joined by Mr. Justice Black and Mr. Justice Douglas. The dissenters thought that "[t]he language of the statute refutes the suggestion that action under color of state law is a necessary ingredient of the cause of action which it recognizes." Further, the dissenters found no constitutional difficulty in according to the statutory words their apparent meaning:

> Congress certainly has the power to create a federal cause of action in favor of persons injured by private individuals through the abridgment of federally created constitutional rights. It seems to me that Congress has done just this in [§ 1985(3)]. This is not inconsistent with the principle underlying the Fourteenth Amendment. That amendment prohibits the respective states from making laws abridging the privileges or immunities of citizens of the United States or denying to any person within the jurisdiction of a state the equal protection of the laws. Cases holding that those clauses are directed only at state action are not authority for the contention that Congress may

[2] "We do not say that no conspiracy by private individuals could be of such magnitude and effect as to work a deprivation of equal protection of the laws, or of equal privileges and immunities under laws. . . . But here nothing of that sort appears. We have a case of a lawless political brawl, precipitated by a handful of white citizens against other white citizens." 341 U.S., at 662.

not pass laws supporting rights which exist apart from the Fourteenth Amendment.[a]

II

Whether or not *Collins v. Hardyman* was correctly decided on its own facts is a question with which we need not here be concerned. But it is clear, in the light of the evolution of decisional law in the years that have passed since that case was decided, that many of the constitutional problems there perceived simply do not exist. Little reason remains, therefore, not to accord to the words of the statute their apparent meaning. That meaning is confirmed by judicial construction of related laws, by the structural setting of § 1985(3) itself, and by its legislative history. And a fair reading of the allegations of the complaint in this case clearly brings them within this meaning of the statutory language. As so construed, and as applied to this complaint, we have no doubt that the statute was within the constitutional power of Congress to enact.

III

We turn, then, to an examination of the meaning of § 1985(3). On their face, the words of the statute fully encompass the conduct of private persons. The provision speaks simply of "two or more persons in any State or Territory" who "conspire or go in disguise on the highway or on the premises of another." Going in disguise, in particular, is in this context an activity so little associated with official action and so commonly connected with private marauders that this clause could almost never be applicable under the artificially restrictive construction of *Collins*. And since the "going in disguise" aspect must include private action, it is hard to see how the conspiracy aspect, joined by a disjunctive, could be read to require the involvement of state officers.

The provision continues, specifying the motivation required "for the purpose of depriving, either directly or indirectly, any person or class of persons of the equal protection of the laws, or of equal privileges and immunities under the laws." This language is, of course, similar to that of § 1 of the Fourteenth Amendment, which in terms speaks only to the states, and judicial thinking about what can constitute an equal protection deprivation has, because of the amendment's wording, focused almost entirely upon identifying the requisite "state action" and defining the offending forms of state law and official conduct. A century of Fourteenth Amendment adjudication has, in other words, made it understandably difficult to conceive of what might constitute a deprivation of the equal protection of the laws by private persons. Yet there is nothing inherent in the phrase that requires the action working the deprivation to come from the state. Indeed, the failure to mention any such requisite can be viewed as an important indication of congressional intent to speak in § 1985(3) of *all* deprivations of "equal protection of the laws" and "equal privileges and immunities under the laws," whatever their source.

The approach of this Court to other Reconstruction civil rights statutes in the years since *Collins* has been to "accord [them] a sweep as broad as [their] language." United States v. Price, 383 U.S. 787, 801 (1966); Jones v. Alfred H. Mayer Co., 392 U.S. 409, 437 (1968). Moreover, very similar lan-

[a] The dissent identified the right alleged to have been violated as the "right to petition the federal government for a redress of grievances." The dissent said that this "right is expressly recognized by the First Amendment" and that the "source of the right in this case is not the Fourteenth Amendment."—[Footnote by eds.]

guage in closely related statutes has early and late received an interpretation quite inconsistent with that given to § 1985(3) in *Collins*. In construing the exact criminal counterpart of § 1985(3), the Court in United States v. Harris, 106 U.S. 629, 637, 639 (1882), observed that the statute was "not limited to take effect only in case [of state action]," but "was framed to protect from invasion by private persons, the equal privileges and immunities under the laws, of all persons and classes of persons." In United States v. Williams, 341 U.S. 70 (1951), the Court considered the closest remaining criminal analogue to § 1985(3), 18 U.S.C. § 241.[4] Mr. Justice Frankfurter's plurality opinion, without contravention from the concurrence or dissent, concluded that "if language is to carry any meaning at all it must be clear that the principal purpose of [§ 241], unlike [18 U.S.C. § 242], was to reach private action rather than officers of a state acting under its authority. Men who 'go in disguise upon the public highway, or upon the premises of another' are not likely to be acting in official capacities." "Nothing in [the] terms [of § 241] indicates that color of state law was to be relevant to prosecution under it."

A like construction of § 1985(3) is reinforced when examination is broadened to take in its companion statutory provisions. There appear to be three possible forms for a state action limitation on § 1985(3)—that there must be action under color of state law, that there must be interference with or influence upon state authorities, or that there must be a private conspiracy so massive and effective that it supplants those authorities and thus satisfies the state action requirement. The Congress that passed the Civil Rights Act of 1871, § 2 of which is the parent of § 1985(3), dealt with each of these three situations in explicit terms in other parts of the same act. An element of the cause of action established by the first section, now 42 U.S.C. § 1983, is that the deprivation complained of must have been inflicted under color of state law. To read any such requirement into § 1985(3) would thus deprive that section of all independent effect. As for interference with state officials, § 1985(3) itself contains another clause dealing explicitly with that situation.[7] And § 3 of the 1871 act provided for military action at the command of the President should massive private lawlessness render state authorities powerless to protect the federal rights of classes of citizens, such a situation being defined by the act as constituting a state denial of equal protection. Given the existence of these three provisions, it is almost impossible to believe that Congress intended, in the dissimilar language of the portion of § 1985(3) now before us, simply to duplicate the coverage of one or more of them.

The final area of inquiry into the meaning of § 1985(3) lies in its legislative history. As originally introduced in the 42nd Congress, the section was solely a criminal provision outlawing certain conspiratorial acts done

---

[4] "If two or more persons conspire to injure, oppress, threaten, or intimidate any citizen in the free exercise or enjoyment of any right or privilege secured to him by the Constitution or laws of the United States, or because of his having so exercised the same; or

"If two or more persons go in disguise on the highway, or on the premises of another, with intent to prevent or hinder his free exercise or enjoyment of any right or privilege so secured—

"They shall be fined not more than $5,000 or imprisoned not more than ten years, or both."

The penalty section was amended in 1968.

[7] "If two or more persons in any State or Territory conspire or go in disguise on the highway or on the premises of another . . . for the purpose of preventing or hindering the constituted authorities of any State or Territory from giving or securing to all persons within such State or Territory the equal protection of the laws. . . . "

with intent "to do any act in violation of the rights, privileges, or immunities of another person. . . . " Cong. Globe, 42nd Cong., 1st Sess.App. 68 (1871). Introducing the bill, the House sponsor, Representative Shellabarger, stressed that "the United States always has assumed to enforce, as against the states, *and also persons*, every one of the provisions of the Constitution." The enormous sweep of the original language led to pressures for amendment, in the course of which the present civil remedy was added. The explanations of the added language centered entirely on the animus or motivation that would be required, and there was no suggestion whatever that liability would not be imposed for purely private conspiracies. Representative Willard, draftsman of the limiting amendment, said that his version "provid[ed] that the essence of the crime should consist in the intent to deprive a person of the equal protection of the laws and of equal privileges and immunities under the laws; in other words, that the Constitution secured, and was only intended to secure, equality of rights and immunities, and that we could only punish by United States laws a denial of that equality." Representative Shellabarger's explanation of the amendment was very similar: "The object of the amendment is . . . to confine the authority of this law to the prevention of deprivations which shall attack the equality of rights of American citizens; that any violation of the right, the animus and effect of which is to strike down the citizen, to the end that he may not enjoy equality of rights as contrasted with his and other citizens' rights, shall be within the scope of the remedies of this section."[8]

Other supporters of the bill were even more explicit in their insistence upon coverage of private action. Shortly before the amendment was introduced, Representative Shanks urged, "I do not want to see [this measure] so amended that there shall be taken out of it the frank assertion of the power of the national government to protect life, liberty, and property, irrespective of the act of the state." At about the same time, Representative Coburn asked: "Shall we deal with individuals, or with the state as a state? If we can deal with individuals, that is a less radical course, and works less interference with local governments. . . . It would seem more accordant with reason that the easier, more direct, and more certain method of dealing with individual criminals was preferable, and that the more thorough method of superseding state authority should only be resorted to when the deprivation of rights and the condition of outlawry was so general as to prevail in all quarters in defiance of or by permission of the local government." After the amendment had been proposed in the House, Senator Pool insisted in support of the bill during Senate debate that "Congress must deal with individuals, not states. It must punish the offender against the rights of the citizen. . . . "

It is thus evident that all indicators—text, companion provisions, and legislative history—point unwaveringly to § 1985(3)'s coverage of private conspiracies. That the statute was meant to reach private action does not, however, mean that it was intended to apply to all tortious, conspiratorial interferences with the rights of others. For, though the supporters of the legislation insisted on coverage of private conspiracies, they were equally emphatic that they did not believe, in the words of Representative Cook, "that Congress has a right to punish an assault and battery when committed by two or more persons within a state." The constitutional shoals that would lie in the path of interpreting § 1985(3) as a general federal tort law

[8] The conspiracy and disguise language of what finally became § 1985(3) appears to have been borrowed from the parent of 18 U.S.C. § 241.

can be avoided by giving full effect to the congressional purpose—by requiring, as an element of the cause of action, the kind of invidiously discriminatory motivation stressed by the sponsors of the limiting amendment. The language requiring intent to deprive of equal protection, or equal privileges and immunities, means that there must be some racial, or perhaps otherwise class-based, invidiously discriminatory animus behind the conspirators' action.[9] The conspiracy, in other words, must aim at a deprivation of the equal enjoyment of rights secured by the law to all.[10]

IV

We return to the petitioners' complaint to determine whether it states a cause of action under § 1985(3) as so construed. To come within the legislation a complaint must allege that the defendants did (1) "conspire to go in disguise on the highway or on the premises of another" (2) "for the purpose of depriving, either directly or indirectly, any person or class of persons of the equal protection of the laws, or of equal privileges and immunities under the laws." It must then assert that one or more of the conspirators (3) did, or caused to be done, "any act in furtherance of the object of [the] conspiracy," whereby another was (4a) "injured in his person or property" or (4b) "deprived of having and exercising any right or privilege of a citizen of the United States."

The complaint fully alleges, with particulars, that the respondents conspired to carry out the assault. It further asserts that "[t]heir purpose was to prevent [the] plaintiffs and other Negro–Americans, through . . . force, violence and intimidation, from seeking the equal protection of the laws and from enjoying the equal rights, privileges and immunities of citizens under the laws of the United States and the state of Mississippi," including a long list of enumerated rights such as free speech, assembly, association, and movement. The complaint further alleges that the respondents were "acting under a mistaken belief that R. G. Grady was a worker for civil rights for Negroes." These allegations clearly support the requisite animus to deprive the petitioners of the equal enjoyment of legal rights because of their race. The claims of detention, threats, and battery amply satisfy the requirement of acts done in furtherance of the conspiracy. Finally, the petitioners—whether or not the nonparty Grady was the main or only target of the conspiracy—allege personal injury resulting from those acts. The complaint, then, states a cause of action under § 1985(3). Indeed, the conduct here alleged lies so close to the core of the coverage intended by Congress that it is hard to conceive of wholly private conduct that would come within the statute if this does not. We must, accordingly, consider whether Congress had constitutional power to enact a statute that imposes liability under federal law for the conduct alleged in this complaint.

---

[9] We need not decide, given the facts of this case, whether a conspiracy motivated by invidiously discriminatory intent other than racial bias would be actionable under the portion of § 1985(3) before us.

[10] The motivation requirement introduced by the word "equal" into the portion of § 1985(3) before us must not be confused with the test of "specific intent to deprive a person of a federal right made definite by decision or other rule of law" articulated by the plurality opinion in Screws v. United States, 325 U.S. 91, 103 (1945), for prosecutions under 18 U.S.C. § 242. Section 1985(3), unlike § 242, contains no specific requirement of "wilfulness." The motivation aspect of § 1985(3) focuses not on scienter in relation to deprivation of rights but on invidiously discriminatory animus.

V

The constitutionality of § 1985(3) might once have appeared to have been settled adversely by United States v. Harris, 106 U.S. 629 (1882), and Baldwin v. Franks, 120 U.S. 678 (1886), which held unconstitutional its criminal counterpart, then § 5519 of the Revised Statutes.[11] The Court in those cases, however, followed a severability rule that required invalidation of an entire statute if any part of it was unconstitutionally overbroad, unless its different parts could be read as wholly independent provisions. This Court has long since firmly rejected that rule in such cases as United States v. Raines, 362 U.S. 17, 20–24 (1960). Consequently, we need not find the language of § 1985(3) now before us constitutional in all its possible applications in order to uphold its facial constitutionality and its application to the complaint in this case

That § 1985(3) reaches private conspiracies to deprive others of legal rights can, of itself, cause no doubts of its constitutionality. It has long been settled that 18 U.S.C. § 241, a criminal statute of far broader phrasing (see n. 4, supra), reaches wholly private conspiracies and is constitutional. E.g., In re Quarles, 158 U.S. 532 (1894); Logan v. United States, 144 U.S. 263, 293–95 (1892); United States v. Waddell, 112 U.S. 76, 77–81 (1884); Ex parte Yarbrough, 110 U.S. 651 (1884). Our inquiry, therefore, need go only to identifying a source of congressional power to reach the private conspiracy alleged by the complaint in this case.

A

Even as it struck down Rev. Stat. § 5519 in *United States v. Harris*, the Court indicated that parts of its coverage would, if severable, be constitutional under the Thirteenth Amendment. And surely there has never been any doubt of the power of Congress to impose liability on private persons under § 2 of that amendment, "for the amendment is not a mere prohibition of state laws establishing or upholding slavery, but an absolute declaration that slavery or involuntary servitude shall not exist in any part of the United States." Civil Rights Cases, 109 U.S. 3, 20 (1883). Not only may Congress impose such liability, but the varieties of private conduct that it may make criminally punishable or civilly remediable extend far beyond the actual imposition of slavery or involuntary servitude. By the Thirteenth Amendment, we committed ourselves as a nation to the proposition that the former slaves and their descendants should be forever free. To keep that promise, "Congress has the power under the Thirteenth Amendment rationally to determine what are the badges and the incidents of slavery, and the authority to translate that determination into effective legislation." *Jones v. Alfred H. Mayer Co.* supra, at 440. We can only conclude that Congress was wholly within its powers under § 2 of the Thirteenth Amendment in creating a statutory cause of action for Negro citizens who have been the victims of conspiratorial, racially discriminatory private action aimed at depriving them of the basic rights that the law secures to all free men.

B

Our cases have firmly established that the right of interstate travel is constitutionally protected, does not necessarily rest on the Fourteenth Amendment, and is assertable against private as well as governmental interference. [E.g.,] Shapiro v. Thompson, 394 U.S. 618, 629–31 (1969). The "right to pass freely from state to state" has been explicitly recognized as

[11] Rev. Stat. § 5519 was repealed in 1909.

"among the rights and privileges of national citizenship." Twining v. New Jersey, 211 U.S. 78, 97 (1908). That right, like other rights of national citizenship, is within the power of Congress to protect by appropriate legislation.

The complaint in this case alleged that the petitioners "were traveling upon the federal, state and local highways in and about" DeKalb, Kemper County, Mississippi. Kemper County is on the Mississippi–Alabama border. One of the results of the conspiracy, according to the complaint, was to prevent the petitioners and other Negroes from exercising their "rights to travel the public highways without restraint in the same terms as white citizens in Kemper County, Mississippi." Finally, the conspiracy was alleged to have been inspired by the respondents' erroneous belief that Grady, a Tennessean, was a worker for Negro civil rights. Under these allegations it is open to the petitioners to prove at trial that they had been engaging in interstate travel or intended to do so, that their federal right to travel interstate was one of the rights meant to be discriminatorily impaired by the conspiracy, that the conspirators intended to drive out-of-state civil rights workers from the state, or that they meant to deter the petitioners from associating with such persons. This and other evidence could make it clear that the petitioners had suffered from conduct that Congress may reach under its power to protect the right of interstate travel.

C

In identifying these two constitutional sources of congressional power, we do not imply the absence of any other. More specifically, the allegations of the complaint in this case have not required consideration of the scope of the power of Congress under § 5 of the Fourteenth Amendment. By the same token, since the allegations of the complaint bring this cause of action so close to the constitutionally authorized core of the statute, there has been no occasion here to trace out its constitutionally permissible periphery.

The judgment is reversed, and the case is remanded to the United States District Court for the Southern District of Mississippi for further proceedings consistent with this opinion.

It is so ordered.

■ MR. JUSTICE HARLAN, concurring.

I agree with the Court's opinion, except that I find it unnecessary to rely on the "right of interstate travel" as a premise for justifying federal jurisdiction under § 1985(3). With that reservation, I join the opinion and judgment of the Court.

NOTES ON GRIFFIN V. BRECKENRIDGE

1. INTRODUCTION

Section 1985(3) is derived from § 2 of the Civil Rights Act of 1871, also known as the Ku Klux Klan Act, § 1 of which became § 1983. Section 1985(3) and § 1983 thus share much of the same legislative history and many of the same objectives. They also share the fact that they were of little significance for almost 100 years following their enactment. Section 1983 was revived by *Monroe v. Pape*. *Griffin* is the analogous case that breathed new life into § 1985(3).

As the *Griffin* Court noted, the text of § 1985(3) states four requirements: (1) a conspiracy of two or more persons; (2) that has as its object depriving "any person or class of persons" of "the equal protection of the laws" or of "equal privileges and immunities under the laws"; and (3) an overt act in furtherance of the conspiracy; (4) that causes injury to another "in his person or property" or that deprives another "of having and exercising any right or privilege of a citizen of the United States." The first, third, and fourth of these provisions are easily satisfied by a wide variety of criminal or tortious behavior: all they require is a conspiracy followed by an overt act that causes injury to persons or property. The crucial element is the second. The statute will have broad or narrow impact depending on how this element is interpreted.

Justice Stewart said in *Griffin* that § 1985(3) was not "intended to apply to all tortious, conspiratorial interferences with the rights of others," and no justice has ever disagreed. As the following materials illustrate, however, the Court has not been very precise as to where, short of "all tortious, conspiratorial interferences with the rights of others," the lines of coverage should be drawn.

2. QUESTIONS AND COMMENTS ON *GRIFFIN V. BRECKENRIDGE*

The biggest problem presented by § 1985(3) is identification of the rights for which the statute provides a remedy. The Court's pronouncements on this question are difficult and confusing. Three aspects of *Griffin* that bear on the question are: (1) whether the statute requires "state action"; (2) the requirement of "invidiously discriminatory animus"; and (3) the sources of power on which the Court relied to uphold the constitutionality of the statute as applied.

(i) State Action

In the *Griffin* Court's words, Collins v. Hardyman, 341 U.S. 651 (1951), had "in effect construed . . . § 1985(3) as reaching only conspiracies under color of state law." This position was unanimously repudiated in *Griffin* on the basis of the text of the statute, as "confirmed by judicial construction of related laws, by the structural setting of § 1985(3) itself, and by its legislative history." The result is that § 1985(3) now applies to the actions of private parties.

The statute's application to private conduct gives rise to the problem of how to contain its reach short of "all tortious, conspiratorial interferences with the rights of others." If § 1985(3) had been interpreted to require state action, the natural source of the rights protected by the statute would be the Fourteenth Amendment. As the *Griffin* Court points out, the problem with this interpretation is § 1983, which already provides relief against state actors who violate the Fourteenth Amendment. Section § 1985(3) would thus be entirely redundant with another civil rights statute enacted at the same time. Even if § 1985(3) had required only the kind of state action anticipated in *Collins* (see footnote 2 in *Griffin*), it would still have been redundant with § 1983.[a]

[a] There is some support for this construction in the legislative history. Section 1985(3), as evidenced by its "go in disguise" language, was primarily aimed at the Ku Klux Klan, and in particular at the inability of the victims of the Klan to achieve redress under state law. Testimony before the Congress revealed, for example, that Klan members often either were members of, or were able to exercise control over, grand and petty juries. An argument could be made in such a situation that the "conspiracy" was large enough, and the inability of state government to protect the rights of Klan victims pervasive enough, so that Klan violence was sufficient "state action" to satisfy even a restrictive reading of the statute. Whether such inef-

Since § 1985(3) does not require state action, there is no redundancy with § 1983—but there is also no catalogue of rights to which § 1985(3) seems naturally to refer. It is not traditional to think of constitutional rights as protections against the misconduct of fellow citizens. The guarantee of "equal protection of the laws," for example, seems to speak directly to state actors. Similarly, it seems odd to regard the First Amendment as protecting against political or religious discrimination by private parties. Applying constitutional rights that exist against government to the actions of private parties would create a host of non-constitutional rights. The Court has taken the view that the statute does not reach that result, nor does it describe with any precision a class of non-constitutional rights that can be asserted against private parties in federal court. The difficulty, then, is how to distinguish the rights protected by § 1985(3) from what would otherwise be garden variety state torts or crimes.

(ii) Discriminatory Animus

The *Griffin* Court sought to confine the private behavior covered by § 1985(3) by saying that "there must be some racial, or perhaps other class-based, invidiously discriminatory animus behind the conspirators' action." Ordinary torts or crimes are not within the scope of § 1985(3) unless they are manifestations of racial discrimination or "perhaps" some other class-based discrimination.

"Perhaps" remains an important ambiguity. It is clear enough that Congress intended § 1985(3) to provide a remedy for racial discrimination, but should other forms of discrimination—based on sex, religion, legitimacy, or alienage, for example—also be covered? Should all of the "suspect classes" that the Fourteenth Amendment has come to protect be used as a measure of the kinds of discrimination covered by § 1985(3)? The "suspect classes" idea was developed in Fourteenth Amendment jurisprudence to limit discrimination by government. Does the shift to private discrimination under § 1985(3) change the inquiry? Do the reasons that underlie the development of Fourteenth Amendment "suspect classes" apply equally well to a prohibition aimed at private conspiracies? Or should § 1985(3) be limited by its historical context to the kind of discrimination, primarily racial, on which the Congress focused in 1871?

(iii) Constitutional Authority

The sources of constitutional authority on which the *Griffin* Court relied to uphold the statute are also relevant to the debate about the kinds of rights protected by § 1985(3). The Court upheld the statute as applied because the plaintiffs asserted two rights that the Court thought Congress clearly had the power to enforce. Interestingly—and perhaps significantly—neither was based on the Fourteenth Amendment.

First, the Court relied on the "right of interstate travel."[b] In this application, the complaint alleged racial discrimination that inhibited the enjoyment

fectiveness of state law could be proved, however—and whether it should be required that it be proved in each case filed under § 1985(3)—is an entirely different matter. Such a proof requirement would likely stultify the remedies provided by the statute.

[b] At least three potential sources of the right to travel have been identified in the cases: the Commerce Clause, the Privileges and Immunities Clause of Art. IV, and the Privileges or Immunities Clause of the Fourteenth Amendment.

of a right protected by federal law but not itself created by § 1985(3). Under this approach, § 1985(3) can be regarded as establishing a cause of action to enforce independently created federal rights when they have been denied on grounds of racial and "perhaps" other class-based discrimination. Does this mean that § 1985(3) can be invoked only if there is a federal right from some independent source that has been discriminatorily denied? If so, § 1985(3) is merely remedial in nature—that is, it *creates* no rights but merely permits civil suit where existing federal rights are denied on grounds of racial and "perhaps" other invidiously discriminatory motives. Does that mean that § 1985(3) remedies racial discrimination only where some other federal provision or statute already forbids it? What if someone acts with a racially discriminatory motive to deny a right under state law? Once a racially discriminatory motive is established, why should it be necessary to identify any additional "rights" of which the plaintiff has been deprived?

Second, the Court apparently regarded it as independently sufficient that Congress could have enacted § 1985(3) under § 2 of the Thirteenth Amendment. Quoting *Jones v. Alfred H. Mayer Co.*, it said that Congress could "rationally" define the "badges" and "incidents" of slavery and could translate that determination into a statute that protected blacks "who have been the victims of conspiratorial, racially discriminatory private action aimed at depriving them of the basic rights that the law secures to all free men." This passage suggests an entirely different theory. The badge-and-incidents language describes the scope of federal legislative power under § 2 of the Thirteenth Amendment, not the self-executing provision of § 1. If § 1985(3) covers all rights that Congress could have created under § 2 of the Thirteenth Amendment, the rights being enforced by § 1985(3) are not created by some independent source of federal law, but by § 1985(3) itself. Congress in § 1985(3) created the right not to be deprived on racially discriminatory grounds of "the basic rights that the law secures to all free men." In other words, perhaps a § 1985(3) action need not be based on the discriminatory deprivation of a federal right that has some independent source. Perhaps § 1985(3) is itself the source of the rights it protects. And perhaps it protects against private deprivation on grounds of race of any right—whether based on state or federal law—generally shared by the public at large, in which case it would be substantially duplicative of §§ 1981 and 1982.

A final dimension of the problem is the relation of the Fourteenth Amendment to the debate about the congressional authority to enact § 1985(3). Note that the Court in *Griffin* explicitly left open the possibility that § 1985(3), even though it reaches private action, might be justified in some other context as an exercise by Congress of its powers under § 5 of the Fourteenth Amendment.[c] Does this suggest that § 1985(3) might extend beyond racial discrimination? Is this why the Fourteenth Amendment might become the source of the kinds of discrimination prohibited by § 1985(3)? One might think the answer to these questions is "yes," since presumably the Court's Thirteenth Amendment rationale for upholding the statute is broad enough to sustain any application in the context of discrimination on grounds of race.

---

[c] Cf. United States v. Guest, 383 U.S. 745 (1966), where six justices indicated in two separate concurring opinions that 18 U.S.C. § 241, the criminal counterpart to § 1985(3), could be upheld under the congressional enforcement power of the Fourteenth Amendment even without any finding of state action. The opinion for the Court upheld the particular indictment at issue on a right to travel theory not unlike the Court's right to travel holding in *Griffin*. It did not address the power of Congress to punish private actors under § 5 of the Fourteenth Amendment.

NOTES ON SUBSEQUENT DECISIONS

1. INTRODUCTION

The various issues raised by *Griffin* have come up in subsequent cases and have been resolved in ways that consistently restrict the scope of the statute. Without questioning the power of Congress to enact a broader law, the Court has narrowly interpreted the rights protected by the statute, the extent to which those rights are protected from private as well as state action, and the discriminatory animus required by the statute. These issues are described in the notes that follow.

2. *UNITED BROTHERHOOD OF CARPENTERS AND JOINERS OF AMERICA V. SCOTT*

This case involved a claim by nonunion workers that they had been injured by a conspiracy to deprive them of their First Amendment rights in violation of § 1985(3). Various unions and private individuals were named as defendants and were found liable by the District Court. The Court of Appeals affirmed, but the Supreme Court reversed. United Brotherhood of Carpenters and Joiners of America v. Scott, 463 U.S. 825 (1983). The Court held that the plaintiffs had failed to prove that the alleged conspiracy had as its object depriving "any person or class of persons" of "the equal protection of the laws" or of "equal privileges and immunities under the laws." Speaking for the Court, Justice White offered two independent reasons for this conclusion.

First, "an alleged conspiracy to infringe First Amendment rights is not a violation of § 1985(3) unless it is proved that the state is involved in the conspiracy or that the aim of the conspiracy is to influence the activity of the state." No such state involvement had been proved in this case. The Court reasoned that some form of state action was necessary because the underlying First Amendment rights, incorporated for application to the states by the Fourteenth Amendment, protected individuals only against encroachment by the government. Although *Griffin* also involved a claim of deprivation of First Amendment rights, the decision was distinguishable because the plaintiffs also alleged rights under the Thirteenth Amendment and the hard-to-locate right to travel among the states, which were also protected from private encroachment.

Second, the Court also held that an intent to discriminate against nonunion workers did not constitute the kind of discriminatory animus required in *Griffin*. The Court found it be "a close question whether § 1985(3) was intended to reach any class-based animus other than animus against Negroes and those who championed their cause, most notably Republicans." Without resolving this question, the Court held that it could not "construe § 1985(3) to reach conspiracies motivated by economic or commercial animus." The Court also noted that the protection of nonunion workers was addressed in great detail by the modern statute regulating collective bargaining, the National Labor Relations Act, 29 U.S.C. § 151 et seq.

Justice Blackmun dissented on both grounds, in an opinion joined by three other justices. On the first ground, he argued that importing a state action requirement into § 1985(3) made it redundant to § 1983. In enacting the statute, Congress emphasized the unequal administration of the laws in the states under reconstruction and sought to prevent any form of interference, whether public or private, with equal exercise and enjoyment of legal rights. On the second ground, Blackmun read the statute "to provide a federal remedy for all *classes* that seek to exercise their legal rights in unprotected circumstances similar to those of the victims of Klan violence." (Emphasis in original.) Blackmun thought that economic classes, such as the economic migrants to the southern states, were among the groups Congress sought to protect.

The Court's recognition that in some circumstances a First Amendment right could be vindicated under § 1985(3) seems to confirm earlier indications that all constitutional rights are cognizable under that statute. But the holding that rights (including First Amendment rights) protected via the Fourteenth Amendment must involve proof "that the state is involved in the conspiracy or that the aim of the conspiracy is to influence the activity of the state" seems to limit § 1985(3) to cases where state action can be proved.

Although the Court also held that "conspiracies against workers who refuse to join a union" is an insufficient "class-based invidiously discriminatory animus," it explicitly reserved decision on whether racial bias is the only form of invidious discrimination covered by § 1985(3). As a result, the only things that are clear are that race counts and bias against non-union workers does not. Is the Court's holding that there is an insufficient class-based bias on these facts persuasive? What are the implications of this part of the Court's opinion on claims of sex discrimination asserted under § 1985(3)?

3. *BRAY V. ALEXANDRIA WOMEN'S HEALTH CLINIC*

In Bray v. Alexandria Women's Health Clinic, 506 U.S. 263 (1993), the Court further restricted the scope of § 1985(3). The case involved a claim of conspiracy to prevent women from seeking abortions by demonstrating in front of abortion clinics in Washington, D.C., and the surrounding area. Writing for the majority, Justice Scalia found no class-based animus against women, based either on the presumed intent or the effect of attempting to prevent abortions. His arguments on this issue ultimately rested on the limited nature of the right to an abortion:

> Whether one agrees or disagrees with the goal of preventing abortion, that goal in itself (apart from the use of unlawful means to achieve it, which is not relevant to our discussion of animus) does not remotely qualify for such harsh description, and for such derogatory association with racism. To the contrary, we have said that "a value judgment favoring childbirth over abortion" is proper and reasonable enough to be implemented by the allocation of public funds, see Maher v. Roe, 432 U.S. 464, 474 (1977), and Congress itself has, with our approval, discriminated against abortion in its provision of financial support for medical procedures, see Harris v. McRae, 448 U.S. 297, 325 (1980). This is not the stuff out of which a § 1985(3) "invidiously discriminatory animus" is created.

Justice Scalia also found no conspiracy to deny "the equal protection of the laws" or "equal privileges and immunities under the laws" within the meaning of § 1985(3). As in *Scott*, the alleged conspiracy was entirely private. It therefore fell within the scope of § 1985(3) only if it involved "an intent to deprive persons of a right guaranteed against private impairment." The constitutional right to an abortion, however, is guaranteed only against government interference. And interference with the right to interstate travel, although it can be infringed by purely private action, was not the object of the conspiracy. As Justice Scalia reasoned:

> Our discussion in *Carpenters* makes clear that it does not suffice for application of § 1985(3) that a protected right be incidentally affected. A conspiracy is not "for the purpose" of denying equal protection simply because it has an effect upon a protected right. The right must be "*aimed at*," *Carpenters*, supra, at 833 (emphasis added); its impairment must be a conscious objective of the enterprise. Just as the "invidiously discriminatory animus" requirement, discussed above, requires that the defendant have taken his action "at least in part 'because of,' not merely 'in spite of,' its adverse effects upon an identifiable group," Personnel Administrator v. Feeney, 442 U.S. 256, 279 (1979), so also the "intent to deprive of a right" requirement demands that the defendant do more than merely be aware of a deprivation of right that he causes, and more than merely accept it; he must act at least in part for the very purpose of producing it. That was not shown to be the case here, and is on its face implausible. Petitioners oppose abortion, and it is irrelevant to their opposition whether the abortion is performed after interstate travel.

Four justices dissented in three separate opinions. Justice Stevens, in an opinion joined by Justice Blackmun, found the requirement of class-based discriminatory animus to be satisfied by both the purpose and the effects of the conspiracy:

> To satisfy the class-based animus requirement of § 1985(3), the conspirators' conduct need not be motivated by hostility toward individual women. As women are unquestionably a protected class, that requirement—as well as the central purpose of the statute—is satisfied if the conspiracy is aimed at conduct that only members of the protected class have the capacity to perform. It is not necessary that the intended effect upon women be the sole purpose of the conspiracy. It is enough that the conspiracy be motivated "at least in part" by its adverse effects upon women. The immediate and intended effect of this conspiracy was to prevent women from obtaining abortions. Even assuming that the ultimate and indirect consequence of petitioners' blockade was the legitimate and nondiscriminatory goal of saving potential life, it is undeniable that the conspirators' immediate purpose was to affect the conduct of women. Moreover, petitioners target women because of their sex, specifically, because of their capacity to become pregnant and to have an abortion.

Justice Stevens also found that the conspiracy was aimed at depriving women who sought an abortion of the right to travel between the states:

> Petitioners' conspiracy had both the purpose and effect of interfering with interstate travel. The number of patients who cross state lines to obtain an abortion obviously depends, to some extent, on the location of the clinic and the quality of its services. In the Washington Metropolitan area, where interstate travel is routine, 20 to 30 percent of the patients at some clinics were from out of state, while at least one clinic obtained over half its patients from other states.

Justice O'Connor, joined by Justice Blackmun, essentially agreed with Justice Stevens' finding of class-based animus against women.

Justice Souter also dissented in part, but based on an entirely different ground. He relied on a separate clause in § 1985(3) which prohibits conspiracies "for the purpose of preventing or hindering the constituted authorities of any State or Territory from giving or securing to all persons within such State or Territory the equal protection of the laws." He interpreted this clause (the "prevention clause") to be broader than the clause prohibiting conspiracies to deprive persons of equal protection and equal privileges and immunities (the "deprivation clause").

Bray presents a situation where the federal remedy, if any, will be supplemental to remedies that are available under state law. Individuals who block access to abortion facilities could be charged with various state crimes (e.g., trespass) and a variety of tort actions could be filed by injured parties in state court. Why was it important to the plaintiffs that a cause of action under § 1985(3) also be available? For a pre-*Bray* analysis of how that decision should have come out, see Randolph M. Scott–McLaughlin, *Bray v. Alexandria Women's Health Clinic*: The Supreme Court's Next Opportunity to Unsettle Civil Rights Law, 66 Tulane L. Rev. 1357 (1992).

4. *GREAT AMERICAN FEDERAL SAVINGS & LOAN ASS'N. V. NOVOTNY*

The question of alternative remedies arose directly in Great American Federal Savings & Loan Ass'n. v. Novotny, 442 U.S. 366 (1979). The Court held in this case that claims cognizable under Title VII of the Civil Rights Act of 1964 could not be asserted under § 1985(3).

Novotny was secretary of the savings and loan, a member of its board of directors, and a loan officer. He was fired, allegedly because he argued at a board meeting that the association was discriminating against its female employees. He filed a complaint with the Equal Employment Opportunity Commission (EEOC) under Title VII of the Civil Rights Act of 1964. After the EEOC gave him a right to sue letter, he filed suit in a federal district court under both Title VII and § 1985(3). The District Court dismissed both claims, but the Court of Appeals reversed, holding that neither claim should have been dismissed. Only the claim under § 1985(3) came before the Supreme Court. Justice Stewart, writing for the majority, held that this claim had been properly dismissed.

The Court first described the elaborate "administrative and judicial process" for resolving claims of employment discrimination under Title VII and then noted: "If a violation of Title VII could be asserted through § 1985(3), a complainant could avoid most if not all of these detailed and specific provisions of the law." The Court framed its holding as follows:

> Section 1985(3) . . . *creates* no rights. It is a purely remedial statute, providing a civil cause of action when some otherwise defined federal right—to equal protection of the laws or equal privileges and immunities under the laws—is breached by a conspiracy in the manner defined by the section. . . . The only question here . . . is whether the rights created by Title VII may be asserted within the *remedial* framework of § 1985(3).
>
> This case thus differs markedly from the cases recently decided by this Court that have related the substantive provisions of last century's civil rights acts to contemporary legislation conferring similar substantive rights. In those cases we have held that substantive rights conferred in the 19th century were not withdrawn, *sub silentio*, by the subsequent passage

of the modern statutes. Thus, in Jones v. Alfred H. Mayer Co., 392 U.S. 409 (1968), we considered the effect of the fair housing provisions of the Civil Rights Act of 1968 on the property rights guaranteed by the Civil Rights Act of 1866, now codified at 42 U.S.C. § 1982. And in Johnson v. Railway Express Agency, 421 U.S. 454 (1975), we held that the passage of Title VII did not work an implied repeal of the substantive rights to contract conferred by the same 19th century statute and now codified at 42 U.S.C. § 1981.[21]

This case, by contrast, does not involve two "independent" rights, and . . . we conclude that § 1985(3) may not be invoked to redress violations of Title VII. It is true that a § 1985(3) remedy would not be coextensive with Title VII, since a plaintiff in an action under § 1985(3) must prove both a conspiracy and a group animus that Title VII does not require. While this incomplete congruity would limit the damage that would be done to Title VII, it would not eliminate it. Unimpaired effectiveness can be given to the plan put together by Congress in Title VII only by holding that deprivation of a right created by Title VII cannot be the basis for a cause of action under § 1985(3).[a]

Justices Powell and Stevens concurred in separate opinions, but each for essentially the same reason: that § 1985(3) should be interpreted to remedy violations of constitutional rights.

Justice White dissented in an opinion joined by Justices Brennan and Marshall. He agreed that Title VII should perhaps be accommodated by requiring that § 1985(3) plaintiffs exhaust administrative remedies prior to filing a § 1985(3) claim, but insisted that both statutes could be applied to the facts of this case:

> Title VII operates both to create new federal rights and to provide a general remedy for the denial thereof, while § 1985(3) operates to provide a separate remedy when the manner of denial is especially invidious and threatening. The Reconstruction Congress that enacted § 1985(3) believed that an especial danger was posed by persons acting with invidious animus and acting in concert—thereby compounding their power and resources—to deny federal rights. Because such private conspiratorial action, the paradigm of which was the activity of the Ku Klux Klan, constituted a serious threat to civil rights and civil order, it was deemed necessary to "giv[e] a civil action to anybody who shall be injured by [such] conspiracy."

Justice White also thought that § 1985(3) was an independent source of rights. Justice White said that because § 1985(3) provided a remedy to "*any person* injured as a result of deprivation of a substantive federal right, it must be seen

[21] Another difference between those cases and this one is to be found in the legislative history of the Civil Rights Act of 1964 and the Civil Rights Act of 1968. [T]he view was consistently expressed that the earlier statutes would not be implicitly repealed. Specific references were made to §§ 1981 and 1982, but, significantly, no notice appears to have been taken of § 1985(3).

[a] In an earlier footnote, the Court said:

> We note the relative narrowness of the issue before the Court. It is unnecessary for us to consider whether a plaintiff would have a cause of action under § 1985(3) where the defendant was not subject to suit under Title VII or a comparable statute. Nor do we think it necessary to consider whether § 1985(3) creates a remedy for statutory rights other than those fundamental rights derived from the Constitution.—[Footnote by eds.]

as itself creating rights in persons other than those to whom the underlying federal right extends." Thus, it followed for White that § 1985(3) allowed people to seek compensation if they were injured by discrimination against others, even if they were not victims of discrimination themselves and even if they had no claim for retaliation under a separate federal statute, such as § 704(a) of Title VII.

The basic question in *Novotny* was whether § 1985(3) is remedial only, as the majority asserts, or whether it can also be an independent source of rights, as claimed by the dissent. Recall that *Griffin* itself was ambiguous on this point. The Court's Thirteenth Amendment holding seems to imply that § 1985(3) is itself the source of the rights against racial discrimination that the statute protects. The Court has never held, and seemed not to so hold in *Griffin*, that the Thirteenth Amendment itself forbids particular forms of private racial discrimination as "badges" or "incidents" of slavery. On the other hand, the Court's right-to-travel holding is consistent with the view that § 1985(3) is remedial only. Are *Griffin* and *Novotny* consistent? Should § 1985(3) be regarded as an independent source of rights? If so, is it sound for Justice White to use § 1985(3) to extend the class of claimants who can sue for violations of Title VII? How would the majority resolve the hypothetical variation of *Novotny* stated above, where it was assumed that Novotny was a supplier of the savings and loan who was discontinued because he objected to the association's discrimination against its female employees?

Consider also the Court's distinction in *Novotny* between § 1981 and § 1982 on the one hand and § 1985(3) on the other. Does it make sense that some of the Reconstruction Civil Rights Acts can be used for injuries covered by modern civil rights statutes while others cannot? Is *Novotny* consistent with *Jones v. Alfred H. Mayer Co.* and *Johnson v. Railway Express Agency*?

5. ALTERNATIVE FEDERAL REMEDIES

Despite the promise of *Griffin*, after this series of decisions, § 1985(3) has become an unwieldy means of protecting civil rights. If state action can easily be established, plaintiffs can rely on the simpler provisions of § 1983. And if they have available some other statute that applies directly to private action, such as Title VII or § 1981, they can—and in some circumstances, they must—rely entirely on that statute.

The latter strategy was the one pursued by abortion clinics and their supporters after *Bray*. They turned to the Racketeering Influenced and Corrupt Organizations Act (RICO), 18 U.S.C. § 1961et seq. This federal statute imposes criminal and civil liability on anyone who engages in or conspires to engage in a "pattern of racketeering activity." The latter term is broadly defined to include two or more of various criminal acts, which need not have led to prior convictions, connected by "continuity and relationship." Sedima, S.P.R.L. v. Imrex Co., 473 U.S. 479, 496 n.14 (1985). The civil remedies include both treble damages and attorneys' fees, making a claim under RICO potentially more valuable to plaintiffs than a civil rights claim. In National Organization for Women, Inc. v. Scheidler, 510 U.S. 249 (1994), the plaintiffs asserted a RICO claim against right-to-life protestors, alleging predicate criminal acts of extortion in using threatened or actual force, violence, or fear to shut down abortion clinics. The Supreme Court held that the plaintiffs had stated a claim under RICO despite the absence of any allegation that the defendants had an economic motive of financial gain from their activities. RICO did not require proof of an economic motive in addition to the predicate crimes and the pattern of racketeering activity.

6. BIBLIOGRAPHY

The series of decisions after *Griffin* led to extensive commentary in the law review literature, most of it critical of the decisions. These articles examine at length the legislative history of § 1985(3), the appropriate modern meaning of § 1985(3), and the impact of the decisions. See Taunya Lovell Banks, The Scope of Section 1985(3) in Light of *Great American Federal Savings and Loan Association v. Novotny*: Too Little Too Late?, 9 Hastings Const. L.Q. 579 (1982); Neil H. Cogan, Section 1985(3)'s Restructuring of Equality: An Essay on Texts, History, Progress, and Cynicism, 39 Rutgers L. Rev. 515 (1987); Ken Gormley, Private Conspiracies and the Constitution: A Modern Vision of 42 U.S.C. § 1985(3), 64 Texas L.Rev. 527 (1985); Janis L. McDonald, Starting from Scratch: A Revisionist View of 42 U.S.C. § 1985(3) and Class–Based Animus, 19 Conn.L.Rev. 471 (1987); Steven F. Shatz, The Second Death of 42 U.S.C. § 1985(3): The Use and Misuse of History in Statutory Interpretation, 27 Boston Coll. L. Rev. 911 (1986); Catherine E. Smith, The Group Dangers of Race–Based Conspiracies, 59 Rutgers L. Rev. 55 (2006); Catherine E. Smith, (Un)Masking Race–Based Intracorporate Conspiracies under the Ku Klux Klan Act, 11 Va. J. Soc. Pol'y & L. 129 (2004); John Valery White, Vindicating Rights in a Federal System: Rediscovering 42 U.S.C. § 1985(3)'s Equality Right, 69 Temple L. Rev. 145 (1997).

NOTES ON 18 U.S.C. §§ 241 AND 242

1. INTRODUCTION

Although these materials focus on civil litigation, brief mention should be made of 18 U.S.C. §§ 241 and 242. Both provide criminal sanctions for behavior analogous to that covered by the civil statutes. Because of the common heritage and similar coverage of these civil and criminal provisions, interpretation of the civil statutes considered in this book has been influenced by cases decided under their criminal counterparts. Moreover, many of the issues arising in the interpretation of §§ 241 and 242 have parallels in one or another of their civil cousins.

This is not to say, of course, that there are not special considerations related to §§ 241 and 242. They are, after all, criminal statutes, and as such are subject to concerns and limitations that do not apply to civil litigation. For example, the constitutional doctrine of vagueness and the related common law doctrine of strict construction have special application to the criminal law. Both doctrines have influenced the interpretation of §§ 241 and 242 in ways that have no parallel in the civil arena.

2. SECTION 241

Section 241 is based on legislation first enacted in the Civil Rights Act of 1870, otherwise known as the Enforcement Act of 1870. Its language is very close to 42 U.S.C. § 1985(3). Section 241 provides:

> If two or more persons conspire to injure, oppress, threaten, or intimidate any citizen in the free exercise or enjoyment of any right or privilege secured to him by the Constitution or laws of the United States, or because of his having so exercised the same; or
>
> If two or more persons go in disguise on the highway, or on the premises of another, with intent to prevent or hinder his free exercise or enjoyment of any right or privilege so secured—
>
> They shall be fined not more than $10,000 or imprisoned not more than ten years, or both; and if death results, they shall be subject to imprisonment for any term of years or for life.

It is settled that § 241, as does § 1985(3), applies to private conspiracies. See United States v. Guest, 383 U.S. 745 (1966). Again like § 1985(3), however, it does not follow from this proposition that the denial of rights that find their source in the Fourteenth Amendment can be punished under § 241 without a showing of state action. Note in addition that § 241 explicitly includes the denial of rights derived from the "laws" of the United States as well as from the Constitution. Unlike § 1985(3), there thus can be no argument that § 241 is limited to the protection of constitutional rights.

These principles were applied in United States v. Johnson, 390 U.S. 563 (1968), where the Court upheld an indictment against private citizens charging "a conspiracy to injure and intimidate three Negroes in the exercise of their right to patronize a restaurant" under the public accommodations provisions of the Civil Rights Act of 1964. The possibility of a "state action" requirement was not even mentioned in the Court's opinion, presumably because the source of the victims' right to service was a federal statute and because it had been established in prior decisions that Congress had the power under the commerce clause to create a right to service in places of public accommodation.

There is, however, debate about the classes of rights covered by § 241. For example, Anderson v. United States, 417 U.S. 211 (1974), involved state election officials convicted of vote fraud. No racial discrimination was alleged. The majority upheld the conviction on the theory that *federal* elections had been affected and that it had "long been settled that § 241 embraces a conspiracy to stuff the ballot box at an election for federal officers." Justice Douglas, joined by Justice Brennan, dissented. He read the record as raising the question "whether a conspiracy to cast fraudulent votes in a *state* election, without any evidence of racial discrimination, could constitute a federal offense under § 241." (Emphasis added.) He concluded that § 241 did not apply in such a case, although he conceded that "the civil protections of the Fourteenth Amendment reach state elections even where there is no racial animus." The dissenters thought, in other words, that § 241 was not intended to apply to purely local vote fraud cases not involving racial discrimination, even though the Fourteenth Amendment may have been violated by the conduct of the state officials. Part of their rationale was the need for strict construction of criminal statutes and the special impact of the federal criminal law on federal-state relations.

3. SECTION 242

Section 242 is based on legislation first enacted in the Civil Rights Act of 1866.[a] As recounted in *Monroe v. Pape*, this statute was the model for what became 42 U.S.C. § 1983. Section 242 provides:

> Whoever, under color of any law, statute, ordinance, regulation, or custom, willfully subjects any inhabitant of any State, Territory, or District to the deprivation of any rights, privileges, or immunities secured or protected by the Constitution or laws of the United States, or to different punishments, pains, or penalties, on account of such inhabitant being an alien, or by reason of his color, or race, than are prescribed for the punishment of citizens, shall be fined not more than $1,000 or imprisoned not more than one year, or both; and if death results shall be subject to imprisonment for any term of years or for life.

The word "willfully" has been construed to require a specific intent, that is, a "purpose to deprive a person of a specific constitutional right . . . made definite by decision or other rule of law. . . . " Screws v. United States, 325 U.S. 91, 101, 103 (1945). This requirement was adopted in order to avoid vagueness concerns that would exist if the statute were regarded as applying to constitutional rights first enunciated after the occurrence of the behavior sought to be punished. As summarized in United States v. Ehrlichman, 546 F.2d 910, 921 (D.C. Cir. 1976), the required "specific intent" under *Screws* can be found if two conditions are met:

> The first is a purely legal determination. Is the constitutional right at issue clearly delineated and plainly applicable under the circumstances of the case? If the trial judge concludes that it is, then the jury must make the second, factual, determination. Did the defendant commit the act in question with the particular purpose of depriving the citizen victim of his enjoyment of the interests protected by that federal right? If both requirements are met, even if the defendant did not in fact recognize the unconstitutionality of his act, he will be adjudged as a matter of law to have acted "willfully". . . .

By parity of reasoning, an "intentional" discrimination asserted as the basis for a civil cause of action under § 1981, § 1982, § 1983, or § 1985(3) will not require that the defendant know that the rights being denied are protected by the Constitution or, as the case may be, by federal law. It will be sufficient that the defendant committed "the act in question with the particular purpose of depriving the citizen victim of his enjoyment of the interests protected by the federal right" at stake.

4. *UNITED STATES V. LANIER*

In United States v. Lanier, 520 U.S. 259 (1997), the Court addressed the specificity with which a constitutional right needs to be identified in prior decisions in order to satisfy the requirement of "fair notice" in a § 242 prosecution. Lanier, a state judge, was charged with 11 violations of § 242 based on a series of sexual assaults. He was convicted on seven of the counts. The Court of Appeals, sitting en banc, reversed his conviction, holding that "criminal liability may be imposed under § 242 only if the constitutional right said to have been

[a] The text of the original statute is set forth in the Notes on the Legislative History of § 1982, supra.

violated is first identified in a decision of [the Supreme] Court (not any other federal, or state, court), and only when the right has been held to apply in 'a factual situation fundamentally similar to the one at bar.' " The Supreme Court granted certiorari and unanimously reversed.

Speaking through Justice Souter, the Court quoted the applicable standard from *Screws*: the fair notice requirement is satisfied "when the accused is charged with violating a 'right which has been made specific either by the express terms of the Constitution or laws of the United States or by decisions interpreting them.' " It then held:

> [C]ontrary to the Court of Appeals, we think it unsound to read *Screws* as reasoning that only this Court's decisions could provide the required warning. . . . Although the Sixth Circuit was concerned, and rightly so, that disparate decisions in various Circuits might leave the law insufficiently certain even on a point widely considered, such a circumstance may be taken into account in deciding whether the warning is fair enough, without any need for a categorical rule that decisions of the Courts of Appeals and other courts are inadequate as a matter of law to provide it.
>
> Nor have our decisions demanded precedents that applied the right at issue to a factual situation that is "fundamentally similar" at the level of specificity meant by the Sixth Circuit in using that phrase. . . . In the civil sphere, we have explained that qualified immunity seeks to ensure that defendants "reasonably can anticipate when their conduct may give rise to liability," Davis v. Scherer, 468 U.S. 183, 195 (1984), by attaching liability only if "the contours of the right violated are sufficiently clear that a reasonable official would understand that what he is doing violates that right," Anderson v. Creighton, 483 U.S. 635, 640 (1987). So conceived, the object of the "clearly established" immunity standard is not different from that of "fair warning" as it relates to law "made specific" for the purpose of validly applying § 242. The fact that one has a civil and the other a criminal law role is of no significance; both serve the same objective, and in effect the qualified immunity test is simply the adaptation of the fair warning standard to give officials (and, ultimately, governments) the same protection from civil liability and its consequences that individuals have traditionally possessed in the face of vague criminal statutes. To require something clearer than "clearly established" would, then, call for something beyond "fair warning."
>
> This is not to say, of course, that the single warning standard points to a single level of specificity sufficient in every instance. In some circumstances, as when an earlier case expressly leaves open whether a general rule applies to the particular type of conduct at issue, a very high degree of prior factual particularity may be necessary. But general statements of the law are not inherently incapable of giving fair and clear warning, and in other instances a general constitutional rule already identified in the decisional law may apply with obvious clarity to the specific conduct in question, even though "the very action in question has not previously been held unlawful," *Anderson*, supra, at 640. As Judge Daughtrey noted in her dissenting opinion in this case, " 'the easiest cases don't even arise. There has never been . . . a § 1983 case accusing welfare officials of selling foster children into slavery; it does not follow that if such a case arose, the of-

> ficials would be immune from damages or criminal liability.' " In sum, as with civil liability under § 1983 or *Bivens*, all that can usefully be said about criminal liability under § 242 is that it may be imposed for deprivation of a constitutional right if, but only if, "in the light of preexisting law the unlawfulness under the Constitution is apparent," *Anderson*, supra, at 640. Where it is, the constitutional requirement of fair warning is satisfied.

The case was remanded for application of this standard.

5. SUBSEQUENT LITIGATION IN *LANIER*

Lanier's actions also illustrate an interesting interaction between § 242 and § 1983. A necessary element of a § 242 violation is that the defendant be proved to have acted "under color of . . . law." Lanier argued that the actions for which he was convicted were not taken under color of law. The Supreme Court declined to address that argument, because the Court of Appeals did not reach the question in its en banc decision; it left the issue to be considered on remand. (Ultimately, the Sixth Circuit dismissed Lanier's appeal of his conviction when he became a fugitive during its pendency.)

Several of the women whom Lanier had sexually assaulted filed a § 1983 action against him, alleging that Lanier had deprived them of their right to personal security and bodily integrity without due process of law and also that he had deprived them of the equal protection of the laws and of their right of access to the courts. Lanier moved to dismiss, asserting, among other things, an affirmative defense of absolute judicial immunity. When the district court denied that motion, Lanier filed an immediate interlocutory appeal.

On appeal, the Sixth Circuit denied Lanier's claim of judicial immunity. Archie v. Lanier, 95 F.3d 438 (6th Cir. 1996). Relying on Mireles v. Waco, 502 U.S. 9, 11 (1991), which had held that judicial immunity does not extend to "liability for nonjudicial actions, i.e., actions not taken in the judge's judicial capacity," the Court of Appeals held that "stalking and sexually assaulting a person, no matter the circumstances, do not constitute 'judicial acts.' The fact that, regrettably, Lanier happened to be a judge when he committed these reprehensible acts is not relevant to the question of whether he is entitled to immunity. Clearly he is not."

Chief Judge Merritt concurred, but noted an incongruity between the result in the civil case and the government's theory in the § 242 criminal prosecution:

> It would seem inconsistent to follow the government and say that Lanier was performing a judicial function under state law for purposes of criminal liability and then turn around and deny Lanier judicial immunity on the ground that he was not performing a judicial function.
>
> The only consistent, sensible approach in this area of law is to say what seems obvious: Sexual assaults have nothing to do with the appearance of carrying out authorized judicial duties, exercising judicial power or performing the function of judging. Yielding to an unruly libido is not the exercise of judicial power, or somehow like or related to the performance of judicial duties. . . . To label Lanier's personal sexual proclivities as "state action" or judicial acts "under color of law" or "clothed with the authority of law" makes an interesting literary figure of speech. But that is

> all it is—a figure of speech, a metaphor. There may be no judicial immunity for such acts in the real world.

Chief Judge Merritt took the position that Lanier had not violated § 242 because "[t]he sexual conduct here was singularly 'personal' and obviously not 'clothed with the authority of law.' "

Is Merritt correct? Consider the ways in which Lanier might be described as having acted under color of state law without having performed a judicial act. As described by the Supreme Court in its *Lanier* decision,

> [t]he two most serious assaults were against a woman whose divorce proceedings had come before Lanier and whose daughter's custody remained subject to his jurisdiction. When the woman applied for a secretarial job at Lanier's courthouse, Lanier interviewed her and suggested that he might have to reexamine the daughter's custody. When the woman got up to leave, Lanier grabbed her, sexually assaulted her, and finally committed oral rape. A few weeks later, Lanier inveigled the woman into returning to the courthouse again to get information about another job opportunity, and again sexually assaulted and orally raped her. On five other occasions Lanier sexually assaulted four other women: two of his secretaries, a Youth Services Officer of the juvenile court over which Lanier presided, and a local coordinator for a federal program who was in Lanier's chambers to discuss a matter affecting the same court.

CHAPTER 5

MODERN CIVIL RIGHTS LEGISLATION: SEX DISCRIMINATION

INTRODUCTION

Civil rights legislation has not been confined to the Reconstruction era. After Brown v. Board of Education, 347 U.S. 483 (1954), civil rights returned to the congressional agenda, culminating in the passage of several major civil rights acts in the 1960s. Most important is the Civil Rights Act of 1964, a statute aimed primarily at racial discrimination but also prohibiting discrimination based on national origin, religion, and sex. This act was quickly followed by other major civil rights legislation: the Voting Rights Act of 1965, the Civil Rights Act of 1968 (prohibiting discrimination in housing), and the Age Discrimination in Employment Act of 1968. All of these statutes have been amended and expanded by subsequent legislation. A late addition to the array of major civil rights acts was the Americans with Disabilities Act of 1990 (ADA), an expansion of the Rehabilitation Act of 1973, which barred discrimination against the disabled by the federal government, recipients of federal funds, and federal contractors. The ADA added coverage of private and public employment, public accommodations, and government services. Finally, Title IX of the Education Amendments of 1972 has assumed particular importance in the law of sex discrimination. It prohibits sex discrimination by any educational program that receives any form of federal financial assistance.

Modern civil rights litigation involves all these statutes, as well as the Reconstruction-era legislation. Civil rights plaintiffs commonly join multiple claims under different statutes in a single lawsuit, a tactic employed in many of the cases in Chapter IV. Any treatment of civil rights litigation as it is practiced today must take account of the modern civil rights statutes. Yet it is not feasible, within the space of a single book, to give a comprehensive account of the large body of law that has developed under these statutes. Whole courses have been devoted to subjects such as employment discrimination, sex-based discrimination, and voting rights.

This chapter concentrates on two statutes that prohibit discrimination on the basis of sex: Title VII of the Civil Rights Act of 1964 and Title IX of the Education Amendments of 1972. Title VII as a prohibition against discrimination on the basis of race has been introduced in the preceding chapter in connection with § 1981. Title VII as a prohibition against sex discrimination raises similar, but distinct issues from those raised by a prohibition against race discrimination. Title VII itself contains an exception for "bona fide occupational qualifications" on the basis of sex, but not for those on the basis of race. Among the Reconstruction-era statutes, § 1983 provides the most general remedy for sex discrimination, but only to enforce the constitutional right to sexual equality under the Equal Protection Clause. Both this constitutional right and the terms of § 1983 are limited by the "state action" concept. Neither Title VII nor Title IX contains any such limitation, and in this respect these statutes greatly expand the remedies for sex discrimination beyond those available under § 1983.

In doing so, Title VII and Title IX raise two issues of general significance. First, how are these statutory prohibitions against sex discrimination related to and influenced by the corresponding prohibition under the Equal Protection Clause? Apart from the question of state action, would cases decided under Title VII or Title IX come out the same way if they had been decided under the Constitution? And second, how do the restrictions on liability in these statutes, particularly liability for damages, compare to the corresponding restrictions under § 1983? Again, would cases decided under Title VII or Title IX come out the same way as cases involving state action decided under § 1983? These two issues are explored in the materials that follow.

On questions of sex discrimination and employment discrimination generally, there is a vast secondary literature. On the law and theory of sex discrimination, Deborah L. Rhode, Justice: Sex Discrimination and the Law (1989); Feminism Confronts Homo Economicus: Gender, Law, and Society (Martha Fineman & Terrance Dougherty, eds. 2005); Feminist Legal Theory (Frances E. Olsen, ed. 1995); Applications of Feminist Legal Theory to Women's Lives: Sex, Violence, Work, and Reproduction (D. Kelly Weisburg, ed. 1996); Feminist Legal Theory: Foundations (D. Kelly Weisburg, ed. 1993). A useful collection of articles appears in Foundations of Employment Discrimination Law (John J. Donohue III, ed., 2d ed. 2003).

1. TITLE VII OF THE CIVIL RIGHTS ACT OF 1964

SUBSECTION A: CLASS–WIDE SEX DISCRIMINATION

Dothard v. Rawlinson

Supreme Court of the United States, 1977.
433 U.S. 321.

■ MR. JUSTICE STEWART delivered the opinion of the Court.

The appellee, Dianne Rawlinson, sought employment with the Alabama Board of Corrections as a prison guard, called in Alabama a "correctional counselor." After her application was rejected, she brought this class suit under Title VII of the Civil Rights Act of 1964, and under 42 U.S.C. § 1983, alleging that she had been denied employment because of her sex in violation of federal law. A three-judge Federal District Court for the Middle District of Alabama decided in her favor. We noted probable jurisdiction of this appeal from the District Court's judgment.

I

At the time she applied for a position as correctional counselor trainee, Rawlinson was a 22–year–old college graduate whose major course of study had been correctional psychology. She was refused employment because she failed to meet the minimum 120–pound weight requirement established by an Alabama statute. The statute also establishes a height minimum of 5 feet 2 inches.

After her application was rejected because of her weight, Rawlinson filed a charge with the Equal Employment Opportunity Commission, and ultimately received a right-to-sue letter. She then filed a complaint in the District Court on behalf of herself and other similarly situated women, challenging the statutory height and weight minima as violative of Title VII and the Equal Protection Clause of the Fourteenth Amendment. A three-judge court was convened. While the suit was pending, the Alabama Board of Corrections adopted Administrative Regulation 204, establishing gender criteria for assigning correctional counselors to maximum-security institutions for "contact positions," that is, positions requiring continual close physical proximity to inmates of the institution. Rawlinson amended her class-action complaint by adding a challenge to Regulation 204 as also violative of Title VII and the Fourteenth Amendment.

Like most correctional facilities in the United States, Alabama's prisons are segregated on the basis of sex. Currently the Alabama Board of Corrections operates four major all-male penitentiaries—Holman Prison, Kilby Corrections Facility, G.K. Fountain Correction Center, and Draper Correctional Center. The Board also operates the Julia Tutwiler Prison for Women, the Frank Lee Youth Center, the Number Four Honor Camp, the State Cattle Ranch, and nine Work Release Centers, one of which is for women. The Julia Tutwiler Prison for Women and the four male penitentiaries are maximum-security institutions. Their inmate living quarters are for the most part large dormitories, with communal showers and toilets that are open to the dormitories and hallways. The Draper and Fountain penitentiaries carry on extensive farming operations, making necessary a large number of strip searches for contraband when prisoners re-enter the prison buildings.

A correctional counselor's primary duty within these institutions is to maintain security and control of the inmates by continually supervising and observing their activities. To be eligible for consideration as a correctional counselor, an applicant must possess a valid Alabama driver's license, have a high school education or its equivalent, be free from physical defects, be between the ages of 20½ years and 45 years at the time of appointment, and fall between the minimum height and weight requirements of 5 feet 2 inches and 120 pounds, and the maximum of 6 feet 10 inches and 300 pounds. Appointment is by merit, with a grade assigned each applicant based on experience and education. No written examination is given.

At the time this litigation was in the District Court, the Board of Corrections employed a total of 435 people in various correctional counselor positions, 56 of whom were women. Of those 56 women, 21 were employed at the Julia Tutwiler Prison for Women, 13 were employed in noncontact positions at the four male maximum-security institutions, and the remaining 22 were employed at the other institutions operated by the Alabama Board of Corrections. Because most of Alabama's prisoners are held at the four maximum-security male penitentiaries, 336 of the 435 correctional counselor jobs were in those institutions, a majority of them concededly in the "contact" classification. Thus, even though meeting the statutory height and weight requirements, women applicants could under Regulation 204 compete equally with men for only about 25% of the correctional counselor jobs available in the Alabama prison system.

II

In enacting Title VII, Congress required "the removal of artificial, arbitrary, and unnecessary barriers to employment when the barriers operate invidiously to discriminate on the basis of racial or other impermissible classification." Griggs v. Duke Power Co., 401 U.S. 424, 431 (1971). The District Court found that the minimum statutory height and weight requirements that applicants for employment as correctional counselors must meet constitute the sort of arbitrary barrier to equal employment opportunity that Title VII forbids. The appellants assert that the District Court erred both in finding that the height and weight standards discriminate against women, and in its refusal to find that, even if they do, these standards are justified as "job related."

A

The gist of the claim that the statutory height and weight requirements discriminate against women does not involve an assertion of purposeful discriminatory motive. It is asserted, rather, that these facially neutral qualification standards work in fact disproportionately to exclude women from eligibility for employment by the Alabama Board of Corrections. We dealt in *Griggs v. Duke Power Co.*, supra, and Albemarle Paper Co. v. Moody, 422 U.S. 405 (1975), with similar allegations that facially neutral employment standards disproportionately excluded Negroes from employment, and those cases guide our approach here.

Those cases make clear that to establish a prima facie case of discrimination, a plaintiff need only show that the facially neutral standards in question select applicants for hire in a significantly discriminatory pattern. Once it is thus shown that the employment standards are discriminatory in effect, the employer must meet "the burden of showing that any given requirement [has] a manifest relationship to the employment in question." *Griggs v. Duke Power Co.*, supra, at 432. If the employer proves that the challenged requirements are job related, the plaintiff may then show that other selection devices without a similar discriminatory effect would also "serve the employer's legitimate interest in 'efficient and trustworthy workmanship.' " *Albemarle Paper Co. v. Moody*, supra, at 425, quoting McDonnell Douglas Corp. v. Green, 411 U.S. 792, 801 (1973).

Although women 14 years of age or older compose 52.75% of the Alabama population and 36.89% of its total labor force, they hold only 12.9% of its correctional counselor positions. In considering the effect of the minimum height and weight standards on this disparity in rate of hiring between the sexes, the District Court found that the 5′2″ requirement would operate to exclude 33.29% of the women in the United States between the ages of 18–79, while excluding only 1.28% of men between the same ages. The 120–pound weight restriction would exclude 22.29% of the women and 2.35% of the men in this age group. When the height and weight restrictions are combined, Alabama's statutory standards would exclude 41.13% of the female population while excluding less than 1% of the male population.[12] Accordingly, the District Court found that Rawlinson had made out a prima facie case of unlawful sex discrimination.

The appellants argue that a showing of disproportionate impact on women based on generalized national statistics should not suffice to estab-

---

[12] Affirmatively stated, approximately 99.76% of the men and 58.87% of the women meet both these physical qualifications. From the separate statistics on height and weight of males it would appear that after adding the two together and allowing for some overlap the result would be to exclude between 2.35% and 3.63% of males from meeting Alabama's statutory height and weight minima. None of the parties has challenged the accuracy of the District Court's computations on this score, however, and the discrepancy is in any event insignificant in light of the gross disparity between the female and male exclusions. . . .

lish a prima facie case. They point in particular to Rawlinson's failure to adduce comparative statistics concerning actual applicants for correctional counselor positions in Alabama. There is no requirement, however, that a statistical showing of disproportionate impact must always be based on analysis of the characteristics of actual applicants. The application process itself might not adequately reflect the actual potential applicant pool, since otherwise qualified people might be discouraged from applying because of a self-recognized inability to meet the very standards challenged as being discriminatory. A potential applicant could easily determine her height and weight and conclude that to make an application would be futile. Moreover, reliance on general population demographic data was not misplaced where there was no reason to suppose that physical height and weight characteristics of Alabama men and women differ markedly from those of the national population.

For these reasons, we cannot say that the District Court was wrong in holding that the statutory height and weight standards had a discriminatory impact on women applicants. The plaintiffs in a case such as this are not required to exhaust every possible source of evidence, if the evidence actually presented on its face conspicuously demonstrates a job requirement's grossly discriminatory impact. If the employer discerns fallacies or deficiencies in the data offered by the plaintiff, he is free to adduce countervailing evidence of his own. In this case no such effort was made.

B

We turn, therefore, to the appellants' argument that they have rebutted the prima facie case of discrimination by showing that the height and weight requirements are job related. These requirements, they say, have a relationship to strength, a sufficient but unspecified amount of which is essential to effective job performance as a correctional counselor. In the District Court, however, the appellants produced no evidence correlating the height and weight requirements with the requisite amount of strength thought essential to good job performance. Indeed, they failed to offer evidence of any kind in specific justification of the statutory standards.[14]

If the job-related quality that the appellants identify is bona fide, their purpose could be achieved by adopting and validating a test for applicants that measures strength directly. Such a test, fairly administered, would fully satisfy the standards of Title VII because it would be one that "measure[s] the person for the job and not the person in the abstract." *Griggs v. Duke Power Co.*, 401 U.S. at 436. But nothing in the present record even approaches such a measurement.

For the reasons we have discussed, the District Court was not in error in holding that Title VII of the Civil Rights Act of 1964, as amended, prohibits application of the statutory height and weight requirements to Rawlinson and the class she represents.

---

[14] [T]he appellants contend that the establishment of the minimum height and weight standards by statute requires that they be given greater deference than is typically given private employer-established job qualifications. The relevant legislative history of the 1972 amendments extending Title VII to the States as employers does not, however, support such a result. Instead, Congress expressly indicated the intent that the same Title VII principles be applied to governmental and private employers alike. Thus for both private and public employers, "[t]he touchstone is business necessity," *Griggs*, 401 U.S. at 431; a discriminatory employment practice must be shown to be necessary to safe and efficient job performance to survive a Title VII challenge.

III

Unlike the statutory height and weight requirements, Regulation 204 explicitly discriminates against women on the basis of their sex. In defense of this overt discrimination, the appellants rely on § 703(e) of Title VII, 42 U.S.C.§ 2000e–2(e), which permits sex-based discrimination "in those certain instances where . . . sex . . . is a bona fide occupational qualification reasonably necessary to the normal operation of that particular business or enterprise."

The District Court rejected the bona-fide-occupational-qualification (BFOQ) defense, relying on the virtually uniform view of the federal courts that § 703(e) provides only the narrowest of exceptions to the general rule requiring equality of employment opportunities. This view has been variously formulated. In Diaz v. Pan American World Airways, 442 F.2d 385, 388 (5th Cir. 1971), the Court of Appeals for the Fifth Circuit held that "discrimination based on sex is valid only when the *essence* of the business operation would be undermined by not hiring members of one sex exclusively." (Emphasis in original.) In an earlier case, Weeks v. Southern Bell Tel. & Tel. Co., 408 F.2d 228, 235 (5th Cir. 1969), the same court said that an employer could rely on the BFOQ exception only by proving "that he had reasonable cause to believe, that is, a factual basis for believing, that all or substantially all women would be unable to perform safely and efficiently the duties of the job involved." See also Phillips v. Martin Marietta Corp., 400 U.S. 542 (1971). But whatever the verbal formulation, the federal courts have agreed that it is impermissible under Title VII to refuse to hire an individual woman or man on the basis of stereotyped characterizations of the sexes, and the District Court in the present case held in effect that Regulation 204 is based on just such stereotypical assumptions.

We are persuaded—by the restrictive language of § 703(e), the relevant legislative history, and the consistent interpretation of the Equal Employment Opportunity Commission—that the BFOQ exception was in fact meant to be an extremely narrow exception to the general prohibition of discrimination on the basis of sex. In the particular factual circumstances of this case, however, we conclude that the District Court erred in rejecting the State's contention that Regulation 204 falls within the narrow ambit of the BFOQ exception.

The environment in Alabama's penitentiaries is a peculiarly inhospitable one for human beings of whatever sex. Indeed, a federal district court has held that the conditions of confinement in the prisons of the State, characterized by "rampant violence" and a "jungle atmosphere," are constitutionally intolerable. Pugh v. Locke, 406 F. Supp. 318, 325 (M.D. Ala. 1976). The record in the present case shows that because of inadequate staff and facilities, no attempt is made in the four maximum-security male penitentiaries to classify or segregate inmates according to their offense or level of dangerousness—a procedure that, according to expert testimony, is essential to effective penological administration. Consequently, the estimated 20% of the male prisoners who are sex offenders are scattered throughout the penitentiaries' dormitory facilities.

In this environment of violence and disorganization, it would be an oversimplification to characterize Regulation 204 as an exercise in "romantic paternalism." Cf. Frontiero v. Richardson, 411 U.S. 677, 684 (1973). In the usual case, the argument that a particular job is too dangerous for women may appropriately be met by the rejoinder that it is the purpose of Title VII to allow the individual woman to make that choice for herself.

More is at stake in this case, however, than an individual woman's decision to weigh and accept the risks of employment in a "contact" position in a maximum-security male prison.

The essence of a correctional counselor's job is to maintain prison security. A woman's relative ability to maintain order in a male, maximum-security, unclassified penitentiary of the type Alabama now runs could be directly reduced by her womanhood. There is a basis in fact for expecting that sex offenders who have criminally assaulted women in the past would be moved to do so again if access to women were established within the prison. There would also be a real risk that other inmates, deprived of a normal heterosexual environment, would assault women guards because they were women. In a prison system where violence is the order of the day, where inmate access to guards is facilitated by dormitory living arrangements, where every institution is understaffed, and where a substantial portion of the inmate population is composed of sex offenders mixed at random with other prisoners, there are few visible deterrents to inmate assaults on women custodians.

Appellee Rawlinson's own expert testified that dormitory housing for aggressive inmates poses a greater security problem than single-cell lockups, and further testified that it would be unwise to use women as guards in a prison where even 10% of the inmates had been convicted of sex crimes and were not segregated from the other prisoners. The likelihood that inmates would assault a woman because she was a woman would pose a real threat not only to the victim of the assault but also to the basic control of the penitentiary and protection of its inmates and the other security personnel. The employee's very womanhood would thus directly undermine her capacity to provide the security that is the essence of a correctional counselor's responsibility.

There was substantial testimony from experts on both sides of this litigation that the use of women as guards in "contact" positions under the existing conditions in Alabama maximum-security male penitentiaries would pose a substantial security problem, directly linked to the sex of the prison guard. On the basis of that evidence, we conclude that the District Court was in error in ruling that being male is not a bona fide occupational qualification for the job of correctional counselor in a "contact" position in an Alabama male maximum-security penitentiary.

The judgment is accordingly affirmed in part and reversed in part, and the case is remanded to the District Court for further proceedings consistent with this opinion.

It is so ordered.

■ MR. JUSTICE REHNQUIST, with whom THE CHIEF JUSTICE and MR. JUSTICE BLACKMUN join, concurring in the result and concurring in part.

I agree with, and join, Parts I and III of the Court's opinion in this case and with its judgment. While I also agree with the Court's conclusion in Part II of its opinion, holding that the District Court was "not in error" in holding the statutory height and weight requirements in this case to be invalidated by Title VII, the issues with which that Part deals are bound to arise so frequently that I feel obliged to separately state the reasons for my agreement with its result. I view affirmance of the District Court in this respect as essentially dictated by the peculiarly limited factual and legal justifications offered below by appellants on behalf of the statutory requirements. For that reason, I do not believe—and do not read the Court's opinion as holding—that all or even many of the height and weight requirements imposed by States on applicants for a multitude of law enforcement agency jobs are pretermitted by today's decision.

I agree that the statistics relied upon in this case are sufficient, absent rebuttal, to sustain a finding of a prima facie violation of § 703(a)(2), in that they reveal a significant discrepancy between the numbers of men, as opposed to women, who are automatically disqualified by reason of the height and weight requirements. The fact that these statistics are national figures of height and weight, as opposed to statewide or pool-of-labor-force statistics, does not seem to me to require us to hold that the District Court erred as a matter of law in admitting them into evidence. . . . It is for the District Court, in the first instance, to determine whether these statistics appear sufficiently probative of the ultimate fact in issue—whether a given job qualification requirement has a disparate impact on some group protected by Title VII. In making this determination, such statistics are to be considered in light of all other relevant facts and circumstances. . . . A reviewing court cannot say as a matter of law that they are irrelevant to the contested issue or so lacking in reliability as to be inadmissible.

If the defendants in a Title VII suit believe there to be any reason to discredit plaintiffs' statistics that does not appear on their face, the opportunity to challenge them is available to the defendants just as in any other lawsuit. They may endeavor to impeach the reliability of the statistical evidence, they may offer rebutting evidence, or they may disparage in arguments or in briefs the probative weight which the plaintiffs' evidence should be accorded. Since I agree with the Court that appellants made virtually no such effort, I also agree with it that the District Court cannot be said to have erred as a matter of law in finding that a prima facie case had been made out in the instant case.

While the District Court's conclusion is by no means *required* by the proffered evidence, I am unable to conclude that the District Court's finding in that respect was clearly erroneous. In other cases there could be different evidence which could lead a District Court to conclude that height and weight *are* in fact an accurate predictor of strength to justify, under all the circumstances, such minima. Should the height and weight requirements be found to advance the job-related qualification of strength to rebut the prima facie case, then, under our cases, the burden would shift back to appellees to demonstrate that other tests, *without* such disparate effect, would also meet that concern. But, here, the District Court permissibly concluded that appellants had not shown enough of a nexus even to rebut the inference.

Appellants, in order to rebut the prima facie case under the statute, had the burden placed on them to advance job-related reasons for the qualification. This burden could be shouldered by offering evidence or by making legal arguments not dependent on any new evidence. The District Court was confronted, however, with only one suggested job-related reason for the qualification—that of strength. Appellants argued only the job-relatedness of actual physical strength; they did not urge that an equally job-related qualification for prison guards is the appearance of strength. As the Court notes, the primary job of correctional counselor in Alabama prisons "is to maintain security and control of the inmates. . . . ," a function that I at least would imagine is aided by the psychological impact on prisoners of the presence of tall and heavy guards. If the appearance of strength had been urged upon the District Court here as a reason for the height and weight minima, I think that the District Court would surely have been entitled to reach a different result than it did. For, even if not perfectly correlated, I would think that Title VII would not preclude a State from saying that anyone under 5′2″ or 120 pounds, no matter how strong in fact, does not have a sufficient appearance of strength to be a prison guard.

But once the burden has been placed on the defendant, it is then up to the defendant to articulate the asserted job-related reasons underlying the use of the minima. McDonnell Douglas Corp. v. Green, 411 U.S. 792, 802 (1973); Griggs v. Duke Power Co., 401 U.S. 424, 431 (1971); Albemarle Paper Co. v. Moody, 422 U.S. 405, 425 (1975). Because of this burden, a reviewing court is not ordinarily justified in relying on arguments in favor of a job qualification that were not first presented to the trial court. As appellants did not even present the "appearance of strength" contention to the District Court as an asserted job-related reason for the qualification requirements, I agree that their burden was not met. The District Court's holding thus did not deal with the question of whether such an assertion could or did rebut appellee Rawlinson's prima facie case.

■ MR. JUSTICE MARSHALL, with whom MR. JUSTICE BRENNAN joins, concurring in part and dissenting in part.

I agree entirely with the Court's analysis of Alabama's height and weight requirements for prison guards, and with its finding that these restrictions discriminate on the basis of sex in violation of Title VII. Accordingly, I join Parts I and II of the Court's opinion. I also agree with much of the Court's general discussion in Part III of the bona-fide-occupational qualification exception contained in § 703(e) of Title VII. The Court is unquestionably correct when it holds "that the BFOQ exception was in fact meant to be an extremely narrow exception to the general prohibition of discrimination on the basis of sex." I must, however, respectfully disagree with the Court's application of the BFOQ exception in this case.

The Court properly rejects two proffered justifications for denying women jobs as prison guards. It is simply irrelevant here that a guard's occupation is dangerous and that some women might be unable to protect themselves adequately. Those themes permeate the testimony of the state officials below, but as the Court holds, "the argument that a particular job is too dangerous for women" is refuted by the "purpose of Title VII to allow the individual woman to make that choice for herself." Some women, like some men, undoubtedly are not qualified and do not wish to serve as prison guards, but that does not justify the exclusion of all women from this employment opportunity. Thus, "[in] the usual case," the Court's interpretation of the BFOQ exception would mandate hiring qualified women for guard jobs in maximum-security institutions. The highly successful experiences of other States allowing such job opportunities, see briefs for the States of California and Washington as amici curiae, confirm that absolute disqualification of women is not, in the words of Title VII, "reasonably necessary to the normal operation" of a maximum-security prison.

What would otherwise be considered unlawful discrimination against women is justified by the Court, however, on the basis of the "barbaric and inhumane" conditions in Alabama prisons, conditions so bad that state officials have conceded that they violate the Constitution. See Pugh v. Locke, 406 F. Supp. 318, 329, 331 (M.D. Ala. 1976). To me, this analysis sounds distressingly like saying two wrongs make a right. It is refuted by the plain words of § 703(e). The statute requires that a BFOQ be "reasonably necessary to the normal operation of that particular business or enterprise." But no governmental "business" may operate "normally" in violation of the Constitution. Every action of government is constrained by constitutional limitations. While those limits may be violated more frequently than we would wish, no one disputes that the "normal operation" of all government functions takes place within them. A prison system operating in blatant violation of the Eighth Amendment is an exception that should be remedied with all possible speed, as Judge Johnson's comprehensive order in *Pugh v.Locke* is designed to do. In the meantime, the existence of such violations should not be legitimatized by calling them "normal." Nor should the Court accept them as justifying conduct that would otherwise violate a statute intended to remedy age-old discrimination.

The Court's error in statutory construction is less objectionable, however, than the attitude it displays toward women. Though the Court recognizes that possible harm to women guards is an unacceptable reason for disqualifying women, it relies instead on an equally speculative threat to prison discipline supposedly generated by the sexuality of female guards. There is simply no evidence in the record to show that women guards would create any danger to security in Alabama prisons significantly greater than that which already exists. All of the dangers—with one exception discussed below—are inherent in a prison setting, whatever the gender of the guards.

The Court first sees women guards as a threat to security because "there are few visible deterrents to inmate assaults on women custodians." In fact, any prison guard is constantly subject to the threat of attack by inmates, and "invisible" deterrents are the guard's only real protection. No prison guard relies primarily on his or her ability to ward off an inmate attack to maintain order. Guards are typically unarmed and sheer numbers of inmates could overcome the normal complement. Rather, like all other law enforcement officers, prison guards must rely primarily on the moral authority of their office and the threat of future punishment for miscreants. As one expert testified below, common sense, fairness, and mental and emotional stability are the qualities a guard needs to cope with the dangers of the job. Well qualified and properly trained women, no less than men, have these psychological weapons at their disposal.

The particular severity of discipline problems in the Alabama maximum-security prisons is also no justification for the discrimination sanctioned by the Court. The District Court found in *Pugh v. Locke* that guards "must spend all their time attempting to maintain control or to protect themselves." If male guards face an impossible situation, it is difficult to see how women could make the problem worse, unless one relies on precisely the type of generalized bias against women that the Court agrees Title VII was intended to outlaw. For example, much of the testimony of appellants' witnesses ignores individual differences among members of each sex and reads like "ancient canards about the proper role of women." Phillips v. Martin Marietta Corp., 400 U.S. 542, 545 (1971). The witnesses claimed that women guards are not strict disciplinarians; that they are physically less capable of protecting themselves and subduing unruly inmates; that inmates take advantage of them as they did their mothers, while male guards are strong father figures who easily maintain discipline, and so on. Yet the record shows that the presence of women guards has not led to a single incident amounting to a serious breach of security in any Alabama institution. And, in any event, "[g]uards rarely enter the cell blocks and dormitories," *Pugh v. Locke*, 406 F. Supp. at 325, where the danger of inmate attacks is the greatest.

It appears that the real disqualifying factor in the Court's view is "[t]he employee's very womanhood." The Court refers to the large number of sex offenders in Alabama prisons, and to "[the] likelihood that inmates would assault a woman because she was a woman." In short, the fundamental justification for the decision is that women as guards will generate sexual assaults. With all respect, this rationale regrettably perpetuates one of the most insidious of the old myths about women—that women, wittingly or not, are seductive sexual objects. The effect of the decision, made I am sure with the best of intentions, is to punish women because their very presence might provoke sexual assaults. It is women who are made to pay the price in lost job opportunities for the threat of depraved conduct by prison inmates. Once again, "[t]he pedestal upon which women have been placed has . . . , upon closer inspection, been revealed as a cage." Sail'er Inn, Inc. v. Kirby, 5 Cal. 3d 1, 20, 485 P.2d 529, 541 (1971). It is particularly ironic that the case is erected here in response to feared misbehavior by imprisoned criminals.

The Court points to no evidence in the record to support the asserted "likelihood that inmates would assault a woman because she was a woman." Perhaps the Court relies upon common sense, or "innate recognition." Brief for Appellants 51. But the danger in this emotionally laden context is that common sense will be used to mask the " 'romantic paternalism' " and persisting discriminatory attitudes that the Court properly eschews. To me, the only matter of innate recognition is that the incidence of sexually motivated attacks on guards will be minute compared to the "likelihood that inmates will assault" a *guard* because he or she is a *guard*.

The proper response to inevitable attacks on both female and male guards is not to limit the employment opportunities of law-abiding women who wish to contribute to their community, but to take swift and sure punitive action against the inmate offenders. Presumably, one of the goals of the Alabama prison system is the eradication of inmates' antisocial behavior patterns so that prisoners will be able to live one day in free society. Sex offenders can begin this process by learning to relate to women guards in a socially acceptable manner. To deprive women of job opportunities because of the threatened behavior of convicted criminals is to turn our social priorities upside down.

Although I do not countenance the sex discrimination condoned by the majority, it is fortunate that the Court's decision is carefully limited to the facts before it. I trust the lower courts will recognize that the decision was impelled by the shockingly inhuman conditions in Alabama prisons, and thus that the "extremely narrow [BFOQ] exception" recognized here will not be allowed "to swallow the rule" against sex discrimination. See *Phillips v. Martin Marietta Corp.*, 400 U.S. at 545. Expansion of today's decision beyond its narrow factual basis would erect a serious roadblock to economic equality for women.

■ MR. JUSTICE WHITE, dissenting.

. . . I have . . . trouble agreeing that a prima facie case of sex discrimination was made out by statistics showing that the Alabama height and weight requirements would exclude a larger percentage of women in the United States than of men. [T]he issue is whether there was discrimination in dealing with actual or potential applicants. . . . I am unwilling to believe that the percentage of women applying or interested in applying for jobs as prison guards in Alabama approximates the percentage of women either in the national or state population. A plaintiff could, of course, show that the composition of the applicant pool was distorted by the exclusion of nonapplicants who did not apply because of the allegedly discriminatory job requirement. But no such showing was made or even attempted here; and although I do not know what the actual fact is, I am not now convinced that a large percentage of the actual women applicants, or of those who are seriously interested in applying, for prison guard positions would fail to satisfy the height and weight requirements. Without a more satisfactory record on this issue, I cannot conclude that appellee Rawlinson has either made out a prima facie case for the invalidity of the restrictions or otherwise proved that she was improperly denied employment as a prison guard. There being no showing of discrimination, I do not reach the question of justification; nor, since she does not meet the threshold requirements for becoming a prison guard, need I deal with the gender-based requirements for contact positions. I dissent from the Court's judgment . . . insofar as it affirms the judgment of the District Court.

NOTES ON DOTHARD V. RAWLINSON

1. THE § 1983 CLAIMS

The plaintiffs in *Dothard* also filed claims under § 1983, alleging that the height and weight requirements and the exclusion of women from contact positions violated the Equal Protection Clause. The District Court ruled for the plaintiffs on these claims as well as on their Title VII claims, but the Supreme Court decided only the Title VII claims. Would the claims under § 1983 and the Equal Protection Clause have come out the same way as the claims under Title VII? The practices challenged in *Dothard*, the different theories of liability, and the remedies available are worth considering separately.

2. THE HEIGHT AND WEIGHT REQUIREMENTS

The Constitution prohibits only intentional discrimination, not neutral practices with discriminatory effects. The height and weight requirements were struck down under Title VII under the theory of disparate impact, which requires the plaintiff to prove only discriminatory effect and then shifts the burden to the defendant to prove that the disputed requirements are "job related for the position in question and consistent with business necessity." 42 U.S.C. § 2000e–2(k)(1)(A)(i). If the defendant meets this burden, then the burden shifts back to the plaintiff to prove that the disputed practices are a pretext for discrimination.

No such theory of liability, with its shifting burdens of proof, is available under the Equal Protection Clause. The Supreme Court required intentional discrimination to establish racial discrimination in violation of the Constitution in Washington v. Davis, 426 U.S. 229 (1976). This conclusion was applied to sex discrimination in Personnel Administrator v. Feeney, 442 U.S. 256 (1979).

In order to establish a constitutional violation, therefore, the plaintiff would have had to prove that the height and weight requirements were *intended* to exclude women from the position as prison guard. Evidence, like that presented in *Dothard* itself, that most women were disqualified by these requirements would have supported an inference of intentional discrimination, but the burden of proof would never have shifted to the defendant. How hard would it have been for the court to find intentional discrimination on the evidence presented, that almost all men (at least 96%) met the height and weight requirements but only about half of women (59%) did? Or does Justice White's criticism of the plaintiff's failure to submit evidence of applicant flow statistics have added force in considering a claim of intentional discrimination? Does the defendants' failure to provide its own statistics or indeed any convincing justification for the height and weight requirements further support a finding of intentional discrimination?

3. DISPARATE IMPACT CLAIMS UNDER TITLE VL;PII

Even in cases decided exclusively under Title VII, the Supreme Court has formulated the elements of a claim of disparate impact differently in different opinions, at one point assimilating them to claims of intentional discrimination. Wards Cove Packing Co. v. Atonio, 490 U.S. 642 (1989). This interpretation of Title VII was largely rejected by Congress in 1991 when it codified the theory of disparate impact in its present form. 42 U.S.C. § 2000e–2(k). The statute now specifies the elements of the plaintiff's case and the defendant's rebuttal in considerable detail. The plaintiff must identify "a particular employment practice" that causes a disparate impact. If the plaintiff succeeds in making this showing, then the defendant must prove that the challenged practice is "job related for the position in question and consistent with business necessity." Most cases stop at either of these first two steps, but cases can proceed to a third step, in which the plaintiff must prove that an alternative practice with less adverse impact could have been adopted by the defendant.

This entire structure of burdens of proof is conducive to class-wide litigation. Although *Dothard* itself was not a class action, the disparate impact claim in this case could have been brought by any woman who sought a job in the Alabama prisons and did not meet the disputed height and weight requirements. In this sense, the decision concerned class-wide liability, as it also did for the exclusion of women from "contact positions." If enough women sought positions in the Alabama prison system, but were denied employment for these reasons, the case could have been certified as a class action under Federal Rule of Civil Procedure 23. A principal case later in this chapter, Wal–Mart Stores, Inc. v. Dukes, 131 S.Ct. 2541 (2011), addresses the question of certification of class actions under Rule 23. Note that under Title VII, a prerequisite to certification is a claim of class-wide liability, such as the claims in *Dothard*.

4. THE EXCLUSION FROM CONTACT POSITIONS

The exclusion of women from contact positions in men's prisons was upheld based on the "bona fide occupational qualification" (BFOQ) provision in Title VII. The Supreme Court thus reached the ironic result that intentional discrimination against women was permissible under Title VII even when neutral practices with discriminatory effects, like the height and weight requirements, were not. The BFOQ allows precisely this result, by creating an exception for employment decisions on the basis of "religion, sex, or national origin in those certain instances where religion, sex, or national origin is a bona fide occupational qualification reasonably necessary to the normal operation of that particular business or enterprise." 42 U.S.C. § 2000e–2(e)(1). Notice that this provision does not apply to racial discrimination. There is no BFOQ for race.

The Equal Protection Clause, of course, contains no explicit exceptions, but judicial decisions have formulated a flexible standard for evaluating sex-based classifications which achieves much the same result. The constitutional standard for sex-based classifications is in marked contrast to the standard of "strict scrutiny" for racial classifications. Any use of race by government must be "narrowly tailored" to serve a "compelling government interest." Adarand Contractors, Inc. v. Pena, 515 U.S. 200, 227 (1995) (opinion of O'Connor, J.). The standard for sex-based classifications is slightly more lenient: "Parties who seek to defend gender-based government action must demonstrate an 'exceedingly persuasive justification' for that action." United States v. Virginia, 518 U.S. 515, 531 (1996). Is the constitutional standard for sex-based classifications more lenient than the standard for racial classifications for the same reasons that there is a BFOQ exception for sex, but not for race?

How would the constitutional standard have applied to the exclusion of women from contact positions? As Justice Marshall pointed out in his dissent, the evidence supporting the exclusion was minimal. Would it have still amounted to an "exceedingly persuasive justification"? It must have, indeed, because otherwise the action by the state in enforcing Regulation 204 (and the Supreme Court's interpretation of the BFOQ exemption) would have been unconstitutional. At the end of the day, is the BFOQ exception simply another way of stating the constitutional standard for judging the acceptability of sex-based classifications? The constitutional prohibition is limited by the state action concept. Should the BFOQ standard be the same for private employers as it is for the states as employers?

Lower court decisions after *Dothard* have not assumed that a BFOQ for prison guards is always available, but have closely examined the sufficiency of the employer's evidence. E.g., United States v. Gregory, 818 F.2d 1114, 1117–18 (4th Cir. 1987), cert. denied, 484 U.S. 847 (1987); see Torres v. Wisconsin Department of Health & Social Services, 859 F.2d 1523 (7th Cir. 1988) (en banc), cert. denied, 489 U.S. 1017 (1989). These cases have also addressed the argument that limiting guards to a single sex was necessary to safeguard the inmates' privacy, finding that other precautions can be taken to protect the limited privacy that inmates receive. A similar argument has been raised by inmates asserting that their constitutional right to privacy was violated by comprehensive surveillance and contact from guards of the opposite sex. See Bonitz v. Fair, 804 F.2d 164 (1st Cir. 1986); Forts v. Ward, 621 F.2d 1210 (2d Cir. 1980).

For a comprehensive review of the BFOQ exception and the theory of sex discrimination generally see Kimberly A. Yuracko, Private Nurses and Playboy Bunnies: Explaining Permissible Sex Discrimination, 92 Cal. L. Rev. 147 (2004); Ann C. McGinley, Harassment of Sex(y) Workers: Applying Title VII to Sexualized Industries, 18 Yale J.L. & Feminism 65 (2006); Symposium: Innate Differences: Responses to the Remarks by Lawrence H. Summers, 11 Cardozo Women's L.J. 497 (2005); Symposium, Women in the Workplace, 13 Duke J. Gender L. & Pol'y 1 (2006).

5. REMEDIES UNDER TITLE VII

As originally enacted, Title VII provided only for equitable relief. It did not authorize the award of damages. Equitable relief, however, was interpreted to include explicitly compensatory remedies, such as orders for hiring, promotions, and reinstatement, as well as awards of back pay and fringe benefits, and even "front pay" for loss of future earnings. 42 U.S.C. § 2000e–5(g). A separate provision authorized the award of attorney's fees. 42 U.S.C. § 2000e–5(k). The absence of the "legal" remedy of compensatory damages was not thought to be a major defect in the statute, and from the plaintiff's perspective, was in some respects advantageous. Black plaintiffs with racial discrimination claims, in particular, were not confronted with the possibility that their claims for damages might be tried before a jury composed mainly, or even entirely, of whites.

The developments under § 1981, recounted in the previous chapter, gradually changed this perception. Under that statute, plaintiffs alleging discrimination on the basis of race or national origin could obtain the full array of appropriate remedies, including compensatory damages as well as equitable relief. This development left plaintiffs who asserted claims of sex discrimination under Title VII at a comparative disadvantage. The Civil Rights Act of 1991 alleviated this disadvantage, but not entirely. The Act added a new section to the code, somewhat confusingly numbered § 1981a (as distinct from § 1981(a)), to augment the remedies available to plaintiffs with claims under Title VII (as well as to those with claims under the Americans with Disabilities Act and the Rehabilitation Act). If these plaintiffs establish a claim of intentional discrimination not covered by § 1981, they may recover damages under the terms of § 1981a.

The remedy under § 1981a is subject to several restrictions. First, it applies only to claims under the designated statutes. Moreover, as already noted, only plaintiffs who do not have a claim under § 1981 can recover damages under § 1981a. This damage remedy is also available only for claims of intentional discrimination. A claim of disparate impact would not be sufficient. Thus, the plaintiff in *Dothard* would still have been restricted to the equitable remedies under Title VII as originally enacted because she prevailed only on her claim that the height and weight requirements had a disparate impact upon women, not on her claim that the explicit exclusion of women from "contact positions" in men's prisons constituted intentional discrimination.

In addition, recovery of punitive damages can be obtained only against private defendants and only upon proof that the defendant acted "with malice or with reckless indifference to the federally protected rights of an aggrieved individual." Recovery of compensatory damages also is limited to amounts that could not be obtained through an award of equitable relief, usually in the form of back pay, under the original provisions of Title VII. Certain kinds of damages are also subject to caps depending on the size of the employer. Awards of punitive damages, damages for future pecuniary losses, and damages for all nonpecuniary losses are capped at various amounts ranging from $50,000 for employers with no more than 100 employees to $300,000 for employers with more than 500 employees.

The interpretation of the caps in § 1981a led to a conflict among the circuits on the question whether awards of "front pay" under Title VII were to be included in determining the amount of monetary relief subject to these caps. "Front pay" is compensation for lost pay awarded from the date of judgment forward, usually to the time when the plaintiff is restored to a position comparable to the one discriminatorily denied to her. Because it involves a prediction of future employment decisions, front pay is necessarily more speculative than back pay, which clearly is excluded from the caps in § 1981a. Awards of front pay, in this respect, more closely resemble an award of damages subject to the caps. The Supreme Court nevertheless held in Pollard v. E.I. du Pont de

Nemours Co., 532 U.S. 843 (2001), that awards of front pay fall outside the caps because they are a form of equitable relief authorized by the original remedial provisions in Title VII, 42 U.S.C. § 2000e–5(g).

6. BIBLIOGRAPHY

The Civil Rights Act of 1991 elicited several comprehensive symposia, as well as articles devoted to narrower topics. Some of the main contributions to the literature are: The Civil Rights Act of 1991: A Symposium, 54 La. L. Rev. 1459 (1994); Symposium: The Civil Rights Act of 1991: Unraveling the Controversy, 45 Rutgers L. Rev. 887 (1993); Symposium: The Civil Rights Act of 1991: Theory and Practice, 68 Notre Dame L. Rev. 911 (1993); Kingsley R. Browne, The Civil Rights Act of 1991: A "Quota Bill," a Codification of *Griggs*, a Partial Return to *Wards Cove*, or All of the Above?, 43 Case Wes. L. Rev. 287 (1993); Note, The Civil Rights Act of 1991 and Less Discriminatory Alternatives in Disparate Impact Litigation, 106 Harv. L. Rev. 1621 (1993).

International Union, UAW v. Johnson Controls, Inc.

Supreme Court of the United States, 1991.
499 U.S. 187.

■ JUSTICE BLACKMUN delivered the opinion of the Court.

In this case we are concerned with an employer's gender-based fetal-protection policy. May an employer exclude a fertile female employee from certain jobs because of its concern for the health of the fetus the woman might conceive?

I

Respondent Johnson Controls, Inc., manufactures batteries. In the manufacturing process, the element lead is a primary ingredient. Occupational exposure to lead entails health risks, including the risk of harm to any fetus carried by a female employee.

Before the Civil Rights Act of 1964, became law, Johnson Controls did not employ any woman in a battery-manufacturing job. In June 1977, however, it announced its first official policy concerning its employment of women in lead-exposure work [warning women of the dangers to unborn children from exposure to lead and encouraging women who sought to have children to avoid jobs involving such exposure].

Five years later, in 1982, Johnson Controls shifted from a policy of warning to a policy of exclusion. Between 1979 and 1983, eight employees became pregnant while maintaining blood lead levels in excess of 30 micrograms per deciliter. This appeared to be the critical level noted by the Occupational Health and Safety Administration (OSHA) for a worker who was planning to have a family. The company responded by announcing a broad exclusion of women from jobs that exposed them to lead:

> [I]t is [Johnson Controls'] policy that women who are pregnant or who are capable of bearing children will not be placed into jobs involving lead exposure or which could expose them to lead through the exercise of job bidding, bumping, transfer or promotion rights.

The policy defined "women . . . capable of bearing children" as "all women except those whose inability to bear children is medically documented." It further stated that an unacceptable work station was one where, "over the past year," an employee had recorded a blood lead level of more than 30 micrograms per deciliter or the work site had yielded an air sample containing a lead level in excess of 30 micrograms per cubic meter.

II

In April 1984, petitioners filed in the United States District Court for the Eastern District of Wisconsin a class action challenging Johnson Controls' fetal-protection policy as sex discrimination that violated Title VII of the Civil Rights Act of 1964. Among the individual plaintiffs were petitioners Mary Craig, who had chosen to be sterilized in order to avoid losing her job, Elsie Nason, a 50–year–old divorcee, who had suffered a loss in compensation when she was transferred out of a job where she was exposed to lead, and Donald Penney, who had been denied a request for a leave of absence for the purpose of lowering his lead level because he intended to become a father. Upon stipulation of the parties, the District Court certified a class consisting of "all past, present and future production and maintenance employees" in United Auto Workers bargaining units at nine of Johnson Controls' plants "who have been and continue to be affected by [the employer's] Fetal Protection Policy implemented in 1982."

The District Court granted summary judgment for defendant-respondent Johnson Controls. Applying a three-part business necessity defense derived from fetal-protection cases in the Courts of Appeals for the Fourth and Eleventh Circuits, the District Court concluded that while "there is a disagreement among the experts regarding the effect of lead on the fetus," the hazard to the fetus through exposure to lead was established by "a considerable body of opinion"; that although "expert opinion has been provided which holds that lead also affects the reproductive abilities of men and women [and] that these effects are as great as the effects of exposure of the fetus . . . a great body of experts are of the opinion that the fetus is more vulnerable to levels of lead that would not affect adults"; and that petitioners had "failed to establish that there is an acceptable alternative policy which would protect the fetus." The court stated that, in view of this disposition of the business necessity defense, it did not "have to undertake a bona fide occupational qualification's (BFOQ) analysis."

The Court of Appeals for the Seventh Circuit, sitting en banc, affirmed the summary judgment by a 7–to–4 vote. The majority held that the proper standard for evaluating the fetal-protection policy was the defense of business necessity; that Johnson Controls was entitled to summary judgment under that defense; and that even if the proper standard was a BFOQ, Johnson Controls still was entitled to summary judgment. . . .

We granted certiorari . . . to address the important and difficult question whether an employer, seeking to protect potential fetuses, may discriminate against women just because of their ability to become pregnant.

III

The bias in Johnson Controls' policy is obvious. Fertile men, but not fertile women, are given a choice as to whether they wish to risk their reproductive health for a particular job. Section 703(a) of the Civil Rights Act of 1964 prohibits sex-based classifications in terms and conditions of employment, in hiring and discharging decisions, and in other employment decisions that adversely affect an employee's status. Respondent's fetal-protection policy explicitly discriminates against women on the basis of their sex. The policy excludes women with childbearing capacity from lead-exposed jobs and so creates a facial classification based on gender. Respondent assumes as much in its brief before this Court.

Nevertheless, the Court of Appeals assumed . . . that sex-specific fetal-protection policies do not involve facial discrimination[,] that because the asserted reason for the sex-based exclusion (protecting women's unconceived offspring) was ostensibly benign, the policy was not sex-based discrimination. That assumption, however, was incorrect.

First, Johnson Controls' policy classifies on the basis of gender and childbearing capacity, rather than fertility alone. Respondent does not seek to protect the unconceived children of all its employees. Despite evidence in the record about the debilitating effect of lead exposure on the male reproductive system, Johnson Controls is concerned only with the harms that may befall the unborn offspring of its female employees. . . . This Court faced a conceptually similar situation in Phillips v. Martin Marietta Corp., 400 U.S. 542 (1971), and found sex discrimination because the policy established "one hiring policy for women and another for men—each having preschool-age children." Johnson Controls' policy is facially discriminatory because it requires only a female employee to produce proof that she is not capable of reproducing.

Our conclusion is bolstered by the Pregnancy Discrimination Act of 1978 (PDA), 42 U.S.C. § 2000e(k), in which Congress explicitly provided that, for purposes of Title VII, discrimination "on the basis of sex" includes discrimination "because of or on the basis of pregnancy, childbirth, or related medical conditions." "The Pregnancy Discrimination Act has now made clear that, for all Title VII purposes, discrimination based on a woman's pregnancy is, on its face, discrimination because of her sex." Newport News Shipbuilding & Dry Dock Co. v. EEOC, 462 U.S. 669, 684 (1983). In its use of the words "capable of bearing children" in the 1982 policy statement as the criterion for exclusion, Johnson Controls explicitly classifies on the basis of potential for pregnancy. Under the PDA, such a classification must be regarded, for Title VII purposes, in the same light as explicit sex discrimination. Respondent has chosen to treat all its female employees as potentially pregnant; that choice evinces discrimination on the basis of sex.

We concluded above that Johnson Controls' policy is not neutral because it does not apply to the reproductive capacity of the company's male employees in the same way as it applies to that of the females. Moreover, the absence of a malevolent motive does not convert a facially discriminatory policy into a neutral policy with a discriminatory effect. Whether an employment practice involves disparate treatment through explicit facial discrimination does not depend on why the employer discriminates but rather on the explicit terms of the discrimination. . . .

In sum, Johnson Controls' policy "does not pass the simple test of whether the evidence shows 'treatment of a person in a manner which but for that person's sex would be different.' " Los Angeles Dept. of Water and Power v. Manhart, 435 U.S. 702, 711 (1978). We hold that Johnson Controls' fetal-protection policy is sex discrimination forbidden under Title VII unless respondent can establish that sex is a "bona fide occupational qualification."

IV

Under § 703(e)(1) of Title VII, an employer may discriminate on the basis of "religion, sex, or national origin in those certain instances where religion, sex, or national origin is a bona fide occupational qualification reasonably necessary to the normal operation of that particular business or enterprise." 42 U.S.C. § 2000e–2(e)(1). We therefore turn to the question whether Johnson Controls' fetal-protection policy is one of those "certain instances" that come within the BFOQ exception.

The BFOQ defense is written narrowly, and this Court has read it narrowly. . . . Our emphasis on the restrictive scope of the BFOQ defense is grounded on both the language and the legislative history of § 703.

The wording of the BFOQ defense contains several terms of restriction that indicate that the exception reaches only special situations. The statute thus limits the situations in which discrimination is permissible to "certain instances" where sex discrimination is "reasonably necessary" to the "normal operation" of the "particular" business. Each one of these terms—certain, normal, particular—prevents the use of general subjective standards and favors an objective, verifiable requirement. But the most telling term is "occupational"; this indicates that these objective, verifiable requirements must concern job-related skills and aptitudes. . . .

Johnson Controls argues that its fetal-protection policy falls within the so-called safety exception to the BFOQ. Our cases have stressed that discrimination on the basis of sex because of safety concerns is allowed only in narrow circumstances. In Dothard v. Rawlinson, 433 U.S. 321 (1977), this Court indicated that danger to a woman herself does not justify discrimination. We there allowed the employer to hire only male guards in contact areas of maximum-security male penitentiaries only because more was at stake than the "individual woman's decision to weigh and accept the risks of employment." We found sex to be a BFOQ inasmuch as the employment of a female guard would create real risks of safety to others if violence broke out because the guard was a woman. Sex discrimination was tolerated because sex was related to the guard's ability to do the job—maintaining prison security. We also required in *Dothard* a high correlation between sex and ability to perform job functions and refused to allow employers to use sex as a proxy for strength although it might be a fairly accurate one. . . .

Justice White ignores the "essence of the business" test and so concludes that "the safety to fetuses in carrying out the duties of battery manufacturing is as much a legitimate concern as is safety to third parties in guarding prisons (*Dothard*) or flying airplanes (Western Airlines, Inc. v. Criswell, 472 U.S. 400 (1985))." By limiting its discussion to cost and safety concerns and rejecting the "essence of the business" test that our case law has established, Justice White seeks to expand what is now the narrow BFOQ defense. Third-party safety considerations properly entered into the BFOQ analysis in *Dothard* and *Criswell* because they went to the core of the employee's job performance. Moreover, that performance involved the central purpose of the enterprise. *Dothard*, 433 U.S. at 335 ("The essence of a correctional counselor's job is to maintain prison security"); *Criswell*, 472 U.S. at 413 (the central mission of the airline's business was the safe transportation of its passengers). Justice White attempts to transform this case into one of customer safety. The unconceived fetuses of Johnson Controls' female employees, however, are neither customers nor third parties whose safety is essential to the business of battery manufacturing. No one can disregard the possibility of injury to future children; the BFOQ, however, is not so broad that it transforms this deep social concern into an essential aspect of battery making.

Our case law, therefore, makes clear that the safety exception is limited to instances in which sex or pregnancy actually interferes with the employee's ability to perform the job. This approach is consistent with the language of the BFOQ provision itself, for it suggests that permissible distinctions based on sex must relate to ability to perform the duties of the job. Johnson Controls suggests, however, that we expand the exception to allow fetal-protection policies that mandate particular standards for pregnant or fertile women. We decline to do so. Such an expansion contradicts not only the language of the BFOQ and the narrowness of its exception but the plain language and history of the Pregnancy Discrimination Act.

The PDA's amendment to Title VII contains a BFOQ standard of its own: unless pregnant employees differ from others "in their ability or inability to work," they must be "treated the same" as other employees "for all employment-related purposes." 42 U.S.C. § 2000e(k). This language clearly sets forth Congress' remedy for discrimination on the basis of pregnancy and potential pregnancy. Women who are either pregnant or potentially pregnant must be treated like others "similar in their ability . . . to work." In other words, women as capable of doing their jobs as their male counterparts may not be forced to choose between having a child and having a job.

Justice White asserts that the PDA did not alter the BFOQ defense. Justice White arrives at this conclusion by ignoring the second clause of the Act which states that "women affected by pregnancy, childbirth, or related medical conditions shall be treated the same for all employment-related purposes . . . as other persons not so affected but similar in their ability or inability to work." 42 U.S.C. § 2000e(k). Until this day, every Member of this Court had acknowledged that "the second clause [of the PDA] could not be clearer: it mandates that pregnant employees 'shall be treated the same for all employment-related purposes' as nonpregnant employees similarly situated with respect to their ability or inability to work." California Federal S. & L. Assn. v. Guerra, 479 U.S. 272, 297 (1987) (White, J., dissenting). Justice White now seeks to read the second clause out of the Act.

The legislative history confirms what the language of the PDA compels. Both the House and Senate Reports accompanying the legislation indicate that this statutory standard was chosen to protect female workers from being treated differently from other employees simply because of their capacity to bear children. . . . The Senate Report . . . states that employers may not require a pregnant woman to stop working at any time during her pregnancy unless she is unable to do her work. Employment late in pregnancy often imposes risks on the unborn child, but Congress indicated that the employer may take into account only the woman's ability to get her job done. With the PDA, Congress made clear that the decision to become pregnant or to work while being either pregnant or capable of becoming pregnant was reserved for each individual woman to make for herself.

We conclude that the language of both the BFOQ provision and the PDA which amended it, as well as the legislative history and the case law, prohibit an employer from discriminating against a woman because of her capacity to become pregnant unless her reproductive potential prevents her from performing the duties of her job. We reiterate our holdings in *Criswell* and *Dothard* that an employer must direct its concerns about a woman's ability to perform her job safely and efficiently to those aspects of the woman's job-related activities that fall within the "essence" of the particular business.

V

We have no difficulty concluding that Johnson Controls cannot establish a BFOQ. Fertile women, as far as appears in the record, participate in the manufacture of batteries as efficiently as anyone else. Johnson Controls' professed moral and ethical concerns about the welfare of the next generation do not suffice to establish a BFOQ of female sterility. Decisions about the welfare of future children must be left to the parents who conceive, bear, support, and raise them rather than to the employers who hire those parents. Congress has mandated this choice through Title VII, as amended by the Pregnancy Discrimination Act. Johnson Controls has attempted to exclude women because of their reproductive capacity. Title VII and the PDA simply do not allow a woman's dismissal because of her failure to submit to sterilization.

Nor can concerns about the welfare of the next generation be considered a part of the "essence" of Johnson Controls' business. Judge Easterbrook in this case pertinently observed: "It is word play to say that 'the job' at Johnson [Controls] is to make batteries without risk to fetuses in the same way 'the job' at Western Air Lines is to fly planes without crashing." Johnson Controls argues that it must exclude all fertile women because it is impossible to tell which women will become pregnant while working with lead. This argument is somewhat academic in light of our conclusion that the company may not exclude fertile women at all; it perhaps is worth noting, however, that Johnson Controls has shown no "factual basis for believing that all or substantially all women would be unable to perform safely and efficiently the duties of the job involved." Weeks v. Southern Bell Tel. & Tel. Co., 408 F.2d 228, 235 (5th Cir. 1969), quoted with approval in *Dothard*, 433 U.S. at 333. Even on this sparse record, it is apparent that Johnson Controls is concerned about only a small minority of women. Of the eight pregnancies reported among the female employees, it has not been shown that any of the babies have birth defects or other abnormalities. The record does not reveal the birth rate for Johnson Controls' female workers but national statistics show that approximately nine percent of all fertile women become pregnant each year. The birthrate drops to two percent for blue collar workers over age 30. See Mary Becker, From *Muller v. Oregon* to Fetal Vulnerability Policies, 53 U. Chi. L. Rev. 1219 (1986). Johnson Controls' fear of prenatal injury, no matter how sincere, does not begin to show that substantially all of its fertile women employees are incapable of doing their jobs.

VI

A word about tort liability and the increased cost of fertile women in the workplace is perhaps necessary. One of the dissenting judges in this case expressed concern about an employer's tort liability and concluded that liability for a potential injury to a fetus is a social cost that Title VII does not require a company to ignore. It is correct to say that Title VII does not prevent the employer from having a conscience. The statute, however, does prevent sex-specific fetal-protection policies. These two aspects of Title VII do not conflict.

More than 40 States currently recognize a right to recover for a prenatal injury based either on negligence or on wrongful death. According to Johnson Controls, however, the company complies with the lead standard developed by OSHA and warns its female employees about the damaging effects of lead. It is worth noting that OSHA gave the problem of lead lengthy consideration and concluded that "there is no basis whatsoever for the claim that women of childbearing age should be excluded from the workplace in order to protect the fetus or the course of pregnancy." 43 Fed. Reg. 52952, 52966 (1978). Instead, OSHA established a series of mandatory protections which, taken together, "should effectively minimize any risk to the fetus and newborn child." Id. at 52966. Without negligence, it would be difficult for a court to find liability on the part of the employer. If, under general tort principles, Title VII bans sex-specific fetal-protection policies, the employer fully informs the woman of the risk, and the employer has not acted negligently, the basis for holding an employer liable seems remote at best.

Although the issue is not before us, Justice White observes that "it is far from clear that compliance with Title VII will preempt state tort liability." [T]he tort liability that Justice White fears will punish employers for *complying* with Title VII's clear command. When it is impossible for an employer to comply with both state and federal requirements, this Court has ruled that federal law pre-empts that of the States. See, e.g., Florida Lime & Avocado Growers, Inc. v. Paul, 373 U.S. 132, 142–43 (1963). . . .

If state tort law furthers discrimination in the workplace and prevents employers from hiring women who are capable of manufacturing the product as efficiently as men, then it will impede the accomplishment of Congress' goals in enacting Title VII. Because Johnson Controls has not argued that it faces any costs from tort liability, not to mention crippling ones, the pre-emption question is not before us. We therefore say no more than that Justice White's speculation appears unfounded as well as premature.

The tort-liability argument reduces to two equally unpersuasive propositions. First, Johnson Controls attempts to solve the problem of reproductive health hazards by resorting to an exclusionary policy. Title VII plainly forbids illegal sex discrimination as a method of diverting attention from an employer's obligation to police the workplace. Second, the spectre of an award of damages reflects a fear that hiring fertile women will cost more. The extra cost of employing members of one sex, however, does not provide an affirmative Title VII defense for a discriminatory refusal to hire members of that gender. Indeed, in passing the PDA, Congress considered at length the considerable cost of providing equal treatment of pregnancy and related conditions, but made the "decision to forbid special treatment of pregnancy despite the social costs associated therewith." Arizona Governing Committee v. Norris, 463 U.S. 1073, 1084, n.14 (1983) (opinion of Marshall, J.).

We, of course, are not presented with, nor do we decide, a case in which costs would be so prohibitive as to threaten the survival of the employer's business. We merely reiterate our prior holdings that the incremental cost of hiring women cannot justify discriminating against them.

VII

. . . It is no more appropriate for the courts than it is for individual employers to decide whether a woman's reproductive role is more important to herself and her family than her economic role. Congress has left this choice to the woman as hers to make.

The judgment of the Court of Appeals is reversed and the case is remanded for further proceedings consistent with this opinion.

It is so ordered.

■ JUSTICE WHITE, with whom THE CHIEF JUSTICE and JUSTICE KENNEDY joins concurring in part and dissenting in part.

The Court properly holds that Johnson Controls' fetal protection policy overtly discriminates against women, and thus is prohibited by Title VII unless it falls within the bona fide occupational qualification (BFOQ) exception, set forth at 42 U.S.C. § 2000e–2(e). The Court erroneously holds, however, that the BFOQ defense is so narrow that it could never justify a sex-specific fetal protection policy. I nevertheless concur in the judgment of reversal because on the record before us summary judgment in favor of Johnson Controls was improperly entered by the District Court and affirmed by the Court of Appeals.

I

In evaluating the scope of the BFOQ defense, the proper starting point is the language of the statute. Title VII forbids discrimination on the basis of sex, except "in those certain instances where . . . sex . . . is a bona fide occupational qualification reasonably necessary to the normal operation of that particular business or enterprise." 42 U.S.C. § 2000e–2(e)(1). For the fetal protection policy involved in this case to be a BFOQ, therefore, the policy must be "reasonably necessary" to the "normal operation" of making batteries, which is Johnson Controls' "particular business." Although that is a difficult standard to satisfy, nothing in the statute's language indicates that it could never support a sex-specific fetal protection policy.[1]

On the contrary, a fetal protection policy would be justified under the terms of the statute if, for example, an employer could show that exclusion of women from certain jobs was reasonably necessary to avoid substantial tort liability. Common sense tells us that it is part of the normal operation of business concerns to avoid causing injury to third parties, as well as to employees, if for no other reason than to avoid tort liability and its substantial costs. This possibility of tort liability is not hypothetical; every State currently allows children born alive to recover in tort for prenatal injuries caused by third parties and an increasing number of courts have recognized a right to recover even for prenatal injuries caused by torts committed prior to conception.

The Court dismisses the possibility of tort liability by no more than speculating that if "Title VII bans sex-specific fetal-protection policies, the employer fully informs the woman of the risk, and the employer has not acted negligently, the basis for holding an employer liable seems remote at best." Such speculation will be small comfort to employers. First, it is far from clear that compliance with Title VII will pre-empt state tort liability, and the Court offers no support for that proposition. Second, although warnings may preclude claims by injured employees, they will not preclude claims by injured children because the general rule is that parents cannot waive causes of action on behalf of their children, and the parents' negligence will not be imputed to the children. Finally, although state tort liability for prenatal injuries generally requires negligence, it will be difficult for

---

[1] The Court's heavy reliance on the word "occupational" in the BFOQ statute is unpersuasive. *Any* requirement for employment can be said to be an occupational qualification, since " 'occupational' " merely means related to a job. See Webster's Third New International Dictionary 1560 (1976). Thus, Johnson Controls' requirement that employees engaged in battery manufacturing be either male or non-fertile clearly is an "occupational qualification." The issue, of course, is whether that qualification is "reasonably necessary to the normal operation" of Johnson Controls' business. It is telling that the Court offers no case support, either from this Court or the lower federal courts, for its interpretation of the word "occupational."

employers to determine in advance what will constitute negligence. Compliance with OSHA standards, for example, has been held not to be a defense to state tort or criminal liability. Moreover, it is possible that employers will be held strictly liable, if, for example, their manufacturing process is considered "abnormally dangerous." See Restatement (Second) of Torts § 869, comment b (1979). . . .

Dothard v. Rawlinson, 433 U.S. 321 (1977), and Western Air Lines, Inc. v. Criswell, 472 U.S. 400 (1985), make clear that avoidance of substantial safety risks to third parties is *inherently* part of both an employee's ability to perform a job and an employer's "normal operation" of its business. Indeed, in both cases, the Court approved the statement in Weeks v. Southern Bell Telephone & Telegraph Co., 408 F.2d 228 (5th Cir. 1969), that an employer could establish a BFOQ defense by showing that "all or substantially all women would be unable to perform *safely* and *efficiently* the duties of the job involved." The Court's statement in this case that "the safety exception is limited to instances in which sex or pregnancy actually interferes with the employee's ability to perform the job," therefore adds no support to its conclusion that a fetal protection policy could never be justified as a BFOQ. On the facts of this case, for example, protecting fetal safety while carrying out the duties of battery manufacturing is as much a legitimate concern as is safety to third parties in guarding prisons (*Dothard*) or flying airplanes (*Criswell*).

Dothard and *Criswell* also confirm that costs are relevant in determining whether a discriminatory policy is reasonably necessary for the normal operation of a business. In *Dothard*, the safety problem that justified exclusion of women from the prison guard positions was largely a result of inadequate staff and facilities. If the cost of employing women could not be considered, the employer there should have been required to hire more staff and restructure the prison environment rather than exclude women. . . . The BFOQ statute, however, reflects "Congress' unwillingness to require employers to change the very nature of their operations." Price Waterhouse v. Hopkins, 490 U.S. 228, 242 (1989) (plurality opinion).

The Pregnancy Discrimination Act (PDA), 42 U.S.C. § 2000e(k), contrary to the Court's assertion, did not restrict the scope of the BFOQ defense. The PDA was only an amendment to the "Definitions" section of Title VII, 42 U.S.C. § 2000e, and did not purport to eliminate or alter the BFOQ defense. Rather, it merely clarified Title VII to make it clear that pregnancy and related conditions are included within Title VII's antidiscrimination provisions. As we have already recognized, "the purpose of the PDA was simply to make the treatment of pregnancy consistent with general Title VII principles." Arizona Governing Committee for Tax Deferred Annuity and Deferred Compensation Plans v. Norris, 463 U.S. 1073, 1085, n.14 (1983). . . .

In enacting the BFOQ standard, "Congress did not ignore the public interest in safety." *Criswell*, supra, at 419. The Court's narrow interpretation of the BFOQ defense in this case, however, means that an employer cannot exclude even *pregnant* women from an environment highly toxic to their fetuses. It is foolish to think that Congress intended such a result, and neither the language of the BFOQ exception nor our cases require it.

II

Despite my disagreement with the Court concerning the scope of the BFOQ defense, I concur in reversing the Court of Appeals because that court erred in affirming the District Court's grant of summary judgment in favor of Johnson Controls. First, the Court of Appeals erred in failing to consider the level of risk-avoidance that was part of Johnson Controls' "normal operation." Although the court did conclude that there was a "substantial risk" to fetuses from lead exposure in fertile women, it merely meant that there was a high risk that some fetal injury would occur absent a fetal protection policy. That analysis, of course, fails to address the *extent* of fetal injury that is likely to occur. If the fetal protection policy insists on a risk-avoidance level substantially higher than other risk levels tolerated by Johnson Controls such as risks to employees and consumers, the policy should not constitute a BFOQ.

Second, even without more information about the normal level of risk at Johnson Controls, the fetal protection policy at issue here reaches too far. This is evident both in its presumption that, absent medical documentation to the contrary, all women are fertile regardless of their age and in its exclusion of presumptively fertile women from positions that might result in a promotion to a position involving high lead exposure. There has been no showing that either of those aspects of the policy is reasonably necessary to ensure safe and efficient operation of Johnson Controls' battery-manufacturing business. Of course, these infirmities in the company's policy do not warrant invalidating the entire fetal protection program.

Third, it should be recalled that until 1982 Johnson Controls operated without an exclusionary policy, and it has not identified any grounds for believing that its current policy is reasonably necessary to its normal operations. Although it is now more aware of some of the dangers of lead exposure, it has not shown that the risks of fetal harm or the costs associated with it have substantially increased. . . .

Finally, the Court of Appeals failed to consider properly petitioners' evidence of harm to offspring caused by lead exposure in males. The court considered that evidence only in its discussion of the business necessity standard, in which it focused on whether *petitioners* had met their burden of proof. The burden of proving that a discriminatory qualification is a BFOQ, however, rests with the employer. Thus, the court should have analyzed whether the evidence was sufficient for petitioners to survive summary judgment in light of *respondent's* burden of proof to establish a BFOQ. Moreover, the court should not have discounted the evidence as "speculative" merely because it was based on animal studies. We have approved the use of animal studies to assess risks, see Industrial Union Dept. v. American Petroleum Institute, 448 U.S. 607, 657, n.64 (1980), and OSHA uses animal studies in establishing its lead control regulations, see United Steelworkers of America, AFL–CIO–CLC v. Marshall, 208 U.S. App. D.C. 60, 128, 647 F.2d 1189, 1257, n.97 (1980). It seems clear that if the Court of Appeals had properly analyzed that evidence, it would have concluded that summary judgment against petitioners was not appropriate because there was a dispute over a material issue of fact.

As Judge Posner observed below:

> The issue of the legality of fetal protection is as novel and difficult as it is contentious and the most sensible way to approach it at this early stage is on a case-by-case basis, involving careful examination of the facts as developed by the full adversary process of a trial. The record in this case is too sparse. The district judge jumped the gun. By affirming on this scanty basis we may be encouraging incautious em-

ployers to adopt fetal protection policies that could endanger the jobs of millions of women for minor gains in fetal safety and health.

But although the defendant did not present enough evidence to warrant the grant of summary judgment in its favor, there is no ground for barring it from presenting additional evidence at trial. Therefore it would be equally precipitate for us to direct the entry of judgment in the plaintiffs' favor.

■ JUSTICE SCALIA, concurring in the judgment.

I generally agree with the Court's analysis, but have some reservations, several of which bear mention.

First, I think it irrelevant that there was "evidence in the record about the debilitating effect of lead exposure on the male reproductive system." Even without such evidence, treating women differently "on the basis of pregnancy" constitutes discrimination "on the basis of sex," because Congress has unequivocally said so. Pregnancy Discrimination Act of 1978, 92 Stat. 2076, 42 U.S.C. § 2000e(k).

Second, the Court points out that "Johnson Controls has shown no factual basis for believing that all or substantially all women would be unable to perform safely . . . the duties of the job involved" (internal quotations omitted). In my view, this is not only "somewhat academic in light of our conclusion that the company may not exclude fertile women at all"; it is entirely irrelevant. By reason of the Pregnancy Discrimination Act, it would not matter if all pregnant women placed their children at risk in taking these jobs, just as it does not matter if no men do so. As Judge Easterbrook put it in his dissent below, "Title VII gives parents the power to make occupational decisions affecting their families. A legislative forum is available to those who believe that such decisions should be made elsewhere."

Third, I am willing to assume, as the Court intimates, that any action required by Title VII cannot give rise to liability under state tort law. That assumption, however, does not answer the question whether an action is required by Title VII (including the BFOQ provision) even if it is subject to liability under state tort law. It is perfectly reasonable to believe that Title VII has *accommodated* state tort law through the BFOQ exception. However, all that need be said in the present case is that Johnson has not demonstrated a substantial risk of tort liability—which is alone enough to defeat a tort-based assertion of the BFOQ exception.

Last, the Court goes far afield, it seems to me, in suggesting that increased cost alone—short of "costs . . . so prohibitive as to threaten survival of the employer's business,"—cannot support a BFOQ defense. I agree with Justice White's concurrence that nothing in our prior cases suggests this, and in my view it is wrong. I think, for example, that a shipping company may refuse to hire pregnant women as crew members on long voyages because the on-board facilities for foreseeable emergencies, though quite feasible, would be inordinately expensive. In the present case, however, Johnson has not asserted a cost-based BFOQ.

I concur in the judgment of the Court.

NOTES ON INTERNATIONAL UNION, UAW V. JOHNSON CONTROLS, INC.

1. DISTINGUISHING *DOTHARD*

Johnson Controls took a far more skeptical attitude than *Dothard* toward the assertion of the BFOQ defense. In *Dothard*, the Court was willing to surmise that women in "contact positions" in male prisons were in greater danger than men. In *Johnson Controls*, the Court rejected scientific evidence that there was at least some risk to the fetus from the mother's exposure to lead. Justice Blackmun, for the majority, concluded that Johnson Controls "may not exclude fertile women at all," but offered the opinion that even if it could, it had shown "no factual basis" for doing so. Justice Scalia agreed with the majority's conclusion, but found the presence or absence of a factual basis for excluding women "entirely irrelevant." Only Justice White would have remanded the case for additional evidence on the level of risk, and even he interpreted the BFOQ to set "a difficult standard to satisfy."

What accounts for the different approach in *Johnson Controls*? The jobs at issue in *Dothard* were narrowly defined. Excluding women from positions as prison guards in men's prisons would not have greatly reduced the opportunities for employment open to women. The jobs at issue in *Johnson Controls* were potentially far more numerous, depending upon the showing required to support a BFOQ defense. On a minimal showing, any job involving exposure to toxic chemicals might have been closed to women. Certainly Johnson Controls took only the most minimal steps to narrow its policy of excluding women, allowing only women who could prove that they were sterile to take jobs involving exposure to lead. A narrower policy supported by stronger evidence of the risks to the fetus would have affected fewer jobs, but its scope would have inevitably remained uncertain. Is there any value to employers to establishing a strong presumption that almost all jobs are open to women and that few can be closed based on the BFOQ? Does the Court's discussion of the preemptive effect of Title VII on state tort law help answer this question?

2. IMPLICATIONS OF THE PREGNANCY DISCRIMINATION ACT

Both Justice Blackmun for the majority and Justice Scalia in his separate opinion relied heavily on the Pregnancy Discrimination Act. The Act added a new provision to Title VII, now codified in 42 U.S.C. § 2000e(k). It reads as follows:

> The terms "because of sex" or "on the basis of sex" include, but are not limited to, because of or on the basis of pregnancy, childbirth, or related medical conditions; and women affected by pregnancy, childbirth, or related medical conditions shall be treated the same for all employment-related purposes, including receipt of benefits under fringe benefit programs, as other person not so affected but similar in their ability or inability to work, and nothing in section 703(h) of this title [concerning equal pay for equal work] shall be interpreted to permit otherwise. This subsection shall not require an employer to pay for health insurance benefits for abortion, except where the life of the mother would be endangered if the fetus were carried to term, or except where medical complications have arisen from an abortion: *Provided*, That nothing herein shall preclude an employer

> from providing abortion benefits or otherwise affect bargaining agreements in regard to abortion.

This provision was added to Title VII to supersede decisions holding that the statute did not prohibit discrimination on the basis of pregnancy as a form of discrimination on the basis of sex. E.g., General Electric Co. v. Gilbert, 429 U.S. 125 (1976). These decisions were based on a constitutional holding that classifications on the basis of pregnancy were not classifications on the basis of sex requiring heightened scrutiny under the Equal Protection Clause. Geduldig v. Aiello, 417 U.S. 484 (1974). In *Geduldig*, the exclusion of pregnancy benefits from a general state disability program was upheld because it was rationally related to legitimate state interests in controlling the costs of the program. In the Court's view, the exclusion of pregnancy did not discriminate on the basis of sex because it did not discriminate against all women, but only against those who were pregnant. Both this decision and its extension to Title VII were widely criticized by women's groups, resulting in the passage of the Pregnancy Discrimination Act.

As Justice White pointed out in his separate opinion, however, the Act only added a definitional provision to Title VII. It did not prohibit all classifications on the basis of pregnancy, but merely made classifications on the basis of pregnancy equivalent to classifications on the basis of sex. The BFOQ exception therefore applies to both. Yet the Court concludes that the Pregnancy Discrimination Act prevents any showing of risk to the fetus sufficient to support a BFOQ. The majority opinion emphasizes the terms of the BFOQ itself and in particular the reference to "occupational qualification." Any risk to the fetus has nothing to do with the occupation of making batteries because the fetus neither participates in the process of manufacture nor uses the batteries produced. Does this reasoning justify the rejection of any evidence, no matter how strong, that exposure to lead would pose risks to the fetus?

3. THE RELEVANCE OF CONSTITUTIONAL DECISIONS ON ABORTION

Justice Scalia endorsed the Court's reasoning that the Pregnancy Discrimination Act makes evidence of risks irrelevant, yet he wrote a separate opinion concurring only in the judgment. Why did he not join Justice Blackmun's opinion for the Court? The answer may lie in the continuing dispute about the constitutional status of abortion. Consider the following passage from the conclusion of Justice Blackmun's opinion:

> It is no more appropriate for the courts than it is for individual employers to decide whether a woman's reproductive role is more important to herself and her family than her economic role. Congress has left this choice to the woman as hers to make.

Is this reasoning more concerned with the scope of the BFOQ under Title VII or with the scope of the right to reproductive freedom under the Constitution? Congress did not address the reproductive role of women in the BFOQ, which speaks only of "bona fide occupational qualifications reasonably necessary to the normal operation of that particular business or enterprise." In the Pregnancy Discrimination Act, Congress addressed the right to abortion only through an exception that left most "health benefits for abortion" to be determined by the employer. Justice Blackmun, of course, wrote the opinion in Roe v. Wade, 410 U.S. 113 (1973), and Justice Scalia has been an outspoken critic of that decision. See Planned Parenthood of Southeastern Pennsylvania v. Casey,

505 U.S. 833, 979 (1992) (Scalia, J., concurring in the judgment in part and dissenting in part).

Perhaps this difference over the constitutional right to an abortion explains why Justice Scalia emphasized the power of Congress to alter the result in *Johnson Controls* and Justice Blackmun did not. Would an amendment to Title VII allowing the employer's policy in *Johnson Controls* be subject to constitutional attack? Perhaps as applied to private employers, it would not, because government action would be lacking; Congress might only have restored to private employers the power to discriminate against women that they possessed before the enactment of Title VII. The same argument, however, could not be made with respect to public employers. Any restriction on the employment of pregnant women by public employers, whether authorized by Congress or not, would raise constitutional questions. Under the holding of *Geduldig v. Aiello*, subjecting classifications on the basis of pregnancy only to the lenient standard of rational basis review, any such restriction would appear to be constitutional. Would it be constitutional if it were considered a sex-based classification subject to the current standard for such classifications, requiring "an exceedingly persuasive justification"? Would any such restriction on the employment of pregnant women be unconstitutional on the independent ground that it infringed the right to an abortion under *Roe v. Wade*?

4. BIBLIOGRAPHY

Much was written about the issue in *Johnson Controls*, both before and after that decision. Almost all of the commentary is favorable to the result reached by the Supreme Court, although different authors give varying emphasis to medical evidence of reproductive hazards (both to men and to women), economic incentives of women in the workplace, and different conceptions of equality from a feminist perspective. Mary Becker, Reproductive Hazards, After *Johnson Controls*, 31 Hous. L. Rev. 43 (1994); Samuel Issacharoff and Elyse Rosenblum, Women and the Workplace: Accommodating the Demands of Pregnancy, 94 Colum. L. Rev. 2154 (1994); Wendy W. Williams, Firing the Woman to Protect the Fetus: The Reconciliation of Fetal Protection Policies with Employment Opportunity Goals under Title VII, 69 Geo. L.J. 641 (1981). For more general discussions of the Pregnancy Discrimination Act, see Joanna L. Grossman, Pregancy, Work, and the Promise of Equal Citizenship, 98 Geo. L.J. 567 (2010); Deborah Dinner, The Costs of Reproduction: History and the Legal Construction of Sex Equality, 46 Harv. C.R.–C.L. L. Rev. 411 (2011).

INTRODUCTORY NOTE ON CLASS ACTIONS

Individual actions are the principal means of enforcing Title VII, but they might be displaced by other means of enforcement, including public actions brought by the federal enforcement agencies and class actions brought on behalf of similarly situated employees or applicants for employment. *Johnson Controls* was one such class action, and other class actions have loomed large in the enforcement of Title VII. In the early years after passage of the statute, class actions took on a prominent role, aptly summarized by the maxim, "Racial discrimination is by definition class discrimination." Oatis v. Crown Zellerbach Corp., 398 F.2d 496, 499 (5th Cir. 1968). In invoking this maxim, courts made it easier for private plaintiffs to obtain certification of a class action, but the Supreme Court has repeatedly re-examined this maxim, beginning with Rodriguez v. East Texas Motor Freight System, Inc. v. Rodriguez, 431 U.S. 395 (1977), and General Telephone Co. of Southwest v. Falcon, 457 U.S. 147 (1982). These decisions emphasized that despite the maxim, "careful attention to the requirements of Fed. Rule Civ. Proc. 23 remains nonetheless indispensable."

The provisions of Rule 23 most commonly invoked in Title VII class actions are the following:

> **(a) Prerequisites to a Class Action.** One or more members of a class may sue or be sued as representative parties on behalf of all only if (1) the class is so numerous that joinder of all members is impracticable, (2) there are questions of law or fact common to the class, (3) the claims or defenses of the representative parties are typical of the claims or defenses of the class, and (4) the representative parties will fairly and adequately protect the interests of the class.
>
> **(b) Class Actions Maintainable.** An action may be maintained as a class action if the prerequisites of subdivision (a) are satisfied, and in addition: . . .
>
> > **(2)** the party opposing the class has acted or refused to act on grounds generally applicable to the class, thereby making appropriate final injunctive relief or corresponding declaratory relief with respect to the class as a whole; or
> >
> > **(3)** the court finds that the questions of law or fact common to the members of the class predominate over any questions affecting only individual members, and that a class action is superior to other available methods for the fair and efficient adjudication of the controversy. The matters pertinent to the findings include: (A) the interest of members of the class in individually controlling the prosecution or defense of separate actions; (B) the extent and nature of any litigation concerning the controversy already commenced by or against members of the class; (C) the desirability or undesirability of concentrating the litigation of the claims in the particular forum; (D) the difficulties likely to be encountered in the management of a class action. . . .

Although formally an issue of procedure, class certification has a profound effect on substantive policy by allowing small claims, which otherwise would be inadequate to support individual litigation, to be aggregated into class claims potentially worth millions of dollars. The exposure to liability on this scale alters the incentives of employers to comply with the law, as well as the dynamics of settlement negotiations after a class has been certified. Employers have greater reason to avoid liability in any form or to limit it by prompt settlement of class-wide claims. Class actions therefore raise fundamental questions about underenforcement—and perhaps overenforcement—of the law. They also raise profound questions about who is to control enforcement—individual plaintiffs and their attorneys or attorneys who seek certification of a class action. The Supreme Court addressed these questions in the next principal case.

Wal–Mart Stores, Inc. v. Dukes

Supreme Court of the United States, 2011.
131 S.Ct. 2541.

■ JUSTICE SCALIA delivered the opinion of the Court.

We are presented with one of the most expansive class actions ever. The District Court and the Court of Appeals approved the certification of a class comprising about one and a half million plaintiffs, current and former female employees of petitioner Wal–Mart who allege that the discretion exercised by their local supervisors over pay and promotion matters violates Title VII by discriminating against women. In addition to injunctive and declaratory relief, the plaintiffs seek an award of backpay. We consider whether the certification of the plaintiff class was consistent with Federal Rules of Civil Procedure 23(a) and (b)(2).

I

A

Petitioner Wal–Mart is the Nation's largest private employer. It operates four types of retail stores throughout the country: Discount Stores, Supercenters, Neighborhood Markets, and Sam's Clubs. Those stores are divided into seven nationwide divisions, which in turn comprise 41 regions of 80 to 85 stores apiece. Each store has between 40 and 53 separate departments and 80 to 500 staff positions. In all, Wal–Mart operates approximately 3,400 stores and employs more than one million people.

Pay and promotion decisions at Wal–Mart are generally committed to local managers' broad discretion, which is exercised "in a largely subjective manner." 222 F.R.D. 137, 145 (ND Cal. 2004). Local store managers may increase the wages of hourly employees (within limits) with only limited corporate oversight. As for salaried employees, such as store managers and their deputies, higher corporate authorities have discretion to set their pay within preestablished ranges.

Promotions work in a similar fashion. Wal–Mart permits store managers to apply their own subjective criteria when selecting candidates as "support managers," which is the first step on the path to management. Admission to Wal–Mart's management training program, however, does require that a candidate meet certain objective criteria, including an above-average performance rating, at least one year's tenure in the applicant's current position, and a willingness to relocate. But except for those requirements, regional and district managers have discretion to use their own judgment when selecting candidates for management training. Promotion to higher office—e.g., assistant manager, co-manager, or store manager—is similarly at the discretion of the employee's superiors after prescribed objective factors are satisfied.

B

The named plaintiffs in this lawsuit, representing the 1.5 million members of the certified class, are three current or former Wal–Mart employees who allege that the company discriminated against them on the basis of their sex by denying them equal pay or promotions, in violation of Title VII of the Civil Rights Act of 1964.

Betty Dukes began working at a Pittsburgh, California, Wal–Mart in 1994. She started as a cashier, but later sought and received a promotion to customer service manager. After a series of disciplinary violations, however, Dukes was demoted back to cashier and then to greeter. Dukes concedes she violated company policy, but contends that the disciplinary actions were in fact retaliation for invoking internal complaint procedures and that male employees have not been disciplined for similar infractions. Dukes also claims two male greeters in the Pittsburgh store are paid more than she is.

Christine Kwapnoski has worked at Sam's Club stores in Missouri and California for most of her adult life. She has held a number of positions, including a supervisory position. She claims that a male manager yelled at her frequently and screamed at female employees, but not at men. The manager in question "told her to 'doll up,' to wear some makeup, and to dress a little better."

The final named plaintiff, Edith Arana, worked at a Wal–Mart store in Duarte, California, from 1995 to 2001. In 2000, she approached the store manager on more than one occasion about management training, but was brushed off. Arana concluded she was being denied opportunity for advancement because of her sex. She initiated internal complaint procedures, whereupon she was told to apply directly to the district manager if she thought her store manager was being unfair. Arana, however, decided against that and never applied for management training again. In 2001, she was fired for failure to comply with Wal–Mart's timekeeping policy.

These plaintiffs, respondents here, do not allege that Wal–Mart has any express corporate policy against the advancement of women. Rather, they claim that their local managers' discretion over pay and promotions is exercised disproportionately in favor of men, leading to an unlawful disparate impact on female employees, see 42 U.S.C. § 2000e–2(k). And, respondents say, because Wal–Mart is aware of this effect, its refusal to cabin its managers' authority amounts to disparate treatment, see § 2000e–2(a). Their complaint seeks injunctive and declaratory relief, punitive damages, and backpay. It does not ask for compensatory damages.

Importantly for our purposes, respondents claim that the discrimination to which they have been subjected is common to *all* Wal–Mart's female employees. The basic theory of their case is that a strong and uniform "corporate culture" permits bias against women to infect, perhaps subconsciously, the discretionary decisionmaking of each one of Wal–Mart's thousands of managers—thereby making every woman at the company the victim of one common discriminatory practice. Respondents therefore wish to litigate the Title VII claims of all female employees at Wal–Mart's stores in a nationwide class action. . . .

C

[R]espondents moved the District Court to certify a plaintiff class consisting of "[a]ll women employed at any Wal–Mart domestic retail store at any time since December 26, 1998, who have been or may be subjected to Wal–Mart's challenged pay and management track promotions policies and practices." As evidence that there were indeed "questions of law or fact common to" all the women of Wal–Mart, as Rule 23(a)(2) requires, respondents relied chiefly on three forms of proof: statistical evidence about pay and promotion disparities between men and women at the company, anecdotal reports of discrimination from about 120 of Wal–Mart's female employees, and the testimony of a sociologist, Dr. William Bielby, who conducted a "social framework analysis" of Wal–Mart's "culture" and personnel practices, and concluded that the company was "vulnerable" to gender discrimination. 603 F.3d 571, 601 (7th Cir. 2010) (en banc).

Wal–Mart unsuccessfully moved to strike much of this evidence. It also offered its own countervailing statistical and other proof in an effort to defeat Rule 23(a)'s requirements of commonality, typicality, and adequate representation. Wal–Mart further contended that respondents' monetary claims for backpay could not be certified under Rule 23(b)(2), first because that Rule refers only to injunctive and declaratory relief, and second because the backpay claims could not be manageably tried as a class without depriving Wal–Mart of its right to present certain statutory defenses. With one limitation not relevant here, the District Court granted respondents' motion and certified their proposed class.

D

A divided en banc Court of Appeals substantially affirmed the District Court's certification order. The majority concluded that respondents' evidence of commonality was sufficient to "raise the common question whether Wal–Mart's female employees nationwide were subjected to a single set of corporate policies (not merely a number of independent discriminatory acts) that may have worked to unlawfully discriminate against them in violation of Title VII." It also agreed with the District Court that the named plaintiffs' claims were sufficiently typical of the class as a whole to satisfy Rule 23(a)(3), and that they could serve as adequate class representatives, see Rule 23(a)(4). With respect to the Rule 23(b)(2) question, the Ninth Circuit held that respondents' backpay claims could be certified as part of a (b)(2) class because they did not "predominat[e]" over the requests for declaratory and injunctive relief, meaning they were not "superior in strength, influence, or authority" to the nonmonetary claims.

Finally, the Court of Appeals determined that the action could be manageably tried as a class action because the District Court could adopt the approach the Ninth Circuit approved in Hilao v. Estate of Marcos, 103 F.3d 767, 782–787 (1996). There compensatory damages for some 9,541 class members were calculated by selecting 137 claims at random, referring those claims to a special master for valuation, and then extrapolating the validity and value of the untested claims from the sample set. The Court of Appeals "s[aw] no reason why a similar procedure to that used in *Hilao* could not be employed in this case." It would allow Wal–Mart "to present individual defenses in the randomly selected 'sample cases,' thus revealing the approximate percentage of class members whose unequal pay or nonpromotion was due to something other than gender discrimination."

We granted certiorari.

II

The class action is "an exception to the usual rule that litigation is conducted by and on behalf of the individual named parties only." Califano v. Yamasaki, 442 U.S. 682, 700–01 (1979). In order to justify a departure from that rule, "a class representative must be part of the class and 'possess the same interest and suffer the same injury' as the class members." East Tex. Motor Freight System, Inc. v. Rodriguez, 431 U.S. 395, 403 (1977) (quoting Schlesinger v. Reservists Comm. to Stop the War, 418 U.S. 208, 216 (1974)). Rule 23(a) ensures that the named plaintiffs are appropriate representatives of the class whose claims they wish to litigate. The Rule's four requirements—numerosity, commonality, typicality, and adequate representation—"effectively 'limit the class claims to those fairly encompassed by the named plaintiff's claims.' " General Telephone Co. of Southwest v. Falcon, 457 U.S. 147, 156 (1982) (quoting General Telephone Co. of Northwest v. EEOC, 446 U.S. 318, 330 (1980)).

A

The crux of this case is commonality—the rule requiring a plaintiff to show that "there are questions of law or fact common to the class." Rule 23(a)(2).[5] That language is easy to misread, since "[a]ny competently crafted class complaint literally raises common 'questions.' " Richard Nagareda, Class Certification in the Age of Aggregate Proof, 84 N.Y.U.L.Rev. 97, 131–132 (2009). For example: Do all of us plaintiffs indeed work for Wal–Mart? Do our managers have discretion over pay? Is that an unlawful employment practice? What remedies should we get? Reciting these questions is not sufficient to obtain class certification. Commonality requires the plaintiff to demonstrate that the class members "have suffered the same injury," *Falcon*, 457 U.S., at 157. This does not mean merely that they have all suffered a violation of the same provision of law. Title VII, for example, can be violated in many ways—by intentional discrimination, or by hiring and promotion criteria that result in disparate impact, and by the use of these practices on the part of many different superiors in a single company. Quite obviously, the mere claim by employees of the same company that they have suffered a Title VII injury, or even a disparate-impact Title VII injury, gives no cause to believe that all their claims can productively be litigated at once. Their claims must depend upon a common contention—for example, the assertion of discriminatory bias on the part of the same supervisor. That common contention, moreover, must be of such a nature that it is capable of classwide resolution—which means that determination of its truth or falsity will resolve an issue that is central to the validity of each one of the claims in one stroke.

> What matters to class certification . . . is not the raising of common "questions"—even in droves—but, rather the capacity of a classwide proceeding to generate common *answers* apt to drive the resolution of the litigation. Dissimilarities within the proposed class are what have the potential to impede the generation of common answers. Nagareda, 84 N.Y.U.L. Rev. at 132.

Rule 23 does not set forth a mere pleading standard. A party seeking class certification must affirmatively demonstrate his compliance with the Rule—that is, he must be prepared to prove that there are *in fact* sufficiently numerous parties, common questions of law or fact, etc. We recognized in *Falcon* that "sometimes it may be necessary for the court to probe behind the pleadings before coming to rest on the certification question," 457 U.S., at 160, and that certification is proper only if "the trial court is satisfied, after a rigorous analysis, that the prerequisites of Rule 23(a) have been satisfied," id., at 161. Frequently that "rigorous analysis" will entail

[5] We have previously stated in this context that "[t]he commonality and typicality requirements of Rule 23(a) tend to merge. Both serve as guideposts for determining whether under the particular circumstances maintenance of a class action is economical and whether the named plaintiff's claim and the class claims are so interrelated that the interests of the class members will be fairly and adequately protected in their absence. Those requirements therefore also tend to merge with the adequacy-of-representation requirement, although the latter requirement also raises concerns about the competency of class counsel and conflicts of interest." General Telephone Co. of Southwest v. Falcon, 457 U.S. 147, 157–58 n.13 (1982). In light of our disposition of the commonality question, however, it is unnecessary to resolve whether respondents have satisfied the typicality and adequate-representation requirements of Rule 23(a).

some overlap with the merits of the plaintiff's underlying claim. That cannot be helped. " '[T]he class determination generally involves considerations that are enmeshed in the factual and legal issues comprising the plaintiff's cause of action.' " *Falcon*, 457 U.S., at 160 (quoting Coopers & Lybrand v. Livesay, 437 U.S. 463, 469 (1978); some internal quotation marks omitted).[6] Nor is there anything unusual about that consequence: The necessity of touching aspects of the merits in order to resolve preliminary matters, e.g., jurisdiction and venue, is a familiar feature of litigation. See Szabo v. Bridgeport Machines, Inc., 249 F.3d 672, 676–677 (7th Cir. 2001) (Easterbrook, J.).

In this case, proof of commonality necessarily overlaps with respondents' merits contention that Wal–Mart engages in a *pattern or practice* of discrimination. That is so because, in resolving an individual's Title VII claim, the crux of the inquiry is "the reason for a particular employment decision," Cooper v. Federal Reserve Bank of Richmond, 467 U.S. 867, 876 (1984). Here respondents wish to sue about literally millions of employment decisions at once. Without some glue holding the alleged *reasons* for all those decisions together, it will be impossible to say that examination of all the class members' claims for relief will produce a common answer to the crucial question *why was I disfavored.*

B

This Court's opinion in *Falcon* describes how the commonality issue must be approached. There an employee who claimed that he was deliberately denied a promotion on account of race obtained certification of a class comprising all employees wrongfully denied promotions and all applicants wrongfully denied jobs. 457 U.S., at 152. We rejected that composite class for lack of commonality and typicality, explaining:

> Conceptually, there is a wide gap between (a) an individual's claim that he has been denied a promotion [or higher pay] on discriminatory grounds, and his otherwise unsupported allegation that the company has a policy of discrimination, and (b) the existence of a class of persons who have suffered the same injury as that individual, such that the individual's claim and the class claim will share common questions of law or fact and that the individual's claim will be typical of the class claims. Id., at 157–58.

Falcon suggested two ways in which that conceptual gap might be bridged. First, if the employer "used a biased testing procedure to evaluate both applicants for employment and incumbent employees, a class action on behalf of every applicant or employee who might have been prejudiced by the test clearly would satisfy the commonality and typicality requirements of Rule 23(a)." Id., at 159, n.15. Second, "[s]ignificant proof that an employer operated under a general policy of discrimination conceivably could justify a class of both applicants and employees if the discrimination manifested it-

[6] A statement in one of our prior cases, Eisen v. Carlisle & Jacquelin, 417 U.S. 156, 177 (1974), is sometimes mistakenly cited to the contrary: "We find nothing in either the language or history of Rule 23 that gives a court any authority to conduct a preliminary inquiry into the merits of a suit in order to determine whether it may be maintained as a class action." But in that case, the judge had conducted a preliminary inquiry into the merits of a suit, not in order to determine the propriety of certification under Rules 23(a) and (b) (he had already done that, see id., at 165), but in order to shift the cost of notice required by Rule 23(c)(2) from the plaintiff to the defendants. To the extent the quoted statement goes beyond the permissibility of a merits inquiry for any other pretrial purpose, it is the purest dictum and is contradicted by our other cases. . . .

self in hiring and promotion practices in the same general fashion, such as through entirely subjective decisionmaking processes." Ibid. We think that statement precisely describes respondents' burden in this case. The first manner of bridging the gap obviously has no application here; Wal–Mart has no testing procedure or other companywide evaluation method that can be charged with bias. The whole point of permitting discretionary decisionmaking is to avoid evaluating employees under a common standard.

The second manner of bridging the gap requires "significant proof" that Wal–Mart "operated under a general policy of discrimination." That is entirely absent here. Wal–Mart's announced policy forbids sex discrimination, and as the District Court recognized the company imposes penalties for denials of equal employment opportunity. The only evidence of a "general policy of discrimination" respondents produced was the testimony of Dr. William Bielby, their sociological expert. Relying on "social framework" analysis, Bielby testified that Wal–Mart has a "strong corporate culture," that makes it " 'vulnerable' " to "gender bias." 222 F.R.D. at 152. He could not, however, "determine with any specificity how regularly stereotypes play a meaningful role in employment decisions at Wal–Mart. At his deposition. . . . Dr. Bielby conceded that he could not calculate whether 0.5 percent or 95 percent of the employment decisions at Wal–Mart might be determined by stereotyped thinking." The parties dispute whether Bielby's testimony even met the standards for the admission of expert testimony under Federal Rule of Civil Procedure 702 and our *Daubert* case, see Daubert v. Merrell Dow Pharmaceuticals, Inc., 509 U.S. 579 (1993).[8] The District Court concluded that *Daubert* did not apply to expert testimony at the certification stage of class-action proceedings. We doubt that is so, but even if properly considered, Bielby's testimony does nothing to advance respondents' case. "[W]hether 0.5 percent or 95 percent of the employment decisions at Wal–Mart might be determined by stereotyped thinking" is the essential question on which respondents' theory of commonality depends. If Bielby admittedly has no answer to that question, we can safely disregard what he has to say. It is worlds away from "significant proof" that Wal–Mart "operated under a general policy of discrimination."

C

The only corporate policy that the plaintiffs' evidence convincingly establishes is Wal–Mart's "policy" of *allowing discretion* by local supervisors over employment matters. On its face, of course, that is just the opposite of a uniform employment practice that would provide the commonality needed for a class action; it is a policy *against having* uniform employment practices. It is also a very common and presumptively reasonable way of doing business—one that we have said "should itself raise no inference of discriminatory conduct," Watson v. Fort Worth Bank & Trust, 487 U.S. 977, 990 (1988).

---

[8] Bielby's conclusions in this case have elicited criticism from the very scholars on whose conclusions he relies for his social-framework analysis. See Monahan, Walker, & Mitchell, Contextual Evidence of Gender Discrimination: The Ascendance of "Social Frameworks," 94 Va. L. Rev. 1715, 1747 (2008) ("[Bielby's] research into conditions and behavior at Wal–Mart did not meet the standards expected of social scientific research into stereotyping and discrimination"); id., at 1745, 1747 ("[A] social framework necessarily contains only general statements about reliable patterns of relations among variables . . . and goes no further. . . . Dr. Bielby claimed to present a social framework, but he testified about social facts specific to Wal–Mart"); id., at 1747–48 ("Dr. Bielby's report provides no verifiable method for measuring and testing any of the variables that were crucial to his conclusions and reflects nothing more than Dr. Bielby's 'expert judgment' about how general stereotyping research applied to all managers across all of Wal–Mart's stores nationwide for the multi-year class period").

To be sure, we have recognized that, "in appropriate cases," giving discretion to lower-level supervisors can be the basis of Title VII liability under a disparate-impact theory—since "an employer's undisciplined system of subjective decisionmaking [can have] precisely the same effects as a system pervaded by impermissible intentional discrimination." Id., at 990–91. But the recognition that this type of Title VII claim "can" exist does not lead to the conclusion that every employee in a company using a system of discretion has such a claim in common. To the contrary, left to their own devices most managers in any corporation—and surely most managers in a corporation that forbids sex discrimination—would select sex-neutral, performance-based criteria for hiring and promotion that produce no actionable disparity at all. Others may choose to reward various attributes that produce disparate impact—such as scores on general aptitude tests or educational achievements, see Griggs v. Duke Power Co., 401 U.S. 424, 431–32 (1971). And still other managers may be guilty of intentional discrimination that produces a sex-based disparity. In such a company, demonstrating the invalidity of one manager's use of discretion will do nothing to demonstrate the invalidity of another's. A party seeking to certify a nationwide class will be unable to show that all the employees' Title VII claims will in fact depend on the answers to common questions.

Respondents have not identified a common mode of exercising discretion that pervades the entire company—aside from their reliance on Dr. Bielby's social frameworks analysis that we have rejected. In a company of Wal–Mart's size and geographical scope, it is quite unbelievable that all managers would exercise their discretion in a common way without some common direction. Respondents attempt to make that showing by means of statistical and anecdotal evidence, but their evidence falls well short.

The statistical evidence consists primarily of regression analyses performed by Dr. Richard Drogin, a statistician, and Dr. Marc Bendick, a labor economist. Drogin conducted his analysis region-by-region, comparing the number of women promoted into management positions with the percentage of women in the available pool of hourly workers. After considering regional and national data, Drogin concluded that "there are statistically significant disparities between men and women at Wal–Mart . . . [and] these disparities . . . can be explained only by gender discrimination." 603 F.3d, at 604 (internal quotation marks omitted). Bendick compared workforce data from Wal–Mart and competitive retailers and concluded that Wal–Mart "promotes a lower percentage of women than its competitors."

Even if they are taken at face value, these studies are insufficient to establish that respondents' theory can be proved on a classwide basis. In *Falcon*, we held that one named plaintiff's experience of discrimination was insufficient to infer that "discriminatory treatment is typical of [the employer's employment] practices." 457 U.S., at 158. A similar failure of inference arises here. As Judge Ikuta observed in her dissent, "[i]nformation about disparities at the regional and national level does not establish the existence of disparities at individual stores, let alone raise the inference that a company-wide policy of discrimination is implemented by discretionary decisions at the store and district level." 603 F.3d, at 637. A regional pay disparity, for example, may be attributable to only a small set of Wal–Mart stores, and cannot by itself establish the uniform, store-by-store disparity upon which the plaintiffs' theory of commonality depends.

There is another, more fundamental, respect in which respondents' statistical proof fails. Even if it established (as it does not) a pay or promotion pattern that differs from the nationwide figures or the regional figures in *all* of Wal–Mart's 3,400 stores, that would still not demonstrate that commonality of issue exists. Some managers will claim that the availability of women, or qualified women, or interested women, in their stores' area does not mirror the national or regional statistics. And almost all of them will claim to have been applying some sex-neutral, performance-based criteria—whose nature and effects will differ from store to store. In the landmark case of ours which held that giving discretion to lower-level supervisors can be the basis of Title VII liability under a disparate-impact theory, the plurality opinion *conditioned* that holding on the corollary that merely proving that the discretionary system has produced a racial or sexual disparity *is not enough.* "[T]he plaintiff must begin by identifying the specific employment practice that is challenged." *Watson*, 487 U.S., at 994; accord, Wards Cove Packing Co. v. Atonio, 490 U.S. 642, 656 (1989) (approving that statement), superseded by statute on other grounds, 42 U.S.C. § 2000e–2(k). That is all the more necessary when a class of plaintiffs is sought to be certified. Other than the bare existence of delegated discretion, respondents have identified no "specific employment practice"—much less one that ties all their 1.5 million claims together. Merely showing that Wal–Mart's policy of discretion has produced an overall sex-based disparity does not suffice.

Respondents' anecdotal evidence suffers from the same defects, and in addition is too weak to raise any inference that all the individual, discretionary personnel decisions are discriminatory. [R]espondents filed some 120 affidavits reporting experiences of discrimination—about 1 for every 12,500 class members—relating to only some 235 out of Wal–Mart's 3,400 stores. 603 F.3d, at 634 (Ikuta, J., dissenting). More than half of these reports are concentrated in only six States (Alabama, California, Florida, Missouri, Texas, and Wisconsin); half of all States have only one or two anecdotes; and 14 States have no anecdotes about Wal–Mart's operations at all. Id., at 634–35, and n.10. Even if every single one of these accounts is true, that would not demonstrate that the entire company "operate[s] under a general policy of discrimination," *Falcon*, at 159, n.15, which is what respondents must show to certify a companywide class.

The dissent misunderstands the nature of the foregoing analysis. It criticizes our focus on the dissimilarities between the putative class members on the ground that we have "blend[ed]" Rule 23(a)(2)'s commonality requirement with Rule 23(b)(3)'s inquiry into whether common questions "predominate" over individual ones. That is not so. We quite agree that for purposes of Rule 23(a)(2) " '[e]ven a single [common] question' " will do . . . (quoting Nagareda, The Preexistence Principle and the Structure of the Class Action, 103 Colum. L. Rev. 149, 176, n.110 (2003)). We consider dissimilarities not in order to determine (as Rule 23(b)(3) requires) whether common questions *predominate*, but in order to determine (as Rule 23(a)(2) requires) whether there *is* "[e]ven a single [common] question." And there is not here. Because respondents provide no convincing proof of a companywide discriminatory pay and promotion policy, we have concluded that they have not established the existence of any common question.

In sum, we agree with Chief Judge Kozinski that the members of the class:

> [H]eld a multitude of different jobs, at different levels of Wal–Mart's hierarchy, for variable lengths of time, in 3,400 stores, sprinkled across 50 states, with a kaleidoscope of supervisors (male and female),

subject to a variety of regional policies that all differed. . . . Some thrived while others did poorly. They have little in common but their sex and this lawsuit. 603 F.3d, at 652 (dissenting opinion).

III

We also conclude that respondents' claims for backpay were improperly certified under Federal Rule of Civil Procedure 23(b)(2). Our opinion in Ticor Title Ins. Co. v. Brown, 511 U.S. 117, 121 (1994) (per curiam) expressed serious doubt about whether claims for monetary relief may be certified under that provision. We now hold that they may not, at least where (as here) the monetary relief is not incidental to the injunctive or declaratory relief.

A

Rule 23(b)(2) allows class treatment when "the party opposing the class has acted or refused to act on grounds that apply generally to the class, so that final injunctive relief or corresponding declaratory relief is appropriate respecting the class as a whole." One possible reading of this provision is that it applies *only* to requests for such injunctive or declaratory relief and does not authorize the class certification of monetary claims at all. We need not reach that broader question in this case, because we think that, at a minimum, claims for *individualized* relief (like the backpay at issue here) do not satisfy the Rule. The key to the (b)(2) class is "the indivisible nature of the injunctive or declaratory remedy warranted—the notion that the conduct is such that it can be enjoined or declared unlawful only as to all of the class members or as to none of them." Nagareda, 84 N.Y.U. L. Rev., at 132. In other words, Rule 23(b)(2) applies only when a single injunction or declaratory judgment would provide relief to each member of the class. It does not authorize class certification when each individual class member would be entitled to a *different* injunction or declaratory judgment against the defendant. Similarly, it does not authorize class certification when each class member would be entitled to an individualized award of monetary damages. . . .

Permitting the combination of individualized and classwide relief in a (b)(2) class is also inconsistent with the structure of Rule 23(b). Classes certified under (b)(1) and (b)(2) share the most traditional justifications for class treatment—that individual adjudications would be impossible or unworkable, as in a (b)(1) class, or that the relief sought must perforce affect the entire class at once, as in a (b)(2) class. For that reason these are also mandatory classes: The Rule provides no opportunity for (b)(1) or (b)(2) class members to opt out, and does not even oblige the District Court to afford them notice of the action. Rule 23(b)(3), by contrast, is an "adventuresome innovation" of the 1966 amendments, Amchem Products, Inc. v. Windsor, 521 U.S. 591, 614 (internal quotation marks omitted), framed for situations "in which 'class-action treatment is not as clearly called for'," id., at 615 (quoting Advisory Committee's Notes, 28 U.S.C. App., p. 697 (1994 ed.)). It allows class certification in a much wider set of circumstances but with greater procedural protections. Its only prerequisites are that "the questions of law or fact common to class members predominate over any questions affecting only individual members, and that a class action is superior to other available methods for fairly and efficiently adjudicating the controversy." Rule 23(b)(3). And unlike (b)(1) and (b)(2) classes, the (b)(3) class is not mandatory; class members are entitled to receive "the best notice that is practicable under the circumstances" and to withdraw from the class at their option. See Rule 23(c)(2)(B).

Given that structure, we think it clear that individualized monetary claims belong in Rule 23(b)(3). The procedural protections attending the (b)(3) class—predominance, superiority, mandatory notice, and the right to opt out—are missing from (b)(2) not because the Rule considers them unnecessary, but because it considers them unnecessary *to a (b)(2) class.* When a class seeks an indivisible injunction benefitting all its members at once, there is no reason to undertake a case-specific inquiry into whether class issues predominate or whether class action is a superior method of adjudicating the dispute. Predominance and superiority are self-evident. But with respect to each class member's individualized claim for money, that is not so—which is precisely why (b)(3) requires the judge to make findings about predominance and superiority before allowing the class. Similarly, (b)(2) does not require that class members be given notice and opt-out rights, presumably because it is thought (rightly or wrongly) that notice has no purpose when the class is mandatory, and that depriving people of their right to sue in this manner complies with the Due Process Clause. In the context of a class action predominantly for money damages we have held that absence of notice and opt-out violates due process. See Phillips Petroleum Co. v. Shutts, 472 U.S. 797, 812 (1985). While we have never held that to be so where the monetary claims do not predominate, the serious possibility that it may be so provides an additional reason not to read Rule 23(b)(2) to include the monetary claims here.

B

Against that conclusion, respondents argue that their claims for backpay were appropriately certified as part of a class under Rule 23(b)(2) because those claims do not "predominate" over their requests for injunctive and declaratory relief. They rely upon the Advisory Committee's statement that Rule 23(b)(2) "does not extend to cases in which the appropriate final relief relates *exclusively or predominantly* to money damages." 39 F.R.D. 69, 102 (1966) (emphasis added). The negative implication, they argue, is that it *does* extend to cases in which the appropriate final relief relates only partially and nonpredominantly to money damages. Of course it is the Rule itself, not the Advisory Committee's description of it, that governs. And a mere negative inference does not in our view suffice to establish a disposition that has no basis in the Rule's text, and that does obvious violence to the Rule's structural features. The mere "predominance" of a proper (b)(2) injunctive claim does nothing to justify elimination of Rule 23(b)(3)'s procedural protections: It neither establishes the superiority of *class* adjudication over *individual* adjudication nor cures the notice and opt-out problems. We fail to see why the Rule should be read to nullify these protections whenever a plaintiff class, at its option, combines its monetary claims with a request—even a "predominating request"—for an injunction. . . .

Finally, respondents argue that their backpay claims are appropriate for a (b)(2) class action because a backpay award is equitable in nature. The latter may be true, but it is irrelevant. The Rule does not speak of "equitable" remedies generally but of injunctions and declaratory judgments. As Title VII itself makes pellucidly clear, backpay is neither. See 42 U.S.C. § 2000e–5(g)(2)(B)(i) and (ii) (distinguishing between declaratory and injunctive relief and the payment of "backpay," see § 2000e–5(g)(2)(A)).

C

. . . Contrary to the Ninth Circuit's view, Wal–Mart is entitled to individualized determinations of each employee's eligibility for backpay. Title VII includes a detailed remedial scheme. If a plaintiff prevails in showing that an employer has discriminated against him in violation of the statute, the court "may enjoin the respondent from engaging in such unlawful employment practice, and order such affirmative action as may be appropriate, [including] reinstatement or hiring of employees, with or without backpay . . . or any other equitable relief as the court deems appropriate." § 2000e–5(g)(1). But if the employer can show that it took an adverse employment action against an employee for any reason other than discrimination, the court cannot order the "hiring, reinstatement, or promotion of an individual as an employee, or the payment to him of any backpay." § 2000e–5(g)(2)(A).

We have established a procedure for trying pattern-or-practice cases that gives effect to these statutory requirements. When the plaintiff seeks individual relief such as reinstatement or backpay after establishing a pattern or practice of discrimination, "a district court must usually conduct additional proceedings . . . to determine the scope of individual relief." Teamsters v. United States, 431 U.S. 324, 361 (1977). At this phase, the burden of proof will shift to the company, but it will have the right to raise any individual affirmative defenses it may have, and to "demonstrate that the individual applicant was denied an employment opportunity for lawful reasons." Id., at 362.

The Court of Appeals believed that it was possible to replace such proceedings with Trial by Formula. A sample set of the class members would be selected, as to whom liability for sex discrimination and the backpay owing as a result would be determined in depositions supervised by a master. The percentage of claims determined to be valid would then be applied to the entire remaining class, and the number of (presumptively) valid claims thus derived would be multiplied by the average backpay award in the sample set to arrive at the entire class recovery—without further individualized proceedings. 603 F.3d, at 625–27. We disapprove that novel project. Because the Rules Enabling Act forbids interpreting Rule 23 to "abridge, enlarge or modify any substantive right," 28 U.S.C. § 2072(b); see Ortiz v. Fibreboard Corp., 527 U.S. 815, 845 (1999), a class cannot be certified on the premise that Wal–Mart will not be entitled to litigate its statutory defenses to individual claims. And because the necessity of that litigation will prevent backpay from being "incidental" to the classwide injunction, respondents' class could not be certified even assuming, arguendo, that "incidental" monetary relief can be awarded to a 23(b)(2) class.

* * *

The judgment of the Court of Appeals is

Reversed.

■ JUSTICE GINSBURG, with whom JUSTICE BREYER, JUSTICE SOTOMAYOR, and JUSTICE KAGAN join, concurring in part and dissenting in part.

The class in this case, I agree with the Court, should not have been certified under Federal Rule of Civil Procedure 23(b)(2). The plaintiffs, alleging discrimination in violation of Title VII, 42 U.S.C. § 2000e et seq., seek monetary relief that is not merely incidental to any injunctive or declaratory relief that might be available. A putative class of this type may be certifiable under Rule 23(b)(3), if the plaintiffs show that common class questions "predominate" over issues affecting individuals—e.g., qualification for, and the amount of, backpay or compensatory damages—and that a class action is "superior" to other modes of adjudication.

Whether the class the plaintiffs describe meets the specific requirements of Rule 23(b)(3) is not before the Court, and I would reserve that matter for consideration and decision on remand. The Court, however, disqualifies the class at the starting gate, holding that the plaintiffs cannot cross the "commonality" line set by Rule 23(a)(2). In so ruling, the Court imports into the Rule 23(a) determination concerns properly addressed in a Rule 23(b)(3) assessment.

I

A

Rule 23(a)(2) establishes a preliminary requirement for maintaining a class action: "[T]here are questions of law or fact common to the class." The Rule "does not require that all questions of law or fact raised in the litigation be common," 1 H. Newberg & A. Conte, Newberg on Class Actions § 3.10, pp. 3–48 to 3–49 (3d ed. 1992); indeed, "[e]ven a single question of law or fact common to the members of the class will satisfy the commonality requirement," Nagareda, The Preexistence Principle and the Structure of the Class Action, 103 Colum. L. Rev. 149, 176, n.110 (2003). See Advisory Committee's 1937 Notes on Fed. Rule Civ. Proc. 23, 28 U.S.C. App., p. 138 (citing with approval cases in which "there was only a question of law or fact common to" the class members). . . .

B

The District Court, recognizing that "one significant issue common to the class may be sufficient to warrant certification," found that the plaintiffs easily met that test. Absent an error of law or an abuse of discretion, an appellate tribunal has no warrant to upset the District Court's finding of commonality. See Califano v. Yamasaki, 442 U.S. 682, 703 (1979) ("[M]ost issues arising under Rule 23 . . . [are] committed in the first instance to the discretion of the district court.").

The District Court certified a class of "[a]ll women employed at any Wal–Mart domestic retail store at any time since December 26, 1998." The named plaintiffs, led by Betty Dukes, propose to litigate, on behalf of the class, allegations that Wal–Mart discriminates on the basis of gender in pay and promotions. They allege that the company "[r]eli[es] on gender stereotypes in making employment decisions such as . . . promotion[s] [and] pay." Wal–Mart permits those prejudices to infect personnel decisions, the plaintiffs contend, by leaving pay and promotions in the hands of "a nearly all male managerial workforce" using "arbitrary and subjective criteria." Further alleged barriers to the advancement of female employees include the company's requirement, "as a condition of promotion to management jobs, that employees be willing to relocate." Absent instruction otherwise, there is a risk that managers will act on the familiar assumption that women, because of their services to husband and children, are less mobile than men. See Dept. of Labor, Federal Glass Ceiling Commission, Good for Business: Making Full Use of the Nation's Human Capital 151 (1995).

Women fill 70 percent of the hourly jobs in the retailer's stores but make up only "33 percent of management employees." 222 F.R.D., at 146. "[T]he higher one looks in the organization the lower the percentage of women." Id., at 155. The plaintiffs' "largely uncontested descriptive statistics" also show that women working in the company's stores "are paid less than men in every region" and "that the salary gap widens over time even for men and women hired into the same jobs at the same time." Ibid.; cf. Ledbetter v. Goodyear Tire & Rubber Co., 550 U.S. 618, 643 (2007) (Ginsburg, J., dissenting).

The District Court identified "systems for . . . promoting in-store employees" that were "sufficiently similar across regions and stores" to conclude that "the manner in which these systems affect the class raises issues that are common to all class members." The selection of employees for promotion to in-store management "is fairly characterized as a 'tap on the shoulder' process," in which managers have discretion about whose shoulders to tap. Vacancies are not regularly posted; from among those employees satisfying minimum qualifications, managers choose whom to promote on the basis of their own subjective impressions.

Wal–Mart's compensation policies also operate uniformly across stores, the District Court found. The retailer leaves open a $2 band for every position's hourly pay rate. Wal–Mart provides no standards or criteria for setting wages within that band, and thus does nothing to counter unconscious bias on the part of supervisors.

Wal–Mart's supervisors do not make their discretionary decisions in a vacuum. The District Court reviewed means Wal–Mart used to maintain a "carefully constructed . . . corporate culture," such as frequent meetings to reinforce the common way of thinking, regular transfers of managers between stores to ensure uniformity throughout the company, monitoring of stores "on a close and constant basis," and "Wal–Mart TV," "broadcas[t] . . . into all stores."

The plaintiffs' evidence, including class members' tales of their own experiences, suggests that gender bias suffused Wal–Mart's company culture. Among illustrations, senior management often refer to female associates as "little Janie Qs." Plaintiffs' Motion for Class Certification. One manager told an employee that "[m]en are here to make a career and women aren't." 222 F.R.D., at 166. A committee of female Wal–Mart executives concluded that "[s]tereotypes limit the opportunities offered to women." Plaintiffs' Motion for Class Certification.

Finally, the plaintiffs presented an expert's appraisal to show that the pay and promotions disparities at Wal–Mart "can be explained only by gender discrimination and not by . . . neutral variables." Using regression analyses, their expert, Richard Drogin, controlled for factors including, inter alia, job performance, length of time with the company, and the store where an employee worked. Id., at 159.[5] The results, the District Court found, were sufficient to raise an "inference of discrimination."

C

The District Court's identification of a common question, whether Wal–Mart's pay and promotions policies gave rise to unlawful discrimination, was hardly infirm. The practice of delegating to supervisors large discretion to make personnel decisions, uncontrolled by formal standards, has long been known to have the potential to produce disparate effects. Manag-

[5] The Court asserts that Drogin showed only average differences at the "regional and national level" between male and female employees. In fact, his regression analyses showed there were disparities *within* stores. The majority's contention to the contrary reflects only an arcane disagreement about statistical method—which the District Court resolved in the plaintiffs' favor. Appellate review is no occasion to disturb a trial court's handling of factual disputes of this order.

ers, like all humankind, may be prey to biases of which they are unaware.[6] The risk of discrimination is heightened when those managers are predominantly of one sex, and are steeped in a corporate culture that perpetuates gender stereotypes.

The plaintiffs' allegations resemble those in one of the prototypical cases in this area, Leisner v. New York Tel. Co., 358 F. Supp. 359, 364–365 (S.D.N.Y. 1973). In deciding on promotions, supervisors in that case were to start with objective measures; but ultimately, they were to "look at the individual as a total individual." Id., at 365 (internal quotation marks omitted). The final question they were to ask and answer: "Is this person going to be successful in our business?" Ibid. (internal quotation marks omitted). It is hardly surprising that for many managers, the ideal candidate was someone with characteristics similar to their own.

We have held that "discretionary employment practices" can give rise to Title VII claims, not only when such practices are motivated by discriminatory intent but also when they produce discriminatory results. See Watson v. Fort Worth Bank & Trust, 487 U.S. 977, 988, 991 (1988). But see ante, at 17 ("[P]roving that [a] discretionary system has produced a . . . disparity *is not enough*."). In *Watson*, as here, an employer had given its managers large authority over promotions. An employee sued the bank under Title VII, alleging that the "discretionary promotion system" caused a discriminatory effect based on race. 487 U.S., at 984 (internal quotation marks omitted). Four different supervisors had declined, on separate occasions, to promote the employee. Id., at 982. Their reasons were subjective and unknown. The employer, we noted "had not developed precise and formal criteria for evaluating candidates"; "[i]t relied instead on the subjective judgment of supervisors." Ibid.

Aware of "the problem of subconscious stereotypes and prejudices," we held that the employer's "undisciplined system of subjective decisionmaking" was an "employment practic[e]" that "may be analyzed under the disparate impact approach." Id., at 990–91. See also Wards Cove Packing Co. v. Atonio, 490 U.S. 642, 657 (1989) (recognizing "the use of 'subjective decision making' " as an "employment practic[e]" subject to disparate-impact attack).

The plaintiffs' allegations state claims of gender discrimination in the form of biased decisionmaking in both pay and promotions. The evidence reviewed by the District Court adequately demonstrated that resolving those claims would necessitate examination of particular policies and practices alleged to affect, adversely and globally, women employed at Wal–Mart's stores. Rule 23(a)(2), setting a necessary but not a sufficient criterion for class-action certification, demands nothing further.

[6] An example vividly illustrates how subjective decisionmaking can be a vehicle for discrimination. Performing in symphony orchestras was long a male preserve. Goldin and Rouse, Orchestrating Impartiality: The Impact of "Blind" Auditions on Female Musicians, 90 Am. Econ. Rev. 715, 715–16, 738 (2000). In the 1970's orchestras began hiring musicians through auditions open to all comers. Reviewers were to judge applicants solely on their musical abilities, yet subconscious bias led some reviewers to disfavor women. Orchestras that permitted reviewers to see the applicants hired far fewer female musicians than orchestras that conducted blind auditions, in which candidates played behind opaque screens.

II

A

The Court gives no credence to the key dispute common to the class: whether Wal–Mart's discretionary pay and promotion policies are discriminatory. "What matters," the Court asserts, "is not the raising of common 'questions,' " but whether there are "[d]issimilarities within the proposed class" that "have the potential to impede the generation of common answers."

The Court blends Rule 23(a)(2)'s threshold criterion with the more demanding criteria of Rule 23(b)(3), and thereby elevates the (a)(2) inquiry so that it is no longer "easily satisfied," 5 J. Moore et al., Moore's Federal Practice § 23.23[2], p. 23–72 (3d ed. 2011). Rule 23(b)(3) certification requires, in addition to the four 23(a) findings, determinations that "questions of law or fact common to class members predominate over any questions affecting only individual members" and that "a class action is superior to other available methods for . . . adjudicating the controversy."

The Court's emphasis on differences between class members mimics the Rule 23(b)(3) inquiry into whether common questions "predominate" over individual issues. And by asking whether the individual differences "impede" common adjudication, ante, at 10 (internal quotation marks omitted), the Court duplicates 23(b)(3)'s question whether "a class action is superior" to other modes of adjudication. Indeed, Professor Nagareda, whose "dissimilarities" inquiry the Court endorses, developed his position in the context of Rule 23(b)(3). See 84 N.Y.U. L. Rev., at 131 (Rule 23(b)(3) requires "some decisive degree of similarity across the proposed class" because it "speaks of common 'questions' that 'predominate' over individual ones"). "The Rule 23(b)(3) predominance inquiry" is meant to "tes[t] whether proposed classes are sufficiently cohesive to warrant adjudication by representation." Amchem Products, Inc. v. Windsor, 521 U.S. 591, 623 (1997). If courts must conduct a "dissimilarities" analysis at the Rule 23(a)(2) stage, no mission remains for Rule 23(b)(3).

Because Rule 23(a) is also a prerequisite for Rule 23(b)(1) and Rule 23(b)(2) classes, the Court's "dissimilarities" position is far reaching. Individual differences should not bar a Rule 23(b)(1) or Rule 23(b)(2) class, so long as the Rule 23(a) threshold is met. See *Amchem Products*, 521 U.S., at 623, n.19 (Rule 23(b)(1)(B) "does not have a predominance requirement"); *Yamasaki*, 442 U.S., at 701 (Rule 23(b)(2) action in which the Court noted that "[i]t is unlikely that differences in the factual background of each claim will affect the outcome of the legal issue"). For example, in Franks v. Bowman Transp. Co., 424 U.S. 747 (1976), a Rule 23(b)(2) class of African–American truckdrivers complained that the defendant had discriminatorily refused to hire black applicants. We recognized that the "qualification[s] and performance" of individual class members might vary. Id., at 772 (internal quotation marks omitted). "Generalizations concerning such individually applicable evidence," we cautioned, "cannot serve as a justification for the denial of [injunctive] relief to the entire class." Ibid.

B

The "dissimilarities" approach leads the Court to train its attention on what distinguishes individual class members, rather than on what unites them. Given the lack of standards for pay and promotions, the majority says, "demonstrating the invalidity of one manager's use of discretion will do nothing to demonstrate the invalidity of another's."

Wal–Mart's delegation of discretion over pay and promotions is a policy uniform throughout all stores. The very nature of discretion is that people will exercise it in various ways. A system of delegated discretion, *Watson* held, is a practice actionable under Title VII when it produces discriminatory outcomes. 487 U.S., at 990–91. A finding that Wal–Mart's pay and promotions practices in fact violate the law would be the first step in the usual order of proof for plaintiffs seeking individual remedies for company-wide discrimination. Teamsters v. United States, 431 U.S. 324, 359 (1977); see Albemarle Paper Co. v. Moody, 422 U.S. 405, 415–423 (1975). That each individual employee's unique circumstances will ultimately determine whether she is entitled to backpay or damages, § 2000e–5(g)(2)(A) (barring backpay if a plaintiff "was refused . . . advancement . . . for any reason other than discrimination"), should not factor into the Rule 23(a)(2) determination.

* * *

The Court errs in importing a "dissimilarities" notion suited to Rule 23(b)(3) into the Rule 23(a) commonality inquiry. I therefore cannot join Part II of the Court's opinion.

NOTES ON WAL–MART STORES, INC. V. DUKES

1. WHAT WAS DECIDED

The Supreme Court unanimously reversed certification of the class under subdivision (b)(2) of Rule 23, dealing with declaratory or injunctive relief. By a vote of five to four, the Court also ruled against eligibility for certification of any class action for failure to satisfy the prerequisite of commonality under subdivision (a)(2). Standing alone, the Court's unanimous holding would have left open for consideration on remand whether the class could be certified as a class action for monetary relief under subdivision (b)(3), a question not specifically discussed either by Justices Scalia or Ginsburg. The five-to-four holding precluded the possibility of certification under (b)(3) because "questions of law or fact common to the class" are among the prerequisites listed in subdivision (a) for certification of *any* class action, whether under (b)(1), (b)(2), or (b)(3). This disputed holding reinforces commonality as a barrier to certification of all kinds of class actions, not just those concerned with employment discrimination. Commentary on the decision has therefore focused on this holding, so much so that Justice Ginsburg's opinion often is characterized simply as a dissent, when in fact she agreed with the majority that the class could not be certified under (b)(2).

The Court's unanimous holding, however, is important in its own right. That is particularly so in employment discrimination class actions, in which the plaintiffs typically seek backpay and damages, in addition to classwide injunctive relief. From now on, any action in which backpay and damages are more than "incidental"—and perhaps any case in which they are present at all—must be certified under subdivision (b)(3). This makes a difference because class actions are harder to certify under (b)(3) than under (b)(2), because class members are entitled to individual notice under (b)(3) but not under (b)(2), and because class members have the right to opt out under (b)(3) but not under (b)(2). Class actions can be certified under (b)(3) only if common questions "predominate over any questions affecting only individual class members." As Justice Ginsburg emphasizes, this "predominance" requirement is much stricter than the requirement of "commonality" under (a)(2). In addition, the requirement of individual notice under (b)(3) can result in significant expense in maintaining a class action, and in a case as large as *Wal–Mart*, with over a million class members, these expenses can be prohibitive. The related right of individual plaintiffs to opt out from (b)(3) class actions creates difficulties in managing the action and can erode the base of class members for which the plaintiffs' attorneys can obtain relief, and any corresponding award of attorney's fees.

If a class action cannot be certified under (b)(3), the obvious alternative now appears to be to assert *only* claims for classwide injunctive or declaratory relief and obtain certification under (b)(2). That prospect leaves the class members to fend for themselves in seeking backpay and damages, which might not be large enough to justify the cost of an individual lawsuit. It also leaves the plaintiffs' attorneys with a drastically reduced prospect of attorney's fees, which depend mainly upon the extent of the relief obtained for the class. Plaintiffs' attorneys undoubtedly would find it easier to obtain certification of a stripped down class action limited to injunctive relief under (b)(2), but they would also find any recovery on behalf of the class (and for themselves) to be stripped down as well. The "money," so to speak, is in monetary recoveries.

2. THE DIFFERENCE BETWEEN THE MAJORITY AND THE DISSENT

Justice Scalia, speaking for the five justices in the majority, held that the requirement of commonality in (a)(2) was not met. Justice Ginsburg, speaking for four justices, would have deferred to the district court's finding that it was. This disagreement goes to both the content of the requirement of commonality, which is discussed below, and to the sufficiency of the evidence in this case, which is discussed in the next note.

On the issue of content, Justice Scalia quoted the late Professor Richard Nagareda for the proposition that the crucial inquiry is "the capacity of a classwide proceeding to generate common *answers* apt to drive the resolution of the litigation." Class-wide questions do not matter unless they are likely to lead to class-wide answers. Finding that they are likely to do so requires an inquiry that goes beyond the pleadings to the factual basis provided by the plaintiffs, a basis that it is itself intertwined with the merits. In footnote 6, Scalia restricted the implications of the important decision in Eisen v. Carlisle & Jacquelin, 417 U.S. 516 (1974), which disapproved of an inquiry into the merits as a preliminary to certification of a class. That holding, Scalia made clear, goes only to a preliminary finding that the plaintiffs' claims are meritorious, not to an examination of the merits of the claim insofar as they reveal whether the requirements of Rule 23 have been satisfied. He emphasized that "rigorous analysis" of the issue of commonality "will entail some overlap with the merits of the plaintiff's underlying claim."

Justice Ginsburg did not deny the need for an examination of the merits insofar as the merits bear on the requirements of Rule 23, but she would have deferred to the district court's assessment of these issues in the absence of "an error of law or an abuse of discretion." She also argues that the majority mistakenly imported into the determination of commonality under (a)(2) the requirements of predominance under (b)(3). She argued, based on considerable lower court precedent, that the existence of common questions of law and fact under (a)(2) should be an easy requirement to meet, whereas the predominance of common questions under (b)(3) involves the kind of "rigorous analysis" that the majority engaged in.

A surprising consequence of Ginsburg's argument is that she did not seem to disagree with Justice Scalia about the disposition of this case, at least not if her reasoning is taken literally. Since the Court was unanimous on the need to certify this case under (b)(3), Justice Ginsburg agreed that it would state the governing standard on remand. But (b)(3), of course, includes the predominance requirement that she accused Justice Scalia of smuggling into (a)(2). On remand, however, the question of predominance would be squarely presented on any view of the rule, and at that point, she would seem no longer to have any reason for objecting to the "rigorous analysis" in which Scalia engaged. Although neither Scalia nor Ginsburg directly addressed the question whether the requirements of (b)(3) were satisfied, Justice Ginsburg might only have wanted to postpone a closer look at the evidence that the majority found wanting. Perhaps, however, she might have evaluated this evidence differently, as discussed in the next note.

3. EVIDENCE OF COMMON QUESTIONS

For the majority, Scalia found no evidence of common questions at all, while Ginsburg found evidence of pervasive gender bias in the subjective decisions made by Wal–Mart's supervisors. Both opinions relied on the same body of evidence submitted by the plaintiffs, which had three main components: anecdotal evidence of particular instances of discrimination; a regression analysis on the low rates at which women were promoted; and a sociological analysis showing a corporate culture "vulnerable" to gender bias.

All three sources of evidence were, according to Scalia, inadequate to overcome the fact that the only common practice challenged by the plaintiffs was "Wal–Mart's 'policy' of *allowing discretion* by local supervisors over employment matters." This "policy *against having* uniform employment practices" could generate common questions of law or fact only with " 'significant proof' that Wal–Mart 'operated under a general policy of discrimination.' " (All italics in original.) According to Scalia, the anecdotal evidence concerned too many supervisors, in too many different stores, making too many different decisions to generate any inference of common practices. It consisted of affidavits of 120 instances of discrimination scattered over 3,400 stores. The regression analysis was also inadequate in his view. It showed, at most, the low rate at which women were promoted in different regions in which Wal–Mart operated, but it failed to identify any common feature of these promotion decisions that caused this discrepancy. And the sociological analysis could not identify the effect of sex-based stereotyping with any precision at all, whether it affected "0.5 percent or 95 percent of the employment decisions at Wal–Mart."

Ginsburg started with a less demanding standard for showing commonality and with an attitude affording greater discretion to the district court. With these differences in approach, she looked at the same evidence as the majority but reached the opposite conclusion. She was more persuaded by the anecdotal evidence, which in her view did not have to identify instances of discrimination in proportion to the scope of the class. She agreed with the district court that the regression analysis was "sufficient to raise an 'inference of discrimination.' " And without specifically examining the evidence of the plaintiff's sociological study, she found evidence of implicit bias in earlier sex discrimination cases and in other studies, and in particular, in one on discrimination in orchestra auditions, cited in footnote 6 of her opinion.

The majority and the dissent seem to differ less in the detailed analysis of the evidence than in their overall attitude towards it. Scalia searched for evidence of a discriminatory policy and found none. Ginsburg looked for a reason to upset the findings of the district court and also found none. Who is right?

The case certainly looks very different depending upon whether a general policy of discrimination must be proved by the plaintiffs or disproved by the defendant. Does Rule 23 effectively require the plaintiffs to prove some general policy in order to proceed as a class action? Should it?

The case also looks very different depending upon assumptions about the prevalence of the particular kind of discrimination alleged. Did Scalia go too far in presuming that Wal–Mart's supervisors made subjective decisions free from pervasive forms of gender bias? Or did he just give Wal–Mart the equivalent of a presumption of innocence in civil proceedings and force the plaintiffs to make some showing of a common policy of discrimination? Conversely, did Justice Ginsburg make the opposite mistake of assuming, without proof, that Wal–Mart's supervisors, who were mostly male, engaged in gender bias? Or did she simply recognize the presence of hidden forms of sex discrimination widely acknowledged to exist in our society?

4. BIBLIOGRAPHY

For articles on the lower court decisions in *Wal–Mart*, particularly on the use of evidence of implicit bias to support class certification, see Melissa Hart & Paul M. Secunda, A Matter of Context: Social Framework Evidence in Employment Discrimination Class Actions, 78 Ford. L. Rev. 37 (2009) ; John Monahan, Laurens Walker & Gregory Mitchell, The Limits of Social Framework Evidence, 8 L. Prob. & Risk 307 (2009) ; Judith Resnik, Fairness in Numbers: A Comment on *AT & T v. Conception*, *Wal–Mart v. Dukes*, and *Turner v. Rogers*, 125 Harv. L. Rev. 78 (2011); Lesley Wexler, *Wal–Mart* Matters, 46 Wake Forest L. Rev. 95 (2011). For the standards for certification, see the article prominently cited in both opinions, Richard Nagareda, Class Certification in the Age of Aggregate Proof, 84 N.Y.U. L. Rev. 97 (2009).

SUBSECTION B: SEXUAL HARASSMENT

Meritor Savings Bank, FSB v. Vinson

Supreme Court of the United States, 1986.
477 U.S. 57.

■ JUSTICE REHNQUIST delivered the opinion of the Court.

This case presents important questions concerning claims of workplace "sexual harassment" brought under Title VII of the Civil Rights Act of 1964.

I

In 1974, respondent Michelle Vinson met Sidney Taylor, a vice president of what is now petitioner Meritor Savings Bank (bank) and manager of one of its branch offices. When respondent asked whether she might obtain employment at the bank, Taylor gave her an application, which she completed and returned the next day; later that same day Taylor called her to say that she had been hired. With Taylor as her supervisor, respondent started as a teller-trainee, and thereafter was promoted to teller, head teller, and assistant branch manager. She worked at the same branch for four years, and it is undisputed that her advancement there was based on merit alone. In September 1978, respondent notified Taylor that she was taking sick leave for an indefinite period. On November 1, 1978, the bank discharged her for excessive use of that leave.

Respondent brought this action against Taylor and the bank, claiming that during her four years at the bank she had "constantly been subjected to sexual harassment" by Taylor in violation of Title VII. She sought injunctive relief, compensatory and punitive damages against Taylor and the bank, and attorney's fees.

At the 11–day bench trial, the parties presented conflicting testimony about Taylor's behavior during respondent's employment. Respondent testified that during her probationary period as a teller-trainee, Taylor treated her in a fatherly way and made no sexual advances. Shortly thereafter, however, he invited her out to dinner and, during the course of the meal, suggested that they go to a motel to have sexual relations. At first she refused, but out of what she described as fear of losing her job she eventually agreed. According to respondent, Taylor thereafter made repeated demands upon her for sexual favors, usually at the branch, both during and after business hours; she estimated that over the next several years she had intercourse with him some 40 or 50 times. In addition, respondent testified that Taylor fondled her in front of other employees, followed her into the women's restroom when she went there alone, exposed himself to her, and even forcibly raped her on several occasions. These activities ceased after 1977, respondent stated, when she started going with a steady boyfriend.

Respondent also testified that Taylor touched and fondled other women employees of the bank, and she attempted to call witnesses to support this charge. But while some supporting testimony apparently was admitted without objection, the District Court did not allow her "to present wholesale evidence of a pattern and practice relating to sexual advances to other female employees in her case in chief, but advised her that she might well be able to present such evidence in rebuttal to the defendants' cases." Respondent did not offer such evidence in rebuttal. Finally, respondent testified that because she was afraid of Taylor she never reported his harassment to any of his supervisors and never attempted to use the bank's complaint procedure.

Taylor denied respondent's allegations of sexual activity, testifying that he never fondled her, never made suggestive remarks to her, never engaged in sexual intercourse with her, and never asked her to do so. He contended instead that respondent made her accusations in response to a business-related dispute. The bank also denied respondent's allegations and asserted that any sexual harassment by Taylor was unknown to the bank and engaged in without its consent or approval.

The District Court denied relief, but did not resolve the conflicting testimony about the existence of a sexual relationship between respondent and Taylor. It found instead that

> [if respondent] and Taylor did engage in an intimate or sexual relationship during the time of [respondent's] employment with [the bank], that relationship was a voluntary one having nothing to do with her

> continued employment at [the bank] or her advancement or promotions at that institution.

The court ultimately found that respondent "was not the victim of sexual harassment and was not the victim of sexual discrimination" while employed at the bank. Although it concluded that respondent had not proved a violation of Title VII, the District Court nevertheless went on to address the bank's liability. After noting the bank's express policy against discrimination, and finding that neither respondent nor any other employee had ever lodged a complaint about sexual harassment by Taylor, the court ultimately concluded that "the bank was without notice and cannot be held liable for the alleged actions of Taylor."

The Court of Appeals for the District of Columbia Circuit reversed . . . and remanded the case for further proceedings. . . . We granted certiorari and now affirm but for different reasons.

II

Title VII of the Civil Rights Act of 1964 makes it "an unlawful employment practice for an employer . . . to discriminate against any individual with respect to his compensation, terms, conditions, or privileges of employment, because of such individual's race, color, religion, sex, or national origin." 42 U.S.C. § 2000e–2(a)(1). The prohibition against discrimination based on sex was added to Title VII at the last minute on the floor of the House of Representatives. 110 Cong. Rec. 2577–2584 (1964). The principal argument in opposition to the amendment was that "sex discrimination" was sufficiently different from other types of discrimination that it ought to receive separate legislative treatment. This argument was defeated, the bill quickly passed as amended, and we are left with little legislative history to guide us in interpreting the Act's prohibition against discrimination based on "sex."

Respondent argues, and the Court of Appeals held, that unwelcome sexual advances that create an offensive or hostile working environment violate Title VII. Without question, when a supervisor sexually harasses a subordinate because of the subordinate's sex, that supervisor "discriminate[s]" on the basis of sex. Petitioner apparently does not challenge this proposition. It contends instead that in prohibiting discrimination with respect to "compensation, terms, conditions, or privileges" of employment, Congress was concerned with what petitioner describes as "tangible loss" of "an economic character," not "purely psychological aspects of the workplace environment." In support of this claim petitioner observes that in both the legislative history of Title VII and this Court's Title VII decisions, the focus has been on tangible, economic barriers erected by discrimination.

We reject petitioner's view. First, the language of Title VII is not limited to "economic" or "tangible" discrimination. The phrase "terms, conditions, or privileges of employment" evinces a congressional intent " 'to strike at the entire spectrum of disparate treatment of men and women' " in employment. Los Angeles Dept. of Water and Power v. Manhart, 435 U.S. 702, 707, n.13 (1978), quoting Sprogis v. United Air Lines, Inc., 444 F.2d 1194, 1198 (7th Cir. 1971). Petitioner has pointed to nothing in the Act to suggest that Congress contemplated the limitation urged here.

Second, in 1980 the EEOC issued Guidelines specifying that "sexual harassment," as there defined, is a form of sex discrimination prohibited by Title VII. As an "administrative interpretation of the Act by the enforcing agency," Griggs v. Duke Power Co., 401 U.S. 424, 433–34 (1971), these

Guidelines, " 'while not controlling upon the courts by reason of their authority, do constitute a body of experience and informed judgment to which courts and litigants may properly resort for guidance,' " General Electric Co. v. Gilbert, 429 U.S. 125, 141–42 (1976), quoting Skidmore v. Swift & Co., 323 U.S. 134, 140 (1944). The EEOC Guidelines fully support the view that harassment leading to noneconomic injury can violate Title VII.

In defining "sexual harassment," the Guidelines first describe the kinds of workplace conduct that may be actionable under Title VII. These include "[u]nwelcome sexual advances, requests for sexual favors, and other verbal or physical conduct of a sexual nature." 29 CFR § 1604.11(a) (1985). Relevant to the charges at issue in this case, the Guidelines provide that such sexual misconduct constitutes prohibited "sexual harassment," whether or not it is directly linked to the grant or denial of an economic quid pro quo, where "such conduct has the purpose or effect of unreasonably interfering with an individual's work performance or creating an intimidating, hostile, or offensive working environment." § 1604.11(a)(3).

In concluding that so-called "hostile environment" (i.e., non quid pro quo) harassment violates Title VII, the EEOC drew upon a substantial body of judicial decisions and EEOC precedent holding that Title VII affords employees the right to work in an environment free from discriminatory intimidation, ridicule, and insult. Rogers v. EEOC, 454 F.2d 234 (5th Cir. 1971), was apparently the first case to recognize a cause of action based upon a discriminatory work environment. In *Rogers*, the Court of Appeals for the Fifth Circuit held that a Hispanic complainant could establish a Title VII violation by demonstrating that her employer created an offensive work environment for employees by giving discriminatory service to its Hispanic clientele. The court explained that an employee's protections under Title VII extend beyond the economic aspects of employment:

> [T]he phrase 'terms, conditions or privileges of employment' in [Title VII] is an expansive concept which sweeps within its protective ambit the practice of creating a working environment heavily charged with ethnic or racial discrimination. . . . One can readily envision working environments so heavily polluted with discrimination as to destroy completely the emotional and psychological stability of minority group workers.

Courts applied this principle to harassment based on race, religion, and national origin. Nothing in Title VII suggests that a hostile environment based on discriminatory *sexual* harassment should not be likewise prohibited. The Guidelines thus appropriately drew from, and were fully consistent with, the existing caselaw.

Since the Guidelines were issued, courts have uniformly held, and we agree, that a plaintiff may establish a violation of Title VII by proving that discrimination based on sex has created a hostile or abusive work environment. As the Court of Appeals for the Eleventh Circuit wrote in Henson v. Dundee, 682 F.2d 897, 902 (11th Cir. 1982):

> Sexual harassment which creates a hostile or offensive environment for members of one sex is every bit the arbitrary barrier to sexual equality at the workplace that racial harassment is to racial equality. Surely, a requirement that a man or woman run a gauntlet of sexual abuse in return for the privilege of being allowed to work and make a living can be as demeaning and disconcerting as the harshest of racial epithets.

Of course, as the courts in both *Rogers* and *Henson* recognized, not all workplace conduct that may be described as "harassment" affects a "term, condition, or privilege" of employment within the meaning of Title VII. For sexual harassment to be actionable, it must be sufficiently severe or pervasive "to alter the conditions of [the victim's] employment and create an abusive working environment." Respondent's allegations in this case—which include not only pervasive harassment but also criminal conduct of the most serious nature—are plainly sufficient to state a claim for "hostile environment" sexual harassment.

The question remains, however, whether the District Court's ultimate finding that respondent "was not the victim of sexual harassment" effectively disposed of respondent's claim. The Court of Appeals recognized, we think correctly, that this ultimate finding was likely based on one or both of two erroneous views of the law. First, the District Court apparently believed that a claim for sexual harassment will not lie absent an economic effect on the complainant's employment. Since it appears that the District Court made its findings without ever considering the "hostile environment" theory of sexual harassment, the Court of Appeals' decision to remand was correct.

Second, the District Court's conclusion that no actionable harassment occurred might have rested on its earlier "finding" that "[i]f [respondent] and Taylor did engage in an intimate or sexual relationship . . . , that relationship was a voluntary one." But the fact that sex-related conduct was "voluntary," in the sense that the complainant was not forced to participate against her will, is not a defense to a sexual harassment suit brought under Title VII. The gravamen of any sexual harassment claim is that the alleged sexual advances were "unwelcome." 29 CFR § 1604.11(a) (1985). While the question whether particular conduct was indeed unwelcome presents difficult problems of proof and turns largely on credibility determinations committed to the trier of fact, the District Court in this case erroneously focused on the "voluntariness" of respondent's participation in the claimed sexual episodes. The correct inquiry is whether respondent by her conduct indicated that the alleged sexual advances were unwelcome, not whether her actual participation in sexual intercourse was voluntary. . . .

[In the next part of its opinion, the Court discussed the issue of the employer's vicarious liability. After reviewing the different standards put forward by the parties, the Court found that the debate over this question to have "a rather abstract quality about it given the state of the record in this case," which contained no findings on the merits of the plaintiff's claim.]

We therefore decline the parties' invitation to issue a definitive rule on employer liability, but we do agree with the EEOC that Congress wanted courts to look to agency principles for guidance in this area. While such common-law principles may not be transferable in all their particulars to Title VII, Congress' decision to define "employer" to include any "agent" of an employer, 42 U.S.C. § 2000e(b), surely evinces an intent to place some limits on the acts of employees for which employers under Title VII are to be held responsible. For this reason, we hold that the Court of Appeals erred in concluding that employers are always automatically liable for sexual harassment by their supervisors. For the same reason, absence of notice to an employer does not necessarily insulate that employer from liability. . . .

Accordingly, the judgment of the Court of Appeals reversing the judgment of the District Court is affirmed, and the case is remanded for further proceedings consistent with this opinion.

It is so ordered.[a]

■ JUSTICE MARSHALL, with whom JUSTICE BRENNAN, JUSTICE BLACKMUN, and JUSTICE STEVENS join, concurring in the judgment.

I fully agree with the Court's conclusion that workplace sexual harassment is illegal, and violates Title VII. Part III of the Court's opinion, however, leaves open the circumstances in which an employer is responsible under Title VII for such conduct. Because I believe that question to be properly before us, I write separately. . . .

The answer supplied by general Title VII law, like that supplied by federal labor law, is that the act of a supervisory employee or agent is imputed to the employer. Thus, for example, when a supervisor discriminatorily fires or refuses to promote a black employee, that act is, without more, considered the act of the employer. The courts do not stop to consider whether the employer otherwise had "notice" of the action, or even whether the supervisor had actual authority to act as he did. Following that approach, every Court of Appeals that has considered the issue has held that sexual harassment by supervisory personnel is automatically imputed to the employer when the harassment results in tangible job detriment to the subordinate employee. . . .

NOTES ON MERITOR SAVINGS BANK, FSB V. VINSON

1. WHAT WAS DECIDED

Meritor Savings Bank addressed two broad questions, but resolved only the first—what constitutes sexual harassment actionable under Title VII. As an initial matter, the Court held that the plaintiff need not allege that the harassment was so severe that she was forced into sexual activity against her will, only that she found it "unwelcome." The plaintiff need only allege that she was subjected to sexual harassment that was "sufficiently severe or pervasive to alter the conditions of [the victim's] employment and create an abusive working environment"—a category of claims dubbed "hostile environment." The plaintiff need not allege "quid pro quo" sexual harassment, in which the grant or denial of economic benefits is conditioned upon the plaintiff's submission to sexual advances. Both forms of sexual harassment are prohibited by Title VII, but in hostile environment cases the plaintiff need not establish any connection between the harassment and concrete economic benefits, such as a raise or promotion.

The second question, discussed by the Court but not resolved, was the circumstances under which an employer can be held liable for sexual harassment by its employees. This question arises in any case in which the harassing employee cannot be immediately identified with the employer. Sexual harassment committed by a sole proprietor or by the president or other high official of an organization can easily be attributed to the employer itself. Harassment by other individuals raises a question under the coverage provisions of Title VII, which apply only to an "employer" as defined by the statute (generally, a public

---

[a] The separate concurring opinion of Justice Stevens has been omitted.—[Footnote by eds.]

employer or a private employer with 15 or more employees), or to "any agent" of an employer. The Court resolved this question only to the extent of rejecting two per se rules, one imposing vicarious liability upon employers for all forms of harassment by their supervisors and one relieving employers entirely of liability in the absence of notice of the harassing conduct. The Court left the law on this question to be developed according to common-law principles.

2. *HARRIS V. FORKLIFT SYSTEMS, INC.*

In Harris v. Forklift Systems, Inc., 510 U.S. 17 (1993), the plaintiff alleged that the president of Forklift Systems had engaged in various forms of sexual harassment. The case therefore presented no question of vicarious liability of the employer. The only question was whether the acts alleged were "sufficiently severe or pervasive to alter the conditions of the victims' employment and create an abusive working environment." As the Court described the facts:

> The Magistrate found that, throughout Harris' time at Forklift, Hardy [the employer's president] often insulted her because of her gender and often made her the target of unwanted sexual innuendoes. Hardy told Harris on several occasions, in the presence of other employees, "You're a woman, what do you know" and "We need a man as the rental manager"; at least once, he told her she was "a dumb ass woman." Again in front of others, he suggested that the two of them "go to the Holiday Inn to negotiate [Harris'] raise." Hardy occasionally asked Harris and other female employees to get coins from his front pants pocket. He threw objects on the ground in front of Harris and other women, and asked them to pick the objects up. He made sexual innuendoes about Harris' and other women's clothing.
>
> In mid-August 1987, Harris complained to Hardy about his conduct. Hardy said he was surprised that Harris was offended, claimed he was only joking, and apologized. He also promised he would stop, and based on this assurance Harris stayed on the job. But in early September, Hardy began anew: While Harris was arranging a deal with one of Forklift's customers, he asked her, again in front of other employees, "What did you do, promise the guy . . . some [sex] Saturday night?" On October 1, Harris collected her paycheck and quit.

Based on these facts, the District Court found no sexual harassment because Hardy's comments, although offensive, were not "so severe as to be expected to seriously affect [Harris'] psychological well-being." The Court of Appeals affirmed. Justice O'Connor, writing for a unanimous Court, reversed:

> [The standard from *Meritor Savings Bank*], which we reaffirm today, takes a middle path between making actionable any conduct that is merely offensive and requiring the conduct to cause a tangible psychological injury. As we pointed out in *Meritor*, "mere utterance of an . . . epithet which engenders offensive feelings in an employee" does not sufficiently affect the conditions of employment to implicate Title VII. Conduct that is not severe or pervasive enough to create an objectively hostile or abusive work environment—an environment that a reasonable person would find hostile or abusive—is beyond Title VII's purview. Likewise, if the victim does not subjectively perceive the environment to be abusive, the conduct has not actually altered the conditions of the victim's employment, and there is no Title VII violation.

> But Title VII comes into play before the harassing conduct leads to a nervous breakdown. A discriminatorily abusive work environment, even one that does not seriously affect employees' psychological well-being, can and often will detract from employees' job performance, discourage employees from remaining on the job, or keep them from advancing in their careers. Moreover, even without regard to these tangible effects, the very fact that the discriminatory conduct was so severe or pervasive that it created a work environment abusive to employees because of their race, gender, religion, or national origin offends Title VII's broad rule of workplace equality. The appalling conduct alleged in *Meritor*, and the reference in that case to environments " 'so heavily polluted with discrimination as to destroy completely the emotional and psychological stability of minority group workers' " merely present some especially egregious examples of harassment. They do not mark the boundary of what is actionable.
>
> We therefore believe the District Court erred in relying on whether the conduct "seriously affect[ed] plaintiff's psychological well-being" or led her to "suffe[r] injury." Such an inquiry may needlessly focus the factfinder's attention on concrete psychological harm, an element Title VII does not require. Certainly Title VII bars conduct that would seriously affect a reasonable person's psychological well-being, but the statute is not limited to such conduct. So long as the environment would reasonably be perceived, and is perceived, as hostile or abusive, there is no need for it also to be psychologically injurious.
>
> This is not, and by its nature cannot be, a mathematically precise test. . . . But we can say that whether an environment is "hostile" or "abusive" can be determined only by looking at all the circumstances. These may include the frequency of the discriminatory conduct; its severity; whether it is physically threatening or humiliating, or a mere offensive utterance; and whether it unreasonably interferes with an employee's work performance. The effect on the employee's psychological well-being is, of course, relevant to determining whether the plaintiff actually found the environment abusive. But while psychological harm, like any other relevant factor, may be taken into account, no single factor is required.

Justice Scalia filed a brief concurring opinion, pointing out a lack of clarity in the standard for liability: " 'Abusive' (or 'hostile,' which in this context I take to mean the same thing) does not seem to me a very clear standard—and I do not think clarity is at all increased by adding the adverb 'objectively' or by appealing to a 'reasonable person's' notion of what the vague word means." Justice Ginsburg also filed a brief concurring opinion emphasizing that, apart from the BFOQ, "Title VII declares discriminatory practices based on race, gender, religion, or national origin equally unlawful." All the justices emphasized that the standard should be framed in ostensibly neutral terms, as what the reaction of a "reasonable person" would be, rather than a "reasonable woman" or a "reasonable man." Does this formal neutrality of the standard make it easier or harder to apply? Or does it just provide some reassurance that the standard itself is nondiscriminatory?

3. THE MEANING OF "SEVERE OR PERVASIVE"

In *Meritor Savings Bank*, the Court did not need to articulate the precise content of the standard for hostile environment sexual harassment. The conduct there was so extreme that it satisfied any plausible standard of severity. *Harris v. Forklift Systems* was different. The Court deliberately set the standard somewhere between conduct that is "merely offensive" and conduct causing "a tangible psychological injury."

The difficulty of establishing "severe or pervasive" harassment based on a single comment or joke was indirectly addressed by the Supreme Court in Clark County School District v. Breeden, 532 U.S. 268 (2001) (per curiam). That case concerned a claim of retaliation arising from an alleged incident of sexual harassment involving a crude description of sexual activity made by an applicant for a job as a school police officer and found in his file. In the presence of the plaintiff, two co-workers chuckled in response to the remark and the plaintiff complained about their behavior, allegedly resulting in retaliation by the employer. The Supreme Court, summarily reversing the decision below, held that co-workers' reaction could not reasonably form the basis for a complaint of sexual harassment and that, accordingly, the plaintiff had no claim of retaliation. The plaintiff, according to the Court, had protested what was, "at worst an 'isolated inciden[t]' that cannot be considered 'extremely serious' as our cases require."

Consider, first, the risks of setting the standard of liability too low. The danger is that Title VII would be transformed into a code of etiquette in the workplace, imposing substantial financial liability for bad manners. From the perspective of employees, it would deter them from engaging in casual discussion whenever there was any risk of offending members of the opposite sex. For employers, it would impose onerous burdens of policing the ways in which individual employees interact with one another. Or, alternatively, it might discourage employers from mixing male and female employees together, possibly leading to a decrease in the employment opportunities of women instead of the increase that Title VII was intended to foster.

As a legal matter, these objections most naturally take the form of an assertion of the right to privacy. What employees do or say to other employees at work is arguably their own business, or at most the business also of their employer. But because places of employment are open to so many people, from co-employees to members of the public, it is difficult to find a strong constitutionally protected interest in individual privacy in the workplace. Critics of the law of sexual harassment have therefore argued, not that sexual harassment law violates the right of privacy, but that it results in a government-imposed regime of employer censorship contrary to the First Amendment. See Kingsley R. Browne, Zero Tolerance for the First Amendment: Title VII's Regulation of Employee Speech, 27 Ohio N.U.L. Rev. 563 (2001); Eugene Volokh, Speech as Conduct: Generally Applicable Laws, Illegal Courses of Conduct, Situation–Altering Utterances, and the Uncharted Zones, 90 Corn. L. Rev. 1277 (2005). Is it a sufficient reply to this argument that the requirement that harassment be "severe or pervasive" eliminates most problems of censorship? Employees who would express themselves through sexual harassment can either choose more moderate means of expression in the workplace or engage in harassing speech elsewhere. The victims of harassment have no such choice, short of quitting their existing jobs and finding new ones. For responses to the First Amendment arguments, see, e.g., Cynthia Estlund, Freedom of Speech in the Workplace and the Problem of Discriminatory Harassment, 75 Tex. L. Rev. 687 (1997); Richard H. Fallon, Jr., Sexual Harassment, Content Neutrality, and the First Amendment Dog That Didn't Bark, 1994 Sup. Ct. Rev. 1.

The opposite problem—setting the standard for liability too high—has also been addressed in the academic literature. Susan Estrich, Sex at Work, 43 Stan. L. Rev. 813 (1991), surveys the cases on both hostile environment and quid pro quo sexual harassment and concludes that judges (predominantly men) tend to apply the standards for liability too strictly to plaintiffs. For instance, she finds that what constitutes a hostile environment is usually determined from the perspective of men, who are inclined to take sexual harassment less seriously than women. For further exploration of this argument, see Anita Bernstein, Treating Sexual Harassment with Respect, 111 Harv. L. Rev. 445 (1997); Nancy Ehrenreich, Pluralist Myths and Powerless Men: The Ideology of Reasonableness in Sexual Harassment Law, 99 Yale L.J. 1177 (1990). Is this argument rendered any less powerful by the fact that more women have become judges and that, after the passage of § 1981a, claims of sexual harassment can be tried to juries, composed of both women and men?

Vicki Schultz, Reconceptualizing Sexual Harassment, 107 Yale L.J. 1683 (1998), argues that the standard of liability has been set too high in a different way. It has focused on harassment related to sexual conduct, preventing plaintiffs from establishing harassment through conduct that is simply hostile to women in the workplace. Sexual desire, on her view, need not have anything to do with sexual harassment, which might involve actions of an entirely nonsexual nature, such as sabotaging the work of female employees. Professor Schultz also seeks to respond to the basic theoretical question of why Title VII prohibits sexual harassment at all. It does not establish a code of sexual behavior, in the workplace or anywhere else. Instead, she argues, the law of sexual harassment should serve the central purpose of the statute: "to enable everyone—regardless of their identities as men or women, or their personae as masculine or feminine—to pursue their chosen endeavors on equal, empowering terms." See also Vicki Schultz, The Sanitized Workplace, 112 Yale L.J. 2061 (2003); Vicki Schultz, Talking About Harassment, 9 J. L. & Pol'y 417 (2001).

The seminal work on the law of sexual harassment, which did much to generate legal recognition of such claims, is Catherine MacKinnon, Sexual Harassment of Working Women (1979). See also Catharine A. MacKinnon, The Logic of Experience: Reflections on the Development of Sexual Harassment Law 90 Geo. L.J. 813 (2002). For a valuable collection of articles on this subject, see Directions in Sexual Harassment Law (Catharine A. MacKinnon and Reva B. Siegel, eds., 2004); see also Theresa M. Beiner, Gender Myths v. Working Realities: Using Social Science to Reformulate Sexual Harassment Law (NYU Press 2005).

4. *ONCALE V. SUNDOWNER OFFSHORE SERVICES, INC.*

The Supreme Court addressed the question of same-sex sexual harassment in Oncale v. Sundowner Offshore Services, Inc., 523 U.S. 75 (1998). The plaintiff in that case worked on an oil platform in the Gulf of Mexico, as part of an eight-man team. After he had been "forcibly subjected to sex-related, humiliating actions against him" and "physically assaulted" by members of the crew, including two supervisors, he complained to other supervisory personnel. They were unsympathetic to his complaints, causing him to quit and then to sue Sundowner in federal court, alleging discrimination on the basis of sex. The district court, however, held that "Mr. Oncale, a male, has no cause of action under Title VII for harassment by male co-workers," and the court of appeals affirmed this decision. The Supreme Court reached the opposite conclusion:

Title VII's prohibition of discrimination "because of . . . sex" protects men as well as women, Newport News Shipbuilding & Dry Dock Co. v. EEOC, 462 U.S. 669, 682 (1983), and in the related context of racial discrimination in the workplace we have rejected any conclusive presumption that an employer will not discriminate against members of his own race. "Because of the many facets of human motivation, it would be unwise to presume as a matter of law that human beings of one definable group will not discriminate against other members of that group." Castaneda v. Partida, 430 U.S. 482, 499 (1977). In Johnson v. Transportation Agency, Santa Clara Cty., 480 U.S. 616 (1987), a male employee claimed that his employer discriminated against him because of his sex when it preferred a female employee for promotion. Although we ultimately rejected the claim on other grounds, we did not consider it significant that the supervisor who made that decision was also a man. If our precedents leave any doubt on the question, we hold today that nothing in Title VII necessarily bars a claim of discrimination "because of . . . sex" merely because the plaintiff and the defendant (or the person charged with acting on behalf of the defendant) are of the same sex. . . .

Respondents and their amici contend that recognizing liability for same-sex harassment will transform Title VII into a general civility code for the American workplace. But that risk is no greater for same-sex than for opposite-sex harassment, and is adequately met by careful attention to the requirements of the statute. Title VII does not prohibit all verbal or physical harassment in the workplace; it is directed only at "*discriminat[ion]* . . . because of . . . sex." We have never held that workplace harassment, even harassment between men and women, is automatically discrimination because of sex merely because the words used have sexual content or connotations. "The critical issue, Title VII's text indicates, is whether members of one sex are exposed to disadvantageous terms or conditions of employment to which members of the other sex are not exposed." Harris v. Forklift Systems, Inc., 510 U.S. 17, 25 (1993) (Ginsburg, J., concurring).

Courts and juries have found the inference of discrimination easy to draw in most male-female sexual harassment situations, because the challenged conduct typically involves explicit or implicit proposals of sexual activity; it is reasonable to assume those proposals would not have been made to someone of the same sex. The same chain of inference would be available to a plaintiff alleging same-sex harassment, if there were credible evidence that the harasser was homosexual. But harassing conduct need not be motivated by sexual desire to support an inference of discrimination on the basis of sex. A trier of fact might reasonably find such discrimination, for example, if a female victim is harassed in such sex-specific and derogatory terms by another woman as to make it clear that the harasser is motivated by general hostility to the presence of women in the workplace. A same-sex harassment plaintiff may also, of course, offer direct comparative evidence about how the alleged harasser treated members of both sexes in a mixed-sex workplace. Whatever evidentiary route the plaintiff chooses to follow, he or she must always prove that the conduct at issue was not merely tinged with offensive sexual connotations, but actually constituted "*discrimina[tion]* . . . because of . . . sex."

And there is another requirement that prevents Title VII from expanding into a general civility code: As we emphasized in *Meritor* and *Harris*, the statute does not reach genuine but innocuous differences in the ways men and women routinely interact with members of the same sex and of the opposite sex. The prohibition of harassment on the basis of sex requires neither asexuality nor androgyny in the workplace; it forbids only behavior so objectively offensive as to alter the "conditions" of the victim's employment. "Conduct that is not severe or pervasive enough to create an objectively hostile or abusive work environment—an environment that a reasonable person would find hostile or abusive—is beyond Title VII's purview." *Harris*, 510 U.S., at 21. We have always regarded that requirement as crucial, and as sufficient to ensure that courts and juries do not mistake ordinary socializing in the workplace—such as male-on-male horseplay or intersexual flirtation—for discriminatory "conditions of employment."

We have emphasized, moreover, that the objective severity of harassment should be judged from the perspective of a reasonable person in the plaintiff's position, considering "all the circumstances." *Harris*, 510 U.S., at 23. In same-sex (as in all) harassment cases, that inquiry requires careful consideration of the social context in which particular behavior occurs and is experienced by its target. A professional football player's working environment is not severely or pervasively abusive, for example, if the coach smacks him on the buttocks as he heads onto the field—even if the same behavior would reasonably be experienced as abusive by the coach's secretary (male or female) back at the office. The real social impact of workplace behavior often depends on a constellation of surrounding circumstances, expectations, and relationships which are not fully captured by a simple recitation of the words used or the physical acts performed. Common sense, and an appropriate sensitivity to social context, will enable courts and juries to distinguish between simple teasing or roughhousing among members of the same sex, and conduct which a reasonable person in the plaintiff's position would find severely hostile or abusive.

5. WHAT IS SEXUAL ABOUT SEXUAL HARASSMENT?

A persistent question about the foundations of the law of sexual harassment has been why it is prohibited at all by Title VII. If the harassment is sex-based only in the sense that it involves actual or threatened sexual conduct, then it seems to fall wholly outside the coverage of the statute, which is concerned only with *discrimination* on the basis of sex as a biological characteristic of an individual, not as a form of conduct. If, on the other hand, it is sex-based only because it is directed at women, then claims of sexual harassment violate the evenhanded policy of the statute, not to protect any one group to the exclusion of another, but only to prohibit discrimination between groups. Even if the gravamen of sexual harassment claims is framed more neutrally—to prohibit harassment of men by women as well as the reverse—such claims would still be confined almost entirely to harassment of women. Instances of sexual harassment of men by women have proved to be relatively rare.

Oncale laid these concerns to rest, first, by recognizing a claim of same-sex sexual harassment, and second, by recognizing that no aspect of the harassment need involve sexual conduct. Why did it take so long for these issues to be resolved? Is it the predominance of cases of men harassing women? Or is it the typically sexual nature of the comments or actions involved in male harassment of women? The opinion in *Meritor Savings Bank* recounted the history of the prohibition against sexual harassment, clearly revealing that it developed from cases of harassment on the basis of race and national origin. Since harassment on these grounds need not involve any particular kind of conduct, so long as it is hostile and discriminatory, it should have been apparent from the beginning that sexual harassment need not involve sexual advances or remarks. Or is the problem simply that "sex" has two different meanings, one referring to a biological characteristic and the other to a form of conduct? After *Oncale*, only "sex" in the first sense is necessarily involved in claims of sexual harassment.

Having laid these concerns to rest, however, the opinion in *Oncale* has raised others in their place. The most puzzling is the "equal opportunity" harasser: a supervisor or co-employee who harasses both men and women equally. The Court emphasized that "[w]hatever evidentiary route the plaintiff chooses to follow, he or she must always prove that the conduct at issue was not merely tinged with offensive sexual connotations, but actually constituted "*discrimina[tion]* . . . because of . . . sex." The opinion in *Oncale* relies heavily on decisions prohibiting other forms of reverse discrimination. On this view, *Oncale* is analogous to cases such as McDonald v. Santa Fe Trail Transportation Co., 427 U.S. 273 (1976), considered in the previous chapter. *McDonald* held that whites could sue for racial discrimination under both Title VII and § 1981. Is same-sex sexual harassment exactly analogous? In particular, would a decision excluding this form of discrimination from the coverage of Title VII raise the same constitutional questions as excluding reverse racial discrimination?

6. DISCRIMINATION ON THE BASIS OF SEXUAL ORIENTATION

Oncale stops short of recognizing any form of protection from harassment on the basis of sexual orientation under Title VII. The closest the Court comes is to allow that the sexual orientation of the *harassing* supervisor or employee, but not of the victim, might be relevant to a claim of same-sex sexual harassment. But if evidence of one actor's sexual orientation is relevant, how could the other's be excluded? And, in practice, won't it prove to be difficult, if not impossible, to distinguish harassment based on the victim's sex from harassment based on the victim's sexual orientation? If a man is a victim of harassment because he is gay, is he also a victim of harassment because he is a man?

The lower federal courts have uniformly rejected this conclusion, interpreting Title VII to prohibit only discrimination on the basis of sex, not discrimination on the basis of sexual orientation. See, e.g., Simonton v. Runyon, 232 F.3d 33, 35 (2d Cir. 2000); Higgins v. New Balance Athletic Shoes, Inc., 194 F.3d 252, 259 (1st Cir. 1999). Bills to amend Title VII to prohibit discrimination on the basis of sexual orientation have been introduced in Congress but have not been passed by either house.

How are these questions of statutory law affected by the changing constitutional law on gay rights? The Court's decision striking down laws prohibiting consensual sex among homosexuals in the privacy of the home was decided solely under the Due Process Clause, based on the absence of any rational relationship between such laws and any legitimate state interest. Lawrence v. Texas, 539 U.S. 558 (2003). Only Justice O'Connor would have decided the case on the ground that such laws discriminate against gays in violation of the

Equal Protection Clause. Although not directly related to Title VII—or, apart from Justice O'Connor, even to a claim of discrimination—would this decision have any effect on the background principles used to interpret Title VII? Does it shed any light on what constitutes discrimination on the basis of sex under that statute?

7. BIBLIOGRAPHY

For articles on the implications of *Oncale*, see Meredith Render, Misogyny, Androgyny, and Sexual Harassment: Sex Discrimination in a Gender–Deconstructed World, 29 Harv. J.L. & Gender 99 (2006); Ronald Turner, Title VII and the Inequality–Enhancing Effects of the Bisexual and Equal Opportunity Harasser Defenses, 7 U. Pa. J. Lab. & Emp. L. 341 (2005); Ronald Turner, The Unenvisaged Case, Interpretive Progression, and the Justiciability of Title VII Same–Sex Sexual Harassment Claims, 7 Duke J. Gender L. & Pol'y 57 (2000); Yvonne Zylan, Finding the Sex in Sexual Harassment: How Title VII and Tort Schemes Miss the Point of Same–Sex Hostile Environment Harassment, 39 U. Mich. J.L. Reform 391 (2006).

Burlington Industries, Inc. v. Ellerth

Supreme Court of the United States, 1998.
524 U.S. 742.

■ JUSTICE KENNEDY delivered the opinion of the Court.

We decide whether, under Title VII of the Civil Rights Act of 1964, an employee who refuses the unwelcome and threatening sexual advances of a supervisor, yet suffers no adverse, tangible job consequences, can recover against the employer without showing the employer is negligent or otherwise at fault for the supervisor's actions.

I

Summary judgment was granted for the employer, so we must take the facts alleged by the employee to be true. The employer is Burlington Industries, the petitioner. The employee is Kimberly Ellerth, the respondent. From March 1993 until May 1994, Ellerth worked as a salesperson in one of Burlington's divisions in Chicago, Illinois. During her employment, she alleges, she was subjected to constant sexual harassment by her supervisor, one Ted Slowik.

In the hierarchy of Burlington's management structure, Slowik was a mid-level manager. Burlington has eight divisions, employing more than 22,000 people in some 50 plants around the United States. Slowik was a vice president in one of five business units within one of the divisions. He had authority to make hiring and promotion decisions subject to the approval of his supervisor, who signed the paperwork. According to Slowik's supervisor, his position was "not considered an upper-level management position," and he was "not amongst the decision-making or policy-making hierarchy." Slowik was not Ellerth's immediate supervisor. Ellerth worked in a two-person office in Chicago, and she answered to her office colleague, who in turn answered to Slowik in New York.

Against a background of repeated boorish and offensive remarks and gestures which Slowik allegedly made, Ellerth places particular emphasis on three alleged incidents where Slowik's comments could be construed as threats to deny her tangible job benefits. In the summer of 1993, while on a business trip, Slowik invited Ellerth to the hotel lounge, an invitation Ellerth felt compelled to accept because Slowik was her boss. When Ellerth gave no encouragement to remarks Slowik made about her breasts, he told her to "loosen up" and warned, "you know, Kim, I could make your life very hard or very easy at Burlington."

In March 1994, when Ellerth was being considered for a promotion, Slowik expressed reservations during the promotion interview because she was not "loose enough." The comment was followed by his reaching over and rubbing her knee. Ellerth did receive the promotion; but when Slowik called to announce it, he told Ellerth, "you're gonna be out there with men who work in factories, and they certainly like women with pretty butts/legs."

In May 1994, Ellerth called Slowik, asking permission to insert a customer's logo into a fabric sample. Slowik responded, "I don't have time for you right now, Kim—unless you want to tell me what you're wearing." Ellerth told Slowik she had to go and ended the call. A day or two later, Ellerth called Slowik to ask permission again. This time he denied her request, but added something along the lines of, "are you wearing shorter skirts yet, Kim, because it would make your job a whole heck of a lot easier."

A short time later, Ellerth's immediate supervisor cautioned her about returning telephone calls to customers in a prompt fashion. In response, Ellerth quit. She faxed a letter giving reasons unrelated to the alleged sexual harassment we have described. About three weeks later, however, she sent a letter explaining she quit because of Slowik's behavior.

During her tenure at Burlington, Ellerth did not inform anyone in authority about Slowik's conduct, despite knowing Burlington had a policy against sexual harassment. In fact, she chose not to inform her immediate supervisor (not Slowik) because " 'it would be his duty as my supervisor to report any incidents of sexual harassment.' " On one occasion, she told Slowik a comment he made was inappropriate.

[When Ellerth sued, the district court granted summary judgment to Burlington.] The Court found Slowik's behavior, as described by Ellerth, severe and pervasive enough to create a hostile work environment, but found Burlington neither knew nor should have known about the conduct. There was no triable issue of fact on the latter point, and the Court noted Ellerth had not used Burlington's internal complaint procedures. Although Ellerth's claim was framed as a hostile work environment complaint, the District Court observed there was a quid pro quo 'component' to the hostile environment. Proceeding from the premise that an employer faces vicarious liability for quid pro quo harassment, the District Court thought it necessary to apply a negligence standard because the quid pro quo merely contributed to the hostile work environment. The District Court also dismissed Ellerth's constructive discharge claim.

The Court of Appeals en banc reversed in a decision which produced eight separate opinions and no consensus for a controlling rationale. . . .

II

At the outset, we assume an important proposition yet to be established before a trier of fact. It is a premise assumed as well, in explicit or implicit terms, in the various opinions by the judges of the Court of Appeals. The premise is: a trier of fact could find in Slowik's remarks numerous threats to retaliate against Ellerth if she denied some sexual liberties.

The threats, however, were not carried out or fulfilled. Cases based on threats which are carried out are referred to often as quid pro quo cases, as distinct from bothersome attentions or sexual remarks that are sufficiently severe or pervasive to create a hostile work environment. The terms quid pro quo and hostile work environment are helpful, perhaps, in making a rough demarcation between cases in which threats are carried out and those where they are not or are absent altogether, but beyond this are of limited utility. . . .

[The Court then noted that the terms "quid pro quo" and "hostile work environment" do not appear in the text of Title VII.] We do not suggest the terms quid pro quo and hostile work environment are irrelevant to Title VII litigation. To the extent they illustrate the distinction between cases involving a threat which is carried out and offensive conduct in general, the terms are relevant when there is a threshold question whether a plaintiff can prove discrimination in violation of Title VII. When a plaintiff proves that a tangible employment action resulted from a refusal to submit to a supervisor's sexual demands, he or she establishes that the employment decision itself constitutes a change in the terms and conditions of employment that is actionable under Title VII. For any sexual harassment preceding the employment decision to be actionable, however, the conduct must be severe or pervasive. Because Ellerth's claim involves only unfulfilled threats, it should be categorized as a hostile work environment claim which requires a showing of severe or pervasive conduct. See Oncale v. Sundowner Offshore Services, Inc., 523 U.S. 75, 81 (1998); Harris v. Forklift Systems, Inc., 510 U.S. 17, 21 (1993). For purposes of this case, we accept the District Court's finding that the alleged conduct was severe or pervasive. The case before us involves numerous alleged threats, and we express no opinion as to whether a single unfulfilled threat is sufficient to constitute discrimination in the terms or conditions of employment.

When we assume discrimination can be proved, however, the factors we discuss below, and not the categories quid pro quo and hostile work environment, will be controlling on the issue of vicarious liability. That is the question we must resolve.

III

We must decide, then, whether an employer has vicarious liability when a supervisor creates a hostile work environment by making explicit threats to alter a subordinate's terms or conditions of employment, based on sex, but does not fulfill the threat. We turn to principles of agency law, for the term "employer" is defined under Title VII to include "agents." 42 U.S.C. § 2000e(b). In express terms, Congress has directed federal courts to interpret Title VII based on agency principles. Given such an explicit instruction, we conclude a uniform and predictable standard must be established as a matter of federal law. We rely "on the general common law of agency, rather than on the law of any particular State, to give meaning to these terms." Community for Creative Non–Violence v. Reid, 490 U.S. 730, 740 (1989). The resulting federal rule, based on a body of case law developed over time, is statutory interpretation pursuant to congressional direction. This is not federal common law in "the strictest sense, i.e., a rule of decision that amounts, not simply to an interpretation of a federal statute . . . , but, rather, to the judicial 'creation' of a special federal rule of decision." Atherton v. FDIC, 519 U.S. 213, 218 (1997). State court decisions, applying state employment discrimination law, may be instructive in applying general agency principles, but, it is interesting to note, in many cases their determinations of employer liability under state law rely in large part on federal court decisions under Title VII.

As *Meritor* acknowledged, the Restatement (Second) of Agency (1957) (hereinafter Restatement), is a useful beginning point for a discussion of general agency principles. . . .

A

Section 219(1) of the Restatement sets out a central principle of agency law:

> A master is subject to liability for the torts of his servants committed while acting in the scope of their employment.

An employer may be liable for both negligent and intentional torts committed by an employee within the scope of his or her employment. Sexual harassment under Title VII presupposes intentional conduct. While early decisions absolved employers of liability for the intentional torts of their employees, the law now imposes liability where the employee's "purpose, however misguided, is wholly or in part to further the master's business." W. Keeton, D. Dobbs, R. Keeton, & D. Owen, Prosser and Keeton on Law of Torts § 70, p. 505 (5th ed. 1984) (hereinafter Prosser and Keeton on Torts). In applying scope of employment principles to intentional torts, however, it is accepted that "it is less likely that a willful tort will properly be held to be in the course of employment and that the liability of the master for such torts will naturally be more limited." F. Mechem, Outlines of the Law of Agency § 394, p. 266 (P. Mechem 4th ed., 1952). The Restatement defines conduct, including an intentional tort, to be within the scope of employment when "actuated, at least in part, by a purpose to serve the [employer]," even if it is forbidden by the employer. Restatement §§ 228(1)(c), 230. For example, when a salesperson lies to a customer to make a sale, the tortious conduct is within the scope of employment because it benefits the employer by increasing sales, even though it may violate the employer's policies. See Prosser and Keeton on Torts § 70, at 505–506. . . .

[Because almost all cases of sexual harassment occur at the instance of the individual supervisor, rather than the employer, the Court concluded as a general matter "that sexual harassment by a supervisor is not conduct within the scope of employment."]

B

Scope of employment does not define the only basis for employer liability under agency principles. In limited circumstances, agency principles impose liability on employers even where employees commit torts outside the scope of employment. The principles are set forth in the much-cited § 219(2) of the Restatement:

> (2) A master is not subject to liability for the torts of his servants acting outside the scope of their employment, unless:
>
> (a) the master intended the conduct or the consequences, or
>
> (b) the master was negligent or reckless, or
>
> (c) the conduct violated a non-delegable duty of the master, or
>
> (d) the servant purported to act or to speak on behalf of the principal and there was reliance upon apparent authority, or he was aided in accomplishing the tort by the existence of the agency relation."

See also § 219, Comment e (Section 219(2) "enumerates the situations in which a master may be liable for torts of servants acting solely for their own purposes and hence not in the scope of employment").

Subsection (a) addresses direct liability, where the employer acts with tortious intent, and indirect liability, where the agent's high rank in the company makes him or her the employer's alter ego. None of the parties contend Slowik's rank imputes liability under this principle. There is no contention, furthermore, that a nondelegable duty is involved. See § 219(2)(c). So, for our purposes here, subsections (a) and (c) can be put aside.

Subsections (b) and (d) are possible grounds for imposing employer liability on account of a supervisor's acts and must be considered. Under subsection (b), an employer is liable when the tort is attributable to the employer's own negligence. Thus, although a supervisor's sexual harassment is outside the scope of employment because the conduct was for personal motives, an employer can be liable, nonetheless, where its own negligence is a cause of the harassment. An employer is negligent with respect to sexual harassment if it knew or should have known about the conduct and failed to stop it. Negligence sets a minimum standard for employer liability under Title VII; but Ellerth seeks to invoke the more stringent standard of vicarious liability.

Subsection 219(2)(d) concerns vicarious liability for intentional torts committed by an employee when the employee uses apparent authority (the apparent authority standard), or when the employee "was aided in accomplishing the tort by the existence of the agency relation" (the aided in the agency relation standard). [The Court first rejected an analysis based on apparent authority because it applies only "where the agent purports to exercise a power which he or she does not have, as distinct from where the agent threatens to misuse actual power."]

D

We turn to the aided in the agency relation standard. In a sense, most workplace tortfeasors are aided in accomplishing their tortious objective by the existence of the agency relation: Proximity and regular contact may afford a captive pool of potential victims. See Gary v. Long, 59 F.3d 1391, 1397 (D.C. Cir. 1995). Were this to satisfy the aided in the agency relation standard, an employer would be subject to vicarious liability not only for all supervisor harassment, but also for all co-worker harassment, a result enforced by neither the EEOC nor any Court of Appeals to have considered the issue. The aided in the agency relation standard, therefore, requires the existence of something more than the employment relation itself.

At the outset, we can identify a class of cases where, beyond question, more than the mere existence of the employment relation aids in commission of the harassment: when a supervisor takes a tangible employment action against the subordinate. . . .

In the context of this case, a tangible employment action would have taken the form of a denial of a raise or a promotion. The concept of a tangible employment action appears in numerous cases in the Courts of Appeals discussing claims involving race, age, and national origin discrimination, as well as sex discrimination. Without endorsing the specific results of those decisions, we think it prudent to import the concept of a tangible employment action for resolution of the vicarious liability issue we consider here. A tangible employment action constitutes a significant change in employment status, such as hiring, firing, failing to promote, reassignment with significantly different responsibilities, or a decision causing a significant change in benefits.

When a supervisor makes a tangible employment decision, there is assurance the injury could not have been inflicted absent the agency relation. A tangible employment action in most cases inflicts direct economic harm. As a general proposition, only a supervisor, or other person acting with the authority of the company, can cause this sort of injury. A co-worker can break a co-worker's arm as easily as a supervisor, and anyone who has regular contact with an employee can inflict psychological injuries by his or her offensive conduct. But one co-worker (absent some elaborate scheme) cannot dock another's pay, nor can one co-worker demote another. Tangible employment actions fall within the special province of the supervisor. The supervisor has been empowered by the company as a distinct class of agent to make economic decisions affecting other employees under his or her control.

Tangible employment actions are the means by which the supervisor brings the official power of the enterprise to bear on subordinates. A tangible employment decision requires an official act of the enterprise, a company act. The decision in most cases is documented in official company records, and may be subject to review by higher level supervisors. E.g., Shager v. Upjohn Co., 913 F.2d 398, 405 (7th Cir. 1990) (noting that the supervisor did not fire plaintiff; rather, the Career Path Committee did, but the employer was still liable because the Committee functioned as the supervisor's "cat's-paw"). The supervisor often must obtain the imprimatur of the enterprise and use its internal processes. See Kotcher v. Rosa & Sullivan Appliance Center, Inc., 957 F.2d 59, 62 (2nd Cir. 1992) ("From the perspective of the employee, the supervisor and the employer merge into a single entity").

For these reasons, a tangible employment action taken by the supervisor becomes for Title VII purposes the act of the employer. Whatever the exact contours of the aided in the agency relation standard, its requirements will always be met when a supervisor takes a tangible employment action against a subordinate. In that instance, it would be implausible to interpret agency principles to allow an employer to escape liability, as *Meritor* itself appeared to acknowledge. . . .

In order to accommodate the agency principles of vicarious liability for harm caused by misuse of supervisory authority, as well as Title VII's equally basic policies of encouraging forethought by employers and saving action by objecting employees, we adopt the following holding in this case and in *Faragher v. Boca Raton*, also decided today. An employer is subject to vicarious liability to a victimized employee for an actionable hostile environment created by a supervisor with immediate (or successively higher) authority over the employee. When no tangible employment action is taken, a defending employer may raise an affirmative defense to liability or damages, subject to proof by a preponderance of the evidence, see Fed. Rule Civ. Proc. 8(c). The defense comprises two necessary elements: (a) that the employer exercised reasonable care to prevent and correct promptly any sexually harassing behavior, and (b) that the plaintiff employee unreasonably failed to take advantage of any preventive or corrective opportunities provided by the employer or to avoid harm otherwise. While proof that an employer had promulgated an anti-harassment policy with complaint procedure is not necessary in every instance as a matter of law, the need for a stated policy suitable to the employment circumstances may appropriately be addressed in any case when litigating the first element of the defense. And while proof that an employee failed to fulfill the corresponding obligation of reasonable care to avoid harm is not limited to showing any unreasonable failure to use any complaint procedure provided by the employer, a demonstration of such failure will normally suffice to satisfy the employer's burden under the second element of the defense. No affirmative defense is available, however, when the supervisor's harassment culminates in a tangible employment action, such as discharge, demotion, or undesirable reassignment.

[The Court then affirmed the court of appeals' decision reversing summary judgment against Ellerth and remanding for further proceedings.]

■ JUSTICE GINSBURG, concurring in the judgment.

I agree with the Court's ruling that "the labels quid pro quo and hostile work environment are not controlling for purposes of establishing employer liability." . . .

■ JUSTICE THOMAS, with whom JUSTICE SCALIA joins, dissenting.

The Court today manufactures a rule that employers are vicariously liable if supervisors create a sexually hostile work environment, subject to an affirmative defense that the Court barely attempts to define. This rule applies even if the employer has a policy against sexual harassment, the employee knows about that policy, and the employee never informs anyone in a position of authority about the supervisor's conduct. As a result, employer liability under Title VII is judged by different standards depending upon whether a sexually or racially hostile work environment is alleged. The standard of employer liability should be the same in both instances: An employer should be liable if, and only if, the plaintiff proves that the employer was negligent in permitting the supervisor's conduct to occur.

I

In race discrimination cases, employer liability has turned on whether the plaintiff has alleged an adverse employment consequence, such as firing or demotion, or a hostile work environment. If a supervisor takes an adverse employment action because of race, causing the employee a tangible job detriment, the employer is vicariously liable for resulting damages. This is because such actions are company acts that can be performed only by the exercise of specific authority granted by the employer, and thus the supervisor acts as the employer. If, on the other hand, the employee alleges a racially hostile work environment, the employer is liable only for negligence: that is, only if the employer knew, or in the exercise of reasonable care should have known, about the harassment and failed to take remedial action. See, e.g., Dennis v. Cty. of Fairfax, 55 F.3d 151, 153 (4th Cir. 1995); Davis v. Monsanto Chemical Co., 858 F.2d 345, 349 (6th Cir. 1988). Liability has thus been imposed only if the employer is blameworthy in some way. See, e.g., *Davis v. Monsanto Chemical Co.*, supra, at 349; Snell v. Suffolk Cty., supra, at 1104; DeGrace v. Rumsfeld, 614 F.2d 796, 805 (1st Cir. 1980).

This distinction applies with equal force in cases of sexual harassment. When a supervisor inflicts an adverse employment consequence upon an employee who has rebuffed his advances, the supervisor exercises the specific authority granted to him by his company. His acts, therefore, are the company's acts and are properly chargeable to it. . . .

If a supervisor creates a hostile work environment, however, he does not act for the employer. As the Court concedes, a supervisor's creation of a hostile work environment is neither within the scope of his employment, nor part of his apparent authority. Indeed, a hostile work environment is antithetical to the interest of the employer. In such circumstances, an employer should be liable only if it has been negligent. That is, liability should attach only if the employer either knew, or in the exercise of reasonable care should have known, about the hostile work environment and failed to take remedial action. . . .

Under a negligence standard, Burlington cannot be held liable for Slowick's conduct. Although respondent alleged a hostile work environment, she never contended that Burlington had been negligent in permitting the harassment to occur, and there is no question that Burlington acted reasonably under the circumstances. The company had a policy against sexual harassment, and respondent admitted that she was aware of the policy but nonetheless failed to tell anyone with authority over Slowick about his behavior. Burlington therefore cannot be charged with knowledge of Slowick's alleged harassment or with a failure to exercise reasonable care in not knowing about it.

NOTES ON BURLINGTON INDUSTRIES, INC. V. ELLERTH

1. *FARAGHER V. CITY OF BOCA RATON*

The Supreme Court decided *Burlington Industries* with a companion case, Faragher v. City of Boca Raton, 524 U.S. 775 (1998), which elaborated on the first of the two elements of the defense available to employers in hostile environment cases. The plaintiffs in *Faragher* were two female lifeguards who worked at a location far removed from the headquarters of the city parks and recreation department, by which they were employed. The plaintiffs alleged that their supervisors at this location, Terry and Silverman, created a hostile environment by repeatedly engaging in uninvited and offensive touching, by making lewd remarks, and by speaking of women in offensive terms. The facts found by the lower courts bore out these allegations, but the court of appeals held that the city could not be held liable for the supervisors' conduct. After elaborating on the justification for the defense recognized in *Burlington Industries* and after summarizing the elements of the defense, the Supreme Court analyzed its application in the following terms:

> Applying these rules here, we believe that the judgment of the Court of Appeals must be reversed. The District Court found that the degree of hostility in the work environment rose to the actionable level and was attributable to Silverman and Terry. It is undisputed that these supervisors "were granted virtually unchecked authority" over their subordinates, "directly controll[ing] and supervis[ing] all aspects of [Faragher's] day-to-day activities." 111 F.3d, at 1544 (Barkett, J., dissenting in part and concurring in part). It is also clear that Faragher and her colleagues were "completely isolated from the City's higher management." Ibid. The City did not seek review of these findings.
>
> While the City would have an opportunity to raise an affirmative defense if there were any serious prospect of its presenting one, it appears from the record that any such avenue is closed. The District Court found that the City had entirely failed to disseminate its policy against sexual

> harassment among the beach employees and that its officials made no attempt to keep track of the conduct of supervisors like Terry and Silverman. The record also makes clear that the City's policy did not include any assurance that the harassing supervisors could be bypassed in registering complaints. Under such circumstances, we hold as a matter of law that the City could not be found to have exercised reasonable care to prevent the supervisors' harassing conduct. Unlike the employer of a small workforce, who might expect that sufficient care to prevent tortious behavior could be exercised informally, those responsible for city operations could not reasonably have thought that precautions against hostile environments in any one of many departments in far-flung locations could be effective without communicating some formal policy against harassment, with a sensible complaint procedure.

Note that the Supreme Court held the city liable despite the fact that the plaintiffs had not complained of the supervisors' conduct to the management of the parks and recreation department. The terms of the defense recognized in *Burlington Industries* require the employer to establish both elements of the defense: both "(a) that the employer exercised reasonable care to prevent and correct promptly any sexually harassing behavior, and (b) that the plaintiff employee unreasonably failed to take advantage of any preventive or corrective opportunities provided by the employer or to avoid harm otherwise." The employer in *Faragher* had failed to satisfy the first element of the defense, and so the plaintiffs' failure to satisfy the second was irrelevant.

The converse situation could also result in liability for the employer. If the plaintiffs satisfy the second element of the defense, by complaining of sexual harassment, the defendant will be held liable even if it satisfied the first element by having a policy against sexual harassment in place and acting promptly on their complaint. The defense consists of two elements, both of which must be met. So, for instance, on the facts of *Meritor Savings Bank*, if the supervisor had committed only one act of harassment, but it was severe enough to create a hostile environment, and the employee had filed a prompt complaint, the employer would still be liable for the single act of harassment. Does this result make sense? Or does it demonstrate that the employer's liability in these circumstances would be limited? What if the single act of harassment were, as was alleged of some of the acts in *Meritor Savings Bank*, a sexual assault? One court refused to hold an employer liable for a single act of harassment if it had acted promptly to remedy it. McCurdy v. Arkansas State Police, 375 F.3d 762 (8th Cir. 2005).

2. THE DEFENSE TO VICARIOUS EMPLOYER LIABILITY

The law under Title VII offers only one analogue to the defense of qualified immunity under § 1983. It is the defense available to employers under *Burlington Industries* and *Faragher*, but it is different in many respects from the defense of qualified immunity.

First, it is a defense for employers, not for employees, who, as discussed below, are not liable at all under Title VII. Second, the defense is restricted in scope: it does not apply to all forms of sexual harassment, but only to cases where there is no "direct" or "indirect" employer liability and no "tangible employment action." Thus the employer is liable, without any defense, for all instances of sexual harassment by its own high officials and for all forms of harassment resulting in "tangible employment action" against the plaintiff.

For the remaining forms of sexual harassment, the employer also is vicariously liable, at least if the harassment is committed by the plaintiff's supervisor. Liability in this situation is strict, in the sense that if the newly formulated defense fails, the employer is automatically held liable for "severe or pervasive" harassment. The defense, however, imports a significant element of fault into the determination of the employer's liability. What should happen when the harassment is by a co-employee and not by a supervisor? The Court's reasoning suggests that the defense is still available, but it leaves open whether the employer is otherwise strictly liable for "severe or pervasive" harassment.

Note that the defense contains two elements, both of which the defendant must satisfy. The defense fails even if the employer exercises reasonable care under the first element, but the employee takes advantage of an effective complaint procedure under the second. So, for instance, on the facts of *Meritor Savings Bank*, if the supervisor had committed only one act of harassment, but it was severe enough to create a hostile environment and the employee had filed a prompt complaint, the employer would still be liable for this single act of harassment. Does this result make sense? Or does it demonstrate that the employer's liability in these circumstances should be limited? What if the single act of harassment were, as was alleged of some of the acts in *Meritor Savings Bank*, a sexual assault?

Judges in the lower federal courts are divided on the question of when the employer's affirmative defense to claims of sexual harassment has been made out under *Ellerth* and *Faragher*. The opinions in Indest v. Freeman Decorating, Inc., 164 F.3d 258 (5th Cir. 1999), 168 F.3d 795 (5th Cir. 1999), are illustrative. In this case, Judge Jones would have held that the employer made out the defense simply by establishing the first element identified in *Ellerth* and *Faragher*: that it took "reasonable care to prevent and correct promptly any sexually harassing behavior," even if the plaintiff acted reasonably in reporting the harassing conduct. Judge Weiner concurred in the judgment for the employer, but he would have read *Ellerth* and *Faragher* literally to require both elements of the defense to be established: reasonable action by the employer and unreasonable action by the harassed employee. A third judge in the case, perhaps bewildered by this unexpected problem, simply concurred in the result without opinion.

Individual liability under § 1983, it is widely believed, usually results in indirect governmental liability through the widespread practice of indemnification of individual government officials by their employers. Supposing that this is true, which statute provides a broader defense to claims of sexual harassment by governmental employers, § 1983 through the defense of qualified immunity to individual liability, or Title VII through the defense to employer liability? Which defense is applicable to a wider range of claims? Which defense is easier for an employer to establish through the adoption of precautionary employment policies? If a plaintiff has a choice, which statute should be used to assert a claim of sexual harassment? Or should a plaintiff routinely file under both statutes? If so, what is the point of maintaining two different systems of rules to impose liability for sexual harassment?

3. LIABILITY OF EMPLOYEES

Liability under Title VII also diverges from liability under § 1983 at the opposite extreme, in which the liability of individual employees or government officers is at issue. The strong trend in the lower court decisions is to impose no liability at all upon individual supervisors and employees under Title VII. See, e.g., Sheridan v. E.I. DuPont de Nemours, 100 F.3d 1061, 1077–78 (3d Cir. 1996); Spencer v. Ripley County State Bank, 123 F.3d 690 (8th Cir. 1997).

These decisions have reasoned, in an argument not yet considered by the Supreme Court, that Congress meant to insulate individual employees from liability when it imposed limits on the liability of employers for damages in § 1981a. If small employers are subject to lower caps on liability than larger employers, and if private employers with fewer than 15 employees are not covered at all by Title VII, then according to this argument, individual employees should not be liable at all. Is this argument strong enough to overcome the literal terms of Title VII defining a covered employer to include both persons with 15 or more employees engaged in commerce and "any agent of such a person"? See 42 U.S.C. § 2000e(b).

The law, as it has evolved under Title VII, makes only the employer liable. Under § 1983, the law goes to almost the opposite extreme: if anyone is liable, it is usually the individual employee. An individual government official or employee, of course, can have a defense of qualified or absolute immunity, as discussed in Chapter I. Nevertheless, this defense of immunity has quite different effects than the rule of no coverage that is developing under Title VII.

4. *JONES V. CLINTON*

In connection with the distinctions addressed in the preceding notes, consider the case of Jones v. Clinton, 993 F. Supp. 1217 (E.D. Ark. 1998), involving allegations of sexual harassment against President Bill Clinton. Paula Corbin Jones claimed that she was the victim of sexual harassment during her employment by the state of Arkansas when she was subjected to a "boorish and offensive" sexual proposition by then-Governor Clinton. The case was brought under § 1983 instead of Title VII because the statute of limitations under Title VII had expired by the time the claim was filed. Sexual harassment by a state official, as a form of intentional discrimination on the basis of sex, violates the Equal Protection Clause and so would support a claim under § 1983. Yet Jones's claim would have given rise to no liability on the part of the state of Arkansas under § 1983, because states are entirely excluded from coverage under that statute. And even if Clinton had been the mayor of a city in Arkansas at the time of the alleged harassment and Jones had been a municipal employee, municipal liability could only have been imposed on the unlikely finding that sexual harassment was "official custom or policy." In the actual case, therefore, the only liability at issue was Clinton's liability in his personal capacity. If the case had reached a trial on the merits, he could have asserted a defense of qualified immunity by showing a reasonable belief that his actions did not violate rights under the Equal Protection Clause. The merits of this defense were not addressed because the District Court granted summary judgment for Clinton, finding no reasonable grounds to infer that sexual harassment had occurred. The case was eventually settled while this ruling was on appeal.

Whatever the merits of the qualified immunity defense, it could not have been raised if *Jones v. Clinton* had been litigated under Title VII. Under the dominant view in the lower federal courts (including the circuit in which the case was brought), Clinton would not have been subjected to individual liability at all. The state of Arkansas would have been liable, however, assuming it had been sued within the limitations period and sexual harassment had been found.[a] Its liability would have been based on a theory of "indirect liability" for the actions of its chief executive. Thus, a Title VII case would have been brought against a different defendant under different substantive rules of liability and different standards for vicarious liability.

Can all this be right? What ought the rules to be? See Barbara Palmer, Judith Baer, Amy Jasperson, and Jacqueline DeLaat, Low–Life–Sleazy–Big–Haired Trailer–Park Girl v. The President: The Paula Jones Case and the Law of Sexual Harassment, 9 Am. U. J. Gender Soc. Pol'y & L. 283 (2001); Ronald Turner, Employer Liability for Supervisory Hostile Environment Sexual Harassment: Comparing Title VII's and Section 1983's Regulatory Regimes, 31 Urb. Law. 503 (1999).

5. BIBLIOGRAPHY

For further analysis of *Burlington Industries* and *Faragher*, see Michael C. Harper, Answering the Title VII Agency Question: A Policy Basis for *Faragher* and *Ellerth*, and J.H. Verkerke, The Triumph of Formalism in the Supreme Court's Recent Employer Liability Decisions, both in Proceedings of N.Y.U. Fifty–First Annual National Conference on Labor: Sexual Harassment in the Workplace (S. Estreicher ed. N.Y.U. 1999); Joanna L. Grossman, The Culture of Compliance: The Final Triumph of Form over Substance in Sexual Harassment Law, 26 Harv. Women's L.J. 3 (2003); Michael C. Harper, Employer Liability for Harassment Under Title VII: A Functional Rationale for *Faragher* and *Ellerth*, 36 San Diego L. Rev. 41 (1999); Ann Juliano and Stewart J. Schwab, The Sweep of Sexual Harassment Cases, 86 Corn. L. Rev. 548 (2001); Kerri Lynn Stone, Consenting Adults?: Why Women Who Submit to Supervisory Sexual Harassment Are Faring Better in Court Than Those Who Say No . . . and Why They Shouldn't, 20 Yale J.L. & Feminism 25 (2008); Noah D. Zatz, Managing the Macaw: Third–Party Harassers, Accommodation, and the Disaggregation of Discriminatory Intent, 109 Colum. L. Rev. 1357 (2009).

2. TITLE IX OF THE EDUCATION AMENDMENTS OF 1972

INTRODUCTORY NOTES ON TITLE IX

1. ENACTMENT AND BASIC PROVISIONS OF TITLE IX

Title IX was modeled on Title VI of the Civil Rights Act of 1964, which prohibits racial discrimination by recipients of federal funds. Title IX applies a similar prohibition to sex discrimination in a provision codified in 20 U.S.C. § 1681(a):

---

[a] The Eleventh Amendment would not have foreclosed state liability. Congress amended Title VII in 1972, explicitly authorizing money damages against states in employment discrimination cases. This statute was upheld in Fitzpatrick v. Bitzer, 427 U.S. 445 (1976), as a valid exercise of congressional power under § 5 of the Fourteenth Amendment.

> No person in the United States shall, on the basis of sex, be excluded from participation in, be denied the benefits of, or be subjected to discrimination under any education program or activity receiving federal financial assistance. . . .

This prohibition is narrower than the corresponding prohibition in Title VI in two respects. First, it applies only to educational programs, so that recipients of federal funds for other purposes fall outside its scope. Nevertheless, the statutory definition of "program or activity" is very broad, resulting in coverage of an entire educational institution if any part of it receives federal funds, even in the limited form of federal scholarships or loans or federal research grants. 20 U.S.C. § 1687. This broad definition was added to the statute to supersede a decision of the Supreme Court that limited the coverage of Title IX to the precise activity receiving federal funds. Grove City College v. Bell, 465 U.S. 555 (1984).

A second limitation on Title IX is that, even within its proper scope, its prohibition against sex discrimination is subject to a number of exceptions. These are more detailed than the BFOQ provision in Title VII and allow various forms of single-sex education, as in military academies and colleges traditionally for men or women alone, and also a variety of single-sex activities associated with education, such as sororities and fraternities, father-son and mother-daughter activities, and scholarships awarded in beauty pageants. 20 U.S.C. § 1681(a)(3)–(a)(9). These exceptions, of course, do not insulate the activities of public institutions from challenges under the Equal Protection Clause. For example, The Virginia Military Institute was forced to admit women despite its traditional policy of admitting only men. United States v. Virginia, 518 U.S. 515 (1996). Title IX also contains a general disclaimer of any form of required affirmative action, although this provision also explicitly allows the use of statistical evidence to prove discrimination. 20 U.S.C. § 1681(b).

The express terms of Title IX authorize only administrative enforcement by the federal departments or agencies that fund educational programs. These departments or agencies are authorized to cut off federal funding to institutions that violate the statute and to enforce the statute "by any other means authorized by law," such as by suing for an injunction. 20 U.S.C. § 1682. Any such suit, however, has to be brought by a duly authorized subdivision of the federal government. Individual victims of discrimination have no right to commence an action under the express terms of Title IX. Nevertheless, the Civil Rights Attorneys Fees Act of 1976, codified at 42 U.S.C. § 1988, authorizes the award of attorney's fees to the prevailing party, other than the United States, in any action to enforce Title IX. This provision seems to be premised on a private cause of action that Title IX does not expressly provide. Whether it should be read as "implying" a private right of action was the subject of the following case.

2. *CANNON V. UNIVERSITY OF CHICAGO*

In Cannon v. University of Chicago, 441 U.S. 677 (1979), the Supreme Court recognized a private right of action for injunctive relief by a woman who alleged discriminatory denial of admission to medical school. Writing for the majority, Justice Stevens relied on a variety of factors to find that a private action, although not expressly recognized in Title IX, was consistent with congressional intent in enacting the statute. All of these factors, although organized around a test for implying private rights of action that the Court has subsequently abandoned, emphasized the parallel between Title IX and Title VI.

First, Title IX created a right not to be discriminated against on the basis of sex, whereas Title VI created a right against racial discrimination. Second, when Congress enacted Title IX in 1972, the courts had already recognized a private remedy under Title VI. As Justice Stevens said: "[D]uring the period between the enactment of Title VI in 1964 and the enactment of Title IX in 1972, this Court had consistently found implied remedies—often in cases much less clear than this." It was only later that the Supreme Court took a stricter approach to implied private rights of action. Third, Stevens noted that Congress had two purposes in enacting Title IX: to prevent the use of federal funds to support discriminatory practices and to protect individual citizens against discrimination. The cut-off of funding would be so severe that it would not likely be invoked for an isolated violation. An injunction would be more effective, and there would be no inconsistency in permitting both remedies. The federal agency charged with enforcing the statute, moreover, had expressed its support of the private remedy as a supplementary means of enforcement. Finally, Justice Stevens reasoned that, ever since the Civil War, the federal government has taken the primary role and the states only a secondary role in protecting against discrimination.

Chief Justice Burger concurred in the judgment without opinion, while Justice Rehnquist, joined by Justice Stewart, wrote a separate concurrence, emphasizing that "[t]he question of the existence of a private right of action is basically one of statutory construction." He concluded that while Congress may well have had reason in the past to believe that the courts would readily create a private cause of action, the situation now was different. The lawmaking branch should be apprized "that the ball, so to speak, may well now be in its court. [T]his Court in the future should be extremely reluctant to imply a cause of action absent . . . specificity on the part of the legislative branch."

In a dissent joined by Justice Blackmun, Justice White argued that Congress specifically intended that there *not* be a private cause of action in this case. In a separate dissent, Justice Powell agreed with that conclusion but launched a much broader attack, arguing that the "mode of analysis we have applied in the recent past cannot be squared with the doctrine of separation of powers." As he reasoned, "When Congress chooses not to provide a private civil remedy, federal courts should not assume the legislative role of creating such a remedy and thereby enlarge their jurisdiction."

3. *FRANKLIN V. GWINNETT COUNTY PUBLIC SCHOOLS*

The decision in *Cannon* left some doubt about how vigorous the private right of action under Title IX would prove to be. The majority opinion looked back to a time when private rights of action were frequently implied under statutes which expressly provided only for public enforcement, an era already past when the case was decided. Not long after the decision in *Cannon*, the standards for implying private rights of action became stricter still, following the reasoning of the concurring opinions and the dissents. Doubts about the vitality of *Cannon*, however, were laid to rest in Franklin v. Gwinnett County Public Schools, 503 U.S. 60 (1992).

That case concerned an action for damages, not the injunction that was sought in *Cannon*. The plaintiff claimed that she had been sexually harassed by her high school coach and teacher and that the school system had responded inadequately to these events. The Supreme Court unanimously concluded that a private action for damages was available under Title IX. Writing for the Court, Justice White said:

> In *Cannon v. University of Chicago*, the Court held that Title IX is enforceable through an implied right of action. We have no occasion here to reconsider that decision. Rather, in this case we must decide what remedies are available in a suit brought pursuant to this implied right. As we have often stated, the question of what remedies are available under a statute that provides a private right of action is "analytically distinct" from the issue of whether such a right exists in the first place. Thus, although we examine the text and history of a statute to determine whether Congress intended to create a right of action, we presume the availability of all appropriate remedies unless Congress has expressly indicated otherwise.

Justice Scalia, joined by Chief Justice Rehnquist and by Justice Thomas, agreed with the Court's result but not its reasoning:

> In my view, when rights of action are judicially "implied," categorical limitation upon their remedial scope may be judicially implied as well. Although we have abandoned the expansive rights-creating approach exemplified by *Cannon*—and perhaps ought to abandon the notion of implied causes of action entirely—causes of action that came into existence under the ancien regime should be limited by the same logic that gave them birth. To require, with respect to a right that is not consciously and intentionally created, that any limitation of remedies must be express, is to provide, in effect, that the most questionable of private rights will also be the most expansively remediable. As the United States puts it, "[w]hatever the merits of 'implying' rights of action may be, there is no justification for treating [congressional] silence as the equivalent of the broadest imaginable grant of remedial authority."
>
> I nonetheless agree with he Court's disposition of this case. Because of legislation enacted subsequent to *Cannon*, it is too late in the day to address whether a judicially implied exclusion of damages under Title IX would be appropriate. The Civil Rights Remedies Equalization Amendment of 1986, 42 U.S.C. § 2000d–7(a)(2), must be read, in my view not only "as a validation of *Cannon*'s holding," but also as an implicit acknowledgment that damages are available.

The statute cited by Justice Scalia, the Civil Rights Remedies Equalization Amendment of 1986, expressly abrogates the immunity of states under the Eleventh Amendment in damage actions under Title IX and other statutes prohibiting discrimination by recipients of federal funds. Plainly, this statute contemplated the existence of damage actions under Title IX and therefore could be read as a "validation" of *Cannon*.

4. *FITZGERALD V. BARNSTABLE SCHOOL COMMITTEE*

Fitzgerald v. Barnstable School Committee, 555 U.S. 246 (2009), concerned the relationship between claims under Title IX and claims under § 1983. The plaintiff alleged that the defendant school district had allowed student-on-student sexual harassment in violation of the Fourteenth Amendment. The

Supreme Court held that the plaintiff's claim, although also covered by Title IX, could be brought under § 1983. To preclude use of § 1983, the Court reasoned, Congress must have "intended the statute's remedial scheme to 'be the exclusive avenue through which a plaintiff may assert [such] claims.' " The Court found no such intention in Title IX for three reasons. First, the remedies under Title IX are confined to a cut-off of federal funds and a limited private right of action. It is not an elaborate scheme that would be frustrated by recognizing overlapping claims under § 1983. Second, the protection against sex discrimination in federally funded schools under Title IX differs in scope from the rights protected under the the Equal Protection Clause, being narrower in some respects and broader in others. There was no evidence that Congress meant to take away the remedy under § 1983 when it protected broader rights under the Constitution. Third, Congress modeled Title IX after Title VI of the Civil Rights Act of 1964, and it was the express intention of Congress for Title IX to be interpreted in the same manner as Title VI. At the time Congress passed Title IX, "the lower courts routinely interpreted Title VI to allow parallel and concurrent § 1983 claims."

In light of this holding, does the damage remedy under Title IX recognized in *Franklin* take on greater or lesser significance? Would most plaintiffs' attorneys now routinely plead claims under both Title IX and § 1983? If so, does this undermine the effect of any limitation on the claims under either statute? For an article discussing the questions raised by *Fitzgerald*, see Rosalie Berger Levinson, Misinterpreting "Sounds of Silence": Why Courts Should Not "Imply" Congressional Preclusion of § 1983 Constitutional Claims, 77 Fordham L. Rev. 775 (2008).

Gebser v. Lago Vista Independent School District

Supreme Court of the United States, 1998.
524 U.S. 274.

■ JUSTICE O'CONNOR delivered the opinion of the Court.

The question in this case is when a school district may be held liable in damages in an implied right of action under Title IX of the Education Amendments of 1972 (Title IX), for the sexual harassment of a student by one of the district's teachers. We conclude that damages may not be recovered in those circumstances unless an official of the school district who at a minimum has authority to institute corrective measures on the district's behalf has actual notice of, and is deliberately indifferent to, the teacher's misconduct.

I

In the spring of 1991, when petitioner Alida Star Gebser was an eighth-grade student at a middle school in respondent Lago Vista Independent School District (Lago Vista), she joined a high school book discussion group led by Frank Waldrop, a teacher at Lago Vista's high school. Lago Vista received federal funds at all pertinent times. During the book discussion sessions, Waldrop often made sexually suggestive comments to the students. Gebser entered high school in the fall and was assigned to classes taught by Waldrop in both semesters. Waldrop continued to make inappropriate remarks to the students, and he began to direct more of his suggestive comments toward Gebser, including during the substantial amount of time that the two were alone in his classroom. He initiated sexual contact with Gebser in the spring, when, while visiting her home ostensibly to give her a book, he kissed and fondled her. The two had sexual intercourse on a number of occasions during the remainder of the school year. Their relationship continued through the summer and into the following school year, and they often had intercourse during class time, although never on school property.

Gebser did not report the relationship to school officials, testifying that while she realized Waldrop's conduct was improper, she was uncertain how to react and she wanted to continue having him as a teacher. In October 1992, the parents of two other students complained to the high school principal about Waldrop's comments in class. The principal arranged a meeting, at which, according to the principal, Waldrop indicated that he did not believe he had made offensive remarks but apologized to the parents and said it would not happen again. The principal also advised Waldrop to be careful about his classroom comments and told the school guidance counselor about the meeting, but he did not report the parents' complaint to Lago Vista's superintendent, who was the district's Title IX coordinator. A couple of months later, in January 1993, a police officer discovered Waldrop and Gebser engaging in sexual intercourse and arrested Waldrop. Lago Vista terminated his employment, and subsequently, the Texas Education Agency revoked his teaching license. During this time, the district had not promulgated or distributed an official grievance procedure for lodging sexual harassment complaints; nor had it issued a formal anti-harassment policy.

Gebser and her mother filed suit against Lago Vista and Waldrop in state court in November 1993, raising claims against the school district under Title IX, 42 U.S.C. § 1983, and state negligence law, and claims against Waldrop primarily under state law. They sought compensatory and punitive damages from both defendants. After the case was removed, the United States District Court for the Western District of Texas granted summary judgment in favor of Lago Vista on all claims, and remanded the allegations against Waldrop to state court. . . .

Petitioners appealed only on the Title IX claim. The Court of Appeals for the Fifth Circuit affirmed. . . . The court first declined to impose strict liability on school districts for a teacher's sexual harassment of a student, reiterating its conclusion [in another case] that strict liability is inconsistent with "the Title IX contract." The court then determined that Lago Vista could not be liable on the basis of constructive notice, finding that there was insufficient evidence to suggest that a school official should have known about Waldrop's relationship with Gebser. Finally, the court refused to invoke the common law principle that holds an employer vicariously liable when an employee is "aided in accomplishing [a] tort by the existence of the agency relation," Restatement (Second) of Agency § 219(2)(d) (1957) (hereinafter Restatement), explaining that application of that principle would result in school district liability in essentially every case of teacher-student harassment.

The court concluded its analysis by reaffirming its holding in Rosa H. v. San Elizario Independent School Dist., 106 F.3d 648 (5th Cir. 1997), that, "school districts are not liable in tort for teacher-student sexual harassment under Title IX unless an employee who has been invested by the school board with supervisory power over the offending employee actually knew of the abuse, had the power to end the abuse, and failed to do so," and ruling that petitioners could not satisfy that standard. . . . We granted certiorari to address the issue, and we now affirm.

II

. . . Petitioners, joined by the United States as amicus curiae, would invoke standards used by the Courts of Appeals in Title VII cases involving a supervisor's sexual harassment of an employee in the workplace. In support of that approach, they point to a passage in Franklin v. Gwinnett County Public Schools, 503 U.S. 60 (1992), in which we stated: "Unquestionably, Title IX placed on the Gwinnett County Public Schools the duty not to discriminate on the basis of sex, and 'when a supervisor sexually harasses a subordinate because of the subordinate's sex, that supervisor "discriminate[s]" on the basis of sex.' Meritor Sav. Bank, FSB v. Vinson, 477 U.S. 57, 64 (1986). We believe the same rule should apply when a teacher sexually harasses and abuses a student." *Meritor* directs courts to look to common-law agency principles when assessing an employer's liability under Title VII for sexual harassment of an employee by a supervisor. Petitioners and the United States submit that, in light of *Franklin*'s comparison of teacher-student harassment with supervisor-employee harassment, agency principles should likewise apply in Title IX actions.

Specifically, they advance two possible standards under which Lago Vista would be liable for Waldrop's conduct. First, relying on a 1997 "Policy Guidance" issued by the Department of Education, they would hold a school district liable in damages under Title IX where a teacher is " 'aided in carrying out the sexual harassment of students by his or her position of authority with the institution,' " irrespective of whether school district officials had any knowledge of the harassment and irrespective of their response upon becoming aware. That rule is an expression of respondeat superior liability, i.e., vicarious or imputed liability, see Restatement § 219(2)(d), under which recovery in damages against a school district would generally follow whenever a teacher's authority over a student facilitates the harassment. Second, petitioners and the United States submit that a school district should at a minimum be liable for damages based on a theory of constructive notice, i.e., where the district knew or "should have known" about harassment but failed to uncover and eliminate it. [S]ee Restatement § 219(2)(b). Both standards would allow a damages recovery in a broader range of situations than the rule adopted by the Court of Appeals, which hinges on actual knowledge by a school official with authority to end the harassment.

Whether educational institutions can be said to violate Title IX based solely on principles of respondeat superior or constructive notice was not resolved by *Franklin*'s citation of *Meritor*. That reference to *Meritor* was made with regard to the general proposition that sexual harassment can constitute discrimination on the basis of sex under Title IX, an issue not in dispute here. In fact, the school district's liability in *Franklin* did not necessarily turn on principles of imputed liability or constructive notice, as there was evidence that school officials knew about the harassment but took no action to stop it. Moreover, *Meritor*'s rationale for concluding that agency principles guide the liability inquiry under Title VII rests on an aspect of that statute not found in Title IX: Title VII, in which the prohibition against employment discrimination runs against "an employer," 42 U.S.C. § 2000e–2(a), explicitly defines "employer" to include "any agent," § 2000e(b). Title IX contains no comparable reference to an educational institution's "agents," and so does not expressly call for application of agency principles.

In this case, moreover, petitioners seek not just to establish a Title IX violation but to recover *damages* based on theories of respondeat superior and constructive notice. It is that aspect of their action, in our view, which is most critical to resolving the case. Unlike Title IX, Title VII contains an express cause of action, § 2000e–5(f), and specifically provides for relief in the form of monetary damages, § 1981a. Congress therefore has directly addressed the subject of damages relief under Title VII and has set out the particular situations in which damages are available as well as the maximum amounts recoverable. § 1981a(b). With respect to Title IX, however, the private right of action is judicially implied, and there is thus no legislative expression of the scope of available remedies, including when it is appropriate to award monetary damages. . . . We made no effort in *Franklin* to delimit the circumstances in which a damages remedy should lie.

III

Because the private right of action under Title IX is judicially implied, we have a measure of latitude to shape a sensible remedial scheme that best comports with the statute. That endeavor inherently entails a degree of speculation, since it addresses an issue on which Congress has not specifically spoken. To guide the analysis, we generally examine the relevant statute to ensure that we do not fashion the parameters of an implied right in a manner at odds with the statutory structure and purpose.

Those considerations, we think, are pertinent not only to the scope of the implied right, but also to the scope of the available remedies. [W]e conclude that it would "frustrate the purposes" of Title IX to permit a damages recovery against a school district for a teacher's sexual harassment of a student based on principles of respondeat superior or constructive notice, i.e., without actual notice to a school district official. Because Congress did not expressly create a private right of action under Title IX, the statutory text does not shed light on Congress' intent with respect to the scope of available remedies. Instead, "we attempt to infer how the [1972] Congress would have addressed the issue had the . . . action been included as an express provision in the" statute.

As a general matter, it does not appear that Congress contemplated unlimited recovery in damages against a funding recipient where the recipient is unaware of discrimination in its programs. When Title IX was enacted in 1972, the principal civil rights statutes containing an express right of action did not provide for recovery of monetary damages at all, instead allowing only injunctive and equitable relief. It was not until 1991 that Congress made damages available under Title VII, and even then, Congress carefully limited the amount recoverable in any individual case, calibrating the maximum recovery to the size of the employer. See 42 U.S.C. § 1981a(b)(3). Adopting petitioners' position would amount, then, to allowing unlimited recovery of damages under Title IX where Congress has not spoken on the subject of either the right or the remedy, and in the face of evidence that when Congress expressly considered both in Title VII it restricted the amount of damages available.

Congress enacted Title IX in 1972 with two principal objectives in mind: "to avoid the use of federal resources to support discriminatory practices" and "to provide individual citizens effective protection against those practices." *Cannon*, supra, at 704. The statute was modeled after Title VI of the Civil Rights Act of 1964, which is parallel to Title IX except that it prohibits race discrimination, not sex discrimination, and applies in all programs receiving federal funds, not only in education programs. See 42 U.S.C. § 2000d et seq. The two statutes operate in the same manner, conditioning an offer of federal funding on a promise by the recipient not to discriminate, in what amounts essentially to a contract between the Government and the recipient of funds.

That contractual framework distinguishes Title IX from Title VII, which is framed in terms not of a condition but of an outright prohibition. Title VII applies to all employers without regard to federal funding and aims broadly to "eradicat[e] discrimination throughout the economy." Landgraf v. USI Film Products, 511 U.S. 244, 254 (1994). Title VII, moreover, seeks to "make persons whole for injuries suffered through past discrimination." Ibid. (internal quotation marks omitted). Thus, whereas Title VII aims centrally to compensate victims of discrimination, Title IX focuses more on "protecting" individuals from discriminatory practices carried out by recipients of federal funds. *Cannon*, supra, at 704. That might explain why, when the Court first recognized the implied right under Title IX in *Cannon*, the opinion referred to injunctive or equitable relief in a private action, but not to a damages remedy.

Title IX's contractual nature has implications for our construction of the scope of available remedies. When Congress attaches conditions to the award of federal funds under its spending power, U.S. Const., Art. I, § 8, cl. 1, as it has in Title IX and Title VI, we examine closely the propriety of private actions holding the recipient liable in monetary damages for noncompliance with the condition. Our central concern in that regard is with ensuring "that the receiving entity of federal funds [has] notice that it will be liable for a monetary award." *Franklin*, supra, at 74. Justice White's opinion announcing the Court's judgment in Guardians Assn. v. Civil Serv. Comm'n of New York City, 463 U.S. 582 (1983), for instance, concluded that the relief in an action under Title VI alleging unintentional discrimination should be prospective only, because where discrimination is unintentional, "it is surely not obvious that the grantee was aware that it was administering the program in violation of the [condition]." 463 U.S., at 598. We confront similar concerns here. If a school district's liability for a teacher's sexual harassment rests on principles of constructive notice or respondeat superior, it will likewise be the case that the recipient of funds was unaware of the discrimination. It is sensible to assume that Congress did not envision a recipient's liability in damages in that situation.

Most significantly, Title IX contains important clues that Congress did not intend to allow recovery in damages where liability rests solely on principles of vicarious liability or constructive notice. Title IX's express means of enforcement—by administrative agencies—operates on an assumption of actual notice to officials of the funding recipient. The statute entitles agencies who disburse education funding to enforce their rules implementing the non-discrimination mandate through proceedings to suspend or terminate funding or through "other means authorized by law." 20 U.S.C. § 1682. Significantly, however, an agency may not initiate enforcement proceedings until it "has advised the appropriate person or persons of the failure to comply with the requirement and has determined that compliance cannot be secured by voluntary means." Ibid. The administrative regulations implement that obligation, requiring resolution of compliance issues "by informal means whenever possible," 34 CFR § 100.7(d) (1997), and prohibiting commencement of enforcement proceedings until the agency has determined that voluntary compliance is unobtainable and "the recipient . . . has been notified of its failure to comply and of the action to be taken to effect compliance," § 100.8(d); see § 100.8(c).

In the event of a violation, a funding recipient may be required to take "such remedial action as [is] deem[ed] necessary to overcome the effects of [the] discrimination." § 106.3. While agencies have conditioned continued funding on providing equitable relief to the victim, the regulations do not appear to contemplate a condition ordering payment of monetary damages, and there is no indication that payment of damages has been demanded as a condition of finding a recipient to be in compliance with the statute. In *Franklin*, for instance, the Department of Education found a violation of Title IX but determined that the school district came into compliance by virtue of the offending teacher's resignation and the district's institution of a grievance procedure for sexual harassment complaints.

Presumably, a central purpose of requiring notice of the violation "to the appropriate person" and an opportunity for voluntary compliance before administrative enforcement proceedings can commence is to avoid diverting education funding from beneficial uses where a recipient was unaware of discrimination in its programs and is willing to institute prompt corrective measures. The scope of private damages relief proposed by petitioners is at odds with that basic objective. When a teacher's sexual harassment is imputed to a school district or when a school district is deemed to have "constructively" known of the teacher's harassment, by assumption the district had no actual knowledge of the teacher's conduct. Nor, of course, did the district have an opportunity to take action to end the harassment or to limit further harassment.

It would be unsound, we think, for a statute's *express* system of enforcement to require notice to the recipient and an opportunity to come into voluntary compliance while a judicially implied system of enforcement permits substantial liability without regard to the recipient's knowledge or its corrective actions upon receiving notice. Moreover, an award of damages in a particular case might well exceed a recipient's level of federal funding. See Tr. of Oral Arg. 35 (Lago Vista's federal funding for 1992–1993 was roughly $120,000). Where a statute's express enforcement scheme hinges its most severe sanction on notice and unsuccessful efforts to obtain compliance, we cannot attribute to Congress the intention to have implied an enforcement scheme that allows imposition of greater liability without comparable conditions.

IV

Because the express remedial scheme under Title IX is predicated upon notice to an "appropriate person" and an opportunity to rectify any violation, 20 U.S.C. § 1682, we conclude, in the absence of further direction from Congress, that the implied damages remedy should be fashioned along the same lines. An "appropriate person" under § 1682 is, at a minimum, an official of the recipient entity with authority to take corrective action to end the discrimination. Consequently, in cases like this one that do not involve official policy of the recipient entity, we hold that a damages remedy will not lie under Title IX unless an official who at a minimum has authority to address the alleged discrimination and to institute corrective measures on the recipient's behalf has actual knowledge of discrimination in the recipient's programs and fails adequately to respond.

We think, moreover, that the response must amount to deliberate indifference to discrimination. The administrative enforcement scheme presupposes that an official who is advised of a Title IX violation refuses to take action to bring the recipient into compliance. The premise, in other words, is an official decision by the recipient not to remedy the violation. That framework finds a rough parallel in the standard of deliberate indifference. Under a lower standard, there would be a risk that the recipient would be liable in damages not for its own official decision but instead for its employees' independent actions. Comparable considerations led to our adoption of a deliberate indifference standard for claims under § 1983 alleging that a municipality's actions in failing to prevent a deprivation of federal rights was the cause of the violation.

Applying the framework to this case is fairly straightforward, as petitioners do not contend they can prevail under an actual notice standard. The only official alleged to have had information about Waldrop's misconduct is the high school principal. That information, however, consisted of a complaint from parents of other students charging only that Waldrop had made inappropriate comments during class, which was plainly insufficient to alert the principal to the possibility that Waldrop was involved in a sexual relationship with a student. Lago Vista, moreover, terminated Waldrop's employment upon learning of his relationship with Gebser. Justice Stevens points out in his dissenting opinion that Waldrop of course had knowledge of his own actions. Where a school district's liability rests on actual notice principles, however, the knowledge of the wrongdoer himself is not pertinent to the analysis. See Restatement § 280.

Petitioners focus primarily on Lago Vista's asserted failure to promulgate and publicize an effective policy and grievance procedure for sexual harassment claims. They point to Department of Education regulations requiring each funding recipient to "adopt and publish grievance procedures providing for prompt and equitable resolution" of discrimination complaints, 34 C.F.R. § 106.8(b) (1997), and to notify students and others "that it does not discriminate on the basis of sex in the educational programs or activities which it operates," § 106.9(a). Lago Vista's alleged failure to comply with the regulations, however, does not establish the requisite actual notice and deliberate indifference. And in any event, the failure to promulgate a grievance procedure does not itself constitute "discrimination" under Title IX. Of course, the Department of Education could enforce the requirement administratively: Agencies generally have authority to promulgate and enforce requirements that effectuate the statute's nondiscrimination mandate, 20 U.S.C. § 1682, even if those requirements do not purport to represent a definition of discrimination under the statute. We have never held, however, that the implied private right of action under Title IX allows recovery in damages for violation of those sorts of administrative requirements.

V

The number of reported cases involving sexual harassment of students in schools confirms that harassment unfortunately is an all too common aspect of the educational experience. No one questions that a student suffers extraordinary harm when subjected to sexual harassment and abuse by a teacher, and that the teacher's conduct is reprehensible and undermines the basic purposes of the educational system. The issue in this case, however, is whether the independent misconduct of a teacher is attributable to the school district that employs him under a specific federal statute designed primarily to prevent recipients of federal financial assistance from using the funds in a discriminatory manner. Our decision does not affect any right of recovery that an individual may have against a school district as a matter of state law or against the teacher in his individual capacity under state law or under 42 U.S.C. § 1983. Until Congress speaks directly on the subject, however, we will not hold a school district liable in damages under Title IX for a teacher's sexual harassment of a student absent actual notice and deliberate indifference. We therefore affirm the judgment of the Court of Appeals.

It is so ordered.

■ JUSTICE STEVENS, with whom JUSTICE SOUTER, JUSTICE GINSBURG, and JUSTICE BREYER join, dissenting.

The question that the petition for certiorari asks us to address is whether the Lago Vista Independent School District (respondent) is liable in damages for a violation of Title IX of the Education Amendments of 1972 (Title IX). The Court provides us with a negative answer to that question because respondent did not have actual notice of, and was not deliberately indifferent to, the odious misconduct of one of its teachers. As a basis for its decision, the majority relies heavily on the notion that because the private cause of action under Title IX is "judicially implied," the Court has "a measure of latitude" to use its own judgment in shaping a remedial scheme. This assertion of lawmaking authority is not faithful either to our precedents or to our duty to interpret, rather than to revise, congressional commands. Moreover, the majority's policy judgment about the appropriate remedy in this case thwarts the purposes of Title IX.

[After arguing in Part I that the majority's decision was inconsistent with *Cannon* and *Franklin*, Justice Stevens continued in Part II of his opinion:]

The Court nevertheless holds that the law does not provide a damages remedy for the Title IX violation alleged in this case because no official of the school district with "authority to institute corrective measures on the district's behalf" had actual notice of Waldrop's misconduct. That holding is at odds with settled principles of agency law, under which the district is responsible for Waldrop's misconduct because "he was aided in accomplishing the tort by the existence of the agency relation." Restatement (Second) of Agency, § 219(2)(d) (1957).[9] This case presents a paradigmatic example of a tort that was made possible, that was effected, and that was repeated over a prolonged period because of the powerful influence that Waldrop had over Gebser by reason of the authority that his employer, the school district, had delegated to him. As a secondary school teacher, Waldrop exercised even greater authority and control over his students than employers and supervisors exercise over their employees. His gross misuse of that authority allowed him to abuse his young student's trust.

Reliance on the principle set out in § 219(2)(b) of the Restatement comports with the relevant agency's interpretation of Title IX. The United

[9] The Court suggests that agency principles are inapplicable to this case because Title IX does not expressly refer to an "agent," as Title VII does. Title IX's focus on the protected class rather than the fund recipient fully explains the statute's failure to mention "agents" of the recipient, however. Moreover, in Meritor Savings Bank, FSB v. Vinson, 477 U.S. 57, (1986), we viewed Title VII's reference to an "agent" as a limitation on the liability of the employer: "Congress' decision to define 'employer' to include any 'agent' of an employer, 42 U.S.C. § 2000e(b), surely evinces an intent to place some limits on the acts of employees for which employers under Title VII are to be held responsible." Id., at 72 (citations omitted).

States Department of Education, through its Office for Civil Rights, recently issued a policy "Guidance" stating that a school district is liable under Title IX if one of its teachers "was aided in carrying out the sexual harassment of students by his or her position of authority with the institution." Dept. of Ed., Office for Civil Rights, Sexual Harassment Guidance: Harassment of Students by School Employees, Other Students, or Third Parties, 62 Fed.Reg. 12034, 12039 (1997). As the agency charged with administering and enforcing Title IX, the Department of Education has a special interest in ensuring that federal funds are not used in contravention of Title IX's mandate. It is therefore significant that the Department's interpretation of the statute wholly supports the conclusion that respondent is liable in damages for Waldrop's sexual abuse of his student, which was made possible only by Waldrop's affirmative misuse of his authority as her teacher.

The reason why the common law imposes liability on the principal in such circumstances is the same as the reason why Congress included the prohibition against discrimination on the basis of sex in Title IX: to induce school boards to adopt and enforce practices that will minimize the danger that vulnerable students will be exposed to such odious behavior. The rule that the Court has crafted creates the opposite incentive. As long as school boards can insulate themselves from knowledge about this sort of conduct, they can claim immunity from damages liability. Indeed, the rule that the Court adopts would preclude a damages remedy even if every teacher at the school knew about the harassment but did not have "authority to institute corrective measures on the district's behalf." It is not my function to determine whether this newly fashioned rule is wiser than the established common-law rule. It is proper, however, to suggest that the Court bears the burden of justifying its rather dramatic departure from settled law, and to explain why its opinion fails to shoulder that burden.

III

The Court advances several reasons why it would "frustrate the purposes" of Title IX to allow recovery against a school district that does not have actual notice of a teacher's sexual harassment of a student. As the Court acknowledges, however, the two principal purposes that motivated the enactment of Title IX were: (1) " 'to avoid the use of federal resources to support discriminatory practices' "; and (2) " 'to provide individual citizens effective protection against those practices.' " It seems quite obvious that both of those purposes would be served—not frustrated—by providing a damages remedy in a case of this kind. To the extent that the Court's reasons for its policy choice have any merit, they suggest that no damages should ever be awarded in a Title IX case—in other words, that our unanimous holding in *Franklin* should be repudiated.

First, the Court observes that at the time Title IX was enacted, "the principal civil rights statutes containing an express right of action did not provide for recovery of monetary damages at all." *Franklin*, however, forecloses this reevaluation of legislative intent; in that case, we "evaluate[d] the state of the law when the Legislature passed Title IX," 503 U.S., at 71, and concluded that "the same contextual approach used to justify an implied right of action more than amply demonstrates the lack of any legislative intent to abandon the traditional presumption in favor of all available remedies," id., at 72. The Court also suggests that the fact that Congress has imposed a ceiling on the amount of damages that may be recovered in Title VII cases, see 42 U.S.C. § 1981a, is somehow relevant to the question whether any damages at all may be awarded in a Title IX case. The short answer to this creative argument is that the Title VII ceiling does not have any bearing on when damages may be recovered from a defendant in a Title IX case. Moreover, this case does not present any issue concerning the amount of any possible damages award.

Second, the Court suggests that the school district did not have fair notice when it accepted federal funding that it might be held liable " 'for a monetary award' " under Title IX. The Court cannot mean, however, that respondent was not on notice that sexual harassment of a student by a teacher constitutes an "intentional" violation of Title IX for which damages are available, because we so held shortly before Waldrop began abusing Gebser. See *Franklin*, supra, at 74–75. Given the fact that our holding in *Franklin* was unanimous, it is not unreasonable to assume that it could have been foreseen by counsel for the recipients of Title IX funds. Moreover, the nondiscrimination requirement set out in Title IX is clear, and this Court held that sexual harassment constitutes intentional sex discrimination long before the sexual abuse in this case began. See *Meritor*, 477 U.S., at 64. Normally, of course, we presume that the citizen has knowledge of the law.

The majority nevertheless takes the position that a school district that accepts federal funds under Title IX should not be held liable in damages for an intentional violation of that statute if the district itself "was unaware of the discrimination." The Court reasons that because administrative proceedings to terminate funding cannot be commenced until after the grant recipient has received notice of its noncompliance and the agency determines that voluntary compliance is not possible, see 20 U.S.C. § 1682, there should be no damages liability unless the grant recipient has actual notice of the violation (and thus an opportunity to end the harassment).

The fact that Congress has specified a particular administrative procedure to be followed when a subsidy is to be terminated, however, does not illuminate the question of what the victim of discrimination on the basis of sex must prove in order to recover damages in an implied private right of action. Indeed, in *Franklin*, we noted that the Department of Education's Office of Civil Rights had declined to terminate federal funding of the school district at issue—despite its finding that a Title IX violation had occurred—because "the district had come into compliance with Title IX" after the harassment at issue. That fact did not affect the Court's analysis, much less persuade the Court that a damages remedy was unavailable. Cf. *Cannon*, 441 U.S., at 711 ("The fact that other provisions of a complex statutory scheme create express remedies has not been accepted as a sufficient reason for refusing to imply an otherwise appropriate remedy under a separate section").

The majority's inappropriate reliance on Title IX's administrative enforcement scheme to limit the availability of a damages remedy leads the Court to require not only actual knowledge on the part of "an official who at a minimum has authority to address the alleged discrimination and to institute corrective measures on the recipient's behalf," but also that official's "refus[al] to take action," or "deliberate indifference" toward the harassment.[13] Presumably, few Title IX plaintiffs who have been victims of intentional discrimination will be able to recover damages under this exceeding-

---

[13] The only decisions the Court cites to support its adoption of such a stringent standard are cases arising under a quite different statute, 42 U.S.C. § 1983.

ly high standard. The Court fails to recognize that its holding will virtually "render inutile causes of action authorized by Congress through a decision that *no* remedy is available." *Franklin*, 503 U.S., at 74.

IV

We are not presented with any question concerning the affirmative defenses that might eliminate or mitigate the recovery of damages for a Title IX violation. It has been argued, for example, that a school district that has adopted and vigorously enforced a policy that is designed to prevent sexual harassment and redress the harms that such conduct may produce should be exonerated from damages liability. The Secretary of Education has promulgated regulations directing grant recipients to adopt such policies and disseminate them to students. A rule providing an affirmative defense for districts that adopt and publish such policies pursuant to the regulations would not likely be helpful to respondent, however, because it is not at all clear whether respondent adopted any such policy, and there is no evidence that such a policy was made available to students, as required by regulation.

A theme that seems to underlie the Court's opinion is a concern that holding a school district liable in damages might deprive it of the benefit of the federal subsidy—that the damages remedy is somehow more onerous than a possible termination of the federal grant. It is possible, of course, that in some cases the recoverable damages, in either a Title IX action or a state-law tort action, would exceed the amount of a federal grant. That is surely not relevant to the question whether the school district or the injured student should bear the risk of harm—a risk against which the district, but not the student, can insure. It is not clear to me why the well-settled rules of law that impose responsibility on the principal for the misconduct of its agents should not apply in this case. As a matter of policy, the Court ranks protection of the school district's purse above the protection of immature high school students that those rules would provide. Because those students are members of the class for whose special benefit Congress enacted Title IX, that policy choice is not faithful to the intent of the policymaking branch of our Government.

I respectfully dissent.

■ JUSTICE GINSBURG, with whom JUSTICE SOUTER, and JUSTICE BREYER join, dissenting.

Justice Stevens' opinion focuses on the standard of school district liability for teacher-on-student harassment in secondary schools. I join that opinion, which reserves the question whether a district should be relieved from damages liability if it has in place, and effectively publicizes and enforces, a policy to curtail and redress injuries caused by sexual harassment. I think it appropriate to answer that question for these reasons: (1) the dimensions of a claim are determined not only by the plaintiff's allegations, but by the allowable defenses; (2) this Court's pathmarkers are needed to afford guidance to lower courts and school officials responsible for the implementation of Title IX.

In line with the tort law doctrine of avoidable consequences, I would recognize as an affirmative defense to a Title IX charge of sexual harassment, an effective policy for reporting and redressing such misconduct. School districts subject to Title IX's governance have been instructed by the Secretary of Education to install procedures for "prompt and equitable resolution" of complaints, 34 CFR § 106.8(b) (1997), and the Department of Education's Office of Civil Rights has detailed elements of an effective grievance process, with specific reference to sexual harassment, 62 Fed.Reg. 12034, 12044–45 (1997).

The burden would be the school district's to show that its internal remedies were adequately publicized and likely would have provided redress without exposing the complainant to undue risk, effort, or expense. Under such a regime, to the extent that a plaintiff unreasonably failed to avail herself of the school district's preventive and remedial measures, and consequently suffered avoidable harm, she would not qualify for Title IX relief.

NOTES ON GEBSER V. LAGO VISTA INDEPENDENT SCHOOL DISTRICT

1. STANDARDS FOR VICARIOUS LIABILITY

Gebser assumes that the same test for what constitutes sexual harassment applies under Title IX as under Title VII, at least insofar as the alleged harassment was unwelcome and was "severe or pervasive." The only issue decided by the Court was whether the school district was liable for this conduct. At this point, the Court departed from standards of vicarious liability under Title VII. The standard under Title IX is one of "reckless indifference": whether "an official who at a minimum has authority to address the alleged discrimination and to institute corrective measures on the recipient's behalf has actual knowledge of discrimination in the recipient's program and fails adequately to respond."

Presumably, this standard applies even if the victim of harassment has suffered some tangible disadvantage, analogous to the "tangible employment action" that provides a basis for vicarious liability in Title VII cases under Burlington Industries, Inc. v. Ellerth, 524 U.S. 742 (1998), and Faragher v. City of Boca Raton, 524 U.S. 775 (1998), both of which are considered in section 1 of this chapter. As an evidentiary matter, of course, a "tangible educational action" may support a finding of vicarious liability under this standard, but it does not automatically do so. Under Title VII, it would. And even in other cases of sexual harassment under Title VII, the employer remains strictly liable unless it can make out the defense formulated in *Faragher*. Justice Ginsburg, in her dissenting opinion, would adopt for Title IX a similar standard for vicarious liability. Would it be identical to the standard under Title VII? Should it?

Under Title IX, the Court adapted the standard of reckless indifference from decisions under § 1983. This left public schools subject to no greater liability under Title IX than they already had under § 1983. Towards the end of its opinion, the Court also mentioned the possibility of joining a § 1983 claim against the individual teacher who engaged in the harassment. This claim, of course, would be subject to a defense of qualified immunity. It is also possible that a case involving employment discrimination, for instance, sexual harassment of one teacher by another, could result in claims under all three statutes. Does it make sense to have broader remedies available against the school district for sexual harassment of one employee by another than for sexual harassment of students by teachers? Or is this just a consequence of the application of Title VII only to employment?

A particularly useful article that surveys the various standards for vicarious liability under Title IX, Title VII, and § 1983 is Catherine Fisk and Erwin

Chemerinsky, Civil Rights Without Remedies: Vicarious Liability Under Title VII, Section 1983, and Title IX, 7 Wm. & Mary Bill Rts. J. 755 (1999).

2. LIMITS ON IMPLIED PRIVATE RIGHTS OF ACTION

In the course of justifying this restrictive standard for vicarious liability, the *Gebser* Court reexamined issues that seemingly were settled by *Cannon* and *Franklin*. The Court emphasized the limited remedies expressly created by the statute, either in the form of a cut-off of federal funds or injunctive relief. Damages, the Court found, were an unusual remedy for civil rights violations at the time Title IX was enacted and would result in potentially unlimited liability regardless of the extent of federal funding. Was Justice Stevens correct in arguing that this reasoning is fundamentally inconsistent with the approach taken in *Cannon* and *Franklin*? If so, what is left of these decisions?

Under the current test for judicial creation of private rights of action, adopted after the decision in *Cannon*, the Court's task "is limited solely to determining whether Congress intended to create the private right of action asserted. . . . " Touche Ross & Co. v. Redington, 442 U.S. 560, 568 (1979). Suppose that under this test, *Cannon* would have come out differently, with no private right of action being added to Title IX. Such a conclusion would be based, under *Touche Ross*, on the view that Congress did not intend to create a private right of action. Is a private action with limited vicarious liability for damages more consistent with this view of congressional intent than a private action without any such limitation? Is the Court limiting the scope of liability, in other words, because it now questions whether it should have implied the remedy in the first place? Recall, however, the basis for Justice Scalia's conclusion in *Franklin*:

> Because of legislation enacted subsequent to *Cannon*, it is too late in the day to address whether a judicially implied exclusion of damages under Title IX would be appropriate. The Civil Rights Remedies Equalization Amendment of 1986, 42 U.S.C. § 2000d–7(a)(2), must be read, in my view not only "as a validation of *Cannon*'s holding," but also as an implicit acknowledgment that damages are available.

Does this change the calculus? What is left of the unlimited availability of remedies said to exist under *Franklin* now that *Gebser* has limited the scope of liability?

3. *JACKSON V. BIRMINGHAM BOARD OF EDUCATION*

The range of claims under Title IX was further expanded by Jackson v. Birmingham Board of Education, 544 U.S. 167 (2005), which recognized a claim for retaliation by a public school teacher who complained about sex discrimination in a high school's athletic program. The Supreme Court emphasized that the school district was on notice that it could be held liable for retaliation based on prior judicial decisions such as *Cannon* and *Gebser* and on longstanding regulations prohibiting retaliation. Because the case came up on a motion to dismiss for failure to state a claim, the plaintiff still had to prove retaliation on remand, and in particular, that his coaching duties were terminated because of his complaints about sex discrimination.

For a discussion of this case that anticipated the Supreme Court's ultimate decision, see Bradford C. Mank, Are Anti–Retaliation Regulations in

Title VI or Title IX Enforceable in a Private Right of Action: Does Sandoval or Sullivan Control this Question?, 35 Seton Hall L. Rev. 47 (2004).

4. THE SOURCE OF FEDERAL LEGISLATIVE POWER

The Court offered another reason for limiting the vicarious liability of recipients of federal funds based on the source of Title IX in the power of Congress to control federal spending. As the Court said:

> When Congress attaches conditions to the award of federal funds under its spending power, U.S. Const. Art. I, § 8, cl.1, as it has in Title IX and Title VI, we examine closely the propriety of private actions holding the recipient liable in monetary damages for noncompliance with the condition.

What is the relevance of the source of congressional power to the question of how Congress has exercised that power? Suppose Congress had explicitly authorized private actions under Title IX. Would the Court have narrowly interpreted an express private right of action to avoid constitutional doubts about the exercise of congressional power? Bear in mind that it was the *Cannon* Court which first recognized a private right of action under Title IX. Would it have done so if it had entertained doubts about the power of Congress to provide explicitly for such actions?

All of these questions seem very remote from the issue of vicarious liability actually decided in *Gebser*. In the end, is the Court just content to have plaintiffs look elsewhere for recoveries based on claims of sexual harassment in educational institutions, to Title VII for employees and § 1983 for students in public schools? Are there constitutional doubts about applying these statutes to educational institutions? Is it because these statutes are not enacted under the spending power?

5. *UNITED STATES V. MORRISON*

In United States v. Morrison, 529 U.S. 598 (2000), the Supreme Court held unconstitutional provisions in The Violence Against Women Act of 1994 that created a private right of action for any victim of "a crime of violence motivated by gender." 42 U.S.C. § 13981. The Court held that these provisions were beyond the powers of Congress. The Court found no basis for the statute under the Commerce Clause because it regulated neither the channels nor the instrumentalities of interstate commerce nor did it regulate any activity that substantially affects interstate commerce. The Court reached the latter conclusion despite substantial congressional findings to the contrary, which elicited dissents from Justices Souter and Breyer.

The Court also held that the statute fell outside the power conferred by § 5 of the Fourteenth Amendment, which provides that "Congress shall have power to enforce, by appropriate legislation, the provisions of this [amendment]." The latter provisions, and particularly the Equal Protection Clause, apply only to state action. The only state action invoked in support of § 13981 came by way of congressional findings that state courts were systematically biased against the victims of gender-motivated violence and so did not afford them full relief for their injuries. No state action, however, was necessarily involved in the conduct giving rise to liability under the statute, as evidenced by the purely private action alleged in *Morrison* itself, which involved sexual assault by individual students at a public university.

The decision in *Morrison*, although it restricts congressional power, does not question the basis for Title IX in congressional authority to regulate recipients of federal funds under the Spending Clause, Article I, § 8, cl. 1. Title IX's coverage is limited to schools that receive federal funds, unlike the coverage of The Violence Against Women Act, which extends to anyone who engages in crimes of sexual violence. Indeed, *Morrison* itself involved a claim under Title IX that was not considered by the Supreme Court but that was remanded by the court of appeals for reconsideration by the district court. Even after *Morrison*, the Supreme Court has recognized that the Spending Clause, together with the Necessary and Proper Clause, gives Congress an independent basis for legislation "to see to it that taxpayer dollars appropriated under that power are in fact spent for the general welfare . . . " Sabri v. United States, 541 U.S. 600 (2004). That case, however, did not involve a prohibition against discrimination, but misappropriation of money from a city that received federal funds. Has the Court avoided questions whether Title IX exceeds congressional power under the Spending Clause by narrowly interpreting the grounds for recovery by private individuals under the statute?

For discussions of the implications of *Morrison*, see John Alan Doran and Christopher Michael Mason, Disproportionate Incongruity: State Sovereign Immunity and the Future of Federal Employment Discrimination Law, 2003 L. Rev. Mich. St. U. Det. C.L. 1; Robert C. Post and Reva B. Siegel, Essay, Equal Protection by Law: Federal Antidiscrimination Legislation After *Morrison* and *Kimel*, 110 Yale L.J. 441 (2000); Ronald D. Rotunda, The Eleventh Amendment, *Garrett*, and Protection for Civil Rights, 53 Ala. L. Rev. 1183 (2002). For discussion of the related topic of congressional power under § 5 of the Fourteenth Amendment, see the Notes on Attempted Circumventions of State Sovereign Immunity in the Introduction, supra.

Davis v. Monroe County Board of Education

Supreme Court of the United States, 1999.
526 U.S. 629.

■ JUSTICE O'CONNOR delivered the opinion of the Court.

Petitioner brought suit against the Monroe County Board of Education and other defendants, alleging that her fifth-grade daughter had been the victim of sexual harassment by another student in her class. Among petitioner's claims was a claim for monetary and injunctive relief under Title IX of the Education Amendments of 1972 (Title IX). The District Court dismissed petitioner's Title IX claim on the ground that "student-on-student," or peer, harassment provides no ground for a private cause of action under the statute. The Court of Appeals for the Eleventh Circuit, sitting en banc, affirmed. We consider here whether a private damages action may lie against the school board in cases of student-on-student harassment. We conclude that it may, but only where the funding recipient acts with deliberate indifference to known acts of harassment in its programs or activities. Moreover, we conclude that such an action will lie only for harassment that is so severe, pervasive, and objectively offensive that it effectively bars the victim's access to an educational opportunity or benefit.

I

Petitioner's Title IX claim was dismissed under Federal Rule of Civil Procedure 12(b)(6) for failure to state a claim upon which relief could be granted. Accordingly, in reviewing the legal sufficiency of petitioner's cause of action, "we must assume the truth of the material facts as alleged in the complaint." Summit Health, Ltd. v. Pinnas, 500 U.S. 322, 325 (1991). . . .

Petitioner's minor daughter, Lucinda, was allegedly the victim of a prolonged pattern of sexual harassment by one of her fifth-grade classmates at Hubbards Elementary School, a public school in Monroe County, Georgia. According to petitioner's complaint, the harassment began in December 1992, when the classmate, G.F., attempted to touch Lucinda's breasts and genital area and made vulgar statements such as " 'I want to get in bed with you' " and " 'I want to feel your boobs.' " Similar conduct allegedly occurred on or about January 4 and January 20, 1993. Lucinda reported each of these incidents to her mother and to her classroom teacher, Diane Fort. Petitioner, in turn, also contacted Fort, who allegedly assured petitioner that the school principal, Bill Querry, had been informed of the incidents. Petitioner contends that, notwithstanding these reports, no disciplinary action was taken against G.F.

G.F.'s conduct allegedly continued for many months. . . . In early February, . . . G.F. again allegedly engaged in harassing behavior, this time while under the supervision of another classroom teacher, Joyce Pippin. Again, LaShonda allegedly reported the incident to the teacher, and again petitioner contacted the teacher to follow up. . . .

The string of incidents finally ended in mid-May, when G.F. was charged with, and pleaded guilty to, sexual battery for his misconduct. The complaint alleges that LaShonda had suffered during the months of harassment, however; specifically, her previously high grades allegedly dropped as she became unable to concentrate on her studies, and, in April 1993, her father discovered that she had written a suicide note. The complaint further alleges that, at one point, LaShonda told petitioner that she " 'didn't know how much longer she could keep [G.F.] off her.' "

Nor was LaShonda G.F.'s only victim; it is alleged that other girls in the class fell prey to G.F.'s conduct. At one point, in fact, a group composed of LaShonda and other female students tried to speak with Principal Querry about G.F.'s behavior. According to the complaint, however, a teacher denied the students' request with the statement, " 'If [Querry] wants you, he'll call you.' "

Petitioner alleges that no disciplinary action was taken in response to G.F.'s behavior toward LaShonda. In addition to her conversations with Fort and Pippin, petitioner alleges that she spoke with Principal Querry in mid-May 1993. When petitioner inquired as to what action the school intended to take against G.F., Querry simply stated, " 'I guess I'll have to threaten him a little bit harder.' " Yet, petitioner alleges, at no point during the many months of his reported misconduct was G.F. disciplined for harassment. Indeed, Querry allegedly asked petitioner why LaShonda " 'was the only one complaining.' "

Nor, according to the complaint, was any effort made to separate G.F. and LaShonda. On the contrary, notwithstanding LaShonda's frequent complaints, only after more than three months of reported harassment was she even permitted to change her classroom seat so that she was no longer seated next to G.F. Moreover, petitioner alleges that, at the time of the events in question, the Monroe County Board of Education (Board) had not instructed its personnel on how to respond to peer sexual harassment and had not established a policy on the issue. . . .

II

Title IX provides, with certain exceptions not at issue here, that

> [n]o person in the United States shall, on the basis of sex, be excluded from participation in, be denied the benefits of, or be subjected to discrimination under any education program or activity receiving Federal financial assistance.

20 U.S.C. § 1681(a). . . . There is no dispute here that the Board is a recipient of federal education funding for Title IX purposes. Nor do respondents support an argument that student-on-student harassment cannot rise to the level of "discrimination" for purposes of Title IX. Rather, at issue here is the question whether a recipient of federal education funding may be liable for damages under Title IX under any circumstances for discrimination in the form of student-on-student sexual harassment.

A

Petitioner urges that Title IX's plain language compels the conclusion that the statute is intended to bar recipients of federal funding from permitting this form of discrimination in their programs or activities. She emphasizes that the statute prohibits a student from being "*subjected to discrimination* under any education program or activity receiving Federal financial assistance." 20 U.S.C. § 1681 (emphasis supplied). It is Title IX's "unmistakable focus on the benefitted class," Cannon v. University of Chicago, 441 U.S. 677, 691 (1979), rather than the perpetrator, that, in petitioner's view, compels the conclusion that the statute works to protect students from the discriminatory misconduct of their peers.

Here, however, we are asked to do more than define the scope of the behavior that Title IX proscribes. We must determine whether a district's failure to respond to student-on-student harassment in its schools can support a private suit for money damages. . . .

We agree with respondents that a recipient of federal funds may be liable in damages under Title IX only for its own misconduct. The recipient itself must "exclud[e] [persons] from participation in, . . . den[y] [persons] the benefits of, or . . . subjec[t] [persons] to discrimination under" its "program[s] or activit[ies]" in order to be liable under Title IX. The Government's enforcement power may only be exercised against the funding recipient, see § 1682, and we have not extended damages liability under Title IX to parties outside the scope of this power.

We disagree with respondents' assertion, however, that petitioner seeks to hold the Board liable for G.F.'s actions instead of its own. Here, petitioner attempts to hold the Board liable for its own decision to remain idle in the face of known student-on-student harassment in its schools. In Gebser v. Lago Vista Independent School Dist., 524 U.S. 274 (1998), we concluded that a recipient of federal education funds may be liable in damages under Title IX where it is deliberately indifferent to known acts of sexual harassment by a teacher. In that case, a teacher had entered into a sexual relationship with an eighth grade student, and the student sought damages under Title IX for the teacher's misconduct. We recognized that the scope of liability in private damages actions under Title IX is circumscribed by [the requirement established in] Pennhurst State School and Hospital v. Halderman, 451 U.S. 1 (1981), . . . that funding recipients have notice of their potential liability. . . .

Gebser thus established that a recipient intentionally violates Title IX, and is subject to a private damages action, where the recipient is deliberately indifferent to known acts of teacher-student discrimination. Indeed, whether viewed as "discrimination" or "subject[ing]" students to discrimination, Title IX "[u]nquestionably . . . placed on [the Board] the duty not" to permit teacher-student harassment in its schools, Franklin v. Gwinnett County Public Schools, 503 U.S. 60, 75 (1992), and recipients violate Title IX's plain terms when they remain deliberately indifferent to this form of misconduct.

We consider here whether the misconduct identified in *Gebser*—deliberate indifference to known acts of harassment—amounts to an intentional violation of Title IX, capable of supporting a private damages action, when the harasser is a student rather than a teacher. We conclude that, in certain limited circumstances, it does. As an initial matter, in *Gebser* we expressly rejected the use of agency principles in the Title IX context, noting the textual differences between Title IX and Title VII. Additionally, the regulatory scheme surrounding Title IX has long provided funding recipients with notice that they may be liable for their failure to respond to the discriminatory acts of certain non-agents. The Department of Education requires recipients to monitor third parties for discrimination in specified circumstances and to refrain from particular forms of interaction with outside entities that are known to discriminate. See, e.g., 34 CFR §§ 106.31(b)(6), 106.31(d), 106.37(a)(2), 106.38(a), 106.51(a)(3) (1998).

The common law, too, has put schools on notice that they may be held responsible under state law for their failure to protect students from the tortious acts of third parties. See Restatement (Second) of Torts § 320, and Comment a (1965). In fact, state courts routinely uphold claims alleging that schools have been negligent in failing to protect their students from the torts of their peers. See, e.g., Rupp v. Bryant, 417 So.2d 658, 666–67 (Fla.1982).

This is not to say that the identity of the harasser is irrelevant. On the contrary, both the "deliberate indifference" standard and the language of Title IX narrowly circumscribe the set of parties whose known acts of sexual harassment can trigger some duty to respond on the part of funding recipients. Deliberate indifference makes sense as a theory of direct liability under Title IX only where the funding recipient has some control over the alleged harassment. A recipient cannot be directly liable for its indifference where it lacks the authority to take remedial action.

The language of Title IX itself—particularly when viewed in conjunction with the requirement that the recipient have notice of Title IX's prohibitions to be liable for damages—also cabins the range of misconduct that the statute proscribes. The statute's plain language confines the scope of prohibited conduct based on the recipient's degree of control over the harasser and the environment in which the harassment occurs. If a funding recipient does not engage in harassment directly, it may not be liable for damages unless its deliberate indifference "subject[s]" its students to harassment. That is, the deliberate indifference must, at a minimum, "cause [students] to undergo" harassment or "make them liable or vulnerable" to it. Moreover, because the harassment must occur "under" "the operations of" a funding recipient, the harassment must take place in a context subject to the school district's control.

These factors combine to limit a recipient's damages liability to circumstances wherein the recipient exercises substantial control over both the harasser and the context in which the known harassment occurs. Only then can the recipient be said to "expose" its students to harassment or "cause" them to undergo it "under" the recipient's programs. We agree with the dissent that these conditions are satisfied most easily and most obviously when the offender is an agent of the recipient. We rejected the use of agency analysis in *Gebser*, however, and we disagree that the term "under" somehow imports an agency requirement into Title IX. As noted above, the theory in *Gebser* was that the recipient was directly liable for its deliberate indifference to discrimination. Liability in that case did not arise because the "teacher's actions [were] treated" as those of the funding recipient; the district was directly liable for its own failure to act. The terms "subjec[t]" and "under" impose limits, but nothing about these terms requires the use of agency principles.

Where, as here, the misconduct occurs during school hours and on school grounds—the bulk of G.F.'s misconduct, in fact, took place in the classroom—the misconduct is taking place "under" an "operation" of the funding recipient. In these circumstances, the recipient retains substantial control over the context in which the harassment occurs. More importantly, however, in this setting the Board exercises significant control over the harasser. We have observed, for example, "that the nature of [the State's] power [over public schoolchildren] is custodial and tutelary, permitting a degree of supervision and control that could not be exercised over free adults." Vernonia School Dist. 47J v. Acton, 515 U.S. 646, 655 (1995). On more than one occasion, this Court has recognized the importance of school officials' "comprehensive authority . . . , consistent with fundamental constitutional safeguards, to prescribe and control conduct in the schools." Tinker v. Des Moines Independent Community School Dist., 393 U.S. 503, 507 (1969). The common law, too, recognizes the school's disciplinary authority. See Restatement (Second) of Torts § 152 (1965). We thus conclude that recipients of federal funding may be liable for "subject[ing]" their students to discrimination where the recipient is deliberately indifferent to known acts of student-on-student sexual harassment and the harasser is under the school's disciplinary authority. . . .

We stress that our conclusion here—that recipients may be liable for their deliberate indifference to known acts of peer sexual harassment—does not mean that recipients can avoid liability only by purging their schools of actionable peer harassment or that administrators must engage in particular disciplinary action. We thus disagree with respondents' contention that, if Title IX provides a cause of action for student-on-student harassment, "nothing short of expulsion of every student accused of misconduct involving sexual overtones would protect school systems from liability or damages." In fact, as we have previously noted, courts should refrain from second guessing the disciplinary decisions made by school administrators. New Jersey v. T. L.O., 469 U.S. 325, 342–43, n.9 (1985).

School administrators will continue to enjoy the flexibility they require so long as funding recipients are deemed "deliberately indifferent" to acts of student-on-student harassment only where the recipient's response to the harassment or lack thereof is clearly unreasonable in light of the known circumstances. The dissent consistently mischaracterizes this standard to require funding recipients to "remedy" peer harassment, and to "ensur[e] that . . . students conform their conduct to" certain rules. Title IX imposes no such requirements. On the contrary, the recipient must merely respond to known peer harassment in a manner that is not clearly unreasonable. This is not a mere "reasonableness" standard, as the dissent assumes. In an appropriate case, there is no reason why courts, on a motion to dismiss, for summary judgment, or for a directed verdict, could not identify a response as not "clearly unreasonable" as a matter of law.

Like the dissent, we acknowledge that school administrators shoulder substantial burdens as a result of legal constraints on their disciplinary authority. To the extent that these restrictions arise from federal statutes, Congress can review these burdens with attention to the difficult position in which such legislation may place our Nation's schools. We believe, however, that the standard set out here is sufficiently flexible to account both for the level of disciplinary authority available to the school and for the potential liability arising from certain forms of disciplinary action. A university might not, for example, be expected to exercise the same degree of control over its students that a grade school would enjoy, and it would be entirely reasonable for a school to refrain from a form of disciplinary action that would expose it to constitutional or statutory claims.

While it remains to be seen whether petitioner can show that the Board's response to reports of G.F.'s misconduct was clearly unreasonable in light of the known circumstances, petitioner may be able to show that the Board "subject[ed]" LaShonda to discrimination by failing to respond in any way over a period of five months to complaints of G.F.'s in-school misconduct from LaShonda and other female students.

B

The requirement that recipients receive adequate notice of Title IX's proscriptions also bears on the proper definition of "discrimination" in the context of a private damages action. We have elsewhere concluded that sexual harassment is a form of discrimination for Title IX purposes and that Title IX proscribes harassment with sufficient clarity to satisfy *Pennhurst*'s notice requirement and serve as a basis for a damages action. See *Gebser v. Lago Vista Independent School Dist.*, 524 U.S., at 281. Having previously determined that "sexual harassment" is "discrimination" in the school context under Title IX, we are constrained to conclude that student-on-student sexual harassment, if sufficiently severe, can likewise rise to the level of discrimination actionable under the statute. The statute's other prohibitions, moreover, help give content to the term "discrimination" in this context. Students are not only protected from discrimination, but also specifically shielded from being "excluded from participation in" or "denied the benefits of" any "education program or activity receiving Federal financial assistance." § 1681(a). The statute makes clear that, whatever else it prohibits, students must not be denied access to educational benefits and opportunities on the basis of gender. We thus conclude that funding recipients are properly held liable in damages only where they are deliberately indifferent to sexual harassment, of which they have actual knowledge, that is so severe, pervasive, and objectively offensive that it can be said to deprive the victims of access to the educational opportunities or benefits provided by the school.

The most obvious example of student-on-student sexual harassment capable of triggering a damages claim would thus involve the overt, physical deprivation of access to school resources. Consider, for example, a case in which male students physically threaten their female peers every day, successfully preventing the female students from using a particular school resource—an athletic field or a computer lab, for instance. District administrators are well aware of the daily ritual, yet they deliberately ignore requests for aid from the female students wishing to use the resource. The district's knowing refusal to take any action in response to such behavior would fly in the face of Title IX's core principles, and such deliberate indifference may appropriately be subject to claims for monetary damages. It is not necessary, however, to show physical exclusion to demonstrate that students have been deprived by the actions of another student or students of an educational opportunity on the basis of sex. Rather, a plaintiff must establish sexual harassment of students that is so severe, pervasive, and objectively offensive, and that so undermines and detracts from the victims' educational experience, that the victim-students are effectively denied equal access to an institution's resources and opportunities. Cf. Meritor Savings Bank, FSB v. Vinson, 477 U.S. 57, 67 (1986).

Whether gender-oriented conduct rises to the level of actionable "harassment" thus "depends on a constellation of surrounding circumstances, expectations, and relationships," Oncale v. Sundowner Offshore Services, Inc., 523 U.S. 75, 82 (1998), including, but not limited to, the ages of the harasser and the victim and the number of individuals involved, see OCR Title IX Guidelines 12041–42. Courts, moreover, must bear in mind that schools are unlike the adult workplace and that children may regularly interact in a manner that would be unacceptable among adults. See, e.g., Brief for National School Boards Association et al. as Amici Curiae 11 (describing "dizzying array of immature . . . behaviors by students"). Indeed, at least early on, students are still learning how to interact appropriately with their peers. It is thus understandable that, in the school setting, students often engage in insults, banter, teasing, shoving, pushing, and gender-specific conduct that is upsetting to the students subjected to it. Damages are not available for simple acts of teasing and name-calling among school children, however, even where these comments target differences in gender. Rather, in the context of student-on-student harassment, damages are available only where the behavior is so severe, pervasive, and objectively offensive that it denies its victims the equal access to education that Title IX is designed to protect.

The dissent fails to appreciate these very real limitations on a funding recipient's liability under Title IX. It is not enough to show, as the dissent would read this opinion to provide, that a student has been "teased," or "called . . . offensive names." Comparisons to an "overweight child who skips gym class because the other children tease her about her size," the student "who refuses to wear glasses to avoid the taunts of 'four-eyes,' " and "the child who refuses to go to school because the school bully calls him a 'scardy-cat' at recess," are inapposite and misleading. Nor do we contemplate, much less hold, that a mere "decline in grades is enough to survive" a motion to dismiss. The drop-off in LaShonda's grades provides necessary evidence of a potential link between her education and G.F.'s misconduct, but petitioner's ability to state a cognizable claim here depends equally on the alleged persistence and severity of G.F.'s actions, not to mention the Board's alleged knowledge and deliberate indifference. We trust that the dissent's characterization of our opinion will not mislead courts to impose more sweeping liability than we read Title IX to require.

Moreover, the provision that the discrimination occur "under any education program or activity" suggests that the behavior be serious enough to have the systemic effect of denying the victim equal access to an educational program or activity. Although, in theory, a single instance of sufficiently severe one-on-one peer harassment could be said to have such an effect, we think it unlikely that Congress would have thought such behavior sufficient to rise to this level in light of the inevitability of student misconduct and the amount of litigation that would be invited by entertaining claims of official indifference to a single instance of one-on-one peer harassment. By limiting private damages actions to cases having a systemic effect on educational programs or activities, we reconcile the general principle that Title IX prohibits official indifference to known peer sexual harassment with the practical realities of responding to student behavior, realities that Congress could not have meant to be ignored. Even the dissent suggests that Title IX liability may arise when a funding recipient remains indifferent to severe, gender-based mistreatment played out on a "widespread level" among students.

The fact that it was a teacher who engaged in harassment in *Franklin* and *Gebser* is relevant. The relationship between the harasser and the victim necessarily affects the extent to which the misconduct can be said to breach Title IX's guarantee of equal access to educational benefits and to have a systemic effect on a program or activity. Peer harassment, in particular, is less likely to satisfy these requirements than is teacher-student harassment.

C

Applying this standard to the facts at issue here, we conclude that the Eleventh Circuit erred in dismissing petitioner's complaint. Petitioner alleges that her daughter was the victim of repeated acts of sexual harassment by G.F. over a five-month period, and there are allegations in support of the conclusion that G.F.'s misconduct was severe, pervasive, and objectively offensive. The harassment was not only verbal; it included numerous acts of objectively offensive touching, and, indeed, G.F. ultimately pleaded guilty to criminal sexual misconduct. Moreover, the complaint alleges that there were multiple victims who were sufficiently disturbed by G.F.'s misconduct to seek an audience with the school principal. Further, petitioner contends that the harassment had a concrete, negative effect on her daughter's ability to receive an education. The complaint also suggests that petitioner may be able to show both actual knowledge and deliberate indifference on the part of the Board, which made no effort whatsoever either to investigate or to put an end to the harassment.

On this complaint, we cannot say "beyond doubt that [petitioner] can prove no set of facts in support of [her] claim which would entitle [her] to relief." Conley v. Gibson, 355 U.S. 41, 45–46 (1957). Accordingly, the judgment of the United States Court of Appeals for the Eleventh Circuit is reversed, and the case is remanded for further proceedings consistent with this opinion.

It is so ordered.

■ JUSTICE KENNEDY, with whom THE CHIEF JUSTICE, JUSTICE SCALIA, and JUSTICE THOMAS join, dissenting.

The Court has held that Congress' power " 'to authorize expenditure of public moneys for public purposes is not limited by the direct grants of legislative power found in the Constitution.' " South Dakota v. Dole, 483 U.S. 203, 207 (1987) (quoting United States v. Butler, 297 U.S. 1, 66 (1936)). As a consequence, Congress can use its Spending Clause power to pursue objectives outside of "Article I's 'enumerated legislative fields' " by attaching conditions to the grant of federal funds. *South Dakota v. Dole*, 483 U.S., at 207. So understood, the Spending Clause power, if wielded without concern for the federal balance, has the potential to obliterate distinctions between national and local spheres of interest and power by permitting the federal government to set policy in the most sensitive areas of traditional state concern, areas which otherwise would lie outside its reach.

A vital safeguard for the federal balance is the requirement that, when Congress imposes a condition on the States' receipt of federal funds, it "must do so unambiguously." Pennhurst State School and Hospital v. Halderman, 451 U.S. 1, 17 (1981). As the majority acknowledges, "legislation enacted . . . pursuant to the spending power is much in the nature of a contract," and the legitimacy of Congress' exercise of its power to condition funding on state compliance with congressional conditions "rests on whether the State voluntarily and knowingly accepts the terms of the 'contract.' " " 'There can, of course, be no knowing acceptance [of the terms of the putative contract] if a State is unaware of the conditions [imposed by the legislation] or is unable to ascertain what is expected of it.' " (Quoting *Pennhurst*, 451 U.S., at 17).

Our insistence that "Congress speak with a clear voice" to "enable the States to exercise their choice knowingly, cognizant of the consequences of their participation," *Pennhurst*, supra, at 17, is not based upon some abstract notion of contractual fairness. Rather, it is a concrete safeguard in the federal system. Only if States receive clear notice of the conditions attached to federal funds can they guard against excessive federal intrusion into state affairs and be vigilant in policing the boundaries of federal power. While the majority purports to give effect to these principles, it eviscerates the clear-notice safeguard of our Spending Clause jurisprudence. . . .

The Court has encountered great difficulty in establishing standards for deciding when to imply a private cause of action under a federal statute which is silent on the subject. We try to conform the judicial judgment to the bounds of likely congressional purpose but, as we observed in Gebser v. Lago Vista Independent School District, 524 U.S. 274 (1998), defining the scope of the private cause of action in general, and the damages remedy in particular, "inherently entails a degree of speculation, since it addresses an issue on which Congress has not specifically spoken."

When the statute at issue is a Spending Clause statute, this element of speculation is particularly troubling because it is in significant tension with the requirement that Spending Clause legislation give States clear notice of the consequences of their acceptance of federal funds. Without doubt, the scope of potential damages liability is one of the most significant factors a school would consider in deciding whether to receive federal funds. Accordingly, the Court must not imply a private cause of action for damages unless it can demonstrate that the congressional purpose to create the implied cause of action is so manifest that the State, when accepting federal funds, had clear notice of the terms and conditions of its monetary liability.

Today the Court fails to heed, or even to acknowledge, these limitations on its authority. The remedial scheme the majority creates today is neither sensible nor faithful to Spending Clause principles. In order to make its case for school liability for peer sexual harassment, the majority must establish that Congress gave grant recipients clear and unambiguous notice that they would be liable in money damages for failure to remedy discriminatory acts of their students. The majority must also demonstrate that the statute gives schools clear notice that one child's harassment of another constitutes "discrimination" on the basis of sex within the meaning of Title IX, and that—as applied to individual cases—the standard for liability will enable the grant recipient to distinguish inappropriate childish behavior from actionable gender discrimination. The majority does not carry these burdens.

. . . In the end, the majority not only imposes on States liability that was unexpected and unknown, but the contours of which are, as yet, unknowable. The majority's opinion purports to be narrow, but the limiting principles it proposes are illusory. The fence the Court has built is made of little sticks, and it cannot contain the avalanche of liability now set in motion. The potential costs to our schools of today's decision are difficult to estimate, but they are so great that it is most unlikely Congress intended to inflict them. . . .

I

I am aware of no basis in law or fact . . . for attributing the acts of a student to a school and, indeed, the majority does not argue that the school acts through its students. Discrimination by one student against another therefore cannot be "under" the school's program or activity as required by Title IX. The majority's imposition of liability for peer sexual harassment thus conflicts with the most natural interpretation of Title IX's "under a program or activity" limitation on school liability. At the very least, my reading undermines the majority's implicit claim that Title IX imposes an unambiguous duty on schools to remedy peer sexual harassment.

. . . In search of a principle, the majority asserts, without much elaboration, that one causes discrimination when one has some "degree of control" over the discrimination and fails to remedy it. . . . To state the majority's test is to understand that it is little more than an exercise in arbitrary line-drawing. The majority does not explain how we are to determine what degree of control is sufficient—or, more to the point, how the States were on clear notice that the Court would draw the line to encompass students. . . .

The majority nonetheless appears to see no need to justify drawing the "enough control" line to encompass students. In truth, however, a school's control over its students is much more complicated and limited than the majority acknowledges. A public school does not control its students in the way it controls its teachers or those with whom it contracts. Most public schools do not screen or select students, and their power to discipline students is far from unfettered.

Public schools are generally obligated by law to educate all students who live within defined geographic boundaries. Indeed, the Constitution of almost every State in the country guarantees the State's students a free primary and secondary public education. In at least some States, moreover, there is a continuing duty on schools to educate even students who are suspended or expelled. Schools that remove a harasser from the classroom and then attempt to fulfill their continuing-education obligation by placing the harasser in any kind of group setting, rather than by hiring expensive tutors for each student, will find themselves at continuing risk of Title IX suits brought by the other students in the alternative education program.

In addition, federal law imposes constraints on school disciplinary actions. This Court has held, for example, that due process requires "[a]t the very minimum," that a student facing suspension "be given some kind of notice and afforded some kind of hearing." Goss v. Lopez, 419 U.S. 565, 579 (1975).

The Individuals with Disabilities Education Act (IDEA), 20 U.S.C. § 1400 et seq., moreover, places strict limits on the ability of schools to take disciplinary actions against students with behavior disorder disabilities, even if the disability was not diagnosed prior to the incident triggering discipline. . . . If, as the majority would have us believe, the behavior that constitutes actionable peer sexual harassment so deviates from the normal teasing and jostling of adolescence that it puts schools on clear notice of potential liability, then a student who engages in such harassment may have at least a colorable claim of severe emotional disturbance within the meaning of IDEA. When imposing disciplinary sanction on a student harasser who might assert a colorable IDEA claim, the school must navigate a complex web of statutory provisions and DOE regulations that significantly limit its discretion.

The practical obstacles schools encounter in ensuring that thousands of immature students conform their conduct to acceptable norms may be even more significant than the legal obstacles. School districts cannot exercise the same measure of control over thousands of students that they do over a few hundred adult employees. The limited resources of our schools must be conserved for basic educational services. Some schools lack the resources even to deal with serious problems of violence and are already overwhelmed with disciplinary problems of all kinds.

Perhaps even more startling than its broad assumptions about school control over primary and secondary school students is the majority's failure to grapple in any meaningful way with the distinction between elementary and secondary schools, on the one hand, and universities on the other. The majority bolsters its argument that schools can control their students' actions by quoting our decision in Vernonia School Dist. 47J v. Acton, 515 U.S. 646, 655 (1995), for the proposition that " 'the nature of [the State's] power [over public school children] is custodial and tutelary, permitting a degree of supervision and control that could not be exercised over free adults.' " Yet the majority's holding would appear to apply with equal force to universities, which do not exercise custodial and tutelary power over their adult students

A university's power to discipline its students for speech that may constitute sexual harassment is also circumscribed by the First Amendment. A number of federal courts have already confronted difficult problems raised by university speech codes designed to deal with peer sexual and racial harassment. See, e.g., UWM Post, Inc. v. Board of Regents of University of Wisconsin System, 774 F.Supp. 1163 (E.D.Wis.1991) (striking down university speech code that prohibited, inter alia, "discriminatory comments" directed at an individual that "intentionally . . . demean" the "sex . . . of the individual" and "[c]reate an intimidating, hostile or demeaning environment for education, university related work, or other university-authorized activity").

The difficulties associated with speech codes simply underscore the limited nature of a university's control over student behavior that may be viewed as sexual harassment. Despite the fact that the majority relies on the assumption that schools exercise a great deal of control over their students to justify creating the private cause of action in the first instance, it does not recognize the obvious limits on a university's ability to control its students as a reason to doubt the propriety of a private cause of action for peer harassment. It simply uses them as a factor in determining whether the university's response was reasonable. . . .

II

Our decision in *Gebser* makes clear that the Spending Clause clear-notice rule requires both that the recipients be on general notice of the kind of conduct the statute prohibits, and—at least when money damages are sought—that they be on notice that illegal conduct is occurring in a given situation.

Title IX, however, gives schools neither notice that the conduct the majority labels peer "sexual harassment" is gender discrimination within the meaning of the Act nor any guidance in distinguishing in individual cases between actionable discrimination and the immature behavior of children and adolescents. The majority thus imposes on schools potentially crushing financial liability for student conduct that is not prohibited in clear terms by Title IX and that cannot, even after today's opinion, be identified by either schools or courts with any precision.

The law recognizes that children—particularly young children—are not fully accountable for their actions because they lack the capacity to exercise mature judgment. It should surprise no one, then, that the schools that are the primary locus of most children's social development are rife with inappropriate behavior by children who are just learning to interact with their peers. The amici on the front lines of our schools describe the situation best:

> Unlike adults in the workplace, juveniles have limited life experiences or familial influences upon which to establish an understanding of appropriate behavior. The real world of school discipline is a rough-and-tumble place where students practice newly learned vulgarities, erupt with anger, tease and embarrass each other, share offensive notes, flirt, push and shove in the halls, grab and offend.

Brief for National School Boards Association et al. as Amici Curiae 10–11.

No one contests that much of this "dizzying array of immature or uncontrollable behaviors by students," is inappropriate, even "objectively offensive" at times, and that parents and schools have a moral and ethical responsibility to help students learn to interact with their peers in an appropriate manner. It is doubtless the case, moreover, that much of this inappropriate behavior is directed toward members of the opposite sex, as children in the throes of adolescence struggle to express their emerging sexual identities.

It is a far different question, however, whether it is either proper or useful to label this immature, childish behavior gender discrimination. Nothing in Title IX suggests that Congress even contemplated this question, much less answered it in the affirmative in unambiguous terms. The majority, nevertheless, has no problem labeling the conduct of fifth graders "sexual harassment" and "gender discrimination." . . .

In reality, there is no established body of federal or state law on which courts may draw in defining the student conduct that qualifies as Title IX gender discrimination. Analogies to Title VII hostile environment harassment are inapposite, because schools are not workplaces and children are not adults. The norms of the adult workplace that have defined hostile environment sexual harassment, see, e.g., Oncale v. Sundowner Offshore Services, Inc., 523 U.S. 75 (1998), are not easily translated to peer relationships in schools, where teenage romantic relationships and dating are a part of everyday life. Analogies to Title IX teacher sexual harassment of students are similarly flawed. A teacher's sexual overtures toward a student are always inappropriate; a teenager's romantic overtures to a classmate (even when persistent and unwelcome) are an inescapable part of adolescence.

The majority admits that, under its approach, "[w]hether gender-oriented conduct rises to the level of actionable 'harassment' . . . 'depends on a constellation of surrounding circumstances, expectations, and relationships, including, but not limited to, the ages of the harasser and the victim and the number of individuals involved.' " The majority does not explain how a school is supposed to discern from this mishmash of factors what is actionable discrimination. [And the] majority does not even purport to explain . . . what constitutes an actionable denial of "equal access to education." Is equal access denied when a girl who tires of being chased by the boys at recess refuses to go outside? When she cannot concentrate during class because she is worried about the recess activities? When she pretends to be sick one day so she can stay home from school? It appears the majority is content to let juries decide. . . .

III

The majority's inability to provide any workable definition of actionable peer harassment simply underscores the myriad ways in which an opinion that purports to be narrow is, in fact, so broad that it will support untold numbers of lawyers who will prove adept at presenting cases that will withstand the defendant school districts' pretrial motions. Each of the barriers to run-away litigation the majority offers us crumbles under the weight of even casual scrutiny.

For example, the majority establishes what sounds like a relatively high threshold for liability—"denial of equal access" to education—and, almost in the same breath, makes clear that alleging a decline in grades is enough to survive 12(b)(6) and, it follows, to state a winning claim. The majority seems oblivious to the fact that almost every child, at some point, has trouble in school because he or she is being teased by his or her peers. The girl who wants to skip recess because she is teased by the boys is no different from the overweight child who skips gym class because the other children tease her about her size in the locker room; or the child who risks flunking out because he refuses to wear glasses to avoid the taunts of "four-eyes"; or the child who refuses to go to school because the school bully calls him a "scaredy-cat" at recess. Most children respond to teasing in ways that detract from their ability to learn. The majority's test for actionable harassment will, as a result, sweep in almost all of the more innocuous conduct it acknowledges as a ubiquitous part of school life.

The string of adjectives the majority attaches to the word "harassment"—"severe, pervasive, and objectively offensive"—likewise fails to narrow the class of conduct that can trigger liability, since the touchstone for determining whether there is Title IX liability is the effect on the child's ability to get an education. Indeed, the Court's reliance on the impact on the child's educational experience suggests that the "objective offensiveness" of a comment is to be judged by reference to a reasonable child at whom the comments were aimed. Not only is that standard likely to be quite expansive, it also gives schools—and juries—little guidance, requiring them to attempt to gauge the sensitivities of, for instance, the average seven year old. . . .

The majority's limitations on peer sexual harassment suits cannot hope to contain the flood of liability the Court today begins. The elements of the Title IX claim created by the majority will be easy not only to allege but also to prove. A female plaintiff who pleads only that a boy called her offensive names, that she told a teacher, that the teacher's response was unreasonable, and that her school performance suffered as a result, appears to state a successful claim.

There will be no shortage of plaintiffs to bring such complaints. Our schools are charged each day with educating millions of children. Of those millions of students, a large percentage will, at some point during their school careers, experience something they consider sexual harassment. . . . The number of potential lawsuits against our schools is staggering.

The cost of defending against peer sexual harassment suits alone could overwhelm many school districts, particularly since the majority's liability standards will allow almost any plaintiff to get to summary judgment, if not to a jury. In addition, there are no damages caps on the judicially implied private cause of action under Title IX. As a result, school liability in one peer sexual harassment suit could approach, or even exceed, the total federal funding of many school districts. Petitioner, for example, seeks damages of $500,000 in this case. Respondent school district received approximately $679,000 in federal aid in 1992–93. The school district sued in *Gebser* received only $120,000 in federal funds a year. Indeed, the entire 1992–93 budget of that district was only $1.6 million. . . .

Even schools that resist overzealous enforcement may find that the most careful and reasoned response to a sexual harassment complaint nonetheless provokes litigation. . . . A school faced with a peer sexual harassment complaint in the wake of the majority's decision may well be beset with litigation from every side. One student's demand for a quick response to her harassment complaint will conflict with the alleged harasser's demand for due process. Another student's demand for a harassment-free classroom will conflict with the alleged harasser's claim to a mainstream placement under the Individuals with Disabilities Education Act or with his state constitutional right to a continuing, free public education. On college campuses, and even in secondary schools, a student's claim that the school should remedy a sexually hostile environment will conflict with the alleged harasser's claim that his speech, even if offensive, is protected by the First Amendment. In each of these situations, the school faces the risk of suit, and maybe even multiple suits, regardless of its response. See Doe v. University of Illinois, 138 F.3d, at 679 (Posner, C. J., dissenting from denial of rehearing en banc) ("Liability for failing to prevent or rectify sexual harassment of one student by another places a school on a razor's edge, since the remedial measures that it takes against the alleged harasser are as likely to expose the school to a suit by him as a failure to take those measures would be to expose the school to a suit by the victim of the alleged harassment"). . . .

In the final analysis, this case is about federalism. Yet the majority's decision today says not one word about the federal balance. . . . Defining the appropriate role of schools in teaching and supervising children who are beginning to explore their own sexuality and learning how to express it to others is one of the most complex and sensitive issues our schools face. Such decisions are best made by parents and by the teachers and school administrators who can counsel with them. The delicacy and immense significance of teaching children about sexuality should cause the Court to act with great restraint before it displaces state and local governments.

Heedless of these considerations, the Court rushes onward, finding that the cause of action it creates is necessary to effect the congressional design. It is not. Nothing in Title IX suggests that Congress intended or contemplated the result the Court reaches today, much less dictated it in unambiguous terms. Today's decision cannot be laid at the feet of Congress; it is the responsibility of the Court. . . .

As its holding makes painfully clear, the majority's watered-down version of the Spending Clause clear-statement rule is no substitute for the real protections of state and local autonomy that our constitutional system requires. If there be any doubt of the futility of the Court's attempt to hedge its holding about with words of limitation for future cases, the result in this case provides the answer. The complaint of this fifth grader survives and the school will be compelled to answer in federal court. We can be assured that like suits will follow—suits, which in cost and number, will impose serious financial burdens on local school districts, the taxpayers who support them, and the children they serve. Federalism and our struggling school systems deserve better from this Court. I dissent.

NOTES ON DAVIS V. MONROE COUNTY BOARD OF EDUCATION

1. DEFINING SEXUAL HARASSMENT

The Court took some care in defining sexual harassment as it applies to cases of one student harassing another. In a variation on the definition under Title VII, the Court said that "a plaintiff must establish sexual harassment of students that is so severe, pervasive, and objectively offensive, and that so undermines and detracts from the victims' educational experience, that the victim-students are effectively denied equal access to an institution's resources and opportunities."

The last element in the quoted definition derives from the language of Title IX requiring equal access, regardless of sex, to all federally funded educational programs. Is this element more difficult to satisfy than the corresponding element under Title VII that the harassment be so severe or pervasive "to alter the terms and conditions of [the victim's] employment and create an abusive working environment"? Meritor Savings Bank v. Vinson, 477 U.S. 57, 67 (1986). Did the majority opinion in *Davis* just transpose this requirement to the educational context? If so, is that a sufficient answer to the dissent's argument that sexual harassment among students is more difficult to define and to identify than sexual harassment among employees?

How important is the specific wording of Title IX in formulating the definition of prohibited harassment? Recall that public schools are covered by § 1983, as well as Title IX. Any plaintiff concerned about a restrictive definition of sexual harassment under Title IX could avoid these restrictions by adding a claim under § 1983. Of course, only vicarious liability of the school is at issue in claims of student-on-student sexual harassment, whether these claims are brought under Title IX or under § 1983. The harassing student is neither a recipient of federal funds under Title IX nor an official acting under color of state law under § 1983, so there can be no claim of individual liability. Should that make a difference in the definition of the underlying prohibited conduct?

2. APPLYING THE STANDARD OF RECKLESS INDIFFERENCE

The majority in *Davis* applied the standard of reckless indifference from *Gebser* to determine the school's vicarious liability. This standard was itself developed in cases of municipal liability under § 1983. Just as the majority was careful to define sexual harassment narrowly, it was also careful to limit the scope of vicarious liability for student-on-student sexual harassment. A recipient of federal funds is liable only "where the recipient is deliberately indifferent to known acts of student-on-student sexual harassment and the harasser is under the school's disciplinary authority." What does the requirement that the harasser be "under the school's disciplinary authority" add to the standard for vicarious liability? Is it more easily satisfied when the harassment occurs in the classroom, as alleged of most of the incidents in *Davis*, or is it satisfied if the harassment merely occurs on school grounds and during school hours? What about the claims of student-on-student harassment at colleges and universities, emphasized by Justice Kennedy in his dissent?

Does the added requirement have its source in the language of Title IX, prohibiting only discrimination by recipients of federal funds, or in constitutional concerns about federalism and the limits of congressional power under the Spending Clause? Again, the ability of plaintiffs to assert claims under § 1983 against public schools, under seemingly the same standard for vicarious liability, casts doubt on the significance of any limitations derived solely from Title IX and its source in congressional power under the Spending Clause. Whatever the arguments based on federalism for limiting liability under Title IX, they seem to apply with equal force to claims under § 1983. What is the common theme that unites these two statutes? The need to avoid imposing liability on units of state government that are not themselves at fault? The limits on the concept of discrimination as a basis for finding liability and remedying inequality?

3. CONSEQUENCES OF THE DECISION

Both the limitations on liability adopted by the majority opinion and the criticism emphasized by the dissent reflect a fear that school districts and courts might be flooded with claims of student-on-student sexual harassment. Is the conduct alleged in *Davis* likely to arise with any frequency? Remember that the harassing student was eventually convicted of sexual assault on the plaintiff, long after the plaintiff had repeatedly complained to school officials of his behavior, or so the plaintiff alleged in the complaint. Is the decision necessarily limited to such extreme facts? Or does it open the door to allegations and evidence that reveal a wide range of disruptive conduct, the "dizzying array of immature or uncontrollable behaviors by students" cited in both the majority opinion and the dissent?

Do students, or their parents, have greater incentives to sue than employees who believe they have been subjected to sexual harassment? Or should the question be asked, not about potential plaintiffs but about their attorneys? Section 1988 authorizes the award of attorney's fees to prevailing plaintiffs in Title IX cases, just as in § 1983 cases. One large difference between the two kinds of cases is that plaintiffs under Title VII usually have an immediate economic stake in keeping their jobs, or if they have quit or been discharged because of sexual harassment, in obtaining recovery of lost wages or salary. Are school children and their parents subject to any similar economic loss because of sexual harassment? Are they more likely than plaintiffs under Title VII to be satisfied with a change in policy that simply eliminates the alleged harassment without any compensation for past wrongdoing? Does this affect the likelihood that they will take their case to court? That they will find an attorney willing to take their case?

4. *ALEXANDER V. SANDOVAL*

After *Gebser* and *Davis*, the tide turned against expansion of remedies against recipients of federal funds. The ability of private litigants to bring claims under Title VI, and by inference, under Title IX, was further restricted by Alexander v. Sandoval, 532 U.S. 275 (2001). As discussed more fully in the Notes on Non–Constitutional Rights Enforceable Under § 1983 in Chapter I, this case held that private litigants could not bring claims of disparate impact based on regulations issued under Title VI, reasoning that such a private right of action could only be based on the statute itself rather than on regulations issued under the statute. The Court did not reach the question whether the regulations prohibiting practices with discriminatory effects were themselves valid. It concluded only that there was no implied private right of action to enforce such regulations. Finding no such basis in the statutory language of Title VI, the Court dismissed the plaintiff's claim. This holding seemingly applies as well to claims under Title IX, to the extent that regulations under that statute prohibit practices with discriminatory effects. For instance, the regulations governing sex discrimination in intercollegiate athletics might be construed to prohibit practices with discriminatory effects, and to that extent, be open to the argument that Title IX provides no private right of action for violation of their terms.

5. *BARNES V. GORMAN*

Imposing further restrictions on claims by private plaintiffs, in Barnes v. Gorman, 536 U.S. 181 (2002), the Supreme Court barred the award of punitive damages on implied rights of action under statutes modeled on Title VI. As in *Alexander v. Sandoval*, the reasoning in this decision plainly reaches claims under Title IX. The specific case concerned a claim under Title II of the Americans with Disabilities Act, which requires recipients of federal funds not to discriminate against the disabled, on the model of the prohibition against racial discrimination in Title VI. The plaintiff in this case, like a private plaintiff under Title IX, asserted an implied right of action based on the defendant's obligation not to discriminate. With particular reference to the remedies made available under Title IX in *Franklin v. Gwinnett County Public Schools*, the Court stated that "*Franklin*, however, did not describe the scope of 'appropriate relief.' We take up this question today." The Court therefore plainly intended its decision to bar the recovery of punitive damages by private plaintiffs under Title IX.

6. BIBLIOGRAPHY

For discussions of sexual harassment under Title IX, see Michelle J. Anderson, The Legacy of the Prompt Complaint Requirement, Corroboration Requirement, and Cautionary Instructions on Campus Sexual Assault, 84 B.U. L. Rev. 945 (2004); Julie Davies, Assessing Institutional Responsibility for Sexual Harassment in Education, 77 Tul. L. Rev. 387 (2002); Nancy Hogshead–Makar and Sheldon Elliot Steinbach, Intercollegiate Athletics'

Unique Environment for Sexual Harassment Claims: Balancing the Realities of Athletics with Preventing Potential Claims, 13 Marq. Sports L. Rev. 173 (2003); Wendy J. Murphy, Using Title IX's "Prompt and Equitable" Hearing Requirements to Force Schools to Provide Fair Judicial Proceedings to Redress Sexual Assault on Campus, 40 New Eng. L. Rev. 1007 (2006); Grayson Sang Walker, The Evolution and Limits of Title IX Doctrine on Peer Sexual Assault, 45 Harv. C.R.–C.L. L. Rev. 95 (2010); Symposium, Title IX and School Bullying, 12 Duke J. Gender L. & Pol'y 1 (2005) (with articles by Paul M. Secunda, Nan Stein, Susan Hanley Kosse and Robert H. Wright).

Several articles and symposia have offered an overall evaluation of Title IX on the occasion of the thirtieth anniversary of its enactment, among them Catherine Pieronek, Title IX Beyond Thirty: A Review of Recent Developments, 30 J. Coll. & Univ. L. 75 (2003); Symposium, Title IX Women, Athletics and the Law (with foreword by Paula A. Monopoli and articles by William C. Duncan, Jocelyn Samuels and Suzanne Sangree), 3 Margins L.J. 209 (2003); Symposium, Title IX at Thirty (with articles by Ted Leland, Karen Peters, Jocelyn Samuels, Kristen Galles, Martha Burk, and Natasha Plumly), 14 Marq. Sports L. Rev. 1 (2003). See also David S. Cohen, Title IX: Beyond Equal Protection, 28 Harv. J.L. & Gender 217 (2005); Lindsay Niehaus, The Title IX Problem: Is It Sufficiently Comprehensive to Preclude § 1983 Actions?, 27 Quinnipiac L. Rev. 499 (2009).

INTRODUCTORY NOTE ON TITLE IX AND ATHLETICS

Title IX has proved to be a major source of litigation over athletics, both at the college level and in high school. Most of the cases has been over the limited athletic opportunities available to female students and mainly the absence of teams and sports for women. Only a few cases have allowed female students to try out for men's team in the absence of a women's team. Mercer v. Duke Univ., 190 F.3d 643 (4th Cir. 1999) (woman allowed to try out to be place kicker on otherwise male football team cannot be excluded from team because of sex); Saint v. Nebraska School Activities Ass'n, 684 F. Supp. 626 (D. Neb. 1988) (granting preliminary injunction to high school girl seeking to try out for boys' wrestling team). These cases, however, are truly exceptional. Sex segregation in athletics has been taken for granted, partly because of a presumed difference in athletic ability between the sexes and partly because of special concerns about mixed teams in contact sports. There has been, in any event, no "sex blind" counterpart to "colorblind" justice in athletics. Attempts to apply a simple analogy from cases of racial equality and integration to sexual equality and sports have failed.

The cases on athletics under Title IX typically do not raise issues analogous to the restricted liability and defenses typical in other civil rights actions or in cases of sexual harassment. Any school that receives federal funds is plainly responsible under Title IX for its athletic program. The main issue in these cases is the correct baseline for assessing the opportunities available to female students. At the college level, this issue has been most controversial in intercollegiate athletics, in which most athletic programs historically have excluded women almost entirely and in which football still is a sport entirely for men without any corresponding women's sport. The large size of football teams and the massive revenue that they produce has complicated the effort to define an appropriate balance between the number of slots on women's teams and the number on men's teams in intercollegiate sports. As a practical matter, few colleges and universities are prepared to abolish their football teams and yet they cannot easily create an equally large number of slots for women in sports in which they alone participate.

This dilemma first led Congress to consider an amendment to Title IX that would have exempted "revenue sports"—football, men's basketball, and now women's basketball—from any requirement under Title IX that colleges and universities provide an equal opportunity to women to compete in intercollegiate athletics. Congress refused to enact this exemption and instead gave authority to the Office of Civil Rights, now in the Department of Education, to promulgate regulations on sex discrimination in intercollegiate athletics. Education Amendments of 1974, Pub. L. No. 93–380 (1974), § 844, 93 Stat. 4093, 4271. The Office of Civil Rights promulgated regulations, summarized in the case that follows, on the allocation of slots between women's and men's teams in intercollegiate sports. These regulations and other statements of regulatory policy have caused colleges and universities to increase the number of women's teams in a variety of sports without, however, offering men's teams in the same sport.

In the case that follows, the university kept the women's varsity swimming team but discontinued the men's team. Other variations in this fact pattern have also emerged. In the leading case of Cohen v. Brown University, 101 F.3d 155 (1st Cir. 1996), the university cut two women's teams and, at the same time, two men's teams in other sports. In a lengthy opinion, the Court of Appeals for the First Circuit held that the university violated Title IX by cutting the women's teams, but not the men's teams, because the cuts caused the percentage of slots on women's teams (less than 37% of the total) to fall significantly below the percentage of women in the university's undergraduate enrollment (almost 48%). This test for equality—requiring proportionality between the slots on women's teams and the percentage of women in the school's overall enrollment—has proved to be controversial. See John C. Weistart, Gender and Sports: Setting a Course for College Athletics: Can Gender Equity Find a Place in Commercialized College Sports?, 3 Duke J. Gender L. & Pol'y 191 (1996); Jerry R. Parkinson, Grappling With Gender Equity, 5 Wm. & Mary Bill of Rts. J. 75 (1996). The test is most controversial when it causes colleges and universities to cut men's teams in order to increase the percentage of positions allocated to women's teams. The following case takes up one challenge to this practice, both under Title IX and the Constitution.

For criticism of the continuing exclusion of women from contact sports, see B. Glenn George, Fifty/Fifty: Ending Sex Segregation in School Sports, 63 Ohio St. L.J. 1107 (2002); Suzanne Sangree, Title IX and the Contact Sports Exemption: Gender Stereotypes in a Civil Rights Statute, 32 Conn. L. Rev. 381 (2000). See also B. Glenn George, Title IX and the Scholarship Dilemma, 9 Marq. Sports L.J. 273 (1999).

For articles generally defending the allocation of athletic opportunities in proportion to enrollments, see Joseph Z. Fleming, Title IX from The Red Rose Crew to Grutter: The Law and Literature of Sports, 14 Fordham Intell. Prop. Media & Ent. L.J. 793 (2004); Kimberly A. Yuracko, One for You and One for Me: Is Title IX's Sex–Based Proportionality Requirement for College Varsity Athletic Positions Defensible?, 97 Nw. U. L. Rev. 731 (2003); Diane Heckman, The Glass Sneaker: Thirty Years of Victories and Defeats Involving

Title IX and Sex Discrimination in Athletics, 13 Fordham Intell. Prop. Media & Ent. L.J. 551 (2003); Patrick N. Findlay, The Case for Requiring a Proportionality Test to Assess Compliance with Title IX in High School Athletics, 23 N. Ill. U. L. Rev. 29 (2002); Deborah Brake, The Struggle for Sex Equality in Sport and the Theory Behind Title IX, 34 U. Mich. J. L. Reform 12 (2000–01). See also Neena K. Chaudhry and Marcia D. Greenberger, Seasons of Change: *Communities for Equity v. Michigan High School Athletic Association*, 13 UCLA Women's L.J. 1 (2003) (arguing for increased opportunities for female high school students).

For criticism of interpretations of Title IX that rely solely upon proportionality of athletic opportunities with overall enrollment figures for male and female students, see Jessica Gavora, Tilting the Playing Field: Schools, Sports, Sex and Title IX (2002); John J. Almond & Daniel A. Cohen. Navigating into the New "Safe Harbor": Model Interest Surveys as a New Tool for Title IX Compliance Programs, 8 Vand. J. Ent. & Tech. L. 1 (2005); Erin E. Buzuvis, Survey Says . . . A Critical Analysis of the New Title IX Policy and a Proposal for Reform, 91 Iowa L. Rev. 821 (2006); Elisa Hatlevig, Title IX Compliance: Looking Past the Proportionality Prong, 12 Sports Law. J. 87 (2005); J. Brad Reich, All the [Athletes] Are Equal, But Some Are More Equal Than Others: An Objective Evaluation of Title IX's Past, Present, and Recommendations for Its Future, 108 Penn St. L. Rev. 525 (2003); Gary R. Roberts, Evaluating Gender Equity Within the Framework of Intercollegiate Athletics' Conflicting Value Systems, 77 Tul. L. Rev. 997 (2003).

Kelley v. Board of Trustees

United States Court of Appeals for the Seventh Circuit, 1994.
35 F.3d 265.

■ CUMMINGS, CIRCUIT JUDGE.

On May 7, 1993, the University of Illinois announced that it intended to terminate four varsity athletic programs, including the men's swimming program, effective July 1, 1993. On May 25, 1993, the plaintiffs, all members of the University of Illinois' men's swimming team prior to its termination, brought suit against the Board of Trustees of the University, its chancellor, athletic director and associate athletic director ("defendants"), alleging that defendants violated Title IX of the Education Amendments of 1972 and the Equal Protection Clause of the Fourteenth Amendment. Plaintiffs' complaint sought damages, as well as an injunction prohibiting the defendants from terminating the men's swimming program, under 42 U.S.C. § 1983 and 42 U.S.C. § 1985(3). In response, defendants filed a motion to dismiss, which the parties agreed to convert to a motion for summary judgment. Plaintiffs moved for a preliminary injunction. After hearing testimony in support of plaintiffs' request for a preliminary injunction and receiving affidavits in support of defendants' motion for summary judgment, the district court granted summary judgment in favor of the defendants and found that the request for a preliminary injunction was therefore moot. Plaintiffs now appeal.

I.

Title IX of the Education Amendments of 1972 provides that

> No person . . . shall, on the basis of sex, be excluded from participation in, be denied the benefits of, or be subjected to discrimination un-

der any education program or activity [other than those specifically described in the Act] receiving Federal financial assistance. . . .

In 1974, Congress requested that the Secretary of the Department of Health, Education and Welfare prepare and publish regulations implementing the provisions of Title IX, "includ[ing,] with respect to intercollegiate athletic activities[,] reasonable provisions considering the nature of particular sports." Pub.L. 93–380, 88 Stat. 484, 612 (1974). Promulgated the following year, the pertinent regulation allows schools to field single-sex teams in certain circumstances[1] but requires that they "provide equal athletic opportunity for . . . both sexes." 34 C.F.R. § 106.41(c). Section 106.41(c) sets out the factors to be examined in determining whether a school provides equal athletic opportunity. Chief among these, and of primary concern here, is "[w]hether the selection of sports and levels of competition effectively accommodate the interests and abilities of members of both sexes." Although § 106.41(c) lists nine other factors, an institution may violate Title IX solely by failing to accommodate effectively the interests and abilities of student athletes of both sexes. See Roberts v. Colorado State Board of Agriculture, 998 F.2d 824, 828 (10th Cir. 1993); Cohen v. Brown University, 991 F.2d 888, 897–98 (1st Cir. 1993).

In 1979, the Department of Health, Education and Welfare, in an effort to encourage self-policing, issued a policy interpretation providing "guidance on what constitutes compliance with the law." 44 Fed.Reg. 71, 413 (1979). According to the policy interpretation, an institution has effectively accommodated the interests of its male and female students if it satisfies any of three benchmarks:

> (1) Whether intercollegiate level participation opportunities for male and female students are provided in numbers substantially proportionate to their respective enrollments; or
>
> (2) Where the members of one sex have been and are underrepresented among intercollegiate athletes, whether the institution can show a history and continuing practice of program expansion which is demonstrably responsive to the developing interest and abilities of the members of that sex; or
>
> (3) Where members of one sex are underrepresented among intercollegiate athletes, and the institution cannot show a continuing practice of program expansion . . . , whether it can be demonstrated that the interests and abilities of the members of that sex have been fully and effectively accommodated by the present program.

44 Fed.Reg. 71, 418 (1979). In essence the policy interpretation establishes a presumption that "effective accommodation" has been achieved if males and females at a school participate in intercollegiate sports in numbers substantially proportionate to the number of students of each sex enrolled at the institution (Benchmark 1). If substantial proportionality has not been achieved, a school must demonstrate either that it has a continuing practice of increasing the athletic opportunities of the underrepresented sex (Benchmark 2) or that its existing programs effectively accommodate the interests of that sex (Benchmark 3).

---

[1] An educational institution may (34 C.F.R. § 106.41(b)): "[O]perate or sponsor separate teams for members of each sex where selection for such teams is based on competitive skill or the activity involved is a contact sport. . . . For the purposes of this part, contact sports include boxing, wrestling, rugby, ice hockey, football, basketball and other sports the purpose or major activity of which involves bodily contact."

II.

In 1982, the Office of Civil Rights of the United States Department of Education determined that the University of Illinois had denied its female students equal athletic opportunities. Relying on the University's representations that it would remedy the disparity within a reasonable period of time, the Office of Civil Rights concluded that the school was not in violation of Title IX. A decade later, however, female participation in intercollegiate athletics at the University of Illinois continued to be disproportionate to female undergraduate enrollment. Thus in 1993, for example, while women comprised 44% of the student body of the University, they accounted for only 23.4% of the school's intercollegiate athletes.

It was against this backdrop that the decision to cut the men's swimming program was made. Faced with a significant deficit in its athletic budget—$600,000 before the receipt of substantial, unanticipated income from a college football bowl game—the University determined that it would need to reduce athletic costs significantly. Determined to field only teams "capable of competing for championships in the Big Ten Conference [the athletic conference to which the University belongs] and the National Collegiate Athletic Association" (Appellees' Br. at 7), the University concluded that it would have to discontinue certain intercollegiate teams in order to eliminate its deficit.

While the University's decision to reduce its athletic offerings was motivated by budget considerations, other considerations—including the need to comply with Title IX—influenced the selection of particular programs to be terminated. . . .

Men's swimming was selected for termination because, among other things, the program was historically weak, swimming is not a widely offered athletic activity in high schools, and it does not have a large spectator following. The University did not eliminate the women's swimming program because the school's legal counsel advised that such action would put the University at risk of violating Title IX.

III.

The University's decision not to terminate the woman's swimming program was—given the requirements of Title IX and the applicable regulation and policy interpretation—extremely prudent. The percentage of women involved in intercollegiate athletics at the University of Illinois is substantially lower than the percentage of women enrolled at the school. If the University had terminated the women's swimming program, it would have been vulnerable to a finding that it was in violation of Title IX. Female participation would have continued to be substantially disproportionate to female enrollment, and women with a demonstrated interest in an intercollegiate athletic activity and demonstrated ability to compete at the intercollegiate level would be left without an opportunity to participate in their sport. The University could, however, eliminate the men's swimming program without violating Title IX since even after eliminating the program, men's participation in athletics would continue to be more than substantially proportionate to their presence in the University's student body. And as the caselaw makes clear, if the percentage of student-athletes of a particular sex is substantially proportionate to the percentage of students of that sex in the general student population, the athletic interests of that sex are presumed to have been accommodated. The University's decision to retain the women's swimming program—even though budget constraints required that the men's program be terminated—was a reasonable response to the requirements of the applicable regulation and policy interpretation.

Plaintiffs contend, however, that the applicable regulation, 34 C.F.R. § 106.41, and policy interpretation, 44 Fed.Reg. 71, 418 (1979), pervert Title IX. Title IX, plaintiffs contend, "ha[s] through some alchemy of bureaucratic regulation been transformed from a statute which prohibits discrimination on the basis of sex into a statute that mandates discrimination against males . . . " (Br. 9). Or, as plaintiffs put it later: "If a university is required by Title IX to eliminate men from varsity athletic competition . . . , then the same Title IX [sh]ould require the university to eliminate women from the academic departments where they are over[-]represented and men from departments where they have been over[-]represented. Such a result would be ridiculous." (Br. 10).

We agree that such a result would be ridiculous. But Congress itself recognized that addressing discrimination in athletics presented a unique set of problems not raised in areas such as employment and academics. See, e.g., Sex Discrimination Regulations, Hearings Before the Subcommittee on Post Secondary Education of the Committee on Education and Labor, 94th Cong. 1st Sess. at 46, 54, 125, 129, 152, 177, 299–300 (1975); 118 Cong.Rec. 5,807 (1972) (statement of Sen. Bayh); 117 Cong.Rec. 30,407 (1971) (same). Congress therefore specifically directed the agency in charge of administering Title IX to issue, with respect to "intercollegiate athletic activities," regulations containing "reasonable provisions considering the nature of particular sports." Pub.L. No. 93–380, 88 Stat. 484, 612. And where Congress has specifically delegated to an agency the responsibility to articulate standards governing a particular area, we must accord the ensuing regulation considerable deference. Chevron U.S.A. v. Natural Resources Defense Council, Inc., 467 U.S. 837, 844 (1984) (Where Congress has expressly delegated to an agency the power to "elucidate a specific provision of a statute by regulation," the resulting regulations should be given "controlling weight unless they are arbitrary, capricious, or manifestly contrary to the statute.").

The regulation at issue here is neither "arbitrary [n]or manifestly contrary to the statute." The regulation provides that notwithstanding Title IX's requirement that "[n]o person . . . shall, on the basis of sex, be excluded from participation in . . . any . . . activity," a school may "sponsor separate teams for members of each sex where selection for such teams is based upon competitive skill or the activity involved is a contact sport." 34 C.F.R. § 106.41(a), (b). Such a provision is not at odds with the purpose of Title IX[5] and we do not understand plaintiffs to argue that it is. And since 34 C.F.R. § 106.41 is not manifestly contrary to the objectives of Title IX, this Court must accord it deference.

Plaintiffs, while they concede the validity of 34 C.F.R. § 106.41, argue that the substantial proportionality test contained in the agency's policy interpretation of that regulation establishes a gender-based quota system, a scheme they allege is contrary to the mandates of Title IX. But the policy interpretation does not, as plaintiffs suggest, mandate statistical balancing. Rather the policy interpretation merely creates a presumption that a school is in compliance with Title IX and the applicable regulation when it

---

[5] Congress would indeed be surprised to learn that Title IX mandated co-ed football teams.

achieves such a statistical balance. Even if substantial proportionality has not been achieved, a school may establish that it is in compliance by demonstrating either that it has a continuing practice of increasing the athletic opportunities of the underrepresented sex or that its existing programs effectively accommodate the interests of that sex.

Moreover, once it is agreed Title IX does not require that all teams be co-ed—a point the plaintiffs concede—and that 34 C.F.R. § 106.41 is therefore a valid regulation, schools must be provided some means of establishing that despite offering single-sex teams, they have provided "equal athletic opportunit[ies] . . . for both sexes." Undoubtedly the agency responsible for enforcement of the statute could have required schools to sponsor a women's program for every men's program offered and vice versa. Requiring parallel teams would certainly have been the simplest method of ensuring equality of opportunity—and plaintiffs would doubtless have preferred this approach since, had it been adopted, the men's swimming program would likely have been saved. It was not unreasonable, however, for the agency to reject this course of action. Requiring parallel teams is a rigid approach that denies schools the flexibility to respond to the differing athletic interests of men and women. It was perfectly acceptable, therefore, for the agency to chart a different course and adopt an enforcement scheme that measures compliance by analyzing how a school has allocated its various athletic resources.

This Court must defer to an agency's interpretation of its regulations if the interpretation is reasonable, Martin v. Occupational Safety & Health Review Comm'n, 499 U.S. 144, 150 (1991), a standard the policy interpretation at issue here meets. Measuring compliance through an evaluation of a school's allocation of its athletic resources allows schools flexibility in meeting the athletic interests of their students and increases the chance that the actual interests of those students will be met. And if compliance with Title IX is to be measured through this sort of analysis, it is only practical that schools be given some clear way to establish that they have satisfied the requirements of the statute. The substantial proportionality contained in Benchmark 1 merely establishes such a safe harbor.

Since the policy interpretation maps out a reasonable approach to measuring compliance with Title IX, this Court does not have the authority to condemn it. Plaintiffs' claim that the University of Illinois violated Title IX when it terminated the men's swimming program is, therefore, rejected. The University's actions were consistent with the statute and the applicable regulation and policy interpretation. And despite plaintiffs' assertions to the contrary, neither the regulation nor the policy interpretation run afoul of the dictates of Title IX.

IV.

Plaintiffs' final argument is that the defendants' decision to eliminate the men's swimming program while retaining the women's program denied them equal protection of law as guaranteed by the Fourteenth Amendment. We do not agree. First, the record makes clear that the University considered gender solely to ensure that its actions did not violate federal law. And insofar as the University actions were taken in an attempt to comply with the requirements of Title IX, plaintiffs' attack on those actions is merely a collateral attack on the statute and regulations and is therefore impermissible. Milwaukee County Pavers Ass'n v. Fiedler, 922 F.2d 419, 424 (7th Cir. 1991).

To the extent that plaintiffs' argument is that Title IX and the applicable regulation—rather than the actions of the defendants—are unconstitutional, it is without merit. While the effect of Title IX and the relevant regulation and policy interpretation is that institutions will sometimes consider gender when decreasing their athletic offerings, this limited consideration of sex does not violate the Constitution. . . . There is no doubt but that removing the legacy of sexual discrimination—including discrimination in the provision of extra-curricular offerings such as athletics—from our nation's educational institutions is an important governmental objective. We do not understand plaintiffs to argue otherwise.

Plaintiffs' complaint appears, instead, to be that the remedial measures required by Title IX and the applicable regulation and policy interpretation are not substantially related to their purported goal. Plaintiffs contend that the applicable rules allow "the University to . . . improve[] its statistics without adding any opportunities for women . . . " (Br. 23), an outcome they suggest is unconstitutional. But to survive constitutional scrutiny, Title IX need not require—as plaintiffs would have us believe—that the opportunities for the underrepresented group be continually expanded. Title IX's stated objective is not to ensure that the athletic opportunities available to women increase. Rather its avowed purpose is to prohibit educational institutions from discriminating on the basis of sex. And the remedial scheme established by Title IX and the applicable regulation and policy interpretation are clearly substantially related to this end. Allowing a school to consider gender when determining which athletic programs to terminate ensures that in instances where overall athletic opportunities decrease, the actual opportunities available to the underrepresented gender do not. And since the remedial scheme here at issue directly protects the interests of the disproportionately burdened gender, it passes constitutional muster. Mississippi University for Women v. Hogan, 458 U.S. 718, 728 (1982) ("[A] gender-based classification favoring one sex can be justified if it intentionally and directly assists members of the sex that is disproportionately burdened."); see also *Cohen*, 991 F.2d at 900–901 (holding that Title IX and the applicable regulation and policy interpretation do not violate the Equal Protection Clause).

V.

Since the district court correctly determined that the University of Illinois decision to terminate the men's swimming program did not violate Title IX or the Equal Protection Clause, its decision is affirmed.

NOTES ON KELLEY V. BOARD OF TRUSTEES

1. CONSISTENCY WITH *GEBSER* AND *DAVIS*

The decision in *Kelley* preceded the decisions of the Supreme Court in *Gebser* and *Davis* by several years. It also concerned quite different issues. Is the court's approach to Title IX consistent with the Supreme Court's approach to private actions endorsed in *Gebser*? In *Kelley*, the Seventh Circuit went so far as to advise the university that its decision "not to terminate the woman's swimming program was—given the requirements of Title IX and the applicable regulation and policy interpretation—extremely prudent." The men's swimming team, by contrast, could be terminated in order to maintain compliance with Title IX. Was that response justified? Is the constitutional principle invoked by the Supreme Court—that conditions imposed as part of the exercise of the congressional spending power must be narrowly construed—equally applicable to interpretation of the conditions themselves as to remedies for their violation?

Kelley could be reconciled with the later decisions in *Gebser* and *Davis* on a number of grounds. First, *Kelley* denied relief under Title IX to the male students who sought to preserve the men's swimming team. This does not, it could be argued, require a broad interpretation of Title IX, since no claim under Title IX was recognized on the actual facts of the case. The Seventh Circuit, however, justified the apparent discrimination against men in cutting the men's swimming team as needed to prevent discrimination against women. It was only for this reason that the men did not succeed on their claim under Title IX.

Second, to the extent that *Kelley* relied on the need to prevent discrimination against women, the court could invoke a regulatory statement by the Office of Civil Rights that was, in turn, supported by an amendment to Title IX explicitly authorizing regulations on the subject of discrimination in intercollegiate sports. The regulatory statement that the court relied on most heavily (containing the three "benchmarks" for compliance) is not a regulation, but a "policy interpretation" of the regulations. Should this kind of agency statement receive the same degree of judicial deference as the regulations that Congress explicitly authorized? The "policy interpretation" did not purport to do anything more than provide guidance about ways to comply with Title IX, in sharp contrast to the multiple factors mentioned in the regulations themselves. If the Office of Civil Rights wanted to transform the three "benchmarks" into a binding interpretation of the statute, shouldn't it have amended its regulations under Title IX?

A more promising distinction rests on the focus in *Kelley* on what Title IX prohibits rather than on what damage remedies it makes available to private plaintiffs. The latter was the focus in *Gebser* and *Davis*. Yet those cases also concerned the extent of an educational institution's responsibility for preventing sexual harassment. The Supreme Court did not concern itself with purely remedial issues. It would be odd, in any event, to adopt a broad interpretation of the prohibition against sex discrimination in Title IX and then limit the remedies that might be used to enforce it. Does a restriction on remedies also affect the nature of the underlying substantive right? For a sustained argument considering these issues, see Daryl J. Levinson, Rights Essentialism and Remedial Equilibration, 99 Colum. L. Rev. 857 (1999).

But even if these grounds for distinguishing *Kelley* fail, the decision might still be correct on other grounds. The history of excluding women entirely from intercollegiate athletics at most schools, and the continued preferred status of football in most athletic programs, may justify a broad interpretation of the statute, and in particular, one that favors the preservation of women's teams over the maintenance of men's teams, even in the same sports.

2. REVERSE DISCRIMINATION UNDER TITLE IX

The statute expressly addresses affirmative action in § 1681(b):

> Nothing contained in [the main prohibition in § 1681(b)] shall be interpreted to require any educational institution to grant preferential or disparate treatment to the members of one sex on account of an imbalance which may exist with respect to the total number or percentage of persons of that sex participating in or receiving the benefits of any federally sup-

ported program or activity, in comparison with the total number or percentage of persons of that sex in any community, State, section, or other area: *Provided*, That this subsection shall not be construed to prevent the consideration in any hearing or proceeding under this title of statistical evidence tending to show that such an imbalance exists with respect to the participation in, or receipt of the benefits of, any such program on activity by the members of one sex.

This provision by itself says nothing about the permissibility of cutting men's teams in order to increase the proportion of slots on women's teams. Yet it does raise problems for the reasoning in *Kelley* that such a step was necessary for the university to maintain compliance with Title IX. How can the test of proportionality with enrollments—the requirement that the percentage of slots on women's teams equal the percentage of women enrolled at the school—not be a requirement imposed "on account of an imbalance"? Does the answer lie in the proviso to § 1681(b) that allows statistical evidence to be used to prove a violation of Title IX? If so, what is the difference between using evidence of imbalance to prove a violation, which is allowed, and treating the imbalance as itself a violation, which is not?

The decisions concerned with claims of discrimination by female students, such as *Cohen v. Brown University*, have construed § 1681(b) narrowly, to prohibit only a finding of violation based only on overall population figures. Comparison with enrollment figures, on this view, remains permissible and substantial deviation from overall enrollment figures can itself constitute a violation of the statute. Was Congress likely to have such a fine distinction in mind when it enacted § 1681(b)? Is it relevant that the percentage of students in most colleges and university approximates their percentage in the general population?

Perhaps decisions like *Cohen* rest ultimately on the need to find some means to compensate for the large role of football in most athletic programs. According to this argument, football is a form of de facto affirmative action in favor of men because it reserves so many athletic slots exclusively for them. Women are therefore entitled to a compensating form of affirmative action by creating teams exclusively for them, even at the expense of men's teams. If this is the motivation for decisions like *Cohen*, how can it be reconciled with the language of § 1681(b)?

3. REVERSE DISCRIMINATION UNDER THE CONSTITUTION

In addition to its holding under Title IX, the Seventh Circuit also held that cutting only the men's swimming team was consistent with the Constitution. For any state college or university, compliance with the Equal Protection Clause will be just as necessary as compliance with Title IX. Otherwise, a state educational institution will be subject to suit under § 1983, as the university was in *Kelley*. Moreover, Title IX itself might be called into question to the extent that it is interpreted to require affirmative action. This claim would be made under the Fifth Amendment insofar as it applies to the Federal Government principles of equal protection that limit states under the Fourteenth Amendment.

Affirmative action on the basis of race has resulted in a line of constitutional decisions culminating in the proposition that all racial classifications by government "must serve a compelling governmental interest, and must be narrowly tailored to further that interest." Adarand Constructors, Inc. v. Pena, 515 U.S. 200, 235 (1995). *Kelley* was decided before this principle became clear and relied on a more lenient constitutional standard for affirmative action: that it must be substantially related to an important governmental objective. This standard, despite the decision in *Adarand*, may still be appropriate for affirmative action in favor of women because sex-based classifications are subject to a more lenient constitutional standard than race-based classifications: sex-based classifications need only have an "exceedingly persuasive justification." United States v. Virginia, 518 U.S. 515, 531 (1996).

Nevertheless, affirmative action that results in the deprivation of benefits or opportunities previously conferred on members of other groups has received especially strict constitutional scrutiny. Thus, the layoff of white employees to protect black employees with lower seniority was held unconstitutional in Wygant v. Jackson Board of Education, 476 U.S. 267 (1986). The same result has also been reached under Title VII, in a case involving interpretation of a consent decree. Firefighter Local Union No. 1784 v. Stotts, 467 U.S. 561, 179–80 (1984). Does this principle, adopted in cases involving racial discrimination in employment, apply equally well to sex discrimination in college sports? On the one hand, cutting an entire men's teams appears to be a more drastic step than laying off a few individuals. A decision about continuing an entire team is all-or-nothing; either a school keeps the entire team for the participating students or it does not. Layoffs of individual employees, however, can be minimized through cutting back on jobs by other means, such as leaving positions unfilled as current employees retire or quit. On the other hand, opportunities to participate in intercollegiate sports do not assume the same economic importance in the lives of most college athletes as does the existence of a job for most employees. Participating in college sports is usually a matter of recreation, not of earning a living.

In terms of the constitutional standard for sex-based classifications, cutting men's teams may be the only way to achieve the goal of increasing athletic opportunities for female students when athletic budgets are limited. Does the need to provide separate teams for women, coupled with budgetary constraints on athletic programs, supply an "exceedingly persuasive justification" for cutting men's teams? If these factors are not sufficient, what would be?

CHAPTER 6

STRUCTURAL REFORM LITIGATION

1. INTRODUCTION

INTRODUCTORY NOTES ON STRUCTURAL REFORM LITIGATION

1. STRUCTURAL REFORM LITIGATION

Most of the cases in this book deal with illegal behavior by government officials. Litigation resulting from so-called "constitutional torts" is often closely analogous to the resolution of ordinary disputes between private parties. Thus, for example, if a plaintiff seeks to recover money damages under § 1983 for an illegal search and seizure, the resulting litigation looks very much like an ordinary tort action. There are one plaintiff, one defendant, one injury, and a settled legal theory that shapes and confines the litigation.

Other cases, however, involve broader attacks on the way government does business. Such suits are typically brought as class actions for injunctive relief. Often they seek systemic reform of government operations or enforcement procedures, relief that far exceeds any preventive or compensatory objective that would make whole any particular plaintiff before the court. Suits of this type have come to be known as "structural reform" or "institutional" or "public law" litigation. They are an important part of the effort to enforce civil rights.

The usual way of describing structural reform litigation is to contrast it with the traditional lawsuit. The traditional lawsuit focuses on the resolution of a particular dispute. It typically involves two parties in a contest over the legal consequences of a specific act or incident. The litigation is retrospective in nature—that is, it involves an assessment of the legal significance of events that have already occurred. The remedy available in such a suit flows logically from the wrong complained of: the plaintiff has suffered injury and seeks damages as compensation for past misconduct or is threatened with injury and seeks an injunction to prevent its recurrence. Once such a remedy is obtained, the litigation is over. It has no continuing life beyond resolution of the dispute that gave it birth.

Structural reform litigation, in contrast, is not merely dispute resolution. It is a means of participating in government. It is an attempt to vindicate constitutional values by changing the conduct of large-scale organizations that affect the rights of many people. Often numerous interests are represented, by intervention or otherwise, in complex and extended judicial proceedings. The remedy sought is systemic in nature—typically an injunction that requires affirmative steps to prevent constitutional violations from occurring. The objective is not merely to prevent recurrence of specific wrongs, but to reform institutional structures so as to reduce the likelihood of future violations.

Such systemic remedies often do not flow logically from particular rights that have been violated. That is to say, the remedies are not necessarily shaped and limited by the particular, proved violations of constitutional rights. Instead, they are fashioned ad hoc to prevent anticipated harms. Litigation to achieve such reforms is prospective in focus, and prospective relief usually implies continuing judicial supervision. The result is often a large-scale, long-term, and sometimes intrusive judicial monitoring of government bureaucracy.

The origins of this development cannot be fully explored here, but a few important factors may be noted:

- The protracted process of school desegregation educated many judges in the need for, and the mechanics of, continuing judicial supervision of state and local governments. In many ways, school desegregation suits became the prototype for a new style of litigation that has since been adapted to other contexts.
- Over the last century, there has been an explosion in the recognition of federal constitutional rights. A natural by-product of this development has been the proliferation of legal theories that can be used to test the validity of government behavior.
- Shifts in the manner in which government power is exercised have given rise to the administrative state. As bureaucracies have exerted greater influence over contemporary life, the courts have made greater efforts to monitor and control their behavior.
- The development of the class action as an effective vehicle for representing collective interests has facilitated large-scale litigation leading to system-wide judicial relief.

By the 1960s a new style of litigation had evolved. "Structural reform" litigation, as it is called here, has played and will continue to play a large role in the enforcement of civil rights. In deciding such cases, the courts are faced with new sets of problems and opportunities.

2. THE PLAN OF THE CHAPTER

Comprehensive treatment of the subject of structural reform litigation would require a separate volume. Such suits have been filed in many contexts and the problems encountered are significantly context-specific. This chapter introduces the subject by presenting a selection of four problems, each of which can be studied independently of the others.

Section 1: School Desegregation. School desegregation is the archetype of structural reform litigation. Beginning with Brown v. Board of Education, 348 U.S. 886 (1954), the federal courts required an end to government-sponsored segregation by race in the public schools. A recurring pattern of judicial insistence and local resistance led to increasingly detailed enforcement decrees. More and more aspects of school policy and management came under judicial supervision. There was not only a general trend toward increasing judicial involvement, but also several shifts in direction, as the courts tried first one approach and then another. School desegregation cases took on a life of their own and evolved in directions that could scarcely have been imagined at the time of *Brown*.

This fascinating history is presented retrospectively in three recent cases dealing with the termination of desegregation decrees. When will a formerly segregated school system be found to have purged itself of the taint of that constitutional violation? When and under what circumstances will the courts relinquish control back to the states? Board of Education of Oklahoma City v. Dowell, 498 U.S. 237 (1991), reaffirmed that desegregation decrees were not intended to operate in perpetuity and suggested that the Oklahoma City schools were entitled to an end of federal judicial supervision. Missouri v. Jenkins, 515 U.S. 70 (1995), addresses how far courts can go in ordering financial expenditures to offset the continuing effects of prior segregation. Finally, United States v. Fordice, 505 U.S. 717 (1992), examines the question of termination of desegregation decrees in the context of higher education. In *Fordice*, the Supreme Court ruled that Mississippi had not yet completed the task of desegregating its institutions of higher education. The issue was complicated by the presence of historically black institutions threatened with a loss of identity by further steps to achieve racial mixing. Together, *Dowell*, *Jenkins*, and *Fordice* recount the past and glimpse the future of desegregation litigation, and illustrate the difficulties now being encountered in the most mature field of structural reform litigation.

Section 2: Enforcing Desegregation Decrees. This section considers the limits on judicial power to enforce desegregation decrees against recalcitrant state or local governments. The issue is addressed in Spallone v. United States, 493 U.S. 265 (1990). In *Spallone*, a divided Supreme Court rejected a trial judge's attempt to hold members of the city council of Yonkers, New York, in personal contempt for refusing to vote for legislation implementing a judicial decree. The Justices agreed that some form of judicial coercion was appropriate, but divided on just what form that coercion should take.

Section 3: Relation of Rights and Remedies in Prison Litigation. This section presents a representative problem in the relation of rights to remedies. Sophisticated observers of modern civil rights litigation have noted a subtle but important interaction between the rights asserted by the plaintiffs and the remedies selected upon proof of their violation. Specifically, the use of system-wide structural decrees to vindicate constitutional rights has led to very specific judicial directives that certain patterns of institutional behavior be changed. These changes then come to be regarded as establishing operational norms for future behavior. Simply put, remedies tend to supplant the underlying rights as the starting point of future litigation.

That phenomenon is evident in school desegregation cases and in a variety of other contexts. The main cases for this section are Rhodes v. Chapman, 452 U.S. 337 (1981), and the more recent decision in Brown v. Plata, 131 S.Ct. 1910 (2011). Both involve the controversial and important context of prisoners' rights litigation. Of course, there are differences among suits aimed at prison reform, but certain features are characteristic of such litigation and, indeed, of structural reform litigation generally. *Rhodes v. Chapman* provides an introduction to the history of prison reform litigation and a vehicle for examining the dynamic interaction of rights and remedies, and *Brown* shows the continuing vitality of prison reform litigation, even in the face of restrictive legislation.

Section 4: Standing. Article III, § 2, of the Constitution provides that the judicial power of the United States shall extend to certain listed "cases" and "controversies." These two words restrict the kinds of claims that can be heard in federal courts. Generically, such matters are referred to as aspects of "justiciability." In theory, they involve preliminary questions to be determined on the pleadings as a threshold condition to determination of the merits of a lawsuit.

The most important of the justiciability doctrines is standing. Traditionally, the law of standing required that the plaintiff show that some personal "legal interest" had been invaded by the defendant. The modern law of standing is far more elaborate. In large part, the change has occurred in response to changes in the shape and structure of modern civil rights litigation. Structural reform suits are designed to coerce systemic change in government operations or procedures, and they create a potential nation of plaintiffs. It therefore becomes increasingly important to decide who has the power to bring such suits.

The Supreme Court's pronouncements on standing have not been uniform, but in recent cases the law of standing has been said to be a blend of "constitutional" and "prudential" considerations. The constitutional limitations purport to state the minimum conditions for adjudication required by the "case or controversy" limitation in Article III, § 2. The "prudential" limitations are imposed by the judiciary on itself in the name of appropriate self-restraint.[a] The constitutional minimum is usually said to comprise three elements: (1) an injury in fact (2) that was caused by or is "fairly traceable" to the defendant and (3) that is "likely" to be redressed by the requested relief.

Standing doctrines are relevant to structural reform litigation in at least two ways. The first is when plaintiffs seek broad relief against government in the name of constitutional or statutory rights that have heretofore not been recognized. This was the problem in the first main case reproduced below. Allen v. Wright, 468 U.S. 737 (1984), involves the "injury in fact" and "causation" components of standing in a suit to require the Internal Revenue Service to revise its procedures for determining the tax-exempt status of racially discriminatory private schools. The case illustrates the operation of standing doctrine as a limitation on litigation at the frontiers of constitutional law.

A second way in which standing influences institutional litigation is illustrated by City of Los Angeles v. Lyons, 461 U.S. 95 (1983). *Lyons* concerns the redressability aspect of standing in a suit seeking a preliminary injunction against the "chokehold" practices of the Los Angeles Police Department. The problem in *Lyons* is not that the plaintiff is asserting a novel constitutional claim—he alleges a perfectly traditional kind of injury. The problem has to do with the remedy, specifically whether in addition to damages Lyons should have standing to seek injunctive relief that will protect the general public from the kind of injury that he suffered.

3. BIBLIOGRAPHY

The phenomenon of structural reform litigation has generated an enormous literature. Generally favorable reviews include Abram Chayes, The Role of the Judge in Public Law Litigation, 89 Harv.L.Rev. 1281 (1976) (an im-

---

[a] The most important prudential limitation is the bar, to which there are many exceptions, against asserting the rights of another. This problem is known as jus tertii or third-party standing. For a representative case on third-party standing, see Singleton v. Wulff, 428 U.S. 106 (1976).

portant early analysis); Abram Chayes, Foreword: Public Law Litigation and the Burger Court, 96 Harv.L.Rev. 4 (1982) (examining subsequent developments in the field); Owen Fiss, Foreword: The Forms of Justice, 93 Harv.L.Rev. 1 (1979) (a classic exposition and defense of structural reform litigation); David Rudenstine, Judicially Ordered Social Reform: Neofederalism and Neonationalism and the Debate over Political Structure, 59 S.Cal.L.Rev. 449 (1986) (relating divisions over structural reform litigation to competing theories of political structure); David Rudenstine, Institutional Injunctions, 4 Cardozo L.Rev. 611 (1983) (arguing that structural injunctions are not inconsistent with federalism and democratic values).

Other authors have expressed cautionary views. See Colin S. Diver, The Judge as Political Powerbroker: Superintending Structural Change in Public Institutions, 65 Va.L.Rev. 43 (1979) (an often-cited critique of the judge's role in structural reform cases); Donald L. Horowitz, The Courts and Social Policy (1977) (a skeptical analysis of the policymaking capacity of courts); Gerald E. Frug, The Judicial Power of the Purse, 126 U.Pa.L.Rev. 715 (1978) (focusing on court orders requiring increased government expenditures); Paul J. Mishkin, Federal Courts as State Reformers, 35 W. & L.L.Rev. 949 (1978) (advocating "restraint" in federal judicial reform of state institutions); Robert F. Nagel, Separation of Power and the Scope of Federal Equitable Remedies, 30 Stan.L.Rev. 661 (1978) (focusing on separation-of-powers concerns); Gerald Rosenberg, The Hollow Hope: Can Courts Bring About Social Change? (1991) (investigating whether and under what circumstances courts can be effective in achieving social reform).

For additional perspectives on structural reform litigation, see Lloyd C. Anderson, Implementation of Consent Decrees in Structural Reform Litigation, 1986 U.Ill.L.Rev. 725 (examining enforcement of complex consent decrees); Lloyd C. Anderson, Release and Resumption of Jurisdiction Over Consent Decrees in Structural Reform Litigation, 42 U.Miami L.Rev. 401 (1987) (discussing judicial retention or release of jurisdiction to enforce consent decrees); Theodore Eisenberg and Stephen C. Yeazell, The Ordinary and the Extraordinary in Institutional Litigation, 93 Harv.L.Rev. 465 (1980) (arguing that the procedures and remedies of structural reform litigation are less "new" than is commonly supposed and that the novelty derives chiefly from the recognition of new rights); William A. Fletcher, The Discretionary Constitution: Institutional Remedies and Judiciary Legitimacy, 91 Yale L.J. 635 (1982) (concluding that the presumptive illegitimacy of essentially political decisions by judges is overcome when the responsible political bodies are "seriously and chronically in default"); Daniel J. Meltzer, Deterring Constitutional Violations by Law Enforcement Officials: Plaintiffs and Defendants as Private Attorneys General, 88 Colum.L.Rev. 247 (1988) (examining judicial remedies designed to deter future misconduct rather than to redress individual grievances; and contrasting the Supreme Court's willingness to recognize such remedies as defenses to criminal prosecution with its reluctance to authorize offensive claims to such remedies in structural reform cases).

See also The Seventh Circuit Symposium: The Federal Courts and the Community, 64 Chi–Kent L.Rev. 435 (1988). Included therein are Linda Hirshman, Foreword: Kicking Over the Traces of Self–Government, 64 Chi-Kent L. Rev. 435 (1988), followed by histories of three major cases written by architects of the litigation. Four commentaries follow: Peter Shane, Rights, Remedies and Restraint, 64 Chi-Kent L. Rev. 531 (1988); Dan Tarlock, Remedying the Irremediable: The Lessons of *Gatreaux,* 64 Chi-Kent L. Rev. 573 (1988); David Strauss, Legality, Activism, and the Patronage Case, 64 Chi-Kent L. Rev. 585 (1988); and Jules Gerard, A Restrained Perspective on Activism, 64 Chi-Kent L. Rev. 605 (1988).

Finally, there is a growing empirical literature, mostly by political scientists, on whether and under what circumstances structural reform litigation actually works to achieve social reform. See, e.g, Gerald Rosenberg, The Hollow Hope: Can Courts Bring About Social Change? (1991), and Donald L. Horowitz, The Courts and Social Policy (1977).

2. SCHOOL DESEGREGATION

Board of Education of Oklahoma City v. Dowell

Supreme Court of the United States, 1991.
498 U.S. 237.

■ CHIEF JUSTICE REHNQUIST delivered the opinion of the Court.

Petitioner Board of Education of Oklahoma City sought dissolution of a decree entered by the District Court imposing a school desegregation plan. The District Court granted relief over the objection of respondents Robert L. Dowell, et al., black students and their parents. The Court of Appeals for the Tenth Circuit reversed, holding that the board would be entitled to such relief only upon " '[n]othing less than a clear showing of grievous wrong evoked by new and unforeseen conditions. . . . ' " We hold that the Court of Appeals' test is more stringent than is required either by our cases dealing with injunctions or by the Equal Protection Clause of the Fourteenth Amendment.

I

This school desegregation litigation began almost 30 years ago. In 1961, respondents, black students and their parents, sued petitioners, the Board of Education of Oklahoma City, to end de jure segregation in the public schools. In 1963, the District Court found that Oklahoma City had intentionally segregated both schools and housing in the past, and that Oklahoma City was operating a "dual" school system—one that was intentionally segregated by race. In 1965, the District Court found that the school board's attempt to desegregate by using neighborhood zoning failed to remedy past segregation because residential segregation resulted in one-race schools. Residential segregation had once been state imposed, and it lingered due to discrimination by some realtors and financial institutions. The District Court found that school segregation had caused some housing segregation. In 1972, finding that previous efforts had not been successful at eliminating state-imposed segregation, the District Court ordered the board to adopt the "Finger Plan," under which kindergartners would be assigned to neighborhood schools unless their parents opted otherwise; children in grades 1–4 would attend formerly all white schools, and thus black children would be bused to those schools; children in grade five would attend formerly all black schools, and thus white children would be bused to those schools; students in the upper grades would be bused to various areas in order to maintain integrated schools; and in integrated neighborhoods there would be stand-alone schools for all grades.

In 1977, after complying with the desegregation decree for five years, the board made a "Motion to Close Case." The District Court held in its "Order Terminating Case":

> The court has concluded that [the Finger Plan] worked and that substantial compliance with the constitutional requirements has been achieved. The school board, under the oversight of the court, has operated the plan properly, and the court does not foresee that the termination of its jurisdiction will result in the dismantlement of the plan or any affirmative action by the defendant to undermine the unitary system so slowly and painfully accomplished over the 16 years during which the cause has been pending before this court. . . .
>
> The school board, as now constituted, has manifested the desire and intent to follow the law. The court believes that the present members and their successors on the board will now and in the future continue to follow the constitutional desegregation requirements.
>
> Now sensitized to the constitutional implications of its conduct and with a new awareness of its responsibility to citizens of all races, the board is entitled to pursue in good faith its legitimate policies without the continuing constitutional supervision of this Court. . . .
>
> Jurisdiction in this case is terminated ipso facto subject only to final disposition of any case now pending on appeal.

This unpublished order was not appealed.

In 1984, the school board faced demographic changes that led to greater burdens on young black children. As more and more neighborhoods became integrated, more stand-alone schools were established, and young black students had to be bused further from their inner-city homes to outlying white areas. In an effort to alleviate this burden and to increase parental involvement, the board adopted the Student Reassignment Plan (SRP), which relied on neighborhood assignments for students in grades K–4 beginning in the 1985–1986 school year. Busing continued for students in grades 5–12. Any student could transfer from a school where he or she was in the majority to a school where he or she would be in the minority. Faculty and staff integration was retained, and an "equity officer" was appointed.

In 1985, respondents filed a "Motion to Reopen the Case," contending that the school district had not achieved "unitary" status and that the SRP was a return to segregation. Under the SRP, 11 of 64 elementary schools would be greater than 90 percent black, 22 would be greater than 90 percent white plus other minorities, and 31 would be racially mixed. The District Court refused to reopen the case, holding that its 1977 finding of unitariness was res judicata as to those who were then parties to the action, and that the district remained unitary. The District Court found that the school board, administration, faculty, support staff, and student body were integrated, and transportation, extracurricular activities and facilities within the district were equal and nondiscriminatory. Because unitariness had been achieved, the District Court concluded [in 1987] that court-ordered desegregation must end.

The Court of Appeals for the Tenth Circuit reversed. It held that, while the 1977 order finding the district unitary was binding on the parties, nothing in that order indicated that the 1972 injunction itself was terminated. The court reasoned that the finding that the system was unitary merely ended the District Court's active supervision of the case, and because the school district was still subject to the desegregation decree, respondents could challenge the SRP. The case was remanded to determine whether the decree should be lifted or modified.

On remand, the District Court found that demographic changes made the Finger Plan unworkable, that the board had done nothing for 25 years to promote residential segregation, and that the school district had bused students for more than a decade in good-faith compliance with the court's orders. The District Court found that present residential segregation was the result of private decisionmaking and economics, and that it was too attenuated to be a vestige of former school segregation. It also found that the district had maintained its unitary status, and that the neighborhood assignment plan was not designed with discriminatory intent. The court concluded that the previous injunctive decree should be vacated and the school district returned to local control.

The Court of Appeals again reversed, holding that " 'an injunction takes on a life of its own and becomes an edict quite independent of the law it is meant to effectuate.' " That court approached the case "not so much as one dealing with desegregation, but as one dealing with the proper application of the federal law on injunctive remedies." Relying on United States v. Swift & Co., 286 U.S. 106 (1932), it held that a desegregation decree remains in effect until a school district can show "grievous wrong evoked by new and unforeseen conditions" and "dramatic changes in conditions unforeseen at the time of the decree that . . . impose extreme and unexpectedly oppressive hardships on the obligor" (quoting Timothy Stoltzfus Jost, From *Swift* to *Stotts* and Beyond: Modification of Injunctions in the Federal Courts, 64 Texas L.Rev. 1101, 1110 (1986)). Given that a number of schools would return to being primarily one-race schools under the SRP, circumstances in Oklahoma City had not changed enough to justify modification of the decree. The Court of Appeals held that, despite the unitary finding, the board had the " 'affirmative duty . . . not to take any action that would impede the process of disestablishing the dual system and its effects' " (quoting Dayton Bd. of Education v. Brinkman, 443 U.S. 526, 538 (1979)).

We granted the board's petition for certiorari to resolve a conflict between the standard laid down by the Court of Appeals in this case and that laid down [in other Circuits]. We now reverse the Court of Appeals.

II

We must first consider whether respondents may contest the District Court's 1987 order dissolving the injunction which had imposed the desegregation decree. Respondents did not appeal from the District Court's 1977 order finding that the school system had achieved unitary status, and petitioners contend that the 1977 order bars respondents from contesting the 1987 order. We disagree, for the 1977 order did not dissolve the desegregation decree, and the District Court's unitariness finding was too ambiguous to bar respondents from challenging later action by the board.

The lower courts have been inconsistent in their use of the term "unitary." Some have used it to identify a school district that has completely remedied all vestiges of past discrimination. Under that interpretation of the word, a unitary school district is one that has met the mandate of Brown v. Board of Education, 349 U.S. 294 (1955), and Green v. New Kent County School Board, 391 U.S. 430 (1968). Other courts, however, have used "unitary" to describe any school district that has currently desegregated student assignments, whether or not that status is solely the result of a court-imposed desegregation plan. In other words, such a school district could be called unitary and nevertheless still contain vestiges of past discrimination. . . .

The District Court's 1977 order is unclear with respect to what it meant by unitary and the necessary result of that finding. We therefore decline to overturn the conclusion of the Court of Appeals that while the 1977 order of the District Court did bind the parties as to the unitary character of the district, it did not finally terminate the Oklahoma City school litigation. . . .

III

The Court of Appeals relied upon language from this Court's decision in *United States v. Swift and Co.*, supra, for the proposition that a desegregation decree could not be lifted or modified absent a showing of "grievous wrong evoked by new and unforeseen conditions." It also held that "compliance alone cannot become the basis for modifying or dissolving an injunction," relying on United States v. W.T. Grant Co., 345 U.S. 629, 633 (1953). We hold that its reliance was mistaken.

In *Swift*, several large meat-packing companies entered into a consent decree whereby they agreed to refrain forever from entering into the grocery business. The decree was by its terms effective in perpetuity. The defendant meat-packers and their allies had over a period of a decade attempted, often with success in the lower courts, to frustrate operation of the decree. It was in this context that the language relied upon by the Court of Appeals in this case was used.

United States v. United Shoe Machinery Corp., 391 U.S. 244 (1968), explained that the language used in *Swift* must be read in the context of the continuing danger of unlawful restraints on trade which the Court had found still existed. "*Swift* teaches . . . a decree may be changed upon an appropriate showing, and it holds that it may not be changed . . . if the purposes of the litigation as incorporated in the decree . . . have not been fully achieved" (emphasis deleted). In the present case, a finding by the District Court that the Oklahoma City School District was being operated in compliance with the commands of the Equal Protection Clause of the Fourteenth Amendment, and that it was unlikely that the school board would return to its former ways, would be a finding that the purposes of the desegregation litigation had been fully achieved. No additional showing of "grievous wrong evoked by new and unforeseen conditions" is required of the school board.

In Milliken v. Bradley (*Milliken II*), 433 U.S. 267, 282 (1977), we said:

> [F]ederal-court decrees must directly address and relate to the constitutional violation itself. Because of this inherent limitation upon federal judicial authority, federal-court decrees exceed appropriate limits if they are aimed at eliminating a condition that does not violate the Constitution or does not flow from such a violation. . . .

From the very first, federal supervision of local school systems was intended as a temporary measure to remedy past discrimination. *Brown II* considered the "complexities arising from the *transition* to a system of public education freed of racial discrimination" in holding that the implementation of desegregation was to proceed "with all deliberate speed" (emphasis added). *Green* also spoke of the "*transition* to a unitary, nonracial system of public education" (emphasis added).

Considerations based on the allocation of powers within our federal system, we think, support our view that the quoted language from *Swift* does not provide the proper standard to apply to injunctions entered in school desegregation cases. Such decrees, unlike the one in *Swift*, are not intended to operate in perpetuity. Local control over the education of children allows citizens to participate in decisionmaking, and allows innovation so that school programs can fit local needs. The legal justification for displacement of local authority by an injunctive decree in a school desegregation case is a violation of the Constitution by the local authorities. Dissolving a desegregation decree after the local authorities have operated in compliance with it for a reasonable period of time properly recognizes that "necessary concern for the important values of local control of public school systems dictates that a federal court's regulatory control of such systems not extend beyond the time required to remedy the effects of past intentional discrimination." Spangler v. Pasadena City Bd. of Education, 611 F.2d 1239, 1245, n.5 (9th Cir. 1979) (Kennedy, J., concurring). . . .

The Court of Appeals, as noted, relied for its statement that "compliance alone cannot become the basis for modifying or dissolving an injunction" on our decision in *United States v. W.T. Grant Co.* That case, however, did not involve the dissolution of an injunction, but the question of whether an injunction should be issued in the first place. This Court observed that a promise to comply with the law on the part of a wrongdoer did not divest a district court of its power to enjoin the wrongful conduct in which the defendant had previously engaged.

A district court need not accept at face value the profession of a school board which has intentionally discriminated that it will cease to do so in the future. But in deciding whether to modify or dissolve a desegregation decree, a school board's compliance with previous court orders is obviously relevant. In this case the original finding of de jure segregation was entered in 1961, the injunctive decree from which the board seeks relief was entered in 1972, and the board complied with the decree in good faith until 1985. Not only do the personnel of school boards change over time, but the same passage of time enables the District Court to observe the good faith of the school board in complying with the decree. The test espoused by the Court of Appeals would condemn a school district, once governed by a board which intentionally discriminated, to judicial tutelage for the indefinite future. Neither the principles governing the entry and dissolution of injunctive decrees, nor the commands of the Equal Protection Clause of the Fourteenth Amendment, require any such Draconian result.

Petitioners urge that we reinstate the decision of the District Court terminating the injunction, but we think that the preferable course is to remand the case to that court so that it may decide, in accordance with this opinion, whether the board made a sufficient showing of constitutional compliance as of 1985, when the SRP was adopted, to allow the injunction to be dissolved. The District Court should address itself to whether the board had complied in good faith with the desegregation decree since it was entered, and whether the vestiges of past discrimination had been eliminated to the extent practicable.[2]

---

[2] As noted above, the District Court earlier found that present residential segregation in Oklahoma City was the result of private decisionmaking and economics, and that it was too attenuated to be a vestige of former school segregation. Respondents contend that the Court of Appeals held this finding was clearly erroneous, but we think its opinion is at least ambiguous

In considering whether the vestiges of de jure segregation had been eliminated as far as practicable, the District Court should look not only at student assignments, but "to every facet of school operations—faculty, staff, transportation, extra-curricular activities and facilities." *Green*, supra, at 435.

After the District Court decides whether the board was entitled to have the decree terminated, it should proceed to decide respondent's challenge to the SRP. A school district which has been released from an injunction imposing a desegregation plan no longer requires court authorization for the promulgation of policies and rules regulating matters such as assignment of students and the like, but it of course remains subject to the mandate of the Equal Protection Clause of the Fourteenth Amendment. If the board was entitled to have the decree terminated as of 1985, the District Court should then evaluate the board's decision to implement the SRP under appropriate equal protection principles. See Washington v. Davis, 426 U.S. 229 (1976); Arlington Heights v. Metropolitan Housing Development Corp., 429 U.S. 252 (1977).

The judgment of the Court of Appeals is reversed, and the case is remanded to the District Court for further proceedings consistent with this opinion.

It is so ordered.

■ JUSTICE SOUTER took no part in the consideration or decision of this case.

■ JUSTICE MARSHALL, with whom JUSTICES BLACKMUN and STEVENS join, dissenting.

Oklahoma gained statehood in 1907. For the next 65 years, the Oklahoma City School Board maintained segregated schools—initially relying on laws requiring dual school systems; thereafter, by exploiting residential segregation that had been created by legally enforced restrictive covenants. In 1972—18 years after this Court first found segregated schools unconstitutional—a federal court finally interrupted this cycle, enjoining the Oklahoma City School Board to implement a specific plan for achieving actual desegregation of its schools.

The practical question now before us is whether, 13 years after that injunction was imposed, the same school board should have been allowed to return many of its elementary schools to their former one-race status. The majority today suggests that 13 years of desegregation was enough. The Court remands the case for further evaluation of whether the purposes of the injunctive decree were achieved sufficient to justify the decree's dissolution. However, the inquiry it commends to the District Court fails to recognize explicitly the threatened reemergence of one-race schools as a relevant "vestige" of de jure segregation.

In my view, the standard for dissolution of a school desegregation decree must reflect the central aim of our school desegregation precedents. In Brown v. Board of Education, 347 U.S. 483, 495 (1954) (*Brown I*), a unanimous Court declared that racially "[s]eparate educational facilities are inherently unequal." This holding rested on the Court's recognition that state-sponsored segregation conveys a message of "inferiority as to th[e] status [of Afro–American school children] in the community that may affect their hearts and minds in a way unlikely ever to be undone." Remedying

on this point. . . . To dispel any doubt, we direct the District Court and the Court of Appeals to treat this question as res nova upon further consideration of this case.

this evil and preventing its recurrence were the motivations animating our requirement that formerly de jure segregated school districts take all feasible steps to eliminate racially identifiable schools. See Green v. New Kent County School Bd., 391 U.S. 430, 442 (1968); Swann v. Charlotte–Mecklenburg Bd. of Education, 402 U.S. 1, 25–26 (1971).

I believe a desegregation decree cannot be lifted so long as conditions likely to inflict the stigmatic injury condemned in *Brown I* persist and there remain feasible methods of eliminating such conditions. Because the record here shows, and the Court of Appeals found, that feasible steps could be taken to avoid one-race schools, it is clear that the purposes of the decree have not yet been achieved and the Court of Appeals' reinstatement of the decree should be affirmed. I therefore dissent.

I

In order to assess the full consequence of lifting the decree at issue in this case, it is necessary to explore more fully than does the majority the history of racial segregation in the Oklahoma City schools. This history reveals nearly unflagging resistance by the board to judicial efforts to dismantle the city's dual education system.

When Oklahoma was admitted to the Union in 1907, its Constitution mandated separation of Afro–American children from all other races in the public school system. In addition to laws enforcing segregation in the schools, racially restrictive covenants, supported by state and local law, established a segregated residential pattern in Oklahoma City. Petitioner Board of Education of Oklahoma City exploited this residential segregation to enforce school segregation, locating "all-Negro" schools in the heart of the city's northeast quadrant, in which the majority of the city's Afro–American citizens resided.

Matters did not change in Oklahoma City after this Court's decision in *Brown I* and Brown v. Board of Education, 349 U.S. 294 (1955) (*Brown II*). Although new school boundaries were established at that time, the board also adopted a resolution allowing children to continue in the schools in which they were placed or to submit transfer requests that would be considered on a case-by-case basis. Because it allowed thousands of white children each year to transfer to schools in which their race was the majority, this transfer policy undermined any potential desegregation.

Parents of Afro–American children relegated to schools in the northeast quadrant filed suit against the board in 1961. Finding that the board's special transfer policy was "designed to perpetuate and encourage segregation," the District Court struck down the policy as a violation of the Equal Protection Clause. Undeterred, the board proceeded to adopt another special transfer policy which, as the District Court found in 1965, had virtually the same effect as the prior policy—"perpetuat[ion] [of] a segregated system."

The District Court also noted that, by failing to adopt an affirmative policy of desegregation, the board had reversed the desegregation process in certain respects. For example, eight of the nine new schools planned or under construction in 1965 were located to serve all-white or virtually all-white school zones. Rather than promote integration through new school locations, the District Court found that the board destroyed some integrated neighborhoods and schools by adopting inflexible neighborhood school attendance zones that encouraged whites to migrate to all-white areas. Because the board's pupil assignments coincided with residential segregation initiated by law in Oklahoma City, the board also preserved and augmented existing residential segregation.

Thus, by 1972, 11 years after the plaintiffs had filed suit and 18 years after our decision in *Brown I*, the school board continued to resist integration and in some respects the board had worsened the situation. Four years after this Court's admonition to formerly de jure segregated school districts to come forward with realistic plans for immediate relief, see *Green*, 391 U.S., at 439, the board still had offered no meaningful plan of its own. Instead, "[i]t rationalize[d] its intransigence on the constitutionally unsound basis that public opinion [was] opposed to any further desegregation." Dowell v. Board of Education of Oklahoma City Public Schools, 338 F.Supp. 1256, 1270 (W.D.Okla.1972). The District Court concluded: "This litigation has been frustratingly interminable, not because of insuperable difficulties of implementation of the commands of the Supreme Court . . . and the Constitution . . . but because of the unpardonable recalcitrance of the . . . board." Consequently, the District Court ordered the board to implement the only available plan that exhibited the promise of achieving actual desegregation—the "Finger Plan" offered by the plaintiffs.

In 1975, after a mere three years of operating under the Finger Plan, the board filed a "Motion to Close Case," arguing that it had " 'eliminated all vestiges of state imposed racial discrimination in its school system.' " In 1977, the District Court granted the board's motion and issued an "Order Terminating Case." The court concluded that the board had "operated the [Finger] Plan properly" and stated that it did not "foresee that the termination of . . . jurisdiction will result in the dismantlement of the [Finger] Plan or any affirmative action by the defendant to undermine the unitary system." The order ended the District Court's active supervision of the school district but did not dissolve the injunctive decree. The plaintiffs did not appeal this order.

The board continued to operate under the Finger Plan until 1985, when it implemented the Student Reassignment Plan (SRP). The SRP superimposed attendance zones over some residentially segregated areas. As a result, considerable racial imbalance reemerged in 33 of 64 elementary schools in the Oklahoma City system with student bodies either greater than 90 percent Afro–American or greater than 90 percent non-Afro–American. More specifically, 11 of the schools ranged from 96.9 percent to 99.7 percent Afro–American, and approximately 44 percent of all Afro–American children in grades K–4 were assigned to these virtually all-Afro–American schools.

In response to the SRP, the plaintiffs moved to reopen the case. Ultimately, the District Court dissolved the desegregation decree, finding that the school district had been "unitary" since 1977 and that the racial imbalances under the SRP were the consequence of residential segregation arising from "personal preferences." The Court of Appeals reversed, finding that the board had not met its burden to establish that "the condition the [decree] sought to alleviate, a constitutional violation, has been eradicated."

II

I agree with the majority that the proper standard for determining whether a school desegregation decree should be dissolved is whether the purposes of the desegregation litigation, as incorporated in the decree, have been fully achieved. I strongly disagree with the majority, however, on what must be shown to demonstrate that a decree's purposes have been fully realized. In my view, a standard for dissolution of a desegregation decree must take into account the unique harm associated with a system of racially identifiable schools and must expressly demand the elimination of such schools.

A

Our pointed focus in *Brown I* upon the stigmatic injury caused by segregated schools explains our unflagging insistence that formerly de jure segregated school districts extinguish all vestiges of school segregation. The concept of stigma also gives us guidance as to what conditions must be eliminated before a decree can be deemed to have served its purpose.

In the decisions leading up to *Brown I*, the Court had attempted to curtail the ugly legacy of Plessy v. Ferguson, 163 U.S. 537 (1896), by insisting on a searching inquiry into whether "separate" Afro–American schools were genuinely "equal" to white schools in terms of physical facilities, curricula, quality of the faculty and certain "intangible" considerations. See, e.g., Sweatt v. Painter, 339 U.S. 629 (1950). In *Brown I*, the Court finally liberated the Equal Protection Clause from the doctrinal tethers of *Plessy*, declaring that "in the field of public education the doctrine of 'separate but equal' has no place. Separate educational facilities are inherently unequal."

The Court based this conclusion on its recognition of the particular social harm that racially segregated schools inflict on Afro–American children.

> To separate them from others of similar age and qualifications solely because of their race generates a feeling of inferiority as to their status in the community that may affect their hearts and minds in a way unlikely ever to be undone. The effect of this separation on their educational opportunities was well stated by a finding in the Kansas case by a court which nevertheless felt compelled to rule against the Negro plaintiffs:
>
> > "Segregation of white and colored children in public schools has a detrimental effect upon the colored children. The impact is greater when it has the sanction of law; for the policy of separating the races is usually interpreted as denoting the inferiority of the Negro group. A sense of inferiority affects the motivation of a child to learn. Segregation with the sanction of law, therefore, has a tendency to [retard] the educational and mental development of Negro children and to deprive them of some of the benefits they would receive in a racial[ly] integrated school system."

Remedying and avoiding the recurrence of this stigmatizing injury have been the guiding objectives of this Court's desegregation jurisprudence ever since. These concerns inform the standard by which the Court determines the effectiveness of a proposed desegregation remedy. In *Green*, a school board sought to implement the mandate of *Brown I* and *Brown II* by adopting a "freedom of choice" plan under which individual students could specify which of two local schools they would attend. The Court held that this plan was inadequate because it failed to redress the effect of segregation upon "every facet of school operations—faculty, staff, transportation, extracurricular activities and facilities." By so construing the extent of a school board's obligations, the Court made clear that the Equal Protection Clause demands elimination of every indicium of a "[r]acial[ly] identifi[able]" school system that will inflict the stigmatizing injury that *Brown I* sought to cure. Accord, *Swann*.

Concern with stigmatic injury also explains the Court's requirement that a formerly de jure segregated school district provide its victims with "make whole" relief. In Milliken v. Bradley, 418 U.S. 717, 746 (1974) (*Milliken I*), the Court concluded that a school desegregation decree must "restore the victims of discriminatory conduct to the position they would have occupied in the absence of such conduct." In order to achieve such "make whole" relief, school systems must redress any effects traceable to former de jure segregation. See Milliken v. Bradley, 433 U.S. 267, 281–88 (1977) (*Milliken II*) (upholding remedial education programs and other measures to redress the substandard communication skills of Afro–American students formerly placed in segregated schools). The remedial education upheld in *Milliken II* was needed to help prevent the stamp of inferiority placed upon Afro–American children from becoming a self-perpetuating phenomenon.

Similarly, avoiding reemergence of the harm condemned in *Brown I* accounts for the Court's insistence on remedies that insure lasting integration of formerly segregated systems. Such school districts are required to "make every effort to achieve the *greatest possible degree of actual desegregation* and [to] be concerned with the elimination of one-race schools." *Swann*, 402 U.S., at 26 (emphasis added). This focus on "achieving and *preserving* an integrated school system," Keyes v. School Dist. No. 1, Denver, Colo., 413 U.S. 189, 251, n.31 (1973) (Powell, J., concurring in part and dissenting in part) (emphasis added), stems from the recognition that the reemergence of racial separation in such schools may revive the message of racial inferiority implicit in the former policy of state-enforced segregation.

Just as it is central to the standard for evaluating the formation of a desegregation decree, so should the stigmatic injury associated with segregated schools be central to the standard for dissolving a decree. The Court has indicated that "the ultimate end to be brought about" by a desegregation remedy is "a unitary, nonracial system of public education." *Green*, 391 U.S., at 436. We have suggested that this aim is realized once school officials have "eliminate[d] from the public schools *all* vestiges of state-imposed segregation," *Swann*, 402 U.S., at 15 (emphasis added), whether they inhere in the school's "faculty, staff, transportation, extracurricular activities and facilities," *Green*, 391 U.S., at 435, or even in "the community and administration['s] attitudes toward [a] school," *Keyes*, 413 U.S., at 196. Although the Court has never explicitly defined what constitutes a "vestige" of state-enforced segregation, the function that this concept has performed in our jurisprudence suggests that it extends to any condition that is likely to convey the message of inferiority implicit in a policy of segregation. So long as such conditions persist, the purposes of the decree cannot be deemed to have been achieved.

B

The majority suggests a more vague and, I fear, milder standard. Ignoring the harm identified in *Brown I*, the majority asserts that the District Court should find that the purposes of the degree have been achieved so long as "the Oklahoma City School District [is now] being operated in compliance with the commands of the Equal Protection Clause" and "it [is] unlikely that the school board would return to its former ways." Insofar as the majority instructs the District Court, on remand, to "conside[r] whether the vestiges of de jure segregation ha[ve] been eliminated as far as practicable," the majority presumably views elimination of vestiges as part of "operat[ing] in compliance with the commands of the Equal Protection

Clause." But as to the scope or meaning of "vestiges," the majority says very little.

By focusing heavily on present and future compliance with the Equal Protection Cause, the majority's standard ignores how the stigmatic harm identified in *Brown I* can persist even after the state ceases actively to enforce segregation. It was not enough in *Green*, for example, for the school district to withdraw its own enforcement of segregation, leaving it up to individual children and their families to "choose" which school to attend. For it was clear under the circumstances that these choices would be shaped by and perpetuate the state-created message of racial inferiority associated with the school district's historical involvement in segregation. In sum, our school-desegregation jurisprudence establishes that the effects of past discrimination remain chargeable to the school district regardless of its lack of continued enforcement of segregation, and the remedial decree is required until those effects have been finally eliminated.

III

Applying the standard I have outlined, I would affirm the Court of Appeals' decision ordering the District Court to restore the desegregation decree. For it is clear on this record that removal of the decree will result in a significant number of racially identifiable schools that could be eliminated.

As I have previously noted,

> Racially identifiable schools are one of the primary vestiges of state-imposed segregation which an effective desegregation decree must attempt to eliminate. . . . A school authority's remedial plan or a district court's remedial decree is to be judged by its effectiveness in achieving this end. *Milliken I*, 418 U.S., at 802–03 (Marshall, J. dissenting).

Against the background of former state-sponsorship of one-race schools, the persistence of racially identifiable schools perpetuates the message of racial inferiority associated with segregation. Therefore, such schools must be eliminated whenever feasible.

It is undisputed that replacing the Finger Plan with a system of neighborhood school assignments for grades K–4 resulted in a system of racially identifiable schools. Under the SRP, over one-half of Oklahoma City's elementary schools now have student bodies that are either 90 percent Afro–American or 90 percent non-Afro–American. Because this principal vestige of de jure segregation persists, lifting the decree would clearly be premature at this point.

The majority equivocates on the effect to be given to the reemergence of racially identifiable schools. It instructs the District Court to consider whether those " 'most important indicia of a segregated system' " have been eliminated, reciting the facets of segregated school operations identified in *Green*—" 'faculty, staff, transportation, extra-curricular activities and facilities.' " And by rendering "res nova" the issue whether residential segregation in Oklahoma City is a vestige of former school segregation, the majority accepts at least as a theoretical possibility that vestiges may exist beyond those identified in *Green*. Nonetheless, the majority hints that the District Court could ignore the effect of residential segregation in perpetuating racially identifiable schools if the court finds residential segregation to be "the result of private decisionmaking and economics." Finally, the majority warns against the application of a standard that would subject formerly segregated school districts to the "Draconian" fate of "judicial tutelage for the indefinite future."

This equivocation is completely unsatisfying. First, it is well established that school segregation "may have a profound reciprocal effect on the racial composition of residential neighborhoods." *Keyes*, 413 U.S., at 202. The record in this case amply demonstrates this form of complicity in residential segregation on the part of the board. The District Court found as early as 1965 that the board's use of neighborhood schools "serve[d] to . . . exten[d] areas of all Negro housing, destroying in the process already integrated neighborhoods and thereby increasing the number of segregated schools." It was because of the school board's responsibility for residential segregation that the District Court refused to permit the board to superimpose a neighborhood plan over the racially isolated northeast quadrant.

Second, there is no basis for the majority's apparent suggestion that the result should be different if residential segregation is now perpetuated by "private decisionmaking." The District Court's conclusion that the racial identity of the northeast quadrant now subsists because of "personal preference[s]" pays insufficient attention to the roles of the state, local officials, and the board in creating what are now self-perpetuating patterns of residential segregation. Even more important, it fails to account for the unique role of the school board in creating "all-Negro" schools clouded by the stigma of segregation—schools to which white parents would not opt to send their children. That such negative "personal preferences" exist should not absolve a school district that played a role in creating such "preferences" from its obligation to desegregate the schools to the maximum extent possible.

I also reject the majority's suggestion that the length of federal judicial supervision is a valid factor in assessing a dissolution. The majority is correct that the Court has never contemplated perpetual judicial oversight of former de jure segregated school districts. Our jurisprudence requires, however, that the job of school desegregation be fully completed and maintained so that the stigmatic harm identified in *Brown I* will not recur upon lifting the decree. Any doubt on the issue whether the school board has fulfilled its remedial obligations should be resolved in favor of the Afro–American children affected by this litigation.

In its concern to spare local school boards the "Draconian" fate of "indefinite" "judicial tutelage," the majority risks subordination of the constitutional rights of Afro–American children to the interest of school board autonomy. The courts must consider the value of local control, but that factor primarily relates to the feasibility of a remedial measure, not whether the constitutional violation has been remedied. *Swann* establishes that if further desegregation is "reasonable, feasible, and workable," then it must be undertaken. In assessing whether the task is complete, the dispositive question is whether vestiges capable of inflicting stigmatic harm exist in the system and whether all that can practicably be done to eliminate those vestiges has been done. The Court of Appeals concluded that "on the basis of the record, it is clear that other measures that are feasible remain available to the Board [to avoid racially identifiable schools]." The school board does not argue that further desegregation of the one-race schools in its system is unworkable and in light of the proven feasibility of the Finger Plan, I see no basis for doubting the Court of Appeals' finding.

We should keep in mind that the court's active supervision of the desegregation process ceased in 1977. Retaining the decree does not require a return to active supervision. It may be that a modification of the decree which will improve its effectiveness and give the school district more flexibility in minimizing busing is appropriate in this case. But retaining the decree seems a slight burden on the school district compared with the risk of not delivering a full remedy to the Afro–American children in the school system.

IV

Consistent with the mandate of *Brown I*, our cases have imposed on school districts an unconditional duty to eliminate any condition that perpetuates the message of racial inferiority inherent in the policy of state-sponsored segregation. The racial identifiability of a district's schools is such a condition. Whether this "vestige" of state-sponsored segregation will persist cannot simply be ignored at the point where a district court is contemplating the dissolution of a desegregation decree. In a district with a history of state-sponsored school segregation, racial separation, in my view, remains inherently unequal.

I dissent.

NOTES ON THE HISTORY OF SCHOOL DESEGREGATION

1. THE REQUIREMENT OF DE JURE SEGREGATION

Near the end of his opinion in *Dowell*, Chief Justice Rehnquist made an elliptical reference to the requirement of de jure segregation. He said that if the District Court found that Oklahoma City School Board was entitled to have the original desegregation decree terminated as of 1985, the court should then examine the decision to end busing in grades K–4 "under appropriate equal protection principles." He cited Washington v. Davis, 426 U.S. 229 (1976), and Arlington Heights v. Metropolitan Housing Development Corp., 429 U.S. 252 (1977), which require proof of intentional discrimination. In the context of school desegregation, the requirement of intentional discrimination is traditionally referred to as "de jure," meaning segregation by the government on purpose. "De facto" is the name given to separation of the races where no such discriminatory purpose can be proved.

Brown v. Board of Education, 347 U.S. 483 (1954), aimed squarely at de jure segregation. The evil attacked there was the formal and categorical separation by law of public school students by race. Educational apartheid was practiced throughout the South and in several border states. Accordingly, early desegregation efforts focused exclusively on that region. By the late 1950s, "massive resistance" had been broken, and southern school districts had abandoned formal policies of segregation. Most adopted so-called "freedom of choice." Under these plans, black students who wished to attend white schools could do so, on application, without legal impediment. For several years, such plans were thought a sufficient response to the mandate of *Brown*. The theory behind freedom of choice was explained by Judge John J. Parker in Briggs v. Elliott, 132 F.Supp. 776, 777 (E.D.S.C. 1955). "The Constitution," said Parker, "does not require integration. It merely forbids discrimination. It does not forbid such segregation that occurs as the result of voluntary action. It merely forbids the use of governmental power to enforce segregation."

However valid in theory, freedom of choice failed utterly in practice. Rapid progress in eliminating one-race schools was made in some border states, but not in the South. Fully 10 years after *Brown*, most southern school districts had only token desegregation, and the vast majority of black children still attended all-black schools. Substantial change came only after passage of the 1964 Civil Rights Act, when the Department of Health, Education, and Welfare began to demand racial mixing as a condition of federal funding.

In 1968, the Supreme Court lost patience. Green v. County School Board, 391 U.S. 430 (1968), required that de jure segregation be eliminated "*now.*" This decision transformed the law of desegregation. No longer was it sufficient, as the lower courts had thought, for the government to stop *requiring* separation by race. Now, the school systems had an *affirmative obligation* to undo the effects of prior segregation. The object was a "unitary" school system without racially identifiable schools.

By requiring that the effects (as well as the fact) of de jure segregation be eliminated, the Court moved toward a de facto remedy. After *Green*, racially identifiable schools in any affected school district showed that the elimination of de jure segregation was incomplete, even though racially identifiable schools where no intent to segregate had been found were not unconstitutional. Racial separation was not in itself unconstitutional. Racial balance and the elimination of one-race schools were required only in school systems with a history of de jure segregation and only as a remedy for that wrong.

2. BUSING

How could a unitary school system be achieved? On the facts of *Green*, it was easy. The county had only two schools, one black and one white, with residents of both races distributed more or less randomly throughout the jurisdiction. All that was required was to split the county into two districts and to send all children, both black and white, to the school in their district. This sort of plan was the rural equivalent of neighborhood schools, and it achieved substantial desegregation throughout the rural and small-town South.

In cities, however, in the South as elsewhere, residential segregation made the job difficult. Neighborhood schools in segregated neighborhoods meant segregated schools. In urban areas, the *Green* mandate to eliminate racially identifiable schools required drastic action. The solution was busing, which the Supreme Court approved in Swann v. Charlotte–Mecklenburg Board of Education, 402 U.S. 1 (1971). As changing judicial attitudes made de jure segregation easier to prove, more and more cities outside the South became subject to busing decrees. See, e.g., Keyes v. School District No. 1, Denver, Colorado, 413 U.S. 189 (1973).

Busing, of course, was enormously controversial, both in the courts and on the streets. Unlike *Brown*, which even in the South came to be accepted as a hallmark of morality and justice, busing never enjoyed popular support. Usually it faced intense and sometimes violent local opposition. The ultimate threat to busing, however, came not from political resistance, but from the demographics of the American city. Even as more and more cities were required to bus, the changing population of those cities—especially the population of school-age children—made racial balance in public schools less and less obtainable. Increasingly, there were not enough white students to go around. As minority enrollment in urban school systems rose from 50 to 60 to 70 percent and higher, redistribution of students within those districts began to seem almost pointless.[a]

The initial response to the changing demographics of urban centers was interdistrict busing. Bringing suburban school districts, most of which were white and many of which were wealthy, into a metropolitan busing plan would increase the pool of white students and make white flight more difficult by extending the reach of the city schools into near-by suburbs. Early cases came from Richmond and Detroit. In both, district judges faced overwhelmingly black inner cities surrounding by a ring of white suburbs. Their solution was to divide the metropolitan areas into pie-shaped wedges and order the exchange of students between predominately black city schools and the predominately white schools in the adjacent suburbs. This sort of plan promised to achieve greater integration—but only by overriding the boundaries of local governments.

In Milliken v. Bradley, 418 U.S. 717 (1974), a bitterly divided Supreme Court rejected this strategy. The Court reiterated that the only basis for ordering busing was to remedy de jure segregation. Racial separation that did not result from official misconduct was no cause for constitutional concern. From this premise, the Court reasoned that the scope of the busing remedy should reflect the scope of the constitutional violation. If only the city were found guilty of de jure segregation, then only the city could be required to bus. If the city and suburbs collaborated in maintaining segregation, then both could be brought within a metropolitan busing plan. In other words, interdistrict busing required proof of an interdistrict violation.

What constituted an interdistrict violation was not entirely clear. The easiest case was where the boundaries between urban and suburban school districts had been gerrymandered to perpetuate segregation. An interdistrict remedy would also be proper where the district lines had historically been ignored to promote segregation, see Newburg Area Council v. Jefferson County Board of Education, 510 F.2d 1358 (6th Cir. 1974), or the government had acted to create and maintain racial segregation as between city and suburbs. See, e.g., Evans v. Buchanan, 393 F.Supp. 428 (D.Del.1975). Absent some version of an interdistrict violation, however, the courts were barred from ordering an interdistrict remedy. The result was that desegregation usually had to be accomplished within the political boundaries of a single school system.

---

[a] Whether and to what extent busing itself contributed to the resegregation of urban school systems are hotly disputed issues. "White flight" is the usual label for whites choosing to live in the suburbs or to send their children to private school in order to avoid busing. Critics of busing tend to exaggerate white flight in order to show the futility of a policy they oppose. Supporters of busing often discount the phenomenon to show that busing works. The empirical evidence is plagued by local variation and debate over methodology and often supports divergent interpretations. Most fair-minded observers, however, would agree on two points.

First, the chief cause of the increasing minority enrollment in urban school systems was a large-scale demographic movement from cities to suburbs. This movement pre-dated busing and cannot plausibly be seen as a response to that policy. Second, busing often exacerbated that development, especially in school districts with substantial minority enrollment and especially in the years immediately following a new court order. For that reason, compulsory transportation as a means of desegregation was more problematic than was at first appreciated. For samplings of the social science literature on these issues, see Christine Rossell, Applied Social Science Research: What Does It Say About the Effectiveness of School Desegregation Plans?, 12 J. Legal Studies 69 (1983); David J. Armour, "White Flight and the Future of School Desegregation," in Walter G. Stephan and Joe R. Feagin, eds., School Desegregation: Past, Present, and Future (1980).

For many American cities, this limitation made it virtually impossible to eliminate all one-race schools.

3. EDUCATIONAL ENHANCEMENTS

In the late 1970s, civil rights activists began to seek an alternative remedy. Foreclosed by precedent and demography from further desegregation through busing, many began to attack the educational consequences of segregation rather than the racial distribution of students. *Brown* had said that separate educational facilities were inherently unequal. Attention now shifted from separateness to inequality. If racial separation were built into the demographics of the American city, inequality need not be. In many American cities, the chief issue became not how to redistribute the declining number of white students among predominantly black schools, but rather how to improve the education offered to black students.

Early Supreme Court approval of such plans came in Milliken v. Bradley (*Milliken II*), 433 U.S. 267 (1977). In the years following, while busing remedies were pursued in some cities, others turned increasingly to educational enhancements (or "sweeteners") as a desegregation remedy. Increased funding for inner-city schools might aid desegregation in two ways: first, by helping to repair the damage inflicted on African–Americans by segregated education; and second, by making inner-city schools more attractive and thereby discouraging white flight. A dramatic example of this approach was considered by the Supreme Court in Missouri v. Jenkins, 495 U.S. 33 (1990), a main case in Section 2 of this Chapter, dealing with the enforcement of desegregation decrees (a 1995 decision by the same name appears immediately below as the next main case).

4. QUESTIONS AND COMMENTS ON *DOWELL*

Implicit in the requirement of de jure segregation as the basis of judicial authority is the prospect that judicial supervision will end when the de jure violation has been remedied. As *Dowell* illustrates, the effects of de jure segregation may be found to have been eliminated, even though de facto segregation continues. Is this appropriate? Or should court-ordered remedies remain in place so long as any segregation continues? Is that what Justice Marshall meant by his contention that desegregation decrees should not be lifted "so long as conditions likely to inflict the stigmatic injury condemned in *Brown I* persist"? Was Marshall saying, in effect, that even de facto segregation should be unconstitutional? Should it be?

5. UNITARINESS LITIGATION

In the past several years, an increasing number of school districts have been declared unitary. In some cases, as in *Dowell*, the school district itself has sought dissolution of the decree. In others, federal courts have declared districts unitary in the course of other litigation, usually suits by parents who demanded race-neutral access to some particularly attractive educational opportunity.

For an interesting example of such litigation, consider the history of the school district involved in Swann v. Charlotte–Mecklenburg Board of Education, 402 U.S. 1 (1971). The Charlotte–Mecklenburg schools remained under court order well into the 1990s. In addition to race-based pupil assignment, the district also implemented a magnet school program. In September 1997, a white parent, William Capacchione, filed suit alleging that his daughter had unconstitutionally been denied admission to a magnet school program on account of her race. Other parents intervened and sought a determination that the school district had attained unitary status. At the same time, counsel for the original *Swann* plaintiffs moved to reactivate that litigation.

The District Court consolidated all these cases, conducted a lengthy trial, and determined that Charlotte–Mecklenburg had achieved unitary status. On that premise, the race-based admissions policy for magnet schools was found to violate equal protection of the laws. The District Court prohibited use of race-based preferences in student assignment and ordered that race-blind assignment policies go into effect in time for the 2000–2001 school year. Capacchione v. Charlotte–Mecklenburg Schools, 57 F. Supp. 2d 228 (W.D.N.C. 1999). The school board appealed, and sought a stay of the order pending the appeal. The Court of Appeals granted that stay. Belk v. Charlotte–Mecklenburg Bd. of Educ., 211 F.3d 853 (4th Cir. 1999). It found that the balance of hardships tilted in favor of the school board, since immediate compliance with the District Court's order would require "redraw[ing] attendance boundaries for virtually every non-magnet school" within the district and perhaps reassigning 50,000 students.

In Charlotte–Mecklenburg, as in some other districts, the school authorities apparently wish to continue using race as a basis for pupil assignment and restrictive admissions in order to achieve integration. Whether such programs can continue after a finding of voluntariness is not clear. In the 1970s, the Supreme Court approved race-based pupil assignments as part of voluntary desegregation plans, see McDaniel v. Barresi, 402 U.S. 39 (1971). *Barresi* has not been overruled, but its continued vitality may be open to question. In any event, *Barresi* only dealt with race-based assignments among presumably comparable schools. The more hotly contested issue is race-based admissions to magnet schools or other specialty programs. In this context, several recent decisions have disapproved race as a criterion for selective admission, outside the remedial context of eliminating de jure segregation. See, e.g., Tuttle v. Arlington County School Board, 195 F.3d 698 (4th Cir. 1999) (striking down a system of admitting students to a special school pursuant to a weighted lottery that increased the chances of African–American applicants); Ho v. San Francisco Unified School District, 147 F.3d 854 (9th Cir. 1998) (suggesting that it might be unconstitutional to continue a consent decree provision capping the number of students of a particular racial or ethnic group who could be assigned to a particularly desirable school). The question whether achieving or maintaining racial balance within a public school system, outside the context of required desegregation, is a sufficiently compelling state interest to justify race-based assignments or admissions has not yet reached the Supreme Court.

For articles discussing the decreased judicial involvement in school desegregation, see Sean F. Reardon, Integrating Neighborhoods, Segregating Schools: The Retreat from School Desegregation in the South, 81 N.C.L. Rev. 1563 (2003); Wendy Parker, The Decline of Judicial Decisionmaking: School Desegregation and District Court Judges, 81 N.C.L. Rev. 1623 (2003).

6. BIBLIOGRAPHY

There is, of course, an enormous and varied literature on school desegregation. A very partial listing of prominent works in that field would include Derrick Bell, The Dialectics of School Desegregation, 32 Ala.L.Rev. 281 (1981) (one of several articles in a symposium on "Judicially Managed Institutional Reform"); Derrick Bell, And We Are Not Saved: The Elusive Quest for Racial Justice (1987); Paul Gewirtz, Remedies and Resistance, 92 Yale L.J. 585 (1983); Gary C. Leedes and James M. O'Fallon, School Desegregation in Richmond: A Case History, 10 U. Rich L.Rev. 1 (1975); James S. Liebman, Desegregation Politics: "All–Out" School Desegregation Explained, 90 Colum.L.Rev. 1463 (1990); James S. Liebman, Implementing *Brown* in the Nineties: Political Reconstruction, Liberal Recollection, and Litigatively Enforced Legislative Reform, 76 Va.L.Rev. 349 (1990); J. Harvie Wilkinson III, From *Brown* to *Bakke*—The Supreme Court and School Integration: 1954–78 (1979).

Missouri v. Jenkins

Supreme Court of the United States, 1995.
515 U.S. 70.

■ CHIEF JUSTICE REHNQUIST delivered the opinion of the Court. . . .

I

A general overview of this litigation is necessary for proper resolution of the issues upon which we granted certiorari. This case has been before the same United States District Judge since 1977. In that year, the KCMSD, the school board, and the children of two school board members brought suit against the state and other defendants. Plaintiffs alleged that the state, the surrounding suburban school districts (SSD's), and various federal agencies had caused and perpetuated a system of racial segregation in the schools of the Kansas City metropolitan area. The District Court realigned the KCMSD as a nominal defendant and certified as a class, present and future KCMSD students. The KCMSD brought a cross-claim against the state for its failure to eliminate the vestiges of its prior dual school system.

After a trial that lasted 7½ months, the District Court dismissed the case against the federal defendants and the SSD's, but determined that the state and the KCMSD were liable for an intradistrict violation, i.e., they had operated a segregated school system within the KCMSD. The District Court determined that prior to 1954 "Missouri mandated segregated schools for black and white children." Furthermore, the KCMSD and the state had failed in their affirmative obligations to eliminate the vestiges of the state's dual school system within the KCMSD.

In June 1985, the District Court issued its first remedial order and established as its goal the "elimination of all vestiges of state imposed segregation." . . . The District Court, pursuant to plans submitted by the KCMSD and the state, ordered a wide range of quality education programs for all students attending the KCMSD. [These included reduced class size, full-day kindergarten, expanded summer school, tutoring, an early childhood development program, and substantial cash grants to each school.] The total cost for these quality education programs has exceeded $220 million.

The District Court also set out to desegregate the KCMSD but believed that "[t]o accomplish desegregation within the boundary lines of a school district whose enrollment remains 68.3% black is a difficult task." Because it had found no interdistrict violation, the District Court could not order mandatory interdistrict redistribution of students between the KCMSD and the SSD's. Milliken v. Bradley, 418 U.S. 717 (1974) (*Milliken I*). . . .

In November 1986, the District Court approved a comprehensive magnet school and capital improvements plan and held the state and the KCMSD jointly and severally liable for its funding. Under the District Court's plan, every senior high school, every middle school, and one-half of the elementary schools were converted into magnet schools. The District Court adopted the magnet-school program to "provide a greater educational opportunity to all KCMSD students," and because it believed "that the proposed magnet plan [was] so attractive that it would draw non-minority students from the private schools who have abandoned or avoided the KCMSD, and draw in additional non-minority students from the suburbs." . . . Since its inception, the magnet school program has operated at a cost, including magnet transportation, in excess of $448 million. . . .

In June 1985, the District Court ordered substantial capital improvements to combat the deterioration of KCMSD's facilities. In formulating its capital-improvements plan, the District Court dismissed as "irrelevant" the "state's argument that the present condition of the facilities [was] not traceable to unlawful segregation." Instead, the District Court focused on its responsibility to "remed[y] the vestiges of segregation" and to "implemen[t] a desegregation plan which w[ould] maintain and attract non-minority members." The initial phase of the capital improvements plan cost $37 million. . . .

In September 1987, the District Court adopted, for the most part, KCMSD's long-range capital improvements plan at a cost in excess of $187 million. The plan called for the renovation of approximately 55 schools, the closure of 18 facilities, and the construction of 17 new schools. The District Court rejected what it referred to as the " 'patch and repair' approach proposed by the state" because it "would not achieve suburban comparability or the visual attractiveness sought by the court as it would result in floor covering with unsightly sections of mismatched carpeting and tile and individual walls possessing different shades of paint." The District Court reasoned that "if the KCMSD schools underwent the limited renovation proposed by the state, the schools would continue to be unattractive and substandard, and would certainly serve as a deterrent to parents considering enrolling their children in KCMSD schools." As of 1990, the District Court had ordered $260 million in capital improvements. Since then, the total cost of capital improvements ordered has soared to over $540 million.

As part of its desegregation plan, the District Court has ordered salary assistance to the KCMSD. In 1987, the District Court initially ordered salary assistance only for teachers within the KCMSD. Since that time, however, the District Court has ordered salary assistance to all but three of the approximately 5,000 KCMSD employees. The total cost of this component of the desegregation remedy since 1987 is over $200 million.

The District Court's desegregation plan has been described as the most ambitious and expensive remedial program in the history of school desegregation. The annual cost per pupil at the KCMSD far exceeds that of the neighboring SSD's or of any school district in Missouri. Nevertheless, the KCMSD, which has pursued a "friendly adversary" relationship with the plaintiffs, has continued to propose ever more expensive programs. As a result, the desegregation costs have escalated and now are approaching an annual cost of $200 million. These massive expenditures have financed

> "high schools in which every classroom will have air conditioning, an alarm system, and 15 microcomputers; a 2,000–square–foot planetarium; green houses and vivariums; a 25–acre farm with an air-conditioned meeting room for 104 people; a Model United Nations wired for language translation; broadcast capable radio and television studios with an editing and animation lab; a temperature controlled art gallery; movie editing and screening rooms; a 3,500–square–foot dust-free diesel mechanics room; 1,875–square–foot elementary school animal rooms for use in a zoo project; swimming pools, and numerous other facilities." Missouri v. Jenkins, 495 U.S. 33, 77 (1990) (*Jenkins II*)(Kennedy, J., concurring in part and concurring in judgment).

Not surprisingly, the cost of this remedial plan has "far exceeded KCMSD's budget, or for that matter, its authority to tax." Id. at 60. The state, through the operation of joint-and-several liability, has borne the brunt of these costs. The District Court candidly has acknowledged that it has "allowed the District planners to dream" and "provided the mechanism for th[ose] dreams to be realized." In short, the District Court "has gone to great lengths to provide KCMSD with facilities and opportunities not available anywhere else in the country."

II

With this background, we turn to the present controversy. . . . Because of the importance of the issues, we granted certiorari to consider the following: (1) whether the District Court exceeded its constitutional authority when it granted salary increases to virtually all instructional and non-instructional employees of the KCMSD, and (2) whether the District Court properly relied upon the fact that student achievement test scores had failed to rise to some unspecified level when it declined to find that the state had achieved partial unitary status as to the quality education programs.

III

. . . Almost 25 years ago, in Swann v. Charlotte–Mecklenburg Bd. of Ed., 402 U.S. 1 (1971), we dealt with the authority of a district court to fashion remedies for a school district that had been segregated in law in violation of the Equal Protection Clause of the Fourteenth Amendment. Although recognizing the discretion that must necessarily adhere in a district court in fashioning a remedy, we also recognized the limits on such remedial power. . . . Three years later, in *Milliken I*, supra, we held that a District Court had exceeded its authority in fashioning interdistrict relief where the surrounding school districts had not themselves been guilty of any constitutional violation. We said that a desegregation remedy "is necessarily designed, as all remedies are, to restore the victims of discriminatory conduct to the position they would have occupied in the absence of such conduct." "[W]ithout an interdistrict violation and interdistrict effect, there is no constitutional wrong calling for an interdistrict remedy." . . .

Three years later, in Milliken v. Bradley, 433 U.S. 267, 280–81 (1977) (*Milliken II*), we articulated a three-part framework derived from our prior cases to guide district courts in the exercise of their remedial authority:

> In the first place, like other equitable remedies, the nature of the desegregation remedy is to be determined by the nature and scope of

> the constitutional violation. The remedy must therefore be related to "the *condition* alleged to offend the Constitution. . . . " *Milliken I*, 418 U.S., at 738. Second, the decree must indeed be *remedial* in nature, that is, it must be designed as nearly as possible "to restore the victims of discriminatory conduct to the position they would have occupied in the absence of such conduct." Id., at 746. Third, the federal courts in devising a remedy must take into account the interests of state and local authorities in managing their own affairs, consistent with the Constitution. . . .

Because "federal supervision of local school systems was intended as a temporary measure to remedy past discrimination," Bd. of Ed. of Oklahoma City v. Dowell, 498 U.S. 237, 247 (1991), we also have considered the showing that must be made by a school district operating under a desegregation order for complete or partial relief from that order. In Freeman v. Pitts, 503 U.S. 467, 491 (1992), we stated that

> [a]mong the factors which must inform the sound discretion of the court in ordering partial withdrawal are the following: [1] whether there has been full and satisfactory compliance with the decree in those aspects of the system where supervision is to be withdrawn; [2] whether retention of judicial control is necessary or practicable to achieve compliance with the decree in other facts of the school system; and [3] whether the school district has demonstrated, to the public and to the parents and students of the once disfavored race, its good-faith commitment to the whole of the courts' decree and to those provisions of the law and the Constitution that were the predicate for judicial intervention in the first place.
>
> The ultimate inquiry is " 'whether the [constitutional violator] ha[s] complied in good faith with the desegregation decree since it was entered, and whether the vestiges of past discrimination ha[ve] been eliminated to the extent practicable.' " Id., at 492.

Proper analysis of the District Court's orders challenged here, then, must rest upon their serving as proper means to the end of restoring the victims of discriminatory conduct to the position they would have occupied in the absence of that conduct and their eventual restoration of "state and local authorities to the control of a school system that is operating in compliance with the Constitution." Id., at 489. We turn to that analysis.

The state argues that the order approving salary increases is beyond the District Court's authority because it was crafted to serve an "interdistrict goal," in spite of the fact that the constitutional violation in this case is "intradistrict" in nature. . . . The proper response to an intradistrict violation is an intradistrict remedy that serves to eliminate the racial identity of the schools within the effected school district by eliminating, as far as practicable, the vestiges of de jure segregation in all facets of their operations.

Here, the District Court has found, and the Court of Appeals has affirmed, that this case involved no interdistrict constitutional violation that would support interdistrict relief. . . . Thus, the proper response by the District Court should have been to eliminate to the extent practicable the vestiges of prior de jure segregation within the KCMSD: a system-wide reduction in student achievement and the existence of 25 racially identifiable schools with a population of over 90% black students.

The District Court and Court of Appeals, however, have felt that because the KCMSD's enrollment remained 68.3% black, a purely intradistrict remedy would be insufficient. . . . But, as noted in *Milliken I*, we have rejected the suggestion "that schools which have a majority of Negro students are not 'desegregated' whatever the racial makeup of the school district's population and however neutrally the district lines have been drawn and administered." . . .

Instead of seeking to remove the racial identity of the various schools within the KCMSD, the District Court has set out on a program to create a school district that was equal to or superior to the surrounding SSD's. Its remedy has focused on "desegregative attractiveness," coupled with "suburban comparability." . . .

The purpose of desegregative attractiveness has been not only to remedy the system-wide reduction in student achievement, but also to attract nonminority students not presently enrolled in the KCMSD. This remedy has included an elaborate program of capital improvements, course enrichment, and extracurricular enhancement not simply in the formerly identifiable black schools, but in schools throughout the district. The District Court's remedial orders have converted every senior high school, every middle school, and one-half of the elementary schools in the KCMSD into "magnet" schools. The District Court's remedial order has all but made the KCMSD itself into a magnet district.

We previously have approved of intradistrict desegregation remedies involving magnet schools. See, e.g., *Milliken II*. Magnet schools have the advantage of encouraging voluntary movement of students within a school district in a pattern that aids desegregation on a voluntary basis, without requiring extensive busing and redrawing of district boundary lines. As a component in an intradistrict remedy, magnet schools also are attractive because they promote desegregation while limiting the withdrawal of white student enrollment that may result from mandatory student reassignment.

The District Court's remedial plan in this case, however, is not designed solely to redistribute the students within the KCMSD in order to eliminate racially identifiable schools within the KCMSD. Instead, its purpose is to attract nonminority students from outside the KCMSD schools. But this interdistrict goal is beyond the scope of the intradistrict violation identified by the District Court. In effect, the District Court has devised a remedy to accomplish indirectly what it admittedly lacks the remedial authority to mandate directly: the interdistrict transfer of students.

In *Milliken I* we determined that a desegregation remedy that would require mandatory interdistrict reassignment of students throughout the Detroit metropolitan area was an impermissible interdistrict response to the intradistrict violation identified. In that case, the lower courts had ordered an interdistrict remedy because " 'any less comprehensive a solution than a metropolitan area plan would result in an all black school system immediately surrounded by practically all white suburban school systems, with an overwhelmingly white majority population in the total metropolitan area.' " We held that before a district court could order an interdistrict remedy, there must be a showing that "racially discriminatory acts of the state or local school districts, or of a single school district have been a substantial cause of interdistrict segregation." Because the record "contain[ed] evidence of de jure segregated conditions only in the Detroit schools" and there had been "no showing of significant violation by the 53 outlying school districts and no evidence of interdistrict violation or effect," we reversed the District Court's grant of interdistrict relief. . . .

What we meant in *Milliken I* by an interdistrict violation was a violation that caused segregation between adjoining districts. Nothing in *Milliken I* suggests that the District Court in that case could have circumvented the limits on its remedial authority by requiring the state of Michigan, a constitutional violator, to implement a magnet program designed to achieve the same interdistrict transfer of students that we held was beyond its remedial authority. Here, the District Court has done just that: created a magnet district of the KCMSD in order to serve the interdistrict goal of attracting nonminority students from the surrounding SSD's and redistributing them within the KCMSD. The District Court's pursuit of "desegregative attractiveness" is beyond the scope of its broad remedial authority.

Respondents argue that the District Court's reliance upon desegregative attractiveness is justified in light of the District Court's statement that segregation has "led to white flight from the KCMSD to suburban districts." [But the] lower courts' "findings" as to "white flight" are . . . inconsistent with the typical supposition, bolstered here by the record evidence, that "white flight" may result from desegregation, not de jure segregation. . . . The record here does not support the District Court's reliance on "white flight" as a justification for a permissible expansion of its intradistrict remedial authority through its pursuit of desegregative attractiveness.

Justice Souter claims that our holding effectively overrules Hills v. Gautreaux, 425 U.S. 284 (1976). In *Gautreaux*, the Federal Department of Housing and Urban Development (HUD) was found to have participated, along with a local housing agency, in establishing and maintaining a racially segregated public housing program. After the Court of Appeals ordered " 'the adoption of a comprehensive metropolitan area plan,' " we granted certiorari to consider the "permissibility in the light of [*Milliken I*] of 'interdistrict relief for discrimination in public housing in the absence of a finding of an inter-district violation.' " Because the "relevant geographic area for the purposes of the [plaintiffs'] housing options [was] the Chicago housing market, not the Chicago city limits," we concluded that "a metropolitan area remedy . . . [was] not impermissible as a matter of law."

Our decision today is fully consistent with *Gautreaux*. A district court seeking to remedy an intradistrict violation that has not "directly caused" significant interdistrict effects, *Milliken I*, 418 U.S., at 744–45, exceeds its remedial authority if it orders a remedy with an interdistrict purpose. This conclusion follows directly from *Milliken II*, decided one year after *Gautreaux*, where we reaffirmed the bedrock principle that "federal-court decrees exceed appropriate limits if they are aimed at eliminating a condition that does not violate the Constitution or does not flow from such a violation." In *Milliken II*, we also emphasized that "federal courts in devising a remedy must taken into account the interests of state and local authorities in managing their own affairs, consistent with the Constitution." *Gautreaux*, however, involved the imposition of a remedy upon a federal agency. Thus, it did not raise the same federalism concerns that are implicated when a federal court issues a remedial order against a state.

The District Court's pursuit of "desegregative attractiveness" cannot be reconciled with our cases placing limitations on a district court's remedial authority. It is certainly theoretically possible that the greater the expenditure per pupil within the KCMSD, the more likely it is that some unknowable number of nonminority students not presently attending schools in the KCMSD will choose to enroll in those schools. . . . But this rationale is not susceptible to any objective limitation. . . . This case provides numerous examples demonstrating the limitless authority of the District Court operating under this rationale. . . . In short, desegregative attractiveness has been used "as the hook on which to hang numerous policy choices about improving the quality of education in general within the KCMSD." *Jenkins II*, 495 U.S., at 76 (Kennedy, J., concurring in part and concurring in judgment).

Nor are there limits to the duration of the District Court's involvement. The expenditures per pupil in the KCMSD currently far exceed those in the neighboring SSD's.[a] Sixteen years after this litigation began, the District Court recognized that the KCMSD has yet to offer a viable method of financing the "wonderful school system being built." Each additional program ordered by the District Court—and financed by the state—to increase the "desegregative attractiveness" of the school district makes the KCMSD more and more dependent on additional funding from the state; in turn, the greater the KCMSD's dependence on state funding, the greater its reliance on continued supervision by the District Court. But our cases recognize that local autonomy of school districts is a vital national tradition and that a district court must strive to restore state and local authorities to the control of a school system operating in compliance with the Constitution.

The District Court's pursuit of the goal of "desegregative attractiveness" results in so many imponderables and is so far removed from the task of eliminating the racial identifiability of the schools within the KCMSD that we believe it is beyond the admittedly broad discretion of the District Court. In this posture, we conclude that the District Court's order of salary increases, which was "grounded in remedying the vestiges of segregation by improving the desegregative attractiveness of the KCMSD" is simply too far removed from an acceptable implementation of a permissible means to remedy previous illegally mandated segregation.

Similar considerations lead us to conclude that the District Court's order requiring the state to continue to fund the quality education programs because student achievement levels were still "at or below national norms at many grade levels" cannot be sustained. The state does not seek from this Court a declaration of partial unitary status with respect to the quality education programs. It challenges the requirement of indefinite funding of a quality education program until national norms are met, based on the assumption that while a mandate for significant education improvement, both in teaching and in facilities, may have been justified originally, its indefinite extension is not.

Our review in this respect is needlessly complicated because the District Court made no findings in its order approving continued funding of the quality education programs. . . . The basic task of the District Court is to decide whether the reduction in achievement by minority students attributable to prior de jure segregation has been remedied to the extent practicable. Under our precedents, the State and the KCMSD are "entitled to a rather precise statement of [their] obligations under a desegregation decree." *Dowell*, 498 U.S., at 246. Although the District Court has determined that "[s]egregation has caused a system wide *reduction* in achieve-

[a] Annual per-pupil costs, excluding capital costs, in the suburban school districts ranged from $2,854 to $5,956. The comparable figure for the KCMSD was $9,412 according to one calculation and $7,665 according to another.—[Footnote by eds.]

ment in the schools of the KCMSD," it never has identified the incremental effect that segregation has had on minority student achievement or the specific goals of the quality education programs.

In reconsidering this order, the District Court should apply our three-part test from *Freeman v. Pitts*, supra. The District Court should consider that the state's role with respect to the quality education programs has been limited to the funding, not the implementation, of those programs. As all the parties agree that improved achievement on test scores is not necessarily required for the state to achieve partial unitary status as to the quality education programs, the District Court should sharply limit, if not dispense with, its reliance on this factor. Just as demographic changes independent of de jure segregation will affect the racial composition of student assignments, so too will numerous external factors beyond the control of the KCMSD and the state affect minority student achievement. So far as these external factors are not the result of segregation, they do not figure in the remedial calculus. Insistence upon academic goals unrelated to the effects of legal segregation unwarrantably postpones the day when the KCMSD will be able to operate on its own.

The District Court also should consider that many goals of its quality education plan already have been attained: the KCMSD now is equipped with "facilities and opportunities not available anywhere else in the country." KCMSD schools received an AAA rating eight years ago, and the present remedial programs have been in place for seven years. It may be that in education, just as it may be in economics, a "rising tide lifts all boats," but the remedial quality education program should be tailored to remedy the injuries suffered by the victims of prior de jure segregation. Minority students in kindergarten through grade 7 in the KCMSD always have attended AAA-rated schools; minority students in the KCMSD that previously attended schools rated below AAA have since received remedial education programs for a period of up to seven years.

On remand, the District Court must bear in mind that its end purpose is not only "to remedy the violation" to the extent practicable, but also "to restore state and local authorities to the control of a school system that is operating in compliance with the Constitution." *Freeman*, 503 U.S., at 489.

The judgment of the Court of Appeals is reversed.

■ JUSTICE O'CONNOR, concurring. . . .

School desegregation remedies are intended, "as all remedies are, to restore the victims of discriminatory conduct to the position they would have occupied in the absence of such conduct." Milliken v. Bradley, 418 U.S. 717, 746 (1974) (*Milliken I*). In the paradigmatic case of an interdistrict violation, where district boundaries are drawn on the basis of race, a regional remedy is appropriate to ensure integration across district lines. So too where surrounding districts contribute to the constitutional violation by affirmative acts intended to segregate the races—e.g., where those districts "arrang[e] for white students residing in the Detroit District to attend schools in Oakland and Macomb Counties." Id., at 746–47. *Milliken I* of course permits interdistrict remedies in these instances of interdistrict violations. Beyond that, interdistrict remedies are also proper where "there has been a constitutional violation within one district that produces a significant segregative effect in another district." Id., at 745. Such segregative effect may be present where a predominantly black district accepts black children from adjacent districts, or perhaps even where the fact of intradistrict segregation actually causes whites to flee the district, for example, to avoid discriminatorily underfunded schools—and such actions produce regional segregation along district lines. In these cases, where a purely intradistrict violation has caused a significant interdistrict segregative effect, certain interdistrict remedies may be appropriate. Where, however, the segregative effects of a district's constitutional violation are contained within that district's boundaries, there is no justification for a remedy that is interdistrict in scope and nature.

Here, where the District Court found that KCMSD students attended schools separated by their race and that facilities have "literally rotted," the District Court of course should order restorations and remedies that would place previously segregated black KCMSD students at par with their white counterparts. . . .

What the District Court did in this case, however, and how it transgressed the constitutional bounds of its remedial powers, is to make desegregative attractiveness the underlying goal of its remedy for the specific purpose of reversing the trend of white flight. However troubling that trend may be, remedying it is within the District Court's authority only it if is "directly caused by the constitutional violation." *Milliken I*, 418 U.S., at 745. . . . The unfortunate fact of racial imbalance and bias in our society, however pervasive or invidious, does not admit of judicial intervention absent a constitutional violation. . . .

■ JUSTICE THOMAS, concurring.

It never ceases to amaze me that the courts are so willing to assume that anything that is predominantly black must be inferior. Instead of focusing on remedying the harm done to those black schoolchildren injured by segregation, the District Court here sought to convert the Kansas City, Missouri, School District (KCMSD) into a "magnet district" that would reverse the "white flight" caused by desegregation. In this respect, I join the Court's decision concerning the two remedial issues presented for review. I write separately, however, to add a few thoughts with respect to the overall course of this litigation. . . .

I

A

The mere fact that a school is black does not mean that it is the product of a constitutional violation. . . .

In the present case, the District Court inferred a continuing constitutional violation from two primary facts: the existence of de jure segregation in the KCMSD prior to 1954, and the existence of de facto segregation today. The District Court found that in 1954, the KCMSD operated 16 segregated schools for black students, and that in 1974 39 schools in the district were more than 90% black. Desegregation efforts reduced this figure somewhat, but the District Court stressed that 24 schools remained "racially isolated," that is, more than 90% black, in 1983–84. For the District Court, it followed that the KCMSD has not dismantled the dual system entirely. . . .

Without more, the District Court's findings could not have supported a finding of liability against the state. It should by now be clear that the existence of one-race schools is not by itself an indication that the state is practicing segregation. The continuing "racial isolation" of schools after de jure segregation has ended may well reflect voluntary housing choices or other private decisions. Here, for instance, the demography of the entire KCMSD has changed considerably since 1954. Though blacks accounted for only 18.9% of KCMSD's enrollment in 1954, by 1983–84, the school district was 67.7% black. That certain schools are overwhelmingly black in a district that is now more than two-thirds black is hardly a sure sign of intentional state action.

. . . The District Court . . . rested the state's liability on the simple fact that the state had intentionally created the dual school system before 1954, and had failed to fulfill "its affirmative duty of disestablishing a dual school system subsequent to 1954." According to the District Court, the schools whose student bodies were more than 90% black constituted "vestiges" of the prior de jure segregation, which the state and the KCMSD had an obligation to eliminate. Later, in the course of issuing its first "remedial" order, the District Court added that a "system wide reduction in student achievement in the schools of . . . KCMSD" was also a vestige of the prior de jure segregation. . . .

When a district court holds the state liable for discrimination almost 30 years after the last official state action, it must do more than show that there are schools with high black populations or low test scores. . . . In fact, where, as here, the finding of liability comes so late in the day, I would think it incumbent upon the District Court to explain how more recent social or demographic phenomena did not cause the "vestiges." This the District Court did not do.

B

Without a basis in any real finding of intentional government action, the District Court's imposition of liability upon the state of Missouri improperly rests upon a theory that racial imbalances are unconstitutional. That is, the court has "indulged the presumption, often irrebuttable in practice, that a presently observed [racial] imbalance has been proximately caused by intentional state action during the prior de jure era." United States v. Fordice, 505 U.S. 717, 745 (1992)(Thomas, J., concurring). In effect, the court found that racial imbalances constituted an ongoing constitutional violation that continued to inflict harm on black students. This position appears to rest upon the idea that any school that is black is inferior, and that blacks cannot succeed without the benefit of the company of whites.

The District Court's willingness to adopt such stereotypes stemmed from a misreading of our earliest school desegregation case. In Brown v. Board of Education, 347 U.S. 483 (1954) (*Brown I*), the Court noted several psychological and sociological studies purporting to show that de jure segregation harmed black students by generating "a feeling of inferiority" in them. Seizing upon this passage in *Brown I*, the District Court asserted that "forced segregation ruins attitudes and is inherently unequal." The District Court suggested that this inequality continues in full force even after the end of de jure segregation. [T]he District Court seemed to believe that black students in the KCMSD would continue to receive an "inferior education" despite the end of de jure segregation, as long as de facto segregation persisted. . . .

[But segregation] was not unconstitutional because it might have caused psychological feelings of inferiority. [S]egregation violated the Constitution because the state classified students based on their race. Of course, segregation additionally harmed black students by relegating them to schools with substandard facilities and resources. But neutral policies, such as local school assignments, do not offend the Constitution when individual private choices concerning work or residence produce schools with high black populations. . . .

Given that desegregation has not produced the predicted leaps forward in black educational achievement, there is no reason to think that black students cannot learn as well when surrounded by members of their own race as when they are in an integrated environment. Indeed, it may very well be that what has been true for historically black colleges is true for black middle and high schools. Despite their origins in "the shameful history of state-enforced segregation," these institutions can be " 'both a source of pride to blacks who have attended them and a source of hope to black families who want the benefits of . . . learning for their children.' " *Fordice*, 505 U.S., at 748 (Thomas, J., concurring). Because of their "distinctive histories and traditions," id., black schools can function as the center and symbol of black communities, and provide examples of independent black leadership, success, and achievement.

Thus, even if the District Court had been on firmer ground in identifying a link between the KCMSD's pre–1954 de jure segregation and the present "racial isolation" of some of the district's schools, mere de facto segregation (unaccompanied by discriminatory inequalities in educational resources) does not constitute a continuing harm after the end of de jure segregation. "Racial isolation" itself is not a harm; only state-enforced segregation is. After all, if separation itself is a harm, and if integration therefore is the only way that blacks can receive a proper education, then there must be something inferior about blacks. Under this theory, segregation injures blacks because blacks, when left on their own, cannot achieve. To my way of thinking, that conclusion is the result of a jurisprudence based upon a theory of black inferiority. . . .

II

. . . The District Court's unwarranted focus on the psychological harm to blacks and on racial imbalances has been only half of the tale. Not only did the court subscribe to a theory of injury that was predicated on black inferiority, it also married this concept of liability to our expansive approach to remedial powers. We have given the federal courts the freedom to use any measure necessary to reverse problems—such as racial isolation or low educational achievement—that have proven stubbornly resistant to government policies. We have not permitted constitutional principles such as federalism or the separation of powers to stand in the way of our drive to reform the schools. Thus, the District Court here ordered massive expenditures by local and state authorities, without congressional or executive authorization and without any indication that such measures would attract whites back to KCMSD or raise KCMSD test scores. The time has come for us to put the genie back in the bottle.

A

The Constitution extends "[t]he judicial Power of the United States" to "all Cases, in Law and Equity, arising under this Constitution, the Laws of the United States, and Treaties made . . . under their Authority." Art. III, §§ 1, 2. I assume for the purposes of this case that the remedial authority of the federal courts is inherent in the "judicial Power," as there is no general equitable remedial power expressly granted by the Constitution or by statute. As with any inherent judicial power, however, we ought to be reluctant to approve its aggressive or extravagant use, and instead we should exercise it in a manner consistent with our history and traditions.

Motivated by our worthy desire to eradicate segregation, however, we have disregarded this principle and given the courts unprecedented authority to shape a remedy in equity. Although at times we have invalidated a decree as beyond the bounds of an equitable remedy, see Milliken v. Bradley, 418 U.S. 717 (1974) (*Milliken I*), these instances have been far outnumbered by the expansions in the equity power. In United States v. Montgomery County Bd. of Ed., 395 U.S. 225 (1969), for example, we allowed federal courts to desegregate faculty and staff according to specific mathematical ratios, with the ultimate goal that each school in the system would have roughly the same proportion of white and black faculty. In Swann v. Charlotte–Mecklenburg Bd. of Ed., 402 U.S. 1 (1971), we permitted federal courts to order busing, to set racial targets for school populations, and to alter attendance zones. And in Milliken v. Bradley, 433 U.S. 267 (1977) (*Milliken II*), we approved the use of remedial or compensatory education programs paid for by the state.

In upholding these court-ordered measures, we indicated that trial judges had virtually boundless discretion in crafting remedies once they had identified a constitutional violation. . . .

Our willingness to unleash the federal equitable power has reached areas beyond school desegregation. Federal courts have used "structural injunctions," as they are known, not only to supervise our nation's schools, but also to manage prisons, mental hospitals, and public housing. See generally D. Horowitz, The Courts and Social Policy 4–9 (1977). Judges have directed or managed the reconstruction of entire institutions and bureaucracies, with little regard for the inherent limitations on their authority.

B

Such extravagant uses of judicial power are at odds with the history and tradition of the equity power and the Framers' design. The available historical records suggest that the Framers did not intend federal equitable remedies to reach as broadly as we have permitted. . . .

At the very least . . . we should exercise the power to impose equitable remedies only sparingly, subject to clear rules guiding its use.

C

Two clear restraints on the use of the equity power—federalism and the separation of powers—derive from the very form of our government. Federal courts should pause before using their inherent equitable powers to intrude into the proper sphere of the states. We have long recognized that education is primarily a concern of local authorities. . . . A structural reform decree eviscerates a state's discretionary authority over its own program and budgets and forces state officials to reallocate state resources and funds to the desegregation plan at the expense of other citizens, other government programs, and other institutions not represented in court. When District Courts seize complete control over the schools, they strip state and local governments of one of their most important governmental responsibilities, and thus deny their existence as independent governmental entities. . . .

The separation of powers imposes additional restraints on the judiciary's exercise of its remedial powers. To be sure, this is not a case of one branch of government encroaching on the prerogatives of another, but rather of the power of the federal government over the states. Nonetheless, what the federal courts cannot do at the federal level they cannot do against the states; in either case, Article III courts are constrained by the inherent constitutional limitations on their powers. There simply are certain things that courts, in order to remain courts, cannot and should not do. There is no difference between courts running school systems or prisons and courts running executive agencies.

In this case, not only did the District Court exercise the legislative power to tax, it also engaged in budgeting, staffing, and educational decisions, in judgments about the location and aesthetic quality of the schools, and in administrative oversight and monitoring. These functions involve a legislative or executive, rather than a judicial power. . . .

D

The dissent's approval of the District Court's treatment of salary increases is typical of this Court's failure to place limits on the equitable remedial power. The dissent frames the inquiry thus: "[t]he only issue, then, is whether the salary increases ordered by the District Court have been reasonably related towards achieving" the goal of remedying a systemwide reduction in student achievement, "keeping in mind the broad discretion enjoyed by the District Court in exercising its equitable powers." In response to its question, the dissent concludes that "it is difficult to see how the District Court abused its discretion" in either the 1992 or 1993 orders and characterizes the lower court's orders as "beyond reproach." When the standard of review is as vague as whether "federal-court decrees . . . directly address and relate to the constitutional violation," *Milliken II*, 433 U.S., at 281–82, it is difficult to ever find a remedial order "unreasonable." Such criteria provide District Courts with little guidance, and provide appellate courts few principles with which to review trial court decisions. If the standard reduces to what one believes is a "fair" remedy, or what vaguely appears to be a good "fit" between violation and remedy, then there is little hope of imposing the constraints on the equity power that the Framers envisioned and that our constitutional system requires.

Contrary to the dissent's conclusion, the District Court's remedial orders are in tension with two common-sense principles. First, the District Court retained jurisdiction over the implementation and modification of the remedial decree, instead of terminating its involvement after issuing its remedy. Although briefly mentioned in Brown v. Board of Education, 349 U.S. 294 (1955) (*Brown II*), as a temporary measure to overcome local resistance to desegregation ("[d]uring this period of transition, the courts will retain jurisdiction"), this concept of continuing judicial involvement has permitted the District Courts to revise their remedies constantly in order to reach some broad, abstract, and often elusive goal. Not only does this approach deprive the parties of finality and a clear understanding of their responsibilities, but it also tends to inject the judiciary into the day-to-day management of institutions and local policies—a function that lies outside of our Article III competence.

Much of the District Court's overreaching in this case occurred because it employed this hit-or-miss method to shape, and reshape, its remedial decree. Using its authority of continuing jurisdiction, the Court pursued its goal of decreasing "racial isolation" regardless of the cost or of the difficulties of engineering demographic changes. Wherever possible, district courts should focus their remedial discretion on devising and implementing a unified remedy in a single decree. . . .

Second, the District Court failed to target its equitable remedies in this case specifically to cure the harm suffered by the victims of segregation. Of course, the initial and most important aspect of any remedy will be to eliminate any invidious racial distinctions in matters such as student assignments, transportation, staff, resource allocation, and activities. This element of most desegregation decrees is fairly straightforward and has not produced many examples of overreaching by the district courts. It is the "compensatory" ingredient in many desegregation plans that has produced many of the difficulties in the case before us.

Having found that segregation "has caused a system wide reduction in student achievement in the schools of the KCMSD," the District Court ordered the series of magnet school plans, educational programs, and capital improvements that the Court criticizes today because of their interdistrict nature. In ordering these programs, the District Court exceeded its authority by benefitting those who were not victims of discriminatory conduct. KCMSD as a whole may have experienced reduced achievement levels, but raising the test scores of the entire district is a goal that is not sufficiently tailored to restoring the victims of segregation to the position they would have occupied absent discrimination. A school district cannot be discriminated against on the basis of its race, because a school district has no race. It goes without saying that only individuals can suffer from discrimination, and only individuals can receive the remedy. . . .

To ensure that district courts do not embark on such broad initiatives in the future, we should demand that remedial decrees be more precisely designed to benefit only those who have been victims of segregation. Race-conscious remedies for discrimination not only must serve a compelling governmental interest (which is met in desegregation cases), but also must be narrowly tailored to further that interest. See Richmond v. J.A. Croson Co., 488 U.S. 469, 509–10 (1989)(plurality opinion). In the absence of special circumstances, the remedy for de jure segregation ordinarily should not include educational programs for students who were not in school (or were even alive) during the period of segregation. Although I do not doubt that all KCMSD students benefit from many of the initiatives ordered by the court below, it is for the democratically accountable state and local officials to decide whether they are to be made available even to those who were never harmed by segregation.

III

This Court should never approve a state's efforts to deny students, because of their race, an equal opportunity for education. But the federal courts also should avoid using racial equality as a pretext for solving social problems that do not violate the Constitution. . . . The desire to reform a school district, or any other institution, cannot so captivate the judiciary that it forgets its constitutionally mandated role. Usurpation of the traditionally local control over education not only takes the judiciary beyond its proper sphere, it also deprives the states and their elected officials of their constitutional powers. At some point, we must recognize that the judiciary is not omniscient, and that all problems do not require a remedy of constitutional proportions.

■ JUSTICE SOUTER, with whom JUSTICE STEVENS, JUSTICE GINSBURG, and JUSTICE BREYER join, dissenting. . . .

I

[In this part of his opinion, Justice Souter argued that the broad question of the legitimacy of the magnet school concept was not "fairly included" in the questions presented in the state's petition for certiorari and therefore should not have been reached. He then turned to the specific issues of reliance on test scores and court-ordered salary increases.]

II

A

The test score question as it comes to us is one of word play, not substance. While the Court insists that the District Court's order of June 17, 1992 (the only order relevant to the test score question on review here), "requir[ed] the state to continue to fund the quality education programs because student achievement levels [in the KCMSD] were still 'at or below national norms at many grade levels . . . ,' " that order contains no discussion at all of student achievement levels in the KCMSD in comparison to national norms, and in fact does not explicitly address the subject of partial unitary status. The reference to test scores "at or below national norms" comes from an entirely different and subsequent order of the District Court (dated Apr. 16, 1993) which is not under review. Its language presumably would not have been quoted to us, if the Court of Appeals's opinion affirming the District Court's June 17, 1992 order had not canvassed subsequent orders and mentioned the District Court's finding of fact that the "KCMSD is still at or below national norms at made grade levels." In any event, what is important here is that none of the District Court's or Court of Appeals's opinions or orders requires a certain level of test scores before unitary status can be found, or indicates that test scores are the only thing standing between the state and a finding of unitary status as to the KCMSD's *Milliken II* programs.[b] . . .

Looking ahead, if indeed the state believes itself entitled to a finding of partial unitary status on the subject of educational programs, there is an orderly procedural course for it to follow. It may frame a proper motion for partial unitary status, and prepare to make a record sufficient to allow the District Court and the Court of Appeals to address the continued need for and efficacy of the *Milliken II* programs.

In the development of a proper unitary status record, test scores will undoubtedly play a role. It is true, as the Court recognizes, that all parties to this case agree that it would be error to require that the students in a school district attain the national average test score as a prerequisite to a finding of partial unitary status, if only because all sorts of causes independent of the vestiges of past school segregation might stand in the way of the goal. That said, test scores will clearly be relevant in determining whether the improvement programs have cured a deficiency in student achievement to the practicable extent. The District Court has noted (in the finding that the Court would read as a dispositive requirement for unitary status) that while students' scores have shown a trend of improvement, they remain at or below national norms. The significance of this fact is subject to assessment. Depending, of course, on other facts developed in the course of unitary status proceedings, the improvement to less than the na-

[b] As Justice Souter elsewhere explained, Milliken v. Bradley, 433 U.S. 267 (1977) (*Milliken II*), held that a district court could correct the deficits resulting from a segregated school system by ordering quality education programs, often called *Milliken II* programs.—[Footnote by eds.]

tional average might reasonably be taken to show that education programs are having a good effect on student achievement, and that further improvement can be expected. On the other hand, if test score changes were shown to have flattened out, that might suggest the impracticability of any additional remedial progress. While the significance of scores is thus open to judgment, the judgment is not likely to be very sound unless it is informed by more of a record than we have in front of us, and the Court's admonition that the District Court should "sharply limit" its reliance on test scores should be viewed in this light.

B

The other question properly before us has to do with the propriety of the District Court's recent salary orders. While the Court suggests otherwise, the District Court did not ground its orders of salary increases solely on the goal of attracting students back to the KCMSD. From the start, the District Court has consistently treated salary increases as an important element in remedying the systemwide reduction in student achievement resulting from segregation in the KCMSD. [T]he Court does not question this remedial goal, which we expressly approved in *Milliken II*. The only issue, then, is whether the salary increases ordered by the District Court have been reasonably related to achieving that goal, keeping in mind the broad discretion enjoyed by the District Court in exercising its equitable powers. . . .

The District Court first ordered KCMSD salary increases, limited to teachers, in 1987, basing its decision on the need to raise the level of student achievement. "[I]t is essential that the KCMSD have sufficient revenues to fund an operating budget which can provide quality education, including a high quality faculty." The state raised no objection to the District Court's order, and said nothing about the issue of salary increases in its 1988 appeal to the Eighth Circuit.

When the District Court's 1987 order expired in 1990, all parties, including the state, agreed to a further order increasing salaries for both instructional and noninstructional personnel through the 1991–1992 school year. In 1992 the District Court merely ordered that salaries in the KCMSD be maintained at the same level for the following year, rejecting the state's argument that desegregation funding for salaries should be discontinued, and in 1993 ordered small salary increases for both instructional and noninstructional personnel through the end of the 1995–1996 school year.

It is the District Court's 1992 and 1993 orders that are before us, and it is difficult to see how the District Court abused its discretion in either instance. The District Court had evidence in front of it that adopting the state's position and discontinuing desegregation funding for salary levels would result in their abrupt drop to 1986–1987 levels, with the resulting disparity between teacher pay in the district and the nationwide level increasing to as much as 40–45 percent, and a mass exodus of competent employees likely taking place. Faced with this evidence, the District Court found that continued desegregation funding of salaries, and small increases in those salaries over time, were essential to the successful implementation of its remedial scheme, including the elevation of student achievement: . . .

> High quality personnel are necessary not only to implement specialized desegregation programs intended to "improve educational op-

portunities and reduce racial isolation," but also to "ensure that there is no diminution in the quality of its regular academic program." . . .

The Court of Appeals affirmed the District Court's orders on the basis of these findings, again taking special note of the importance of adequate salaries to the remedial goal of improving student achievement:

> [Q]uality education programs and magnet schools [are] a part of the remedy for the vestiges of segregation causing a system wide reduction in student achievement in the KCMSD schools. . . . The significant finding of the [district] court with respect to the earlier funding order was that the salary increases were essential to comply with the court's desegregation orders, and that high quality teachers, administrators, and staff must be hired to improve the desegregative attractiveness of KCMSD. . . .

[T]he Court does not question the District Court's salary orders insofar as they relate to the objective of raising the level of student achievement in the KCMSD, but rather overlooks that basis for the orders altogether. The Court suggests that the District Court rested its approval of salary increases only on the object of drawing students into the district's schools and rejects the increases for that reason. It seems clear, however, that the District Court and the Court of Appeals both viewed the salary orders as serving two complementary but distinct purposes, and to the extent that the District Court concludes on remand that its salary orders are justified by reference to the quality of education alone, nothing in the Court's opinion precludes those orders from remaining in effect.

III

The two discrete questions that we actually accepted for review are, then, answerable on their own terms without any need to consider whether the District Court's use of the magnet school concept in its remedial plan is itself constitutionally vulnerable. . . .

But there is more to fuel dissent. . . . We have most recently summed up the obligation to correct the condition of de jure segregation by saying that "the duty of a former de jure district is to take 'whatever steps might be necessary to convert to a unitary system in which racial discrimination would be eliminated root and branch.' " *Freeman*, 503 U.S., at 486, quoting Green v. School Bd. of New Kent County, 391 U.S. 430, 437–38 (1968). Although the fashioning of judicial remedies to this end has been left, in the first instance, to the equitable discretion of the district courts, in Milliken v. Bradley, 418 U.S. 717 (1974) (*Milliken I*) we established an absolute limitation on this exercise of equitable authority. "[W]ithout an interdistrict violation and interdistrict effect, there is no constitutional wrong calling for an interdistrict remedy." Id., at 745.

The Court proceeds as if there is no question but that this proscription applies to this case. But the proscription does not apply. We are not dealing here with an interdistrict remedy in the sense that *Milliken I* used that term. In the *Milliken I* litigation, the District Court had ordered 53 surrounding school districts to be consolidated with the Detroit school system, and mandatory busing to be started within the enlarged district, even though the court had not found that any of the suburban districts had acted in violation of the Constitution. . . . It was this imposition of remedial measures on more than the one wrongdoing school district that we termed an "interdistrict remedy":

> We . . . turn to address, for the first time, the validity of a remedy mandating cross-district or interdistrict consolidation to remedy a condition of segregation found to exist in only one district.

Id., at 744. . . .

We did not hold, however, that any remedy that takes into account conditions outside of the district in which a constitutional violation has been committed is an "interdistrict remedy" and as such improper in the absence of an "interdistrict violation." To the contrary, by emphasizing that remedies in school desegregation cases are grounded in traditional equitable principles, we left open the possibility that a district court might subject a proven constitutional wrongdoer to a remedy with intended effects going beyond the district of the wrongdoer's violation, when such a remedy is necessary to redress the harms flowing from the constitutional violation.

The Court, nonetheless, reads *Milliken I* quite differently. It reads the case as categorically forbidding imposition of a remedy on a guilty district with intended consequences in a neighboring innocent district, unless the constitutional violation yielded segregative effects in that innocent district.

Today's decision therefore amounts to a redefinition of the terms of *Milliken I* and consequently to a substantial expansion of its limitation on the permissible remedies for prior segregation. The Court has not only rewritten *Milliken I*; it has effectively overruled a subsequent case. . . .

Two terms after *Milliken*, we decided Hills v. Gautreaux, 425 U.S. 284 (1976), a unanimous opinion by Justice Stewart. The District Court in *Gautreaux* had found that the United States Department of Housing and Urban Development (HUD) and the Chicago Housing Authority (CHA) had maintained a racially segregated system of public housing within the city of Chicago, in violation of various constitutional and statutory provisions. The issue before us was whether "the remedial order of the federal trial court [might] extend beyond Chicago's territorial boundaries." Id., at 286. [O]ur express understanding of the question we were deciding [was]: "the permissibility in light of *Milliken* of 'inter-district relief for discrimination in public housing in the absence of a finding of an inter-district violation.' " Id., at 292. . . .

We held that a district court may indeed subject a governmental perpetrator of segregative practices to an order for relief with intended consequences beyond the perpetrator's own subdivision, even in the absence of effects outside that subdivision, so long as the decree does not bind the authorities of other governmental units that are free of violations and segregative effects:

> [*Milliken*'s] holding that there had to be an interdistrict violation or effect before a federal court could order the crossing of district boundary lines reflected the substantive impact of a consolidation remedy on separate and independent school districts. The District Court's desegregation order in *Milliken* was held to be an impermissible remedy not because it envisioned relief against a wrongdoer extending beyond the city in which the violation occurred but because it contemplated a judicial decree restructuring the operation of local governmental entities that were not implicated in any constitutional violation. . . .

Id., at 296.

In the face of *Gautreaux*'s language, the Court claims that it was only because the " 'relevant geographic area for the purposes of the [plaintiffs'] housing options [was] the Chicago housing market, not the Chicago city limits' " that we held that " 'a metropolitan area remedy [was] not impermissible as a matter of law.' " But that was only half the explanation. Requiring a remedy outside the city in the wider metropolitan area was permissible not only because that was the area of the housing market even for people who lived within the city (thus relating the scope of the remedy to the violation suffered by the victims) but also because the trial court could order a remedy in that market without binding a governmental unit innocent of the violation and free of its effects. In "reject[ing] the contention that, since HUD's constitutional and statutory violations were committed in Chicago, *Milliken* precludes an order against HUD that will affect its conduct in the greater metropolitan area," we stated plainly that "[t]he critical distinction between HUD and the suburban school districts in *Milliken* is that HUD has been found to have violated the Constitution. . . . Nothing in the *Milliken* decision suggests a per se rule that federal courts lack authority to order parties found to have violated the Constitution to undertake boundaries of the city where the violation occurred." Id., at 298.

On its face, the District Court's magnet school concept falls entirely within the scope of equitable authority recognized in *Gautreaux*. In *Gautreaux*, the fact that the CHA and HUD had the authority to operate outside the limits of the city of Chicago meant that an order to fund or build housing beyond those limits would "not necessarily entail coercion of uninvolved governmental units. . . . " Id. Here, by the same token, the District Court has not sought to "consolidate or in any way restructure" the SSDs, or, indeed, to subject them to any remedial obligation at all. The District Court's remedial measures go only to the operation and quality of schools within the KCMSD, and the burden of those measures accordingly falls only on the two proven constitutional wrongdoers in this case, the KCMSD and the state. . . .

Gautreaux's holding is now effectively overruled, for the Court's opinion can be viewed as correct only on that assumption. But there is no apparent reason to reverse that decision, which represented the judgment of a unanimous Court, seems to reflect equitable common sense, and has been in the reports for two decades. . . .

■ JUSTICE GINSBURG, dissenting.

I join Justice Souter's illuminating dissent and emphasize a consideration key to this controversy.

The Court stresses that the present remedial programs have been in place for seven years. But compared to more than two centuries of firmly entrenched official discrimination, the experience with the desegregation remedies ordered by the District Court has been evanescent.

In 1724, Louis XV of France issued the Code Noir, the first slave code for the Colony of Louisiana, an area that included Missouri. When Missouri entered the union in 1821, it entered as a slave state.

Before the Civil War, Missouri law prohibited the creation or maintenance of schools for educating blacks: "No person shall keep or teach any school for the instruction of Negroes or mulattoes, in reading or writing, in this state." Act of Feb. 16, 1847, § 1.

Beginning in 1865, Missouri passed a series of laws requiring separate public schools for blacks. The Missouri Constitution first permitted, then required, separate schools.

After this Court announced its decision in Brown v. Board of Education, 347 U.S. 483 (1954), Missouri's Attorney General declared these provisions mandating segregated schools unenforceable. The statutes were repealed in 1957 and the constitutional provision was rescinded in 1976. Nonetheless, 30 years after *Brown*, the District Court found that "the inferior education indigenous of the state-compelled dual school system has lingering effects in the Kansas City, Missouri, School District," 593 F.Supp., at 1492. The District Court concluded that "the state . . . cannot defend its failure to affirmatively act to eliminate the structure and effects of its past dual system on the basis of restrictive state law." Id., at 1510. Just ten years ago, in June 1985, the District Court issued its first remedial order.

Today, the Court declares illegitimate the goal of attracting nonminority students to the Kansas city, Missouri, School District and thus stops the District Court's effort to integrate a school district that was, in the 1984/1985 school year, sorely in need and 68.3% black. Given the deep, inglorious history of segregation in Missouri, to curtail desegregation at this time and in this manner is an action at once too swift and too soon.

NOTES ON MISSOURI V. JENKINS

1. HISTORY OF THE *JENKINS* LITIGATION[a]

At the time of *Brown,* Missouri schools were segregated by law. Within a few years, formal segregation was gone, but racially identifiable schools lingered in Kansas City. Efforts to address this problem within the confines of the KCMSD were at first inadequate and later futile. In 1958–1959, the KCMSD enrollment was 22.5 percent African–American, and the system retained majority white enrollment until 1970. During that time, school-by-school racial balance could have been achieved, but was not. As late as 1974, 80 percent of African–American students in the KCMSD attended schools that were more than 90 percent African–American. Redistribution of students and the closing of some predominantly African–American schools increased the mix, but these changes were undercut by steadily declining white enrollment. By 1983–1984, white enrollment had dropped to less than one-third of the total, and the trend continued. No feasible plan for redistributing those students could hope to eliminate predominantly one-race schools in Kansas City.

The local response was a suit for interdistrict busing. In Kansas City, as in so many urban centers, the increasingly black inner city was surrounded by largely white outlying areas. If the suburbs could be made to exchange students with the KCMSD, racial balance could be achieved, and the political support of wealthy suburbs might be enlisted to help fund urban schools. The suit was filed by the KCMSD (and some students) seeking to establish misconduct by itself and others (the state, various federal agencies, and surrounding school districts in Missouri and Kansas) that would justify *inter*district busing. The allegation of *intra*district segregation was added only later, after the KCMSD

[a]The facts stated here are taken primarily from the extensive opinions of the Eighth Circuit. See Jenkins v. Missouri, 807 F.2d 657 (8th Cir.1986), and Jenkins v. Missouri, 855 F.2d 1295 (8th Cir.1988).

had been realigned as a party defendant. Despite this realignment, it seems clear that, from the beginning, the interests of the KCMSD lay with the desegregation plaintiffs rather than with the other government defendants.

First and foremost, KCMSD wanted relief from the racial imbalance and economic isolation of the center city; it wanted metropolitan busing. This the District Court refused to order. It found the suburban school districts had eliminated all vestiges of segregation and had achieved unitary school systems within four years (usually within one year) of *Brown*. The Court also found that no action by the suburbs or by the *other* government defendants had caused significant continuing interdistrict segregation. The racial disparity between city and suburbs did not result in appreciable degree from government action, but from social and economic conditions for which the defendants were not directly responsible. In other words, there was no interdistrict violation. Therefore, there could be no interdistrict busing.

Attention then turned to what could be done within the KCMSD to undo the lingering effects of the inferior education indigenous to segregated school systems. The magnet school plan and the capital improvements program were ordered to address that problem. The rationale was succinctly explained by the Eighth Circuit:

> The District Court's remedial orders were based on the elementary principle that the victims of unconstitutional segregation must be made whole, and that to make them whole it will be necessary to improve their educational opportunities and to reduce their racial isolation. The foundation of the plans adopted was the idea that improving the KCMSD as a system would at the same time compensate the blacks for the education they had been denied and attract whites from within and without the KCMSD to formerly black schools. The long-term goal of the District Court's effort was therefore: "to make available to *all* KCMSD students educational opportunities equal to or greater than those presently available in the average Kansas City, Missouri metropolitan suburban school district."

2. *JENKINS I* AND *II*

The KCMSD desegregation litigation first reached the Supreme Court in 1989, but *Jenkins I*, 491 U.S. 274 (1989), concerned only attorney's fees. The next year the case returned. *Jenkins II*, 495 U.S. 33 (1990), dealt with the question whether the District Court could increase local property taxes in order to pay for the desegregation order. This decision, which is described in the next Section, held that federal courts could not directly raise taxes but could order local governments to do so, even in ways or amounts not authorized by state law. On the broader question of the validity of the underlying desegregation order, the Court specifically denied review. Thus, although the Court had at least two prior opportunities, the fundamental issue of scope of remedial authority was not reached until 1995.

3. QUESTIONS AND COMMENTS

Aside from the complexities of extended litigation and haphazard Supreme Court review, *Jenkins* raises fundamental questions about desegregation remedies. Justice Thomas's concurrence calls for sharp restraints on remedial discretion. Even if the Court was not willing to go so far, it did confine desegregation remedies to the situs of constitutional violation. Is the disagreement between majority and dissent at bottom a continuing dispute about *Milliken v. Bradley*, or does *Jenkins*, as the dissenters claim, extend that case to new ground? Either way, the ruling has broad implications for urban America.[b]

4. SUBSEQUENT DEVELOPMENTS IN *JENKINS*

In 1997, the District Court approved a settlement between KCMSD and the state, providing that the state would pay the district $320 million over three years, and in return, would be dismissed from the litigation. Jenkins v. Missouri, 959 F. Supp. 1151 (W.D. Mo.), aff'd, 122 F.3d 588 (8th Cir. 1997). Pursuant to that settlement, the state was dismissed as a party in 1999, and the District Court set a hearing date to determine whether KCMSD had attained unitary status.

A few months later, the State Board of Education voted to withdraw accreditation of KCMSD as of May 1, 2000 because of poor student test scores. In response, KCMSD filed a motion seeking to bar the state's action on the ground that it would interfere with the remedial decree in *Jenkins*. At the end of a hearing devoted to that motion, the district court sua sponte declared the KCMSD unitary. In an en banc opinion, the Court of Appeals reversed and remanded the case for a fuller evidentiary hearing. Jenkins v. State of Missouri, 216 F.3d 720 (8th Cir. 2000). The Court of Appeals noted that "once there has been a finding that a defendant established an unlawful dual school system in the past, there is a presumption that current disparities of the sort listed in Green v. County School Board, 391 U.S. 430, 435 (1968), are the result of the defendant's unconstitutional conduct. Therefore, the burden of proving unitariness rests on the constitutional violator." It then held that the Due Process Clause meant that "[t]he parties are entitled to notice and an opportunity to prepare for a unitary status hearing. . . . The sua sponte ruling of the District Court, in spite of its several earlier orders setting the unitary status hearing some two months later, deprived the Jenkins Class of this constitutional guarantee." It thus remanded the case for such a hearing.

United States v. Fordice

Supreme Court of the United States, 1992.
505 U.S. 717.

■ JUSTICE WHITE delivered the opinion of the Court.

In 1954, this Court held that the concept of "separate but equal'" has no place in the field of public education. Brown v. Board of Education (*Brown I*), 347 U.S. 483, 495 (1954). The following year, the Court ordered an end to segregated public education "with all deliberate speed." Brown v. Board of Education (*Brown II*), 349 U.S. 294, 301 (1955). Since these decisions, the Court has had many occasions to evaluate whether a public school district has met its affirmative obligation to dismantle its prior de jure segregated system in elementary and secondary schools. In this case we decide what standards to apply in determining whether the state of Mississippi has met this obligation in the university context.

---

[b] For criticism of *Jenkins* as reflecting an unarticulated ambition to end court-ordered desegregation, see Bradley W. Joondeph, *Missouri v. Jenkins* and the De Facto Abandonment of Court–Enforced Desegregation, 71 Wash. L. Rev. 597 (1996).

I

Mississippi launched its public university system in 1848 by establishing the University of Mississippi, an institution dedicated to the higher education exclusively of white persons. In succeeding decades, the state erected additional post-secondary, single-race educational facilities. Alcorn State University opened its doors in 1871 as "an agricultural college for the education of Mississippi's black youth." Creation of four more exclusively white institutions followed: Mississippi State University (1880), Mississippi University for Women (1885), University of Southern Mississippi (1912), and Delta State University (1925). The state added two more solely black institutions in 1940 and 1950: in the former year, Jackson State University, which was charged with training "black teachers for the black public schools," and in the latter year, Mississippi Valley State University, whose functions were to educate teachers primarily for rural and elementary schools and to provide vocational instruction to black students.

Despite this Court's decisions in *Brown I* and *Brown II*, Mississippi's policy of de jure segregation continued. The first black student was not admitted to the University of Mississippi until 1962, and then only by court order. For the next 12 years the segregated public university system in the state remained largely intact. Mississippi State University, Mississippi University for Women, University of Southern Mississippi, and Delta State University each admitted at least one black student during these years, but the student composition of these institutions was still almost completely white. During this period, Jackson State and Mississippi Valley State were exclusively black; Alcorn State had admitted five white students by 1968.

In 1969, the United States Department of Health, Education and Welfare (HEW) initiated efforts to enforce Title VI of the Civil Rights Act of 1964. HEW requested that the state devise a plan to disestablish the formerly de jure segregated university system. In June 1973, the Board of Trustees of State Institutions of Higher Learning submitted a Plan of Compliance, which expressed the aims of improving educational opportunities for all Mississippi citizens by setting numerical goals on the enrollment of other-race students at state universities, hiring other-race faculty members, and instituting remedial programs and special recruitment efforts to achieve those goals. HEW rejected this plan as failing to comply with Title VI because it did not go far enough in the areas of student recruitment and enrollment, faculty hiring, elimination of unnecessary program duplication, and institutional funding practices to ensure that "a student's choice of institution or campus, henceforth, will be based on other than racial criteria." The board reluctantly offered amendments, prefacing its reform pledge to HEW with this statement: "With deference, it is the position of the Board of Trustees . . . that the Mississippi system of higher education is in compliance with Title VI of the Civil Rights Act of 1964." At this time, the racial composition of the state's universities had changed only marginally from the levels of 1968, which were almost exclusively single-race.[2] Though HEW refused to accept the modified plan, the board adopted it anyway. But even the limited effects of this plan in disestablishing the prior de jure seg-

[2] For the 1974–1975 school year, black students comprised 4.1 percent of the full-time undergraduate enrollments at University of Mississippi; at Mississippi State University, 7.5 percent; at University of Southern Mississippi, 8.0 percent; at Delta State University, 12.6 percent; at Mississippi University for Women, 13.0 percent. At Jackson State, Alcorn State, and Mississippi Valley State, the percentages of black students were 96.6 percent, 99.9 percent, and 100 percent, respectively.

regated system were substantially constricted by the state legislature, which refused to fund it until fiscal year 1978, and even then at well under half the amount sought by the board.

Private petitioners initiated this lawsuit in 1975. They complained that Mississippi had maintained the racially segregative effects of its prior dual system of post-secondary education in violation of the Fifth, Ninth, Thirteenth, and Fourteenth Amendments, 42 U.S.C. §§ 1981 and 1983, and Title VI of the Civil Rights Act of 1964, 42 U.S.C. § 2000d. Shortly thereafter, the United States filed its complaint in intervention, charging that state officials had failed to satisfy their obligation under the Equal Protection Clause of the and Title VI to dismantle Mississippi's dual system of higher education.

After this lawsuit was filed, the parties attempted for 12 years to achieve a consensual resolution of their differences through voluntary dismantlement by the state of its prior separated system. The Board of Trustees implemented reviews of existing curricula and program "mission" at each institution. In 1981, the board issued "Mission Statements" that identified the extant purpose of each public university. These "missions" were clustered into three categories: comprehensive, urban, and regional. "Comprehensive" universities were classified as those with the greatest existing resources and program offerings. All three such institutions (University of Mississippi, Mississippi State, and Southern Mississippi) were exclusively white under the prior de jure segregated system. The board authorized each to continue offering doctoral degrees and to assert leadership in certain disciplines. Jackson State, the sole urban university, was assigned a more limited research and degree mission, with both functions geared toward its urban setting. It was exclusively black at its inception. The "regional" designation was something of a misnomer, as the board envisioned those institutions primarily in an undergraduate role, rather than a "regional" one in the geographical sense of serving just the localities in which they were based. Only the universities classified as "regional" included institutions that, prior to desegregation, had been either exclusively white—Delta State and Mississippi University for Women—or exclusively black—Alcorn State and Mississippi Valley.

By the mid–1980s, 30 years after *Brown*, more than 99 percent of Mississippi's white students were enrolled at University of Mississippi, Mississippi State, Southern Mississippi, Delta State, and Mississippi University for Women. The student bodies at these universities remained predominantly white, averaging between 80 and 91 percent white students. Seventy-one percent of the state's black students attended Jackson State, Alcorn State, and Mississippi Valley, where the racial composition ranged from 92 to 99 percent black.

II

By 1987, the parties concluded that they could not agree on whether the state had taken the requisite affirmative steps to dismantle its prior de jure segregated system. They proceeded to trial. Both sides presented voluminous evidence on a full range of educational issues spanning admissions standards, faculty and administrative staff recruitment, program duplication, on-campus discrimination, institutional funding disparities, and satellite campuses. Petitioners argued that in various ways the state continued to reinforce historic, race-based distinctions among the universities. Respondents argued generally that the state had fulfilled its duty to disestablish its state-imposed segregative system by implementing and maintaining good-faith, nondiscriminatory race-neutral policies and practices in student admission, faculty hiring, and operations. Moreover, they suggested, the state had attracted significant numbers of qualified black students to those universities composed mostly of white persons. Respondents averred that the mere continued existence of racially identifiable universities was not unlawful given the freedom of students to choose which institution to attend and the varying objectives and features of the state's universities.

At trial's end, based on the testimony of 71 witnesses and 56,700 pages of exhibits, the District Court entered extensive findings of fact. The court first offered a historical overview of the higher education institutions in Mississippi and the developments in the system between 1954 and the filing of this suit in 1975. It then made specific findings recounting post–1975 developments, including a description at the time of trial, in those areas of the higher education system under attack by plaintiffs: admission requirements and recruitment; institutional classification and assignment of missions; duplication of programs; facilities and finance; the land grant institutions; faculty and staff; and governance.

The court's conclusions of law followed. As an overview, the court outlined the common ground in the case: "Where a state has previously maintained a racially dual system of public education established by law, it assumes an 'affirmative duty' to reform those policies and practices which required or contributed to the separation of the races." Noting that courts unanimously hold that the affirmative duty to dismantle a racially dual structure in elementary and secondary schools also governs in the higher education context, the court observed that there was disagreement whether Green v. New Kent County School Bd., 391 U.S. 430 (1968), applied in all of its aspects to formerly dual systems of higher education, i.e., whether "some level of racial mixture at previously segregated institutions of higher learning is not only desirable but necessary to 'effectively' desegregate the system." Relying [inter alia] on its understanding of our . . . decision in Bazemore v. Friday, 478 U.S. 385 (1986), the court concluded that in the higher education context, "the affirmative duty to desegregate does not contemplate either restricting choice or the achievement of any degree of racial balance." Thus, the court stated: "While student enrollment and faculty and staff hiring patterns are to be examined, greater emphasis should instead be placed on current state higher education policies and practices in order to insure that such policies and practices are racially neutral, developed and implemented in good faith, and do not substantially contribute to the continued racial identifiability of individual institutions."

When it addressed the same aspects of the university system covered by the fact-findings in light of the foregoing standard, the court found no violation of federal law in any of them. "In summary, the court finds that current actions on the part of the defendants demonstrate conclusively that the defendants are fulfilling their affirmative duty to disestablish the former de jure segregated system of higher education."

The Court of Appeals reheard the case en banc and affirmed the decision of the District Court. With a single exception, it did not disturb the District Court's findings of fact or conclusions of law. The en banc majority agreed that "Mississippi was . . . constitutionally required to eliminate invidious racial distinctions and dismantle its dual system." That duty, the court held, had been discharged since "the record makes clear that Mississippi has adopted and implemented race neutral policies for operating its colleges and universities and that all students have real freedom of choice to attend the college or university they wish. . . . "

We granted the respective writs of certiorari filed by the United States and the private petitioners.

III

The District Court, the Court of Appeals, and respondents recognize and acknowledge that the state of Mississippi had the constitutional duty to dismantle the dual school system that its laws once mandated. . . .

Our decisions establish that a state does not discharge its constitutional obligations until it eradicates policies and practices traceable to its prior de jure dual system that continue to foster segregation. Thus we have consistently asked whether existing racial identifiability is attributable to the state, and examined a wide range of factors to determine whether the state has perpetuated its formerly de jure segregation in any facet of its institutional system.

The Court of Appeals concluded that the state had fulfilled its affirmative obligation to disestablish its prior de jure segregated system by adopting and implementing race-neutral policies governing its college and university system. Because students seeking higher education had "real freedom" to choose the institution of their choice, the state need do no more. Even though neutral policies and free choice were not enough to dismantle a dual system of primary or secondary schools, *Green v. New Kent County School Board*, the Court of Appeals thought that universities "differ in character fundamentally" from lower levels of schools, sufficiently so that our decision in *Bazemore v. Friday*, justified the conclusion that the state had dismantled its former dual system.

Like the United States, we do not disagree with the Court of Appeals' observation that a state university system is quite different in very relevant respects from primary and secondary schools. Unlike attendance at the lower level schools, a student's decision to seek higher education has been a matter of choice. The state historically has not assigned university students to a particular institution. Moreover, like public universities throughout the country, Mississippi's institutions of higher learning are not fungible—they have been designated to perform certain missions. Students who qualify for admission enjoy a range of choices of which institution to attend. Thus, as the Court of Appeals stated, "it hardly needs mention that remedies common to public school desegregation, such as pupil assignments, busing, attendance quotas, and zoning, are unavailable when persons may freely choose whether to pursue an advanced education and, when the choice is made, which of several universities to attend."

We do not agree with the Court of Appeals or the District Court, however, that the adoption and implementation of race-neutral policies alone suffice to demonstrate that the state has completely abandoned its prior dual system. That college attendance is by choice and not by assignment does not mean that a race-neutral admissions policy cures the constitutional violation of a dual system. In a system based on choice, student attendance is determined not simply by admissions policies, but also by many other factors. Although some of these factors clearly cannot be attributed to state policies, many can be. Thus, even after a state dismantles its segregative admissions policy, there may still be state action that is traceable to the state's prior de jure segregation and that continues to foster segregation. The Equal Protection Clause is offended by "sophisticated as well as simple-minded modes of discrimination." Lane v. Wilson, 307 U.S. 268, 275 (1939). If policies traceable to the de jure system are still in force and have discriminatory effects, those policies too must be reformed to the extent practicable and consistent with sound educational practices.[4] We also disagree with respondents that the Court of Appeals and District Court properly relied on our decision in *Bazemore v. Friday*. *Bazemore* neither requires nor justifies the conclusions reached by the two courts below.

Bazemore raised the issue whether the financing and operational assistance provided by a state university's extension service to voluntary 4–H and Homemaker Clubs was inconsistent with the Equal Protection Clause because of the existence of numerous all-white and all-black clubs. Though prior to 1965 the clubs were supported on a segregated basis, the District Court had found that the policy of segregation had been completely abandoned and that no evidence existed of any lingering discrimination in either services or membership; any racial imbalance resulted from the wholly voluntary and unfettered choice of private individuals. In this context, we held inapplicable the *Green* Court's judgment that a voluntary choice program was insufficient to dismantle a de jure dual system in public primary and secondary schools, but only after satisfying ourselves that the state had not fostered segregation by playing a part in the decision of which club an individual chose to join.

Bazemore plainly does not excuse inquiry into whether Mississippi has left in place certain aspects of its prior dual system that perpetuate the racially segregated higher education system. If the state perpetuates policies and practices traceable to its prior system that continue to have segregative effects—whether by influencing student enrollment decisions or by fostering segregation in other facets of the university system—and such policies are without sound educational justification and can be practicably eliminated, the state has not satisfied its burden of proving that it has dismantled its prior system. Such policies run afoul of the Equal Protection Clause, even though the state has abolished the legal requirement that whites and blacks be educated separately and has established racially neutral policies not animated by a discriminatory purpose. Because the standard applied by the District Court did not make these inquiries, we hold that the Court of Appeals erred in affirming the District Court's ruling that the state had brought itself into compliance with the Equal Protection Clause in the operation of its higher education system.

IV

Had the Court of Appeals applied the correct legal standard, it would have been apparent from the undisturbed factual findings of the District Court that there are several surviving aspects of Mississippi's prior dual

---

[4] To the extent we understand private petitioners to urge us to focus on present discriminatory effects without addressing whether such consequences flow from policies rooted in the prior system, we reject this position. Private petitioners contend that the state must not only cease its legally authorized discrimination, it must also "eliminate its continuing effects insofar as practicable." Though they seem to disavow as radical a remedy as student reassignment in the university setting, their focus on "student enrollment, faculty and staff employment patterns, [and] black citizens' college-going and degree-granting rates" would seemingly compel remedies akin to those upheld in *Green v. New Kent County School Board*, were we to adopt their legal standard. As will become clear, however, the inappropriateness of remedies adopted in *Green* by no means suggests that the racial identifiability of the institutions in a university system is irrelevant to deciding whether a state such as Mississippi has satisfactorily dismantled its prior de jure dual system or that the state need not take additional steps to ameliorate such identifiability.

system which are constitutionally suspect; for even though such policies may be race-neutral on their face, they substantially restrict a person's choice of which institution to enter and they contribute to the racial identifiability of the eight public universities. Mississippi must justify these policies or eliminate them.

It is important to state at the outset that we make no effort to identify an exclusive list of unconstitutional remnants of Mississippi's prior de jure system. In highlighting, as we do below, certain remnants of the prior system that are readily apparent from the findings of fact made by the District Court and affirmed by the Court of Appeals,[8] we by no means suggest that the Court of Appeals need not examine, in light of the proper standard, each of the other policies now governing the state's university system that have been challenged or that are challenged on remand in light of the standard that we articulate today. With this caveat in mind, we address four policies of the present system: admission standards, program duplication, institutional mission assignments, and continued operation of all eight public universities.

We deal first with the current admissions policies of Mississippi's public universities. As the District Court found, the three flagship historically white universities in the system—University of Mississippi, Mississippi State University, and University of Southern Mississippi—enacted policies in 1963 requiring all entrants to achieve a minimum composite score of 15 on the American College Testing Program (ACT). The court described the "discriminatory taint" of this policy, an obvious reference to the fact that, at the time, the average ACT score for white students was 18 and the average score for blacks was 7. The District Court concluded, and the en banc Court of Appeals agreed, that present admissions standards derived from policies enacted in the 1970s to redress the problem of student unpreparedness. Obviously, this mid-passage justification for perpetuating a policy enacted originally to discriminate against black students does not make the present admissions standards any less constitutionally suspect.

The present admission standards are not only traceable to the de jure system and were originally adopted for a discriminatory purpose, but they also have present discriminatory effects. Every Mississippi resident under 21 seeking admission to the university system must take the ACT. Any applicant who scores at least 15 qualifies for automatic admission to any of the five historically white institutions except Mississippi University for Women, which requires a score of 18 for automatic admission unless the student has a 3.0 high school grade average. Those scoring less than 15 but at least 13 automatically qualify to enter Jackson State University, Alcorn State University, and Mississippi Valley State University. Without doubt, these requirements restrict the range of choices of entering students as to which institution they may attend in a way that perpetuates segregation. Those scoring 13 or 14, with some exceptions, are excluded from the five historically white universities and if they want a higher education must go to one of the historically black institutions or attend junior college with the

[8] In this sense, it is important to reiterate that we do not disturb the findings of no discriminatory purpose in the many instances in which the courts below made such conclusions. The private petitioners and the United States, however, need not show such discriminatory intent to establish a constitutional violation for the perpetuation of policies traceable to the prior de jure segregative regime which have continuing discriminatory effects. As for present policies that do not have such historical antecedents, a claim of violation of the cannot be made out without a showing of discriminatory purpose.

hope of transferring to a historically white institution.[9] Proportionately more blacks than whites face this choice: in 1985, 72 percent of Mississippi's white high school seniors achieved an ACT composite score of 15 or better, while less than 30 percent of black high school seniors earned that score. It is not surprising then that Mississippi's universities remain predominantly identifiable by race. . . .

Another constitutionally problematic aspect of the state's use of the ACT test scores is its policy of denying automatic admission if an applicant fails to earn the minimum ACT score specified for the particular institution, without also resorting to the applicant's high school grades as an additional factor in predicting college performance. The United States produced evidence that the American College Testing Program (ACTP), the administering organization of the ACT, discourages use of ACT scores as the sole admissions criterion on the ground that it gives an incomplete "picture" of the student applicant's ability to perform adequately in college. One ACTP report presented into evidence suggests that "it would be foolish" to substitute a three-or four-hour test in place of a student's high school grades as a means of predicting college performance. The record also indicated that the disparity between black and white students' high school grade averages was much narrower than the gap between their average ACT scores, thereby suggesting that an admissions formula which included grades would increase the number of black students eligible for automatic admission to all of Mississippi's public universities.[10]

The United States insists that the state's refusal to consider information which would better predict college performance than ACT scores alone is irrational in light of most states' use of high school grades and other indicators along with standardized test scores. The District Court observed that the Board of Trustees was concerned with grade inflation and the lack of comparability in grading practices and course offerings among the state's diverse high schools. Both the District Court and the Court of Appeals found this concern ample justification for the failure to consider high school grade performance along with ACT scores. In our view, such justification is inadequate because the ACT requirement was originally adopted for discriminatory purposes, the current requirement is traceable to that decision and seemingly continues to have segregative effects, and the state has so far failed to show that the "ACT-only" admission standard is not susceptible to elimination without eroding sound educational policy.

A second aspect of the present system that necessitates further inquiry is the widespread duplication of programs. "Unnecessary" duplication refers, under the District Court's definition, "to those instances where two or more institutions offer the same nonessential or noncore program. Under this definition, all duplication at the bachelor's level of nonbasic liberal arts and sciences course work and all duplication at the master's level and

---

9 The District Court's finding that "[v]ery few black students, if any, are actually denied admission to a Mississippi university as a first-time freshman for failure to achieve the minimal ACT score" ignores the inherent self-selection that accompanies public announcement of "automatic" admissions standards. It is logical to think that some percentage of black students who fail to score 15 do not seek admission to one of the historically white universities because of this automatic admission standard.

10 In 1985, 72 percent of white students in Mississippi scored 15 or better on the ACT, whereas only 30 percent of black students achieved that mark, a difference of nearly 2½ times. By contrast, the disparity among grade averages was not nearly so wide. 43.8 percent of white high school students and 30.5 percent of black students averaged at least a 3.0, and 62.2 percent of whites and 49.2 percent of blacks earned at least a 2.5 grade point average. . . .

above are considered to be unnecessary." The District Court found that 34.6 percent of the 29 undergraduate programs at historically black institutions are "unnecessarily duplicated" by the historically white universities, and that 90 percent of the graduate programs at the historically black institutions are unnecessarily duplicated at the historically white institutions. In its conclusions of law on this point, the District Court nevertheless determined that "there is no proof" that such duplication "is directly associated with the racial identifiability of institutions," and that "there is no proof that the elimination of unnecessary program duplication would be justifiable from an educational standpoint or that its elimination would have a substantial effect on student choice."

The District Court's treatment of this issue is problematic from several different perspectives. First, the court appeared to impose the burden of proof on the plaintiffs to meet a legal standard the court itself acknowledged was not yet formulated. It can hardly be denied that such duplication was part and parcel of the prior dual system of higher education—the whole notion of "separate but equal" required duplicative programs in two sets of schools—and that the present unnecessary duplication is a continuation of that practice. *Brown* and its progeny, however, established that the burden of proof falls on the state, and not the aggrieved plaintiffs, to establish that it has dismantled its prior de jure segregated system. The court's holding that petitioners could not establish the constitutional defect of unnecessary duplication, therefore, improperly shifted the burden away from the state. Second, implicit in the District Court's finding of "unnecessary" duplication is the absence of any educational justification and the fact that some if not all duplication may be practicably eliminated. Indeed, the District Court observed that such duplication "cannot be justified economically or in terms of providing quality education." Yet by stating that "there is no proof" that elimination of unnecessary duplication would decrease institutional racial identifiability, affect student choice, and promote educationally sound policies, the court did not make clear whether it had directed the parties to develop evidence on these points, and if so, what that evidence revealed. Finally, by treating this issue in isolation, the court failed to consider the combined effects of unnecessary program duplication with other policies, such as differential admissions standards, in evaluating whether the state had met its duty to dismantle its prior de jure segregated system.

We next address Mississippi's scheme of institutional mission classification, and whether it perpetuates the state's formerly de jure dual system. The District Court found that, throughout the period of de jure segregation, University of Mississippi, Mississippi State University, and University of Southern Mississippi were the flagship institutions in the state system. They received the most funds, initiated the most advanced and specialized programs, and developed the widest range of curricular functions. At their inception, each was restricted for the education solely of white persons. The missions of Mississippi University for Women (MUW) and Delta State University (DSU), by contrast, were more limited than their other all-white counterparts during the period of legalized segregation. MUW and DSU were each established to provide undergraduate education solely for white students in the liberal arts and such other fields as music, art, education, and home economics. When they were founded, the three exclusively black universities were more limited in their assigned academic missions than the five all-white institutions. Alcorn State, for example, was designated to serve as "an agricultural college for the education of Mississippi's black youth." Jackson State and Mississippi Valley State were established to train black teachers. . . .

In 1981, the state assigned certain missions to Mississippi's public universities as they then existed. It classified University of Mississippi, Mississippi State, and Southern Mississippi as "comprehensive" universities having the most varied programs and offering graduate degrees. Two of the historically white institutions, Delta State University and Mississippi University for Women, along with two of the historically black institutions, Alcorn State University and Mississippi Valley State University, were designated as "regional" universities with more limited programs and devoted primarily to undergraduate education. Jackson State University was classified as an "urban" university whose mission was defined by its urban location.

The institutional mission designations adopted in 1981 have as their antecedents the policies enacted to perpetuate racial separation during the de jure segregated regime. The Court of Appeals expressly disagreed with the District Court by recognizing that the "inequalities among the institutions largely follow the mission designations, and the mission designations to some degree follow the historical racial assignments." It nevertheless upheld this facet of the system as constitutionally acceptable based on the existence of good-faith racially neutral policies and procedures. That different missions are assigned to the universities surely limits to some extent an entering student's choice as to which university to seek admittance. While the courts below both agreed that the classification and mission assignments were made without discriminatory purpose, the Court of Appeals found that the record "supports the plaintiffs' argument that the mission designations had the effect of maintaining the more limited program scope at the historically black universities." We do not suggest that absent discriminatory purpose the assignment of different missions to various institutions in a state's higher education system would raise an equal protection issue where one or more of the institutions become or remain predominantly black or white. But here the issue is whether the state has sufficiently dismantled its prior dual system; and when combined with the differential admission practices and unnecessary program duplication, it is likely that the mission designations interfere with student choice and tend to perpetuate the segregated system. On remand, the court should inquire whether it would be practicable and consistent with sound educational practices to eliminate any such discriminatory effects of the state's present policy of mission assignments.

Fourth, the state attempted to bring itself into compliance with the Constitution by continuing to maintain and operate all eight higher educational institutions. The existence of eight instead of some lesser number was undoubtedly occasioned by state laws forbidding the mingling of the races. And as the District Court recognized, continuing to maintain all eight universities in Mississippi is wasteful and irrational. The District Court pointed especially to the facts that Delta State and Mississippi Valley are only 35 miles apart and that only 20 miles separate Mississippi State and Mississippi University for Women. It was evident to the District Court that "the defendants undertake to fund more institutions of higher learning than are justified by the amount of financial resources available to the state," but the court concluded that such fiscal irresponsibility was a policy choice of the legislature rather than a feature of a system subject to constitutional scrutiny.

Unquestionably, a larger rather than a smaller number of institutions from which to choose in itself makes for different choices, particularly when examined in the light of other factors present in the operation of the system, such as admissions, program duplication, and institutional mission designations. Though certainly closure of one or more institutions would decrease the discriminatory effects of the present system, based on the present record we are unable to say whether such action is constitutionally required. Elimination of program duplication and revision of admissions criteria may make institutional closure unnecessary. However, on remand this issue should be carefully explored by inquiring and determining whether retention of all eight institutions itself affects student choice and perpetuates the segregated higher education system, whether maintenance of each of the universities is educationally justifiable, and whether one or more of them can be practicably closed or merged with other existing institutions.

Because the former de jure segregated system of public universities in Mississippi impeded the free choice of prospective students, the state in dismantling that system must take the necessary steps to ensure that this choice now is truly free. The full range of policies and practices must be examined with this duty in mind. That an institution is predominantly white or black does not in itself make out a constitutional violation. But surely the state may not leave in place policies rooted in its prior officially-segregated system that serve to maintain the racial identifiability of its universities if those policies can practicably be eliminated without eroding sound educational policies.

If we understand private petitioners to press us to order the upgrading of Jackson State, Alcorn State, and Mississippi Valley solely so that they may be publicly financed, exclusively black enclaves by private choice, we reject that request. The state provides these facilities for all its citizens and it has not met its burden under *Brown* to take affirmative steps to dismantle its prior de jure system when it perpetuates a separate, but "more equal" one. Whether such an increase in funding is necessary to achieve a full dismantlement under the standards we have outlined, however, is a different question, and one that must be addressed on remand.

Because the District Court and the Court of Appeals failed to consider the state's duties in their proper light, the cases must be remanded. To the extent that the state has not met its affirmative obligation to dismantle its prior dual system, it shall be adjudged in violation of the Constitution and Title VI and remedial proceedings shall be conducted. The decision of the Court of Appeals is vacated, and the cases are remanded for further proceedings consistent with this opinion.

■ JUSTICE O'CONNOR, concurring.

I join the opinion of the Court, which requires public universities, like public elementary and secondary schools, to affirmatively dismantle their prior de jure segregation in order to create an environment free of racial discrimination and to make aggrieved individuals whole. I write separately to emphasize that it is Mississippi's burden to prove that it has undone its prior segregation, and that the circumstances in which a state may maintain a policy or practice traceable to de jure segregation that has segregative effects are narrow. In light of the state's long history of discrimination, and the lost educational and career opportunities and stigmatic harms caused by discriminatory educational systems, the courts below must carefully examine Mississippi's proffered justifications for maintaining a remnant of de jure segregation to ensure that such rationales do not merely mask the perpetuation of discriminatory practices. . . . Only by eliminating a remnant that unnecessarily continues to foster segregation or by negating insofar as possible its segregative impact can the state satisfy its constitutional obligation to dismantle the discriminatory system that should, by now, be only a distant memory.

■ JUSTICE THOMAS, concurring.

"We must rally to the defense of our schools. We must repudiate this unbearable assumption of the right to kill institutions unless they conform to one narrow standard." W.E.B. Du Bois, Schools, 13 The Crisis 111, 112 (1917).

I agree with the Court that a state does not satisfy its obligation to dismantle a dual system of higher education merely by adopting race-neutral policies for the future administration of that system. Today, we hold that "[i]f policies traceable to the de jure system are still in force and have discriminatory effects, those policies too must be reformed to the extent practicable and consistent with sound educational policies." I agree that this statement defines the appropriate standard to apply in the higher-education context. I write separately to emphasize that this standard is far different from the one adopted to govern the grade-school context in Green v. New Kent County School Bd., 391 U.S. 430 (1968), and its progeny. In particular, because it does not compel the elimination of all observed racial imbalance, it portends neither the destruction of historically black colleges nor the severing of those institutions from their distinctive histories and traditions.

In *Green*, we held that the adoption of a freedom-of-choice plan does not satisfy the obligations of a formerly de jure grade-school system should the plan fail to decrease, if not eliminate, the racial imbalance within that system. Although racial imbalance does not itself establish a violation of the Constitution, our decisions following *Green* indulged the presumption, often irrebuttable in practice, that a presently observed imbalance has been proximately caused by intentional state action during the prior de jure era. As a result, we have repeatedly authorized the district courts to reassign students, despite the operation of facially neutral assignment policies, in order to eliminate or decrease observed racial imbalances. See, e.g., Swann v. Charlotte–Mecklenburg Board of Ed., 402 U.S. 1 (1971).

Whatever the merit of this approach in the grade-school context, it is quite plainly not the approach that we adopt today to govern the higher-education context. We explicitly reject the use of remedies as "radical" as student reassignment—i.e., "remedies akin to those upheld in *Green*." Of necessity, then, we focus on the specific policies alleged to produce racial imbalance, rather than on the imbalance itself. Thus, a plaintiff cannot obtain relief merely by identifying a persistent racial imbalance, because the district court cannot provide a reassignment remedy designed to eliminate that imbalance directly. Plaintiffs are likely to be able to identify, as these plaintiffs have identified, specific policies traceable to the de jure era that continue to produce a current racial imbalance. As a practical matter, then, the district courts administering our standard will spend their time determining whether such policies have been adequately justified—a far narrower, more manageable task than that imposed under *Green*.

A challenged policy does not survive under the standard we announce today if it began during the prior de jure era, produces adverse impacts, and persists without sound educational justification. When each of these elements has been met, I believe, we are justified in not requiring proof of a present specific intent to discriminate. . . . Although we do not formulate our standard in terms of a burden shift with respect to intent, the factors we do consider—the historical background of the policy, the degree of its adverse impact, and the plausibility of any justification asserted in its defense—are precisely those factors that go into determining intent under Washington v. Davis, 426 U.S. 229 (1976). Thus, if a policy remains in force, without adequate justification and despite tainted roots and segregative effect, it appears clear—clear enough to presume conclusively—that the state has failed to disprove discriminatory intent.

We have no occasion to elaborate upon what constitutes an adequate justification. Under *Green*, we have recognized that an otherwise unconstitutional policy may be justified if it serves "important and legitimate ends," Dayton Bd. of Ed. v. Brinkman, 443 U.S. 526, 538 (1979), or if its elimination is not "practicable," Board of Ed. of Oklahoma City v. Dowell, 498 U.S. 237, 250 (1991). As Justice Scalia points out, our standard appears to mirror these formulations rather closely. Nonetheless, I find most encouraging the Court's emphasis on "sound *educational* practices" (emphasis added) [and "sound educational justification" and "sound educational policy"]. From the beginning, we have recognized that desegregation remedies cannot be designed to ensure the elimination of any remnant at any price, but rather must display "a practical flexibility" and "a facility for adjusting and reconciling public and private needs." Brown v. Board of Ed., 349 U.S. 294, 300 (1955). Quite obviously, one compelling need to be considered is the educational need of the present and future students in the Mississippi university system, for whose benefit the remedies will be crafted.

In particular, we do not foreclose the possibility that there exists "sound educational justification" for maintaining historically black colleges as such. Despite the shameful history of state-enforced segregation, these institutions have survived and flourished. Indeed, they have expanded as opportunities for blacks to enter historically white institutions have expanded. Between 1954 and 1980, for example, enrollment at historically black colleges increased from 70,000 to 200,000 students, while degrees awarded increased from 13,000 to 32,000. See Susan Hill, National Center for Education Statistics, The Traditionally Black Institutions of Higher Education 1860 to 1982, pp. xiv–xv (1985). These accomplishments have not gone unnoticed: "The colleges founded for Negroes are both a source of pride to blacks who have attended them and a source of hope to black families who want the benefits of higher learning for their children. They have exercised leadership in developing educational opportunities for young blacks at all levels of instruction, and, especially in the South, they are still regarded as key institutions for enhancing the general quality of the lives of black Americans." Carnegie Commission on Higher Education, From Isolation to Mainstream: Problems of the Colleges Founded for Negroes 11 (1971).

I think it undisputable that these institutions have succeeded in part because of their distinctive histories and traditions; for many, historically black colleges have become "a symbol of the highest attainments of black culture." Jean L. Preer, Lawyers v. Educators: Black Colleges and Desegregation in Public Higher Education 2 (1982). Obviously, a state cannot maintain such traditions by closing particular institutions, historically white or historically black, to particular racial groups. Nonetheless, it hardly follows that a state cannot operate a diverse assortment of institutions—including historically black institutions—open to all on a race-neutral basis, but with established traditions and programs that might disproportionately appeal to one race or another. No one, I imagine, would argue that such institutional diversity is without "sound educational justification," or that it is even remotely akin to program duplication, which is designed to separate the races for the sake of separating the races. The Court at least hints at the importance of this value when it distinguishes *Green* in part on the ground that colleges and universities "are not fungible." Although I agree that a state is not constitutionally required to maintain its historically black institutions as such, I do not understand our opinion to hold that a state is forbidden from doing so. It would be ironic, to say the least, if the institutions that sustained blacks during segregation were themselves destroyed in an effort to combat its vestiges.

■ JUSTICE SCALIA, concurring in the judgment in part and dissenting in part.

With some of what the Court says today, I agree. I agree, of course, that the Constitution compels Mississippi to remove all discriminatory barriers to its state-funded universities. Brown v. Board of Education, 347 U.S. 483 (1954) (*Brown I*). I agree that the Constitution does not compel Mississippi to remedy funding disparities between its historically black institutions (HBIs) and historically white institutions (HWIs). And I agree that Mississippi's American College Testing Program (ACT) requirements need further review. I reject, however, the effectively unsustainable burden the Court imposes on Mississippi, and all states that formerly operated segregated universities, to demonstrate compliance with *Brown I*. That requirement, which resembles what we prescribed for primary and secondary schools in Green v. New Kent County School Board, 391 U.S. 430 (1968), has no proper application in the context of higher education, provides no genuine guidance to states and lower courts, and is as likely to subvert as to promote the interests of those citizens on whose behalf the present suit was brought.

I

Before evaluating the Court's handiwork, it is no small task simply to comprehend it. The Court sets forth not one, but seemingly two different tests for ascertaining compliance with *Brown I*—though in the last analysis they come to the same. The Court initially announces the following test, in part III of its opinion: all policies (i) "traceable to [the state's] prior [de jure] system" (ii) "that continue to have segregative effects—whether by influencing student enrollment decisions or by fostering segregation in other facets of the university system—"must be eliminated (iii) to the extent "practicabl[e]" and (iv) consistent with "sound educational" practices. When the Court comes to applying its test, however, in part IV of the opinion, "influencing student enrollment decisions" is not merely one example of a "segregative effec[t]," but is elevated to an independent and essential requirement of its own. The policies that must be eliminated are those that (i) are legacies of the dual system, (ii) "contribute to the racial identifiability" of the state's universities (the same as (i) and (ii) in part III), and in addition (iii) do so in a way that "*substantially restrict[s] a person's choice of which institution to enter*" (emphasis added).

What the Court means by "substantially restrict[ing] a person's choice of which institution to enter" is not clear. During the course of the discussion in part IV the requirement changes from one of strong coercion ("substantially restrict," "interfere"), to one of middling pressure ("restrict," "limi[t]"), to one of slight inducement ("inherent[ly] self-selec[t]," "affect"). If words have any meaning, in this last stage of decrepitude the requirement is so frail that almost anything will overcome it. Even an open-admissions policy would fall short of ensuring that student choice is unaffected by state action. The Court's results also suggest that the "restricting-choice" requirement is toothless. Nothing else would explain how it could be met by Mississippi's mission designations, program duplication, and operation of all eight formerly de jure colleges. Only a test aimed at state action that "affects" student choice could implicate policies such as these, which in no way restrict the decision where to attend college. (Indeed, program duplication and continuation of the eight schools have quite the opposite effect; they multiply, rather than restrict, limit, or impede the available choices.) At the end of the day, then, the Court dilutes this potentially useful concept to the point of such insignificance that it adds nothing to the Court's test except confusion. It will be a fertile source of litigation.

Almost as inscrutable in its operation as the "restricting-choice" requirement is the requirement that challenged state practices perpetuate de facto segregation. That is "likely" met, the Court says, by Mississippi's mission designations. Yet surely it is apparent that by designating three colleges of the same prior disposition (HWIs) as the only comprehensive schools, Mississippi encouraged integration; and that the suggested alternative of elevating an HBI to comprehensive status (so that blacks could go there instead of to the HWIs) would have been an invitation to continuing segregation. It appears, moreover, that even if a particular practice does not, in isolation, rise to the minimal level of fostering segregation, it can be aggregated with other ones, and the composite condemned. It is interesting to speculate how university administrators are going to guess which practices a district judge will choose to aggregate; or how district judges are going to guess when disaggregation is lawful.

The Court appears to suggest that a practice that has been aggregated and condemned may be disaggregated and approved so long as it does not itself "perpetuat[e] the segregated higher education system"—which seems, of course, to negate the whole purpose of aggregating in the first place. The Court says:

> Elimination of program duplication and revision of admissions criteria may make institutional closure unnecessary. . . . [O]n remand, this issue should be carefully explored by inquiring and determining whether retention of all eight institutions itself . . . perpetuates the segregated higher education system, whether maintenance of each of the universities is educationally justifiable, and whether one or more of them can be practicably closed or merged with other existing institutions.

Perhaps the Court means, however, that even if retention of all eight institutions is found by itself not to "perpetuat[e] the segregated higher education system," it must still be found that such retention is "educationally justifiable," or that none of the institutions can be "practicably closed or merged." It is unclear.

Besides the ambiguities inherent in the "restricting choice" requirement and the requirement that the challenged state practice or practices perpetuate segregation, I am not sanguine that there will be comprehensible content to the to-be-defined-later (and, make no mistake about it, outcome-determinative) notions of "sound educational justification" and "im-

Once that has been done, however, it is not just unprecedented, but illogical as well, to establish that former de jure states continue to deny equal protection of the law to students whose choices among public university offerings are unimpeded by discriminatory barriers. Unless one takes the position that *Brown I* required states not only to provide equal access to their universities but also to correct lingering disparities between them, that is, to remedy institutional noncompliance with the "equal" requirement of *Plessy*, a state is in compliance with *Brown I* once it establishes that it has dismantled all discriminatory barriers to its public universities. Having done that, a state is free to govern its public institutions of higher learning as it will, unless it is convicted of discriminating anew—which requires both discriminatory intent and discriminatory causation. See Washington v. Davis, 426 U.S. 229 (1976).

That analysis brings me to agree with the judgment that the Court of Appeals must be reversed in part—for the reason (quite different from the Court's) that Mississippi has not borne the burden of demonstrating that intentionally discriminatory admissions standards have been eliminated. It has been established that Mississippi originally adopted ACT assessments as an admissions criterion because that was an effective means of excluding blacks from the HWIs. Given that finding, the District Court should have required Mississippi to prove that its continued use of ACT requirements does not have a racially exclusionary purpose and effect—a not insubstantial task, see Freeman v. Pitts, 503 U.S. 467, 503 (1992) (Scalia, J., concurring).

III

I must add a few words about the unanticipated consequences of today's decision. Among petitioners' contentions is the claim that the Constitution requires Mississippi to correct funding disparities between its HBIs and HWIs. The Court rejects that—as I think it should, since it is students and not colleges that are guaranteed equal protection of the laws. But to say that the Constitution does not require equal funding is not to say that the Constitution prohibits it. The citizens of a state may conclude that if certain of their public educational institutions are used predominantly by whites and others predominantly by blacks, it is desirable to fund those institutions more or less equally.

Ironically enough, however, today's decision seems to prevent adoption of such a conscious policy. What the Court says about duplicate programs is as true of equal funding: the requirement "was part and parcel of the prior dual system." Moreover, equal funding, like program duplication, facilitates continued segregation—enabling students to attend schools where their own race predominates without paying a penalty in the quality of education. Nor could such an equal-funding policy be saved on the basis that it serves what the Court calls a "sound educational justification." The only conceivable educational value it furthers is that of fostering schools in which blacks receive their education in a "majority" setting; but to acknowledge that as a "value" would contradict the compulsory-integration philosophy that underlies *Green*. Just as vulnerable, of course, would be all other programs that have the effect of facilitating the continued existence of predominantly black institutions: elevating an HBI to comprehensive status (but see ante, where the Court explicably suggests that this action may be required); offering a so-called Afrocentric curriculum, as has been done recently on an experimental basis in some secondary and primary schools, see Sonia F. Jarvis, *Brown* and the Afrocentric Curriculum, 101

Yale L.J. 1285, 1287, and n.12 (1992); preserving eight separate universities, which is perhaps Mississippi's single policy most segregative in effect; or providing funding for HBIs as HBIs, see 20 U.S.C. §§ 1060–1063c, which does just that.

But this predictable impairment of HBIs should come as no surprise: for incidentally facilitating—indeed, even tolerating—the continued existence of HBIs is not what the Court's test is about, and has never been what *Green* is about. What the Court's test is designed to achieve is the elimination of predominantly black institutions. While that may be good social policy, the present petitioners, I suspect, would not agree; and there is much to be said for the Court of Appeals' perception that "if no [state] authority exists to deny [the student] the right to attend the institution of his choice, he is done a severe disservice by remedies which, in seeking to maximize integration, minimize diversity and vitiate his choices." But whether or not the Court's antagonism to unintegrated schooling is good policy, it is assuredly not good constitutional law. There is nothing unconstitutional about a "black" school in the sense, not of a school that blacks must attend and that whites cannot, but of a school that, as a consequence of private choice in residence or in school selection, contains, and has long contained, a large black majority. (The Court says this, but does not appear to mean it). In a perverse way, in fact, the insistence, whether explicit or implicit, that such institutions not be permitted to endure perpetuates the very stigma of black inferiority that *Brown I* sought to destroy. Not only Mississippi but Congress itself seems out of step with the drum that the Court beats today, judging by its passage of an act entitled "Strengthening Historically Black Colleges and Universities," which authorizes the Education Department to provide money grants to historically black colleges. 20 U.S.C. §§ 1060–1063c. The implementing regulations designate Alcorn State University, Jackson State University, and Mississippi Valley State University as eligible recipients.

* * *

The Court was asked to decide today whether, in the provision of university education, a state satisfies its duty under *Brown I* by removing discriminatory barriers to admissions. That question required us to choose between the standards established in *Green* and *Bazemore*, both of which cases involved (as, for the most part, this does) free-choice plans that failed to end de facto segregation. Once the confusion engendered by the Court's something-for-all, guidance-to-none opinion has been dissipated, compare O'Connor, J., concurring, with Thomas, J., concurring, it will become apparent that, essentially, the Court has adopted *Green*.

I would not predict, however, that today's opinion will succeed in producing the same result as *Green*—viz., compelling the states to compel racial "balance" in their schools—because of several practical imperfections: because the Court deprives district judges of the most efficient (and perhaps the only effective) *Green* remedy, mandatory student assignment; because some contradictory elements of the opinion (its suggestion, for example, that Mississippi's mission designations foster, rather than deter, segregation) will prevent clarity of application; and because the virtually standardless discretion conferred upon district judges will permit them to do pretty much what they please. What I do predict is a number of years of litigation-driven confusion and destabilization in the university systems of all the formerly de jure states, that will benefit neither blacks nor whites, neither predominantly black institutions nor predominantly white ones. Nothing good will come of this judicially ordained turmoil, except the public recognition that any Court that would knowingly impose it must hate segregation. We must find some other way of making that point.

NOTES ON DESEGREGATING HIGHER EDUCATION

1. HISTORY OF THE *FORDICE* LITIGATION

The *Fordice* litigation was begun in 1975 as a class action on behalf of black Mississippians. The United States intervened as a plaintiff. The case was tried in 1987, when attempts at a negotiated settlement finally ran aground. By that time, most lower-court opinions agreed that states had an affirmative obligation—analogous to that imposed in *Green*—to eliminate the vestiges of a dual system of higher education. In *Fordice*, the Fifth Circuit took the contrary view, that because college students are not assigned by the government to particular institutions, freedom of choice is sufficient.[a] In *Fordice*, the Supreme Court rejected this position and required that Mississippi take additional steps to eliminate racial identifiability in its institutions of higher education.

How should that be done? The simplest way is to close institutions. That Mississippi operates eight colleges and universities is itself a legacy of de jure segregation. When the dual systems for blacks and whites merged into one, the continued operation of eight institutions became, as the District Court found, highly problematic. But closure would likely affect historically black institutions. Such institutions are generally smaller than their white counterparts and have been less well funded. They therefore have smaller and less adequate facilities. Moreover, historically white institutions have generally been more successful in attracting black students than the other way around. The most direct and efficient means of bringing both races into the same classrooms would therefore seem to be to close one or more historically black institutions, effectively forcing those students to attend historically white schools.

This prospect made strange bedfellows. As explained by Drew S. Days III in *Brown* Blues: Rethinking the Integrative Ideal, 34 Wm. & Mary L. Rev. 53, 65 (1992):

> Black higher education groups were at odds with federal agencies and the NAACP Legal Defense Fund . . . regarding the wisdom of pressing desegregation of public colleges and universities. Black college presidents, faculty, and alumni were undoubtedly mindful of the burdens the black community had been forced to bear during desegregation of public primary and secondary systems. They feared that desegregation of higher education would result, at best, in whites displacing black teachers and administrators, as well as black students. At worst, given the relative inferiority of their institutions, desegregation might result in the closing of schools, or the absorption of traditionally black institutions into historically white schools. In either event, institutions important to the black community would lose their identity, and opportunities in higher education for black administrators, faculty, and students would be significantly diminished.

---

[a] This position of the lower courts is scathingly criticized by Wendy R. Brown in The Convergence of Neutrality and Choice: The Limits of the State's Affirmative Duty to Provide Equal Educational Opportunity, 60 Tenn. L. Rev. 63 (1992).

What the historically black colleges and universities really wanted, according to one source, is that the constitutional obligation to desegregate would somehow be interpreted to require increased funding for historically black institutions. See *Washington Post*, June 27, 1992, page A11. That hope seems to have been dashed. "If we understand private petitioners to press us to order the upgrading of Jackson State, Alcorn State, and Mississippi Valley solely that they may be publicly financed, exclusively black enclaves by private choice," said the Justices, "we reject that request. The state provides these facilities for all of its citizens and it has not met its burden to dismantle its prior de jure system when it perpetuates a separate but 'more equal' one." Is that the right answer? Does it follow from *Brown*?

After indicating that funding parity for historically black institutions is not constitutionally required, the Court nevertheless held out the possibility that funding increases might be necessary "to achieve a full dismantlement" of the dual system. Under what circumstances might that be true? In dissent, Justice Scalia suggested to the contrary that the Court's analysis might actually prevent equal funding for historically black institutions. Is that true? Could it justified by *Brown*?

The Justices were most unclear about the future of Mississippi's historically black institutions: "Though certainly closure of one or more institutions would decrease the discriminatory effects of the present system, based on the present record we are unable to say whether such action is constitutionally required." In determining what is constitutionally required, should the District Court take into account the desire of the black community to maintain and improve historically black institutions? Or is that concern fundamentally inconsistent with the constitutional mandate?

2. BIBLIOGRAPHY

Scholarly reaction to the *Fordice* decision has been intense and interesting. For a passionate defense of historically black institutions, see Wendy Brown–Scott, Race Consciousness in Higher Education: Does "Sound Educational Policy" Support the Continued Existence of Historically Black Colleges?, 43 Emory L.J. 1 (1994). For an excellent history of the origins and evolution of historically black institutions of higher education and an endorsement of their continued relevance in a post-*Brown* world, see Leland Ware, The Most Visible Vestige: Black Colleges After Fordice, 35 B.C.L. Rev. 633 (1994). At least one scholar was moved by *Fordice* to question *Brown* itself. See Alex M. Johnson, Jr., Bid White, Tonk, and *United States v. Fordice*: Why Integrationism Fails African–Americans Again, 81 Calif. L. Rev. 1401 (1993). Foreseeing the closure or consolidation of historically black institutions, Johnson argues that "the Court's willingness to countenance such a remedy stems from its assumption that the type of integration mandated by *Brown v. Board of Education* is in the best interests of the African–American community. History has revealed otherwise." Instead, Johnson supports a concept of voluntary integration. In his view, historically black colleges must be maintained at increased funding levels, while at the same time guaranteeing African–Americans equal opportunity at historically white institutions. Thus, African–American students will themselves select when integration should occur: "It is only when those students are sufficiently mature, confident, and equipped to enter the predominantly white society that meaningful integration will occur."

3. *FORDICE* ON REMAND

On remand the District Court issued an elaborate opinion that satisfied neither side. Ayers v. Fordice, 879 F.Supp. 1419 (N.D.Miss.1995). On the one hand, the court refused, as the Supreme Court has suggested it should, to order funding "equity" between historically white and historically black institutions. Funding differences based on differences in programs (especially the higher cost of graduate education) were allowed to continue. On the other hand, the court rejected the state's plan to close one historically black institution (Mississippi Valley State University) and merge it into a neighboring white school (Delta State University) in the hope of creating a new institution (to be called Delta Valley University) without racial identity. The two schools were only 35 miles apart and had similar programs. The court agreed that maintaining both institutions "tends to shape student choice by race and thereby perpetuates segregation." Nonetheless, the court found the merger proposal "unsupported at this time by sufficient research" and ordered further study to determine whether consolidation was "the only educationally feasible solution."

The major change ordered by the court concerned admissions. Plaintiffs had sought "open admissions" at regional universities and abandonment of the ACT. The court rejected those claims and endorsed the state's plan to adopt a state-wide admissions policy governing all universities. The new policy lowered admissions standards at historically white institutions and increased the numbers of eligible blacks, but raised admissions standards at historically black institutions and decreased the numbers of eligible applicants. Special remediation programs were proposed to avoid an overall decline in minority college enrollment.

Does the court's order make sense as desegregation? In particular, why must the state show that consolidation of institutions was the "*only* educationally feasible solution"? Should the state have authority to take any action that would ameliorate racial identifiability, or does the history of de jure segregation give the court power to ensure that the interests of historically black institutions are adequately considered?

3. ENFORCING DESEGREGATION DECREES

Spallone v. United States

Supreme Court of the United States, 1990.
493 U.S. 265.

■ CHIEF JUSTICE REHNQUIST delivered the opinion of the Court.

This case is the most recent episode of a lengthy lawsuit in which the City of Yonkers was held liable for intentionally enhancing racial segregation in housing in Yonkers. The issue here is whether it was a proper exercise of judicial power for the District Court to hold petitioners, four Yonkers city councilmembers, in contempt for refusing to vote in favor of legislation implementing a consent decree earlier approved by the city. We hold that in the circumstances of this case, the District Court abused its discretion.

I

In 1980, the United States filed a complaint alleging, inter alia, that the two named defendants—the City of Yonkers and the Yonkers Community Development Agency—had intentionally engaged in a pattern and practice of housing discrimination, in violation of Title VII of the Civil Rights Act of 1968 and the Equal Protection Clause of the Fourteenth Amendment. The government and plaintiff-intervenor National Association for the Advancement of Colored People (NAACP) asserted that the city had, over a period of three decades, selected sites for subsidized housing in order to perpetuate residential racial segregation. The plaintiffs' theory was that the city had equated subsidized housing for families with minority housing, and thus disproportionately restricted new family housing projects to areas of the city—particularly southwest Yonkers—already predominately populated by minorities.

The District Court found the two named defendants liable, concluding that the segregative effect of the city's actions had been "consistent and extreme," and that "the desire to preserve existing patterns of segregation ha[d] been a significant factor in the sustained community opposition to subsidized housing in East Yonkers and other overwhelmingly white areas of the city." The District Court in its remedial decree . . . required affirmative steps to disperse public housing throughout Yonkers. Part IV of the order noted that the city previously had committed itself to provide acceptable sites for 200 units of public housing as a condition for receiving 1983 Community Development Block Grant funds from the federal government, but had failed to do so. Consequently, it required the city to designate sites for 200 units of public housing in East Yonkers. . . . Part VI directed the city to develop by November 1986 a long-term plan "for the creation of additional subsidized family housing units . . . in existing residential areas in east or northwest Yonkers." The court did not mandate specific details of the plan such as how many subsidized units must be developed, where they should be constructed, or how the city should provide for the units.

Under the charter of the City of Yonkers all legislative powers are vested in the city council, which consists of an elected mayor and six councilmembers, including petitioners. The city, for all practical purposes, therefore, acts through the city council when it comes to the enactment of legislation. Pending appeal of the District Court's liability and remedial orders, however, the city did not comply with Parts IV and VI of the remedial order. . . . The United States and the NAACP then moved for an adjudication of civil contempt and the imposition of coercive sanctions, but the District Court declined to take that action. Instead, it secured an agreement from the city to appoint an outside housing advisor to identify sites for the 200 units of public housing and to draft a long-term plan.

In December 1987, the Court of Appeals for the Second Circuit affirmed the District Court's judgment in all respects, and we subsequently denied certiorari. Shortly after the Court of Appeals' decision, in January 1988, the parties agreed to a consent decree that set forth "certain actions which the City of Yonkers [would] take in connection with a consensual implementation of Parts IV and VI" of the housing remedy order. The decree was approved by the city council in a five-to-two vote (petitioners Spallone and Chema voting no), and entered by the District Court as a consent judgment on January 28, 1988. Sections 12 through 18 of the decree established the framework for the long-term plan and are the underlying bases for the contempt orders at issue in this case. Perhaps most significant was § 17, in which the city agreed to adopt, within 90 days, legislation conditioning the construction of all multifamily housing on the inclusion of at least 20 percent assisted units, granting tax abatements and density bonuses to developers, and providing for zoning changes to allow the placement of housing developments.

For several more months, however, the city continued to delay action toward implementing the long-term plan. [On June 13, 1988, the District Court entered an order] which provided greater detail for the legislation prescribed by § 17 of the decree. After several weeks of further delay the court, after a hearing held on July 26, 1988, entered an order requiring the City of Yonkers to enact on or before August 1, 1988, the "legislative package" described in a section of the earlier consent decree; the second paragraph provided:

> It is further ORDERED that, in the event the City of Yonkers fails to enact the legislative package on or before August 1, 1988, the City of Yonkers shall be required to show cause at a hearing before this court at 10:00 a.m. on August 2, 1988, why it should not be held in contempt, and each individual city council member shall be required to show cause at a hearing before this court at 10:00 a.m. on August 2, 1988, why he should not be held in contempt.

Further provisions of the order specified escalating daily amounts of fines in the event of contempt, and provided that if the legislation were not enacted before August 10, 1988, any councilmember who remained in contempt should be committed to the custody of the United States Marshal for imprisonment. The specified daily fines for the city were $100 for the first day, to be doubled for each consecutive day of noncompliance; the specified daily fine for members of the city council was $500 per day.

Notwithstanding the threat of substantial sanctions, on August 1 the city council defeated a resolution of intent to adopt the legislative package, known as the Affordable Housing Ordinance, by a vote of four to three (petitioners constituting the majority). On August 2, the District Court [held both the city and the councilmembers in contempt.]

On August 17, the Court of Appeals stayed the contempt sanctions pending appeal. Shortly thereafter, the court affirmed the adjudications of contempt against both the city and the councilmembers, but limited the fines against the city so that they would not exceed $1 million per day. . . .

Both the city and the councilmembers requested this Court to stay imposition of sanctions pending filing and disposition of petitions for certiorari. We granted a stay as to petitioners, but denied the city's request. With the city's daily contempt sanction approaching $1 million per day, the city council finally enacted the Affordable Housing Ordinance on September 9, 1988, by a vote of five to two, petitioners Spallone and Fagan voting no. Because the contempt orders raise important issues about the appropriate exercise of the federal judicial power against individual legislators, we granted certiorari and now reverse.

II

The issue before us is relatively narrow. There can be no question about the liability of the City of Yonkers for racial discrimination. . . . Nor do we have before us any question as to the District Court's remedial order. . . . Our focus, then, is only on the District Court's order of July 26 imposing contempt sanctions on the individual petitioners if they failed to vote in favor of the ordinance in question.

Petitioners contend that the District Court's orders violate their rights to freedom of speech under the First Amendment, and they also contend that they are entitled as legislators to absolute immunity for actions taken in discharge of their legislative responsibilities. We find it unnecessary to reach either of these questions, because we conclude that the portion of the District Court's order of July 26 imposing contempt sanctions against the petitioners if they failed to vote in favor of the court-proposed ordinance was an abuse of discretion under traditional equitable principles. . . .

In selecting a means to enforce the consent judgment, the District Court was entitled to rely on the axiom that "courts have inherent power to enforce compliance with their lawful orders through civil contempt." Shillitani v. United States, 384 U.S. 364, 370 (1966). When a district court's order is necessary to remedy past discrimination, the court has an additional basis for the exercise of broad equitable powers. See Swann v. Charlotte–Mecklenburg Bd. of Ed., 402 U.S. 1, 15 (1971). But while "remedial powers of an equity court must be adequate to the task, . . . they are not unlimited." Whitcomb v. Chavis, 403 U.S. 124, 161 (1971). "[T]he federal courts in devising a remedy must take into account the interests of state and local authorities in managing their own affairs, consistent with the Constitution." Milliken v. Bradley, 433 U.S. 267, 280–81 (1977). And the use of the contempt power places an additional limitation on a district court's discretion, for as the Court of Appeals recognized, "in selecting contempt sanctions, a court is obliged to use the 'least possible power adequate to the end proposed.' " United States v. City of Yonkers, 856 F.2d 444, 454 (2d Cir.1988).

Given that the city had entered a consent judgment committing itself to enact legislation implementing the long-term plan, we certainly cannot say it was an abuse of discretion for the District Court to have chosen contempt sanctions against the city, as opposed to petitioners, as a means of ensuring compliance. The city, as we have noted, was a party to the action from the beginning, had been found liable for numerous statutory and constitutional violations, and had been subjected to various elaborate remedial decrees which had been upheld on appeal. Petitioners, the individual city councilmen, on the other hand, were not parties to the action, and they had not been found individually liable for any of the violations upon which the remedial decree was based. Although the injunctive portion of that decree was directed not only to the city but to "its officers, agents, employees, successors and all persons in active concert or participation with any of them," the remaining parts of the decree ordering affirmative steps were directed only to the city.

It was, in fact, the city which capitulated. After the Court of Appeals had briefly stayed the imposition of sanctions in August, and we granted a stay as to petitioners but denied it to the city in September, the city council on September 9, 1988, finally enacted the Affordable Housing Ordinance by a vote of five to two. While the District Court could not have been sure in late July that this would be the result, the city's arguments against imposing sanctions on it pointed out the sort of pressure that such sanctions would place on the city. After just two weeks of fines, the city's emergency financial plan required it to curtail sanitation services (resulting in uncollected garbage), eliminate part-time school crossing guards, close all public libraries and parks and lay off approximately 477 employees. In the ensuing four weeks, the city would have been forced to lay off another 1100 city employees.

Only eight months earlier, the District Court had secured compliance with an important remedial order through the threat of bankrupting fines against the city alone. . . .

The nub of the matter, then, is whether in the light of the reasonable probability that sanctions against the city would accomplish the desired result, it was within the court's discretion to impose sanctions on the petitioners as well under the circumstances of this case.

In Tenney v. Brandhove, 341 U.S. 367 (1951), we held that state legislators were absolutely privileged in their legislative acts in an action against them for damages. We applied this same doctrine of legislative immunity to regional legislatures in Lake Country Estates, Inc. v. Tahoe Regional Planning Agency, 440 U.S. 391, 404–05 (1979), and to actions for both damages and injunctive relief in Supreme Court of Virginia v. Consumers Union of United States, Inc., 446 U.S. 719, 731–34 (1980). The holdings in these cases do not control the question whether local legislators such as petitioners should be immune from contempt sanctions imposed for failure to vote in favor of a particular legislative bill. But some of the same considerations on which the immunity doctrine is based must inform the District Court's exercise of its discretion in a case such as this. "Freedom of speech and action in the legislature," we observed, "was taken as a matter of course by those who severed the Colonies from the Crown and founded our nation." *Tenney,* 341 U.S., at 372.

In perhaps the earliest American case to consider the import of the legislative privilege, the Supreme Judicial Court of Massachusetts, interpreting a provision of the Massachusetts Constitution granting the rights of freedom of speech and debate to state legislators, recognized that "the privilege secured by it is not so much the privilege of the house as an organized body, *as of each individual member composing it, who is entitled to this privilege, even against the declared will of the house.* For he does not hold this privilege at the pleasure of the house; but derives it from the will of the people. . . . " Coffin v. Coffin, 4 Mass. 1, 27 (1808). This theme underlies our cases interpreting the speech or debate clause and the federal common law of legislative immunity, where we have emphasized that any restriction on a legislator's freedom undermines the "public good" by interfering with the rights of the people to representation in the democratic process. The District Court was quite sensitive to this fact; it observed:

> I know of no parallel for a court to say to an elected official, "You are in contempt of court and subject to personal fines and may eventually be subject to personal imprisonment because of a manner in which you cast a vote." I find that extraordinary.

Sanctions directed against the city for failure to take actions such as required by the consent decree coerce the city legislators and, of course, restrict the freedom of those legislators to act in accordance with their current view of the city's best interests. But we believe there are significant differences between the two types of fines. The imposition of sanctions on individual legislators is designed to cause them to vote, not with a view to the interest of their constituents or of the city, but with a view solely to their own personal interests. Even though an individual legislator took the extreme position—or felt that his constituents took the extreme position—that even a huge fine against the city was preferable to enacting the Affordable Housing Ordinance, monetary sanctions against him individually would motivate him to vote to enact the ordinance simply because he did not want to be out of pocket financially. Such fines thus encourage legislators, in effect, to declare that they favor an ordinance not in order to avoid bankrupting the city for which they legislate, but in order to avoid bankrupting themselves.

This sort of individual sanction effects a much greater perversion of the normal legislative process than does the imposition of sanctions on the city for the failure of these same legislators to enact an ordinance. In that case, the legislator is only encouraged to vote in favor of an ordinance that he would not otherwise favor by reason of the adverse sanctions imposed on the city. A councilman who felt that his constituents would rather have the city enact the Affordable Housing Ordinance than pay a "bankrupting fine" would be motivated to vote in favor of such an ordinance because the sanctions were a threat to the fiscal solvency of the city for whose welfare he was in part responsible. This is the sort of calculus in which legislators engage regularly.

We hold that the District Court, in view of the "extraordinary" nature of the imposition sanctions against the individual councilmen, should have proceeded with such contempt sanctions first against the city alone in order to secure compliance with the remedial orders. Only if that approach failed to produce compliance within a reasonable time should the question of imposing contempt sanctions against petitioners have been considered. "This limitation accords with the doctrine that a court must exercise '[t]he least possible power adequate to the end proposed.' " *Shillitani v. United States,* 384 U.S., supra, at 371.

■ JUSTICE BRENNAN with whom JUSTICE MARSHALL, JUSTICE BLACKMUN, and JUSTICE STEVENS join, dissenting.

I understand and appreciate the Court's concern about the District Court's decision to impose contempt sanctions against local officials acting in a legislative capacity. We must all hope that no court will ever again face the open and sustained defiance of established constitutional values and valid judicial orders that prompted Judge Sand's invocation of the contempt power in this manner. But I firmly believe that its availability for such use, in extreme circumstances, is essential. As the District Court was aware:

> The issues transcend Yonkers. They go to the very foundation of the system of constitutional government. If Yonkers can defy the orders of a federal court in any case, but especially a civil rights case, because compliance is unpopular, and if that situation is tolerated, then our constitutional system of government fails. The issues before the court this morning are no less significant than that.

The Court today recognizes that it was appropriate for the District Court to hold in contempt and fine the City of Yonkers to encourage the city councilmembers to comply with their prior promise to redress the city's history of racial segregation. Yet the Court also reprimands the District Court for simultaneously fining the individual councilmembers whose continuing defiance was the true source of the impasse, holding that personal sanctions should have been considered only after the city sanctions first proved fruitless.

I cannot accept this parsimonious view of the District Court's discretion to wield the power of contempt. Judge Sand's intimate contact for many years with the recalcitrant councilmembers and his familiarity with the city's political climate gave him special insight into the best way to coerce compliance when all cooperative efforts had failed. From our detached vantage point, we can hardly judge as well as he which coercive sanctions or combination thereof were most likely to work quickly and least disruptively. Because the Court's ex post rationalization of what Judge Sand should have done fails to do justice either to the facts of the case or the art of judging, I must dissent.

I

[Justice Brennan's detailed factual history is omitted.]

II

. . . The Court's disfavor of personal sanctions rests on two premises: (1) Judge Sand should have known when he issued the contempt order that there was a "reasonable probability that sanctions against the city [alone] would accomplish the desired result"; and (2) imposing personal fines "effects a much greater perversion of the normal legislative process than does the imposition of sanctions on the city." Because personal fines were both completely superfluous to and more intrusive than sanctions against the city alone, the Court reasons, the personal fines constituted an abuse of discretion. Each of these premises is mistaken.

A

While acknowledging that Judge Sand "could not have been sure in late July that this would have been the result," the Court confidently concludes that Judge Sand should have been *sure enough* that fining the city would eventually coerce compliance that he should not have personally fined the councilmembers as well. In light of the information available to Judge Sand in July, the Court's confidence is chimerical. Although the escalating city fines eventually would have seriously disrupted many public services and employment, the Court's failure even to consider the possibility that the councilmembers would maintain their defiant posture despite the threat of fiscal insolvency bespeaks an ignorance of Yonkers' history of entrenched discrimination and an indifference to Yonkers' political reality.

The Court first fails to adhere to our longstanding recognition that the "district court has firsthand experience with the parties and is best qualified to deal with the 'flinty, intractable realities of day-to-day implementation of constitutional commands.'" United States v. Paradise, 480 U.S. 149, 184 (1987) (quoting Swann v. Charlotte–Mecklenburg Board of Education, 402 U.S. 1, 6 (1971)). Deference to the court's exercise of discretion is particularly appropriate where, as here, the record clearly reveals that the court employed extreme caution before taking the final step of holding the councilmembers personally in contempt. Judge Sand patiently weathered a whirlwind of evasive maneuvers and misrepresentations; considered and rejected alternative means of securing compliance other than contempt sanctions; and carefully considered the ramifications of personal fines. In the end, he readily acknowledged:

I know of no parallel for a court to say to an elected official: "You are in contempt of court and subject to personal fines and may eventually be subject to personal imprisonment because of a manner in which you cast a vote." I find that extraordinary.

I find it so extraordinary that at great cost in terms of time and in terms of money and energy and implementation of court's orders, I have sought alternatives to that. But they have all been unsuccessful. . . .

After according no weight to Judge Sand's cautious and contextual judgment despite his vastly superior vantage point, the Court compounds its error by committing two more. First, the Court turns a blind eye to most of the evidence available to Judge Sand suggesting that, because of the councilmembers' continuing intransigence, sanctions against the city alone might not coerce compliance and that personal sanctions would significantly increase the chance of success. Second, the Court fails to acknowledge that supplementing city sanctions with personal ones likely would secure compliance more promptly, minimizing the overall disruptive effect of the city sanctions on city services generally and long-term compliance with the consent decree in particular.

As the events leading up to the contempt order make clear, the recalcitrant councilmembers were extremely responsive to strong segments of their constituencies that were vociferously opposed to racial residential integration. Councilmember Fagan, for example, explained that his vote against the Housing Ordinance required by the consent decree "was an act of defiance. The people clearly wanted me to say no to the judge." Councilmember Spallone declared openly that "I will be taking on the judge all the way down the line. I made a commitment to my people and that commitment remains." Moreover, once Yonkers had gained national attention over its refusal to integrate, many residents made it clear to their representatives on the council that they preferred bankrupt martyrdom to integration. As a contemporaneous article observed, "[t]he defiance councilmen are riding a wave of resentment among their white constituents that is so intense that many insist they are willing to see the city bankrupted. . . . " *N.Y. Times*, Aug. 5, 1988. It thus was not evident that petitioners opposed bankrupting the city; at the very least, capitulation by any individual councilmember was widely perceived as political suicide. As a result, even assuming that each recalcitrant member sought to avoid city bankruptcy, each still had a very strong incentive to play "chicken" with his colleagues by continuing to defy the contempt order while secretly hoping that at least one colleague would change his position and suffer the wrath of the electorate. As Judge Sand observed, "[w]hat we have here is competition to see who can attract the greatest notoriety, who will be the political martyr . . . *without regard to what is in the best interests of the City of Yonkers*" (emphasis added). . . .

The Court, in addition to ignoring all of this evidence before concluding that city sanctions alone would eventually coerce compliance, also inexplicably ignores the fact that imposing personal fines in addition to sanctions against the city would not only help ensure but actually *hasten* compliance. City sanctions, by design, impede the normal operation of local government. Judge Sand knew that each day the councilmembers remained in contempt, the city would suffer an ever-growing financial drain that threatened not only to disrupt many critical city services but also to frustrate the long-term success of the underlying remedial scheme. Fines assessed against the public fisc directly "diminish the limited resources which the city has to comply with the decree," United States v. Providence, 492 F.Supp. 602, 610 (D.R.I.1980), and more generally curtail various public services with a likely disparate impact on poor and minority residents.

Given these ancillary effects of city sanctions, it seems to me entirely appropriate—indeed obligatory—for Judge Sand to have considered not just whether city sanctions alone would *eventually* have coerced compliance, but also *how promptly* they would have done so. The Court's implicit conclusion that personal sanctions were redundant both exaggerates the likelihood that city sanctions alone would have worked at all and also fails to give due weight to the importance of speed, because supplementing the city sanctions with personal sanctions certainly increased the odds for prompt success. At the very least, personal sanctions made political martyrdom a much more unattractive option for the councilmembers. In light of the tremendous stakes at issue, I cannot fault Judge Sand for deciding to err on the side of being safe rather than sorry. . . .

B

The Court purports to bolster its judgment by contending that personal sanctions against councilmembers effect a greater interference than city sanctions with the "interests of . . . local authorities in managing their own affairs." Without holding today that the doctrine of absolute legislative immunity itself is applicable to local (as opposed to state and regional) legislative bodies, the Court declares that the principle of legislative independence underlying this doctrine "must inform the District Court's exercise of its discretion in a case such as this." . . .

The doctrine of legislative immunity recognizes that, when acting collectively to pursue a vision of the public good through legislation, legislators must be free to represent their constituents "without fear of outside interference" that would result from private lawsuits. Supreme Court of Virginia v. Consumers Union of the United States, Inc., 446 U.S. 719, 731 (1980). Of course, legislators are bound to respect the limits placed on their discretion by the federal Constitution; they are duty-bound not to enact laws they believe to be unconstitutional, and their laws will have no effect to the extent that courts believe them to be unconstitutional. But when acting "in the sphere of legitimate legislative activity," Tenney v. Brandhove, 341 U.S. 367, 376 (1951)—i.e., formulating and expressing their vision of the public good within self-defined constitutional boundaries—legislators are to be "immune from deterrents to the uninhibited discharge of their legislative duty." Id. at 377. Private lawsuits threaten to chill robust representation by encouraging legislators to avoid controversial issues or stances in order to protect themselves "not only from the consequences of litigation's results but also from the burden of defending themselves." *Supreme Court of Virginia,* 446 U.S., at 732. To encourage legislators best to represent their constituents' interests, legislators must be afforded immunity from private suit.

But once a federal court has issued a valid order to remedy the effects of a prior, specific constitutional violation, the representatives are no longer "acting in a field where legislators traditionally have power to act." *Tenney,* 341 U.S., at 379. At this point, the Constitution itself imposes an overriding definition of the "public good," and a court's valid command to obey constitutional dictates is not subject to override by any countervailing preference of the polity, no matter how widely and ardently shared. Local legislators, for example, may not frustrate valid remedial decrees merely because they or their constituents would rather allocate public funds for other uses. More to the point here, legislators certainly may not defy court-ordered remedies for racial discrimination merely because their constituents prefer to maintain segregation. . . .

III

The Court's decision today that Judge Sand abused his remedial discretion by imposing personal fines simultaneously with city fines creates no new principle of law; indeed, it invokes no principle of any sort. But it directs a message to district judges that, despite their repeated and close contact with the various parties and issues, even the most delicate remedial choices by the most conscientious and deliberate judges are subject to being second-guessed by this Court. I hope such a message will not daunt the courage of district courts who, if ever again faced with such protracted defiance, must carefully yet firmly secure compliance with their remedial orders. But I worry that the Court's message will have the unintended effect of emboldening recalcitrant officials continually to test the ultimate reach of the remedial authority of the federal courts, thereby postponing the day when all public officers finally accept that "the responsibility of those who exercise power in a democratic government is not to reflected inflamed public feeling but to help form its understanding." Cooper v. Aaron, 358 U.S. 1, 26 (1958) (Frankfurter, J., concurring).

NOTES ON ENFORCING DESEGREGATION DECREES

1. *JENKINS II*

Desegregation of the Kansas City, Missouri, School District (KCMSD) has produced three Supreme Court decisions styled *Missouri v. Jenkins*. The first, *Jenkins I*, 491 U.S. 274 (1989), concerned attorney's fees. *Jenkins III*, 515 U.S. 70 (1995), which appears in the preceding Section as a main case, concerned the broad question whether the District Court had overstepped its bounds in ordering expensive improvements in KCMSD schools in order to attract white students. *Jenkins II*, 495 U.S. 33 (1990), dealt with a narrower issue of enforcement.

The desegregation remedies ordered by the District Court were very expensive. Even though the state was required to bear three-fourths of the costs, the KCMSD was unable to pay its share. The District Court therefore ordered an increase in the local property taxes from $2.05 to $4.00 per $100 of assessed valuation, despite the fact that state law allowed local property taxes to be raised to that level only on referendum approval by two-thirds of the voters. For reasons that seemed puzzling at the time and in retrospect seem even more so, the Supreme Court granted review limited to the question of the property tax increase. On the broader question of the validity of the underlying desegregation order, review was specifically denied. The only issue before the Court in *Jenkins II* was, therefore, whether courts could raise taxes.

The Justices were unanimous in concluding that the District Court had abused its discretion by directly imposing a tax increase. This ruling, however, turned out to be largely procedural. Speaking through Justice White, the Court affirmed judicial authority to compel a locality to raise its own taxes, even in ways or amounts not permitted by state law. Thus, the District Court could do indirectly what it could not do directly, a conclusion that provoked disagreement from Justice Kennedy, joined by the Chief Justice and by Justices O'Connor and Scalia. Although Justices Kennedy et al. objected vociferously to "judicial taxation," they seemed chiefly concerned about the extravagance (as they saw it) of the underlying order. Whether they would have contested judicial authority to compel increased taxes if they had not objected to the underlying order was unclear. Cf. Griffin v. County School Bd. of Prince Edward County, 377 U.S. 218 (1964).

2. *JENKINS* AND *SPALLONE*

Jenkins and *Spallone* make an interesting pair. In *Jenkins,* the Court held it permissible for the District Court to raise local taxes to fund a desegregation decree. In *Spallone,* the Court held that it was error for the District Court to hold individual city officers in contempt for refusing to implement a court order. Are the two decisions consistent? If the trial court in *Jenkins* had required local officials to raise property taxes and if they had refused, what could the District Court have done? Could the officials then have been held in contempt? If so, what is the problem with *Spallone*? If not, how else could the taxes be raised?

The majority in *Spallone* thought that there was an important difference between holding local officials in contempt and holding the local government itself in contempt. And they thought it better to act against the city than the individuals. Could an argument be made that this is backwards? As the dissent argues, who suffers if city services are terminated because money is needed to pay the federal contempt fine? And if capitulation by the individuals is required in order to lift the contempt against the city, is it realistic to suggest that an important component of legislative independence has been preserved?

Would these problems be better addressed if the choice among remedies were left to the district and circuit courts to be worked out on the facts of each case? What is the Supreme Court's role in such matters? What did the Court actually accomplish in *Jenkins* and *Spallone*?

For wide-ranging discussion of remedies for federal constitutional violations, with particular focus on *Jenkins* and *Spallone,* see Barry Friedman, When Rights Encounter Reality: Enforcing Federal Remedies, 65 So.Cal.L.Rev. 735 (1992). See also D. Bruce La Pierre, Enforcement of Judgments Against States and Local Governments: Judicial Control over the Power to Tax, 61 G.W.L. Rev. 299 (1993) (providing a comprehensive analysis of the rule in *Jenkins II*).

4. PRISONS

INTRODUCTORY NOTES ON CRUEL AND UNUSUAL PUNISHMENT

1. BACKGROUND

The Eighth Amendment to the Constitution prohibits "cruel and unusual punishments." Originally, the amendment applied only to the federal government, see, e.g., In re Kemmler, 136 U.S. 436 (1890), and only to particular methods of punishment, see, e.g., Weems v. United States, 217 U.S. 349 (1910); Trop v. Dulles, 356 U.S. 66 (1958). By the end of the 1960s, however, the Supreme Court had held that the Due Process Clause of the Fourteenth Amendment incorporates the protections of the Eighth Amendment and makes them applicable to the states. Robinson v. California, 370 U.S. 660 (1962). Shortly thereafter, federal district courts and courts of appeals, faced with appalling conditions in state prison systems, began to hold that the Eighth Amendment prohibited cruel and unusual conditions of confinement, as well as cruel and unusual forms of punishment. See, e.g., Jackson v. Bishop, 404 F.2d 571 (8th Cir. 1968) (enjoining the use of corporal punishment in an Arkansas prison); Jordan v. Fitzharris, 257 F. Supp. 674 (N.D. Cal. 1966) (forbidding the use of unventilated, unlit, bare concrete "strip cells" for solitary confinement in a California prison).

Following such decisions as *Jackson*, *Jordan*, and Holt v. Sarver, 309 F. Supp. 362 (E.D. Ark. 1970), discussed later in this Section, § 1983 lawsuits against prison officials soared. In 1966, the first year in which data concerning state prisoner rights cases was kept as a specific category, there were 218 lawsuits filed. In 1995, there were 40,569 civil rights lawsuits filed by inmates against prison officials, an increase of over 18,000 percent. According to a report by the Bureau of Justice Statistics, there was then about one pending § 1983 lawsuit for every thirty inmates in state prisons. See Roger A. Hanson and Henry W.K. Daley, Challenging the Conditions of Prisons and Jails: A Report on Section 1983 Litigation 2 (1995). Many of these lawsuits involve discrete claims by individual inmates, seeking damages for the use of excessive force by guards, a failure to protect them against violence by other inmates, denials of due process in disciplinary hearings, and the like. But there are also a large number of structural reform lawsuits in which prisoners seek ongoing supervision or regulation of prison practices. By the mid–1980s, roughly one quarter of the nation's 903 state prisons (including at least one in each of 43 states and the District of Columbia) and 15 percent of the nation's 3300 local jails were operating under court orders. The prisons under court order housed 42 percent of the nation's state prisoners, and the jails under court order housed 44 percent of the nation's jail inmates. See Margo Schlanger, Beyond the Hero Judge: Institutional Reform Litigation as Litigation, 97 Mich. L. Rev. 1994, 2004 (1999).

The Supreme Court set out the contours of the Eighth Amendment's coverage of prison conditions in a series of decisions. Taken together, the cases identify both a subjective and an objective component to Eighth Amendment claims. The subjective component focuses on the state of mind possessed by the relevant prison officials, while the objective component concerns the question whether the deprivation a prisoner suffered is sufficiently serious.

2. *ESTELLE V. GAMBLE*

Estelle v. Gamble, 429 U.S. 97 (1976), involved a claim by a Texas state inmate that prison officials had failed to provide adequate medical treatment for a back injury. In an opinion by Justice Marshall, the Court recognized that the government had an "obligation to provide medical care for those whom it is punishing by incarceration" because a failure to provide care "may actually produce physical 'torture or a lingering death,' the evils of most immediate concern to the drafters of the [Eighth] Amendment" or "may result in pain and suffering which no one suggests would serve any penological purpose. . . . The infliction of such unnecessary suffering is inconsistent with contemporary standards of decency," the touchstone of an Eighth Amendment claim. But the Court limited its holding to cases of "deliberate indifference to serious medical needs":

> [A]n inadvertent failure to provide adequate medical care cannot be said to constitute "an unnecessary and wanton infliction of pain" or to be "repugnant to the conscience of mankind." Thus, a complaint that a physician has been negligent in diagnosing or treating a medical condition does not state a valid claim of medical mistreatment under the Eighth Amendment. Medical malpractice does not become a constitutional violation merely be-

cause the victim is a prisoner. In order to state a cognizable claim, a prisoner must allege acts or omissions sufficiently harmful to evidence deliberate indifference to serious medical needs. It is only such indifference that can offend "evolving standards of decency" in violation of the Eighth Amendment.

3. *WILSON V. SEITER*

In Wilson v. Seiter, 504 U.S. 294 (1991), the Court extended the *Estelle v. Gamble* framework to all Eighth Amendment challenges. Wilson was an inmate in an Ohio correctional facility. He alleged a variety of unsafe and unhealthy conditions at the facility and sought declaratory and injunctive relief, as well as $900,000 in compensatory and punitive damages. The Court, in an opinion by Justice Scalia, held that an intent requirement was implicit in the Eighth Amendment's use of the word "punishment" and thus that all Eighth Amendment claims require a culpable state of mind. The defendant prison officials argued that the appropriate standard of intent for claims of cruel and unusual prison conditions had been set out in the Court's decision in Whitley v. Albers, 475 U.S. 312 (1986), which held that a prisoner challenging an excessive use of physical force—the plaintiff was shot by prison officials attempting to quell a prison riot—must show that force was "maliciously and sadistically [applied] for the very purpose of causing harm." The *Wilson* Court rejected that standard as unduly stringent:

> Where (as in *Whitley*) officials act in response to a prison disturbance, their actions are necessarily taken "in haste, under pressure," and balanced against "competing institutional concerns for the safety of prison staff or other inmates.". . . . In contrast, "the State's responsibility to attend to the medical needs of prisoners does not ordinarily clash with other equally important governmental responsibilities," *Whitley*, 475 U.S., at 320, so that in that context, as *Estelle* held, "deliberate indifference" would constitute wantonness. . . .
>
> [W]hether [official conduct] can be characterized as "wanton" depends upon the constraints facing the official. From that standpoint, we see no significant distinction between claims alleging inadequate medical care and those alleging inadequate "conditions of confinement." Indeed, the medical care a prisoner receives is just as much a "condition" of his confinement as the food he is fed, the clothes he is issued, the temperature he is subjected to in his cell, and the protection he is afforded against other inmates. There is no indication that, as a general matter, the actions of prison officials with respect to these nonmedical conditions are taken under materially different constraints than their actions with respect to medical conditions. Thus, as retired Justice Powell has concluded: "Whether one characterizes the treatment received by [the prisoner] as inhumane conditions of confinement, failure to attend to his medical needs, or a combination of both, it is appropriate to apply the 'deliberate indifference' standard articulated in *Estelle*." LaFaut [v. Smith, 834 F.2d 389,] 391–92 [(4th Cir. 1987).]

4. *FARMER V. BRENNAN*

The Supreme Court clarified the meaning of the "deliberate indifference" requirement in Farmer v. Brennan, 511 U.S. 825 (1994). Farmer was a pre-operative transsexual inmate in a federal penitentiary who was placed in the general prison population, where he was beaten and raped. He brought a *Bivens* action seeking compensatory and punitive damages as well as an injunction barring any future confinement in a high-security facility. The Court, in an opinion by Justice Souter, explained that "deliberate indifference describes a state of mind more blameworthy than negligence. [T]he cases are also clear that it is satisfied by something less than acts or omissions for the very purpose of causing harm or with knowledge that harm will result." The Court saw deliberate indifference as equivalent to "recklessness," as that concept is understood in criminal law:

> We hold . . . that a prison official cannot be found liable under the Eighth Amendment for denying an inmate humane conditions of confinement unless the official knows of and disregards an excessive risk to inmate health or safety; the official must both be aware of facts from which the inference could be drawn that a substantial risk of serious harm exists, and he must also draw the inference. . . . The Eighth Amendment does not outlaw cruel and unusual "conditions"; it outlaws cruel and unusual "punishments." An act or omission unaccompanied by knowledge of a significant risk of harm might well be something society wishes to discourage, and if harm does result society might well wish to assure compensation. The common law reflects such concerns when it imposes tort liability on a purely objective basis. But an official's failure to alleviate a significant risk that he should have perceived but did not, while no cause for commendation, cannot under our cases be condemned as the infliction of punishment.

The Court further commented that the concept of deliberate indifference required in Eighth Amendment cases was subjective and could be proved "in the usual ways, including inference from circumstantial evidence." "[A] factfinder may conclude," said the Court, "that a prison official knew of a substantial risk from the very fact that the risk was obvious." Finally, the Court emphasized that prison officials cannot escape liability by arguing that, while they were aware of a substantial risk, they did not foresee the precise way in which it would materialize.

Note that the "deliberate indifference" standard for Eighth Amendment claims is significantly different from the "deliberate indifference" standard used in failure to train cases such as City of Canton v. Harris, 489 U.S. 378 (discussed in Chapter I). In *Canton*, the Court held that a municipality can be liable for failure to train its employees when the municipality's failure shows "a deliberate indifference to the rights of its inhabitants." The Court observed that "it may happen that in light of the duties assigned to specific officers or employees the need for more or different training is so obvious, and the inadequacy so likely to result in the violation of constitutional rights, that the policymakers of the city can reasonably be said to have been deliberately indifferent to the need"—an objective, rather than a subjective standard. As the *Farmer* Court explained,

> *Canton*'s objective standard, however, is not an appropriate test for determining the liability of prison officials under the Eighth Amendment as interpreted in our cases. Section 1983, which merely provides a cause of action, "contains no state-of-mind requirement independent of that necessary to state a violation of the underlying constitutional right." Daniels v.

Williams, 474 U.S. 327, 330 (1986). And while deliberate indifference serves under the Eighth Amendment to ensure that only inflictions of punishment carry liability, the "term was used in the *Canton* case for the quite different purpose of identifying the threshold for holding a city responsible for the constitutional torts committed by its inadequately trained agents," Collins v. Harker Heights, 503 U.S. 115, 124 (1992), a purpose the *Canton* Court found satisfied by a test permitting liability when a municipality disregards "obvious" needs. Needless to say, moreover, considerable conceptual difficulty would attend any search for the subjective state of mind of a governmental entity, as distinct from that of a governmental official. For these reasons, we cannot accept petitioner's argument that *Canton* compels the conclusion here that a prison official who was unaware of a substantial risk of harm to an inmate may nevertheless be held liable under the Eighth Amendment if the risk was obvious and a reasonable prison official would have noticed it.

5. RELATION OF RIGHT TO REMEDY IN PRISON REFORM

Aside from decisions defining the subjective component of a claim of cruel and unusual punishment, the Court has also grappled with the objective component of the question—what conditions qualify as cruel and unusual punishment—and with the proper remedial scope for such violations. The two questions are interrelated. Indeed, in no arena has the interdependency of rights and remedies been more dramatically revealed than in structural reform litigation concerning conditions of confinement in prison.

Rhodes v. Chapman

Supreme Court of the United States, 1981.
452 U.S. 337.

■ JUSTICE POWELL delivered the opinion of the Court.

The question presented is whether the housing of two inmates in a single cell at the Southern Ohio Correctional Facility is cruel and unusual punishment prohibited by the Eighth and Fourteenth Amendments.

I

Respondents Kelly Chapman and Richard Jaworski are inmates at the Southern Ohio Correctional Facility (SOCF), a maximum-security state prison in Lucasville, Ohio. They were housed in the same cell when they brought this action in the District Court for the Southern District of Ohio on behalf of themselves and all inmates similarly situated at SOCF. Asserting a cause of action under 42 U.S.C. § 1983, they contended that "double celling" at SOCF violated the Constitution. The gravamen of their complaint was that double celling confined cellmates too closely. It also was blamed for overcrowding at SOCF, said to have overwhelmed the prison's facilities and staff. As relief, respondents sought an injunction barring petitioners, who are Ohio officials responsible for the administration of SOCF, from housing more than one inmate in a cell, except as a temporary measure.

The District Court made extensive findings of fact about SOCF on the basis of evidence presented at trial and the court's own observations during an inspection that it conducted without advance notice. These findings describe the physical plant, inmate population, and effects of double celling. Neither party contends that these findings are erroneous.

SOCF was built in the early 1970's. In addition to 1,620 cells, it has gymnasiums, workshops, schoolrooms, "dayrooms," two chapels, a hospital ward, commissary, barber-shop, and library. Outdoors, SOCF has a recreation field, visitation area, and garden. The District Court described this physical plant as "unquestionably a top-flight, first-class facility."

Each cell at SOCF measures approximately 63 square feet. Each contains a bed measuring 36 by 80 inches, a cabinet-type night stand, a wall-mounted sink with hot and cold running water, and a toilet that the inmate can flush from inside the cell. Cells housing two inmates have a two-tiered bunk bed. Every cell has a heating and air circulation vent near the ceiling, and 960 of the cells have a window that inmates can open and close. All of the cells have a cabinet, shelf, and radio built into one of the walls, and in all of the cells one wall consists of bars through which the inmates can be seen.

The "dayrooms" are located adjacent to the cellblocks and are open to inmates between 6:30 a.m. and 9:30 p.m. According to the District Court, "[t]he day rooms are in a sense part of the cells and they are designed to furnish that type of recreation or occupation which an ordinary citizen would seek in his living room or den." Each dayroom contains a wall-mounted television, card tables, and chairs. Inmates can pass between their cells and the dayrooms during a 10–minute period each hour, on the hour, when the doors to the dayrooms and cells are opened.

As to the inmate population, the District Court found that SOCF began receiving inmates in late 1972 and double celling them in 1975 because of an increase in Ohio's statewide prison population. At the time of trial, SOCF housed 2,300 inmates, 67 percent of whom were serving life or other long-term sentences for first-degree felonies. Approximately, 1,400 inmates were double celled. Of these, about 75 percent had the choice of spending much of their waking hours outside their cells, in the dayrooms, school, workshops, library, visits, meals, or showers. The other double-celled inmates spent more time locked in their cells because of a restrictive classification.[3]

The remaining findings by the District Court addressed respondents' allegation that overcrowding created by double celling overwhelmed SOCF's facilities and staff. The food was "adequate in every respect," and respondents adduced no evidence "whatsoever that prisoners have been underfed or that the food facilities have been taxed by the prison population." The air ventilation system was adequate, the cells were substantially free of offensive odor, the temperature in the cellblocks was well controlled, and the noise in the cellblocks was not excessive. Double celling had not reduced significantly the availability of space in the dayrooms or visitation facilities,[4] nor had it rendered inadequate the resources of the library or

---

[3] Inmates who requested protective custody but could not substantiate their fears were classified as "limited activity" and were locked in their cells all but six hours a week. Inmates classified as "voluntarily idle" and newly arrived inmates awaiting classification had only four hours a week outside their cells. Inmates housed in administrative isolation for disciplinary reasons were allowed out of their cells for two hours a week to attend religious services, a movie, or the commissary.

[4] The court noted that SOCF is one of the few maximum-security prisons in the country to permit contact visitation for all inmates.

schoolrooms.[5] Although there were isolated incidents of failure to provide medical or dental care, there was no evidence of indifference by the SOCF staff to inmates' medical or dental needs. As to violence, the court found that the number of acts of violence at SOCF had increased with the prison population, but only in proportion to the increase in population. Respondents failed to produce evidence establishing that double celling itself caused greater violence, and the ratio of guards to inmates at SOCF satisfied the standard of acceptability offered by respondents' expert witness. Finally, the court did find that the SOCF administration, faced with more inmates than jobs, had "water[ed] down" jobs by assigning more inmates to each job than necessary and by reducing the number of hours that each inmate worked; it also found that SOCF had not increased its staff of psychiatrists and social workers since double celling had begun.

Despite these generally favorable findings, the District Court concluded that double celling at SOCF was cruel and unusual punishment. The court rested its conclusion on five considerations. One, inmates at SOCF are serving long terms of imprisonment. In the court's view, that fact "can only accent[uate] the problems of close confinement and overcrowding." Two, SOCF housed 38 percent more inmates at the time of trial than its "design capacity." In reference to this, the court asserted: "Overcrowding necessarily involves excess limitation of general movement as well as physical and mental injury from long exposure." Three, the court accepted as contemporary standards of decency several studies recommending that each person in an institution have at least 50–55 square feet of living quarters.[7] In contrast, double-celled inmates at SOCF share 63 square feet. Four, the court asserted that "[a]t the best a prisoner who is double celled will spend most of his time in the cell with his cellmate." Five, SOCF has made double celling a practice; it is not a temporary condition.[9]

On appeal to the Court of Appeals for the Sixth Circuit, petitioners argued that the District Court's conclusion must be read, in light of its findings, as holding that double celling is per se unconstitutional. The Court of Appeals disagreed; it viewed the District Court's opinion as holding only that double celling is cruel and unusual punishment under the circumstances at SOCF. It affirmed, without further opinion, on the ground that the District Court's findings were not clearly erroneous, its conclusions of law were "permissible from the findings," and its remedy was a reasonable response to the violations found. We granted the petition for certiorari because of the importance of the question to prison administration. We now reverse.

---

[5] The court found that adequate lawbooks were available, even to inmates in protective or disciplinary confinement, to allow effective access to court. As to school, no inmate who was "ready, able, and willing to receive schooling has been denied the opportunity," although there was some delay before an inmate received the opportunity to attend.

[7] The District Court cited, e.g., American Correctional Assn., Manual of Standards for Adult Correctional Institutions, Standard No. 4142, p. 27 (1977) (60–80 square feet); National Sheriffs' Assn., A Handbook on Jail Architecture 63 (1975) (70–80 square feet); National Council on Crime and Delinquency, Model Act for the Protection of the Rights of Prisoners, § 1, 18 Crime & Delinquency 4, 10 (1972) (50 square feet).

[9] Rather than order that petitioners either move respondents into single cells or release them, as respondents urged, the District Court initially ordered petitioners to "proceed with reasonable dispatch to formulate, propose, and carry out some plan which will terminate double celling at SOCF." Petitioners submitted five plans, each of which the court rejected. It then ordered petitioners to reduce the inmate population at SOCF by 25 men per month until the population fell to the prison's approximate design capacity of 1,700.

II

We consider here for the first time the limitation that the Eighth Amendment, which is applicable to the states through the Fourteenth Amendment, Robinson v. California, 370 U.S. 660 (1962), imposes upon the conditions in which a state may confine those convicted of crimes. It is unquestioned that "[c]onfinement in a prison . . . is a form of punishment subject to scrutiny under the Eighth Amendment standards." Hutto v. Finney, 437 U.S. 678, 685 (1978). But until this case, we have not considered a disputed contention that the conditions of confinement at a particular prison constituted cruel and unusual punishment. Nor have we had an occasion to consider specifically the principles relevant to assessing claims that conditions of confinement violate the Eighth Amendment. We look, first, to the Eighth Amendment precedents for the general principles that are relevant to a state's authority to impose punishment for criminal conduct.

A

The Eighth Amendment, in only three words, imposes the constitutional limitation upon punishments: they cannot be "cruel and unusual." The Court has interpreted these words "in a flexible and dynamic manner," Gregg v. Georgia, 428 U.S. 153, 171 (1976) (joint opinion), and has extended the amendment's reach beyond the barbarous physical punishments at issue in the Court's earliest cases. Today, the Eighth Amendment prohibits punishments which, although not physically barbarous, "involve the unnecessary and wanton infliction of pain," *Gregg v. Georgia*, 428 U.S., at 173, or are grossly disproportionate to the severity of the crime, Coker v. Georgia, 433 U.S. 584 (1977) (plurality opinion); Weems v. United States, 217 U.S. 349 (1910). Among "unnecessary and wanton" inflictions of pain are those that are "totally without penological justification." *Gregg v. Georgia*, 428 U.S., at 183.

No static "test" can exist by which courts determine whether conditions of confinement are cruel and unusual, for the Eighth Amendment "must draw its meaning from the evolving standards of decency that mark the progress of a maturing society." Trop v. Dulles, 356 U.S. 86, 101 (1958) (plurality opinion). The Court has held, however, that "Eighth Amendment judgments should neither be nor appear to be merely the subjective views" of judges. Rummel v. Estelle, 445 U.S. 263, 275 (1980). To be sure, "the Constitution contemplates that in the end [a court's] own judgment will be brought to bear on the question of the acceptability" of a given punishment. *Coker v. Georgia*, 433 U.S., at 592 (plurality opinion). But such " 'judgment[s] should be informed by objective factors to the maximum possible extent.' " *Rummel v. Estelle*, 435 U.S., at 274–75, quoting *Coker v. Georgia*, 433 U.S., at 592 (plurality opinion). For example, when the question was whether capital punishment for certain crimes violated contemporary values, the Court looked for "objective indicia" derived from history, the action of state legislatures, and the sentencing by juries. *Gregg v. Georgia*, 428 U.S., at 176–87; *Coker v. Georgia*, 433 U.S., at 593–96. Our conclusion in Estelle v. Gamble, 429 U.S. 97, 103 (1976), that deliberate indifference to an inmate's medical needs is cruel and unusual punishment rested on the fact, recognized by the common law and state legislatures, that "[a]n inmate must rely on prison authorities to treat his medical needs; if the authorities fail to do so, those needs will not be met."

These principles apply when the conditions of confinement compose the punishment at issue. Conditions must not involve the wanton and unnecessary infliction of pain, nor may they be grossly disproportionate to the severity of the crime warranting imprisonment. In *Estelle v. Gamble*, we held that the denial of medical care is cruel and unusual because, in the worst case, it can result in physical torture, and, even in less serious cases, it can result in pain without any penological purpose. In Hutto v. Finney, 437 U.S. 678 (1978), the conditions of confinement in two Arkansas prisons constituted cruel and unusual punishment because they resulted in unquestioned and serious deprivation of basic human needs. Conditions other than those in *Gamble* and *Hutto*, alone or in combination, may deprive inmates of the minimal civilized measure of life's necessities. Such conditions could be cruel and unusual under the contemporary standard of decency that we recognized in *Gamble*. But conditions that cannot be said to be cruel and unusual under contemporary standards are not unconstitutional. To the extent that such conditions are restrictive and even harsh, they are part of the penalty that criminal offenders pay for their offenses against society.

B

In view of the District Court's findings of fact, its conclusion that double celling at SOCF constitutes cruel and unusual punishment is insupportable. Virtually every one of the court's findings tends to *refute* respondents' claim. The double celling made necessary by the unanticipated increase in prison population did not lead to deprivations of essential food, medical care, or sanitation. Nor did it increase violence among inmates or create other conditions intolerable for prison confinement. Although job and educational opportunities diminished marginally as a result of double celling, limited work hours and delay before receiving education do not inflict pain, much less unnecessary and wanton pain; deprivations of this kind simply are not punishments. We would have to wrench the Eighth Amendment from its language and history to hold that delay of these desirable aids to rehabilitation violates the Constitution.

The five considerations on which the District Court relied also are insufficient to support its constitutional conclusion. The court relied on the long terms of imprisonment served by inmates of SOCF; the fact that SOCF housed 38 percent more inmates than its "design capacity"; the recommendation of several studies that each inmate have at least 50–55 square feet of living quarters; the suggestion that double-celled inmates spend most of their time in their cells with their cellmates; and the fact that double celling at SOCF was not a temporary condition. These general considerations fall far short in themselves of proving cruel and unusual punishment, for there is no evidence that double celling under these circumstances either inflicts unnecessary or wanton pain or is grossly disproportionate to the severity of crimes warranting imprisonment.[13] At most, these considerations amount to a theory that double celling inflicts pain. Perhaps they re-

[13] Respondents and the District Court erred in assuming that opinions of experts as to desirable prison conditions suffice to establish contemporary standards of decency. As we noted in Bell v. Wolfish, 441 U.S. 520, 543–44 (1979), such opinions may be helpful and relevant with respect to some questions, but "they simply do not establish the constitutional minima; rather, they establish goals recommended by the organization in question." See U.S. Dept. of Justice, Federal Standards for Prisons and Jails 1 (1980). Indeed, generalized opinions of experts cannot weigh as heavily in determining the contemporary standards of decency as "the public attitude toward a given sanction." Gregg v. Georgia, 428 U.S. 153, 173 (1976) (joint opinion). We could agree that double celling is not desirable, especially in view of the size of these cells. But there is no evidence in this case that double celling is viewed generally as violating decency. Moreover, though small, the cells in SOCF are exceptionally modern and functional; they are heated and ventilated and have hot and cold running water and a sanitary toilet. Each cell also has a radio.

flect an aspiration toward an ideal environment for long-term confinement. But the Constitution does not mandate comfortable prisons, and prisons of SOCF's type, which house persons convicted of serious crimes, cannot be free of discomfort. Thus, these considerations properly are weighed by the legislature and prison administration rather than a court. There being no constitutional violation,[15] the District Court had no authority to consider whether double celling in light of these considerations was the best response to the increase in Ohio's statewide prison population.

III

This Court must proceed cautiously in making an Eighth Amendment judgment because, unless we reverse it, "[a] decision that a given punishment is impermissible under the Eighth Amendment cannot be reversed short of a constitutional amendment," and thus "[r]evisions cannot be made in the light of further experience." *Gregg v. Georgia*, 428 U.S., at 176. In assessing claims that conditions of confinement are cruel and unusual, courts must bear in mind that their inquiries "spring from constitutional requirements and that judicial answers to them must reflect that fact rather than a court's idea of how best to operate a detention facility." *Bell v. Wolfish*, 441 U.S., at 539.

Courts certainly have a responsibility to scrutinize claims of cruel and unusual confinement, and conditions in a number of prisons, especially older ones, have justly been described as "deplorable" and "sordid." Id., at 562. When conditions of confinement amount to cruel and unusual punishment, "federal courts will discharge their duty to protect constitutional rights." Procunier v. Martinez, 416 U.S. 396, 405–06 (1974). In discharging this oversight responsibility, however, courts cannot assume that state legisla-

---

[15] The dissenting opinion states that "the facility described by [the Court] is not the one involved in this case." The incorrectness of this statement is apparent from an examination of the facts set forth at length above and the District Court's detailed findings of fact.

In several instances, the dissent selectively relies on testimony without acknowledging that the District Court gave it little or no weight. For example, the dissent emphasizes the testimony of experts as to psychological problems that "may be expected" from double celling; it also relies on similar testimony as to an increase in tension and aggression. The dissent fails to mention, however, that the District Court also referred to the testimony by the prison superintendent and physician that "there has been no increase [in violence] other than what one would expect from increased numbers [of inmates]." More telling is the fact—ignored by the dissent—that the District Court resolved this conflict in the testimony by holding "that there had been no increase in violence or criminal activity increase due to double celling; there has been [an increase] due to increased population." This holding was based on uncontroverted prison records, required to be maintained by the Ohio Department of Corrections and described by the District Court as being "detail[ed] and bespeak[ing] credibility."

There is some ambiguity in the opinion of the District Court concerning the amount of time that double-celled inmates were required to remain in their cells. The dissent relies only on selective findings that most inmates are out of their cells only 10 hours a day and that others are out only four-six hours a week. The dissent fails to note that the first of these findings is flatly inconsistent with a prior, twice-repeated, finding by the court that inmates "have to be locked in their cell with their cellmate only from about 9:00 p.m. to 6:30 a.m.," leaving them free to move about for some 14 hours. Moreover, it is unquestioned—and also not mentioned by the dissent—that the inmates who spend most of their time locked in their cells are those who have a "restrictive classification." . . .

The dissent also makes much of the fact that SOCF was housing 38 percent more inmates at the time of trial than its "rated capacity." According to the United States Bureau of Prisons, at least three factors influence prison population: the number of arrests, prosecution policies, and sentencing and parole decisions. Because these factors can change rapidly, while prisons require years to plan and build, it is extremely difficult to calibrate a prison's "rated" or "design capacity" with predictions of prison population. The question before us is not whether the designer of SOCF guessed incorrectly about future prison population, but whether the actual conditions of confinement at SOCF are cruel and unusual.

tures and prison officials are insensitive to the requirements of the Constitution or to the perplexing sociological problems of how best to achieve the goals of the penal function in the criminal justice system: to punish justly, to deter future crime, and to return imprisoned persons to society with an improved chance of being useful, law-abiding citizens.

In this case, the question before us is whether the conditions of confinement at SOCF are cruel and unusual. As we find that they are not, the judgment of the Court of Appeals is reversed.

It is so ordered.

■ JUSTICE BRENNAN, with whom JUSTICE BLACKMUN and JUSTICE STEVENS join, concurring in the judgment.

Today's decision reaffirms that "[c]ourts certainly have a responsibility to scrutinize claims of cruel and unusual punishment." With that I agree. I also agree that the District Court's findings in this case do not support a judgment that the practice of double celling in the Southern Ohio Correctional Facility is in violation of the Eighth Amendment. I write separately, however, to emphasize that today's decision should in no way be construed as a retreat from careful judicial scrutiny of prison conditions, and to discuss the factors courts should consider in undertaking such scrutiny.

I

Although this Court has never before considered what prison conditions constitute "cruel and unusual punishment" within the meaning of the Eighth Amendment, such questions have been addressed repeatedly by the lower courts. In fact, individual prisons or entire prison systems in at least 24 states have been declared unconstitutional under the Eighth and Fourteenth Amendments, with litigation underway in many others. Thus, the lower courts have learned from repeated investigation and bitter experience that judicial intervention is *indispensable* if constitutional dictates—not to mention considerations of basic humanity—are to be observed in the prisons.

No one familiar with litigation in this area could suggest that the courts have been overeager to usurp the task of running prisons, which, as the Court today properly notes, is entrusted in the first instance to the "legislature and prison administration rather than a court." And certainly, no one could suppose that the courts have ordered creation of "comfortable prisons" on the model of country clubs. To the contrary, "the soul-chilling inhumanity of conditions in American prisons has been thrust upon the judicial conscience." Inmates of Suffolk County Jail v. Eisenstadt, 360 F.Supp. 676, 684 (D.Mass.1973).

Judicial opinions in this area do not make pleasant reading. For example, in Pugh v. Locke, 406 F.Supp. 318 (M.D.Ala.1976), Chief Judge Frank Johnson described in gruesome detail the conditions then prevailing in the Alabama penal system. The institutions were "horrendously overcrowded," to the point where some inmates were forced to sleep on mattresses spread on floors in hallways and next to urinals. The physical facilities were "dilapidat[ed]" and "filthy," the cells infested with roaches, flies, mosquitoes, and other vermin. Sanitation facilities were limited and in ill repair, emitting an "overpowering odor"; in one instance over 200 men were forced to share one toilet. Inmates were not provided with toothpaste, toothbrush, shampoo, shaving cream, razors, combs, or other such necessities. Food was "unappetizing and unwholesome," poorly prepared and often infested with insects, and served without reasonable utensils. There were no meaningful vocational, educational, recreational, or work programs. A United States health officer described the prisons as "wholly unfit for human habitation according to virtually every criterion used for evaluation by public health inspectors." Perhaps the worst of all was the "rampant violence" within the prison. Weaker inmates were "repeatedly victimized" by the stronger; robbery, rape, extortion, theft, and assault were "everyday occurrences among the general inmate population." Faced with this record, the court—not surprisingly—found that the conditions of confinement constituted cruel and unusual punishment, and issued a comprehensive remedial order affecting virtually every aspect of prison administration.

Unfortunately, the Alabama example is neither aberrational nor anachronistic. Last year, in Ramos v. Lamm, 639 F.2d 559 (10th Cir. 1980), for example, the Tenth Circuit declared conditions in the maximum-security unit of the Colorado State Penitentiary at Cannon City unconstitutional. The living areas of the prison were "unfit for human habitation"; the food unsanitary and "grossly inadequate"; the institution "fraught with tension and violence," often leading to injury and death; the health care "blatant[ly] inadequat[e]" and "appalling"; and various restrictions of prisoners' rights to visitation, mail, and access to courts in violation of basic constitutional rights. Similar tales of horror are recounted in dozens of other cases.

Overcrowding and cramped living conditions are particularly pressing problems in many prisons. Out of 82 court orders in effect concerning conditions of confinement in federal and state correctional facilities as of March 31, 1978, 26 involved the issue of overcrowding. . . .

The problems of administering prisons within constitutional standards are indeed " 'complex and intractable,' " but at their core is a lack of resources allocated to prisons. Confinement of prisoners is unquestionably an expensive proposition; the average direct current expenditure at adult institutions in 1977 was $5,461 per inmate; the average cost of constructing space for an additional prisoner is estimated at $25,000 to $50,000. Oftentimes, funding for prisons has been dramatically below that required to comply with basic constitutional standards. . . .

Over the last decade, correctional resources, never ample, have lagged behind burgeoning prison populations. . . . A major infusion of money would be required merely to keep pace with prison populations.

Public apathy and the political powerlessness of inmates have contributed to the pervasive neglect of the prisons. Chief Judge Henley observed that the people of Arkansas "knew little or nothing about their penal system" prior to the *Holt* litigation, despite "sporadic and sensational" exposes. Holt v. Sarver, 309 F.Supp. 362 (E.D.Ark.1970). Prison inmates are "voteless, politically unpopular, and socially threatening." Norval Morris, The Snail's Pace of Prison Reform, in Proceedings of the 100th Annual Congress of Correction of the American Correctional Assn. 36, 42 (1970). Thus, the suffering of prisoners, even if known, generally "moves the community in only the most severe and exceptional cases." Ibid. As a result even conscientious prison officials are "[c]aught in the middle," as state legislatures refuse "to spend sufficient tax dollars to bring conditions in outdated prisons up to minimally acceptable standards." Johnson v. Levine, 450 F.Supp. 648, 654 (D.Md.1978). After extensive exposure to this process, Chief Judge Pettine came to view the "barbaric physical conditions" of Rhode Island's prison system as "the ugly and shocking outward manifestations of a deeper dysfunction, an attitude of cynicism, hopelessness, predatory selfishness, and callous indifference that appears to infect, to one degree or another, almost everyone who comes into contact with the [prison]." Palmigiano v. Garrahy, 443 F.Supp. 956, 984 (D.R.I.1977).

Under these circumstances, the courts have emerged as a critical force behind efforts to ameliorate inhumane conditions. Insulated as they are from political pressures, and charged with the duty of enforcing the Constitution, courts are in the strongest position to insist that unconstitutional conditions be remedied, even at significant financial cost. . . .

Progress toward constitutional conditions of confinement in the nation's prisons has been slow and uneven, despite judicial pressure. Nevertheless, it is clear that judicial intervention has been responsible, not only for remedying some of the worst abuses by direct order, but also for "forcing the legislative branch of government to reevaluate correction policies and to appropriate funds for upgrading penal systems." 3 American Prisons and Jails 163. . . .

Even prison officials have acknowledged that judicial intervention has helped them to obtain support for needed reform. The Commissioner of Corrections of New York City, a defendant in many lawsuits challenging jail and prison conditions, has stated: "Federal courts may be the last resort for us. . . . If there's going to be change, I think the federal courts are going to have to force cities and states to spend more money on their prisons. . . . I look on the courts as a friend." Stephen Gettinger, "Cruel and Unusual" Prisons, 3 Corrections Magazine 3, 5 (Dec. 1977). . . .

II

The task of the courts in cases challenging prison conditions is to "determine whether a challenged punishment comports with human dignity." Furman v. Georgia, 408 U.S. 238, 282 (1972) (Brennan, J., concurring). . . .

In performing this responsibility, this Court and the lower courts have been especially deferential to prison authorities "in the adoption and execution of policies and practices that in their judgment are needed to preserve internal order and discipline and to maintain institutional security." Bell v. Wolfish, 441 U.S. 520, 547 (1979). Many conditions of confinement, however, including overcrowding, poor sanitation, and inadequate safety precautions, arise from neglect rather than policy. There is no reason of comity, judicial restraint, or recognition of expertise for courts to defer to negligent omissions of officials who lack the resources or motivation to operate prisons within limits of decency. Courts must and do recognize the primacy of legislative and executive authorities in the administration of prisons; however, if the prison authorities do not conform to constitutional minima, the courts are under an obligation to take steps to remedy the violations.

The first aspect of judicial decisionmaking in this area is scrutiny of the actual conditions under challenge. It is important to recognize that various deficiencies in prison conditions "must be considered together." *Holt v. Sarver*, 309 F. Supp., at 373. The individual conditions "exist in combination; each affects the other; and taken together they [may] have a cumulative impact on the inmates." Ibid. Thus, a court considering an Eighth Amendment challenge to conditions of confinement must examine the totality of the circumstances. Even if no single condition of confinement would be unconstitutional in itself, "exposure to the cumulative effect of prison conditions may subject inmates to cruel and unusual punishment." Laaman v. Helgemoe, 437 F.Supp. 269, 322–23 (D.N.H.1977).

Moreover, in seeking relevant information about conditions in a prison, the court must be open to evidence and assistance from many sources, including expert testimony and studies on the effect of particular conditions on prisoners. For this purpose, public health, medical, psychiatric, psychological, penological, architectural, structural, and other experts have proved useful to the lower courts in observing and interpreting prison conditions.

More elusive, perhaps, is the second aspect of the judicial inquiry: application of realistic yet humane standards to the conditions as observed. Courts have expressed these standards in various ways . . . , but in the end the court attempting to apply them is left to rely upon its own experience and on its knowledge of contemporary standards.

In determining when prison conditions pass beyond legitimate punishment and become cruel and unusual, the "touchstone is the effect upon the imprisoned." *Laaman v. Helgemoe*, 437 F. Supp., at 323. The court must examine the effect upon inmates of the condition of the physical plant (lighting, heat, plumbing, ventilation, living space, noise levels, recreation space); sanitation (control of vermin and insects, food preparation, medical facilities, lavatories and showers, clean places for eating, sleeping, and working); safety (protection from violent, deranged, or diseased inmates, fire protection, emergency evacuation); inmate needs and services (clothing, nutrition, bedding, medical, dental, and mental health care, visitation time, exercise and recreation, educational and rehabilitative programming); and staffing (trained and adequate guards and other staff, avoidance of placing inmates in positions of authority over other inmates). When "the cumulative impact of the conditions of incarceration threatens the physical, mental, and emotional health and well-being of the inmates and/or creates a probability of recidivism and future incarceration," the court must conclude that the conditions violate the Constitution. Id., at 323.

III

A reviewing court is generally limited in its perception of a case to the findings of the trial court. . . .

I have not the slightest doubt that 63 square feet of cell space is not enough for two men. I understand that every major study of living space in prisons has so concluded. That prisoners are housed under such conditions is an unmistakable signal to the legislators and officials of Ohio: either more prison facilities should be built or expanded, or fewer persons should be incarcerated in prisons. Even so, the findings of the District Court do not support a conclusion that the conditions at the Southern Ohio Correctional Facility—cramped though they are—constitute cruel and unusual punishment.

The "touchstone" of the Eighth Amendment inquiry is "the effect upon the imprisoned." The findings of the District Court leave no doubt that the prisoners are adequately sheltered, fed, and protected, and that opportunities for education, work, and rehabilitative assistance are available. One need only compare the District Court's description of conditions at the Southern Ohio Correctional Facility with descriptions of other major state and federal facilities, see supra, to realize that this prison, crowded though it is, is one of the better, more humane large prisons in the nation.[15] . . .

---

15 If it were true that any prison providing less than 63 square feet of cell space per inmate were a per se violation of the Eighth Amendment, then approximately two-thirds of all federal, state, and local inmates today would be unconstitutionally confined.

The District Court may well be correct *in the abstract* that prison overcrowding and double celling such as existed at the Southern Ohio Correctional Facility generally [result] in serious harm to the inmates. But cases are not decided in the abstract. A court is under the obligation to examine the *actual effect* of challenged conditions upon the well-being of the prisoners. The District Court in this case was unable to identify any actual signs that the double celling at the Southern Ohio Correctional Facility has seriously harmed the inmates there; indeed, the court's findings of fact suggest that crowding at the prison has not reached the point of causing serious injury. Since I cannot conclude that the totality of conditions at the facility offends constitutional norms, and am of the view that double celling it itself not per se impermissible, I concur in the judgment of the Court.

■ JUSTICE BLACKMUN concurring in the judgment. . . .

I perceive, as Justice Brennan obviously does in view of his separate writing, a possibility that the Court's opinion in this case today might be regarded, because of some of its language, as a signal to prison administrators that the federal courts now are to adopt a policy of general deference to such administrators and to state legislatures, deference not only for the purpose of determining contemporary standards of decency, but for the purpose of determining whether conditions at a particular prison are cruel and unusual within the meaning of the Eighth Amendment. That perhaps was the old attitude prevalent several decades ago. I join Justice Brennan's opinion because I, too, feel that the federal courts must continue to be available to those state inmates who sincerely claim that the conditions to which they are subjected are violative of the amendment. . . .

■ JUSTICE MARSHALL, dissenting.

From reading the Court's opinion in this case, one would surely conclude that the Southern Ohio Correctional Facility (SOCF) is a safe, spacious prison that happens to include many two-inmate cells because the state has determined that that is the best way to run a prison. But the facility described by the majority is not then one involved in this case. SOCF is overcrowded, unhealthful, and dangerous. None of these conditions results from a considered policy judgment on the part of the state. . . . No one argued at trial and no one has contended here that double celling was a legislative policy judgment. No one has asserted that prison officials imposed it as a disciplinary or a security matter. And no one has claimed that the practice has anything whatsoever to do with "punish[ing] justly," "deter[ring] future crime," or "return[ing] imprisoned persons to society with an improved chance of being useful law-abiding citizens." The evidence and the District Court's findings clearly demonstrate that the *only* reason double celling was imposed on inmates at SOCF was that more individuals were sent there than the prison was ever designed to hold. . . .

In a doubled cell, each inmate has only some 30–35 square feet of floor space.[3] Most of the windows in the Supreme Court building are larger than that. The conclusion of every expert who testified at trial and of every serious study of which I am aware is that a long-term inmate must have to himself, at the very least, 50 square feet of floor space—an area smaller than that occupied by a good-sized automobile—in order to avoid serious

[3] The bed alone, which is bunk-style in the doubled cells, takes up approximately 20 square feet. Thus, the actual amount of floor space per inmate, without making allowance for any other furniture in the room, is some 20–24 square feet, an area about the size of a typical door.

mental, emotional, and physical deterioration. The District Court found that as a fact. Even petitioners, in their brief in this Court, concede that double celling as practiced at SOCF is "less than desirable."

The Eighth Amendment "embodies 'broad and idealistic concepts of dignity, civilized standards, humanity, and decency,' " against which conditions of confinement must be judged. Estelle v. Gamble, 429 U.S. 97, 102 (1976), quoting Jackson v. Bishop, 404 F.2d 571, 579 (8th Cir. 1968). Thus the state cannot impose punishment that violates "the evolving standards of decency that mark the progress of a maturing society." Trop v. Dulles, 356 U.S. 86, 101 (1958) (plurality opinion). For me, the legislative judgment and the consistent conclusions by those who have studied the problem provide considerable evidence that those standards condemn imprisonment in conditions so crowded that serious harm will result. The record amply demonstrates that those conditions are present here. It is surely not disputed that SOCF is severely overcrowded. The prison is operating at 38 percent above its design capacity.[5] It is also significant that some two-thirds of the inmates at SOCF are serving lengthy or life sentences, for, as we have said elsewhere, "the length of confinement cannot be ignored in deciding whether the confinement meets constitutional standards." Hutto v. Finney, 437 U.S. 678, 686 (1978). Nor is double celling a short-term response to a temporary problem. The trial court found, and it is not contested, that double celling, if not enjoined, will continue for the foreseeable future. The trial court also found that most of the double-celled inmates spend most of their time in their cells.[6]

---

5 . . . In its opinion today, the Court at least mentions that SOCF is operating at 38 percent above its rated capacity, but it dismisses that rating as "[p]erhaps" reflecting "an aspiration toward an ideal environment for long-term confinement." "The question before us," the majority adds, "is not whether the designer of SOCF guessed incorrectly about future prison population, but whether the actual conditions of confinement at SOCF are cruel and unusual." Rated capacity, the majority argues, is irrelevant because of the numerous factors that influence prison population. Actually, it is the factors that influence prison population that are irrelevant. By definition, rated capacity represents "the number of inmates that a confinement unit, facility, or entire correctional agency can hold." If prison population, for whatever reason, exceeds rated capacity, then the prison must accommodate more people that it is designed to hold—in short, it is overcrowded. . . .

6 . . . The majority assumes that the trial court's finding that most inmates are out of their cells only 10 hours each day is "flatly inconsistent" with its finding that regulations permit most inmates to be out of their cells up to 14 hours each day. The majority goes on to reject the first finding in favor of the second. A more reasonable course would be to read these two findings in such a way as to give meaning to both. Thus I read the District Court's opinion as finding that although most inmates are permitted out of their cells up to 14 hours each day, conditions in the prison are such that many choose not to do so.

The majority also attaches importance to the fact that the inmates who are locked in their cells for all but four to six hours a week are in a "restrictive classification." It is not clear to me why this matters. The inmates who are out of their cells only four to six hours each week are in three categories: "receiving," a category in which new inmates are placed for "a couple of weeks"; "voluntarily idle," which presumably means what says; and "limited activity," for those inmates who have requested, but have not received, protective custody. It is not immediately apparent why classification in any of these categories justifies imposition of otherwise cruel and unusual punishment. In particular, the state surely lacks authority to force an individual to choose between possibility of rape or other physical harm (the presumed reason for the request for protective custody) and unconstitutionally cramped quarters. The majority asserts, incorrectly, that some of these inmates have committed rule infractions. In fact, inmates who commit infractions are out of their cells only *two* hours each week. Although this dissent has not addressed their particular plight, it is beyond question that if punishment is cruel and unusual, then the mere fact that an individual prisoner has committed a rule infraction does not warrant its imposition.

It is simply not true, as the majority asserts, that "there is no evidence that double celling under these circumstances either inflicts unnecessary or wanton pain or is grossly disproportionate to the severity of crimes warranting imprisonment." The District Court concluded from the record before it that long exposure to these conditions will "*necessarily*" involve "excess limitation of general movement as well as physical and mental injury. . . . "[7] And, of course, of all the judges who have been involved in this case, the trial judge is the only one who has actually visited the prison. That is simply an additional reason to give in this case the deference we have always accorded to the careful conclusions of the finder of fact. There is not a shred of evidence to suggest that anyone who has given the matter serious thought has ever approved, as the majority does today, conditions of confinement such as those present at SOCF. I see no reason to set aside the concurrent conclusions of two courts that the overcrowding and double celling here in issue are sufficiently severe that they will, if left unchecked, caused deterioration in respondents' mental and physical health. These conditions in my view go well beyond contemporary standards of decency and therefore violate the Eighth and Fourteenth Amendments. . . .

A society must punish those who transgress its rules. When the offense is severe, the punishment should be of proportionate severity. But the punishment must always be administered within the limitations set down by the Constitution. With the rising crime rates of recent years, there has been an alarming tendency toward a simplistic penological philosophy that if we lock the prison doors and throw away the keys, our streets will somehow be safe. In the current climate, it is unrealistic to expect legislators to care whether the prisons are overcrowded or harmful to inmate health. It is at that point—when conditions are deplorable and the political process offers no redress—that the federal courts are required by the Constitution to play a role. I believe that this vital duty was properly discharged by the District Court and the Court of Appeals in this case. The majority today takes a step toward abandoning that role altogether. I dissent.

NOTES ON THE RELATION OF RIGHTS AND REMEDIES IN PRISON CASES

1. INTRODUCTION

The prison cases illustrate a complex relationship between rights and remedies in certain kinds of institutional reform litigation, an interesting chapter in the evolution of constitutional rights. Additionally, they reveal an increasing tension between the lower courts and a divided Supreme Court.

2. *HOLT V. SARVER*

The prototype for prison reform suits was Holt v. Sarver, 309 F.Supp. 362 (E.D.Ark.1970) (*Holt II*). In earlier cases, specific practices of the Arkansas prison system had been declared unconstitutional. These cases, and a legislative investigation spawned by them, revealed conditions of squalor and degradation. Inmates were housed in large barracks, where sexual and other assaults were common. Liquor and drugs were available and commonly used. Iso-

[7] In its findings, the District Court credited expert testimony that "close quarters" would likely increase the incidence of schizophrenia and other mental disorders and that the double celling imposed in this case had led to increases in tension and in "aggressive and anti-social characteristics." . . .

lation cells and other facilities were overcrowded, and food, health care, and sanitation were inadequate. Virtually no effort was made at rehabilitation. Worst of all was the pervasive control of inmates by other inmates. The Arkansas prisons were run by a skeleton staff of civilians, augmented by inmate "trusties." Trusties guarded other inmates and performed important administrative functions. Their authority over inmates of lesser rank was great and largely uncontrolled. As a result, interaction between ordinary inmates and trusty guards was characterized by extortion, violence, and indifference to inmate welfare. As the court summarized, "just about every abuse which the [trusty] system is capable of producing has been produced and is being practiced in this state."

In *Holt II*, class actions were brought to challenge the continuation of such conditions. As a result, correctional officials were ordered "to make a prompt and reasonable start" toward eliminating unconstitutional conditions of confinement. The court supplemented that directive with more specific descriptions of required reforms and demanded prompt submission of a report and plan "showing what, if anything, [the officials] have done . . . , what they plan to do, and when they plan to do it." Additional hearings and court orders followed. In 1973 the District Court tried to end its continuing supervision of the Arkansas prisons, but the Eighth Circuit reversed. Finney v. Arkansas Bd. of Correction, 505 F.2d 194 (8th Cir. 1974). Later hearings revealed that some conditions had deteriorated since 1973 and that many evils had not been corrected. The District Court then entered additional orders placing limits on the number of persons to be confined in one cell, requiring that each prisoner have a bunk, discontinuing an unwholesome diet, and setting a 30–day maximum for sentences of punitive isolation.

The last of these features (as well as an award of attorney's fees under 42 U.S.C. § 1988) was upheld by the Supreme Court in Hutto v. Finney, 437 U.S. 678 (1978). The Court made plain that its approval of the 30–day limit was based specifically on the conditions of punitive isolation and more generally on the history of the Arkansas prison litigation:

> The question before the trial court was whether past constitutional violations had been remedied. The court was entitled to consider the severity of those violations in assessing the constitutionality of conditions in the isolation cells. The court took note of the inmates' diet, the continued overcrowding, the rampant violence, the vandalized cells, and the "lack of professionalism and good judgment on the part of maximum security personnel." The length of time each inmate spent in isolation was simply one consideration among many. We find no error in the court's conclusion that, taken as a whole, conditions in the isolation cells continued to violate the prohibition against cruel and unusual punishment.
>
> In fashioning a remedy, the District Court had ample authority to go beyond earlier orders and to address each element contributing to the violation. The District Court had given the Department repeated opportunities to remedy the cruel and unusual conditions in the isolation cells. If petitioners had fully complied with the court's earlier orders, the present time limit might well have been unnecessary. But taking the long and unhappy history of the litigation into account, the court was justified in en-

tering a comprehensive order to insure against the risk of inadequate compliance.[a]

3. THE PATTERN OF PRISON REFORM SUITS

Holt v. Sarver was an early example of a kind of litigation that was later to become almost commonplace. Several such cases are quoted in Justice Brennan's concurrence in *Rhodes*. Among the most famous is Pugh v. Locke, 406 F.Supp. 318 (M.D.Ala.1976), where then-District Court Judge Frank M. Johnson, finding Alabama prison conditions deplorable, undertook detailed and continuing judicial supervision of their reform. As Justice Brennan summarized, the remedial order eventually issued in that case covered "virtually every aspect of prison administration."[b] Moreover, such problems were not confined to a few jurisdictions. By the end of the 1970s, prisons in approximately half the states were subject to court-ordered reform.

In these suits, certain characteristics have emerged as typical. The cases usually have been brought as class actions in order to broaden the focus of the litigation beyond discrete allegations of injury to particular prisoners. Federal courts traditionally had followed a "hands-off" policy regarding state prison administration, but a close look at the intolerable, often appalling, conditions inside many prisons led to a change in attitude. Initial intervention typically sprang from a simple perception that "something had to be done." All too often state officials were unable or unwilling to correct the problems, and it was clear that nothing would be done if the federal courts abstained from action. The frequent results were hearings focusing on deplorable conditions, a court order designed to deal with the situation, complaints of non-compliance, further hearings, additional orders, additional complaints, and so on.

An important feature of this process is the focus of the courts on the cumulative effect of the conditions under which prisoners are confined. Specific conditions of confinement do not exist in isolation, but only as part of a totality of circumstances that in sum define the impact of the prison experience. It is natural, therefore, to address the acceptability of a particular aspect of confinement in the context of the overall condition of the prison. This approach led to a broadening of the judicial focus. Conditions that may not in isolation violate the Eighth Amendment may take on a different cast when aggregated. Decisions such as *Holt II* and *Pugh v. Locke* and the trial court decision in *Rhodes v. Chapman* relied heavily on the totality of the circumstances to justify court-ordered reform of specific prison practices.

In Wilson v. Seiter, 504 U.S. 294 (1991), the Supreme Court tried to put a brake on this reasoning. The Court held that although "[s]ome conditions of confinement may establish an Eighth Amendment violation 'in combination' when each would not do so alone," this would be true "only when they have a mutually enforcing effect that produces the deprivation of a single, identifiable human need such as food, warmth, or exercise—for example, a low cell temper-

---

[a] A chronicle and history of the *Holt* litigation and of the conditions in Arkansas prisons can be found in Owen M. Fiss and Doug Rendleman, Injunctions 528–752 (2d ed. 1984). The authors also include extensive treatment of prison reform litigation in Texas (pages 752–804) and a bibliography on the structural injunction (pages 827–30).

[b] A detailed history of this litigation may be found in Ira P. Robbins and Michael B. Buser, Punitive Conditions of Prison Confinement: An Analysis of *Pugh v. Locke* and Federal Court Supervision of State Prison Administration Under the Eighth Amendment, 29 Stan.L.Rev. 893 (1977).

ature at night combined with a failure to issue blankets." But it rejected the theory that "all prison conditions are a seamless web for Eighth Amendment purposes. Nothing so amorphous as 'overall conditions' can rise to the level of cruel and unusual punishment when no specific deprivation of a single human need exists."

4. THE DECLINE OF THE "TAILORING PRINCIPLE"

Remedies useful to reform the totality of conditions may not be narrowly addressed to specific objectionable practices. Instead, the remedies may be structural and institutional; they may address the underlying organization and financial arrangements that are responsible for the general condition of the prison. There is, therefore, a decline in what Owen Fiss calls the "tailoring principle"—the traditional idea that the remedy must fit the violation.[c] No longer does the scope of the remedy follow ineluctably from the definition of the right. Instead, the remedy may be designed to restructure an organization so as to reduce the future threat to constitutional rights.

An example of this phenomenon is the judicial response to the problem of inmate violence. No aspect of prison life is more difficult to control, nor more dreadful to tolerate, than inmate assault of other inmates. Remedies for discrete instances of inmate violence might include ordering protective custody or awarding damages against a careless guard. More widespread problems, however, require systemic remedies. Not surprisingly, courts have learned to evaluate the level of inmate violence in an institution and to develop structural reforms. Most commonly, courts have ordered increased hiring of guards and a classification of inmates to separate the vulnerable from the aggressive. Sometimes, court orders have extended to such matters as overcrowding and aspects of prison architecture.[d]

Judicial participation in framing such widespread decrees has also led to a blurring of traditional notions of right and remedy. Prison reform suits vindicate the Eighth Amendment right against cruel and unusual conditions of confinement. That "right," however, is usually stated at a high level of abstraction. More detailed, and hence more meaningful, are the precise remedies ordered to vindicate that right. Over time, particular remedies tend to assume a life of their own and are asserted as independent rights. The process is described in Note, Complex Enforcement: Unconstitutional Prison Conditions, 94 Harv.L.Rev. 626, 638–40 (1981):[*]

> The tendency in complex enforcement is for remedies to become part of the substantive law, as "rights" in themselves or, more generally, as the normative criteria by which a system's lawfulness is judged. This transformation of remedies into norms has occurred through two developments.
>
> First, complex remedies have tended to converge, with certain categories of affirmative requirements becoming more or less standard. For example, courts have concluded that violence in prisons cannot be contained without minimally rational classification systems and adequately trained personnel. Similarly, they have routinely required prisons relying on out-

---

[c] See Owen M. Fiss, Foreword: The Forms of Justice, 93 Harv.L.Rev. 1, 46 et seq. (1979).

[d] See generally James E. Robertson, Surviving Incarceration: Constitutional Protection from Inmate Violence, 35 Drake L.Rev. 101 (1985–86).

side medical care to maintain current medical records and provide quick access to receiving facilities. . . .

Second, as these affirmative requirements have become standard, they have ceased to be merely remedial responses to wrongs independently identified. Rather, they occupy an ambiguous status: while they are not constitutional rights as such, they seem to represent the criteria of legality and therefore are more than mere remedies. . . .

Whatever the label, however, these standard features now function as the more or less essential elements—the normative criteria—of an "adequate" prison. The substantive inquiry no longer focuses on whether actual abuses suffered by inmates shock the conscience. Instead, it focuses on the substantial *risk* of harm to which inmates are exposed. The court asks whether the prison has met its "affirmative duty" to provide reasonable safety and adequate medical care—in short to operate a prison "countenanced by the Constitution." These standard remedial features comprise the criteria of what is reasonable, and thus define with specificity the prison's affirmative duties. A failure to meet them, without more, constitutes the violation. So, for example, a staff shortage and inadequate medical records, formerly viewed as causes of wrongful conditions, become themselves "deprivations" violative of the Eighth Amendment.

5. QUESTIONS AND COMMENTS ON *RHODES V. CHAPMAN*

The effect of *Chapman* for other prisons is unclear. As has been noted, most prisons "are not shiny or new, and bear little resemblance to the top-flight, first class facility involved in *Chapman*." Susan Herman, Institutional Litigation in the Post–*Chapman* World, 12 N.Y.U.Rev. of Law & Social Change 299, 301 (1983–84). For example, one commentator reported that "[b]etween the June 1981 announcement of *Rhodes* and September 1983, federal district courts [ruled] on 11 cases in which allegations of unconstitutional overcrowding among the general prison population were at issue. All but two of these decisions held that overcrowding as practiced inflicted cruel and unusual punishment." James E. Robertson, When the Supreme Court Commands, Do the Lower Federal Courts Obey? The Impact of *Rhodes v. Chapman* on Correctional Litigation, 7 Hamline L.Rev. 79, 91–92 (1984).

Are these decisions necessarily inconsistent with *Rhodes v. Chapman*? Are they faithful to its spirit? More generally, does *Chapman* signal the illegitimacy of the subtle process of transforming remedies that may be appropriate in some contexts into constitutional rights that can be asserted independently of context? If so, is it right? How does it inform the approach that the lower federal courts should follow in future prison reform suits?

6. *LEWIS V. CASEY*

In addition to structural reform under the Eighth Amendment, courts have also issued structural injunctions to correct other constitutional violations. In Lewis v. Casey, 518 U.S. 343 (1996), the Supreme Court reviewed one such injunction. In 1990, 22 inmates in various Arizona state prisons filed a class action, alleging that prison officials were denying them their constitutional right of access to the courts, recognized by the Supreme Court in Bounds v. Smith, 430 U.S. 817 (1977). Following a three-month bench trial, the District Court found that the plaintiffs lacked adequate access to the courts because of inadequate legal library facilities. In particular, the District Court found that two groups of inmates—"lockdown prisoners," who were denied physical access to the law library, and illiterate or non-English-speaking inmates, who were not provided with adequate assistance—were especially hampered. Ultimately, the District Court promulgated a 25 page injunction that "specified in minute detail the times that libraries were to be kept open, the number of hours of library use to which each inmate was entitled (10 per week), the minimal educational requirements for prison librarians (a library science degree, law degree, or paralegal degree), the content of a videotaped legal-research course for inmates (to be prepared by persons appointed by the special master but funded by ADOC), and similar matters." The Court of Appeals affirmed the District Court's finding of a *Bounds* violation and its injunction.

The Supreme Court, in an opinion by Justice Scalia, reversed. First, it narrowed the right recognized by *Bounds* to make clear that "prison law libraries and legal assistance programs are not ends in themselves, but only the means for ensuring a reasonably adequate opportunity to present claimed violations of fundamental constitutional rights to the courts." Thus, the Court "disclaim[ed]" the suggestion in *Bounds* that states were required not only to enable an inmate to file his claim in a procedurally adequate form, but was also required to "enable the prisoner to discover grievances, and to litigate effectively once in court. . . . These elaborations upon the right of access to the courts have no antecedent in our pre-*Bounds* cases. . . . To demand the conferral of such sophisticated legal capabilities upon a mostly uneducated and indeed largely illiterate prison population is effectively to demand permanent provision of counsel, which we do not believe the Constitution requires."

Second, it held that the actual injuries suffered by the plaintiffs did not support the sweeping injunction issued by the District Court: "The remedy must of course be limited to the inadequacy that produced the injury in fact that the plaintiff has established." At the trial, the District Court had found actual injury on the part of only one named plaintiff, Bartholic, and the cause of that injury was the defendants' failure to the special services that Bartholic would have needed, in light of his illiteracy, to avoid dismissal of his case. "At the outset, therefore, we can eliminate from the proper scope of this injunction provisions directed at special services or special facilities required by non-English speakers, by prisoners in lockdown, and by the inmate population at large. If inadequacies of this character exist, they have not been found to have harmed any plaintiff in this lawsuit, and hence were not the proper object of this District Court's remediation." And even as to that injury, the Court held that it was not widespread enough to justify systemwide relief.

Finally, the Court criticized the process by which the District Court developed its order for failing to give adequate consideration to the views of state prison authorities: "[T]he strong considerations of comity that require giving a state court system that has convicted a defendant the first opportunity to correct its own errors . . . also require giving the States the first opportunity to correct the errors made in the internal administration of their prisons." (Quoting Preiser v. Rodriguez, 411 U.S. 475, 492, (1973).)

In concurrence, Justice Thomas would have gone even further. He would have overruled *Bounds* altogether. He wrote to "reiterate my observation in Missouri v. Jenkins, 515 U.S. 70 (1995)," that the federal judiciary has for the last half century been exercising "equitable" powers and issuing structural decrees entirely out of line with its constitutional mandate. He argued that principles of federalism and separation of powers should drastically limit the equitable power of federal courts.

Justice Souter, joined by Justices Ginsburg and Breyer, agreed with the majority that the District Court had not made adequate factual findings to support the injunction and that the injunction was imposed through a process that failed to give adequate deference to prison authorities, but took issue with the Court's position that *Bounds* claims required showing that the prisoner's underlying legal claim—the one he sought to raise in the pleading he was unable to file—was nonfrivolous: "I, in contrast, would go no further than to require that a prisoner have some concrete grievance or gripe about the conditions of his confinement, the validity of his conviction, or perhaps some other problem for which he would seek legal redress . . . (even though a claim based on that grievance might well fail sooner or later in the judicial process)." Thus, Justice Souter would have adopted a more liberal actual injury standard. Justice Souter also dissented from the Court's partial overruling of *Bounds*:

> I cannot concur in the suggestion that *Bounds* should be overruled to the extent that it requires States choosing to provide law libraries for court access to make them available for a prisoner's use in the period between filing a complaint and its final disposition. *Bounds* stated the obvious reasons for making libraries available for these purposes, and developments since *Bounds* have confirmed its reasoning. With respect to habeas claims, for example, the need for some form of legal assistance is even more obvious now than it was then, because the restrictions developed since *Bounds* have created a "substantial risk" that prisoners proceeding without legal assistance will never be able to obtain review of the merits of their claims. Nor should discouragement from the number of frivolous prison suits lead us to doubt the practical justifiability of providing assistance to a pro se prisoner during trial. In the past few years alone, we have considered the petitions of several prisoners who represented themselves at trial and on appeal, and who ultimately prevailed. See, e. g., Farmer v. Brennan, 511 U.S. 825 (1994); Helling v. McKinney, 509 U.S. 25 (1993); Hudson v. McMillian, 503 U.S. 1 (1992).

Justice Stevens dissented. He pointed to Arizona's long history of failure to provide adequate access to legal materials and took issue with the Court's characterization of the process by which the District Court developed its remedial decree.

7. BIBLIOGRAPHY

For additional treatment of the Supreme Court's approach to prisoner rights, see Malcolm M. Feeley and Edward L. Rubin, Judicial Policy Making and the Modern State: How the Courts Reformed America's Prisons (1998); Emily Calhoun, The Supreme Court and the Constitutional Rights of Prisoners: A Reappraisal, 4 Hast. Con. L.Q. 219 (1977) (detailing the Court's "extreme deference" to decisions of prison administrators); and William A. Fletcher, The Discretionary Constitution: Institutional Remedies and Judiciary Legitimacy, 91 Yale L.J. 635, 683–88 (1982) (suggesting that "when a prison system has a long history of atrocious conditions and political neglect, and, possibly more important, when the district court has attempted over a long period to get prison officials to correct the unconstitutional conditions, the district court may properly exercise a degree of remedial discretion it should not otherwise exercise"). For a fascinating history of the Alabama prison litigation, see Larry W. Yackle, Reform and Regret: The Story of Federal Judicial Involvement in the Alabama Prison System (1989).

For generally favorable reviews of institutional reform suits, see Robert D. Goldstein, A *Swann* Song for Remedies: Equitable Relief in the Burger Court, 13 Harv.C.R.–C.L.L.Rev. 1 (1978) (criticizing the reassertion of a close relation between right and remedy as a limit on the discretion of the district judge); and David Rudenstine, Institutional Injunctions, 4 Cardozo L.Rev. 611 (1983) (endorsing court-ordered reforms of prisons and other institutions as not inconsistent with values of federalism and democratic process). For a more skeptical view, see Paul J. Mishkin, Federal Courts as State Reformers, 35 W. & L.L.Rev. 949 (1978) (emphasizing as the "most significant" feature of such cases the "expansive definition of constitutional rights in terms which imply an institutional remedy"). For analysis of the interaction of rights and remedies in structural reform litigation, see Barry Friedman, When Rights Encounter Reality: Enforcing Federal Remedies, 65 So. Cal. L. Rev. 735 (1992). For criticism of the Supreme Court's attack on judicial activism in prison cases, see Melvin Gutterman, The Contours of Eighth Amendment Prison Jurisprudence: Conditions of Confinement, 48 S.M.U. L. Rev. 373 (1995). For comprehensive analysis of public interest advocacy in prison reform litigation, see Susan P. Sturm, The Legacy and Future of Corrections Litigation, 142 U. Pa. L. Rev. 639 (1993). For a discussion of the role of litigators in prison reform cases, see Margo Schlanger, Beyond the Hero Judge, Institutional Reform Litigation as Litigation, 97 Mich. L. Rev. 1994 (1999). Finally, for discussion of the appropriate standards for modifying or dissolving structural injunctions in prison cases, see Sarah N. Welling and Barbara W. Jones, Prison Reform Issues for the Eighties: Modification and Dissolution of Injunctions in the Federal Courts, 20 Conn.L.Rev. 865 (1988).

For an influential account of prison reform litigation, see Malcolm M. Feeley and Edward L. Rubin, Judicial Policy Making and the Modern State: How the Courts Reformed America's Prisons (1998, paperback ed. 2000). Finally, for an extensive empirical study of inmate litigation in the federal courts, both before and after the Prison Litigation Reform Act of 1996, see Margo Schlanger, Inmate Litigation, 116 Harv. L. Rev. 1555 (2003).

INTRODUCTORY NOTE ON THE PRISON LITIGATION REFORM ACT

In 1996, Congress passed the Prison Litigation Reform Act (PLRA), Pub. L. No. 104–134, 110 Stat. 1321. The Act made a number of changes with respect to prisoner litigation in federal courts, including significant limitations on the ability of prisoners to proceed in forma pauperis (that is, without paying court fees) and on the award of attorney's fees. In addition, the PLRA barred prisoners from bringing § 1983 damages lawsuits for mental or emotional injuries "without a prior showing of physical injury." PLRA § 803(d) (amending 42 U.S.C. § 1997e).

Of particular salience to structural reform litigation was § 802 of the PLRA. It amended 18 U.S.C. § 3626 to provide:

(a) REQUIREMENTS FOR RELIEF.—

(1) PROSPECTIVE RELIEF.—(A) Prospective relief in any civil action with respect to prison conditions shall extend no further than necessary to correct the violation of the Federal right of a particular plaintiff or plaintiffs. The court shall not grant or approve any prospective relief unless the court finds that such relief is narrowly drawn, extends no further than necessary to correct the violation of the Federal right, and is the least intrusive means necessary to correct the violation of the Federal right. The court shall give substantial weight to any adverse impact on public safety or the operation of a criminal justice system caused by the relief.

(B) The court shall not order any prospective relief that requires or permits a government official to exceed his or her authority under State or local law or otherwise violates State or local law, unless—

(i) Federal law permits such relief to be ordered in violation of State or local law;

(ii) the relief is necessary to correct the violation of a Federal right; and

(iii) no other relief will correct the violation of the Federal right.

(C) Nothing in this section shall be construed to authorize the courts, in exercising their remedial powers, to order the construction of prisons or the raising of taxes, or to repeal or detract from otherwise applicable limitations on the remedial powers of the courts.

To what extent does this provision of the PLRA merely codify existing law after *Rhodes*? Does subsection (C) set out a different legal standard for prison cases than for school cases? Is this a permissible exercise of congressional power?

Section 802(a) also substantially restricted the ability of federal courts to enter consent judgments, providing that "[i]n any civil action with respect to prison conditions, the court shall not enter or approve a consent decree unless it complies with the limitations on relief set forth in subsection (a)," that is, the need-narrowness-intrusiveness criteria.

Consider the substantial effects of § 802(a)'s restriction of consent judgments. A large number of structural injunctions were the result of settlements, rather than fully litigated cases. As one recent commentator observes:

> The ordinary litigation incentives favoring settlement operate strongly for parties and judges in structural reform cases. Settlement saves the enormous expense and uncertainty of trial and appeal, and it gives the parties augmented control over the specifics of a remedy. More speculatively, defendants who agree to a decree may transform themselves in the eyes of the public, and even in their own eyes, from "lawbreakers to law implementers." And there are also more situation-specific incentives. Plaintiffs or their counsel, and judges, may push especially hard for settlement if they believe that necessary institutional change requires the cooperation of the defendants, which is more easily obtained by consent than by judicial fiat. Another frequently remarked dynamic favoring settlement in institutional reform cases . . . is the high level of cooperation by defendants. The explanation seems clear: defendants, who are government officials operating under fiscal and political constraints, frequently win by

losing. The result of a consent decree can be more resources and freedom from entrenched restrictions on changes in policy and practice. "The court is making me do it" trumps many ordinary political considerations. In the particular context of prison litigation, defendants were often themselves interested in the professionalization, and concurrent bureaucratization, of the prisons under their supervision. Finally, with a consent decree, defendant officials can even gain a power, unavailable through the ordinary political process, to bind their successors. For all these reasons, settlements of various kinds do indeed seem to be the primary source of judgments in prison and jail cases; the litigation has frequently been, to use Marc Galanter's coinage, "litigotiation"—"the strategic pursuit of a settlement through mobilizing the court process."

Margo Schlanger, Beyond the Hero Judge, Institutional Reform Litigation as Litigation, 97 Mich. L. Rev. 1994, 2011–13 (1999). If defendants are forced to concede liability, are they more likely to litigate to the hilt? Will admissions of liability for purposes of a consent judgment open defendants up to § 1983 damages liability as well?

Section 802(a) also explicitly limited the authority of federal courts to order prisoners to be released—a common order in cases involving prison overcrowding—unless the court had previously entered an order for less intrusive relief that failed to remedy the deprivation of the federal right sought to be remedied through the prisoner release order and the defendant is given a reasonable amount of time to comply. It required that three-judge district courts be used to issue such orders and that the court find by "clear and convincing" evidence—rather than merely by a preponderance—that "crowding is the primary cause of the violation of a Federal right; and no other relief will remedy the violation of the Federal right."

Finally, in a provision that has prompted substantial litigation, § 802 of the PLRA codified a standard for terminating injunctive relief:

(1) TERMINATION OF PROSPECTIVE RELIEF.—(A) In any civil action with respect to prison conditions in which prospective relief is ordered, such relief shall be terminable upon the motion of any party or intervener—

(i) 2 years after the date the court granted or approved the prospective relief;

(ii) 1 year after the date the court has entered an order denying termination of prospective relief under this paragraph; or

(iii) in the case of an order issued on or before the date of enactment of the Prison Litigation Reform Act, 2 years after such date of enactment. . . .

(2) IMMEDIATE TERMINATION OF PROSPECTIVE RELIEF.—In any civil action with respect to prison conditions, a defendant or intervener shall be entitled to the immediate termination of any prospective relief if the relief was approved or granted in the absence of a finding by the court that the relief is narrowly drawn, extends no further than necessary to correct the violation of the Federal right, and is the least intrusive means necessary to correct the violation of the Federal right.

(3) LIMITATION.—Prospective relief shall not terminate if the court makes written findings based on the record that prospective relief remains necessary to correct a current or ongoing violation of the Federal right, extends no further than necessary to correct the violation of the Federal right, and that the prospective relief is narrowly drawn and the least intrusive means to correct the violation. . . .

The PLRA also set out a set of specific procedures for termination motions, including a provision automatically "staying," that is, terminating, any prospective relief subject to a pending motion, within a relatively short time after the motion is filed.[a]

For an extended examination of the PLRA's effects on individual claims by prisoners, see Margo Schlanger, Prison Litigation, 116 Harv. L. Rev. 1555 (2003). Schlanger finds that while the PLRA reduced new federal filings by prisoners by over 40%, it also made constitutionally meritorious cases harder to bring and harder to win. She concludes that, as an effort to cope with the high volume of prisoner claims, most with a low probability of success, the PLRA has introduced as many problems as it has solved. In particular, its provisions for inmate payment of filing fees, reduced attorney's fees to prevailing plaintiffs, and exhaustion of administrative remedies have reduced the volume of meritorious and nonmeritorious claims alike, decreasing the effect of prisoner litigation as a deterrent to abusive prison conditions.

Brown v. Plata

Supreme Court of the United States, 2011.
131 S.Ct. 1910.

■ JUSTICE KENNEDY delivered the opinion of the Court.[a]

This case arises from serious constitutional violations in California's prison system. The violations have persisted for years. They remain uncorrected. The appeal comes to this Court from a three-judge District Court order directing California to remedy two ongoing violations of the Cruel and Unusual Punishments Clause, a guarantee binding on the States by the Due Process Clause of the Fourteenth Amendment. The violations are the subject of two class actions in two Federal District Courts. The first involves the class of prisoners with serious mental disorders. That case is *Coleman v. Brown*. The second involves prisoners with serious medical conditions. That case is *Plata v. Brown*. The order of the three-judge District Court is applicable to both cases.

After years of litigation, it became apparent that a remedy for the constitutional violations would not be effective absent a reduction in the prison system population. The authority to order release of prisoners as a remedy to cure a systemic violation of the Eighth Amendment is a power reserved to a three-judge district court, not a single-judge district court. 18 U.S.C. § 3626(a). In accordance with that rule, the *Coleman* and *Plata* District Judges independently requested that a three-judge court be convened. The

[a] The constitutionality of the automatic stay provision was challenged unsuccessfully in Miller v. French, 530 U.S. 327 (2000).

[a] The Court's opinion is replete with citations to various appendices, which reproduced materials in the record of the case. Citations to the record have been omitted (as is the usual practice in this book), and quotations from the appendices have been presented as if they came directly from the underlying sources. [Footnote by eds.]

Chief Judge of the Court of Appeals for the Ninth Circuit convened a three-judge court composed of the *Coleman* and *Plata* District Judges and a third, Ninth Circuit Judge. Because the two cases are interrelated, their limited consolidation for this purpose has a certain utility in avoiding conflicting decrees and aiding judicial consideration and enforcement. . . .

The appeal presents the question whether the remedial order issued by the three-judge court is consistent with requirements and procedures set forth in a congressional statute, the Prison Litigation Reform Act of 1995 (PLRA), 18 U.S.C. § 3626. The order leaves the choice of means to reduce overcrowding to the discretion of state officials. But absent compliance through new construction, out-of-state transfers, or other means—or modification of the order upon a further showing by the State—the State will be required to release some number of prisoners before their full sentences have been served. High recidivism rates must serve as a warning that mistaken or premature release of even one prisoner can cause injury and harm. The release of prisoners in large numbers—assuming the State finds no other way to comply with the order—is a matter of undoubted, grave concern.

At the time of trial, California's correctional facilities held some 156,000 persons. This is nearly double the number that California's prisons were designed to hold, and California has been ordered to reduce its prison population to 137.5% of design capacity. By the three-judge court's own estimate, the required population reduction could be as high as 46,000 persons. Although the State has reduced the population by at least 9,000 persons during the pendency of this appeal, this means a further reduction of 37,000 persons could be required. . . . The population reduction potentially required is . . . of unprecedented sweep and extent.

Yet so too is the continuing injury and harm resulting from these serious constitutional violations. For years the medical and mental health care provided by California's prisons has fallen short of minimum constitutional requirements and has failed to meet prisoners' basic health needs. Needless suffering and death have been the well-documented result. Over the whole course of years during which this litigation has been pending, no other remedies have been found to be sufficient. Efforts to remedy the violation have been frustrated by severe overcrowding in California's prison system. Short term gains in the provision of care have been eroded by the long-term effects of severe and pervasive overcrowding.

Overcrowding has overtaken the limited resources of prison staff; imposed demands well beyond the capacity of medical and mental health facilities; and created unsanitary and unsafe conditions that make progress in the provision of care difficult or impossible to achieve. The overcrowding is the "primary cause of the violation of a Federal right," 18 U.S.C. § 3626(a)(3)(E)(i), specifically the severe and unlawful mistreatment of prisoners through grossly inadequate provision of medical and mental health care.

This Court now holds that the PLRA does authorize the relief afforded in this case and that the court-mandated population limit is necessary to remedy the violation of prisoners' constitutional rights. The order of the three-judge court, subject to the right of the State to seek its modification in appropriate circumstances, must be affirmed.

I

A

The degree of overcrowding in California's prisons is exceptional. California's prisons are designed to house a population just under 80,000, but at the time of the three-judge court's decision the population was almost double that. The State's prisons had operated at around 200% of design capacity for at least 11 years. Prisoners are crammed into spaces neither designed nor intended to house inmates. As many as 200 prisoners may live in a gymnasium, monitored by as few as two or three correctional officers. As many as 54 prisoners may share a single toilet.

The Corrections Independent Review Panel, a body appointed by the Governor and composed of correctional consultants and representatives from state agencies, concluded that California's prisons are "severely overcrowded, imperiling the safety of both correctional employees and inmates."[1] . . .

Prisoners in California with serious mental illness do not receive minimal, adequate care. Because of a shortage of treatment beds, suicidal inmates may be held for prolonged periods in telephone-booth sized cages without toilets. A psychiatric expert reported observing an inmate who had been held in such a cage for nearly 24 hours, standing in a pool of his own urine, unresponsive and nearly catatonic. Prison officials explained they had "no place to put him." Other inmates awaiting care may be held for months in administrative segregation, where they endure harsh and isolated conditions and receive only limited mental health services. Wait times for mental health care range as high as 12 months. In 2006, the suicide rate in California's prisons was nearly 80% higher than the national average for prison populations; and a court-appointed Special Master found that 72.1% of suicides involved "some measure of inadequate assessment, treatment, or intervention, and were therefore most probably foreseeable and/or preventable."

Prisoners suffering from physical illness also receive severely deficient care. California's prisons were designed to meet the medical needs of a population at 100% of design capacity and so have only half the clinical space needed to treat the current population. A correctional officer testified that, in one prison, up to 50 sick inmates may be held together in a 12–by 20–foot cage for up to five hours awaiting treatment. The number of staff is inadequate, and prisoners face significant delays in access to care. A prisoner with severe abdominal pain died after a 5–week delay in referral to a specialist; a prisoner with "constant and extreme" chest pain died after an 8–hour delay in evaluation by a doctor; and a prisoner died of testicular cancer after a "failure of MDs to work up for cancer in a young man with 17 months of testicular pain."[3] Doctor Ronald Shansky, former medical direc-

---

[1] A similar conclusion was reached by the Little Hoover Commission, a bipartisan and independent state body, which stated that "[o]vercrowded conditions inside the prison walls are unsafe for inmates and staff," Solving California's Corrections Crisis: Time is Running Out 17 (Jan.2007). . . .

[3] Because plaintiffs do not base their case on deficiencies in care provided on any one occasion, this Court has no occasion to consider whether these instances of delay—or any other particular deficiency in medical care complained of by the plaintiffs—would violate the Constitution under Estelle v. Gamble, 429 U.S. 97, 104–05 (1976), if considered in isolation. Plaintiffs rely on systemwide deficiencies in the provision of medical and mental health care that, taken as a whole, subject sick and mentally ill prisoners in California to "substantial risk of serious harm" and cause the delivery of care in the prisons to fall below the evolving standards

tor of the Illinois state prison system, surveyed death reviews for California prisoners. He concluded that extreme departures from the standard of care were "widespread," and that the proportion of "possibly preventable or preventable" deaths was "extremely high." Many more prisoners, suffering from severe but not life-threatening conditions, experience prolonged illness and unnecessary pain.

B

These conditions are the subject of two federal cases. The first to commence, *Coleman v. Brown,* was filed in 1990. *Coleman* involves the class of seriously mentally ill persons in California prisons. Over 15 years ago, in 1995, after a 39–day trial, the *Coleman* District Court found "overwhelming evidence of the systematic failure to deliver necessary care to mentally ill inmates" in California prisons. Coleman v. Wilson, 912 F.Supp. 1282 (E.D.Cal.). The prisons were "seriously and chronically understaffed," and had "no effective method for ensuring . . . the competence of their staff." The prisons had failed to implement necessary suicide-prevention procedures, "due in large measure to the severe understaffing." Mentally ill inmates "languished for months, or even years, without access to necessary care." "They suffer from severe hallucinations, [and] they decompensate into catatonic states." The court appointed a Special Master to oversee development and implementation of a remedial plan of action.

In 2007, 12 years after his appointment, the Special Master in *Coleman* filed a report stating that, after years of slow improvement, the state of mental health care in California's prisons was deteriorating. The Special Master ascribed this change to increased overcrowding. The rise in population had led to greater demand for care, and existing programming space and staffing levels were inadequate to keep pace. Prisons had retained more mental health staff, but the "growth of the resource [had] not matched the rise in demand." At the very time the need for space was rising, the need to house the expanding population had also caused a "reduction of programming space now occupied by inmate bunks." The State was "facing a four to five-year gap in the availability of sufficient beds to meet the treatment needs of many inmates/patients." "[I]ncreasing numbers of truly psychotic inmate/patients are trapped in [lower levels of treatment] that cannot meet their needs." The Special Master concluded that many early "achievements have succumbed to the inexorably rising tide of population, leaving behind growing frustration and despair."

C

The second action, *Plata v. Brown,* involves the class of state prisoners with serious medical conditions. After this action commenced in 2001, the State conceded that deficiencies in prison medical care violated prisoners' Eighth Amendment rights. The State stipulated to a remedial injunction. The State failed to comply with that injunction, and in 2005 the court appointed a Receiver to oversee remedial efforts. The court found that "the California prison medical care system is broken beyond repair," resulting in an "unconscionable degree of suffering and death." The court found: "[I]t is an uncontested fact that, on average, an inmate in one of California's prisons needlessly dies every six to seven days due to constitutional deficiencies in the [California prisons'] medical delivery system." And the court made findings regarding specific instances of neglect, including the following:

---

of decency that mark the progress of a maturing society. Farmer v. Brennan, 511 U.S. 825, 834 (1994).

> [A] San Quentin prisoner with hypertension, diabetes and renal failure was prescribed two different medications that actually served to exacerbate his renal failure. An optometrist noted the patient's retinal bleeding due to very high blood pressure and referred him for immediate evaluation, but this evaluation never took place. It was not until a year later that the patient's renal failure was recognized, at which point he was referred to a nephrologist on an urgent basis; he should have been seen by the specialist within 14 days but the consultation never happened and the patient died three months later.

Prisons were unable to retain sufficient numbers of competent medical staff and would "hire any doctor who had a license, a pulse and a pair of shoes." Medical facilities lacked "necessary medical equipment" and did "not meet basic sanitation standards." "Exam tables and counter tops, where prisoners with . . . communicable diseases are treated, [were] not routinely disinfected."

In 2008, three years after the District Court's decision, the Receiver described continuing deficiencies in the health care provided by California prisons:

> Timely access is not assured. The number of medical personnel has been inadequate, and competence has not been assured. . . . Adequate housing for the disabled and aged does not exist. The medical facilities, when they exist at all, are in an abysmal state of disrepair. Basic medical equipment is often not available or used. Medications and other treatment options are too often not available when needed. . . . Indeed, it is a misnomer to call the existing chaos a "medical delivery system"—it is more an act of desperation than a system.

A report by the Receiver detailed the impact of overcrowding on efforts to remedy the violation. . . . "[O]vercrowding, and the resulting day to day operational chaos of the [prison system], creates regular 'crisis' situations which . . . take time [and] energy . . . away from important remedial programs." Overcrowding had increased the incidence of infectious disease and had led to rising prison violence and greater reliance by custodial staff on lockdowns, which "inhibit the delivery of medical care and increase the staffing necessary for such care." . . .

D

The *Coleman* and *Plata* plaintiffs, believing that a remedy for unconstitutional medical and mental health care could not be achieved without reducing overcrowding, moved their respective District Courts to convene a three-judge court empowered under the PLRA to order reductions in the prison population. The judges in both actions granted the request, and the cases were consolidated before a single three-judge court. The State has not challenged the validity of the consolidation in proceedings before this Court, so its propriety is not presented by this appeal.

The three-judge court heard 14 days of testimony and issued a 184–page opinion, making extensive findings of fact. The court ordered California to reduce its prison population to 137.5% of the prisons' design capacity within two years. Assuming the State does not increase capacity through new construction, the order requires a population reduction of 38,000 to 46,000 persons. Because it appears all but certain that the State cannot complete sufficient construction to comply fully with the order, the prison population will have to be reduced to at least some extent. The court did not order the State to achieve this reduction in any particular manner. Instead, the court ordered the State to formulate a plan for compliance and submit its plan for approval by the court.

The State appealed to this Court pursuant to 28 U.S.C. § 1253, and the Court postponed consideration of the question of jurisdiction to the hearing on the merits.

II

As a consequence of their own actions, prisoners may be deprived of rights that are fundamental to liberty. . . . To incarcerate, society takes from prisoners the means to provide for their own needs. Prisoners are dependent on the State for food, clothing, and necessary medical care. A prison's failure to provide sustenance for inmates "may actually produce physical 'torture or a lingering death.' " Estelle v. Gamble, 429 U.S. 97, 103 (1976) (quoting In re Kemmler, 136 U.S. 436, 447 (1890)). Just as a prisoner may starve if not fed, he or she may suffer or die if not provided adequate medical care. A prison that deprives prisoners of basic sustenance, including adequate medical care, is incompatible with the concept of human dignity and has no place in civilized society.

If government fails to fulfill this obligation, the courts have a responsibility to remedy the resulting Eighth Amendment violation. Courts must be sensitive to the State's interest in punishment, deterrence, and rehabilitation, as well as the need for deference to experienced and expert prison administrators faced with the difficult and dangerous task of housing large numbers of convicted criminals. Courts nevertheless must not shrink from their obligation to "enforce the constitutional rights of all 'persons,' including prisoners." Cruz v. Beto, 405 U.S. 319, 321 (1972) (per curiam). Courts may not allow constitutional violations to continue simply because a remedy would involve intrusion into the realm of prison administration.

Courts faced with the sensitive task of remedying unconstitutional prison conditions must consider a range of available options, including appointment of special masters or receivers and the possibility of consent decrees. When necessary to ensure compliance with a constitutional mandate, courts may enter orders placing limits on a prison's population. By its terms, the PLRA restricts the circumstances in which a court may enter an order "that has the purpose or effect of reducing or limiting the prison population." 18 U.S.C. § 3626(g)(4). The order in this case does not necessarily require the State to release any prisoners. The State may comply by raising the design capacity of its prisons or by transferring prisoners to county facilities or facilities in other States. Because the order limits the prison population as a percentage of design capacity, it nonetheless has the "effect of reducing or limiting the prison population."

Under the PLRA, only a three-judge court may enter an order limiting a prison population. § 3626(a)(3)(B). Before a three-judge court may be convened, a district court first must have entered an order for less intrusive relief that failed to remedy the constitutional violation and must have given the defendant a reasonable time to comply with its prior orders. § 3626(a)(3)(A). The party requesting a three-judge court must then submit "materials sufficient to demonstrate that [these requirements] have been met." § 3626(a)(3)(C). If the district court concludes that the materials are, in fact, sufficient, a three-judge court may be convened.

The three-judge court must then find by clear and convincing evidence that "crowding is the primary cause of the violation of a Federal right" and that "no other relief will remedy the violation of the Federal right." 18

U.S.C. § 3626(a)(3)(E). As with any award of prospective relief under the PLRA, the relief "shall extend no further than necessary to correct the violation of the Federal right of a particular plaintiff or plaintiffs." § 3626(a)(1)(A). The three-judge court must therefore find that the relief is "narrowly drawn, extends no further than necessary . . . , and is the least intrusive means necessary to correct the violation of the Federal right." Ibid. In making this determination, the three-judge court must give "substantial weight to any adverse impact on public safety or the operation of a criminal justice system caused by the relief." Ibid. Applying these standards, the three-judge court found a population limit appropriate, necessary, and authorized in this case.

This Court's review of the three-judge court's legal determinations is de novo, but factual findings are reviewed for clear error. See Anderson v. Bessemer City, 470 U.S. 564, 573–74 (1985). . . . The three-judge court's finding of fact maybe reversed only if this Court is left with a " 'definite and firm conviction that a mistake has been committed.' " Id., at 573 (quoting United States v. United States Gypsum Co., 333 U.S. 364, 395 (1948).

A

The State contends that it was error to convene the three-judge court without affording it more time to comply with the prior orders in *Coleman* and *Plata*. . . .

Before a three-judge court may be convened to consider whether to enter a population limit, the PLRA requires that the court have "previously entered an order for less intrusive relief that has failed to remedy the deprivation of the Federal right sought to be remedied." 18 U.S.C. § 3626(a)(3)(A)(i). This provision refers to "an order." It is satisfied if the court has entered one order, and this single order has "failed to remedy" the constitutional violation. The defendant must also have had "a reasonable amount of time to comply with the previous court orders." § 3626(a)(3)(A)(ii). This provision refers to the court's "orders." It requires that the defendant have been given a reasonable time to comply with all of the court's orders. Together, these requirements ensure that the "last resort remedy" of a population limit is not imposed "as a first step." Inmates of Occoquan v. Barry, 844 F.2d 828, 843 (D.C. Cir. 1988).

The first of these conditions, the previous order requirement of § 3626(a)(3)(A)(i), was satisfied in *Coleman* by appointment of a Special Master in 1995, and it was satisfied in *Plata* by approval of a consent decree and stipulated injunction in 2002. . . .

The State claims . . . that the second condition, the reasonable time requirement of § 3626(a)(3)(A)(ii), was not met because other, later remedial efforts should have been given more time to succeed. In 2006, the *Coleman* District Judge approved a revised plan of action calling for construction of new facilities, hiring of new staff, and implementation of new procedures. That same year, the *Plata* District Judge selected and appointed a Receiver to oversee the State's ongoing remedial efforts. When the three-judge court was convened, the Receiver had filed a preliminary plan of action calling for new construction, hiring of additional staff, and other procedural reforms.

Although both the revised plan of action in *Coleman* and the appointment of the Receiver in *Plata* were new developments in the courts' remedial efforts, the basic plan to solve the crisis through construction, hiring, and procedural reforms remained unchanged. These efforts had been ongoing for years; the failed consent decree in *Plata* had called for implementation of new procedures and hiring of additional staff; and the *Coleman* Special Master had issued over 70 orders directed at achieving a remedy through construction, hiring, and procedural reforms. . . .

Having engaged in remedial efforts for 5 years in *Plata* and 12 in *Coleman,* the District Courts were not required to wait to see whether their more recent efforts would yield equal disappointment. When a court attempts to remedy an entrenched constitutional violation through reform of a complex institution, such as this statewide prison system, it may be necessary in the ordinary course to issue multiple orders directing and adjusting ongoing remedial efforts. Each new order must be given a reasonable time to succeed, but reasonableness must be assessed in light of the entire history of the court's remedial efforts. A contrary reading of the reasonable time requirement would in effect require district courts to impose a moratorium on new remedial orders before issuing a population limit. This unnecessary period of inaction would delay an eventual remedy and would prolong the courts' involvement, serving neither the State nor the prisoners. Congress did not require this unreasonable result when it used the term "reasonable."

. . . The *Coleman* and *Plata* courts acted reasonably when they convened a three-judge court without further delay.

B

Once a three-judge court has been convened, the court must find additional requirements satisfied before it may impose a population limit. The first of these requirements is that "crowding is the primary cause of the violation of a Federal right." 18 U.S.C. § 3626(a)(3)(E)(i).

1

The three-judge court found the primary cause requirement satisfied by the evidence at trial. The court found that overcrowding strains inadequate medical and mental health facilities; overburdens limited clinical and custodial staff; and creates violent, unsanitary, and chaotic conditions that contribute to the constitutional violations and frustrate efforts to fashion a remedy. The three-judge court also found that "until the problem of overcrowding is overcome it will be impossible to provide constitutionally compliant care to California's prison population."

The parties dispute the standard of review applicable to this determination. With respect to the three-judge court's factual findings, this Court's review is necessarily deferential. It is not this Court's place to "duplicate the role" of the trial court. *Anderson*, 470 U.S., at 573. The ultimate issue of primary cause presents a mixed question of law and fact; but there, too, "the mix weighs heavily on the 'fact' side." Lilly v. Virginia, 527 U.S. 116, 148 (1999) (Rehnquist, C. J., concurring in judgment). Because the "district court is 'better positioned' . . . to decide the issue," our review of the three-judge court's primary cause determination is deferential. Salve Regina College v. Russell, 499 U.S. 225, 233 (1991).

The record documents the severe impact of burgeoning demand on the provision of care. At the time of trial, vacancy rates for medical and mental health staff ranged as high as 20% for surgeons, 25% for physicians, 39% for nurse practitioners, and 54.1% for psychiatrists. These percentages are based on the number of positions budgeted by the State. Dr. Ronald Shansky, former medical director of the Illinois prison system, concluded that these numbers understate the severity of the crisis because the State has not budgeted sufficient staff to meet demand. . . .

Even on the assumption that vacant positions could be filled, the evidence suggested there would be insufficient space for the necessary additional staff to perform their jobs. The *Plata* Receiver, in his report on overcrowding, concluded that even the "newest and most modern prisons" had been "designed with clinic space which is only one-half that necessary for the real-life capacity of the prisons." . . .

This shortfall of resources relative to demand contributes to significant delays in treatment. Mentally ill prisoners are housed in administrative segregation while awaiting transfer to scarce mental health treatment beds for appropriate care. One correctional officer indicated that he had kept mentally ill prisoners in segregation for "6 months or more." Other prisoners awaiting care are held in tiny, phone-booth sized cages. The record documents instances of prisoners committing suicide while awaiting treatment.

Delays are no less severe in the context of physical care. Prisons have backlogs of up to 700 prisoners waiting to see a doctor. A review of referrals for urgent specialty care at one prison revealed that only 105 of 316 pending referrals had a scheduled appointment, and only 2 had an appointment scheduled to occur within 14 days. Urgent specialty referrals at one prison had been pending for six months to a year.

Crowding also creates unsafe and unsanitary living conditions that hamper effective delivery of medical and mental health care. A medical expert described living quarters in converted gymnasiums or dayrooms, where large numbers of prisoners may share just a few toilets and showers, as "breeding grounds for disease." Cramped conditions promote unrest and violence, making it difficult for prison officials to monitor and control the prison population. . . .

Increased violence also requires increased reliance on lockdowns to keep order, and lockdowns further impede the effective delivery of care. In 2006, prison officials instituted 449 lockdowns. The average lockdown lasted 12 days, and 20 lockdowns lasted 60 days or longer. During lockdowns, staff must either escort prisoners to medical facilities or bring medical staff to the prisoners. Either procedure puts additional strain on already overburdened medical and custodial staff. Some programming for the mentally ill even may be canceled altogether during lockdowns, and staff may be unable to supervise the delivery of psychotropic medications.

The effects of overcrowding are particularly acute in the prisons' reception centers, intake areas that process 140,000 new or returning prisoners every year. Crowding in these areas runs as high as 300% of design capacity. Living conditions are "toxic," and a lack of treatment space impedes efforts to identify inmate medical or mental health needs and provide even rudimentary care. The former warden of San Quentin reported that doctors in that prison's reception center "were unable to keep up with physicals or provid[e] any kind of chronic care follow-up." Inmates spend long periods of time in these areas awaiting transfer to the general population. Some prisoners are held in the reception centers for their entire period of incarceration.

Numerous experts testified that crowding is the primary cause of the constitutional violations. The former warden of San Quentin and former acting secretary of the California prisons concluded that crowding "makes it virtually impossible for the organization to develop, much less implement, a plan to provide prisoners with adequate care." The former executive director of the Texas Department of Criminal Justice testified that "[e]verything revolves around overcrowding" and that "overcrowding is the primary cause of the medical and mental health care violations." The former head of corrections in Pennsylvania, Washington, and Maine testified that overcrowding is "overwhelming the system both in terms of sheer numbers, in terms of the space available, in terms of providing healthcare." And the current secretary of the Pennsylvania Department of Corrections testified that "the biggest inhibiting factor right now in California being able to deliver appropriate mental health and medical care is the severe overcrowding."

2

The State attempts to undermine the substantial evidence presented at trial, and the three-judge court's findings of fact, by complaining that the three-judge court did not allow it to present evidence of current prison conditions. This suggestion lacks a factual basis. . . .

The three-judge court's opinion cited and relied on this evidence of current conditions. The court relied extensively on the expert witness reports. The court cited the most current data available on suicides and preventable deaths in the California prisons. The court relied on statistics on staff vacancies that dated to three months before trial, and statistics on shortages of treatment beds for the same period. These are just examples of the extensive evidence of current conditions that informed every aspect of the judgment of the three-judge court. The three-judge court did not abuse its discretion when it also cited findings made in earlier decisions of the *Plata* and *Coleman* District Courts. Those findings remained relevant to establish the nature of these longstanding, continuing constitutional violations.

It is true that the three-judge court established a cutoff date for discovery a few months before trial. The order stated that site inspections of prisons would be allowed until that date, and that evidence of "changed prison conditions" after that date would not be admitted. The court also excluded evidence not pertinent to the issue whether a population limit is appropriate under the PLRA, including evidence relevant solely to the existence of an ongoing constitutional violation. The court reasoned that its decision was limited to the issue of remedy and that the merits of the constitutional violation had already been determined. The three-judge court made clear that all such evidence would be considered "[t]o the extent that it illuminates questions that are properly before the court."

Both rulings were within the sound discretion of the three-judge court. Orderly trial management may require discovery deadlines and a clean distinction between litigation of the merits and the remedy. . . .

The State does not point to any significant evidence that it was unable to present and that would have changed the outcome of the proceedings. To the contrary, the record and opinion make clear that the decision of the three-judge court was based on current evidence pertaining to ongoing constitutional violations.

3

The three-judge court acknowledged that the violations were caused by factors in addition to overcrowding and that reducing crowding in the prisons would not entirely cure the violations. This is consistent with the reports of the *Coleman* Special Master and *Plata* Receiver, both of whom concluded that even a significant reduction in the prison population would not remedy the violations absent continued efforts to train staff, improve facilities, and reform procedures.[8] The three-judge court nevertheless found that overcrowding was the primary cause in the sense of being the foremost cause of the violation.

This understanding of the primary cause requirement is consistent with the text of the PLRA. The State in fact concedes that it proposed this very definition of primary cause to the three-judge court. "Primary" is defined as "[f]irst or highest in rank, quality, or importance; principal." American Heritage Dictionary 1393 (4th ed.2000). Overcrowding need only be the foremost, chief, or principal cause of the violation. . . .

A finding that overcrowding is the "primary cause" of a violation is therefore permissible, despite the fact that additional steps will be required to remedy the violation.

C

The three-judge court was also required to find by clear and convincing evidence that "no other relief will remedy the violation of the Federal right." § 3626(a)(3)(E)(ii).

The State argues that the violation could have been remedied through a combination of new construction, transfers of prisoners out of State, hiring of medical personnel, and continued efforts by the *Plata* Receiver and *Coleman* Special Master. The order in fact permits the State to comply with the population limit by transferring prisoners to county facilities or facilities in other States, or by constructing new facilities to raise the prisons' design capacity. And the three-judge court's order does not bar the State from undertaking any other remedial efforts. If the State does find an adequate remedy other than a population limit, it may seek modification or termination of the three-judge court's order on that basis. The evidence at trial, however, supports the three-judge court's conclusion that an order limited to other remedies would not provide effective relief.

The State's argument that out-of-state transfers provide a less restrictive alternative to a population limit must fail because requiring out-of-state transfers itself qualifies as a population limit under the PLRA. Such an order "has the purpose or effect of reducing or limiting the prison population, or . . . directs the release from or nonadmission of prisoners to a prison." § 3626(g)(4). The same is true of transfers to county facilities. Transfers provide a means to reduce the prison population in compliance with the three-judge court's order. They are not a less restrictive alternative to that order.

Even if out-of-state transfers could be regarded as a less restrictive alternative, the three-judge court found no evidence of plans for transfers in numbers sufficient to relieve overcrowding. . . .

---

8 The *Plata* Receiver concluded that those who believed a population reduction would be a panacea were "simply wrong." The Receiver nevertheless made clear that "the time this process will take, and the cost and the scope of intrusion by the Federal Court cannot help but increase, and increase in a very significant manner, if the scope and characteristics of [California prison] overcrowding continue." The *Coleman* Special Master likewise found that a large release of prisoners, without other relief, would leave the violation "largely unmitigated" even though deficiencies in care "are unquestionably exacerbated by overcrowding" and "defendants' ability to provide required mental health services would be enhanced considerably by a reduction in the overall census" of the prisons.

Construction of new facilities, in theory, could alleviate overcrowding, but the three-judge court found no realistic possibility that California would be able to build itself out of this crisis. At the time of the court's decision the State had plans to build new medical and housing facilities, but funding for some plans had not been secured and funding for other plans had been delayed by the legislature for years. Particularly in light of California's ongoing fiscal crisis, the three-judge court deemed "chimerical" any "remedy that requires significant additional spending by the state." . . .

The three-judge court also rejected additional hiring as a realistic means to achieve a remedy. The State for years had been unable to fill positions necessary for the adequate provision of medical and mental health care, and the three-judge court found no reason to expect a change. Although the State points to limited gains in staffing between 2007 and 2008, the record shows that the prison system remained chronically understaffed through trial in 2008. The three-judge court found that violence and other negative conditions caused by crowding made it difficult to hire and retain needed staff. The court also concluded that there would be insufficient space for additional staff to work even if adequate personnel could somehow be retained. Additional staff cannot help to remedy the violation if they have no space in which to see and treat patients.

The three-judge court also did not err, much less commit clear error, when it concluded that, absent a population reduction, continued efforts by the Receiver and Special Master would not achieve a remedy. Both the Receiver and the Special Master filed reports stating that overcrowding posed a significant barrier to their efforts. . . .

The State claims that, even if each of these measures were unlikely to remedy the violation, they would succeed in doing so if combined together. Aside from asserting this proposition, the State offers no reason to believe it is so. Attempts to remedy the violations in *Plata* have been ongoing for 9 years. In *Coleman,* remedial efforts have been ongoing for 16. At one time, it may have been possible to hope that these violations would be cured without a reduction in overcrowding. A long history of failed remedial orders, together with substantial evidence of overcrowding's deleterious effects on the provision of care, compels a different conclusion today.

The common thread connecting the State's proposed remedial efforts is that they would require the State to expend large amounts of money absent a reduction in overcrowding. The Court cannot ignore the political and fiscal reality behind this case. California's Legislature has not been willing or able to allocate the resources necessary to meet this crisis absent a reduction in overcrowding. There is no reason to believe it will begin to do so now, when the State of California is facing an unprecedented budgetary shortfall. . . .

D

The PLRA states that no prospective relief shall issue with respect to prison conditions unless it is narrowly drawn, extends no further than necessary to correct the violation of a federal right, and is the least intrusive means necessary to correct the violation. 18 U.S.C. § 3626(a). When determining whether these requirements are met, courts must "give substantial weight to any adverse impact on public safety or the operation of a criminal justice system."

1

The three-judge court acknowledged that its order "is likely to affect inmates without medical conditions or serious mental illness." This is because reducing California's prison population will require reducing the number of prisoners outside the class through steps such as parole reform, sentencing reform, use of good-time credits, or other means to be determined by the State. Reducing overcrowding will also have positive effects beyond facilitating timely and adequate access to medical care, including reducing the incidence of prison violence and ameliorating unsafe living conditions. According to the State, these collateral consequences are evidence that the order sweeps more broadly than necessary.

The population limit imposed by the three-judge court does not fail narrow tailoring simply because it will have positive effects beyond the plaintiff class. Narrow tailoring requires a " 'fit' between the [remedy's] ends and the means chosen to accomplish those ends." Board of Trustees of State Univ. of N.Y. v. Fox, 492 U.S. 469, 480 (1989). The scope of the remedy must be proportional to the scope of the violation, and the order must extend no further than necessary to remedy the violation. This Court has rejected remedial orders that unnecessarily reach out to improve prison conditions other than those that violate the Constitution. Lewis v. Casey, 518 U.S. 343, 357 (1996). But the precedents do not suggest that a narrow and otherwise proper remedy for a constitutional violation is invalid simply because it will have collateral effects.

Nor does anything in the text of the PLRA require that result. The PLRA states that a remedy shall extend no further than necessary to remedy the violation of the rights of a "particular plaintiff or plaintiffs." 18 U.S.C. § 3626(a)(1)(A). This means only that the scope of the order must be determined with reference to the constitutional violations established by the specific plaintiffs before the court.

This case is unlike cases where courts have impermissibly reached out to control the treatment of persons or institutions beyond the scope of the violation. Even prisoners with no present physical or mental illness may become afflicted, and all prisoners in California are at risk so long as the State continues to provide inadequate care. Prisoners in the general population will become sick, and will become members of the plaintiff classes, with routine frequency; and overcrowding may prevent the timely diagnosis and care necessary to provide effective treatment and to prevent further spread of disease. Relief targeted only at present members of the plaintiff classes may therefore fail to adequately protect future class members who will develop serious physical or mental illness. Prisoners who are not sick or mentally ill do not yet have a claim that they have been subjected to care that violates the Eighth Amendment, but in no sense are they remote bystanders in California's medical care system. They are that system's next potential victims.

A release order limited to prisoners within the plaintiff classes would, if anything, unduly limit the ability of State officials to determine which prisoners should be released. As the State acknowledges in its brief, "release of seriously mentally ill inmates [would be] likely to create special dangers because of their recidivism rates." The order of the three-judge court gives the State substantial flexibility to determine who should be released. If the State truly believes that a release order limited to sick and mentally ill inmates would be preferable to the order entered by the three-judge court, the State can move the three-judge court for modification of the order on that basis. The State has not requested this relief from this Court.

The order also is not overbroad because it encompasses the entire prison system, rather than separately assessing the need for a population limit at every institution. . . . Although the three-judge court's order addresses the entire California prison system, it affords the State flexibility to accommodate differences between institutions. There is no requirement that every facility comply with the 137.5% limit. Assuming no constitutional violation results, some facilities may retain populations in excess of the limit provided other facilities fall sufficiently below it so the system as a whole remains in compliance with the order. This will allow prison officials to shift prisoners to facilities that are better able to accommodate overcrowding, or out of facilities where retaining sufficient medical staff has been difficult. The alternative—a series of institution-specific population limits—would require federal judges to make these choices. Leaving this discretion to state officials does not make the order overbroad. . . .

As the State implements the order of the three-judge court, time and experience may reveal targeted and effective remedies that will end the constitutional violations even without a significant decrease in the general prison population. The State will be free to move the three-judge court for modification of its order on that basis, and these motions would be entitled to serious consideration. At this time, the State has not proposed any realistic alternative to the order. The State's desire to avoid a population limit, justified as according respect to state authority, creates a certain and unacceptable risk of continuing violations of the rights of sick and mentally ill prisoners, with the result that many more will die or needlessly suffer. The Constitution does not permit this wrong.

2

In reaching its decision, the three-judge court gave "substantial weight" to any potential adverse impact on public safety from its order. The court devoted nearly 10 days of trial to the issue of public safety, and it gave the question extensive attention in its opinion. Ultimately, the court concluded that it would be possible to reduce the prison population "in a manner that preserves public safety and the operation of the criminal justice system."

The PLRA's requirement that a court give "substantial weight" to public safety does not require the court to certify that its order has no possible adverse impact on the public. A contrary reading would depart from the statute's text by replacing the word "substantial" with "conclusive." . . . [T]he PLRA contemplates that courts will retain authority to issue orders necessary to remedy constitutional violations, including authority to issue population limits when necessary. A court is required to consider the public safety consequences of its order and to structure, and monitor, its ruling in a way that mitigates those consequences while still achieving an effective remedy of the constitutional violation.

This inquiry necessarily involves difficult predictive judgments regarding the likely effects of court orders. Although these judgments are normally made by state officials, they necessarily must be made by courts when those courts fashion injunctive relief to remedy serious constitutional violations in the prisons. These questions are difficult and sensitive, but they are factual questions and should be treated as such. Courts can, and should, rely on relevant and informed expert testimony when making factual findings. It was proper for the three-judge court to rely on the testimony of prison officials from California and other States. Those experts testified on the basis of empirical evidence and extensive experience in the field of prison administration.

The three-judge court credited substantial evidence that prison populations can be reduced in a manner that does not increase crime to a significant degree. . . .

Expert witnesses produced statistical evidence that prison populations had been lowered without adversely affecting public safety in a number of jurisdictions, including certain counties in California, as well as Wisconsin, Illinois, Texas, Colorado, Montana, Michigan, Florida, and Canada. Washington's former secretary of corrections testified that his State had implemented population reduction methods, including parole reform and expansion of good time credits, without any "deleterious effect on crime." In light of this evidence, the three-judge court concluded that any negative impact on public safety would be "substantially offset, and perhaps entirely eliminated, by the public safety benefits" of a reduction in overcrowding.

The court found that various available methods of reducing overcrowding would have little or no impact on public safety. Expansion of good-time credits would allow the State to give early release to only those prisoners who pose the least risk of reoffending. Diverting low-risk offenders to community programs such as drug treatment, day reporting centers, and electronic monitoring would likewise lower the prison population without releasing violent convicts.[12] The State now sends large numbers of persons to prison for violating a technical term or condition of their parole, and it could reduce the prison population by punishing technical parole violations through community-based programs. This last measure would be particularly beneficial as it would reduce crowding in the reception centers, which are especially hard hit by overcrowding. The court's order took account of public safety concerns by giving the State substantial flexibility to select among these and other means of reducing overcrowding. . . .

During the pendency of this appeal, the State in fact began to implement measures to reduce the prison population. These measures will shift "thousands" of prisoners from the state prisons to the county jails by "mak[ing] certain felonies punishable by imprisonment in county jail" and "requir[ing] that individuals returned to custody for violating their conditions of parole 'serve any custody term in county jail.' " These developments support the three-judge court's conclusion that the prison population can be reduced in a manner calculated to avoid an undue negative effect on public safety.

III

Establishing the population at which the State could begin to provide constitutionally adequate medical and mental health care, and the appropriate time frame within which to achieve the necessary reduction, requires a degree of judgment. The inquiry involves uncertain predictions regarding the effects of population reductions, as well as difficult determinations re-

12 Expanding such community-based measures may require an expenditure of resources by the State to fund new programs or expand existing ones. The State complains that the order therefore requires it to "divert" savings that will be achieved by reducing the prison population and that setting budgetary priorities in this manner is a "severe, unlawful intrusion on the State authority." This argument is not convincing. The order does not require the State to use any particular approach to reduce its prison population or allocate its resources.

garding the capacity of prison officials to provide adequate care at various population levels. Courts have substantial flexibility when making these judgments. " 'Once invoked, "the scope of a district court's equitable powers . . . is broad, for breadth and flexibility are inherent in equitable remedies." ' " Hutto v. Finney, 437 U.S., at 687 n.9 (quoting Milliken v. Bradley, 433 U.S. 267, 281 (1977), in turn quoting Swann v. Charlotte–Mecklenburg Bd. of Ed., 402 U.S. 1, 15 (1971)).

Nevertheless, the PLRA requires a court to adopt a remedy that is "narrowly tailored" to the constitutional violation and that gives "substantial weight" to public safety. 18 U.S.C. § 3626(a). When a court is imposing a population limit, this means the court must set the limit at the highest population consistent with an efficacious remedy. The court must also order the population reduction achieved in the shortest period of time reasonably consistent with public safety.

A

The three-judge court concluded that the population of California's prisons should be capped at 137.5% of design capacity. This conclusion is supported by the record. Indeed, some evidence supported a limit as low as 100% of design capacity. The chief deputy secretary of Correctional Healthcare Services for the California prisons testified that California's prisons "were not designed and made no provision for any expansion of medical care space beyond the initial 100% of capacity." Other evidence supported a limit as low as 130% [citing expert testimony]. . . .

According to the State, this testimony expressed the witnesses' policy preferences, rather than their views as to what would cure the constitutional violation. Of course, courts must not confuse professional standards with constitutional requirements. Rhodes v. Chapman, 452 U.S. 337, 348 n.13 (1981). But expert opinion may be relevant when determining what is obtainable and what is acceptable in corrections philosophy. Nothing in the record indicates that the experts in this case imposed their own policy views or lost sight of the underlying violations. To the contrary, the witnesses testified that a 130% population limit would allow the State to remedy the constitutionally inadequate provision of medical and mental health care. When expert opinion is addressed to the question of how to remedy the relevant constitutional violations, as it was here, federal judges can give it considerable weight.

The Federal Bureau of Prisons (BOP) has set 130% as a long-term goal for population levels in the federal prison system. The State suggests the expert witnesses impermissibly adopted this professional standard in their testimony. But courts are not required to disregard expert opinion solely because it adopts or accords with professional standards. Professional standards may be "helpful and relevant with respect to some questions." *Chapman*, 452 U.S., at 348 n.13. The witnesses testified that a limit of 130% was necessary to remedy the constitutional violations, not that it should be adopted because it is a BOP standard. If anything, the fact that the BOP views 130% as a manageable population density bolsters the three-judge court's conclusion that a population limit of 130% would alleviate the pressures associated with overcrowding and allow the State to begin to provide constitutionally adequate care.

Although the three-judge court concluded that the "evidence in support of a 130% limit is strong," it found that some upward adjustment was warranted in light of "the caution and restraint required by the PLRA." The three-judge court noted evidence supporting a higher limit. In particular, the State's Corrections Independent Review Panel had found that 145% was the maximum "operable capacity" of California's prisons, although the relevance of that determination was undermined by the fact that the panel had not considered the need to provide constitutionally adequate medical and mental health care, as the State itself concedes. After considering, but discounting, this evidence, the three-judge court concluded that the evidence supported a limit lower than 145%, but higher than 130%. It therefore imposed a limit of 137.5%.

This weighing of the evidence was not clearly erroneous. The adversary system afforded the court an opportunity to weigh and evaluate evidence presented by the parties. The plaintiffs' evidentiary showing was intended to justify a limit of 130%, and the State made no attempt to show that any other number would allow for a remedy. There are also no scientific tools available to determine the precise population reduction necessary to remedy a constitutional violation of this sort. The three-judge court made the most precise determination it could in light of the record before it. The PLRA's narrow tailoring requirement is satisfied so long as these equitable, remedial judgments are made with the objective of releasing the fewest possible prisoners consistent with an efficacious remedy. In light of substantial evidence supporting an even more drastic remedy, the three-judge court complied with the requirement of the PLRA in this case.

B

The three-judge court ordered the State to achieve this reduction within two years. At trial and closing argument before the three-judge court, the State did not argue that reductions should occur over a longer period of time. The State later submitted a plan for court approval that would achieve the required reduction within five years, and that would reduce the prison population to 151% of design capacity in two years. The State represented that this plan would "safely reach a population level of 137.5% over time." The three-judge court rejected this plan because it did not comply with the deadline set by its order.

The State first had notice that it would be required to reduce its prison population in February 2009, when the three-judge court gave notice of its tentative ruling after trial. The 2–year deadline, however, will not begin to run until this Court issues its judgment. When that happens, the State will have already had over two years to begin complying with the order of the three-judge court. The State has used the time productively. At oral argument, the State indicated it had reduced its prison population by approximately 9,000 persons since the decision of the three-judge court. After oral argument, the State filed a supplemental brief indicating that it had begun to implement measures to shift "thousands" of additional prisoners to county facilities.

Particularly in light of the State's failure to contest the issue at trial, the three-judge court did not err when it established a 2–year deadline for relief. . . .

The three-judge court, however, retains the authority, and the responsibility, to make further amendments to the existing order or any modified decree it may enter as warranted by the exercise of its sound discretion. "The power of a court of equity to modify a decree of injunctive relief is long-established, broad, and flexible." New York State Assn. for Retarded Children, Inc. v. Carey, 706 F.2d 956, 967 (2d Cir. 1983) (Friendly, J.). A court that invokes equity's power to remedy a constitutional violation by an injunction mandating systemic changes to an institution has the continuing duty and responsibility to assess the efficacy and consequences of its order. Experience may teach the necessity for modification or amendment of an earlier decree. To that end, the three-judge court must remain open to a showing or demonstration by either party that the injunction should be altered to ensure that the rights and interests of the parties are given all due and necessary protection.

Proper respect for the State and for its governmental processes require that the three-judge court exercise its jurisdiction to accord the State considerable latitude to find mechanisms and make plans to correct the violations in a prompt and effective way consistent with public safety. In order to "give substantial weight to any adverse impact on public safety," 18 U.S.C. § 3626(a)(1)(A), the three-judge court must give due deference to informed opinions as to what public safety requires, including the considered determinations of state officials regarding the time in which a reduction in the prison population can be achieved consistent with public safety. An extension of time may allow the State to consider changing political, economic, and other circumstances and to take advantage of opportunities for more effective remedies that arise as the Special Master, the Receiver, the prison system, and the three-judge court itself evaluate the progress being made to correct unconstitutional conditions. At the same time, both the three-judge court and state officials must bear in mind the need for a timely and efficacious remedy for the ongoing violation of prisoners' constitutional rights.

The State may wish to move for modification of the three-judge court's order to extend the deadline for the required reduction to five years from the entry of the judgment of this Court, the deadline proposed in the State's first population reduction plan. The three-judge court may grant such a request provided that the State satisfies necessary and appropriate preconditions designed to ensure that measures are taken to implement the plan without undue delay. Appropriate preconditions may include a requirement that the State demonstrate that it has the authority and the resources necessary to achieve the required reduction within a 5–year period and to meet reasonable interim directives for population reduction. The three-judge court may also condition an extension of time on the State's ability to meet interim benchmarks for improvement in provision of medical and mental health care.

The three-judge court, in its discretion, may also consider whether it is appropriate to order the State to begin without delay to develop a system to identify prisoners who are unlikely to reoffend or who might otherwise be candidates for early release. Even with an extension of time to construct new facilities and implement other reforms, it may become necessary to release prisoners to comply with the court's order. To do so safely, the State should devise systems to select those prisoners least likely to jeopardize public safety. An extension of time may provide the State a greater opportunity to refine and elaborate those systems.

The State has already made significant progress toward reducing its prison population, including reforms that will result in shifting "thousands" of prisoners to county jails. As the State makes further progress, the three-judge court should evaluate whether its order remains appropriate. If significant progress is made toward remedying the underlying constitutional violations, that progress may demonstrate that further population reductions are not necessary or are less urgent than previously believed. Were the State to make this showing, the three-judge court in the exercise of its discretion could consider whether it is appropriate to extend or modify this timeline.

Experience with the three-judge court's order may also lead the State to suggest other modifications. The three-judge court should give any such requests serious consideration. The three-judge court should also formulate its orders to allow the State and its officials the authority necessary to address contingencies that may arise during the remedial process.

These observations reflect the fact that the three-judge court's order, like all continuing equitable decrees, must remain open to appropriate modification. They are not intended to cast doubt on the validity of the basic premise of the existing order. The medical and mental health care provided by California's prisons falls below the standard of decency that inheres in the Eighth Amendment. This extensive and ongoing constitutional violation requires a remedy, and a remedy will not be achieved without a reduction in overcrowding. The relief ordered by the three-judge court is required by the Constitution and was authorized by Congress in the PLRA. The State shall implement the order without further delay.

The judgment of the three-judge court is affirmed.

It is so ordered.

■ JUSTICE SCALIA, with whom JUSTICE THOMAS joins, dissenting.

Today the Court affirms what is perhaps the most radical injunction issued by a court in our Nation's history: an order requiring California to release the staggering number of 46,000 convicted criminals.

There comes before us, now and then, a case whose proper outcome is so clearly indicated by tradition and common sense, that its decision ought to shape the law, rather than vice versa. One would think that, before allowing the decree of a federal district court to release 46,000 convicted felons, this Court would bend every effort to read the law in such a way as to avoid that outrageous result. Today, quite to the contrary, the Court disregards stringently drawn provisions of the governing statute, and traditional constitutional limitations upon the power of a federal judge, in order to uphold the absurd.

The proceedings that led to this result were a judicial travesty. I dissent because the institutional reform the District Court has undertaken violates the terms of the governing statute, ignores bedrock limitations on the power of Article III judges, and takes federal courts wildly beyond their institutional capacity.

I

A

The Prison Litigation Reform Act (PLRA) states that "[p]rospective relief in any civil action with respect to prison conditions shall extend no further than necessary to correct the violation of the Federal right of a particular plaintiff or plaintiffs"; that such relief must be "narrowly drawn, [and] exten [d] no further than necessary to correct the violation of the Federal right"; and that it must be "the least intrusive means necessary to correct the violation of the Federal right." 18 U.S.C. § 3626(a)(1)(A). In deciding whether these multiple limitations have been complied with, it is necessary to identify with precision what is the "violation of the Federal right of a particular plaintiff or plaintiffs" that has been alleged. What has been alleged here, and what the injunction issued by the Court is tailored (narrowly or not) to remedy is the running of a prison system with inadequate medical facilities. That may result in the denial of needed medical treatment to "a particular [prisoner] or [prisoners]," thereby violating (according to our cases) his or their Eighth Amendment rights. But the mere existence of the inadequate system does not subject to cruel and unusual punishment the entire prison population in need of medical care, including those who receive it.

The Court acknowledges that the plaintiffs "do not base their case on deficiencies in care provided on any one occasion"; rather, "[p]laintiffs rely on systemwide deficiencies in the provision of medical and mental health care that, taken as a whole, subject sick and mentally ill prisoners in California to 'substantial risk of serious harm' and cause the delivery of care in the prisons to fall below the evolving standards of decency that mark the progress of a maturing society" [see n.3]. But our judge-empowering "evolving standards of decency" jurisprudence (with which, by the way, I heartily disagree, see, e.g., Roper v. Simmons, 543 U.S. 551, 615–16 (2005) (Scalia, J., dissenting)) does not prescribe (or at least has not until today prescribed) rules for the "decent" running of schools, prisons, and other government institutions. It forbids "indecent" treatment of individuals—in the context of this case, the *denial of medical care* to those who need it. And the persons who have a constitutional claim for denial of medical care are those who are denied medical care—not all who face a "substantial risk" (whatever that is) of being denied medical care.

The *Coleman* litigation involves "the class of seriously mentally ill persons in California prisons," and the *Plata* litigation involves "the class of state prisoners with serious medical conditions." The plaintiffs do not appear to claim—and it would absurd to suggest—that every single one of those prisoners has personally experienced "torture or a lingering death" as a consequence of that bad medical system. Indeed, it is inconceivable that anything more than a small proportion of prisoners in the plaintiff classes have personally received sufficiently atrocious treatment that their Eighth Amendment right was violated—which, as the Court recognizes, is why the plaintiffs do not premise their claim on "deficiencies in care provided on any one occasion." Rather, the plaintiffs' claim is that they are all part of a medical system so defective that some number of prisoners will inevitably be injured by incompetent medical care, and that this number is sufficiently high so as to render the system, as a whole, unconstitutional.

But what procedural principle justifies certifying a class of plaintiffs so they may assert a claim of systemic unconstitutionality? I can think of two possibilities, both of which are untenable. The first is that although some or most plaintiffs in the class do not *individually* have viable Eighth Amendment claims, the class as a whole has collectively suffered an Eighth Amendment violation. That theory is contrary to the bedrock rule that the sole purpose of classwide adjudication is to aggregate claims that are individually viable. . . .

The second possibility is that every member of the plaintiff class *has* suffered an Eighth Amendment violation merely by virtue of being a patient in a poorly-run prison system, and the purpose of the class is merely to aggregate all those individually viable claims. This theory has the virtue of being consistent with procedural principles, but at the cost of a gross substantive departure from our case law. Under this theory, each and every prisoner who happens to be a patient in a system that has systemic weaknesses . . . has suffered cruel or unusual punishment, even if that person cannot make an individualized showing of mistreatment. Such a theory of the Eighth Amendment is preposterous. And we have said as much in the past: "If . . . a healthy inmate who had suffered no deprivation of needed medical treatment were able to claim violation of his constitutional right to medical care . . . simply on the ground that the prison medical facilities were inadequate, the essential distinction between judge and executive would have disappeared: it would have become the function of the courts to assure adequate medical care in prisons." Lewis v. Casey, 518 U.S. 343, 350 (1996).

Whether procedurally wrong or substantively wrong, the notion that the plaintiff class can allege an Eighth Amendment violation based on "systemwide deficiencies" is assuredly wrong. It follows that the remedy decreed here is also contrary to law, since the theory of systemic unconstitutionality is central to the plaintiffs' case. The PLRA requires plaintiffs to establish that the systemwide injunction entered by the District Court was "narrowly drawn" and "extends no further than necessary" to correct "the violation of the Federal right of a particular plaintiff or plaintiffs." If (as is the case) the only viable constitutional claims consist of individual instances of mistreatment, then a remedy reforming the system as a whole goes far beyond what the statute allows.

It is also worth noting the peculiarity that the vast majority of inmates most generously rewarded by the release order—the 46,000 whose incarceration will be ended—do not form part of any aggrieved class even under the Court's expansive notion of constitutional violation. Most of them will not be prisoners with medical conditions or severe mental illness; and many will undoubtedly be fine physical specimens who have developed intimidating muscles pumping iron in the prison gym.

B

Even if I accepted the implausible premise that the plaintiffs have established a systemwide violation of the Eighth Amendment, I would dissent from the Court's endorsement of a decrowding order. That order is an example of what has become known as a "structural injunction." As I have previously explained, structural injunctions are radically different from the injunctions traditionally issued by courts of equity, and presumably part of "the judicial Power" conferred on federal courts by Article III:

> The mandatory injunctions issued upon termination of litigation usually required "a single simple act." H. McClintock, Principles of Equity § 15, pp. 3233 (2d ed.1948). . . . Compliance with these "single act" mandates could, in addition to being simple, be quick; and once it was achieved the contemnor's relationship with the court came to an end, at least insofar as the subject of the order was concerned. Once the document was turned over or the land conveyed, the litigant's obligation to the court, and the court's coercive power over the litigant, ceased. . . . The court did not engage in any ongoing supervision of the litigant's conduct, nor did its order continue to regulate its behavior.

Mine Workers v. Bagwell, 512 U.S. 821, 841–42 (1994) (Scalia, J., concurring).

Structural injunctions depart from that historical practice, turning judges into long-term administrators of complex social institutions such as schools, prisons, and police departments. Indeed, they require judges to play a role essentially indistinguishable from the role ordinarily played by executive officials. Today's decision not only affirms the structural injunction but vastly expands its use, by holding that an entire system is unconstitutional because it *may produce* constitutional violations.

The drawbacks of structural injunctions have been described at great length elsewhere. See, e.g., *Lewis*, 518 U.S. at 385 (Thomas, J., concurring); Missouri v. Jenkins, 515 U.S. 70, 124–33 (1995) (Thomas, J., concurring). This case illustrates one of their most pernicious aspects: that they force judges to engage in a form of factfinding-as-policymaking that is outside the traditional judicial role. The factfinding judges traditionally engage in involves the determination of past or present facts based (except for a limited set of materials of which courts may take "judicial notice") exclusively upon a closed trial record. That is one reason why a district judge's factual findings are entitled to plain-error review: because having viewed the trial first hand he is in a better position to evaluate the evidence than a judge reviewing a cold record. In a very limited category of cases, judges have also traditionally been called upon to make some predictive judgments: which custody will best serve the interests of the child, for example, or whether a particular one-shot injunction will remedy the plaintiff's grievance. When a judge manages a structural injunction, however, he will inevitably be required to make very broad empirical predictions necessarily based in large part upon policy views—the sort of predictions regularly made by legislators and executive officials, but inappropriate for the Third Branch.

This feature of structural injunctions is superbly illustrated by the District Court's proceeding concerning the decrowding order's effect on public safety. The PLRA requires that, before granting "[p]rospective relief in [a] civil action with respect to prison conditions," a court must "give substantial weight to any adverse impact on public safety or the operation of a criminal justice system caused by the relief." 18 U.S.C. § 3626(a)(1)(A). Here, the District Court discharged that requirement by making the "factual finding" that "the state has available methods by which it could readily reduce the prison population to 137.5% design capacity or less without an adverse impact on public safety or the operation of the criminal justice system." . . . It "reject[ed] the testimony that inmates released early from prison would commit additional new crimes," finding that "shortening the length of stay through earned credits would give inmates incentives to participate in programming designed to lower recidivism," and that "slowing the flow of technical parole violators to prison, thereby substantially reducing the churning of parolees, would by itself improve both the prison and parole systems, and public safety." It found that "the diversion of offenders to community correctional programs has significant beneficial effects on public safety" and that "additional rehabilitative programming would result in a significant population reduction while improving public safety."

The District Court cast these predictions (and the Court today accepts them) as "factual findings," made in reliance on the procession of expert witnesses that testified at trial. Because these "findings" have support in the record, it is difficult to reverse them under a plain-error standard of review. And given that the District Court devoted nearly 10 days of trial and 70 pages of its opinion to this issue, it is difficult to dispute that the District Court has discharged its statutory obligation to give "substantial weight to any adverse impact on public safety."

But the idea that the three District Judges in this case relied solely on the credibility of the testifying expert witnesses is fanciful. *Of course* they were relying largely on their own beliefs about penology and recidivism. And *of course* different district judges, of different policy views, would have "found" that rehabilitation would not work and that releasing prisoners would increase the crime rate. I am not saying that the District Judges rendered their factual findings in bad faith. I am saying that it is impossible for judges to make "factual findings" without inserting their own policy judgments, when the factual findings *are* policy judgments. What occurred here is no more judicial factfinding in the ordinary sense than would be the factual findings that deficit spending will not lower the unemployment rate, or that the continued occupation of Iraq will decrease the risk of terrorism. Yet, because they have been branded "factual findings" entitled to deferential review, the policy preferences of three District Judges now govern the operation of California's penal system.

It is important to recognize that the dressing-up of policy judgments as factual findings is not an error peculiar to this case. It is an unavoidable concomitant of institutional-reform litigation. When a district court issues an injunction, it must make a factual assessment of the anticipated consequences of the injunction. And when the injunction undertakes to restructure a social institution, assessing the factual consequences of the injunction is necessarily the sort of predictive judgment that our system of government allocates to other government officials.

But structural injunctions do not simply invite judges to indulge policy preferences. They invite judges to indulge *incompetent* policy preferences. Three years of law school and familiarity with pertinent Supreme Court precedents give no insight whatsoever into the management of social institutions. Thus, in the proceeding below the District Court determined that constitutionally adequate medical services could be provided if the prison population was 137.5% of design capacity. This was an empirical finding it was utterly unqualified to make. Admittedly, the court did not generate that number entirely on its own; it heard the numbers 130% and 145% bandied about by various witnesses and decided to split the difference. But the ability of judges to spit back or even average-out numbers spoon-fed to them by expert witnesses does not render them competent decisionmakers in areas in which they are otherwise unqualified.

The District Court also relied heavily on the views of the Receiver and Special Master, and those reports play a starring role in the Court's opinion today. . . . The use of these reports is even less consonant with the traditional judicial role than the District Court's reliance on the expert testimony at trial. The latter, even when, as here, it is largely the expression of policy judgments, is at least subject to cross-examination. Relying on the un-cross-examined findings of an investigator, sent into the field to prepare a factual report and give suggestions on how to improve the prison system, bears no resemblance to ordinary judicial decisionmaking. . . .

C

My general concerns associated with judges' running social institutions are magnified when they run prison systems, and doubly magnified when they force prison officials to release convicted criminals. . . .

As the author of today's opinion explained earlier this Term, granting a writ of habeas corpus " 'disturbs the State's significant interest in repose for concluded litigation, denies society the right to punish some admitted offenders, and intrudes on state sovereignty to a degree matched by few exercises of federal judicial authority.' " Harrington v. Richter, 562 U.S.

___, ___, 131 S.Ct. 770 (2011) (quoting Harris v. Reed, 489 U.S. 255, 282 (1989) (Kennedy, J., dissenting)). Recognizing that habeas relief must be granted sparingly, we have reversed the Ninth Circuit's erroneous grant of habeas relief to individual California prisoners four times this Term alone. [Citations omitted.] And yet here, the Court affirms an order granting the functional equivalent of 46,000 writs of habeas corpus, based on its paean to courts' "substantial flexibility when making these judgments." It seems that the Court's respect for state sovereignty has vanished in the case where it most matters.

II

The Court's opinion includes a bizarre coda noting that "[t]he State may wish to move for modification of the three-judge court's order to extend the deadline for the required reduction to five years." The District Court, it says, "may grant such a request provided that the State satisfies necessary and appropriate preconditions designed to ensure the measures are taken to implement the plan without undue delay". . . .

The legal effect of this passage is unclear—I suspect intentionally so. If it is nothing but a polite remainder to the State and to the District Court that the injunction is subject to modification, then it is entirely unnecessary. As both the State and the District Court are undoubtedly aware, a party is *always* entitled to move to modify an equitable decree, and the PLRA contains an express provision authorizing District Courts to modify or terminate prison injunctions. See 18 U.S.C. § 3626(b).

I suspect, however, that this passage is a warning shot across the bow, telling the District Court that it had *better* modify the injunction if the State requests what we invite it to request. Such a warning, if successful, would achieve the benefit of a marginal reduction in the inevitable murders, robberies, and rapes to be committed by the released inmates. But it would achieve that at the expense of intellectual bankruptcy, as the Court's "warning" is entirely alien to ordinary principles of appellate review of injunctions. When a party moves for modification of an injunction, the district court is entitled to rule on that motion first, subject to review for abuse of discretion if it declines to modify the order. Horne v. Flores, 557 U.S. 433 (2009). . . .

Of course what is really happening here is that the Court, overcome by common sense, disapproves of the results reached by the District Court, but cannot remedy them (it thinks) by applying ordinary standards of appellate review. It has therefore selected a solution unknown in our legal system: A deliberately ambiguous set of suggestions on how to modify the injunction, just deferential enough so that it can say with a straight face that it is "affirming," just stern enough to put the District Court on notice that it will likely get reversed if it does not follow them. In doing this, the Court has aggrandized itself, grasping authority that appellate courts are not supposed to have, and using it to enact a compromise solution with no legal basis other than the Court's say-so. That we are driven to engage in these extralegal activities should be a sign that the entire project of permitting district courts to run prison systems is misbegotten.

But perhaps I am being too unkind. The Court, or at least a majority of the Court's majority, must be aware that the judges of the District Court are likely to call its bluff, since they know full well it cannot possibly be an abuse of discretion to refuse to accept the State's proposed modifications in an injunction that has just been approved *(affirmed)* in its present form. An injunction, after all, does not have to be perfect; only good enough for government work, which the Court today says this *is*. So perhaps the coda is nothing more than a ceremonial washing of the hands—making it clear for all to see, that if the terrible things sure to happen as a consequence of this outrageous order do happen, they will be none of this Court's responsibility. After all, did we not want, and indeed even suggest, something better?

III

In view of the incoherence of the Eighth Amendment claim at the core of this case, the nonjudicial features of institutional reform litigation that this case exemplifies, and the unique concerns associated with mass prisoner releases, I do not believe this Court can affirm this injunction. I will state my approach briefly: In my view, a court may not order a prisoner's release unless it determines that the prisoner is suffering from a violation of his constitutional rights, and that his release, and no other relief, will remedy that violation. . . .

This view follows from the PLRA's text that I discussed at the outset, 18 U.S.C. § 3626(a)(1)(A). "[N]arrowly drawn" means that the relief applies only to the "particular [prisoner] or [prisoners]" whose constitutional rights are violated; "extends no further than necessary" means that prisoners whose rights are not violated will not obtain relief; and "least intrusive means necessary to correct the violation of the Federal right" means that no other relief is available.

I acknowledge that this reading of the PLRA would severely limit the circumstances under which a court could issue structural injunctions to remedy allegedly unconstitutional prison conditions. . . . [M]y approach may invite the objection that the PLRA appears to contemplate structural injunctions in general and mass prisoner-release orders in particular. The statute requires courts to "give substantial weight to any adverse impact on public safety or the operation of a criminal justice system caused by the relief" and authorizes them to appoint Special Masters, § 3626(a)(1)(A), (f), provisions that seem to presuppose the possibility of a structural remedy. It also sets forth criteria under which courts may issue orders that have "the purpose or effect of reducing or limiting the prisoner population." § 3626(g)(4).

I do not believe that objection carries the day. In addition to imposing numerous limitations on the ability of district courts to order injunctive relief with respect to prison conditions, the PLRA states that "[n]othing in this section shall be construed to . . . repeal or detract from otherwise applicable limitations on the remedial powers of the courts." § 3626(a)(1)(C). The PLRA is therefore best understood as an attempt to constrain the discretion of courts issuing structural injunctions—not as a mandate for their use. For the reasons I have outlined, structural injunctions, especially prisoner-release orders, raise grave separation-of-powers concerns and veer significantly from the historical role and institutional capability of courts. It is appropriate to construe the PLRA so as to constrain courts from entering injunctive relief that would exceed that role and capability.

* * *

The District Court's order that California release 46,000 prisoners extends "further than necessary to correct the violation of the Federal right of a particular plaintiff or plaintiffs" who have been denied needed medical care. 18 U.S.C. § 3626(a)(1)(A). It is accordingly forbidden by the PLRA—besides defying all sound conception of the proper role of judges.

■ JUSTICE ALITO, with whom THE CHIEF JUSTICE joins, dissenting.

The decree in this case is a perfect example of what the Prison Litigation Reform Act of 1995 (PLRA) was enacted to prevent.

The Constitution does not give federal judges the authority to run state penal systems. Decisions regarding state prisons have profound public safety and financial implications, and the States are generally free to make these decisions as they choose.

The Eighth Amendment imposes an important—but limited—restraint on state authority in this field. The Eighth Amendment prohibits prison officials from depriving inmates of "the minimal civilized measure of life's necessities." Rhodes v. Chapman, 452 U.S. 337, 347 (1981). Federal courts have the responsibility to ensure that this constitutional standard is met, but undesirable prison conditions that do not violate the Constitution are beyond the federal courts' reach.

In this case, a three-judge court exceeded its authority under the Constitution and the PLRA. The court ordered a radical reduction in the California prison population without finding that the current population level violates the Constitution.

Two cases were before the three-judge court, and neither targeted the general problem of overcrowding. . . . Both of the cases were brought not on behalf of all inmates subjected to overcrowding, but rather in the interests of much more limited classes of prisoners, namely, those needing mental health treatment and those with other serious medical needs. But these cases were used as a springboard to implement a criminal justice program far different from that chosen by the state legislature. Instead of crafting a remedy to attack the specific constitutional violations that were found—which related solely to prisoners in the two plaintiff classes—the lower court issued a decree that will at best provide only modest help to those prisoners but that is very likely to have a major and deleterious effect on public safety.

The three-judge court ordered the premature release of approximately *46,000 criminals—the equivalent of three Army divisions.*

The approach taken by the three-judge court flies in the face of the PLRA. Contrary to the PLRA, the court's remedy is not narrowly tailored to address proven and ongoing constitutional violations. And the three-judge court violated the PLRA's critical command that any court contemplating a prisoner release order must give "substantial weight to any adverse impact on public safety." 18 U.S.C. § 3626(a)(1)(A). The three-judge court would have us believe that the early release of 46,000 inmates will not imperil—and will actually improve—public safety. Common sense and experience counsel greater caution.

I would reverse the decision below for three interrelated reasons. First, the three-judge court improperly refused to consider evidence concerning present conditions in the California prison system. Second, the court erred in holding that no remedy short of a massive prisoner release can bring the California system into compliance with the Eighth Amendment. Third, the court gave inadequate weight to the impact of its decree on public safety.

I

Both the PLRA and general principles concerning injunctive relief dictate that a prisoner release order cannot properly be issued unless the relief is necessary to remedy an ongoing violation. . . . Proof of past violations will not do; nor is it sufficient simply to establish that *some* violations continue. The scope of permissible relief depends on the scope of any continuing violations, and therefore it was essential for the three-judge court to make a reliable determination of the extent of any violations as of the time its release order was issued. Particularly in light of the radical nature of its chosen remedy, nothing less than an up-to-date assessment was tolerable.

The three-judge court, however, relied heavily on outdated information and findings and refused to permit California to introduce new evidence. Despite evidence of improvement,[1] the three-judge court relied on old findings made by the single-judge courts, including a finding made 14 years earlier. The three-judge court highlighted death statistics from 2005, while ignoring the "significant and continuous decline since 2006," California Prison Health Care Receivership Corp., K. Imai, Analysis of Year 2008 Death Reviews 31 (Dec.2009) (hereinafter 2008 Death Reviews). And the court dwelled on conditions at a facility that has since been replaced.

Prohibiting the State from introducing evidence about conditions as of the date when the prisoner release order was under consideration, the three-judge court explicitly stated that it would not "evaluate the state's continuing constitutional violations." Instead, it based its remedy on constitutional deficiencies that, in its own words, were found "years ago."[2] . . .

The majority approves the three-judge court's refusal to receive fresh evidence based largely on the need for "[o]rderly trial management." The majority reasons that the three-judge court had closed the book on the question of constitutional violations and had turned to the question of remedy. As noted, however, the extent of any continuing constitutional violations was highly relevant to the question of remedy.

The majority also countenances the three-judge court's reliance on dated findings. The majority notes that the lower court considered recent reports by the Special Master and Receiver, but the majority provides no persuasive justification for the lower court's refusal to receive hard, up-to-date evidence about any continuing violations. With the safety of the people of California in the balance, the record on this issue should not have been closed.

The majority repeats the lower court's error of reciting statistics that are clearly out of date. The Court notes the lower court's finding that as of 2005 "an inmate in one of California's prisons needlessly dies every six to seven days." Yet by the date of the trial before the three-judge court, the death rate had been trending downward for 10 quarters, and the number of likely preventable deaths fell from 18 in 2006 to 3 in 2007, a decline of 83

---

1 Before requesting the appointment of a three-judge court, the District Court in *Coleman* recognized "commendable progress" in the State's effort to provide adequate mental health care, and the District Court in *Plata* acknowledged that "the Receiver has made much progress since his appointment." The report of the Special Master to which the Court refers, identifies a "generally positive trend."

2 For this reason, it is simply not the case that "evidence of current conditions . . . informed every aspect of the judgment of the three-judge court," as the majority insists.

percent. Between 2001 and 2007, the California prison system had the 13th lowest average mortality rate of all 50 state systems.

The majority highlights past instances in which particular prisoners received shockingly deficient medical care. But such anecdotal evidence cannot be given undue weight in assessing the current state of the California system. The population of the California prison system (156,000 inmates at the time of trial) is larger than that of many medium-sized cities, and an examination of the medical care provided to the residents of many such cities would likely reveal cases in which grossly deficient treatment was provided. Instances of past mistreatment in the California system are relevant, but prospective relief must be tailored to present and future, not past, conditions.

II

Under the PLRA, a court may not grant any prospective relief unless the court finds that the relief is narrowly drawn, extends no further than necessary to correct the "violation of [a] Federal right, and is the least intrusive means necessary to correct the violation of the Federal right." § 3626(a)(1)(A). In addition, the PLRA prohibits the issuance of a prisoner release order unless the court finds "by clear and convincing evidence that . . . crowding is the primary cause of the violation of a Federal right" and that "no other relief will remedy the violation of the Federal right." § 3626(a)(3)(E).

These statutory restrictions largely reflect general standards for injunctive relief aimed at remedying constitutional violations by state and local governments. "The power of the federal courts to restructure the operation of local and state governmental entities is not plenary. . . . Once a constitutional violation is found, a federal court is required to tailor the scope of the remedy to fit the nature and extent of the constitutional violation." Dayton Bd. of Ed. v. Brinkman, 433 U.S. 406, 419–20 (1977) (internal quotation marks omitted).

Here, the majority and the court below maintain that no remedy short of a massive release of prisoners from the general prison population can remedy the State's failure to provide constitutionally adequate health care. This argument is implausible on its face and is not supported by the requisite clear and convincing evidence.

It is instructive to consider the list of deficiencies in the California prison health care system that are highlighted in today's opinion for this Court and in the opinion of the court below. The deficiencies noted by the majority here include the following: "[e]xam tables and counter tops, where prisoners with . . . communicable diseases are treated, [are] not routinely disinfected"; medical facilities "are in an abysmal state of disrepair"; medications "are too often not available when needed"; "[b]asic medical equipment is often not available or used"; prisons "would 'hire any doctor who had a license, a pulse and a pair of shoes' "; and medical and mental health staff positions have high vacancy rates. The three-judge court pointed to similar problems (citing, among other things, staffing vacancies, too few beds for mentally ill prisoners, and an outmoded records management system).

Is it plausible that none of these deficiencies can be remedied without releasing 46,000 prisoners? Without taking that radical and dangerous step, exam tables and counter tops cannot properly be disinfected? None of the system's dilapidated facilities can be repaired? Needed medications and equipment cannot be purchased and used? Staff vacancies cannot be filled? The qualifications of prison physicians cannot be improved? A better records management system cannot be developed and implemented?

I do not dispute that general overcrowding *contributes* to many of the California system's healthcare problems. But it by no means follows that reducing overcrowding is the only or the best or even a particularly good way to alleviate those problems. Indeed, it is apparent that the prisoner release ordered by the court below is poorly suited for this purpose. The release order is not limited to prisoners needing substantial medical care but instead calls for a reduction in the system's overall population. Under the order issued by the court below, it is not necessary for a single prisoner in the plaintiff classes to be released. Although some class members will presumably be among those who are discharged, the decrease in the number of prisoners needing mental health treatment or other forms of extensive medical care will be much smaller than the total number of prisoners released, and thus the release will produce at best only a modest improvement in the burden on the medical care system.

The record bears this out. The Special Master stated dramatically that even releasing 100,000 inmates (two-thirds of the California system's entire inmate population!) would leave the problem of providing mental health treatment "largely unmitigated." Similarly, the Receiver proclaimed that "those . . . who think that population controls will solve California's prison health care problems . . . are simply wrong."

The State proposed several remedies other than a massive release of prisoners, but the three-judge court, seemingly intent on attacking the broader problem of general overcrowding, rejected all of the State's proposals. In doing so, the court made three critical errors.

First, the court did not assess those proposals and other remedies in light of conditions proved to exist at the time the release order was framed. Had more recent evidence been taken into account, a less extreme remedy might have been shown to be sufficient.

Second, the court failed to distinguish between conditions that fall below the level that may be desirable as a matter of public policy and conditions that do not meet the minimum level mandated by the Constitution. To take one example, the court criticized the California system because prison doctors must conduct intake exams in areas separated by folding screens rather than in separate rooms, creating conditions that "do not allow for appropriate confidentiality." But the legitimate privacy expectations of inmates are greatly diminished, and this Court has never suggested that the failure to provide private consultation rooms in prisons amounts to cruel and unusual punishment.

Third, the court rejected alternatives that would not have provided "immediate" relief. But nothing in the PLRA suggests that public safety may be sacrificed in order to implement an immediate remedy rather than a less dangerous one that requires a more extended but reasonable period of time.

If the three-judge court had not made these errors, it is entirely possible that an adequate but less drastic remedial plan could have been crafted. . . . Many of the problems noted above plainly could be addressed without releasing prisoners and without incurring the costs associated with a large-scale prison construction program. Sanitary procedures could be improved; sufficient supplies of medicine and medical equipment could be purchased;

an adequate system of records management could be implemented; and the number of medical and other staff positions could be increased. Similarly, it is hard to believe that staffing vacancies cannot be reduced or eliminated and that the qualifications of medical personnel cannot be improved by any means short of a massive prisoner release. Without specific findings backed by hard evidence, this Court should not accept the counterintuitive proposition that these problems cannot be ameliorated by increasing salaries, improving working conditions, and providing better training and monitoring of performance.

While the cost of a large-scale construction program may well exceed California's current financial capabilities, a more targeted program, involving the repair and perhaps the expansion of current medical facilities (as opposed to general prison facilities), might be manageable. . . .

When the State proposed to make a targeted transfer of prisoners in one of the plaintiff classes (i.e., prisoners needing mental health treatment), one of the District Judges blocked the transfers for fear that the out-of-state facilities would not provide a sufficiently high level of care. The District Judge even refused to allow out-of-state transfers for prisoners who volunteered for relocation. And the court did this even though there was not even an allegation, let alone clear evidence, that the States to which these prisoners would have been sent were violating the Eighth Amendment. . . .

Finally, as a last resort, a much smaller release of prisoners in the two plaintiff classes could be considered. Plaintiffs proposed not only a systemwide population cap, but also a lower population cap for inmates in specialized programs. The three-judge court rejected this proposal, and its response exemplified what went wrong in this case. One judge complained that this remedy would be deficient because it would protect only the members of the plaintiff classes. The judge stated:

> The only thing is we would be protecting the class members. And maybe that's the appropriate thing to do. I mean, that's what this case is about, but it would be . . . difficult for me to say yes, and the hell with everybody else.

Overstepping his authority, the judge was not content to provide relief for the classes of plaintiffs on whose behalf the suit before him was brought. Nor was he content to remedy the only constitutional violations that were proved—which concerned the treatment of the members of those classes. Instead, the judge saw it as his responsibility to attack the general problem of overcrowding.

III

Before ordering any prisoner release, the PLRA commands a court to "give substantial weight to any adverse impact on public safety or the operation of a criminal justice system caused by the relief." § 3626(a)(1)(A). This provision unmistakably reflects Congress' view that prisoner release orders are inherently risky.

In taking this view, Congress was well aware of the impact of previous prisoner release orders [discussing the experience in Philadelphia, where police subsequently rearrested many released prisoners]. Despite the record of past prisoner release orders, the three-judge court in this case concluded that loosing 46,000 criminals . . . would actually improve public safety. In reaching this debatable conclusion, the three-judge court relied on the testimony of selected experts, and the majority now defers to what it characterizes as the lower court's findings of fact on this controversial public policy issue.

This is a fundamental and dangerous error. When a trial court selects between the competing views of experts on broad empirical questions such as the efficacy of preventing crime through the incapacitation of convicted criminals, the trial court's choice is very different from a classic finding of fact and is not entitled to the same degree of deference on appeal. . . .

The three-judge court acknowledged that it "ha[d] not evaluated the public safety impact of each individual element" of the population reduction plan it ordered the State to implement. The majority argues that the three-judge court nevertheless gave substantial weight to public safety because its order left "details of implementation to the State's discretion." Yet the State had told the three-judge court that, after studying possible population reduction measures, it concluded that "reducing the prison population to 137.5% within a two-year period cannot be accomplished without unacceptably compromising public safety." The State found that public safety required a 5–year period in which to achieve the ordered reduction.

Thus, the three-judge court approved a population reduction plan that neither it nor the State found could be implemented without unacceptable harm to public safety. And this Court now holds that the three-judge court discharged its obligation to "give substantial weight to any adverse impact on public safety," § 3626(a)(1)(A), by deferring to officials who did not believe the reduction could be accomplished in a safe manner. I do not believe the PLRA's public-safety requirement is so trivial.

The members of the three-judge court and the experts on whom they relied may disagree with key elements of the crime-reduction program that the State of California has pursued for the past few decades, including "the shift to inflexible determinate sentencing and the passage of harsh mandatory minimum and three-strikes laws." And experts such as the Receiver are entitled to take the view that the State should "rethin[k] the place of incarceration in its criminal justice system." But those controversial opinions on matters of criminal justice policy should not be permitted to override the reasonable policy view that is implicit in the PLRA—that prisoner release orders present an inherent risk to the safety of the public.

* * *

The prisoner release ordered in this case is unprecedented, improvident, and contrary to the PLRA. In largely sustaining the decision below, the majority is gambling with the safety of the people of California. Before putting public safety at risk, every reasonable precaution should be taken. The decision below should be reversed, and the case should be remanded for this to be done.

I fear that today's decision, like prior prisoner release orders, will lead to a grim roster of victims. I hope that I am wrong.

In a few years, we will see.

NOTE ON STRUCTURAL REFORM AFTER THE PLRA

As the Supreme Court began to hand down the first restrictive decisions in structural reform cases, scholars began to lament the passing of this form of litigation. As *Brown v. Plata* suggests, however, the obituary was premature. For documentation of the continued importance of structural reform decrees, see, e.g., Charles F. Sabel & William H. Simon, Destabilization Rights: How Public Law Litigation Succeeds, 117 Harv. L. Rev. 1015 (2004), which refers to the "protean persistence of public law litigation" and says that the movement is "still-growing." In the area of correctional institutions, the frequency of structural reform decrees has declined under the PLRA but by no means to insignificance. See Margo Schlanger, Civil Rights Injunctions Over Time: A Case Study of Jail and Prison Court Orders, 81 N.Y.U.L. Rev. 550 (2006), which provides detailed description and comprehensive analysis of both the quantity and content of structural reform decrees in this area.

As these and other sources confirm, structural reform injunctions persist but not in the same magnitude or form as once was true. At least some observers thought there had been significant evolution in the content of structural reform decrees, in prisons and elsewhere. A brief description summarizing the academic literature appears in John C. Jeffries, Jr. & George A. Rutherglen, Structural Reform Revisited, 95 Cal. L. Rev. 1387, 1411–12 (2007) (footnotes omitted):

> There has been, however, an important qualitative change in the nature of structural reform litigation. Early cases saw broad claims leading to broad relief which tended to mature into specific regulation of everything in sight. The style of relief has aptly been termed "command and control" [Sabel & Simon, supra, at 1019]. More recent cases are likely to be narrower and more focused, to involve heavier investment in demonstrating causal links between challenged conditions and constitutional violations, and to result in decrees of a different character. Newer decrees typically avoid the "kitchen sink" approach to institutional reform in favor of orders that identify goals the defendants are expected to achieve and specify standards and procedures for measurement of performance. Data collection, monitoring and reporting requirements, performance measures, and mechanisms for on-going re-evaluation and auditing are often prominently featured. As a result, structural reform injunctions have been more fine-grained, more process-oriented, and therefore in important ways less intrusive.
>
> Thanks to the remarkable efforts of dedicated scholars, more information is available than ever before about the incidence, targets, strategies, and successes of structural reform litigation. This information is of course valuable to scholars but primarily important to practitioners in the field. Consultation among the parties, which has always been necessary to resolving litigation on this scale, has led to the exchange of information and experience on which remedies actually work. Remedies effective in one case are copied in another. As the scope and contentiousness of institutional reform litigation have diminished, so has the force of the objections that it usurps processes better left to state and local government. At least where Congress has not acted to restrict injunctive relief, structural reform litigation has not markedly declined, but instead has stabilized as a form of litigation with a range of generally accepted remedies adopted in a few leading cases and imitated elsewhere.

5. STANDING

Allen v. Wright

Supreme Court of the United States, 1984.
468 U.S. 737.

■ JUSTICE O'CONNOR delivered the opinion of the Court.

Parents of black public school children allege in this nationwide class action that the Internal Revenue Service (IRS) has not adopted sufficient standards and procedures to fulfill its obligation to deny tax-exempt status to racially discriminatory private schools. They assert that the IRS thereby harms them directly and interferes with the ability of their children to receive an education in desegregated public schools. The issue before us is whether plaintiffs have standing to bring this suit. . . . We hold that they do not.

I

The Internal Revenue Service denies tax-exempt status under §§ 501(a) and (c)(3) of the Internal Revenue Code—and hence eligibility to receive charitable contributions deductible from income taxes under §§ 170(a)(1) and (c)(2) of the Code—to racially discriminatory private schools. Rev.Rul. 71–447, 1972–2 Cum.Bull. 230.[1] The IRS policy requires that a school applying for tax-exempt status show that it "admits the students of any race to all the rights, privileges, programs, and activities generally accorded or made available to students at that school and that the school does not discriminate on the basis of race in administration of its educational policies, admissions policies, scholarship and loan programs, and athletic and other school-administered programs." To carry out this policy, the IRS has established guidelines and procedures for determining whether a particular school is in fact racially nondiscriminatory. Rev. Proc. 75–50, 1975–6 Cum.Bull. 587. Failure to comply with the guidelines "will ordinarily result in the proposed revocation of" tax-exempt status.

The guidelines provide that "[a] school must show affirmatively both that it has adopted a racially nondiscriminatory policy as to students that is made known to the general public and that since the adoption of that policy it has operated in a bona fide manner in accordance therewith." The school must state its nondiscrimination policy in its organizational charter, and in all of its brochures, catalogues, and other advertisements to prospective students. The school must make its nondiscrimination policy known to the entire community served by the school and must publicly disavow any contrary representations made on its behalf once it becomes aware of them. The school must have nondiscriminatory policies concerning all programs and facilities, including scholarships and loans, and the school must annually certify, under penalty of perjury, compliance with these requirements.

The IRS rules require a school applying for tax-exempt status to give a breakdown along racial lines of its student body and its faculty and admin-

---

[1] As the Court explained last term in Bob Jones University v. United States, 461 U.S. 574, 577–79 (1983), the IRS announced this policy in 1970 and formally adopted it in 1971. This change in prior policy was prompted by litigation over tax exemptions for racially discriminatory private schools in the state of Mississippi, litigation that resulted in the entry of an injunction against the IRS largely if not entirely coextensive with the position the IRS had voluntarily adopted. Green v. Connally, 330 F.Supp. 1150 (D.D.C.), summarily aff'd sub nom. Coit v. Green, 404 U.S. 997 (1971) (entering permanent injunction).

istrative staff, as well as of scholarships and loans awarded. They also require the applicant school to state the year of its organization, and to list "incorporators, founders, board members, and donors of land or buildings," and state whether any of the organizations among these have an objective of maintaining segregated public or private school education. The rules further provide that, once given an exemption, a school must keep specified records to document the extent of compliance with the IRS guidelines. Finally, the rules announce that any information concerning discrimination at a tax-exempt school is officially welcomed.

In 1976 respondents challenged these guidelines and procedures in a suit filed in federal District Court against the Secretary of the Treasury and the Commissioner of Internal Revenue. The plaintiffs named in the complaint are parents of black children who, at the time the complaint was filed, were attending public schools in seven states in school districts undergoing desegregation. They brought this nationwide class action "on behalf of themselves and their children, and . . . on behalf of all other parents of black children attending public school systems undergoing, or which may in the future undergo, desegregation pursuant to court order [or] HEW regulations and guidelines, under state law, or voluntarily." They estimated that the class they seek to represent includes several million persons.

Respondents allege in their complaint that many racially segregated private schools were created or expanded in their communities at the time the public schools were undergoing desegregation. According to the complaint, many such private schools, including 17 schools or school systems identified by name in the complaint (perhaps some 30 schools in all), receive tax exemptions either directly or through the tax-exempt status of "umbrella" organizations that operate or support the schools. Respondents allege that, despite the IRS policy of denying tax-exempt status to racially discriminatory private schools and despite the IRS guidelines and procedures for implementing that policy, some of the tax-exempt racially segregated private schools created or expanded in desegregating districts in fact have racially discriminatory policies. Respondents allege that the IRS grant of tax exemptions to such racially discriminatory schools is unlawful.

Respondents allege that the challenged government conduct harms them in two ways. The challenged conduct

> (a) constitutes tangible federal financial aid and other support for racially segregated educational institutions, and
>
> (b) fosters and encourages the organization, operation and expansion of institutions providing racially segregated educational opportunities for white children avoiding attendance in desegregating public school districts and thereby interferes with the efforts of federal courts, HEW and local school authorities to desegregate public school districts which have been operating racially dual school systems.

Thus, respondents do not allege that their children have been the victims of discriminatory exclusion from the schools whose tax exemptions they challenge as unlawful. Indeed, they have not alleged at any stage of this litigation that their children have ever applied or would ever apply to any private school. Rather, respondents claim a direct injury from the mere fact of the challenged government conduct and, as indicated by the restriction of the plaintiff class to parents of children in desegregating school districts, injury to their children's opportunity to receive a desegregated education. The latter injury is traceable to the IRS grant of tax exemptions to racially discriminatory schools, respondents allege, chiefly because contributions to such schools are deductible from income taxes . . . and the "deductions facilitate the raising of funds to organize new schools and expand existing schools in order to accommodate white students avoiding attendance in desegregating public school districts."

Respondents request only prospective relief. They ask for a declaratory judgment that the challenged IRS tax-exemption practices are unlawful. They also ask for an injunction requiring the IRS to deny tax exemptions to a considerably broader class of private schools than the class of racially discriminatory private schools. Under the requested injunction, the IRS would have to deny tax-exempt status to all private schools

> which have insubstantial or non-existent minority enrollments, which are located in or serve desegregating public school districts, and which either—
>
> (1) were established or expanded at or about the time the public school district in which they are located or which they serve were desegregating;
>
> (2) have been determined in adversary judicial or administrative proceedings to be racially segregated; or
>
> (3) cannot demonstrate that they do not provide racially segregated educational opportunities for white children avoiding attendance in desegregating public school systems.

Finally, respondents ask for an order directing the IRS to replace its 1975 guidelines with standards consistent with the requested injunction.

In May 1977 the District Court permitted intervention as a defendant by petitioner Allen, the head of one of the private school systems identified in the complaint. Thereafter, progress in the lawsuit was stalled for several years. During this period, the Internal Revenue Service reviewed its challenged policies and proposed new Revenue Procedures to tighten requirements for eligibility for tax-exempt schools. In 1979, however, Congress blocked any strengthening of the IRS guidelines at least until October 1980.[16] The District Court thereupon considered and granted the defendants' motion to dismiss the complaint, concluding that respondents lack standing, that the judicial task proposed by respondents is inappropriately intrusive for a federal court, and that awarding the requested relief would be contrary to the will of Congress expressed in the 1979 ban on strengthening the IRS guidelines.

The United States Court of Appeals for the District of Columbia reversed, concluding that respondents have standing to maintain this lawsuit. . . . The Court of Appeals also held that the 1979 congressional actions were not intended to preclude judicial remedies and that the relief

[16] Section 615 of the Act, known as the Dornan Amendment, specifically forbade the use of funds to carry out the IRS's proposed Revenue Procedures. Section 103 of the Act, known as the Ashbrook Amendment, more generally forbade the use of funds to make the requirements for tax-exempt status of private schools more stringent than those in effect prior to the IRS's proposal of its new Revenue Procedures.

These provisions expired on October 1, 1980, but [the] Dornan and Ashbrook amendments were reinstated for the period December 16, 1980, through September 30, 1981. For fiscal year 1982, Congress specifically denied funding for carrying out not only administrative actions but also court orders entered after the date of the IRS's proposal of its first revised Revenue Procedure. No such spending restrictions are currently in force.

requested by respondents could be fashioned "without large scale judicial intervention in the administrative process." . . .

We granted certiorari and now reverse.

II

A

Article III of the Constitution confines the federal courts to adjudicating actual "cases" and "controversies." As the Court [has] explained . . . , the "case or controversy" requirement defines with respect to the judicial branch the idea of separation of powers on which the federal government is founded. The several doctrines that have grown up to elaborate that requirement are "founded in concern about the proper—and properly limited—role of the courts in a democratic society." Warth v. Seldin, 422 U.S. 490, 498 (1975).

> All of the doctrines that cluster about Article III—not only standing but mootness, ripeness, political question, and the like—relate in part, and in different though overlapping ways, to an idea, which is more than an intuition but less than a rigorous and explicit theory, about the constitutional and prudential limits to the powers of an unelected, unrepresentative judiciary in our kind of government.

Vander Jagt v. O'Neill, 699 F.2d 1166, 1178–79 (D.C. Cir. 1982) (Bork, J., concurring). The case-or-controversy doctrines state fundamental limits on federal judicial power in our system of government.

The Article III doctrine that requires a litigant to have "standing" to invoke the power of a federal court is perhaps the most important of these doctrines. "In essence the question of standing is whether the litigant is entitled to have the court decide the merits of the dispute or of particular issues." *Warth v. Seldin*, supra, at 498. Standing doctrine embraces several judicially self-imposed limits on the exercise of federal jurisdiction, such as the general prohibition on a litigant's raising another person's legal rights, the rule barring adjudication of generalized grievances more appropriately addressed in the representative branches, and the requirement that a plaintiff's complaint fall within the zone of interests protected by the law invoked. The requirement of standing, however, has a core component derived directly from the Constitution. A plaintiff must allege personal injury fairly traceable to the defendant's allegedly unlawful conduct and likely to be redressed by the requested relief.

Like the prudential component, the constitutional component of standing doctrine incorporates concepts concededly not susceptible of precise definition. The injury alleged must be, for example, " 'distinct and palpable,' " and not "abstract" or "conjectural" or "hypothetical." The injury must be "fairly" traceable to the challenged action, and relief from the injury must be "likely" to follow from a favorable decision. See Simon v. Eastern Kentucky Welfare Rights Org., 426 U.S. 26, 38 (1976).

The absence of precise definitions, however, as this Court's extensive body of case law on standing illustrates, hardly leaves courts at sea in applying the law of standing. Like most legal notions, the standing concepts have gained considerable definition from developing case law. In many cases the standing question can be answered chiefly by comparing the allegations of the particular complaint to those made in prior standing cases. More important, the law of Article III standing is built on a single basic idea—the idea of separation of powers. It is this fact which makes possible the gradual clarification of the law through judicial application. Of course, both federal and state courts have long experience in applying and elaborating in numerous contexts the pervasive and fundamental notion of separation of powers.

Determining standing in a particular case may be facilitated by clarifying principles or even clean rules developed in prior cases. Typically, however, the standing inquiry requires careful judicial examination of a complaint's allegations to ascertain whether the particular plaintiff is entitled to an adjudication of the particular claims asserted. Is the injury too abstract, or otherwise not appropriate, to be considered judicially cognizable? Is the line of causation between the illegal conduct and injury too attenuated? Is the prospect of obtaining relief from the injury as a result of a favorable ruling too speculative? These questions and any others relevant to the standing inquiry must be answered by reference to the Article III notion that federal courts may exercise power only "in the last resort, and as a necessity," and only when adjudication is "consistent with a system of separated powers and [the dispute is one] traditionally thought to be capable of resolution through the judicial process." Flast v. Cohen, 392 U.S. 83, 97 (1968).

B

Respondents allege two injuries in their complaint to support their standing to bring this lawsuit. First, they say that they are harmed directly by the mere fact of government financial aid to discriminatory private schools. Second, they say that the federal tax exemptions to racially discriminatory private schools in their communities impair their ability to have their public schools desegregated. . . . We conclude that neither suffices to support respondents' standing. The first fails under clear precedents of this Court because it does not constitute judicially cognizable injury. The second fails because the alleged injury is not fairly traceable to the assertedly unlawful conduct of the IRS.

1

Respondents' first claim of injury can be interpreted in two ways. It might be a claim simply to have the government avoid the violation of law alleged in respondents' complaint. Alternatively, it might be a claim of stigmatic injury, or denigration, suffered by all members of a racial group when the government discriminates on the basis of race.[20] Under neither interpretation is this claim of injury judicially cognizable.

This Court has repeatedly held that an asserted right to have the government act in accordance with law is not sufficient, standing alone, to confer jurisdiction on a federal court. In Schlesinger v. Reservists Committee to Stop the War, 418 U.S. 208 (1974), for example, the Court rejected a claim of citizen standing to challenge Armed Forces Reserve commissions held by members of Congress as violating the incompatibility clause of Art. I, § 6, Cl. 2 of the Constitution. As citizens, the Court held, plaintiffs alleged nothing but "the abstract injury in nonobservance of the Constitution." . . . Respondents here have no standing to complain simply that their government is violating the law.

Neither do they have standing to litigate their claims based on the stigmatizing injury often caused by racial discrimination. There can be no

[20] [W]e assume, without deciding, that the challenged government tax exemptions are the equivalent of government discrimination.

doubt that this sort of noneconomic injury is one of the most serious consequences of discriminatory government action and is sufficient in some circumstances to support standing. Our cases make clear, however, that such injury accords a basis for standing only to "those persons who are personally denied equal treatment" by the challenged discriminatory conduct.

In Moose Lodge No. 107 v. Irvis, 407 U.S. 163 (1972), the Court held that the plaintiff had no standing to challenge a club's racially discriminatory membership policies because he had never applied for membership. In O'Shea v. Littleton, 414 U.S. 488 (1974), the Court held that the plaintiffs had no standing to challenge racial discrimination in the administration of their city's criminal justice system because they had not alleged that they had been or would likely be subject to the challenged practices. The Court denied standing on similar facts in Rizzo v. Goode, 423 U.S. 362 (1976). In each of those cases, the plaintiffs alleged official racial discrimination comparable to that alleged by respondents here. Yet standing was denied in each case because the plaintiffs were not personally subject to the challenged discrimination. Insofar as their first claim of injury is concerned, respondents are in exactly the same position. . . .

The consequences of recognizing respondents' standing on the basis of their first claim of injury illustrate why our cases plainly hold that such injury is not judicially cognizable. If the abstract stigmatic injury were cognizable, standing would extend nationwide to all members of the particular racial groups against which the government was alleged to be discriminating by its tax exemption to a racially discriminatory school, regardless of the location of that school. A black person in Hawaii could challenge the grant of a tax exemption to a racially discriminatory school in Maine. Recognition of standing in such circumstances would transform the federal courts into "no more than a vehicle for the vindication of the value interests of concerned bystanders." United States v. SCRAP, 412 U.S. 669, 687 (1973). Constitutional limits on the role of the federal courts preclude such a transformation.

2

It is in their complaint's second claim of injury that respondents allege harm to a concrete, personal interest that can support standing in some circumstances. The injury they identify—their children's diminished ability to receive an education in a racially integrated school—is, beyond any doubt, not only judicially cognizable but . . . one of the most serious injuries recognized in our legal system. Despite the constitutional importance of curing the injury alleged by respondents, however, the federal judiciary may not redress it unless standing requirements are met. In this case, respondents' second claim of injury cannot support standing because the injury alleged is not fairly traceable to the government conduct respondents challenge as unlawful.

The illegal conduct challenged by respondents is the IRS's grant of tax exemptions to some racially discriminatory schools. The line of causation between that conduct and desegregation of respondents' schools is attenuated at best. From the perspective of the IRS, the injury to respondents is highly indirect and "results from the independent action of some third party not before the court," *Simon v. Eastern Kentucky Welfare Rights Org.*, supra, at 42. . . .

The diminished ability of respondents' children to receive a desegregated education would be fairly traceable to unlawful IRS grants of tax exemptions only if there were enough racially discriminatory private schools receiving tax exemptions in respondents' communities for withdrawal of those exemptions to make an appreciable difference in public-school integration. Respondents have made no such allegation. It is, first, uncertain how many racially discriminatory private schools are in fact receiving tax exemptions. Moreover, it is entirely speculative, as respondents themselves conceded in the Court of Appeals, whether withdrawal of a tax exemption from any particular school would lead the school to change its policies. It is just as speculative whether any given parent of a child attending such a private school would decide to transfer the child to public school as a result of any changes in educational or financial policy made by the private school once it was threatened with loss of tax-exempt status. It is also pure speculation whether, in a particular community, a large enough number of the numerous relevant school officials and parents would reach decisions that collectively would have a significant impact on the racial composition of the public schools. . . .

The idea of separation of powers that underlies standing doctrine explains why our cases preclude the conclusion that respondents' alleged injury "fairly can be traced to the challenged action" of the IRS. That conclusion would pave the way generally for suits challenging, not specifically identifiable government violations of law, but the particular programs agencies establish to carry out their legal obligations. Such suits, even when premised on allegations of several instances of violations of law, are rarely if ever appropriate for federal-court adjudication.

> Carried to its logical end, [respondents'] approach would have the federal courts as virtually continuing monitors of the wisdom and soundness of executive action; such a role is appropriate for the Congress acting through its committees and the 'power of the purse'; it is not the role of the judiciary, absent actual present or immediately threatened injury resulting from unlawful government action.

Laird v. Tatum, 408 U.S. 1, 15 (1972).

The same concern for the proper role of the federal courts is reflected in cases like *O'Shea v. Littleton*, *Rizzo v. Goode*, and City of Los Angeles v. Lyons, 461 U.S. 95 (1983). In all three cases plaintiffs sought injunctive relief directed at certain statewide law enforcement practices. The Court held in each case that, absent an allegation of a specific threat of being subject to the challenged practices, plaintiffs had no standing to ask for an injunction. Animating this Court's holdings was the principle that "[a] federal court . . . is not the proper forum to press" general complaints about the way in which government goes about its business. Id. at 111–12.

Case-or-controversy considerations, the Court observed in *O'Shea v. Littleton*, supra, at 499, "obviously shade into those determining whether the complaint states a sound basis for equitable relief." The latter set of considerations should therefore inform our judgment about whether respondents have standing. Most relevant to this case is the principle articulated in *Rizzo v. Goode*, supra, at 378–79:

> When a plaintiff seeks to enjoin the activity of a government agency . . . his case must contend with "the well established rule that the government has traditionally been granted the widest latitude in the 'dispatch of its own internal affairs.' "

When transported into the Article III context, that principle, grounded as it is in the idea of separation of powers, counsels against recognizing standing in a case brought not to enforce specific legal obligations whose violation works a direct harm, but to seek a restructuring of the apparatus established by the executive branch to fulfill its legal duties. The Constitution, after all, assigns to the executive branch, and not to the judicial branch, the duty to "take Care that the Laws be faithfully executed." Art. II, § 3. We could not recognize respondents' standing in this case without running afoul of that structural principle.

C

The Court of Appeals relied for its contrary conclusion on Gilmore v. City of Montgomery, 417 U.S. 556 (1974), Norwood v. Harrison, 413 U.S. 455 (1973), and on Coit v. Green, 404 U.S. 997 (1971), summarily affirming Green v. Connally, 330 F.Supp. 1150 (D.D.C.1971). . . . None of these cases, however, requires that we find standing in this lawsuit.

In *Gilmore v. City of Montgomery*, the plaintiffs asserted a constitutional right, recognized in an outstanding injunction, to use the city's public parks on a nondiscriminatory basis. They alleged that the city was violating that equal protection right by permitting racially discriminatory private schools and other groups to use the public parks. The Court recognized plaintiffs' standing to challenge this city policy insofar as the policy permitted the exclusive use of the parks by racially discriminatory private schools: the plaintiffs had alleged direct cognizable injury to their right to nondiscriminatory access to the public parks.

Standing in *Gilmore* thus rested on an allegation of direct deprivation of a right to equal use of the parks. . . . The *Gilmore* Court did not rest its finding of standing on an abstract denigration injury, and no problem of attenuated causation attended the plaintiffs' claim of injury.

In *Norwood v. Harrison*, parents of public school children in Tunica County, Mississippi, filed a statewide class action challenging the state's provision of textbooks to students attending racially discriminatory private schools in the state. The Court held the state's practice unconstitutional because it breached "the state's acknowledged duty to establish a unitary school system." The Court did not expressly address the basis for the plaintiffs' standing.

In *Gilmore*, however, the Court identified the basis for standing in *Norwood*: "The plaintiffs in *Norwood* were parties to a school desegregation order and the relief they sought was directly related to the concrete injury they suffered." Through the school-desegregation decree, the plaintiffs had acquired a right to have the state "steer clear" of any perpetuation of the racially dual school system that it had once sponsored. The interest acquired was judicially cognizable because it was a personal interest, created by law, in having the state refrain from taking specific actions. The plaintiffs' complaint alleged that the state directly injured that interest by aiding racially discriminatory private schools. Respondents in this lawsuit, of course, have no injunctive rights against the IRS that are allegedly being harmed by the challenged IRS action.

Unlike *Gilmore* and *Norwood, Coit v. Green* cannot easily be seen to have based standing on an injury different in kind from any asserted by respondents here. The plaintiffs in *Coit*, parents of black school children in Mississippi, sued to enjoin the IRS grant of tax exemptions to racially discriminatory private schools in the state. Nevertheless, *Coit* in no way mandates the conclusion that respondents have standing.

First, the decision has little weight as a precedent on the law of standing. This Court's decision in *Coit* was merely a summary affirmance; for that reason alone it could hardly establish principles contrary to those set out in opinions issued after full briefing and argument. Moreover, when the case reached this Court, the plaintiffs and the IRS were no longer adverse parties; and the ruling that was summarily affirmed did not include a ruling on the issue of standing, which had been briefly considered in a prior ruling of the District Court. . . .

In any event, the facts in the *Coit* case are sufficiently different from those presented in this lawsuit that the absence of standing here is unaffected by the possible propriety of standing there. In particular, the suit in *Coit* was limited to the public schools of one state. Moreover, the District Court found, based on extensive evidence before it . . . , that large numbers of segregated private schools had been established in the state for the purpose of avoiding a unitary public school system; that the tax exemptions were critically important to the ability of such schools to succeed; and that the connection between the grant of tax exemptions to discriminatory schools and desegregation of the public schools in the particular state was close enough to warrant the conclusion that irreparable injury to the interest in desegregated education was threatened if the tax exemptions continued. What made possible those findings was the fact that, when the Mississippi plaintiffs filed their suit, the IRS had a policy of granting tax exemptions to racially discriminatory private schools; thus, the suit was initially brought, not simply to reform executive branch enforcement procedures, but to challenge a fundamental IRS policy decision, which affected numerous identifiable schools in the state of Mississippi.

The limited setting, the history of school desegregation in Mississippi at the time of the *Coit* litigation, the nature of the IRS conduct challenged at the outset of the litigation, and the District Court's particular findings, which were never challenged as clearly erroneous, amply distinguish the *Coit* case from respondents' lawsuit. Thus, we need not consider whether standing was properly found in *Coit*. Whatever the answer to that question, respondents' complaint, which aims at nationwide relief and does not challenge particular identified unlawful IRS actions, alleges no connection between the asserted desegregation injury and the challenged IRS conduct direct enough to overcome the substantial separation-of-powers barriers to a suit seeking an injunction to reform administrative procedures.

"The necessity that the plaintiff who seeks to invoke judicial power stand to profit in some personal interest remains an Article III requirement." *Simon v. Eastern Kentucky Welfare Rights Org.*, supra, at 39. Respondents have not met this fundamental requirement. The judgement of the Court of Appeals is accordingly reversed, and the injunction issued by that court is vacated.

■ JUSTICE MARSHALL took no part in the decision of this case.

■ JUSTICE BRENNAN, dissenting. . . .

One could hardly dispute the proposition that Article III of the Constitution, by limiting the judicial power to "cases" or "controversies," embodies the notion that each branch of our national government must confine its actions to those that are consistent with our scheme of separated powers. But simply stating that unremarkable truism provides little, if any, illumination of the standing inquiry that must be undertaken by a federal court faced with a particular action filed by particular plaintiffs. . . .

The Court's attempt to obscure the standing question must be seen, therefore, as no more than a cover for its failure to recognize the nature of the specific claims raised by the respondents in these cases. By relying on generalities concerning our tripartite system of government, the Court is able to conclude that the respondents lack standing to maintain this action without acknowledging the precise nature of the injuries they have alleged. In so doing, the Court displays a startling insensitivity to the historical role played by the federal courts in eradicating race discrimination from our nation's schools. . . . Because I cannot join in such misguided decisionmaking, I dissent.

I

The respondents, suing individually and on behalf of their minor children, are parents of black children attending public schools in various school districts across the nation. Each of these school districts, the respondents allege, was once segregated and is now in the process of desegregating pursuant to court order, federal regulations or guidelines, state law, or voluntary agreement. Moreover, each contains one or more private schools that discriminate against black school children and that operate with the assistance of tax exemptions unlawfully granted to them by the Internal Revenue Service (IRS).

To eliminate this federal financial assistance for discriminating schools, the respondents seek a declaratory judgment that current IRS practices are inadequate both in identifying racially discriminatory schools and in denying requested tax exemptions or revoking existing exemptions for any schools so identified. In particular, they allege that existing IRS guidelines permit schools to receive tax exemptions simply by adopting and certifying—but not implementing—a policy of nondiscrimination. Pursuant to these ineffective guidelines,[2] many private schools that discriminate on the basis of race continue to benefit illegally from their tax-exempt status and the resulting charitable deductions granted to taxpayers who contribute to such schools. The respondents therefore seek a permanent injunction requiring the IRS to deny tax exemptions [as set forth in the opinion of the Court]. The requested relief is substantially similar to the enforcement guidelines promulgated by the IRS itself in 1978 and 1979, before congressional action temporarily stayed, and the agency withdrew, the amended procedures.

II

Persons seeking judicial relief from an Article III court must have standing to maintain their cause of action. At a minimum, the standing requirement is not met unless the plaintiff has "such a personal stake in the outcome of the controversy as to assure that concrete adverseness which sharpens the presentation of issues upon which the court so largely

---

[2] [W]e must accept as true the factual allegations made by the respondents. It nonetheless should be noted that significant evidence exists to support the respondents' claim that the IRS guidelines are ineffective. Indeed, the Commissioner of the IRS admitted as much in testimony before Congress: "This litigation prompted the Service once again to review its procedures in this area. It focused our attention on the adequacy of existing policies and procedures as we moved to formulate a litigation position. *We concluded that the Service's procedures were ineffective in identifying schools which in actual operation discriminate against minority students*, even though the schools may profess an open enrollment policy and comply with the yearly publication requirements of Revenue Procedure 75–50." . . . Tax–Exempt Status of Private Schools: Hearings Before the Subcommittee on Oversight of the House Committee on Ways and Means, 96th Cong., 1st. Sess., 5 (1979) (statement of Jerome Kurtz, Commissioner of Internal Revenue) (emphasis added).

depends. . . . " Baker v. Carr, 369 U.S. 186, 204 (1962). Under the Court's cases, this "personal stake" requirement is satisfied if the person seeking redress has suffered, or is threatened with, some "distinct and palpable injury," and if there is some causal connection between the asserted injury and the conduct being challenged.

A

In these cases, the respondents have alleged at least one type of injury that satisfies the constitutional requirement of "distinct and palpable injury."[3] In particular, they claim that the IRS' grant of tax-exempt status to racially discriminatory private schools directly injures their children's opportunity and ability to receive a desegregated education. . . .

The Court acknowledges that this alleged injury is sufficient to satisfy constitutional standards. It does so only grudgingly, however, without emphasizing the significance of the harm alleged. Nonetheless, we have consistently recognized throughout the last 30 years that the deprivation of a child's right to receive an education in a desegregated school is a harm of special significance. . . .

B

Fully explicating the injury alleged helps to explain why it is fairly traceable to the government conduct challenged by the respondents. . . . Viewed in light of the injuries they claim, the respondents have alleged a direct causal relationship between the government action they challenge and the injury they suffer: their inability to receive an education in a racially integrated school is directly and adversely affected by the tax-exempt status granted by the IRS to racially discriminatory schools in their respective school districts. Common sense alone would recognize that the elimination of tax-exempt status for racially discriminatory private schools would serve to lessen the impact that those institutions have in defeating efforts to desegregate the public schools. . . .

Moreover, the Court has previously recognized the existence, and constitutional significance, of such direct relationships between unlawfully segregated school districts and government support for racially discriminatory private schools in those districts. In Norwood v. Harrison, 413 U.S. 455 (1973), for example, we considered a Mississippi program that provided textbooks to students attending both public and private schools, without regard to whether any participating school had racially discriminatory policies. In declaring that program constitutionally invalid, we noted that "a state may not induce, encourage or promote private persons to accomplish what it is constitutionally forbidden to accomplish." We then spoke directly to the financial aid provided by the state textbook program and the constitutional rights asserted by the students and their parents:

> The District Court laid great stress on the absence of a showing by appellants that "any child enrolled in private school, if deprived of free textbooks, would withdraw from private school and subsequently enroll in the public schools." . . . *We do not agree with the District Court in its analysis of the legal consequences of this uncertainty, for the Constitution does not permit the state to aid discrimination even when there is no precise causal relationship between state financial aid to a private school and the continued well-being of that school. A state*

[3] Because I conclude that the second injury alleged by the respondents is sufficient to satisfy constitutional requirements, I do not need to reach what the Court labels the "stigmatic injury." . . .

> *may not grant the type of tangible financial aid here involved if that aid has a significant tendency to facilitate, reinforce, and support private discrimination.*" (Emphasis added.)

Thus, *Norwood* explicitly stands for the proposition that government aid to racially discriminatory schools is a direct impediment to school desegregation.

The Court purports to distinguish *Norwood* from the present litigation because " '[t]he plaintiffs in *Norwood* were parties to a school desegregation order' " and therefore "had acquired a right to have the state 'steer clear' of any perpetuation of the racially dual school system that it had once sponsored," whereas the "[r]espondents in this lawsuit . . . have no injunctive rights against the IRS that are allegedly being harmed." . . . Given that many of the school districts identified in the respondents' complaint have also been the subject of court-ordered integration, the standing inquiry in these cases should not differ. And, although, the respondents do not specifically allege that they are named parties to any outstanding desegregation orders, that is undoubtedly due to the passage of time since the orders were issued, and not to any difference in the harm they suffer.

Even accepting the relevance of the Court's distinction, moreover, that distinction goes to the injury suffered by the respective plaintiffs and not to the causal connection between the harm alleged and the governmental action challenged. The causal relationship existing in *Norwood* between the alleged harm (i.e., interference with the plaintiffs' injunctive rights to a desegregated school system) and the challenged government action (i.e., free textbooks provided to racially discriminatory schools) is indistinguishable from the causal relationship existing in the present cases, unless the Court intends to distinguish the lending of textbooks from the granting of tax-exempt status. . . . [8]

Similarly, although entitled to less weight than a decision after full briefing and oral argument on the merits, our summary affirmance in Coit v. Green, 404 U.S. 997 (1971), is directly relevant to the standing of the respondents in this litigation. . . .

Given these precedents, the Court is forced to place primary reliance on our decision in Simon v. Eastern Kentucky Welfare Rights Org., 426 U.S. 26 (1976). In that case, the Court denied standing to plaintiffs who challenged an IRS revenue ruling that granted charitable status to hospitals even though they failed to operate to the extent of their financial ability when refusing medical services for indigent patients. The Court found that the injury alleged was not one "that fairly can be traced to the challenged action of the defendant." In particular, it was "purely speculative" whether the denial of access to hospital services alleged by the plaintiffs fairly could be traced to the government's grant of tax-exempt status to the relevant hospitals, primarily because hospitals were likely making their service decisions without regard to the tax implications.

Even accepting the correctness of the causation analysis included in that decision, however, it is plainly distinguishable from the case at hand. The respondents in this case do not challenge the denial of any service by a tax-exempt institution; admittedly, they do not seek access to racially discriminatory private schools. Rather, the injury they allege, and the injury that clearly satisfies constitutional requirements, is the deprivation to their

---

[8] Our subsequent decision in Gilmore v. City of Montgomery, 417 U.S. 556 (1974), heavily relied on our decision in *Norwood*. . . .

children's opportunity and ability to receive an education in a racially integrated school district. This injury, as the Court admits, and as we have previously held in *Norwood v. Harrison*, is of a kind that is directly traceable to the governmental action being challenged. The relationship between the harm alleged and the governmental action cannot simply be deemed "purely speculative," as was the causal connection at issue in *Simon*. . . .

III

More than one commentator has noted that the causation component of the Court's standing inquiry is no more than a poor disguise for the Court's view of the merits of the underlying claims.[10] The Court today does nothing to avoid that criticism. What is most disturbing about today's decision, therefore, is not the standing analysis applied, but the indifference evidenced by the Court to the detrimental effects that racially segregated schools, supported by tax-exempt status from the federal government, have on the respondents' attempt to obtain an education in a racially integrated school system. I cannot join such indifference, and would give the respondents a chance to prove their case on the merits.

■ JUSTICE STEVENS, with whom JUSTICE BLACKMUN joins, dissenting.

Three propositions are clear to me: (1) respondents have adequately alleged "injury in fact"; (2) their injury is fairly traceable to the conduct that they claim to be unlawful; and (3) the "separation of powers" principle does not create a jurisdictional obstacle to the consideration of the merits of their claim.

I

Respondents, the parents of black school children, have alleged that their children are unable to attend fully desegregated schools because large numbers of white children in the areas in which respondents reside attend private schools which do not admit minority children. The Court, Justice Brennan, and I all agree that this is an adequate allegation of "injury in fact." . . .

II

In the final analysis, the wrong the respondents allege that the government has committed is to subsidize the exodus of white children from schools that would otherwise be racially integrated. The critical question in this case, therefore, is whether respondents have alleged that the government has created that kind of subsidy.

In answering that question, we must of course assume that respondents can prove what they have alleged. Furthermore, at this stage of the case we must put to one side all questions about the appropriateness of a nationwide class action. The controlling issue is whether the causal connection between the injury and the wrong has been adequately alleged.

. . . Only last term we explained the effect of . . . preferential [tax] treatment:

> Both tax exemptions and tax deductibility are a form of subsidy that is administered through the tax system. A tax exemption has much the same effect as a cash grant to the organization of the amount

[10] See, e.g., Laurence Tribe, American Constitutional Law § 3–21 (1978); Abram Chayes, Foreword: Public Law Litigation and the Burger Court, 96 Harv.L.Rev. 1, 14–22 (1982); Gene R. Nichol, Jr., Causation as a Standing Requirement: The Unprincipled Use of Judicial Restraint, 69 Ky.L.J. 185 (1980–81); Mark V. Tushnet, The New Law of Standing: A Plea for Abandonment, 62 Corn.L.Rev. 663 (1977).

> of tax it would have to pay on its income. Deductible contributions are similar to cash grants of the amount of a portion of the individual's contributions.

Regan v. Taxation With Representation of Washington, Inc., 461 U.S. 540, 544 (1983).

The purpose of this scheme, like the purpose of any subsidy, is to promote the activity subsidized. . . . If the granting of preferential tax treatment would "encourage" private segregated schools to conduct their "charitable" activities, it must follow that the withdrawal of the treatment would "discourage" them, and hence promote the process of desegregation.

We have held that when a subsidy makes a given activity more or less expensive, injury can fairly be traced to the subsidy for purposes of standing analysis because of the resulting increase or decrease in the ability to engage in the activity. Indeed, we have employed exactly this causation analysis in the same context at issue here—subsidies given private schools that practice racial discrimination. Thus, in Gilmore v. City of Montgomery, 417 U.S. 556 (1974), we easily recognized the causal connection between official policies that enhanced the attractiveness of segregated schools and the failure to bring about or maintain a desegregated public school system. Similarly, in Norwood v. Harrison, 413 U.S. 455 (1973), we concluded that the provision of textbooks to discriminatory private schools "has a significant tendency to facilitate, reinforce, and support private discrimination." . . .

This causation analysis is nothing more than a restatement of elementary economics: when something becomes more expensive, less of it will be purchased. . . . If racially discriminatory private schools lose the "cash grants" that flow from the operation of the statutes, the education they provide will become more expensive and hence less of their services will be purchased. [T]he withdrawal of the subsidy for segregated schools means the incentive structure facing white parents who seek such schools for their children will be altered. Thus, the laws of economics, not to mention the laws of Congress embodied in §§ 170 and 501(c)(3), compel the conclusion that the injury respondents have alleged—the increased segregation of their children's schools because of the ready availability of private schools that admit whites only—will be redressed if these schools' operations are inhibited through the denial of preferential tax treatment.

III

Considerations of tax policy, economics, and pure logic all confirm the conclusion that respondents' injury in fact is fairly traceable to the government's allegedly wrongful conduct. The Court therefore is forced to introduce the concept of "separation of powers" into its analysis. The Court writes that the separation of powers "explains why our cases preclude the conclusion" that respondents' injury is fairly traceable to the conduct they challenge.

The Court could mean one of three things by its invocation of the separation of powers. First, it could simply be expressing the idea that if the plaintiff lacks Article III standing to bring a lawsuit, then there is no "case or controversy" within the meaning of Article III and hence the matter is not within the area of responsibility assigned to the judiciary by the Constitution. . . . While there can be no quarrel with this proposition, in itself it provides no guidance for determining if the injury respondents have alleged is fairly traceable to the conduct they have challenged.

Second, the Court could be saying that it will require a more direct causal connection when it is troubled by the separation of powers implications of the case before it. That approach confuses the standing doctrine with the justiciability of the issues that respondents seek to raise. The purpose of the standing inquiry is to measure the plaintiff's stake in the outcome, not whether a court has the authority to provide it with the outcome it seeks. . . .

Thus, the " 'fundamental aspect of standing' is that it focuses primarily on the *party* seeking to get his complaint before the federal court rather than 'on the issues he wishes to have adjudicated,' " United States v. Richardson, 418 U.S. 166, 174 (1974) (emphasis in original). The strength of the plaintiff's interest in the outcome has nothing to do with whether the relief it seeks would intrude upon the prerogatives of other branches of government; the possibility that the relief might be inappropriate does not lessen the plaintiff's stake in obtaining that relief. If a plaintiff presents a nonjusticiable issue, or seeks relief that a court may not award, then its complaint should be dismissed for those reasons, and not because the plaintiff lacks a stake in obtaining that relief and hence has no standing. Imposing an undefined but clearly more rigorous standard for redressability for reasons unrelated to the causal nexus between the injury and the challenged conduct can only encourage undisciplined, ad hoc litigation, a result that would be avoided if the Court straightforwardly considered the justiciability of the issues respondents seek to raise, rather than using those issues to obfuscate standing analysis.

Third, the Court could be saying that it will not treat as legally cognizable injuries that stem from an administrative decision concerning how enforcement resources will be allocated. This surely is an important point. Respondents do seek to restructure the IRS' mechanisms for enforcing the legal requirement that discriminatory institutions not receive tax-exempt status. Such restructuring would dramatically affect the way in which the IRS exercises its prosecutorial discretion. The executive requires latitude to decide how best to enforce the law, and in general the Court may well be correct that the exercise of that discretion, especially in the tax context, is unchallengeable.

However, as the Court also recognizes, this principle does not apply when suit is brought "to enforce specific legal obligations whose violation works a direct harm." . . . Here, respondents contend that the IRS is violating a specific constitutional limitation on its enforcement discretion. There is a solid basis for that contention. In *Norwood*, we wrote:

> A state's constitutional obligation requires it to steer clear, not only of operating the old dual system of racially segregated schools, but also of giving significant aid to institutions that practice racial or other invidious discrimination.

Gilmore echoed this theme:

> [A]ny tangible state assistance, outside the generalized services government might provide to private segregated schools in common with other schools, and with all citizens, is constitutionally prohibited if it has "a significant tendency to facilitate, reinforce, and support private discrimination." . . .

Respondents contend that these cases limit the enforcement discretion enjoyed by the IRS. They establish, respondents argue, that the IRS cannot provide "cash grants" to discriminatory schools through preferential tax treatment without running afoul of a constitutional duty to refrain from "giving significant aid" to these institutions. Similarly, respondents claim that the Internal Revenue Code itself, as construed in Bob Jones University v. United States, 461 U.S. 574 (1983), constrains enforcement discretion.[12] It has been clear since Marbury v. Madison, 1 Cranch (5 U.S.) 137 (1803), that "[i]t is emphatically the province and duty of the judicial department to say what the law is." Deciding whether the Treasury has violated a specific legal limitation on its enforcement discretion does not intrude upon the prerogative of the executive, for in so deciding we are merely saying "what the law is." Surely the question whether the Constitution or the Code limits enforcement discretion is one within the judiciary's competence, and I do not believe that the question whether the law, as enunciated in *Gilmore, Norwood*, and *Bob Jones*, imposes such an obligation upon the IRS is so insubstantial that respondents' attempt to raise it should be defeated for lack of subject-matter jurisdiction on the ground that it infringes the executive's prerogatives.

In short, I would deal with the question of the legal limitations on the IRS' enforcement discretion on the merits, rather than by making the untenable assumption that the granting of preferential tax treatment to segregated schools does not make those schools more attractive to white students and hence does not inhibit the process of desegregation. I respectfully dissent.

NOTES ON ALLEN V. WRIGHT

1. QUESTIONS AND COMMENTS ON *ALLEN V. WRIGHT*

Justice O'Connor's opinion for the Court in *Allen* rejected as insufficient to establish standing two alleged injuries suffered by the plaintiffs. The first was that all members of the public are injured when the government does not obey the law. The second was that all blacks are stigmatized when the government discriminates on the basis of race. Is it factually accurate to say that neither of these characterizations describes a real injury? If not, why are these injuries not cognizable in a court of law?

The *Allen* Court was nonetheless unanimous in concluding that the plaintiffs had suffered an injury sufficient to confer standing to sue. As Justice O'Connor said, it was "their children's diminished ability to receive an education in a racially integrated school" that sufficed to get the plaintiffs over the first standing hurdle. Even though a sufficient injury to establish standing had been alleged, however, the Court held that the plaintiffs lacked standing because their injury was not caused by the government conduct of which they complained. Does the concept of causation used by the majority reflect a factual conclusion or a legal conclusion? That is, does the majority mean to say that the IRS policy was factually irrelevant to the injury asserted by the plaintiffs? Or does it mean to say that whatever causal relationship that exists is a constitutionally insufficient basis for filing a lawsuit? Where might such "proximate cause" principles come from? From the "case" or "controversy" language of Article III? From separation of powers principles?

Justice Stevens joins issue with the majority on whether it is better to resolve the issues in *Allen* through an interpretation of the constitutional re-

[12] In *Bob Jones* we clearly indicated that the Internal Revenue Code not only permits but in fact requires the denial of tax-exempt status to racially discriminatory private schools. . . .

quirements for standing or through a resolution of the merits of the plaintiffs' claims. As Justice Stevens recognizes, a holding that the plaintiffs have standing does not necessarily mean that they will win on the merits, even if they can establish as true all of the facts asserted in their complaint. Would it have been better to resolve *Allen* on the merits? Is standing an undesirable procedural hurdle? Or are there advantages in creating an independent law of standing to act as a preliminary screening device for claims at the frontiers of constitutional law?

2. BIBLIOGRAPHY

The issue of standing has generated an enormous literature. Among the many articles criticizing the modern law of standing are Lee A. Albert, Justiciability and Theories of Judicial Review: A Remote Relationship, 50 S.Cal.L.Rev. 1139 (1977); Lee A. Albert, Standing to Challenge Administrative Action: An Inadequate Surrogate for Claim for Relief, 83 Yale L.J. 425 (1974); David P. Currie, Misunderstanding Standing, 1981 Supreme Court Rev. 41 (1981); Donald L. Doernberg, "We the People": John Locke, Collective Constitutional Rights, and Standing to Challenge Government Action, 73 Cal.L.Rev. 52 (1985); Richard H. Fallon, Jr., Of Justiciability, Remedies, and Public Law Litigation: Notes on the Jurisprudence of *Lyons*, 59 N.Y.U.L.Rev. 1 (1984); William A. Fletcher, The Structure of Standing, 98 Yale L.J. 221 (1988); C. Douglas Floyd, The Justiciability Decisions of the Burger Court, 60 Notre Dame Law. 862 (1985); James C. Hill and Thomas E. Baker, Dam Federal Jurisdiction!, 32 Emory L.J. 1 (1983); David A. Logan, Standing to Sue: A Proposed Separation of Powers Analysis, 1984 Wis.L.Rev. 37 (1984); Gene R. Nichol, Jr., Injury and the Disintegration of Article III, 74 Cal.L.Rev. 1915 (1986); Gene R. Nichol, Jr., Abusing Standing: A Comment on *Allen v. Wright*, 133 U.Pa.L.Rev. 635 (1985); Gene R. Nichol, Jr., Rethinking Standing, 72 Cal.L.Rev. 68 (1984); Antonin Scalia, The Doctrine of Standing as an Essential Element of Separation of Powers, 17 Suffolk U.L.Rev. 881 (1983); Eric J. Segall, Standing Between the Court and the Commentators: A Necessity Rationale for Public Actions, 54 U. Pitt. L. Rev. 351 (1993); and Mark V. Tushnet, The New Law of Standing: A Plea for Abandonment, 62 Corn. L.Rev. 663 (1977).

City of Los Angeles v. Lyons

United States Supreme Court, 1983.
461 U.S. 95.

■ JUSTICE WHITE delivered the opinion of the Court. . . .

I

This case began on February 7, 1977, when respondent, Adolph Lyons, filed a complaint for damages, injunction, and declaratory relief in the United States District Court for the Central District of California. The defendants were the City of Los Angeles and four of its police officers. The complaint alleged that on October 6, 1976, at 2 a.m., Lyons was stopped by the defendant officers for a traffic or vehicle code violation and that although Lyons offered no resistance or threat whatsoever, the officers, without provocation or justification, seized Lyons and applied a "chokehold"[1]—

[1] The police control procedures at issue in this case are referred to as "control holds," "chokeholds," "strangleholds," and "neck restraints." All these terms refer to two basic control procedures: the "carotid" hold and the "bar arm" hold. In the "carotid" hold, an officer posi-

either the "bar arm control" hold or the "carotid-artery control" hold or both—rendering him unconscious and causing damage to his larynx. . . . Count V, with which we are principally concerned here, sought a preliminary and permanent injunction against the city barring the use of the control holds. That count alleged that the city's police officers, "pursuant to the authorization, instruction and encouragement of defendant City of Los Angeles, regularly and routinely apply these choke holds in innumerable situations where they are not threatened by the use of any deadly force whatsoever," that numerous persons have been injured as the result of the application of the chokeholds, that Lyons and others similarly situated are threatened with irreparable injury in the form of bodily injury and loss of life, and that Lyons "justifiably fears that any contact he has with Los Angeles Police officers may result in his being choked and strangled to death without provocation, justification or other legal excuse." . . . Injunctive relief was sought against the use of the control holds "except in situations where the proposed victim of said control reasonably appears to be threatening the immediate use of deadly force." . . .

The District Court [issued] a preliminary injunction. [It] found that Lyons had been stopped for a traffic infringement and that without provocation or legal justification the officers involved had applied a "department-authorized chokehold which resulted in injuries to the plaintiff." The court further found that the department authorizes the use of the holds in situations where no one is threatened by death or grievous bodily harm, that officers are insufficiently trained, that the use of the holds involves a high risk of injury or death as then employed, and that their continued use in situations where neither death nor serious bodily injury is threatened "is unconscionable in a civilized society." The court concluded that such use violated Lyons' substantive due process rights under the Fourteenth Amendment. A preliminary injunction was entered enjoining "the use of both the carotid artery and bar arm holds under circumstances which do not threaten death or serious bodily injury." An improved training program and regular reporting and recordkeeping were also ordered.[3] The Court of Appeals affirmed. . . . We granted certiorari and now reverse.

II

Since our grant of certiorari, circumstances pertinent to the case have changed. Originally, Lyons' complaint alleged that at least two deaths had occurred as a result of the application of chokeholds by the police. His first amended complaint alleged that 10 chokehold-related deaths had occurred. By May 1982, there had been five more such deaths. On May 6, 1982, the Chief of Police in Los Angeles prohibited the use of the bar-arm chokehold in any circumstances. A few days later, on May 12, 1982, the Board of Police Commissioners imposed a six-month moratorium on the use of the ca-

---

tioned behind a subject places one arm around the subject's neck and holds the wrist of that arm with his other hand. The officer, by using his lower forearm and bicep muscle, applies pressure concentrating on the carotid arteries located on the sides of the subject's neck. The "carotid" hold is capable of rendering the subject unconscious by diminishing the flow of oxygenated blood to the brain. The "bar arm" hold, which is administered similarly, applies pressure at the front of the subject's neck. "Bar arm" pressure causes pain, reduces the flow of oxygen to the lungs, and may render the subject unconscious.

[3] By its terms, the injunction was to continue in force until the court approved the training program to be presented to it. It is fair to assume that such approval would not be given if the program did not confine the use of the strangleholds to those situations in which their use, in the view of the District Court, would be constitutional. Because of successive stays entered by the Court of Appeals and by this Court, the injunction has not gone into effect.

rotid-artery chokehold except under circumstances where deadly force is authorized.[4]

[Lyons argues] that in light of changed conditions, an injunctive decree is now unnecessary because he is no longer subject to a threat of injury. He urges that the preliminary injunction should be vacated. The city, on the other hand, while acknowledging that subsequent events have significantly changed the posture of this case, . . . asserts that the case is not moot because the moratorium is not permanent and may be lifted at any time.

We agree with the city that the case is not moot, since the moratorium by its terms is not permanent. Intervening events have not "irrevocably eradicated the effects of the alleged violation." County of Los Angeles v. Davis, 440 U.S. 625, 631 (1979). We nevertheless hold, for another reason, that the federal courts are without jurisdiction to entertain Lyons' claim for injunctive relief.

III

. . . In O'Shea v. Littleton, 414 U.S. 488 (1974), . . . a class of plaintiffs [claimed] that they had been subjected to discriminatory enforcement of the criminal law. Among other things, a county magistrate and judge were accused of discriminatory conduct in various respects, such as sentencing members of plaintiff's class more harshly than other defendants. . . . We [held that] the complaint [failed] to allege a case or controversy. Although it was claimed . . . that particular members of the plaintiff class had actually suffered from the alleged unconstitutional practices, we observed that "[p]ast exposure to illegal conduct does not in itself show a present case or controversy regarding injunctive relief . . . if unaccompanied by any continuing, present adverse effects." Past wrongs were evidence bearing on "whether there is a real and immediate threat of repeated injury." But the prospect of future injury rested "on the likelihood that [plaintiffs] will again be arrested for and charged with violations of the criminal law and will again be subjected to bond proceedings, trial, or sentencing before petitioners." The most that could be said for plaintiffs' standing was "that *if* [plaintiffs] proceed to violate an unchallenged law and *if* they are charged, held to answer, and tried in any proceedings before petitioners, they will be subjected to the discriminatory practices that petitioners are alleged to have followed." We could not find a case or controversy in those circumstances: the threat to the plaintiffs was not "sufficiently real and immediate to show an existing controversy simply because they anticipate violating lawful criminal statutes and being tried for their offenses. . . . " It was to be assumed that "[plaintiffs] will conduct their activities within the law and so avoid prosecution and conviction as well as exposure to the challenged course of conduct said to be followed by petitioners."

We further observed that case-or-controversy considerations "obviously shade into those determining whether the complaint states a sound basis for equitable relief," and went on to hold that even if the complaint presented an existing case or controversy, an adequate basis for equitable relief against petitioners had not been demonstrated:

---

[4] The Board of Police Commissioners directed the Los Angeles Police Department (LAPD) staff to use and assess the effectiveness of alternative control techniques and report its findings to the board every two months. Prior to oral argument in this case, two such reports had been submitted, but the board took no further action. On November 9, 1982, the board extended the moratorium until it had the "opportunity to review and evaluate" a third report from the Police Department. Insofar as we are advised, the third report has yet to be submitted.

> [Plaintiffs] have failed, moreover, to establish the basic requisites of the issuance of equitable relief in these circumstances—the likelihood of substantial and immediate irreparable injury, and the inadequacy of remedies at law. We have already canvassed the necessarily conjectural nature of the threatened injury to which [plaintiffs] are allegedly subjected. And if any of the [plaintiffs] are ever prosecuted and face trial, or if they are illegally sentenced, there are available state and federal procedures which could provide relief from the wrongful conduct alleged.

Another relevant decision for present purposes is Rizzo v. Goode, 423 U.S. 362 (1976), a case in which plaintiffs alleged widespread illegal and unconstitutional police conduct aimed at minority citizens and against city residents in general. The Court reiterated the holding in *O'Shea* that past wrongs do not in themselves amount to that real and immediate threat of injury necessary to make out a case or controversy. The claim of injury rested upon "what one of a small, unnamed minority of policemen might do to them in the future because of that unknown policeman's perception" of departmental procedures. This hypothesis was "even more attenuated than those allegations of future injury found insufficient in *O'Shea* to warrant [the] invocation of federal jurisdiction." The Court also held that plaintiffs' showing at trial of a relatively few instances of violations by individual police officers, without any showing of a deliberate policy on behalf of the named defendants, did not provide a basis for equitable relief. . . .

IV

No extension of *O'Shea* and *Rizzo* is necessary to hold that respondent Lyons has failed to demonstrate a case or controversy with the city that would justify the equitable relief sought.[6] Lyons' standing to seek the injunction requested depended on whether he was likely to suffer future injury from the use of the chokeholds by police officers. . . . That Lyons may have been illegally choked by the police on October 6, 1976, while presumably affording Lyons standing to claim damages against the individual officers and perhaps against the city, does nothing to establish a real and immediate threat that he would again be stopped for a traffic violation, or for any other offense, by an officer or officers who would illegally choke him into unconsciousness without any provocation or resistance on his part. The additional allegation in the complaint that the police in Los Angeles routinely apply chokeholds in situations where they are not threatened by the use of deadly force falls far short of the allegations that would be necessary to establish a case or controversy between these parties.

In order to establish an actual controversy in this case, Lyons would have had not only to allege that he would have another encounter with the police but also to make the incredible assertion either (1) that *all* police officers in Los Angeles *always* choke any citizen with whom they happen to have an encounter, whether for the purpose of arrest, issuing a citation, or for questioning, or (2) that the city ordered or authorized police officers to act in such manner. Although Count V alleged that the city authorized the use of the control holds in situations where deadly force was not threatened, it did not indicate why Lyons might be realistically threatened by police officers who acted within the strictures of the city's policy. If, for ex-

---

[6] The city states in its brief that . . . "[t]he parties agreed and advised the District Court that the respondent's damages claim could be severed from his effort to obtain equitable relief." Respondent does not suggest otherwise. This case, therefore, as it came to us, is on all fours with *O'Shea* and should be judged as such.

ample, chokeholds were authorized to be used only to counter resistance to an arrest by a suspect, or to thwart an effort to escape, any future threat to Lyons from the city's policy or from the conduct of police officers would be no more real than the possibility that he would again have an encounter with the police and that either he would illegally resist arrest or detention or the officers would disobey their instructions and again render him unconscious without any provocation.[7]

Under *O'Shea* and *Rizzo*, these allegations were an insufficient basis to provide a federal court with jurisdiction to entertain Count V of the complaint.[8] . . . For several reasons—each of them infirm in our view—the Court of Appeals [thought that *O'Shea* and *Rizzo* were distinguishable.]

First, the Court of Appeals thought that Lyons was more immediately threatened than the plaintiffs in those cases since . . . Lyons need only be stopped for a minor traffic violation to be subject to the strangleholds. But even assuming that Lyons would again be stopped for a traffic or other violation in the reasonably near future, it is untenable to assert, and the complaint made no such allegation, that strangleholds are applied by the Los Angeles police to every citizen who is stopped or arrested regardless of the conduct of the person stopped. We cannot agree that the "odds" that Lyons would not only again be stopped for a traffic violation but would also be subjected to a chokehold without any provocation whatsoever are sufficient to make out a federal case for equitable relief. We note that five months elapsed between October 6, 1976, and the filing of the complaint, yet there was no allegation of further unfortunate encounters between Lyons and the police.

---

[7] The centerpiece of Justice Marshall's dissent is that Lyons had standing to challenge the city's policy because to recover damages he would have to prove that what allegedly occurred on October 6, 1976, was pursuant to city authorization. We agree completely that for Lyons to succeed in his damages action, it would be necessary to prove that what happened to him—that is, as alleged, he was choked without any provocation or legal excuse whatsoever—was pursuant to a city policy. For several reasons, however, it does not follow that Lyons had standing to seek the injunction prayed for in Count V.

First, Lyons alleges [that the city authorizes] the use of chokeholds "in situations where [the officers] are threatened by far less than deadly force." This is not equivalent to the unbelievable assertion that the city either orders or authorizes application of the chokeholds where there is no resistance or other provocation.

Second, even if such an allegation is thought to be contained in the complaint, it is belied by the record made on the application for preliminary injunction.

Third, even if the complaint must be read as containing an allegation that officers are authorized to apply the chokeholds where there is no resistance or other provocation, it does not follow that Lyons has standing to seek an injunction against the application of the restraint holds in situations that he has not experienced, as for example, where the suspect resists arrest or tries to escape but does not threaten the use of deadly force. Yet that is precisely the scope of the injunction that Lyons [sought].

Fourth, and in any event, to have a case or controversy with the city . . . , Lyons would have to credibly allege that he faced a realistic threat from the future application of the city's policy. Justice Marshall nowhere confronts this requirement—the necessity that Lyons demonstrate that he, himself, will not only again be stopped by the police but will also be choked without any provocation or legal excuse. Justice Marshall plainly does not agree with that requirement, and he was in dissent in *O'Shea v. Littleton*. We are at issue in that respect.

[8] As previously indicated, Lyons alleged that he feared he would be choked in any, future encounter with the police. The reasonableness of Lyons' fear is dependent upon the likelihood of a recurrence of the allegedly unlawful conduct. It is the *reality* of the threat of repeated injury that is relevant to the standing inquiry, not the plaintiff's subjective apprehensions. The emotional consequences of a prior act simply are not a sufficient basis for an injunction absent a real and immediate threat of future injury by the defendant. Of course, emotional upset is a relevant consideration in a damages action.

Of course, it may be that among the countless encounters between the police and the citizens of a great city such as Los Angeles, there will be certain instances in which strangleholds will be illegally applied and injury and death unconstitutionally inflicted on the victim. As we have said, however, it is no more than conjecture to suggest that in every instance of a traffic stop, arrest, or other encounter between the police and a citizen, the police will act unconstitutionally and inflict injury without provocation or legal excuse. And it is surely no more than speculation to assert either that Lyons himself will again be involved in one of those unfortunate instances, or that he will be arrested in the future and provoke the use of a chokehold by resisting arrest, attempting to escape, or threatening deadly force or serious bodily injury.

Second, the Court of Appeals viewed *O'Shea* and *Rizzo* as cases in which the plaintiffs sought "massive structural" relief against the local law enforcement systems and therefore [thought] that the holdings in those cases were inapposite to cases such as this where the plaintiff, according to the Court of Appeals, seeks to enjoin only an "established," "sanctioned" police practice assertedly violative of constitutional rights. *O'Shea* and *Rizzo*, however, cannot be so easily confined to their facts. If Lyons has made no showing that he is realistically threatened by a repetition of his experience of October 1976, then he has not met the requirements for seeking an injunction in a federal court, whether the injunction contemplates intrusive structural relief or the cessation of a discrete practice.

The Court of Appeals also asserted that Lyons "had a live and active claim" against the city "if only for a period of a few seconds" while the stranglehold was being applied to him and that for two reasons the claim had not become moot so as to disentitle Lyons to injunctive relief: First, because under normal rules of equity, a case does not become moot merely because the complained of conduct has ceased; and second, because Lyons' claim is "capable of repetition but evading review" and therefore should be heard. We agree that Lyons had a live controversy with the city. Indeed, he still has a claim for damages against the city that appears to meet all Article III requirements. Nevertheless, the issue here is not whether that claim has become moot but whether Lyons meets the preconditions for asserting an injunctive claim in a federal forum. The equitable doctrine that cessation of the challenged conduct does not bar an injunction is of little help in this respect, for Lyons' lack of standing does not rest on the termination of the police practice but on the speculative nature of his claim that he will again experience injury as the result of that practice even if continued.

The rule that a claim does not become moot where it is capable of repetition, yet evades review, is likewise inapposite. Lyons' claim that he was illegally strangled remains to be litigated in his suit for damages; in no sense does that claim "evade" review. Furthermore, the capable-of-repetition doctrine applies only in exceptional situations, and generally only where the named plaintiff can make a reasonable showing that he will again be subjected to the alleged illegality. As we have indicated, Lyons has not made this demonstration.

The record and findings . . . do not improve Lyons' position with respect to standing. . . . There was no finding that Lyons faced a real and immediate threat of again being illegally choked. The city's policy was described as authorizing the use of the strangleholds "under circumstances where no one is threatened with death or grievous bodily harm." That policy was not further described, but the record before the court contained the department's existing policy with respect to the employment of chokeholds. Nothing in that policy, contained in a police department manual, suggests that the chokeholds, or other kinds of force for that matter, are authorized absent some resistance or other provocation by the arrestee or other suspect.[9] On the contrary, police officers were instructed to use chokeholds only when lesser degrees of force do not suffice and then only "to gain control of a suspect who is violently resisting the officer or trying to escape." . . .

V

Lyons fares no better if it be assumed that his pending damages suit affords him Article III standing to seek an injunction as a remedy for the claim arising out of the October 1976 events. The equitable remedy is unavailable absent a showing of irreparable injury, a requirement that cannot be met where there is no showing of any real or immediate threat that the plaintiff will be wronged again. . . . The speculative nature of Lyons' claim of future injury requires a finding that this prerequisite of equitable relief has not been fulfilled. . . . Absent a sufficient likelihood that he will again be wronged in a similar way, Lyons is no more entitled to an injunction than any other citizen of Los Angeles; and a federal court may not entertain a claim by any or all citizens who no more than assert that certain practices of law enforcement officers are unconstitutional. Cf. Schlesinger v. Reservists Committee to Stop the War, 418 U.S. 208 (1974). . . .

We decline the invitation to slight the preconditions for equitable relief; for as we have held, recognition of the need for a proper balance between state and federal authority counsels restraint in the issuance of injunctions against state officers engaged in the administration of the states' criminal laws in the absence of irreparable injury which is both great and immediate. *O'Shea*, supra, at 499; Younger v. Harris, 401 U.S. 37, 46 (1971). . . . In exercising their equitable powers federal courts must recognize "[t]he special delicacy of the adjustment to be preserved between federal equitable power and state administration of its own law." Stefanelli v. Minard, 342 U.S. 117, 120 (1951). The Court of Appeals failed to apply these factors properly and therefore erred in finding that the District Court had not abused its discretion in entering an injunction in this case.

As we noted in *O'Shea*, withholding injunctive relief does not mean that the "federal law will exercise no deterrent effect in these circumstances." If Lyons has suffered an injury barred by the federal Constitution, he has a remedy for damages under § 1983. Furthermore, those who deliberately deprive a citizen of his constitutional rights risk conviction under the federal criminal laws.

Beyond these considerations the state courts need not impose the same standing or remedial requirements that govern federal-court proceedings. The individual states may permit their courts to use injunctions to oversee the conduct of law enforcement authorities on a continuing basis. But this

---

[9] The dissent notes that a LAPD training officer stated that the police are authorized to employ the control holds whenever an officer "feels" that there is about to be a bodily attack. The dissent's emphasis on the word "*feels*" apparently is intended to suggest that LAPD officers are authorized to apply the holds whenever they "feel" like it. If there is a distinction between permitting the use of the holds when there is a "threat" of serious bodily harm, and when the officer "feels" or believes there is about to be a bodily attack, the dissent has failed to make it clear. The dissent does not, because it cannot, point to any written or oral pronouncement by the LAPD or any evidence showing a pattern of police behavior that would indicate that the official policy would permit the application of the control holds on a suspect who was not offering, or threatening to offer, physical resistance.

is not the role of a federal court, absent far more justification than Lyons has proffered in this case.

The judgment of the Court of Appeals is accordingly

Reversed.

■ JUSTICE MARSHALL, with whom JUSTICE BRENNAN, JUSTICE BLACKMUN, and JUSTICE STEVENS join, dissenting.

The District Court found that the City of Los Angeles authorizes its police officers to apply life-threatening chokeholds to citizens who pose no threat of violence, and that respondent, Adolph Lyons, was subjected to such a chokehold. The Court today holds that a federal court is without power to enjoin the enforcement of the city's policy, no matter how flagrantly unconstitutional it may be. Since no one can show that he will be choked in the future, no one—not even a person who, like Lyons, has almost been choked to death—has standing to challenge the continuation of the policy. The city is free to continue the policy indefinitely as long as it is willing to pay damages for the injuries and deaths that result. I dissent from this unprecedented and unwarranted approach to standing.

There is plainly a "case or controversy" concerning the constitutionality of the city's chokehold policy. The constitutionality of that policy is directly implicated by Lyons' claim for damages against the city. . . . Lyons therefore has standing to challenge the city's chokehold policy and to obtain whatever relief a court may ultimately deem appropriate. None of our prior decisions suggests that his requests for particular forms of relief raise any additional issues concerning his standing. . . .

I

A

Respondent Adolph Lyons is a 24–year–old Negro male who resides in Los Angeles. According to the uncontradicted evidence in the record, at about 2 a.m. on October 6, 1976, Lyons was pulled over to the curb by two officers of the Los Angeles Police Department (LAPD) for a traffic infraction because one of his taillights was burned out. The officers greeted him with drawn revolvers as he exited from his car. Lyons was told to face his car and spread his legs. He did so. He was then ordered to clasp his hands and put them on top of his head. He again complied. After one of the officers completed a patdown search, Lyons dropped his hands, but was ordered to place them back above his head, and one of the officers grabbed Lyons' hands and slammed them onto his head. Lyons complained about the pain caused by the ring of keys he was holding in his hand. Within 5 to 10 seconds, the officer began to choke Lyons by applying a forearm against his throat. As Lyons struggled for air, the officer handcuffed him, but continued to apply the chokehold until he blacked out. When Lyons regained consciousness, he was lying face down on the ground, choking, gasping for air, and spitting up blood and dirt. He had urinated and defecated. He was issued a traffic citation and released.

On February 7, 1977, Lyons commenced this action under § 1983 against the individual officers and the city . . . seeking damages and declaratory and injunctive relief. He claimed that he was subjected to a chokehold without justification and that defendant officers were "carrying out the official policies, customs and practices of the Los Angeles police department and the city of Los Angeles." . . . Lyons alleged that the city authorizes the use of chokeholds "in innumerable situations where [the police] are not threatened by the use of any deadly force whatsoever."

B

Although the city instructs its officers that use of a chokehold does not constitute deadly force, since 1975 no less than 16 persons have died following the use of a chokehold by an LAPD police officer. Twelve have been Negro males.[3] The evidence submitted to the District Court established that for many years it has been the official policy of the city to permit police officers to employ chokeholds in a variety of situations where they face no threat of violence. In reported "altercations" between LAPD officers and citizens the chokeholds are used more frequently than any other means of physical restraint. Between February 1975 and July 1980, LAPD officers applied chokeholds on at least 975 occasions, which represented more than three-quarters of the reported altercations.

It is undisputed that chokeholds pose a high and unpredictable risk of serious injury or death. Chokeholds are intended to bring a subject under control by causing pain and rendering him unconscious. Depending on the position of the officer's arm and the force applied, the victim's voluntary or involuntary reaction, and his state of health, an officer may inadvertently crush the victim's larynx, trachea, or hyoid. The result may be death caused by either cardiac arrest or asphyxiation.[7] An LAPD officer described

---

[3] Thus in a city where Negro males constitute 9 percent of the population, they have accounted for 75 percent of the deaths resulting from the use of chokeholds. . . .

[7] The physiological effects of the chokeholds were described as follows by Dr. A. Griswold, an expert in pathology:

> From a medical point of view, the bar arm control is extremely dangerous in an unpredictable fashion. Pressure from a locked forearm across the neck sufficient to compress and close the trachea applied for a sufficient period of time to cause unconsciousness from asphyxia must, to an anatomical certainty, also result in . . . a very high risk of a fractured hyoid bone or crushed larynx. The risk is substantial, but at the same time, unpredictable.
>
> It depends for one thing on which vertical portion of the neck the forearm pressure is exerted. . . .
>
> Another factor contributing to unpredictability is the reaction of the victim. [The] pressure exerted in a bar arm control . . . can result in a laryngeal spasm or seizure which simply shuts off the tracheal air passage, leading to death by asphyxiation. Also, it must result in transmission to the brain of nerve messages that there is immediate, acute danger of death. This transmission immediately sets up a "fight or flee" syndrome wherein the body reacts violently to save itself or escape. Adrenalin output increases enormously; blood oxygen is switched to muscles and strong, violent struggle ensues which is to a great extent involuntary. From a medical point of view, there would be no way to distinguish this involuntary death struggle from a wilful, voluntary resistance. Thus, an instruction to cease applying the hold when "resistance ceases" is meaningless. . . .
>
> The LAPD [operates under a] misconception . . . that the length of time for applying the hold is the sole measure of risk. This is simply not true. If sufficient force is applied, the larynx can be crushed or hyoid fractured with death ensuing, in seconds. An irreversible laryngeal spasm can also occur in seconds.
>
> From a medical point of view, the carotid control is extremely dangerous in a manner that is at least as equally unpredictable as the bar arm control.
>
> . . . When applied with sufficient pressure, this control will crush the carotid sheath against the bony structure of the neck, foreseeably shutting down the supply of oxygenated blood to the brain and leading to unconsciousness in approximately 10 to 15 seconds.
>
> However, pressure on both carotid sheaths also results in pressure, if inadvertent or unintended, on both of the vagus nerves. The vagus nerves (right and left) arise in the brain and are composed of both sensory and motor fibers. . . . Stimulation of these nerves by pressure can activate reflexes within the vagus system that can result in immediate heart stoppage (cardiac arrest). . . . There is also evidence that cardiac arrest can

the reaction of a person to being choked as "do[ing] the chicken," in reference apparently to the reactions of a chicken when its neck is wrung. The victim experiences extreme pain. His face turns blue as he is deprived of oxygen, he goes into spasmodic convulsions, his eyes roll back, his body wriggles, his feet kick up and down, and his arms move about wildly.

Although there has been no occasion to determine the precise contours of the city's chokehold policy, the evidence submitted to the District Court provides some indications. LAPD Training Officer Terry Speer testified that an officer is authorized to deploy a chokehold whenever he "*feels* that there's about to be a bodily attack made on him." (Emphasis added.) A training bulletin states that "[c]ontrol holds . . . allow officers to subdue *any* resistance by the suspects." In the proceedings below the city characterized its own policy as authorizing the use of chokeholds " 'to gain control of a suspect who is violently resisting the officer *or trying to escape*,' " to "subdue *any* resistance by the suspects," and to permit an officer, "where . . . resisted, but *not necessarily threatened with serious bodily harm or death*, . . . to subdue a suspect who forcibly resists an officer." (Emphasis added.)

The training given LAPD officers provides additional revealing evidence of the city's chokehold policy. Officer Speer testified that in instructing officers concerning the use of force, the LAPD does not distinguish between felony and misdemeanor suspects. Moreover, the officers are taught to maintain the chokehold until the suspect goes limp, despite substantial evidence that the application of a chokehold invariably induces a "fight or flee" syndrome, producing an *involuntary* struggle by the victim which can easily be misinterpreted by the officer as willful resistance that must be overcome by prolonging the chokehold and increasing the force applied. In addition, officers are instructed that the chokeholds can be safely deployed for up to three or four minutes. Robert Jarvis, the city's expert who has taught at the Los Angeles Police Academy for the past 12 years, admitted that officers are never told that the bar-arm control can cause death if applied for just two seconds. Of the nine deaths for which evidence was submitted to the District Court, the average duration of the choke where specified was approximately 40 seconds.

C

In determining the appropriateness of a preliminary injunction, the District Court . . . found that "[d]uring the course of this confrontation, said officers, without provocation or legal justification, applied a *department-authorized* chokehold which resulted in injuries to plaintiff." The court found that the "City of Los Angeles and the department authorize the use of these holds under circumstances where no one is threatened by death or grievous bodily harm." (Emphasis added.) The court concluded that the use of the chokeholds constitutes "deadly force," and that the city may not constitutionally authorize the use of such force "in situations where death or serious bodily harm is not threatened." On the basis of this conclusion, the District Court entered a preliminary injunction enjoining "the use of both the carotid-artery and bar arm holds under circumstances which do not threaten death or serious bodily injury."[10] As the Court of Ap-

result from simultaneous pressure on both vagus nerves regardless of the intensity or duration of the pressure.

[10] The preliminary injunction provided that the city itself could lift the injunction by obtaining court approval of a training program, and also required the city to keep records of all uses of chokeholds and to make those records available.

peals noted, "[a]ll the trial judge has done, so far, is to tell the city that its police officers may not apply life threatening strangleholds to persons stopped in routine police work unless the application of such force is necessary to prevent serious bodily harm to an officer."

II

. . . The Court errs in suggesting that Lyons' prayer for injunctive relief . . . concerns a policy that was not responsible for his injuries and that therefore could not support an award of damages. Ante n.7. . . . The Court apparently finds Lyons' complaint wanting because, although it alleges that he was choked without provocation and that the officers acted pursuant to an official policy, it fails to allege in haec verba that the city's policy authorizes the choking of suspects without provocation. I am aware of no case decided since the abolition of the old common-law forms of action, and the Court cites none, that in any way supports this crabbed construction of the complaint. . . .

The Court also errs in asserting that even if the complaint sufficiently alleges that the city's policy authorizes the use of chokeholds without provocation, such an allegation is in any event "belied by the record made on the application for preliminary injunction." This conclusion flatly contradicts the District Court's express factual finding . . . that the officers applied a "*department-authorized* chokehold which resulted in injuries to plaintiff." (Emphasis added.) . . .

III

Since Lyons' claim for damages plainly gives him standing, and since the success of that claim depends upon a demonstration that the city's chokehold policy is unconstitutional, it is beyond dispute that Lyons has properly invoked the District Court's authority to adjudicate the constitutionality of the city's chokehold policy. . . . The Court nevertheless holds that a federal court has no power under Article III to adjudicate Lyons' request, in the same lawsuit, for injunctive relief with respect to that very policy. This anomalous result is not supported either by precedent or by the fundamental concern underlying the standing requirement. Moreover, by fragmenting a single claim into multiple claims for particular types of relief and requiring a separate showing of standing for each form of relief, the decision today departs from this Court's traditional conception of standing and of the remedial powers of the federal courts.

A

It is simply disingenuous for the Court to assert that its decision requires "[n]o extension" of O'Shea v. Littleton, 414 U.S. 488 (1974), and Rizzo v. Goode, 423 U.S. 362 (1976). In contrast to this case *O'Shea* and *Rizzo* involved disputes focusing solely on the threat of future injury which the plaintiffs in those cases alleged they faced. In *O'Shea* the plaintiffs did not allege past injury and did not seek compensatory relief.[13] In *Rizzo*, the plaintiffs sought only declaratory and injunctive relief and alleged past in-

---

The District Court refrained from determining the precise nature of the city's policy given the limited nature of its inquiry at the preliminary injunction stage.

[13] Although counsel for the plaintiffs in *O'Shea* suggested at oral argument that certain plaintiffs had been exposed to illegal conduct in the past, in fact "[n]o damages were sought against the petitioners . . . nor were any specific instances involving the individually named respondents set forth in the claim against these judicial officers." The Court referred to the absence of past injury repeatedly.

stances of police misconduct only in an attempt to establish the substantiality of the threat of future injury. . . .

These decisions do not support the Court's holding today. As the Court recognized in *O'Shea*, standing under Article III is established by an allegation of " 'threatened or actual injury.' " Because the plaintiffs in *O'Shea* [and] *Rizzo* did not seek to redress past injury, their standing to sue depended entirely on the risk of future injury they faced. Apart from the desire to eliminate the possibility of future injury, the plaintiffs in those cases had no other personal stake in the outcome of the controversies.

By contrast, Lyons' request for prospective relief is coupled with his claim for damages based on past injury. In addition to the risk that he will be subjected to a chokehold in the future, Lyons has suffered past injury. Because he has a live claim for damages, he need not rely solely on the threat of future injury to establish his personal stake in the outcome of the controversy. In the cases relied on by the majority, the Court simply had no occasion to decide whether a plaintiff who has standing to litigate a dispute must clear a separate standing hurdle with respect to each form of relief sought.[17]

B

. . . Because Lyons has a claim for damages against the city, and because he cannot prevail on that claim unless he demonstrates that the city's chokehold policy violates the Constitution, his personal stake in the outcome of the controversy adequately assures an adversary presentation of his challenge to the constitutionality of the policy.[18] Moreover, the resolution of this challenge will be largely dispositive of his requests for declaratory and injunctive relief. No doubt the requests for injunctive relief may raise additional questions. But these questions involve familiar issues relating to the appropriateness of particular forms of relief, and have never been thought to implicate a litigant's standing to sue. The denial of standing separately to seek injunctive relief therefore cannot be justified by the basic concern underlying the Article III standing requirement.

C

By fragmenting the standing inquiry and imposing a separate standing hurdle with respect to each form of relief sought, the decision today departs significantly from this Court's traditional conception of the standing requirement and the remedial powers of the federal courts. We have never required more than that a plaintiff have standing to litigate a claim.

---

[17] The Court's reliance on *Rizzo* is misplaced for another reason. In *Rizzo* the Court concluded that the evidence presented at trial failed to establish an "affirmative link between the occurrence of the various incidents of police misconduct and the adoption of any plan or policy by [defendants]." Because the misconduct being challenged was, in the Court's view, the result of the behavior of unidentified officials not named as defendants rather than any policy of the named defendants—the city Managing Director, and the Police Commissioner—the Court had "serious doubts" whether a case or controversy existed between the plaintiffs and those defendants. Here, by contrast, Lyons has clearly established a case or controversy between himself and the city concerning the constitutionality of the city's policy. . . .

[18] It is irrelevant that the District Court has severed Lyons' claim for damages for his claim for injunctive relief. If the District Court, in deciding whether to issue an injunction, upholds city's policy against constitutional attack, this ruling will be res judicata with respect to Lyons' claim for damages. The severance of the claims therefore does not diminish Lyons' incentive to establish the unconstitutionality of the policy.

It is unnecessary to decide here whether the standing of a plaintiff who alleges past injury that is legally redressable depends on whether he specifically seeks damages.

Whether he will be entitled to obtain particular forms of relief should he prevail has never been understood to be an issue of standing. . . .

1

Our cases uniformly state that the touchstone of the Article III standing requirement is the plaintiff's personal stake in the underlying dispute, not in the particular types of relief sought. . . . The personal stake of a litigant depends, in turn, on whether he has alleged a legally redressable injury. In determining whether a plaintiff has a sufficient personal stake in the outcome of a controversy, this Court has asked whether he "personally has suffered some actual *or* threatened injury," Gladstone, Realtors v. Village of Bellwood, 441 U.S. 91, 99 (1979) (emphasis added), whether the injury "fairly can be traced to the challenged action," Simon v. Eastern Kentucky Welfare Rights Org., 426 U.S. 26, 41 (1976), and whether plaintiff's injury "is likely to be redressed by a favorable decision." Id., at 38. These well-accepted criteria for determining whether a plaintiff has established the requisite personal stake do not fragment the standing inquiry into a series of discrete questions about the plaintiff's stake in each of the particular types of relief sought. Quite the contrary, they ask simply whether the plaintiff has a sufficient stake in seeking a judicial resolution of the controversy.

Lyons has alleged past injury and a risk of future injury and has linked both to the city's chokehold policy. Under established principles, the only additional question in determining standing under Article III is whether the injuries he has alleged can be remedied or prevented by *some* form of judicial relief. Satisfaction of this requirement ensures that the lawsuit does not entail the issuance of an advisory opinion without the possibility of any judicial relief, and that the exercise of a court's remedial powers will actually redress the alleged injury.[20] Therefore Lyons needs to demonstrate only that, should he prevail on the merits, "the exercise of the Court's remedial powers would redress the claimed injuries." Duke Power Co. v. Carolina Environmental Study Group, Inc., 438 U.S. 59, 74 (1978). Lyons has easily made this showing here, for monetary relief would plainly provide redress for his past injury, and prospective relief would reduce the likelihood of any future injury. Nothing more has ever been required to establish standing. . . . Until now, questions concerning remedy were relevant to the threshold issue of standing only in the limited sense that some relief must be possible. . . .

2

The Court's fragmentation of the standing inquiry is also inconsistent with the way the federal courts have treated remedial issues since the merger of law and equity. The federal practice has been to reserve considera-

[20] This limited inquiry into remedy, which addresses two *jurisdictional* concerns, provides no support for the Court's requirement that standing be separately demonstrated with respect to each particular form of relief sought. First, a court must have the power to fashion some appropriate remedy. This concern, an aspect of the more general case-or-controversy requirement, reflects the view that the adjudication of rights which a court is powerless to enforce is tantamount to an advisory opinion. See Aetna Life Ins. Co. v. Haworth, 300 U.S. 227, 241 (1937). Second, a court must determine that there is an available remedy which will have a "substantial probability," Warth v. Seldin, 422 U.S. 490, 508 (1975), of redressing the plaintiff's injury. This latter concern is merely a recasting of the causal nexus that must exist between the alleged injury and the action being challenged, and ensures that the granting of judicial relief will not be an exercise in futility. These considerations are summarized by the requirement that a plaintiff need only allege an injury that is "legally redress*able*." (Emphasis added.)

tion of the appropriate relief until after a determination of the merits, not to foreclose certain forms of relief by a ruling on the pleadings. The prayer for relief is no part of the plaintiff's cause of action. . . .

IV

Apart from the question of standing, the only remaining question presented in the petition for certiorari is whether the preliminary injunction issued by the District Court must be set aside because it "constitute[s] a substantial interference in the operation of a municipal police department." In my view it does not.

[T]he city argues that the District Court ignored the principles of federalism set forth in Rizzo v. Goode, 423 U.S. 362 (1976). The city's reliance on *Rizzo* is misplaced. That case involved an injunction which "significantly revis[ed] the internal procedures of the Philadelphia police department." The injunction required the police department to adopt " 'a comprehensive program for dealing adequately with civilian complaints' " to be formulated in accordance with extensive "guidelines" established by the District Court. Those guidelines specified detailed revisions of police manuals and rules of procedure, as well as the adoption of specific procedures for processing, screening, investigating, and adjudicating citizen complaints. In addition, the District Court supervised the implementation of the comprehensive program, issuing detailed orders concerning the posting and distribution of the revised police procedures and the drawing up of a "Citizen's Complaint Report" in a format designated by the court. The District Court also reserved jurisdiction to review the progress of the police department. This Court concluded that the sweeping nature of the injunctive relief was inconsistent with "the principles of federalism."

The principles of federalism simply do not preclude the limited preliminary injunction issued in this case. Unlike the permanent injunction at issue in *Rizzo*, the preliminary injunction involved here entails no federal supervision of the LAPD's activities. The preliminary injunction merely forbids the use of chokeholds absent the threat of deadly force, permitting their continued use where such a threat does exist. This limited ban takes the form of a preventive injunction, which has traditionally been regarded as the least intrusive form of equitable relief. Moreover, the city can remove the ban by obtaining approval of a training plan. Although the preliminary injunction also requires the city to provide records of the uses of chokeholds to respondent and to allow the court access to such records, this requirement is hardly onerous, since the LAPD already maintains records concerning the use of chokeholds.

A district court should be mindful that "federal-court intervention in the daily operation of a large city's police department . . . is undesirable and to be avoided if at all possible." *Rizzo*, supra, at 381 (Blackmun, J., dissenting). The modest interlocutory relief granted in this case differs markedly, however, from the intrusive injunction involved in *Rizzo*, and simply does not implicate the federalism concerns that arise when a federal court undertakes to "supervise the functioning of the police department."

V

Apparently because it is unwilling to rely solely on its unprecedented rule of standing, the Court goes on to conclude that, even if Lyons has standing, "[t]he equitable remedy is unavailable." . . . With the single exception of *Rizzo v. Goode*, all of the cases relied on by the Court concerned injunctions against state criminal proceedings. The rule of Younger

v. Harris, 401 U.S. 37 (1971), that such injunctions can be issued only in extraordinary circumstances in which the threat of injury is "great and immediate" reflects the venerable rule that equity will not enjoin a criminal prosecution, the fact that constitutional defenses can be raised in such a state prosecution, and an appreciation of the friction that injunctions against state judicial proceedings may produce.

Our prior decisions have repeatedly emphasized that where an injunction is not directed against a state criminal or quasi-criminal proceeding, "the relevant principles of equity, comity, and federalism" that underlie the *Younger* doctrine "have little force." Steffel v. Thompson, 415 U.S. 452, 462, (1974). Outside the special context in which the *Younger* doctrine applies, we have held that the appropriateness of injunctive relief is governed by traditional equitable considerations. See Doran v. Salem Inn, Inc., 422 U.S. 922, 930 (1975). Whatever the precise scope of the *Younger* doctrine may be, the concerns of comity and federalism that counsel restraint when a federal court is asked to enjoin a state criminal proceeding simply do not apply to an injunction directed solely at a police department.

If the preliminary injunction granted by the District Court is analyzed under general equitable principles, rather than the more stringent standards of *Younger v. Harris*, it becomes apparent that there is no rule of law that precludes equitable relief and requires that the preliminary injunction be set aside. . . .

The District Court concluded, on the basis of the facts before it, that Lyons was choked without provocation pursuant to an unconstitutional city policy. Given the necessarily preliminary nature of its inquiry, there was no way for the District Court to know the precise contours of the city's policy or to ascertain the risk that Lyons, who had alleged that the policy was being applied in a discriminatory manner, might again be subjected to a chokehold. But in view of the court's conclusion that the unprovoked choking of Lyons was pursuant to a city policy, Lyons has satisfied "the usual basis for injunctive relief, 'that there exists some cognizable danger of recurrent violation.' " Rondeau v. Mosinee Paper Corp., 422 U.S. 49, 59 (1975), quoting United States v. W. T. Grant Co., 345 U.S. 629, 633 (1953). The risk of serious injuries and deaths to other citizens also supported the decision to grant a preliminary injunction. Courts of equity have much greater latitude in granting injunctive relief "in furtherance of the public interest than . . . when only private interests are involved." Virginian R. Co. v. Railway Employees, 300 U.S. 515, 522 (1937). In this case we know that the District Court would have been amply justified in considering the risk to the public, for after the preliminary injunction was stayed, five additional deaths occurred prior to the adoption of a moratorium. See n.3, supra. Under these circumstances, I do not believe that the District Court abused its discretion. . . .

Here it is unnecessary to consider the propriety of a permanent injunction. The District Court has simply sought to protect Lyons and other citizens of Los Angeles pending a disposition of the merits. It will be time enough to consider the propriety of a permanent injunction when and if the District Court grants such relief.

VI

The Court's decision removes an entire class of constitutional violations from the equitable powers of a federal court. It immunizes from prospective equitable relief any policy that authorizes persistent deprivations of constitutional rights as long as no individual can establish with substantial certainty that he will be injured, or injured again, in the future. The Chief Justice asked in Bivens v. Six Unknown Fed. Narcotics Agents, 403 U.S. 388, 419 (1971) (dissenting opinion), "what would be the judicial response to a police order authorizing 'shoot to kill' with respect to every fugitive"? His answer was that it would be "easy to predict our collective wrath and outrage." We now learn that wrath and outrage cannot be translated into an order to cease the unconstitutional practice, but only an award of damages to those who are victimized by the practice and live to sue and to the survivors of those who are not so fortunate. Under the view expressed by the majority today, if the police adopt a policy of "shoot to kill," or a policy of shooting one out of 10 suspects, the federal courts will be powerless to enjoin its continuation. The federal judicial power is now limited to levying a toll for such a systematic constitutional violation.

NOTES ON CITY OF LOS ANGELES V. LYONS

1. QUESTIONS AND COMMENTS ON *LYONS*

The first question addressed in *Lyons* was whether the case was mooted by the moratorium on chokeholds announced after the grant of certiorari. Mootness has been described as "the doctrine of standing set in a time frame: The requisite personal interest that must exist at the commencement of the litigation (standing) must continue throughout its existence (mootness)." Henry Monaghan, Constitutional Adjudication: The Who and When, 82 Yale L.J. 1363, 1384 (1973). If, during the course of litigation, the requisite live controversy between the contending parties ceases to exist, the case will be dismissed as moot.

Plainly, *Lyons* was not moot with respect to the claim for damages. Lyons had already been injured and the extent to which he was entitled to compensation for that injury could not have been affected by the city's subsequent chokehold policy. But the only question before the Supreme Court was whether Lyons was entitled to a preliminary injunction forbidding the use of chokeholds. The Court held that this aspect of the case was not moot because the moratorium was "not permanent" and had not " 'irrevocably eradicated the effects of the alleged violation.' " If this was so, then why did Lyons lack standing? The Court could be described as holding that the injunction "case or controversy" between Lyons and the city was not moot, even though there was no "case or controversy" over the injunction to begin with. Is this what the Court meant? How can the relation between the Court's mootness and standing holdings be reconciled?

The dissent's argument on the standing issue is straightforward: Lyons alleges that he was choked and that the city is responsible because the conduct of its police officers was pursuant to official city policy. This plainly suffices to establish the "injury in fact" and "causation" components of the standing inquiry, and whether the plaintiff's injury can be remedied by an injunction rather than damages presents not a question of standing but of remedies.[a] Why

---

[a] This position is defended by Richard Fallon, Jr., in Of Justiciability, Remedies, and Public Law Litigation: Notes on the Jurisprudence of *Lyons*, 59 N.Y.U.L.Rev. 1 (1984). Fallon describes the majority as embracing a notion of "remedial standing"—that is, "a requirement that any requested remedy must be effective in redressing the injury on which standing is predicated, or some other injury sufficient to support standing." To him, it is "unnecessary and unfortunate" to regard the issue "of remedial efficacy as part of the standing inquiry" because the "constitutionalization of remedial standing intrudes into the domain of mootness" and it

did the majority reject this position? Does the majority ask any questions on the standing inquiry that would not be asked in determining whether to grant equitable relief? If not, what advantage is gained by dealing with them as questions of standing?

In the final paragraphs of its opinion, the Court added that Lyons was in any event not entitled to an injunction because he had not shown a sufficient need for one and because principles of federalism counseled restraint. Is the dissent's response to this position persuasive? How important to this debate is the fact that it was a *preliminary* injunction, not a *permanent* injunction, that was before the Court?

2. *RIZZO V. GOODE*

On the standing issue, the Court relied on O'Shea v. Littleton, 414 U.S. 488 (1974), and Rizzo v. Goode, 423 U.S. 362 (1976). *O'Shea* is described adequately in the Court's opinion. *Rizzo* is described more fully below.

Two actions against the Philadelphia Mayor, City Managing Director, and Police Commissioner were consolidated for trial. The plaintiffs were certified to represent a class consisting of all citizens of Philadelphia and an "included" class of all black citizens of Philadelphia. The gravamen of the suit was that the city did not have an effective procedure for handling citizen complaints about police misconduct. The District Court heard 250 witnesses over 21 days. They testified to approximately 40 alleged instances of police misconduct for which, in the plaintiffs view, the officers involved had not been adequately disciplined. Although there was some dispute about how many of these allegations were confirmed by the evidence, the Supreme Court agreed arguendo that there were 19 cases "occurring in the city of Philadelphia over a year's time in which numbers of police officers violated citizens' constitutional rights." The Court added:

> The District Court . . . found that the evidence did not establish the existence of any policy on the part of the named [defendants] to violate the legal and constitutional rights of the plaintiff classes, but it did find that evidence of departmental procedure indicated a tendency to discourage the filing of civilian complaints and to minimize the consequences of police misconduct.

The District Court directed that the defendants draft a "comprehensive program" for dealing with citizen complaints that adhered to detailed criteria. As the Supreme Court described in a footnote:

"diminishes the power of courts, and potentially the capacity of Congress, to protect federal rights and to provide remedies for their violation." For similar views, see Linda Fisher, Caging *Lyons:* The Availability of Injunctive Relief in Section 1983 Actions, 18 Loyola U.Chi.L.J. 1085 (1987), concluding that "[c]oncerns about recurrence are more suitably raised during consideration of the merits of an injunctive claim."

For further criticism of *Lyons*, see Laura E. Little, It's About Time: Unraveling Standing and Equitable Ripeness, 41 Buff. L. Rev. 933 (1993). Little argues that the *Lyons* Court was "ill-advised" to undertake a separate standing inquiry for equitable relief. "Threshold questions about whether a controversy is sufficiently concrete to justify federal court jurisdiction should be analytically distinct from issues bearing on whether a particular remedy is appropriate in a case." Rather, the question whether the threat of harm is sufficiently ripe to warrant an injunction should be analyzed as an issue of "equitable ripeness"—that is, as part of the law of remedies to be determined after, not before, development of a factual record.

> A judgment of considerable detail was [entered]. The existing procedure for handling complaints, embodied in the 2–page "directive 127," was expanded to an all-encompassing 14–page document reflecting the revisions suggested by the District Court's "guidelines." Directive 127 as revised was ordered by the District Court to be promulgated as such by the Police Commissioner and posted in various public areas, with copies provided anyone who either requested one or inquired generally into the procedure for lodging complaints. A "Citizen's Complaint Report" was ordered drawn up in a format designated by the court, with copies to be printed and available in sufficient quantities to the public in several locations. The department was further ordered to propose a police recruit training manual reflective of the court's "guidelines," with [the plaintiffs] then having the chance to proffer alternative suggestions. Finally, the department was directed to maintain adequate statistical records and annual summaries to provide a basis for the court's "evaluation" of the program as ordered; the court reserved jurisdiction to review [the defendant's] progress in these areas and to grant further relief as might be appropriate.

The Third Circuit affirmed on appeal, but the Supreme Court reversed. Speaking for the Court, Justice Rehnquist began with the following observations:

> The findings of fact made by the District Court . . . disclose a central paradox which permeates that court's legal conclusions. Individual police officers *not named as parties* to the action were found to have violated the constitutional rights of particular individuals, only a few of whom were parties plaintiff. As the facts developed, there was no affirmative link between the occurrence of the various incidents of police misconduct and the adoption of any plan or policy by [the defendants]—express or otherwise—showing their authorization or approval of such misconduct. Instead, the *sole* causal connection found by the District Court between [the defendants] and the individual [plaintiffs] was that in the absence of a change in police disciplinary procedures, the incidents were likely to continue to occur, *not* with respect to them but as to the members of the classes they represented. In sum, the genesis of this lawsuit—a heated dispute between individual citizens and certain policemen—has evolved into an attempt by the federal judiciary to resolve a "controversy" between the entire citizenry of Philadelphia and the [defendant] elected and appointed officials over what steps might, in the Court of Appeals' words, "appear to have the potential for prevention of future police misconduct."

Justice Rehnquist then gave three reasons for reversal. First, the Court had "serious doubts whether on the facts as found there was made out the requisite Article III case or controversy between the individually named [plaintiffs] and [defendants]." After drawing an analogy to *O'Shea*, Rehnquist concluded by observing that "insofar as the individual [plaintiffs] are concerned, we think they lacked the requisite 'personal stake in the outcome,' i.e., the order overhauling police disciplinary procedures."

Second, the Court said that relief against the named defendants was unavailable under § 1983 since they had not personally subjected any plaintiffs to the denial of any constitutional rights or in any way caused the denial of such rights. The District Court had found some 20 incidents in a city of three million inhabitants with a police force of 7500. Even the District Court thought that "the problems disclosed by the record . . . are fairly typical of [those] afflicting police departments in major urban areas." In this context, the Court concluded that no cause of action under § 1983 was stated because no sufficient pattern of behavior was shown to justify holding the defendant officials responsible for the actions of a small minority of police officers.

Finally, and "beyond considerations concerning the existence of a live controversy and threshold statutory liability," the Court felt obliged to address "an additional and novel" claim. Specifically, the plaintiffs asserted that:

> [G]iven the citizenry's "right" to be protected from unconstitutional exercises of police power, and the "need for protection from such abuses," [the plaintiffs] have a right to mandatory equitable relief in some form when those in supervisory positions do not institute steps to reduce the incidence of unconstitutional police misconduct. The scope of equity power, it is proposed, should be extended to the fashioning of prophylactic procedures for a state agency designed to minimize this kind of misconduct on the part of a handful of its employees.

> The Court found two problems with this theory. First, it departed from the "settled rule that in federal equity cases 'the nature of the violation determines the scope of the remedy.' " Second, it offended "important considerations of federalism":

> [T]he principles of federalism which play such an important part in governing the relationship between federal courts and state governments, though initially expounded and perhaps entitled to their greatest weight in cases where it was sought to enjoin a criminal prosecution in progress, have not been limited either to that situation or indeed to a criminal proceeding itself. We think these principles likewise have applicability where injunctive relief is sought not against the judicial branch of the state government, but against those in charge of state or local governments such as [the defendants] here. . . . When it injected itself by injunctive decree into the internal disciplinary affairs of this state agency, the District Court departed from these precepts.

Justice Blackmun, joined by Justices Brennan and Marshall, dissented.[b] Justice Blackmun began with the observation that "federal court intervention in the daily operation of a large city's police department . . . is undesirable and to be avoided if at all possible." Here, however, the District Court engaged in "a careful and conscientious resolution" of the matters alleged in the complaint and made "detailed findings of fact, now accepted by both sides." The remedy, moreover, "evolved with the defendant officials' consent, reluctant though that assent may have been, and it was one that the police department concededly could live with." "No one . . . disputes the apparent efficacy of the relief or the fact that it effectuated a betterment in the system and should serve to lessen the number of instances of deprival of constitutional rights. . . . "

The dissent then responded directly to the three concerns raised by the majority. On the standing issue, *O'Shea* was thought distinguishable because there the plaintiffs had not alleged a prior injury at the hands of the defendants. Moreover, the dissent accepted the District Court's conclusion that a "pattern" of constitutional violations had been shown and thought this finding relevant to the existence of a "case or controversy." On the question of "threshold

[b] Justice Stevens did not participate.

statutory liability," the dissent thought that § 1983 extended to *injunctive* relief for failure to supervise, even though other questions would be presented if money damages were sought or if the officials were entirely unaware of any constitutional violations. On the federalism point, the dissent concluded:

> I would regard what was accomplished in this case as one of those rightly rare but nevertheless justified instances . . . of federal court "intervention" in a state or municipal executive area. The facts, the deprival of constitutional rights, and the pattern are all proved in sufficient degree. And the remedy is carefully delineated, worked out within the administrative structure rather than superimposed by edict upon it, and essentially, and concededly, "livable." . . . It is a matter of regret that the Court sees fit to nullify what so meticulously and thoughtfully has been evolved to satisfy an existing need relating to constitutional rights that we cherish and hold dear.

3. CONCLUDING QUESTIONS AND COMMENTS

Rizzo was a highly controversial decision. Was it correctly decided? Was it persuasive authority for the Court's result in *Lyons*?

APPENDIX A

THE CONSTITUTION OF THE UNITED STATES OF AMERICA

We the People of the United States, in Order to form a more perfect Union, establish Justice, insure domestic Tranquility, provide for the common defence, promote the general Welfare, and secure the Blessings of Liberty to ourselves and our Posterity, do ordain and establish this Constitution for the United States of America.

ARTICLE I.

SECTION 1. All legislative Powers herein granted shall be vested in a Congress of the United States, which shall consist of a Senate and House of Representatives.

SECTION 2. The House of Representatives shall be composed of Members chosen every second Year by the People of the several States, and the Electors in each State shall have the Qualifications requisite for Electors of the most numerous Branch of the State Legislature.

No Person shall be a Representative who shall not have attained to the Age of twenty five Years, and been seven Years a Citizen of the United States, and who shall not, when elected, be an Inhabitant of that State in which he shall be chosen.

Representatives and direct Taxes shall be apportioned among the several States which may be included within this Union, according to their respective Numbers, which shall be determined by adding to the whole Number of free Persons, including those bound to Service for a Term of Years, and excluding Indians not taxed, three fifths of all other Persons. The actual Enumeration shall be made within three Years after the first Meeting of the Congress of the United States, and within every subsequent Term of ten Years, in such Manner as they shall by Law direct. The Number of Representatives shall not exceed one for every thirty Thousand, but each State shall have at Least one Representative; and until such enumeration shall be made, the State of New Hampshire shall be entitled to chuse three, Massachusetts eight, Rhode Island and Providence Plantations one, Connecticut five, New–York six, New Jersey four, Pennsylvania eight, Delaware one, Maryland six, Virginia ten, North Carolina five, South Carolina five, and Georgia three.

When vacancies happen in the Representation from any State, the Executive Authority thereof shall issue Writs of Election to fill such Vacancies.

The House of Representatives shall chuse their Speaker and other Officers; and shall have the sole Power of Impeachment.

SECTION 3. The Senate of the United States shall be composed of two Senators from each State, chosen by the Legislature thereof, for six Years; and each Senator shall have one Vote.

Immediately after they shall be assembled in Consequence of the first Election, they shall be divided as equally as may be into three Classes. The Seats of the Senators of the first Class shall be vacated at the Expiration of the second Year, of the second Class at the Expiration of the fourth Year, and of the third Class at the Expiration of the sixth Year, so that one third may be chosen every second Year; and if Vacancies happen by Resignation, or otherwise, during the Recess of the Legislature of any State, the Executive thereof may make temporary Appointments until the next Meeting of the Legislature, which shall then fill such Vacancies.

No Person shall be a Senator who shall not have attained to the Age of thirty Years, and been nine Years a Citizen of the United States, and who shall not, when elected, be an Inhabitant of that State for which he shall be chosen.

The Vice President of the United States shall be President of the Senate, but shall have no Vote, unless they be equally divided.

The Senate shall chuse their other Officers, and also a President pro tempore, in the Absence of the Vice President, or when he shall exercise the Office of President of the United States.

The Senate shall have the sole Power to try all Impeachments. When sitting for that Purpose, they shall be on Oath or Affirmation. When the President of the United States is tried, the Chief Justice shall preside: And no Person shall be convicted without the Concurrence of two thirds of the Members present.

Judgment in Cases of Impeachment shall not extend further than to removal from Office, and disqualification to hold and enjoy any Office of honor, Trust or Profit under the United States: but the Party convicted shall nevertheless be liable and subject to Indictment, Trial, Judgment and Punishment, according to Law.

SECTION 4. The Times, Places and Manner of holding Elections for Senators and Representatives, shall be prescribed in each State by the Legislature thereof; but the Congress may at any time by Law make or alter such Regulations, except as to the Places of chusing Senators.

The Congress shall assemble at least once in every Year, and such Meeting shall be on the first Monday in December, unless they shall by Law appoint a different Day.

SECTION 5. Each House shall be the Judge of the Elections, Returns and Qualifications of its own Members, and a Majority of each shall constitute a Quorum to do Business; but a smaller Number may adjourn from day to day, and may be authorized to compel the Attendance of absent Members, in such Manner, and under such Penalties as each House may provide.

Each House may determine the Rules of its Proceedings, punish its Members for disorderly Behaviour, and, with the Concurrence of two thirds, expel a Member.

Each House shall keep a Journal of its Proceedings, and from time to time publish the same, excepting such Parts as may in their Judgment require Secrecy; and the Yeas and Nays of the Members of either House on any question shall, at the Desire of one fifth of those Present, be entered on the Journal.

Neither House, during the Session of Congress, shall, without the Consent of the other, adjourn for more than three days, nor to any other Place than that in which the two Houses shall be sitting.

SECTION 6. The Senators and Representatives shall receive a Compensation for their Services, to be ascertained by Law, and paid out of the Treasury of the United States. They shall in all Cases, except Treason, Felony and Breach of the Peace, be privileged from Arrest during their Attendance at the Session of their respective Houses, and in going to and returning from the same; and for any Speech or Debate in either House, they shall not be questioned in any other Place.

No Senator or Representative shall, during the Time for which he was elected, be appointed to any civil Office under the Authority of the United States, which shall have been created, or the Emoluments whereof shall have been encreased during such time; and no Person holding any Office under the United States, shall be a Member of either House during his Continuance in Office.

SECTION 7. All Bills for raising Revenue shall originate in the House of Representatives; but the Senate may propose or concur with amendments as on other Bills.

Every Bill which shall have passed the House of Representatives and the Senate, shall, before it become a Law, be presented to the President of the United States; If he approve he shall sign it, but if not he shall return it, with his Objections to that House in which it shall have originated, who shall enter the Objections at large on their Journal, and proceed to reconsider it. If after such Reconsideration two thirds of that House shall agree to pass the Bill, it shall be sent, together with the Objections, to the other House, by which it shall likewise be reconsidered, and if approved by two thirds of that House, it shall become a Law. But in all such Cases the Votes of both Houses shall be determined by Yeas and Nays, and the Names of the Persons voting for and against the Bill shall be entered on the Journal of each House respectively. If any Bill shall not be returned by the President within ten Days (Sunday excepted) after it shall have been presented to him, the Same shall be a Law, in like Manner as if he had signed it, unless the Congress by their Adjournment prevent its Return, in which Case it shall not be a Law.

Every Order, Resolution, or Vote to which the Concurrence of the Senate and House of Representatives may be necessary (except on a question of Adjournment) shall be presented to the President of the United States; and before the Same shall take Effect, shall be approved by him, or being disapproved by him, shall be repassed by two thirds of the Senate and House of Representatives, according to the Rules and Limitations prescribed in the Case of a Bill.

SECTION 8. The Congress shall have Power To lay and collect Taxes, Duties, Imposts and Excises, to pay the Debts and provide for the common Defence and general Welfare of the United States; but all Duties, Imposts and Excises shall be uniform throughout the United States;

To borrow Money on the credit of the United States;

To regulate Commerce with foreign Nations, and among the several States, and with the Indian Tribes;

To establish an uniform Rule of Naturalization, and uniform Laws on the subject of Bankruptcies throughout the United States;

To coin Money, regulate the Value thereof, and of foreign Coin, and fix the Standard of Weights and Measures;

To provide for the Punishment of counterfeiting the Securities and current Coin of the United States;

To establish Post Offices and post Roads;

To promote the Progress of Science and useful Arts, by securing for limited Times to Authors and Inventors the exclusive Right to their respective Writings and Discoveries;

To constitute Tribunals inferior to the supreme Court;

To define and punish Piracies and Felonies committed on the high Seas, and Offences against the Law of Nations;

To declare War, grant Letters of Marque and Reprisal, and make Rules concerning Captures on Land and Water;

To raise and support Armies, but no Appropriation of Money to that Use shall be for a longer Term than two Years;

To provide and maintain a Navy;

To make Rules for the Government and Regulation of the land and naval Forces;

To provide for calling forth the Militia to execute the Laws of the Union, suppress Insurrections and repel Invasions;

To provide for organizing, arming, and disciplining, the Militia, and for governing such Part of them as may be employed in the Service of the United States, reserving to the States respectively, the Appointment of the Officers, and the Authority of training the Militia according to the discipline prescribed by Congress;

To exercise exclusive Legislation in all Cases whatsoever, over such District (not exceeding ten Miles square) as may, by Cession of particular States, and the Acceptance of Congress, become the Seat of the Government of the United States, and to exercise like Authority over all Places purchased by the Consent of the Legislature of the State in which the Same shall be, for the Erection of Forts, Magazines, Arsenals, dock-Yards, and other needful Buildings;—And

To make all Laws which shall be necessary and proper for carrying into Execution the foregoing Powers, and all other Powers vested by this Constitution in the Government of the United States, or in any Department or Officer thereof.

SECTION 9. The Migration or Importation of such Persons as any of the States now existing shall think proper to admit, shall not be prohibited by the Congress prior to the Year one thousand eight hundred and eight, but a Tax or duty may be imposed on such Importation, not exceeding ten dollars for each Person.

The Privilege of the Writ of Habeas Corpus shall not be suspended, unless when in Cases of Rebellion or Invasion the public Safety may require it.

No Bill of Attainder or ex post facto Law shall be passed.

No Capitation, or other direct, Tax shall be laid, unless in Proportion to the Census or Enumeration herein before directed to be taken.

No Tax or Duty shall be laid on Articles exported from any State.

No Preference shall be given by any Regulation of Commerce or Revenue to the Ports of one State over those of another; nor shall Vessels bound to, or from, one State, be obliged to enter, clear, or pay Duties in another.

No Money shall be drawn from the Treasury, but in Consequence of Appropriations made by Law; and a regular Statement and Account of the Receipts and Expenditures of all public Money shall be published from time to time.

No Title of Nobility shall be granted by the United States: And no Person holding any Office of Profit or Trust under them, shall, without the Consent of the Congress, accept of any present, Emolument, Office, or Title, of any kind whatever, from any King, Prince or foreign State.

SECTION 10. No State shall enter into any Treaty, Alliance, or Confederation; grant Letters of Marque and Reprisal; coin Money; emit Bills of Credit; make any Thing but gold and silver Coin a Tender in Payment of Debts; pass any Bill of Attainder, ex post facto Law, or Law impairing the Obligation of Contracts, or grant any Title of Nobility.

No State shall, without the Consent of the Congress, lay any Imposts or Duties on Imports or Exports, except what may be absolutely necessary for executing its inspection Laws: and the net Produce of all Duties and Imposts, laid by any State on Imports or Exports, shall be for the Use of the Treasury of the United States; and all such Laws shall be subject to the Revision and Controul of the Congress.

No State shall, without the Consent of Congress, lay any Duty of Tonnage, keep Troops, or Ships of War in time of Peace, enter into any Agreement or Compact with another State, or with a foreign Power, or engage in War, unless actually invaded, or in such imminent Danger as will not admit of delay.

ARTICLE II.

SECTION 1. The executive Power shall be vested in a President of the United States of America. He shall hold his Office during the Term of four Years, and, together with the Vice President, chosen for the same Term, be elected, as follows:

Each State shall appoint, in such Manner as the Legislature thereof may direct, a Number of Electors, equal to the whole Number of Senators and Representatives to which the State may be entitled in the Congress: but no Senator or Representative, or Person holding an Office of Trust or Profit under the United States, shall be appointed an Elector.

The Electors shall meet in their respective States, and vote by Ballot for two Persons, of whom one at least shall not be an Inhabitant of the same State with themselves. And they shall make a List of all the Persons voted for, and of the Number of Votes for each; which List they shall sign and certify, and transmit sealed to the Seat of the Government of the United States, directed to the President of the Senate. The President of the Senate shall, in the Presence of the Senate and House of Representatives, open all the Certificates, and the Votes shall then be counted. The Person having the greatest Number of Votes shall be the President, if such Number be a Majority of the whole Number of Electors appointed; and if there be more than one who have such Majority, and have an equal Number of Votes, then the House of Representatives shall immediately chuse by Ballot one of them for President; and if no Person have a Majority, then from the five highest on the List the said House shall in like Manner chuse the President. But in chusing the President, the Votes shall be taken by States, the Representation from each State having one Vote; a quorum for this Purpose shall consist of a Member or Members from two thirds of the States, and a Majority of all the States shall be necessary to a Choice. In every Case, after the Choice of the President, the Person having the greatest Number of Votes of the Electors shall be the Vice President. But if there should remain two or more who have equal Votes, the Senate shall chuse from them by Ballot the Vice President.

The Congress may determine the Time of chusing the Electors, and the Day on which they shall give their Votes; which Day shall be the same throughout the United States.

No Person except a natural born Citizen, or a Citizen of the United States, at the time of the Adoption of this Constitution, shall be eligible to the Office of President; neither shall any Person be eligible to that Office who shall not have attained to the Age of thirty five Years, and been fourteen Years a Resident within the United States.

In Case of the Removal of the President from Office, or of his Death, Resignation, or Inability to discharge the Powers and Duties of the said Office, the Same shall devolve on the Vice President, and the Congress may by Law provide for the Case of Removal, Death, Resignation or Inability, both of the President and Vice President, declaring what Officer shall then act as President, and such Officer shall act accordingly, until the Disability be removed, or a President shall be elected.

The President shall, at stated Times, receive for his Services, a Compensation, which shall neither be encreased nor diminished during the Period for which he shall have been elected, and he shall not receive within that Period any other Emolument from the United States, or any of them.

Before he enter on the Execution of his Office, he shall take the following Oath or Affirmation:—"I do solemnly swear (or affirm) that I will faithfully execute the Office of President of the United States, and will to the best of my Ability, preserve, protect and defend the Constitution of the United States."

SECTION 2. The President shall be Commander in Chief of the Army and Navy of the United States, and of the Militia of the several States, when called into the actual Service of the United States; he may require the Opinion, in writing, of the principal Officer in each of the executive Departments, upon any Subject relating to the Duties of their respective Offices, and he shall have Power to grant Reprieves and Pardons for Offences against the United States, except in Cases of Impeachment.

He shall have Power, by and with the Advice and Consent of the Senate, to make Treaties, provided two thirds of the Senators present concur; and he shall nominate, and by and with the Advice and Consent of the Senate, shall appoint Ambassadors, other public Ministers and Consuls, Judges of the supreme Court, and all other Officers of the United States, whose Appointments are not herein otherwise provided for, and which shall be established by Law: but the Congress may by Law vest the Appointment of such inferior Officers, as they think proper, in the President alone, in the Courts of Law, or in the Heads of Departments.

The President shall have Power to fill up all Vacancies that may happen during the Recess of the Senate, by granting Commissions which shall expire at the End of their next Session.

SECTION 3. He shall from time to time give to the Congress Information of the State of the Union, and recommend to their Consideration such Measures as he shall judge necessary and expedient; he may, on extraordinary Occasions, convene both Houses, or either of them, and in Case of Disagreement between them, with Respect to the Time of Adjournment, he may adjourn them to such Time as he shall think proper; he shall receive Ambassadors and other public Ministers; he shall take Care that the Laws be faithfully executed, and shall Commission all the Officers of the United States.

SECTION 4. The President, Vice President and all Civil Officers of the United States, shall be removed from Office on Impeachment for, and Conviction of, Treason, Bribery, or other high Crimes and Misdemeanors.

ARTICLE III.

SECTION 1. The judicial Power of the United States, shall be vested in one supreme Court, and in such inferior Courts as the Congress may from time to time ordain and establish. The Judges, both of the supreme and inferior Courts, shall hold their Offices during good Behaviour, and shall, at stated Times, receive for their Services, a Compensation, which shall not be diminished during their Continuance in Office.

SECTION 2. The judicial Power shall extend to all Cases, in Law and Equity, arising under this Constitution, the Laws of the United States, and Treaties made, or which shall be made, under their Authority;—to all Cases affecting Ambassadors, other public Ministers and Consuls;—to all Cases of admiralty and maritime Jurisdiction;—to Controversies to which the United States shall be a Party;—to Controversies between two or more States;—between a State and Citizens of another State;—between Citizens of different States;—between Citizens of the same State claiming Lands under Grants of different States, and between a State, or the Citizens thereof, and foreign States, Citizens or Subjects.

In all Cases affecting Ambassadors, other public Ministers and Consuls, and those in which a State shall be Party, the Supreme Court shall have original Jurisdiction. In all the other Cases before mentioned, the supreme Court shall have appellate Jurisdiction, both as to Law and Fact, with such Exceptions, and under such Regulations as the Congress shall make.

The Trial of all Crimes, except in Cases of Impeachment, shall be by Jury; and such Trial shall be held in the State where the said Crimes shall have been committed; but when not committed within any State, the Trial shall be at such Place or Places as the Congress may by Law have directed.

SECTION 3. Treason against the United States, shall consist only in levying War against them, or in adhering to their Enemies, giving them Aid and Comfort. No Person shall be convicted of Treason unless on the Testimony of two Witnesses to the same overt Act, or on Confession in open Court.

The Congress shall have Power to declare the Punishment of Treason, but no Attainder of Treason shall work Corruption of Blood, or Forfeiture except during the Life of the Person attainted.

ARTICLE IV.

SECTION 1. Full Faith and Credit shall be given in each State to the public Acts, Records, and judicial Proceedings of every other State. And the

Congress may by general Laws prescribe the Manner in which such Acts, Records and Proceedings shall be proved, and the Effect thereof.

SECTION 2. The Citizens of each State shall be entitled to all Privileges and Immunities of Citizens in the several States.

A Person charged in any State with Treason, Felony, or other Crime, who shall flee from Justice, and be found in another State, shall on Demand of the executive Authority of the State from which he fled, be delivered up, to be removed to the State having Jurisdiction of the Crime.

No Person held to Service or Labour in one State, under the Laws thereof, escaping into another, shall, in Consequence of any Law or Regulation therein, be discharged from such Service or Labour, but shall be delivered up on Claim of the Party to whom such Service or Labour may be due.

SECTION 3. New States may be admitted by the Congress into this Union; but no new State shall be formed or erected within the Jurisdiction of any other State; nor any State be formed by the Junction of two or more States, or Parts of States, without the Consent of the Legislatures of the States concerned as well as of the Congress.

The Congress shall have Power to dispose of and make all needful Rules and Regulations respecting the Territory or other Property belonging to the United States; and nothing in this Constitution shall be so construed as to Prejudice any Claims of the United States, or of any particular State.

SECTION 4. The United States shall guarantee to every State in this Union a Republican Form of Government, and shall protect each of them against Invasion; and on Application of the Legislature, or of the Executive (when the Legislature cannot be convened) against domestic Violence.

ARTICLE V.

The Congress, whenever two thirds of both Houses shall deem it necessary, shall propose Amendments to this Constitution, or, on the Application of the Legislatures of two thirds of the several States, shall call a Convention for proposing Amendments, which, in either Case, shall be valid to all Intents and Purposes, as Part of this Constitution, when ratified by the Legislatures of three fourths of the several States, or by Conventions in three fourths thereof, as the one or the other Mode of Ratification may be proposed by the Congress; Provided that no Amendment which may be made prior to the Year One thousand eight hundred and eight shall in any Manner affect the first and fourth Clauses in the Ninth Section of the first Article; and that no State, without its Consent, shall be deprived of its equal Suffrage in the Senate.

ARTICLE VI.

All Debts contracted and Engagements entered into, before the Adoption of this Constitution, shall be as valid against the United States under this Constitution, as under the Confederation.

This Constitution, and the Laws of the United States which shall be made in Pursuance thereof; and all Treaties made, or which shall be made, under the Authority of the United States, shall be the supreme Law of the Land; and the Judges in every State shall be bound thereby, any Thing in the Constitution or Laws of any State to the Contrary notwithstanding.

The Senators and Representatives before mentioned, and the Members of the several State Legislatures, and all executive and judicial Officers, both of the United States and of the several States, shall be bound by Oath or Affirmation, to support this Constitution; but no religious Test shall ever be required as a Qualification to any Office or public Trust under the United States.

ARTICLE VII.

The Ratification of the Conventions of nine States, shall be sufficient for the Establishment of this Constitution between the States so ratifying the Same.

* * *

ARTICLES IN ADDITION TO, AND AMENDMENT OF, THE CONSTITUTION OF THE UNITED STATES OF AMERICA, PROPOSED BY CONGRESS, AND RATIFIED BY THE SEVERAL STATES, PURSUANT TO THE FIFTH ARTICLE OF THE ORIGINAL CONSTITUTION.

AMENDMENT I [1791].

Congress shall make no law respecting an establishment of religion, or prohibiting the free exercise thereof; or abridging the freedom of speech, or of the press; or the right of the people peaceably to assemble, and to petition the Government for a redress of grievances.

AMENDMENT II [1791].

A well regulated Militia, being necessary to the security of a free State, the right of the people to keep and bear Arms, shall not be infringed.

AMENDMENT III [1791].

No Soldier shall, in time of peace be quartered in any house, without the consent of the Owner, nor in time of war, but in a manner to be prescribed by law.

AMENDMENT IV [1791].

The right of the people to be secure in their persons, houses, papers, and effects, against unreasonable searches and seizures, shall not be violated, and no Warrants shall issue, but upon probable cause, supported by Oath or affirmation, and particularly describing the place to be searched, and the persons or things to be seized.

AMENDMENT V [1791].

No person shall be held to answer for a capital, or otherwise infamous crime, unless on a presentment or indictment of a Grand Jury, except in cases arising in the land or naval forces, or in the Militia, when in actual service in time of War or public danger; nor shall any person be subject for the same offence to be twice put in jeopardy of life or limb; nor shall be compelled in any criminal case to be a witness against himself, nor be deprived of life, liberty, or property, without due process of law; nor shall private property be taken for public use, without just compensation.

AMENDMENT VI [1791].

In all criminal prosecutions, the accused shall enjoy the right to a speedy and public trial, by an impartial jury of the State and district wherein the crime shall have been committed, which district shall have been previously ascertained by law, and to be informed of the nature and cause of the accusation; to be confronted with the witnesses against him; to have compulsory process for obtaining Witnesses in his favor, and to have the Assistance of Counsel for his defence.

AMENDMENT VII [1791].

In Suits at common law, where the value in controversy shall exceed twenty dollars, the right of trial by jury shall be preserved, and no fact tried by a jury, shall be otherwise re-examined in any Court of the United States, than according to the rules of the common law.

AMENDMENT VIII [1791].

Excessive bail shall not be required, nor excessive fines imposed, nor cruel and unusual punishments inflicted.

AMENDMENT IX [1791].

The enumeration in the Constitution, of certain rights, shall not be construed to deny or disparage others retained by the people.

AMENDMENT X [1791].

The powers not delegated to the United States by the Constitution, nor prohibited by it to the States, are reserved to the States respectively, or to the people.

AMENDMENT XI [1798].

The Judicial power of the United States shall not be construed to extend to any suit in law or equity, commenced or prosecuted against one of the United States by Citizens of another State, or by Citizens or Subjects of any Foreign State.

AMENDMENT XII [1804].

The Electors shall meet in their respective states and vote by ballot for President and Vice–President, one of whom, at least, shall not be an inhabitant of the same state with themselves; they shall name in their ballots the person voted for as President, and in distinct ballots the person voted for as Vice–President, and they shall make distinct lists of all persons voted for as President, and of all persons voted for as Vice–President, and of the number of votes for each, which lists they shall sign and certify, and transmit sealed to the seat of the government of the United States, directed to the President of the Senate;—The President of the Senate shall, in the presence of the Senate and House of Representatives, open all the certificates and the votes shall then be counted;—The person having the greatest number of votes for President, shall be the President, if such number be a majority of the whole number of Electors appointed; and if no person have such majority, then from the persons having the highest numbers not exceeding three on the list of those voted for as President, the House of Representatives shall choose immediately, by ballot, the President. But in choosing the President, the votes shall be taken by states, the representation from each state having one vote; a quorum for this purpose shall consist of a member or members from two-thirds of the states, and a majority of all the states shall be necessary to a choice. And if the House of Representatives shall not choose a President whenever the right of choice shall devolve upon them, before the fourth day of March next following, then the Vice–President shall act as President, as in the case of the death or other constitutional disability of the President—The person having the greatest number of votes as Vice–President, shall be the Vice–President, if such number be a majority of the whole number of Electors appointed, and if no person have a majority, then from the two highest numbers on the list, the Senate shall choose the Vice–President; a quorum for the purpose shall consist of two-thirds of the whole number of Senators, and a majority of the whole number shall be necessary to a choice. But no person constitutionally ineligible to the office of President shall be eligible to that of Vice–President of the United States.

AMENDMENT XIII [1865].

SECTION 1. Neither slavery nor involuntary servitude, except as a punishment for crime whereof the party shall have been duly convicted, shall exist within the United States, or any place subject to their jurisdiction.

SECTION 2. Congress shall have power to enforce this article by appropriate legislation.

AMENDMENT XIV [1868].

SECTION 1. All persons born or naturalized in the United States, and subject to the jurisdiction thereof, are citizens of the United States and of the State wherein they reside. No State shall make or enforce any law which shall abridge the privileges or immunities of citizens of the United States; nor shall any State deprive any person of life, liberty, or property, without due process of law; nor deny to any person within its jurisdiction the equal protection of the laws.

SECTION 2. Representatives shall be apportioned among the several States according to their respective numbers, counting the whole number of persons in each State, excluding Indians not taxed. But when the right to vote at any election for the choice of electors for President and Vice President of the United States, Representatives in Congress, the Executive and Judicial officers of a State, or the members of the Legislature thereof, is denied to any of the male inhabitants of such State, being twenty-one years of age, and citizens of the United States, or in any way abridged, except for participation in rebellion, or other crime, the basis of representation therein shall be reduced in the proportion which the number of such male citizens shall bear to the whole number of male citizens twenty-one years of age in such State.

SECTION 3. No person shall be a Senator or Representative in Congress, or elector of President and Vice President, or hold any office, civil or military, under the United States, or under any State, who, having previously taken an oath, as a member of Congress, or as an officer of the United States, or as a member of any State legislature, or as an executive or judicial officer of any State, to support the Constitution of the United States, shall have engaged in insurrection or rebellion against the same, or given aid or comfort to the enemies thereof. But Congress may by a vote of two-thirds of each House, remove such disability.

SECTION 4. The validity of the public debt of the United States, authorized by law, including debts incurred for payment of pensions and bounties for services in suppressing insurrection or rebellion, shall not be questioned. But neither the United States nor any State shall assume or pay any debt or obligation incurred in aid of insurrection or rebellion against the United States, or any claim for the loss of emancipation of any slave; but all such debts, obligations and claims shall be held illegal and void.

SECTION 5. The Congress shall have power to enforce, by appropriate legislation, the provisions of this article.

AMENDMENT XV [1870].

SECTION 1. The right of citizens of the United States to vote shall not be denied or abridged by the United States or by any State on account of race, color, or previous condition of servitude.

SECTION 2. The Congress shall have power to enforce this article by appropriate legislation.

AMENDMENT XVI [1913].

The Congress shall have power to lay and collect taxes on incomes, from whatever source derived, without apportionment among the several States, and without regard to any census or enumeration.

AMENDMENT XVII [1913].

The Senate of the United States shall be composed of two Senators from each State, elected by the people thereof, for six years; and each Senator shall have one vote. The electors in each State shall have the qualifications requisite for electors of the most numerous branch of the State legislatures.

When vacancies happen in the representation of any State in the Senate, the executive authority of such State shall issue writs of election to fill such vacancies: *Provided,* That the legislature of any State may empower the executive thereof to make temporary appointments until the people fill the vacancies by election as the legislature may direct.

This amendment shall not be so construed as to affect the election or term of any Senator chosen before it becomes valid as part of the Constitution.

AMENDMENT XVIII [1919].

SECTION 1. After one year from the ratification of this article the manufacture, sale, or transportation of intoxicating liquors within, the importation thereof into, or the exportation thereof from the United States and all territory subject to the jurisdiction thereof for beverage purposes is hereby prohibited.

SECTION 2. The Congress and the several States shall have concurrent power to enforce this article by appropriate legislation.

SECTION 3. This article shall be inoperative unless it shall have been ratified as an amendment to the Constitution by the legislatures of the several States, as provided in the Constitution, within seven years from the date of the submission hereof to the States by the Congress.

AMENDMENT XIX [1920].

The right of citizens of the United States to vote shall not be denied or abridged by the United States or by any State on account of sex.

Congress shall have power to enforce this article by appropriate legislation.

AMENDMENT XX [1933].

SECTION 1. The terms of the President and Vice President shall end at noon on the 20th day of January, and the terms of Senators and Representatives at noon on the 3d day of January, of the years in which such terms would have ended if this article had not been ratified; and the terms of their successors shall then begin.

SECTION 2. The Congress shall assemble at least once in every year, and such meeting shall begin at noon on the 3d day of January, unless they shall by law appoint a different day.

SECTION 3. If, at the time fixed for the beginning of the term of the President, the President elect shall have died, the Vice President elect shall become President. If a President shall not have been chosen before the time fixed for the beginning of his term, or if the President elect shall have failed to qualify, then the Vice President elect shall act as President until a President shall have qualified; and the Congress may by law provide for the case wherein neither a President elect nor a Vice President elect shall have qualified, declaring who shall then act as President, or the manner in which one who is to act shall be selected, and such person shall act accordingly until a President or Vice President shall have qualified.

SECTION 4. The Congress may by law provide for the case of the death of any of the persons from whom the House of Representatives may choose a President whenever the right of choice shall have devolved upon them, and for the case of the death of any of the persons from whom the Senate may choose a Vice President whenever the right of choice shall have devolved upon them.

SECTION 5. Sections 1 and 2 shall take effect on the 15th day of October following the ratification of this article.

SECTION 6. This article shall be inoperative unless it shall have been ratified as an amendment to the Constitution by the legislatures of three-fourths of the several States within seven years from the date of its submission.

AMENDMENT XXI [1933].

SECTION 1. The eighteenth article of amendment to the Constitution of the United States is hereby repealed.

SECTION 2. The transportation or importation into any State, Territory, or possession of the United States for delivery or use therein of intoxicating liquors, in violation of the laws thereof, is hereby prohibited.

SECTION 3. This article shall be inoperative unless it shall have been ratified as an amendment to the Constitution by conventions in the several States, as provided in the Constitution, within seven years from the date of the submission hereof to the States by the Congress.

AMENDMENT XXII [1951].

SECTION 1. No person shall be elected to the office of the President more than twice, and no person who has held the office of President, or acted as President, for more than two years of a term to which some other person was elected President shall be elected to the office of the President more than once. But this Article shall not apply to any person holding the office of President when this Article was proposed by the Congress, and shall not prevent any person who may be holding the office of President, or acting as President, during the term within which this Article becomes operative from holding the office of President or acting as President during the remainder of such term.

SECTION 2. This article shall be inoperative unless it shall have been ratified as an amendment to the Constitution by the legislatures of three-fourths of the several States within seven years from the date of its submission to the States by the Congress.

AMENDMENT XXIII [1961].

SECTION 1. The District constituting the seat of Government of the United States shall appoint in such manner as the Congress may direct:

A number of electors of President and Vice President equal to the whole number of Senators and Representatives in Congress to which the District would be entitled if it were a State, but in no event more than the least populous State; they shall be in addition to those appointed by the States, but they shall be considered, for the purposes of the election of President and Vice President, to be electors appointed by a State; and they shall meet in the District and perform such duties as provided by the twelfth article of amendment.

SECTION 2. The Congress shall have power to enforce this article by appropriate legislation.

AMENDMENT XXIV [1964].

SECTION 1. The right of citizens of the United States to vote in any primary or other election for President or Vice President, for electors for President or Vice President, or for Senator or Representative in Congress, shall not be denied or abridged by the United States or any State by reason of failure to pay any poll tax or other tax.

SECTION 2. The Congress shall have power to enforce this article by appropriate legislation.

AMENDMENT XXV [1967].

SECTION 1. In case of the removal of the President from office or of his death or resignation, the Vice President shall become President.

SECTION 2. Whenever there is a vacancy in the office of the Vice President, the President shall nominate a Vice President who shall take office upon confirmation by a majority vote of both Houses of Congress.

SECTION 3. Whenever the President transmits to the President pro tempore of the Senate and the Speaker of the House of Representatives his written declaration that he is unable to discharge the powers and duties of his office, and until he transmits to them a written declaration to the contrary, such powers and duties shall be discharged by the Vice President as Acting President.

SECTION 4. Whenever the Vice President and a majority of either the principal officers of the executive departments or of such other body as Congress may by law provide, transmit to the President pro tempore of the Senate and the Speaker of the House of Representatives their written declaration that the President is unable to discharge the powers and duties of his office, the Vice President shall immediately assume the powers and duties of the office as Acting President.

Thereafter, when the President transmits to the President pro tempore of the Senate and the Speaker of the House of Representatives his written declaration that no inability exists, he shall resume the powers and duties of his office unless the Vice President and a majority of either the principal officers of the executive department or of such other body as Congress may by law provide, transmit within four days to the President pro tempore of the Senate and the Speaker of the House of Representatives their written declaration that the President is unable to discharge the powers and duties of his office. Thereupon Congress shall decide the issue, assembling within forty-eight hours for that purpose if not in session. If the Congress, within twenty-one days after receipt of the latter written declaration, or, if Congress is not in session, within twenty-one days after Congress is required to assemble, determines by two-thirds vote of both Houses that the President is unable to discharge the powers and duties of his office, the Vice President shall continue to discharge the same as Acting President; otherwise, the President shall resume the powers and duties of his office.

AMENDMENT XXVI [1971].

SECTION 1. The right of citizens of the United States, who are eighteen years of age or older, to vote shall not be denied or abridged by the United States or by any State on account of age.

SECTION 2. The Congress shall have power to enforce this article by appropriate legislation.

AMENDMENT XXVII [1992].

No law varying the compensation for the services of the Senators and Representatives shall take effect until an election of Representatives shall have intervened.

APPENDIX B

SELECTED FEDERAL STATUTES

I. TITLE 18, U.S.C.:

§ 241. Conspiracy against rights

If two or more persons conspire to injure, oppress, threaten, or intimidate any person in any State, Territory, Commonwealth, Possession, or District in the free exercise or enjoyment of any right or privilege secured to him by the Constitution or laws of the United States, or because of his having so exercised the same; or

If two or more persons go in disguise on the highway, or on the premises of another, with intent to prevent or hinder his free exercise or enjoyment of any right or privilege so secured—

They shall be fined under this title or imprisoned not more than ten years, or both; and if death results from the acts committed in violation of this section or if such acts include kidnapping or an attempt to kidnap, aggravated sexual abuse or an attempt to commit aggravated sexual abuse, or an attempt to kill, they shall be fined under this title or imprisoned for any term of years or for life, or both, or may be sentenced to death.

§ 242. Deprivation of rights under color of law

Whoever, under color of any law, statute, ordinance, regulation, or custom, willfully subjects any person in any State, Territory, Commonwealth, Possession, or District to the deprivation of any rights, privileges, or immunities secured or protected by the Constitution or laws of the United States, or to different punishments, pains, or penalties, on account of such person being an alien, or by reason of his color, or race, than are prescribed for the punishment of citizens, shall be fined under this title or imprisoned not more than one year, or both; and if bodily injury results from the acts committed in violation of this section or if such acts include the use, attempted use, or threatened use of a dangerous weapon, explosives, or fire, shall be fined under this title or imprisoned not more than ten years, or both; and if death results from the acts committed in violation of this section or if such acts include kidnapping or an attempt to kidnap, aggravated sexual abuse, or an attempt to commit aggravated sexual abuse, or an attempt to kill, shall be fined under this title, or imprisoned for any term of years or for life, or both, or may be sentenced to death.

II. TITLE 20, U.S.C.:

§ 1681. Sex

(a) Prohibition against discrimination; exceptions

No person in the United States shall, on the basis of sex, be excluded from participation in, be denied the benefits of, or be subjected to discrimination under any education program or activity receiving Federal financial assistance, except that:

(1) Classes of educational institutions subject to prohibition

In regard to admissions to educational institutions, this section shall apply only to institutions of vocational education, professional education, and graduate higher education, and to public institutions of undergraduate higher education;

(2) Educational institutions commencing planned change in admissions

In regard to admissions to educational institutions, this section shall not apply (A) for one year from June 23, 1972, nor for six years after June 23, 1972, in the case of an educational institution which has begun the process of changing from being an institution which admits only students of one sex to being an institution which admits students of both sexes, but only if it is carrying out a plan for such a change which is approved by the Secretary of Education or (B) for seven years from the date an educational institution begins the process of changing from being an institution which admits only students of only one sex to being an institution which admits students of both sexes, but only if it is carrying out a plan for such a change which is approved by the Secretary of Education, whichever is the later;

(3) Educational institutions of religious organizations with contrary religious tenets

This section shall not apply to an educational institution which is controlled by a religious organization if the application of this subsection would not be consistent with the religious tenets of such organization;

(4) Educational institutions training individuals for military services or merchant marine

This section shall not apply to an educational institution whose primary purpose is the training of individuals for the military services of the United States, or the merchant marine;

(5) Public educational institutions with traditional and continuing admissions policy

In regard to admissions this section shall not apply to any public institution of undergraduate higher education which is an institution that traditionally and continually from its establishment has had a policy of admitting only students of one sex;

(6) Social fraternities or sororities; voluntary youth service organizations

This section shall not apply to membership practices—

(A) of a social fraternity or social sorority which is exempt from taxation under section 501(a) of Title 26, the active membership of which consists primarily of students in attendance at an institution of higher education, or

(B) of the Young Men's Christian Association, Young Women's Christian Association, Girl Scouts, Boy Scouts, Camp Fire Girls, and voluntary youth service organizations which are so exempt, the membership of which has traditionally been limited to persons of one sex and principally to persons of less than nineteen years of age;

(7) Boy or Girl conferences

This section shall not apply to—

(A) any program or activity of the American Legion undertaken in connection with the organization or operation of any Boys State conference, Boys Nation conference, Girls State conference, or Girls Nation conference; or

(B) any program or activity of any secondary school or educational institution specifically for—

(i) the promotion of any Boys State conference, Boys Nation conference, Girls State conference, or Girls Nation conference; or

(ii) the selection of students to attend any such conference;

(8) Father-son or mother-daughter activities at educational institutions

This section shall not preclude father-son or mother-daughter activities at an educational institution, but if such activities are provided for students of one sex, opportunities for reasonably comparable activities shall be provided for students of the other sex; and

(9) Institution of higher education scholarship awards in "beauty" pageants

This section shall not apply with respect to any scholarship or other financial assistance awarded by an institution of higher education to any individual because such individual has received such award in any pageant in which the attainment of such award is based upon a combination of factors related to the personal appearance, poise, and talent of such individual and in which participation is limited to individuals of one sex only, so long as such pageant is in compliance with other nondiscrimination provisions of Federal law.

(b) Preferential or disparate treatment because of imbalance in participation or receipt of Federal benefits; statistical evidence of imbalance

Nothing contained in subsection (a) of this section shall be interpreted to require any educational institution to grant preferential or disparate treatment to the members of one sex on account of an imbalance which may exist with respect to the total number or percentage of persons of that sex participating in or receiving the benefits of any federally supported program or activity, in comparison with the total number or percentage of persons of that sex in any community, State, section, or other area: Provided, That this subsection shall not be construed to prevent the consideration in any hearing or proceeding under this chapter of statistical evidence tending to show that such an imbalance exists with respect to the participation in, or receipt of the benefits of, any such program or activity by the members of one sex.

(c) "Educational institution" defined

For purposes of this chapter an educational institution means any public or private preschool, elementary, or secondary school, or any institution of vocational, professional, or higher education, except that in the case of an educational institution composed of more than one school, college, or department which are administratively separate units, such term means each such school, college, or department.

§ 1682. Federal administrative enforcement; report to Congressional committees

Each Federal department and agency which is empowered to extend Federal financial assistance to any education program or activity, by way of grant, loan, or contract other than a contract of insurance or guaranty, is authorized and directed to effectuate the provisions of section 1681 of this title with respect to such program or activity by issuing rules, regulations, or orders of general applicability which shall be consistent with achievement of the objectives of the statute authorizing the financial assistance in connection with which the action is taken. No such rule, regulation, or order shall become effective unless and until approved by the President. Compliance with any requirement adopted pursuant to this section may be effected

(1) by the termination of or refusal to grant or to continue assistance under such program or activity to any recipient as to whom there has been an express finding on the record, after opportunity for hearing, of a failure to comply with such requirement, but such termination or refusal shall be limited to the particular political entity, or part thereof, or other recipient as to whom such a finding has been made, and shall be limited in its effect to the particular program, or part thereof, in which such noncompliance has been so found, or

(2) by any other means authorized by law:

Provided, however, That no such action shall be taken until the department or agency concerned has advised the appropriate person or persons of the failure to comply with the requirement and has determined that compliance cannot be secured by voluntary means. In the case of any action terminating, or refusing to grant or continue, assistance because of failure to comply with a requirement imposed pursuant to this section, the head of the Federal department or agency shall file with the committees of the House and Senate having legislative jurisdiction over the program or activity involved a full written report of the circumstances and the grounds for such action. No such action shall become effective until thirty days have elapsed after the filing of such report.

§ 1683. Judicial review

Any department or agency action taken pursuant to section 1682 of this title shall be subject to such judicial review as may otherwise be provided by law for similar action taken by such department or agency on other grounds. In the case of action, not otherwise subject to judicial review, terminating or refusing to grant or to continue financial assistance upon a finding of failure to comply with any requirement imposed pursuant to section 1682 of this title, any person aggrieved (including any State or political subdivision thereof and any agency of either) may obtain judicial review of such action in accordance with chapter 7 of Title 5, and such action shall not be deemed committed to unreviewable agency discretion within the meaning of section 701 of that title.

III. TITLE 28, U.S.C.:

§ 1331. Federal question; amount in controversy; costs

The district courts shall have original jurisdiction of all civil actions arising under the Constitution, laws, or treaties of the United States.

§ 1343. Civil rights and elective franchise

(a) The district courts shall have original jurisdiction of any civil action authorized by law to be commenced by any person:

(1) To recover damages for injury to his person or property, or because of the deprivation of any right or privilege of a citizen of the United States, by any act done in furtherance of any conspiracy mentioned in section 1985 of Title 42;

(2) To recover damages from any person who fails to prevent or to aid in preventing any wrongs mentioned in section 1985 of Title 42 which he had knowledge were about to occur and power to prevent;

(3) To redress the deprivation, under color of any State law, statute, ordinance, regulation, custom or usage, of any right, privilege or immunity secured by the Constitution of the United States or by any Act of Congress providing for equal rights of citizens or of all persons within the jurisdiction of the United States;

(4) To recover damages or to secure equitable or other relief under any Act of Congress providing for the protection of civil rights, including the right to vote.

(b) For purposes of this section—

(1) the District of Columbia shall be considered to be a State; and

(2) any Act of Congress applicable exclusively to the District of Columbia shall be considered to be a statute of the District of Columbia.

§ 1443. Civil rights cases

Any of the following civil actions or criminal prosecutions, commenced in a State court may be removed by the defendant to the district court of the United States for the district and division embracing the place wherein it is pending:

(1) Against any person who is denied or cannot enforce in the courts of such State a right under any law providing for the equal civil rights of citizens of the United States, or of all persons within the jurisdiction thereof;

(2) For any act under color of authority derived from any law providing for equal rights, or for refusing to do any act on the ground that it would be inconsistent with such law.

§ 1738. State and Territorial statutes and judicial proceedings; full faith and credit

The Acts of the legislature of any State, Territory, or Possession of the United States, or copies thereof, shall be authenticated by affixing the seal of such State, Territory or Possession thereto.

The records and judicial proceedings of any court of any such State, Territory or Possession, or copies thereof, shall be proved or admitted in other courts within the United States and its Territories and Possessions by the attestation of the clerk and seal of the court annexed, if a seal exists, together with a certificate of a judge of the court that the said attestation is in proper form.

Such Acts, records and judicial proceedings or copies thereof, so authenticated, shall have the same full faith and credit in every court within the United States and its Territories and Possessions as they have by law or usage in the courts of such State, Territory or Possession from which they are taken.

§ 2283. Stay of State court proceedings

A court of the United States may not grant an injunction to stay proceedings in a State court except as expressly authorized by Act of Congress, or where necessary in aid of its jurisdiction, or to protect or effectuate its judgments.

IV. TITLE 42, U.S.C.:

§ 1981. Equal rights under the law

(a) Statement of equal rights

All persons within the jurisdiction of the United States shall have the same right in every State and Territory to make and enforce contracts, to sue, be parties, give evidence, and to the full and equal benefit of all laws and proceedings for the security of persons and property as is enjoyed by white citizens, and shall be subject to like punishment, pains, penalties, taxes, licenses, and exactions of every kind, and to no other.

(b) Definition

For purposes of this section, the term "make and enforce contracts" includes the making, performance, modification, and termination of contracts, and the enjoyment of all benefits, privileges, terms, and conditions of the contractual relationship.

(c) Protection against impairment

The rights protected by this section are protected against impairment by nongovernmental discrimination and impairment under color of State law.

§ 1981a. Damages in cases of intentional discrimination in employment

(a) Right of recovery

(1) Civil rights

In an action brought by a complaining party under section 706 or 717 of the Civil Rights Act of 1964 [42 U.S.C. 2000e–5] against a respondent who engaged in unlawful intentional discrimination (not an employment practice that is unlawful because of its disparate impact) prohibited under section 703, 704, or 717 of the Act [42 U.S.C. 2000e–2 or 2000e–3] and provided that the complaining party cannot recover under section 1981 of this title, the complaining party may recover compensatory and punitive damages as allowed in subsection (b) of this section, in addition to any relief authorized by section 706(g) of the Civil Rights Act of 1964, from the respondent.

(2) Disability

In an action brought by a complaining party under the powers, remedies, and procedures set forth in section 706 or 717 of the Civil Rights Act of 1964 (as provided in section 107(a) of the Americans with Disabilities Act of 1990 [42 U.S.C. 12117(a)], and section 794a(a)(1) of Title 29, respectively) against a respondent who engaged in unlawful intentional discrimination (not an employment practice that is unlawful because of its disparate impact) under section 791 of Title 29 and the regulations implementing section 791 of Title 29, or who violated the requirements of section 791 of Title 29 or the regulations implementing section 791 of Title 29 concerning the provision of a reasonable accommodation, or section 102 of the Americans with Disabilities Act of 1990 [42 U.S.C. 12112], or committed a violation of section 102(b)(5) of the Act, against an individual, the complaining party may recover compensatory and punitive damages as allowed in subsection (b) of this section, in addition to any relief authorized by section 706(g) of the Civil Rights Act of 1964, from the respondent.

(3) Reasonable accommodation and good faith effort

In cases where a discriminatory practice involves the provision of a reasonable accommodation pursuant to section 102(b)(5) of the Americans with Disabilities Act of 1990 or regulations implementing section 791 of Title 29, damages may not be awarded under this section where the covered entity demonstrates good faith efforts, in consultation with the person with the disability who has informed the covered entity that accommodation is needed, to identify and make a reasonable accommodation that would provide such individual with an equally effective opportunity and would not cause an undue hardship on the operation of the business.

(b) Compensatory and punitive damages

(1) Determination of punitive damages

A complaining party may recover punitive damages under this section against a respondent (other than a government, government agency or political subdivision) if the complaining party demonstrates that the respondent engaged in a discriminatory practice or discriminatory practices with malice or with reckless indifference to the federally protected rights of an aggrieved individual.

(2) Exclusions from compensatory damages

Compensatory damages awarded under this section shall not include backpay, interest on backpay, or any other type of relief authorized under section 706(g) of the Civil Rights Act of 1964.

(3) Limitations

The sum of the amount of compensatory damages awarded under this section for future pecuniary losses, emotional pain, suffering, inconvenience, mental anguish, loss of enjoyment of life, and other nonpecuniary losses, and the amount of punitive damages awarded under this section, shall not exceed, for each complaining party—

(A) in the case of a respondent who has more than 14 and fewer than 101 employees in each of 20 or more calendar weeks in the current or preceding calendar year, $50,000;

(B) in the case of a respondent who has more than 100 and fewer than 201 employees in each of 20 or more calendar weeks in the current or preceding calendar year, $100,000; and

(C) in the case of a respondent who has more than 200 and fewer than 501 employees in each of 20 or more calendar weeks in the current or preceding calendar year, $200,000; and

(D) in the case of a respondent who has more than 500 employees in each of 20 or more calendar weeks in the current or preceding calendar year, $300,000.

(4) Construction

Nothing in this section shall be construed to limit the scope of, or the relief available under, section 1981 of this title.

(c) Jury trial

If a complaining party seeks compensatory or punitive damages under this section—

(1) any party may demand a trial by jury; and

(2) the court shall not inform the jury of the limitations described in subsection (b)(3) of this section.

(d) Definitions

As used in this section:

(1) Complaining party

The term "complaining party" means—

(A) in the case of a person seeking to bring an action under subsection (a)(1) of this section, the Equal Employment Opportunity Commission, the Attorney General, or a person who may bring an action or proceeding under title VII of the Civil Rights Act of 1964 [42 U.S.C. 2000e et seq.]; or

(B) in the case of a person seeking to bring an action under subsection (a)(2) of this section, the Equal Employment Opportunity Commission, the Attorney General, a person who may bring an action or proceeding under section 794a(a)(1) of Title 29, or a person who may bring an action or proceeding under title I of the Americans with Disabilities Act of 1990 [42 U.S.C. 12101 et seq.].

(2) Discriminatory practice

The term "discriminatory practice" means the discrimination described in paragraph (1), or the discrimination or the violation described in paragraph (2), of subsection (a) of this section.

§ 1982. Property rights of citizens

All citizens of the United States shall have the same right, in every State and Territory, as is enjoyed by white citizens thereof to inherit, purchase, lease, sell, hold, and convey real and personal property.

§ 1983. Civil action for deprivation of rights

Every person who, under color of any statute, ordinance, regulation, custom, or usage, of any State or Territory or the District of Columbia, subjects, or causes to be subjected, any citizen of the United States or other person within the jurisdiction thereof to the deprivation of any rights, privileges, or immunities secured by the Constitution and laws, shall be liable to the party injured in an action at law, suit in equity, or other proper proceeding for redress, except that in any action brought against a judicial officer for an act or omission taken in such officer's judicial capacity, injunctive relief shall not be granted unless a declaratory decree was violated or declaratory relief was unavailable. For the purposes of this section, any Act of Congress applicable exclusively to the District of Columbia shall be considered to be a statute of the District of Columbia.

§ 1985. Conspiracy to interfere with civil rights

(1) Preventing officer from performing duties

If two or more persons in any State or Territory conspire to prevent, by force, intimidation, or threat, any person from accepting or holding any office, trust, or place of confidence under the United States, or from discharging any duties thereof; or to induce by like means any officer of the United States to leave any State, district, or place, where his duties as an officer are required to be performed, or to injure him in his person or property on account of his lawful discharge of the duties of his office, or while engaged in the lawful discharge thereof, or to injure his property so as to molest, interrupt, hinder, or impede him in the discharge of his official duties;

(2) Obstructing justice; intimidating party, witness, or juror

If two or more persons in any State or Territory conspire to deter, by force, intimidation, or threat, any party or witness in any court of the United States from attending such court, or from testifying to any matter pending therein, freely, fully, and truthfully, or to injure such party or witness in his person or property on account of his having so attended or testified, or to influence the verdict, presentment, or indictment of any grand or petit juror in any such court, or to injure such juror in his person or property on account of any verdict, presentment, or indictment lawfully assented to by him, or of his being or having been such juror; or if two or more persons conspire for the purpose of impeding, hindering, obstructing, or defeating, in any manner, the due course of justice in any State or Territory, with intent to deny to any citizen the equal protection of the laws, or to injure him or his property for lawfully enforcing, or attempting to enforce, the right of any person, or class of persons, to the equal protection of the laws;

(3) Depriving persons of rights or privileges

If two or more persons in any State or Territory conspire or go in disguise on the highway or on the premises of another, for the purpose of depriving, either directly or indirectly, any person or class of persons of the equal protection of the laws, or of equal privileges and immunities under the laws; or for the purpose of preventing or hindering the constituted authorities of any State or Territory from giving or securing to all persons within such State or Territory the equal protection of the laws; or if two or more persons conspire to prevent by force, intimidation, or threat, any citizen who is lawfully entitled to vote, from giving his support or advocacy in a legal manner, toward or in favor of the election of any lawfully qualified person as an elector for President or Vice President, or as a Member of Congress of the United States; or to injure any citizen in person or property on account of such support or advocacy; in any case of conspiracy set forth in this section, if one or more persons engaged therein do, or cause to be done, any act in furtherance of the object of such conspiracy, whereby another is injured in his person or property, or deprived of having and exercising any right or privilege of a citizen of the United States, the party so injured or deprived may have an action for the recovery of damages occasioned by such injury or deprivation, against any one or more of the conspirators.

§ 1986. Action for neglect to prevent

Every person who, having knowledge that any of the wrongs conspired to be done, and mentioned in section 1985 of this title, are about to be committed, and having power to prevent or aid in preventing the commission of the same, neglects or refuses so to do, if such wrongful act be committed, shall be liable to the party injured, or his legal representatives, for all damages caused by such wrongful act, which such person by reasonable diligence could have prevented; and such damages may be recovered in an action on the case; and any number of persons guilty of such wrongful neglect or refusal may be joined as defendants in the action; and if the death of any party be caused by any such wrongful act and neglect, the legal representatives of the deceased shall have such action therefor, and may recover not exceeding $5,000 damages therein, for the benefit of the widow of the deceased, if there be one, and if there be no widow, then for the benefit of the next of kin of the deceased. But no action under the provisions of this section shall be sustained which is not commenced within one year after the cause of action has accrued.

§ 1988. Proceedings in vindication of civil rights; attorney's fees; expert fees

(a) Applicability of statutory and common law

The jurisdiction in civil and criminal matters conferred on the district courts by the provisions of titles 13, 24, and 70 of the Revised Statutes for the protection of all persons in the United States in their civil rights, and for their vindication, shall be exercised and enforced in conformity with the laws of the United States, so far as such laws are suitable to carry the same into effect; but in all cases where they are not adapted to the object, or are deficient in the provisions necessary to furnish suitable remedies and punish offenses against law, the common law, as modified and changed by the constitution and statutes of the State wherein the court having jurisdiction of such civil or criminal cause is held, so far as the same is not inconsistent with the Constitution and laws of the United States, shall be extended to and govern the said courts in the trial and disposition of the cause, and, if it is of a criminal nature, in the infliction of punishment on the party found guilty.

(b) Attorney's fees

In any action or proceeding to enforce a provision of sections 1981, 1981a, 1982, 1983, 1985, and 1986 of this title, title IX of Public Law 92–318, the Religious Freedom Restoration Act of 1993, the Religious Land Use and Institutionalized Persons Act of 2000, title VI of the Civil Rights Act of 1964, or section 13981 of this title, the court, in its discretion, may allow the prevailing party, other than the United States, a reasonable attorney's fee as part of the costs, except that in any action brought against a judicial officer for an act or omission taken in such officer's judicial capacity such officer shall not be held liable for any costs, including attorney's fees, unless such action was clearly in excess of such officer's jurisdiction.

(c) Expert fees

In awarding an attorney's fee under subsection (b) of this section in any action or proceeding to enforce a provision of section 1981 or 1981a of this title, the court, in its discretion, may include expert fees as part of the attorney's fee.

§ 1997e. Suits by prisoners

(a) Applicability of administrative remedies

No action shall be brought with respect to prison conditions under section 1983 of this title, or any other Federal law, by a prisoner confined in any jail, prison, or other correctional facility until such administrative remedies as are available are exhausted.

(b) Failure of State to adopt or adhere to administrative grievance procedure

The failure of a State to adopt or adhere to an administrative grievance procedure shall not constitute the basis for an action under section 1997a or 1997c of this title.

(c) Dismissal

(1) The court shall on its own motion or on the motion of a party dismiss any action brought with respect to prison conditions under section 1983 of this title, or any other Federal law, by a prisoner confined in any jail, prison, or other correctional facility if the court is satisfied that the action is frivolous, malicious, fails to state a claim upon which relief can be granted, or seeks monetary relief from a defendant who is immune from such relief.

(2) In the event that a claim is, on its face, frivolous, malicious, fails to state a claim upon which relief can be granted, or seeks monetary relief from a defendant who is immune from such relief, the court may dismiss the underlying claim without first requiring the exhaustion of administrative remedies.

(d) Attorney's fees

(1) In any action brought by a prisoner who is confined to any jail, prison, or other correctional facility, in which attorney's fees are authorized under section 1988 of this title, such fees shall not be awarded, except to the extent that—

(A) the fee was directly and reasonably incurred in proving an actual violation of the plaintiff's rights protected by a statute pursuant to which a fee may be awarded under section 1988 of this title; and

(B)(i) the amount of the fee is proportionately related to the court ordered relief for the violation; or

(ii) the fee was directly and reasonably incurred in enforcing the relief ordered for the violation.

(2) Whenever a monetary judgment is awarded in an action described in paragraph (1), a portion of the judgment (not to exceed 25 percent) shall be applied to satisfy the amount of attorney's fees awarded against the defendant. If the award of attorney's fees is not greater than 150 percent of the judgment, the excess shall be paid by the defendant.

(3) No award of attorney's fees in an action described in paragraph (1) shall be based on an hourly rate greater than 150 percent of the hourly rate established under section 3006A of Title 18 for payment of court-appointed counsel.

(4) Nothing in this subsection shall prohibit a prisoner from entering into an agreement to pay an attorney's fee in an amount greater than the amount authorized under this subsection, if the fee is paid by the individual rather than by the defendant pursuant to section 1988 of this title.

(e) Limitation on recovery

No Federal civil action may be brought by a prisoner confined in a jail, prison, or other correctional facility, for mental or emotional injury suffered while in custody without a prior showing of physical injury.

(f) Hearings

(1) To the extent practicable, in any action brought with respect to prison conditions in Federal court pursuant to section 1983 of this title, or any other Federal law, by a prisoner confined in any jail, prison, or other correctional facility, pretrial proceedings in which the prisoner's participation is required or permitted shall be conducted by telephone, video conference, or other telecommunications technology without removing the prisoner from the facility in which the prisoner is confined.

(2) Subject to the agreement of the official of the Federal, State, or local unit of government with custody over the prisoner, hearings may be conducted at the facility in which the prisoner is confined. To the extent practicable, the court shall allow counsel to participate by telephone, video conference, or other communications technology in any hearing held at the facility.

(g) Waiver of reply

(1) Any defendant may waive the right to reply to any action brought by a prisoner confined in any jail, prison, or other correctional facility under section 1983 of this title or any other Federal law. Notwithstanding any other law or rule of procedure, such waiver shall not constitute an admission of the allegations contained in the complaint. No relief shall be granted to the plaintiff unless a reply has been filed.

(2) The court may require any defendant to reply to a complaint brought under this section if it finds that the plaintiff has a reasonable opportunity to prevail on the merits.

(h) "Prisoner" Defined

As used in this section, the term "prisoner" means any person incarcerated or detained in any facility who is accused of, convicted of, sentenced for, or adjudicated delinquent for, violations of criminal law or the terms and conditions of parole, probation, pretrial release, or diversionary program.

§ 2000e [§ 701 of Title VII]. Definitions

For the purposes of this subchapter—

(a) The term "person" includes one or more individuals, governments, governmental agencies, political subdivisions, labor unions, partnerships, associations, corporations, legal representatives, mutual companies, joint-stock companies, trusts, unincorporated organizations, trustees, trustees in cases under Title 11, or receivers.

(b) The term "employer" means a person engaged in an industry affecting commerce who has fifteen or more employees for each working day in each of twenty or more calendar weeks in the current or preceding calendar year, and any agent of such a person, but such term does not include (1) the United States, a corporation wholly owned by the Government of the United States, an Indian tribe, or any department or agency of the District of Columbia subject by statute to procedures of the competitive service (as defined in section 2102 of Title 5), or (2) a bona fide private membership club (other than a labor organization) which is exempt from taxation under section 501(c) of Title 26, except that during the first year after March 24, 1972, persons having fewer than twenty-five employees (and their agents) shall not be considered employers.

(c) The term "employment agency" means any person regularly undertaking with or without compensation to procure employees for an employer or to procure for employees opportunities to work for an employer and includes an agent of such a person.

(d) The term "labor organization" means a labor organization engaged in an industry affecting commerce, and any agent of such an organization, and includes any organization of any kind, any agency, or employee representation committee, group, association, or plan so engaged in which employees participate and which exists for the purpose, in whole or in part, of dealing with employers concerning grievances, labor disputes, wages, rates of pay, hours, or other terms or conditions of employment, and any conference, general committee, joint or system board, or joint council so engaged which is subordinate to a national or international labor organization.

(e) A labor organization shall be deemed to be engaged in an industry affecting commerce if

(1) it maintains or operates a hiring hall or hiring office which procures employees for an employer or procures for employees opportunities to work for an employer, or

(2) the number of its members (or, where it is a labor organization composed of other labor organizations or their representatives, if the aggregate number of the members of such other labor organization) is

(A) twenty-five or more during the first year after March 24, 1972, or

(B) fifteen or more thereafter, and such labor organization—

(1) is the certified representative of employees under the provisions of the National Labor Relations Act, as amended [29 U.S.C. 151 et seq.], or the Railway Labor Act, as amended [45 U.S.C. 151 et seq.];

(2) although not certified, is a national or international labor organization or a local labor organization recognized or acting as the representative of employees of an employer or employers engaged in an industry affecting commerce; or

(3) has chartered a local labor organization or subsidiary body which is representing or actively seeking to represent employees of employers within the meaning of paragraph (1) or (2); or

(4) has been chartered by a labor organization representing or actively seeking to represent employees within the meaning of paragraph (1) or (2) as the local or subordinate body through which such employees may enjoy membership or become affiliated with such labor organization; or

(5) is a conference, general committee, joint or system board, or joint council subordinate to a national or international labor organization, which includes a labor organization engaged in an industry affecting commerce within the meaning of any of the preceding paragraphs of this subsection.

(f) The term "employee" means an individual employed by an employer, except that the term "employee" shall not include any person elected to public office in any State or political subdivision of any State by the qualified voters thereof, or any person chosen by such officer to be on such officer's personal staff, or an appointee on the policy making level or an immediate adviser with respect to the exercise of the constitutional or legal powers of the office. The exemption set forth in the preceding sentence shall not include employees subject to the civil service laws of a State government, governmental agency or political subdivision. With respect to employment in a foreign country, such term includes an individual who is a citizen of the United States.

(g) The term "commerce" means trade, traffic, commerce, transportation, transmission, or communication among the several States; or between a State and any place outside thereof; or within the District of Columbia, or a possession of the United States; or between points in the same State but through a point outside thereof.

(h) The term "industry affecting commerce" means any activity, business, or industry in commerce or in which a labor dispute would hinder or obstruct commerce or the free flow of commerce and includes any activity or industry "affecting commerce" within the meaning of the Labor–Management Reporting and Disclosure Act of 1959 [29 U.S.C. 401 et seq.], and further includes any governmental industry, business, or activity.

(i) The term "State" includes a State of the United States, the District of Columbia, Puerto Rico, the Virgin Islands, American Samoa, Guam, Wake Island, the Canal Zone, and Outer Continental Shelf lands defined in the Outer Continental Shelf Lands Act [43 U.S.C. 1331 et seq.].

(j) The term "religion" includes all aspects of religious observance and practice, as well as belief, unless an employer demonstrates that he is unable to reasonably accommodate to an employee's or prospective employee's religious observance or practice without undue hardship on the conduct of the employer's business.

(k) The terms "because of sex" or "on the basis of sex" include, but are not limited to, because of or on the basis of pregnancy, childbirth, or related medical conditions; and women affected by pregnancy, childbirth, or related medical conditions shall be treated the same for all employment-related purposes, including receipt of benefits under fringe benefit programs, as other persons not so affected but similar in their ability or inability to work, and nothing in section 2000e–2(h) of this title shall be interpreted to permit otherwise. This subsection shall not require an employer to pay for health insurance benefits for abortion, except where the life of the mother would be endangered if the fetus were carried to term, or except where medical complications have arisen from an abortion: Provided, That nothing herein shall preclude an employer from providing abortion benefits or otherwise affect bargaining agreements in regard to abortion.

(l) The term "complaining party" means the Commission, the Attorney General, or a person who may bring an action or proceeding under this subchapter.

(m) The term "demonstrates" means meets the burdens of production and persuasion.

(n) The term "respondent" means an employer, employment agency, labor organization, joint labor-management committee controlling apprenticeship or other training or retraining program, including an on-the-job training program, or Federal entity subject to section 2000e–16 of this title.

§ 2000e–2 [§ 703 of Title VII]. Unlawful employment practices

(a) Employer practices

It shall be an unlawful employment practice for an employer—

(1) to fail or refuse to hire or to discharge any individual, or otherwise to discriminate against any individual with respect to his compensation, terms, conditions, or privileges of employment, because of such individual's race, color, religion, sex, or national origin; or

(2) to limit, segregate, or classify his employees or applicants for employment in any way which would deprive or tend to deprive any individual of employment opportunities or otherwise adversely affect his status as an employee, because of such individual's race, color, religion, sex, or national origin.

(b) Employment agency practices

It shall be an unlawful employment practice for an employment agency to fail or refuse to refer for employment, or otherwise to discriminate against, any individual because of his race, color, religion, sex, or national origin, or to classify or refer for employment any individual on the basis of his race, color, religion, sex, or national origin.

(c) Labor organization practices

It shall be an unlawful employment practice for a labor organization—

(1) to exclude or to expel from its membership, or otherwise to discriminate against, any individual because of his race, color, religion, sex, or national origin;

(2) to limit, segregate, or classify its membership or applicants for membership, or to classify or fail or refuse to refer for employment any individual, in any way which would deprive or tend to deprive any individual of employment opportunities, or would limit such employment opportunities or otherwise adversely affect his status as an employee or as an applicant for employment, because of such individual's race, color, religion, sex, or national origin; or

(3) to cause or attempt to cause an employer to discriminate against an individual in violation of this section.

(d) Training programs

It shall be an unlawful employment practice for any employer, labor organization, or joint labor-management committee controlling apprenticeship or other training or retraining, including on-the-job training programs to discriminate against any individual because of his race, color, religion, sex, or national origin in admission to, or employment in, any program established to provide apprenticeship or other training.

(e) Businesses or enterprises with personnel qualified on basis of religion, sex, or national origin; educational institutions with personnel of particular religion

Notwithstanding any other provision of this subchapter,

(1) it shall not be an unlawful employment practice for an employer to hire and employ employees, for an employment agency to classify, or refer for employment any individual, for a labor organization to classify its membership or to classify or refer for employment any individual, or for an

employer, labor organization, or joint labor-management committee controlling apprenticeship or other training or retraining programs to admit or employ any individual in any such program, on the basis of his religion, sex, or national origin in those certain instances where religion, sex, or national origin is a bona fide occupational qualification reasonably necessary to the normal operation of that particular business or enterprise, and

(2) it shall not be an unlawful employment practice for a school, college, university, or other educational institution or institution of learning to hire and employ employees of a particular religion if such school, college, university, or other educational institution or institution of learning is, in whole or in substantial part, owned, supported, controlled, or managed by a particular religion or by a particular religious corporation, association, or society, or if the curriculum of such school, college, university, or other educational institution or institution of learning is directed toward the propagation of a particular religion.

(f) Members of Communist Party or Communist-action or Communist-front organizations

As used in this subchapter, the phrase "unlawful employment practice" shall not be deemed to include any action or measure taken by an employer, labor organization, joint labor-management committee, or employment agency with respect to an individual who is a member of the Communist Party of the United States or of any other organization required to register as a Communist-action or Communist-front organization by final order of the Subversive Activities Control Board pursuant to the Subversive Activities Control Act of 1950.

(g) National security

Notwithstanding any other provision of this subchapter, it shall not be an unlawful employment practice for an employer to fail or refuse to hire and employ any individual for any position, for an employer to discharge any individual from any position, or for an employment agency to fail or refuse to refer any individual for employment in any position, or for a labor organization to fail or refuse to refer any individual for employment in any position, if—

(1) the occupancy of such position, or access to the premises in or upon which any part of the duties of such position is performed or is to be performed, is subject to any requirement imposed in the interest of the national security of the United States under any security program in effect pursuant to or administered under any statute of the United States or any Executive order of the President; and

(2) such individual has not fulfilled or has ceased to fulfill that requirement.

(h) Seniority or merit system; quantity or quality of production; ability tests; compensation based on sex and authorized by minimum wage provisions

Notwithstanding any other provision of this subchapter, it shall not be an unlawful employment practice for an employer to apply different standards of compensation, or different terms, conditions, or privileges of employment pursuant to a bona fide seniority or merit system, or a system which measures earnings by quantity or quality of production or to employees who work in different locations, provided that such differences are not the result of an intention to discriminate because of race, color, religion, sex, or national origin, nor shall it be an unlawful employment practice for an employer to give and to act upon the results of any professionally developed ability test provided that such test, its administration or action upon the results is not designed, intended or used to discriminate because of race, color, religion, sex or national origin. It shall not be an unlawful employment practice under this subchapter for any employer to differentiate upon the basis of sex in determining the amount of the wages or compensation paid or to be paid to employees of such employer if such differentiation is authorized by the provisions of section 206(d) of Title 29.

(i) Businesses or enterprises extending preferential treatment to Indians

Nothing contained in this subchapter shall apply to any business or enterprise on or near an Indian reservation with respect to any publicly announced employment practice of such business or enterprise under which a preferential treatment is given to any individual because he is an Indian living on or near a reservation.

(j) Preferential treatment not to be granted on account of existing number or percentage imbalance

Nothing contained in this subchapter shall be interpreted to require any employer, employment agency, labor organization, or joint labor-management committee subject to this subchapter to grant preferential treatment to any individual or to any group because of the race, color, religion, sex, or national origin of such individual or group on account of an imbalance which may exist with respect to the total number or percentage of persons of any race, color, religion, sex, or national origin employed by any employer, referred or classified for employment by any employment agency or labor organization, admitted to membership or classified by any labor organization, or admitted to, or employed in, any apprenticeship or other training program, in comparison with the total number or percentage of persons of such race, color, religion, sex, or national origin in any community, State, section, or other area, or in the available work force in any community, State, section, or other area.

(k) Burden of proof in disparate impact cases

(1)(A) An unlawful employment practice based on disparate impact is established under this subchapter only if—

(i) a complaining party demonstrates that a respondent uses a particular employment practice that causes a disparate impact on the basis of race, color, religion, sex, or national origin and the respondent fails to demonstrate that the challenged practice is job related for the position in question and consistent with business necessity; or

(ii) the complaining party makes the demonstration described in subparagraph (C) with respect to an alternative employment practice and the respondent refuses to adopt such alternative employment practice.

(B)(i) With respect to demonstrating that a particular employment practice causes a disparate impact as described in subparagraph (A)(i), the complaining party shall demonstrate that each particular challenged employment practice causes a disparate impact, except that if the complaining party can demonstrate to the court that the elements of a respondent's decisionmaking process are not capable of separation for analysis, the decisionmaking process may be analyzed as one employment practice.

(ii) If the respondent demonstrates that a specific employment practice does not cause the disparate impact, the respondent shall not be required to demonstrate that such practice is required by business necessity.

(C) The demonstration referred to by subparagraph (A)(ii) shall be in accordance with the law as it existed on June 4, 1989, with respect to the concept of "alternative employment practice".

(2) A demonstration that an employment practice is required by business necessity may not be used as a defense against a claim of intentional discrimination under this subchapter.

(3) Notwithstanding any other provision of this subchapter, a rule barring the employment of an individual who currently and knowingly uses or possesses a controlled substance, as defined in schedules I and II of section 102(6) of the Controlled Substances Act (21 U.S.C. 802(6)), other than the use or possession of a drug taken under the supervision of a licensed health care professional, or any other use or possession authorized by the Controlled Substances Act or any other provision of Federal law, shall be considered an unlawful employment practice under this subchapter only if such rule is adopted or applied with an intent to discriminate because of race, color, religion, sex, or national origin.

(l) Prohibition of discriminatory use of test scores

It shall be an unlawful employment practice for a respondent, in connection with the selection or referral of applicants or candidates for employment or promotion, to adjust the scores of, use different cutoff scores for, or otherwise alter the results of, employment related tests on the basis of race, color, religion, sex, or national origin.

(m) Impermissible consideration of race, color, religion, sex, or national origin in employment practices

Except as otherwise provided in this subchapter, an unlawful employment practice is established when the complaining party demonstrates that race, color, religion, sex, or national origin was a motivating factor for any employment practice, even though other factors also motivated the practice.

(n) Resolution of challenges to employment practices implementing litigated or consent judgments or orders

(1)(A) Notwithstanding any other provision of law, and except as provided in paragraph (2), an employment practice that implements and is within the scope of a litigated or consent judgment or order that resolves a claim of employment discrimination under the Constitution or Federal civil rights laws may not be challenged under the circumstances described in subparagraph (B).

(B) A practice described in subparagraph (A) may not be challenged in a claim under the Constitution or Federal civil rights laws—

(i) by a person who, prior to the entry of the judgment or order described in subparagraph (A), had—

(I) actual notice of the proposed judgment or order sufficient to apprise such person that such judgment or order might adversely affect the interests and legal rights of such person and that an opportunity was available to present objections to such judgment or order by a future date certain; and

(II) a reasonable opportunity to present objections to such judgment or order; or

(ii) by a person whose interests were adequately represented by another person who had previously challenged the judgment or order on the same legal grounds and with a similar factual situation, unless there has been an intervening change in law or fact.

(2) Nothing in this subsection shall be construed to—

(A) alter the standards for intervention under rule 24 of the Federal Rules of Civil Procedure or apply to the rights of parties who have successfully intervened pursuant to such rule in the proceeding in which the parties intervened;

(B) apply to the rights of parties to the action in which a litigated or consent judgment or order was entered, or of members of a class represented or sought to be represented in such action, or of members of a group on whose behalf relief was sought in such action by the Federal Government;

(C) prevent challenges to a litigated or consent judgment or order on the ground that such judgment or order was obtained through collusion or fraud, or is transparently invalid or was entered by a court lacking subject matter jurisdiction; or

(D) authorize or permit the denial to any person of the due process of law required by the Constitution.

(3) Any action not precluded under this subsection that challenges an employment consent judgment or order described in paragraph (1) shall be brought in the court, and if possible before the judge, that entered such judgment or order. Nothing in this subsection shall preclude a transfer of such action pursuant to section 1404 of Title 28.

§ 2000e–5 [§ 706 of Title VII]. Enforcement provisions

(a) Power of Commission to prevent unlawful employment practices

The Commission is empowered, as hereinafter provided, to prevent any person from engaging in any unlawful employment practice as set forth in section 2000e–2 or 2000e–3 of this title.

(b) Charges by persons aggrieved or member of Commission of unlawful employment practices by employers, etc.; filing; allegations; notice to respondent; contents of notice; investigation by Commission; contents of charges; prohibition on disclosure of charges; determination of reasonable cause; conference, conciliation, and persuasion for elimination of unlawful practices; prohibition on disclosure of informal endeavors to end unlawful practices; use of evidence in subsequent proceedings; penalties for disclosure of information time for determination of reasonable cause

Whenever a charge is filed by or on behalf of a person claiming to be aggrieved, or by a member of the Commission, alleging that an employer, employment agency, labor organization, or joint labor-management committee controlling apprenticeship or other training or retraining, including on-the-job training programs, has engaged in an unlawful employment practice, the Commission shall serve a notice of the charge (including the date, place and circumstances of the alleged unlawful employment practice) on such employer, employment agency, labor organization, or joint labor-management committee (hereinafter referred to as the "respondent") within ten days, and shall make an investigation thereof. Charges shall be in writing under oath or affirmation and shall contain such information and be in such form as the Commission requires. Charges shall not be made public by the Commission. If the Commission determines after such investigation that there is not reasonable cause to believe that the charge is true, it shall dismiss the charge and promptly notify the person claiming to be aggrieved and the respondent of its action. In determining whether reasonable cause exists, the Commission shall accord substantial weight to final findings and orders made by State or local authorities in proceedings commenced under State or local law pursuant to the requirements of subsections (c) and (d) of this section. If the Commission determines after such investigation that there is reasonable cause to believe that the charge is true, the Commission shall endeavor to eliminate any such alleged unlawful employment practice by informal methods of conference, conciliation, and persuasion. Nothing said or done during and as a part of such informal endeavors may be made public by the Commission, its officers or employees, or used as evidence in a subsequent proceeding without the written consent of the persons concerned. Any person who makes public information in violation of this subsection shall be fined not more than $1,000 or imprisoned for not more than one year, or both. The Commission shall make its determination on reasonable cause as promptly as possible and, so far as practicable, not later than one hundred and twenty days from the filing of the charge or, where applicable under subsection (c) or (d) of this section, from the date upon which the Commission is authorized to take action with respect to the charge.

(c) State or local enforcement proceedings; notification of State or local authority; time for filing charges with Commission; commencement of proceedings

In the case of an alleged unlawful employment practice occurring in a State, or political subdivision of a State, which has a State or local law prohibiting the unlawful employment practice alleged and establishing or authorizing a State or local authority to grant or seek relief from such practice or to institute criminal proceedings with respect thereto upon receiving notice thereof, no charge may be filed under subsection (a) of this section by the person aggrieved before the expiration of sixty days after proceedings have been commenced under the State or local law, unless such proceedings have been earlier terminated, provided that such sixty-day period shall be extended to one hundred and twenty days during the first year after the effective date of such State or local law. If any requirement for the commencement of such proceedings is imposed by a State or local authority other than a requirement of the filing of a written and signed statement of the facts upon which the proceeding is based, the proceeding shall be deemed to have been commenced for the purposes of this subsection at the time such statement is sent by registered mail to the appropriate State or local authority.

(d) State or local enforcement proceedings; notification of State or local authority; time for action on charges by Commission

In the case of any charge filed by a member of the Commission alleging an unlawful employment practice occurring in a State or political subdivision of a State which has a State or local law prohibiting the practice alleged and establishing or authorizing a State or local authority to grant or seek relief from such practice or to institute criminal proceedings with respect thereto upon receiving notice thereof, the Commission shall, before taking any action with respect to such charge, notify the appropriate State or local officials and, upon request, afford them a reasonable time, but not less than sixty days (provided that such sixty-day period shall be extended to one hundred and twenty days during the first year after the effective day of such State or local law), unless a shorter period is requested, to act under such State or local law to remedy the practice alleged.

(e) Time for filing charges; time for service of notice of charge on respondent; filing of charge by Commission with State or local agency; seniority system

(1) A charge under this section shall be filed within one hundred and eighty days after the alleged unlawful employment practice occurred and notice of the charge (including the date, place and circumstances of the alleged unlawful employment practice) shall be served upon the person against whom such charge is made within ten days thereafter, except that in a case of an unlawful employment practice with respect to which the person aggrieved has initially instituted proceedings with a State or local agency with authority to grant or seek relief from such practice or to institute criminal proceedings with respect thereto upon receiving notice thereof, such charge shall be filed by or on behalf of the person aggrieved within three hundred days after the alleged unlawful employment practice occurred, or within thirty days after receiving notice that the State or local agency has terminated the proceedings under the State or local law, whichever is earlier, and a copy of such charge shall be filed by the Commission with the State or local agency.

(2) For purposes of this section, an unlawful employment practice occurs, with respect to a seniority system that has been adopted for an intentionally discriminatory purpose in violation of this subchapter (whether or not that discriminatory purpose is apparent on the face of the seniority provision), when the seniority system is adopted, when an individual becomes subject to the seniority system, or when a person aggrieved is injured by the application of the seniority system or provision of the system.

(3)(A) For purposes of this section, an unlawful employment practice occurs, with respect to discrimination in compensation in violation of this subchapter, when a discriminatory compensation decision or other practice is adopted, when an individual becomes subject to a discriminatory compensation decision or other practice, or when an individual is affected by application of a discriminatory compensation decision or other practice, including each time wages, benefits, or other compensation is paid, resulting in whole or in part from such a decision or other practice.

(B) In addition to any relief authorized by section 1981a of this title, liability may accrue and an aggrieved person may obtain relief as provided in subsection (g)(1), including recovery of back pay for up to two years preceding the filing of the charge, where the unlawful employment practices that have occurred during the charge filing period are similar or related to unlawful employment practices with regard to discrimination in compensation that occurred outside the time for filing a charge.

(f) Civil action by Commission, Attorney General, or person aggrieved; preconditions; procedure; appointment of attorney; payment of fees, costs, or security; intervention; stay of Federal proceedings; action for appropriate temporary or preliminary relief pending final disposition of charge; jurisdiction and venue of United States courts; designation of judge to hear and determine case; assignment of case for hearing; expedition of case; appointment of master

(1) If within thirty days after a charge is filed with the Commission or within thirty days after expiration of any period of reference under subsection (c) or (d) of this section, the Commission has been unable to secure from the respondent a conciliation agreement acceptable to the Commission, the Commission may bring a civil action against any respondent not a government, governmental agency, or political subdivision named in the charge. In the case of a respondent which is a government, governmental agency, or political subdivision, if the Commission has been unable to secure from the respondent a conciliation agreement acceptable to the Commission, the Commission shall take no further action and shall refer the case to the Attorney General who may bring a civil action against such respondent in the appropriate United States district court. The person or persons aggrieved shall have the right to intervene in a civil action brought by the Commission or the Attorney General in a case involving a government, governmental agency, or political subdivision. If a charge filed with the Commission pursuant to subsection (b) of this section is dismissed by the Commission, or if within one hundred and eighty days from the filing of such charge or the expiration of any period of reference under subsection (c) or (d) of this section, whichever is later, the Commission has not filed a civil action under this section or the Attorney General has not filed a civil action in a case involving a government, governmental agency, or political subdivision, or the Commission has not entered into a conciliation agreement to which the person aggrieved is a party, the Commission, or the Attorney General in a case involving a government, governmental agency, or political subdivision, shall so notify the person aggrieved and within ninety days after the giving of such notice a civil action may be brought against the respondent named in the charge (A) by the person claiming to be aggrieved or (B) if such charge was filed by a member of the Commission, by any person whom the charge alleges was aggrieved by the alleged unlawful employment practice. Upon application by the complainant and in such circumstances as the court may deem just, the court may appoint an attorney for such complainant and may authorize the commencement of the action without the payment of fees, costs, or security. Upon timely application, the court may, in its discretion, permit the Commission, or the Attorney General in a case involving a government, governmental agency, or political subdivision, to intervene in such civil action upon certification that the case is of general public importance. Upon request, the court may, in its discretion, stay further proceedings for not more than sixty days pending the termination of State or local proceedings described in subsections (c) or (d)

of this section or further efforts of the Commission to obtain voluntary compliance.

(2) Whenever a charge is filed with the Commission and the Commission concludes on the basis of a preliminary investigation that prompt judicial action is necessary to carry out the purposes of this Act, the Commission, or the Attorney General in a case involving a government, governmental agency, or political subdivision, may bring an action for appropriate temporary or preliminary relief pending final disposition of such charge. Any temporary restraining order or other order granting preliminary or temporary relief shall be issued in accordance with rule 65 of the Federal Rules of Civil Procedure. It shall be the duty of a court having jurisdiction over proceedings under this section to assign cases for hearing at the earliest practicable date and to cause such cases to be in every way expedited.

(3) Each United States district court and each United States court of a place subject to the jurisdiction of the United States shall have jurisdiction of actions brought under this subchapter. Such an action may be brought in any judicial district in the State in which the unlawful employment practice is alleged to have been committed, in the judicial district in which the employment records relevant to such practice are maintained and administered, or in the judicial district in which the aggrieved person would have worked but for the alleged unlawful employment practice, but if the respondent is not found within any such district, such an action may be brought within the judicial district in which the respondent has his principal office. For purposes of sections 1404 and 1406 of Title 28, the judicial district in which the respondent has his principal office shall in all cases be considered a district in which the action might have been brought.

(4) It shall be the duty of the chief judge of the district (or in his absence, the acting chief judge) in which the case is pending immediately to designate a judge in such district to hear and determine the case. In the event that no judge in the district is available to hear and determine the case, the chief judge of the district, or the acting chief judge, as the case may be, shall certify this fact to the chief judge of the circuit (or in his absence, the acting chief judge) who shall then designate a district or circuit judge of the circuit to hear and determine the case.

(5) It shall be the duty of the judge designated pursuant to this subsection to assign the case for hearing at the earliest practicable date and to cause the case to be in every way expedited. If such judge has not scheduled the case for trial within one hundred and twenty days after issue has been joined, that judge may appoint a master pursuant to rule 53 of the Federal Rules of Civil Procedure.

(g) Injunctions; appropriate affirmative action; equitable relief; accrual of back pay; reduction of back pay; limitations on judicial orders

(1) If the court finds that the respondent has intentionally engaged in or is intentionally engaging in an unlawful employment practice charged in the complaint, the court may enjoin the respondent from engaging in such unlawful employment practice, and order such affirmative action as may be appropriate, which may include, but is not limited to, reinstatement or hiring of employees, with or without back pay (payable by the employer, employment agency, or labor organization, as the case may be, responsible for the unlawful employment practice), or any other equitable relief as the court deems appropriate. Back pay liability shall not accrue from a date

more than two years prior to the filing of a charge with the Commission. Interim earnings or amounts earnable with reasonable diligence by the person or persons discriminated against shall operate to reduce the back pay otherwise allowable.

(2)(A) No order of the court shall require the admission or reinstatement of an individual as a member of a union, or the hiring, reinstatement, or promotion of an individual as an employee, or the payment to him of any back pay, if such individual was refused admission, suspended, or expelled, or was refused employment or advancement or was suspended or discharged for any reason other than discrimination on account of race, color, religion, sex, or national origin or in violation of section 2000e–3(a) of this title.

(B) On a claim in which an individual proves a violation under section 2000e–2(m) of this title and a respondent demonstrates that the respondent would have taken the same action in the absence of the impermissible motivating factor, the court—

(i) may grant declaratory relief, injunctive relief (except as provided in clause (ii)), and attorney's fees and costs demonstrated to be directly attributable only to the pursuit of a claim under section 2000e–2(m) of this title; and

(ii) shall not award damages or issue an order requiring any admission, reinstatement, hiring, promotion, or payment, described in subparagraph (A).

(h) Provisions of chapter 6 of Title 29 not applicable to civil actions for prevention of unlawful practices

The provisions of chapter 6 of Title 29 shall not apply with respect to civil actions brought under this section.

(i) Proceedings by Commission to compel compliance with judicial orders

In any case in which an employer, employment agency, or labor organization fails to comply with an order of a court issued in a civil action brought under this section, the Commission may commence proceedings to compel compliance with such order.

(j) Appeals

Any civil action brought under this section and any proceedings brought under subsection (i) of this section shall be subject to appeal as provided in sections 1291 and 1292, Title 28.

(k) Attorney's fee; liability of Commission and United States for costs

In any action or proceeding under this subchapter the court, in its discretion, may allow the prevailing party, other than the Commission or the United States, a reasonable attorney's fee (including expert fees) as part of the costs, and the Commission and the United States shall be liable for costs the same as a private person.